July 17-21, 2016
Pisa, Italy

Association for Computing Machinery

Advancing Computing as a Science & Profession

SIGIR'16

Proceedings of the 39th International ACM SIGIR conference on Research and Development in Information Retrieval

Sponsored by:

ACM SIGIR

Association for
Computing Machinery

Advancing Computing as a Science & Profession

The Association for Computing Machinery
2 Penn Plaza, Suite 701
New York, New York 10121-0701

Notice to Past Authors of ACM-Published Articles
ACM intends to create a complete electronic archive of all articles and/or other material previously published by ACM. If you have written a work that has been previously published by ACM in any journal or conference proceedings prior to 1978, or any SIG Newsletter at any time, and you do NOT want this work to appear in the ACM Digital Library, please inform permissions@acm.org, stating the title of the work, the author(s), and where and when published.

ISBN: 978-1-4503-4290-2 (Digital)

ISBN: 978-1-4503-4614-6 (Print)

Additional copies may be ordered prepaid from:

ACM Order Department
PO Box 30777
New York, NY 10087-0777, USA

Phone: 1-800-342-6626 (USA and Canada)
+1-212-626-0500 (Global)
Fax: +1-212-944-1318
E-mail: acmhelp@acm.org
Hours of Operation: 8:30 am – 4:30 pm ET

Printed in the USA

General Chairs' Welcome

It is our great pleasure to welcome you to SIGIR 2016, the 39th International ACM SIGIR Conference on Research and Development in Information Retrieval. SIGIR is back in Pisa, Italy, after exactly 30 years from the 1986 edition; at that time the proceedings were still in paper form, the conference did not have its own web page, Wi-Fi in the lecture rooms was not provided, and delegates tweeting about their impressions were still rare. Notwithstanding the lack of the modern commodities above, those who participated in that edition tell us stories of a lively and thoroughly enjoyable event; we hope to live up to that tradition and offer you five days of engaging scientific events, networking opportunities, and social fun.

The conference will start on July 17 with a day of (full-day and half-day) tutorials, plus the Doctoral Consortium. SIGIR 2016 will enter its main phase in the three days that follow, when the main conference (July 18-20) and the SIRIP Industry Track (July 20) will take place. The stimulating technical program set up includes two valuable and insightful keynote talks opening the first and the third day of the main conference:

- *Understanding Human Language: Can NLP and Deep Learning Help?* by Christopher Manning, Stanford University;
- *Big Data in Climate: Opportunities and Challenges for Machine Learning,* by Vipin Kumar, University of Minnesota.

The last day of the conference (July 21) will be entirely devoted to workshops.

We would like to take this opportunity to thank everybody who helped us in setting up SIGIR 2016. First of all, we would like to give heartfelt thanks to our sponsor, ACM SIGIR, and our corporate supporters: Baidu (Platinum Supporter), Appen, Bloomberg, Booking.com, eBay, Facebook, Google, Huawei, IBM, Microsoft, Yahoo! (Silver Supporters), and Yandex (Bronze Supporter). All of them provided generous sponsorship, which allowed us to keep the registration fees (believe it or not...) as low as possible and fund a lot of student travels. Thanks also to the National Research Council of Italy and to the Qatar Computing Research Institute for supporting our organizational work.

Putting everything together was a hard teamwork. We want to thank everybody involved in making SIGIR 2016 an exciting event. First and foremost, we want to thank our Program Chairs Javed Aslam, Ian Ruthven, and Justin Zobel, not only for chairing the selection of the full papers, but also for painstakingly overseeing the rest of the scientific program. Many thanks also to the Short Papers Chairs Ben Carterette, Carlos Castillo, and Jaana Kekäläinen, who had to deal with an inordinate amount of short paper submissions under tighter-than-usual time constraints; to the Tutorials Chairs Evangelos Kanoulas and Tie-Yan Liu; to the Workshops Chairs Aristides Gionis and Edie Rasmussen; to the Demo Chair Craig Macdonald; to the Doctoral Consortium Chairs Brian Davison and Kira Radinski; to the SIRIP Industry Track Chairs Jussi Karlgren and Gilad Mishne; to the Sponsorship Chairs Fabrizio Falchi and Jimmy Huang; and to the Awards Chair Norbert Fuhr. All of them went to great lengths to ensure the high quality of this conference. Quite aside from the people who held chairing roles, lots of other people contributed to the scientific success of SIGIR 2016: many thanks to the members of the Senior Program Committee, to the members of the first-tier Program Committee, to the mentors of the Doctorial Consortium Committee, and to all those who reviewed, in any capacity, full papers, short papers, tutorial and workshop proposals, demo papers.

Last but not least, we would like to thank all the members of the local organizing team at the National Research Council of Italy; in order to keep the registration fees as low as possible, no professional conference organization company was called in to help, and they took 100% of the organization upon them. We would thus like our two Local Chairs Andrea Esuli and Chiara Renso; our Treasurer Giulio Galesi; our Publications Chair Claudio Lucchese; our Publicity Chair Nicola Tonellotto; our Webmaster Franco Maria Nardini; our Student Volunteers Coordinators Alejandro Moreo Fernández and, again, Franco Maria Nardini. Thanks also to (in no particular order) Catherine Bosio, Matteo Catena, Francesca Donati, and Sara Montesi for helping in various phases of the organization. They all invested tremendous efforts into making SIGIR 2016 an exciting and enjoyable event. It is due to them that the organization of SIGIR 2016 was not just hard work, but also a pleasure.

We look forward to welcoming you in Pisa, Tuscany, possibly the most enchanting region of Italy, surely the richest of artistic heritage and landscapes. Due to its history and the extraordinary quality of food and wines, it is an unforgettable place to visit. We hope that you will be rewarded by the technical challenges of SIGIR 2016 but you will get also a chance to explore our region and enjoy its vibrant atmosphere!

Raffaele Perego
ISTI-CNR, Italy

Fabrizio Sebastiani
Qatar Computing Research Institute, HBKU, Qatar

SIGIR 2016 Program Chairs' Preface

Welcome to SIGIR 2016, the 39th Annual International ACM-SIGIR Conference on Research and Development in Information Retrieval, the premier conference in the area. We are grateful to all those who chose to submit their research papers to SIGIR 2016 and gave the Program Committee an opportunity to evaluate their work for potential inclusion in the program. We are also grateful to the 61 Senior Program Committee Members, 244 Program Committee Members, and many additional reviewers for providing significant time and effort to selecting this year's conference program. This pool of committed SIGIR volunteers comes from 24 countries and over 180 institutions.

The PC reviewed 341 papers for the full paper track, and accepted 62 with an acceptance rate of 18%. The top countries in terms of accepted papers (taking all author affiliations of each paper equally into account) were the U.S.A. (34%), and China (23%) with the most successful countries (as measured by how likely authors from that country were to have their papers accepted) were Russia (55% of authors had their paper accepted), Israel (50%), and Germany (45%). With 1236 authors overall, 313 were from the U.S.A and 283 from China; and 289 from the next six most represented countries combined.

As has been customary for many years, SIGIR 2016 employed a two-tier double-blind review process. At least three reviewers reviewed each paper, and then the Primary Area Chair of the paper led a discussion, which was used as the basis of the meta-review. The Secondary Area Chair assigned to each paper double-checked the reviews and discussion and, in some cases, provided an additional review. The PC chairs carefully examined the reviews and associated discussion, asking for additional reviews where necessary to provide a fuller discussion or additional expert opinion.

The SIGIR 2016 PC meeting operated as a virtual meeting, held over several days, in order to facilitate the involvement of as many Senior PC members as possible. Prior to the PC meeting the PC chairs proposed a list of "clear accepts" and "clear rejects" where the meta-reviews and reviews clearly indicated a decision. Over the four days of the PC meeting, the chairs indicated which undecided papers were open for discussion, led the discussion on these papers, and made the final decision when discussions moved towards completion; overall nearly half of the submitted papers were reviewed by the chairs or at the meeting. We are grateful for the involvement of the Senior PC members in supporting this PC meeting, especially those very committed members who participated in almost every discussion. The virtual PC meeting was supplemented by a small physical meeting of the Senior PC members who attended the ECIR 2016 conference, which took place during the same week.

The short paper track received 339 submissions and accepted 104 papers for what promises to be a strong short paper track. Thanks are due to Ben Carterette, Carlos Castillo, and Jaana Kekäläinen, the track chairs, for arranging and managing a thorough review process for so many papers – a huge effort for which we are very grateful.

The tutorial track reviewed 20 submissions and accepted 2 full-day tutorials and 10 half-day tutorials. We are grateful to Evangelos Kanoulas and Tie-Yan Liu for leading the selection of a diverse and high quality tutorial program.

The workshops track received 12 submissions and selected 7 workshop proposals. We thank Aristides Gionis and Edie Rasmussen for their efforts in producing a great set of workshops.

The demos track received 35 submissions of which 21 were accepted. Many thanks are due to Craig Macdonald for chairing this track and providing us with an array of interesting demos.

Brian D. Davison and Kira Radinsky organised the Doctoral Consortium, a vitally important part of the SIGIR program. Thanks to their efforts, the event received 23 submissions from doctoral students and accepted 15 of these for presentation and discussion at the consortium.

This year's industry track is the SIGIR Symposium on IR in Practice (SIRIP 2016) co-chaired by Jussi Karlgren and Gilad Mishne. Their efforts in organizing SIRIP and producing an interesting set of speakers from diverse backgrounds are gratefully acknowledged.

Finally, special thanks to Norbert Fuhr for chairing the panel to select the Best Paper and Best Student Paper.

We hope you find this program stimulating and thought provoking, and that the conference provides you with an opportunity to share ideas with other researchers, practitioners and students from institutions all around the world.

Javed Aslam
SIGIR 2016 PC Co-Chair
Northeastern University

Justin Zobel
SIGIR 2016 PC Co-Chair
University of Melbourne

Ian Ruthven
SIGIR 2016 PC Co-Chair
University of Strathclyde

Table of Contents

Session: Learning-to-rank

Session Chair: Mattew Lease *(University of Texas at Austin)*

Session: Music and Math

Session Chair: Jaap Kamps *(University of Amsterdam)*

Session: Microblog

Session Chair: Mark D. Smucker *(University of Waterloo)*

Session: Web Search

Session Chair: David Hawking *(Microsoft Research)*

Session: Question Answering
Session Chair: Hideo Joho *(University of Tsukuba)*

Session: Learning
Session Chair: Emine Yilmaz *(University College London)*

Session: Efficiency I
Session Chair: Alistair Moffat *(University of Melbourne)*

Session: Recommendation Systems I
Session Chair: Oren Kurland *(Technion)*

Session: User Needs
Session Chair: Diane Kelly *(University of North Carolina at Chapel Hill)*

Session: Privacy, Advertising, and Products

Session Chair: Grace Hui Yang *(Georgetown University)*

Session: Novelty and Diversity

Session Chair: Charlie L.A. Clarke *(University of Waterloo)*

Session: Entities and Knowledge Graphs

Session Chair: Jamie Callan *(Carnegie Mellon University)*

Session: SIRIP I: Big companies, big data

Session Chair: Gilad Mishne *(Color Genomics)*

Session: Evaluation II

Session Chair: Tetsuya Sakai *(Waseda University)*

Session: Events

Session Chair: Fernando Diaz *(Microsoft Research)*

Session: SIRIP II: Small companies, big ideas

Session Chair: Gilad Mishne *(Color Genomics)*

Session: Recommendation Systems II

Session Chair: Josiane Mothe *(Institut de Recherche en Informatique de Toulouse)*

Session: Image and Multimodal Search

Session Chair: Gabriella Pasi *(Universitá degli Studi di Milano Bicocca)*

Session: SIRIP III: Modeling and Evaluation

Session Chair: Jussi Karlgren *(Gavagai & KTH)*

Session: Behavior Models and Applications

Session Chair: David Elsweiler *(University of Regensburg)*

Session: Efficiency II

Session Chair: Alistair Moffat *(University of Melbourne)*

Volumn 2

Session: Short Collection Papers

Session: Short Research Papers

Demonstrations

Session Chair: Craig Macdonald *(University of Glasgow)*

Doctoral Consortium

Tutorials

Workshops

SIGIR 2016 Conference Organization

General Chairs: Raffaele Perego *(ISTI-CNR, Italy)*
Fabrizio Sebastiani *(Qatar Computing Research Institute, HBKU, Qatar)*

Program Chairs: Javed Aslam *(Northeastern University, US)*
Ian Ruthven *(University of Strathclyde, UK)*
Justin Zobel *(University of Melbourne, Australia)*

Short Papers Chairs: Ben Carterette *(University of Delaware, US)*
Carlos Castillo *(Eurecat Technology Centre of Catalonia, Spain)*
Jaana Kekalainen *(University of Tampere, Finland)*

Tutorials Chairs: Evangelos Kanoulas *(University of Amsterdam, Netherlands)*
Tie-Yan Liu *(Microsoft Research, China)*

Workshops Chairs: Aristides Gionis *(Aalto University, Finland)*
Edie Rasmussen *(University of British Columbia, Canada)*

Demo Chair: Craig Macdonald *(University of Glasgow, UK)*

Industry Track Chairs: Jussi Karlgren *(Gavagai & KTH, Sweden)*
Gilad Mishne *(Color Genomics, US)*

Doctoral Consortium Chairs: Brian Davison *(Lehigh University, US)*
Kira Radinsky *(SalesPredict, Israel)*

Awards Chair: Norbert Fuhr *(University of Duisburg-Essen, Germany)*

Local Arrangements Chairs: Andrea Esuli *(ISTI-CNR, Italy)*
Chiara Renso *(ISTI-CNR, Italy)*

Sponsorships Chairs: Fabrizio Falchi *(ISTI-CNR, Italy)*
Jimmy Huang *(York University, Canada)*

Proceedings Chair: Claudio Lucchese *(ISTI-CNR, Italy)*

Publicity Chair: Nicola Tonellotto *(ISTI-CNR, Italy)*

Treasurer: Giulio Galesi *(ISTI-CNR, Italy)*

Volunteer Coordinators: Alejandro Moreo Fernández *(ISTI-CNR, Italy)*
Franco Maria Nardini *(ISTI-CNR, Italy)*

Webmaster: Franco Maria Nardini *(ISTI-CNR, Italy)*

Senior Program Committee:

Eugene Agichtein *(Emory University, USA)*
James Allan *(University of Massachusetts Amherst, USA)*
Leif Azzopardi *(University of Glasgow, UK)*
Krisztian Balog *(University of Stavanger, Norway)*
Peter Bruza *(Queensland University of Technology, Australia)*
Jamie Callan *(Carnegie Mellon University, USA)*
David Carmel *(Yahoo Research, Israel)*
Yi Chang *(Yahoo Research, USA)*
Charles L.A. Clarke *(University of Waterloo, Canada)*
Kevyn Collins-Thompson *(University of Michigan, USA)*
Nick Craswell *(Microsoft, USA)*
Fabio Crestani *(Università della Svizzera Italiana, Switzerland)*
Bruce Croft *(University of Massachusetts Amherst, USA)*
Ronan Cummins *(University of Cambridge, UK)*
Maarten de Rijke *(University of Amsterdam, The Netherlands)*
Arjen P. de Vries *(Radboud University, The Netherlands)*
Fernando Diaz *(Microsoft Research, USA)*
David Elsweiler *(University of Regensburg, Germany)*
Hui Fang *(University of Delaware, USA)*
Evgeniy Gabrilovich *(Google, USA)*
Jianfeng Gao *(Microsoft Research, USA)*
Shlomo Geva *(Queensland University of Technology, Australia)*
Marcos Goncalves *(UFMG, Brazil)*
Julio Gonzalo *(UNED, Spain)*
Claudia Hauff *(TU Delft, The Netherlands)*
Djoerd Hiemstra *(University of Twente, The Netherlands)*
Xian-Sheng Hua *(Alibaba Group, China)*
Jimmy Huang *(York University, Canada)*
Hideo Joho *(University of Tsukuba, Japan)*
Gareth Jones *(Dublin City University, Ireland)*
Jaap Kamps *(University of Amsterdam, The Netherlands)*
Diane Kelly *(University of North Carolina at Chapel Hill, USA)*
Wessel Kraaij *(Leiden University, The Netherlands)*
Oren Kurland *(Technion, Israel)*
Wai Lam *(Chinese University of Hong Kong, China)*
Matthew Lease *(University of Texas at Austin, USA)*
Hang Li *(Huawei Technologies, China)*
Stephane Marchand-Maillet *(University of Geneva, Switzerland)*
Massimo Melucci *(University of Padua, Italy)*
Donald Metzler *(Google, USA)*
Stefano Mizzaro *(University of Udine, Italy)*
Josiane Mothe *(Institut de Recherche en Informatique de Toulouse, France)*
Isabelle Moulinier *(Thomson Reuters, USA)*
Edleno S. Moura *(Institute of Computing - UFAM, Brazil)*
Vanessa Murdock *(Microsoft Research, USA)*

Program Committee (continued):

Marc Bron *(Yahoo, UK)*
George Buchanan *(City University London, UK)*
Iván Cantador *(Universidad Autónoma de Madrid, Spain)*
Rob Capra *(University of North Carolina at Chapel Hill, USA)*
Mark Carman *(Monash University, Australia)*
Claudio Carpineto *(Fondazione Ugo Bordoni, Italy)*
Marc-Allen Cartright *(Google, USA)*
James Caverlee *(Texas A&M University, USA)*
Soumen Chakrabarti *(IIT Bombay, Italy)*
Kevin C. Chang *(University of Illinois at Urbana-Champaign, USA)*
Ruey-Cheng Chen *(RMIT University, Australia)*
Yi Chen *(NJIT, USA)*
Ed H Chi *(Google, USA)*
Francisco Claude *(Universidad Diego Portales, Chile)*
Stéphane Clinchant *(Xerox Research Center Europe, France)*
Jack G. Conrad *(Thomson Reuters, USA)*
Gordon V. Cormack *(University of Waterloo, Canada)*
J. Shane Culpepper *(RMIT University, Australia)*
Tonya Custis *(Thomson Reuters, USA)*
Altigran S. da Silva *(Universidade Federal do Amazonas, Brazil)*
Jeff Dalton *(Google, USA)*
Van Dang *(Google, USA)*
Gianluca Demartini *(University of Sheffield, UK)*
Emanuele Di Buccio *(University of Padua, Italy)*
Giorgio Maria Di Nunzio *(University of Padua, Italy)*
Laura Dietz *(University of Mannheim, Germany)*
Shuai Ding *(Google, USA)*
Debora Donato *(StumbleUpon, USA)*
Dietmar H. Dorr *(Google, USA)*
Zhicheng Dou *(Renmin University of China, China)*
Doug Downey *(Northwestern University, USA)*
Andy Edmonds *(Adobe, USA)*
Miles Efron *(University of Illinois, USA)*
Carsten Eickhoff *(ETH Zurich, Switzerland)*
Yuan Fang *(Institute for Infocomm Research, Singapore)*
Yi Fang *(Santa Clara University, USA)*
Nicola Ferro *(University of Padua, Italy)*
Marcus C. Fontoura *(Microsoft, USA)*
Dayne Freitag *(SRI International, USA)*
Ingo Frommholz *(University of Bedfordshire, UK)*
Patrick Gallinari *(Université Pierre et Marie Curie, France)*
Debasis Ganguly *(Dublin City University, Ireland)*
Bin Gao *(Microsoft Research, China)*
Eric Gaussier *(Université Joseph Fourier, France)*
Lorraine Goeuriot *(Université Grenoble Alpes, France)*

Program Committee (continued):

Nazli Goharian *(Georgetown University, USA)*
Peter B. Golbus *(Wayfair, USA)*
Brigitte Grau *(LIMSI-CNRS and ENSIIE, France)*
Vincent Guigue *(Université Pierre et Marie Curie, France)*
Mustafa Ghulam *(University of Bedfordshire, UK)*
Jiafeng Guo *(Institute of Computing Technology, Chinese Academy of Sciences, China)*
Maxim Gurevich *(Bento Labs, USA)*
Cathal Gurrin *(Dublin City University, Ireland)*
Ido Guy *(Yahoo Research, Israel)*
Martin Halvey *(University of Strathclyde, UK)*
Allan Hanbury *(TU Wien, Austria)*
Sanda M. Harabagiu *(University of Texas at Dallas, USA)*
Morgan Harvey *(Northumbria University, UK)*
Ahmed Hassan *(Microsoft Research, USA)*
David Hawking *(Microsoft Research, Australia)*
Ben He *(University of Chinese Academy of Sciences, China)*
Daqing He *(University of Pittsburgh, USA)*
Jiyin He *(CWI, The Netherlands)*
Yunlong He *(Yahoo Research, USA)*
Liangjie Hong *(Yahoo Research, USA)*
Winston H. Hsu *(National Taiwan University, Taiwan)*
Jeff Huang *(Brown University, USA)*
Xuanjing Huang *(Fudan University, China)*
Samuel Huston *(Google, USA)*
Radu-Tudor Ionescu *(University of Bucharest, Romania)*
Adam Jatowt *(Kyoto University, Japan)*
Jiepu Jiang *(University of Massachusetts Amherst, USA)*
Jing Jiang *(Singapore Management University, Singapore)*
Joemon M. Jose *(University of Glasgow, UK)*
Min-Yen Kan *(National University of Singapore, Singapore)*
Mohan Kankanhalli *(National University of Singapore, Singapore)*
Evangelos Kanoulas *(University of Amsterdam, The Netherlands)*
Makoto Kato *(Kyoto University, Japan)*
Enver Kayaaslan *(Turgut Ozal University, Turkey)*
Heikki Keskustalo *(University of Tampere, Finland)*
Julia Kiseleva *(Eindhoven University of Technology, The Netherlands)*
Weize Kong *(University of Massachusetts Amherst, USA)*
Alexander Kotov *(Wayne State University, USA)*
Udo Kruschwitz *(University of Essex, UK)*
Anagha Kulkarni *(San Francisco State University, USA)*
Susana Ladra *(University of A Coruña, Spain)*
Dmitry Lagun *(Google, USA)*
Will Lamond *(Wayfair, USA)*
Sylvain Lamprier *(LIP6 - UPMC, France)*

Program Committee (continued):

Léa Laporte *(LIRIS - INSA Lyon, France)*
Ray R Larson *(University of California, USA)*
Martha Larson *(Delft University of Technology, The Netherlands)*
Dawn Lawrie *(Loyola University Maryland, USA)*
Chia-Jung Lee *(Microsoft Research, USA)*
Jochen L. Leidner *(Thomson Reuters, UK)*
Daniel Lemire *(Université du Québec, Canada)*
Liangda Li *(Yahoo Research, USA)*
Min Li *(Alibaba, China)*
Kewen Liao *(University of Melbourne, Australia)*
Christina Lioma *(University of Copenhagen, Denmark)*
Jialu Liu *(University of Illinois at Urbana-Champaign, USA)*
Tie-Yan Liu *(Microsoft Research, China)*
Yiqun Liu *(Tsinghua University, China)*
Claudio Lucchese *(ISTI-CNR, Italy)*
Robert WP Luk *(The Hong Kong Polytechnic University, China)*
Mihai Lupu *(TU Wien, Austria)*
Yuanhua Lv *(Microsoft Research, USA)*
Hao Ma *(Microsoft Research, USA)*
Andrew MacFarlane *(City University London, UK)*
Prasenjit Majumder *(DAIICT, India)*
Amin Mantrach *(Yahoo Research, USA)*
Ilya Markov *(University of Amsterdam, The Netherlands)*
Yosi Mass *(IBM Research Lab, Israel)*
Julian McAuley *(University of California San Diego, USA)*
Richard McCreadie *(University of Glasgow, UK)*
Gayle McElvain *(Thomson Reuters, USA)*
Kevin McGuinness *(Dublin City University, Ireland)*
Paul McNamee *(Johns Hopkins University, USA)*
Qiaozhu Mei *(University of Michigan, USA)*
Edgar Meij *(Yahoo Research, Spain)*
Mandar Mitra *(Indian Statistical Institute, India)*
Alessandro Moschitti *(Qatar Computing Research Institute, HBKU, Qatar)*
Yashar Moshfeghi *(University of Glasgow, UK)*
Franco Maria Nardini *(ISTI-CNR, Italy)*
Roberto Navigli *(Sapienza University of Rome, Italy)*
Michael L. Nelson *(Old Dominion University, USA)*
Chong-Wah Ngo *(City University of Hong Kong, China)*
Dong Nguyen *(University of Twente, The Netherlands)*
Alexandros Ntoulas *(Samsung Research America, USA)*
Pan Pan *(Alibaba Group, China)*
Laurence A.F. Park *(Western Sydney University, Australia)*
Gabriella Pasi *(Università degli Studi di Milano Bicocca, Italy)*
Virgil Pavlu *(Northeastern University, USA)*
Jan Pedersen *(Microsoft Research, USA)*

Program Committee (continued):

Vassilis Plachouras *(Thomson Reuters, UK)*
Barbara Poblete *(University of Chile, Chile)*
Martin Potthast *(Bauhaus-Universität, Germany)*
Kunal Punera *(RelateIQ, USA)*
Filip Radlinski *(Microsoft Research, UK)*
Fiana Raiber *(Technion, Israel)*
Karthik Raman *(Google, USA)*
Edie Rasmussen *(University of British Columbia, Canada)*
Yongli Ren *(RMIT University, Australia)*
Haggai Roitman *(IBM Research, Israel)*
Dmitri Roussinov *(University of Strathclyde, UK)*
Eric SanJuan *(University of Avignon, France)*
Rodrygo Santos *(Universidade Federal de Minas Gerais, Brazil)*
Jacques Savoy *(University of Neuchatel, Switzerland)*
Ralf Schenkel *(University of Passau, Germany)*
Anne Schuth *(Blendle, The Netherlands)*
Pavel Serdyukov *(Yandex, Russia)*
Chirag Shah *(Rutgers University, USA)*
Anna Shtok *(Technion IIT, Israel)*
Gianmaria Silvello *(University of Padua, Italy)*
Laurianne Sitbon *(Queensland University of Technology, Australia)*
Catherine L. Smith *(Kent State University, USA)*
Aya Soffer *(IBM Research, Israel)*
Alessandro Sordoni *(Université de Montréal, Canada)*
Laure Soulier *(Université Pierre et Marie Curie, France)*
Alessandro Sperduti *(University of Padua, Italy)*
Mingxuan Sun *(Louisiana State University, USA)*
Idan Szpektor *(Yahoo Research, Israel)*
S.M.M. Tahaghoghi *(Microsoft Research, USA)*
Jiliang Tang *(Yahoo Research, USA)*
Gabriele Tolomei *(Yahoo Research, UK)*
Anastasios Tombros *(Queen Mary University of London, UK)*
Dolf Trieschnigg *(Mydatafactory, The Netherlands)*
Manos Tsagkias *(904Labs, The Netherlands)*
Theodora Tsikrika *(Centre for Research and Technology Hellas, Greece)*
Emre Velipasaoglu *(OpsClarity, USA)*
Adriano Veloso *(Universidade Federal de Minas Gerais, Brazil)*
Rossano Venturini *(University of Pisa, Italy)*
Bin Wang *(Institute of Information Engineering, Chinese Academy of Sciences, China)*
Hongning Wang *(University of Virginia, USA)*
Jian Wang *(LinkedIn, USA)*
Jun Wang *(University College London, UK)*
Lidan Wang *(IBM Research, USA)*
Meng Wang *(Hefei University of Technology, China)*

Program Committee (continued):

Quan Wang *(Institute of Information Engineering, Chinese Academy of Sciences, China)*
Shuaiqiang Wang *(University of Jyväskylä, Finland)*
Ingmar Weber *(Qatar Computing Research Institute, HBKU, Qatar)*
Wouter Weerkamp *(904Labs, The Netherlands)*
Gerhard Weikum *(Max Planck Institute for Informatics, Germany)*
Ji-Rong Wen *(Renmin University of China, China)*
Robert West *(Stanford University, USA)*
Wei Wu *(Microsoft Research, China)*
Xuansong Xie *(Taobao, China)*
Chenyan Xiong *(Carnegie Mellon University, USA)*
Jun Xu *(Institute of Computing Technology, Chinese Academy of Sciences, China)*
Tan Xu *(AT&T Labs, USA)*
Xiaobing Xue *(Twitter, USA)*
Makoto Yamada *(Kyoto University, Japan)*
Zheng Ye *(Maluuba Research, Canada)*
Reyyan Yeniterzi *(Ozyegin University, Turkey)*
Xing Yi *(Yahoo Research, USA)*
Dawei Yin *(Yahoo Research, USA)*
Elad Yom-Tov *(Microsoft Research, Israel)*
Minoru Yoshida *(University of Tokushima, Japan)*
Dell Zhang *(Birkbeck, University of London, UK)*
Lanbo Zhang *(Twitter, USA)*
Min Zhang *(Tsinghua University, China)*
Qi Zhang *(Fudan University, China)*
Yi Zhang *(University of California Santa Cruz, USA)*
Le Zhao *(Houzz, USA)*
Xiaowei Zhao *(Alibaba Group, China)*
Ke Zhou *(Yahoo Research, UK)*
Mianwei Zhou *(Yahoo Research, USA)*
Nivio Ziviani *(Universidade Federal de Minas Gerais, Brazil)*
Guido Zuccon *(Queensland University of Technology, Australia)*

Program Committee additional reviewers:

Saeid Balaneshin-kordan *(Wayne State University, USA)*
Gianni Barlacchi *(University of Trento, Italy)*
Daniele Bonadiman *(University of Trento, Italy)*
Dongho Choi *(Rutgers University, USA)*
Yagmur Gizem Cinar *(Université Grenoble Alpes, France)*
Arman Cohan *(Georgetown University, USA)*
Eva D'hondt *(LIMSI-CNRS, France)*
Nan Du *(Georgia Institute of Technology, USA)*
Matthew Ekstrand-Abueg *(Northeastern University, USA)*
Mustafa Ghulam *(University of Bedfordshire, UK)*
Simon Gog *(Karlsruhe Institute of Technology, Germany)*

Program Committee additional reviewers (continued):

Parantapa Goswami *(Université Grenoble Alpes, France)*
David Graus *(University of Amsterdam, Netherlands)*
Artem Grotov *(University of Amsterdam, Netherlands)*
Longkun Guo *(Fuzhou University, China)*
Xiangnan He *(National University of Singapore, Singapore)*
Damien Jose *(Microsoft Research, USA)*
Denis Kotkov *(University of Jyväskylä, Finland)*
Will Lamond *(Wayfair, USA)*
Long Le *(Rutgers University, USA)*
Cheng Li *(Northeastern University, USA)*
Babak Loni *(Delft University of Technology, Netherlands)*
Xiaolu Lu *(RMIT University, Australia)*
Rui Luo *(University College London, UK)*
Craig Macdonald *(University of Glasgow, UK)*
Joel Mackenzie *(RMIT University, Australia)*
Maria Maistro *(University of Padua, Italy)*
Kleanthis Malialis *(University College London, UK)*
Stefania Marrara *(Università degli Studi di Milano Bicocca, Italy)*
Ziad Matni *(Rutgers University, USA)*
Corren McCoy *(Old Dominion University, USA)*
Avihai Mejer *(Yahoo Research, Israel)*
Pavel Metrikov *(Northeastern University, USA)*
Jun Miao *(York University, Canada)*
Matthew Mitsui *(Rutgers University, USA)*
Jose G. Moreno *(LIMSI-CNRS, France)*
Massimo Nicosia *(University of Trento, Italy)*
Fedor Nikolaev *(Wayne State University, USA)*
Joao Palotti *(Technical University of Vienna, Austria)*
Gaurav Pandey (*University of Jyväskylä, Finland)*
Denis Parra *(Pontificia Universidad Católica de Chile, Chile)*
Casper Petersen *(University of Copenhagen, Denmark)*
Giulio Ermanno Pibiri *(University of Pisa, Italy)*
Yuval Pinter *(Yahoo Research, Israel)*
Yongrui (Louie) Qin *(Univeristy of Huddersfield, UK)*
Adam Roegiest *(University of Waterloo, Canada)*
Yao Shen *(Nanjing University of Aeronautics and Astronautics, China)*
Martijn Spitters *(Blendle, Netherlands)*
Jian-Tao Sun *(Microsoft Research, USA)*
Xing Tan *(York University, Canada)*
Kateryna Timoshenko *(University of Trento, Italy)*
Gilad Tsur *(Yahoo Research, Israel)*
Antonio Uva *(University of Trento, Italy)*
Oscar Valdivia-Verdugo *(Cloner SpA, Chile)*
Marco Viviani *(Università degli Studi di Milano Bicocca, Italy)*
Sheng Wang *(RMIT University, Australia)*

Program Committee additional reviewers (continued):

Yao Wu *(Simon Fraser University, Canada)*
Yixin Wu *(University College London, UK)*
Yu Wu *(Beihang University, China)*
Chen Xing *(Nankai University, China)*
Lina Yao *(University of New South Wales, Australia)*
Aston Zhang *(University of Illinois at Urbana-Champaign, USA)*
Weinan Zhang *(University College London, UK)*
Yongfeng Zhang (*University of California Santa Cruz, USA)*
Jessie Zhao *(York University, Canada)*
Qi Zhao *(University of California Santa Cruz, USA)*
Masrour Zoghi *(University of Amsterdam, Netherlands)*

Short Papers Committee:

Jatowt Adam *(Kyoto University, Japan)*
Mikhail Ageev *(Moscow State University, Russia)*
Dyaa Albakour *(Signal Media, UK)*
Omar Alonso *(Microsoft Research, USA)*
Ismail S. Altingovde *(Middle East Technical University, Turkey)*
Jisun An *(Qatar Computing Research Institute, HBKU, Qatar)*
Paavo Arvola *(University of Tampere, Finland)*
KhudaBukhsh Ashiqur *(Carnegie Mellon University, USA)*
Mossaab Bagdouri *(University of Maryland, USA)*
Ashraf Bah Rabiou *(University of Delaware, USA)*
Rafael E. Banchs *(Institute for Infocomm Research, Singapore)*
Zhifeng Bao *(RMIT University, Australia)*
Bodo Billerbeck *(Microsoft Research, Australia)*
Danushka Bollegala *(University of Liverpool, UK)*
Gloria Bordogna *(Consiglio Nazionale delle Ricerche, Italy)*
Arbi Bouchoucha *(Yellow Pages Group, Canada)*
Mohand Boughanem *(IRIT, University Paul Sabatier, France)*
Leonid Boytsov *(Carnegie Mellon University, USA)*
Davide Buscaldi *(LIPN, Université Paris 13, France)*
Fidel Cacheda *(University of A Coruña, Spain)*
Rui Cai *(Microsoft Research, China)*
Fazli Can *(Bilkent University, Turkey*)
Cornelia Caragea *(University of North Texas, USA)*
Mark Carman *(Monash University, Australia)*
Marc-Allen Cartright *(Google Inc., USA)*
Praveen Chandar *(IBM Research Cambridge, USA)*
Francine Chen *(FX Palo Alto Laboratory, USA)*
Hsin-Hsi Chen *(National Taiwan University, Taiwan)*
Stefano Cresci *(IIT-CNR, Italy)*
Bin Cui *(Peking University, China)*
Sally Jo Cunningham *(University of Waikato, New Zealand)*
Emanuele Di Buccio *(University of Padua, Italy)*
Giorgio Maria Di Nunzio *(University of Padua, Italy)*

Short Papers Committee (continued):

Laura Dietz *(University of Mannheim, Germany)*
Bekir Taner Dincer *(Mugla University, Turkey)*
Carsten Eickhoff *(ETH Zurich, Switzerland)*
Tamer Elsayed *(Qatar University, Qatar)*
Yi Fang *(Santa Clara University, USA)*
Katayoun Farrahi *(Goldsmiths, Uni. of London, UK)*
Hakan Ferhatosmanoglu *(Bilkent University, Turkey)*
Nicola Ferro *(University of Padua, Italy)*
Luanne Freund *(University of British Columbia, Canada)*
Ingo Frommholz *(University of Bedfordshire, UK)*
Patrick Gallinari *(Université Pierre et Marie Curie, France)*
Debasis Ganguly *(Dublin City University, Ireland)*
Bin Gao *(Microsoft Research, China)*
Wei Gao *(Qatar Computing Research Institute, HBKU, Qatar)*
Susan Gauch *(University of Arkansas, USA)*
Tatiana Gossen *(Otto-von-Guericke University Magdeburg, Germany)*
Brigitte Grau *(LIMSI-CNRS and ENSIIE, France)*
David Graus *(University of Amsterdam, The Netherlands)*
Artem Grotov *(University of Amsterdam, The Netherlands)*
Morgan Harvey *(Northumbria University, UK)*
Ben He *(University of Chinese Academy of Sciences, China)*
Xiangnan He *(National University of Singapore, Singapore)*
Frank Hopfgartner *(University of Glasgow, UK)*
Jiepu Jiang *(University of Massachusetts Amherst, USA)*
Joemon Jose *(University of Glasgow, UK)*
Marko Junkkari *(University of Tampere, Finland)*
Nattiya Kanhabua *(Aalborg University, Denmark)*
Evangelos Kanoulas *(University of Amsterdam, The Netherlands)*
Bahar Karaoglan *(Ege University, Turkey)*
Liadh Kelly *(Trinity College Dublin, Ireland)*
Heikki Keskustalo *(University of Tampere, Finland)*
Yubin Kim *(Carnegie Mellon University, USA)*
Julia Kiseleva *(Technical University of Eindhoven, The Netherlands)*
Alexander Kotov *(Wayne State University, USA)*
Kriste Krstovski *(University of Massachusetts Amherst, USA)*
Udo Kruschwitz *(University of Essex, UK)*
Sanna Kumpulainen *(Tampere University of Technology, Finland)*
Hui Li *(University of Maryland, College Park, USA)*
Chenliang Li *(Wuhan University, China)*
Shangsong Liang *(University College London, UK)*
Christina Lioma *(University of Copenhagen, Denmark)*
Jiyun Luo *(Georgetown University, USA)*
Andrew MacFarlane *(City University London, UK)*
Takuya Maekawa *(Osaka University, Japan)*
Walid Magdy *(Qatar Computing Research Institute, HBKU, Qatar)*

Short Papers Committee (continued):

Maria Maistro *(University of Padua, Italy)*
Ilya Markov *(University of Amsterdam, The Netherlands)*
Mónica Marrero *(National Supercomputing Center, Spain)*
Paul McNamee *(Johns Hopkins University, USA)*
Edgar Meij *(Yahoo Rsearch, Spain)*
Aditya Mogadala *(Karlsruhe Institute of Technology, Germany)*
Alessandro Moschitti *(Qatar Computing Research Institute, HBKU, Qatar)*
Preslav Nakov *(Qatar Computing Research Institute, HBKU, Qatar)*
Michael L. Nelson *(Old Dominion University, USA)*
Dong Nguyen *(Twente University, The Netherlands)*
Daan Odijk *(University of Amsterdam, The Netherlands)*
Neil O'Hare *(Yahoo Research, Spain)*
Alexandra Olteanu *(EPFL, Switzerland)*
Jiaul Paik *(University of Maryland, College Park, USA)*
Dipasree Pal *(Indian Statistical Institute, Kolkata, India)*
Filipa Peleja *(Universidade Nova de Lisboa, Portugal)*
Casper Petersen *(University of Copenhagen, Denmark)*
Karen Pinel-Sauvagnat *(IRIT, France)*
Laura Po *(University of Modena and Reggio Emilia, Italy)*
Filip Radlinski *(Microsoft Research, UK)*
Zhaochun Ren *(University of Amsterdam, The Netherlands)*
Haggai Roitman *(IBM Research Lab, Haifa, Israel)*
Karankumar Sabhnani *(University of Delaware, USA)*
Maya Sappelli *(TNO, The Netherlands)*
Anne Schuth *(Blendle, The Netherlands)*
Jangwon Seo *(Google, USA)*
Jialie Shen *(Singapore Management University, Singapore)*
Michael Shuhmacher *(University of Mannheim, Germany)*
Gianmaria Silvello *(University of Padua, Italy)*
Yang Song *(Microsoft Research, USA)*
Ruihua Song *(Microsoft Research, China)*
Laure Soulier *(Université Pierre et Marie Curie, France)*
Damiano Spina *(RMIT University, Australia)*
Aixin Sun *(Nanyang Technological University, Singapore)*
S.M.M. Tahaghoghi *(Microsoft Research, USA)*
Carla Teixeira Lopes *(University of Porto, Portugal)*
James A. Thom *(RMIT University, Australia)*
Bart Thomee *(Yahoo Research, USA)*
Anastasios Tombros *(Queen Mary University of London, UK)*
Ricardo Torres *(University of Campinas, Brazil)*
Christophe Van Gysel *(University of Amsterdam, The Netherlands)*
Olga Vechtomova *(University of Waterloo, Canada)*
Suzan Verberne *(Radboud University, The Netherlands)*
Stephen Wan *(CSIRO, Australia)*
Changhu Wang *(Microsoft Research, China)*

Short Papers Committee (continued):

Hongning Wang *(University of Virginia, USA)*
Lidan Wang *(University of Illinois, USA)*
Wouter Weerkamp *(904Labs, The Netherlands)*
Xing Wei *(Inmobi Inc., USA)*
Christa Womser-Hacker *(University of Hildesheim, Germany)*
Tan Xu *(AT&T, USA)*
Zheng Ye *(Maluuba, Waterloo, Canada)*
Masaharu Yoshioka *(Hokkaido University, Japan)*
Xiaojun (Jenny) Yuan *(Univ. at Albany, The State Univ. of New York, USA)*
Mustafa Zengin *(University of Delaware, USA)*
Dong Zhou *(Hunan University of Science and Technology, China)*
Ke Zhou *(Yahoo Research, UK)*
Guido Zuccon *(Queensland University of Technology, Australia)*

Short Papers Committee additional reviewers:

Eva D'hondt *(LIMSI-CNRS, France)*
Maram Hasanain *(Qatar University, Qatar)*
K. Dilek Onal *(Middle East Technical University, Turkey)*
Rifat Ozcan *(Turgut Ozal University, Turkey)*
Jose Moreno *(LIMSI-CNRS, France)*

Demonstrations Committee:

Omar Alonso *(Microsoft Research, USA)*
Krisztian Balog *(University of Stavanger, Norway)*
Laura Dietz *(University of Mannheim, Germany)*
Dina Demner-Fushman *(NLM/NIH, USA)*
Henry Field *(Endicott College, USA)*
John Foley *(University of Massachusetts Amherst, USA)*
Ana Freire *(Universitat Pompeu Fabra, Spain)*
Grant Ingersoll *(Lucidworks, USA)*
Udo Kruschwitz *(University of Essex, UK)*
Sarvnaz Karimi *(CSIRO, Australia)*
Jochen Leidner *(Thomson Reuters, UK)*
Teerapong Leelanupab *(King Mongkuts Institute of Tech. Ladkrabang, Thailand)*
Richard McCreadie *(University of Glasgow, UK)*
Stefano Mizzaro *(University of Udine, Italy)*
Sean Moran *(University of Glasgow, UK)*
Iadh Ounis *(University of Glasgow, UK)*
Vassilis Plachouras *(Thomson Reuters, UK)*
Javier Parapar *(University of A Coruña, Spain)*
Jeremy Pickens *(Catalyst, USA)*
Rodrygo Santos *(Universidade Federal de Minas Gerais, Brazil)*
Jialie Shen *(Singapore Management University, Singapore)*
Luchen Tan *(University of Waterloo, Canada)*
Bin Wang *(Chinese Academy of Sciences, China)*
Tan Xu *(AT&T Research, USA)*
Guido Zuccon *(Queensland University of Technology, Australia)*

Tutorials Committee: Ben Carterette *(University of Delaware, US)*
Hsin-Hsi Chen *(National Taiwan University, Taiwan)*
Djoerd Hiemstra *(University of Twente, The Netherlands)*
Katja Hofmann (*Microsoft Research, USA*)
Gareth Jones *(Dublin City University, Ireland)*
Jaap Kamps (*University of Amsterdam, The Netherlands)*
Gary Marchionini *(University of North Carolina at Chapel Hill, USA)*
Edgar Meij *(Yahoo Research, Spain)*
Vanessa Murdock *(Microsoft Research, USA)*
Douglas Oard (*University of Maryland, USA)*
Tao Qin *(Microsoft Research, China)*
Mark Sanderson *(RMIT University, Australia)*
Pavel Serdyukov *(Yandex, Russia)*
Mark D. Smucker *(University of Waterloo, Canada)*
Ian Soboroff (*NIST, USA*)
Emine Yilmaz *(University College London, UK)*
Min Zhang *(Tsinghua University, China)*

SIGIR 2016 Sponsors & Supporters

Sponsors:

SIGIR Special Interest Group on Information Retrieval

acm Association for Computing Machinery

Platinum Supporters:

Baidu 百度

Silver Supporters:

appen

Bloomberg

Booking.com

ebay

facebook

Silver Supporters:

Google™

HUAWEI

IBM®

Microsoft

YAHOO!

Bronze Supporters:

Yandex

Institutional Supporters:

Consiglio Nazionale
delle Ricerche

معهد قطر لبحوث الحوسبة
Qatar Computing Research Institute
عضو في مؤسسة قطر
Member of Qatar Foundation

Publisher Supporters:

M&C
MORGAN & CLAYPOOL
PUBLISHERS

now
the essence of knowledge

Springer

A Complete & Comprehensive Movie Review Dataset (CCMR)

Xuezhi Cao , Weiyue Huang, Yong Yu
Apex Data and Knowledge Management Lab
Shanghai Jiao Tong University
cxz,hwy,yyu@apex.sjtu.edu.cn

ABSTRACT

Online review sites are widely used for various domains including movies and restaurants. These sites now have strong influences towards users during purchasing processes. There exist plenty of research works for review sites on various aspects, including item recommendation, user behavior analysis, etc. However, due to the lack of complete and comprehensive dataset, there are still problems that remain to be solved. Therefore, in this paper we assemble and publish such dataset (CCMR) for the community. CCMR outruns existing datasets in terms of completeness, comprehensiveness and scale. Besides describing the dataset and its collecting methodology, we also propose several potential research topics that are made possible by having this dataset. Such topics include: (i) a statistical approach to reduce the impacts from fake reviews and (ii) analyzing and modeling the influences of public opinions towards users during rating actions. We further conduct preliminary analysis and experiments for both directions to show that they are promising.

CCS Concepts

•**Information systems** → **Test collections; Spam detection; Personalization;**

Keywords

Test Collection, User Behavior, Review Sites

1. INTRODUCTION

Online review sites are now widely used for various domains. For example we have IMDb and MovieLens for movies, Yelp for restaurants, TripAdvisor for hotels and attractions. When making choices, nowadays lots of people refer to these review sites for guidance. These sites have significant influences towards users during their purchasing processes.

Due to the importance, there are plenty of research works in this direction. Most of existing works focus on rating prediction and user behavior analysis. For rating predictions, the goal is to improve user experiences by implementing corresponding recommender systems [8]. Matrix factorization is the most widely used technique for this task [3]. For user behavior analysis, researches mainly focus on detecting malicious users and bots in review sites (or fake review detection) [7]. Because higher rating in review sites may lead to more purchases, some merchants hire malicious users or bots to give untruthful ratings. These fake reviews highly jeopardize the user experiences and bring review sites into disrepute. There are research works that tackle this by rating pattern analysis [2], linguistic analysis [5] and other techniques.

Despite the satisfying research outcomes, there are still research problems remain to be solved. For example, most existing works on fake review detection focus on identifying each malicious user or fake review instance instead of targeting directly at the final aggregated ratings, which are the most important information the review sites provide for users. Also, there is no work on analyzing the influences of public opinions towards users (users are aware of the aggregated rating for the item before rating it in most sites). For these directions, one major obstacle is the lack of suitable dataset. To model the aggregated ratings, we requires complete rating logs. To analyze the influences of public opinions, we need snapshots of aggregated ratings right before each rating action. However, currently there is no dataset that satisfies these requirements.

Therefore, we assemble and publish a complete and comprehensive dataset CCMR for the community. Here complete indicates complete logs over all users instead of only a subset of users, and comprehensive indicates the availability of side information such as timestamps, item-side information, review texts and snapshots of the aggregated ratings.

In the following sections, we first describe the dataset and its collecting methodology, and then compare it with existing datasets. Further, we propose two potential topics that benefit from CCMR. We also conduct preliminary analysis and experiments according to these topics.

2. CCMR DATASET

The CCMR dataset can be freely accessed online[1]. For privacy concerns, we reorder the user ids as well as the movie ids in CCMR. For review texts, we replace each word with corresponding word id.

CCMR consists of movie rating logs from one of China's largest movie review sites. The data is collected and dumped in May, 2015. All rating logs before the collection time are

[1]http://dataset.apexlab.org/ccmr

SIGIR '16, July 17-21, 2016, Pisa, Italy

DOI: http://dx.doi.org/10.1145/2911451.2914669

Table 1: CCMR Compare with Existing Datasets

	EachMovie	Book-Crossing [10]	MovieLens	Netflix [1]	**CCMR**
# Users	72,916	278,858	240,000	480,000	4,920,695
# Items	1,628	271,379	33,000	18,000	190,129
# Rating Actions	2,811,983	1,149,780	22,000,000	100,000,000	283,775,314
Timestamp	√	×	√	√	√
Item Info	×	√	√(partial)	×	√
Full Log	×	×	×	×	√
Aggregated Stats	×	×	×	×	√

included. In total, it covers 190,129 movies and 4,920,695 active users (with at least one rating action). Among those users and movies, we have 283,775,314 rating actions. On average we have 1,471.92 rating logs per movie and 58.10 per active user. Besides the rating matrix, we also include the corresponding review text, the date of the rating action as well as the snapshot of aggregated statistics for the target movie right before the rating action. For aggregated statistics, -1 is given when no statistic is available due to insufficient rating histories. We list and explain all data columns for rating logs in Table 2. For each movie, we also provide director(s), actors, movie genre (action/romance/etc.), release date and nation.

Table 2: Data Columns in CCMR - Rating Logs

Column	**Description**
user_id	Re-ordered to 0-4,920,694.
movie_id	Re-ordered to 0-190,128.
rating	1-5 scale, and 0 indicates user mark it as watched but no rating is given.
date	Date of the rating action
review_text	Review text of the rating action.
stat_avg	Average rating of the movie right before the rating action.
stat_distrib_1 ... stat_distrib_5	Rating distribution of the movie right before the rating action. (Given in percentage)

We plot the distribution of user's rating counts as well as movie's with log-log plots in Figure 1, from which we can notice the power law or the long tail phenomenon. We can also notice that in log-log plot for user, there is an unusual streak above the main streak, i.e. an unusual large number of users have exactly the same number of rating logs. By detailed analysis, ratings from each of these users are mostly conducted on the same day. So they are highly likely the malicious users or bots.

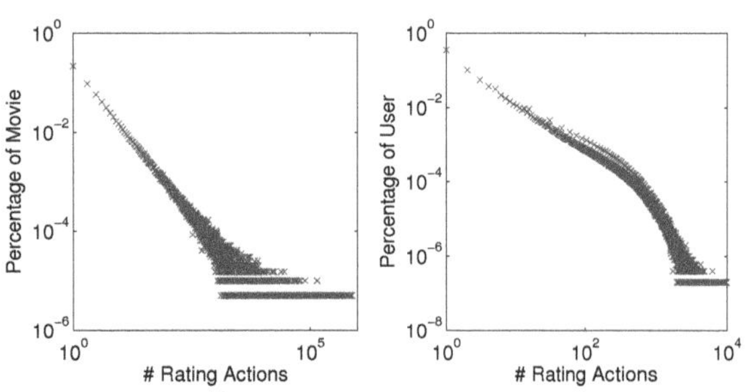

Figure 1: Log-Log Plot for Movie/User Action Frequency

One of the most well known task based on rating logs is rating prediction, which is also the core for recommender systems in item-based sites. Matrix factorization is the most widely accepted and used technique for this task [3]. As this task has been heavily studied, there also exist several well assembled datasets, e.g. Book-Crossing, EachMovie and MovieLens from GroupLens[2] and the Netflix dataset [1]. Comparing to these datasets, CCMR's advantage is its scale, completeness and comprehensiveness. Therefore, CCMR can be employed for wider scenarios and research topics. A detailed comparison is listed in Table 1.

3. FAKE REVIEWS

Because review sites now play important parts during user's purchasing processes, the ratings are critical for the product's revenues. Driven by benefits, some merchants hire malicious users or bots to generate fake reviews to increase the rating of their products or to discredit their competitors. As analyzed previously (Figure 1), malicious users widely exist and have noticeable influences on the overall statistics.

Fake reviews not only have negative impact on user experiences but also bring the review sites disrepute. Therefore, this problem has aroused people's attention and heated discussion. There are works aiming at identifying the fake reviews or malicious users. Jindal et al. focus on unusual review patterns in [2]. Linguistic features in the review text are also considered in [5]. Mukherjee et al. further go beyond single user and target at group spammers [6].

Despite the promising performance of existing works, they only focus on identifying specific user or review instance. On the other hand, users normally do not go through each review instance in detail. Instead, most users only focus on the aggregated ratings. So we can eliminate the fake reviews' influences by directly recovering the unbiased aggregated ratings. Another advantage of this is that spammers can not easily find the rules and evolve accordingly while they can for traditional approaches. Therefore, this would be a great future direction for fake review detection. However, to the best of our knowledge, currently there is no research work following this direction.

One major reason is that currently we have no suitable dataset to conduct this topic. We need the complete rating logs to model the aggregated ratings, while current datasets only provide logs over a subset of users instead of complete logs.

Another problem is the lack of ground truth (the unbiased public opinion towards the item). By analyzing the identified fake reviews (by analysis in Figure 1 and existing techniques), we find that most fake reviews are close to the

[2]http://grouplens.org/datasets/movielens/

movie's release date (few weeks). Specifically, we define f_k to be the ratio of fake reviews posted within k days after the release date ($f_{+\infty}$=1), and n_k accordingly for normal reviews. We plot f_k/n_k in Figure 2 to show that fake reviews significantly shift towards the release date comparing to normal reviews. This finding also matches with intuition because only the ratings in first few weeks are crucial for the movie's box office. Therefore we consider the aggregated rating at a long time (years) after the movie's release date as a good approximation of the unbiased public opinion.

So the task can be formally stated as: given rating logs within k days after the movie's release date, estimate the unbiased public rating (approximated by the aggregated rating at least one year after release date). We model the task as regression problem and employ linear regression for it. For features, we include the average ratings on day 1, day 2 up to day k, and also movie-side information including directors, actors, genre and nations. Except for the real-valued average ratings, one-hot encoding is used for the categorical information.

For comparison, we implement baseline method by directly use the average rating as the estimation, which is the method used in most review sites. By using Mean Absolute Error (MAE) as the metric, we show the results in Figure 3. As we can notice, performance of linear regression is noticeably better than the baseline. We believe there still exist much space for improvement by employing more advanced techniques. The results also indicate that the task is rather challenging, especially for the very first few days.

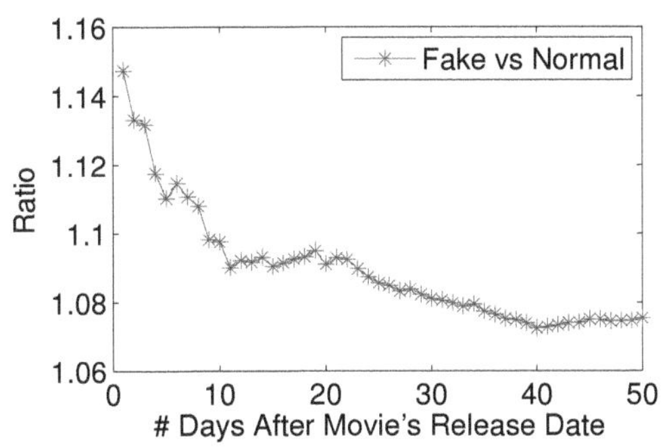

Figure 2: Review Distribution, Fake vs Normal

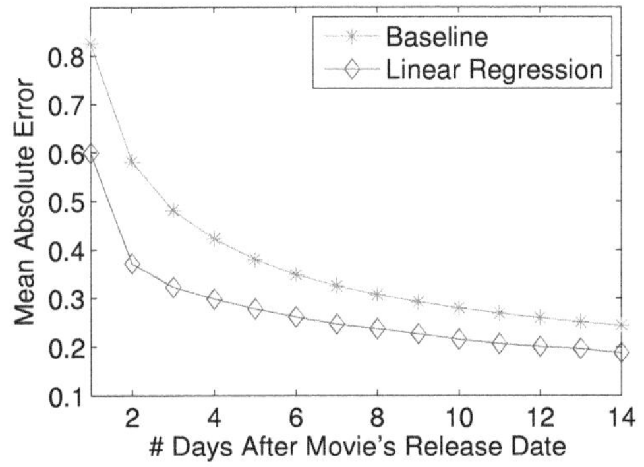

Figure 3: Preliminary Result for Recovering Truthful Rating

4. INFLUENCE OF PUBLIC OPINION

In this section we focus on behavior analysis over legitimate users instead of malicious users. We propose another future direction: to analyze and model the influences of public opinions towards each individual user in review sites.

The users are aware of the public opinion towards the item before rating it. Recall the online rating process. In most scenarios, users conduct the rating actions on the item's detail page, in which the aggregated rating (given by average rating and rating distribution) is normally highlighted. However, there is no research analyzing whether and to what extent are users influenced by such public opinions.

There are several works in similar directions. Krishnan et al. define this influence as Social Influence Bias (SIB) in [4], and find statistically significant evidence of SIB on a political-related rating system (a rather small dataset and specific scenario). Behavior patterns behind voting actions is targeted in [9]. They claimed that user actually votes for whether the instance is ranked lower/higher than it deserves according to his/her opinion.

However, there is no work modeling this in large-scale review sites. The main reason is that no existing dataset provides the snapshots of the aggregated ratings before each rating action. By assembling CCMR, we provide such dataset for the community.

To show the existence of such influence (or SIB) in review sites, we conduct the following preliminary analysis. We randomly select popular movies with rather large variation in their aggregated rating. For each movie, we represent their rating logs as (r_i, p_i) where r_i indicates the rating of ith action and p_i indicates the public opinion (the aggregated rating) right before the action. We group the logs by similar p_i, and report the rating results from each group by averaging. If users are not effected by public opinion, then r_i and p_i should be independent and the mean of r_i within each group should be the same, which represents the true public opinion towards the movie. We plot the results for three movies in Figure 4. As we can see, dependency exists. The phenomenon widely exists in most movies. Therefore, we claim that the public opinion do have an noticeable influence on users.

To gain more insight, we model the user's final rating by linear combination over user's actual preferences and the public opinion. The combination parameter for each user varies as some users are susceptible while the others are not. We further integrate the model with traditional matrix factorization (MF) [3]. The overall model as well as the loss function are now as follows:

$$
\begin{aligned}
r_{ij} &= (1 - w_i)U_i \cdot V_j + w_i p_{ij} \\
\mathcal{L}(w, U, V) &= \sum_{ij} (R_{ij} - r_{ij})^2 + \gamma(|w| + |U| + |v|)
\end{aligned} \tag{1}
$$

where r_{ij} is the predicted rating for user i on movie j. $U_i \cdot V_j$ models the user's true preferences by user and item's latent factor according to MF. p_{ij} is the public opinion for movie j just before the user i rates it. w_i is the parameter indicating to what extent user i is influenced by public opinion. Large w_i indicates the user to be more susceptible.

Evaluating it as rate prediction model, it has slight improvement comparing to MF. A relative improvement of 1.74% is achieved according to RMSE metric. As our goal is to understand the influence of public opinion instead of rating prediction, we focus on parameter w_i. We plot the

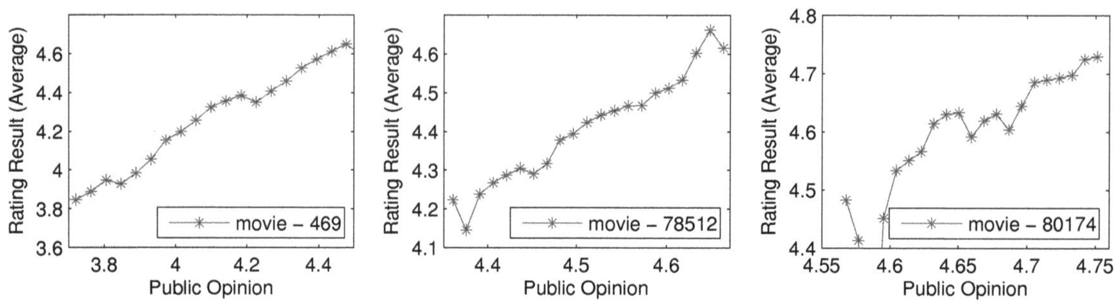

Figure 4: Influence of Public Opinion on User Ratings

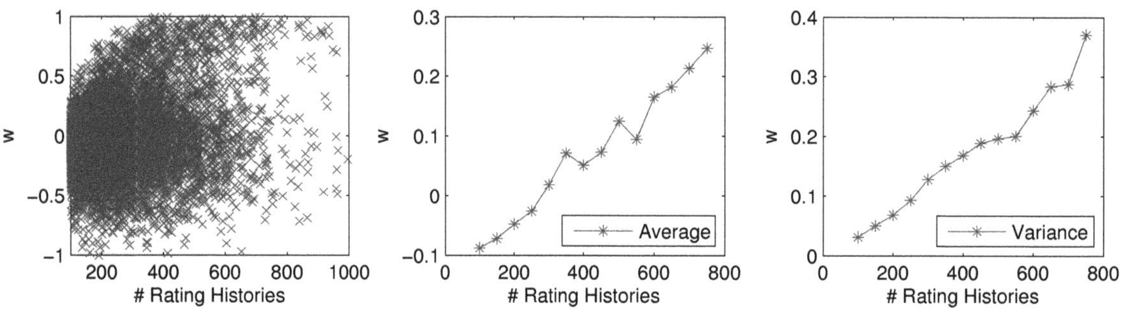

Figure 5: w vs # Rating Histories

analytical results regarding w_i and the number of rating actions made by user i in Figure 5. On the left we plot each user instance. For users with few actions, the distribution seems like Gaussian. However, when shifting to users with heavy activities, the distribution begins to fan out, especially to higher w. To be clear, we also plot the mean and variance of w for users with different activity level. From which we conclude that users with heavy activities are tend to be more conservative and susceptible to public opinions. And for normal users, the susceptible level is mostly due to the user's personality.

By these preliminary analysis, we show that influences of public opinion do exist and there are interesting phenomenons in user behaviors. We believe that following this direction, there are plenty of behavior patterns to be revealed. By understanding such patterns, we can model user preferences more accurately and further improve personalized services such as recommender systems.

5. CONCLUSION

In this paper we assemble and publish a benchmark dataset CCMR for the community. CCMR is a complete and comprehensive movie review dataset with over 283 million rating actions made by 4.9 million users over 190k movies. The data is complete as it includes actions from all users instead of only users in sampled subset. For comprehensiveness, we provide timestamp, item-side information as well as the snapshot of aggregated statistics for the item before each rating action. Therefore, our dataset CCMR can support a wider range of tasks. Further, we propose two novel tasks that are made possible by employing CCMR dataset. One is to eliminate effect of fake reviews by directly recovering the unbiased aggregated rating, and the other is to analyze and model the influences of public opinions towards each user. We also conduct preliminary analysis and experiments for these tasks. We will keep maintaining and updating this dataset. For any suggestions to extend the dataset, please contact the first author.

6. REFERENCES

[1] J. Bennett and S. Lanning. The netflix prize. In *Proceedings of KDD cup and workshop*, volume 2007, page 35, 2007.

[2] N. Jindal, B. Liu, and E.-P. Lim. Finding unusual review patterns using unexpected rules. In *CIKM*, pages 1549–1552. ACM, 2010.

[3] Y. Koren, R. Bell, and C. Volinsky. Matrix factorization techniques for recommender systems. *Computer*, (8):30–37, 2009.

[4] S. Krishnan, J. Patel, M. J. Franklin, and K. Goldberg. A methodology for learning, analyzing, and mitigating social influence bias in recommender systems. In *RecSys*, pages 137–144. ACM, 2014.

[5] T. Lappas. Fake reviews: The malicious perspective. In *Natural Language Processing and Information Systems*, pages 23–34. Springer, 2012.

[6] A. Mukherjee, B. Liu, J. Wang, N. Glance, and N. Jindal. Detecting group review spam. In *WWW companion*, pages 93–94. ACM, 2011.

[7] A. Mukherjee, V. Venkataraman, B. Liu, and N. S. Glance. What yelp fake review filter might be doing? In *ICWSM*, 2013.

[8] P. Resnick and H. R. Varian. Recommender systems. *Communications of the ACM*, 40(3):56–58, 1997.

[9] R. Sipos, A. Ghosh, and T. Joachims. Was this review helpful to you?: it depends! context and voting patterns in online content. In *WWW*, pages 337–348. ACM, 2014.

[10] C.-N. Ziegler, S. M. McNee, J. A. Konstan, and G. Lausen. Improving recommendation lists through topic diversification. In *WWW*, pages 22–32. ACM, 2005.

A Cross-Platform Collection of Social Network Profiles

Maria Han Veiga
Inst. of Computational Science
University of Zurich, Switzerland
hmaria@physik.uzh.ch

Carsten Eickhoff
Dept. of Computer Science
ETH Zurich, Switzerland
ecarsten@inf.ethz.ch

ABSTRACT

The proliferation of Internet-enabled devices and services has led to a shifting balance between digital and analogue aspects of our everyday lives. In the face of this development there is a growing demand for the study of privacy hazards, the potential for unique user de-anonymization and information leakage between the various social media profiles many of us maintain. To enable the structured study of such adversarial effects, this paper presents a dedicated dataset of cross-platform social network personas (*i.e.*, the same person has accounts on multiple platforms). The corpus comprises 850 users who generate predominantly English content. Each user object contains the online footprint of the same person in three distinct social networks: Twitter, Instagram and Foursquare. In total, it encompasses over 2.5M tweets, 340k check-ins and 42k Instagram posts. We describe the collection methodology, characteristics of the dataset, and how to obtain it. Finally, we discuss a common use case, cross-platform user identification.

CCS Concepts

•**Information systems** → *Test collections;*

Keywords

Collection; Data set; Online Social Networks

1. INTRODUCTION

The field of computational social science and data-driven research is growing in importance [9], and with this trend, there is a need for common academic benchmarking collections to facilitate a robust and reproducible research environment. In practice, however, datasets are often obtained via ad-hoc collection, or on the basis of proprietary data.

While originally Online Social Networks (OSNs) focused on allowing users to communicate, connect with others and share content, nowadays the term includes platforms which are primarily user-centric, allowing members to broadcast personal thoughts and content. [8] finds that OSNs are among the most frequently visited Web sites for a large population of users. In consequence, they can be used to study human behaviour at a large scale. Furthermore, because many OSNs are public by default and provide APIs to access their content, they have become good candidates for data collection to be used to study problems such as user/topic modelling, user identification or information leakage.

In this paper, we introduce a collection of 850 users and their online footprint (part of their generated content and user profiles) spread across three social networks: Twitter, Instagram and Foursquare. It is our objective to provide a dataset on which privacy-sensitive methods and the defense against them can be tested. The construction of this dataset was initially carried out during a research project studying cross platform privacy loss arising from public information sharing on social networks [4]. In Table 1, a comparison of our dataset with other existing corpora is given.

Our data collection method relies on linking users across three popular OSN platforms. Twitter is a microblogging platform whose main content comes in *tweets*, posts limited to 140 characters which can contain text, video or images, links to external Web sites, references to other users and *hashtags* (terms starting with the # symbol used to mark keywords or topics in a tweet). Instagram is a photo sharing platform. Its main content are photos or videos along with optional textual descriptors. Foursquare is a location service platform concentrating on the notion of *check-ins*.

The paper makes the following novel contributions (1) We describe the methodology and release the code to construct a user-centric cross-OSN dataset. (2) We release a dataset of 850 profile triples across the aforementioned OSNs.

The remainder of this paper is structured as follows: in Section 2, we present the methodology used to create the collection. Section 3 presents key statistics and qualitative aspects of the dataset. Section 4 discusses the task of cross-platform user identification as an example use case before sketching a range of further conceivable use cases and tasks.

2. METHOD

We use Twitter, Instagram and Foursquare mainly due to the ease of crawling and publicly accessible APIs, but also because the content generated by the users in these distinct social networks is diverse and representative of a comprehensive range of OSN use cases. In [11], the authors find that on Twitter, the top types of content users share are: personal information, random thoughts, opinions/complaints and facts (*e.g.* news). While on Instagram, the ma-

SIGIR '16, July 17–21, 2016, Pisa, Italy.

DOI: http://dx.doi.org/10.1145/2911451.2914666

Table 1: **An overview of existing datasets containing cross-OSN user profiles.**

Features	MNA [7]	MAH [12]	About.me [10]	Cross OSN
OSNs	Twitter, Foursquare	Twitter, BlogCatalog	Flickr, Google+, Instagram, Tumblr, Twitter, Youtube	Instagram, Twitter Foursquare
# Users	500	2710	15,595	850
Content type	User IDs, posts, friends graph	User IDs, friends graph	User IDs, post IDs	User IDs, post IDs
Availability	Unknown	Unknown	Available	Available

jority of the posted pictures can be put in 1 of 8 categories, with the leading categories being *selfies* and *friends* [5]. On Foursquare, users share their location in terms of venues, which carries not only information in the form of raw geographic coordinates, but often also the venue's name and function.

In order to obtain profiles from different OSNs belonging to the same person, we first use the Twitter Search API to search for specific post patterns (*e.g.*, https://instagr.am/p/*), in order to identify users who cross-post content from other platforms on Twitter. A graphical depiction of the collection process is shown in Figure 1.

The data was collected in January and February 2016. While we were able to find over 5000 profile triples, only approximately 20% of these triples fulfill our criteria of actively using the three selected OSNs, posting predominantly in English and sharing content publicly. After enforcing these requirements, our dataset contains a total of 850 distinct user profiles.

2.1 English predominance

We focused on profiles with predominantly English content as the initial study for which the data was collected was a natural language processing task that would have suffered from excessive amounts of cross-language content.

In order to guarantee that the majority of the content is posted in English, we use the method described in Algorithm 1. We set the ratio to be 0.1 and $K = 100$ for our collection. The purpose is not to exclude users that occasionally post in a non-English language, but to make sure the data set does not contain too many strictly non English-speaking users.

Data: twitter timeline
Result: true or false
initialization;
for *K posts* **do**
| count(english posts);
end
if *count.total/K* < *ratio* **then**
| disregard user;
else
| crawl timeline;
end

Algorithm 1: English check

2.2 Spam detection

To increase the confidence that users are authentic personal accounts instead of spammers that merely redistribute content from other users, we have a simple heuristic described in Algorithm 2. We take the timeline of the user from the respective OSN and we check whether the majority of the posts come from the same user name. In our collection, the threshold is set to 30%. Suspected spammer triples are flagged but, for completeness, remain in the dataset.

Data: Instagram or Foursquare timeline
Result: spammerFlag
initialization;
for *posts* **do**
| count(author of post);
end
if *counter.max/total posts* < *threshold* **then**
| spammerFlag=1;
else
| spammerFlag=0;
end

Algorithm 2: Identity check

3. DATASET

Our 850 authentic English-speaking users produced approximately 2.5M tweets, 340k check-ins and 42k Instagram posts[1]. Four users were flagged as spammers under the rule described in Section 2.2.

Figure 2 shows the distribution of tweets per user. Figures 3 and 4 show the distribution of number of check-ins and Instagram posts per user, respectively.

The Twitter API restricts access to at most 3200 tweets per profile (including re-tweets) [13]. Because we exclude direct re-tweets from our data set, the majority of the Twitter profiles we collect contain between 3000 and 3200 tweets. For each Instagram profile, we recover the most recent posts through the Instagram API and complement them with existing content which has been posted on Twitter. For each Foursquare profile, we recover those check-ins that were cross-posted on the retrieved Twitter timeline.

In this dataset, we observe check-ins from 111 countries, spawning 669 venue types. The most visited venue types are shown in Figure 5.

3.1 Properties

For each user we store Twitter, Instagram and Foursquare IDs along with the tweet and post IDs of all shared content. The Foursquare data is represented as a list of tuples (*venue_id*, *tweet_id*), where *tweet_id* is the tweet announcing the check-in. An example of the collected user data is shown in Table 2. For copyright reasons, we do not distribute the content but instead provide the scripts to crawl the data [1]. Using these scripts, the following can be retrieved:

[1]http://cake.da.inf.ethz.ch/OSN-sigir2016/

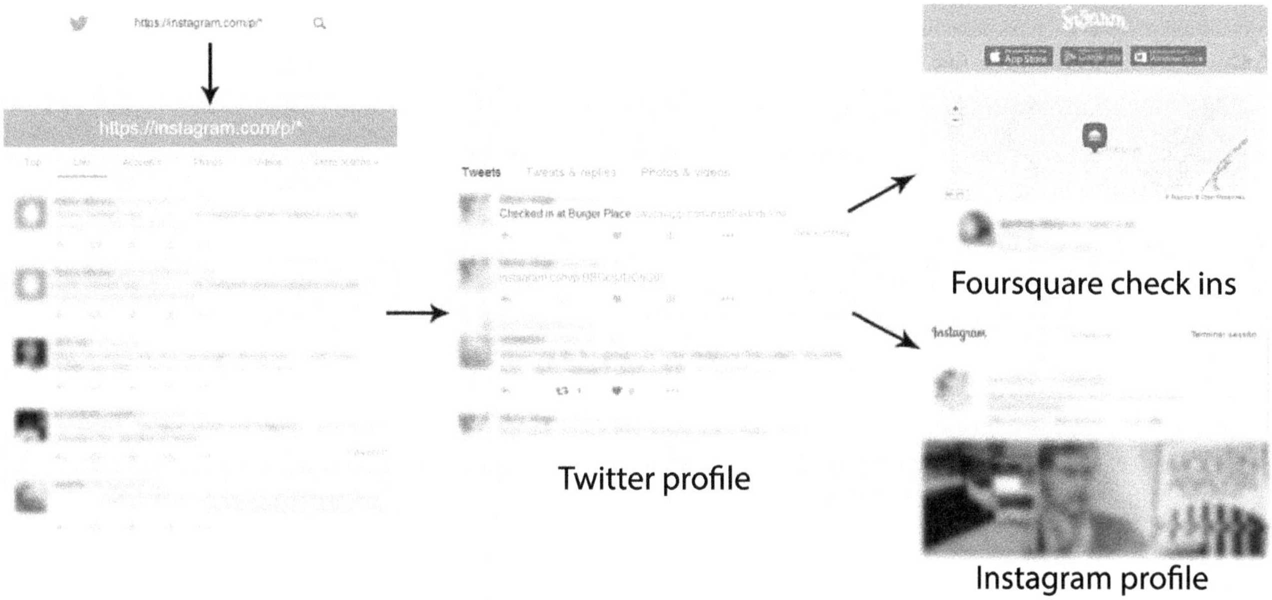

Figure 1: Dataset collection. We use Twitter's search API to find posts with the pattern of a Foursquare check-in or an Instagram post. If a profile contains both, we crawl the Foursquare check-ins and Instagram profile through their respective APIs.

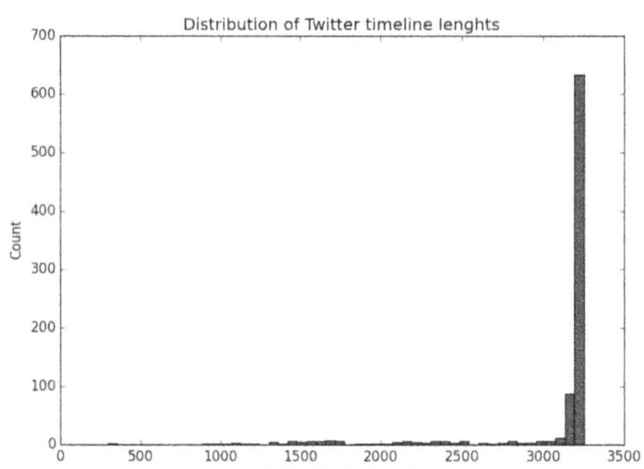

Figure 2: Histogram of tweets per user

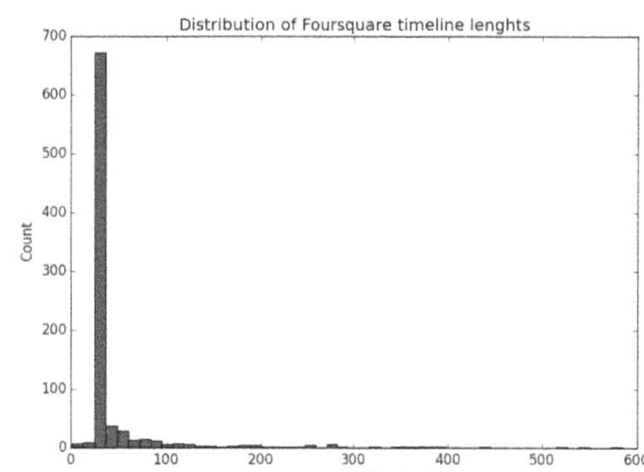

Figure 4: Histogram of Instagram posts per user

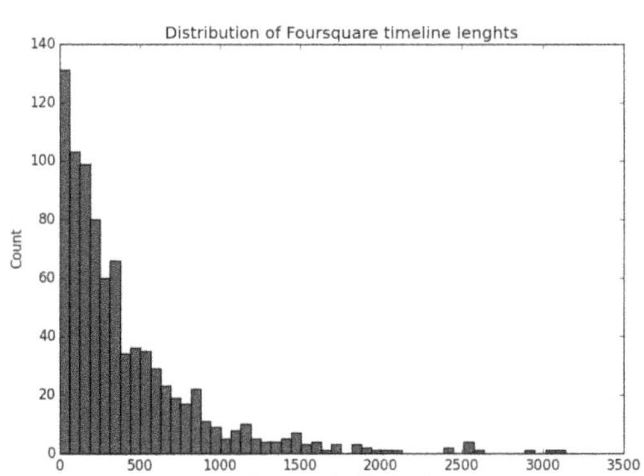

Figure 3: Histogram of Foursquare posts per user

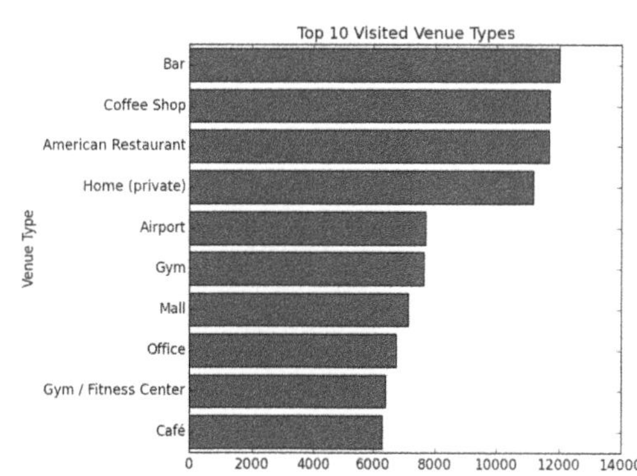

Figure 5: Top 10 visited venue types

Table 2: Example of provided and retrievable data.

Feature	Description	Retrieves
TWITTER		
ID	Integer	Twitter profile
Timeline	List of tweet IDs	Tweet object
INSTAGRAM		
ID	Integer	Instagram profile
Timeline	List of post shortcodes	Instagram object
FOURSQUARE		
ID	User unique identifier	–
Timeline	List of pairs (tweet_id,venue_id)	Venue object

- From Twitter: using the user ID, a profile object that contains information such as the name, location, date of creation of account, and with the post ID, a the tweet object, containing the tweet and metadata [13].
- From Instagram: using the user ID, a profile object containing information such as the name, location, date of creation of account, and with the post shortcode from Instagram, an Instagram object containing the link with the image and related metadata [6].
- From Foursquare: using the venue ID, the venue object can be retrieved, containing information such as venue type, venue name and location [3].

4. DISCUSSION

In this section we present a use case for this dataset in a cross-OSN user identification task. Then, we elaborate on other tasks that can find this collection useful.

4.1 User Identification

The task of user identification is concerned with matching profiles from different domains belonging to the same natural person [14]. In this scenario, we use Instagram and Twitter as our data sources. A simple, yet powerful baseline algorithm is used, which compares the similarity of the nicknames on the respective platforms.

By assigning minimal Levenshtein distance between user names and choosing the one with the lowest edit distance, we attain a matching accuracy of 70.1%. If the user names are preprocessed by converting them to lowercase (as in both these social networks the letter case does not make a difference), we attain an accuracy of 72.8%. One can think of many more advanced schemes tracking common topics or writing styles across social networks.

4.2 Content generation and spreading

In [2], the authors study how users behave across Pinterest and Twitter. Other papers study Twitter or Instagram alone [11, 5]. It would be interesting to study the behaviour of users in these OSNs while having access to their multiple profiles. This could help answer whether some topics are OSN-specific or whether the activity in one profile can indicate future activity in another profile.

4.3 Cross-OSN inference

Following the idea that an activity on one platform can indicate future activity on another one, an interesting study would be to see whether it is possible to infer information from one OSN regarding another one. For example, whether it is possible to predict topics, interests or intentions. An example of this type of work can be found in [4], where the authors use Twitter timelines to infer venue type visits.

4.4 Aggregated OSN topic modelling

Because OSNs can carry different information depending on their functionality, the access to several profiles from the same user across different platforms might give an advantage when modelling the user. These user models can be used for targeted advertisement or recommender systems. An interesting task would be to compare whether the inclusion of different profiles can benefit the models or not.

5. CONCLUSION

In this paper, we described the collection, structure and properties of a benchmarking corpus of cross-platform OSN user profiles useful for a wide range of privacy-related research questions. It encompasses hundreds of user triples, millions of tweets and thousands of Instagram and Foursquare posts. In order to reduce the inherent amount of noise in the dataset, we ensure a focus on English-speaking users and perform spammer identification. To the best of our knowledge, this dataset is the first of its kind both in nature as well as scale.

6. REFERENCES

[1] *CrossOSN-crawler code repository.* https://github.com/hanveiga/CrossOSN-crawler.

[2] R. O. et al. Of Pins and Tweets: Investigating how users behave across image- and text-based social networks. In *ICWSM 2014.*

[3] Foursquare. *Foursquare API overview*, 2015 (accessed May 2, 2015). https://developer.foursquare.com/overview/.

[4] M. I. Han Veiga. *Task Driven Information Valuation.* Zürich, 2015.

[5] Y. Hu, L. Manikonda, and S. Kambhampati. What we instagram: A first analysis of instagram photo content and user types.

[6] Instagram. *Instagram API overview*, 2015 (accessed May 2, 2015). https://www.instagram.com/developer.

[7] X. Kong, J. Zhang, and P. S. Yu. Inferring anchor links across multiple heterogeneous social networks. In *CIKM 2013.*

[8] R. Kumar and A. Tomkins. A characterization of online browsing behavior. In *WWW 2010.*

[9] D. Lazer, A. Pentland, and et al. Computational social science. *Science*, 323(5915):721–723, 2009.

[10] B. H. Lim, D. Lu, T. Chen, and M.-Y. Kan. #mytweet via instagram: Exploring user behaviour across multiple social networks. In *ASONAM 2015.*

[11] M. Naaman, J. Boase, and C.-H. Lai. Is it really about me?: Message content in social awareness streams. In *CSCW 2010.*

[12] S. Tan, Z. Guan, D. Cai, X. Qin, J. Bu, and C. Chen. Mapping users across networks by manifold alignment on hypergraph.

[13] Twitter. *Twitter Rest API overview*, 2015 (accessed May 2, 2015). https://dev.twitter.com/rest/public.

[14] R. Zafarani and H. Liu. Connecting users across social media sites: A behavioral-modeling approach. In *KDD 2013.*

A Test Collection for Matching Patients to Clinical Trials

Bevan Koopman[1,2], Guido Zuccon[2]
[1]Australian e-Health Research Centre, CSIRO, Brisbane, Australia
[2]Queensland University of Technology (QUT), Brisbane, Australia
bevan.koopman@csiro.au, g.zuccon@qut.edu.au

ABSTRACT

We present a test collection to study the use of search engines for matching eligible patients (the query) to clinical trials (the document). Clinical trials are experiments conducted in the development of new medical treatments, drugs or devices. Recruiting candidates for a trial is often a time-consuming and resource intensive effort, and imposes delays or even the cancellation of trials.

The collection described in this paper provides: i) a large corpus of clinical trials; ii) 60 patient case reports used as topics; iii) multiple query representations for a single topic (long, short and ad-hoc); iv) a user provided estimate of how many trials they expect each patient topic would be eligible for; and v) relevance assessments by medical professionals. The availability of such a collection allows researchers to investigate, among other questions: i) the effectiveness of retrieval methods for this task, ii) how multiple representations of an information affect retrieval iii) what influences relevance assessments in this context, iv) whether automated matching of patients to trials improves patient recruitment. The collection is available at http://doi.org/10.4225/08/5714557510C17.

CCS Concepts

•**Information systems → Information retrieval; Test collections;**

Keywords

Information Retrieval, Clinical Trials, Test Collections

1. INTRODUCTION

Clinical trials are experiments done in the development of new treatments, drugs or medical devices. They are a critical step for medical advancement and are a regulatory requirement before new medical advances can be used in practise. However, recruiting a sufficient number of eligible patients to participate in a trial can be a major obstacle [9]. If suitable patients cannot be found then trials may be cancelled or significantly delayed. Even if sufficient patients are found, the recruitment process can be time consuming and resource intensive. Automating and improving this difficult manual process has the potential to improve the running of a clinical trial. In addition, certain patients can benefit from finding and being included into specific trials, e.g., to have access to potentially life-saving treatment options. However, often treating doctors are not aware of trials that may benefit specific patients.

Large collections of clinical trials are published online (e.g., ClinicalTrials.gov contained approx. 200,000 trails in 2015), with details of the inclusion and exclusion criteria of eligible patients. At the same time, a patient's conditions are also documented in electronic form (for example, in electronic patient records). Matching patients to clinical trials is essentially an information retrieval task: the query is the patient details (either in the form of electronic patient records or ad-hoc queries) and the documents are the clinical trials currently recruiting patients.

While research exists on automated matching of patients to trials [10], much of the evaluation is done on small, private datasets and on specific diseases. This paper aims to address this gap by developing a large-scale, heterogeneous test collection of clinical trial documents and associated patient queries. The availability of such a collection allows researchers to investigate: i) the effectiveness of retrieval methods for this task, ii) how multiple representations of an information affect retrieval iii) what influences relevance assessments in this context, iv) whether automated matching of patients to trials improves patient recruitment.

2. RELATED WORK

Sustained focus on medical information retrieval has led to the development of a number of other relevant test collections. Within TREC, there have been two medical related tracks relevant to this work: the Medical Records Track (MedTrack) and the Clinical Decision Support (CDS Track).

The MedTrack task involved searching a collection of electronic patient records for patients that meet a certain criteria (the query) [12]. One use case was that the query indicated the inclusion criteria for a clinical trial, while the documents were patients to be retrieved that matched that criteria. Thus, Medtrack could be viewed as the opposite, trial-centric (trial is the query and patient is the document) to the patient-centric task considered here. Another important difference that sets this work apart is that real clinical trials were used; instead Medtrack used only ad-hoc queries to describe the patient (e.g., topic# 115 "Adult patients who are admitted with an asthma exacerbation").

In the TREC CDS task the topics were patient case re-

SIGIR '16, July 17-21, 2016, Pisa, Italy
© 2016 ACM. ISBN 978-1-4503-4069-4/16/07...$15.00
DOI: http://dx.doi.org/10.1145/2911451.2914672

```
A 51-year-old woman is seen in clinic for advice on os-
teoporosis. She has a past medical history of signifi-
cant hypertension and diet-controlled diabetes mellitus.
She currently smokes 1 pack of cigarettes per day. She
was documented by previous LH and FSH levels to be in
menopause within the last year. She is concerned about
breaking her hip as she gets older and is seeking advice
on osteoporosis prevention.
```

Figure 1: Example patient case (topic# 201429).

ports and were used to search for medical journal articles that would help uncover the diseases, tests and treatments relevant to the patient case [11]. The patient case reports were verbose: on average 78 words per topic (an example report is shown in Figure 1). TREC CDS is intended for searching medical literature for clinical decision support; however, the patient case reports are general descriptions of a patient past and current medical history. The patient case reports can, therefore, also be used to search for clinical trials. For this reason, we use the same patient case reports from TREC CDS as our topics in this test collection to search for clinical trials. This also has the added advantage of being able to link a patient with both clinical trials from this collection and associated medical literature from the TREC CDS collection.

Other medical collections do exist in the TREC Genomics Track and in the CLEF eHealth Lab; however, these are focused on genomic search and consumer health search and, therefore, not detailed here.

3. CREATION OF THE COLLECTION

3.1 Document Collection

A collection of 204,855 publicly available clinical trails was crawled from ClinicalTrials.gov.[1] Trials are made available in a specific XML format, however, large portions (including the inclusion and exclusion criteria) are free-text.[2] These represent the documents to be searched.

3.2 Query Topics

As query topics, we adopted the topics previously used by the TREC CDS [11], comprising 60 patient case reports (30 from 2014 and 30 from 2015). Each topic describes a patient with certain conditions and observations. Each patient case topic had two forms: a description (on average 78 words) and a shorter summary (on average 22 words).

As noted above, the topics were verbose patient case reports. Automatically matching these case reports to clinical trials was the first use case — here the user simply supplies the case report and does not author a query. However, an alternative use case exists as a traditional ad-hoc retrieval scenario where the user authors a short keyword query. To cover this second use case we showed four medical assessors each patient case report and asked them to provide ad-hoc keyword queries that they would issue to a search engine to find clinical trials for the given patient. A total of 489 unique queries were produced, on average 8.2 (sd=3.2) keyword queries per topic. In addition, assessors were asked the following question for each topic: "How many clinical trials do you expect this patient would be eligible for?" The answer to this was recorded and was used in the INST evaluation measure [5][3] we will detail in Section 3.4.

3.3 Pooling and Judging

A number of baseline retrieval models were run to form the pool. These included: BM25, Language Model (Direchlet and Jelinek-Mercer), Divergence From Randomness (BB2 and DLH) and TF-IDF.[4] While this was only a small number of systems, we note that Moffat et al. found that query variations are as strong as system variations in producing a diverse document pool [6]; thus, we overcame the limit of having a small number of systems by including a large number of query variations. Specifically, each baseline system listed above was run with the following queries for each topic: i) the patient case report description; ii) the patient case report summary; and iii) the ad-hoc keyword queries provided by our medical assessors (8.2 queries on average). This equates to an average of 61 runs per topic (10.2 queries per topic * 6 baseline methods). This provided a diverse set of retrieved documents to form the pool.

To maximise the time and minimise costs associated with employing medical assessors it was important to maximise the chance of sampling important documents for assessment. A standard approach to form the pool is to include all documents that are highly ranked by participating systems. However, Moffat et al. [7] noted that not all documents provide the same benefit and instead propose an alternative method based on the Ranked Biased Precision (RBP) evaluation measure. Documents were ranked according to RBP across all queries; documents that were retrieved by multiple, different systems in top-ranked positions would appear higher in the RBP ranking. The pool was then formed based on the available assessment budget by setting a cut-off point of 4,000 documents in the RBP ranking — documents above the cut-off were included in the pool.

The documents and queries were uploaded to the Relevation! relevance assessment system [2] and four medical assessors were engaged to conduct the relevance assessment according to a three-point scale: 0) *Would not refer this patient for this clinical trial*; 1) *Would consider referring this patient to this clinical trial upon further investigation*; and 2) *Highly likely to refer this patient for this clinical trial.* Queries were divided amongst the four assessors; a control query (topic #20158) was used to familiarise assessors with the task and to record inter-coder reliability (agreement found to be 70%). This highlights the difficulty intrinsic in judging relevance in the medical domain, as identified by other studies [3]. Reasons for assessors disagreement will be investigated in future work.

3.4 The Task and Evaluation Measures

The task of matching patients to trials has three specific use cases; we use these to set the evaluation measures.

The first use case is in a General Practitioner (GP) setting where the GP opens a patient's record as part of a consultation and a search is automatically initiated to find relevant clinical trials that the GP may refer the patient to. In this scenario the GP is time-pressured and would likely only review a small number of results, stopping when a sin-

[1] This represents all the trials available on 16th Dec., 2015.

[2] More details on the format and download options can be found at: https://clinicaltrials.gov/ct2/resources/download.

[3] We are thankful to the authors of [5] for sharing their sample implementation of INST.

[4] The Terrier IR system was used for all models and parameters left to Terrier defaults [4].

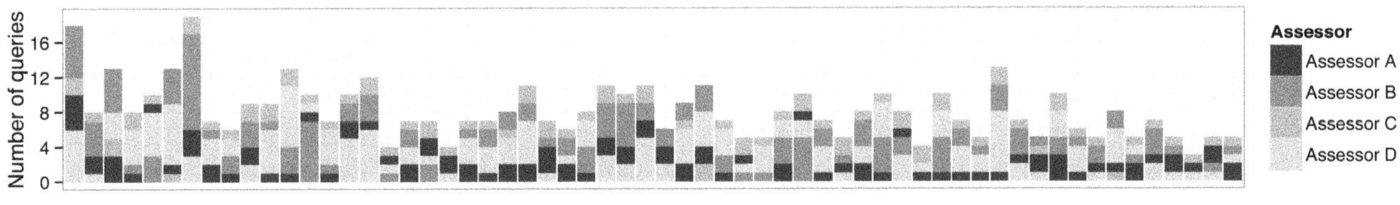

Figure 2: Number of queries supplied by each assessors for each topic.

gle relevant trial is found. Thus for this scenario we adopted Mean Reciprocal Rank (MRR) as the evaluation measure.

The second use case is also set within a general medical professional (GP or other) but where the user is specifically searching for clinical trials and may dedicate more time and effort to the task. In this case they may issue an ad-hoc query themselves and be willing to evaluate a few more results. For this scenario we adopted Precision at 5 (P@5) as the evaluation measure.

The final use case is for medical specialists or patients themselves searching for trials. Here both types of users may conduct longer search sessions and review far more results. They may use both short ad-hoc queries and more verbose patient case reports. In addition, both users would have an expectation about how many clinical trials they would be eligible for. This would influence their search behaviour: for rare diseases, they may expect to find a very small number of trials and would therefore not persist in examining results at greater rank depths. In contrast, for common diseases, they would expect to find many relevant trials and would therefore persist to greater rank depths. This notion of expected number of (relevant) results is directly modelled by T in the INST evaluation measure [5]; thus we adopted INST for this scenario. INST is a weighted precision metric where the likelihood of the user assessing a document at a specific rank depends on the rank position, the expected number of relevant documents, and the actual number of relevant documents encountered up to that rank. According to INST, the expected depth at which the user would stop viewing documents falls between approximately $T+0.25$ (all encountered documents are relevant) and $2T+0.5$ (no encountered documents are relevant) [5].

4. ANALYSIS OF THE COLLECTION

4.1 Test Collection Statistics

The collection contains 204,855 clinical trial documents. There are 60 topics made up of three types: patient case descriptions, patient case summaries and assessor provided ad-hoc queries, totalling an average of 10.2 queries per topic. A total of 4,000 documents were judged (67 per topic, min=13, max=153, mean=63, sd=27).

The number of ad-hoc queries provided by the assessors differed per topic and per assessor, as shown in Figure 2. Some assessors entered multiple short queries, while others preferred single longer queries. The average query length was 4.5 words, sd=2.5 words.

Assessors were also asked how many clinical trials they expected a patient would be eligible for. This was represented as T in the INST evaluation measure. The values of T for each topic, across the four assessors, is shown in Figure 3. Values of T varied across topics, thus indicating the different information needs assessors derived from different patients. Although T varied across topics, individual assessors displayed similar trends across topics; e.g., assessor D typically chose lower values of T and assessor C displayed

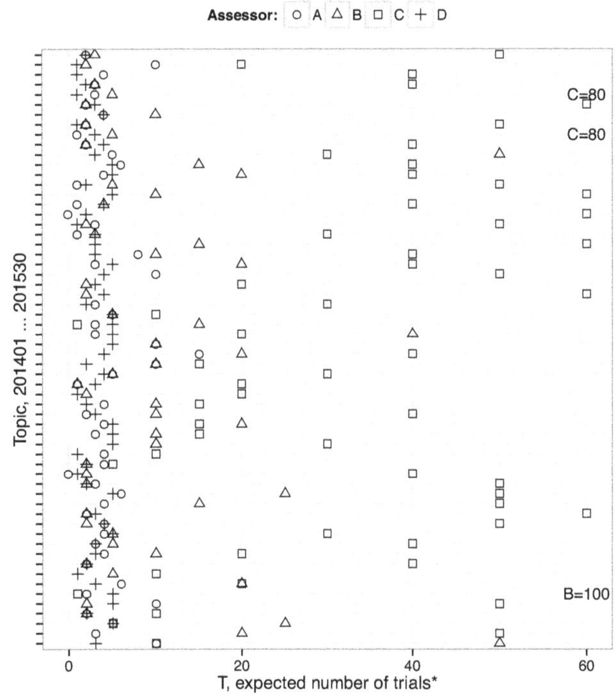

*x-axis truncated at $T = 60$ excluding outliners $T = 80, 80, 100$.

Figure 3: T, the users' expected number of clinical trials for a patient topic.

higher values of T. This resulted in values of T that varied across assessors for a single topic. Qualitative feedback from assessors indicated estimating T was challenging and subjective. The assessors were asked about their rationale for determining values of T. We found that regardless of the value of T, assessors indicated that the main rationale was how rare or common the patient's medical condition was; secondary to that was the likelihood that clinical trails were currently being conducted on the patient's condition.

4.2 Retrieval Results Analysis

The relevance assessments we collected were used to evaluate six standard baselines. The purpose of the evaluation was twofold. On one hand, the retrieval systems were used to form the pool for assessments, thus the evaluation reports how effective the systems that contributed to the pool were. On the other hand, this evaluation serves to demonstrate the type of research questions this collection can contribute to investigate, e.g., what type of queries (verbose, summaries, ad-hoc) are most effective for searching for clinical trials.

For each system, runs were created using three different topic types: i) verbose patient case report descriptions; ii) shorter patient case report summaries; and iii) short ad-hoc keyword queries. Note that ad-hoc queries generated more than one run per topic per system, i.e., on average each system generated 8.2 runs per topic. We therefore averaged the effectiveness of a system over all ad-hoc queries for a topic.

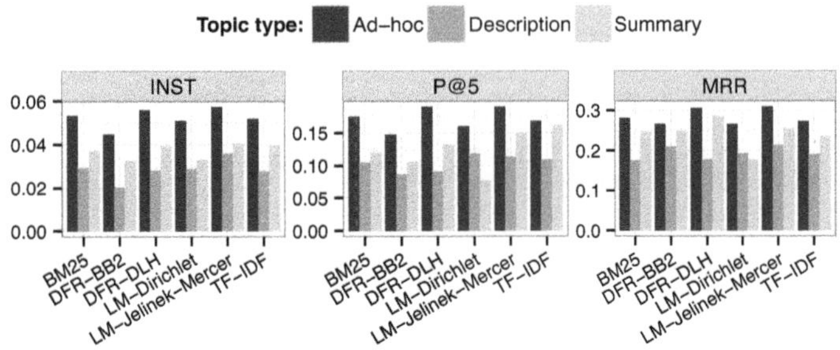

Figure 4: Retrieval results for different baselines and topic representations.

Retrieval results are shown in Figure 4. We firstly observe that there was high variability of performance across the topic types. The assessor-provided ad-hoc queries proved most effective overall, followed by summary patient case reports and finally the full description patient case reports were the least effective topic type.

There was also variability across different baseline methods. The best method for ad-hoc queries was clearly the Jelinek-Mercer language model. For the longer summaries and descriptions the best method varied: TF-IDF proving effective for summaries, while no method clearly stood out for descriptions. This observation suggests that different baseline methods are best suited to different use cases.

Overall, we note that there was more variability across topic types than across baseline methods. This is inline with the results of Moffat et al. [6] that found query variability was as significant as system variability.

5. DISCUSSION

The test collection described in this paper is clearly aimed at focusing research on matching eligible patients to clinical trails; however, it also provides the basis for exploring a number of other research aspects:

Query representations and variations. The collection provides multiple representations for a single topics: descriptions, summaries and ad-hoc queries (on average 8.2 per topic). The availability of multiple representations makes it possible to investigate whether specific retrieval methods are more suitable to different representations, e.g., ad-hoc vs verbose. The ad-hoc queries themselves expose different ways of formulating the same information need, each leading to different effectiveness for the same retrieval method. Along with the TREC-8 Query Track [1] and the CLEF 2015 eHealth [8], our collection is a rare example of a test collection with multiple query variations.

Expected number of relevant results (T). Assessors indicated how many trials they expected the patient would have been eligible for. This data can serve the evaluation (e.g., through INST) but also allows exploring the perception about the results assessors expected to obtain. In particular, we observed that T greatly varied across topics and across assessors (this latter result was in contrast to previous studies [6]). Finally, this is the first collection that provides a user's estimate of the number of relevant documents they believe are required for each topic.

What makes a clinical trial relevant. The collection makes available data to understand what characterises relevance when judging the eligibility of a patient to a clinical trial. It also provides evidence to the fact that judging the eligibility of a clinical trial is often challenging when only summary information about patients is available.

6. CONCLUSIONS

This paper presented a test collection aimed at helping the development of systems to automatically match eligible patients to clinical trials. The collection can be used to discriminate between different systems on this task. The limited number of assessments may make the evaluation less reliable for new systems that greatly differ from those used to form the pool. Nevertheless, the value of the collection is the insights it provides into research questions related to, e.g., the effectiveness of different query representations (and variations), how assessors judge relevance of patients to clinical trials, etc. The collection presents several original aspects. This is the first publicly available, large scale collection for matching patients to clinical trials — an important task for medical advancement. The collection is also the first that provides estimates of the number of expected relevant documents for each query topic (T), and is one of the few that provides multiple query representations and variations.

Future work will consider increasing the number of assessed documents, including increasing the number of systems used to form the pool, especially when specialised systems to search clinical trials become available. We also plan to expand the analysis of query variations and the effect query representations have on system effectiveness. Finally, another line of future research will consider the analysis of assessor disagreement (both for relevance and for the value of T) to gain further insights about how users perceive relevance for this task. The collection is available at http://doi.org/10.4225/08/5714557510C17 and our INST implementation at https://github.com/ielab/inst_eval.

7. REFERENCES

[1] C. Buckley and J. A. Walz. The TREC-8 Query Track. In *TREC*, 1999.

[2] B. Koopman and G. Zuccon. Relevation!: An open source system for information retrieval relevance assessment. In *SIGIR*, Gold Coast, Australia, July 2014.

[3] B. Koopman and G. Zuccon. Why assessing relevance in medical IR is demanding. In *MedIR at SIGIR*, 2014.

[4] C. Macdonald, R. McCreadie, R. L. Santos, and I. Ounis. From puppy to maturity: Experiences in developing terrier. *Proc. of OSIR at SIGIR*, pages 60–63, 2012.

[5] A. Moffat, P. Bailey, F. Scholer, and P. Thomas. INST: An adaptive metric for information retrieval evaluation. In *ADCS*, Sydney, Australia, 2015.

[6] A. Moffat, F. Scholer, P. Thomas, and P. Bailey. Pooled evaluation over query variations: Users are as diverse as systems. In *CIKM*, 2015.

[7] A. Moffat, W. Webber, and J. Zobel. Strategic system comparisons via targeted relevance judgments. In *SIGIR*, pages 375–382. ACM, 2007.

[8] J. Palotti, G. Zuccon, L. Goeuriot, L. Kelly, A. Hanbury, G. J. Jones, M. Lupu, and P. Pecina. Clef ehealth evaluation lab 2015, task 2: Retrieving information about medical symptoms. CLEF, 2015.

[9] L. T. Penberthy, B. A. Dahman, V. I. Petkov, and J. P. DeShazo. Effort required in eligibility screening for clinical trials. *Journal of Oncology Practice*, 8(6):365–370, 2012.

[10] T. R. Pressler, P.-Y. Yen, J. Ding, J. Liu, P. J. Embi, and P. R. O. Payne. Computational challenges and human factors influencing the design and use of clinical research participant eligibility pre-screening tools. *BMC Medical Informatics & Decision Making*, 12:47–47, 2012.

[11] M. S. Simpson, E. M. Voorhees, and W. Hersh. Overview of the TREC clinical decision support track. In *TREC*, 2014.

[12] E. M. Voorhees and W. R. Hersh. Overview of the TREC 2012 Medical Records Track. In *TREC*, 2012.

ArabicWeb16: A New Crawl for Today's Arabic Web

Reem Suwaileh[1], Mucahid Kutlu[1], Nihal Fathima[1], Tamer Elsayed[1], Matthew Lease[2]
[1] Department of Computer Science and Engineering, Qatar University, Qatar
{reem.suwaileh, mucahidkutlu, nihal.fathima, telsayed}@qu.edu.qa
[2] School of Information, University of Texas at Austin, USA
ml@utexas.edu

ABSTRACT

Web crawls provide valuable snapshots of the Web which enable a wide variety of research, be it distributional analysis to characterize Web properties or use of language, content analysis in social science, or Information Retrieval (IR) research to develop and evaluate effective search algorithms. While many English-centric Web crawls exist, existing public Arabic Web crawls are quite limited, limiting research and development. To remedy this, we present *ArabicWeb16*, a new public Web crawl of roughly 150M Arabic Web pages with significant coverage of dialectal Arabic as well as Modern Standard Arabic. For IR researchers, we expect ArabicWeb16 to support various research areas: ad-hoc search, question answering, filtering, cross-dialect search, dialect detection, entity search, blog search, and spam detection.

Keywords

Multi-Dialect; Web Collection; Arabic Retrieval; Ad-hoc Search; Evaluation

1. INTRODUCTION

A central requirement of the Cranfield method for evaluating Information Retrieval (IR) systems is a document collection [7], which is also essential for system development. More specifically, advancing the state-of-the-art in the area of Web search mandates the availability of a large-scale Web collection that is representative of the size and diversity of the Web. A variety of English-centric Web crawls have been previously performed such as VLC2 [11], WT10g [1], Gov2 [4], ClueWeb09 [5], and ClueWeb12[1]. ClueWeb12 intentionally eliminated non-English content.

Approximately 370 million people are estimated to live in the Arab World today, yet the ability of researchers to support this population and their various dialects[2] by advancing the state-of-the-art in Arabic IR (and Arabic Web search in particular) has been greatly restricted by the lack of available Arabic data [9]. Fifteen years ago, the TREC Cross-Language Track created a test collection of Modern Standard Arabic (MSA) news articles from Agence France Press' (AFP) [10]. Great at the time, this test collection has become rather dated and small by today's standards.

The ClueWeb09 Web crawl consists of about 1B Webpages in 10 languages, including 29.2M (2.9%) Arabic pages. This Arabic subset (denoted by *ArClueWeb09*) constitutes the only and largest Arabic Web crawl available for IR research. While this makes it a wonderful resource to researchers, it nevertheless presents several notable limitations.

Most obviously, the contents of this 2009 Web crawl have become somewhat dated in relation to understanding and supporting today's Arabic Web, especially in regard to rapid growth in social media use since then. Secondly, given its coverage of Arabic content was only incidental in crawling, it offers only limited coverage of even the Arabic Web as of 2009. Thirdly, the above two factors conspire to greatly limit its coverage of dialectal Arabic. Finally, our analysis of the ArClueWeb09 subset leads us to estimate that perhaps 14% of its pages are not actually Arabic, with less accurate tools for automatic language detection available in 2009 vs. today. For whatever reason, we know of no analysis having been reported on the content of ArClueWeb09, nor of any IR studies having used it. Taken together, these factors suggest a strong need for an updated crawl of today's Arabic Web that is far more representative of its current state and better supporting research, especially on Arabic IR.

Common Crawl's[3] most recent November 2015 boasts over 1.82 billion URLs, but past analysis suggests that, similar to ClueWeb09, English content dominates the crawl [12]. While Common Crawl could be mined to identify and extract a useful Arabic subset akin to ArClueWeb09, this would address only recency, not coverage.

To address the above concerns, we believe a focused Arabic Web crawl is vital to enable and encourage research on today's Arabic Web. Beyond achieving a massive and modern crawl, we sought to ensure broad coverage of dialectal Arabic. To the best of our knowledge, our new public Web crawl, *ArabicWeb16*, is now the the largest and most representative snapshot of today's Arabic Web. ArabicWeb16 includes about 150M pages crawled over the month of January 2016. To obtain ArabicWeb16, please check the ArabicWeb16 project Web page[4].

[1]lemurproject.org/clueweb12
[2]en.wikipedia.org/wiki/Varieties_of_Arabic
[3]commoncrawl.org
[4]http://qufaculty.qu.edu.qa/telsayed/arabicweb16

SIGIR '16, July 17 - 21, 2016, Pisa, Italy

ISBN 978-1-4503-4069-4/16/07...$15.00
DOI: http://dx.doi.org/10.1145/2911451.2914677

2. CRAWLING PROCESS

Inspired by seed selection of ClueWeb09[5], we constructed our Web crawl using seeds collected from a range of sources (e.g., Wikipedia, Alexa, ArClueWeb09, and Twitter) and selection methods (manual selection and BootCaT [2]) (Section 2.1). We modified Heritrix[6] to prioritize Arabic pages in crawling, and we applied a 3-step language detection pipeline to identify Arabic content (Section 2.2). We also excluded certain types of content during crawling, as well as post-processed data to remove duplicates and further filter out non-Arabic content, among others (Section 2.3).

2.1 Seed Selection

We have collected around 27M seed URLs via several sources and methods:

Wikipedia: Given Wikipedia's high quality, diversity of topics, and authenticity, we downloaded its Arabic pages on October 2nd 2015 and used Wikipedia Extractor[7] to extract approximately 382K URLs of articles.

Manual Selection: We manually harvested around 6.1K popular Arabic websites. These websites are of various categories such as directories, forums, news sources, governmental, academic and question-answering websites. They were obtained from pre-compiled lists on the Web (e.g., Wikipedia) or by issuing Arabic queries against Google.

Alexa: Alexa[8] provides country-specific website rankings based on estimated daily unique visitors per month. We collected the top 500 websites of 12 Arab countries. We obtained roughly 670 seed pages after eliminating duplicates and non-Arabic pages among all countries.

ArClueWeb09: Since ArClueWeb09 contains a relatively large and diverse set of Arabic pages (29M pages), we believed it to be a good addition to our seed list. We performed a cleaning process on this dataset that includes language detection, *Blacklist*[9] URL filtering, and inappropriate-content filtering. From our cleaning process, we found that 2.9M pages were non-Arabic and 95K web pages were either blacklisted or contain inappropriate content. This resulted in 26.1M seed web pages.

Twitter: To support research related to Arabic microblog IR tasks, we collected webpages linked from Twitter. We crawled tweets for one month (Nov. 9th to Dec. 9th 2015) via Twitter's API. We then extracted URLs from Arabic tweets and filtered out URLs of tweets and blacklisted pages. This process resulted in 348K seed pages.

BootCaT [2]: We collected a set of MSA and dialectal queries. The MSA queries contain ArClueWeb09 queries and category names from the DMOZ Open Directory Project[10] and Wikipedia.

In order to collect dialectal queries, we conducted an informal survey among Arab participants. We also used an available list from the *Al-mo3jam* website[11] for each Arab country. In order to avoid biasing data collection toward any one dialect, we randomly selected dialectal words for each country such that the number of selected dialectal words per country is proportional to the estimated size of its internet user population.

We performed an extensive filtering to remove duplicates, non-Arabic queries, queries with more than 5 words, any English word written in Arabic letters, such as ماي سبيس (*MySpace*) and inappropriate terms. The final list of queries contains around 5600 MSA and 1104 dialectal queries. We ran all queries against Google and Bing search engines where we set the language to Arabic and enabled safe mode to eliminate inappropriate content. We retrieved the first 20 results from each search, yielding approximately 24K URLs after eliminating duplicates.

2.2 Language-Focused Crawling

Prioritized Crawling: The relatively small size of ArClueWeb09 (only 3% of ClueWeb09) exemplifies that general Web crawls yield relatively low harvest rate of Arabic pages. Therefore, we modified Heritrix via a method similar to *soft-focusing* [6], decreasing the priority of URLs extracted from non-Arabic pages (as opposed to completely eliminating them). This ensured coverage of Arabic pages that are accessible only through non-Arabic pages. In addition to decreasing priority, our method also increases the cost of pages extracted from non-Arabic pages. If the crawler cannot identify any Arabic pages crawled from a host after a threshold number of attempts, it eliminates that host.

Language Detection: To prioritize the URLs in the crawler's queues, we detect the language of each page once downloaded. In addition to pure Arabic pages, we also considered multilingual pages related to Arabic (*e.g.*, a page with few Arabic sentences) as Arabic pages.

To detect the language of a page, we applied a 3-stage pipeline (from most-to-least trusted stages). For a given Web page, our algorithm first checks the HTML code of the page. If tagged as Arabic, we consider it so. Otherwise, we run *LangDetect* [14], also used in ClueWeb12, on the page. If it is still not detected as Arabic, Persian, nor Urdu (languages using Arabic characters), we perform a character analysis. If the page contains Arabic (but not Persian or Urdu) characters, we consider it to be Arabic.

2.3 Crawler Execution Details

Having observed ClueWeb switched crawlers from Nutch[12] in 2009 to Heritrix in 2012, we conducted pilot evaluations with both and ultimately selected Heritrix due to reliability and ease of use and modification. However, since Heritrix does not support distributed crawling (unlike Nutch), it was necessary to add a post-processing step to remove duplicate pages crawled by different Heritrix instances.

Crawling was performed on an 11-node cluster, each having 24 cores (2.5 GHz) and 128GB of RAM. We dedicated 3 nodes for ArClueWeb09, 3 nodes for Wikipedia, and 1 node for Twitter seeds. Rest of seeds were distributed evenly over the remaining 4 nodes. We used default parameter configuration of Heritrix and employed 25 threads on each node.

We began crawling on January 1st, 2016 and stopped on January 30th, 2016. During crawling, we excluded non-textual multimedia, compressed data, pages over 100MB, and Twitter content. In addition to removing duplicates in post-processing, we also filtered out non-target pages (*e.g.*, non-Arabic pages, DNS servers, robot.txt files) and pages

[5] boston.lti.cs.cmu.edu/Data/web08-bst/planning.html
[6] webarchive.jira.com/wiki/display/Heritrix/Heritrix
[7] medialab.di.unipi.it/wiki/Wikipedia_Extractor
[8] www.alexa.com
[9] urlblacklist.com
[10] dmoz.org/World/Arabic
[11] ar.mo3jam.com
[12] nutch.apache.org

that return 3xx, 4xx or 5xx error codes. Crawled pages are stored in compressed WARC files.

3. ArabicWeb16 DATASET

Table 1 presents statistics characterizing ArabicWeb16 and ArClueWeb09 Web crawls. ArabicWeb16 is seen to be 5x larger than ArClueWeb09 with respect to number of pages (150M vs. 30M Arabic pages), and 11x larger with respect to storage requirements of uncompressed files (11TB vs. 1TB). In terms of overlap, 2016 versions of 1.5M pages from ArClueWeb09 can be found in ArabicWeb16. Pages from ArClueWeb09 missing in ArabicWeb16 may arise from several causes: the pages no longer existing, being eliminated due to not being detected as Arabic or other filtering criteria (see Section 2.3), or simply having not yet been crawled.

Table 1: ArabicWeb16 & ArClueWeb09 Statistics

	ArabicWeb16	ArClueWeb09
Data Size	10.8 TB	0.97 TB
Pages	150.9M	29.2M
Domains	768,516	196,776
Dialectal Pages	31.4M	6.2M
Est. AR Pages	97%	86.1%

To evaluate the accuracy of our automatic language detection pipeline, we checked for false positives (pages misdetected as Arabic) by manually inspecting 1000 random pages in ArabicWeb16. We found that 97% of them are indeed Arabic, showing our method's reliability. We also replicated the same method for analyzing ArClueWeb09. Of the 1000 random pages, we found 86.1% were Arabic.

3.1 Diversity of Domains

Table 1 shows that ArabicWeb16 covers nearly 4x more domains than ArClueWeb09 (768K vs. 197K). We further counted the number of pages per domain to construct the histogram in Figure 1. For each given page count shown on the x-axis (in log-scale), the y-axis shows the number of domains (in log-scale) having that many pages. The distribution is roughly similar between ArabicWeb16 and ArClueWeb09, with the greater domain and page count of ArabicWeb16 vs. ArClueWeb09 being somewhat obscured by the histogram bucketing. It is interesting to note ArabicWeb16's far greater prevalence of domains having only a single page, whereas ArClueWeb09 finding more domains with 10-99 pages. We also analyzed the top 100 domains in ArabicWeb16 and, interestingly, found that more than 50% are forums. Overall, the diversity seen in pages per domain suggests ArabicWeb16 will be useful for researchers interested in working with domains of varying depth.

3.2 Diversity of Dialects

With regard to coverage of dialectal Arabic, we estimate the distribution of dialectal content vs. MSA in our crawl by training a multi-class *Naïve Bayes* classifier using the `Scikit-learn` [13] library. We distinguish MSA from 4 common geographical dialects: Egyptian, Gulf, Levantine and Maghrebi. Using several dialectal Arabic datasets [8, 3], we sampled a balanced dataset for MSA and each dialect, roughly 7k tweets and comments per category. Since our training dataset is not covering all Arabic dialects, we introduced a 6th category, named *others*, and classified pages as *others* if their classification confidence score is < 0.5.

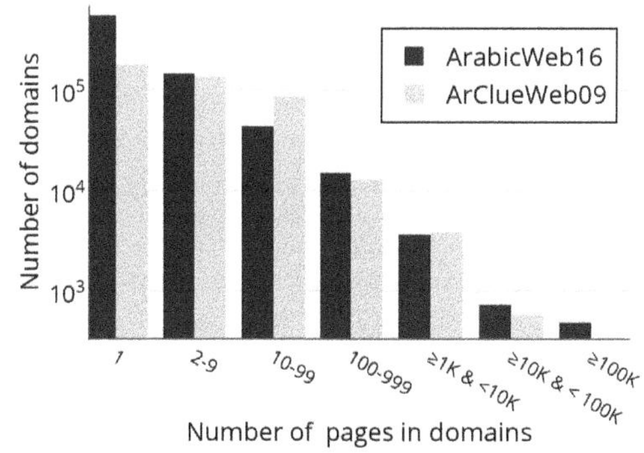

Figure 1: Histogram of pages per domain (log-scale)

We classified the first 150 Arabic words from each page. Table 2 shows the dialectal distribution in both datasets. In ArClueWeb09, we applied our post-processing step (see Section 2.3) and ran the classifier on that filtered dataset.

Table 2: Distribution of MSA and Dialects

Dialect	ArabicWeb16	ArClueWeb09
MSA	119M (79%)	19.9M (76%)
Egyptian	9M (6%)	1.5M (6%)
Gulf	7.6M (5%)	2.7M (10%)
Levantine	7M (5%)	1.5M (6%)
Maghrebi	5M (3%)	0.4M (1.6%)
Others	2.8M (2%)	0.1M (< 1%)

ArabicWeb16 has 5 times more pages with dialects than ArClueWeb09, that is, the ratio of dialectal content is proportional to the ratio of dataset sizes. However, considering the number of internet users of each country[13], the distribution of dialects in ArabicWeb16 is a better representative of dialects. For instance, while Egypt has the highest number of internet users among Arab countries, pages with Egyptian dialect is also more than others in ArabicWeb16, which is not the case in ArClueWeb09.

3.3 Diversity of Page Content

To estimate the proportion of different Web page types in ArabicWeb16, we asked CrowdFlower.com *contributors* to classify pages into the following category schema we defined:

Informational: Web pages whose main purpose is to provide information (*e.g.*, Wikipedia). Information can vary from scientific articles to event schedules.

Discussion & Opinion: Web pages with discussions, opinions, interviews, etc., often on social platforms.

News and Media: Web pages that provide different topics of news and articles from around the world.

Online Services: Web pages for online applications, or platforms for payment and shopping. These Web pages may list services or products to buy or use, user-guides, etc.

Organizational: Institutional Web pages describing owners' interests, activities, news or services, etc.

Entertainment: Web pages with a main purpose to provide entertainment to users (*e.g.*, games, movies).

Other: Web pages not fitting any of the above types.

We randomly sampled 1000 pages from ArabicWeb16 and ArClueWeb09. Broken links and non-Arabic web pages were

[13]internetlivestats.com/internet-users/

identified and excluded from the task in both datasets. We limited the job to Arabic-speakers and moderately-rated contributors who passed test questions with $\geq 80\%$ accuracy.

We requested 3 judgments per page. The overall *Fleiss's Kappa* inter-annotator agreement values for ArabicWeb16 and ArClueWeb09 are 0.57 (moderate agreement) and 0.37 (fair agreement), respectively.

Table 3 presents the number of pages receiving ≥ 2 agreeing labels for each page type. The number of annotated pages in ArClueWeb09 is 5x smaller (as its size). This is mainly because of higher percentage of broken links and non-Arabic pages. We notice that ArabicWeb16 has more pages annotated as Discussion & Opinion. This can be due to the increasing popularity of social media platforms (*e.g.*, tumblr) in recent years. Overall, ArabicWeb16 appears to provide better diversity in terms of page content.

Table 3: Distribution of Different Web page Types

Web page Type	ArabicWeb16	ArClueWeb09
Informational	113 (12.80%)	23 (12.92%)
Discuss. & Opinion	295 (33.41%)	37 (20.79%)
News and Media	93 (10.53%)	9 (5.06%)
Online Services	36 (4.08%)	7 (3.93%)
Organizational	8 (0.91%)	2 (1.12%)
Entertainment	28 (3.17%)	4 (2.25%)
Other	310 (35.11%)	96 (53.93%)

4. ENABLING NEW RESEARCH

A primary goal in constructing ArabicWeb16 is to enable further research in Arabic IR by providing a sound dataset that supports various IR tasks. We envision ArabicWeb16 can be employed for research related to (at least) the following areas: ad-hoc web search, question answering, filtering, cross-dialect search, dialect detection, spam detection, entity-oriented search, and blog track tasks.

To further elaborate, ArabicWeb16 contains many forums, including question-answering sites given as seeds, as well as many informational pages such as Wikipedia, which can usefully support question answering research. In addition, the large dialectal content clearly supports cross-dialect search. While we filtered blacklisted pages in selection of seeds, we intentionally did not filter out spams. Leaving spam present in ArabicWeb16 makes it useful for (Arabic) spam detection research. Finally, ArabicWeb16 contains approximately 19M blog pages (as determined by checking domain names), clearly providing significant content for blog search research.

5. CONCLUSION AND FUTURE WORK

The ever-increasing scale of the Web, shifting patterns of user search and information-sharing behaviors, and emergency of new types of content (e.g., blogs and tweets) creates an ever-growing need to continuously adapt and refine IR methods. Progress in Arabic IR has been impaired in recent years vs. other languages due to lack of suitable data supporting research. Creating a vast Arabic IR collection will therefore create new opportunities and pave way for more further advancements and enhancements in Arabic IR.

Our ongoing work includes construction of search topics and collection of corresponding relevance judgments in order to provide researchers not just with documents to search, but a complete test collection for IR experimentation.

Acknowledgments

This work was made possible by NPRP grant# NPRP 7-1313-1-245 from the Qatar National Research Fund (a member of Qatar Foundation). The statements made herein are solely the responsibility of the authors. We thank the Texas Advanced Computing Center (TACC) at the University of Texas at Austin for computing resources enabling this research.

6. REFERENCES

[1] P. Bailey, N. Craswell, and D. Hawking. Engineering a multi-purpose test collection for web retrieval experiments. *Information Processing & Management*, 39(6):853–871, 2003.

[2] M. Baroni and S. Bernardini. BootCaT: Bootstrapping Corpora and Terms from the Web. In *Proceedings of the Language Resources and Evaluation Conf. (LREC)*, 2004.

[3] H. Bouamor, N. Habash, and K. Oflazer. A Multidialectal Parallel Corpus of Arabic. In *Proceedings of the Language Resources and Evaluation Conference (LREC)*, pages 1240–1245, 2014.

[4] C. Buckley, D. Dimmick, I. Soboroff, and E. Voorhees. Bias and the limits of pooling for large collections. *Information retrieval*, 10(6):491–508, 2007.

[5] J. Callan, M. Hoy, C. Yoo, and L. Zhao. The ClueWeb09 Dataset, 2009. Presentation Nov. 19, 2009 at NIST TREC. Slides online at boston.lti.cs.cmu.edu/classes/11-742/S10-TREC/TREC-Nov19-09.pdf.

[6] S. Chakrabarti, M. Van den Berg, and B. Dom. Focused crawling: a new approach to topic-specific Web resource discovery. *Computer Networks*, 31(11):1623–1640, 1999.

[7] C. W. Cleverdon. The evaluation of systems used in information retrieval. In *Proceedings of the international conference on scientific information*, volume 1, pages 687–698. National Academy of Sciences, 1959.

[8] R. Cotterell and C. Callison-Burch. A Multi-Dialect, Multi-Genre Corpus of Informal Written Arabic. In *Proceedings of the Language Resources and Evaluation Conference (LREC)*, pages 241–245, 2014.

[9] K. Darwish and W. Magdy. Arabic Information Retrieval. *Foundations and Trends in Information Retrieval*, 7(4):239–342, 2014.

[10] F. C. Gey and D. W. Oard. The TREC-2001 Cross-Language Information Retrieval Track: Searching Arabic Using English, French or Arabic Queries. In *Proc. of the Tenth Text REtrieval Conference (TREC 10)*, 2001.

[11] D. Hawking, E. Voorhees, N. Craswell, and P. Bailey. Overview of the TREC-8 Web Track. In *Proceedings of the Eighth Text REtrieval Conference (TREC 8)*, 1999.

[12] V. Kolias, I. Anagnostopoulos, and E. Kayafas. Exploratory Analysis of a Terabyte Scale Web Corpus. *arXiv preprint arXiv:1409.5443*, 2014.

[13] F. Pedregosa, G. Varoquaux, A. Gramfort, et al. Scikit-learn: Machine learning in python. *The Journal of Machine Learning Research*, 12:2825–2830, 2011.

[14] N. Shuyo. Language detection library for java, 2010. http://code.google.com/p/language-detection/.

Building Test Collections for Evaluating Temporal IR

Hideo Joho
University of Tsukuba,
Tsukuba, Japan
hideo@slis.tsukuba.ac.jp

Adam Jatowt
Kyoto University, Kyoto, Japan
adam@dl.kuis.kyoto-u.ac.jp

Roi Blanco
University of A Coruña
rblanco@udc.es

Haitao Yu
University of Tsukuba,
Tsukuba, Japan
yuhaitao@slis.tsukuba.ac.jp

Shuhei Yamamoto
University of Tsukuba,
Tsukuba, Japan
yamahei@ce.slis.tsukuba.ac.jp

ABSTRACT

Research on temporal aspects of information retrieval has recently gained considerable interest within the Information Retrieval (IR) community. This paper describes our efforts for building test collections for the purpose of fostering temporal IR research. In particular, we overview the test collections created at the two recent editions of Temporal Information Access (Temporalia) task organized at NTCIR-11 and NTCIR-12, report on selected results and discuss several observations we made during the task design and implementation. Finally, we outline further directions for constructing test collections suitable for temporal IR.

CCS Concepts

•**Information systems → Test collections;**

Keywords

Temporal IR; test collections; temporal query intents; temporal search result diversification

1. INTRODUCTION

Topical document relevance has traditionally been the key concern in the development and evaluation of Information Retrieval (IR) systems. Recently, however, IR community has been interested in exploring other dimensions which underlie effective search processes such as the novelty, diversity, coverage, and/or readability. Timeliness is one such quality aspect of documents which, to a significant degree, determines user satisfaction, at least, for the subset of queries whose underlying search intents contain strong temporal component (e.g., `Pisa weather`, `Olympics 2020`). In consequence, Temporal IR [1, 7] has started to emerge as one challenge of information retrieval in which time and temporality play crucial roles.

SIGIR '16, July 17-21, 2016, Pisa, Italy

DOI: http://dx.doi.org/10.1145/2911451.2914673

Table 1: Number of formal runs (number of teams) in subtasks of Temporalia-1 and Temporalia-2. Number of teams increased by 40% in Temporalia-2.

Task	TQIC	TID	TIR	TDR
Temporalia-1 EN	17 (6)	-	19 (6)	-
Temporalia-2 EN	-	30 (12)	-	9 (3)
Temporalia-2 CH	-	7 (3)	-	0 (0)

Time-related aspects can be actually bound to many components in the architecture of a search engine system and to many steps of a retrieval process. For example, temporality may be already estimated on the level of input queries (query issue time and temporal intent class). Documents can be associated with different types of time (e.g., publication time, content focus time or content modification time) allowing construction of temporally-aware search indexes. Finally, retrieval mechanisms can output results according to the match between the temporal aspects of query intents and the estimated time scopes of documents [3].

While some prior attempts tried to survey the growing field of Temporal IR [1, 7] or to investigate the actual user needs and tactics while searching for information of temporal character [4], the community lacks common evaluation grounds and standardized test beds for effective comparison and evaluation of search technologies.

Temporal Information Access (*Temporalia*)[1] tasks hosted at NTCIR-11 [5] and NTCIR-12 [6] aimed to fill in this gap. Both *Temporalia-1* and *Temporalia-2* consisted of two subtasks focusing on two crucial components necessary for designing an effective time-aware IR process. *Temporal Query Intent Categorization* (*TQIC*) in Temporalia-1 and *Temporal Intent Disambiguation* (*TID*) in Temporalia-2 dealt with the problem of recognizing temporal class of search queries. On the other hand, *Temporal Information Retrieval* (*TIR*) and *Temporally Diversified Retrieval* (*TDR*) in Temporalia-1 and Temporalia-2, respectively, concentrated on evaluating document retrieval for information needs with underlying temporal aspect. While English was our primary focus, the second edition of Temporalia extended also the evaluation to Chinese. Tab. 1 shows the overall participation in both editions of the task, while Tab. 2 summarizes the resulting test collections.

[1]http://ntcirtemporalia.github.io/

Table 2: Collection statistics.

Collection	Language	Description	Size
Temporalia-1 TQIC	EN	Queries with temporal classes	300
Temporalia-1 TIR	EN	Topics with temporal subtopics	50
Temporalia-2 TID	EN	Queries with distribution over temporal classes	300
Temporalia-2 TID	CH	Queries with distribution over temporal classes	300
Temporalia-2 TDR	EN	Topics with temporal subtopics	50
Temporalia-2 TDR	CH	Topics with temporal subtopics	50

Table 3: Example queries for the TID subtask (Dry Run) with query submission date of May 1, 2013.

Query	Past	Recency	Future	Atem.
Australian Open	0.091	0.0	0.455	0.455
NBA Finals	0.1	0.0	0.4	0.5
NBA playoff schedule	0.0	0.2	0.6	0.2
price of oil	0.0	0.9	0.0	0.1
how to lose weight	0.0	0.1	0.0	0.9
time in India	0.0	1.0	0.0	0.0
history of volleyball	1.0	0.0	0.0	0.0

2. RELATED TEST COLLECTIONS

Although many tasks at TREC, CLEF or NTCIR have been devoted to query analysis and document retrieval, only a few of them particularly focused on temporal aspects in search. Furthermore, temporal notions in other tasks were typically limited to the timeliness and recency requirements put on extracted information. *TempSum* and *KBA* are the most relevant ones.

TREC's *Temporal Summarization task*[2] (*TempSum*) is composed of two subtasks: *Sequential Update Summarization* and *Value Tracking*. Sequential Update Summarization asks to find timely, sentence-level, reliable, relevant and non-redundant updates about developing events, while Value Tracking requires tracking values of event-related attributes (e.g., fatalities count) being of high importance to the event. Both subtasks have clear temporal character since the updates have to be not only relevant but also timely. Although, we also test ranking methods for the "recency" class of search needs in our tasks, we do not limit the scope to the information needs about recent or ongoing events, or to a particular type of attribute-like information. Hence, any temporal query category may become an input, and the results are output as lists of ranked documents rather than information pieces.

One of its subtasks, *Streaming Slot Filling*, tracks the attributes and relations of a selected entity over time. Similarly to TempSum, the temporal information need is in the form of a recency requirement. In addition, only documents related to a particular entity such as a person or organization are deemed relevant.

3. TEMPORAL INFORMATION ACCESS

First we discuss time categorization used in Temporalia. Several categorizations of time are possible such as ones according to calendar, frequency, periodicity, distance, etc. However, the most common and the most natural distinction is the division of timeline into the past, present and future from the viewpoint of a speaker or information searcher. Therefore, we have constructed our task around this natural

[2]http://www.trec-ts.org/

Table 4: Example topic for TDR subtask (Dry Run).

Title	Father's day
Description	I am from a country where Father's Day is not a common custom, and I would like to learn more about Father's day and its relation to the role of father in society.
Past question	What is the history and origin of the Father's day?
Recency question	What famous persons has lately done during Father's day?
Future question	What is the future outlook for the problem of fatherlessness and how the father's role is supposed to change?
Atemporal question	What is Father's day?
Search date	1 Mar 2013 GMT+0:00

time distinction assuming the query issuing time as a center (i.e., point "now"). In addition, we provided an atemporal class for queries without any obvious time focus. The four classes are defined below. We also show example queries with their per-class probability distributions in Tab. 3.

Past: class of queries about past entities or events. Content relevant to past-related queries is not expected to change significantly over time.

Recency: class of queries about present or recent entities or events. Relevant content for queries belonging to the Recency class generally changes frequently and quickly hence the search results are expected to contain timely and up-to-date documents.

Future: class of queries about predicted, scheduled or expected events. Search results should contain documents with future-related information when compared to the query issuing time.

Atemporal: class characterizing queries without any clear temporal intent. Search results returned for atemporal queries are not expected to be related to time, neither, their content should change much over time. Navigational queries are considered to be atemporal.

3.1 Temporal Intent Detection

In both the task editions we have approached the problem of detecting temporal classes of intent underlying search queries. According to the well-known study conducted in 2008 on the AOL query dataset [10], about 1.5% of queries have been found to contain explicit temporal expressions (e.g., `Tokyo Olympics 1964`, `popular songs 2000s`). Although this rate may seem small at first, it amounts to quite a large number of searches, and it does not cover queries which lack clear temporal expressions which contain strong implicit temporal component (e.g., `Berlin Wall`, `economic forecast` or `Tokyo Olympics`).

Given the set of query strings associated with their submitting times, participants had to develop systems to de-

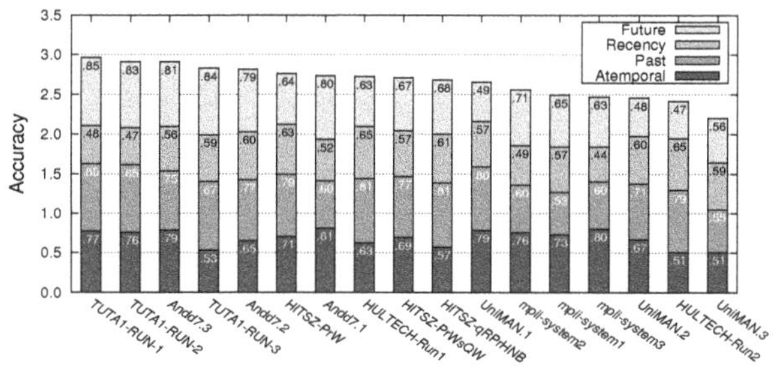

Figure 1: Performance in TQIC subtask.

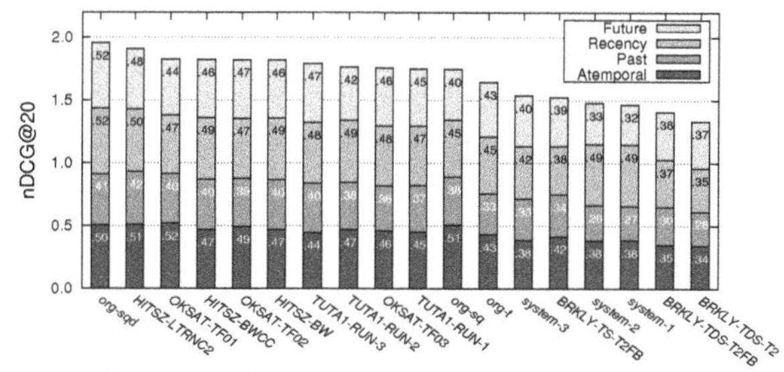

Figure 2: Performance in TIR subtask.

		Estimated class				
		Atemporal	Past	Recency	Future	total
Answer class	Atemporal	783 (67.7%)	111(9.6%)	193(16.7%)	69(6.0%)	1,156
	Past	147(13.1%)	836(74.2%)	61(5.4%)	82(7.3%)	1,126
	Recency	154(13.5%)	28(2.5%)	638(55.9%)	322(28.2%)	1,142
	Future	51(4.4%)	18(1.6%)	299(25.9%)	786(68.1%)	1,154
	total	1,135(24.8%)	993(21.7%)	1,191(26.0%)	1,259(27.5%)	4,578

Figure 3: Confusion matrix in TQIC subtask.

termine either the dominant temporal class (past, recency, future and atemporal) of each of the queries (TQIC subtask in Temporalia-1) or their per-class distribution (TID subtask in Temporalia-2). Queries for both the dry and formal runs were created based on seed set of temporal expressions and were then collected from search engine query logs or search suggestions given by major search engines. We have then administered crowdsourcing tasks for determining the distribution of queries across the temporal classes. Each query received 20 judgments.

The performance of submitted runs in TQIC was measured by the average rate of queries with correct temporal classes and, in TID, by (i) the averaged per-class absolute loss as well as (ii) by the cosine similarity between the ground truth temporal class distribution and the distribution estimated by the participating systems.

In Fig.1 we show the system performance in Temporalia-1 TQIC subtask. Temporalia-2 TID results will be reported at NTCiR-12 Conference, June 2016, Tokyo, Japan.

3.2 Temporal Ranking

The second problem relates to ranking results for queries containing temporal requirement. First, *Temporal Information Retrieval* (TIR) at Temporalia-1 asked participants to retrieve a set of documents for a search topic that incorporates time factor. In addition to a standard search topic data (i.e., title, description, and sub topics), TIR search topic contained the query submitting date information to indicate the relationship between the query and searcher.

Temporally Diversified Retrieval (TDR) extended TIR by requiring participants to separately retrieve ranked lists of documents relevant to each of four temporal intent classes for a given topic. Participants were also asked to return a set of documents that is temporally diversified for the same topic. TDR participants received a set of topic descriptions, query issuing time, and indicative search questions for each of temporal classes (Past, Recency, Future, and Atemporal). The objective of the indicative search questions was to demonstrate one possible subtopic under a particular temporal class. In Tab. 4 we show an example topic with its subtopics.

For the evaluation, the standard Cranfield methodology was used. In particular, a pool of potentially relevant documents was created based on the top-ranked documents from participants' submitted runs. Then each document in the pool was assessed through online crowdsourcing (3 judgments per document for each class), and its relevance grade was judged. Given a ranked list generated for a specific temporal subtopic, the system performance was evaluated using Precision, Q-measure and nDCG metric. For a diversified ranked list generated to satisfy all possible temporal classes, the performance was evaluated using α-nDCG and D#-nDCG.

In Fig.2 we show the system performance in Temporalia-1's TIR subtask. Temporalia-2's TDR results will be reported at NTCIR-12 Conference.

3.2.1 Document Collections

Both, Temporalia-1 and Temporalia-2 used the same document corpus for English called *LivingKnowledge News and Blogs Annotated Sub-collection* constructed by the LivingKnowledge project and distributed by the Internet Memory Foundation [9]. This collection of approximately 20GB size spans the time period from May 2011 to March 2013 and contains around 3.8M documents from about 1,500 different blogs and news sources. We chose this collection since it has a relatively long temporal span of documents. To facilitate information extraction, we have indicated sentence boundaries as well as mentions of named entities, and we have also disambiguated detected temporal expressions.

Temporalia-2 has also introduced Chinese language. SogouCA [3] and SogouT [4] document collections were used for the dry run and formal run, respectively. Three kinds of annotations were provided: sentence splitting, named entities, and time annotations.

4. DISCUSSIONS

In this section we discuss several observations obtained during the task design and we outline some future directions:

Challenges with Recency and Future classes: Recency and Future classes seem to be the most challenging when it comes to recognizing temporal intent. The mean classification accuracy for these classes were 0.565 and 0.678, respectively, compared to 0.687 and 0.733 for the Atemporal and Past classes, respectively. This can be also seen in Fig. 3, which shows the confusion matrix for TQIC subtask.

Balancing queries over temporal classes: When creating test sets for TID subtask we faced the problem with

[3] http://www.sogou.com/labs/dl/ca.html
[4] http://www.sogou.com/labs/dl/t-e.html

Team	Runs	Num. of features	External data sources	External tools	Classifiers
HITSZ	3	3 features + ngrams and POS ngrams	Web search results (titles, snippets)	POS tagger, NER	Classifier voting & rule-based method
HULTECH	2	11 features	Web search results (snippets)	TempoWordnet, GTE	Ensemble learning (8 classifiers)
TUTA1 (top)	3	3 feature groups	AOL 500K query session	POS tagger, SUTime, NER	Semi-supervised & supervised classifiers (Log. Reg., SVMLin)
Andd7	3	3 features + bag of words	-	Porter Stemmer	SVM, NB, DT & their agreement
MPII	3	6 feature groups + ngrams	DMOZ directory	2 thesauri, POS tagger, NER	NB, DT & simulated annealing
UniMan	3	19 features	Wikipedia	POS tagger, TempoWordnet, ManTIME	SVM & Random Forrest

Figure 4: Overview of techniques used in TQIC.

constructing a query set that would be appropriately balanced over query classes. For example, Atemporal class was ubiquitous for each query making it difficult to find many queries without substantial probability score in the Atemporal class. Relatedly, the combinations in which relatively high rate was observed in the Future as well as in the Past class were quite rare. All these issues made the construction of symmetrical test set collections a difficult challenge.

Sources of temporal signals: Participants used variety of external sources and tools for capturing temporal signals. For a rough overview, we show in Fig. 4 the types of temporal signals and techniques used by the participating teams in the TQIC subtask.

Relation to search result diversification tasks: *IMine* [8] and *Intent* [12] tasks focus on various aspects of search result diversification in IR. For example, *Query Understanding* (*QU*) and *Vertical Incorporating* (*VI*) subtasks in *IMine-2* require to identify the subtopics of a query or diversify organic results respectively. Temporal intent detection and temporal diversification of results could be then regarded as attempts at enforcing higher level diversification, i.e., diversification not on the level of subtopics but, on the level of temporal classes, each of which typically covers several possible subtopics that share the same temporal orientation.

Task participation: As indicated in Tab. 1, the number of participating teams in Temporalia-2 increased by 40% from Temporalia-1. This demonstrates the need for and benefits of Temporalia's test collections. As for the subtask breakdown, tasks related to estimating temporal query classes were more popular than ones for retrieving documents. Besides the presumed difficulty of indexing the document collection, the need to cope with large data sizes as well as with the content of varying subtopics, the other reasons for this preference could come from the problems with estimating temporality of large text chunks in contrast to short query strings that can be rather easily manipulated. We also note that Chinese language TDR failed to attract any participation in contrast to Chinese language TID. This may suggest that the additional difficulty of processing large amounts of ideograms in documents might have outweighed the benefits of solving the task in a language less commonly researched within the IR community.

Future of Temporal IR evaluation: Estimating focus time of documents [1, 3], which is the time to which documents refer to, could be one possible subtask in the future. Another challenge is estimating document creation time. In this context, we note that *SemEval2015* introduced *Diachronic Text Evaluation* task [11] which required to identify time interval when a given piece of news text (typically spanning between tens to a couple of hundred of words) was published on the time scale of 1700 and 2010.

We think that the combination of the document creation and focus time coupled with the estimated query's temporality and its issuing date should offer sufficient for judging temporal correspondence of documents to the query. Finally, future challenges could be designed to testing temporal query suggestion or retrieval mechanisms over long term document archives.

5. CONCLUSIONS

In this paper we have reported the results of our recent efforts towards building test collections for fostering Temporal IR and related applications in the context of Temporalia-1 and Temporalia-2 tasks at NTCIR-11/12. Both tasks focused on two important objectives. The first one is to test methods for recognizing temporal aspects behind query intent. The second objective is to facilitate comparison of document ranking methods according to temporal classes of queries. Unlike other test collections, Temporalia's test collections are designed to let researchers compare performance of their systems across major temporal classes.

Acknowledgments This work was supported in part by MEXT Grant-in-Aid for Young Scientists B (#24700239 and #22700096), and by the JST research promotion program Sakigake. The authors also thank the NTCIR project at NII.

6. REFERENCES

[1] R. Campos, G. Dias, A.M. Jorge, and A. Jatowt. Survey of Temporal Information Retrieval and Related Applications. In: *ACM Comp. Surv.*, 15:1–15:41, 2014.

[2] C. Clarke, M. Kolla, G. Cormack, O. Vechtomova, A. Ashkan, S. Buttcher, and I. MacKinnon. Novelty and Diversity in Information Retrieval Evaluation. In: *Proc. of 31st SIGIR*, 659–666, 2008.

[3] A. Jatowt, C.M. Au Yeung and K. Tanaka. Estimating Document Focus Time. In: *CIKM'13*, 2273–2278.

[4] H. Joho, A. Jatowt, and R. Blanco. Temporal Information Searching Behaviour and Strategies. In: *Inf. Proc. & Manag.*, 51(6):834-850 (2015).

[5] H. Joho, A. Jatowt, R. Blanco, H. Naka and S. Yamamoto. Overview of NTCIR-11 Temporal Information Access (Temporalia) Task. In: *Proc. of NTCIR-11*, 2014.

[6] H. Joho, A. Jatowt, R. Blanco, H. Yu and S. Yamamoto. Overview of NTCIR-12 Temporal Information Access (Temporalia-2) Task. In: *Proc. of NTCIR-12*, to appear, 2016.

[7] N. Kanhabua, R. Blanco and K. Nørväg. Temporal Information Retrieval. In: *Foundations and Trends in Information Retrieval*, 9(2):91–208, 2014.

[8] Y. Liu, R. Song, M. Zhang, Z. Dou, T. Yamamoto, M. P. Kato, H. Ohshima, K. Zhou. Overview of the NTCIR-11 IMine Task. In: *Proc. of NTCIR-11*, 2014.

[9] M. Matthews, P. Tolchinsky, R. Blanco, J. Atserias, P. Mika, and H. Zaragoza. Searching through Time in the New York Times. In: *Proc. of HCIR 2010*, 41–44, 2010.

[10] S. Nunes, C. Ribeiro, and G. David. Use of Temporal Expressions in Web Search. In: *Proc. of ECIR 2008*, 580–584, 2008.

[11] O. Popescu, and C. Strapparava. SemEval2015, Task 7: Diachronic Text Evaluation. In: *Proc. of the International Workshop on Semantic Evaluation.*, 2015.

[12] T. Sakai, Z. Dou, T. Yamamoto, Y. Liu, M. Zhang, M. P. Kato, R. Song, M. Iwata Summary of the NTCIR-10 INTENT-2 Task: Subtopic Mining and Search Result Diversification. In: *Proc. of IGIR 2013*, 761–764, 2013.

DAJEE: A Dataset of Joint Educational Entities for Information Retrieval in Technology Enhanced Learning

Vladimir Estivill-Castro
School of ICT
Griffith University
170 Kessels road, Nathan
QLD, 4111, Australia
v.estivill-castro@griffith.edu.au

Carla Limongelli
Dept. of Computer Science and Automation
Roma Tre University
Via della Vasca Navale, 79
Rome, Italy
limongel@dia.uniroma3.it

Matteo Lombardi, Alessandro Marani
School of ICT
Griffith University
170 Kessels road, Nathan
QLD, 4111, Australia
{matteo.lombardi,alessandro.marani}@griffithuni.edu.au

ABSTRACT

In the Technology Enhanced Learning (TEL) community, the problem of conducting reproducible evaluations of recommender systems is still open, due to the lack of exhaustive benchmarks. The few public datasets available in TEL have limitations, being mostly small and local.

Recently, Massive Open Online Courses (MOOC) are attracting many studies in TEL, mainly because of the huge amount of data for these courses and their potential for many applications in TEL. This paper presents *DAJEE*, a dataset built from the crawling of MOOCs hosted on the Coursera platform. *DAJEE* offers information on the usage of more than 20,000 resources in 407 courses by 484 instructors, with a conjunction of different educational entities in order to store the courses' structure and the instructors' teaching experiences.

Keywords

TEL dataset, Educational Dataset, MOOC, Coursera

1. INTRODUCTION

The increasing trend of contributions on Information Retrieval (IR) and recommender systems in TEL brought to the attention of the research community the lack of large and exhaustive datasets for a reproducible and significant evaluation of those systems [1, 5].

At the same time, the idea of Massive Open Online Courses (MOOCs) has raised the interest of the TEL community [2, 1]. These courses are publicly available worldwide and usually offer a very qualitative learning service. One of the largest and popular platform hosting MOOCs is Coursera [2] of Stanford University. On Coursera there are hundreds of high-quality courses delivered by prestigious universities all around the world. It is not difficult to see MOOCs platforms, specially Coursera, as a potential dataset of educational resources and data in general. Although usually MOOCs resources do not include metadata, it is still possible to derive some educational traits of resources from the data about courses. Other information about courses and instructors can be extracted too.

Hence, this paper presents *DAJEE*, a DAtaset of Joint Educational Entities, to gather this information from MOOCs and provide an important asset for IR applications in TEL.

1.1 Other datasets in TEL

Presently, the most used datasets in TEL are based on Learning Objects (LO) available on Learning Object Repositories (LORs). One of the most popular LOR is MERLOT[1] [5], referencing to more than 40.000 LOs on the Web. MERLOT does not store the materials, just the URL and the metadata. However, there is some concern about the completeness of the metadata of LOs in LORs [6], and the inability of current schemata of metadata to provide useful information for the recommendation of LOs [3].

Similarly to MERLOT, this contribution presents a reference dataset of teaching resources, where only the data about the resources are stored in the repository. Unlike MERLOT and other LORs, our dataset also stores contextual information about how resources have been practically used in courses by instructors, with a clear distinction of the different educational entities (lessons, concepts and resources). A LO indeed can vary from a very small lesson about one concept to an entire course. Instead, the goal of this dataset is to provide educational data of resources, courses, lessons and instructors independently, so that a wider variety of IR systems in TEL can be proposed and evaluated with such a dataset.

2. EDUCATIONAL DATA IN COURSERA

At the moment, Coursera is recognised as the largest platform hosting MOOCs with more than 1,700 courses delivered by 147 institutions[2]. The Coursera APIs v1[3] deliver little information, only a few attributes of about 100 courses. For these reasons, we have developed a crawler of data from Coursera in order to build a dataset of teaching resources. The dataset actually stores the URL to the resources on

[1]https://www.merlot.org

[2]Source: https://www.coursera.org on 22/01/2016

[3]https://tech.coursera.org/app-platform/catalog/ accessed on 22/01/2016

SIGIR '16, July 17-21, 2016, Pisa, Italy

© 2016 ACM. ISBN 978-1-4503-4069-4/16/07...$15.00

DOI: http://dx.doi.org/10.1145/2911451.2914670

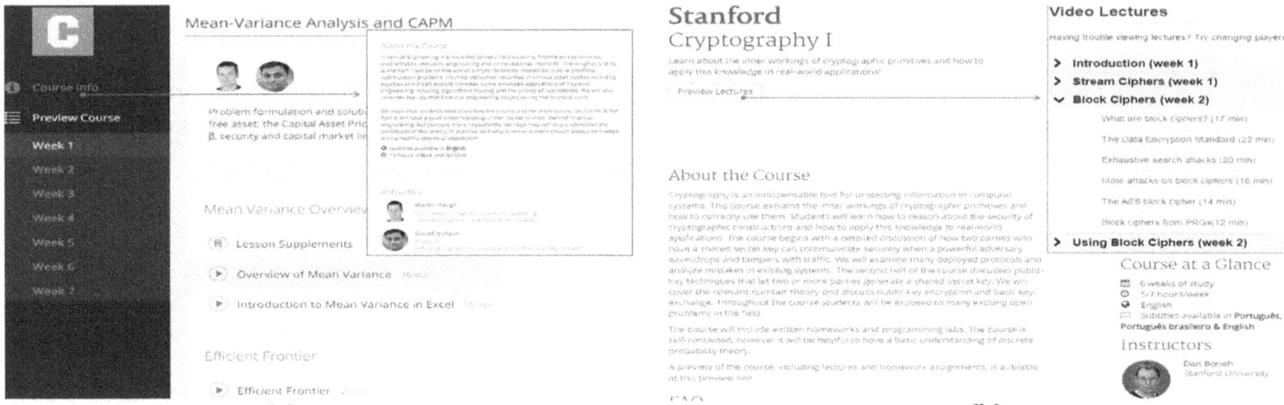

(a) (b)

Figure 1: An example of learn-type (a) and course-type (b) format of courses in Coursera.

Coursera, not the resources themselves, with information about i) the resources, ii) the courses where they have been delivered, and iii) the instructors who delivered them on Coursera. We briefly present the structure of Coursera[4] and the data that we have been able to crawl.

The courses are divided into weeks, which are, in essence, lessons. Usually, a course has a presentation page with a section for the abstract, the course syllabus and instructors among other information. In Coursera we have found two types of courses: *learn* and *course*; this distinction is stated directly in the URL of the courses. The course-type courses offer a more informative presentation page reporting also the category of a course (not available for the other type). Instead, the learn-type courses have a more meaningful internal structure, where a concept can be associated with more than one resource. In course-type courses, resources are directly delivered in lessons with no mention of concepts, so for those courses we considered the title of the resources as the target concept. Independently of the course type, not all courses have a preview of their content and structure. When there is a preview, the content of the course can be accessed without enrolling; it is sufficient to be logged in on Coursera. Figure 1a shows the structure of a learn-type course with a preview available. As we can see, i) the course has at least one instructor, ii) it is divided into weeks or lessons, iii) each lesson is divided into concepts and iv) the concepts contain the resources. Such structure is maintained in our dataset.

The resources delivered on Coursera are mostly videos, but in learn-type courses there are other types of resources. Interestingly, most of the videos have downloadable transcripts; valuable data for applying text-mining and IR tools.

This analysis of Coursera unveiled the potential of a big and well-characterized dataset of teaching resources. Hence, we designed and implemented a crawler for extracting resources and educational data around them. An educational entity from Coursera was saved in this dataset, upon condition that all the compulsory attributes (reported in bold in Section 3) were extracted. In addition, some learn-type courses allowed access only to the first week of the course, so only the data of the first lesson have been crawled. Moreover, some instructors did not present their affiliation in their page, so they have not been included in the set of instructors of a course. Consequently, a course resulting with no instructors has not been recorded in the dataset. Table 1 reports the amount of the crawled data that are in *DAJEE*.

[4]The structure presented here is related to the time of the crawling design, implementation and running that took place in from August to November 2015.

Entity	Number of crawled instances
University	99
Instructor	484
Course	407
Category	46 (10 root categories)
Lesson	2,365
Concept	8,716
Resource	22,663

Table 1: Summary of educational entities of Coursera included in *DAJEE*.

2.1 Some considerations of resources types and purposes in Coursera

Resource type	Title Prefix	URL Suffix
Exam	Quiz	-
Peer	Assignment Review Classmates	- give-feedback
Quiz	Practice Quiz	-
Programming	Assignment	-

Table 2: Pattern of resource titles and URL for some resource types in Coursera.

While exploring the resources delivered on Coursera, we found a number of different resource types, mostly in learn-type courses. This difference is reported directly in the URL of the resource, corresponding to this pattern:
$.../ < course\_URL > / < resource\_type > /....$
So, during the crawling phase, the type of a resource is extracted from the URL and associated with the resource, with two exceptions. The type *lecture* has been renamed to *video* because a lecture was always delivered with video resources. The crawled resources of type *supplement* always refer to further reading or insights, so the type for those resources is *document* and the purpose is *supplement.* With these con-

siderations, the types of resources available in *DAJEE* are: *exam*, *peer*, *quiz*, *document*, *video* and *programming*.

In addition, when analysing the title of the crawled resources, we identified a pattern that is applied to all the resource types, with the exception of videos and supplements. The first terms of the title specify the purpose of the resource with this pattern: $< resource\_purpose >:< resource\_title >$. Moreover, all the resources of type *peer* have their URL ending with $/give-feedback$. Table 2 summarises these patterns used for attaining the purpose of the resources, where a title prefix is the substring until the first occurrence of colon, and the URL suffix is the substring from the last occurrence of '/'. Taking into account the latter considerations, the dataset offers resources for the following purposes: *presenting*, *examination*, *supplement*, *feedback*, *assessing* and *practice quiz*.

3. THE DAJEE DATASET

DAJEE is a MySql Database (DB) that hosts the data of the educational entities reported in Table 1 and described afterwards. For a better understanding, Figure 2 shows the E-R diagram of the DB reporting all the entities in *DAJEE*. We chose a low level of normalization of the DB because it is for consulting purposes only. Bear in mind that the bold attributes of an entity had to be crawled from Coursera, otherwise the entity would not have been included in the dataset. Furthermore, if a course did not have the compulsory data, then all the related entities were discarded.

3.1 University

It just reports the ***name*** and ***URL*** of the universities of courses and instructors. It also has an *id* field for being identified within the DB; this is the key of this entity.

3.2 Instructor

It also has an *id* field as key. Other information is about the ***name***, ***university***, *position* in the university (it can be *NULL*) and the *website* (it may be empty). In addition, the pair *name* and *university* must be unique.

3.3 Course

This entity has many attributes, being one of the most informative entity in Coursera. These are the attributes: *id* (key), ***title***, ***URL***, ***course_code***, ***language***, ***id_university***, *length*, *length_description* (*NULL*), *short_description* (it can be empty), *description* and *subtitles* (it can be empty). More in depth, the *course_code* is extracted from *URL* and uniquely identifies courses in Coursera. The length is not always reported in the presentation page of the course. If not available, it is determined as the sum of the duration of the resources delivered in the course. The field *length_description* is an indicative duration of the course; usually they show either the following wording, "6 weeks of study, 5-7 hours/week" or the following one, "4-6 hours/week". The attribute *short_description* is extracted for only the course-type courses (41 courses) when provided; it is not reported for learn-type courses. Finally, *category* is a comma-separated list of ids of the table *Category*.

3.4 Category

This entity represents a category with the following attributes: *id* (key), *id_root_category* (equal to -1 if the category is root) and ***name***.

3.5 Concept

This entity is very simple and consists of *id* (key), ***name*** and *language* (can be empty). The name of a concept is composed by the title of the concept (as found on the webpage) and the name of the lesson, following this pattern: $< concept\_name >::< lesson\_name >$. We chose such representation since some concepts have very generic titles; it is more expressive to include the name of the lesson, with an easy separation using two colons. The language of a concept is not specified on Coursera, but it has been derived analysing the transcripts of its video resources. If no video resources are associated with the concept, then *language* is empty.

3.6 Lesson

This entity is a container of concepts and it is not directly reported in Coursera. It is recognized from headers of a course web-page that either contains the concepts, for learn-type courses (refer to Figure 1a), or resources, for course-type courses (see Figure 1b). In case of learn-type courses, a lesson matches with a week, while for course-type courses that may not be the case. The following attributes exist for this entity: *id* (key), ***name***, ***concepts***, ***prerequisites***, *description*, ***id_cm*** (id of the concept map), ***version_cm*** (version of the concept map). *Concepts* is a collection of id of the table *concept*, separated by a comma, and it refers to the concepts taught in the lesson. *Prerequisites* reports the list of ids of the previous lessons (for Coursera only one), in order to keep trace of the sequencing of the lessons as found in the course. *Description* of a lesson is not always available on Coursera, but it is never empty in the dataset. The descriptions of lessons start with a prefix reporting the number of the week in which the lesson is delivered (i.e. week 1 - descriptionText). We adopted this approach because a week in course-type courses usually refers to more than one container (headers) of concepts, as Figure 1b shows. Finally, the attributes *id_cm* and *version_cm* identify the concept map of a course.

3.7 Concept Map

In education, a concept map is a very powerful way to represent the course domain, namely the concepts taught in a course and their arrangement. In this dataset, a concept map (table *conceptmap*) consists of the concepts and their sequencing in a course on Coursera, connecting a course with its concepts. A concept map is related to only one course, thus the *id* consists of the prefix "coursera:" and the course code (e.g. coursera:positive-psychology). The prefix is helpful to distinguish possible matching of course codes from other MOOCs platforms. With a different crawling of the same platform, we may find some differences for a concept map, so the attribute *version* identifies a particular arrangement of the map. To sum up, a concept map is uniquely identified by ***id*** and ***version***. For an id of a concept map, there is a record for each concept of the map, reporting the id of the *concept* (*conceptID*) and the id of the previous *concept* (*prerequisite*), if any.

3.8 Teaching Context

This entity connects together *concept maps*, *instructors* and *courses* via the following attributes: ***id_cm***, ***version_cm***, ***id_course*** and ***id_instructor***(foreign keys to the respective tables).

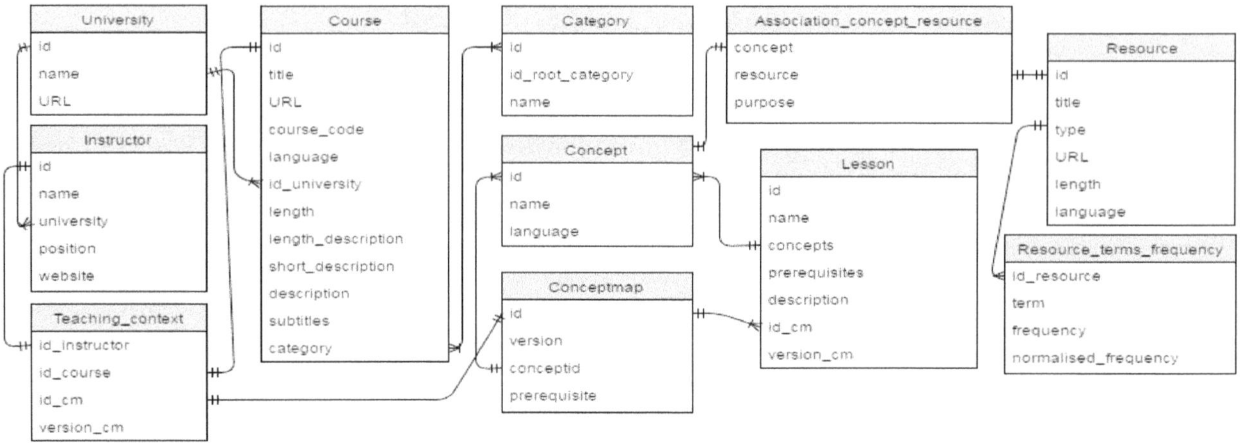

Figure 2: The Entity-Relationship diagram of the current version of the dataset.

3.9 Resource

A *resource* entity has the following attributes: *id* (key), ***title***, ***type***, ***URL***, *length* and *language*. The attribute *type* consists of six values introduced in Section 2.1. The length can be zero, specially for *document* and *programming* resources where the duration was never specified. The language of a resource is determined by extracting the language of the transcript using the tool Apache Tika[5]. If the transcript was not available or not provided, the language of the concept to which it belongs was assigned (it can be empty).

3.10 Resources Terms Frequency

For copyright issues, the transcripts of the video resources are not included in this dataset. However, the table named *resource_terms_ frequency* provides the *frequency* and *normalised frequency* of each stemmed term in the transcript of a resource. The stop words are not included in this table. For further text analysis, the plain transcript can be easily downloaded from the web-page of the resource, following the *URL* in table *resource*.

3.11 Association Concept - Resource

This is a relationship with attributes connecting *concept* and *resource*. The table that implements the relationship that a resource *is for* a concept is named *association_concept_ resource*. The key of this table consists of ***concept*** and ***resource*** (foreign keys), and the attribute is ***purpose***. The purposes available in *DAJEE* are reported in Section 2.1.

4. CONCLUSIONS

This paper presents *DAJEE*, a dataset for TEL applications obtained from the crawling of data in MOOCs hosted on Coursera. *DAJEE* presently refers to more than 20.000 resources, which is already half of the number of LOs in MERLOT. In the future, the number of resources is expected to increase significantly with the crawling of other MOOCs platforms.

DAJEE provides data about lessons, courses and instructors when resources have been delivered. Therefore, data mining and IR techniques can be employed to extract the teaching patterns and preferences of instructors by analysing the resources and their arrangement in courses. Text-mining tools can also be applied to the transcripts of resources for discovering further knowledge about instructors and courses. This knowledge can be helpful for supporting course design and lesson planning [4], helping in the creation of learning activities [3] among other applications. Moreover, *DAJEE* is expected to be useful for conducting a comparative and reproducible evaluation of recommender systems in TEL [5, 1]. Finally, it may also help to address the *cold start* problem of recommender systems [7] in TEL.

DAJEE can be accessed publicly for research purposes only, following the authors' approval. Researchers can apply for it by filling in the form at http://144.6.235.142/dajee.

[5]https://tika.apache.org/

5. REFERENCES

[1] Drachsler, H., Verbert, K., Santos, O. C., and Manouselis, N. Panorama of recommender systems to support learning. In *Recommender systems handbook*. Springer, 2015, pp. 421–451.

[2] Kay, J., Reimann, P., Diebold, E., and Kummerfeld, B. Moocs: So many learners, so much potential... *IEEE Intelligent Systems*, 3 (2013), 70–77.

[3] Krieger, K. Creating learning material from web resources. In *The Semantic Web. Latest Advances and New Domains*. Springer, 2015, pp. 721–730.

[4] Limongelli, C., Lombardi, M., Marani, A., Sciarrone, F., and Temperini, M. A recommendation module to help teachers build courses through the moodle learning management system. *New Review of Hypermedia and Multimedia* (2015), 1–25.

[5] Lombardi, M., and Marani, A. A comparative framework to evaluate recommender systems in technology enhanced learning: a case study. In *Advances in Artificial Intelligence and Its Applications*. Springer, 2015, pp. 155–170.

[6] Palavitsinis, N., Manouselis, N., and Sanchez-Alonso, S. Metadata quality in learning object repositories: a case study. *The Electronic Library 32*, 1 (2014), 62–82.

[7] Shani, G., and Gunawardana, A. Evaluating recommendation systems. In *Recommender systems handbook*. Springer, 2011, pp. 257–297.

Evaluating Retrieval over Sessions: The TREC Session Track 2011–2014

Ben Carterette
University of Delaware,
Newark, DE, USA
carteret@cis.udel.edu

Paul Clough
University of Sheffield,
Sheffield, UK
p.d.clough@sheffield.ac.uk

Mark Hall
Edge Hill University, Ormskirk,
UK
hallmark@edgehill.ac.uk

Evangelos Kanoulas
University of Amsterdam,
Amsterdam, The Netherlands
e.kanoulas@uva.nl

Mark Sanderson
RMIT University, Melbourne,
Australia
mark.sanderson@rmit.edu.au

ABSTRACT

Information Retrieval (IR) research has traditionally focused on serving the best results for a single query— so-called ad hoc retrieval. However, users typically search iteratively, refining and reformulating their queries during a session. A key challenge in the study of this interaction is the creation of suitable evaluation resources to assess the effectiveness of IR systems over sessions. This paper describes the TREC Session Track, which ran from 2010 through to 2014, which focussed on forming test collections that included various forms of implicit feedback. We describe the test collections; a brief analysis of the differences between datasets over the years; and the evaluation results that demonstrate that the use of user session data significantly improved effectiveness.

1. INTRODUCTION

One of the commonest IR system evaluation methodologies is the Cranfield approach [4] using test collections to conduct controlled, systematic, and repeatable evaluations [7]. The focus of such evaluation is on how well an IR system can locate and rank relevant documents from a single query. In practice, however, users typically reformulate queries in response to search results or as their information need alters over time [9]. Retrieval evaluation should compute system success over multiple query-response interactions [10].

The TREC Session Track[1] was an attempt to evaluate IR systems over multi-query sessions. In 2010, the track produced test collections and evaluation measures for studying retrieval over sessions [11]; from 2011 on [12, 13, 1, 2], the track focused more on providing participants with user data with which to improve retrieval. The resulting collections consist of document collections, topics, and relevance assessments, as well as log data from user sessions.

[1]http://ir.cis.udel.edu/sessions/

SIGIR '16, July 17-21, 2016, Pisa, Italy

DOI: http://dx.doi.org/10.1145/2911451.2914675

The track's test collections are described here and compared: including studying the effects of the search engines used to build the collections, user variability, and topic analysis. Participant results indicate that certain types of search benefit significantly from exploiting session information.

2. SESSION TRACK OVERVIEW

The aim of the track was to test if the retrieval effectiveness of a query could be improved by using previous queries, ranked results, and user interactions. We constructed four test collections comprising N sessions of varying length, each the result of a user attempting to satisfy one of T pre-defined topics. Each session numbered $1..i..N$ consisted of:

- m_i blocks of user interactions (the session's *length*);
- the *current query* q_{m_i} in the session;
- $m_i - 1$ blocks of interactions in the session prior to the current query, composed of:
  1. the user queries in the session, q_1, q_2, ..., q_{m_i-1};
  2. the ranked list of URLs seen by the user for each of those queries;
  3. the set of clicked URLs/snippets.

Ranking algorithms were evaluated on the current query under two conditions: A one-off ad hoc query; or a query using some or all of the prior logged data. The latter condition had several different sub-conditions that varied year to year: ("RL" refers to Ranked List):

- RL1: The baseline condition: an ad hoc query
- RL2-1: RL1 plus previous session queries
- RL2-2: RL2-1 plus rankings (URLs, titles, snippets)
- RL2-3: RL2-2 plus user data (clicks, dwell times)
- RL3: Using all data in the session log (in particular, other sessions on the same topic)

The focus of the track was on the degree to which a group improved their retrieval system's baseline effectiveness (RL1) by incorporating some or all of the additional log data.

3. TEST COLLECTIONS

Table 1 shows statistics of the Session track collections. The ClueWeb09 collection was used in 2011 and 2012, and the ClueWeb12 collection in 2013 and 2014.

Topics: While not a part of a true log of user search activity, we felt it was important to define topic descriptions for overall sessions so as to make relevance assessing

Table 1: Four years of TREC Session Track test collections and evaluations

	2011	2012	2013	2014
collection	ClueWeb09	ClueWeb09	ClueWeb12	ClueWeb12
topic properties				
topic set size	62	48	61	60‡
topic cat. dist.	known-item†	10 exploratory, 6 interpretive, 20 known-item, 12 known-subj	10 exploratory, 9 interpretive, 32 known-item, 10 known-subj	15 exploratory, 15 interpretive, 15 known-item, 15 known-subj
session properties				
user population	U. Sheffield	U. Sheffield	U. Sheffield + IR researchers	MTurk
search engine	BOSS+CW09 filter	BOSS+CW09 filter	indri	indri
total sessions	76	98	133	1,257
sessions per topic	1.2	2.0	2.2	21.0
mean length (in queries)	3.7	3.0	3.7	3.7
median time between queries	68.5s	66.7s	72.2s	25.6s
relevance judgments				
topics judged	62	48	49	51
total judgments	19,413	17,861	13,132	16,949
evaluation by nDCG@10				
mean RL1	0.3015	0.1847	0.1373	0.1719
mean RL2-1	0.3083	0.1950	–§	–§
mean RL2-2	0.2941	0.2140	–§	–§
mean RL2-3	0.3077	0.2303	0.1832	0.1885
mean RL3	–§	–§	0.1834	0.2002
max RL* - RL1	0.1800	0.1770	0.1230	0.1507

† 2011 topics were not categorized, but a retrospective analysis suggests most of them fit the "known-item" label best.
‡ 2014 topics were reused 2012 and 2013 topics.
§ The RL2-1 and RL2-2 conditions were eliminated for 2013 and 2014; the RL3 condition was introduced in 2013.

simpler. The challenge was to construct topics that were likely to require multiple query reformulations. In 2011, we did this by adapting multi-faceted TREC 2007 Question Answering track topics. Because of the nature of the QA track, many topics modelled "fact-finding" tasks answerable by a single document. In 2012-2013, we developed topics according to a task categorization scheme [15] with four classes: *known-item*; *known-subject*; *interpretive*; and *exploratory*. In 2014, we reused topics from 2012-2013 selecting fifteen topics from the four categories, biasing selection to topics that had longer user sessions and more clicks.

Sessions: Assessing the impact of session data on retrieval effectiveness required capturing user-system interactions, including queries, rankings, and clicks. We describe the users and search engines employed to generate the data.

Users: In 2011-2013, the primary user group were staff and students at the University of Sheffield. Using a university-wide email, we invited participants to search on as many topics as they had time for. In 2013 we solicited additional participants from the Session Track and SIG-IRList mailing lists. In 2014 we used a crowdsourcing platform (Mechanical Turk) taking a similar approach to past work for crowdsourcing interactions [18].

Search process: Users were shown a topic description, a search box for entering queries, and a list of ten ranked results with a pagination control to navigate to further results. Each retrieved item was represented by its title, URL, and snippet. Additionally, there was a "Save" button that users were instructed to use to collect those documents that helped them satisfy their information need. We experimented with additional components, such as a list of queries issued, but did not observe a difference in users' behaviour.

Search engine: In 2011-2012 we used Yahoo!'s BOSS (Build your Own Search System) API to search the live web. We filtered URLs returned by BOSS against those in the ClueWeb09 collection so that users would only see pages that were present in the publicly-available corpus. A large number of pages returned by BOSS did not match any URL in ClueWeb09. In 2013-2014, we switched to indri search with a home-built index of ClueWeb12. The indri index included each of the twenty ClueWeb12 segments (ClueWeb12_00 through ClueWeb12_19) indexed using the Krovetz stemmer and no stopword list. The indexes searched contained only text from title fields, anchor text from incoming links ("inlink" text), and page URLs. Each query was incorporated into an indri structured query language template and a retrieval score was computed from a query-likelihood model for the full document representation and three weighted combinations of query-likelihood field models with unordered-window within-field models. The "inlink" model was weighted 50 times higher than the title model, and 100 times higher than the URL model. This query template is the product of manual search and investigation of retrieved results.

The system logged all interactions with the user, including the queries issued, which documents were ranked (including URL, title, and snippet), which documents the user viewed, and which they saved as relevant to the task (note however that the latter are not the relevance judgments). This log data was then used to create the sessions.

4. EVALUATION

We used topical relevance judgments in order to compute measures of effectiveness like nDCG@10 for each topic. Since the Session Track examines whether session log data can be exploited, the evaluation examined the *change* in effectiveness from the baseline (RL1) to using some data (RL2) to using a full query log (RL3). In addition, since each topic may be the subject of more than one session, and

2013 \ 2014	4	3	2	1	0	-2
nav - 4	1	0	0	0	0	0
key - 3	0	1	2	7	4	0
hi - 2	0	4	28	52	14	2
rel - 1	1	12	75	89	64	0
not - 0	4	5	50	161	337	11
junk -2	0	0	0	0	4	5

Table 2: Agreement on relevance grades

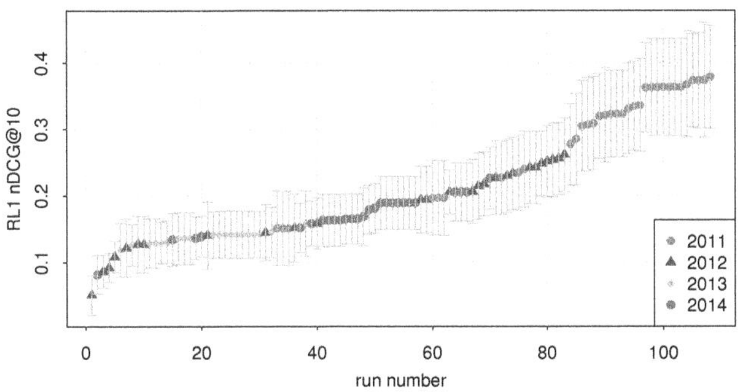

Figure 1: Mean nDCG@10 (with error bars showing ±2 standard error) for all 108 submitted runs' RL1 baseline.

each session may use different queries, the evaluation was over *sessions* rather than over topics.

Documents were selected for judging by pooling the top-10 results from all the submitted RLs along with all documents that were retrieved and viewed by the users. TREC NIST assessors (*not* the original users) judged each pooled document with respect to the topic description. All original user actions were invisible to the assessors; judgments were made solely on the topical similarity to the topic description on a 6-grade scale. Over four years, 66,548 relevance judgments were made to 60,500 unique pages identified by URL: 33,686 pages from ClueWeb09 ; 26,814 from ClueWeb12. A total of 19,179 (29%) documents were judged relevant (grade 1 or higher) and 47,369 (71%) judged nonrelevant.

Since the topics for 2014 were taken from the 2012 & 2013 Session Tracks and in the last two years the document collection was ClueWeb12, we have documents with multiple assessments. Table 2 shows assessor agreement. Assessors were much more likely to say a document judged non-relevant in 2013 was relevant in 2014 than vice versa.

Results: Figure 1 shows nDCG@10 for all groups' baseline RL1 submissions, sorted by nDCG@10 and coded by year. It is evident that 2011 had the best baseline effectiveness (average nDCG@10 of 0.30), followed by 2012 (0.18), then 2014 (0.17), and finally 2013 (0.14) had the lowest baseline effectiveness. The change from 2011 to 2012 reflects a shift to more difficult topics: the 2012 known-subject and interpretive topic categories proved to be significantly more difficult than the 2011 known-item topics. The change from 2012 to 2013 reflects a change in the underlying search technology from Yahoo! BOSS to the Indri-based system.

Figure 2 shows the improvement over each submitted run's RL1 baseline sorted by that improvement. Improvement from the RL1 baseline does not show any trend by year—for 2011, the average improvement was 0.04, for 2012 it was 0.05, for 2013 it was 0.05, and for 2014 it dropped to 0.02.

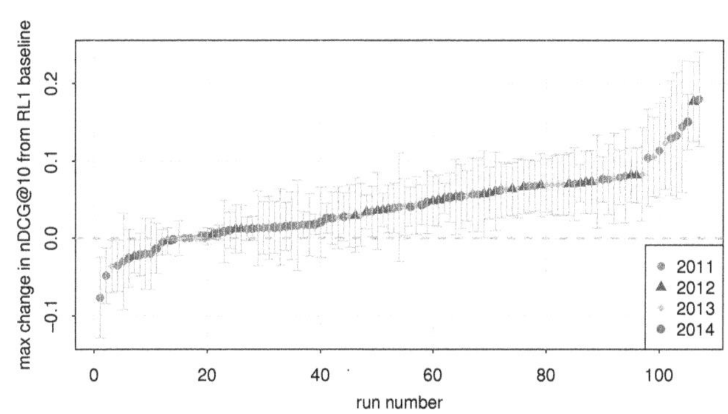

Figure 2: Largest measured improvement in nDCG@10 from RL1 to any other condition for all 108 submitted runs, with error bars showing ±2 standard errors.

From these results, we conclude that it is possible to use session history to improve effectiveness over basic ad hoc retrieval, and moreover that it does not take a lot of session history to do so. Further evidence is offered in [6, 5, 17]. A study of particular interest due to the fact that it was conducted both over a Session track collection and a commercial search engine proprietary collection is that by Raman et al. [16]; the session collection enabled them to demonstrate the effectiveness of their algorithm in accordance to the proprietary test collection.

5. ANALYSIS

In this section we perform some basic analysis of the Session Track collections and evaluation results.

Topic categories: We investigated the degree to which systems were able to improve effectiveness for each of our four topic classes. We look at the average improvement from the RL1 baseline, and find the maximum average improvement to any other RL condition for each run.

The overall mean improvements are 0.04, 0.07, 0.04, and 0.05 for known-item, known-subject, exploratory, and interpretive respectively, though only the differences between known-subject and the others were statistically significant.This suggests that known-subject topics benefit most from access to session history, but the details are more subtle. Exploratory topics tend to have the largest improvements for individual systems: the five largest improvements in exploratory topics are 5–10% larger than the five largest in known-subject topics. Exploratory topics also show the greatest benefit from the use of more log data: from RL1 to RL2, exploratory topics only increase an average of 0.03 (compare to 0.05 for known-subject topics, the largest improvement), but from RL2 to RL3 they increase by 0.05 (compare to 0.04 for known-subject topics, the second-largest improvement).

Topic variability: Most IR test collections have only one instantiation of a topic (an exception is the TREC Query track). Since we may have multiple sessions for any given topic, the Session Track gives us a chance to analyze variability in effectiveness within topics.

Figure 3 shows how much effectiveness varies over the different user sessions of a single topic. Each plot on the x-axis is a topic, the y-axis is a boxplot of the range in nDCG@10 changes from RL1 to any other RL. A taller box means more variability. A point or box plotted further up the y-axis indicates higher average change in nDCG@10 across the sessions

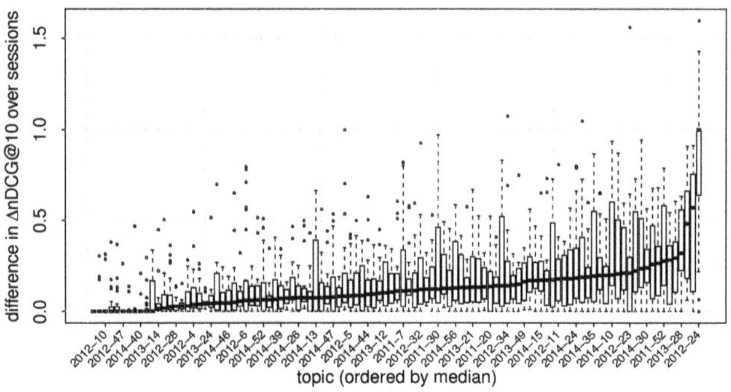

Figure 3: Variability over sessions and system effectiveness for selected topics.

of a topic. An extreme case is topic 24 from 2012 (the right most topic on the plot). There were five sessions recorded for this topic (numbers 48–52); one group improved from 0.00 in RL1 to 0.91 in RL3 on one session, but fell from 0.81 in RL1 to 0.00 in RL2 on another. Many other groups had similarly large differences across sessions on this topic.

The result indiactes that there is a substantial variability in topics, separate from the variability in system effectiveness, due to the way the users performs their search and formulates their query. Previous user study showed this as well [14]. It may be beneficial to include multiple versions of the same topic in standard test collections, so as to better capture interactions between topic and system variability.

6. CONCLUSION

This paper describes the four test collections produced for the TREC Session Track that have been used to assess the use of implicit feedback on retrieval performance within sessions. The key result from the track is that aggregate data from all participant submissions shows that retrieval effectiveness was improved for ad hoc retrieval using data based on session history data. It also appears that the more detailed the session data, the greater the improvement.

Through analyzing aspects of the test collections, such as topic categories and variability, we demonstrate how the resources can be used to investigate implicit feedback and offer reusable and publicly-accessible resources for evaluating IR systems across sessions.

7. ACKNOWLEDGEMENTS

This work was supported in part by the Australian Research Council's Discovery Projects scheme (DP130104007), the National Science Foundation (NSF) under grant number IIS-1350799, and the Google Faculty Research Award scheme. Any opinions, findings and conclusions or recommendations expressed in this material are the authors' and do not necessarily reflect those of the sponsors.

8. REFERENCES

[1] B. Carterette, E. Kanoulas, A. Bah, M. Hall, and P. D. Clough. Overview of the TREC 2013 Session track. In *Proceedings of TREC*, 2013.

[2] B. Carterette, E. Kanoulas, A. Bah, M. Hall, and P. D. Clough. Overview of the TREC 2014 Session track (notebook version). In *Proceedings of TREC*, 2014.

[3] B. Carterette, E. Kanoulas, P. D. Clough, and M. Sanderson, editors. *Proceedings of the ECIR 2011 Workshop on Information Retrieval Over Query Sessions*, Available at http://ir.cis.udel.edu/ECIR11Sessions.

[4] C. W. Cleverdon. The significance of the cranfield tests on index languages. In *Proceedings of SIGIR*, pages 3–12, 1991.

[5] D. Guan and H. Yang. Is the first query the most important: An evaluation of query aggregation schemes in session search. In *Proceedings of AIRS*, pages 86–99. 2014.

[6] D. Guan, S. Zhang, and H. Yang. Utilizing query change for session search. In *Proceedings of SIGIR*, pages 453–462, 2013.

[7] D. Harman. *Information Retrieval Evaluation.* Synthesis Lectures on Information Concepts, Retrieval, and Services. Morgan & Claypool Publishers, 2011.

[8] P. Ingwersen and K. Järvelin. *The Turn: Integration of Information Seeking and Retrieval in Context (The Information Retrieval Series).* Springer-Verlag New York, Inc., Secaucus, NJ, USA, 2005.

[9] B. J. Jansen, D. L. Booth, and A. Spink. Patterns of query reformulation during Web searching. *J. Am. Soc. Inf. Sci. Technol.*, 60(7):1358–1371, July 2009.

[10] K. Järvelin. Explaining user performance in information retrieval: Challenges to ir evaluation. In *Proceedings of ICTIR*, pages 289–296, 2009.

[11] E. Kanoulas, B. Carterette, P. Clough, and M. Sanderson. Session track overview. In *Proceedings of the 19th Text REtreival Conference (TREC)*, 2010.

[12] E. Kanoulas, B. Carterette, M. Hall, P. D. Clough, and M. Sanderson. Overview of the TREC 2011 Session track. In *Proceedings of TREC*, 2011.

[13] E. Kanoulas, B. Carterette, M. Hall, P. D. Clough, and M. Sanderson. Overview of the TREC 2012 Session track. In *Proceedings of TREC*, 2012.

[14] K. S. Kim. Information-seeking on the web: Effects of user and task variables. *Library and Information Science Research*, 23(3), 2011.

[15] Y. Li and N. J. Belkin. A faceted approach to conceptualizing tasks in information seeking. *Inf. Process. Manage.*, 44(6):1822–1837, Nov. 2008.

[16] K. Raman, P. N. Bennett, and K. Collins-Thompson. Toward whole-session relevance: Exploring intrinsic diversity in web search. In *Proceedings of SIGIR*, pages 463–472, 2013.

[17] S. Zhang, D. Guan, and H. Yang. Query change as relevance feedback in session search. In *Proceedings of SIGIR*, pages 821–824, 2013.

[18] G. Zuccon, T. Leelanupab, S. Whiting, E. Yilmaz, J. Jose, and L. Azzopardi. Crowdsourcing interactions: Capturing query sessions through crowdsourcing. In *Proceedings of ECIR*, 2011.

EveTAR: A New Test Collection for Event Detection in Arabic Tweets

Hind Almerekhi[*], Maram Hasanain, Tamer Elsayed
Computer Science and Engineering Department, Qatar University, Doha, Qatar
halmerekhi@qf.org.qa, {maram.hasanain, telsayed}@qu.edu.qa

ABSTRACT

Research on event detection in Twitter is often obstructed by the lack of publicly-available evaluation mechanisms such as test collections; this problem is more severe when considering the scarcity of them in languages other than English. In this paper, we present *EveTAR*, the *first* publicly-available test collection for event detection in *Arabic* tweets. The collection includes a crawl of 590M Arabic tweets posted in a month period and covers 66 *significant* events (in 8 different categories) for which more than 134k relevance judgments were gathered using crowdsourcing with high average inter-annotator agreement (Kappa value of 0.6).

We demonstrate the usability of the collection by evaluating 3 state-of-the-art event detection algorithms. The collection is also designed to support other retrieval tasks, as we show in our experiments with ad-hoc search systems.

Keywords

Evaluation; Crowdsourcing; Twitter; Ad-hoc Search

1. INTRODUCTION

The overwhelming popularity of Twitter led several parts of the world (e.g., the Arab region) to use it as a medium for continuous exchange of short messages (i.e., tweets). While it became essential for everyday Arab users, popular Arabic news agencies (e.g., AlJazeera and AlArabiya) are also using it extensively to continuously update their followers on critical events and news as they happen. The Arab social media report[1] shows that, as of March 2014, an average of 17M Arabic tweets are posted every day. Such tweets are extremely noisy, full of typos and redundancy, making it difficult to manually identify events [8]. With the growing events in the Arab region, the need for automatic tools that can reliably track the huge stream of tweets and detect events before being publicly announced is increasing.

[*]Also affiliated with Qatar Foundation, Doha, Qatar.
[1]http://www.arabsocialmediareport.com

SIGIR '16, July 17–21, 2016, Pisa, Italy.
© 2016 ACM. ISBN 978-1-4503-4069-4/16/07...$15.00
DOI: http://dx.doi.org/10.1145/2911451.2914681

To design and develop high quality event detection systems, evaluation mechanisms, such as *test collections*, are evidently required. A test collection typically consists of a set of documents (tweets), topics (events), and relevance judgments (labels) that specify which documents are relevant to the topics [14]. The problem of detecting events in Twitter has been extensively studied [2, 13, 15], however most of event detection systems were tested on English tweets. To the best of our knowledge, Alsaedi and Burnap [1] presented the only study that tackles the problem of event detection in Arabic tweets, however, no test collection was publicly-available for further research.

This paper presents *EveTAR*, the *first* publicly-available test collection for event detection in *Arabic* tweets. More specifically, the collection was designed for the problem of detecting *significant* events. A significant event is defined as an occurrence that happens at a particular time in a specific location and is discussed by the media (e.g., covered by an online news article). This definition is similar to definitions introduced in [8]. However, we emphasize event significance, which is often neglected in most event definitions [1, 2, 12]. *EveTAR* covers 66 manually-identified significant events occurred in the month of January 2015. More than 134k potentially-relevant tweets to the events were judged through crowdsourcing. The design of *EveTAR* allows for the evaluation of systems that are built for other tasks, such as ad-hoc search and filtering. It can also be extended to support other tasks such as summarization.

In building *EveTAR*, we address three research questions:

- **RQ1:** How can we design a test collection that is reusable and supports multiple tasks?
- **RQ2:** How can we use crowdsourcing in building a reliable test collection?
- **RQ3:** How well do existing state-of-the-art event detection techniques perform on Arabic tweets?

Our contribution in this study is 3-fold:

1. *EveTAR* is the *first* test collection for the task of event detection in Arabic tweets.
2. We make the full test collection publicly-available for research[2], including ids of 590M Arabic tweets, 66 events and 134K relevance judgments, inter-annotator agreements, queries used to identify potentially-relevant tweets for the events, and documented design of the crowdsourcing tasks.

[2]http://qufaculty.qu.edu.qa/telsayed/evetar

3. We demonstrate that our test collection can be used to evaluate existing state-of-the-art event detection systems in addition to ad-hoc search systems.

2. RELATED WORK

In this section, we discuss some of the existing test collections for event detection and compare them with *EveTAR*.

The study of Alsaedi and Burnap [1] is the first on event detection in Arabic tweets, focusing on detecting events in Abu Dhabi. Around 1M Arabic tweets were collected and labelled by 3 annotators, however, the dataset was not made publicly-available. Additionally, it was restricted to events in Abu Dhabi, which introduces a bias towards types of events that happen in that location.

Petrović et al. [13] built a test collection consisting of 50M English tweets for the task of First Story Detection. Given a set of manually-crafted events, authors recruited expert annotators to collect on-topic tweets for those events. The need for expert annotators makes the creation of the test collection expensive and limits its scale. Furthermore, the authors identified 27 events with 3K relevant tweets only, making it difficult to use the collection for conducting large-scale evaluation of event detection over the Twitter stream.

On a larger scale, McMinn et al. [8] built a publicly-available test collection for evaluating event detection. The authors crawled around 120M English tweets, covering more than 500 events identified using automatic and manual ways, and collected labels for over 150K tweets. We consider their approach as a basis for our work, however, we followed a slightly different approach to construct *EveTAR* with manual identification of events. On average, *EveTAR* has more tweets per event when compared to their collection. Additionally, we designed our test collection to be general enough to support additional tasks like ad-hoc search.

Contrasting *EveTAR* to other event detection test collections, we find it the largest (with 590M tweets) compared to collections described in [3], [6], [9] and [10]. Moreover, events in *EveTAR* were not limited to a specific location as opposed to test collections in [2] or [3] for example.

3. BUILDING EveTAR

We built *EveTAR* based on the following pipeline: collecting the tweet dataset, identifying events in this dataset, extracting potentially-relevant tweets for those events, and finally obtaining their relevance judgments.

3.1 Collecting a Tweet Dataset

We used Twitter's streaming API to collect a dataset of 590M Arabic tweets over the month of January 2015. Tweets were collected by tracking 400 most frequently-used Arabic words extracted from a previously-crawled Twitter stream.

3.2 Identifying Events

Following the approach of McMinn et al. [8], we manually collected a set of 357 events in the month of January 2015 listed over both the English[3] and Arabic[4] Wikipedia's Current Events Portal (WCEP). We then applied our significance criteria over two phases. In the first, we only kept events for which we found at least one online *Arabic* news article discussing the event; only 71 events satisfied that condition. For each of those events, we used Twitter's online search service to manually try to find at least 20 non-redundant tweets related to the event. We restricted the search to 5 days starting 2 days prior to the event date. Eventually, 66 events satisfied the condition, comprising our final list of events. For each of those, we prepared a complete representation as shown in the translated example below:

ID	E12
Title	Discovery of tomb of Egyptian queen Khentakawess III
Date	January 04, 2015
Location	Abusir, Egypt
Category	Arts and Culture
Reference	http://cnn.it/1O6grQK
Keywords	Khentakawess, Egyptian queen, archaeologist
Description	A Czech archeological team discovered the tomb of an Egyptian queen named Khentakawess III who lived during the 5th dynasty.

The final events fall into 8 WCEP categories; Table 1 shows their distribution. Interestingly, the majority belong to Armed Conflicts and Attacks.

Table 1: Distribution of events

Category (Events)	Category (Events)
Armed Conflicts & Attacks (45)	Sports (5)
Business & Economy (1)	Arts & Culture (2)
International Relations (3)	Law & Crime (2)
Disasters & Accidents (3)	Politics & Elections (5)

The above event representation is sufficient to evaluate event detection systems that represent events by any combination of date/time, location, and set of keywords. However, in designing *EveTAR*, we elected to enrich the above representation by adding a list of tweets related (or relevant) to each event. That serves two purposes; first, it helps evaluate several event detection systems that represent an event by a list of tweets, and second, it enables the evaluation of other types of retrieval systems such as ad-hoc search or filtering systems that rely on producing lists of tweets per topic.

We obtained those tweets over 2 steps. We first extracted a list of potentially-relevant tweets for each event from our dataset, then used crowdsourcing to obtain relevance judgments on them; both are described in the following sections.

3.3 Extracting Tweets of Events

For each event, we manually crafted a list of keyword and phrase queries, ran them against a Lucene-constructed index of the dataset, and collected the resulted tweets (up to 10k per event). After removing exact tweet-text duplicates, we finally got a set of 134,069 potentially-relevant tweets.

3.4 Collecting Relevance Judgments

For efficiently labeling that large set of potential event-related tweets, we used CrowdFlower crowdsourcing platform[5]. We ran a set of pilot studies before launching the final labeling tasks, one per event. In each task, annotators were given an introduction to the task, the title, description and date of the event, and the content of a corresponding Arabic news article. Annotators were then asked to label each of the candidate tweets as relevant to the event or not.

[3] https://en.wikipedia.org/wiki/Portal:Current_events

[4] https://ar.wikipedia.org/wiki/بوابة:أحداث_جارية

[5] http://www.crowdflower.com

Before annotators can start labeling, they were required to pass a qualification test by correctly labeling a minimum of 8 out of 10 gold tweets. Gold tweets were randomly sampled from the collection of potentially-relevant tweets per event. Once they start labeling, annotators had to maintain a minimum accuracy of 80% over gold tweets within the task to continue labeling. An average of 8 annotators were blocked while labeling for an event, and only labels from trusted annotators where included in *EveTAR*. We chose to have each tweet annotated by 3 annotators to ensure a majority label. We also restrict the annotators to be Arabic-speaking with an intermediate level per CrowdFlower's ranking of annotators. An average of 59 hours were spent per event.

To decide the final label of a tweet out of the 3 given labels, we adopted a trust-based voting scheme that utilizes the trust scores provided by CrowdFlower per annotator (describing her accuracy in the current task). We chose the label that has the highest sum of trust scores over corresponding annotators. For all events, 51,424 tweets were labeled as relevant and 82,645 were non-relevant, based on the above voting scheme.

We also computed an overall trust score per tweet using the following Equation[6]:

$$\text{Tweet Trust Score} = \frac{\max(\sum_{i=1}^{r} trust_i, \sum_{i=1}^{n} trust_i)}{\sum_{i=1}^{n+r} trust_i} \quad (1)$$

where r and n are the number of annotators labeling the tweet as relevant or non-relevant respectively, and $trust_i$ is the trust score for an annotator. Averaging this overall trust score over all tweets and all events results in an average quality score of 0.94 out of 1.

We measure the quality of the obtained labels by computing the inter-annotator agreement using Fleiss' Kappa [16] per event. We chose this measure over the widely-used Cohen's Kappa as it allows measuring annotators' agreement when having more than 2 annotators labeling a single data item. In literature, the value of Kappa has been mapped into 6 categories based on how strong the agreement is [16]. Figure 1 illustrates the distribution of events over Fleiss' Kappa categories. Over all events, we got an average Kappa of 0.60, which is considered a moderate agreement. Moreover, more than half of the events got a substantial to an almost perfect agreement. Additionally, eliminating the 3 events with slight annotator agreement results in an average agreement of 0.62, which is considered *substantial*. We observed that events with slight agreement tend to be less popular in the media than those with almost perfect agreement.The figure also shows a slight drop in the values of the average trust score per event with decreasing Kappa values.

4. USING EveTAR

In this section, we demonstrate the usability of *EveTAR* for event detection in addition to other retrieval tasks, taking ad-hoc search as an example.

4.1 Evaluating Event Detection

We experimented with *EveTAR* to show how it can be used to evaluate state-of-the-art event detection algorithms

[6]The equation is stemming from the one used by CrowdFlower to report confidence in the aggregated label given for a data item, see: http://bit.ly/20NmFkU

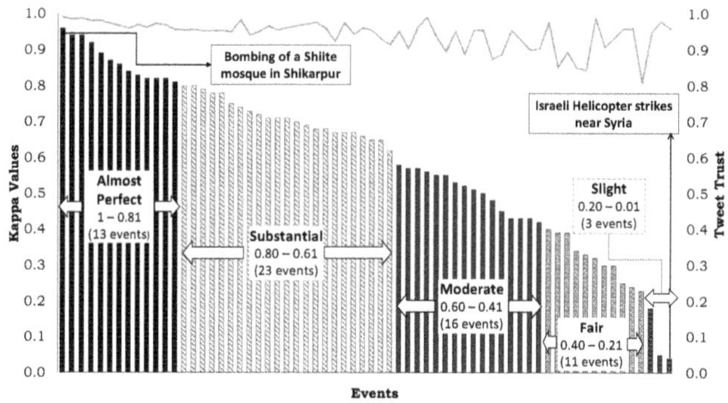

Figure 1: Distribution of events over Fleiss' Kappa categories and average trust scores.

over Arabic tweets. We used an open-source implementation of 3 event detection algorithms provided by SONDY platform[7], namely MABED [4], EDCoW [17], and Peaky Topics [15]. We ran the algorithms using SONDY's default parameter settings.

In a real setting, we should run those algorithms on the full dataset (590M tweets), but due to time limitation and to be able to compute both recall and precision of event detection, we only ran the algorithms on the labeled subset (134K tweets). We evaluated the output of each algorithm by *manually* comparing the output events with the labeled events (based on their descriptions). Moreover, we also *automatically* evaluated the output using the approach of Petrović [11]. Performance was evaluated using the standard precision (P), recall (R) and F_1 measures.

To compare event detection over *EveTAR* with another available test collection, we used McMinn et al. English test collection [8]. We crawled a subset of the collection, that was created similar to *EveTAR*, of 23K judged tweets covering 361 events. We ran and evaluated the same algorithms using the setup explained above. Results over both collections are summarized in Table 2. The label (A) next to some algorithms indicates the automatic evaluation.

Table 2: Event detection performance with *EveTAR* and an English collection

Algorithm	*EveTAR*			*McMinn et al.*		
	P	R	F_1	P	R	F_1
EDCoW	0.09	0.15	0.11	0.17	0.05	0.07
Peaky Topics	0.11	0.80	0.19	0.17	**0.58**	0.26
Peaky Topics(A)	0.10	0.71	0.16	0.08	0.29	0.13
MABED	0.42	0.64	0.51	0.89	0.24	0.38
MABED(A)	**0.61**	**0.92**	**0.73**	**1.0**	0.28	**0.43**

Over both collections and using both manual and automatic evaluation, MABED consistently exhibited the best performance. Moreover, automatic evaluation of MABED showed that the results are somewhat close to those using the manual method. The same observation stands with Peaky Topics when using *EveTAR*. We believe using automatic evaluation more accurately reflects detection performance as it compares identified events with the ground truth on a tweet-level, not to mention its efficiency. These

[7]mediamining.univ-lyon2.fr/people/guille/sondy.php

results demonstrate that *EveTAR* can be used to automatically evaluate event detection systems.

While F_1 numbers over *EveTAR* (especially for MABED) are relatively high, this is probably an artifact of using only the judged subset of tweets instead of the full dataset for testing. Another factor we noticed is that the default value of a MABED parameter that indicates the number of events to be detected was 100, which is coincidentally close enough to the number of events in *EveTAR*.

4.2 Evaluating Ad-hoc Search

In addition to event detection, *EveTAR* is designed to support evaluation of other tasks like ad-hoc search, as it provides a short query and a list of relevant tweets per topic (i.e., event). Using *EveTAR*, we experimented with two ad-hoc search systems, denoted by query likelihood (QL) and query expansion (QE), which were adopted by one of the top teams in the ad-hoc search task in TREC-2013 microblog track [5, 7]. We ran the search systems (using their reported parameter values) over the Lucene index of the 590M tweets. Both MAP and P@30 measures were used to evaluate the performance of the systems as summarized in Table 3.

Table 3: Ad-hoc search performance with *EveTAR*

Model	*MAP*	*P@30*
QL	0.1283	0.3783
QE	0.1207	0.3384

We notice that P@30 values for both models are in range of those reported in [7], however, MAP values are much lower than expected. The difference in ad-hoc search performance between *EveTAR* and the English collection in [7] might be due to the very big difference in dataset size, as the English dataset is much smaller than *EveTAR*. Surprisingly, the QE model is performing worse than QL; we believe that the lack of proper Arabic text normalization on tweets used to select expansion terms might cause a poor selection of terms for expansion. Further experiments are needed to understand the performance of ad-hoc search systems over *EveTAR*.

5. CONCLUSION & FUTURE WORK

In this paper, we present our work on constructing *EveTAR*, the first publicly-available Arabic test collection for event detection. The collection includes 66 events manually-identified during the month of January 2015. We used crowdsourcing to collect a total of 134K labeled tweets. We demonstrate the usage of our collection in manually and automatically evaluating state-of-the-art event detection algorithms. We also show how *EveTAR* can be used to automatically evaluate other tasks such as ad-hoc search.

There are several possible directions for future work. First, the experimental results obtained in demonstrating the usage of *EveTAR* are just preliminary; therefore we still need to further study the performance of event detection and ad-hoc search systems over Arabic tweets. Second, we plan to run more extensive studies to evaluate systems built for other retrieval tasks (e.g., tweet filtering) over our collection. Finally, we would like to explore the possibility of extending *EveTAR* with more events using the automatically-identified potential events by event detection systems.

Acknowledgments

This work was made possible by NPRP grant# NPRP 6-1377-1-257 from the Qatar National Research Fund (a member of Qatar Foundation). The statements made herein are solely the responsibility of the authors.[8]

6. REFERENCES

[1] N. Alsaedi and P. Burnap. Arabic event detection in social media. In *Computational Linguistics and Intelligent Text Processing*, pages 384–401. 2015.

[2] H. Becker, M. Naaman, and L. Gravano. Beyond trending topics: Real-world event identification on Twitter. In *ICWSM'11*, pages 438–441, 2011.

[3] T. Gottron, O. Radcke, and R. Pickhardt. On the temporal dynamics of influence on the social semantic web. In *Semantic Web and Web Science*, pages 75–87. 2013.

[4] A. Guille and C. Favre. Mention-anomaly-based event detection and tracking in Twitter. In *IEEE/ACM International Conference on Advances in Social Networks Analysis and Mining*, pages 375–382, 2014.

[5] M. Hasanain, L. Al-Marri, and T. Elsayed. QU at TREC-2013: Expansion Experiments for Microblog Ad hoc Search. In *TREC-2013*, 2014.

[6] F. Kunneman and A. van den Bosch. Event detection in Twitter: A machine-learning approach based on term pivoting. In *BNAIC'14*, 2014.

[7] J. Lin and M. Efron. Overview of the TREC-2013 Microblog Track. In *TREC-2013*, 2013.

[8] A. J. McMinn, Y. Moshfeghi, and J. M. Jose. Building a large-scale corpus for evaluating event detection on Twitter. In *CIKM'13*, pages 409–418, 2013.

[9] T. Mitra and E. Gilbert. Credbank: A large-scale social media corpus with associated credibility annotations. In *ICWSM'15*, 2015.

[10] R. Parikh and K. Karlapalem. ET: Events from Tweets. In *WWW'13 Companion*, pages 613–620, 2013.

[11] S. Petrović. *Real-time event detection in massive streams*. PhD thesis, School of Informatics, University of Edinburgh, 2013.

[12] S. Petrović, M. Osborne, and V. Lavrenko. Streaming first story detection with application to Twitter. In *NAACL HLT'10*, pages 181–189, 2010.

[13] S. Petrović, M. Osborne, and V. Lavrenko. Using paraphrases for improving first story detection in news and Twitter. In *NAACL HLT'12*, pages 338–346, 2012.

[14] M. Sanderson. *Test collection based evaluation of information retrieval systems*. Now Publishers Inc, 2010.

[15] D. A. Shamma, L. Kennedy, and E. F. Churchill. Peaks and persistence: modeling the shape of microblog conversations. In *CSCW'11*, pages 355–358, 2011.

[16] J. Sim and C. C. Wright. The kappa statistic in reliability studies: use, interpretation, and sample size requirements. *Physical therapy*, 85(3):257–268, 2005.

[17] J. Weng and B.-S. Lee. Event detection in Twitter. In *ICWSM'11*, pages 401–408, 2011.

[8]The first author was not funded by the grant.

GNMID14: A Collection of 110 Million Global Music Identification Matches

Cameron Summers, Greg Tronel, Jason Cramer, Aneesh Vartakavi, Phillip Popp
Gracenote, Emeryville, CA, USA
csummers, gtronel, jcramer, avartakavi, ppopp@gracenote.com

ABSTRACT

A new dataset is presented composed of music identification matches from Gracenote, a leading global music metadata company. Matches from January 1, 2014 to December 31, 2014 have been curated and made available as a public dataset called Gracenote Music Identification 2014, or GNMID14, at the following address: https://developer.gracenote.com/mid2014. This collection is the first significant music identification dataset and one of the largest music related datasets available containing more than 110M matches in 224 countries for 3M unique tracks, and 509K unique artists. It features geotemporal information (i.e. country and match date), genre and mood metadata. In this paper, we characterize the dataset and demonstrate its utility for Information Retrieval (IR) research.

Keywords

dataset; collection; music; geotemporal; content identification; fingerprint; mood; genre; music similarity; music consumption behavior

1. INTRODUCTION

The marriage of the internet and audio fingerprinting technology allowed, for the first time, massive numbers of people to identify a recorded music track. Using a device such as a smartphone, a person can easily identify a recorded track being played and discover information like the artist's home country or even purchase the recording. A byproduct of this identification process is a record that includes information such as timestamp, location on geo-enabled devices, and track metadata of the identified music, and in aggregation, these records create a unique music consumption signal.

Datasets of other music consumption signals, such as internet radio or microblogs (e.g. Twitter), have been successfully used in a variety of information retrieval applications [9, 5]. They link contextual information with music content, enriching retrieval interactions in search and recommendation systems, and they enable personalization when user information is available [10]. However, no significant public datasets exist for music identification, which provides a different perspective on music consumption behavior. Here we introduce a dataset to fill this gap called the Gracenote Music Identification 2014 dataset, or GNMID14. Its unique signal, large size and rich metadata such as mood, date, and location make it a valuable resource on which to perform IR experiments for music. In the following section, we describe existing related datasets. Section 3 characterizes the dataset and proposes potential uses. Section 4 presents suggested applications. Section 5 presents results of an example application. And Section 6 summarizes and discusses future work.

SIGIR '16, July 17 - 21, 2016, Pisa, Italy

ISBN 978-1-4503-4069-4/16/07...$15.00

DOI: http://dx.doi.org/10.1145/2911451.2914679

2. RELATED DATASETS

While no significant public datasets exist for music identification at the time of this publication, there are several datasets worth comparing in terms of content, size, geotemporal context, and track metadata. 30Music [12] - 31M Last.fm user listening events - and #nowPlaying [14] - 58M Twitter logs of listening streams - compare most closely in content and size of MID14 but lack geographical information. Additionally, the structure inherent to music identification arguably makes the associated track metadata cleaner because fingerprints uniquely identify a track with its metadata in a database. In contrast, matching large amounts of text from Twitter logs has a number of challenges [14] and Last.fm metadata comes from user tags, which can be noisy [6].

The Million Musical Tweet Dataset (MMTD) [4] is another listening event dataset from Twitter and includes geotemporal data like that of GNMID14. However, it is about 100 times smaller in size and is subject to similar issues with Twitter text matching. The Million Song Dataset (MSD) [1] uniquely provides audio features among large music datasets as well as some complementary datasets for satellite applications. Compared to GNMID14, MSD differs most notably in its absence of geotemporal information and smaller scale. Each of these other datasets provide user information where GNMID14 does not, however, making them well-suited for personalization applications. But for content-based information retrieval applications, GNMID14 fills a gap as a large dataset with a unique music consumption signal and contextual information.

Beyond the music domain several text-based datasets exist that include geographical and temporal information such as those used in tasks at Text Retrieval Conference (TREC) and Semantic Evaluation (SemEval) [8, 13, 2]. Geotemporal information has fueled great strides in general information retrieval tasks[11], and we hope that this dataset can similarly move research forward in the music domain.

3. THE GNMID14 DATASET

A music identification event consists of a query against a database containing music fingerprints. A typical query scenario involves a user hearing music being played aloud, recording that music with a device such as cell phone, sending the query for identification, and then reviewing information about the identified music. The data in GNMID14 is the resulting positive matches from these music identification queries for the whole year 2014. We refer the reader to [3] for a closer review audio fingerprinting technology.

3.1 Curation

GNMID14 was created through curation of a raw export of matches from 2014 of the music identification database. As this data is not a current product of the company, it is provided to the research community with fewer curation steps than is typically applied when data is licensed to another company. However, the authors believe that the resulting data is still cleaner than what is typically available to researchers using large datasets in the music domain.

The initial export included the following fields: Date, Country, Track ID, User ID, and from this several curation steps were performed. First, entries with incomplete or missing fields were removed. All entries from users with greater than 1000 total matches were also removed to reduce the likelihood of non-human users. Next, the User ID was dropped in its entirety to avoid privacy issues encountered in other large datasets [7]. Next, duplicate tracks were removed as extensively as possible using a combination of text and fingerprint analysis. Finally metadata - track name, artist name, 25 artist-level genres and 26 track-level moods - was mapped to each Track ID.

3.2 Statistics

Table 1 provides some basic statistics on GNMID14. As outlined in the table, cover for genre and mood [1] are less than 100% of the total tracks. While this is typical of music metadata at this scale, this coverage is relatively high.

Figure 1 and Figure 2 show the distribution of genre and mood across matches. Additionally, Figure 3 and Figure 4 show the distribution of genre and mood across tracks. Lastly, Table 2 shows the top 10 countries with the most matches in the dataset.

Table 1: GNMID14 Statistics

Countries	224
Unique Tracks	3,061,121
Unique Artists	509,005
Matches	111,105,707
Matches with Genres	90%
Matches with Mood	94%

[1]Genre is editorially labeled and mood is machine generated.

Figure 1: Distribution of genres across matches

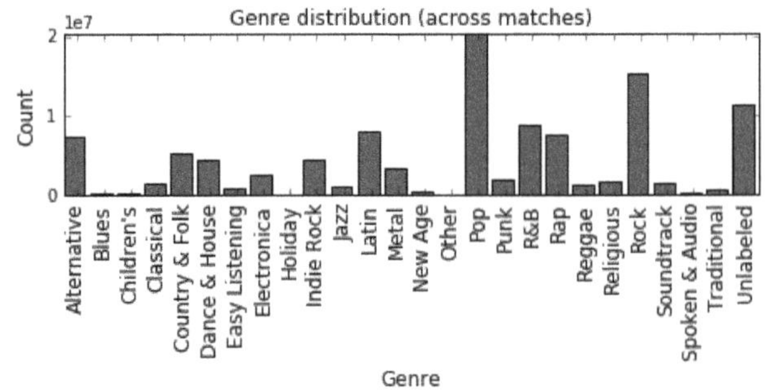

Figure 2: Distribution of moods across matches

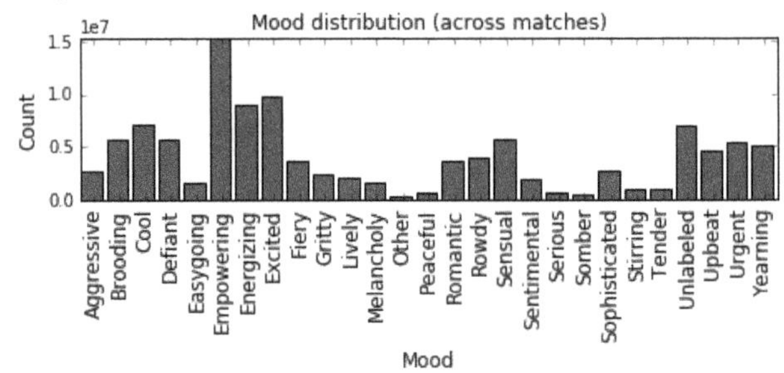

Figure 3: Distribution of genres across tracks

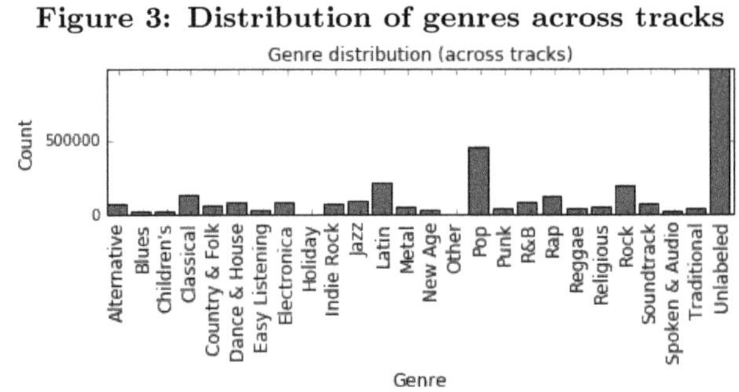

Figure 4: Distribution of moods across tracks

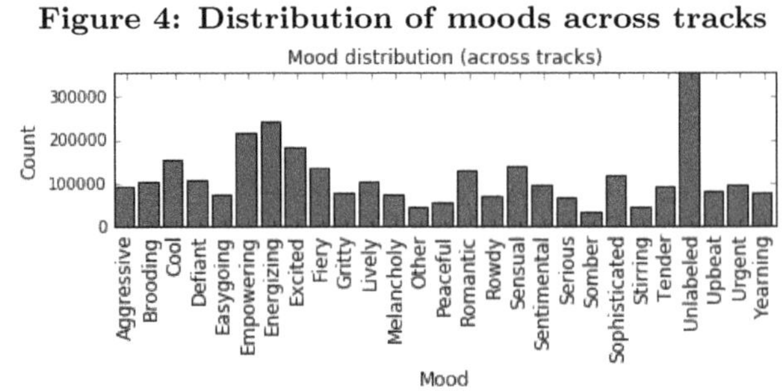

4. SUGGESTED APPLICATIONS

This dataset offers a rich environment for variety of studies of the world's music. General analysis of elements in the dataset such as temporal genre distributions or geographic

Table 2: Countries by Number of Matches

Number of Matches	Country Code
18,026,281	USA
4,828,753	MEX
3,176,338	DEU
2,886,882	BRA
1,975,424	RUS
1,974,358	ESP
1,752,407	FRA
1,658,587	GBR
1,642,353	COL
1,511,542	CHL

artist distributions may yield useful results for IR applications. The temporal nature of the data allows for prediction of artist or genre popularity or geographical movement of a track. Also, an understanding of the relationship between a music identification signal and a user listening signal would help the IR community select the appropriate music consumption dataset for their research.

5. GEOGRAPHIC SIMILARITY

To demonstrate the utility of GNMID14 we present a novel similarity metric for retrieving tracks in the dataset. Due to various characteristics such as language, origin, and genre, a track will have a distinct geographic popularity distribution. For example, a track sung in Japanese by a Japanese artist may have many listens in Japan and fewer listens elsewhere. It can be useful and interesting in a search or recommendation system to find songs with a similar popularity distribution across countries. This provides another way of exploring the data beyond that of a more traditional similarity metric such as retrieving tracks of the same genre.

5.1 Methods

To find similar tracks we first represent each track in a vectorized "bag-of-countries" form and use a vector similarity metric, in this case Euclidean distance, to compute the similarity of the tracks.

Specifically, for track x_i with total listens in countries $[c_1, c_2, ..., c_n]$, we calculate a normalized geographic listening distribution, $\hat{x_i}$, to account for differences in track popularity in (1).

$$\hat{x_i} = < \frac{c_1}{\sum^n c_k}, \frac{c_2}{\sum^n c_k}, ..., \frac{c_n}{\sum^n c_k} > \quad (1)$$

We then calculate the Euclidean distance, d_{ij}, between track $\hat{x}_i$ and $\hat{x}_j$ as

$$d_{ij} = \left\| \hat{x}_i - \hat{x}_j \right\|_2^2 \quad (2)$$

.

For a given seed track x_s, we rank the remaining tracks in ascending order by distance to the seed track d_{sj} and retrieve the N highest ranking results.

5.2 Results

Three seed tracks were chosen from GNMID14 to show a variety of behaviors of retrieval using the similarity metric in (2). Figure 5 shows a comparison of sparse country listening distributions between the seed track "Dark Horse" by Katy Perry and the retrieved track with the smallest distance, "Black Ice" by AC/DC. Countries with low counts have been omitted for clearer visualization. As is clearly seen in the Figure 5, these tracks exhibit very similar distributions with heavy activity in the United States and secondary activity in Brazil and Mexico. Additionally, Table 3 shows the top 5 tracks with most similar listening distributions.

Similarly, Figure 6 and Table 4 show the track distribution comparison for the most similar track and top 5 most similar tracks, respectively, for the seed track "Yamulemaeu" by Joe Arroyo y La Verdad. And Figure 7 and Table 5 show the track distribution comparison for the most similar track and top 5 most similar tracks, respectively for the seed track "Y(JR GROOVE Remix)" by MBLAQ.

Figure 5: Geographical distributions of "Dark Horse" and most similar track

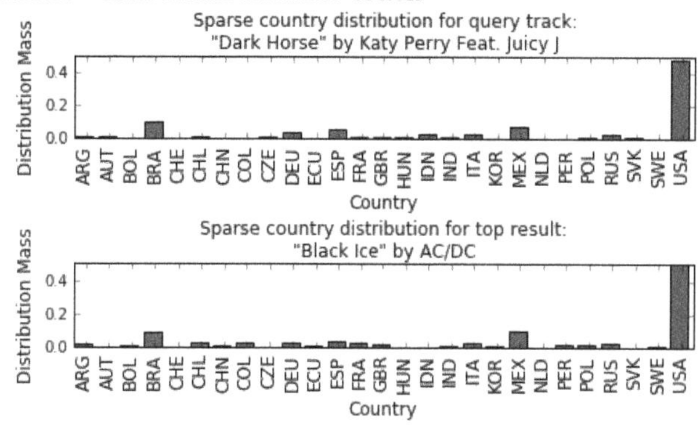

Figure 6: Geographical distributions of "Yamulemaeu" and most similar track

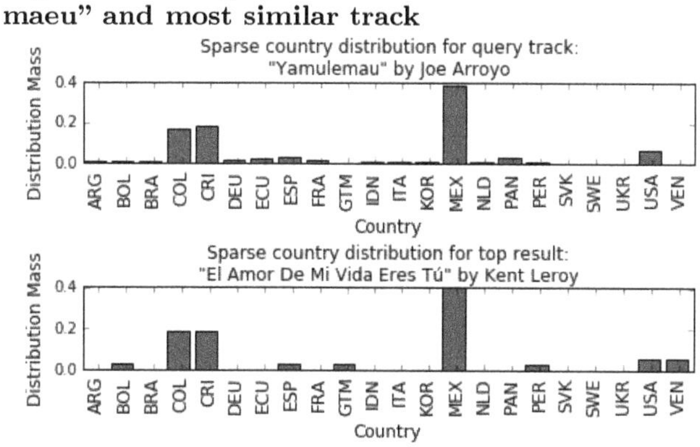

5.3 Discussion

The most similar tracks retrieved for the first two seed tracks, whose most similar tracks are shows in Table 3 and Table 4, give a sense of geography and language and yet cross boundaries in other content dimensions such as artist origin and genre. The third seed track by MBLAQ, a South Korean artist, presents an interesting result where there is no activity in South Korea. Still, this retrieves other tracks from Korean pop artists with similar popularity in other parts of the world.

Figure 7: Geographical distributions of "Y(JR GROOVE Remix)" and most similar track

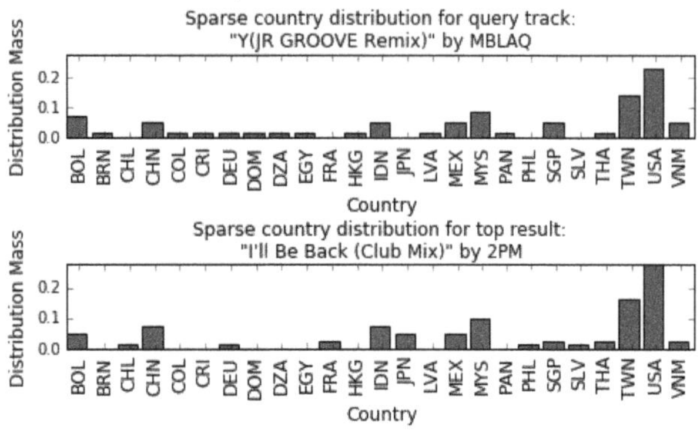

Table 3: Top 5 Similar Tracks for "Dark Horse" by Katy Perry feat. Juicy J

Rank	Track	Artist
1	Black Ice	AC/DC
2	Even In Death	Evanescence
3	Try	P!nk
4	By The Way	Red Hot Chili Peppers
5	Duality	Slipknot

Table 4: Top 5 Similar Tracks for "Yamulemau" by Joe Arroyo

Rank	Track	Artist
1	El Amor De Mi Vida Eres Tú	Kent Leroy
2	Cuatro Cirios.	Javier Solís
3	Sola Con Mi Soledad	Maricela
4	Te Llamo Para Despedirme	Sergio Denis
5	Necesito Una Compañera	Los 3 Grandes Compositores

Table 5: Top 5 Similar Tracks for "Y(JR GROOVE Remix)" by MBLAQ

Rank	Track	Artist
1	I'll Be Back (Club Mix)	2PM
2	I REMEMBER	B.A.P, Dae Hyen
3	Purple Line	東方神起
4	야누스 (Janus)	보이프렌드
5	Catch Me	東方神起

6. CONCLUSIONS

This paper presented a novel dataset of music identification matches that fills a gap in available datasets for music information retrieval. The results of a small investigation into a geographical similarity metric for music tracks showed the utility of the dataset for IR related tasks. Moving forward, additional metadata may be added to enhance the utility of the dataset, and pending interest from the research community, additional data may be released.

7. REFERENCES

[1] T. Bertin-Mahieux, D. P. Ellis, B. Whitman, and P. Lamere. The million song dataset. In *ISMIR 2011: Proceedings of the 12th International Society for Music Information Retrieval Conference, October 24-28, 2011, Miami, Florida*, pages 591–596. University of Miami, 2011.

[2] R. Campos, G. Dias, A. M. Jorge, and A. Jatowt. Survey of temporal information retrieval and related applications. *ACM Computing Surveys (CSUR)*, 47(2):15, 2014.

[3] P. Cano, E. Batlle, T. Kalker, and J. Haitsma. A review of audio fingerprinting. *Journal of VLSI signal processing systems for signal, image and video technology*, 41(3):271–284, 2005.

[4] D. Hauger, M. Schedl, A. Košir, and M. Tkalcic. The million musical tweets dataset: What can we learn from microblogs. In *Proceedings of the 14th International Society for Music Information Retrieval Conference (ISMIR 2013)*, 2013.

[5] Y. Kim, B. Suh, and K. Lee. # nowplaying the future billboard: mining music listening behaviors of twitter users for hit song prediction. In *Proceedings of the first international workshop on Social media retrieval and analysis*, pages 51–56. ACM, 2014.

[6] P. Lamere. Social tagging and music information retrieval. *Journal of new music research*, 37(2):101–114, 2008.

[7] A. Narayanan and V. Shmatikov. How to break anonymity of the netflix prize dataset. *arXiv preprint cs/0610105*, 2006.

[8] M. Sanderson. *Test collection based evaluation of information retrieval systems.* Now Publishers Inc, 2010.

[9] M. Schedl. Leveraging microblogs for spatiotemporal music information retrieval. In *Advances in Information Retrieval*, pages 796–799. Springer, 2013.

[10] M. Schedl, A. Vall, and K. Farrahi. User geospatial context for music recommendation in microblogs. In *Proceedings of the 37th international ACM SIGIR conference on Research & development in information retrieval*, pages 987–990. ACM, 2014.

[11] G. Tassey, B. R. Rowe, D. W. Wood, A. N. Link, and D. A. Simoni. Economic impact assessment of nist's text retrieval conference (trec) program. *Report prepared for National Institute of Technology (NIST)*, 2010.

[12] R. Turrin, M. Quadrana, A. Condorelli, R. Pagano, and P. Cremonesi. 30music listening and playlists dataset.

[13] P. S. Yu, X. Li, and B. Liu. On the temporal dimension of search. In *Proceedings of the 13th international World Wide Web conference on Alternate track papers & posters*, pages 448–449. ACM, 2004.

[14] E. Zangerle, M. Pichl, W. Gassler, and G. Specht. # nowplaying music dataset: Extracting listening behavior from twitter. In *Proceedings of the First International Workshop on Internet-Scale Multimedia Management*, pages 21–26. ACM, 2014.

Longitudinal Navigation Log data on a Large Web Domain

Suzan Verberne
Radboud University, Nijmegen, the Netherlands
s.verberne@cs.ru.nl

Bram Arends
Radboud University, Nijmegen, the Netherlands
b.j.w.t.arends@student.ru.nl

Wessel Kraaij
TNO, the Hague
Radboud University, Nijmegen, the Netherlands
Leiden Institute of Advanced Computer Science, Leiden University
kraaijw@acm.org

Arjen de Vries
Radboud University
Nijmegen, the Netherlands
arjen@acm.org

ABSTRACT

We have collected the access logs for our university's web domain over a time span of 4.5 years. We now release the pre-processed data of a 3-month period for research into user navigation behavior. We preprocessed the data so that only successful GET requests of web pages by non-bot users are kept. The resulting 3-month collection comprises 9.6M page visits (190K unique URLs) by 744K unique visitors.

CCS Concepts

•**Information systems** → **Web log analysis; Traffic analysis;** *Web searching and information discovery;*

Keywords

data collection; access logs; navigation behavior; link analysis; graph clustering

1. INTRODUCTION

Finding information on the web requires a combination of searching and browsing. Browsing a large web domain can sometimes be challenging because traditional navigation structures do not support a complex hierarchy of pages and the possibility of multiple entry points [4]. In this paper we address the navigation behavior of users on a so-called *mega-site*. Mega-sites are extremely large, many levels deep, made up of many subsections, cater to many audiences and have multiple entry points [4]. Organizations with mega-sites are typically large organizations with many divisions and multiple target groups. Universities are prototypical examples of such organizations.

We present a newly released data collection that comprises longitudinal navigation log data on a mega-site: a university web domain. The complete data set consists of 4.5 years of access data. A first set of 3 months will now be released as a resource for research. The data collection is unique in two ways: (1) its size: the pre-processed data of only 3 months comprises almost 10 Million page visits; (2) its richness: all information from the original access log entries, including URL strings, referrers and timestamps, has been preserved.

The data collection is valuable for a range of research topics: user navigation, browsing and stopping behavior, evaluation of clustering techniques on large (directed) graphs, evaluation of link prediction and page recommendation techniques, clustering of web users based on their online activities, evaluation of content-based and navigation-based user profiles, and the evaluation of usability of mega-sites.

In this paper, we describe the preprocessing of the data, present some statistics of the resulting data collection and show two examples of research that can be conducted with this data collection: link prediction and graph clustering.

SIGIR '16, July 17-21, 2016, Pisa, Italy
© 2016 ACM. ISBN 978-1-4503-4069-4/16/07...$15.00
DOI: http://dx.doi.org/10.1145/2911451.2914667

Table 1: Statistics for the data collection, showing the cumulative effect of filtering applied to the raw log files.

# of entries in raw sample	164,923,821
# of entries after success status filtering	121,840,127
# of entries after request type filtering	115,866,318
# of entries after file type filtering	12,963,852
# of entries after web bot filtering	9,633,438
# of entries after anonymization	9,555,418
# of unique users in sample	744,340
# of unique URLs in sample	190,457

2. DATA

We have been collecting (and are still collecting) server access logs since September 2011 on the web domain of our university. The data is constantly growing, with a speed of more than 50 Million page visits per month. The data that we make available for research covers three months of navigation logs: from October 1st to December 31st 2014. The raw data comprises 156M page visits (1.3M unique URLs).

2.1 Preprocessing

The log data are formatted as Apache log files.[1] We filtered the raw data as follows: We removed all requests that did not result in a successful response (status codes starting

[1]See https://httpd.apache.org/docs/1.3/logs.html for a definition of the format.

```
8567899994 - - [01/Oct/2014:00:08:04 +0100] "GET http://www.ru.nl/facilitairbedrijf/horeca/refter-0/weekmenu-refter/menu-deze-week? HTTP/1.1" 200 4138 "-
4051463049 - - [01/Oct/2014:00:08:06 +0100] "GET http://www.ru.nl/docentenacademie/educatieve-minor/aanmelden/voorlichting-intake/ HTTP/1.1" 200 17740 "h
1458578703 - - [01/Oct/2014:00:08:06 +0100] "GET http://www.ru.nl/overons/organisatie/organisatiegids/ HTTP/1.1" 200 59891 "-"
4051463049 - - [01/Oct/2014:00:08:07 +0100] "GET http://www.ru.nl/? HTTP/1.1" 200 1694 "http://www.ru.nl/docentenacademie/educatieve-minor/aanmelden/voor
1458578703 - - [01/Oct/2014:00:08:09 +0100] "GET http://www.ru.nl/deutsch/ HTTP/1.1" 200 50113 "-"
1996730999 - - [01/Oct/2014:00:08:09 +0100] "GET http://www.ru.nl/radboudintolanguages/taaltrainingen/frans/ HTTP/1.1" 200 36980 "-"
1458578703 - - [01/Oct/2014:00:08:09 +0100] "GET http://www.ru.nl/english/ HTTP/1.1" 200 71544 "-"
1458578703 - - [01/Oct/2014:00:08:10 +0100] "GET http://www.ru.nl/alumni/vind-studiegenoten/alumni_netwerk/ HTTP/1.1" 200 35677 "-"
5198472765 - - [01/Oct/2014:00:08:11 +0100] "GET http://www.ru.nl/ouders/studiekeuze/ouders-coach/ HTTP/1.1" 200 49792 "http://www.ru.nl/ouders/studiekeu
1458578703 - - [01/Oct/2014:00:08:12 +0100] "GET http://www.ru.nl/opleidingen/ HTTP/1.1" 200 71659 "-"
1458578703 - - [01/Oct/2014:00:08:12 +0100] "GET http://www.ru.nl/algemeen/informatie-cookies/ HTTP/1.1" 200 63960 "-"
8883787189 - - [01/Oct/2014:00:08:13 +0100] "GET http://www.ru.nl/blackboard/ HTTP/1.1" 200 14354 "https://www.google.nl/"
1458578703 - - [01/Oct/2014:00:08:14 +0100] "GET http://www.ru.nl/algemeen/sitemap/ HTTP/1.1" 200 64653 "-"
1458578703 - - [01/Oct/2014:00:08:14 +0100] "GET http://www.ru.nl/algemeen/overige_informatie/disclaimer/ HTTP/1.1" 200 64279 "-"
```

Figure 1: Screenshot of small portion of the filtered data with masked IP addresses in the first column.

with 3 or higher); all requests that are no GET requests; and all requests for images and other files that do not result from a navigational process.[2] In addition, we removed all requests that supposedly come from web bots, using the regular expression `.*(Yahoo! Slurp|bingbot|Googlebot).*` on the log entry. We anonymized the data by taking the following measures:

- We replaced all occurrences of the same IP address by a unique random identifier (a 10-digit string).
- We removed the last part of each log entry – the User-Agent HTTP request header – which is the identifying information that the client browser reports about itself.[3]
- If the referrer is a search engine, we removed everything after the substring `/search?`. We are aware that queries can provide valuable information about pages in the domain [2], but queries are also known to potentially be personally identifiable information [1]; for that reason, we will postpone a decision on releasing filtered query information, and first gain experience with the external usage of the data without search queries.
- We removed requests for URLs that only occur once in the 3-month-dataset to reduce the chance of unmasking specific users. This is an additional security step since extremely low-frequent URLs are highly specific and therefore often unique for a person.

The effect of each of the filtering steps is shown in Table 1. The information that is retained per entry is: unique user id, timestamp, GET request (URL), status code, the size of the object returned to the client, and the referrer URL. A sample of the resulting data is shown in Figure 1. The sample illustrates that the content (URLs and referrers) is multilingual: predominantly Dutch, and English and German in smaller proportions.

2.2 Statistics on the resulting collection

The final size of the collection is 9.6M page visits (190K unique URLs) by 744K unique visitors. Figure 2 shows the distribution of the number of occurrences of GET requests in the collection, on a log-log scale. The plot indicates the expected long-tail (power law) distribution: very few pages occur highly frequently, and many occur infrequently.

[2]All files with one of the extensions `axd`, `aspx`, `bmp`, `doc`, `docx`, `jpg`, `jpeg`, `gif`, `css`, `js`, `png`, `sav`, `swf`, `ttf`, `txt`, `xls`, `xlsx`, `xml`, `zip`, `ppt`, `pptx`, `ico`

[3]The Electronic Frontier Foundation shows the potential of this information: https://panopticlick.eff.org/

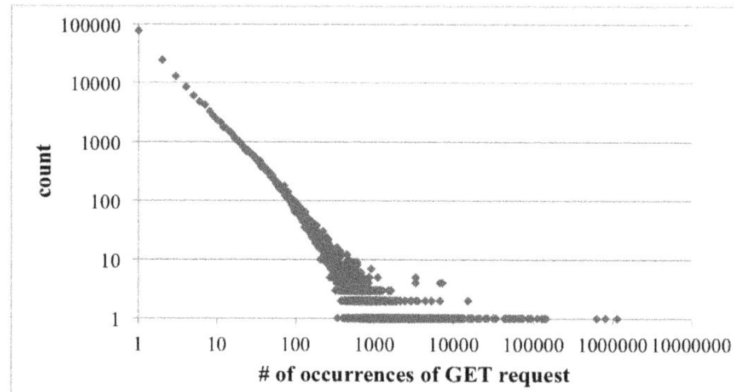

Figure 2: Distribution of the number of occurrences of unique GET requests in the collection.

2.3 Availability

The data collection is available to researchers through DANS (Data Archiving and Networked Services).[4] Users of the dataset are asked to sign a data agreement stating that they will use the dataset for research purposes, that they will not attempt to discover the identities of the persons whose navigation behavior is logged in the collection, and that they will erase the data after completion of their research.

3. EXAMPLE RESULTS

In this section, we describe the results of two experiments with the data, one addressing the task of link prediction and one addressing the task of URL clustering. Both tasks have only been evaluated before on much smaller datasets. The results presented here demonstrate the utility of the new data collection for the evaluation and validation of graph methods on large data sets.

3.1 Link prediction

Our first goal was to investigate how well we could predict the next request of a user based on the navigation behavior of other users. This task is called link prediction. Link prediction can be employed for recommending relevant pages to the user and/or webmaster and thereby improving the user experience on a web domain. We use a subset of our data for our experiments: one week of logs (7 days) were used as training data, and one day (the 8th day) was used as test data. This resulted in a training set with 35,000 unique URLs and 85,000 unique users. Although this is a

[4]http://dx.doi.org/10.17026/dans-28m-mwht

very small portion of our data, it is much larger than the data sets used in previous work on link prediction, with 100 to 1000 unique URLs [8, 11].

Method. We adopted the most commonly used method for link prediction: Markov chains [8, 11]. A Markov chain describes a system of transitions between states, where the probability of going to a state only depends on the previous state. In our model, the states represent the visited pages and the transitions represent the probability of a user visiting two pages directly after each other.

Let $s(t-1)$ be the vector representing the state during time $t-1$, and A the transition matrix with the probabilities of going from one state to another. Then the probability of going to $s(t)$ is computed with:

$$s(t) = s(t-1)A \tag{1}$$

The transition matrix A is computed with:

$$A(s, s') = \frac{C(s, s')}{\sum_{s''} C(s, s'')} \tag{2}$$

where $A(s, s')$ is the probability of going from state s to state s', and $C(s, s')$ is the number of times s preceeds s' in the training data [8]. The resulting transition matrix for our data is sparse.

We investigated the effect of the history size (using 1, 2 or 3 previously visited pages) on the quality of prediction of the next page. We compared two interpolation strategies from the literature [8, 11] for combining the previous stages:

$$s(t) = a_1 i_{t-1} A + a_2 i_{t-2} A^2 + ... \qquad \text{(summation)}$$

$$s(t) = \max(a_1 i_{t-1} A,\ a_2 i_{t-2} A^2,\ ...) \qquad \text{(maximization)}$$

where $s(t)$ denotes the probability of going to state s during time t, i_t is the vector representing the state, with a probability 1 at that state at that time, and a_i are user specified weights; we use uniform weights in our experiment.

Experimental setup. The requests in the training and test data were grouped by user and sorted by timestamp, resulting in a full path of requested pages per user. We divided these paths into sessions: after at least thirty minutes of inactivity a new session was started. We used sessions from 1,000 randomly selected users from the test data for evaluation; we repeated the experiment five times with a different random seed and report the average accuracy over the seeds. We vary the size of the history (1, 2 or 3 previous pages) and the interpolation strategy for previous stages (summation or maximization).

For each page in the test data that has sufficient history in its session, our algorithms try to predict the next visited page. Note that the interpolation over previous stages functions as a back-off strategy for missing links in the training data: if we try to predict the navigation sequence $A \rightarrow B \rightarrow C$, after seeing $A \rightarrow B$ in the test data, it might be that the path $A \rightarrow B \rightarrow C$ is not present in the training data, but the path $B \rightarrow C$ is. In both interpolation strategies, the probability of $B \rightarrow C$ is a factor in prediction. However, if C does not occur in the training data at all, predicting C is not possible. In our experiment, 3% of the URLs in the test data does not occur in the training data.

Results. We let the Markov chain return the page predictions in decreasing order of probability. We evaluated the prediction quality in terms of Success@1 and Success@3:

Table 2: Evaluation of link prediction (Success@1 and Success@3 scores, averaged over 5 random data seeds), using two strategies for combining the previous states and three history sizes (number of previous pages used).

History size	Summation		Maximization	
	S@1	S@3	S@1	S@3
1	64.3%	82.9%	64.3%	82.9%
2	46.9%	61.2%	46.7%	61.1%
3	79.4%	90.0%	80.3%	90.3%

the proportion of predictions with the correct next URL returned in the top-1 or the top-3 respectively. The results, presented in Table 2, show that there is no clear preference for one interpolation method over the other. If we use a history of three URLs in the session, 90% of the returned URL suggestions has the correct next URL in the top-3. This is a result that would be useful in a recommendation setting on the web domain: providing the user with three suggestions for the next URL to visit.

Interestingly, the results for a history of two URLs are worse than the results for a history of one URL, even though the interpolation of previous stages ensures a back-off mechanism. We speculate that there are many sessions with two URLs – the first URL serving as history for the second – and these are relatively easy to predict, compared to the sessions with three URLs, where there is more variety in the history: If $A \rightarrow B \rightarrow C$ is not present in the training data, but $A \rightarrow B \rightarrow X$ and $A \rightarrow B \rightarrow Y$ are, with high probabilities, then the back-off probability of $B \rightarrow C$ cannot compensate for the wrong X and Y predictions.

This initial result shows the potential of link prediction on the navigation graph, and provides future directions for research into the use of Markov chains on large directed graphs, and the modeling of user navigation behavior.

3.2 Web page clustering

In a second study, we investigated the clustering of web pages based on the transitions of visitors between URLs. In previous work, techniques for clustering navigation patterns were only evaluated on smaller data sets [9, 10]. Most graph clustering techniques that can handle large graphs have been developed for undirected graphs (for community detection) [6, 5]. Spectral clustering methods are often used to cluster directed graphs, but applying them to large graphs is not feasible [5].

Method. A solution to our problem is provided by Rosvall and Bergstrom (2008) [7]. They use a random walk method to find a good clustering, by compressing the bit sequence of a random walk with Huffman coding. Huffman coding is a compression technique that assigns short codewords to common bit sequences and long codewords to rare ones; the most frequently visited nodes in a random walk get the shortest codes. The average number of bits to describe one step in the graph is a measure for the quality of the clustering. The idea is that a good clustering will result in a better compression for the bit sequence than a bad clustering, because when performing a random walk, one is more likely to stay in a good cluster for a long time before leaving. A clustering that minimizes the entropy of the bit sequence would be optimal. Finding the minimal entropy can be achieved with the Louvain algorithm, which greedily

Table 3: The first 6 URLs from the five largest clusters found by clustering the navigation paths as directed graphs.

1	http://www.ru.nl/?
	http://www.ru.nl
	http://www.ru.nl/vm_syllabus_plus/rooster
	http://www.ru.nl/algemene_onderdelen/zoeken/
	http://www.ru.nl/vacatures/details/details_v
	http://www.ru.nl/vacatures/alle-vacatures
2	http://www.ru.nl/studereninnijmegen/?
	http://www.ru.nl/studereninnijmegen/opleiding
	http://www.ru.nl/studereninnijmegen
	http://www.ru.nl/studereninnijmegen/voorlicht
	http://www.ru.nl/studereninnijmegen/vm/zoeken
	http://www.ru.nl/studereninnijmegen/opleiding
3	http://www.ru.nl/ubn/?
	http://www.ru.nl/ubn
	http://www.ru.nl/ubn/literatuur_zoeken/zoeks
	http://www.ru.nl/ubn/literatuur_zoeken/onder
	http://www.ru.nl/ubn/literatuur_zoeken/vakge
	http://www.ru.nl/ubn/literatuur_zoeken/vakge
4	http://www.ru.nl/nieuws/?
	http://www.ru.nl/nieuws
	http://www.ru.nl/nieuws/@797633/rotonde-oke
	http://www.ru.nl/nieuws/persberichten-0/vm/o
	http://www.ru.nl/nieuws/opinie/columns/colum
	http://www.ru.nl/nieuws/dossiers/dossiers
5	http://www.ru.nl/students/?
	http://www.ru.nl/students/masters/masters-pr
	http://www.ru.nl/students/masters/masters-pr
	http://www.ru.nl/students/masters/admission/
	http://www.ru.nl/students/masters/financial-
	http://www.ru.nl/students/bachelors/bachelor

minimizes the entropy in $O(n \log n)$ (with n being the number of nodes). In the case of sparse graphs, its complexity appears to be linear with the number of nodes [3].

We cluster the transition matrix A from the Markov chain, in order to get a clustering of the web pages in the data collection. The already available transition probabilities from one node to another are used to construct the random walk. One parameter that needs to be set is the teleportation probability, which is the probability to jump to a random node in the graph at any time. This is needed when the random walk gets stuck in dead ends or cycles. We set the teleportation probability to 0.15, which is the same value as in Google's PageRank algorithm and proposed in the paper by Rosvall and Bergstrom [7].

Experimental setup. We again used the sample of one week for these experiments, comprising 35,000 unique URLs. Note that we only use transitions between pages for the clustering, not the URL strings or the content of the URLs.

Results. 2,915 clusters were generated for the set of URLs in our sample. The majority of clusters contains only one or two URLs, which is probably caused by the sparsity of the graph. We manually went through the clusters and we found that the 20 largest clusters represent sensible groups of URLs. As illustration, Table 3 shows the first 8 URLs from the five largest clusters. Clusters 2, 3, 4 and 5 turn out to comprise specific subdomains. Cluster 1 (which is the largest cluster) contains general and often-visited pages.

This initial result provides future directions for research into the development of clustering techniques on large directed graphs, especially for modeling user navigation behavior, and clustering users into visitor groups.

4. CONCLUSIONS

We have prepared a data collection of user interaction logs with a university web site. The collection comprises 3 months of data, filtered for unsuccessful requests, download file types and web bots, and anonymized while preserving unique visitor IDs. The size of the preprocessed data is 9.6M page visits (190K unique URLs) by 744K unique visitors. The data collection allows for research on, among other things, user navigation, browsing and stopping behavior and web user clustering. We have conducted two exploratory studies on a one-week subset of the data, directed at link prediction and graph clustering. The results show the potential of the data, especially given its size and its richness.

For experiments that require larger data sets it will be possible to release more data in the future: we have been collecting data for 4.5 years and the raw data is growing at a speed of 50 Million page visits per month.[5] In addition, we will investigate the possibility to release the domain's query logs together with the navigation log data.

Acknowledgements

This publication was supported by the Dutch national program COMMIT (project P7 SWELL).

5. REFERENCES

[1] Adar, E.: User 4xxxxx9: Anonymizing query logs. In: Proc of Query Log Analysis Workshop, International Conference on World Wide Web. (2007)

[2] Antonellis, I., Garcia-Molina, H., Karim, J.: Tagging with queries: How and why? In: Second ACM International Conference on Web Search and Data Mining WSDM 2009, Late Breaking Results Session, Infolab (February 2009)

[3] Blondel, V.D., Guillaume, J.L., Lambiotte, R., Lefebvre, E.: Fast unfolding of communities in large networks. Journal of Statistical Mechanics: Theory and Experiment **2008**(10) (2008) P10008

[4] Boag, P.: Navigation for mega-sites. Smashing Magazine (2013) Accessed on January 20, 2016.

[5] Fortunato, S.: Community detection in graphs. Physics Reports **486**(3) (2010) 75–174

[6] Malliaros, F.D., Vazirgiannis, M.: Clustering and community detection in directed networks: A survey. Physics Reports **533**(4) (2013) 95–142

[7] Rosvall, M., Bergstrom, C.T.: Maps of random walks on complex networks reveal community structure. Proceedings of the National Academy of Sciences **105**(4) (2008) 1118–1123

[8] Sarukkai, R.R.: Link prediction and path analysis using Markov chains. Computer Networks **33**(1) (2000) 377–386

[9] Smith, K.A., Ng, A.: Web page clustering using a self-organizing map of user navigation patterns. Decision Support Systems **35**(2) (2003) 245–256

[10] Xu, J., Liu, H.: Web user clustering analysis based on K-Means algorithm. In: Information Networking and Automation (ICINA), 2010 International Conference on. Volume 2., IEEE (2010) V2–6

[11] Zhu, J., Hong, J., Hughes, J.G.: Using Markov chains for link prediction in adaptive web sites. In: Soft-Ware 2002: Computing in an Imperfect World. Springer (2002) 60–73

[5] Please contact the authors if you are interested in obtaining a larger collection.

New Collection Announcement: Focused Retrieval Over the Web

Ivan Habernal[⋆]
habernal@ukp.informatik.tu-darmstadt.de

Maria Sukhareva[⋆]
sukhareva@ukp.informatik.tu-darmsdtadt.de

Fiana Raiber[†]
fiana@tx.technion.ac.il

Anna Shtok[†]
annabel@tx.technion.ac.il

Oren Kurland[†]
kurland@ie.technion.ac.il

Hadar Ronen[‡]
hadarg@gmail.com

Judit Bar-Ilan[‡]
Judit.Bar-Ilan@biu.ac.il

Iryna Gurevych[⋆]
gurevych@ukp.informatik.tu-darmsdtadt.de

[⋆]UKP Lab, Technische Universität Darmstadt, Germany

[†]Faculty of Industrial Engineering and Management, Technion, Israel

[‡]Department of Information Science, Bar-Ilan University, Israel

ABSTRACT

Focused retrieval (a.k.a., passage retrieval) is important at its own right and as an intermediate step in question answering systems. We present a new Web-based collection for focused retrieval. The document corpus is the Category A of the ClueWeb12 collection. Forty-nine queries from the educational domain were created. The 100 documents most highly ranked for each query by a highly effective learning-to-rank method were judged for relevance using crowdsourcing. All sentences in the relevant documents were judged for relevance.

Categories and Subject Descriptors: H.3.0 [Information Storage and Retrieval] General

Keywords: focused retrieval

1. INTRODUCTION

Many retrieval applications and tasks rely on *passage retrieval*; that is, retrieving document parts (passages), rather than whole documents, in response to expressions of information needs. Question answering systems, for example, often apply passage retrieval in response to the question at hand [7, 1]. Then, an answer is compiled from the top retrieved passages. In *focused retrieval* systems, the result list retrieved for a query is composed of sentences [10, 25, 24] or more generally passages [2, 3, 4, 6, 9].

To advance the development of passage retrieval methods — e.g., in light of the recent resurgence of interest in Web question answering [1] — collections for evaluating passage retrieval effectiveness are called for. In this paper we describe a new such Web-based collection.

The document corpus is category A of the English ClueWeb12 collection which contains about 733 million documents. Forty-nine short keyword queries, accompanied by descriptions of the information need, were created based on questions posted on community question answering sites and questionnaires. The queries are from the education domain and are of topical nature. They represent various information needs of parents (henceforth, the target group). Furthermore, educational topics are of interest to a wide range of additional users, such as education experts, journalists, policy makers, and students.

For each query, a document list was retrieved using a highly effective learning-to-rank method. All sentences in documents in the list were judged for relevance using crowdsourcing. The final collection as well as the data processing pipeline are publicly available.[1]

2. RELATED COLLECTIONS

The Novelty tracks of TREC [10, 25, 24] used relevance judgments for sentences and the HARD (High Accuracy Retrieval from Documents) tracks [2, 3, 4] used relevance judgments for passages. These tracks rely on old (mainly) newswire TREC document corpora and are rarely used nowadays. In contrast, our dataset is based on the newest Web collection of TREC (ClueWeb12).

The task in the TREC Question Answering (QA) track was to provide a short, concise answer to a factoid question [26]. In contrast, our queries are opinion-seeking and cannot necessarily be answered by a short string. The annotators in the TREC QA track evaluated the short answer string, while our annotators were asked to determine the relevance to a query of each sentence in the top retrieved documents.

[1]The dataset can be downloaded at: http://ie.technion.ac.il/~kurland/dip2016corpus/; the code used to process the data can be found at: https://github.com/UKPLab/sigir2016-collection-for-focused-retrieval.

SIGIR '16, July 17-21, 2016, Pisa, Italy

© 2016 ACM. ISBN 978-1-4503-4069-4/16/07...$15.00

DOI: http://dx.doi.org/10.1145/2911451.2914682

There is a Wikipedia-based INEX (Initiative for the Evaluation of XML Retrieval) collection with relevance judgments provided for parts of documents with respect to queries [6, 9]. The relevance judgment regime that was found to be the most robust with respect to inter-annotator agreement rates was highlighting all and only relevant text in each document [21]. We adopt a similar (binary) relevance judgment regime, but use crowdsourcing to produce judgments rather than trained annotators as was the case in INEX. Furthermore, we use a noisy Web collection (ClueWeb12) rather than the well edited Wikipedia collection.

A recently introduced collection provides relevance judgments for "answer passages" [13]: passages in the documents most highly ranked in response to a query are judged with respect to TREC topics (specifically, their descriptions) that are of a question form/type; the document collection is TREC's GOV2. In contrast, the queries we have developed are not necessarily of question form (e.g., many of the queries are of topical nature), and we use the much larger and noisier ClueWeb12 collection.

3. COLLECTION DESCRIPTION

3.1 Queries

To ensure high variability of queries, as well as their pertinence to the target group (parents), we combined two approaches for query compilation. The first approach relied on exploiting existing Question-Answering Web portals and the second approach utilized a user questionnaire.

To sample users' information needs from QA sites, we used Yahoo L6 Question Answering Collection[2] [23] and selected about 150k questions from the Education section which contains nine categories. Questions from each category were projected onto a latent 300-dimensional semantic space using `word2vec` [18] and independently clustered into $k/10$ clusters (where k is a number of question in the category) using the CLUTO software package[3] with the Repeated Bisection clustering method [27]. We randomly sampled 10 questions from each of the 5 largest clusters, and conducted a survey with eight participants whose task was to formulate a query/queries that would best represent the information needs reflected by that cluster. This process yielded roughly 200 queries in total, from which 39 queries were randomly selected. The selected queries were enriched with a specification of what relevant information is to be expected from the system; these specifications are similar to the *narratives* used in TREC.

Although the Yahoo QA set is very rich, it usually covers US-specific topics. We thus created an additional Google Forms based online questionnaire of 20 parental issues and distributed it among 51 non-US parents of children aged 1-21. The instructions were to rank each issue according to the level of interest that causes participants to search for online information, on a scale from 1 (not interested at all) to 5 (very interested). For the 10 top ranked queries, a description was added.

The final query set (examples of query titles are presented in Table 3) consists of 49 queries combined from the two

Query ID: 1017, **Query Title:** student loans

Relevant info	Irrelevant info
• Eligibility criteria for student loans. • Categories of student loans. • Where to apply for student loans. • Conditions for student loans.	• Completely unrelated topics. • Information on loans which are not for educational purposes. • Information about financial aid options which are not loans. • Information on the effect of student loans on higher education prices and global economy.

Table 1: Example of a query.

aforementioned approaches.[4] Following common practice, a query is composed of a short title and information need description. To make the annotation task easier for non-expert judges, we presented the information need description in a table. The table provides context that cannot be inferred from the title alone, and examples of relevant and irrelevant information that the annotator may encounter (see an example in Table 1).

3.2 Document collection

The full ClueWeb12 dataset (category A), which contains about 733 million documents, was used for creating the collection. For the retrieval stage, the documents and the queries were stemmed using the Krovetz stemmer via the Indri toolkit[5] which was also used for retrieval. The 100 documents most highly ranked with respect to a query were annotated. (Details of the retrieval method are provided below.) Some of the (Web) documents are noisy and hard to read. Thus, we pre-processed all documents before the annotation. Specifically, we applied a state-of-the-art boilerplate removal tool [22] and a sentence splitter [16]. As a result of applying the boilerplate, a few documents became empty and were removed from the lists to be annotated.

3.3 Data annotation

3.3.1 Initial document retrieval

We first ranked all the documents in the dataset with respect to a query using the negative cross entropy between the unsmoothed unigram language model induced from the query and the Dirichlet-smoothed unigram language model induced from each of the documents [15]. Following common practice [8], documents assigned with a score below 70 by Waterloo's spam classifier were filtered out from this initial ranking top down until 1000 presumably non-spam documents were accumulated. The remaining documents were then re-ranked to produce the final document ranking.

To re-rank the documents, a learning-to-rank approach was applied with 130 features. Most of these features were used in Microsoft's learning-to-rank datasets[6] with the following exceptions. Instead of the two quality features (QualityScore and QualityScore2), which are not available for the ClueWeb12 dataset, we used query-independent document quality measures that were shown to be highly effective

[2]Provided by Yahoo! Webscope, http://research.yahoo.com/Academic_Relations

[3]http://www.cs.umn.edu/~karypis/cluto

[4]We removed one query from the 50 selected queries as it asked for a site containing only links, which has a very different nature from the topical queries in the rest of the corpus.

[5]www.lemurproject.org/indri

[6]www.research.microsoft.com/en-us/projects/mslr

Documents			4,820
Sentences			628,026
Workers			2,041
Sentences/HIT	1...40	41...80	81...120
HITs	2199	1800	4,130
Average duration (sec)	67	87	150

Table 2: Annotation details.

for spam classification [20] and Web retrieval [5]. Specifically, we used as features the ratio between the number of stopwords and non-stopwords in a document, the percentage of stopwords in a stopwords list that appear in the document and the entropy of the term distribution in a document. As is the case with the features used in Microsoft's datasets, these quality measures were computed for the entire document, its body, title, URL and anchor text. We used the score assigned to a document by Waterloo's spam classifier [8] as an additional quality measure. Hence, Waterloo's spam classifier served both for filtering out documents from the initial document ranking and as a feature in the learning-to-rank model. Additional features used in Microsoft's datasets that were not considered here are the Boolean Model, Vector Space Model, LMIR.ABS, Outlink number, SiteRank, Query-URL click count, URL click count, and URL dwell time.

To integrate the features we used SVM^{rank} [12] applied with a linear kernel and default free-parameter values. The titles of topics 201-250 from TREC 2013 were used as queries to train the model. The Dirichlet smoothing parameter in LMIR.DIR, which served both for creating the initial ranking and as a feature in the learning-to-rank model, was set to $\mu = 1000$. We used LMIR.JM with $\lambda = 0.1$; for BM25, we set $k1 = 1$ and $b = 0.5$. The INQUERY list was used for computing the two stopword-based quality measures.

3.3.2 Crowdsourcing document annotations

Data preparation.

Although the majority of documents (≈74%) are no longer than 120 sentences, the document length distribution is heavy-tailed: 73% of the sentences are in documents containing over 120 sentences (e.g., the longest document contains over 4500 sentences). It has been frequently pointed out in previous work on crowdsourcing that unlike traditional annotation approaches, a so-called "fun factor" can strongly affect the annotation quality and workers' response. In some cases it played even a more important role than the size of the reward [19, 14]. Thus, during a pilot study, three experts were instructed to provide their feedback on how many sentences they can annotate without significant loss of concentration. Based on their observations, the length of a single *Human Intelligence Task (HIT)* was limited to 120 sentences. If a document contained more than 120 sentences, it was split on paragraph borders so that each split segment would have no more than 120 sentences. If a document or a split segment contained less than 80 or less than 40 sentences, it was grouped in medium and short HIT groups, respectively. Table 2 sums up the annotation setup details.

Annotation setup.

We performed crowdsourcing using the *Amazon Mechanical Turk* platform. The task was designed as follows: the workers were invited to read a document from top to bottom. Each document was split into sentences and no paragraph marking was preserved. The workers were to judge each sentence individually as relevant or not to a given query. The instructions asked workers to base their decision on two lists of relevant and irrelevant examples (Table 1). If a worker decided that a sentence or several sentences were relevant then they should highlight it by either clicking on it or dragging the mouse over the relevant sentences.[7] We also provided a link to guidelines[8] with an extended definition of what should be considered relevant. According to the guidelines, a sentence can be either:

- Clearly relevant, if it is informative and relevant regardless of its context.
- Relevant in context, if it is only relevant to a query in the context of a clearly informative sentence that either precedes or succeeds it.
- Clearly irrelevant, if it does not fall into any of the two aforementioned categories.

Workers were asked to highlight only sentences that are clearly relevant and relevant in context.

Quality control.

In order to be allowed to work on a HIT, workers were required to have two Amazon Mechanical Turk Qualifications: 1. They must be based in the US. 2. They must have acceptance rate higher than 95%. Rather than generating the gold data through a majority vote over five workers' decisions, we integrated MACE, an unsupervised tool for quality prediction of non-expert annotations [11], in our publicly available pipeline and extended the guideline by a warning about automatic cheater detection. Later on, 64 workers were blocked from working on the HITs based on the competence scores assigned by MACE.

Results.

Table 2 provides a summary of the resulting dataset. The dataset includes 4820 annotated documents and over 600k annotated sentences (5 assignments per sentence) for 49 queries. The total cost of the annotation was 3880 US Dollars. The workers' response varied depending on the length of the documents. The best response was observed for short HITs with an average annotation speed of 288 HITs a day, while long HITs were annotated with an average speed of 174 HITs a day. Although we did not explicitly instruct workers to submit any qualitative user feedback, the annotation interface had a comment field which was mostly designed to provide a convenient way for workers to report technical problems. Interestingly, we received over 2000 commented HITs (10% of the total) with multiple positive feedback about the content of the annotated documents. Many workers pointed out that they found articles useful and educational and, hence, enjoyed working on the task despite a modest reward. This demonstrates, again, the importance of the entertainment component for the success of a crowdsourcing annotation task, as it is very likely that the high agreement between annotators (see Section 3.4) is a direct

[7]http://tinyurl.com/jdxuyyl
[8]http://tinyurl.com/zvwjm2p

consequence of the fact that many workers were attentively reading documents because of their personal interest in the documents' content.

3.4 Collection statistics

For each annotated document, we computed observed annotation agreement using the *DKPro Agreement* package [17].[9] The minimal units for agreement computation were sentences, each with two categories per annotator (relevant or non-relevant). Average agreement over all documents judged is 0.725 and standard deviation is 0.175 (where agreement ranges between 0 and 1). Interestingly, we found that the average (over sentences) agreement on non-relevant documents is statistically significantly higher than that on relevant documents: 0.880 vs 0.706 respectively[10]. Presumably, when the document is relevant the annotators may comprehend it differently as the task of marking relevant sentences is challenging; in contrast, it is easier to agree on irrelevant documents, especially if these are off topic.

Overall, the documents retrieved for 49 queries were annotated. Per query, about 98 documents on average were annotated on a sentence level. On average, about 87 documents and about 4618 sentences per query were judged relevant. Overall, about 89% of the annotated documents are relevant and about 36% of the sentences are relevant. The Normalized Discounted Cumulative Gain (NDCG) at top 30 documents is 0.924 and the precision at top 5 ranks is 0.943; these performance numbers attest to the high effectiveness of the retrieval.

Query ID	Query Title
1001	Alternative ADHD treatments
1002	Cellphone for 12 years old kids
1003	Dealing with kids that skip classes
1004	Child depression
1005	Discipline for 8 year old daughter
1006	Discipline issues in elementary school
1007	Getting rid of childhood phobia
1008	Handling conflicts between children
1010	Homeschooling legal issues

Table 3: Examples of the queries used.

4. SUMMARY

We presented a novel Web-based collection for query-based focused retrieval (a.k.a. passage retrieval) with sentence-level relevance judgments. The document corpus is the Category A of the ClueWeb12 collection; forty-nine queries from the educational domain are used.

Acknowledgments. We thank the reviewers for their comments. This paper is based upon work supported in part by the German Research Foundation (DFG) via the German-Israeli Project Cooperation (DIP, grant DA 1600/1-1), the Volkswagen Foundation as part of the Lichtenberg-Professorship Program under grant № I/82806, and the Technion-Microsoft Electronic Commerce Research Center.

[9]The dynamic nature of assigning HITs to workers in crowdsourcing as well as splitting long documents into several HITs do not allow us to compute traditional inter-annotator statistics like Cohen's κ, Krippendorff's α or Fleiss' π, as these measures expect a fixed set of the same annotators over the entire data.

[10]We used two tailed permutation test at 95% confidence level to test the difference.

5. REFERENCES

[1] E. Agichtein, D. Carmel, C. L. A. Clarke, P. Paritosh, D. Pelleg, and I. Szpektor. Web question answering: Beyond factoids: SIGIR 2015 workshop. In *Proc. of SIGIR*, page 1143, 2015.

[2] J. Allan. HARD track overview in TREC 2003: High accuracy retrieval from documents. In *Proc. of TREC*, pages 24–37, 2003.

[3] J. Allan. HARD track overview in TREC 2004 - high accuracy retrieval from documents. In *Proc. of TREC*, 2004.

[4] J. Allan. HARD track overview in TREC 2005 high accuracy retrieval from documents. In *Proc. of TREC*, 2005.

[5] M. Bendersky, W. B. Croft, and Y. Diao. Quality-biased ranking of web documents. In *Proc. of WSDM*, pages 95–104, 2011.

[6] T. Chappell and S. Geva. Overview of the INEX 2010 focused relevance feedback track. In *Proc. of INEX*, pages 303–312, 2010.

[7] K. Collins-Thompson, J. Callan, E. Terra, and C. L. Clarke. The effect of document retrieval quality on factoid question answering performance. In *Proc. of SIGIR*, pages 574–575, 2004.

[8] G. V. Cormack, M. D. Smucker, and C. L. A. Clarke. Efficient and effective spam filtering and re-ranking for large web datasets. *Journal of Information Retrieval*, 14(5):441–465, 2011.

[9] S. Geva, J. Kamps, and R. Schenkel, editors. *Focused Retrieval of Content and Structure, INEX 2011*, volume 7424 of *Lecture Notes in Computer Science*. Springer, 2012.

[10] D. Harman. Overview of the TREC 2002 novelty track. In *Proc. of TREC*, 2002.

[11] D. Hovy, T. Berg-Kirkpatrick, A. Vaswani, and E. Hovy. Learning whom to trust with mace. In *Proc. NAACL-HLT*, pages 1120–1130, 2013.

[12] T. Joachims. Training linear svms in linear time. In *Proc. of KDD*, pages 217–226, 2006.

[13] M. Keikha, J. H. Park, and W. B. Croft. Evaluating answer passages using summarization measures. In *Proceedings of SIGIR*, pages 963–966, 2014.

[14] A. Kumaran, M. Densmore, and S. Kumar. Online gaming for crowd-sourcing phrase-equivalents. In *Proc. of COLING*, pages 1238–1247, 2014.

[15] J. D. Lafferty and C. Zhai. Document language models, query models, and risk minimization for information retrieval. In *Proc. of SIGIR*, pages 111–119, 2001.

[16] C. D. Manning, M. Surdeanu, J. Bauer, J. Finkel, S. J. Bethard, and D. McClosky. The Stanford CoreNLP natural language processing toolkit. In *Proc. of ACL*, pages 55–60, 2014.

[17] C. M. Meyer, M. Mieskes, C. Stab, and I. Gurevych. DKPro Agreement: An Open-Source Java Library for Measuring Inter-Rater Agreement. In *Proc. of COLING: System Demonstrations*, pages 105–109, Dublin, Ireland, 2014.

[18] T. Mikolov, I. Sutskever, K. Chen, G. S. Corrado, and J. Dean. Distributed representations of words and phrases and their compositionality. In *NIPS 26*, pages 3111–3119. 2013.

[19] Z. Nevěřilová. Annotation game for textual entailment evaluation. In *Proc. of CICLing 2014*, pages 340–350. Springer Berlin Heidelberg, 2014.

[20] A. Ntoulas, M. Najork, M. Manasse, and D. Fetterly. Detecting spam web pages through content analysis. In *Proc. of WWW*, pages 83–92, 2006.

[21] B. Piwowarski, A. Trotman, and M. Lalmas. Sound and complete relevance assessment for xml retrieval. *ACM Trans. Inf. Syst.*, 27(1):1:1–1:37, 2008.

[22] J. Pomikálek. *Removing boilerplate and duplicate content from web corpora*. PhD thesis, Masaryk university, Faculty of informatics, Brno, Czech Republic, 2011.

[23] C. Shah and J. Pomerantz. Evaluating and predicting answer quality in community QA. In *Proc. of SIGIR*, pages 411–418, 2010.

[24] I. Soboroff. Overview of the TREC 2004 novelty track. In *Proc. of TREC*, 2004.

[25] I. Soboroff and D. Harman. Overview of the TREC 2003 novelty track. In *Proc. of TREC*, pages 38–53, 2003.

[26] E. Voorhees and D. Tice. Building a Question Answering Test Collection. In *Proc. of SIGIR*, 2000.

[27] Y. Zhao and G. Karypis. Criterion functions for document clustering: Experiments and analysis. Technical report, Department of Computer Science, University of Minnesota, Minneapolis, 2002.

NTCIR Lifelog: The First Test Collection for Lifelog Research

Cathal Gurrin
Dublin City University, Ireland
cathal.gurrin@dcu.ie

Hideo Joho
University of Tsukuba, Japan
hideo@slis.tsukuba.ac.jp

Frank Hopfgartner
University of Glasgow, UK
frank.hopfgartner@glasgow.ac.uk

Liting Zhou
Dublin City University, Ireland
becky.zhou@dcu.ie

Rami Albatal
Heystaks Ltd., Ireland
rami.albatal@heystaks.com

ABSTRACT

Test collections have a long history of supporting repeatable and comparable evaluation in Information Retrieval (IR). However, thus far, no shared test collection exists for IR systems that are designed to index and retrieve multimodal lifelog data. In this paper we introduce the first test collection for personal lifelog data, which has been employed for the NTCIR12-Lifelog task. In this paper, the requirements for the test collection are motivated, the process of creating the test collection is described, along with an overview of the test collection. Finally suggestions are given for possible applications of the test collection.

Keywords

lifelog, test collection, information retrieval, multimodal, evaluation

1. INTRODUCTION

One aspect of IR that has been gathering increasing attention in recent years is the concept of lifelogging. Lifelogging is defined as a form of pervasive computing, consisting of a unified digital record of the totality of an individual's experiences, captured multi-modally through digital sensors and stored permanently as a personal multimedia archive [3]. Lifelogging typically generates multimedia archives of life-experience data in an enormous (potentially multi-decade) lifelog. Therefore a lifelog needs to be organised and searchable to be of value to the individual / lifelogger, hence there have been calls for a test collection of lifelog data [6].

However, the design and construction of a lifelog test collection is not trivial. Jones and Teeven [9], in the context of personal information management (PIM), state that *"the design of shared test collections for PIM evaluation requires some creative thinking, because such collections must differ from more traditional shared test collections"*. Although an increased level of individual information has been incorporated into the design of recent test collections (e.g., Contextual Suggestion Track at TREC [2]), the scope of individual information represented by "user profiles" is far too limited to evaluate lifelog systems.

The contribution of this paper is a description of the requirements for a lifelog test collection (Section 2) and a description of the first lifelog test collection (Section 3) that has been employed in the Lifelog Task[1] of the NTCIR-12 Evaluation Forum. This is followed (Section 4) by a short list of potential applications of the test collection.

2. CREATING THE TEST COLLECTION

The basic structure of test collections used for IR research is based on the standard three components of 1) a collection of domain-representative documents, 2) a set of queries (called topics) that are representative of the domain of application, and 3) a set of relevance judgements. This section describes requirements that are particularly relevant to lifelog test collections. Moreover, we share our experiences of generating a test collection of personal lifelog data.

2.1 Requirements for the Test Collection

Prior to generating the test collection we defined requirements for the collection based on our experiences of developing prototype lifelogging applications and relevant literature concerning lifelogging and human memory, such as [11].

Validity of the Collection.

In order to allow for statistically significant studies in the field of lifelogging, a test collection needs to contain (a sample of) a dataset that is large enough to represent real-world data of lifeloggers. Since many lifeloggers use visual data to record daily activities and reflect upon their behaviour (e.g., [1]), we needed visual lifelogs captured from wearable cameras along with metadata describing the daily life of the lifelogger, such as locations and physical activities. Similarly, realistic topics are required representing real-world information needs, based on the experience of individuals who engage in lifelogging.

Privacy by Design.

In the field of lifelogging, personal sensor data (especially camera or audio data) will carry privacy concerns [10, 4].

[1]http://ntcir-lifelog.computing.dcu.ie/ (Visited: 25 Mar 2016)

SIGIR '16, July 17-21, 2016, Pisa, Italy
© 2016 ACM. ISBN 978-1-4503-4069-4/16/07...$15.00
DOI: http://dx.doi.org/10.1145/2911451.2914680

Number of Lifeloggers	3
Size of the Collection (GB)	18.18GB
Size of the Collection (Images)	88,124 images
Size of the Collection (Long-stay Semantic Locations)	130 locations
Size of the Collection (Visual Concept Metadata)	825MB
Size of the Collection (Visual Concepts Detected)	1,000
Number of Known Item (LSAT) Topics	48
Number of Insight Analytics (LIT) Topics	10

Table 1: Statistics of NTCIR-12 Lifelog Data

Therefore, we must consider the principles of privacy-by-design when creating the test collection. This means removing user-identifiable data from the collection, yet maintaining the usefulness of the data for the proposed purpose of supporting experimental IR research.

Facilitation of Research Activities.

In order to encourage comparative evaluation over lifelog data, the dataset needs to include sufficient metadata so as to lower the overhead for participation, hence allowing researchers interested in a broad range of IR-related applications to utilise the test collection. Moreover, a reusable test collection is required that can support a number of years of ongoing research activities. Addressing these issues, a lifelog dataset requires a set of relevance judgements that can be utilised both as a source of data for comparative evaluation as well as being later utilised as a source of training data for future lifelog system experimentation.

2.2 Process of Creating the Test Collection

Given the requirements for the lifelog test collection to be as realistic as possible, there were a number of steps that were taken to ensure that this was the case, while at the same time respecting the concept of privacy-by-design and the personal nature of the rich media data being donated by a number of lifeloggers.

Low-overhead Multimodal Data Capture.

Due to the long-term, always-on, nature of lifelog data gathering, it was important to reduce the overhead on the lifelogger of gathering the data. Hence, the data was gathered using only two logging devices, the OMG Autograper wearable camera and a smartphone running the Moves app[2]. The OMG Autographer is worn on a lanyard around the neck, is orientated towards the activity the wearer is engaged in and can operate for a full-day on a battery charge. This camera takes photos passively (i.e., without explicit user intervention) and as such, it gathers a detailed digital trace of the activities of the wearer at about two images per minute. This camera is a later generation of the Microsoft Sensecam wearable camera [7]. The Moves app is a smartphone app that automatically records user activity in terms of semantic locations and physical activities (e.g. waking, cycling, running, transport), without requiring any user intervention. This app was installed on the personal smartphones used by the lifeloggers. The moves data was exported from the Moves cloud-service after the data gathering process was complete.

Temporal Alignment.

It was important to ensure temporal alignment of the sensor data, given that it is from two distinct devices. It was necessary to check and resolve alignment problems (typically in the order of 1-2 minutes) for one lifelogger by cross-referencing reported timestamps from the Autographer camera with clocks captured daily in the real-world.

Data Filtering for Privacy Preservation.

Given the personal nature of lifelog data, it was necessary to give the lifeloggers an opportunity to remove any data that they may be uncomfortable sharing. This involved a manual inspection of all their lifelog data before sharing it with us. Following this, all images were reviewed by one trusted individual with oversight of the entire collection to ensure that no potentially embarrassing or offensive images were accidentally included in the collection.

Anonymisation of the Dataset.

Two steps were taken to ensure privacy of both the lifeloggers and individuals (subjects and bystanders) captured in the lifelog, by removing identifiable content. Firstly, each recognisable face in every image was blurred in a manual process, which ensured no false positives or missed faces. A second step was to resize every image down to 1024 x 768 resolution which had the effect of both reducing the disk-size of the collection, but also rendering the majority of any on-screen text captured by the lifelogging camera to be illegible. Since privacy extends beyond content of images, the Moves app automatically converts all locations from absolute GPS locations into semantic locations, which resulted in potentially sensitive absolute addresses being labeled with generic names such as 'home' or 'work', thereby making it more unlikely that the lifeloggers could be identified.

Figure 1: Sample Wearable Camera images from the Test Collection

[2]https://moves-app.com, Visited 1 June 2016

3. DETAILS OF THE TEST COLLECTION

3.1 The Dataset

The NTCIR Lifelog test collection consists of data from three lifeloggers for a period of about one month each. The lifeloggers would all have had involvement with a university, but in different roles. The lifeloggers gathered data in an all-day gathering process; thereby gathering a wide range of daily activities. The data volume was roughly equally distributed per lifelogger. The data consists of a collection of wearable camera images (taken by an OMG Autographer camera) as shown in Figure 1; in total there were 88,124 images in the test collection. It also contains 130 semantic locations (e.g., Starbucks cafe, Dublin Airport, home, work) which were the places where the lifeloggers went (and lingered for some time) during their month of data gathering. Additionally, the physical activities (e.g., walking, transport, cycling) of the lifelogger during this month were included on a minute-by-minute basis. All data is accompanied by XML markup at the minute level of granularity. An example of the XML description is shown in Figure 2.

```
<minute id="906">
  <location>Work</location>
  <activity>walking</activity>
  <images>
   <image>
    <image-path>/u1/2015-02-18/
     20150218/150615e.jpg</image-path>
    <image-id>u1_2015-02-18_150615_1
    </image-id>
   </image>
   <image>
    <image-path>/u1/2015-02-18/
     20150218/150652e.jpg</image-path>
    <image-id>u1_2015-02-18\150652_2
    </image-id>
   </image>
  </images>
</minute>
```

Figure 2: An example of the XML data description for one minute

Given the fact that lifelog data is typically visual in nature, and to lower the barriers to participation for non-computer vision researchers, the output of the CAFFE visual concept detector [8] was included in the test collection as a source of additional visual metadata. This software provided labels and probabilities of occurrence for 1,000 everyday objects in every image (objects such as school bus, pizza, radio, ostrich, bridegroom, desktop computer, etc.). A summary of the test collection is shown in Table 1.

3.2 The Topics

Aside from the data, the test collection includes a set of topic descriptions that are representative of the real-world information needs of lifeloggers and represent the *Retrieval* and *Reflection* reasons for accessing memories [11]. Some topics have a single correct result, whereas others require a number of relevant events to be returned for every topic.

TITLE: Tower Bridge
DESCRIPTION: Find the moment(s) when I was looking at Tower Bridge in London.
NARRATIVE: To be considered relevant, the full span of Tower Bridge must be visible. Moments of crossing the Tower Bridge or showing some subset of Tower Bridge are not considered relevant.

Figure 3: LSAT Topic Example

The 48 search topics, called LSAT (Lifelog Semantic Access) Topics, were suggested by the three lifeloggers and they represent the challenge of *Retrieval* from memories. These topics were evaluated in terms of traditional IR effectiveness measurements such as Precision, Recall, MAP and NDCG. An example of an LSAT topic is shown in Figure 3. Table 2 shows ten example LSAT topics, the number of relevant results for each topic, and the recall performance of the best official automatic and interactive runs. For further details, the reader is referred to the more detailed Lifelog task overview paper from the NTCIR-12 proceedings [5].

Topic Title	Relevant	Automatic	Inter
Photographing a Lake	2	2	0
Tower Bridge	1	1	1
Driving a Rental Car	19	0	5
Lost	1	1	N/A
Man in a Burberry Coat	1	1	0
Antiques Store	3	3	3
Building a Computer	14	1	1
Bus to the Airport	1	1	1
Checking the Menu	3	0	0
Car Repair	1	0	1

Table 2: Ten sample topics from the NTCIR-12 Lifelog collection, showing the number of relevant events, the recall performance of the best performing automatic and interactive runs.

Additionally, there are ten exploratory topics representing the challenge of supporting *Reflection* from memories. These are called LIT (Lifelog Insight) Topics and are not evaluated in a traditional sense, rather, participants were encouraged to prepare insights (in any form) and demonstrate them directly to other participants at the NTCIR-12 Conference. An example of an LIT topic is shown in Figure 4.

TITLE: Early Morning Commute
DESCRIPTION: Early Provide insights on the methods of, and duration, each lifelogger spends commuting to work.
NARRATIVE: Commuting to work or university, via whatever means, is relevant. Commuting to a meeting in a location that is not the user's normal place of work is also relevant if it could be considered to be a morning commute to work. Commuting home is not relevant. General travelling is not relevant.

Figure 4: LIT Topic Example

3.3 The Relevance Assessments

The pooling method of creating relevance judgements is the typical approach for large-datasets in IR. Specifically with regard to the LSAT task, however, the relevance judgements were manual (non-pooled), and were generated by the lifeloggers and reviewed by the task organisers. The data was segmented into topic-specific events manually and at evaluation time, submissions in the form of image IDs (smallest unit of retrieval) were mapped onto events and the events judged as relevant or not relevant. If there were more than one image from any given event identified as relevant, then only the top ranked image (from that event) was selected for evaluation.

In addition, so as to make the test collection as useful as possible for a wide-range of researchers, we also provided relevance judgements for the LSAT task on a per-image basis, as the smallest unit of retrieval possible from this test collection.

Since the LIT task was an exploration-focused task, rather than a retrieval-focused task, there were no relevance judgements prepared for the LIT task. Instead, the LIT task participants presented their findings, techniques and insights in oral and poster session at NTCIR-12.

4. POTENTIAL RESEARCH CHALLENGES

Having a large collection of annotated personal data, such as this lifelog test collection, opens up a number of research opportunities:

- Multi-modal search and retrieval over archives of personal data.
- Lifelog-specific access, addressing many applications of memory, as defined by [11].
- Activity recognition from real-world data, in terms of both physical and real-world activities.
- Visual concept extraction, from real-world all-day wearable camera data (with additional supporting metadata).
- Time-series analysis of all-day personal data over extended time-periods from one, or multiple users.
- Generating insights & analytics from real-world datasets of wearable personal sensing.
- Contextual analysis of real-world user activities, to support exploratory approaches to contextual information access.
- Privacy-aware retrieval, to explore the privacy concerns surrounding search and retrieval from large lifelog archives.

The NTCIR-12 Lifelog test collection can be used to facilitate such research challenges of lifelog data. Both the document collection and query data will be released to research communities after the NTCIR-12 conference and will be made available to researchers who sign up to a (standard) data-release agreement.

5. CONCLUSION

This paper reported the design and construction of the first test collection for lifelog research. A document collection and information needs of the NTCIR Lifelog test collection are highly individual and multimodal when compared to conventional test collections.

Research conducted by participants of NTCIR-12 Lifelog Task was presented at the NTCIR-12 Conference, June 7-10, 2016 at Tokyo, Japan, and at a parallel workshop at the University of Glasgow. Based on our experiences and feedback from participants, we will prepare a new test collection for NTCIR-13, which will incorporate additional sources of contextual data (e.g., audio, computer interactions, physical accelerations/movement, biometrics) and the provision of more raw-metadata, as opposed to the semantic data that was provided with this collection.

6. ACKNOWLEDGMENTS

We acknowledge the financial support of Science Foundation Ireland (SFI) under grant number SFI/12/RC/2289 and the input of the DCU ethics committee and the risk & compliance officer.

7. REFERENCES

[1] S. Chowdhury, P. J. McParlane, M. S. Ferdous, and J. Jose. "my day in review": Visually summarising noisy lifelog data. In *ICMR'15*, pages 607–610. ACM, 2015.

[2] A. Dean-Hall, C. L. A. Clarke, J. Kamps, P. Thomas, and E. M. Voorhees. Overview of the TREC 2014 contextual suggestion track. In *TREC'14*, 2014.

[3] M. Dodge and R. Kitchin. "Outlines of a world coming into existence": Pervasive computing and the ethics of forgetting. *Environment and Planning B*, 34(3):431–445, 2007.

[4] C. Gurrin, R. Albatal, H. Joho, and K. Ishii. A privacy by design approach to lifelogging. In *Digital Enlightenment Yearbook 2014*, pages 49–73. IOS Press, 2014.

[5] C. Gurrin, H. Joho, F. Hopfgartner, L. Zhou, and R. Albatal. Overview of NTCIR-12 lifelog task. In *Proceedings of NTCIR-12 Conference*. NII, 2016.

[6] C. Gurrin, A. F. Smeaton, and A. R. Doherty. Lifelogging: Personal big data. *Foundations and Trends in Information Retrieval*, 8(1):1–125, 2014.

[7] S. Hodges, L. Williams, E. Berry, S. Izadi, J. Srinivasan, A. Butler, G. Smyth, N. Kapur, and K. R. Wood. Sensecam: A retrospective memory aid. In *UbiComp 2006*, pages 177–193, 2006.

[8] Y. Jia, E. Shelhamer, J. Donahue, S. Karayev, J. Long, R. Girshick, S. Guadarrama, and T. Darrell. Caffe: Convolutional architecture for fast feature embedding. In *ACM MM*, pages 675–678, 2014.

[9] W. Jones and J. Teevan. *Personal information management*. University of Washington Press, 2011.

[10] N. Li and F. Hopfgartner. To log or not to log? SWOT analysis of self-tracking. In *Lifelogging - Interd. Approaches to Unravel the Phenomenon of Digital Self-Tracking*. Springer VS, 2016.

[11] A. J. Sellen and S. Whittaker. Beyond total capture: A constructive critique of lifelogging. *Commun. ACM*, 53(5):70–77, May 2010.

SOGOU-2012-CRAWL: A Crawl of Search Results in the Sogou 2012 Chinese Query Log

Stewart Whiting & Joemon M. Jose
School of Computing Science,
University of Glasgow,
Scotland, UK.
{stewh,jj}@dcs.gla.ac.uk

Omar Alonso
Microsoft Corp.
Mountain View,
California, USA.
omalonso@microsoft.com

ABSTRACT

In 2012, Sogou, a major Chinese web search engine released a large-scale query log containing 43.5M user interactions, including submitted queries and clicked web page search results. This query log offers a deep sample of queries over a two day period from 30th December 2011 to 1st January 2012. In August 2013, we identified 1.4M predominantly Chinese language unique search result URLs that were clicked at least three times in this query log. We crawled the HTML content of these URLs to construct the supplementary SOGOU-2012-CRAWL dataset, which we release in this work. A real large-scale query log with accompanying crawl such as this offers several opportunities for reproducible information retrieval (IR) research, including query classification, intent modelling and indexing strategy. In this paper we first detail the query log and crawl dataset construction and characteristics. Following this, to demonstrate potential applications we use the crawl to indicatively analyse various time-based patterns in web content and search behaviour. In particular, we study the distribution of language-independent date expressions in the crawled web content. Based on this, we propose a simple approach for modelling the past/present/future temporal intent of queries based on the date the query was submitted by the user, and the dates appearing in the clicked search results. We observe several prominent temporal patterns which may lead to novel time-aware IR approaches.

1. INTRODUCTION

A great deal of research in information retrieval (IR) is based on analysing the past behaviour of real IR system users. Such user interaction is captured in a *query log* which comprises a rich time-stamped record of past user actions such as query input, result clicks and result page navigation. From the lowest-level interactions, higher-level task-oriented aspects such as information seeking sessions, topic focus, intent and implicit relevance can be observed, studied and modelled.

Unfortunately, despite their research value, few query logs are available for researchers outside industrial labs due to privacy concerns and commercial sensitivity. Indeed, the most recent large-scale English-language query logs are AOL [9] and MSN 2006 [3].

SIGIR '16, July 17-21, 2016, Pisa, Italy

DOI: http://dx.doi.org/10.1145/2911451.2914668

More recent query logs are available for learning to rank tasks - however their queries and result domains/URLs have been mapped to arbitrary tokens to ensure privacy, thereby making content-based analysis impossible.

In recent years, Sogou[1], a major Chinese portal and web search engine, has made several large-scale Chinese web search engine query logs openly available for research. While this means that some analysis inevitably requires Chinese language skills, many findings are likely to be generalisable to IR systems in other languages since they are based on language-independent behavioural, temporal and textual statistical distributions.

To the best of our knowledge, there is no sufficiently large nor recent query log with accompanying result crawl openly available. A query log without result crawl impedes deeper content analysis of search results for tasks such as query classification, intent modelling and indexing strategies. Hence, in this work we present a supplementary result crawl dataset to augment the Sogou 2012 query log with the full HTML content of clicked result URLs – thereby offering many opportunities for novel research.

The Sogou 2012 query log contains 43.5M low-level interactions (e.g., queries submitted, results clicked with their ranking, and result page inspection depth) from 0:05am 30th December 2011 to 4:58pm 1st January 2012. Accordingly, the query log offers considerable depth into search activity over a relatively short period, as opposed to a small sample of search activity over a longer period as is more common in previous datasets. The query log only contains search results clicked - so analysis of non-clicked results cannot be performed. The dataset we prepared and present in this paper, named SOGOU-2012-CRAWL, is a crawl of 1.4M search results clicked in this Sogou query log. We detail the construction and release of this dataset in Section 2.

To indicatively demonstrate the potential of SOGOU-2012-CRAWL for IR research, we study some of its language-independent content and query-biased temporal dimensions. In particular, we consider the following questions: (i) to what extent do web pages contain dates? (ii) how are the dates distributed in those web pages? (iii) can the temporal intent of a query (or similarly, its *topic*) be determined based on the dates contained in clicked, and therefore assumed implicitly relevant web pages?

2. SOGOU-2012-CRAWL DATASET

In this section we detail the construction of the SOGOU-2012-CRAWL dataset. We have made this supplementary crawl dataset available to download as a 15Gb archive of HTML page snap-

[1] http://www.sogou.com

shots[2]. The Sogou 2012 query log itself must be downloaded directly from the Sogou labs website[3].

Because of the long-tail popularity distribution of result clicks, there is a very large number of results clicked only once or twice in the query log. From a practical perspective, since our crawler was based geographically in Europe we found that network speed, reliability and time outs to servers located inside China posed several crawling technical difficulties. To alleviate these issues by reducing the number of web pages we needed to download, we only crawled search result URLs that were clicked three or more times by users (for any given search query). Accordingly, we identified 1.41M unique search results for crawling.

In August 2013, we successfully crawled 1.22M of the URLs (87% success rate) to form the SOGOU-2012-CRAWL dataset. Although not always the case, we have to assume the URLs have not changed since the the result click as the vast majority of the documents are not in the Internet Archive[4] for the result click date. This assumption will undoubtedly be invalid for news sites which change daily – so temporally sensitive analysis (such as that we perform in the following sections) must be conducted with care.

Several data cleaning stages were employed to prepare the final crawl dataset for release. Many result URLs were unable to be crawled because the server was uncontactable (e.g., server offline), an error page was returned (e.g., 401, 404, 500 HTTP errors), or had a robots.txt entry that excluded crawling. In these cases, the result URL still appear in the crawl dataset but with content of '[notavailable]' to signify a crawling issue.

Several character set encodings are commonly used in China – in particular UTF8, GBK and GB2312. In many cases, the character set reported by HTTP headers or HTML head tags, and the actual content encoding were mismatched. We used various techniques to detect this, and encode the final crawl dataset consistently in UTF8.

3. CRAWL TEMPORAL ANALYSIS

To demonstrate the potential value of the SOGOU-2012-CRAWL dataset, we perform preliminary analysis of its temporal characteristics. First we extract and analyse the dates present in result pages in the crawl as a whole – that is, without considering the related query times. More interestingly, in Section 4 we consider the temporal information provided by the crawl and the query log together. With that in mind, we further study how the dates present in clicked result URLs correspond with the real-time of the search queries, in order to model query-biased temporal search intents.

3.1 Related Work

In this section, we present existing work related to temporal analysis of information seeking and web content in IR. *When* a query is posed to a system provides an implicit temporal clue, since it offers a signal of the user's current interest in a particular query topic. Likewise, temporal clues such as dates and times contained in relevant content also provide an anchor in time for that relevance. Past work has mostly examined these elements independently.

The popularity of many queries is subject to periodic temporal trends [1], as well as event-driven temporal activity arising from one-off events. Explicit temporal expressions are included in up to 1.5-2% of web queries [8], such as "`world cup 2012`" and "`nyc weekend events`". [10] consider these temporal expressions in a relevance model. Further, [7] do the same for query topics which implicitly express a temporal expression (e.g., "`brazil world cup`"). [2] integrate temporal expressions in documents into a time-aware probabilistic retrieval model.

[6] identify and classify temporal information needs based on the relevant document timestamp distribution to improve retrieval. [5] studied how 150M web pages changed over 11 weeks. They found longer documents tended to have more frequent and extensive changes made to them, and for web pages that change regularly, they do so consistently over time. Acknowledging web page content is often dynamic, [4] incorporate content dynamics into a relevance model to improve navigational query effectiveness.

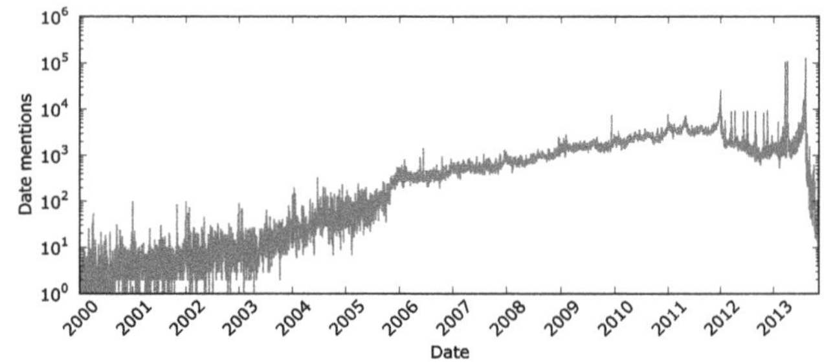

Figure 1: Frequency distribution (from 2000-01-01 to 2013-12-31) of dates contained in 1.22M search result pages crawled from Sogou 2012 result click URLs. Plotted with a log_{10} y-axis frequency scale.

3.2 Extracting Temporal Expressions

For temporal analysis, we must first extract temporal expressions (in this case, date expressions) appearing in the crawled result pages. Dates can be expressed in many cultural short- and long-forms. In written Chinese language, dates are typically in big-Endian Chinese year/month/day date formats, e.g. `YYYY-MM-DD`, `YYYY.MM.DD` and `YYYY年MM月DD日`.

From the complete crawl dataset, we extracted 5.41M dates between 2000-01-01 to 2014-12-31, inclusive, from a total of 313,211 web pages. All temporal analysis presented in this paper is based on these extracted dates – and in the next section, the queries that were used to find the pages containing those dates. For the purpose of this work, we relied on simple temporal expression extraction based on regular expressions. Future work will employ full multi-lingual and diverse temporal expression tagging, such as that provided by HeidelTime [11], to improve coverage and accuracy.

Overall, 25.7% of the crawled result web pages contain at least one date, with an average of 17.27 (±59.7) and median of 5 dates per page. Note the wide dispersion in the number of dates in each web page – the majority of documents contain a few dates, while a smaller amount have a very large number of dates. Web pages with a single date are likely to be timestamped content, such as a news article or blog post. Likewise, documents with several dates may be continually revised information, such as blog posts with comments, or similarly threaded discussion boards.

The frequency distribution of all the extracted dates over time is presented in Figure 1. Evident is the rising frequency of dates up to the end of 2011 – the period of time covered by the query log. Following this, the frequency of dates declines quickly, although some of this volume may be attributed to the delayed crawling. Occasional spikes likely represent major upcoming predictable events being discussed (e.g., major sporting events, public holidays etc.).

[2] http://www.stewh.com/sogou-2012-crawl

[3] http://www.sogou.com/labs - note that this site is available in English and Chinese language versions.

[4] http://www.archive.org

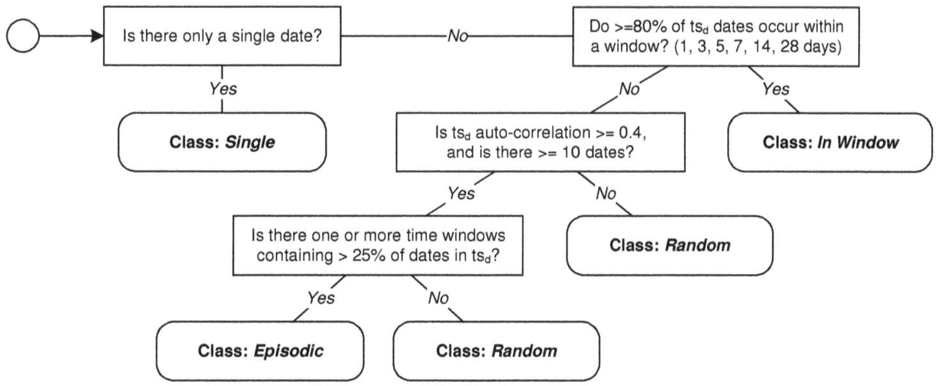

Figure 2: Heuristic-based decision tree classifier for categorising crawled search result pages into temporal date distributions.

3.3 Document Dates Distribution Classes

In the next step of temporal analysis we characterise the distribution of dates occurring in each *individual* web page in the crawl. To that end, in this section we propose a classifier for 4 common document date distribution classes we have observed: *Single*, *In Window*, *Episodic* or *Random*. Each of these classes is conceptually defined as follows:

Single - web page contains a single date expression.

In Window - web page contains multiple date references, with $\geqslant$ 80% of dates occurring within an n day period ($n = 1, 3, 5, 7, 14, 28$ days). An 80% (rather than 100%) threshold permits more robust tolerance to outlying dates (for instance, a '*today*' date on a page containing mainly past timestamped discussion).

Episodic - web page has significant trends in date distribution, with 1 or more defined bursts.

Random - web page contains multiple dates, but with no immediate apparent temporal pattern.

3.4 Classifier Implementation

We use a classifier to label each web page containing dates with one of the above temporal classes. To that end, we first define ts_d as the time series of dates present in the document d in the our crawl. ts_d is modelled as vector of length 5,475 (i.e., for the 365 days $\times 15$ years, between 2000-01-01 and 2014-12-31). Consequently, the ith index of the ts_d vector refers to number of dates in the document on the day 2000-01-01, plus i days.

We use a decision tree (shown in Figure 2) incorporating various heuristics to determine the class of each page, based entirely on features extracted from ts_d. Auto-correlation is the cross-correlation of the signal with a lagged version of itself (1 day in this case). It is effective for measuring temporal uniformity, and co-ordinated bursts of dates [6]. Single and In Window (1 day window) classes are in essence the same, except that the In Window class applies to pages which have multiple instances of the same date.

3.5 Results and Discussion

In Table 1, we present the results of classifying 313,211 web pages containing at least one date. Almost 16% of these pages have a discernible pattern comprising multiple dates contained within them. Single and In Window classes account for almost all documents, with results presented in Table 2 showing a windows of 1-3 days are most common for those pages. As such, we find that for the almost 50% of search result web pages containing non-randomly distributed dates, the majority contain either a single date, or several dates contained in a short period of days.

Table 1: Date distribution classification results for the 313,211 search result pages containing dates.

Class	Instances	%
Single	98,177	31.1%
In Window	47,831	15.3%
Episodic	3,317	1.1%
Random	163,886	52.3%

Table 2: Classification window sizes for the 47,831 search result pages containing multiple dates in a window of 28 or less days.

Window Size	Instances	%
1 day	25,249	52.8%
3 days	5,217	10.9%
5 days	2,276	4.8%
7 days	2,884	6.0%
14 days	6,733	14.1%
28 days	5,472	11.4%

4. QUERY-BIASED TEMPORAL INTENTS

In many cases, users search for topics or similiarly, events, anchored in the past, present or future with respect to the present time [6, 7]. We seek to identify these intents by examining the dates present in the search results of clicked (and therefore, assumed relevant) search results. Rather than classifying the distribution of dates present in a single document, in this section we study the distribution of dates contained in the assumed relevant documents for a topic (that is, clicked search results) – with respect to the real-time of the query (which we refer to as q_τ).

The Sogou 2012 query log contains 42.17M search result clicks in total. 3.11M (7.4%) of these are for documents which were classified as Single/In Window/Episodic in the previous section (i.e., have a non-random date distribution)[5].

Considering each query q and the day it was used as unique (i.e., q_i will be counted twice if it appears on two separate days), there are 10.1M queries in the dataset. 1.1M queries (10.9%) have one or more clicked search result which contains at least one date.

We define the *query-biased temporal intent* (or, $q_{intent,\tau}$) in terms of the average difference (Δ, in days) between q_τ and dates appearing in clicked documents (weighted by their click proportion).

[5]Recall, we only crawled search result URLs with 3 or more clicks, so the long-tail may substantially increase this percentage.

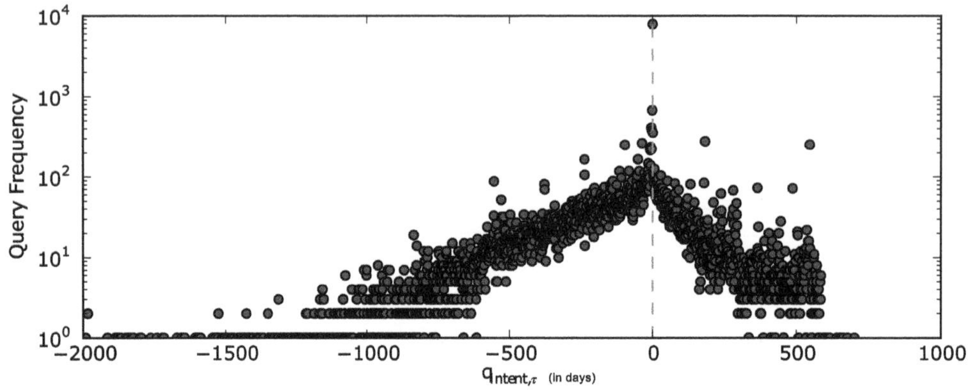

Figure 3: $q_{intent,\tau}$ (that is, temporal intent in terms of days past/present/future from query time) distribution of 1.1M queries in Sogou 2012. Data points less than -2000 days removed to improve graph clarity. Vertical marker at $x = 0$ denotes '*today*' temporal intents.

This means $q_{intent,\tau}$ may be negative (i.e., an intent in the *past*), positive (i.e., an intent in the *future*), or zero (i.e., an intent *now/today*). Note that $q_{intent,\tau}$ may also be undefined in the case that there are no dates present in any of its clicked documents. $q_{intent,\tau}$ is formalised as follows. For each query q_i occurring at time q_t (we specify time by day, e.g., 2011-12-30), we compute $q_{intent,\tau}$ as:

$$q_{intent,\tau} = \frac{\sum_{d_i \in D_q} \sum_{\tau_i \in dates(d_i)} \Delta(\tau_i, q_\tau)}{\sum_{d_i \in D_q} |dates(d_i)|} \qquad (1)$$

Where D_q is the set of all document results d_i (including duplicates) clicked for q_i, i.e., $D_q = \{d_1, d_2 \ldots d_i\}$. $dates(d_i)$ is the set of dates τ_i (including duplicates) present in d_i, i.e., $dates(d_i) = \{\tau_1, \tau_2 \ldots \tau_i\}$. Finally, $\Delta(x, y)$ is the total days between two dates.

4.1 Results and Discussion

In Figure 3, we show the $q_{intent,\tau}$ distribution of 1.1M queries with clicked search results which contain dates in Sogou 2012. A distinctive distribution of past, present and future query-biased temporal intents is evident. Most notably, there is a search tendency centred around '*today*' dates (that is, the time of the query interaction, i.e., 30th December 2011 to 1st January 2012), with very recent past and upcoming future dates also common. The steady decline in queries with far mid- to long-term past and future intents is also apparent. There are notably more search intents for past topics, with the majority of intents going back the past 1,000 days. In comparison, the majority of future intents goes forward 500 days. Outliers are likely notable past/future events, for example the 2012 London Olympics. These event topics attract lots of different queries and have many dates mentioned in search results referring to published event schedules.

5. DISCUSSION AND CONCLUSION

In this paper we present a major new dataset – a supplementary crawl of the web search results clicked in the open, large-scale and predominantly Chinese language Sogou 2012 query log. We name this dataset SOGOU-2012-CRAWL, and release it to the research community for future work.

While there are several query logs openly available for reproducible research, to the best of our knowledge, there is no recent large-scale query log accompanied by the content of clicked search results. As a result, this dataset opens up several new opportunities for information retrieval research challenges such as query classification, intent modelling and indexing strategy.

To characterise the crawl, and demonstrate its value for language-independent IR research, we indicatively analysed various time-based patterns in web content and search behaviour. We first studied the distribution of language-independent date expressions in the crawled web content. Further, we propose a simple approach for modelling the past/present/future temporal intent of queries based on the date the query was submitted by the user, and the dates appearing in the clicked search result pages. Based on this model we observe several notable query-biased temporal intent patterns. In particular, we note that users' temporal interests are mainly concentrated on information related to *now*. However, we find there are a large number of interests which extend into the future, and likewise, up to 1,000 days into the past (shown in Figure 3). This asymmetric double long-tail distribution may offer opportunities for detecting and supporting time-aware information needs, so we leave further analysis and modelling to future work.

6. REFERENCES

[1] S. M. Beitzel, E. C. Jensen, A. Chowdhury, O. Frieder, and D. Grossman. Temporal analysis of a very large topically categorized web query log. *J. Am. Soc. Inf. Sci. Technol.*, 58(2):166–178, 2007.

[2] K. Berberich, S. Bedathur, O. Alonso, and G. Weikum. A language modeling approach for temporal information needs. ECIR'2010, pages 13–25, Berlin, Heidelberg, 2010. Springer-Verlag.

[3] N. Craswell, R. Jones, G. Dupret, and E. Viegas. Wscd '09: Proceedings of the 2009 workshop on web search click data. New York, NY, USA, 2009. ACM.

[4] J. L. Elsas and S. T. Dumais. Leveraging temporal dynamics of document content in relevance ranking. WSDM '10, pages 1–10, New York, NY, USA, 2010. ACM.

[5] D. Fetterly, M. Manasse, M. Najork, and J. Wiener. A large-scale study of the evolution of web pages. WWW '03, pages 669–678, New York, NY, USA, 2003. ACM.

[6] R. Jones and F. Diaz. Temporal profiles of queries. *ACM Trans. Inf. Syst.*, 25(3):14–es, 2007.

[7] N. Kanhabua and K. Nørvåg. Determining time of queries for re-ranking search results. ECDL'10, pages 261–272, Berlin, Heidelberg, 2010. Springer-Verlag.

[8] S. Nunes, C. Ribeiro, and G. David. Use of temporal expressions in web search. ECIR'08, pages 580–584, Berlin, Heidelberg, 2008.

[9] G. Pass, A. Chowdhury, and C. Torgeson. A picture of search. InfoScale '06, New York, NY, USA, 2006. ACM.

[10] J. Strötgen, O. Alonso, and M. Gertz. Identification of top relevant temporal expressions in documents. TempWeb '12, pages 33–40, New York, NY, USA, 2012. ACM.

[11] J. Strötgen and M. Gertz. Heideltime: High quality rule-based extraction and normalization of temporal expressions. SemEval '10, pages 321–324, Stroudsburg, PA, USA, 2010. ACL.

The BOLT IR Test Collections of Multilingual Passage Retrieval from Discussion Forums

Ian Soboroff
National Institute of Standards and Technology
Gaithersburg, MD
ian.soboroff@nist.gov

Kira Griffitt and Stephanie Strassel
Linguistic Data Consortium
Philadelphia, PA
kiragrif@ldc.upenn.edu, strassel@ldc.upenn.edu

ABSTRACT

This paper describes a new test collection for passage retrieval from multilingual, informal text. The task being modeled is that of a monolingual English-speaking user who wishes to search discussion forum text in a foreign language. The system retrieves relevant short passages of text and presents them to the user, translated into English. The test collection contains more than 2 billion words of discussion thread text, 250 queries representing complex informational search needs, and manual relevance judgments of forum post passages, pooled from real systems. This information retrieval test collection is the first to combine multilingual search, passage retrieval, and informal online genre text.

1. INTRODUCTION

The DARPA Broad Operational Language Translation (BOLT) program was "aimed at enabling communications with non-English-speaking populations and identifying information in foreign-language resources."[2] As part of the program, performers were tasked to complete a multilingual passage retrieval task: in response to a textual query in English, retrieve relevant passages from English, Arabic and Chinese discussion forums, translated into English.

To evaluate this task, we constructed a test collection of 2 million discussion forum threads totalling nearly 70 million posts and 250 search topics with free-text information need statements. The information needs represent users looking for information about, relationships between, effects of, and opinions about current events and socially prominent subjects. Systems participating in the BOLT program retrieved short passages in response to each query and translated them into English. These passages were manually judged for relevance by bilingual speakers with access to the original documents in their original language. The first 100 topics have an average of 185 judged passages each, and the latter 150 topics have an average of 486 judged passages. The combination of multilinguality, passage retrieval, and informal online discussion text makes this test collection unique.

SIGIR '16, July 17 - 21, 2016, Pisa, Italy

ACM ISBN 978-1-4503-4069-4/16/07...$15.00

DOI: http://dx.doi.org/10.1145/2911451.2914674

Passage retrieval has been extensively studied in information retrieval [4], information extraction [9], and question answering [7]. As shown in the TREC HARD track [1], passage retrieval tasks can be complicated to specify. They also present a challenge to reproducibility: unless systems retrieve the exact same passages as were judged, interpreting passage-level relevance judgments is not straightforward.

2. EVALUATION TASK

The BOLT IR task is to retrieve short relevant passages of text from informal text in response to a natural language English sentence representing a complex information need. We imagine an English-speaking intelligence analyst searching across multiple languages. The analyst is looking to survey diverse views and different relationships among people, both document authors and people mentioned in the documents. Because the documents in the collection are in multiple languages, passages in languages other than English must be translated to English for the end user.

We have found it helpful to describe this task as an imaginary interface for the analyst that presents retrieved snippets in context; the user can select a snippet to drill down to the full document, and switch back and forth between the translated text and the original (presumably with a native speaker or linguist assisting). Because the user views the retrieved passages in context, it is not critical that passages exactly contain just the relevant information, nor do they need to disambiguate or coreference things mentioned in the passage. Because the native language is one step lower in the drill-down, translation quality is inherent in the task and affects the interaction. This perspective was reflected in the BOLT IR evaluation which did not require passages to contain only relevant content, and which measured retrieval effectiveness separately from translation quality. Although we do not report details of the evaluation in this paper, these considerations are important for understanding the relevance assessments.

3. DOCUMENT COLLECTION

The document collection is a set of two million online discussion forum threads collected by the Linguistic Data Consortium (LDC) containing 2.3 billion words of text. The threads are available in the original HTML and also in a cleaned XML format which was used in all stages of building the collection. The threads come from a number of different forums on different subjects. The threads come from three different identified language sources: English, Arabic, and Mandarin Chinese. The Arabic subcollection is intended to

Language	English	Mandarin	Arabic
number of tokens	694,914,443	1,050,254,101	616,719,471
number of threads	457,970	789,077	773,861
average messages per thread	13.23	50.77	30.82
average thread size in bytes	14,651.2	5,769.3	11,380.5

Topic set	P2	P3
number of topics	100	150
avg relevant passages per topic	114.56	252.46

Table 1: Statistics on the BOLT IR collection. In Mandarin, 1.5 tokens = 1 word, otherwise 1 token = 1 word.

target the Egyptian Arabic dialect, but the posts often contain Modern Standard Arabic and/or other Arabic dialects.

From a total forum crawl of roughly 3 billion words, LDC selected a subset of roughly 700 million words from each language to form the final collection. Table 1 gives statistics on the size of the collection.

4. TOPICS

The user's information needs that give rise to the queries are called "topics". The topics were developed by LDC annotators, which included native speakers of Mandarin and Egyptian as well as English speakers. The topics were developed using a collection exploration process: the annotator thought of a topic and did preliminary searches to determine whether the topic had any relevant information in the collection. The annotator then formulated a query for their topic, and surveyed the relevant threads that were returned by a basic text search tool. Based on this survey, they made a qualitative judgment about the prevalence of relevant information in the corpus, and developed topics where their judgment was that the topic was not likely to be highly productive for the corpus. As part of the query, the annotator could indicate that they only wanted information in Arabic, Chinese, or English, or would accept results from any language. This factor was a constraint on relevant information.

After arriving at a right-sized topic, the annotator wrote a textual description and rules of interpretation for assessing relevance. The topics were classified according to two informal taxonomies: the subject of the topic ("asks-about", which could be a person, location, organization, movement, event, or abstract entity, ...), and the kind of information desired ("asks-for": which could be statements or opinions, relationships, effects, information about, participants or members of, ...). The annotator also noted from which languages they expected the majority of relevant information to come, based on their searching. In contrast to the language-target restriction in the query, this expectation was not a restriction on relevance; relevant information could come from any language, as long as the query allowed it. Lastly, the annotator included one or more examples of relevant passages from their search. Figure 1 shows an example topic. Systems only had access to the topic number, the `query`, and the `language-target` information, but the complete topic statement was developed ahead of time and used for reference during assessment.

There were three BOLT IR evaluations over the course of three phases of the program. The first phase was highly exploratory, whereas the latter two, which we call P2 and P3, resulted in comparable collections following roughly the same rules for topic development and relevance assessment. In phase 3, topics tended to have more relevant passages due to the pooling procedure used (see below), but they actually have a greater variance in relevance because effort was put towards creating topics in P3 with small ($<$ 100 passages) relevant sets.

5. POOLING

In response to the topic, evaluation systems automatically retrieved a ranked list of up to 1000 citations from the document collection. A citation is defined to be an English passage of no more than 250 characters, with a pointer back to the original source text. In Figure 1, the `thread`, `post`, `offset`, and `length` is the pointer for first example citation. System outputs followed this format, with threads and posts counting from 1 and offsets starting at 0 within the cleaned XML formatted collection. Citations were required to be English, and so Arabic or Chinese passages needed to be translated before they could be returned to the user; systems conceivably could do this at any time prior to returning results, including automatically translating the entire corpus at the start. Citations could not cross post or thread boundaries.

We combined the top 100 citations from each evaluation system to form a pool.[8] Pooling usually drops duplicated documents, but in this case, we planned for the assessors to judge the citation text as well as the pointer, so many close duplicates needed to be kept in the pool. To make it easier for the assessors to be consistent across near-duplicate cases, we combined all citations with greater than 95% token bigram overlap into equivalence classes. Neither near-duplication nor relevance are actually transitive, so assessments made to equivalence classes were hand-checked to make sure we didn't propagate judgments too far.

The pooling method can only be as effective as the diversity of the constituent system outputs, and indeed in phase 2 we were concerned that because the evaluation only has a limited number of participants, the estimates of recall we computed were biased high. For phase 3, we solicited a range of system outputs from each evaluation participant, including baselines which would not be measured but which served to enrich the pool. This resulted in nearly twice the number of relevant citations compared with phase 2. Because this occurred despite the aforementioned effort to limit the number of relevant citations in phase 3, we are hopeful that the phase 3 relevance judgments represent a more reusable collection with better recall estimates. Section 7 discusses recall further.

```
<topic number="BIR_300158">
  <query>What do people say about self-publishing?</query>
  <description>This query asks for statements and opinions about self-publishing.</description>
  <language-target lang="none"/>
  <properties>
    <asks-about target="practice-or-custom"/>
    <asks-for response="statements-or-opinions"/>
    <languages eng="T" arz="F" cmn="F"/>
  </properties>
  <rule number="1">Answers must be about self-publishing.</rule>
  <cite number="1" thread="bolt-eng-DF-275-201910-15807137" post="5" offset="133" length="125" rel="yes">
   Meaning that if they ask you to pay them, you're also getting scammed (or self-publishing, which also
   tends to be a scam...).</cite>
</topic>
```

Figure 1: An example topic from phase 3. Systems were presented with the query and language-target clauses.

6. ASSESSMENT PROCESS

Rather than making a simple relevance judgment for each citation, the assessor followed a decision-points annotation model [5] derived from the application scenario described in section 2, in order to tease apart relevance from translation quality. [3] First, the assessor decided whether the citation was clear enough to make a relevance judgment, or if they felt they probably understood the citation but wanted to refer to the original language text, or if the citation was completely incomprehensible. Incomprehensible citations were not assessed further.

For comprehensible citations, the assessor judged whether the citation satisfied the topic's rules of interpretation for relevance, and further whether the citation provided useful information to the user. Citations were judged to be not useful if for example they merely restated the query. If the assessor needed to refer to the original language citation, either because they wished to see greater context or wanted to confirm their understanding of the translation, they decided whether the original Mandarin or Arabic text was relevant and useful as above, and then returned to the translated citation to make a judgment of relevance for the citation itself. In phase 3, the assessor further noted whether they felt they were being generous in their judgment.

This multi-stage process allowed the assessor to separately consider translation acceptability from relevance. Resources did not permit us to do deep assessment of translations, as might be expected of an MT corpus, but by folding translation acceptability into the relevance assessment process, it is possible to subset the data to use only the most acceptable translations or to allow relevance within the original citation context.

In the BOLT evaluation, systems received credit for citations that were understandable, relevant and useful, even if the source language needed to be checked to make that judgment. Having these fine-grained assessments with a rule for giving credit means that later users of this data can choose to give credit for stricter or looser scenarios.

We presented a topic's citation pool to the assessor in random order to avoid system bias effects. A single citation was judged for all citations in a near-duplicate equivalent class, and equivalence classes were checked for consistency in a second pass.

The assessor judging the citations for a particular topic was not necessarily the topic's creator. In particular, citations that came from Mandarin or Arabic were assessed by a native speaker. A subset of the topics were selected to be fully assessed by a second assessor.

In phase 3, the assessor additionally noted whether the source text for Arabic citations included Egyptian Arabic or not. This annotation was made following the realization that Egyptian writers frequently code-switch between dialectal and standard Arabic, and that the line between a passage being in Modern Standard Arabic or Egyptian dialect was hard to draw. Although the assessor did not mark the code-switch boundaries, we hope that this data might be useful for training systems to differentiate the two dialects of Arabic.

7. NOTES ON USAGE

The BOLT IR test collections are straightforward to use to measure the effectiveness of post and thread retrieval. Measuring passage retrieval is more complex, because retrieved passages may not directly correspond to the passages that were judged by our assessors. Also note that the assessor did not judge the source language text when the translated citation was sufficient. In general, the reusability of passage-level assessments is not well understood and deserves more study.

A more significant issue is assessment coverage and recall estimation. Because our pools were limited to DARPA contractors being evaluated on the IR task, it's likely that there are many relevant posts that were not pooled and hence not judged. Experimenters should be cautious in handling unjudged retrieved posts, especially for systems that do find judged relevant posts around those same ranks. Retrieval measures that are robust to missing judgments, such as those proposed by Sakai [6] or Yilmaz et al [10], may be useful here.

8. BASELINE PERFORMANCE

While this paper is not an evaluation report, we would like to give an indication of reasonable baseline performance which may be expected on this collection. We do this here by anonymizing the BOLT submissions and reporting precision and recall of retrieved forum posts.

The official measures in BOLT included variants of precision and recall based on character counts for citations. Since

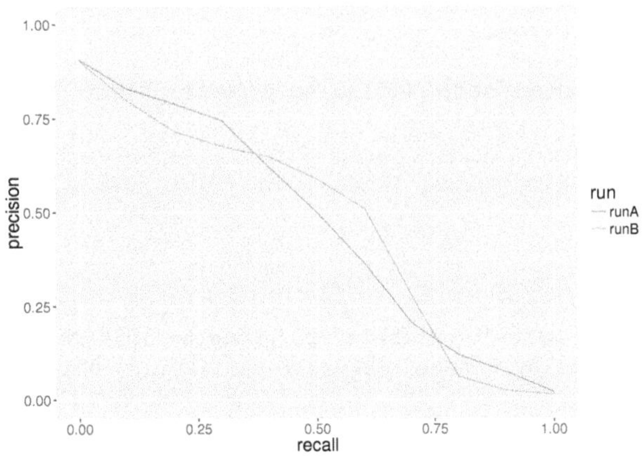

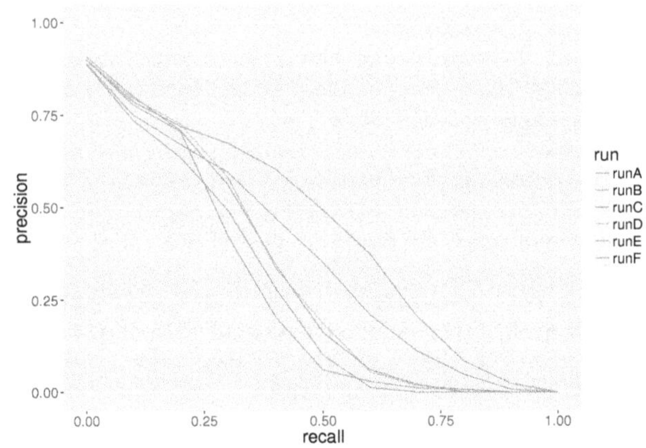

Figure 2: Recall-precision plots for post retrieval performance of several anonymized submissions in the BOLT program, phase 2 (left) and phase 3 (right).

as we note in the previous section, reusing this collection for passage retrieval evaluation requires some significant effort, we convert the original BOLT submissions to simpler post retrieval runs by ranking posts according to the highest ranked passage retrieved from that post. A post is considered to be relevant if any relevant passage is known from that post. Because all these systems were pooled, we are not affected by unjudged posts.

Please note that these systems were not optimized for this measure, and while these measures are reasonable to compute for this collection, they are not the best comparisons of these specific runs, which were developed to solve the passage retrieval task rather than the post retrieval task. The purpose of these scores is solely to provide indicators of reasonable state-of-the-art performance on a post retrieval task using this data. Figure 2 plots interpolated precision at standard recall points, as reported by the `trec_eval` tool[1]. Mean average precision for the P2 runs is 0.45 and 0.46, and for the P3 runs ranges from 0.25 to 0.42.

9. CONCLUSION

The BOLT IR collections, built as part of DARPA's Broad Operational Language Translation program, are new test collections that can be used to measure multilingual retrieval from informal discussion forum text. Furthermore, as the annotations are at the passage level, the collection provides a basis for considering how to create reusable collections for passage retrieval evaluation. The corpora described in this paper have been distributed to performers in the DARPA BOLT program, and are expected to be published in LDC's catalog in 2016.

Although three collections were built over the course of the program, we only consider the latter two, from phases 2 and 3, to be reusable as IR test collections. The collection built for phase 1 represented a learning curve in designing the passage retrieval task and assessment process, and while that data is likely quite useful to researchers it should be regarded with caution as an IR test collection.

Finally, this paper has been submitted as part of a new SIGIR call for short papers on datasets and test collections, and as such we hope it can be regarded as a proposed template for such papers. In particular, we recommend that papers describing IR test collections provide specific guidance on usage and report baseline effectiveness scores.

10. REFERENCES

[1] J. Allan. HARD track overview in TREC 2005: High accuracy retrieval from documents. In *Proceedings of TREC 2005*, pages 52–68. NIST, 2006.

[2] BOLT program home page. http://www.darpa.mil/program/broad-operational-language-translation, retrieved on Feb 1, 2016.

[3] K. Griffitt and S. Strassel. The query of everything: Developing open-domain, natural language queries for BOLT information retrieval. In *Proceedings of LREC 2016*, Portorož, Slovenia, 2016.

[4] M. Kaszkiel and J. Zobel. Passage retrieval revisited. In *Proceedings of SIGIR 1997*, Philadelphia, PA, 1997.

[5] J. Medero, K. Maeda, S. Strassel, and C. Walker. An efficient approach for gold-standard annotation: Decision points for complex tasks. In *Proceedings of LREC 2006*, Genoa, Italy, 2006.

[6] T. Sakai and N. Kando. On information retrieval metrics designed for evaluation with incomplete relevance assessments. *Information Retrieval*, 11(5):447–470, March 2008.

[7] S. Tellex, B. Katz, J. Lin, A. Fernandes, and G. Martin. Quantitative evaluation of passage retrieval algorithms for question answering. In *Proceedings of SIGIR 2003*, Toronto, Canada, 2003.

[8] E. M. Voorhees and D. K. Harman, editors. *TREC: Experiment and Evaluation in Information Retrieval.* MIT Press, 2005.

[9] W. Xu, R. Grishman, and L. Zhao. Passage retrieval for information extraction using distant supervision. In *Proceedings of the 5th International Joint Conference on Natural Language Processing*, Chiang Mai, Thailand, 2011.

[10] E. Yilmaz, E. Kanoulas, and J. A. Aslam. A simple and efficient sampling method for estimating AP and NDCG. In *Proceedings of SIGIR 2008*, Singapore, 2008.

[1]https://github.com/usnistgov/trec_eval/

The Factoid Queries Collection

Ido Guy
Ben Gurion University of the Negev, Israel
Yahoo Research, Israel
idoguy@acm.org

Dan Pelleg
Yahoo Research, Israel
pellegd@acm.org

ABSTRACT

We present a collection of over 15,000 queries, issued to commercial web search engines, whose answer is a single fact. The collection was produced based on queries landing on questions within a large community question answering website, each with a best answer no longer than 3 words and an explicit reference to a Wikipedia page. We describe the collection generation process and provide a variety of descriptive characteristics, demonstrating the collection's uniqueness compared to existing datasets and its potential use for research of factoid question answering and retrieval.

Keywords: dataset; fact retrieval; factoid question answering

1 INTRODUCTION

In recent years, commercial search engines have started to provide inline results to factoid questions, which present a short answer (e.g., a number, a unit, or a few words) directly on the search results page (SERP) [5]. This is part of a broader trend of presenting search results, such as weather, sport scores, or dictionary definitions, directly on the SERP, sparing the user the need to click. Commercial search engines put considerable effort to satisfy this kind of need, usually under the "card" paradigm, where a dedicated module is built to respond to a particular type of query [7].

Despite the increasing popularity of such fact retrieval, little has been published about the technology behind it, and, in particular, little is known about how web search users formulate factoid queries and express "factual" information needs. Previous research collections synthesized queries by making assumptions on the actual query distribution; most noticeably, these queries were generally thought of as starting with one of the WH-question words[1] [3, 4, 6]. Yet, as we will later show, this common perception is inaccurate, as many factual queries "in the wild" do not match this pattern. In addition, synthesis of the queries, however accurate, gives no information about their distribution. Without click logs, there is no way to determine which facts are more popular, and what phrasing is more commonly used to query for them.

[1]Who, where, why, when, how, what, and which.

SIGIR '16, July 17-21, 2016, Pisa, Italy

DOI: http://dx.doi.org/10.1145/2911451.2914676

In this paper, we present the *FactQueries* collection[2]: a collection of 15,557 queries that landed on factoid question pages within the Yahoo Answers Community Questions Answering (CQA) website. Factoid questions were identified by considering questions with best answers that include no more than 3 words and an explicit link within the "source" field to English Wikipedia. The factuality of the questions and the correctness of the corresponding answers were validated by manual judgment. We then fetched, for each factoid question, up to 5 queries from commercial web search engines that landed on the question's page. Each entry in the collection includes a query, the corresponding question's title and best answer, an integer indicating the query's landing frequency on the question's page, the answer's source field, and a link to the question's page on Yahoo Answers.

The *FactQueries* collection reflects queries by web search users that are formulated to retrieve factual answers. To the best of our knowledge, it is the first to include web search queries that express factual intent and are not restricted to predefined patterns. The collection offers the following contributions:

- It includes queries from commercial web search engines, exactly as they were generated by users. Over 70% of the questions have multiple landing queries, demonstrating the diverse ways users may query for the same fact.
- It includes an indication of the frequency of each query.
- Nearly 60% of the queries are not phrased as WH-questions, reflecting the difference between query language and question language.
- As opposed to other datasets, the generation process of *FactQueries* did not apply any restrictions on the question or query, but rather on the answer. It therefore reflects a broader set of topics and questions for facts web users are interested in, which span the diverse categories of Yahoo Answers, from Science and Mathematics to Music and Entertainment.
- While the collection includes a link to the knowledge source (Wikipedia), it is not restricted to facts that map to a knowledge graph structure [3, 4]. On the other hand, the collection's facts are not as complex as trivia questions that deliberately combine multiple facts [8], as these are not typically pursued by web search users.
- The correctness of the answer is validated both by the Yahoo Answers "best answer" mechanism and in-house annotators, reducing the likelihood of wrong answers, such as recently reported for existing factoid datasets [2].

[2]http://webscope.sandbox.yahoo.com/catalog.php?datatype=l&did=76

2 COLLECTION GENERATION

The collection was generated based on questions from the Yahoo Answers (YA) CQA website, which satisfy the following two preconditions:

1. The text of the question's "best answer" contains between 1 to 3 words (based on white-space tokenization). Note that this precondition implies that the question has a best answer, chosen either by the asker or by the community [1].
2. The "source" field of the best answer includes a link to English Wikipedia. Note that this precondition implies that the question has a non-empty source field (Yahoo Answers allows answerers to add their source(s) in an optional field below the answer's text).

We conjectured that these two stipulations would yield a subset of answers likely to be factual. Applying these two preconditions on the entire set of Yahoo Answers non-deleted English questions, posted between 2006 and 2014, produced a set of over 31,000 different questions. We applied additional rule-based filtering to detect answer text that does not contain the actual answer, including reference pointing (e.g., answers that contain "try", "check", "go to", "wikipedia", "http://", "visit", "hope this helps", or "there you go"), multiple choice selection (e.g., "yes", "nope", or starting with "2.", "c ", or "3)"), and expression of doubt (e.g., "think", "believe", "maybe", "probably", "i"). This filtering left us with nearly 19,000 questions. For 7,500 of these questions, we had a non-empty set of "landing queries", i.e., queries from commercial web search engines that resulted in a click on their YA page. The landing queries we inspected were issued between 2012 and 2014.

We sent this set of 7,500 questions to manual judgment by 25 professional in-house annotators ("editors"). Each question was evaluated by a single editor. The editors were given the question's title, its (up-to-3-words) best answer, the link to the question's page, and the link(s) provided in the source field of the best answer. They were asked the following questions:

- Q1: Does the entry describe a question that has exactly one factual answer, which can be expressed in a few words?
- Q2: If Q1 is affirmative, is the provided answer correct?

In addition, the editors were given the following notes with regards to Q1:

- We seek facts, not opinions. So for a question like "What is the best book series by J.K. Rowling?", Q1 should be negative.
- If the answer requires a longer explanation than a few words, Q1 should be negative.
- For classic Yes/No questions, Q1 should be negative (e.g., "Is Sidney the capital of Australia?").
- We are not looking for lists. If there is more than one answer, Q1 should be negative (e.g., "What is the cast of Star Wars?" or "Who are Barack Obama's Children?").

For determining the answer's correctness (Q2), editors were instructed to use Wikipedia and, if needed, a web search.

Overall, for 79.7% of the 7,500 questions given to editors, Q1 was affirmative, i.e., they were indicated to contain a factual question (19.8% negative, 0.5% "don't know"). This high portion indicates that our methodology for extracting factual questions is effective, to the degree of achieving almost 80% precision without human interference. Out of the questions indicated to be factual, for 86.4% the answer was

question	editor's comment
Who was the african american that discovered penicillin?	question is wrong
How much do 3ds cost on black friday?	no definitive answer
What was Alexander Graham Bell's Most unknown invention?	opinion-based
What is it called when a person thinks they are always right?	no definitive answer
Who Played Michael Jackson in The Jacksons: American Dream?	different actors for each age
Lands discovered between 17-19 century?	list
What is an RDF file, and how do I use it?	detailed answer required
How old is Ke Huy Quan?	time-dependent
Where was ezra J. warner born?	two persons with that name
Did 50 cent real get shot 9 times?	yes/no question

Table 1: Example questions marked non-factual.

question	best answer	editor's comment
How many seasons does the cartoon winx have?	3 seasons.	answer is outdated
Who invented the muffin?	Fannie Merritt Farmer	no definitive answer
World War 2 Total Deaths?	Approx. 72 million	estimated number
What is the legal smoking age in italy?	it is 14.	should be 18

Table 2: Example questions marked factual but incorrect.

indicated to be correct (Q2 affirmative). Table 1 lists a few examples for question titles marked non-factual (Q1 negative), while table 2 lists a few examples for question titles marked as factual, but with incorrect answers (Q1 affirmative and Q2 negative). For the collection, we only considered questions for which both Q1 and Q2 were affirmative (68.9% of the original set of questions).

Figure 1 shows the portion of questions marked as factual (Q1 affirmative) and answers marked as correct (Q1 and Q2 affirmative) according to the answer length in words. The portion of factual answers decreases from 82.4% for 1-word and 81.1% for 2-word answers, to 74% for 3-word answers, indicating that as answers become longer, they are less likely to be factual.

After selecting our subset of questions based on the feedback from annotators, we sampled a list of up to 5 landing queries per question. We filtered out a small subset of the queries, such as queries that included "yahoo answers" or very long queries. This left us with a set of 15,557 queries, referring to 4,691 distinct YA questions. Each query is represented as a tab-separated line in the collection, with the following fields:

1. **Query**. The query's text as logged by the search engine.
2. **Occurrence Score (*OcSc*)**. An integer between 1 and 10 representing the occurrence frequency of the query's landing on the YA page (a larger integer indicates a higher landing frequency)[3].
3. **Question Title**. The title of the question in YA.
4. **Answer**. The best answer for the question (1-3 words).
5. **Source**. The source field for the answer, which includes at least one URL of an English Wikipedia page.
6. **URL**. The URL of the Yahoo Answers page. In addition to the information directly included in this collection, the Yahoo Answers page may provide additional information, such as the question's description, the question's

[3]Generated by manual bucketing, to obscure sensitive data.

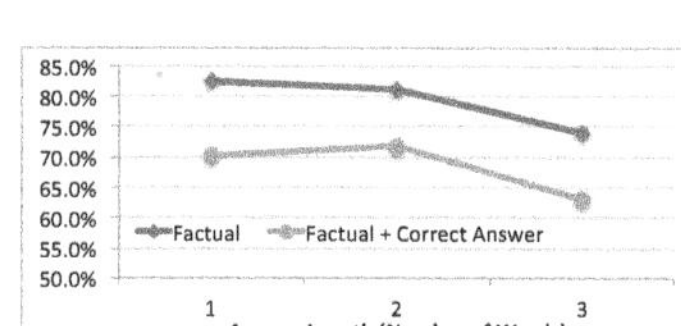

Figure 1: Percentage of questions marked factual and answers marked correct by answer length.

Question's Title	Best Answer	Query	*OcSc*
What is altitude of Ouray, Colorado?	7,792 ft	ouray colorado elevation	8
		ouray altitude	7
		altitude of ouray	2
		altitude ouray	1
		ouray altitude co	1
What is it called when you dance on a ribbon in the air?	Aerial silk	what is it called when you dance on a ribbon	8
		What is ribbon dancing called	7
		ribbon dancing in air	2
		what is dancing with ribbons in the air called	1
		air ribbon dancing	1
What episode of the simpsons does homer smoke weed?	Weekend at Burnsie's	simpsons weed episode	10
		homer smokes weed	10
		simpsons weed episodes	6
		the simpsons episode homer smokes weed	6
		homer simpson smoke weed	5

Table 3: Collection examples.

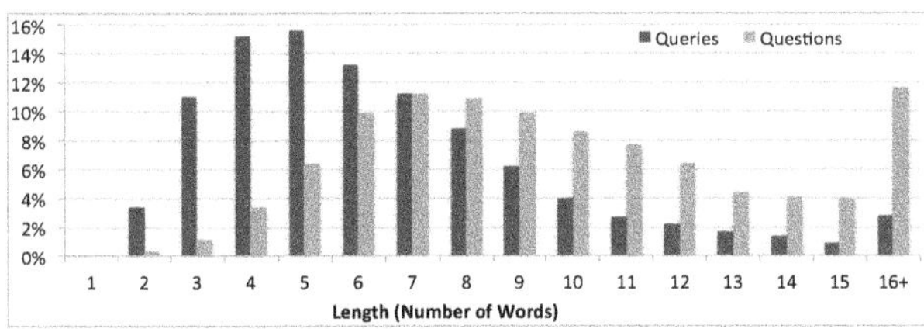

Figure 2: Query and Question Length Distribution.

category, other answers, votes on the answers, links to the profile page of the asker and answerers, and more.

It should be noted that the matching of the landing queries to their corresponding questions was not manually verified. We generally observed a good match across the collection, but the *OcSc* can be used for filtering to queries with more "landing evidence".

Table 3 includes a few examples from the collection. The examples demonstrate differently-phrased queries that landed on the same YA page for three different questions.

3 COLLECTION CHARACTERISTICS

In this section, we describe the characteristics of the collection. We first focus on queries and then discuss questions.

3.1 Queries

The average length of a query in the collection is 6.6 words (stdev: 3.5, median: 6, max: 53). Figure 2 shows the detailed distribution. The portions of 1-word queries (0.02%) and 2-word queries (3.33%) are very low, whereas 11.4% of the queries contain more than 10 words. This distribution of query length is in accordance with previous findings reported for queries that landed on CQA websites [9].

Table 4 shows the distribution of queries per question in the collection. As can be seen, 28.4% of the questions have only one landing query, while almost half have 5 queries, which is the maximum number allowed for this collection.

The next analysis focuses on the portion of question queries [11]. The "queries" row of Table 5 shows the distribution of queries starting with a WH-word. The most popular WH-word, by a large margin, is "what", opening over 20% of all queries in the collection, followed by "who" and "how" (half of the latter start with "how many"). On the other hand, not even one query starts with "why", which typically represents broader, open-ended types of questions [10].

1	2	3	4	5
28.4%	11.5%	7.1%	6.0%	47.0%

Table 4: Queries per Question Distribution.

	What	Who	How	When	Which	Where	Why	Total
Queries	20.9%	7.0%	5.4%	3.1%	2.9%	1.6%	0	40.9%
Questions	42.9%	12.8%	5.7%	4.2%	4.2%	1.7%	0.1%	71.6%

Table 5: Distribution of queries and questions starting with WH-words.

	1	2	3	4	5	6	7	8	9	10
All	62.9%	11.4%	4.8%	4.8%	3.6%	3.1%	2.7%	2.7%	2.4%	1.6%
1 query	83.4%	8.6%	2.8%	1.4%	0.8%	0.7%	0.6%	0.5%	0.8%	0.5%
5 queries	55.4%	11.9%	5.5%	6.0%	4.6%	4.0%	3.7%	3.6%	3.3%	2.1%
5 queries, 1st	7.9%	12.1%	8.3%	11.5%	10.3%	9.9%	10.5%	10.6%	10.7%	8.3%
5 queries, 5th	97.5%	1.7%	0.5%	0.1%	0.1%	0.0%	0.0%	0.0%	0.0%	0.0%

Table 6: Distribution of query occurrence score.

As a sanity check to the collection generation process, we also inspected yes/no queries. Overall, very few queries follow a yes/no pattern [11]: no queries start with "was", "did", "does", "are", "do", "will", "would", "should", "can", or "could". Very small portions of the queries start with "is" (4 in total) and "were" (10 queries), with many of the latter resulting from misspelling of the more common "where". In total, it can be seen that only slightly over 40% of the queries are question queries, leaving nearly 60% of the queries not phrased as classic questions. Considering queries that contain a WH-word anywhere in the text, although these are often not WH-questions (e.g., "person who studies music"), the portion grows to 47.6%. Other common words to open a query in the collection are "the" (4.4% of the queries), "a" (1.6%), "name" (0.8%), "in" (0.7%), "movie" (0.7%), and "first" (0.4%).

As mentioned in Section 2, the occurrence score, marked *OcSc*, represents the frequency of the query in our inspected log, and ranges from 1 to 10. Table 6 shows the distribution of the *OcSc* across all queries ("All" row). The majority of the queries (62.9%) have an *OcSc* of 1, while lower portions have higher *OcSc*, down to 1.6% for *OcSc* of 10. For questions with 1 query, as can be seen in the respective row of Table 6, the *OcSc* is typically lower, while for questions with 5 queries, the *OcSc* is higher across all queries. The two lowest rows of Table 6 show the *OcSc* distribution of the 1st query (the one with highest *OcSc*) and the 5th query (lowest *OcSc*) for questions with 5 landing queries. It can be seen that the *OcSc* for the 1st query is distributed roughly evenly across the 10 buckets, while the *OcSc* score of the 5th query is all but minimal.

3.2 Questions

The average question title length is 10 words (stdev: 4.2, median: 9, max: 24). The full distribution is shown in Figure 2, as compared to the query length distribution. The correlation between the question length and the average length of its landing queries is positive, but not extremely high ($r=0.36$, $p<0.001$). As can be seen in Table 5 (bottom row), a substantially higher portion of the questions (over 70%) start with a WH-word, with "what" alone opening 42.9% of the questions, and "why" opening as few as 4 questions.

As previously mentioned, the source field of the best answer is provided as part of the collection. While this field usually contains a single URL, the user interface does not strictly impose it and in some cases the field may include multiple URLs and even some free-form text. In rare cases (2.9% of the questions), the field is null due to various processing issues. For the rest of the questions (4,555 in total), 95.5% have exactly one URL in their source field (linking to English Wikipedia), while 4.5% have multiple URLs (up

	Zero	Avg	Std	Max
# other answers	32.1%	2.4	3.5	55
description length (words)	42.9%	16.2	31.6	665
# best answer's upvotes	65.8%	0.56	1.11	26
# best answer's downvotes	91.6%	0.11	0.44	6

Table 7: Additional question characteristics

Category Name	% Questions	Freq-Ratio
Entertainment & Music	31.7%	**2.23**
Science & Mathematics	22.0%	**3.98**
Education & Reference	9.0%	1.96
Arts & Humanities	8.6%	**2.44**
Society & Culture	4.3%	0.56
Sports	3.8%	0.91
Politics & Government	3.5%	0.73
Health	2.3%	0.29
Travel	2.2%	1.03
Computers & Internet	2.1%	0.36

Table 8: Most common top-level categories.

to 4, except one case with 7), to a total of 455 URLs. Of these, 67% link to English Wikipedia, while the rest link to a variety of websites (114 in total), with `imdb.com` (14 URLs) and `youtube.com` (12 URLs) the most popular. Inspecting all the URLs to English Wikipedia within the source field, including the cases where the field contains multiple URLs (a total of 4,651 URLs), we see that they cover 4,391 different Wikipedia values. The vast majority of these values (95%) appear exactly once in *FactQueries*, 4.2% appear twice, 0.7% appear 3 times, and 0.1% (5 values) appear 4 times in the collection: Adenosine triphosphate, Cellular respiration, DNA, List of Bleach episodes, and Generation Y.

Table 7 shows several statistics of question metadata not directly included in the collection, including the number of answers aside from the best answer, the length of the question's description (body), and the number of upvotes and downvotes the best answer received.

Questions on Yahoo Answers are assigned to categories, in a 3-level taxonomy with over 1500 nodes [1]. The collection's questions span all 26 top-level categories of Yahoo Answers. Table 8 shows the 10 most common top-level categories, alongside the corresponding portion of questions in the collection. The two most common categories, jointly covering over 50% of the questions, are Entertainment & Music and Science & Mathematics. The top-level categories with the smallest portions in the collection are Pregnancy & Parenting (8 questions), Dining Out (4), and Local Businesses (3).

Since some categories are more frequent than others on YA, it is also interesting to inspect the frequency of the category in the collection relative to its general YA frequency. The "Freq-Ratio" column of Table 8 indicates the ratio between the portion of category questions in *FactQueries* and on YA in general (considering over 150M non-deleted English questions with a best answer). A ratio greater than 1 indicates higher frequency of the category across *FactQueries*' questions than across all YA's questions. The categories with highest ratio are Science & Mathematics (3.98), Arts & Humanities (2.44), and Entertainment & Music (2.23). The three categories with the lowest ratio (not shown in the table) are Beauty & Style (0.12), Pregnancy & Parenting (0.05), and Family & Relationships (0.02).

Thus far, we inspected the top-level categories in the YA taxonomy. To gain a more fine-grained sense of the collection's topics, we also examine the specific categories assigned to questions (any category in the taxonomy, at any level, can be assigned to a question). Table 9 shows the 15 most common categories within *FactQueries*. The most popular categories are Movies, Biology, Celebrities, History, Chemistry, and Comics, reflecting the mix of science and entertainment. The categories with the highest freq-ratio are Geography, Trivia, Comedy, and Biology. The categories with the lowest freq-ratio among the 30 most common YA categories are Polls & Surveys, Hair, Diet & Fitness, Pregnancy, Singles & Dating, Friends, and Marriage & Divorce (the last two without any associated questions in the collection).

Category Name	Top-level Category	% Qstns	Freq-Ratio
Movies	Entertainment & Music	6.5%	5.20
Biology	Science & Mathematics	4.9%	**10.07**
Celebrities	Entertainment & Music	4.8%	5.60
History	Arts & Humanities	4.7%	7.63
Chemistry	Science & Mathematics	4.5%	5.78
Comics & Animation	Entertainment & Music	4.0%	4.98
Words & Wordplay	Education & Reference	3.6%	3.97
Geography	Science & Mathematics	3.0%	**19.70**
Homework Help	Education & Reference	2.3%	1.84
Other - Music	Entertainment & Music	2.3%	2.81
Comedy	Entertainment & Music	2.0%	**10.92**
Books & Authors	Arts & Humanities	1.9%	1.77
Astronomy & Space	Science & Mathematics	1.8%	5.72
Drama	Entertainment & Music	1.7%	6.15
Trivia	Education & Reference	1.7%	**15.16**

Table 9: Most common categories.

4 CONCLUSION

The *FactQueries* collection provides researchers and practitioners with over 15,000 queries used by web search users to find answers to a variety of factual questions. The factual nature of the questions and the correctness of the answers were validated in a large editorial effort. The collection strives to help the community better understand the domain of factoid queries, which plays an interesting role in today's web search.

5 REFERENCES

[1] L. A. Adamic, J. Zhang, E. Bakshy, and M. S. Ackerman. Knowledge sharing and Yahoo Answers: Everyone knows something. In *Proc. WWW*, pages 665–674, 2008.

[2] H. Bast and E. Haussmann. More accurate question answering on freebase. In *Proc. CIKM*, pages 1431–1440, 2015.

[3] J. Berant, A. Chou, R. Frostig, and P. Liang. Semantic parsing on freebase from question-answer pairs. In *Proc. EMNLP*, pages 1533âĂŞ–1544, 2013.

[4] Q. Cai and A. Yates. Large-scale semantic parsing via schema matching and lexicon extension. In *Proc. ACL*, pages 423–433, 2013.

[5] A. Chuklin and P. Serdyukov. Good abandonments in factoid queries. In *Proc. WWW Companion*, pages 483–484, 2012.

[6] H. T. Dang, D. Kelly, and J. J. Lin. Overview of the trec 2007 question answering track. In *Proc. TREC*, 2007.

[7] I. Guy. Searching by talking: Analysis of voice queries on mobile web search. In *Proc. SIGIR*, 2016.

[8] A. Kalyanpur, S. Patwardhan, B. Boguraev, A. Lally, and J. Chu-Carroll. Fact-based question decomposition in deepqa. *IBM Journal of Research and Development*, 56(3.4):13:1–13:11, 2012.

[9] G. Tsur, D. Carmel, Y. Pinter, and I. Szpektor. Identifying queries with question intent. In *Proc. WWW*, pages 783–793, 2016.

[10] S. Verberne. Paragraph retrieval for why-question answering. In *Proc. SIGIR*, pages 922–922, 2007.

[11] R. W. White, M. Richardson, and W. Yih. Questions vs. queries in informational search tasks. In *Proc. WWW*, pages 135–136, 2015.

The LExR Collection for Expertise Retrieval in Academia

Vitor Mangaravite, Rodrygo L. T. Santos, Isac S. Ribeiro,
Marcos André Gonçalves, Alberto H. F. Laender
{mangaravite, rodrygo, isacsandin, mgoncalv, laender}@dcc.ufmg.br
Department of Computer Science
Universidade Federal de Minas Gerais
Belo Horizonte, MG, Brazil

ABSTRACT

Expertise retrieval has been the subject of intense research over the past decade, particularly with the public availability of benchmark test collections for expertise retrieval in enterprises. Another domain which has seen comparatively less research on expertise retrieval is academic search. In this paper, we describe the Lattes Expertise Retrieval (LExR) test collection for research on academic expertise retrieval. LExR has been designed to provide a large-scale benchmark for two complementary expertise retrieval tasks, namely, *expert profiling* and *expert finding*. Unlike currently available test collections, which fully support only one of these tasks, LExR provides graded relevance judgments performed by expert judges separately for each task. In addition, LExR is both cross-organization and cross-area, encompassing candidate experts from all areas of knowledge working in research institutions all over Brazil. As a result, it constitutes a valuable resource for fostering new research directions on expertise retrieval in an academic setting.

Keywords

Academic search; expertise retrieval

1. INTRODUCTION

The need for expertise emerges whenever proficient knowledge is required about a particular topic. Two information retrieval tasks have been proposed to address complementary sides of this need: *expert profiling* and *expert finding* [3]. Expert profiling can be seen as a summarization task, aimed at identifying the topics of expertise of a given person. In turn, expert finding (often referred to as expert search) can be seen as a ranking task, aimed at identifying expert persons given a topic of interest. These two complementary tasks have been the subject of substantial research over the past decade, which contributed to approaches for summarizing, ranking, and evaluating expertise.

One of the key driving forces for the progress of research on expertise retrieval has been the availability of public benchmark test collections. The TREC Enterprise track contributed two such test collections suitable for expert finding in an enterprise setting. In particular, the World Wide Web Consortium (W3C) test collection [5] includes W3C working group members as candidate experts, whereas the CSIRO Enterprise Research Collection (CERC) [1] includes CSIRO employees as candidate experts. Test collections developed for expert finding in an academic setting have also been made publicly available. For instance, the UvT test collection [2] and its extended version TU [4] include employees of Tilburg University, the Netherlands, as candidate experts. In turn, the ArnetMiner test collection [10] includes researchers with a DBLP page as candidate experts. Other non-public test collections for expertise retrieval have also been developed [3, see Section 4.2.4]. Table 1 describes core properties and salient statistics of these test collections.

As shown in the top half of Table 1, most of the existing expertise retrieval test collections encompass candidate experts from a single organization. The only exception is the ArnetMiner test collection, which includes computer science researchers from multiple organizations as candidate experts. On the other hand, both the ArnetMiner as well as the W3C test collections encompass candidate experts from a single knowledge area, namely, computer science and web standards, respectively. In addition, none of these test collections fully supports both the expert profiling as well as the expert finding tasks. Indeed, W3C, CERC, and ArnetMiner focus on expert finding, with only CERC including relevance judgments performed by expert judges. In contrast, UvT and TU primarily focus on expert profiling, with expert finding supported via pseudo relevance judgments adapted from expert profiling judgments. Moreover, except for TU's support of expert profiling, none of these test collections provides graded relevance judgments, which could enable more discriminative ranking comparisons [9].

In this paper, we introduce the Lattes Expertise Retrieval (LExR) test collection, a new test collection for expertise retrieval in academia. As described in the bottom half of Table 1, LExR addresses the strengths and weaknesses of previous test collections in order to provide a comprehensive, large-scale benchmark for evaluating expertise retrieval approaches. In particular, it is both cross-organization and cross-area, encompassing candidate experts from all knowledge areas working in research institutions all over Brazil. In addition, it includes graded relevance judgments performed by the experts themselves as opposed to external judges. Moreover, additional cross-expert judgments are included for expert finding, which provide improved cov-

SIGIR '16, July 17-21, 2016, Pisa, Italy
© 2016 ACM. ISBN 978-1-4503-4069-4/16/07... $15.00
DOI: http://dx.doi.org/10.1145/2911451.2914678

	domain	year	cross-organization	cross-area	expert profiling	free topics	expert judging	graded judging	expert finding	expert judging	graded judging	#candidates	#documents	#queries	#qrels	size
W3C [5]	enterprise	2004							✔			1,092	331,037	99	9,860	5.70
CERC [1]	enterprise	2007		✔					✔	✔		3,500	370,715	127	2,862	4.20
UvT [2]	academia	2006		✔	✔		✔		✔			1,168	36,699	743/1,491	4,318	0.31
TU [4]	academia	2008		✔	✔		✔	✔	✔			977	32,567	239/1,266	2,112	1.11
ArnetMiner [10]	academia	2008	✔						✔	✔		1,033,050	1,632,440	13	1,781	0.85
LExR	academia	2015	✔	✔	✔	✔	✔	✔	✔	✔	✔	206,697	11,942,014	1,450 /235	50,802 /1,635	7.51

Table 1: Core properties and salient statistics of publicly available test collections for expertise retrieval. Whenever two figures are present for #queries or #qrels, they correspond to the expert profiling and expert finding tasks, respectively. The uncompressed collection sizes are measured in GB.

erage of relevant experts for a given topic as well as better consensus on the relevance grades assigned to each expert by multiple judges. As a result, LExR coherently supports both expert profiling and expert finding, enabling the investigation of a variety of research questions related to expertise retrieval in academia. In the remainder of this paper, we discuss the methodology behind the construction of the LExR test collection and its salient characteristics. The full test collection is available for download from http://www.lbd.dcc.ufmg.br/lbd/collections.

2. LExR TEST COLLECTION

The LExR test collection is based upon the Lattes platform,[1] an internationally renowned initiative for managing information about science, technology, and innovation for individual researchers and research institutions in Brazil [6]. LExR was developed to provide a unified yet coherent benchmark for research on expert profiling and expert finding in academia. In the remainder of this section, we describe the methodology behind the construction of LExR. In particular, Section 2.1 describes the acquisition of documentary evidence of expertise for a large set of academic experts, whereas Section 2.2 describes the process of obtaining relevance judgments for expert profiling and finding.

2.1 Candidates and Documents

The Lattes platform currently stores the academic curricula of nearly 4.5 million individuals involved in research activities in Brazil. Each curriculum comprises information about an individual's academic life, including his or her current and past affiliations, earned degrees, academic services, student supervisions, research projects, and scientific publications. To start off with a large set of promising experts, we obtained the curricula of 206,697 individuals with a doctorate degree and at least one publication. Figure 1 shows the distribution of candidate experts per broad area of interest, as informed in their curriculum (for now, ignore the red bars). As shown in the figure, *exact and earth sciences* contribute the majority of candidate experts in the collection (36%), followed by *biology* (27%) and *health sciences* (16%). The least represented area is *linguistics, languages, and arts*, which account for less than 1% of all candidates.

[1]http://lattes.cnpq.br/

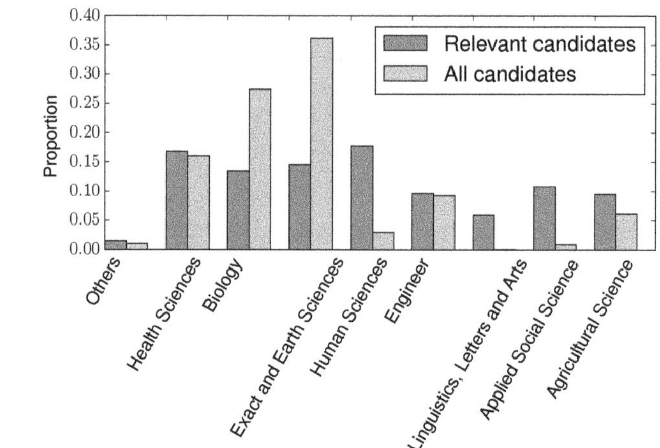

Figure 1: Candidate experts per area of interest.

In order to simulate a general-purpose academic search scenario, we retained only metadata records associated with scientific publications, which are typically available in online repositories such as digital libraries and academic social networks. The resulting 11,942,014 documents comprise multiple types of publication, including books and book chapters (8%), journal articles (20%), conference papers (46%), and other published material (26%). Most documents are written in Portuguese (61%), followed by English (22%), Spanish (9%), and other languages (8%). Among relevant candidates in our ground-truth, English documents are prevalent (51%), followed by Portuguese (37%), Spanish (6%), and other languages (5%). For each document with a digital object identifier (DOI), we further attempted to recover its abstract by scraping the landing page associated with its DOI. Given the enormous amount of publishers in our corpus (precisely, 2,836), we handcrafted scrapers for the 22 most prolific ones, which account for 80% of all documents with a DOI. Factoring in download failures, we were able to recover the abstract for a total of 413,356 documents. Another 69,866 abstracts were recovered using the Mendeley API.[2] Figure 2 shows the distribution of profile sizes in terms of the number of

[2]http://dev.mendeley.com/

documents as well as the number of tokens in each profile. In both cases, we can observe a long-tail distribution with most candidates having relatively small profiles and a few candidates having very large profiles.

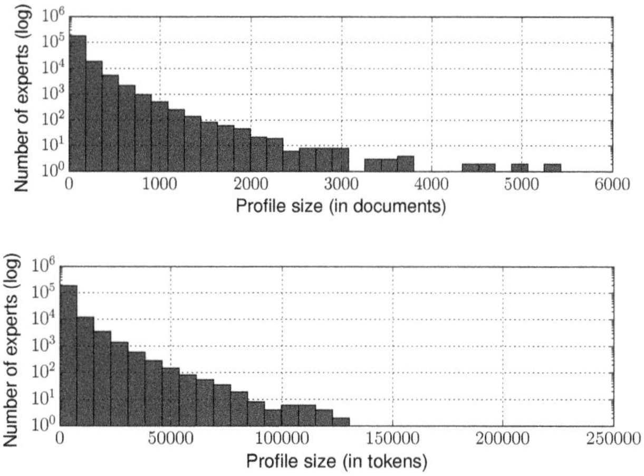

Figure 2: Distribution of profile sizes.

2.2 Queries and Relevance Judgments

For a test collection to provide a realistic benchmark for evaluation, a set of queries should be selected that are representative of real user information needs [9]. Although we do not have direct access to expert finding users in our scenario, we do have access to expert profiling users, namely, the experts themselves. In this section, we describe the process of producing queries and relevance judgments for both the expert profiling and the expert finding tasks.

2.2.1 *Expert Profiling*

Early test collections for expert finding such as the W3C test collection [1] lacked knowledgeable judges to assess the relevance of candidate experts [3]. For expert profiling, the most knowledgeable judge to assess an expert's profile is arguably the expert him or herself. Indeed, even when expertise profiles are meant to be used by others, as is the case in academic and professional online social networks, they must be typically approved by the profiled expert beforehand. With this in mind, we invited a subset of 5,355 of the most prominent researchers from our set of candidates to participate in our expert profiling judgments. These included researchers from 123 research consortia awarded by the Brazilian government with a five-year grant (starting from 2008) to foster networks of collaborative research in several areas considered strategic for the country.

In contrast to previous expert profiling test collections, such as UvT [2] and TU [4], we did not impose a predefined set of topics of expertise for each expert to choose from. Instead, each of the 5,355 invited experts was presented with a list of suggested topics obtained by pooling nine standard content-based tag recommenders operating on different fields of the expert's publications, namely, titles, abstracts, and keywords [8]. In particular, each expert was presented with up to 60 suggested topics in no particular order, selected in a round-robin fashion from the top 50 tags returned by each recommender. Of the 5,355 invited experts, 1,450 (27%) responded to our invitation and provided relevance judgments on the suggested topics of their expertise, with the option to inform us of further topics not among the suggested ones. Relevance judgments were performed on a graded scale, with 0, 1, and 2 indicating an irrelevant, relevant, and highly relevant topic for the expert's profile, respectively. Altogether, these 1,450 experts (queries) identified 50,802 somewhat relevant topics (qrels) that make our benchmark for expert profiling. Table 2 shows a breakdown of the average number of qrels of various relevance grades per query. On average, each expert in our benchmark has a total of 27 relevant topics of expertise in his or her profile.

expert profiling		expert finding	
grade	avg. qrels	grade	avg. qrels
1	10.90 (39%)	1	1.90 (20%)
2	16.73 (61%)	2	3.25 (34%)
		3	4.41 (46%)

Table 2: Average number of relevants of various grades per expert profiling and expert finding query.

2.2.2 *Expert Finding*

While relevance judgments for expert profiling could be trivially converted into judgments for expert finding (and vice versa), the resulting judgments would likely lack in coverage and coherence. To illustrate this situation, Figure 3 depicts a direct conversion of expert profiling judgments (represented by directed edges running from experts to topics, weighted by the relevance grade assigned in each judgment) into expert finding judgments (represented by transposed edges running from topics to experts).

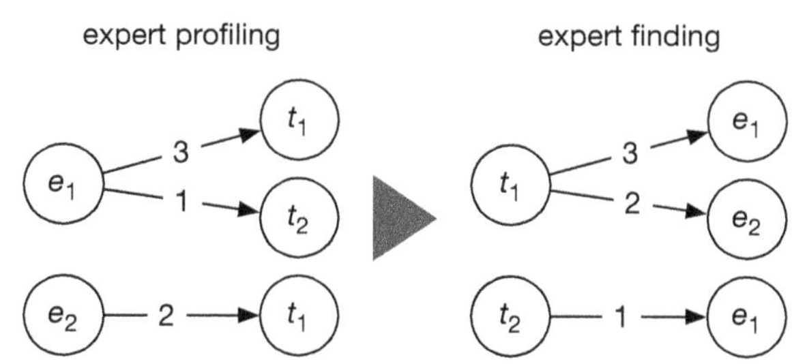

Figure 3: Asymmetric conversion between expert profiling and expert finding relevance judgments.

From Figure 3, a coverage problem may arise in the resulting expert finding judgments to the extent that further relevant experts on topics t_1 and t_2 will be missing, unless they have been previously included in the expert profiling judgments. Likewise, in a typical situation where expert profiling judgments are performed by different judges (ideally, each expert would judge his or her own profile), relevance grades assigned to the same topic will not be comparable to one another, thus resulting incoherent expert finding judgments. As an illustrative example, a boastful yet unknowledgeable candidate e_1 may assign him or herself a relevance grade 3 for topic t_1, whereas a modest yet proficient candidate e_2 may assign him or herself a grade 2 for the same topic. When converted into expert finding judgments, these assignments may convey the wrong impression about these candidates' relative expertise on topic t_1.

To overcome such an asymmetry, we conducted a second round of judgments aimed specifically at the expert finding task. To this end, we invited a subset of the researchers that had contributed judgments on their own expertise profiles to judge the expertise of others. To avoid overly specific topics, we discarded 102 of the 1,450 original respondents with a single topic of expertise shared by at most one other researcher. As a result, for each topic of his or her expertise, each of the invited 1,348 researchers (acting as a judge) was presented with a list of at least two other candidates that had also declared themselves somewhat experts on the topic. A link to the full curriculum of each candidate was also provided to aid in the judgment. The judge was then asked to determine the expertise of each candidate on the topic following a graded scale, with 0, 1, 2, and 3 indicating an unknowledgeable, somewhat knowledgeable, very knowledgeable, and expert person on the topic, respectively. Of the 1,348 invited researchers, 513 (38%) agreed to act as judges for this second round of relevance judgments.

To enforce a minimum level of support and an improved consensus on the judged experts, we retained 235 topics that had at least three self-declared experts (in the expert profiling judgments) subsequently considered as experts by at least two judges (in the expert finding judgments). The final relevance grade for an expert was computed as the rounded mean of the grades received from all judges. Analogously, we estimated the disagreement about an expert as the standard deviation around the expert's unrounded mean grade. Per-topic disagreement values were then obtained by averaging the disagreements observed for all experts associated with each topic. Figure 4 shows the distributions of disagreement considering all topics, as well as subsets of topics with experts from an increasing number of areas of interest.

As shown in the 'All' group in Figure 4, disagreement values vary considerably across topics, with an average of 0.29 ± 0.02. Interestingly, the more knowledge areas covered by a topic, the higher the disagreement observed for this topic, with topics covering five or more areas showing the highest average disagreement (0.37 ± 0.07). In total, the 235 obtained topics (queries) were associated with 1,635 experts (qrels) in our benchmark for expert finding. As shown in Table 2, this makes an average of over five experts per query. In addition, these experts are more evenly distributed across knowledge areas, as highlighted by the red bars in Figure 1.

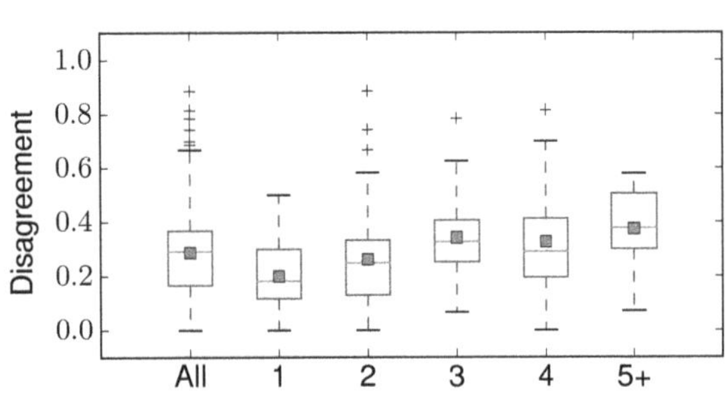

Figure 4: Judging disagreement distributions for all topics and for subsets of topics with experts from an increasing number of knowledge areas.

3. CONCLUSIONS

The public availability of benchmark test collections has fostered intense research on expertise retrieval over the past decade, particularly in the enterprise domain. In this paper, we described a new test collection for expertise retrieval in the academic domain, which has not seen as much research progress in comparison. In particular, the Lattes Expertise Retrieval (LExR) test collection provides a large-scale benchmark for the evaluation of two complementary expertise retrieval tasks, namely, expert profiling and expert finding.[3] Moreover, it is the first publicly available test collection that fully supports both tasks, with dedicated graded relevance judgments performed by real experts for each task separately. In addition, it is both cross-organization and cross-area, encompassing candidate experts from all areas of knowledge working in research institutions spread all over Brazil. Together, these features make LExR a unique and valuable resource for the research community.

Acknowledgments

This work was partially funded by projects InWeb (MCT/CNPq 573871/2008-6) and MASWeb (FAPEMIG/PRONEX APQ-01400-14), and by the authors' individual grants from CNPq and FAPEMIG.

4. REFERENCES

[1] P. Bailey, N. Craswell, I. Soboroff, and A. P. de Vries. The CSIRO enterprise search test collection. *SIGIR Forum*, 41(2):42–45, 2007.

[2] K. Balog, T. Bogers, L. Azzopardi, M. de Rijke, and A. van den Bosch. Broad expertise retrieval in sparse data environments. In *Proc. of SIGIR*, pages 551–558, 2007.

[3] K. Balog, Y. Fang, M. de Rijke, P. Serdyukov, and L. Si. Expertise retrieval. *Found. Trends Inf. Retr.*, 6(2–3):127–256, 2012.

[4] R. Berendsen, M. de Rijke, K. Balog, T. Bogers, and A. van den Bosch. On the assessment of expertise profiles. *J. Am. Soc. Inf. Sci. Technol.*, 64(10):2024–2044, 2013.

[5] N. Craswell, A. P. de Vries, and I. Soboroff. Overview of the TREC 2005 Enterprise track. In *Proc. of TREC*, 2005.

[6] J. Lane. Let's make science metrics more scientific. *Nature*, 464(7288):488–489, 2010.

[7] V. Mangaravite and R. L. T. Santos. On information-theoretic document-person associations for expert search in academia. In *Proc. of SIGIR*, 2016.

[8] I. S. Ribeiro, R. L. T. Santos, M. A. Gonçalves, and A. H. F. Laender. On tag recommendation for expertise profiling: A case study in the scientific domain. In *Proc. of WSDM*, pages 189–198, 2015.

[9] M. Sanderson. Test collection based evaluation of information retrieval systems. *Found. Trends Inf. Retr.*, 4(4):247–375, 2010.

[10] J. Tang, J. Zhang, L. Yao, J. Li, L. Zhang, and Z. Su. ArnetMiner: extraction and mining of academic social networks. In *Proc. of KDD*, pages 990–998, 2008.

[3]Reference results for both tasks can be found in [7, 8].

UQV100: A Test Collection with Query Variability

Peter Bailey
Microsoft,
Australia
pbailey@microsoft.com

Alistair Moffat
The University of Melbourne,
Australia
ammoffat@unimelb.edu.au

Falk Scholer
RMIT University,
Australia
falk.scholer@rmit.edu.au

Paul Thomas
Microsoft,
Australia
pathom@microsoft.com

ABSTRACT

We describe the UQV100 test collection, designed to incorporate variability from users. Information need "backstories" were written for 100 topics (or sub-topics) from the TREC 2013 and 2014 Web Tracks. Crowd workers were asked to read the backstories, and provide the queries they would use; plus effort estimates of how many useful documents they would have to read to satisfy the need. A total of 10,835 queries were collected from 263 workers. After normalization and spell-correction, 5,764 unique variations remained; these were then used to construct a document pool via Indri-BM25 over the ClueWeb12-B corpus. Qualified crowd workers made relevance judgments relative to the backstories, using a relevance scale similar to the original TREC approach; first to a pool depth of ten per query, then deeper on a set of targeted documents.

The backstories, query variations, normalized and spell-corrected queries, effort estimates, run outputs, and relevance judgments are made available collectively as the UQV100 test collection. We also make available the judging guidelines and the gold hits we used for crowd-worker qualification and spam detection.

We believe this test collection will unlock new opportunities for novel investigations and analysis, including for problems such as task-intent retrieval performance and consistency (independent of query variation), query clustering, query difficulty prediction, and relevance feedback, among others.

1. INTRODUCTION

Test collection-based evaluation is the most widely used methodology for measuring the effectiveness of information retrieval systems. A typical test collection consists of a set of queries, a collection of documents to search over, and a set of relevance judgments that indicate, for query-document pairs, whether the document was a topically related resource for that query. To evaluate a search system, a ranked answer list is generated for each query, and the relevance of each item is determined with reference to the available judgments [3]. Finally, the relevance information is condensed into a single number, based on a chosen effectiveness metric, which may take into account features such as the number of relevant answers that were retrieved, at what positions in the ranked list the relevant answers were located, and so on.

SIGIR '16, July 17–21, 2016, Pisa, Italy

ACM 978-1-4503-4069-4/16/07 ... $15.00.
http://dx.doi.org/10.1145/2911451.2914671.

Collection-based evaluation has several advantages: it supports reproducible experimentation; and, while constructing a test collection is typically resource-intensive in terms of time and labor – particularly the creation of relevance judgments – it is then inexpensive to run any number of further experiments using the same framework. However, there are also limitations in terms of the realism of the evaluation. For example, the user is almost entirely removed from the evaluation, and is represented via a single search query that instantiates the underlying information need.

The TREC Query Track studied the impact on effectiveness evaluation of multiple user-generated search queries, all aiming to resolve the same underlying information need. Analysis concluded that "topics are extremely variable; queries dealing with the same topic are extremely variable" while "systems were only somewhat variable" [4]. A specific concern is the coverage that existing collections offer when widely varying queries are admitted, even for a single topic. Moffat et al. [10] examine the adequacy of relevance judgments in a standard single-query test collection in the face of such query variations; their results demonstrate that a large proportion of documents retrieved for the variable queries are unjudged, including many near the top of their rankings. Our purpose in this work is to address the challenge posed by this earlier work, and develop a test collection that explicitly includes query variability as a factor.

2. THE COLLECTION

Corpus, Topics, and Backstories ClueWeb12-B [11] was used as an underlying corpus due to its wide availability, scale, coverage of modern Web documents, and additional annotations. One hundred topics from the 2013 and 2014 TREC Web tracks [5, 6] were taken as the basis for information-need statements (background stories, or "backstories", written by us), in a manner similar to that described by Bailey et al. [2]. Topic numbers 201–300 were used; where a topic contained subtopics, one of them was selected as the focus of the backstory, and the others were ignored. An example backstory is shown below, for topic 215 (*maryland department of natural resources*), subtopic 2 (*How do you get a Maryland fishing license?*):

> *Having heard of the pristine environment in Maryland, you have long dreamed of taking a fishing holiday there. However, you think that you may need a fishing license in Maryland. How do you get one?*

	Mean	Min.	Max.
Raw queries per worker	41.2	1	100
Raw queries per backstory	72.5	35	106
Normalized queries per backstory	61.0	22	101
Spell corrected queries per backstory	57.7	19	101

Table 1: Query counts through the data simplification process.

Each backstory provides a brief motivating context, hopefully with some degree of realism, that helps individuals imagine themselves in a similar information-seeking situation and informs their query and effort responses [2]. The wording makes use of anaphora (co-referencing entities via pronouns) to avoid offering obvious queries.

Query Variations and Effort Estimates We developed two crowd worker interfaces. Both presented the backstory, and then asked the worker to enter the first query they would use to access information via a search engine in response to the backstory, and for estimates of the effort (in terms of number of useful documents, and number of queries) that they anticipated needing to satisfy the information need. We varied from the radio-button interface described by Bailey et al. [2]. In one interface we asked for effort estimates using graphical slider widgets ranging from 0 to 101 for the estimate of the number of useful documents required, and 1 to 11 for the number of queries that would need to be issued. In the other interface, we provided text entry fields requiring integer non-negative numbers. These two interfaces were released to two different English-speaking crowds.

As is often the case with crowds, a number of low quality workers participated. A mixture of methods was used to identify suspicious data, including noting workers who entered the same query text for multiple responses, or who provided undeviating effort estimates regardless of the backstory. Data from these workers was removed. At the conclusion of the cleaning process we had data from 263 individuals, spread across the 100 backstories. The count of workers per backstory averaged 108 (min: 105, max: 113) and there were a total of 10,835 individual queries and effort estimates provided. Each query was normalized to lowercase, with extraneous whitespace and trailing punctuation removed, and passed through the Bing search engine's spelling service to generate a final canonical form of each worker's query. This was done to avoid differences arising in how systems might handle such basic query normalization and spell correction of the query variations, and to reflect how queries would be pre-processed in a live system. It also reduced the total number of unique query variations (Table 1).

For example, for the Maryland fishing license backstory listed earlier, there were 53 unique spell-corrected query variations obtained. The average effort estimate in terms of useful documents required was 2.7 (which lies in the lowest decile of the 100 backstories). There were 13 variations which occurred more than once, of which 7 occurred only twice. The most popular query was "*maryland fishing license*" which occurred 14 times. Many of the single occurrence variations are expressed in more natural language forms, such as "*how do i get a fishing license in maryland*", "*who can get a fishing license in maryland*", and "*is a fishing license needed in maryland*". Only 8% of occurrences were identical to the corresponding TREC title query. In these regards, our collection process provided similar query diversity as is reported by Bailey et al. [2].

Relevance Judgments The 2013 and 2014 TREC Web collections include NIST-generated relevance judgments covering the 100 topic/subtopic pairs, based on the sets of 61 and 30 participating system runs, many of which will have run the nominal "title" query associated with the topic. The TREC judgments use a six-category scale with four ordinal relevance levels for informational tasks; a category for navigational tasks; and a final category for spam [6]. Analysis of the NIST relevance judgments indicates that these definitions were not strictly followed. For example, topic 298 had approximately 50% of the documents given the *Home Page* label for the entire collection, all of which came from pages on the official website of the Jehovah's Witnesses; yet many of these pages are only of marginal relevance. We adapted the TREC category names and descriptions to provide slightly clearer expression of what each category label should capture, and added more information about what a searcher might do after reading a document in this category. Our assessors would receive little training, and so the judging guidelines and qualification test had to suffice. The new rating categories were: *Essential*; *Very Useful*; *Mostly Useful*; *Slightly Useful*; *Not Useful*; and *Junk*. The lowest, rating *Slightly Useful*, includes good-quality pages containing links to documents that would probably have useful information, even if they did not include the requisite information themselves. We believe this reflects real user behavior in web search activities. The full description of each rating is available in the judging guidelines provided as part of the collection.

For effectiveness metrics that use ordinal (graded) relevance, the *Junk* category should be merged with the *Not Useful* category, after which the scale can be applied directly as a five-level ordinal relevance scale. For metrics that require binary relevance judgments, our recommendation is to fold the *Junk* and *Not Useful* categories into a single *Not Relevant* category, and to fold the remaining levels into a single *Relevant* category.

Quality Control A total of 120 documents were randomly selected from those topic/subtopic-document pairs available in the original TREC qrels files that did not appear in our top-10 pools. These were stratified-sampled to obtain an even spread of TREC relevance labels. Each of the topic/subtopics was replaced by the corresponding backstory, and then each document was judged by two of the authors with respect to the judging guidelines. Any disagreements were discussed, and a final label agreed. Five of the pairs were subsequently discarded, due to genuine disagreement and potential for confusion, leaving a set of 115 "gold" judgments to draw from.

Judgments were then sourced via a crowd worker platform. From the gold set of backstory-document labels, a set of 27 were selected, again attempting to stratify as evenly as possible across the label categories. Before being asked to provide ratings, workers had to correctly rate documents from at least four of seven randomly chosen test questions (from the set of 27), and had up to three attempts. Additional random injections from the remaining gold judgments were used by the crowd-sourcing system to calibrate ongoing worker quality levels, and eliminate workers failing to meet standards without incurring unnecessary costs. There was no intentional overlap between the workers who provided the original query variations and effort estimates and those carrying out judging.

Aptness of Relevance Judgments A critical question that arises is that of how to assess what we denote as *aptness*, the extent to which a set of relevance judgments is fit for scoring a set of runs generated by systems and/or queries. Moffat and Zobel [7] introduce the notion of a *residual*, a numeric quantification of the extent of the (upward) uncertainty of a score that arises from the presence of unjudged documents. Residuals can be calculated for any weighted-precision effectiveness metric, including Reciprocal Rank (RR), by taking the difference between the "all unjudged documents are non-relevant" and the "all unjudged documents are maximally relevant" run scores. The greater the residual, the less apt the judgments.

Figure 1a illustrates this approach. To construct the graph, the

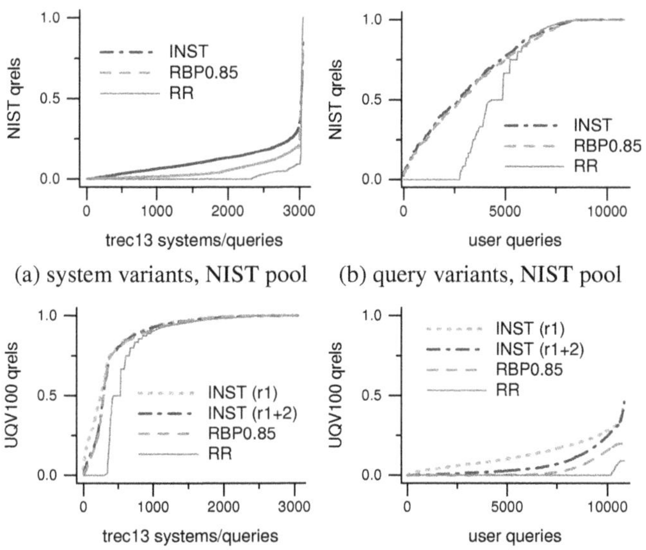

(a) system variants, NIST pool (b) query variants, NIST pool

(c) system variants, UQV pool (d) query variants, UQV pool

Figure 1: Residuals for (left column) $50 \times 61 = 3{,}050$ TREC runs from 2013, and for (right column) 10,835 user-generated queries including repeats. Residual scores for three metrics are shown in each pane, computed using (top row) the NIST qrels selecting only the query subtopic used to generate the corresponding backstory, and using (bottom row) the new UQV100 qrels. All runs are relative to the ClueWeb12-B collection, and all metrics were evaluated over the top 200 documents retrieved; with Indri/BM25 used to construct runs for the user query variants in the right column. In the bottom row, the additional INST line shows the first round of judgments; both rounds were used for RBP and RR.

$50 \times 61 = 3{,}050$ combinations between TREC 2013 contributing systems and topics were scored using the NIST-provided qrels file and four different metrics, including the INST mechanism of Bailey et al. [2], and residuals computed. Those residual were then independently sorted for each metric, and plotted by ascending value. The relatively low residuals shown in Figure 1a for the RR and RBP0.85 provides evidence of the aptness of the judgments for the evaluation of the contributing runs. But when using the user-supplied T values (which average at 4.7), INST has an expected search depth of 8.6, and the higher residuals show that the available judgments are not such a good fit. Moffat et al. [9] discuss INST in detail, including the relationship between T, expected search depth, and residual.

Use of NIST Judgments for Query Variants Figure 1b was generated using the same methodology as Figure 1a, but using the 10,385 user queries (5,764 distinct). The NIST-supplied qrels are again used; what is clear is that the judgments are no longer apt, and that none of these three metrics, not even RR, should be used to generate effectiveness scores for these runs. Indeed, residuals of over 0.5 arise for more than half of the queries. Even if by chance the lower-end scores for some metric displayed some particular attribute (for example, gave rise to a statistically significant system comparison), it would be risky to trust such a conclusion.

Working With INST We are interested in exploring the implications of using Bailey et al.'s INST metric when forming a test collection. INST is designed to be sensitive to the user's search goal, and is parameterized by a value T, the expected number of useful documents that will be required. For example, when $T = 1$, the user is anticipating needing to retrieve one relevant document, and the information need may well be navigational or factoid in nature. Higher values of T correspond to richer information needs.

The effort-influenced variability embedded in INST means that it is desirable to judge different topics to different depths, rather than use a uniform pool. Moreover, INST is an adaptive metric and becomes increasingly top-weighted as relevant documents are encountered. In combination, these two factors suggest a two-stage judgment process: first, uniform pooling to a relatively shallow depth, followed by a *gap analysis* to determine the topics, and document within topics, where further judgment effort should be applied in order to ensure that all residuals were broadly comparable to within the limits of the judgment budget. In doing so, we are in part implementing the mechanism described by Moffat et al. [8].

Depth	Total pool	Per run	Per document
1	2,741	0.25	0.25
2	5,157	0.48	0.24
5	11,755	1.08	0.22
10	21,895	2.02	0.20
20	40,478	3.74	0.19
50	91,556	8.45	0.17
100	170,166	15.71	0.16
200	316,171	29.18	0.15

Table 2: Pool sizes over 10,835 topic-query combinations. The final two columns give per run and per retrieved document averages.

Collecting New Judgments: Round 1 Table 2 lists the uniform pool sizes that were generated from the user queries, with the final two columns normalized first on a per topic-query basis, and then second on a per-document retrieved basis. Despite the fact that there are nominally only 100 different information needs covered by these queries, and despite the fact that on average each query occurs twice, even at depth 10 fully 20% of the documents retrieved must be judged in order to cover the pool.

A first round of crowd-worker judgments was collected using a uniform pool depth of 10 and three-way overlap judging, based on the use of Indri/BM25 to construct runs against the ClueWeb12-B corpus for each of the 10,385 spell-corrected query variants (5,764 distinct). A median label from the (in almost all cases) three individual judge labels (after removing ratings that indicated a judge was unable to provide a label due to page load failure or other reasons) was assigned. Results are reported using this median label; in the collection data resources we also provide a re-estimated label based on the Community BCC algorithm described by Venanzi et al. [12].

Collecting New Judgments: Round 2 We then scored each run using INST, and for each document-topic combination, computed the sum over the runs of the residuals associated with that document [8]. That list of document-topic pairs was then sorted into decreasing order, and a further 5,501 documents taken from the front of it and judged, with aggregate per-document residuals of between 1.653 and 0.051. This targeted process had the effect of applying deeper pooling on topics with higher T values, and on topics where there were comparatively few relevant documents identified. Note that the adaptive and goal-sensitive nature of INST means that we are unable to determine which additional judgments were required without the initial round of judgments being completed.

Figure 1c and 1d show the application of the new qrels, with two lines plotted for INST showing the further improvement in average residual delivered by the Round 2 judgments. Using the full set of

UQV100 judgments, more precise measurement of effectiveness for the query variants can be achieved (Figure 1d), because that facet is the basis of the pooling. But the ability to accurately evaluate different retrieval systems has been significantly compromised (Figure 1c) compared to the NIST judgments arising from pooling across systems. Determining how best to cater to the cross-product of these competing requirements is a clear direction for future work.

As a future extension we plan to incorporate further variability by using one or more systems that vary considerably from the Indri/BM25 system we have used here. We will update the collection progressively as further labels become available.

Observations on Judgments The final set of 27,396 judgments represent all 100 topics, and reflect contributions from 179 judges, after qualification tests and anti-spam measures were applied. Each topic was judged by 42 judges on average (range 17–68). With each topic/document pair having been judged (for the most part) three times, we computed an inter-assessor agreement as Krippendorff's $\alpha = 0.26$, or 0.24 with binary labels.

We emphasize that the TREC and UQV100 judgments are different, should not be aggregated, and are not interchangeable. TREC judgments were created by well-qualified, specialist analysts against TREC judging guidelines and topic descriptions; each judge would read hundreds of documents per topic. UQV100 judgments were made by judges from a more diverse population, working under very different constraints, against UQV100 judging guidelines and backstories – which may incur some topic intent drift – and judges would read many fewer documents per topic on average. UQV100 judgments were also subject to automated quality control tests as well as post-hoc data cleaning.

3. POTENTIAL USES

We present three possible uses of UQV100, beyond the obvious example of using it to investigate system performance on a per query or per backstory basis. When assessing the latter, we recommend averaging the query-level performance across all query variations belonging to a specific backstory first, and then averaging these across the 100 backstories (double-averaging).

Query Clustering While commercial web search engines have large query logs and can use these to examine query–query relationships via within-session re-formulations or co-clicks on the web graph, there is no equivalent in current test collections available to the broader IR community. The UQV100 collection supports some new investigations in query clustering by having so many query variations per backstory. As observed in an extensive investigation of query clustering [1], there are various practical applications of improved query clustering abilities. Even in commercial web search engines, there are difficulties in finding many examples of queries to cluster for rare queries; however this dataset contains many rare queries in each backstory cluster. Either the raw or spell-corrected query variations could be used in this application.

Query Transformations and Difficulty Prediction Performance has been shown to vary widely by the query variation [2], yet the information seeking task remains the same. With many different query variations, each with performance scores, it is now possible to examine which query variations within a cluster have the best performance, and hence investigate what query transformations on low-performing queries lead to better results. An alternative to this investigation would be to use the collection for learning to predict query difficulty [14], given each cluster has a range of scores.

Relevance Feedback Blind relevance feedback approaches have been well studied [13]. The UQV100 collection can support new analysis of such algorithms, given the large number of query variations per cluster. The analysis can examine either individual queries, or the entire set of variations, and may provide additional opportunities for exploring how structural or syntactic elements of query expression (for example, presence of natural language structures, stop-words, term count, and so on) can lead to altered performance of relevance feedback.

4. CONCLUSIONS

We have constructed a substantial new information retrieval test collection (UQV100), using the ClueWeb12-B corpus as the underlying set of documents. The additional resources for the test collection consist of: 100 backstories and their paired TREC topic/subtopic id; corresponding normalized and spell-corrected query variations (an average of 58 per backstory) and effort estimates; judging guidelines; gold hits for qualification and quality control for future judgments of unjudged documents; top-k document ID rankings for all queries using Indri/BM25 against ClueWeb12-B; and relevance judgments (as per judging guidelines) for as a minimum the top-10 pooled documents for each query variation relative to the corresponding backstory. These resources are all freely available from `http://dx.doi.org/10.4225/49/5726E597B8376`.

Acknowledgment This work was supported by the Australian Research Council's *Discovery Projects* Scheme (project DP140102655). Xiaolu Lu (RMIT University) provided helpful assistance.

References

[1] R. Baeza-Yates, C. Hurtado, and M. Mendoza. Improving search engines by query clustering. *JASIST*, 58(12):1793–1804, 2007.

[2] P. Bailey, A. Moffat, F. Scholer, and P. Thomas. User variability and IR system evaluation. In *Proc. SIGIR*, pages 625–634, 2015.

[3] C. Buckley and E. M. Voorhees. Retrieval system evaluation. In E. M. Voorhees and D. K. Harman, editors, *TREC: Experiment and Evaluation in Information Retrieval*, chapter 3, pages 53–75. MIT Press, 2005.

[4] C. Buckley and J. Walz. The TREC-8 query track. In *Proc. TREC*, 1999. NIST Special Publication 500-246.

[5] K. Collins-Thompson, P. N. Bennett, F. Diaz, C. L. A. Clarke, and E. M. Voorhees. TREC 2013 web track overview. In *Proc. TREC*, 2013. NIST Special Publication 500-302.

[6] K. Collins-Thompson, C. Macdonald, P. N. Bennett, F. Diaz, and E. M. Voorhees. TREC 2014 web track overview. In *Proc. TREC*, 2014. NIST Special Publication 500-308.

[7] A. Moffat and J. Zobel. Rank-biased precision for measurement of retrieval effectiveness. *ACM Trans. Inf. Sys.*, 27(1):2.1–2.27, 2008.

[8] A. Moffat, W. Webber, and J. Zobel. Strategic system comparisons via targeted relevance judgments. In *Proc. SIGIR*, pages 375–382, 2007.

[9] A. Moffat, P. Bailey, F. Scholer, and P. Thomas. INST: An adaptive metric for information retrieval evaluation. In *Proc. Aust. Doc. Comp. Symp.*, pages 5:1–5:4, 2015.

[10] A. Moffat, F. Scholer, P. Thomas, and P. Bailey. Pooled evaluation over query variations: Users are as diverse as systems. In *Proc. CIKM*, pages 1759–1762, 2015.

[11] The Lemur Project. The ClueWeb12 Dataset, 2012. URL `www.lemurproject.org/clueweb12.php/`.

[12] M. Venanzi, J. Guiver, G. Kazai, P. Kohli, and M. Shokouhi. Community-based Bayesian aggregation models for crowdsourcing. In *Proc. WWW*, pages 155–164, 2014.

[13] J. Xu and W. B. Croft. Query expansion using local and global document analysis. In *Proc. SIGIR*, pages 4–11, 1996.

[14] E. Yom-Tov, S. Fine, D. Carmel, and A. Darlow. Learning to estimate query difficulty: Including applications to missing content detection and distributed information retrieval. In *Proc. SIGIR*, pages 512–519, 2005.

A Dynamic Recurrent Model for Next Basket Recommendation

Feng Yu, Qiang Liu[*], Shu Wu, Liang Wang, Tieniu Tan
Center for Research on Intelligent Perception and Computing
National Laboratory of Pattern Recognition
Institute of Automation, Chinese Academy of Sciences
{feng.yu, qiang.liu, shu.wu, wangliang, tnt}@nlpr.ia.ac.cn

ABSTRACT

Next basket recommendation becomes an increasing concern. Most conventional models explore either sequential transaction features or general interests of users. Further, some works treat users' general interests and sequential behaviors as two totally divided matters, and then combine them in some way for next basket recommendation. Moreover, the state-of-the-art models are based on the assumption of Markov Chains (MC), which only capture local sequential features between two adjacent baskets. In this work, we propose a novel model, Dynamic REcurrent bAsket Model (DREAM), based on Recurrent Neural Network (RNN). DREAM not only learns a dynamic representation of a user but also captures global sequential features among baskets. The dynamic representation of a specific user can reveal user's dynamic interests at different time, and the global sequential features reflect interactions of all baskets of the user over time. Experiment results on two public datasets indicate that DREAM is more effective than the state-of-the-art models for next basket recommendation.

Keywords

Next basket recommendation; recurrent neural network

1. INTRODUCTION

In real-world scenarios, a customer always purchases a series of baskets of items at different time. This recommendation task in e-commerce sites is formulated as the next basket recommendation, which has received much attention recently [1, 3].

In general, there are two distinct approaches for next basket recommendation. One perspective is the collaborative filtering (CF) models, which capture users' general interests but have difficulty in considering sequential features of historical transactions. Matrix factorization (MF) is a successful CF model [4]. Through factorizing a user-item matrix constructed by the whole historical transaction data, users' general interests can be represented by latent vectors. For instance, a sportsman always buy various athletic equipment, the latent vector may tell that he is interested in sport and we can recommend sports items. Moreover, some sequential recommendation models mainly based on MC [2], which extract sequential features from historical transactions and then predict next purchase based on these sequential behaviors.

As a consequence, a more appropriate way to next basket recommendation is to capture above sequential behaviors and user general interests in a hybrid model. Factorizing Personalized Markov Chains (FPMC) can model sequential behaviors between every two adjacent baskets, and user general interests is shaped by items in baskets [7]. Actually there are multiple interacting factors influencing users' next purchase in real commercial scenarios. FPMC just utilizes a linear operation on multiple factors, and cannot depict the interactions among multiple factors. Hierarchical Representation Model (HRM) seems to partially solve the problem of how to summarize multiple interacting factors through a nonlinear *max pooling* operation [9]. Nevertheless, all the MC based methods (including above FPMC and HRM) have the same deficiency that these recommenders can only model local sequential behaviors between every two adjacent baskets, and some of which may be irrelevant sometimes. For instance, a user u bought a ultrabook in basket $B^u_{t_1}$ (a basket of user u at time t_1, similarly hereinafter), some food in $B^u_{t_2}$ and accessories of the ultrabook in $B^u_{t_3}$, there does not exist any relevance between every two adjacent baskets. Hence, we need to model global sequential behaviors to make the best of all relations among sequential baskets like the above $B^u_{t_1}$ and $B^u_{t_3}$. For this reason, we plan to model global sequential features among all sequential baskets of a user.

In order to mine global sequential features in complex commercial scenarios and reveal dynamic representations of users' interests, deep neural network is employed in this work. As stated above, local sequential features extracted by HRM is not capable enough to model relations among apart baskets, while a recurrent operation of a deep RNN architecture can capture global sequential features from all baskets of a user. Recently, RNN approaches to word embedding for sentence modeling [5], sequential click prediction [10] have achieved much success in respective fields. We propose a dynamic recurrent model, i.e., DREAM, for next bas-

*The first two authors contributed equally to this paper.

SIGIR '16, July 17–21, 2016, Pisa, Italy

© 2016 ACM. ISBN 978-1-4503-4069-4/16/07...$15.00

DOI: http://dx.doi.org/10.1145/2911451.2914683

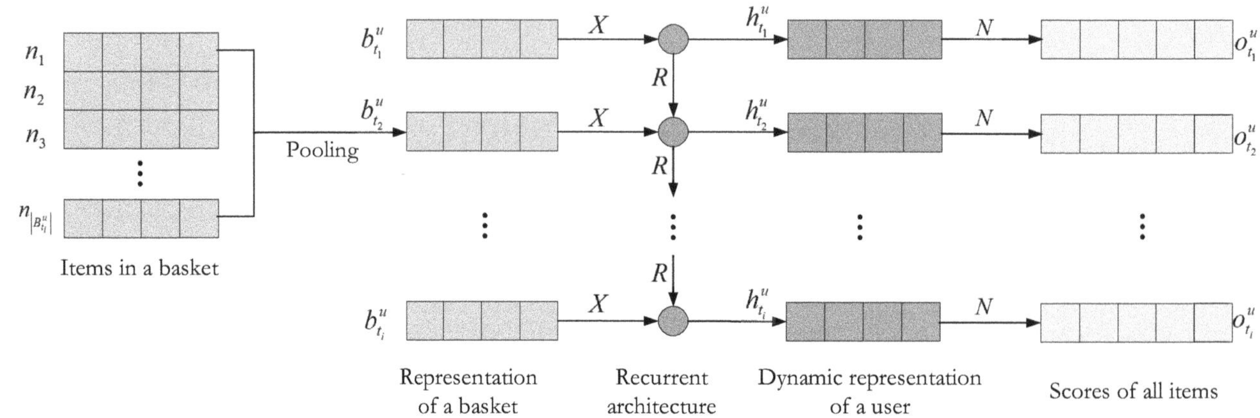

Figure 1: The framework of DREAM. Pooling operation on the items in a basket to get the representation of the basket. The input layer comprises a series of basket representations of a user. Dynamic representation of the user can be obtained in the hidden layer. Finally the output layer shows scores of this user towards all items.

ket recommendation. An input instance of DREAM model consists a series of baskets of items, which are sequential transactions of a specific user. Pooling and matrix operations can offer each user a dynamic representation with different baskets over time. Moreover, the recurrent structure can obtain some global sequential features for all users from overall historical transaction data. Our experiment results on two real-world datasets reveal that the DREAM model achieves great improvement for next basket recommendation comparing with the state-of-the-art models such as FPMC, HRM.

In this work, we take advantage of the whole historical sequential transaction data to gain comprehensive understanding of users' purchase interests and consequently recommend items that each user most probably purchase in the next visit. The main contributions of this work are as follows. We investigate the dynamic representation of each user and the global sequential behaviors of item-purchase history. Experiments on two datasets are conducted to validate the effectiveness of DREAM model. To the best of our knowledge, DREAM is the first approach that attempts to incorporate dynamic representation and global sequential behaviors for enhancing the performance of next basket recommendation.

2. THE PROPOSED APPROACH

In this section, we formulate the task of next basket recommendation and then introduce the proposed DREAM model in detail.

2.1 Problem Formulation

In the scenario of next basket recommendation, there are a mass of users, and each user purchases a series of baskets of items. Let $\boldsymbol{N}$ be the representations of items, and $\boldsymbol{n}_v \in \mathbb{R}^d$ indicates the latent representations of item v. For a user u, the historical transactions B^u are composed of a collection of baskets $\{B^u_{t_1}, B^u_{t_2}, ...\}$ in time order, where $B^u_{t_i}$ is a basket of items purchased by user u at time t_i. For next basket recommendation with historical transaction data, we formalize the problem as predicting a ranking list of items for each user at a specific time t_i.

2.2 DREAM

The general framework of DREAM is illustrated in Figure 1. An input instance of the proposed model are a sequence of baskets. For one basket $B^u_{t_i}$ of the user u, there are a variety of items, $B^u_{t_i} = \{\boldsymbol{n}^u_{t_i,j} \in \mathbb{R}^d | j = 1, 2, ..., |B^u_{t_i}|\}$. $\boldsymbol{n}^u_{t_i,j}$ is the latent representation of the j-th item in basket $B^u_{t_i}$ and $|B^u_{t_i}|$ means the number of items in basket $B^u_{t_i}$. Now, we can generate the latent vector representation $\boldsymbol{b}^u_{t_i}$ for a basket $B^u_{t_i}$ by aggregating representation vectors of these items. In this work, we adopt two kinds of aggregation operation, i.e., *max pooling* and *average pooling*.

For the *max pooling* operation, we aggregate a group of vectors through taking the maximum value of every dimension among all those vectors. Then each dimension of $\boldsymbol{b}^u_{t_i}$ is formulated as

$$b^u_{t_i,k} = max\left(n^u_{t_i,1,k}, n^u_{t_i,2,k}, ...\right), \tag{1}$$

where $b^u_{t_i,k}$ is the k-th dimension of a basket-representing vector $\boldsymbol{b}^u_{t_i}$, $n^u_{t_i,j,k}$ means the value of k-th dimension of the vector representation of the j-th item $(\boldsymbol{n}^u_{t_i,j})$ in basket $B^u_{t_i}$.

The *average pooling* is a similar operation but replaces maximum with average. In other words, the *average pooling* is to aggregate a group of vectors through taking the average value of every dimension of all those vectors, which can be formulated in a similar way as

$$\boldsymbol{b}^u_{t_i} = \frac{1}{|B^u_{t_i}|} \sum\nolimits_{j=1}^{|B^u_{t_i}|} \boldsymbol{n}^u_{t_i,j}. \tag{2}$$

These above representations of baskets can form the input layer of a recurrent architecture.

As is shown in Figure 1, the vector representation of a hidden layer $\boldsymbol{h}^u_{t_i}$ is the dynamic representation of user u at time t_i. The recurrent connection weight matrix $\boldsymbol{R}$ helps to propagate sequential signals between every two adjacent hidden state $\boldsymbol{h}^u_{t_{i-1}}$ and $\boldsymbol{h}^u_{t_i}$ [10]. $\boldsymbol{X}$ is a transition matrix between latent vector representations of baskets and a user's interests. Then, the vector representation of the hidden layer can be computed as:

$$\boldsymbol{h}^u_{t_i} = f\left(\boldsymbol{X}\boldsymbol{b}^u_{t_i} + \boldsymbol{R}\boldsymbol{h}^u_{t_{i-1}}\right), \tag{3}$$

where $\boldsymbol{b}^u_{t_i}$ is a latent vector representation of the user's basket at time t_i, and $\boldsymbol{h}^u_{t_{i-1}}$ is the dynamic representation of the previous time t_{i-1}. $f(x)$ is a activation function, here we choose a *sigmoid* function $f(x) = \frac{1}{1+e^{-x}}$. Finally the model can output a user's scores $\boldsymbol{o}_{u,t_i}$ towards all items at time t_i. The output $\boldsymbol{o}_{u,t_i}$ can be calculated through multiplication of item matrix $\boldsymbol{N}$ and a user's dynamic representation $\boldsymbol{h}^u_{t_i}$, which is formulated as follows:

$$\boldsymbol{o}_{u,t_i} = \boldsymbol{N}^T \boldsymbol{h}^u_{t_i}. \tag{4}$$

Therefore $o_{u,t_i,v}$, i.e., an element of $\boldsymbol{o}_{u,t_i}$, represents the score of a transaction between a user u and an item v at time t_i. A higher score indicates that the user is more likely to purchase the corresponding item.

2.3 Objective Function

In the learning process of DREAM, we adopt Bayesian Personalized Ranking (BPR) [6]. BPR is a state-of-the-art pairwise ranking framework for the implicit feedback data. The basic assumption is that a user prefers an item in basket at a specific time than a negative item sample. The negative items can be any other items apart from those in the basket. In this way, we need to maximize the following probability:

$$p\left(u, t, v \succ v'\right) = \sigma\left(o_{u,t,v} - o_{u,t,v'}\right), \tag{5}$$

where v' denotes a negative item sample, and $\sigma(x)$ is a nonlinear function which is chosen as $\sigma(x) = \frac{1}{1+e^{-x}}$. Adding up all the log likelihood and the regularization term, the objective function can be written as follows:

$$J = \sum \ln\left(1 + e^{-\left(o_{u,t,v} - o_{u,t,v'}\right)}\right) + \frac{\lambda}{2}\|\Theta\|^2, \tag{6}$$

where $\Theta = \{\boldsymbol{N}, \boldsymbol{R}, \boldsymbol{X}\}$ denotes all the parameters to be learnt, λ is a parameter to control the power of regularization. Furthermore, the objective function can be optimized by Back Propagation Through Time (BPTT) [8]. BPTT is to iteratively repeat the calculation of derivations of J with respect to different parameters and obtain these gradients of all the parameters in the end. Then we update parameters utilizing Stochastic Gradient Descent (SGD) until converge.

Notice that the DREAM model utilize an iterative method in learning users' representation vectors. That is to say, for any new transactions, we can update users' representation vectors based current ones. Some state-of-the-art models, such as HRM, need to factorize a new built user-item matrix to get users' representation vectors. Therefore this iterative learning method may be more practical in real-world applications.

3. EXPERIMENTS

3.1 Datasets and Baselines

To evaluate the performance of our method on the task of next basket recommendation, we perform experiments on two real-world datasets, i.e., Ta-Feng[1] and T-mall[2]. The Ta-Feng dataset contains numerous baskets of purchased items from a grocery store, where each basket encapsulates the items purchased by one user in a period of time. This dataset is a public dataset which contains 817,741 transactions belonging to 32,266 users and 23,812 items. The T-mall dataset is a public online e-commerce dataset released by Alibaba group[3], which contains 4,298 transactions of 884 users and 9,531 brands. The slight difference between these two datasets is that the T-mall dataset records the transactions based on brands and each brand may covers a series of items. The above datasets are preprocessed to obtain k-*core* subsets [7], i.e. each user u purchased in total at least k items $\left(\sum_{t_i} \left|B^u_{t_i}\right| \geqslant k\right)$ and vice versa each item was purchased by at least k users. We set $k = 10$ for the Ta-Feng dataset, and $k = 3$ for the relatively smaller T-Mall dataset.

Several baseline and state-of-the-art methods on next-basket recommendation are used for empirical comparison. (1) **TOP** recommends the top popular items to each user. (2) **MC** is a Markov chain model based on sequential transaction information of a user. The prediction function is as follows:

$$p\left(i \in B^u_{t_i} | B^u_{t_{i-1}}\right) := \frac{1}{\left|B^u_{t_{i-1}}\right|} \sum_{j \in B^u_{t_{i-1}}} p\left(i \in B^u_{t_i} | j \in B^u_{t_{i-1}}\right)$$

(3) **NMF** is a collaborative filtering method, which applies Nonnegative Matrix Factorization over the user-item matrix. For implementation, we adopt the released codes from NMF: DTU Toolbox[4]. (4) **FPMC** [7] is a hybrid model combining MC and MF for next basket recommendation, which can capture both sequential effects and general interests of users. (5) **HRM** [9] is a state-of-the-art hierarchical representation model, which can capture general users' interests and sequential effects. Besides, with various nonlinear operations, HRM can capture all those factors more properly than previous models.

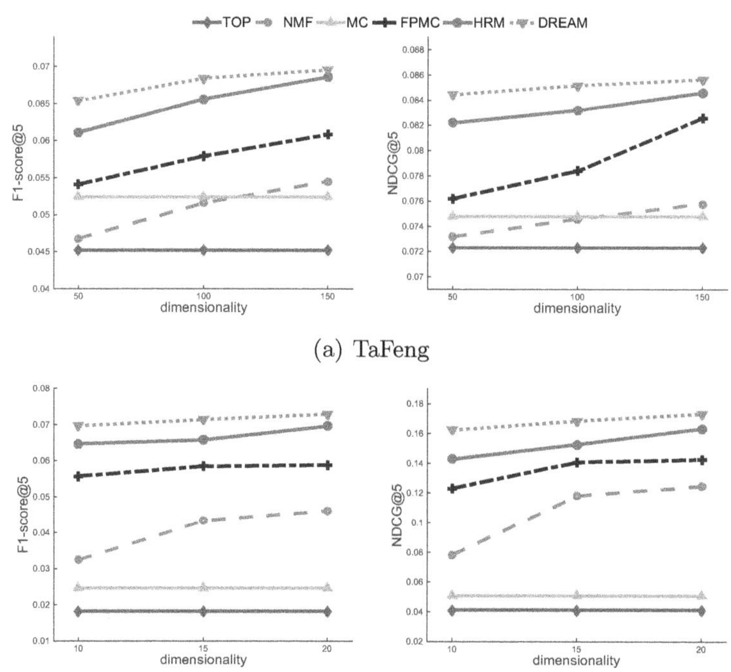

(a) TaFeng

(b) Tmall

Figure 2: Experiment Results of different methods on two datasets.

[1]http://recsyswiki.com/wiki/Grocery shopping datasets
[2]http://102.alibaba.com/competition/addDiscovery/index.htm
[3]http://www.alibabagroup.com/cn/global/home
[4]http://cogsys.imm.dtu.dk/toolbox/nmf/

Table 1: Performance comparison of two pooling operations on two datasets

Methods	Ta-Feng						Tmall					
	d=50		d=100		d=150		d=10		d=15		d=20	
	f1-score	NDCG	f1-score	NDCG	f1-score	NDCG	f1-score	NDCG	f1-score	NDCG	f1-score	NDCG
Avg-Pooling	0.061	0.082	0.064	0.081	0.067	0.083	0.058	0.141	0.063	0.154	0.066	0.160
Max-Pooling	**0.065**	**0.084**	**0.068**	**0.085**	**0.070**	**0.086**	**0.070**	**0.162**	**0.071**	**0.168**	**0.073**	**0.173**

3.2 Metrics and Setup

For recommendation, we generate a ranking list of K items ($K = 5$) for each user u. In order to measure the performance of next basket recommendation, we adopt two evaluation metrics, i.e., $F1$-*score* and Normalized Discounted Cumulative Gain ($NDCG$). $F1$-*score* calculates the harmonic mean of the precision and recall measurements. $NDCG$ is a cumulative measure of ranking quality, which is more sensitive to the relevance of higher ranked items. For both metrics, the larger the value, the better the performance.

On both datasets, we use the last transaction of each user as the testing data and all the rest transactions as the training data. The vector representations of items are randomly initialized. Moreover, performance results of different methods are compared along with varying dimensions d of the representation. We illustrate the results with dimensions $\{50, 100, 150\}$ for the Ta-Feng dataset, and $\{10, 15, 20\}$ for the relatively smaller T-Mall dataset.

3.3 Results and Analyses

First, the performance of DREAM model are compared with the state-of-the-art methods. As illustrated in Figure 2, in general, the performance ranking of next basket recommendation methods is as follows, DREAM, HRM, FPMC, NMF, MC and TOP. Since the baseline TOP just list the popular items and does not utilize the features of separate baskets, this method is the weakest one among all methods. Despite the fact that NMF and MC leverage only one kind of feature, either sequential behaviors or users' general interests, we can observe that the NMF model achieve better performance than that of the MC model, especially on the sparse T-mall data. It may be because that MC cannot reveal the collaborative information among users. On the sparse user-item matrix of T-mall, collaborative information is more important to generate the accurate interests of users than the sparse sequential behaviors. On both datasets, the HRM model outperforms the FPMC model. Though FPMC and HRM both utilize sequential behaviors, the nonlinear operations among multiple factors of HRM earn it a better performance, while the FPMC model's linear independence assumption of interaction relationship of items in a basket makes it inapplicable in complex commercial scenarios. The proposed DREAM model can consistently outperform all comparing models in terms of both metrics on two datasets. These results show that the dynamic representation of user with a recurrent architecture is effective in capturing sequential features and dynamic interests of users. Besides, richer nonlinear operations such as *pooling* and activation functions contribute to a better representations of baskets.

Then, we assess performances of the DREAM model with *max pooling* and *average pooling*. As illustrated in Table 1, DREAM with *max pooling* can outperform DREAM with *average pooling* on both datasets with $F1$-*score*@5 and $NDCG$@5. It demonstrates that *max pooling* gains advantage over *average pooling* in modeling interactions among multiple factors. Obviously, as a linear operation, *average pooling* takes an average representation of a basket, indicating that each item in a basket measures the basket representation in an independent way. In real-world scenario, many items we purchase are interactive, that is to say, one item influences whether we purchase another item, then the whole items we purchase can help shape our interests. Consequently a better solution is to learn the elaborate interaction relationship of a basket of items through a nonlinear operation. *Max pooling* is a nonlinear operation, which takes a key representation of a basket and is more capable to learn those complicated interactions than a linear operation.

4. CONCLUSIONS

In this paper, we have proposed a dynamic recurrent basket model based on RNN for next basket recommendation. Our model can merge users' current interests and global sequential features into users' recurrent and dynamic representation. Moreover, it shows that the nonlinear operation on learning the representation of a basket does well in capturing elaborate interactions among multiple factors of items. Extensive experiments on two public datasets demonstrated the effectiveness of the proposed model.

5. ACKNOWLEDGMENTS

This work is jointly supported by National Basic Research Program of China (2012CB316300), and National Natural Science Foundation of China (61403390, U1435221, 61525306).

6. REFERENCES

[1] G. Adomavicius and A. Tuzhilin. Toward the next generation of recommender systems: A survey of the state-of-the-art and possible extensions. *TKDE*, 17(6):734–749, 2005.

[2] S. Chen, J. L. Moore, D. Turnbull, and T. Joachims. Playlist prediction via metric embedding. In *SIGKDD*, pages 714–722, 2012.

[3] A. Gatzioura and M. Sanchez-Marre. A case-based recommendation approach for market basket data. *IEEE Intelligent Systems*, 30(1):20–27, 2015.

[4] Y. Koren, R. Bell, and C. Volinsky. Matrix factorization techniques for recommender systems. *IEEE Computer*, (8):30–37, 2009.

[5] T. Mikolov, S. Kombrink, L. Burget, J. H. Černocký, and S. Khudanpur. Extensions of recurrent neural network language model. In *ICASSP*, pages 5528–5531, 2011.

[6] S. Rendle, C. Freudenthaler, Z. Gantner, and L. Schmidt-Thieme. Bpr: Bayesian personalized ranking from implicit feedback. In *UAI*, pages 452–461, 2009.

[7] S. Rendle, C. Freudenthaler, and L. Schmidt-Thieme. Factorizing personalized markov chains for next-basket recommendation. In *WWW*, pages 811–820, 2010.

[8] D. E. Rumelhart, G. E. Hinton, and R. J. Williams. Learning representations by back-propagating errors. *Cognitive modeling*, 5:3, 1988.

[9] P. Wang, J. Guo, Y. Lan, J. Xu, S. Wan, and X. Cheng. Learning hierarchical representation model for nextbasket recommendation. In *SIGIR*, pages 403–412, 2015.

[10] Y. Zhang, H. Dai, C. Xu, J. Feng, T. Wang, J. Bian, B. Wang, and T.-Y. Liu. Sequential click prediction for sponsored search with recurrent neural networks. In *AAAI*, pages 1369–1376, 2014.

A Simple Enhancement for Ad-hoc Information Retrieval via Topic Modelling

Fanghong Jian[1], Jimmy Xiangji Huang, Jiashu Zhao[2], Tingting He[3] and Po Hu[3]
Information Retrieval and Knowledge Management Research Lab
[1]National Engineering Research Center for E-Learning, [3]School of Computer Science, Central China Normal University, Wuhan, China; [2]School of Information Technology, York University, Toronto, Canada
jhuang@yorku.ca, jfhrecoba@mails.ccnu.edu.cn, jessie@cse.yorku.ca

ABSTRACT

Traditional information retrieval (IR) models, in which a document is normally represented as a bag of words and their frequencies, capture the term-level and document-level information. Topic models, on the other hand, discover semantic topic-based information among words. In this paper, we consider term-based information and semantic information as two features of query terms and propose a simple enhancement for ad-hoc IR via topic modeling. In particular, three topic-based hybrid models, LDA-BM25, LDA-MATF and LDA-LM, are proposed. A series of experiments on eight standard datasets show that our proposed models can always outperform significantly the corresponding strong baselines over all datasets in terms of MAP and most of datasets in terms of P@5 and P@20. A direct comparison on eight standard datasets also indicates our proposed models are at least comparable to the state-of-the-art approaches.

Keywords

Probabilistic Model; Dirichlet Language Model; LDA

1. INTRODUCTION

Many traditional IR models are based on the assumption that query terms are independent of each other, where a document is represented as a bag of words. Nevertheless this assumption may not hold in practice. Each document may contain several different topics and terms appeared in the document might belong to different topics, which represent different semantic information. Many researchers have been working on term topic information in IR [1, 10, 15, 16]. However, the nature of the associations among query terms still awaits further study. Some cluster-based approaches consider each document has only one topic [10], which is not reasonable to model large collection of documents. Topic-based document representation is effective in the language modeling (LM) framework [1, 15, 16]. But there is no generality in BM25 [2, 6, 20] and MATF (Multi Aspect TF) [13] based frameworks.

In this paper, we present three hybrid models for enhancing traditional IR model via topic modelling. In our proposed approach, term-based information and semantic information are considered as two features of query terms. Latent Dirichlet Allocation (LDA) [3] is utilized to combine these two features and enhance three well-known traditional IR models BM25 [2], MATF [13] and Dirichlet LM [18]. In particular, three hybrid models, denoted as LDA-BM25, LDA-MATF and LDA-LM, are proposed respectively. The main contributions of this paper are as follows. First we propose three simple but effective IR models by combining traditional IR models with topic model. Second we conduct extensive experiments to confirm the effectiveness of our proposed models.

The remainder of this paper is organized as follows. We describe the related work and propose three topic-based hybrid models for ad-hoc IR in Section 2 and 3 respectively. In Section 4, we set up our experimental environment on eight TREC collections. In Section 5, the experimental results are presented and discussed. Finally, we conclude our work briefly and present future research directions in Section 6.

2. RELATED WORK

Since the 1990s, researchers started to investigate how to integrate term association into IR models [8, 12, 16, 19, 20]. The query-term associations have been modeled by different approaches according to the distance of the query terms in documents. For example, Buttcher et al. (2006) [4] used a proximity accumulator to associate each query term. Lv and Zhai (2009) [11] proposed a positional language model (PLM) that incorporated the term proximity in a model-based approach using term-propagation functions. Metzler et al. (2005) [12] proposed a Markov Random Fields (MRF) model which modeled the joint distribution over queries and documents. Song et al. (2011) [14] proposed Proximity Probabilistic Model (PPM) which used a position-dependent term count to represent both the number of occurrences of a term and the term counts propagated from other terms. Recently, topic models have been widely used to explore latent term association in knowledge discovery and other related area. Liu and Croft (2004) [10] proposed cluster-based retrieval models under the language modeling framework, which were used to smooth the probabilities in the document model. In their approach, a document is supposed to contain only one topic, which is not reasonable to model large collection of documents. Azzopardi et al. (2004) [1] showed that it was effective to use the LDA model [3] to smooth the probabilities in the document model on several small collections. Wei and Croft (2006) [15] also discussed the applications of LDA in large collections, and presented a detailed evalua-

SIGIR '16, July 17-21, 2016, Pisa, Italy
© 2016 ACM. ISBN 978-1-4503-4069-4/16/07...$15.00
DOI: http://dx.doi.org/10.1145/2911451.2914750

tion of the effectiveness. Yi and Allan (2009) [17] explored the utility of Mixture of Unigrams (MU) model, LDA and Pachinko Allocation Model (PAM) [9] for IR. They showed that topic models were effective for document smoothing. More rigorous topic models like LDA provided gains over cluster-based models and more elaborate topic models that capture topic dependencies provided no additional gains. Although it is effective to integrate topic models into the language modeling framework, how to integrate topical information into other traditional IR models is not clear.

3. OUR APPROACH

For enhancing performance, topic model is integrated into traditional retrieval models. First, the latent semantic information of query terms in a document is extracted via topic modeling. Then, the term-based information is obtained through traditional retrieval models. The documents that are more related to the query according to both semantic topic-based information and term-based information are boosted in the ranking process. For clarification, Table 1 outlines the notations used throughout the paper.

Table 1: Notations

Notations	Description
c	collection
d	document
q	query
q_i	query term
dl	length of document
$avdl$	average document length
N	number of indexed documents in collection
n	number of indexed documents containing a term
tf	within-document term frequency
qtf	within-query term frequency
z	topic
K_t	number of topics
p, p_{ml}	probability function
w', w'', w	weighting function
b, k_1, k_3	parameter in BM25
μ	Dirichlet prior in Dirichlet LM
α, β	hyperparameter in LDA

3.1 Topic-based Hybrid Model

Traditional retrieval models only capture term-based information. On the other hand, topic models acquire semantic information between words. In this paper, we propose enhanced retrieval models that consider not only term frequency, document frequency and document length, but also term topics information. We treat term-based information and semantic topic-based information as two features for query terms. The enhanced retrieval models combine these two features.

Given a query q, for each term q_i in query q, $w(q_i, d)$ is the enhanced weight for document d. In order to capture the two kinds of information, we use a parameter λ to balance their importance. So the weight of a query term for a document is as follows.

$$w(q_i, d) = (1 - \lambda) \cdot w''(q_i, d) + \lambda \cdot w'(q_i, d) \qquad (1)$$

where $w''(q_i, d)$ represents the explicit term-based related information in traditional retrieval model for document d, $w'(q_i, d)$ is the implicit semantic information in topic model. Finally, a document's weight for a query is given by the sum of its weight for each term in the query. When λ equals to 0, the hybrid models become traditional IR models such as BM25 and LM. When λ equals to 1, the hybrid models become topic models. Because traditional IR models and topic models are normalized independently, the value of λ changes with different combinations. It is well known that BM25, MATF and Dirichlet LM are the state-of-the-art traditional IR models and LDA is a simple but effective topic model. Therefore, we use BM25, MATF and Dirichlet LM as the traditional models and we use LDA as the topic model.

3.2 Topic Model

In general, topic model is used to capture latent semantic information of terms in document. There are a lot of topic models, such as probabilistic Latent Semantic Indexing (pLSI) [7], LDA [3] and PAM [9]. LDA is a simple and effective topic model, and is broadly used. In this paper, we use LDA as our topic model.

LDA model can generate the probability of topics in a document and the probability of words in a topic, which can obtain the generated probability of words in a document. We take the probability of a query term in a document as its implicit semantic information in the document. The probability is larger, the term is more related with the document. In order to be the same magnitude with weights in traditional models, the weight of a query term for a document in LDA uses log value of the generated probability as follows.

$$w'(q_i, d) = \log p(q_i|d) = \log \left(\sum_{z=1}^{K_t} p(q_i|z) p(z|d) \right) \qquad (2)$$

The LDA model can not be solved by exact inference and use Gibbs Sampling for parameter estimation like in [5].

3.3 Traditional Information Retrieval Models

Traditional information retrieval models are mainly classified into classic probabilistic model, vector space model and statistical language model. There are several well-known strong baselines in each class, considering BM25, MATF and Dirichlet LM respectively.

In BM25, the weight of a query term is related to its within-document term frequency and query term frequency. The corresponding weighting function is as follows.

$$w''(q_i, d) = \frac{(k_1 + 1) * tf}{K + tf} * \log \frac{(N - n + 0.5)}{(n - 0.5)} * \frac{(k_3 + 1) * qtf}{k_3 + qtf} \qquad (3)$$

where w'' is the weight of a query term, the k_is are tuning constants and K equals to $k_1 * ((1 - b) + b * dl/avdl)$.

In 2013, Jiaul H. Paik [13] proposed a novel TF-IDF term weighting scheme MATF that employed two different within document term frequency normalizations to capture two different aspects of term saliency. One component of the term frequency is effective for short queries, while the other performs better on long queries. The final weight is measured by taking a weighted combination of these components, which is determined on the basis of the length of the corresponding query. Experiments carried out on a set of news and web datasets show that MATF outperforms several well-known state-of-the-art TF-IDF baselines with significantly large margin.

Dirichlet LM presented by Zhai and Lafferty in 2001 [18] used the likelihood probability of query terms in a document to rank relevance between query and document. In order to better computing, the weight of a query term uses the log value of the probability as follows.

$$w''(q_i, d) = \log p(q_i|d) = \log \left(\frac{dl}{dl + \mu} p_{ml}(q_i|d) + \frac{\mu}{dl + \mu} p_{ml}(q_i|c) \right) \qquad (4)$$

4. EXPERIMENTAL SETTING

We conduct experiments on eight standard collections, which include AP88-89 with queries 51-100, AP88-90 with queries 51-150, FBIS with queries 351-450, FT(91-94) with queries 301-400, LA with queries 301-400, SJMN(1991) with queries 51-150, WSJ(87-92) with queries 151-200 and WT2G with queries 401-450. These datasets are different in size and genre [15, 19]. Queries without judgments are removed.

	Eval Metric	AP88-89	AP88-90	FBIS	FT	LA	SJMN	WSJ	WT2G
BM25	MAP	0.2710	0.2198	0.2606	0.2600	0.2490	0.1965	0.3156	0.3156
	P@5	0.4360	0.4566	**0.3735**	0.3726	0.3571	0.3404	0.5240	0.5280
	P@20	0.3860	0.3894	0.2685	0.2389	0.2194	0.2564	0.4410	0.3930
LDA-BM25	MAP	0.3021* (+11.476%)	**0.2617*** (+19.064%)	**0.2661** (+2.111%)	0.2769* (+6.500%)	0.2592* (+4.96%)	0.2297* (+16.902%)	**0.3471*** (+9.981%)	0.3230 (+2.345%)
	P@5	0.5020 (+15.138%)	**0.5232*** (+14.595%)	0.3679 (-1.499%)	0.3621 (-2.818%)	0.3673 (+2.856%)	0.3809 (+11.889%)	**0.5520** (+5.344%)	**0.5360** (+1.515%)
	P@20	**0.4388*** (+13.679%)	**0.4505*** (+15.693%)	0.2691 (+0.223%)	0.2416 (+1.130%)	0.2291* (+5.105%)	0.2915 (+13.697%)	**0.4640*** (+5.215%)	0.4030 (+2.545%)
MATF	MAP	0.2771	0.2238	0.2553	0.2660	0.2502	0.2095	0.3029	0.3340
	P@5	0.4531	0.4707	0.3605	**0.3789**	0.3571	0.3723	0.5240	0.5240
	P@20	0.3980	0.4086	0.2673	0.2426	0.2240	0.2809	0.3950	0.4110
LDA-MATF	MAP	**0.3041*** (+9.744%)	**0.2617*** (+16.935%)	0.2634* (+3.173%)	**0.2781*** (+4.549%)	0.2586* (+3.357%)	**0.2309*** (+10.215%)	0.3343* (+10.366%)	**0.3393** (+1.587%)
	P@5	0.4898 (+8.100%)	0.5131 (+9.008%)	0.3580 (-0.693%)	0.3621 (-4.434%)	**0.3694** (+3.444%)	**0.3915** (+5.157%)	0.5200 (-0.763%)	**0.5360** (+2.290%)
	P@20	0.4378* (+10.000%)	0.4465* (+9.276%)	**0.2784** (+4.153%)	**0.2453** (+1.113%)	**0.2337*** (+4.330%)	**0.2989** (+6.408%)	0.4300* (+8.861%)	**0.4150** (+0.973%)
LM	MAP	0.2672	0.2157	0.2525	0.2571	0.2427	0.2009	0.3047	0.3118
	P@5	0.4571	0.4465	0.3506	0.3684	0.3429	0.3532	0.5120	0.5000
	P@20	0.4041	0.4146	0.2500	0.2311	0.2235	0.2697	0.3910	0.3920
LDA-LM	MAP	0.2980* (+11.527%)	0.2560* (+18.683%)	0.2628* (+4.079%)	0.2774* (+7.896%)	**0.2603*** (+7.252%)	0.2254* (+12.195%)	0.3344* (+9.747%)	0.3165* (+1.507%)
	P@5	**0.5102*** (+11.617%)	0.5010* (+12.206%)	0.3630 (+3.537%)	0.3600 (-2.280%)	**0.3694*** (+7.728%)	0.3830* (+8.437%)	0.5200 (+1.563%)	0.5080 (+1.600%)
	P@20	0.4276* (+5.815%)	0.4414* (+6.464%)	0.2599* (+3.960%)	0.2426* (+4.976%)	0.2286 (+2.282%)	0.2904* (+7.675%)	0.4320* (+10.486%)	0.3950 (+0.765%)

Table 2: Comparison with baselines. The best result obtained on each dataset is in bold. "*" denotes statistically significant improvements over corresponding baselines (Wilcoxon signed-rank test with $p < 0.05$). The percentages below are the percentage improvement of proposed models over corresponding baselines.

For all test collections used, each term is stemmed by using Porter's English stemmer. Standard English stopwords are removed. The official TREC evaluation measure is used in our experiments, namely Mean Average Precision (MAP). To investigate top retrieved documents, P@5 and P@20 are also used for evaluation. All statistical tests are based on Wilcoxon Matched-pairs Signed-rank test.

For fair comparisons, we use the following parameter settings for both the baselines and our proposed models, which are popular in the IR domain for building strong baselines. First, in BM25, setting k_1, k_3 and b to 1.2, 8 and 0.35 respectively gave the best MAP for most datasets in [20]. Second, in Dirichlet LM, $\mu = 1000$ was shown in [15] to achieve best MAP for most datasets. Finally, in LDA model, we use symmetric Dirichlet priors with $\alpha = 50/K_t$ and $\beta = 0.01$, which are common settings in the literature and shown in [15] that retrieval results were not very sensitive to the values of these parameters. The number of topics K_t is set to be 400 as recommended in [15].

5. EXPERIMENTAL RESULTS

5.1 Comparison with Baselines

We first investigate the performance of our proposed topic-based models compared with the corresponding strong baselines BM25, MATF and Dirichlet LM. The experimental results are presented in Table 2. As shown by the results, our proposed models outperform the corresponding baselines on almost all datasets in terms of MAP, P@5 and P@20. Statistically significant improvement can be observed on most of datasets in terms of MAP and P@20. According to the results in Table 2, each hybrid model has its advantage on some aspects. However, there is no single hybird model that can achieve the best performance on all the datasets.

5.2 Parameter Sensitivity

An important issue that may affect the robustness of our proposed models is the sensitivity of their parameter λ to retrieval performance. Since the weights of query terms in traditional retrieval models and topic model are normalized independently, the value of λ reflects the influence of using topic-based model. Figure 1 plots the evaluation metrics MAP obtained by the proposed hybrid models over λ values ranging from 0 to 1 on all the datasets. It is clear that hybrid models perform better than either traditional models or topic model on all data sets. As we can see from Figure 1, our proposed models LDA-BM25, LDA-MATF and LDA-LM generally perform well over different datasets when λ has a smaller value.

We also study the performance of our proposed topic-based models with different number of topics compared with the corresponding baselines in terms of MAP. In Figure 2, the traditional models are shown as straight lines since the performance does not change over the number of topics. All the results are presented in Figure 2, which shows that our proposed models with different number of topics outperform corresponding baselines in terms of MAP over all datasets. Figure 2 shows that the proposed hybrid models tend to perform better when the number of topics increases. When the number of topics reaches a certain value, the retrieval performance tends to become more stable. The performance tendency of our proposed models with different number of topics is surprisingly consistent on all the datasets. Similar trends for λ and with different number of topics can also be observed in terms of P@5 and P@20.

5.3 Comparison with CRTER2 and LBDM

In addition, we compare our proposed models with two state-of-the-art approaches. Zhao etc. [19, 20] showed that bigram cross term model (CRTER2) is at least comparable to major probabilistic proximity models PPM [14] and BM25TP [4] in BM25-based framework. Xing and Allan [17], which is most close to our proposed model LDA-LM, showed their LDA-based model (LBDM) [15] achieved the best performance in topic-based LM framework. So we make a direct comparison with CRTER2 and LBDM. The results in terms of MAP are presented in Table 3. "↑" denotes LDA-BM25 outperforms CRTER2, while "⇑" denotes LDA-LM outperforms LBDM. Among eight datasets, LDA-BM25 wins five times and LDA-LM wins four times. By comparison, we can conclude that our proposed models LDA-BM25 and LDA-LM are at least comparable to the state-of-the-art models CRTER2 and LBDM.

Table 3: Comparison with CRTER2 and LBDM

	CRTER2	LDA-BM25	LBDM	LDA-LM
AP88-89	0.2789	0.3021↑	0.3051	0.2980
AP88-90	0.2268	0.2617↑	0.2535	0.2560⇑
FBIS	0.2738	0.2661	0.2636	0.2628
FT	0.2717	0.2769↑	0.2750	0.2774⇑
LA	0.2604	0.2592	0.2630	0.2603
SJMN	0.2095	0.2297↑	0.2234	0.2254⇑
WSJ	0.3406	0.3471↑	0.3359	0.3344
WT2G	0.3359	0.3230	0.3108	0.3165⇑

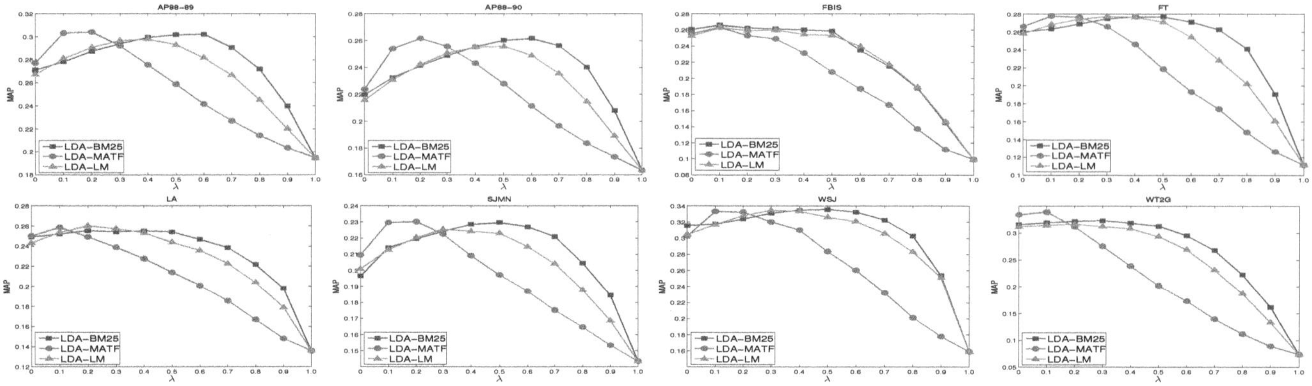

Figure 1: Parameter sensitivity of λ on all data sets

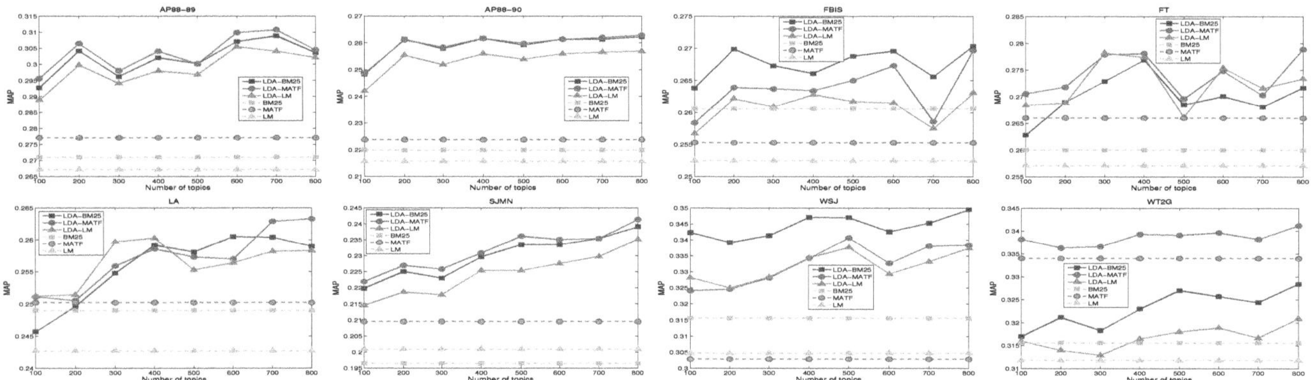

Figure 2: Parameter sensitivity of the number of topics on all data sets

6. CONCLUSIONS AND FUTURE WORK

In this paper, a simple enhancement for ad-hoc IR is proposed by combining traditional retrieval model and topic model. Specifically, we present three hybrid models LDA-BM25, LDA-MATF and LDA-LM for enhancing traditional IR models via topic modeling. These three models capture both term-based information and latent semantic topic-based information at the same time. Experimental results on eight standard datasets show that the proposed models are effective, and outperform the corresponding strong baselines on most of datasets in terms of MAP, P@5 and P@20. Meanwhile, our proposed models are at least comparable to the state-of-the-art `CRTER2` and topic-based model `LBDM`. Additionally, we carefully analyze the influence of λ to our proposed models and the performance of our proposed models with different number of topics.

There are several interesting future research directions to further explore. We would like to study the optimal topic number on each dataset. It is also interesting to conduct an in-depth study on the combination traditional IR model with topic model and find the best combination. We also plan to evaluate our models on more datasets including some real datasets and apply our models into real world applications.

7. ACKNOWLEDGMENTS

This research is supported by a Discovery grant from the Natural Sciences & Engineering Research Council (NSERC) of Canada, an NSERC CREATE award and also supported by the National Natural Science Foundation of China. We thank anonymous reviewers for their thorough comments.

8. REFERENCES

[1] L. Azzopardi, M. Girolami, and C. J. Van Rijsbergen. Topic Based Language Models for ad hoc Information Retrieval. In *Proceedings of the International Joint Conference on Neural Networks*, pages 3281–3286, 2004.

[2] M. Beaulieu, M. Gatford, X. Huang, S. Robertson, S. Walker, and P. Williams. Okapi at TREC-5. In *Proc. of TREC*, pages 143–166, 1996.

[3] D. M. Blei, A. Y. Ng, and M. I. Jordan. Latent Dirichlet Allocation. *Journal of Machine Learning Research*, 3:993–1022, 2003.

[4] S. Buttcher, C. L. A. Clarke, and B. Lushman. Term Proximity Scoring for Ad-hoc Retrieval on Very Large Text Collections. In *Proceedings of the 29th ACM SIGIR*, pages 621 – 622, 2006.

[5] T. L. Griffiths and M. Steyvers. Finding Scientific Topics. In *Proceeding of the National Academy of Sciences*, pages 5228–5235, 2004.

[6] B. He, J. X. Huang, and X. Zhou. Modeling term proximity for probabilistic information retrieval models. *Information Sciences*, 181(14):3017–3031, 2011.

[7] T. Hofmann. Probabilistic Latent Semantic Indexing. In *Proceedings of the 22nd ACM SIGIR*, pages 50–57, 1999.

[8] Q. Hu, J. X. Huang, and X. Hu. Modeling and Mining Term Association for Improving Biomedical Information Retrieval Performance. *BMC Bioinformatics*, 13(2):18 pages, 2012.

[9] W. Li and A. McCallum. Pachinko Allocation: DAG-Structured Mixture Models of Topic Correlations. In *Proc. of ICML*, pages 577–584, 2006.

[10] X. Liu and W. B. Croft. Cluster-Based Retrieval Using Language Models. In *Proceedings of the 27th ACM SIGIR*, pages 186–193, 2004.

[11] Y. Lv and C. Zhai. Positional Language Models for Information Retrieval. In *Proceedings of the 32nd ACM SIGIR*, pages 299–306, 2009.

[12] D. Metzler and W. B. Croft. A Markov Random Field Model for Term Dependencies. In *Proceedings of the 28th ACM SIGIR*, pages 472–479, 2005.

[13] J. H. Paik. A Novel TF-IDF Weighting Scheme for Effective Ranking. In *Proc. of the 36th ACM SIGIR*, pages 343–352, 2013.

[14] R. Song, L. Yu, J. R. Wen, and H. W. Hon. A Proximity Probabilistic Model for Information Retrieval. *Tech. Rep., Microsoft Research*, 2011.

[15] X. Wei and W. B. Croft. LDA-Based Document Models for Ad-hoc Retrieval. In *Proc. of the 29th ACM SIGIR*, pages 178–185, 2006.

[16] X. Wei and W. B. Croft. Modeling Term Associations for Ad-Hoc Retrieval Performance within Language Modeling Framework. In *Proceedings of the 29th European Conference on IR research*, pages 52–63, 2007.

[17] X. Yi and J. Allan. A Comparative Study of Utilizing Topic Models for Information Retrieval. In *Proceedings of the 31st European Conference on IR Research on Advances in Information Retrieval (ECIR'09)*, pages 29–41, 2009.

[18] C. Zhai and J. Lafferty. A Study of Smoothing Methods for Language Models Applied to Information Retrieval. *ACM TOIS*, 22(2):179–214, 2004.

[19] J. Zhao, J. X. Huang, and B. He. CRTER: Using Cross Terms to Enhance Probabilistic IR. In *Proc. of the 34th ACM SIGIR*, pages 155–164, 2011.

[20] J. Zhao, J. X. Huang, and Z. Ye. Modeling Term Associations for Probabilistic Information Retrieval. *ACM Trans. Inf. Syst.*, 32(2):1–47, 2014.

An Empirical Study of Learning to Rank for Entity Search

Jing Chen
Language Technologies Institute
Carnegie Mellon University
Pittsburgh, PA 15213, USA
jingc1@cs.cmu.edu

Chenyan Xiong
Language Technologies Institute
Carnegie Mellon University
Pittsburgh, PA 15213, USA
cx@cs.cmu.edu

Jamie Callan
Language Technologies Institute
Carnegie Mellon University
Pittsburgh, PA 15213, USA
callan@cs.cmu.edu

ABSTRACT

This work investigates the effectiveness of learning to rank methods for entity search. Entities are represented by multi-field documents constructed from their RDF triples, and field-based text similarity features are extracted for query-entity pairs. State-of-the-art learning to rank methods learn models for ad-hoc entity search. Our experiments on an entity search test collection based on DBpedia confirm that learning to rank methods are as powerful for ranking entities as for ranking documents, and establish a new state-of-the-art for accuracy on this benchmark dataset.

Keywords

Entity Search, Learning to rank, Knowledge Base, DBpedia

1. INTRODUCTION

Publicly available knowledge bases such as DBpedia, Freebase, and Wikipedia are beginning to be used for tasks such as document ranking, card retrieval, and question answering [3, 4, 5]. A key component in many such systems is ad-hoc entity retrieval - using a query to retrieve one or more entities that satisfy some underlying information need. Several methods of representing and ranking entities have been developed recently, however the problem is far from solved.

Recent knowledge bases store information in RDF triples. A triple is a piece of information about the entity, for example its name, alias, category, description or relationship to another entity. Some prior research represents each entity as a structured document by grouping RDF triples into fields [1, 6] or a tree [2]. This allows entities to be retrieved by typical document retrieval algorithms such as BM25, query likelihood, or sequential dependency models.

This work investigates the effectiveness of learning to rank (LeToR) models, the state-of-the-art in ranking documents, for entity search. It represents entities following the previous state-of-the-art's multi-field representations [6], extracts text similarity features for query-entity pairs, and studies the effectiveness of state-of-the-art learning to rank models for ranking entities. Experimental results on an entity search test collection based on DBpedia [1] confirm that learning to rank is as powerful for entity ranking as for document ranking, and significantly improves the previous state-of-the-art. Results also indicate that learning to rank models with text similarity features are especially effective on keyword queries.

Our analysis further shows the influence of query types on learning to rank models. Different types of queries use different parts of an entity's representation. It is more effective to learn different models for different types of queries than to use a single model for all types of queries.

2. LEARNING TO RANK ENTITIES

The first question in entity search is how to represent entities. We follow Zhiltsov et al. [6] and group RDF triples into five fields: `Name`, which contains the entity's names; `Cat`, which contains its categories; `Attr`, which contains all attributes except name; `RelEn`, which includes the names of its neighbor entities; and `SimEn`, which contains its aliases. We include all the RDF triples in DBpedia in the fields.

In state-of-the-art learning to rank systems for document ranking, most features are the scores of common unsupervised ranking algorithms applied to different document representations (fields). The different ranking algorithms and representations provide different views of the relevance of the document to the query. The multiple perspectives represented by these features are the backbone of any learning to rank system.

This approach can be applied to entity search by extracting features for query-entity pairs. We use the following ranking algorithms on each of an entity's five fields: `Language model` with Dirichlet smoothing ($\mu = 2500$), `BM25` (default parameters), `coordinate match`, `cosine similarity`, and `sequential dependency model (SDM)`. We also include Zhiltsov et al's. [6] `fielded sequential dependency model (FSDM)` score for the full document as a feature. As a result, there are in total 26 features as listed in Table 2.

With features extracted for all query-entity pairs, all learning to rank models developed for ranking documents can be used to rank entities. We use two widely-used LeToR models: `RankSVM`, which is a SVM-based pairwise method, and `Coordinate Accent`, which is a gradient-based listwise method that directly optimizes mean average precision (MAP). Both of these LeToR algorithms are robust and effective on a variety of datasets.

SIGIR '16, July 17 - 21, 2016, Pisa, Italy

ISBN 978-1-4503-4069-4/16/07...$15.00

DOI: http://dx.doi.org/10.1145/2911451.2914725

Table 1: Query sets used in experiments.

Query Set	Queries	Search Task
SemSearch ES	130	Retrieve one entity
ListSearch	115	Retrieve a list of entities
INEX-LD	100	Mixed keyword queries
QALD-2	140	Natural language questions

Table 2: Query-entity features used in learning to rank.

Features	Dimension
FSDM	1
SDM on all fields	5
BM25 on all fields	5
Language model on all fields	5
Coordinate match on all fields	5
Cosine similarity on all fields	5

3. EXPERIMENTAL METHODOLOGY

This section describes our experiment methodology in studying the effectiveness of learning to rank in entity search.

Dataset: Our experiments are conducted on the entity search test collection provided by Balog and Neumayer [1], which others also have used for research on entity retrieval [2, 6]. The dataset has 485 queries with relevance judgments on entities from DBpedia version 3.7. These queries come from seven previous competitions and are merged into four groups based on their search tasks [6]. Table 1 lists the four query groups used in our experiments.

Base Retrieval Model: We use the `fielded sequential dependency model` (FSDM) as the base retrieval model to enable direct comparison with prior work [6]. All learning to rank methods are used to rerank the top 100 entities per query retrieved by FSDM.

Ranking Models: RankSVM implementation is provided by SVMLight toolkit[1]. `Coordinate Ascent` implementation is provided by RankLib[2]. Both methods are trained and tested using five fold cross validation. We use linear kernel in RankSVM. For each fold, hyper-parameters are selected by another five fold cross validation on the *training* partitions only. The 'c' of RankSVM is selected from the range $1-100$ using a step size of 1. The number of random restarts and iterations of `Coordinate Ascent` are selected from the ranges $1-10$ and $10-50$ respectively using a step size of 1.

Baselines: The main baseline is FSDM, the previous state-of-the-art for the benchmark [6]. We also include SDM-CA and MLM-CA [6] results as they perform well in the test collection.

Evaluation Metrics: All methods are evaluated by MAP@100, P@10 and P@20 following previous work [6]. We also report NDCG@20. Statistical significance tests are performed by Fisher Randomization (permutation) tests with $p < 0.05$.

4. EVALUATION RESULTS

We first present experimental results for learning to rank on entity search. Then we provide analysis of the importance of features and fields, and the influence of different query types on LeToR models.

[1]https://www.cs.cornell.edu/people/tj/svm_light/svm_rank.html

[2]http://sourceforge.net/p/lemur/wiki/RankLib/

4.1 Overall Performance

The ranking performances of learning to rank models are listed in Table 3a. We present results separately for each query group and also combine the query groups together, shown in the `All` section of Table 3a. Relative performances over FSDM are shown in parenthesis. †, ‡, § indicate statistical significance over SDM-CA, MLM-CA, and FSDM respectively. The best performing method for each metric is marked **bold**. Win/Tie/Loss are the number of queries improved, unchanged and hurt, also compared with FSDM.

The results demonstrate the power of learning to rank for entity search. On all query sets and all evaluation metrics, both learning methods outperform FSDM, defining a new state-of-the-art in entity search. The overall improvements on all queries can be as large as 8%. On `SemSearch ES`, `ListSearch` and `INEX-LD`, where the queries are keyword queries like 'Charles Darwin', LeToR methods show significant improvements over FSDM. However, on QALD-2, whose queries are questions such as 'Who created Wikipedia', simple text similarity features are not as strong.

Similar trends are also found in individual query performances. Figure 1 compares the best learning method, RankSVM, with FSDM at each query. The x-axis lists all queries, ordered by relative performance. The y-axis is the relative performance of RankSVM over FSDM on NDCG@20. On keyword queries more than half of the queries are improved while only about a quarter of the queries are hurt. On questions (QALD-2), about the same number of queries are improved and hurt. A more effective method of handling natural question queries was developed recently by Lu et al. in which queries are parsed using question-answering techniques [2]. That method achieves 0.25 in P@10, but performs worse than FSDM on keyword queries. Section 4.3 further studies the influence of query types on entity-ranking accuracy.

4.2 Field and Feature Study

The second experiment studies the contribution of fields and feature groups to learning to rank models. For each field or feature group, we compare the accuracy of models when used without field or features from that group to those with all features. The change in accuracy indicates the contribution of the corresponding field or feature group. The field and feature studies for RankSVM are shown in Figures 2a and 2b respectively. The x-axis is the field or feature group studied. The y-axis is the performance difference between the two conditions (All versus held out). Larger values indicate greater contributions. Figure 2a organizes features by the fields they are extracted from, including Name, Cat, Attr, RelEn, and SimEn. Figure 2b organizes features into five groups, with one retrieval model per group. `SDM related` contains FSDM and SDM scores as they are very correlated.

Figure 2a shows that RankSVM favors different fields for different query sets. The Name field is useful for `ListSearch` and QALD-2, but does not contribute much to the other two query sets. RelEn provides the most gain to keyword queries, but is not useful at all for the natural language question queries in QALD-2. For feature groups we find that `SDM related` features are extremely important and provide the most gains across all query sets. This result is expected because all of the queries are relatively long queries and often contain phrases, which is where SDM is the most useful.

Table 3: Accuracy of learning to rank methods on entity search. Relative improvements over FSDM are shown in parentheses. Win/Tie/Loss show the number of queries improved, unchanged and hurt, comparing with FSDM. $\dagger, \ddagger, \S$ indicate statistical significance over SDM-CA, MLM-CA, and FSDM respectively. The best method for each metric is marked **bold**.

(a) Overall accuracy on each query group. All section combines the evaluation results of the other four sections.

	MAP@100	P@10	P@20	NDCG@20	Win/Tie/Loss
	SemSearch ES				
SDM-CA	0.254 (-34.2%)	0.202 (-29.3%)	0.148 (-27.0%)	0.355 (-29.5%)	26/15/89
MLM-CA	0.320† (-17.1%)	0.250† (-12.6%)	0.178† (-12.3%)	0.443† (-12.0%)	30/32/68
FSDM	0.386†‡ -	0.286†‡ -	0.203†‡ -	0.503†‡ -	-
RankSVM	**0.410**†‡§ (+6.3%)	**0.304**†‡§ (+6.2%)	**0.213**†‡§ (+4.5%)	**0.527**†‡§ (+4.7%)	65/27/38
Coordinate Ascent	0.396†‡ (+2.6%)	0.295†‡ (+3.2%)	0.206†‡ (+1.1%)	0.511†‡ (+1.5%)	48/32/50
	ListSearch				
SDM-CA	0.197 (-3.0%)	0.252 (-1.4%)	0.202 (-0.6%)	0.296 (+1.7%)	55/23/37
MLM-CA	0.190 (-6.6%)	0.252 (-1.4%)	0.192 (-5.3%)	0.275 (-5.3%)	39/28/48
FSDM	0.203 -	0.256 -	0.203 -	0.291 -	-
RankSVM	0.224†‡§ (+10.3%)	**0.303**†‡§ (+18.7%)	**0.235**†‡§ (+15.9%)	**0.332**†‡§ (+14.3%)	61/23/31
Coordinate Ascent	**0.225**†‡§ (+10.5%)	0.300†‡§ (+17.3%)	0.229†‡§ (+12.9%)	0.328†‡§ (+12.9%)	62/21/32
	INEX-LD				
SDM-CA	0.117‡ (+5.2%)	0.258 (-1.9%)	0.199 (-7.2%)	0.284 (-0.9%)	43/7/50
MLM-CA	0.102 (-8.2%)	0.238 (-9.5%)	0.190 (-11.4%)	0.261 (-8.8%)	34/13/53
FSDM	0.111‡ -	0.263‡ -	0.214†‡ -	0.287‡ -	-
RankSVM	**0.126**‡§ (+12.9%)	**0.282**‡ (+7.2%)	**0.231**†‡§ (+7.7%)	**0.317**†‡§ (+10.6%)	55/9/36
Coordinate Ascent	0.121‡§ (+8.9%)	0.275‡ (+4.6%)	0.224†‡ (+4.4%)	0.306†‡§ (+6.7%)	53/7/40
	QALD-2				
SDM-CA	0.184 (-6.0%)	0.106 (-22.0%)	0.090 (-19.2%)	0.244‡ (-6.8%)	36/66/38
MLM-CA	0.152 (-22.4%)	0.103 (-24.6%)	0.084 (-24.3%)	0.206 (-21.3%)	17/78/45
FSDM	0.195‡ -	0.136†‡ -	0.111‡ -	0.262‡ -	-
RankSVM	0.197‡ (+0.8%)	0.136†‡ (0.0%)	0.113†‡ (+1.6%)	0.266‡ (+1.6%)	31/74/35
Coordinate Ascent	**0.208**‡ (+6.6%)	**0.141**†‡ (+3.2%)	**0.115**†‡ (+2.9%)	**0.278**‡ (+5.9%)	40/71/29
	All				
SDM-CA	0.192 (-16.9%)	0.198 (-14.3%)	0.155 (-13.7%)	0.294 (-13.1%)	160/111/214
MLM-CA	0.196 (-15.3%)	0.206 (-11.0%)	0.157 (-12.4%)	0.297 (-12.1%)	120/151/214
FSDM	0.231†‡ -	0.231†‡ -	0.179†‡ -	0.339†‡ -	-
RankSVM	**0.246**†‡§ (+6.5%)	**0.251**†‡§ (+8.7%)	**0.193**†‡§ (+7.8%)	**0.362**†‡§ (+7.0%)	212/133/140
Coordinate Ascent	0.245†‡§ (+5.8%)	0.248†‡§ (+7.2%)	0.189†‡§ (+5.4%)	0.358†‡§ (+5.7%)	203/131/151

(b) Accuracy of learning to rank models when queries from different groups are all trained and tested together. Relative accuracy and Win/Tie/Loss are compared with the same model but trained and tested separately on each query group.

	MAP@100	P@10	P@20	NDCG@20	Win/Tie/Loss
RankSVM	0.234 (-4.9%)	0.238 (-5.3%)	0.185 (-4.0%)	0.347 (-4.3%)	153/136/196
Coordinate Ascent	0.233 (-4.7%)	0.232 (-6.2%)	0.179 (-5.1%)	0.344 (-3.8%)	148/129/208

4.3 Query Type Differences

Previous experiments found that when different models are trained for different types of queries, each model favors different types of evidence. However, in live query traffic different types of queries are mixed together. The third experiment investigates the accuracy of a learning to rank entities system in a more realistic setting. The four query sets are combined into one query set, and new models are trained and tested using five fold cross validation as before.

Table 3a All shows the average accuracy when different models are trained for each of the four types of query. Table 3b shows the accuracy when a single model is trained for all types of queries. Despite being trained with more data, both learning to rank algorithms produce less effective models for the diverse query set than for the four smaller, focused query sets. Nonetheless, a single learned model is as accurate as the average accuracy of four carefully-tuned, query-set-specific FSDM models.

This results suggests that diverse query streams may benefit from query classification and type-specific entity ranking models. They may also benefit from new types of features or more sophisticated ranking models.

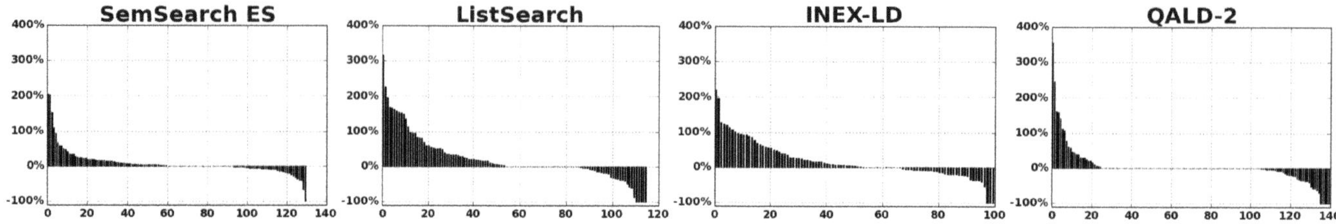

Figure 1: Query-level relative accuracy of four query groups. The X-axis lists all queries, ordered by relative accuracy. The Y-axis is the relative accuracy of `RankSVM` compared with `FSDM` using NDCG@20. A positive value indicates an improvement and a negative value indicates a loss.

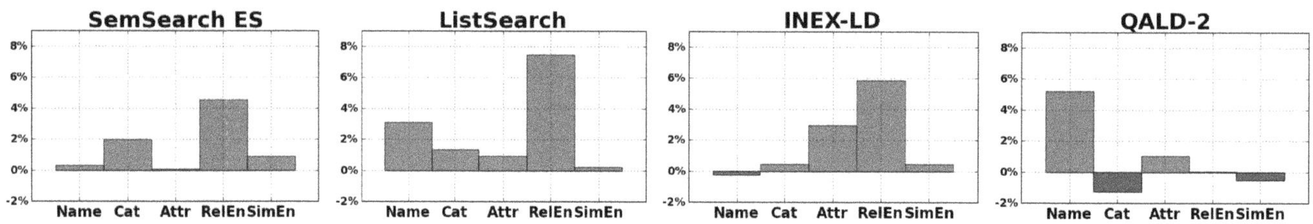

(a) Influence of fields

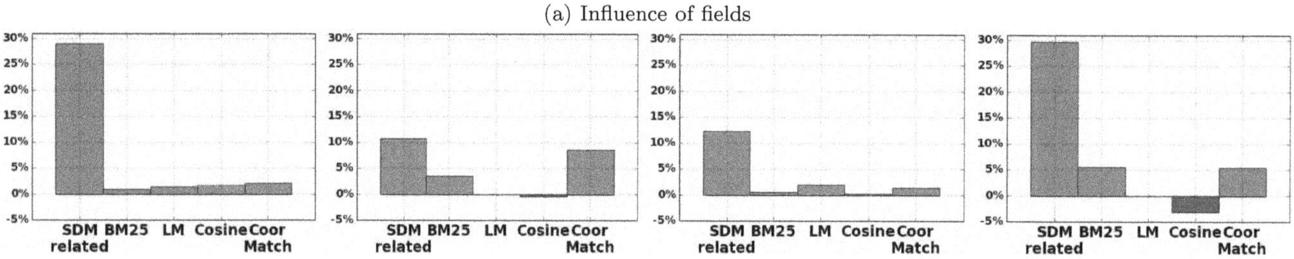

(b) Influence of feature groups

Figure 2: The contribution of fields and feature groups to `RankSVM`'s performance. The X-axis lists the fields or feature groups. The Y-axis is the relative NDCG@20 difference between `RankSVM` used with all fields or feature groups and without the corresponding field or feature group. Larger values indicate greater contribution.

5. CONCLUSIONS AND FUTURE WORK

This paper uses learning to rank models, the state-of-the-art in document ranking, for more accurate ad-hoc entity ranking. Entities are represented by multi-field documents constructed from RDF triples. How well a query matches an entity document is estimated by text similarity features and a learned model. Experiments on an entity-oriented test collection reveal the power of learning to rank for entity retrieval. Moreover, statistically significant improvements over the previous state-of-the-art are observed on all evaluation metrics.

Further analysis reveals that query types play an important role in the effectiveness of learned models. Text similarity features are very helpful for keyword queries, but less effective with longer natural language question queries. Learned models for different query types favor different entity fields because each query type targets different RDF predicates. This difference between query types is a new challenge to the use of entities in diverse search environments, because currently a single learned model does not provide much gain on average. An interesting future research direction is to automatically detect the type of entity search required for a query or task, and then use a model adapted for that type or task.

6. ACKNOWLEDGMENTS

This research was supported by National Science Foundation (NSF) grant IIS-1422676. Any opinions, findings and conclusions expressed in this paper are the authors' and do not necessarily reflect those of the sponsors.

7. REFERENCES

[1] K. Balog and R. Neumayer. A test collection for entity search in dbpedia. In *Proceedings of the 36th international ACM SIGIR conference on Research and development in information retrieval (SIGIR 2013)*, pages 737–740. ACM, 2013.

[2] C. Lu, W. Lam, and Y. Liao. Entity retrieval via entity factoid hierarchy. In *Proceedings of the 53rd Annual Meeting of the Association for Computational Linguistics (ACL 2015)*, pages 514–523. ACL, 2015.

[3] J. Pound, P. Mika, and H. Zaragoza. Ad-hoc object retrieval in the web of data. In *Proceedings of the 19th international conference on World wide web (WWW 2010)*, pages 771–780. ACM, 2010.

[4] C. Xiong and J. Callan. Esdrank: Connecting query and documents through external semi-structured data. In *Proceedings of the 24th ACM International Conference on Information and Knowledge Management (CIKM 2015)*, pages 951–960. ACM, 2015.

[5] C. Xiong and J. Callan. Query expansion with freebase. In *Proceedings of the 2015 International Conference on The Theory of Information Retrieval (ICTIR 2015)*, pages 111–120. ACM, 2015.

[6] N. Zhiltsov, A. Kotov, and F. Nikolaev. Fielded sequential dependence model for ad-hoc entity retrieval in the web of data. In *Proceedings of the 38th International ACM SIGIR Conference on Research and Development in Information Retrieval (SIGIR 2015)*, pages 253–262. ACM, 2015.

An Exploration of Evaluation Metrics for Mobile Push Notifications

Luchen Tan, Adam Roegiest, Jimmy Lin, and Charles L. A. Clarke
David R. Cheriton School of Computer Science
University of Waterloo, Ontario, Canada
{luchen.tan, aroegies, jimmylin}@uwaterloo.ca, claclark@gmail.com

ABSTRACT

How do we evaluate systems that filter social media streams and send users updates via push notifications on their mobile phones? Such notifications must be relevant, timely, and novel. In this paper, we explore various evaluation metrics for this task, focusing specifically on measuring relevance. We begin with an analysis of metrics deployed at the TREC 2015 Microblog evaluations. A simple change to the metrics, reflecting a different assumption, dramatically alters system rankings. Applying another metric, previously used in the TREC Microblog evaluations, again yields different system rankings. We find little correlation between a number of "reasonable" evaluation metrics, which suggests that system effectiveness depends on how you measure it—an undesirable state in IR evaluation. However, we argue that existing evaluation metrics can be generalized into a framework that uses the same underlying contingency table, but places different weights and penalties. Although we stop short of proposing the "one true metric", this framework can guide the future development of a family of metrics that more accurately models user needs.

1. INTRODUCTION

This paper explores the problem of evaluating push notification techniques on social media streams in a filtering application. We assume an infinite stream of social media posts such as Twitter, against which the user issues an arbitrary number of standing queries representing "interest profiles", analogous to topics in traditional ad hoc retrieval. For example, the user might be interested in poll results for the 2016 U.S. presidential elections and wishes to be notified whenever new results are published. The system's task is to identify relevant tweets from the stream and send those updates directly to the user's mobile phone via push notifications. Since such notifications are often associated with an auditory or visual cue upon arrival, each imposes a nontrivial cognitive burden on the user (even if ignored). Thus, careful control of the volume of notifications is critical to successful push strategies. This paper explores evaluation metrics for such a task.

SIGIR '16, July 17 - 21, 2016, Pisa, Italy

ISBN 978-1-4503-4069-4/16/07...$15.00
DOI: http://dx.doi.org/10.1145/2911451.2914694

At a high level, push notifications should be relevant, timely (provide updates as soon after the actual event occurrence as possible), and novel (users should not be pushed multiple notifications that say the same thing). Accordingly, an evaluation metric should reward systems for updates that satisfy these three main criteria. As the design space is vast, in this short paper we focus on relevance, adopting existing notions of novelty and timeliness.

We start with an analysis of metrics from the TREC 2015 Microblog track, which operationalized such a push notification task, and then re-assess submitted runs after making a minor tweak to reflect a different assumption about the user model. We then re-assess submitted runs using variants of a metric that has been applied in previous iterations of the same evaluation. Using score and rank correlations, we compare system effectiveness as measured by each metric. Our results are surprising: we find little correlation between the different metrics. This means that the answer to "which system is better" depends on how you measure it, which is undesirable from an evaluation perspective.

The contribution of this paper is twofold. First, we present the novel and surprising finding discussed above: any number of reasonable evaluation metrics give rise to significantly different system rankings. We discuss and analyze why, tracing the issue to the handling of days for which there are no relevant tweets. Second, we argue that the different existing evaluation metrics we applied can be generalized into a framework that uses the same underlying contingency table, but places different weights and penalties. Although we do not propose the "one true metric", we believe this framework can guide the future development of an evaluation metric that more accurately models user needs.

2. BACKGROUND

The application described in the introduction was operationalized in the TREC 2015 Microblog track as the so-called "scenario A" variant of the real-time filtering task [3]. Over the official evaluation period, which spanned ten days during July 2015, participating systems "listened" to Twitter's live tweet sample stream to identify relevant tweets with respect to 225 topics, 51 of which were later assessed. Each system identified up to ten tweets per day, which were putatively delivered to hypothetical users. In total, 14 groups submitted 37 runs to the evaluation. Data from this evaluation provides the starting point for our analysis.

The assessment workflow for the track was as follows:

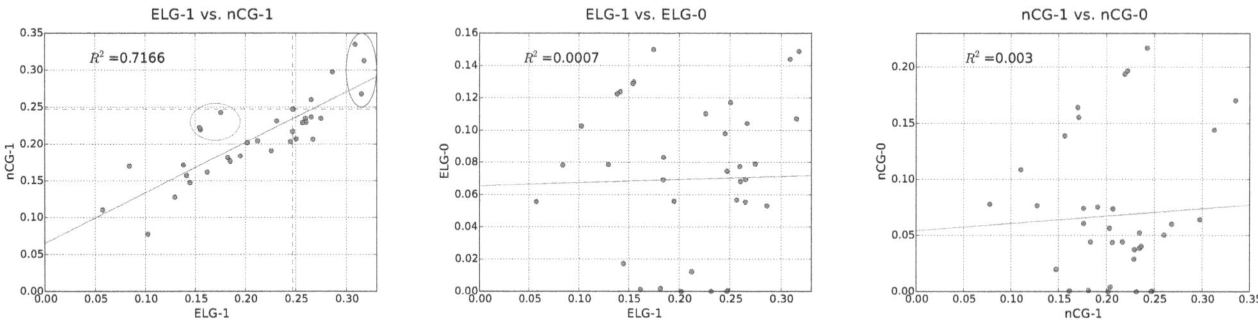

Figure 1: ELG-1 vs. nCG-1 (left), ELG-1 vs. ELG-0 (middle), and nCG-1 vs. nCG-0 (right) for all submitted runs. Plots show that the treatment of "silent days" has a large impact on system scores.

first, tweets returned by the systems were assessed for relevance using a traditional pooling process. Relevant documents were then semantically clustered into groups containing tweets that share substantively similar information. We refer the reader to previous papers for more details [5].

The two metrics used to evaluate system runs were expected latency-discounted gain (ELG) and normalized cumulative gain (nCG). These two metrics are computed for each topic for each day in the evaluation period (explained in detail below). The score for a topic is the average of the daily scores in the evaluation period. The score of a system run is the average of the scores across all topics.

Expected latency-discounted gain (ELG) was adapted from the TREC Temporal Summarization track [2]:

$$\frac{1}{N}\sum \mathrm{G}(t) \qquad (1)$$

where N is the number of tweets returned and $\mathrm{G}(t)$ is the gain of each tweet: non-relevant tweets receive a gain of 0, relevant tweets receive a gain of 0.5, and highly-relevant tweets receive a gain of 1.0.

A key aspect of this metric is its handling of redundancy and timeliness: a system only receives credit for returning one tweet from each cluster. Furthermore, a latency penalty is applied to all tweets, computed as $\mathrm{MAX}(0, (100-d)/100)$, where the delay d is the time elapsed (in minutes, rounded down) between the tweet creation time and the putative time the tweet was delivered. That is, if the system delivers a relevant tweet within a minute of the tweet being posted, the system receives full credit. Otherwise, credit decays linearly such that after 100 minutes, the system receives no credit even if the tweet was relevant.

The second metric is normalized cumulative gain (nCG):

$$\frac{1}{\mathcal{Z}}\sum \mathrm{G}(t) \qquad (2)$$

where $\mathcal{Z}$ is the maximum possible gain (given the ten tweet per day limit). The gain of each individual tweet is computed as above (with the latency penalty). Note that gain is not discounted (as in nDCG) because the notion of document ranks is not meaningful in this context.

Due to the setup of the task and the nature of interest profiles, it is possible (and indeed observed empirically) that for some days, no relevant tweets appear in the judgment pool. In terms of evaluation metrics, a system should be rewarded for correctly identifying these cases and not pushing non-relevant content. If there are *no* relevant tweets for a particular day and the system returns zero tweets, it receives a score of one (i.e., perfect score) for that day; otherwise, the system receives a score of zero for that day. This applies to both ELG and nCG.

It is worth mentioning that despite superficial similarities, our task is very different from document filtering in the context of topic detection and tracking (TDT) [1]. TDT is concerned with identifying *all* documents related to a particular event—with an intelligence analyst in mind—which requires keeping track of false alarms and missed detections. In contrast, we are focused on identifying a small set of the most relevant updates to push to users, grounded in interactions with mobile devices. Furthermore, in TDT, systems must make online decisions as soon as documents arrive, whereas in our case systems can choose to push older content (subjected to the latency penalty), thus giving rise to the possibility of algorithms operating on bounded buffers. For these various reasons, TDT evaluation tools such as the decision error tradeoff (DET) curve and derivative metrics provide inspiration, but are not directly applicable.

3. ANALYSIS OF "SILENT DAYS"

In Figure 1 (left), we show a scatterplot of the official ELG scores (which we call ELG-1 for reasons that will become clear shortly) vs. nCG (specifically, nCG-1, for the same reasons). Although there is an overall correlation between ELG-1 and nCG-1 across all submitted runs, we do note that in particular cases ELG-1 and nCG-1 are capturing different aspects of effectiveness: for example, the top three runs in terms of ELG-1 (circled in blue) exhibit relatively large differences in nCG-1. There are also cases in which systems achieve high nCG-1 relative to their ELG-1 scores (the runs circled in red).

One interesting aspect of ELG-1 and nCG-1 is their handling of days in which there are no relevant documents: for rhetorical convenience, we call days in which there are no relevant tweets for a particular topic (in the pool) "silent days", in contrast to "eventful days" (where there are relevant tweets). In both ELG-1 and nCG-1, for a "silent day", the only two possible scores are one (if the system remained silent) or zero (if the system pushed any tweet). This means that an empty run (a system that never returns anything) may have a non-zero score based on how many silent days there are in each topic. As it turns out, an empty run will score 0.2471 in ELG-1 and nCG-1, shown as dotted lines in Figure 1 (left). Since this was the first year of this TREC evaluation, systems achieved high scores by simply returning few results, in many cases for totally idiosyncratic reasons—for example, the misconfiguration of a score threshold.

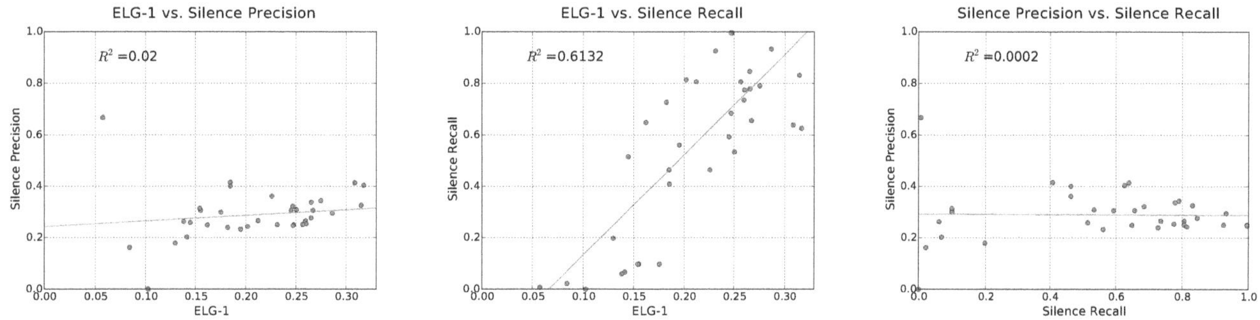

Figure 2: Characterizing the effects of "silent days": silence precision vs. ELG-1 (left), silence recall vs. ELG-1 (middle), and silence precision vs. silence recall (right). Systems score well by learning when to "shut up".

As an alternative, what if we did not reward systems for remaining silent? That is, on a silent day, all systems receive a zero score, no matter what they did. We call these variant metrics ELG-0 and nCG-0 (in contrast to ELG-1 and nCG-1). We can justify this from the user perspective in that for a silent day, the user does not obtain any relevant information regardless of system output (since there *are* no relevant documents). In this case, how would the user know to "reward" a system for remaining silent? That is, properly determining a silent day requires global knowledge (e.g., from pooling), which no individual user has access to.

In Figure 1, we show scatterplots of ELG-1 vs. ELG-0 (middle) and nCG-1 vs. nCG-0 (right). We see no discernible relationship between each pair of metrics, which suggests that the handling of silent days *is the most critical part of each metric*, in that different (reasonable) formulations yield dramatically different results and system rankings. In fact, we would go as far as saying that effectiveness under ELG-1 and nCG-1 is primarily dominated by a system's ability to identify the silent days. Under both metrics, systems do well by learning when to "shut up".

This observation is further illustrated by the scatterplots in Figure 2, where we show silence precision vs. ELG-1 (left), silence recall vs. ELG-1 (middle), and silence precision vs. silence recall (right) for all runs. Silence precision and recall follow the usual definitions of precision and recall, but with respect to identifying the silent days. Since each topic has an equal number of days, there is no difference between micro- and macro-averaging. Across all the topics, 24.7% of all days are completely silent, while another 6.7% have relevant but redundant material. We see that there is a slightly positive (but very weak) correlation between ELG-1 and silence precision. The middle graph, in effect, shows that systems achieve a high ELG-1 score by achieving a high silence recall—i.e., getting a good score is dominated by a system knowing when to "shut up". Although systems with comparable silence recall can differ substantially in ELG-1, we were surprised by how much of the variance in the official metric can be explained by silence recall alone.

The right graph in Figure 2 shows the tradeoffs systems make with respect to precision and recall. On the right edge of the plot are cases where the systems are almost always quiet, achieving nearly perfect recall; in the left lower corner is a system that never "shuts up", and hence its precision and recall are both zero. It is interesting to note that some systems perform poorly in both precision *and* recall—they don't push content when there's relevant content and don't "shut up" when there's no relevant content.

To our knowledge, we are the first to make this observation about the huge impact of silent vs. eventful days in the current evaluation of push notification. However, we withhold judgment as to whether the current TREC metrics represent the "right" approach: from the user perspective, since push notifications are associated with high cognitive effort (because they may interrupt the user), perhaps we should force systems to focus on learning when to "shut up". On the other hand, having such highly binarized scores on the silent days creates many issues for system tuning, since it creates discontinuities in the objective. We observe similar issues when trying to optimize a metric such as precision at rank one for question answering.

4. GAIN AND PAIN

What are other reasonable ways in which we can evaluate the push notification task? A simple and intuitive utility-based metric would be to reward "gain" based on delivery of relevant information and to deduct "pain" based on delivery of non-relevant information. In fact, the TREC 2012 Microblog track employed exactly such a metric, called T11U [4], itself derived from the linear utility metrics used in the TREC filtering tracks.

We adopt a slightly different but mathematically equivalent formulation as follows:

$$\text{T11U} = \alpha \cdot \mathcal{G} - (1 - \alpha) \cdot N_x \quad (3)$$

where $\mathcal{G}$ is total gain, N_x is the number of non-relevant documents pushed, and α controls the relative weight of gain vs. pain. Note that in T11U, the total gain factors in different relevance grades, the latency penalty, and the treatment of redundant tweets in exactly the same way as ELG.

In Figure 3, we show a scatterplot of ELG-1 vs. T11U with $\alpha = 0.66$, which was the value used in TREC 2012. This value can be understood as setting the gain of a relevant notification (highest relevance grade, no temporal penalty, not redundant) equal to the pain of returning two non-relevant updates. With this setting, we do see reasonable positive correlation between ELG-1 and T11U overall, but this correlation is highly misleading. According to T11U, very few systems achieve positive utility overall—that is, the gain from pushing relevant content is not sufficient to offset the pain from pushing non-relevant content. Furthermore, the relatively large cluster of runs which score around zero in T11U vary widely in ELG-1, from around 0.2 to over 0.3, with the highest T11U score being somewhere in the middle of this band. In other words, poorly-performing systems

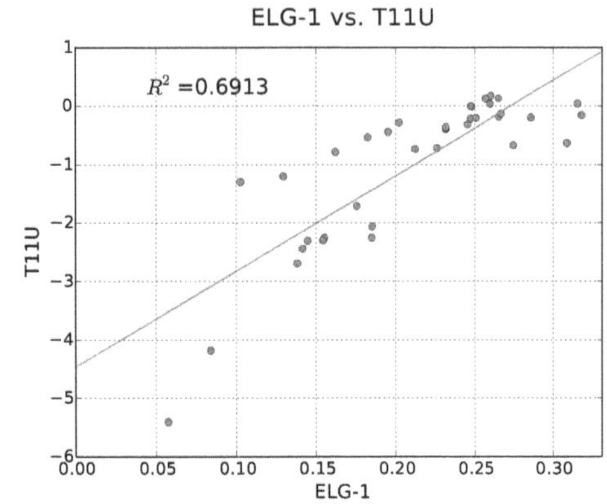

Figure 3: ELG-1 vs. T11U.

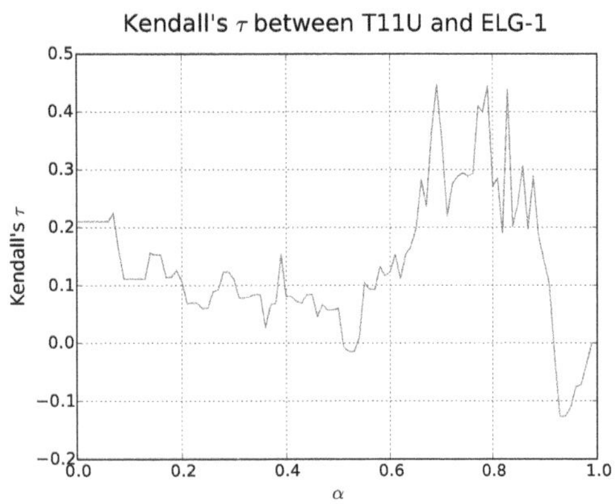

Figure 4: Kendall's τ between T11U and ELG-1 for different values of α.

score low in both ELG-1 and T11U, but beyond that, T11U and ELG-1 exhibit a weak correlation at best.

Of course, absolute scores and relative system rankings depend on the α parameter that balances gain vs. pain, and the setting of $\alpha = 0.66$ was arbitrary. What would the evaluation results look like for different settings of α? The answer is shown in Figure 4, where we sweep the α parameter and compute Kendall's τ with respect to ELG-1 for each setting. The results show that Kendall's τ varies substantially, ranging from moderate correlation to non-existent and even slightly negative correlation. We have shown above that high correlations can be misleading, and this plot shows that $\alpha = 0.66$ is around the highest Kendall's τ we can obtain regardless. These results suggest that T11U and ELG-1 are measuring quite different aspects of effectiveness.

5. TOWARD A GENERAL FRAMEWORK

Let us take stock of our findings so far: we have evaluated runs from the TREC 2015 Microblog track using official as well as alternative metrics (ELG-1, ELG-0, nCG-1, nCG-0, and T11U). In comparing the metrics, we observe many inconsistencies in terms of both system scores and relative rankings. In other words, "which system is better" depends on what measure we use. From an evaluation perspective, this is not desirable because researchers lack consistent guidance for algorithm development.

To address this issue, we propose a general evaluation framework built around the contingency table shown in Table 1. At the core, our framework is utility-based in that gain is rewarded for pushing relevant content ($+G_E$) and pain is deducted for pushing non-relevant content ($-P_E$ and $-P_0$). However, a key insight is the explicit separation of eventful and silent days, which our ELG-1 vs. ELG-0 experiments have shown to be critical in system evaluations.

System action	"eventful days"	"silent days"
Pushed relevant	$+G_E$	-
Pushed not-relevant	$-P_E$	$-P_0$
Stayed silent	$-S_E$	$+S_0$

Table 1: The contingency table for a general evaluation framework for push notifications.

Our evaluation framework is general in that the metrics we have examined in this paper can be viewed as specific instantiations of the parameters in Table 1. For example, T11U sets G_E and P_E (based on α) but ignores the final row, and furthermore does not make the distinction between eventful and silent days. ELG-1 and ELG-0 make different choices on S_0, how systems should be rewarded for staying silent on silent days, but both set P_E and P_0 to zero. That is, no pain is deducted for pushing non-relevant content.

Using the framework presented in Table 1 as a guide, we can imagine a family of metrics beyond those already presented. For example, we might augment T11U by creating a distinction between eventful and silent days, thus arriving at a metric that is closer to ELG-1 or ELG-0. We might set P_E differently from P_0 to create more nuanced distinctions in a T11U-like metric. Different ratios between these weights also give rise to emphasis on different aspects of the push notification problem.

The question remains on how to properly set the gain and pain weights in the contingency table—and we presently provide no concrete answer, expect to say that further studies in user modeling are necessary. For example, we have presented two plausible scenarios (ELG-1 and ELG-0) for the treatment of silent systems on silent days: a user study is necessary to decide which alternative (or neither) matches user preferences. Although the development of the "one true metric" is beyond the limited scope of this short paper, our framework contributes to a step toward that goal.

Acknowledgments. This work was supported in part by the U.S. National Science Foundation under awards IIS-1218043 and CNS-1405688 and the Natural Sciences and Engineering Research Council of Canada (NSERC). Any opinions, findings, conclusions, or recommendations expressed are those of the authors and do not necessarily reflect the views of the sponsors.

6. REFERENCES

[1] J. Allan. *Topic Detection and Tracking: Event-Based Information Organization.* Kluwer, 2002.

[2] J. Aslam, M. Ekstrand-Abueg, V. Pavlu, F. Diaz, R. McCreadie, and T. Sakai. TREC 2014 Temporal Summarization Track overview. *TREC*, 2014.

[3] J. Lin, M. Efron, Y. Wang, G. Sherman, and E. Voorhees. Overview of the TREC-2015 Microblog Track. *TREC*, 2015.

[4] I. Soboroff, I. Ounis, C. Macdonald, and J. Lin. Overview of the TREC-2012 Microblog Track. *TREC*, 2012.

[5] Y. Wang, G. Sherman, J. Lin, and M. Efron. Assessor differences and user preferences in tweet timeline generation. *SIGIR*, 2015.

An Improved Multileaving Algorithm for Online Ranker Evaluation

Brian Brost[1], Ingemar J. Cox[1,2], Yevgeny Seldin[1], Christina Lioma[1]
[1] University of Copenhagen
[2] University College London
brian.brost@di.ku.dk, ingemar@ieee.org, seldin@di.ku.dk, c.lioma@di.ku.dk

ABSTRACT

Online ranker evaluation is a key challenge in information retrieval. An important task in the online evaluation of rankers is using implicit user feedback for inferring preferences between rankers. Interleaving methods have been found to be efficient and sensitive, i.e. they can quickly detect even small differences in quality. It has recently been shown that multileaving methods exhibit similar sensitivity but can be more efficient than interleaving methods. This paper presents empirical results demonstrating that existing multileaving methods either do not scale well with the number of rankers, or, more problematically, can produce results which substantially differ from evaluation measures like NDCG. The latter problem is caused by the fact that they do not correctly account for the similarities that can occur between rankers being multileaved. We propose a new multileaving method for handling this problem and demonstrate that it substantially outperforms existing methods, in some cases reducing errors by as much as 50%.

1. INTRODUCTION

Online evaluation using interleaving is an increasingly popular paradigm in ranker evaluation and has been found to be efficient and sensitive [4]. Here efficient means that relatively little click feedback is required to reliably distinguish rankers, and sensitive means that interleaving can distinguish between rankers with very similar retrieval quality. In addition to these requirements an important criterion for evaluating interleaving methods is that they be unbiased, in the sense that they do not systematically favour certain rankers independently of their actual quality.

Multileaving methods were recently introduced [2, 3] and potentially offer substantial improvements over interleaving in terms of efficiency, since they can compare sets of rankers of arbitrary size at each comparison. They were also found to be similarly sensitive to interleaving [3].

Section 2 describes related work, including two state of the art methods, Team Draft Multileave (TDM) and Probabilistic Multileave (PM). We observe that TDM does not scale well as the number of rankers in the comparison set increases, limiting its efficiency. We show that PM can fail to properly account for ranker similarities, introducing bias. Section 3 then describes our proposed solution and Section 4 provides experimental results demonstrating the new algorithm's superiority. Our contributions are to produce a new multileaving method which outperforms current methods and to identify that PM can be biased.

SIGIR '16, July 17 - 21, 2016, Pisa, Italy

ISBN 978-1-4503-4069-4/16/07...$15.00
DOI: http://dx.doi.org/10.1145/2911451.2914706

2. RELATED WORK

Multileaving consists of two stages. First we create the multileaved list by sampling from the individual ranked lists, and then we credit rankers based on user clicks on the multileaved list and thereby infer a preference ordering of the rankers. Three multileaving methods have been proposed, namely, Team Draft Multileave (TDM) [3], Optimised Multileave [3] and Probabilistic Multileave (PM) [2]. We describe the two best performing methods, TDM and PM.

TDM creates the multileaved list in rounds. In each round a random ordering of the rankers is decided and the top document that has not yet appeared in the multileaving is drawn from each ranker. This process is then repeated until the multileaved list is of sufficient length. In the credit inference stage of TDM, rankers are credited for each click on a document drawn from the corresponding ranker. This credit does not consider the position of the document in the ranker's retrieved list. A matrix, M, of pair-wise preferences between pairs of rankers is then inferred based on which ranker was given more credit.

Since rankers are only credited for clicks on documents drawn from the corresponding ranker, TDM does not scale well to comparing more rankers than there are documents in the multileaved list. Since users of search engines typically only inspect the first results page, the multileaved list is effectively only of length 10. We are often interested in comparing significantly more than just 10 rankers, so there is a need for multileaving methods which scale better to larger comparison sets.

PM also creates the multileaved list in rounds. In each round a random ordering of the rankers is decided. Then, a document is probabilistically selected from the ranker, where the probability of drawing a document d from ranker R_j is determined solely by the document's rank and is given by Equation 1, where $r_j(d)$ is the rank of document d in ranker R_j, and D is the set of documents ranked by R_j.

$$P(d|R_j) = \frac{\frac{1}{r_j(d)^3}}{\sum_{d' \in D} \frac{1}{r_j(d')^3}} \tag{1}$$

Note that when a document is drawn, the document is removed from all the rankers' retrieved lists. In the next round, the probabilities of the remaining documents are recalculated according to Equation 1, where the rankings, $r_j(d)$, are now determined in the absence of previously chosen documents.

In the credit inference stage, PM considers all possible assignments of documents to rankers that could have occurred, and weight each assignment based on its probability. An assignment, a, has probability, $P(a)$, given by

$$P(a) = \prod_{r=1}^{L} P(d_r|R_{\alpha(r)})P(R_{\alpha(r)}) \quad (2)$$

where L, is the length of the multileaved list, $P(d_r|R_{\alpha(r)})$, is the probability of drawing document d_r from the assigned ranker, $R_{\alpha(r)}$ and is given by Equation 1, and $P(R_{\alpha(r)})$ is given by $1/|R|$. For an assignment, a, Ranker R_j is given credit, $o_j(a)$ equal to the number of assigned documents clicked on. The total credit, $o_j(A)$, assigned to ranker R_j, is given by $o_j(A) = \sum_{a \in A} o_j(a)P(a)$, where A is the set of all possible assignments. A matrix, M, of pair-wise preferences between pairs of rankers is then inferred based on which ranker was given more credit.

PM can be biased since rankers can benefit from the presence of documents contributed by similar rankers, and these rankers will therefore perform better according to PM than they actually do in practice. To illustrate this problem, consider the following simple example: three rankers and their corresponding retrieved lists: $(R_1 : D_1, D_2)$ $(R_2 : D_2, D_1)$, and $(R_3 : D_2, D_1)$. The possible multileavings of length two, are $\{D_1, D_2\}$ and $\{D_2, D_1\}$. The former multileaving occurs with probability 0.3704, and the latter occurs with probability 0.6296. Assume that D_1 and D_2 are both relevant and always clicked on, i.e. all three rankers have equal performance. Even though the rankers are equally good, R_1 will lose to the other two rankers with probability 0.6296 due to the fact that when the multileaving $\{D_1, D_2\}$ occurs, R_1 is given more credit in the credit inference stage of PM and if $\{D_2, D_1\}$ occurs, R_2 and R_3 are given more credit. Thus, for PM, the presence of similar rankers introduces bias and distorts the outcome of comparisons. Similar rankers benefit because their assignments are weighted higher.

3. SAMPLE-ONLY SCORED MULTILEAVE

We propose a multileaving method called Sample-only Scored Multileave (SOSM) which scales well with the number of rankers being compared, without introducing bias. The main difference relative to PM is that the score attributed to each ranker *only* depends on how each ranker ranks the sample of documents contained in the multileaving, *not* how each ranker ranks documents in their original retrieved lists. In this way, if a document is preferentially sampled, it will not disproportionally disadvantage other rankers provided they rank the sample well.

The process of creating the multileaved list in SOSM is identical to that in TDM described in Section 2.

To infer preferences, each ranker ranks the documents in the multileaved list such that $r'_j(d)$ denotes the order of document d in the multileaved list according to ranker R_j. Letting D_M denote the documents of the multileaved list, the score of document d for ranker R_j is given in Equation 3. Letting C denote the clicked documents, ranker R_j is credited with $\sum_{d \in C} s(d|R_j)$, where

$$s(d|R_j) = \frac{\frac{1}{r'_j(d)^3}}{\sum_{d' \in D_M} \frac{1}{r'_j(d')^3}} \quad (3)$$

A matrix, M, of preferences between pairs of rankers is then inferred based on which ranker was given more credit. Note the similarity between our scoring function in Equation 3, and that of Equation 1 used by PM. The only difference is that in the denominator we only sum over the documents contained in the multileaved list.

SOSM scales well with the number of rankers being compared, as verified experimentally in Section 4, and is also unbiased. It is simple to verify that SOSM is unbiased, according to the definition of bias given in [1]. Additionally, we verify the unbiasedness of SOSM experimentally in Section 4.

4. EXPERIMENTAL EVALUATION

In our problem setup, we are given a set of rankers R whose performance we want to evaluate on a dataset using click feedback [3]. Multileaving methods output an $|R| \times |R|$ matrix M after each comparison, where M_{ij} is 1 if the multileaving method inferred a preference for ranker R_i over R_j, 0 if it inferred a preference for ranker R_j over R_i and 0.5 if no preference was inferred between the rankers. We then define $\hat{M}(t)$ such that $\hat{M}_{ij}$ is the average over t multileaved comparisons of M_{ij}.

The mean NDCG@10 for held out queries in the dataset is assumed to be ground truth. We define an $|R| \times |R|$ preference matrix P in which P_{ij} is 1 if ranker R_i has a higher NDCG@10 than ranker R_j, 0 if R_j has a higher score than R_i, and 0.5 if the two rankers have the same score.

For a given pair of rankers, we consider the multileaving method to have made an error after t comparisons if $\hat{M}_{ij}(t)$ and P_{ij} are not equal. We wish to minimize the percentage of errors made,

$$E(t) = \frac{\sum_{i,j \in R} sgn(\hat{M}_{ij}(t) - 0.5) \neq sgn(P_{ij} - 0.5)}{|R|(|R| - 1)} \quad (4)$$

For these experiments we compare feature rankers from the MSLR-WEB30k [6], YLR1 and YLR2 [5] datasets. Feature rankers can be rankers like PageRank or the BM25 score of the body of a document. Feature rankers were also used for the experimental setup in [3, 2].

We use a simulated user setup. For each iteration we randomly sample with replacement a query from the pool of queries of the dataset. The rankers being compared are then multileaved, and clicks on the multileaved list are generated from three different probabilistic user models: the perfect, navigational and informational click models as described in [1].

For each dataset the queries are split into a training and test set. For a given run on k rankers, we randomly sample k feature rankers from the given dataset and compute NDCG@10 for each of these rankers on the test query set. These NDCG@10 scores are used to create a ground truth preference matrix P against which we can measure the percentage errors E defined in Equation 4. For each iteration we then randomly sample a query from the training set, multileave the k rankers using each multileaving method, and compute E for each method. We then investigate how E

develops at each iteration. Additionally we show the percentage errors of the NDCG@10 score computed only from the queries so far used for multileaving. This serves as a lower bound on the error that can reasonably be obtained. For PM we fix the sample size parameter at 10,000 as in [2].

Findings:

Table 1 enumerates the percentage error after 2,000 and 10,000 iterations when multileaving 5, 40 or 100 rankers for the three click models. In almost all cases SOSM is superior. The two exceptions occur when comparing only 5 rankers. In this case, TDM is marginally better than SOSM for the informational click model, and equivalent for the perfect click model. For 40 or 100 rankers, SOSM substantially outperforms TDM and PM. For example, with 100 rankers and the informational click model, the error rates are reduced by 50% from 32% to 16% after 10,000 iterations.

Figure 1 shows how the performances of the multileaving methods are affected by the click model used. For all three click models, SOSM outperforms both TDM and PM. This is most pronounced for the navigational model, where the percentage error for TDM and PM is 50% greater than that of SOSM (30% compared to 20%).

Figure 2 shows the sensitivity of the multileaving methods to different choices of dataset. We repeat the experiment from Figure 1(b) using two other datasets. All three algorithms (TDM, PM, SOSM) perform similarly across datasets. In all cases, SOSM exhibits superior performance.

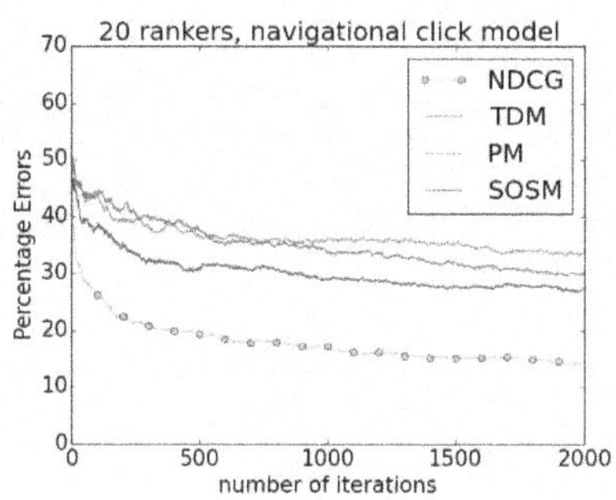

(a) YLR1

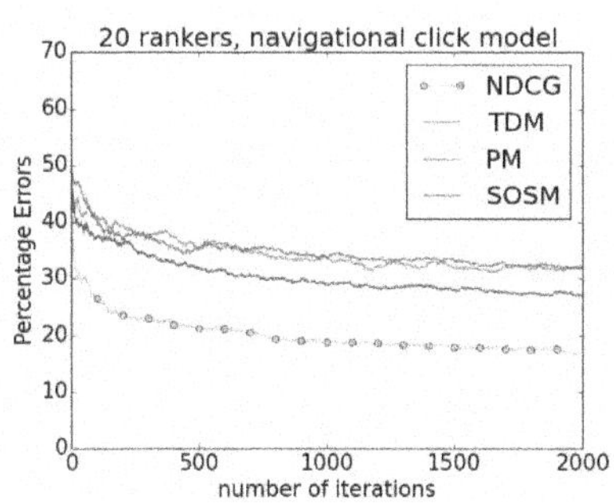

(b) YLR2

Figure 2: Percentage errors (averaged over 25 runs) versus the number of iterations on random subsets of 20 rankers for the YLR1 (a) and YLR2 (b) datasets using a navigational click model.

Figure 3 shows how the performances of the multileaving methods vary with the number of rankers being compared. We show the percentage error after 2,000 iterations, as a function of the number k of rankers that are multileaved. For a given k, a random subset of rankers is selected and

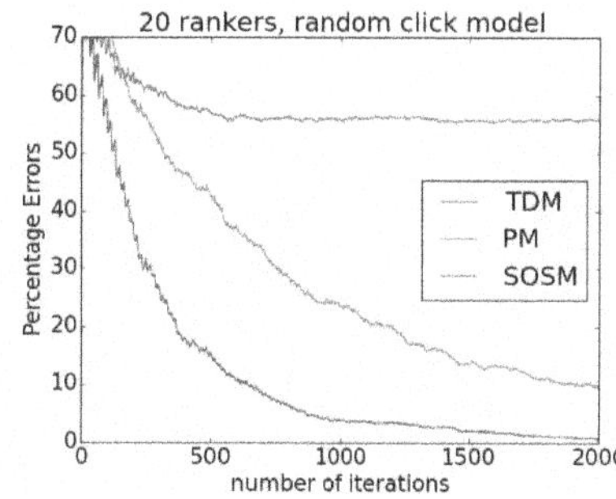

(a) random click model

Figure 4: Percentage errors (averaged over 25 runs) versus the number of iterations on random subsets of 20 rankers for the MSLR dataset using a random click model.

multileaved for 2,000 iterations. The same subset is used for PM, TDM and SOSM. This is repeated 25 times, each time with a different random subset of k rankers. The results in Figure 3 are the average of these 25 runs. We observe that for SOSM and PM the error remains relatively stable as the number of rankers increases. However, for TDM the error is increasing and we observe that its performance becomes worse than PM for large numbers of rankers. This is due to the fact that during the scoring phase, TDM is unable to assign credit to more than the 10 rankers from which the multileaved documents originated.

Figure 4 tests if the multileaving methods are biased. In Section 2, we showed that PM could exhibit bias under certain conditions. For this experiment we use a random click model, i.e. clicks are random and independent of document relevance. In this case, we expect that the elements of the pairwise preference matrix should converge to 0.5, i.e. there is no observed preference between rankers i and j. In this case, an error is declared if the value of $\hat{M}_{ij}(t)$ deviates from 0.5 by more than 0.03. Figure 4 shows that PM exhibits very strong bias, with error rates of about 60%.[1] TDM's behaviour is much better, but after 2000 iterations some bias is still present. In contrast, the percentage error decreases much quicker in SOSM, and is almost zero after just 2000 iterations.

5. CONCLUSION AND FUTURE WORK

We identified and experimentally verified weaknesses in the scalability of TDM and the unbiasedness of PM. We then proposed a new algorithm, SOSM, that corrects these problems. Experimental results using simulated users (perfect, navigational, informational click models), on three different datasets confirmed that (i) SOSM scales well with the number of rankers to be multileaved, (ii) is unbiased, and (iii) has significantly less error than prior methods. In some cases error rates were reduced by half.

The residual error needs investigating but is likely to be partly due to (i) establishing a ground truth based on NDCG@10, which is not used as the scoring function in Equation 3, and

[1]Note that in [2] no such bias was detected. However, in [2] the set of multileaved rankers was not picked randomly. Further, personal communication with an author of [2] confirmed the existence of a software bug in PM which we corrected for these experiments.

Table 1: Percentage error, E, after 2,000 and 10,0000 iterations for each multileaving method for 5, 40 and 100 rankers and three click models. The best performing method is bolded and * indicates a statistically significant difference with $p < 0.01$ to both the baseline methods according to paired t-tests.

	Iterations	2,000			10,000		
Click Model	Method / # Rankers	TDM	PM	SOSM	TDM	PM	SOSM
Perfect	5 rankers	**18%**	23%	**18%**	14%	18%	**14%**
	40 rankers	23%	28%	**17%***	18%	28%	**15%***
	100 rankers	30%	29%	**18%***	21%	28%	**16%***
Navigational	5 rankers	27%	30%	**22%**	24%	25%	**16%**
	40 rankers	34%	30%	**24%***	26%	31%	**22%***
	100 rankers	39%	31%	**25%***	29%	29%	**21%***
Informational	5 rankers	**18%**	29%	20%	**16%**	32%	18%
	40 rankers	37%	32%	**22%***	27%	32%	**15%***
	100 rankers	42%	33%	**21%***	34%	32%	**16%***

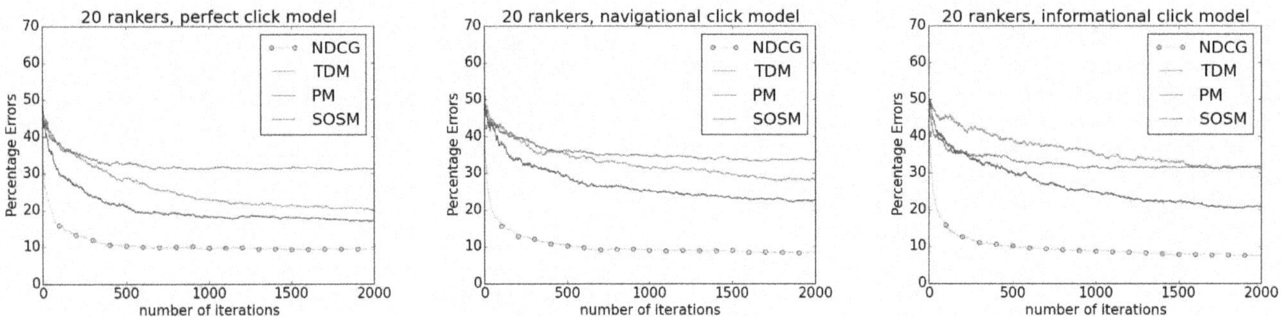

(a) perfect click model (b) navigational click model (c) informational click model

Figure 1: Percentage errors (averaged over 25 runs) versus the number of iterations on random subsets of 20 rankers for the MSLR dataset using perfect (a), navigational (b), and informational (c) click models.

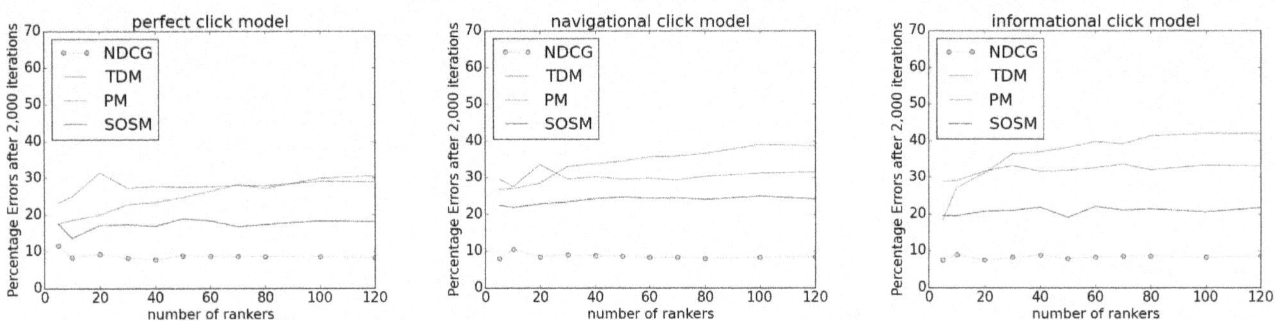

(a) perfect click model (b) navigational click model (c) informational click model

Figure 3: Percentage errors after 2,000 iterations (averaged over 25 runs) versus the number of rankers being compared on 25 random subsets of k rankers for the MSLR dataset with perfect (a), navigational (b), and informational (c) click models.

(ii) the ground truth data is computed on "test" data that is not used during the multileave experiments.

Future work will investigate scoring functions allowing the multileaving method to optimise for specific evaluation measures such as NDCG@10 or to agree with specific measures of user satisfaction.

6. REFERENCES

[1] K. Hofmann, S. Whiteson, and M. D. Rijke. Fidelity, soundness, and efficiency of interleaved comparison methods. *TOIS*, 31(4):17.1-17.39, 2013.

[2] A. Schuth, R.-J. Bruintjes, F. Büttner, J. van Doorn, C. Groenland, H. Oosterhuis, C.-N. Tran, B. Veeling, J. van der Velde, R. Wechsler, et al. Probabilistic multileave for online retrieval evaluation. *SIGIR*, pages 955–958, 2015.

[3] A. Schuth, F. Sietsma, S. Whiteson, D. Lefortier, and M. de Rijke. Multileaved comparisons for fast online evaluation. *CIKM*, pages 71–80. 2014.

[4] O. Chapelle, T. Joachims, F. Radlinski and Y. Yue, and M. de Rijke. Large-scale validation and analysis of interleaved search evaluation. *TOIS*, 30(1):6.1-6.41, 2012.

[5] O. Chapelle and Y. Chang. Yahoo! Learning to Rank Challenge Overview. *JMLR*, 14:1-24, 2011

[6] Microsoft Learning to Rank Datasets, 2012 http://research.microsoft.com/en-us/projects/mslr/default.aspx

An Unsupervised Approach to Anomaly Detection in Music Datasets

Yen-Cheng Lu[1] Chih-Wei Wu[2] Chang-Tien Lu[1] Alexander Lerch[2]
[1]Department of Computer Science, Virginia Tech
[2]Center for Music Technology, Georgia Institute of Technology
[1]{kevinlu, ctlu}@vt.edu, [2]{cwu307, alexander.lerch}@gatech.edu

ABSTRACT

This paper presents an unsupervised method for systematically identifying anomalies in music datasets. The model integrates categorical regression and robust estimation techniques to infer anomalous scores in music clips. When applied to a music genre recognition dataset, the new method is able to detect corrupted, distorted, or mislabeled audio samples based on commonly used features in music information retrieval. The evaluation results show that the algorithm outperforms other anomaly detection methods and is capable of finding problematic samples identified by human experts. The proposed method introduces a preliminary framework for anomaly detection in music data that can serve as a useful tool to improve data integrity in the future.

Keywords

Anomaly detection; music information retrieval; unsupervised

1. INTRODUCTION

Music information retrieval (MIR) is an active research area that integrates knowledge from a number of different fields, including Electrical Engineering, Computer Science, Psychology, and Musicology [7]. Many previous studies in this area have adopted machine learning techniques and applied them to audio data to build an intelligent system that understands music. The evaluation of such systems, as described by Schedl et al. [7], requires different datasets and annotations depending on the tasks. However, since the annotation process for music data is both complex and subjective, the quality of the annotations created by human experts can vary considerably from dataset to dataset, potentially introducing errors into the system and adversely affecting the performance. Finding a way to enhance the correctness of these datasets is thus crucial for the further improvement of MIR systems.

A typical example of the types of problems encountered concerns the Music Genre Recognition (MGR). According to Sturm [10], the most frequent used dataset in MGR is GTZAN [12], and many existing systems are evaluated based on their performance in classifying GTZAN audio data into its annotated genre class. However, Sturm points out that this dataset actually contains a significant fraction of corrupted files, repeated clips, and misclassified genre labels. These are clearly undesirable for the proper training of an MGR system.

In the data mining community, the corruptions listed above are referred to as anomalies or outliers. Identifying these outliers in a given dataset could be formulated as an anomaly detection problem [3]. Although anomaly detection methods are widely applied in various types of datasets, they are rarely discussed in the MIR community.

In this paper, we propose an unsupervised approach to address this problem and to detect the anomalies in music datasets. A statistics-based model is developed to capture the normal behavior of feature representations. Adding a Student-t prior to the latent error variable in the model maintains the robustness of the estimation of the normal behavior and absorbs the anomalous effects into this latent variable. The contributions of this paper are summarized as follows:

- **An unsupervised music anomaly detection approach:** An unsupervised approach for detecting anomalies in music datasets is proposed. No anomaly label is required.
- **A categorical anomaly detection model:** A regression based categorical anomaly detection model using a robust estimation strategy is also proposed. Furthermore, an approach to approximate the analytically intractable inference is also developed.
- **Benchmark experiments:** Results on the benchmark dataset demonstrated that the proposed approach outperforms existing state-of-the-art methods.

2. METHOD

2.1 Feature Extraction

In this paper, a set of baseline features based on Tzanetakis and Cook's features [12] is extracted for comparison with prior work in this area. The extracted features can be divided into three categories: spectral, temporal and rhythmic. All of these features are extracted using a block-wise analysis method. The process begins by down-mixing the audio signal to a mono signal, that is then segmented into overlapping blocks (block size: 23 ms, hop size: 11 ms). The temporal features are computed from the time domain signal of each block directly. The spectral features are computed from the

SIGIR '16, July 17-21, 2016, Pisa, Italy

DOI: http://dx.doi.org/10.1145/2911451.2914700

magnitude spectrum of each block using a Hann window. The rhythmic features are extracted from the beat histogram of the entire time domain signal. The selected features are as follows (for details of the implementations, please refer to [5]):

- **Spectral Features** ($d = 16$): Spectral Centroid (SC), Spectral Roll-off (SR), Spectral Flux (SF), 13 Mel Frequency Cepstral Coefficients (MFCCs)
- **Temporal Features** ($d = 1$): Zero Crossing Rate (ZCR)
- **Rhythmic Features** ($d = 8$): Period0 (P0), Amplitude0 (A0), RatioPeriod1 (RP1), Amplitude1 (A1), RatioPeriod2 (RP2), Amplitude2 (A2), RatioPeriod3 (RP3), Amplitude3 (A3).

Spectral and temporal features are aggregated in texture windows of length 0.743 s following the standard procedure as outlined in [12]. The mean and standard deviation of the features within a window are then computed to create a new feature vector. Finally, all the resulting feature vectors are reaggregated with their mean and standard deviation, generating a single feature vector that represents each individual recording in the dataset.

2.2 Model Design

Given N feature vectors $X = \{X_1, ..., X_N\}$ and their corresponding categories $Y = \{Y_1, ..., Y_N\}$, where each $Y_n \in \{C_1, C_2, ..., C_M\}$, we formulate the relation of Y and X based on a linear assumption. The input-output relationship can be represented as a regression model:

$$g(Y) = X\beta + \varepsilon, \tag{1}$$

where g is the categorical link function, β is the regression coefficient matrix, and ε is a random variable that represents the white-noise vector of each instance. The link function g is a logit function that is paired with a category C_M, i.e., $\ln\left(P(Y_n = C_m)/P(Y_n = C_M)\right) = X_n\beta_m + \varepsilon_{nm}$. Since the probabilities of the categories will sum to one, we can derive the following modeling equations:

$$P(Y_n = C_m) = \frac{\exp\{X_n\beta_m + \varepsilon_{nm}\}}{1 + \sum_{l=1}^{M-1}\exp\{X_n\beta_l + \varepsilon_{nl}\}} \tag{2}$$

and

$$P(Y_n = C_M) = \frac{1}{1 + \sum_{l=1}^{M-1}\exp\{X_n\beta_l + \varepsilon_{nl}\}} \tag{3}$$

The coefficient vector β usually represents the decision boundary in a classification problem. Here, β is used to capture the normal behavior of the data. Following the convention, we assume that each β_m obeys a Gaussian distribution with a predefined mean vector and a predefined covariance matrix Σ_β, i.e.,

$$\beta_m \sim N(\beta_m | \mathbf{0}, \Sigma_\beta) \tag{4}$$

In traditional regression applications, the error factor ε is generally assumed to follow a Gaussian distribution. However, a Gaussian distribution lacks tolerance for anomalies since the probability distribution is near zero at points far away from the distribution mean. In the study of robust statistics, it is suggested to assume that this random variable follows a heavy-tailed distribution in order to improve the capability of capturing anomalies [11].

In this work, we assume that the error is a zero-mean Student-t random variable, which has been shown to be a useful way to improve the robustness of the logistic regression model [6]. The probability density function is as the following:

$$p(\varepsilon|\sigma_\varepsilon^2, df) = \frac{\Gamma(\frac{df+1}{2})}{\Gamma(\frac{df}{2})\sqrt{\pi df \sigma_\varepsilon^2 \varepsilon}}\left(1 + \frac{\varepsilon^2}{df\sigma_\varepsilon^2}\right)^{1(\frac{df+1}{2})} \tag{5}$$

where σ^2 is the scaling parameter, and df is the number of the degrees of freedom. We utilize the Student-t variable as an "error-buffer" here to absorb the error introduced by the anomaly instances, thus allowing us to easily differentiate between the anomalies and errors.

2.3 Approximate Inference

Since the response is a categorical variable, the inference becomes intractable. We make a Bayesian assumption to the model and use the variational-EM algorithm [1] to approximate the inference. We start from the joint distribution of the model:

$$p(Y, \beta, \varepsilon) \propto p(Y|\beta, \varepsilon)p(\beta)p(\varepsilon) \tag{6}$$

Suppose there is a proposal distribution $q(Y, \varepsilon, \beta)$ that approximates p, s.t. $q \simeq p$. Based on the structure of the model, we can factorize q into two parts, i.e., $q(\varepsilon)$ and $q(\beta)$. The estimation of the variational variables is updated by maximizing the optimal factors until the convergence criterion is satisfied. For each individual update we apply iterated re-weighted least squares (IRLS) to find the optimum. Applying the Taylor expansion to the log expectations above, we can obtain a quadratic form in $\ln q = -\frac{1}{2}\nu^T Q \nu + \nu^T b$, where ν represent the target variable to update, and

$$b(\nu) = \nabla\nabla_\nu q(\nu) - \nabla_\nu q(\nu) \tag{7}$$

$$Q(\nu) = \nabla\nabla_\nu q(\nu) \tag{8}$$

In each iteration, we update the value of ν by

$$\nu^{(new)} = Q^{-1}(\nu^{(old)})b(\nu^{(old)}) \tag{9}$$

Thus, by iteratively updating β and ε, with estimating the gradient and Hessian in each iteration, the process will converge to a local optimum of these variables.

2.4 Anomaly Detection Process

The full process, shown in Algorithm 1, consists of feature extraction and anomaly identification. It begins by taking the music clips and extracting their features. The anomaly identification process then takes the extracted feature vectors

Algorithm 1 Detection Process

Require: Dataset of music clips D
Ensure: The anomalous instances

```
set [Y, X] = extractFeatures(D)
set β* = β0, ε* = 0
while Not converge do
    set β* = argmax_β(p(β|X, Y, ε*))
    set ε* = argmax_ε(p(ε|X, Y, β*))
    set L = ln(p(θ|X, Y, ε*))
end while
set AnomalySet = φ
for all ε*_n in ε* do
    if ε*_n > ErrorThreshold then
        put n in AnomalySet
    end if
end for
return AnomalySet
```

Method	P	R	F	AUC
Linear Detection	**0.59**	**0.55**	**0.57**	**0.91**
Clustering	0.23	0.23	0.23	0.74
KNN	0.27	0.26	0.27	0.78
LOF	0.26	0.25	0.25	0.74

Table 1: Average Detection Rate for Injected Data

and the corresponding categories as the input, and returns a set of indices of the anomalous instances as the output.

The process starts by taking the MGR dataset D and performing a feature extraction to obtain the feature vector X and its corresponding class labels Y. Next, the anomaly detection method starts with initial values of the variables β_0 and ε_0. The process iteratively updates the model variables β and ε using the approach introduced above (lines 3–7). After the variables have converged, the error variable ε is checked to identify anomalies (lines 8–13). As a reasonable assumption, similar to the analysis of Gaussian distributions, instances with ε greater than 3 times of the standard deviation are labeled anomalies.

3. EXPERIMENT

3.1 Experimental Design

The experiments were conducted on the popular GTZAN dataset [12]. This dataset consists of 10 music genres (blues, classical, country, disco, hip-hop, jazz, metal, pop, reggae, and rock), each with 100 audio tracks. All tracks consist of a 30-second excerpt of complex mixtures of music.

For this study, two sets of experiments were conducted to test the performance of the proposed method and three other benchmark methods. In the first experiment, we used a purified GTZAN dataset that excludes the conspicuous misclassified and jitter music clips reported in [9]. An injection process was performed by randomly choosing 5% of the instances in each genre, and randomizing their genre labels to create outliers. Sturm's report identifies around 50 conspicuous files, which corresponds to about 5% of the total number of files in the dataset. We generated 10 random realizations of the dataset, and evaluated the measures with the average for this 10-run batch. This experiment simulates the best-case scenario, where the dataset is clean and all genres are well separated in feature space. The results thus serve as a sanity check for all the methods.

In the second experiment, we applied our method to the full GTZAN dataset directly. The outliers identified were then compared with the list reported in [9]. This experiment is effectively a real-world scenario in which case the automated anomaly detection methods are expected to find the outliers identified by human experts. Two sets of features represent the dataset, one is the feature set as described in Sect. 2 and the other a minimal feature set using only 13 MFCCs, as reported in the work of Hansen et al. [4].

3.2 Benchmark Methods

We compared the results obtained using our approach with those of three unsupervised benchmark methods. Due to the small number of true anomaly labels and their uneven distributions across different genres, the application of a supervised anomaly classifier was deemed not feasible and thus excluded in this experiment.

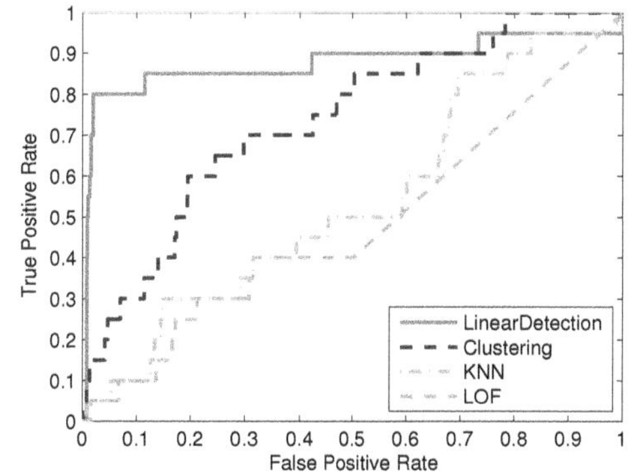

Figure 1: ROC curves on injected data

1. *Clustering*: an intuitive method for detecting misclassified music clips is to group them into M clusters. Ideally, all of the music clips in the same cluster should belong to the same genre so the instances with different category indices than the majority are labeled as anomalies. In this experiment, we used k-means clustering with the centroids initialized using the mean of each genre.
2. *k-Nearest Neighbor* (KNN): the KNN-based method calculates the distance from each instance to its k-nearest neighbor and marks those points with high average distances to their neighbors as anomalies. In our experiment, values for k between 1 and 20 were tested and the value with the best result were chosen. We set $k = 10$ in the injection set and $k = 1$ in the expert-label set.
3. *Local Outlier Factor* (LOF): LOF [2] is one of the most popular anomaly detection methods. Similar to the KNN method, it calculates the local density of each instance that can be estimated from the distance of its k-nearest neighbors. This approach compares an object's local density to its neighbors' and identifies the objects with significant lower local densities as anomalies. The value of k was chosen using the same approach as for the *KNN* method. We set $k = 15$ in both the injection experiment and the expert-label experiment.

3.3 Experimental Results

Our evaluation of the results obtained for the four methods was based on four standard metrics: precision P, recall R, F-measure F, and Area Under ROC Curve AUC. The first set of experiments was conducted on the injected data set. As shown in Table 1, the proposed method outperformed the three benchmark methods on all of the metrics.

Figure 1 shows the ROC curves for injected data. In the figure, *LinearDetection* refers to the proposed method, which is based on a linear assumption. Since our method has the best performance with respect to the AUC, the anomaly scores given by our approach provides the most useful information for ranking the significance of the detected anomalies. The advantage of the proposed method is that the regression model captures the input-output relationship between the features and the genres, while the benchmark methods rely solely on the distribution of features and may thus fail to capture the actual pattern.

We also compared our feature set with a minimal feature set containing only MFCCs, as used in [4]. As shown in Table 2, the performance metric for all the methods dropped

Method	*P*	*R*	*F*	*AUC*
Linear Detection	**0.52**	**0.40**	**0.45**	**0.87**
Clustering	0.08	0.07	0.07	0.61
KNN	0.12	0.11	0.12	0.68
LOF	0.13	0.13	0.13	0.70

Table 2: Average detection rate for injected data with only MFCCs features

Method	*P*	*R*	*F*	*AUC*
Linear Detection	**0.18**	**0.23**	**0.20**	**0.63**
Clustering	0.08	0.07	0.07	0.41
KNN	0.10	0.09	0.10	0.50
LOF	0.10	0.09	0.10	0.51

Table 3: Detection rates for GTZAN data (Sturm's anomalies)

in this case. In particular, the performance of the *Clustering* method wa significantly dropped. This observation suggests that in MFCC feature space, the genres overlap substantially and cannot be separated by clustering.

In the second set of experiments, the anomaly detection process was applied to the full GTZAN dataset and aim to detect the misclassified music clips reported by Sturm [9]. The results are shown in Table 3. Although our method still outperformed the benchmark methods, the performance decreased noticeably compared to the injection setup. Based on the metrics utilized here, none of these methods are able to detect anomalies with high accuracy. Comparing our results with the anomalies reported in [9], we found that our method is able to detect the jitter clips (*reggae*: No. 87), and some of the obviously misclassified clips, including *reggae*: No. 88, *disco*: No. 41, *pop*: No. 81, *hip-hop*: No. 31, all of which achieved high anomaly score with our method. Interestingly, we also found that neither our method nor any of the benchmark methods could successfully detect anomalies in the metal genre (*metal*: Nos. 46–57). These music clips are in fact punk rock but are annotated as metal in the GTZAN dataset. It can be observed that the extracted features for these music clips are very similar to other metal clips. This implies that the features used for this approach are not able to sufficiently differentiate *punk rock* from *metal*. One important task for future work is therefore to improve the identification of representative features to allow for better differentiation between similar genres.

It should also be pointed out that while people mostly agree on the genre labels *hip-hop* and *blues*, they tend to disagree on the category *rock* [8], demonstrating the inherent ambiguity of many music genres. This trend can be observed in Table 4, where the detection rates for *metal* and *rock* are the lowest among all the genres. This is most likely due to the inherent ambiguity in these genre categories, which could result in inconsistent patterns in the feature space and thus increase the difficulty of anomaly detection. All of the methods failed to detect the alternative rock clips reported by Sturm (*metal*: Nos. 96–99); the feature vectors of these clips are generally similar to those of other metal music clips. To the best of our understanding, these clips can also be categorized as nu-metal, which is a sub-category of metal music in the taxonomy of genre. This again highlights the natural ambiguity involved in classifying music. One potential solution is to develop a multi-class modeling method to tolerate this ambiguity and suggest alternative classes that might also be applicable to individual music clips.

Genre	# Anomalies	# Positives	*P*	*R*
Blues	0	1	N/A	N/A
Classical	0	0	N/A	N/A
Country	4	8	0.13	0.25
Disco	7	9	0.33	0.42
Hip-hop	2	6	0.17	0.50
Jazz	2	0	N/A	0.00
Metal	16	1	0.00	0.00
Pop	3	6	0.33	0.67
Reggae	7	10	0.30	0.43
Rock	2	15	0.00	0.00

Table 4: Detection rate on GTZAN data by genre

4. CONCLUSION

In this paper, we have presented an unsupervised approach for automatic anomaly detection in music datasets. The proposed approach incorporates a novel statistical model to identify suspect files in existing music datasets with no training data required. The experimental results demonstrated that our method outperformed other benchmark anomaly detection approaches when applied to the GTZAN dataset. In the future, more features will be investigated to find better and meaningful representations for anomaly detection in music datasets.

5. REFERENCES

[1] C. M. Bishop. *Pattern Recognition and Machine Learning (Information Science and Statistics)*. Springer-Verlag New York, Inc., Secaucus, NJ, USA, 2006.

[2] M. M. Breunig, H.-P. Kriegel, R. T. Ng, and J. Sander. Lof: identifying density-based local outliers. *SIGMOD Record*, 29(2):93–104, May 2000.

[3] V. Chandola, A. Banerjee, and V. Kumar. Anomaly detection: A survey. *ACM Computer Survey*, 41(3):15:1–15:58, July 2009.

[4] L. Hansen, T. Lehn-SchiÃÿler, K. Petersen, J. Arenas-Garcia, J. Larsen, and S. Jensen. Learning and clean-up in a large scale music database. In *European Signal Processing Conference (EUSIPCO)*, pages 946–950, 2007.

[5] A. Lerch. *An Introduction to Audio Content Analysis: Applications in Signal Processing and Music Informatics*. John Wiley and Sons, 2012.

[6] C. Liu. *Robit Regression: A Simple Robust Alternative to Logistic and Probit Regression*, pages 227–238. John Wiley & Sons, Ltd, 2005.

[7] M. Schedl, E. Gómez, and J. Urbano. *Music Information Retrieval: Recent Developments and Applications*, volume 8. Now Publishers Inc., Hanover, MA, USA, 2014.

[8] M. Sordo, O. Celma, M. Blech, and E. Guaus. The Quest for Musical Genres: Do the Experts and the Wisdom of Crowds Agree? In *Int. Conference on Music Information Retrieval (ISMIR)*, pages 255–260, 2008.

[9] B. L. Sturm. An analysis of the GTZAN music genre dataset. In *Proceedings of the second international ACM workshop on Music Information Retrieval with user-centered and multimodal strategies*, 2012.

[10] B. L. Sturm. The State of the Art Ten Years After a State of the Art: Future Research in Music Information Retrieval. *Journal of New Music Research*, 2013.

[11] D. E. Tyler. Robust statistics: Theory and methods. *Journal of the American Statistical Association*, 103:888–889, 2008.

[12] G. Tzanetakis and P. Cook. Musical genre classification of audio signals. *IEEE Transactions on Speech and Audio Processing*, 10(5):293–302, 2002.

Anonymizing Query Logs by Differential Privacy

Sicong Zhang, Hui Yang, Lisa Singh
Department of Computer Science
Georgetown University
sz303@georgetown.edu, huiyang@cs.georgetown.edu, Lisa.Singh@georgetown.edu

ABSTRACT

Query logs are valuable resources for Information Retrieval (IR) research. However, because they are also rich in private and personal information, the huge concern of leaking user privacy prevents query logs from being shared from the search companies to the broad research community. Bothered by the lack of good research data for years, the authors of this paper are motivated to explore ways to generate anonymized query logs that can still be effectively used to support the search task. We introduce a framework to anonymize query logs by differential privacy, the latest development in privacy research. The framework is empirically evaluated against multiple search algorithms on their retrieval utility, measured in standard IR evaluation metrics, using the anonymized logs. The experiments show that our framework is able to achieve a good balance between retrieval utility and privacy.

Keywords

Privacy-Preserving Information Retrieval, Query Log Anonymization, Differential Privacy

1. INTRODUCTION

Query logs are essential research resources for Information Retrieval (IR), especially for the field of Web search. However, releasing query logs without proper anonymization may lead to serious violations of users' privacy. This was the case in 2006 when American Online (AOL) released an insufficiently anonymized version of their query log [1]. Table 1 shows a sample of this AOL query log.

Existing work on query log anonymization has attempted to protect the privacy of search logs in many ways. For instance, [1, 3] used clustering techniques and k-anonymity, which assumes each query to be issued by at least k different users, to anonymize query logs. The limitation of a k-anonymity approach is that its privacy guarantee can be easily broken when an adversary knows information about the users from an unexpected source. When an adversary knows about the user more than what the k-anonymity algorithm assumes, the adversary could join the unexpected source with existing ones and break the privacy guarantee. A stronger privacy notation is thus needed in query log anonymization.

SIGIR '16, July 17–21, 2016, Pisa, Italy.

DOI: http://dx.doi.org/10.1145/2911451.2914732

Table 1: A Sample of the AOL Query Log during March 2006, from User 2178.

Query	Rank	Clicked URL
weatherchannel	1	http://www.weatherchannel.com.au
weatherchannel	5	http://www.weatherchannel.com.ru
honda accord check engine light...	1	http://www.automedia.com
fuel additives check engine light...	1	http://www.smogtips.com
...		

In this paper, we propose to use differential privacy [6, 8] to anonymize a query log. Differential privacy is the state-of-the-art approach which provides a strong privacy notion. It has been widely used in the database and data mining communities. Differential privacy provides guarantees which can be theoretically proved that every individual user in the datasets would not be identified. Unlike k-anonymity, differential privacy does not make assumptions about the amount and scope of an adversary's background knowledge.

A query log anonymization mechanism $A(Q)$ satisfies (ϵ, δ)-*differential privacy* if for all neighboring query logs Q_1 and Q_2, and for all possible outputs Q^* the following inequality holds: $Pr[A(Q_1) = Q^*] \le e^\epsilon \times Pr[A(Q_2) = Q^*] + \delta$, where ϵ and δ are two model parameters related to the level of privacy guarantees. The smaller their values, the better the privacy guarantee. Specifically, a differentially private algorithm achieves ϵ-differential privacy if $\delta = 0$, which is even stronger than (ϵ, δ)-differential privacy.

In addition, most existing work in query log anonymization [8] measured the utility of the anonymization output in terms of the size of the remaining logs, without measuring a utility that is directly related to retrieval performance. It is thus difficult to tell how much utility is left in the query logs after anonymization in terms of how useful the logs is when we use them to retrieve relevant documents in a Web search algorithm. In this paper, we propose the retrieval utility function from the viewpoint of a search engine to report the actual usefulness of query logs after anonymization by differential privacy. Our approach achieves ϵ-differential privacy with $\delta = 0$.

To evaluate our approach, we experiment on the task of document retrieval with the anonymized query log using two Web search algorithms, a query-click model [4] and an implicit feedback model [2]. We then calculate the utility of the anonymized query log using retrieval effectiveness measures such as nDCG [7]. The results show that our framework is able to generate anonymized query logs that maintain a good level of retrieval utility. In another experiment on the

Table 2: Samples of the anonymized AOL query log.

Part 1: Query Counts		Part 2: Click-Through Counts			Part 3: Query Transitions Counts		
Query	*Counts*	*Query*	*Clicked-through URL*	*Counts*	*Query*	*Next Query*	*Counts*
weather	13826	weather	http://www.weather.com	4190	weather	aol weather	44
weather channel	1175	weather	http://weather.yahoo.com	1035	weather	weather channel	25
aol weather	284	aol weather	http://weather.aol.com	30	weather	las vegas weather	9
las vegas weather	126	aol weather	http://aolsvc.weather.aol.com	16	aol weather	aol yellow pages	5
...		...			...		

tradeoff between privacy and utility, the framework is shown to be able to achieve a good balance between the two.

2. PROBLEM FORMULATION

This section presents our formulation of the query log anonymization problem.

Query Log Q: Query log Q is a textual document that records query data between the search engine and its users. Usually, it contains a record for each user including the user's id, the query, a ranked list of URLs that the search engine returns to the user, click-through information, and timestamps for all user actions.

Web Search Using Query Logs: Given a query q and a query log Q, the task of Web Search is to provide a ranked list of documents or URLs D that is relevant to q, from a set of documents or URLs that are built into a pre-indexed corpus C. Most Web search algorithms fit into this setting. User clicks, query reformulations, time spent examining the returned documents, and clicked documents on similar queries shared by multiple users are often the key elements used in a modern Web search algorithm.

The Task of Query Log Anonymization: Given an input query log Q, the task is to produce a version of the log in which the identifiable data is removed and the remaining data is adequately anonymized so as to reduce the likelihood of re-identification of users. The output of this task is an anonymized query log Q', with a guaranteed degree of privacy.

Privacy Function A: An anonymized query log Q' is generated by applying a privacy function A on the original query log Q. That is, $Q' = A(Q)$. Usually, A is parameterized to indicate the level of privacy that Q' can achieve. For example, in differential privacy, ϵ is the parameter in A, i.e., $Q' = A(\epsilon, Q)$. Smaller ϵ values indicate higher levels of privacy protection.

Utility Function U: In privacy-related research, the remaining utility of the data after applying a privacy function on it is an indispensable part of the research. Usually, a utility function U needs to be domain specific to be able to evaluate the usefulness of the data in a domain. The utility function can be applied on both the original data $U(Q)$ and the anonymized data $U(Q')$ to compare the utility deduction.

Utility Function for Web Search: In the context of information retrieval, a utility function U could be a two-step process – the first is to use the query log for document retrieval, i.e., to retrieve a set of ranked documents D for any $q \in Q$, where $D = R(q), q \in D$ and R is a retrieval algorithm. The second is to use IR evaluation metrics E to measure how good the retrieved document list D is with respect to each q being evaluated; that is $E : E(D)$. Therefore, the utility function of a query log Q can be represented as $U(Q) = E(R(Q))$, where E is a retrieval effectiveness measure for search results generated by R.

Goal: The goal of a successful query log anonymization algorithm is to have $|U(Q) - U(Q')| < \sigma$, where σ is kept small. At the same time, a successful query log anonymization algorithm should ensure that the privacy level $\epsilon : Q' = A(\epsilon, Q)$ is small enough to provide high privacy guarantee.

3. FORMAT OF ANONYMIZED LOG

In order to improve the privacy level of query logs to match the specifications of differential privacy, a search record might be removed or modified into a set of statistics. However, we need to be aware that such changes made on the original data only make sense if the remaining logs can provide enough information to be useful, in our case, to still be able to support Web Search. This section explains the output format of query log anonymization in our framework.

Firstly, we need to keep queries, which are central in query logs. They are kept in the textual format as they are. Low-frequency queries are removed since they are too unique and greatly increase the chance to break privacy guarantee if they stay. Next, the click-throughs are also key data in a query log. However, they can only be released in a statistical format in order to apply differential privacy on the log. Therefore, we aggregate all the click-throughs and show them as summary counts (see Table 1). Furthermore, highly identifiable features such as the user ids are removed during anonymization. Therefore, they are not shown up in the output log. Finally, we also maintain query transitions in a query log, allowing researchers to develop more advanced web search algorithms for multiple search queries in sessions.

The following format is proposed for an anonymized query log (shown in Table 2). Each anonymized query log Q' consists of three parts. The first part contains the released search queries and their corresponding frequencies in Q. Notice that all queries in Q' are in plain text, allowing researchers the opportunity to develop full-text retrieval algorithms. The second part contains click through data for each of the released query-URL pairs. Each line shows a query, a clicked URL for this query, and the number of clicks for the query-URL pair. The last part of Q' contains information about the query transitions in Q. Each line shows a pair of adjacent queries and the frequency of this query transition. To achieve differential privacy [6], all of the statistics in Q' could be modified with Laplacian noise [10].

4. ANONYMIZING QUERY LOG

We care about both the privacy levels and the utility it remains after being private. On the privacy side, our query log anonymization algorithm is a significant improvement upon [8] where their approach provides an (ϵ, δ)-differential privacy while we can achieve ϵ-differential privacy. We achieve this by making use of an external stochastic query pool to expand the query set. On the utility side, we are probably the first to use the IR evaluation metrics to measure the utility of an anonymized query log.

The main steps of anonymizing a query log Q are:
1) Remove Sensitive Data. We remove unique queries (frequency less than 5) or queries containing unique terms. This is to filter out sensitive data such as SSN or bank account numbers. **2) Limit User Activities.** We only keep the first q_f number of queries and the first c_f number of URL clicks for a user who has been logged in Q. The remaining set of search records forms Q_{clean}. **3) Expand the Query Set.** We define a query pool Q_p as the collection of potential queries to add into a query log. Query log owners, such as search engine companies could extend a to-be-released query log with more queries sampled from search records outside of this to-be-released log. Theoretically, every sufficiently frequent query gets a chance to be included in the expanded set. In this paper, we simulate this process by using high-frequency n-grams in general English [5]. We refer the combined set of queries as Q^+, where $Q^+ = Q_{clean} + Q_p$. **4) Select Final Set of Queries.** We use $Lap(b)$ as the Laplacian noise with parameter b [6]. We define the fuzzed query counts as the original query counts plus the corresponding Laplacian noise. We choose to release a query q when its fuzzed query counts $(M(q, Q^+) + Lap(b))$ is greater than a threshold K. Here $M(q, Q^+)$ is the frequency of the query q in Q^+. Note that the added queries can also be released with fuzzed query counts if the counts are greater than the threshold. The final query set generated after this step is referred to as $Q_{reduced}$. **5) Generate Log Statistics.** As presented in section 3, we release the query counts and click counts for each URL. All counts are fuzzed with Laplacian noise. **6) Generate Query Transitions.** We also release the query transition information to preserve sequential information of the query logs. We release adjacent query transitions from Q_{clean} with fuzzed counts, if both queries are included in $Q_{reduced}$.

5. UTILITY OF WEB SEARCH

As we defined in Section 2, the utility function of a query log Q in the context of IR is $U(Q) = E(R(Q))$, which is a nested function of two parts, retrieval and IR evaluation.

Part 1: Retrieval The first part is to use the query log Q for document retrieval, i.e., to retrieve a set of ranked documents D for any $q \in Q$. This step produces ranking lists which we denote as $R(Q)$. In this preliminary work, we test our approach of generating Q' using two click-based Web search algorithms. One is a random walk algorithm based on the query-click graph, and the other uses clicks as implicit feedback. Both of them do not require access to document content.

The first retrieval algorithm is based on a random walk model, a variation of a popular web search algorithm proposed by Craswell et al. [4]. In the graph, nodes are queries and documents (URLs), while the transitions include clicked documents from a query, adjacent queries in the original log, and self-loops to a node itself. The transition probability $P(k|j)$ from a query node j to a document node or another query node k is calculated by:

$$P(k|j) = \begin{cases} (1-s)C_{jk}/\Sigma_i C_{ji} & ,\forall k \neq j \\ s & ,k = j \end{cases} \quad (1)$$

where, C_{jk} is the weight between node j and k given by Q', and s is the self-transition probability. If both nodes j and k are query nodes, weight C_{jk} is defined as the query transition counts from j to k in Q'; otherwise, if j is a query node while k is a document node, weight C_{jk} is defined as the click-through counts for this query-document pair in Q'. In our approach, we set the self loop probability $s = 0.1$. Considering the cost of computation, each time step we start from a test query node, random walk three steps before stopping. After that, we can rank documents in descending order by the probability of being the stopping node.

The second retrieval algorithm we implemented is based on implicit feedback from user clicks, which is a variant of [2]. Given a query q, the relevance score $S(d)$ for each document d is calculated as:

$$S(d) = \begin{cases} \lambda \frac{1}{I_d+1} + (1-\lambda)\frac{1}{O_d+1}, & \text{if implicit feedback exists for d} \\ \frac{1}{O_d+1}, & \text{otherwise} \end{cases} \quad (2)$$

where λ is a parameter to weight the importance of user click. O_d is the original rank which is ranked using the order of click-through counts of document d with the query q, according to Q'. I_d is the rank of d from Q_{Test} when the user made the click. In our approach, we empirically set $\lambda = 0.6$. Finally, the documents are ranked in the descending order of $S(d)$ scores for each individual query q.

Part 2: IR Evaluation The second part is to apply IR evaluation metrics on those retrieved documents and to generate a final set of numerical scores to indicate the level of retrieval utility. We apply the evaluation metrics E to the ranked list R. We evaluate the search results using standard IR evaluation metrics such as nDCG [7] and MAP (Mean Average Precision) [9].

Table 3: Statistics of the AOL query log.

Statistics	Counts
Total number of records	36,389,567
Log size (GB)	2.2
# of unique user IDs	657,426
# of unique queries	10,154,742
# of clicks	19,442,629
Avg. clicks per user	29.57

Table 4: Utilities with Random Walk. Two-tailed t-tests ($p < 0.01$) show that no significant difference of utility scores before and after anonymization.

Query Log	nDCG@10	P@5	P@10	MAP
Original	0.6658	0.1484	0.0779	0.6395
Anonymized	0.6675	0.1486	0.0777	0.6424

6. EXPERIMENTS

We use the AOL query log [1] for our experiments. Table 3 presents the major statistics of AOL query log. For each parameter setting, the experiments are conducted in the following order: (1) A 5-fold cross validation is used to partition the data. In each run, we use 80% of the data as the training set Q and the remaining as the test set Q_{Test}; (2)

Table 5: **Utilities with Implicit Feedback. Two-tailed t-tests ($p < 0.01$) show that no significant difference of utility scores before and after anonymization.**

Query Log	nDCG@10	P@5	P@10	MAP
Original	0.6919	0.1535	0.0796	0.6725
Anonymized	0.6897	0.1527	0.0790	0.6711

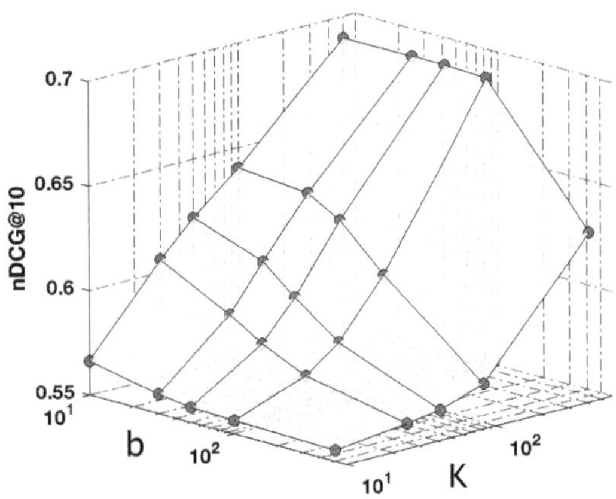

Figure 1: Relationships between noise b, query cutoff K and utility score $nDCG@10$.

The proposed ϵ-differentially private query log anonymization framework is applied to anonymize the query log. (3) Documents are retrieved using the algorithms as described in Section 5 for queries in Q_{Test}; (4) These retrieval algorithms are also run on the original log Q to compare their performance against that when the anonymized log Q' is used. We report the utility scores in nDCG@10 [7], Precision@5,@10, and MAP.

6.1 Utility by Retrieval Effectiveness

We first compare retrieval results using the original query log (Q) and the anonymized query log (Q'). Table 4 compares the performances of the Random Walk algorithm on query logs before and after anonymization while Table 5 compares the performances of the Implicit Feedback algorithm on query logs before and after anonymization. The anonymized query log used in both tables is the same and was generated with the settings $\epsilon = 29.99$, query counts threshold $K = 500$, and noise scale $b = 10$. Within each of the two tables, statistical significance tests (two-tailed t-tests, $p < 0.01$) show that the performances on query logs before and after anonymization are not significantly different from each other. This confirms that the retrieval effectiveness of our anonymized query log is comparable to the retrieval effectiveness of the un-anonymized version.

6.2 Privacy-Utility Tradeoff

More privacy guarantee would consume more utility of an anonymized query log. Here we also study the privacy-utility tradeoff with different parameter settings. Figure 1 shows the utility score (measured in nDCG@10) for the Implicit Feedback algorithms using Q' with different values for the query cutoff threshold K and the noise level b. Fixing all the other parameters including the log size, we range both K and b from 10 to 500. Figure 1 plots the trends between the utility scores and the parameter values. Each data point represents the average from a 5-fold cross-validation experiments. We observe that as the noise level b increases, the utility scores $nDCG@10$ decreases. We also observe that the utility score is less sensitive to b when b is much smaller than K. This matches our intuition that larger noise (comparing with K) will reduce retrieval performance and cause decreased utility.

7. CONCLUSIONS

In this paper, we introduce a framework for anonymizing search query logs and evaluating their Web search utility. We apply differential privacy, which is a strong privacy notation, to anonymize the logs. The experiments show that the Web search algorithms using the anonymized logs do not perform significantly different from those using the original logs. Since the high-level privacy has been guaranteed by our ϵ-differentially private anonymization algorithm, we suggest that search engine companies might be able to use less strict parameter settings and still maintain high utility. By proposing a new query log anonymization algorithm and a novel utility evaluation framework, our work makes an important step towards releasing Web query logs.

8. ACKNOWLEDGMENTS

This research was supported by NSF grant CNS-1223825, NSF grant IIS-145374, and DARPA grant FA8750-14-2-0226. Any opinions, findings, conclusions, or recommendations expressed in this paper are of the authors, and do not necessarily reflect those of the sponsor.

References

[1] E. Adar. User 4xxxxx9: Anonymizing query logs. In *Query Logs Workshop at the WWW'07.*

[2] E. Agichtein, E. Brill, and S. Dumais. Improving web search ranking by incorporating user behavior information. In *SIGIR '06.*

[3] C. Carpineto and G. Romano. Semantic search log k-anonymization with generalized k-cores of query concept graph. In *ECIR'13.*

[4] N. Craswell and M. Szummer. Random walks on the click graph. In *SIGIR '07.*

[5] M. Davies. N-grams data from the corpus of contemporary american english (coca). *Downloaded from http://www.ngrams.info*, 23:2012, 2011.

[6] C. Dwork. Differential privacy: A survey of results. In *Theory and Applications of Models of Computation*, pages 1–19. Springer, 2008.

[7] K. Järvelin and J. Kekäläinen. Cumulated gain-based evaluation of ir techniques. *ACM Trans. Inf. Syst.*, 20(4):422–446, Oct. 2002.

[8] A. Korolova, K. Kenthapadi, N. Mishra, and A. Ntoulas. Releasing search queries and clicks privately. In *WWW '09.*

[9] S. Robertson. A new interpretation of average precision. In *SIGIR '08.*

[10] R. Sarathy and K. Muralidhar. Evaluating laplace noise addition to satisfy differential privacy for numeric data. *Trans. Data Privacy*, 4(1):1–17, Apr. 2011.

Audio Features Affected by Music Expressiveness

Experimental Setup and Preliminary Results on Tuba Players

Alberto Introini
Dipartimento di Informatica
Università degli Studi di Milano
39, Via Comelico, Milano, Italy

Giorgio Presti
Dipartimento di Informatica
Università degli Studi di Milano
39, Via Comelico, Milano, Italy
giorgio.presti@unimi.it

Giuseppe Boccignone
Dipartimento di Informatica
Università degli Studi di Milano
39, Via Comelico, Milano, Italy

ABSTRACT

Within a Music Information Retrieval perspective, the goal of the study presented here is to investigate the impact on sound features of the musician's *affective intention*, namely when trying to intentionally convey emotional contents via expressiveness. A preliminary experiment has been performed involving 10 tuba players. The recordings have been analysed by extracting a variety of features, which have been subsequently evaluated by combining both classic and machine learning statistical techniques. Results are reported and discussed.

1. INTRODUCTION

The sound and music computing literature has investigated several approaches relevant for *Music Information Retrieval* (MIR) tasks. A prominent one is the identification of emotions expressed by music so as to facilitate emotion-based music organization, indexing, and retrieval (see [1] for a discussion). Yet, when such perspective is embraced a deceptively simple question should be answered: which facets of music (such as: harmony, rhythm and timbre) and which combinations of these features can be effectively exploited for emotion identification?

In order to make a principled step in such direction, here we present a preliminary study on how audio features are likely to be modulated while musicians try to intentionally convey emotional contents through expressiveness.

Reviews made by [7] and [20] revealed that there is not a dominant feature among the others able to distinguish different emotions, instead a large set of features is necessary to get some result. As to expressivenes, [10] found a set of relevant *score-independent* features (such as: *Roughness*, *Attack time*, *Peak level* and *Notes per second*). In [4] a great variety of features is used to achieve emotion classification and are also related to which emotion they outline, e.g. *Dynamics*, *Timbre* and *Articulation*. Research in [19] was aimed at finding which aspects of the signal other than *brightness* and *attack time* were relevant in timbre-evoked emotions, and determined the relevance of *odd-even ratio*, a feature strictly related to the harmonic properties of the signal. Eventually, [17] suggest the choice of *tempo*, *dynamics*, and *articulation* as key feature-classes for studying music expressiveness, while demonstrating that musicians play in a different way whether they are trying to *express* an emotion rather than when *feeling* an emotion.

In the study reported here, as a novel contribution, we set up an experiment leading the musician to mostly exploit on *emotional contagion* and *auditory sensations* rather than *musical expectancy*, *episodic memories* or others subjective phenomena. Then, we have exploited a mix of statistical analysis (*ANalysis Of VAriance*, ANOVA) and machine learning techniques [2], such as dimensionality reduction (*Principal Component Analysis*, PCA) and automatic classification (*Support Vector Machines*, SVM), to analyse the emotional content conveyed by the audio features.

SIGIR '16, July 17 - 21, 2016, Pisa, Italy

ISBN 978-1-4503-4069-4/16/07... $15.00

DOI: http://dx.doi.org/10.1145/2911451.2914690

2. BACKGROUND AND RATIONALES

The music ability to elicit emotions intrigues researchers since a long time [3]. Juslin and Västfjäll reviewed several works related to this topic, and, most important, identified six mechanisms through which music can evoke emotions [6]:

1. Brain stem reflexes: Emotion is induced by *sound* itself because one or more acoustical characteristics of the music are taken by the brain stem to signal a potentially important event; reflexes account for the impact of *auditory sensations*

2. Evaluative conditioning: Listened music is repeatedly paired with other positive or negative stimuli.

3. Emotional contagion: The listener "perceives" the emotional expression of the music, and then "mimics" this expression internally, which leads to an induction of the same emotion by means of either peripheral feedback from muscles, or a more direct activation of the relevant emotional representations in the brain.

4. Visual imagery: The listener conjures up visual images while listening to the music; experienced emotions are the result of a close interaction between the music and the images.

5. Episodic memory: The music evokes a memory of a particular event in the listener's life.

6. Music expectancies: A specific feature violates, delays, or confirms the listener's expectations about the continuation of the music.

It is clear that mechanisms 2, 4, 5 and 6 are strictly subjective, while 1 and 3 rely on some degree of objective (or at least shared) aspects.In particular, emotional contagion

Figure 1: The *ad hoc* composed music fragment

is likely to be deeply rooted in simulation and motor-based mechanisms of emotion and thus relying on a shared manifold between subjects [18]. Under this rationale, 1 and 3 have been considered the mechanisms to be principally elicited in setting up the experiment.

3. EXPERIMENTAL SETUP

Ten tuba players have been asked to play 7 times a music fragment composed *ad hoc*, each time trying to express one different emotion among the six *basic emotions* namely, *anger, disgust, fear, happiness, sadness* and *surprise* [5], plus a neutral performance. This approach is different from [15], since the mechanisms we are investigating are closer to low-level affect processing rather than that involved in *music expectancies* [6].

The players came from different geographical areas and cultural and musical backgrounds: a tuba teacher, a graduated professional, a graduating student, a semi-pro, 3 young mid-level students and 3 amateurs. Each performer had sufficient skills to perform the melodic fragment: being able to express emotions regardless of the technical aspects was a basic condition in order to add expressiveness to the performance.

Materials: Instrument and Music Fragment. Materials choice aimed at maximizing the influence of shared mechanisms (*brain stem reflexes* and *emotional contagion*) over acoustic outcomes with respect to other mechanisms (cfr. Section 2).

In such precise perspective, we chose the tuba since its sound is generated by the musician and then amplified, tuned and filtered by the instrument: this allows the artist to take control over many aspects of the timbre, enabling great expressiveness. Further, the " embodied" characteristics of how tuba sound is produced are intimately connected to low-level aspects of affect production Of course, many other brasses share the same advantages, but our knowledge of this instrument allowed to conduct a sound analysis taking into account its potential and capabilities. What is important here is that brasses are instruments the most close to the human voice from both a technical and a timbral point of view.

A music fragment (shown in Figure 1) has been composed *ad hoc*. It presents no hints about known tunes, this should avoid emotions evoked by *episodic memories* and likely *evaluative conditionings*. Moreover, it sounds more like a *succession of pitches* rather than a *melody*, almost resembling a serial sequence: this should help avoiding any *music expectancy*. Just a small variance in note durations has been introduced to let some room for the performer to add expressiveness without stimulating much rhythmic expectancies. Note that the score has been written with neither key signatures nor time indications, dynamics and agogics. Performers are used to read scores containing tempo, phrasing and articulation signs; a score like this should guarantee more degrees of freedom to the interpreters.

Data acquisition. Once the performer was comfortable with the setup, 7 performances have been recorded: 6 while the musician tried to express basic emotions and a *neutral* one, which served as a baseline reference.

To prevent systematic bias in collecting data due to a common sequence pattern, the 6 basic emotions have been considered in random order. For each emotion the performer has been given some time to enter the right mood, and then the performance was recorded and listened back until the musician was satisfied of the outcome.

The neutral recording was the last task, made after a small debriefing phase and with a metronome to a fixed tempo of 85 BPM: the attention given to the metronome and to a rigorous execution was meant to leave no space for emotions in the performance, thus flattening the expressiveness. To prevent influences between musicians, they were not allowed to listen to others' performance before the experiment ended.

All recordings have been made in the same environment (a small concert hall), with the same equipment and with the same settings. The aim was limiting the influence of ambience on musicians while keeping the level differences consistent across the performances.

All signals have been recorded as mono PCM 44.100kHz 24bit files, the hardware and software tools used are: an *AKG C 419* Clip Microphone for wind instruments; an *M-AUDIO MobilePre USB* sound card; a laptop PC running *Cockos Reaper v4.77 x64* digital audio workstation. To prevent biases in the computation of some features, each recorded track has been manually processed in order to set leading and trailing silence to 0.5 seconds. Since the microphone was attached to the instrument, almost no reverberation was captured by the recordings (e.g. the ratio of *dry* vs. *wet* signal is very high).

4. DATA ANALYSIS AND RESULTS

Feature extraction has been performed within the Matlab environment, using both toolboxes (such as the *MIRToolbox* [9] and the *Timbre Toolbox* [11]) and custom algorithms, such as [13]. Table 1 shows the complete feature set together with the results obtained. Below we briefly discuss how each feature maps over the tuba performance.

- **Beats Per Minute (BPM)** corresponds to the speed of the execution.
- **Root Mean Square (RMS)** is a measure of the signal energy; here it reflects how *loud* the instrument has been played.
- **Low Energy (LOW)** is the percentage of signal with a level below the average [16]. This is a good measure of the amount of amplitude modulation and *legatos*.
- **Attack leap (ATK)** is a measure of the dynamic range of the attack phase of the sound [9]. This is influenced by transients, *staccatos* and abrupt dynamic changes, in opposition to *legatos* and soft attacks.
- **Harmonic energy (HAE), Noise Energy (NOE), Noisiness (NSN)** and **Harmonic Spectral Deviation (HRD)** measure the periodic vs. non-periodic component of the sound [11, 8]; in our context is intended to measure the balance between pitched notes and buzz.
- **Brightness (EBF)** by and large measures the amount of high-frequencies in the signal. Many algorithms have been proposed to measure brightness, for our task the one described in [13] and implemented in [14] gives the best results. Many aspects of sound production may influence EBF.

- **Tristimulus (T1-3)**, a concept borrowed from colour perception studies, is triple which in MIR is used for measuring the contribution of the fundamental, the second and third harmonic, and all the remaining components on the overall sound [12]. In our context, T1 and T3 can be thought as how many harmonics are excited.
- **Inharmonicity (INH)** and **Roughness (ROH)** are respectively a measure of the partials that fall outside the harmonic series and a measure of the intrinsic dissonance of the sound [11]. They both measure harshness of sound and may be good indicators of *sforzato*, *singing through the instrument* or other peculiar techniques.
- **Odd-Even Ratio (OER)** is the ratio between the energy of odd and even harmonics. Usually it depends only on the instrument, but it may also reflect the intention of the performer to obtain a *softer* or a *bitter* sound.

Folllowing [11], time-varying features are collapsed into scalar values through their medians (M) and interquartile ranges (IQR). Since a certain amount of subjectivity and cultural differences are present also in the *contagion* mechanism, and since the technical skills of the performers were not as uniform as expected, all features were normalized by performer. This allowed to evaluate the relation among different emotions rather than the artist's skills or instrument manufacture. The only feature that was considered by its non-normalized value is BPM (denoted $\mathbf{BPM_{nn}}$ in Table 1), since it showed some predictive accuracy also in the non-normalized version.

ANOVA was performed on each feature to test statistical significance when distinguishing between emotions. All features can be considered statistically significant ($p < 0.05$), except for $\mathrm{ATK_{IQR}}$ and $\mathrm{HRD_{IQR}}$, which were thus discarded from further analyses. We also analysed the feature space to test when and where features means were significantly different among the emotions; in other words we investigated which classes were distinguished by each feature. The outcomes are graphically shown in Table 1, each dot meaning that the feature can help distinguishing the corresponding pair of classes. The table shows that each pair of emotions is distinguishable by at least one feature.

A redundancy analysis over the remaining 24 features was then performed via PCA [2], showing that 4 principal components (PCs) have an eigenvalue greater than one, explaining 82.1% of the variance. To explain more than 90%, 7 PCs are necessary. An ANOVA test run over all PCs revealed that $\mathrm{PC_{1\text{-}3}}$ are useful to differentiate basic emotions, but none of the remaining are statistically significant. Moreover, always according to ANOVA, no PC can help distinguishing *disgust* vs. *surprise*. Feature coefficients related to $\mathrm{PC_{1\text{-}3}}$ are shown in Table 1.

To assess the goodness of ANOVA and PCA results in terms of predictive accuracy, we automatically classified recordings through an SVM [2], then we considered the F-Scores obtained from the confusion matrices generated according to a *leave-one-out* strategy [2] over the 70 available recordings.

The test considered: the whole feature set (called 24F in Table 2), sets of relevant PCs (respectively 7PC, 4PC, and 3PC) and different subsets of features.

Clearly, according to ANOVA, we expect to see lower F-scores for emotions with less features binding them. As to PCA, a failure in isolating the right components will result in better F-Scores when using feature subset rather than PCs sets.

SVM behaved as expected for what concerns the 24F set, presenting smaller F-Scores for *fear*, *disgust* and *surprise*, while holding a greater accuracy in other classes, thus confirming ANOVA results. SVM scores seem to be higher with reduced feature sets, suggesting the need of dimensionality reduction. Unfortunately PCA seems to fail to isolate the right components: 7F, 4F, and 3F present better results than 7PC, 4PC, and 3PC.

5. CONCLUSIONS

We outlined an experiment to investigate the effect of expressiveness on audio features, where a set of musicians was asked to play a music fragment composed *ad hoc* while trying to express different emotions. Overall preliminary results look promising.

Recorded data have been processed by extracting 26 features subsequently analysed via ANOVA, PCA and an SVM classifier. The ANOVA test discarded 2 features and gave a broad view of which features can distinguish each pair of emotions. PCA on the one hand revealed the presence of redundancy but, on the other hand for what concerns our goals, failed in isolating the correct descriptors, probably due to the small size of our dataset (70 recordings and 24 features). Different dimensionality reduction techniques will be explored in future works. SVM classification confirmed the reliability of ANOVA results, in particular the confusion between some classes of emotions, which needs to be addressed to understand whether the cause of the cluttering is a matter of chosen features or a matter of eliciting mechanisms.

In the experiment we considered a brass instrument (tuba). The rationale for this choice was motivated in Section 3. An issue to be further investigated is how the results translate to other classes of instruments such as stringed, keyboards and percussions.

6. REFERENCES

[1] M. Barthet, G. Fazekas, and M. Sandler. Multidisciplinary perspectives on music emotion recognition: Implications for content and context-based models. In *Proc. Int. Symp. Comp. Music Modeling and Retrieval (CMMR)*, pages 492–507, 2012.

[2] C. M. Bishop. *Pattern Recognition and Machine Learning*. Springer-Verlag New York, Inc., 2006.

[3] M. Budd et al. *Music and the emotions: The philosophical theories*. Routledge, 2002.

[4] T. Eerola, O. Lartillot, and P. Toiviainen. Prediction of multidimensional emotional ratings in music from audio using multivariate regression models. In *ISMIR*, pages 621–626, 2009.

[5] P. Ekman and K. Scherer. Expression and the nature of emotion. *Approaches to emotion*, 3:19–344, 1984.

[6] P. N. Juslin and D. Västfjäll. Emotional responses to music: The need to consider underlying mechanisms. *Behavioral and brain sciences*, 31(05):559–575, 2008.

[7] Y. E. Kim, E. M. Schmidt, R. Migneco, B. G. Morton, P. Richardson, J. Scott, J. A. Speck, and D. Turnbull. Music emotion recognition: A state of the art review. In *Proc. ISMIR*, pages 255–266. Citeseer, 2010.

Table 1: 26 chosen features, with emotion pairs and PCA coefficients.
A: Anger, D: Disgust, F: Fear, H: Happiness, S: Sadness, U: Surprise, N: Neutral.

	AS	AN	SU	AH	UN	AF	HN	HS	FN	SD	SN	DF	HF	AD	AU	HU	DN	UF	HD	DU	SF	#	PC1	PC2	PC3
BPM	•		•		•					•							•	•	•	•		8	0,17	0,03	**0,41**
BPM-nn			•	•	•			•		•									•			6	0,17	0,06	**0,41**
RMS	•	•	•	•		•		•	•					•	•							9	**0,25**	-0,21	-0,07
LOW	•	•	•	•	•		•									•					•	8	0,23	0,16	-0,01
ATK-M	•	•	•		•					•												5	0,18	-0,01	**0,30**
ATK-IQR																						0	-	-	-
EBF-M	•	•	•	•		•		•	•			•		•	•			•				11	**0,24**	-0,22	-0,05
EBF-IQR	•	•	•	•	•		•						•									7	**0,24**	0,07	-0,04
T1-M	•	•	•	•		•		•	•		•											8	-0,23	**0,26**	0,06
T1-IQR	•					•	•				•	•					•					6	-0,02	**0,35**	-0,13
T3-M	•	•	•	•		•		•	•				•		•							9	**0,26**	-0,16	-0,16
T3-IQR	•	•		•		•			•							•			•			7	0,18	-0,10	-0,32
HAE-M		•		•	•		•			•	•		•									7	-0,23	-0,22	0,12
HAE-IQR		•		•	•											•						4	-0,20	-0,17	**0,26**
NOE-M		•		•	•		•			•	•		•			•						8	-0,22	-0,22	0,18
NOE-IQR				•																		1	-0,16	-0,11	**0,35**
NSN-M	•	•	•		•									•						•		6	**0,24**	0,17	0,19
NSN-IQR	•	•	•		•	•	•	•		•				•								9	**0,25**	0,08	0,20
HRD-M		•	•		•		•			•	•		•			•						8	-0,21	-0,26	0,09
HRD-IQR																						0	-	-	-
INH-M	•	•	•		•		•															5	0,23	0,18	0,13
INH-IQR	•	•	•					•		•												5	0,22	0,04	**0,22**
ROH-M	•					•			•			•			•							5	0,11	-0,32	-0,09
ROH-IQR	•	•		•		•			•			•		•	•							8	0,22	-0,22	-0,15
OER-M	•		•			•		•	•		•	•					•	•				9	-0,18	**0,30**	-0,07
OER-IQR	•					•	•	•	•		•	•					•	•				9	-0,05	**0,38**	-0,08
PC1	•	•	•	•	•	•	•	•		•				•			•	•			•	13			
PC2	•				•	•			•		•	•	•		•							8			
PC3				•			•	•					•			•			•			6			
	20	18	16	15	14	13	11	11	10	9	8	7	7	6	6	6	5	5	4	2	2	#			

Table 2: *F*-Scores of SVM classification
SVM trained with different sets of features and PCs.

	24F	7F	7PC	4F	4PC	3F	3PC
Ang	78%	**100%**	58%	72%	69%	62%	69%
Hap	60%	60%	57%	63%	73%	71%	64%
Sad	67%	76%	42%	**80%**	63%	62%	55%
Dis	32%	67%	35%	40%	0%	27%	14%
Sur	21%	63%	35%	50%	27%	71%	27%
Fea	32%	56%	33%	50%	21%	0%	0%
Neu	82%	83%	67%	83%	77%	69%	71%

7F: BPM, RMS, $T1_M$, $T1_{IQR}$ HAE_M OER_M. ROH_M.
4F: BPM, EBF_{IQR}, EBF_M, HRD_M; **3F:** NSN_{IQR}, NOE_M, $T3_M$

[8] J. Krimphoff et al. Characterization of the timbre of complex sounds. 2. Acoustic analysis and psychophysical quantification. *J. de Physique*, 4:625–628, 1994.

[9] O. Lartillot, P. Toiviainen, and T. Eerola. A Matlab toolbox for music information retrieval. In *Data analysis, machine learning and applications*, pages 261–268. Springer, 2008.

[10] L. Mion and G. D. Poli. Score-independent audio features for description of music expression. *IEEE Trans. Audio, Speech, and Language Processing*, 16(2):458–466, 2008.

[11] G. Peeters, B. L. Giordano, P. Susini, N. Misdariis, and S. McAdams. The timbre toolbox: Extracting audio descriptors from musical signals. *J. Acoustical Society of America*, 130(5):2902–2916, 2011.

[12] H. F. Pollard and E. V. Jansson. A tristimulus method for the specification of musical timbre. *Acta Acustica united with Acustica*, 51(3):162–171, 1982.

[13] G. Presti and D. Mauro. Continuous Brightness Estimation (CoBE): Implementation and its possible applications. In *10th Proc. Int. Symp. Comp. Music Modeling and Retrieval (CMMR)*, pages 967–974, 2013.

[14] G. Presti, D. Mauro, and G. Haus. TRAP: TRAnsient Presence detection exploiting continuous brightness estimation (CoBE). In *Proceedings of the 12th Sound and Music Computing Conference (SMC 2015), Maynooth, Ireland*, pages 379–385, 2015.

[15] E. Schubert. Update of the hevner adjective checklist. *Perceptual and motor skills*, 96(3c):1117–1122, 2003.

[16] G. Tzanetakis and P. Cook. Musical genre classification of audio signals. *IEEE Trans. Speech and Audio Processing,*, 10(5):293–302, 2002.

[17] A. G. Van Zijl, P. Toiviainen, O. Lartillot, and G. Luck. The sound of emotion: The effect of performers' experienced emotions on auditory performance characteristics. *Music Perception: An Interdisciplinary Journal*, 32(1):33–50, 2014.

[18] J. Vitale, M.-A. Williams, B. Johnston, and G. Boccignone. Affective facial expression processing via simulation: A probabilistic model. *Biologically Inspired Cognitive Architectures Journal*, 10:30–41, 2014.

[19] B. Wu, A. Horner, and C. Lee. Musical timbre and emotion: The identification of salient timbral features in sustained musical instrument tones equalized in attack time and spectral centroid. In *Proc. 40th Int. Comp. Music Conf.(ICMC)*, pages 928–934, 2014.

[20] Y.-H. Yang and H. H. Chen. Machine recognition of music emotion: A review. *ACM Trans. Intelligent Systems and Technology (TIST)*, 3(3):40, 2012.

Automatic Identification and Contextual Reformulation of Implicit System-Related Queries

Adam Fourney
Microsoft Research
Redmond, WA, USA
adamfo@microsoft.com

Susan T. Dumais
Microsoft Research
Redmond, WA, USA
sdumais@microsoft.com

ABSTRACT

Web search functionality is increasingly integrated into operating systems, software applications, and other interactive environments that extend beyond the traditional web browser. In particular, intelligent virtual assistants (e.g., Microsoft Cortana or Apple Siri) often "fall-back" to generic web search in cases where utterances fall outside the set of scenarios known to the agent. In this paper we analyze a 3 month log of web search queries posed via the Cortana virtual assistant. We report that, in this environment, users frequently ask questions that implicitly pertain to the systems or devices from which they are searching (e.g., asking: [how do I take a screenshot]). Unfortunately, accurately answering these *implicit system queries* poses significant challenges to general web search engines, due in part to the lack of available context. We show that such queries: (1) can be detected with high precision, (2) are common, and (3) can be automatically reformulated to substantially improve retrieval performance in these fall-through scenarios.

CCS Concepts

•**Information systems** → **Query intent;** *Reformulation;*

Keywords

Implicit system search; virtual assistants

1. INTRODUCTION

Web search queries are often short and underspecified. To compensate, contemporary web search engines consider the contexts in which queries arise in an effort to better infer searchers' information needs [2]. For example, one can often expect to be directed to local establishments when searching [`where can I get sushi`], despite the query's failure to explicitly communicate a desire for geographic localization. Such queries are said to be implicitly localizable [11], and gains in retrieval performance can be achieved from strategies as simple as learning when to automatically reformulate requests to include mentions of a user's known location [4] (e.g., rewriting the former example to read: [`where can I get sushi in Pisa Italy`]).

Figure 1: When asked [`where can I find missed calls`], both the iPhone virtual assistant (Siri, left), and Windows Phone virtual assistant (Cortana, right) elect to perform a web search. Lacking an awareness of system context, the search engine returns results for Android.

Increasingly, web search engines field queries from a range of new environments, including: operating systems [8], desktop applications [7], and virtual assistants (such as Siri [1], or Cortana [9]). Such integrations alter or extend the contexts in which queries may originate, thus posing new challenges in this space. For example, a user may ask [`where can I get sushi`] in one session, and [`where can I find missed calls`] in the next. This latter example, together with such queries as [`how do I mute this phone`], and [`set up voice mail`], typify a class of queries which implicitly pertain to the systems, platforms or devices from which they originate. In contrast to their implicitly localizable counterparts, these *implicit system queries* continue to suffer from their underspecificity, and web search engines often respond with results that are not relevant to their device context. For instance, iOS or Windows Phone users may be misdirected to resources about Android smart phones (Figure 1).

In this paper, we take inspiration from work done with implicit local search, and present methods for detecting and refining implicit system queries. The discussion is grounded

SIGIR '16, July 17-21, 2016, Pisa, Italy
© 2016 ACM. ISBN 978-1-4503-4069-4/16/07...$15.00
DOI: http://dx.doi.org/10.1145/2911451.2914701

by considering 3 months of spoken web search queries issued to the Bing.com search engine via the Cortana virtual assistant on Windows Phone devices. We begin by situating our work with respect to past research, then describe our dataset. We then separately consider two classes of implicit system searches, namely: *semi-implicit* system queries, in which a user's device is specified via a pronominal reference (e.g., "`can this phone be a hot spot`"); and *fully implicit* system queries, which lack such lexical cues (e.g., "`how do I enable a hot spot`"). The paper concludes with a discussion of future work.

2. BACKGROUND

To ground the remainder of the discussion, we consider web search queries posed to virtual assistants on smart phone devices. Virtual assistants allow users to engage in a conversational style of spoken interaction to access a device's commands, settings, and integrated services. Virtual assistants can also be asked to query the web, and often default to this behavior when a user's intent is unclear. Whether issuing commands or performing a web search, users are encouraged, by convention and instruction [1, 9], to structure their utterances as if they were talking with a person.

As we will show, this confounding of command & control functionality with web search, results in an environment where implicit system queries are common, and where web search results leave much to be desired. In the literature, there are two general strategies for coping with these challenges: Working from the top-down, recent research [5, 10] has sought to develop general classifiers that can detect *orphaned utterances* – queries in domains that one might suspect to be covered by virtual assistants, but which instead fall-back to a generic web search. Many of these orphaned utterances are device-related, and their detection can help to identify common ill-served intents.

Working from the bottom-up, earlier work has sought to leverage system context to improve the retrieval performance of underspecified system-related searches [3, 12]. For example, Ekstrand et al. demonstrate how software version information, together with details of a system's state, can be leveraged when evaluating web search queries related to image editing software [3]. These bottom-up efforts show promise, but assume all queries posed to the retrieval engine are system-related. This assumption is violated by intelligent virtual assistants that field queries about many topics.

The work presented in this paper represents a hybrid approach, striving first to detect implicit system queries, then to augment those queries with contextual details of the user's system. As noted in the introduction, our approach is most similar to work done in implicit local search [4, 11].

3. DATASET

Our dataset consists of 3 months of spoken queries issued to the Bing.com search engine via the Cortana virtual assistant. The dataset contains tens of millions of English language queries, originating from within the United States, collected from July 1st, 2015 through September 30th, 2015. Prior to analyses, queries were normalized by removing punctuation, and by converting text to lowercase. Additionally, compound nouns containing the word "`phone`" were normalized as follows: Compound nouns synonymous with phone, such as "`telephone`" or "`mobile phone`", were converted to the base word "`phone`". The remaining phone-related compound nouns were tokenized such that each appears as a single term (e.g., "`phone number`" becomes "`phone_number`", "`phone bill`" becomes "`phone_bill`", etc.) This normalization facilitates phrase-based matching strategies, which, as we show in the next section, are an effective means for detecting semi-implicit system queries.

4. SEMI-IMPLICIT SYSTEM QUERIES

To motivate our further study of implicit system queries, we consider the subset of queries that betray their system-related nature, but which otherwise leave implicit the identities of the systems to which they pertain. Examples, include: [`can this phone be a hot spot`], [`how to silence the phone`], and [`set my phone's quiet hours`]. We refer to such queries as *semi-implicit*. In the remainder of this section, we demonstrate that semi-implicit queries can be reliably detected with simple heuristics, that they occur frequently in the logs, and that simple query alteration strategies can substantially improve retrieval performance.

4.1 Detection and Alteration Heuristics

We identify semi-implicit queries heuristically by identifying searches that: (1) have been posed by more than one user, and (2) contain indicator phrases such as "`my phone`", "`this phone`" or "`the phone`". The first condition, which restricts analysis to non-unique queries, serves as a heavy-handed filter for excluding searches which may have been issued accidentally (e.g., pocket dialing), or which may contain speech recognition errors. Roughly half of the distinct queries in our dataset are excluded by this filter.

In addition to detecting semi-implicit queries, we explore two reformulation strategies that aim to improve the quality of retrieved results. The first strategy replaces indicator phrases with the model names of the users' smart phones, as determined from client meta data (e.g., the "`UserAgent`" header). Alternatively, the second reformulation strategy replaces indicator phrases with the names of the devices' operating platforms (e.g., "Windows Phone", "iOS", etc.) Finally, we consider a third approach which directly interleaves the results retrieved by the first two alterations. The merged results alternate between device- and platform-specific responses (with duplicates removed).

4.2 Precision of Indicator Phrases

To estimate the precision of our detection criteria, we randomly sampled 100 queries identified by each of the indicator phrases listed in Table 1a. We then presented crowd workers with a contextualized scenario, and tasked them with labeling the results. An example labeling task is as follows:

> *Sarah activates her smart phone's voice interface and says: "how do I silence the phone". You observe that Sarah is using a Lumia 640 smart phone, which runs the Windows Phone operating system. When Sarah spoke the phrase "the phone", was she talking about her Lumia 640?*

We obtained 5 judgments for each of the 300 queries, and used a majority voting criteria to derive a final set of labels. We find that, within our sample, the precisions of the heuristic classifiers ranges from 0.89 to 0.96 (Table 1a). Moreover, we inspected queries labeled as false positives,

(a) semi-implicit system queries	precision
containing "*my phone*" (sample N = 100)	0.96
containing "*this phone*" (sample N = 100)	0.90
containing "*the phone*" (sample N = 100)	0.89
(b) fully implicit system queries	**precision**
queries selected via LR test (sample N = 300)	0.90

Table 1: Precision of semi-implicit (a) and fully implicit (b) indicator phrases, as judged by a panel of independent human labelers.

and found that such searches were frequently difficult to interpret (e.g., [`look the phone`], and [`ok my phone`]). Such queries may constitute non-unique speech input errors or false activations.

4.3 Impact to Search Traffic

Applying the query detection heuristics to the complete 3 month query log reveals that users are 1.52 times more likely to refer to their devices with semi-implicit phrases like "`my phone`", or "`the phone`", than to *explicitly* mention the type of device they are using. (Table 2a,c). Moreover, when semi-implicit phrases were used, searchers were only about half as likely to click on a search result. These differences are highly statistically significant (χ^2 goodness of fit, $p \ll 0.0001$), and, together, strongly support this paper's focus on improving the retrieval performance of implicit system queries.

4.4 Retrieval Performance

Finally, we characterize the retrieval performance of the automatic query alteration strategies outlined above. For each of the 300 sampled queries (i.e., those mentioned in section 4.2), we retrieved web search results with: the unaltered query, the device-specific alteration, and the platform-specific alteration. Crowd workers again provided judgments – this time rating relevance on a 5-point scale ranging from Poor to Perfect. We focus on the top three search results in each condition, as the phones in our dataset could only display two or three results at a time (Figure 1). Table 3a reports the mean nDCG@3 for the various conditions, as well as the number of individual queries whose nDCG@3 scores were improved (wins) or hindered (losses) by the alteration. We found that, on average, reformulations outperformed unaltered queries across all treatment conditions. Moreover, we found that between 66% - 82% of individual queries benefited from reformulation (only 13% - 22% were impacted negatively). All win/loss ratios reported in table 3a are highly statistically significant (sign test, $p \ll 0.0001$). In more practical terms: across all queries, the median relevance of the *topmost* search result was 4 (excellent) in all treatment conditions, but was only 2 (fair) for the unaltered query baseline. These findings speak to the efficacy of simple, but targeted, reformulation strategies in this context.

(a) semi-implicit system queries	relative search volume	relative CTR
contains "*my phone*"	1.08	0.54
contains "*this phone*"	0.26	0.64
contains "*the phone*"	0.19	0.24
any of the three	1.52	0.52
(b) fully implicit system queries		
queries selected via LR test	8.68	0.45
(c) explicit system system queries		
mentions device's operating platform	0.73	1.04
mentions device's hardware model	0.28	0.89
either of the two	1.00	1.00

Table 2: Normalized search volume and click-through rates (CTR) of queries classified as (a) semi-, or (b) fully implicit system queries in the 3 month dataset. Values are normalized with respect to queries that *explicitly* mentioned the operating platform or hardware model of the device from which they originated (c).

5. FULLY IMPLICIT SYSTEM QUERIES

We now turn our attention to *fully implicit system queries*, which provide no overt indication of their system-related nature. Examples of fully implicit system queries include [`how do I take a screenshot`], and [`change the wallpaper`]. We present a fully unsupervised log-based approach for detection and alteration of such queries.

5.1 Detecting Fully Implicit System Queries

When faced with unsatisfactory search results for implicit system-related queries, users often reformulate their searches by adding additional details of their system context. Mir-

	Mean nDCG@3				# Wins / No Change / Losses		
(a) semi-implicit system queries	no alteration	platform	device	interleaved	platform	device	interleaved
containing "*my phone*" (N = 100)	0.43	0.55	**0.69**	0.64	66/14/20	**80/4/16**	77/3/20
containing "*this phone*" (N = 100)	0.39	0.54	**0.71**	0.66	67/13/20	**82/5/13**	76/3/21
containing "*the phone*" (N = 100)	0.39	0.52	**0.66**	0.63	66/12/22	78/3/19	**80/1/19**
(b) fully implicit system queries							
queries selected via LR test (N = 300)	0.57	0.68	0.68	**0.69**	**180/44/76**	181/32/87	196/17/87

Table 3: Retrieval performance for various reformulation strategies, applied to semi-implicit (a) and fully implicit (b) system queries. The leftmost columns report mean nDCG @ 3. The rightmost columns report the number of individual queries whose nDCG @ 3 score increased (wins), remained unchanged, or decreased (losses) after reformulation. All win/loss ratios, in both (a) and (b), are highly statistically significant (sign test, $p \ll 0.0001$).

roring past work [6], we leverage the likelihood ratio test to detect these non-accidental reformulations. We define a *query pair*, $\langle q_1, q_2 \rangle$, to be a pair of successive queries, issued by the same user, occurring no more than 30 minutes apart in the log dataset. The second query, q_2 is then abstracted as a boolean event, s_2, which occurs whenever q_2 mentions a user's system, platform or device by name. We then consider the goodness of fit of two competing hypotheses that explain the observed occurrence frequencies of $\langle q_1, s_2 \rangle$ pairs:

$$H_0 : P(s_2|q_1) = P(s_2|\neg q_1)$$
$$H_1 : P(s_2|q_1) \neq P(s_2|\neg q_1)$$

The first hypothesis, H_0, asserts that s_2 occurs independently from q_1. Conversely, H_1 asserts a dependence; and, in practice, we find that $P(s_2|q_1) >> P(s_2|\neg q_1)$. The likelihood ratio test statistic, $\chi^2 = -2\ log\ (L(H_0)/L(H_1))$, can be computed directly from observed data, and is known to be asymptotically Chi-squared distributed, with 1 degree of freedom [6]. In this paper, we reject H_0 when the test statistic is larger than 28.00. This corresponds to a p-value $< 10^{-7}$, and is strong evidence that q_1 requires an explicit system reformulation. Once discovered, such queries are placed in a lookup table used to identify future instances.

5.2 Empirical Results

As before, we report values for precision (Table 1b), traffic impact (Table 2b), and retrieval performance (Table 3b). By many measures, implicit system searches perform similarly to semi-implicit queries. Notably, classifier precision is again judged to be 0.90, and the query alteration strategies again lead to mean nDCG@3 values approaching 0.7 in all three conditions. For implicit system queries, reformulation improved between 60% - 65% of all individual queries (wins), and negatively impacted 25% - 29% of queries (losses). The slightly lower win/loss ratio, compared to semi-implicit queries, can be attributed to the higher baseline performance in the fully implicit case. The chief distinction between semi- and fully implicit system queries, however, is one of traffic volume: We find that fully implicit system searchers occur 5.7 times more frequently than semi-implicit searches, and 8.6 times more frequently than those that explicitly specify a device or platform.

6. CONCLUSION & FUTURE WORK

When users speak queries to intelligent virtual assistants, their utterances often implicitly pertain to the devices from which they originate. In this paper, we have we have shown that such queries: (1) can be reliably detected, (2) account for a meaningful proportion of search traffic, and (3) can be reformulated to greatly improve retrieval performance. Nevertheless, our analysis is limited in several ways, and there are numerous opportunities for future research. We elaborate below.

Citing a desire to filter accidental query activations and speech recognition errors, our methods consider only queries that have been issued by more than one person. However, we believe there is little risk in lifting this restriction, as user are unlikely to attend to search results in cases of false activation. Further study is necessary to more fully investigate this issue.

We are also sensitive to the possibility that users may use virtual assistants to query about *other* devices or platforms, and that the proposed reformulation strategies may hinder such efforts. In our log dataset we found that users *explicitly* query about their own devices roughly 4 times as often as they query about other platforms. We hypothesize that this difference is even more dramatic for implicit system queries – especially in scenarios where queries contain phrases such as "`this phone`", or "`my phone`". Again, further study could help to elucidate these factors.

We also recognize that, just as there are degrees of geographic locality (e.g., country, state, county, address), so too are there degrees of system locality (platform, product line, device model, etc.) On average, our results suggest that reformulations should be as specific as possible (i.e., prefer model over platform). However, there are individual cases where more general reformulations yield superior results. This suggests opportunities for the development of more nuanced classifiers that can determine the type of reformulation needed to best address an implicit system query.

Finally, while we focus on queries issued to virtual assistants, we feel that implicit system searches will become an important class of queries moving forward, especially as web search is integrated into new applications and environments.

7. REFERENCES

[1] Apple Corporation. iOS - Siri - Apple. http://www.apple.com/ios/siri/, 2015.

[2] P. N. Bennett, R. W. White, W. Chu, S. T. Dumais, P. Bailey, F. Borisyuk, and X. Cui. Modeling the Impact of Short- and Long-term Behavior on Search Personalization. In *Proc. SIGIR '12*, pages 185–194, New York, NY, USA, 2012. ACM.

[3] M. Ekstrand, W. Li, T. Grossman, J. Matejka, and G. Fitzmaurice. Searching for Software Learning Resources Using Application Context. In *Proc. UIST '11*, pages 195–204, New York, NY, USA, 2011. ACM.

[4] L. Gravano, V. Hatzivassiloglou, and R. Lichtenstein. Categorizing Web Queries According to Geographical Locality. In *Proc. CIKM '03*, pages 325–333, New York, NY, USA, 2003. ACM.

[5] D. Hakkani-Tur, Y.-C. Ju, G. Zweig, and G. Tur. Clustering Novel Intents in a Conversational Interaction System with Semantic Parsing. In *Proceedings of Interspeech*. ISCA, Sept. 2015.

[6] R. Jones, B. Rey, O. Madani, and W. Greiner. Generating Query Substitutions. In *Proc. WWW '06*, pages 387–396, New York, NY, USA, 2006. ACM.

[7] Microsoft Corporation. Do things quickly with Tell Me. https://support.office.com/en-us/article/Do-things-quickly-with-Tell-Me, 2015.

[8] Microsoft Corporation. Search for anything, anywhere - Windows Help. http://windows.microsoft.com/en-us/windows-10/getstarted-search-for-anything-cortana, 2015.

[9] Microsoft Corporation. What can I say to Cortana? http://www.windowsphone.com/en-us/how-to/wp8/cortana/what-can-i-say-to-cortana, 2015.

[10] G. Tur, A. Deoras, and D. Hakkani-Tur. Detecting Out-Of-Domain Utterances Addressed to a Virtual Personal Assistant. In *Proceedings of Interspeech*. ISCA, Sept. 2014.

[11] M. J. Welch and J. Cho. Automatically Identifying Localizable Queries. In *Proc. SIGIR '08*, pages 507–514, New York, NY, USA, 2008. ACM.

[12] J.-R. Wen, N. Lao, and W.-Y. Ma. Probabilistic Model for Contextual Retrieval. In *Proc. SIGIR '04*, pages 57–63, New York, NY, USA, 2004. ACM.

Axiomatic Analysis for Improving the Log-Logistic Feedback Model

Ali Montazeralghaem[†], Hamed Zamani[‡], and Azadeh Shakery[†]
[†]School of Electrical and Computer Engineering, College of Engineering, University of Tehran, Iran
[‡]Center for Intelligent Information Retrieval, College of Information and Computer Sciences, University of Massachusetts Amherst, MA 01003
{ali.montazer,shakery}@ut.ac.ir zamani@cs.umass.edu

ABSTRACT

Pseudo-relevance feedback (PRF) has been proven to be an effective query expansion strategy to improve retrieval performance. Several PRF methods have so far been proposed for many retrieval models. Recent theoretical studies of PRF methods show that most of the PRF methods do not satisfy all necessary constraints. Among all, the log-logistic model has been shown to be an effective method that satisfies most of the PRF constraints. In this paper, we first introduce two new PRF constraints. We further analyze the log-logistic feedback model and show that it does not satisfy these two constraints as well as the previously proposed "relevance effect" constraint. We then modify the log-logistic formulation to satisfy all these constraints. Experiments on three TREC newswire and web collections demonstrate that the proposed modification significantly outperforms the original log-logistic model, in all collections.

CCS Concepts

•Information systems → Query representation; Query reformulation;

Keywords

Pseudo-relevance feedback; axiomatic analysis; theoretical analysis; query expansion; semantic similarity

1. INTRODUCTION

Pseudo-relevance feedback (PRF) refers to a query expansion strategy to address the vocabulary mismatch problem in information retrieval (IR). PRF assumes that a number of top-retrieved documents are relevant to the initial query. Based on this assumption, it updates the query model using these pseudo-relevant documents to improve the retrieval performance. PRF has been shown to be highly effective in many retrieval models [1, 5, 8, 10].

Several PRF models with different assumptions and formulations have so far been proposed. Clinchant and Gaussier [2] theoretically analyzed a number of effective PRF models. To this end, they proposed five constraints (axioms) for PRF models and showed that the log-logistic feedback model [1] is the only PRF model (among the studied ones) that satisfies all the constraints. They also showed that its performance is superior to the other PRF methods, including the mixture model [10] and the geometric relevance model [9]. Effectiveness of the log-logistic model motivates us, in this paper, to study this state-of-the-art PRF model.

Recently, Pal et al. [8] proposed a sixth constraint for PRF models to improve the PRF performance in the divergence from randomness framework. This constraint, which is called "relevance effect", indicates that the terms in the feedback documents with high relevance scores (i.e., relevance of document to the initial query) should have higher weights in the feedback model compared to those with exactly similar statistics, but appear in the documents with lower relevance scores. Formally writing, if a term w occurs in two documents $d_1, d_2 \in F$ (F denotes the set of feedback documents) such that d_1 is more relevant to the initial query than d_2. Then, we can say that the feedback weight of w given the $F - \{d_1\}$ feedback documents is lower than the weight of the same word in the $F - \{d_2\}$ feedback documents [8]. It can be shown that the log-logistic feedback model does not satisfy the relevance effect constraint.

In this paper, we propose two additional constraints for PRF models. The first constraint considers the semantic similarity of feedback terms to the initial query. Although previous work, such as [4], proposed similar constraints for retrieval models, to the best of our knowledge, it is the first time to study a semantic-related constraint for the PRF task. The second constraint indicates that the weight of each term w in the feedback model not only depends on the distribution of w in the feedback documents, but is also related to the distribution of the other terms in those documents. We further show that the log-logistic model does not satisfy the two proposed constraints. We then propose a modification to the log-logistic feedback model to satisfy the proposed constraints as well as the relevance effect constraint [8].

We evaluate the modified log-logistic model using three standard TREC collections: AP (Associated Press 1988-89), Robust (TREC 2004 Robust track), and WT10g (TREC 9-10 Web track). The experimental results demonstrate that the proposed method significantly outperforms the original log-logistic feedback model in all collections. The proposed method is also shown to be more robust than the original log-logistic model, especially in the web collection.

SIGIR '16, July 17-21, 2016, Pisa, Italy

DOI: http://dx.doi.org/10.1145/2911451.2914768

2. METHODOLOGY

In this section, we introduce two constraints that (pseudo) relevance feedback methods should satisfy (in addition to those proposed in [2, 8]). We further analyze the log-logistic model, a state-of-the-art feedback model, and figure out that this model does not satisfy the proposed constraints as well as the "relevance effect" constraint introduced in [8]. Based on these observations, we modify the log-logistic feedback model to satisfy all the constraints.

We first introduce our notation. Let $FW(w; F, P_w, Q)$ be the *feedback weight* function that assigns a real-value weight to each feedback term w for a given query Q. F and P_w respectively denote the set of feedback documents for the query Q and a set of term-dependent parameters. For simplicity, we henceforth use $FW(w)$. In the following equations, TF and IDF denote term frequency and inverse document frequency, respectively. The notation $|\cdot|$ is also used for query/document length or size of a given set.

2.1 Constraints

In this subsection, we introduce two constraints for feedback models.

[Semantic effect] Let Q be a single-term query (i.e., $Q = \{q\}$), w_1 and w_2 be two terms such that $IDF(w_1) = IDF(w_2)$, $\forall D \in F : TF(w_1, D) = TF(w_2, D)$, and

$$sem(q, w_1) < sem(q, w_2)$$

where $sem(\cdot,\cdot)$ denotes the semantic similarity of the given terms. Then, we can say:

$$FW(w_1) < FW(w_2)$$

The intuition behind this constraint is that the feedback terms should be semantically similar to the initial query.

[Distribution effect] Let w_1 and w_2 be two vocabulary terms such that $TF(w_1, D_1) = TF(w_2, D_2)$, $TF(w_1, D_2) = TF(w_2, D_1) = 0$, and $|D_1| = |D_2|$, where D_1 and D_2 are two documents in the feedback set F. Also, assume that w_1 and w_2 do not occur in other feedback documents, and

$$UniqueTerms(D_1) < UniqueTerms(D_2)$$

where $UniqueTerms(\cdot)$ denotes the number of unique terms in the given document. Then, we can say:[1]

$$FW(w_1) < FW(w_2)$$

In other words, this constraint implies that for computing the feedback weight of a term w, the distribution of other terms in the feedback documents should also be considered.

2.2 Modifying the Log-Logistic Model

The feedback weight of each term w in the log-logistic feedback model [1] is computed as follows:

$$FW(w) = \frac{1}{|F|}\sum_{D\in F} FW(w, D) = \frac{1}{|F|}\sum_{D\in F} \log\left(\frac{t(w, D) + \lambda_w}{\lambda_w}\right) \quad (1)$$

where $\lambda_w = \frac{N_w}{N}$ (N_w and N denote the number of documents in the collection that contain w and the total number of documents in the collection, respectively), and $t(w, D) = TF(w, D)\log(1+c\frac{avg_l}{|D|})$ (avg_l denotes the average document length and c is a free hyper-parameter). It is shown that the log-logistic model satisfies all the PRF constraints introduced in [2]. It can be easily proved that this model cannot satisfy the constraints proposed in this paper. In more detail, there is no semantic-related or relevance-related components in the log-logistic formulation and thus it cannot satisfy the proposed "semantic effect" and the "relevance effect" [8] constraints. In addition, the log-logistic formula does not consider the distribution of other terms in computing the weight of each term w, and thus it does not satisfy the "distribution effect" constraint.

To satisfy the "semantic effect" constraint, we modify the log-logistic feedback weight function as follows:

$$FW_{sem}(w) = FW(w) * \beta * \frac{1}{|Q|}\sum_{q\in Q}\frac{s(w, q)}{s(q, q)} \quad (2)$$

where $s(\cdot,\cdot)$ denotes the semantic similarity between the given two terms. The parameter β controls the effect of semantic similarity in the feedback weight function. The semantic weighting component comes from the query-growth function, which was previously proposed by Fang and Zhai [4]. Note that in Equation (2), we can ignore the $1/|Q|$ term and the β parameter, since they are equal for all terms and the feedback weighting function will be normalized. Several methods have so far been proposed to incorporate semantic similarity of terms in various retrieval tasks. In this paper, we consider the mutual information as a basic semantic similarity metric to compute $s(\cdot,\cdot)$. The mutual information (MI) of two terms w and w' is computed as follows:

$$I(X_w, X_{w'}) = \sum_{X_w, X_{w'}\in\{0,1\}} p(X_w, X_{w'}) \log\frac{p(X_w, X_{w'})}{p(X_w)p(X_{w'})}$$

where X_w and $X_{w'}$ are two binary random variables that represent the presence or absence of the terms w and w' in each document. A simple way to compute the mutual information is to consider the whole collection; but, this choice may not be ideal for ambiguous terms. Another way is to compute the mutual information from the pseudo-relevant documents. However, the top-retrieved documents could be a biased corpus for this goal. Therefore, similar to [4], we extract the mutual information from a corpus containing the top m retrieved documents and $r \times m$ documents randomly selected from the collection, where r is a free parameter that controls the generality of mutual information scores.

To satisfy the "distribution effect" constraint, we re-define the function $t(w, D)$ as follows:

$$t^*(w, D) = \frac{t(w, D)}{\log(\frac{|D|}{ut(D)})} \quad (3)$$

where $ut(D)$ denotes the number of unique terms in the document D. A similar approach for modifying the raw TF formula was previously used in [7].

To satisfy the "relevance effect" constraint, we re-define the function $FW(w, D)$ (see Equation (1)) as follows:

$$FW^*(w, D) = FW(w, D) * RS(Q, D) \quad (4)$$

where $RS(Q, D)$ denotes the relevance score of the document D to the query Q. This function can be computed using the relevance score of D in the first ranking phase in PRF. A similar idea was previously proposed by Lavrenko and Croft [5]. They used the query likelihood similarity as a posterior probability in the relevance models. Lv and

[1]The intuition behind this constraint comes from the definition of *information* in information theory literature.

Table 1: Collections statistics.

ID	Collection	Queries (title only)	#docs	doc length	#qrels
AP	Associated Press 88-89	TREC 1-3 Ad Hoc Track, topics 51-200	165k	287	15,838
Robust	TREC Disks 4 & 5 minus Congressional Record	TREC 2004 Robust Track, topics 301-450 & 601-700	528k	254	17,412
WT10g	TREC Web Collection	TREC 9-10 Web Track, topics 451-550	1692k	399	5931

Table 2: Performance of the proposed modifications and the baselines. Superscripts 0/1 denote that the MAP improvements over NoPRF/LL are statistically significant. The highest value in each column is marked in bold.

Method	AP			Robust			WT10g		
	MAP	P@10	RI	MAP	P@10	RI	MAP	P@10	RI
NoPRF	0.2642	0.4260	–	0.2490	0.4237	–	0.2080	0.3030	–
LL	0.3385	0.4622	0.15	0.2829	0.4393	0.33	0.2127	0.3187	0.08
LL+Sem	0.3422^{0}	0.4702	0.18	0.2940^{01}	0.4474	0.31	0.2247	0.3188	0.10
LL+Rel	0.3425^{0}	0.4681	**0.20**	0.2897^{01}	**0.4490**	0.35	0.2289^{01}	**0.3289**	0.17
LL+Dis	0.3386^{0}	0.4671	0.16	0.2831^{0}	0.4401	0.32	0.2194	0.3207	0.13
LL+All	$\mathbf{0.3445^{01}}$	**0.4722**	**0.20**	$\mathbf{0.2979^{01}}$	0.4486	**0.36**	$\mathbf{0.2300^{01}}$	0.3177	**0.19**

Zhai [6] also used a similar technique to improve the divergence minimization feedback model [10].

Considering the aforementioned modifications, we can rewrite the log-logistic feedback weighting formula as follows:

$$FW^*(w) = \frac{1}{|F|}\sum_{D\in F}\left(\log(\frac{t^*(w,D)+\lambda_w}{\lambda_w}) * RS(Q,D) * \sum_{q\in Q}\frac{s(w,q)}{s(q,q)}\right) \quad (5)$$

3. EXPERIMENTS

3.1 Experimental Setup

We used three standard TREC collections in our experiments: AP (Associated Press 1988-89), Robust (TREC Robust Track 2004 collection), and WT10g (TREC Web Track 2001-2002). The first two collections are newswire collections, and the third collection is a web collection with more noisy documents. The statistics of these datasets are reported in Table 1. We consider the title of topics as queries. All documents are stemmed using the Porter stemmer. Stopwords are removed in all the experiments. We used the standard INQUERY stopword list. All experiments were carried out using the Lemur toolkit[2].

3.1.1 Parameter Setting

The number of feedback documents, the number of feedback terms, the feedback coefficient and the parameter that controls the generally of mutual information scores (parameter r) are set using 2-fold cross validation over each collection. We sweep the number of feedback documents and feedback terms between $\{10, 25, 50, 75, 100\}$, the feedback coefficient between $\{0, 0.1, \cdots, 1\}$, and the parameter r between $\{2, 4, 6, 8, 10\}$.

3.1.2 Evaluation Metrics

To evaluate retrieval effectiveness, we use mean average precision (MAP) of the top-ranked 1000 documents as the main evaluation metric. In addition, we also report the precision of the top 10 retrieved documents (P@10). Statistically significant differences of performance are determined using the two-tailed paired t-test computed at a 95% confidence level over average precision per query.

To evaluate the robustness of methods, we consider the robustness index (RI) [3] which is defined as $\frac{N_+ - N_-}{N}$, where N denotes the number of queries and N_+/N_- shows the number of queries improved/decreased by the feedback method.[3] The RI value is always in the $[-1, 1]$ interval and the method with higher value is more robust.

3.2 Results and Discussion

In this subsection, we first evaluate the proposed modifications to the log-logistic model. We further study the sensitivity of the proposed method to the free parameters.

3.2.1 Evaluating the Modified Log-Logistic Model

We consider two baselines: (1) the document retrieval method without feedback (NoPRF), and (2) the original log-logistic feedback model (LL). Although several other PRF methods have already been proposed, since in this paper, we propose a modification of the log-logistic model, we do not compare the proposed method with other existing PRF models.

To study the effect of each constraint in the retrieval performance, we modify the log-logistic model based on each constraint, separately. LL+Sem, LL+Rel, and LL+Dis denote the modified log-logistic model based on the "semantic effect", the "relevance effect", and the "distribution effect" constraints, respectively. We also modify the log-logistic model by considering all of these constraints (called LL+All) as introduced in Equation (5). The results obtained by the baselines and those achieved by the proposed modifications are reported in Table 2. According to this table, LL outperforms the NoPRF baseline in all cases, which shows the effectiveness of the log-logistic model. The improvements on the WT10g collection is lower than those on the AP and the Robust collections. This observation demonstrates that the

[2]http://lemurproject.org/

[3]To avoid the influence of very small average precision changes in the RI value, we only consider the improvements/losses higher than 10% (relatively).

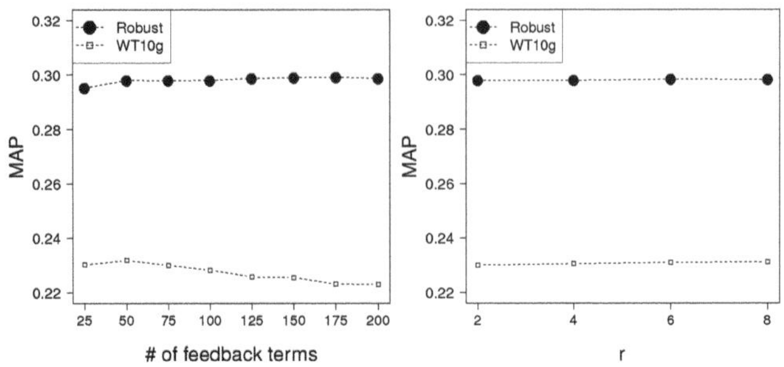

Figure 1: Sensitivity of the proposed method to the number of feedback terms and the parameter r.

log-logistic model is less effective and robust in improving the retrieval performance in the web collection, compared to the newswire collections. LL+Sem and LL+Rel perform better than LL in terms of MAP and P@10, in all collections. The MAP improvements are statistically significant in many cases, especially in the LL+Rel method. Except in one case (i.e., LL+Sem in Robust), both LL+Sem and LL+Rel models are shown to be more robust than the LL baseline. It is worth noting that we use very simple modifications to satisfy these two constraints, and thus using more accurate methods to satisfy these constraints can potentially improve the performance. LL+Dis method in general performs comparable to or sometimes slightly better than the LL baseline. The results achieved on the WT10g collection shows that LL+Dis can be more effective in noisy conditions, such as web collections. Overall, although the theoretical analysis shows that PRF methods should satisfy the "distribution effect" constraint, it does not substantially affect the retrieval performance in the AP and the Robust collections. The reason is that the values of $\frac{|D|}{ut(D)}$ (see Equation (3)) are very close to each other for different documents, especially in newswire collections. Thus, our modification to the log-logistic regarding the "distribution effect" constraint cannot substantially affect the retrieval performance.

As shown in Table 2, the LL+All method, which is our final modification to the log-logistic model, outperforms both baselines in all collections in terms of MAP and P@10. The MAP improvements are always statistically significant. The LL+All method is also shown to be more robust than the LL method, in particular in the WT10g collection.

3.2.2 *Parameter Sensitivity*

In this set of experiments, we fix one of the parameters r (the generality control parameter for mutual information) and n (the number of feedback terms), and then sweep the other one to show the sensitivity of the method to the input parameters. The results are reported in Figure 1.[4] According to this figure, the method is quite stable w.r.t. the changes in the values of these two parameters, especially for the parameter r. The results also indicate that by increasing the number of feedback terms, performance in the Robust collection generally increases, but in the WT10g collection it is not the case. The reason could be related to the noisy nature of this collection compared to the newswire collections.

[4] For the sake of visualization, we only report the results for the Robust and the WT10g collections. The behaviour of the method in AP is similar to the Robust collection.

4. CONCLUSIONS AND FUTURE WORK

In this paper, we proposed two new constraints for pseudo-relevance feedback models. The first constraint considers semantic similarity of the feedback terms to the initial query. The second constraint focuses on the effect of distribution of all terms in the feedback documents on each term. We further studied the log-logistic model, a state-of-the-art feedback model, and showed that this model does not satisfy the proposed constraints as well as the previously proposed "relevance effect" constraint [8]. We then modified the log-logistic model to satisfy all of these constraints. The proposed modification was evaluated using three TREC newswire and web collections. Experimental results suggest that the modified model significantly outperforms the original log-logistic model, in all collections.

An interesting future direction is to study other feedback methods, such as the language model-based feedback methods, and modify them in order to satisfy the constraints. In this paper, we only consider simple approaches to satisfy the constraints, such as using mutual information for capturing semantic similarities. Future work can focus on more complex and accurate approaches to improve the retrieval performance.

5. ACKNOWLEDGEMENTS

This work was supported in part by the Center for Intelligent Information Retrieval. Any opinions, findings and conclusions or recommendations expressed in this material are those of the authors and do not necessarily reflect those of the sponsor.

6. REFERENCES

[1] S. Clinchant and E. Gaussier. Information-based Models for Ad Hoc IR. In *SIGIR '10*, pages 234–241, 2010.

[2] S. Clinchant and E. Gaussier. A Theoretical Analysis of Pseudo-Relevance Feedback Models. In *ICTIR '13*, pages 6–13, 2013.

[3] K. Collins-Thompson. Reducing the Risk of Query Expansion via Robust Constrained Optimization. In *CIKM '09*, pages 837–846, 2009.

[4] H. Fang and C. Zhai. Semantic Term Matching in Axiomatic Approaches to Information Retrieval. In *SIGIR '06*, pages 115–122, 2006.

[5] V. Lavrenko and W. B. Croft. Relevance Based Language Models. In *SIGIR '01*, pages 120–127, 2001.

[6] Y. Lv and C. Zhai. Revisiting the Divergence Minimization Feedback Model. In *CIKM '14*, pages 1863–1866, 2014.

[7] J. H. Paik. A Novel TF-IDF Weighting Scheme for Effective Ranking. In *SIGIR '13*, pages 343–352, 2013.

[8] D. Pal, M. Mitra, and S. Bhattacharya. Improving Pseudo Relevance Feedback in the Divergence from Randomness Model. In *ICTIR '15*, pages 325–328, 2015.

[9] J. Seo and W. B. Croft. Geometric Representations for Multiple Documents. In *SIGIR '10*, pages 251–258, 2010.

[10] C. Zhai and J. Lafferty. Model-based Feedback in the Language Modeling Approach to Information Retrieval. In *CIKM '01*, pages 403–410, 2001.

Balancing Relevance Criteria through Multi-Objective Optimization

Joost van Doorn[1]
joost.vandoorn@student.uva.nl

Daan Odijk[1]
d.odijk@uva.nl

Diederik M. Roijers[1,2]
diederik.roijers@cs.ox.ac.uk

Maarten de Rijke[1]
derijke@uva.nl

[1]Informatics Institute, University of Amsterdam, Amsterdam, The Netherlands
[2]Department of Computer Science, University of Oxford, Oxford, United Kingdom

ABSTRACT

Offline evaluation of information retrieval systems typically focuses on a single effectiveness measure that models the utility for a typical user. Such a measure usually combines a behavior-based rank discount with a notion of document utility that captures the single relevance criterion of topicality. However, for individual users relevance criteria such as credibility, reputability or readability can strongly impact the utility. Also, for different information needs the utility can be a different mixture of these criteria. Because of the focus on single metrics, offline optimization of IR systems does not account for different preferences in balancing relevance criteria.

We propose to mitigate this by viewing multiple relevance criteria as objectives and learning a set of rankers that provide different trade-offs w.r.t. these objectives. We model document utility within a gain-based evaluation framework as a weighted combination of relevance criteria. Using the learned set, we are able to make an informed decision based on the values of the rankers and a preference w.r.t. the relevance criteria. On a dataset annotated for readability and a web search dataset annotated for sub-topic relevance we demonstrate how trade-offs between can be made explicit. We show that there are different available trade-offs between relevance criteria.

Keywords

Multi-objective optimization; Learning to rank

1. INTRODUCTION

The primary goal of information retrieval (IR) systems is to satisfy the information need of a user. Search engines today are fairly successful in finding topically relevant pages. To achieve this most search engines are optimized to rank documents based on their topical relevance to the query. In an offline optimization setting relevance is typically determined by experts, and evaluated with utility-based metrics such as nDCG, which tends to focus on optimizing a single aspect of utility. In online optimization, feedback is collected implicitly for all relevance criteria. However, this approach may ignore differences between individual users and information needs by aggregating across all users and queries. Often aggregation works well, but not always. E.g., users that have limited vocabularies (e.g., children) can benefit from search results optimized for their reading level. When people look for medical information on the web they would benefit from accurate and reliable information, more so than when looking for information on a Star Wars movie.

Utility depends on many factors aside from topicality; criteria such as credibility, reputability and readability are also important [14]. While their importance is typically secondary to topicality, there clearly is a benefit in many use cases. A learning to rank approach [16] can be used to learn an optimal ranker for a specified weighted preference over criteria. Similarly, data fusion techniques can combine ranked lists that are optimized for a certain notion of utility. But what if we want to optimize for multiple criteria, without knowing their relative importance beforehand? For instance, how should we balance relevance and readability if we do not know who our user will be? Or relevance and sub-topic relevance?

We draw inspiration from multi-objective optimization techniques to answer these questions, i.e., to find a set of rankers for which each solution is optimal for a different trade-off in the relevance criteria. We combine the multi-objective technique *Optimistic Linear Support (OLS)* [12] with multiple utility-based metrics in a learning-to-rank setting. We consider two scenarios with two relevance criteria for which we optimize a set of rankers. We evaluate our approach on two datasets, one annotated for relevance and readability, and one annotated for relevance and diversity. To learn our rankers we apply dueling bandit gradient descent with a point-wise ranking function. To optimize for diversity we subsequently apply MMR and cluster-based ranking.

2. BACKGROUND

The concept of relevance is core to IR and a much debated subject. Park [9] gives an extensive analysis on the nature of relevance in IR, and argues that relevance is intrinsically related to the selection process by the user. Cooper [4] states that each query could represent a set of specific questions as part of the information need, where documents are relevant if they provide an answer to one of these specific questions. Schamber [14] identifies major criterion groups for relevance: aboutness, currency, availability, clarity and credibility. There is a general trend that relevance cannot be attributed to just one factor such as topicality, but is multi-factored [9].

Many metrics have been proposed to measure the effectiveness of an IR system; we focus on metrics based on the concept of utility [2, 4]. The utility of an IR system depends on all factors that determine the usefulness for each specific user. Cooper [4] defines utility as "A catch all concept involving not only topic relatedness

SIGIR '16, July 17 - 21, 2016, Pisa, Italy

ISBN 978-1-4503-4069-4/16/07...$15.00

DOI: http://dx.doi.org/10.1145/2911451.2914708

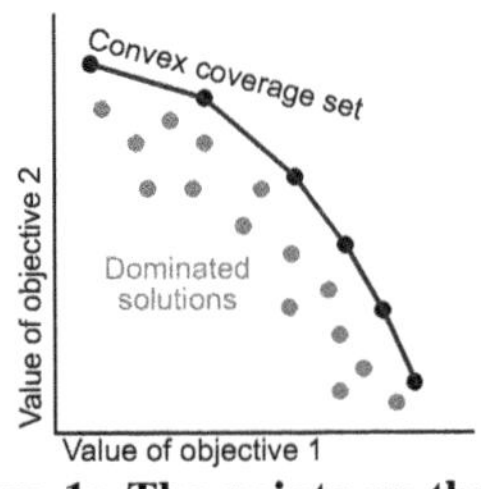

Figure 1: The points on the line represent solutions in the coverage set, the others are dominated.

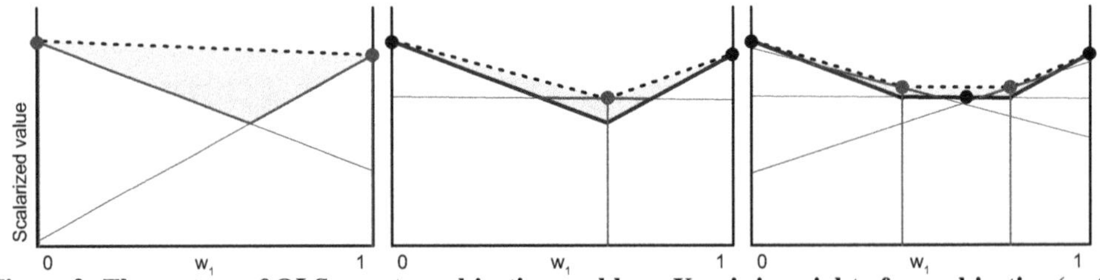

Figure 2: Three steps of OLS on a two-objective problem. X-axis is weight of one objective (note: $w_2 = 1 - w_1$), y-axis the scalarized value. Blue area highlights difference between upper bound and convex value. As more solutions are added to the CCS, the difference is iteratively reduced.

but also quality, novelty, importance, credibility, and many other things." Utility-based metrics combine a notion of utility with specific assumptions about user behavior [2]. Each document has a specific numerical utility value for an information need. Additionally, a discount function is used on the document's rank, under the assumption that more effort is needed to reach lower ranked documents, and it is less likely for the user to reach these documents. Many metrics, therefore, boil down to the same basic formula to estimate the utility of the ranked list, composed of a sum of the product of document utility and a discount factor [3]:

$$M = \sum_{k=1}^{K} gain(rel_k) \times discount(k) \quad (1)$$

Extensions focus on multiple criteria. E.g., Dai et al. [5] present an extension of nDCG for freshness and relevance. Zuccon [17] proposes on an extension of rank-based precision for readability.

Similarly, diversity and novelty metrics also take into account multiple criteria in the form of subtopic relevance [3]. The underlying assumption is that there are multiple subtopics (or categories) for each query, and each user will be interested in results for at least one of these subtopics. Relevance assessments are provided for each of the subtopics belonging to a query separately. These are combined based on the probability $p(i|q)$ of intent i being intended by the user for query q [1]. α-nDCG extends (1) with a weighted sum over subtopics, given p_i as the probability of each subtopic:

$$\alpha\text{-nDCG} = \frac{1}{N} \sum_{i=1}^{M} p_i \sum_{k=1}^{K} gain_i^k \times discount(k) \quad (2)$$

While there has been previous work that combines multiple relevance criteria in the utility-based evaluation framework, to the best of our knowledge, no previous work uses multi-objective optimization techniques on information retrieval problems, i.e., existing methods do not return a *set* of alternative rankers with different available trade-offs with respect to the different relevance criteria.

3. MULTI-OBJECTIVE OPTIMIZATION

Scalarization function. We assume that a ranker has a value for each different relevance criterion, i.e., each ranker has an associated value vector $\mathbf{V}$, with a value, V_i in each criterion i. We follow [11] and assume that the preference of an individual user with respect to these criteria can be expressed in terms of an unknown *scalarization function* f, that collapses the value vector to a scalar utility: $f(\mathbf{V}, \mathbf{w})$, where $\mathbf{w}$ is a vector that parameterizes f. We are unable to observe this function directly. Instead, we aim to find a *coverage set* [11] of rankers, that contains an optimal trade-off for each possible preference (i.e., f and $\mathbf{w}$) that a user might have, see Fig. 1.

We assume that f is linear (where weighted means: $\sum_i^C w_i = 1$):

$$f(\mathbf{V}, \mathbf{w}) = \mathbf{w}^T \mathbf{V}, \quad (3)$$

i.e., the utility for the user is a *weighted* sum over relevance criteria.

Metrics as objectives. To formulate our own scalarization function we can combine (1) with (3):

$$M = \sum_{i=1}^{C} w_i \sum_{k=1}^{K} gain_i(doc_k) \times discount(k) \quad (4)$$

This definition is similar to the definition of α-nDCG of (2), where instead of a sum over topics we have a sum over C relevance criteria. In α-nDCG, the metric M would subsequently be normalized. It is, however, not desirable to normalize the linear scalarized value function as this would remove the convex property of the value vector that is required for efficient optimization using OLS. The linear scalarization function does require values that are comparable in their magnitude, therefore, the individual value functions are normalized with normalization value N_i instead, giving:

$$V_i = \frac{1}{N_i} \sum_{k=1}^{K} gain_i(doc_k) \times discount(k) \quad (5)$$

Convex coverage set. Because each criterion contributes positively to the scalarization function, and we are interested in the *relative* importance of each criterion, we can assume that $\mathbf{w}$ is a positive vector that sums to 1 in order to determine a coverage set. A coverage set that covers all possible linear scalarizations is called a convex coverage set (CCS) [11]. To compute the (approximate) CCS, we build on the Optimistic Linear Support (OLS) framework for multi-objective optimization [12]. Fig. 2 illustrates the OLS procedure; OLS computes a CCS by solving a multi-objective problem as a series of single-objective problems, i.e., problems that are scalarized using different $\mathbf{w}$. At each iteration, OLS tries to find a new ranker, thereby incrementally building a CCS. We can use existing single-objective optimization techniques to find rankers for a given $\mathbf{w}$. We use Dueling Bandit Gradient Descent (DBGD) [16].

Each ranker found in an iteration of OLS has an associated value vector $\mathbf{V}$. For each $\mathbf{w}$, the scalarized value of a ranker is $V_{\mathbf{w}} = \mathbf{w} \cdot \mathbf{V}$. Given a partial CCS, i.e., the set S of rankers and associated $\mathbf{V}$ found so far, we define the scalarized value function as a function of $\mathbf{w}$:

$$V_S^*(\mathbf{w}) = \max_{\mathbf{V} \in S} \mathbf{w} \cdot \mathbf{V},$$

i.e., the scalarized value function is the convex upper surface of the vectors in Fig. 2. OLS selects the next $\mathbf{w}$ from the *corner weights* of $V_S^*(\mathbf{w})$, i.e., those $\mathbf{w}$ where $V_S^*(\mathbf{w})$ changes slope. In Fig. 2 the corner weights evaluated in that iteration are indicated by the blue vertical lines. The maximal possible improvement in scalarized value on the partial CCS is indicated by the dashed lines above $V_S^*(\mathbf{w})$. Once it reaches a corner weight, OLS is provably optimal as long as the single-objective method it employs to solve the scalarized problems is exact [12]. In practice, exact single-objective subroutines are not required; we can safely use DBGD, but with lesser guarantees of the optimality of the solution [13].

Reuse and iterated search scheme. A limitation of applying standard OLS is that for every corner weight DBGD needs to be run. This can be expensive, depending on the size of the dataset. However, this can be mitigated by hot-starting the single-objective optimization algorithm with parts of previously found solutions (following [13]). For each new corner weight, we multi-start DBGD, starting from the rankers that were found at the 3 closest corner weights so far. It is possible that DBGD does not find a new best solution, even though such a solution might still exist. If this is the case for a number of iterations, we take a random pertubation step. DBGD is stopped automatically after 40,000 iterations, or if no improvement has been found after 20 random pertubations. To our knowledge, this is the first time such a Multi-Start/Iterated Local Search scheme [7] has been combined with OLS.

4. EXPERIMENTAL SET-UP

To demonstrate how multi-objective optimization for balancing multiple relevance criteria works in practice, we perform experiments on two datasets: (i) balancing readability and topical relevance in a health setting (CLEF eHealth 2015 task 2 [8]), and (ii) balancing diversity and topical relevance in a web search dataset annotated for sub-topic relevance (TREC 2012 Web Track diversity task). While our runs are competitive, our main goal is to find multiple solutions that balance different relevance criteria, which we report in the form of a CCS.

CLEF eHealth. CLEF eHealth 2015 task 2 provides annotations for two objectives. It is composed of 5 training queries and 67 test queries; annotations are provided for relevance only for the training queries, and both relevance and understandability for the test queries. As the extra understandability annotations are required to optimize for both relevance and understandability at the same time we only use the test set queries for optimization. To measure readability document text is extracted using boilerpipe [6]. Since simple readability metrics do not correlate well with actual readability in the medical domain [15], another approach to readability is required. We compiled a list of medical terms and counted their occurrences. This list was taken from an English Wikipedia page, for which all words contained in the 20k English word list from the Google Trillion Word Corpus were filtered out.[1] Using this feature, and, additionally, the Coleman-Liau index, Gunning fog index, and document length, we trained an SVM to predict the understandability score. For the CLEF eHealth 2015 task 2 the usual metrics are RBP, uRBP and uRBPgr. In preliminary experiments we found a strong correlation between RBP and uRBP, like [17]. Hence, we optimize for nDCG using relevance annotations (nDCG_{rel}), and also for nDCG using understandability annotations ($\text{nDCG}_{\text{read}}$). We normalize $\text{nDCG}_{\text{read}}$ so that the value is in the same range as nDCG_{rel}.

TREC Web Diversity. The TREC 2012 Web Track diversity task comes with 50 queries, with sub topic relevance assessments provided for the first 20 documents produced by the participating systems. TREC 2010 and 2011 Web Track diversity task queries were used for training. For diversity we use MMR and cluster-based ranking [10] with cosine similarity on TF-IDF vectors. We only apply MMR on the first T clusters. Documents are first scored based on relevance, subsequently, MMR and cluster-based ranking rerank the documents for diversity, which produces a $rank_i$ for each document i. Using $rank_i$, the final ranking is determined based on $(1 - w_d)score_i + w_d \frac{1}{rank_i}$, where w_d is a parameter that balances diversity and relevance. The usual metrics reported for the TREC Diversity task are nDCG and α-nDCG. For optimization we use both nDCG and α-nDCG to optimize for both relevance and diversity. As clustering introduces a lot of randomness, we average over 5 runs of DBGD. For value functions V_{rel} and V_{div}, we normalize the values of nDCG and α-nDCG, respectively, to $[0, 1]$.

5. RESULTS

CLEF eHealth 2015 task 2. For this task, we simultaneously optimize for readability and relevance, using nDCG for both metrics.

[1]For this list see: github.com/JoostvDoorn/moo-sigir2016

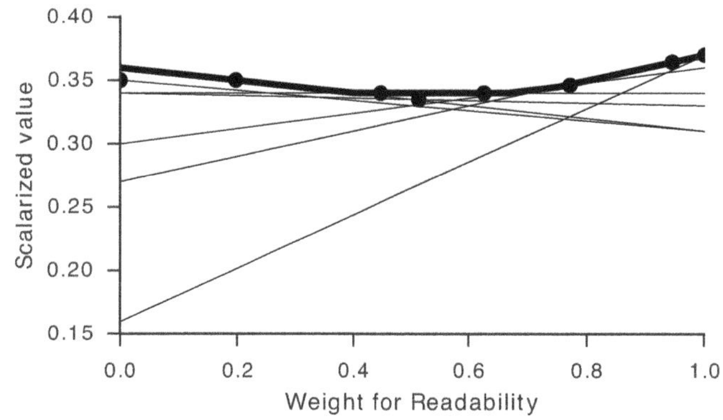

Figure 3: The CCS found on CLEF eHealth 2015, with a scalarized value based on relevance and readability. Absolute left having maximum weight on relevance, and absolute right maximum weight on readability.

The scalarized value of a solution was calculated using a weighted interpolation between value functions V_{rel} and V_{read} (Eq. 3).

The convex coverage set (CCS), constructed using OLS, is shown in Fig. 3. OLS finds eight solutions of which six are not dominated. The set of solutions is reported in Table 1 with their RBP and uRBP scores. We note that our best uRBP score is above the second run for the original task and the best nDCG_{rel} is in the top-5 out of 110 runs. We observe that we are able to find solutions that optimally combine the nDCG_{rel} and $\text{nDCG}_{\text{read}}$ objectives given different preferences for readability. E.g., with a w_{read} of 0.626, we obtain a 5% increase in $\text{nDCG}_{\text{read}}$, with an 8% loss compared the best solution in terms of nDCG_{rel} ($w_{read} = 0.197$). uRBP combines both objectives, and is highly correlated to RBP [17]. Due to this correlation, using RBP with uRBP would not find all rankers that offer the best available trade-offs between relevance and readability; the solution would be biased toward relevance. We therefore conclude that uRBP is not suitable for all possible preferences that a user might have.

Table 1: Evaluation of the solutions from the CCS on eHealth.

w_{read}	nDCG_{rel}	$\text{nDCG}_{\text{read}}$	RBP	uRBP	uRBPgr
0.000	0.350	0.783	0.392	**0.342**	0.337
0.197	**0.364**	0.777	**0.397**	0.340	**0.339**
0.448	0.344	0.807	0.371	0.327	0.324
0.514	0.343	0.804	0.372	0.327	0.324
0.626	0.335	0.814	0.369	0.326	0.324
0.771	0.298	0.832	0.333	0.294	0.294
0.944	0.266	**0.840**	0.304	0.270	0.269
1.000	0.157	**0.840**	0.189	0.160	0.159

To further analyze the effect of different weights for the readability objective, we analyze the annotations at each position in the ranking averaged over topics. Fig. 4 shows for three solutions in the CCS. The ranker optimized for readability does not show documents with higher relevance annotations in the top positions, whereas the other rankers are able to place more relevant documents at the top (similarly for readability). We observe that each ranker is suitable for their specific scalarization function, and as such our method is effective in balancing different relevance criteria.

TREC 2012 diversity task. For this task, we simultaneously optimize for overall relevance and sub-topic relevance by linearly combining value functions based on nDCG and α-nDCG. The CCS from OLS is shown in Fig. 5. The results from the points in the CCS on the TREC 2012 diversity task are shown in Table 2. Fewer solutions were found for the CCS compared to the readability task,

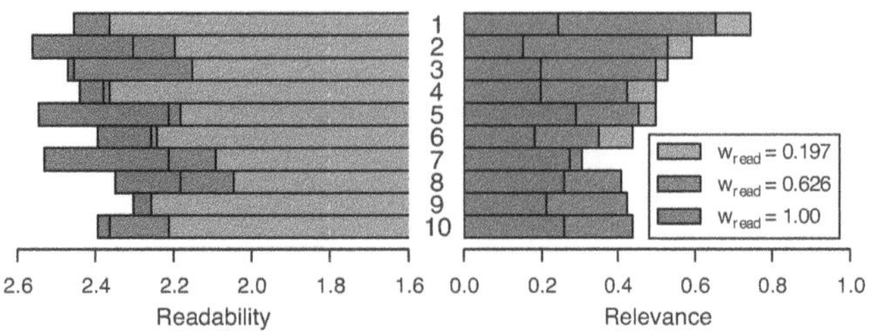

Figure 4: Average readability and relevance annotations on each rank for three different solutions in the CCS.

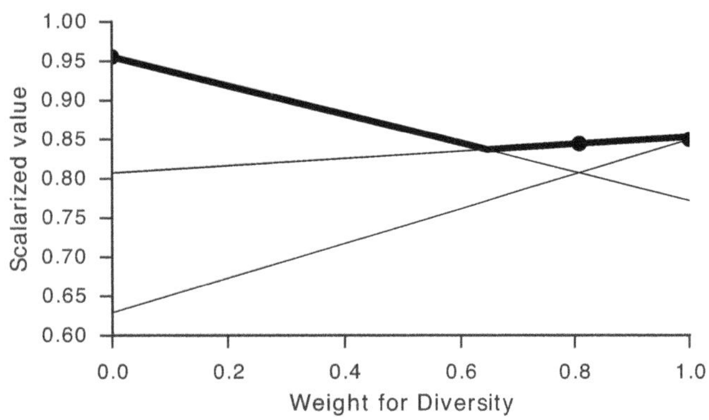

Figure 5: The CCS found on the TREC 2010 and 2011 datasets, with a scalarized value based on relevance and diversity. Absolute left having maximum weight on relevance, and absolute right maximum weight on diversity.

furthermore the differences between the values in Table 5 are also quite small, suggesting only a small trade-off between the objectives. As such this setting seems less suitable for our method. In terms of α-nDCG, the solutions on the test set (TREC 2012) are mid-performers compared to the original participants (the best solution is above the fourth of nine participants). The overall nDCG score would have ranked second. During training (TREC 2010–2011), the intermediate solution that OLS found obtains the same α-nDCG score with an increase in nDCG, compared to the solution optimized only for α-nDCG, see Fig. 5. We therefore conclude that our approach finds more balanced and better solutions, than if we would optimize for a single objective.

Table 2: Evaluation of the solutions from the CCS on the TREC 2012 dataset.

w_{div}	nDCG	α-nDCG
0.000	**0.236**	0.489
0.808	0.229	**0.493**
1.000	0.204	0.480

6. DISCUSSION

We demonstrated how to optimize rankings for multiple objectives by proposing a multi-objective approach based on optimistic linear support and DBGD for learning to rank. Because DBGD may get stuck in a local minimum we proposed an iterated local search schema for DBGD, and reuse of rankers inside OLS in order to make our algorithm more efficient. Using this approach, we have found multiple optimal rankers on the CLEF eHealth 2015 task 2 and on the TREC diversity task that offer different trade-offs w.r.t. different relevance criteria. These multiple optimal rankers are more flexible than a one-size-fits-all ranker produced by a standard learning to rank approach, and our work therefore forms an important step for flexibly optimizing search when multiple criteria are in play.

As to future work, one important issue is exposing different solutions to the user, or using different solutions to select the desired one. Exposing the user to multiple solutions can be done using additional user interface elements, or based on profiling of the user or adapting per query. The number of user interface controls provided in generic search engines is very minimal; specialized search engines are more likely to benefit from optimizing their controls based on these multi-objective criteria. Future work may also investigate what a good scalarization function is, as others may exist and be more suited, and which metrics are more suitable for linear combination. Many current evaluation metrics are highly correlated with relevance and as such may not always provide the flexibility to get a large CCS.

Acknowledgments. This research was supported by Ahold, Amsterdam Data Science, the Bloomberg Research Grant program, the Dutch national program COMMIT, Elsevier, the European Community's Seventh Framework Programme (FP7/2007-2013) under grant agreement nr 312827 (VOX-Pol), the ESF Research Network Program ELIAS, the Royal Dutch Academy of Sciences (KNAW) under the Elite Network Shifts project, the Microsoft Research Ph.D. program, the Netherlands eScience Center under project number 027.012.105, the Netherlands Institute for Sound and Vision, the Netherlands Organisation for Scientific Research (NWO) under project nrs 612.001.109, 727.011.005, 612.001.116, HOR-11-10, 640.006.013, 612.-066.930, CI-14-25, SH-322-15, 652.002.001, 612.001.551, the Yahoo Faculty Research and Engagement Program, and Yandex. All content represents the opinion of the authors, which is not necessarily shared or endorsed by their respective employers and/or sponsors.

REFERENCES

[1] R. Agrawal, S. Gollapudi, A. Halverson, and S. Ieong. Diversifying search results. In *WSDM'09*, pages 5–14. ACM, 2009.

[2] B. Carterette. System effectiveness, user models, and user utility: a conceptual framework for investigation. In *SIGIR'11*, pages 903–912. ACM, 2011.

[3] C. L. Clarke, N. Craswell, I. Soboroff, and A. Ashkan. A comparative analysis of cascade measures for novelty and diversity. In *WSDM'11*, pages 75–84. ACM, 2011.

[4] W. S. Cooper. A definition of relevance for information retrieval. *Information Storage and Retrieval*, 7(1):19–37, 1971.

[5] N. Dai, M. Shokouhi, and B. D. Davison. Learning to rank for freshness and relevance. In *SIGIR'11*, pages 95–104. ACM, 2011.

[6] C. Kohlschütter, P. Fankhauser, and W. Nejdl. Boilerplate detection using shallow text features. In *WSDM'10*, pages 441–450. ACM, 2010.

[7] H. R. Lourenço, O. C. Martin, and T. Stützle. *Iterated local search.* Springer, 2003.

[8] J. Palotti, G. Zuccon, L. Goeuriot, L. Kelly, A. Hanbury, G. J. Jones, M. Lupu, and P. Pecina. CLEF eHealth evaluation lab 2015, task 2: Retrieving information about medical symptoms. In *CLEF '15*. Springer, 2015.

[9] T. K. Park. The nature of relevance in information retrieval: An empirical study. *The Library Quarterly*, 63(3):318–351, 1993.

[10] F. Raiber and O. Kurland. The Technion at TREC 2013 web track: Cluster-based document retrieval. Technical report, Technion, Israel, 2013.

[11] D. M. Roijers, P. Vamplew, S. Whiteson, and R. Dazeley. A survey of multi-objective sequential decision-making. *Journal of Artificial Intelligence Research*, 48:67–113, 2013.

[12] D. M. Roijers, S. Whiteson, and F. A. Oliehoek. Computing convex coverage sets for faster multi-objective coordination. *Journal of Artificial Intelligence Research*, 52:399–443, 2015.

[13] D. M. Roijers, S. Whiteson, and F. A. Oliehoek. Point-based planning for multi-objective POMDPs. In *IJCAI'15*, 2015.

[14] L. Schamber and J. Bateman. User criteria in relevance evaluation: Toward development of a measurement scale. In *ASIS'96*, volume 33, pages 218–25. ERIC, 1996.

[15] X. Yan, D. Song, and X. Li. Concept-based document readability in domain specific information retrieval. In *CIKM'06*, pages 540–549. ACM, 2006.

[16] Y. Yue and T. Joachims. Interactively optimizing information retrieval systems as a dueling bandits problem. In *ICML'09*, pages 1201–1208. ACM, 2009.

[17] G. Zuccon. Understandability biased evaluation for information retrieval. In *ECIR'16*. Springer, 2016.

Build Emotion Lexicon from the Mood of Crowd via Topic-Assisted Joint Non-negative Matrix Factorization

Kaisong Song[1], Wei Gao[2], Ling Chen[3], Shi Feng[1,4], Daling Wang[1,4], Chengqi Zhang[3]
[1]School of Computer Science and Engineering, Northeastern University, Shenyang, China
[2]Qatar Computing Research Institute, Hamad Bin Khalifa University, Doha, Qatar
[3]Centre for Quantum Computation and Intelligent Systems, University of Technology, Sydney, Australia
[4]Key Laboratory of Medical Image Computing (Northeastern University), Ministry of Education, China
kaisongsong@gmail.com, {fengshi, wangdaling}@cse.neu.edu.cn
wgao@qf.org.qa, {ling.chen, chengqi.zhang}@uts.edu.au

ABSTRACT

In the research of building emotion lexicons, we witness the exploitation of crowd-sourced affective annotation given by readers of online news articles. Such approach ignores the relationship between topics and emotion expressions which are often closely correlated. We build an emotion lexicon by developing a novel joint non-negative matrix factorization model which not only incorporates crowd-annotated emotion labels of articles but also generates the lexicon using the topic-specific matrices obtained from the factorization process. We evaluate our lexicon via emotion classification on both benchmark and built-in-house datasets. Results demonstrate the high-quality of our lexicon.

Keywords

emotion lexicon; joint NMF; emotion classification

1. INTRODUCTION

A basic task in sentiment analysis is classifying the sentiment polarity (positive or negative) of the given subjective text [8, 11, 13]. However, the binary scheme may be oversimplified. Recently, *emotion analysis* represents a natural evolution of *sentiment analysis* by modeling finer-grained emotions, e.g., happy, sad, angry, etc. [9, 14].

Emotion lexicons are the essential resources for emotion analysis. Compared to sentiment lexicons such as SentiWordNet[1] [1], where each entry is typically labeled with sentiment polarity, emotion lexicons are more complex in the sense that each entry may convey a mixture of multiple emotions which bear different emotion intensity[2] [14].

Most of the existing lexicon construction approaches [3, 12, 15] are based upon a set of hand-coded seed words. Consequently, the quality of lexicons is sensitive to the manual seed selection. Today, many news websites (e.g., rappler.com, corriere.it, etc.) allow users to express their feelings about an article with a simple click on a given set of emoticons. Figure 1 shows the emotion distribution based on such kind of votes from the crowd regarding an article on rappler.com via an GUI called "mood meter" which is embedded in each of its web page.

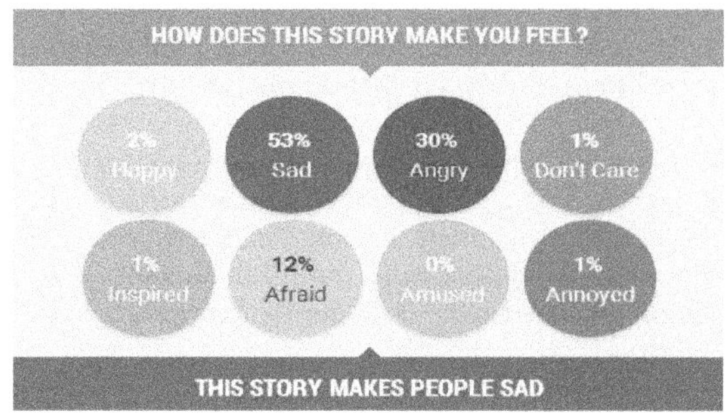

Figure 1: The emotion distribution generated by "mood meter" on a news article

Staiano and Guerini [14] proposed a compositional semantics method that utilized crowd-based affective annotation, where they represented words and emotions in a high-dimensional space based on their occurrences in the document. A deficiency is that they ignored the versatility of affections among various contexts. It cannot distinguish accurately the emotion of words by disregarding different topics where words exist. Since documents and topics are of many-to-many correspondence in a collection, it would be more useful to consider emotions at topic level. Some researchers tried to model topic and sentiment simultaneously [4, 8] for joint sentiment-topic analysis. However, no work has considered topics when building emotion lexicons.

Intuitively, emotion expressions are pertinent to the topics in which they reside. For example, "predictable" suggests happiness for stock market, but for a movie it implies disappointment or even anger. We expect that topic-assisted workaround can produce finer-grained and more accurate entries for emotion lexicons. In this paper, we develop a novel joint non-negative matrix factorization model which associates words with emotions in a low-dimensional semantic space based on hidden topics. An emotion lexicon is built from word-topic and emotion-topic factor matrices, which result from the joint model, using matrix composition.

[1]http://sentiwordnet.isti.cnr.it/
[2]git.io/MqyoIg

SIGIR '16, July 17 - 21, 2016, Pisa, Italy

ISBN 978-1-4503-4069-4/16/07... $15.00
DOI: http://dx.doi.org/10.1145/2911451.2914759

2. RELATED WORK

Emotion lexicons are typically built based on a set of seed words [3, 12, 14, 15]. Xu et al. [15] proposed a graph-based algorithm which ranked words according to a few manually selected seed words. Song et al. [12] and Feng et al. [3] improved this method by supplementing seed words with graphical emoticons or combined their effects. Differently, Staiano and Guerini [14] proposed a compositional semantics method using crowd-annotated articles crawled from the Internet. In this paper, we also resort to crowd-annotated articles while we incorporate topic-emotion relationship for lexicon construction which was not considered previously.

Non-negative matrix factorization (NMF) has been widely used in image or text representation. Lee and Seung [5] investigated the properties of the algorithm and emphasized the clustering aspect. Xu et al. [16] applied standard NMF to document clustering. In recent years, different extensions [7, 10] have been proposed for solving sentiment analysis and sentiment lexicon construction. Li et al. [7] creatively applied orthogonal NMF, proposed by Ding et al. [2], to sentiment classification by incorporating lexical prior knowledge. Peng and Park [10] proposed a constrained symmetric NMF method for sentiment lexicon construction, which considers synonyms and antonyms simultaneously.

Lee et al. [6] used a generic semi-supervised NMF (SSNMF) method which jointly incorporates the data matrix and the (partial) class label matrix into NMF. We base our model on SSNMF for lexicon construction by incorporating different factorization schemes for the supervision matrix, which naturally results in a lexicon from the estimated factor matrices. To our knowledge, this is the first attempt for building fine-grained emotion lexicon based on NMF models.

3. PRELIMINARIES

We first introduce a compositional semantics method [14] for building an emotion lexicon from crowd-annotated news. Then, we review semi-supervised NMF [6] which paves the way for developing our lexicon generation method.

3.1 Compositional Semantics Method (CS)

Let $D = \{d_1, \ldots, d_{|D|}\}$ be a set of documents, and $W = \{w_1, \ldots, w_{|W|}\}$ be the complete vocabulary set of the whole corpus. We define a word-document matrix $\mathbf{M}_{WD}$ of size $|W| \times |D|$, using (w, d) as index and $M_{WD(w,d)}$ as entry value based on raw frequencies *f*, normalized frequencies *nf* or *tf-idf*. Given emotion set $E = \{e_1, \ldots, e_{|E|}\}$, we can represent emotion labels from crowd-annotated resources as a document-emotion matrix $\mathbf{M}_{DE}$ of size $|D| \times |E|$ whose entry values are based on crowd-sourced affective annotation (see Figure 1). Staiano and Guerini [14] built a word-emotion matrix $\mathbf{M}_{WE}$ using the compositional semantics (CS) method by multiplying matrices $\mathbf{M}_{WD}$ and $\mathbf{M}_{DE}$:

$$\mathbf{M}_{WE} = \mathbf{M}_{WD}\mathbf{M}_{DE} \tag{1}$$

An emotion lexicon can be obtained by first applying column-wise normalization to $\mathbf{M}_{WE}$ and then scaling its row-wise data that sums up to one.

3.2 Semi-Supervised NMF (SSNMF)

Non-negative Matrix Factorization (NMF) [5] is an unsupervised algorithm widely used in image or text representation. A generic semi-supervised NMF (SSNMF) algorithm [6] was proposed to incorporate the data matrix $\mathbf{X} = [x_1, \ldots, x_n] \in \mathbb{R}_+^{m\times n}$, where m is the dimension of data vectors, and the class label matrix $\mathbf{Y} = [y_1, \ldots, y_n] \in \mathbb{R}_+^{c\times n}$, where c is the number of classes. The objective function, which involves the non-negative two-factor decomposition of $\mathbf{X}$ and $\mathbf{Y}$ sharing a common factor matrix $\mathbf{S} \in \mathbb{R}_+^{k\times n}$, is to minimize the following:

$$\mathcal{J} = ||\mathbf{U} \odot (\mathbf{X} - \mathbf{AS})||^2 + \alpha||\mathbf{V} \odot (\mathbf{Y} - \mathbf{BS})||^2 \tag{2}$$

where α is a tradeoff parameter adjusting the importance of the supervised term, $\mathbf{A} \in \mathbb{R}_+^{m\times k}$ and $\mathbf{B} \in \mathbb{R}_+^{c\times k}$ are basis matrices for $\mathbf{X}$ and $\mathbf{Y}$, $\mathbf{U}$ and $\mathbf{V}$ are weights matrices, both of which can be fixed as *all-ones matrices* to make an NMF that fully uses labeled data [6]. Notation $||.||^2$ denotes the squared sum of all the elements in the matrix and $\odot$ represents element-wise product.

4. OUR JOINT NMF MODEL

Inspired from SSNMF, we can jointly model the hidden topics and the explicit crowd-based emotions of articles by customizing the factorization process. Let $T = \{t_1, ..., t_{|T|}\}$ be a set of topics in low-dimensional space with $|T| \ll \min\{|D|, |W|\}$. Given the word-document matrix $\mathbf{M}_{WD}$ and document-emotion matrix $\mathbf{M}_{DE}$, we decompose them based on equation 2 by minimizing:

$$\mathcal{J} = ||\mathbf{M}_{WD} - \mathbf{M}_{WT}\mathbf{M}_{DT}^{\intercal}||^2 + \alpha||\mathbf{M}_{DE}^{\intercal} - \mathbf{M}_{ET}\mathbf{M}_{DT}^{\intercal}||^2 \tag{3}$$

to learn the three topic-specific factor matrices $\mathbf{M}_{WT}$, $\mathbf{M}_{DT}$ and $\mathbf{M}_{ET}$, where $\mathbf{M}_{ET}$ represents the strength that emotions are associated with topics. Then, we can get the word emotion distributions by using a *variant* of compositional semantics approach (see equation 1) as below:

$$\mathbf{M}'_{WE} = \mathbf{M}_{WT}\mathbf{M}_{ET}^{\intercal} \tag{4}$$

A deficiency of directly applying SSNMF is that the emotion modeling is still coarse-grained for lexicon construction which is concerned about word-level emotion. We enhance the model by modeling the emotions of subjective texts using a weighted linear combination of emotion words, which will result in an additional term of the 3-factor decomposition of $\mathbf{M}_{DE}$ based on formula 3 as follow:

$$\mathcal{J}' = \mathcal{J} \ + \ \beta||\mathbf{M}_{DE} - \mathbf{M}_{WD}^{\intercal}\mathbf{M}_{WT}\mathbf{M}_{ET}^{\intercal}||^2 \tag{5}$$

where β is a tradeoff parameter, $\mathbf{M}_{WD}$ is fixed and considered as word weights, and $\mathbf{M}_{WT}$ and $\mathbf{M}_{ET}$ are variables whose product happens to be $\mathbf{M}'_{WE}$. With the last term, the joint model aims to improve the estimation of the topic-specific factor matrices by approximating the document-level emotions $\mathbf{M}_{DE}$ based on the word-level emotions $\mathbf{M}'_{WE}$.

Computation: Factor matrices $\mathbf{M}_{WT}$, $\mathbf{M}_{ET}$ and $\mathbf{M}_{DT}$ are first randomly initialized, and then updated iteratively by the following updating formulas:

$$\mathbf{M}_{WT} \leftarrow \mathbf{M}_{WT} \odot \frac{\mathbf{M}_{WD}\mathbf{M}_{DT} + \beta\mathbf{M}_{WE}\mathbf{M}_{ET}}{\mathbf{M}_{WT}\mathbf{M}_{DT}^{\intercal}\mathbf{M}_{DT} + \beta\mathbf{M}_{WW}\mathbf{M}_{WT}\mathbf{M}_{ET}^{\intercal}\mathbf{M}_{ET}}$$

$$\mathbf{M}_{ET} \leftarrow \mathbf{M}_{ET} \odot \frac{\alpha\mathbf{M}_{DE}^{\intercal}\mathbf{M}_{DT} + \beta\mathbf{M}_{WE}^{\intercal}\mathbf{M}_{WT}}{\alpha\mathbf{M}_{ET}\mathbf{M}_{DT}^{\intercal}\mathbf{M}_{DT} + \beta\mathbf{M}_{ET}\mathbf{M}_{WT}^{\intercal}\mathbf{M}_{WW}\mathbf{M}_{WT}}$$

$$\mathbf{M}_{DT} \leftarrow \mathbf{M}_{DT} \odot \frac{\mathbf{M}_{WD}^{\intercal}\mathbf{M}_{WT} + \alpha\mathbf{M}_{DE}\mathbf{M}_{ET}}{\mathbf{M}_{DT}\mathbf{M}_{WT}^{\intercal}\mathbf{M}_{WT} + \alpha\mathbf{M}_{DT}\mathbf{M}_{ET}^{\intercal}\mathbf{M}_{ET}}$$

where $\mathbf{M}_{WW} = \mathbf{M}_{WD}\mathbf{M}_{WD}^{\intercal}$, $\mathbf{M}_{WE} = \mathbf{M}_{WD}\mathbf{M}_{DE}$, and the divisions are all element-wise. The update formulas can be easily induced based on the derivatives in [6].

Example entries	afraid	amused	angry	annoyed	dont_care	happy	inspired	sad
crime#n	.000 (.119)	.000 (.088)	**.994** (**.272**)	.000 (.104)	.000 (.085)	.006 (.096)	.000 (.094)	.000 (.142)
dead#a	.000 (**.218**)	.000 (.059)	.000 (.173)	.000 (.080)	.000 (.075)	.000 (.055)	.000 (.057)	**1.00** (**.283**)
criminal#a	.001 (.145)	.000 (.092)	**1.00** (**.233**)	.000 (.137)	.000 (.086)	.000 (.117)	.000 (.059)	.000 (.131)
interesting#a	.000 (.034)	**1.00** (**.252**)	.000 (.046)	.000 (.098)	.000 (.142)	.000 (.181)	.000 (**.206**)	.000 (.041)
monitor#v	**.511** (**.238**)	.000 (.098)	**.485** (.157)	.000 (.124)	.000 (.078)	.004 (.109)	.000 (.097)	.000 (.099)
funny#a	.000 (.055)	**.977** (**.278**)	.000 (.065)	.000 (.125)	.001 (**.203**)	.022 (.110)	.000 (.093)	.043 (.071)
sad#a	.000 (.050)	.000 (.081)	.000 (.112)	.000 (.104)	.000 (.172)	.000 (.071)	.000 (.109)	**1.00** (**.301**)

Table 1: Example entries in our constructed emotion lexicon. Emotion scores higher than 20% are highlighted for readability purposes. The brackets enclose the scores given by the CS method as a baseline

Emotion	afraid	amused	angry	annoyed
votes$_{avg.}$	7.8%	10.6%	10.9%	5.9%
Emotion	dont_care	happy	inspired	sad
votes$_{avg.}$	5.9%	34.1%	10.3%	14.5%

Table 2: Emotion distribution over Rappler dataset

Lexicon Construction: Given $\mathbf{M}_{WT}$ and $\mathbf{M}_{ET}$ represented in the $|T|$-dimensional topic space, we can build a word-emotion matrix $\mathbf{M}'_{WE}$ based on equation 4. After normalizing its entries, we obtain a $|E|$-dimensional vector for each word w:

$$\overline{\mathbf{M}'_{WE(w,.)}} = \frac{1}{Z_w} \langle \mathbf{M}'_{WE(w,1)}, \cdots, \mathbf{M}'_{WE(w,|E|)} \rangle \quad (6)$$

where each element $\mathbf{M}'_{WE(w,e)}$ indexed by (w, e) represents the emotion score of word w belonging to emotion category $e \in E$, and $Z_w = \sum_{e \in E} \frac{\mathbf{M}'_{WE(w,e)}}{\sqrt{\sum_{w \in W} \mathbf{M}'^{2}_{WE(w,e)}}}$ is the normalization term for w (column-wise normalization ensures that different columns for all the emotions are comparable).

Our created emotion lexicon contains 31,806 entries in total. Table 1 presents several example entries. Similar to [14], we lemmatize and Part-of-Speech (PoS) tag all the documents (PoS we considered are adjective, noun, verb and adverb), and we only keep those *lemma#PoS* entries in the lexicon which also appear in WordNet for eliminating noise words. We can see that each entry has at least one main emotion (e.g., *monitor#v* has two main emotions of *afraid* and *angry*), and our lexicon differentiates the emotions better by assigning discriminative weighting scores as compared to the CS baseline.

5. EXPERIMENTAL EVALUATION

5.1 Data Resources

To build our lexicon, we crawled 31,107 English news articles published before 2015-11-06 from *rappler.com*. We used Standford CoreNLP[3], an integrated suite of natural language processing tools, to tokenize, PoS tag and lemmatize all text data. In Table 2, we report the average percentage of votes for each emotion over all the documents in the corpus. From Table 2, we find that the emotion of *happy* has a lot more votes than the others, which reflects that readers' emotion preference is consistent to the general observation – positive sentiment dominates in real-world data. The crawled resources and generated lexicons have been made publicly available[4].

To evaluate the lexicon, we applied it for emotion classification on news headlines as [14] did. We used two datasets:

[3]http://nlp.stanford.edu/software/corenlp.shtml
[4]https://sites.google.com/site/emolexdata/

Rappler	angry	sad	afraid	happy	inspired	other
SemEval	anger	sadness	fear	joy	surprise	–

Table 3: Emotion label mapping over two test sets

(1) A benchmark dataset from SemEval-2007[5] on identifying "Affective Text", which contains $1k$ annotated headlines. As SemEval-2007 test set consists of only six emotions, we adopted an emotion mapping method as displayed in Table 3 to map them to our pre-defined emotions in the lexicon. (2) A built-in-house dataset with total $31k$ headlines of the crawled *Rappler* articles.

We implement the algorithms using Matlab and run them on a high performance Linux cluster.

5.2 Experiments and Results

We evaluate the quality of the emotion lexicons in two ways: (1) we examine the quality of lexicons created by our method and other competitive methods using the crawled *Rappler* news articles via an emotion classification task; (2) we compare our created lexicons with publicly available state-of-the-art lexicons in similar size.

5.2.1 Parameter Setting

We tune the number of topics $|T|$ by performing a grid search over all values of $10 * x$ with $x \in \{1, 2, ..., 30\}$. The tradeoff parameters α and β are tuned over all values in $\{0.1, 1, 10, 100\}$. The tuning is based on the performance of emotion classification on the headlines in SemEval's trial set and a held-out set which consists of 20% headlines randomly selected from the Rappler articles. Finally, we set $|T| = 250$, $\alpha = 1$ and $\beta = 10$. We set the number of iterations as 300, which is large enough for ensuring convergence according to our observation on the drop of $\mathcal{J}$ and $\mathcal{J}'$ values.

5.2.2 Comparison of Lexicon Building Methods

For emotion classification, we use a straight-forward voting-based algorithm [12, 14] to assign emotion labels to a test headline h. We conduct element-wise sum over the emotion words in the headline by looking up the lexicon and then average the sums by word counts, i.e., $\overline{V_h} = \frac{1}{Z_h} < \sum_w \overline{\mathbf{M}'_{WE(w,1)}}, ..., \sum_w \overline{\mathbf{M}'_{WE(w,|E|)}} >$ where Z_h is the number of emotion words in h. We then normalize $\overline{V_h}$ with the min-max normalization and map each emotion element into a binary decision with fixed thresholds. We set threshold at 0.5 for SemEval-2007 test set and 0.35 for Rappler test set, empirically[6]. We use F-1 measure to assess the classification performance on each emotion. Tables 4 and 5 show the re-

[5]http://nlp.cs.swarthmore.edu/semeval/tasks/
[6]We set a lower threshold for Rappler test set since only a single emotion in each news receives more than 50% votes

Method		fear	anger	joy	sadness	surprise
CS	*f*	.301	.080	**.292**	.349	.096
	nf	.329	.090	.291	.386	.081
	tf-idf	.338	.090	.289	.354	.094
Joint ($\mathcal{J}$)	*f*	.288	.098	.231	.383	.099
	nf	.306	.087	.256	.387	.095
	tf-idf	**.372**	.091	.283	.357	.132
Joint ($\mathcal{J}'$)	*f*	.309	.101	.252	.350	.082
	nf	.349	**.105**	.222	**.393**	.058
	tf-idf	.361	.082	.270	.359	**.133**

Table 4: SemEval-2007 emotion classification (F1)

Method		afraid	amused	angry	annoyed
CS	*f*	.304	.293	.361	.160
	nf	.324	.292	.375	.162
	tf-idf	.341	.277	.377	.145
Joint ($\mathcal{J}$)	*f*	.331	.289	.370	**.208**
	nf	.325	.302	.360	.191
	tf-idf	.338	.267	.366	.138
Joint ($\mathcal{J}'$)	*f*	.333	.279	.371	.198
	nf	**.351**	**.311**	**.386**	.198
	tf-idf	.328	.274	.368	.148
Method		dont_care	happy	inspired	sad
CS	*f*	.142	.653	.297	.429
	nf	.143	.652	.291	.445
	tf-idf	.133	**.654**	.284	.427
Joint ($\mathcal{J}$)	*f*	.177	.596	.270	.430
	nf	.172	.613	**.300**	.434
	tf-idf	.129	.624	.266	.416
Joint ($\mathcal{J}'$)	*f*	.191	.608	.275	.400
	nf	**.199**	.596	.298	**.461**
	tf-idf	.152	.613	.268	.419

Table 5: Rappler emotion classification (F1)

sults by averaging 20 independent runs (with random initial matrices) on *SemEval* and *Rappler* test sets, respectively.

Our joint models perform better than CS for most emotions especially under *nf* configuration. This indicates that normalized frequency can prevent the bias towards long documents and our method considering topic is effective. Moreover, joint model $\mathcal{J}'$ also performs $\mathcal{J}$ at most cases, implying the usefulness of considering word-level emotion in decomposition. Surprisingly, the results under *tf-idf* configuration are unstable, which suggests that introducing *idf* is sub-optimal. This is because frequent emotion words, e.g., "good", receive low $tf * idf$, thus are not learned well.

5.2.3 Comparison with Available Emotion Lexicons

We compare our lexicons with the original lexicons released by Staiano and Guerini [14]. We assess them via emotion classification on the larger built-in-house *Rappler* test set. Figure 2 demonstrates that our lexicon configured as *nf* achieves the best results on nearly all emotions, which suggests the high usability of our created lexicon.

6. CONCLUSIONS

We present a joint NMF method which incorporates crowd-based emotion labels on articles and generates topic-specific factor matrices for building emotion lexicons via compositional semantics. Experiments conducted on the benchmark and built-in-house datasets demonstrate our method outperforms the competitive methods on emotion classification. Moreover, our created lexicon outperforms the competitive counterpart on emotion classification task. Our future work will study emotion-specific word embeddings for lexicon construction using deep learning.

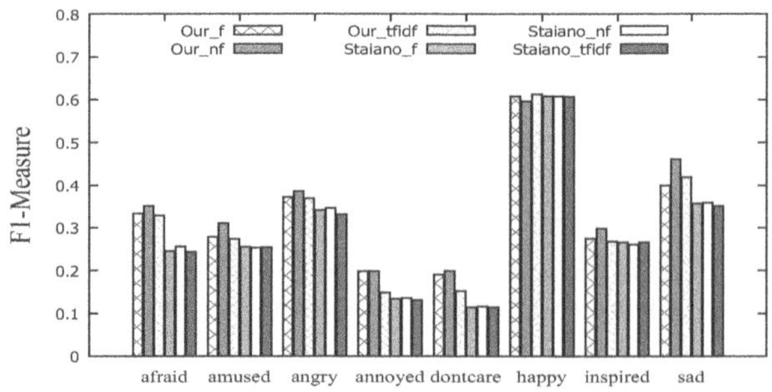

Figure 2: Comparison among different lexicons

Acknowledgments

This work is supported by the National Natural Science Foundation of China (61370074, 61402091), the Fundamental Research Funds for the Central Universities (N130604002, N140404012) and the ARC Discovery Project (DP140100545).

7. REFERENCES

[1] S. Baccianella, A. Esuli, and F. Sebastiani. Sentiwordnet 3.0: An enhanced lexical resource for sentiment analysis and opinion mining. In *LREC*, pages 2200–2204, 2010.

[2] C. H. Q. Ding, T. Li, W. Peng, and H. Park. Orthogonal nonnegative matrix t-factorizations for clustering. In *SIGKDD*, pages 126–135, 2006.

[3] S. Feng, K. Song, D. Wang, and G. Yu. A word-emoticon mutual reinforcement ranking model for building sentiment lexicon from massive collection of microblogs. *World Wide Web*, 18(4):949–967, 2015.

[4] Y. He, C. Lin, W. Gao, and K.-F. Wong. Dynamic joint sentiment-topic model. *ACM Trans. Intell. Syst. Technol.*, 5(1):6:1–6:21, 2013.

[5] D. D. Lee and H. S. Seung. Learning the parts of objects by non-negative matrix factorization. *Nature*, 401, 1999.

[6] H. Lee, J. Yoo, and S. Choi. Semi-supervised nonnegative matrix factorization. *IEEE Signal Process. Lett.*, 17(1):4–7, 2010.

[7] T. Li, Y. Zhang, and V. Sindhwani. A non-negative matrix tri-factorization approach to sentiment classification with lexical prior knowledge. In *ACL*, pages 244–252, 2009.

[8] Q. Mei, X. Ling, M. Wondra, H. Su, and C. Zhai. Topic sentiment mixture: modeling facets and opinions in weblogs. In *WWW*, pages 171–180, 2007.

[9] S. M. Mohammad and P. D. Turney. Crowdsourcing a word-emotion association lexicon. *Computational Intelligence*, 29(3):436–465, 2013.

[10] W. Peng and D. H. Park. Generate adjective sentiment dictionary for social media sentiment analysis using constrained nonnegative matrix factorization. In *ICWSM*, pages 273–280, 2011.

[11] K. Song, L. Chen, W. Gao, S. Feng, D. Wang, and C. Zhang. Persentiment: A personalized sentiment classification system for microblog users. In *WWW (Companion Volume)*, pages 255–258, 2016.

[12] K. Song, S. Feng, W. Gao, D. Wang, L. Chen, and C. Zhang. Build emotion lexicon from microblogs by combining effects of seed words and emoticons in a heterogeneous graph. In *Hypertext*, pages 283–292, 2015.

[13] K. Song, S. Feng, W. Gao, D. Wang, G. Yu, and K.-F. Wong. Personalized sentiment classification based on latent individuality of microblog users. In *IJCAI*, pages 2277–2283, 2015.

[14] J. Staiano and M. Guerini. Depeche mood: a lexicon for emotion analysis from crowd annotated news. In *ACL*, pages 427–433, 2014.

[15] G. Xu, X. Meng, and H. Wang. Build chinese emotion lexicons using a graph-based algorithm and multiple resources. In *COLING*, pages 1209–1217, 2010.

[16] W. Xu, X. Liu, and Y. Gong. Document clustering based on non-negative matrix factorization. In *SIGIR*, pages 267–273, 2003.

Burst Detection in Social Media Streams for Tracking Interest Profiles in Real Time

Cody Buntain
Dept. of Computer Science
University of Maryland
College Park, Maryland, USA
cbuntain@cs.umd.edu

Jimmy Lin
David R. Cheriton School of Computer Science
University of Waterloo
Waterloo, Ontario, Canada
jimmylin@uwaterloo.ca

ABSTRACT

This work presents RTTBurst, an end-to-end system for ingesting descriptions of user interest profiles and discovering new and relevant tweets based on those interest profiles using a simple model for identifying bursts in token usage. Our approach differs from standard retrieval-based techniques in that it primarily focuses on identifying noteworthy moments in the tweet stream, and "summarizes" those moments using selected tweets. We lay out the architecture of RTTBurst, our participation in and performance at the TREC 2015 Microblog track, and a method for combining and potentially improving existing TREC systems. Official results and post hoc experiments show that our simple targeted burst detection technique is competitive with existing systems. Furthermore, we demonstrate that our burst detection mechanism can be used to improve the performance of other systems for the same task.

CCS Concepts

•**Information systems** → **Summarization;** *Social tagging systems;* •**Human-centered computing** → *Social networking sites;*

Keywords

burst detection, real-time tracking, twitter

1. INTRODUCTION

A significant power of social media is the velocity with which new information is posted and shared. If a user is interested in recent posts about a particular item, event, or topic, she can search for a few relevant keywords in a social network and track the newest developments. For instance, one can track tweets mentioning "goal" on Twitter during the 2014 World Cup to identify when goals are scored [4]. If a user wants to track these interesting events on current social media platforms, however, she must remain online and manually filter through many duplicate posts. Many approaches have been proposed to address this need [3, 7, 8, 9], as explored at the 2015 Text Retrieval Conference (TREC) [6] organized by the National Institute of Standards and Technology (NIST).

SIGIR '16, July 17-21, 2016, Pisa, Italy

DOI: http://dx.doi.org/10.1145/2911451.2914733

This paper describes a simple scoring method that uses burst detection to address this social media tracking problem. By identifying rapid increases (i.e., "bursts") in relevant social media posts, one can theoretically rely on the social network to determine interesting data for a given set of interests. We describe this approach, which we call RTTBurst, and its use of real-time burst detection on Twitter's social media stream. Besides documenting our techniques, RTTBurst was one of the systems participating in the TREC 2015 Microblog track, and we discuss its performance relative to similarly purposed systems. Lastly, RTTBurst's architecture is quite different from the other TREC systems, allowing us to demonstrate its use as an additional filtering step to increase other systems' performance.

This work makes the following contributions:

- Presents a real-time streaming algorithm for discovering and summarizing relevant moments on Twitter,
- Details RTTBurst's performance relative to similar real-time systems, and
- Demonstrates that burst detection can enhance other real-time tracking systems.

2. RELATED WORK

Identifying important events from the ever-growing body of digital media has fascinated researchers for over twenty years, starting from digital newsprint to blogs and now social media [1]. Early event detection research followed the work of Kleinberg [5] by identifying bursty keywords from digital newspapers and clustering those keywords to identify bursty events. These works inspired our exploration of burst detection, but they often used complex models, were not designed for big datasets, and were not designed for real-time use.

A recently published survey by Atefeh and Khreich [2] explores many of the avenues used for modern event detection in social media. They laid out many of the issues in analyzing Twitter (e.g., high levels of noise, mixed language, spelling/grammar mistakes, etc.) and presented a classification of event detection techniques. The classes cover three dimensions: unspecified vs. specified event information, new vs. retrospective detection, and unsupervised vs. supervised learning methods. Our work falls in the new-event-detection, unsupervised learning classes but represents a hybrid in the unspecified vs. specified dimension. RTTBurst was originally developed on an open-domain model and was adapted to the interest tracking domain. It allows the user to pre-specify a topic of interest but leverages temporal signatures to identify new, unanticipated events related to that topic. This hybridization is well-suited for the TREC 2015 Microblog track, which focused on identifying new, topically relevant information on Twitter in real time.

As mentioned in the track's 2015 overview paper by Lin et al. [6], this filtering task's goal was to identify new tweets relevant to a set of given interest profiles, each of which was comprised of an identifier, title, a brief description, and a narrative describing the topic of interest. The evaluation occurred in July of 2015 over ten days and was broken across two tasks: a mobile notification task that enforced a limit of 10 tweets per topic per day and penalized tweets based on the delay between posting and reporting (Scenario A), and a daily digest task with the relaxed constraint of 100 messages per day and no temporal penalty (Scenario B). For the evaluation, NIST created 225 topics, 51 of which were later assessed.

3. METHODS

RTTBurst's high-level pipeline is composed of several stages, from collecting the Twitter stream, to finding bursty tokens, to using these tokens to extract the most interesting tweets. Each of these stages is described below.

Processing the Twitter Stream. For input, RTTBurst used Twitter's unfiltered public sample stream, corresponding to approximately 1% of the full stream (though larger samples should also work), and the user's interest profiles. After extracting search keywords $k \in P_i$ from the set of interest profile titles P, RTTBurst leveraged Apache Spark's[1] Twitter receiver to collect all tweets from the public sample stream and tokenized them using CMU's ARK TweetNLP tokenizer.[2] We then applied a series of filters to remove non-English tweets and low-quality tweets based on the number of hashtags, web links, token counts, and whether the tweet contained the string "follow" (motivated by the large amount of "follow-me" spam on Twitter).

After this first round of quality-based pruning, RTTBurst then calculated the intersection between each tweet's token set and the set of all search keywords $\cup_i P_i$ and kept only those tweets with a non-empty intersection (i.e., only those tweets that contained at least one keyword from at least one interest profile). These tokenized tweets were then converted into a time-stamped inverted index matching tokens to the *users* who tweeted them.

Identifying Bursty Tokens. This time-stamped inverted index allowed us to capture changes in a token's usage over time. We maintained a sliding window over all tweets generated by the Twitter streaming API within the past two minutes and incremented the window by 60-second time slices. Each window therefore overlapped with the previous 60 seconds to smooth the input.

For each two-minute window, we calculated the number of users tweeting with each token and stored this frequency over the previous N windows. We normalized these frequencies by the number of unique tokens in the past N windows and used add-one additive smoothing to correct for tokens with zero occurrences in a single window. Following the features set forth in the paper by Buntain et al. [3], we then used linear regression to fit a line to the natural logarithm of this frequency data. By transforming this frequency data to logarithmic space, exponential curves will appear linear, simplifying the linear regression step, and the steeper the slope of the best-fit line, the steeper the exponential growth of the token's usage. Based on this fit, we then scored each token by the product of the slope of the best-fit line and its coefficient of determination R^2. Since R^2 coefficient is in the range $[0, 1]$, this product reduced scores for highly deviant frequency curves. In this manner, tokens experiencing large bursts in usage, which we would expect to exhibit exponential growth, were scored highly. We then discarded all tokens with scores below a burst threshold γ and any token whose length is less than four characters.

[1]https://spark.apache.org

[2]http://www.cs.cmu.edu/~ark/TweetNLP/

Moment Summarization. Every sixty seconds, RTTBurst identified a new (possibly empty) set of bursty tokens, which corresponded to noteworthy moments in the relevant interest profile. For the TREC Microblog track, however, returning these bursty tokens was not sufficient for summarizing the moment, since the evaluation was based on judgments over individual tweets. Rather, our system used tweets to summarize these moments, similar to the ReDites system [7].

To this end, every sixty seconds, RTTBurst parsed all tweets in the previous N windows to create a subset of tweets containing these bursty tokens. We then calculated a Jaccard similarity score for each tweet in this subset by comparing the tweet to tweets returned to the user in previous windows. Any new tweet whose Jaccard similarity was above our threshold $J_t = 0.7$ was discarded, and the remaining tweets were sorted by their similarity scores in decreasing order. Finally, the top M least similar tweets containing bursty tokens from the past N windows were assigned to the relevant interest profiles and stored.

Before pushing a tweet to the user, however, RTTBurst performed one last pass through the tweets to select those that were most relevant to the given interest profile. For each candidate tweet stored up to this point, RTTBurst then selected only those tweets that contained at least X tokens from the relevant interest profile. All other tweets were then discarded.

In summary, for Scenario A of the TREC Microblog track, the top 10 most dissimilar tweets containing bursty tokens and at least two tokens from the relevant interest profile were returned to the user per day. Scenario B followed the same pipeline with the additional relaxation of returning the top 100 most dissimilar tweets.

3.1 Ensembles with RTTBurst

While analyzing results after the official TREC 2015 evaluation, we noticed a significant dissimilarity between the tweets returned by RTTBurst and those returned by the other systems. This observation led to an interesting question: If we apply the burst detection approach of RTTBurst to the output of another more traditional information retrieval system, could we increase the system's performance? To explore this question, we designed a simple gating mechanism that, given a set of tweets returned by system A, used RTTBurst to keep only those tweets that contained a bursty token.

Following from this question of using RTTBurst to filter other systems, we also investigated whether RTTBurst could be used to create ensembles of these information tracking and summarization systems. That is, given the output of two TREC systems A and B, would applying RTTBurst to their combined output yield higher scores? For this investigation, we constructed a simple system that takes the union of any two systems' returned tweets and then applies RTTBurst's gating mechanism to filter the results. To ensure that RTTBurst did not benefit simply from combining multiple systems, we also conducted an experiment that scored the outputs of each pair of systems, without any gating by RTTBurst. Duplicate tweets were removed from this paired output, the output was ordered by delivery time, and only the first tweets within the scenario A daily limits were scored.

4. RESULTS

We divide our results into two sets: The first covers RTTBurst's relative performance results from the real-time Microblog track tasks as scored by NIST (including some post hoc testing), and the second covers results from our ensemble experiments.

Table 1: Optimized Parameters, Tweets Delivered to Users, and Scores (Best in Bold)

Parameters			Scenario A				Scenario B		
Window Size (N)	Top M Tweets	Burst Threshold γ	Delivered Tweets	Unjudged Tweets	ELG	nCG	Delivered Tweets	Unjudged Tweets	nDCG
† 30	10	0.07	1	0	0.2471	0.2471	1	0	0.2471
37	13	0.036854	29	15	**0.2549**	0.2464	29	15	0.2420
18	34	0.138824	15	7	0.2525	**0.2494**	15	7	0.2479
37	48	0.067306	6	1	0.2506	0.2479	6	1	**0.2489**

† – Parameters used for TREC 2015 evaluation

4.1 RTTBurst Performance

RTTBurst's TREC evaluation version originally lacked several tweet quality metrics (i.e., it did not filter out tweets with many hashtags, many links, or few tokens) and did not include mechanisms for preventing duplicate tweet content from being reported to the user. This official run crystallized the need for these quality metrics as our system caught a significant amount of spam in this early run. For example, while the original RTTBurst implementation did prevent the same tweet ID from being reported twice, two different tweets with the same content could still be reported, and many Twitter bots spammed the same tweet content with only slight differences (one token at the end of the tweet might differ from one spam tweet to the next).

Following the TREC evaluation period and the release of the NIST-judged tweets, we implemented these quality metrics and performed a series of post hoc parameter optimization experiments. Parameter optimization used a randomized parameter search over window size $N \in [7, 43]$, maximum tweets delivered per minute $N \in [10, 50]$, and burst thresholds $\gamma \in [0.015, 0.18]$. For each parameter set, we recorded the number of tweets RTTBurst flagged for delivery to the user (across all topics), the number of these tweets that did not have associated relevance judgments from NIST (unjudged tweets), and their scores. Table 1 shows the top-scoring sets for both scenarios from the official run (indicated by the †) and our parameter optimization (see the track overview paper [6] for details on the scoring methodology). Official scores placed RTTBurst 11th out of 32 automatic runs in Scenario A (ranked by ELG) and 4th out of 38 in Scenario B. After parameter optimization, RTTBurst would move up one rank in Scenario A and would remain in fourth in Scenario B. Note that randomized parameter optimization produced more scored tweets than the official run, which was essentially silent. It is worthwhile to note that RTTBurst is exceedingly conservative in the emission of tweets, and that this approach occupies a completely different point in the tradeoff space compared to standard retrieval-based systems.

4.2 Gating with RTTBurst

Applying RTTBurst's gating mechanism to a single Scenario A system resulted in an average increase in ELG and nCG by 17% and 13% respectively but decreased the ELG of the best-performing system [10] by about 19%. A two-sided t-test on the original scores and the gated scores determined this increase in ELG was statistically significant ($t(33) = 3.28$, $p < 0.01$). In total, RTTBurst increased the performance of 22 systems and decreased the performance of 13 systems, as shown in Figure 1a. For Scenario B, gating with RTTBurst resulted in a 9% decrease in nDCG@10.

For system pairs, comparing an individual system with its highest-scoring pair (that is, pairing it to all other systems and taking the one that achieves the highest ELG) yielded an 11% average ELG increase. Only three systems achieved higher scores without pairing. Using RTTBurst to gate these pairs yielded a 24% increase in ELG over the individual, ungated systems, and five systems performed worse than their unpaired, ungated counterparts. Differences in single system ELG and paired, gated system scores are shown in Figure 1b.

For completeness, we also compared the best pairs' ELG to a silent system (Figure 2a) and the best gated pairs of systems (Figure 2b). Note that these figures show absolute scores as opposed to score differences. We see that the best pairs of systems did not perform as well as a silent system, but applying RTTBurst as an additional gating filter raised all pairs up to or above the score for a silent system.

5. DISCUSSION

Results from our experiments and the official Microblog track exhibited a correlation between higher scores and fewer reported tweets. This link was first apparent given the score for a system that returns no tweets at all: an ELG, nCG, and nDCG@10 of 0.2471, which placed in the upper third of rankings in both TREC scenarios. During our parameter optimization experiments, we saw more evidence of this trend in a strongly negative, nearly linear correlation ($R^2 = 0.8172$) between the more tweets RTTBurst returned and the score produced by the TREC evaluations. This preference towards silence might explain why gating with RTTBurst increased the average score in Scenario A: Summed across all topics, gating reduced the average number of tweets delivered by two orders of magnitude (from 1,600 tweets to a mere 57).

Such a significant reduction in the number of delivered tweets suggested another issue regarding similarity of results returned by the original systems and their gated counterparts. From Figure 2, all systems' scores tended to converge to the same value; this convergence would be easily explained if all systems were converging to the same set of tweets. To examine this potential issue, we calculated the Jaccard similarity among the returned tweets for each system and then among the gated systems: For the original systems, the average similarity across all systems was 0.045, and for our gated systems, average similarity was 0.55. Therefore, gains made from gating with RTTBurst are not the result of reducing all output to a common set of tweets. This result suggests bursts provide a valuable relevance signal.

While this convergence is a positive effect for many systems, we must address why RTTBurst decreases the top performing run [10] by 19%. One possibility is the absence of query expansion techniques. RTTBurst was originally designed as an open-domain system without tracking capabilities, and the modifications to track interest profiles did not include data-driven synonyms or identify related keywords that could expand the filtered data. RTTBurst therefore potentially discarded many relevant tweets, something that future versions of the system should address. Another possibility, however, is an imbalance in the "bursty-ness" of some topics; thresholds for bursts about celebrities may be too high for more esoteric topics.

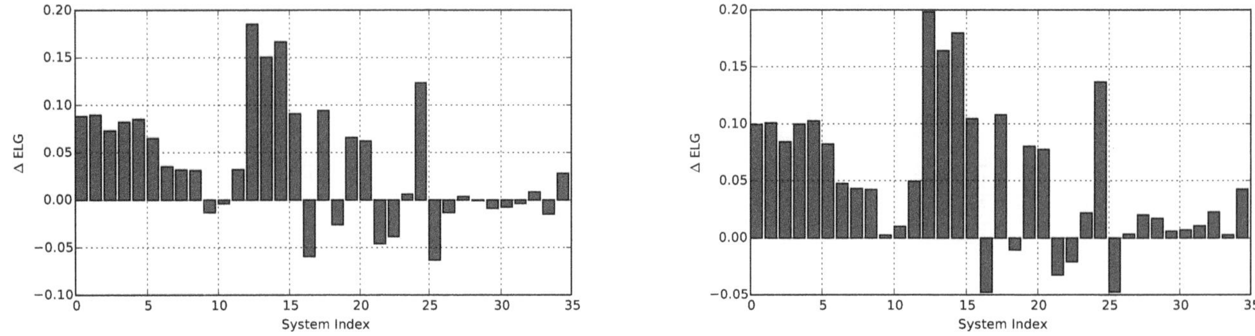

(a) Single System vs. Gated System

(b) Single System vs. Paired, Gated System

Figure 1: Performance Differences in ELG. Systems arranged alphabetically.

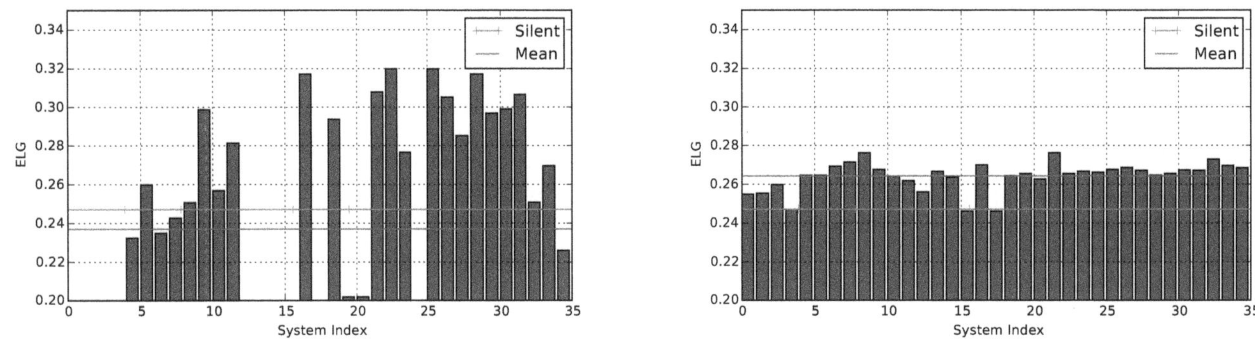

(a) ELG of Best System Pairs vs. Silent System

(b) ELG of Best Gated System Pairs vs. Silent System

Figure 2: Average ELG vs. Silent System. Systems arranged alphabetically.

This work is also limited by unjudged tweets in the returned tweet sets, which makes a true performance comparison between official and post hoc runs difficult. That is, while the NIST assessors provided relevance judgments for approximately 94k tweets, the Twitter sample stream over the TREC evaluation period contains around 40 million tweets, so it is highly likely post hoc runs of RTTBurst may return tweets without these judgments. This limitation may be the driving force behind the connection between returned tweet set size and low scores. Going forward, we need to explore better methods for scoring these unjudged tweets or comparing judged and unjudged tweets and scores via similarity propagation, self-learning, or a similar method.

6. CONCLUSIONS

RTTBurst is a hybrid end-to-end system that uses a simple burst-detection technique to identify tweets a user may find interesting. This paper laid out RTTBurst's architecture, our participation in and performance at the TREC 2015 Microblog track, and a method for combining and potentially improving the performance of existing TREC systems. While not as effective as the best systems, RTTBurst did perform well and shows potential in hybrid or combined approaches. Further steps could be taken to integrate modern information retrieval techniques like query expansion and spam detection to increase RTTBurst's performance. Given RTTBurst's simple model and its stream-oriented processing, it is at least a useful tool that can be easily integrated into other approaches.

Acknowledgments. This work was supported in part by the National Science Foundation under awards IIS-1218043 and CNS-1405688. Any opinions, findings, conclusions, or recommendations expressed are those of the authors and do not necessarily reflect the views of the sponsors.

7. REFERENCES

[1] J. Allan, R. Papka, and V. Lavrenko. On-line new event detection and tracking. *SIGIR*, 1998.

[2] F. Atefeh and W. Khreich. A survey of techniques for event detection in Twitter. *Computational Intelligence*, 31(1):132–164, 2015.

[3] C. Buntain, J. Lin, and J. Golbeck. Discovering Key Moments in Social Media Streams. *CCNC*, 2016.

[4] L. Cipriani. Goal! Detecting the most important World Cup moments. Technical report, Twitter, 2014.

[5] J. Kleinberg. Bursty and hierarchical structure in streams. *KDD*, 2002.

[6] J. Lin, M. Efron, Y. Wang, G. Sherman, and E. Voorhees. Overview of the TREC-2015 Microblog Track. *TREC*, 2015.

[7] M. Osborne, S. Moran, R. McCreadie, A. Von Lunen, M. Sykora, E. Cano, N. Ireson, C. Macdonald, I. Ounis, Y. He, and Others. Real-Time Detection, Tracking, and Monitoring of Automatically Discovered Events in Social Media. *ACL*, 2014.

[8] J. Rogstadius, M. Vukovic, C. A. Teixeira, V. Kostakos, E. Karapanos, and J. A. Laredo. Crisistracker: Crowdsourced social media curation for disaster awareness. *IBM Journal of Research and Development*, 57(5), 2013.

[9] T. Sakaki, M. Okazaki, and Y. Matsuo. Earthquake shakes Twitter users: real-time event detection by social sensors. *WWW*, 2010.

[10] L. Tan, A. Roegiest, and C. L. A. Clarke. University of Waterloo at TREC 2015 Microblog track. *TREC*, 2015.

Cluster-based Joint Matrix Factorization Hashing for Cross-Modal Retrieval

Dimitrios Rafailidis
Department of Informatics
Aristotle University of Thessaloniki
Thessaloniki, Greece
draf@csd.auth.gr

Fabio Crestani
Faculty of Informatics
Università della Svizzera italiana (USI)
Lugano, Switzerland
fabio.crestani@usi.ch

ABSTRACT

Cross-modal retrieval has been an emerging topic over the last years, as modern applications have to efficiently search for multimedia documents with different modalities. In this study, we propose a cross-modal hashing method by following a cluster-based joint matrix factorization strategy. Our method first builds clusters for each modality separately and then generates a cross-modal cluster representation for each document. We formulate a joint matrix factorization process with the constraint that pushes the documents' representations of the different modalities and the cross-modal cluster representations into a common consensus matrix. In doing so, we capture the inter-modality, intra-modality and cluster-based similarities in a unified latent space. Finally, we present an efficient way to generate the hash codes using the maximum entropy principle and compute the binary codes for external queries. In our experiments with two publicly available data sets, we show that the proposed method outperforms state-of-the-art hashing methods for different cross-modal retrieval tasks.

CCS Concepts

•Information systems → Multimedia information systems;

Keywords

Hashing; cross-modal retrieval; matrix factorization

1. INTRODUCTION

In multimedia applications, hashing techniques have been widely used for large-scale similarity search, such as locality sensitive hashing [4], iterative quantization [5] and spectral hashing [8]. The key idea is to design hash functions and learn similarity preserving binary codes for data representation with low storage cost and fast query speed. In the aforementioned hashing methods, given a query from one modality, for example an image-query, results are efficiently retrieved from an image database. In this study, we focus on cross-modal hashing, for example, given a query from an image modality, how to return the most relevant results from a textual modality. The rich representation of a document with different modalities has many applications; for instance, in a real-world multimedia application, given an image-query, a search engine can return relevant text documents to describe its details.

To handle the large amount of available multimedia content with different modalities in modern applications, several cross-modal hashing methods have been proposed [1, 6, 11, 13]. The main challenge of cross-modal hashing is how to learn the binary codes by capturing both the inter-modality and intra-modality similarities [2, 12]. For instance, [1] constructs a unified space and learns groups of hash functions with eigendecomposition and AdaBoost to ensure that if two documents with different modalities are relevant, then their corresponding hash codes are similar. [6] extends spectral hashing to cross-modal retrieval by formulating the learning of binary codes as a tractable eigenvalue problem. [11] presents an iterative scheme to learn a shared hamming space using a graph regularization formulation and a set of binary classifiers. [13] constructs heterogeneous hamming spaces and then connect them, while preserving the local structure using an anchor-based representation. Finally, [12] considers inter-modality and intra-modality consistency to generate a common hamming space, and integrates a linear regression model to learn hash functions so that the binary codes for new documents can be efficiently generated.

In [2], authors make the first attempt to compute hash codes using joint/collective matrix factorization with a latent factor model. Each matrix corresponds to the documents' representations for each modality, and then by jointly factorizing the matrices unified hash codes are generated. By revealing the associations between the different modalities and computing the similarities in each modality, the joint matrix factorization hashing method of [2] achieves high cross-modal retrieval accuracy. Nonetheless, the baseline joint matrix factorization that is used in [2] does not preserve the similarities that documents have in their neighborhoods/clusters in the same modality, nor considers the associations that the neighborhoods have in the different modalities.

To capture the inter-modality and intra-modality similarities at a neighborhood-based level, in this study we introduce a cluster-based joint matrix factorization method for cross-modal hashing. Our method consists of three steps, firstly we propose an efficient way to generate cross-modal

SIGIR '16, July 17-21, 2016, Pisa, Italy

DOI: http://dx.doi.org/10.1145/2911451.2914710

cluster representations for the documents. In the second step, we incorporate the generated cross-modal cluster representations into a joint factorization technique to compute the inter-modality and intra-modality similarities of the documents in the different modalities. This is achieved by formulating a joint matrix factorization process with the constraint that pushes the documents' representations of the different modalities and the cross-modal cluster representations into a common consensus matrix. Finally, we calculate the unified hash codes based on the maximum entropy principle [8], as well as the projection matrices to generate hash codes for external documents that do not belong to the database. Our experiments on two benchmark data sets demonstrate the superiority of the proposed hashing method over competitive hashing methods for different cross-modal retrieval tasks.

2. PROBLEM FORMULATION

In the remainder of the paper, we use the following notation, numbers are denoted by lower case letters e.g., a; matrices by plain upper case letters e.g., A; sets by calligraphic upper case letters e.g., $\mathcal{A}$; and vectors by lower case bold letters e.g., $\mathbf{a}$.

Let n be the number of documents and m the number of modalities. Given $j = 1 \ldots m$ and $i = 1 \ldots n$, each i-th document is represented in the j-th modality by a d_j-dimensional feature vector:

$$\mathbf{x}_i^{(j)} = [x_1^{(j)}, x_2^{(j)}, \ldots, x_{d_j}^{(j)}] \in \Re^{1 \times d_j}$$

with $d_j \neq d_{j'}$ for two different modalities j and j'. In the j-th modality, the n feature vectors are stored in a matrix $X^{(j)} \in \Re^{d_j \times n}$, where the i-th column is the feature vector $\mathbf{x}_i^{(j)}$. In our method, we assume that the inter-modality and intra-modality similarities are calculated in a unified hash code with length k for each document i:

$$\mathbf{b}_i = [y_1, y_2, \ldots, y_k] \in \{0,1\}^{1 \times k}$$

The problems that our cross-modal hashing method faces are formally defined as follows:

DEFINITION 1. *(Internal Documents' Hash Codes)* *"To compute a consensus binary matrix $B \in \{0,1\}^{k \times n}$, where the i-th column corresponds to the unified hash code $\mathbf{b}_i$ of an internal document i."*

DEFINITION 2. *(External Documents' Hash Codes)* *"To calculate m projection matrices $P^{(j)} \in \Re^{k \times d_j}$, with $j = 1, \ldots, m$, so as for any external document i that does not belong to B, given its representation $\mathbf{x}_i^{(j)}$ in modality j to generate the respective hash code $\mathbf{b}_i$."*

In the following Section, we detail each step of our method.

3. PROPOSED APPROACH

3.1 Cross-Modal Cluster Representations

$\forall\ j=1, \ldots, m$ we cluster the n feature vectors $\mathbf{x}^{(j)}$ with power iteration [7]. Thus, we have m different clusterings:

$$\begin{cases} \mathcal{C}_1^{(1)}, \mathcal{C}_2^{(1)}, \ldots, \mathcal{C}_{q1}^{(1)} \\ \mathcal{C}_1^{(2)}, \mathcal{C}_2^{(2)}, \ldots, \mathcal{C}_{q2}^{(2)} \\ \vdots \\ \mathcal{C}_1^{(m)}, \mathcal{C}_2^{(m)}, \ldots, \mathcal{C}_{qm}^{(m)} \end{cases} \tag{1}$$

where q_j is the number of clusters in the j-th modality, with $q_j \neq q_{j'}$ for two modalities j, j'. Also, $\mathcal{C}_w^{(j)}$ denotes the w-th cluster of the j-th modality, with $w \in 1, \ldots q_j^{(j)}$. Let $Z \in \Re^{q \times n}$ be the cross-modal cluster matrix, with q=$q_1 + q_2 +, \ldots, q_m$. $\forall\ c$=$1, \ldots, q$ we set $Z(c,i)$=1, if a document i belongs to cluster c, and 0 otherwise. The i-th column of Z is a representation (feature vector) of document i based on all the generated clusters in the m modalities. Hence, if two documents, e.g. i and p, belong to the same clusters in most of the m modalities, then the respective i-th and p-th columns (representations) of the cross-modal cluster matrix Z will be similar.

3.2 Joint Matrix Factorization

3.2.1 *Intra-modality and Cluster-based Similarities in Individual Matrix Factorization*

To capture the intra-modality similarities of the n documents, $\forall\ j$=$1, \ldots, m$ we consider the following matrix factorization of $X(j)$:

$$X^{(j)} \approx U^{(j)} V^{(j)} \tag{2}$$

with $U^{(j)} \in \Re^{d_j \times k}$, $V^{(j)} \in \Re^{k \times n}$ and k being the number of latent factors in matrix factorization, equal to the length of the hash codes $\mathbf{b_i}$. In addition, we consider the matrix factorization of the cross-modal cluster matrix Z as follows: $Z \approx U_z V_z$, with $U_z \in \Re^{q \times k}$ and $V^{(j)} \in \Re^{k \times n}$, to capture the associations of the n documents at the cluster-based level. Given the m matrices $X^{(j)}$ and the cross-modal cluster matrix Z, in total we have $m + 1$ individual matrix factorizations:

$$\begin{cases} X^{(1)} \approx U^{(1)} V^{(1)} \\ X^{(2)} \approx U^{(2)} V^{(2)} \\ \vdots \\ X^{(m)} \approx U^{(m)} V^{(m)} \end{cases} \tag{3}$$
$$Z \approx U_z V_z$$

As presented in Section 3.1, the cluster assignments are non-negative ($Z \geq 0$), with the feature vectors also being non-negative in each matrix $X^{(j)} \geq 0$; consequently, each matrix factorization in Eq. (3) is subject to:

$$U^{(1)}, \ldots U^{(m)} \geq 0, \quad V^{(1)}, \ldots V^{(m)} \geq 0, \quad U_z, V_z \geq 0$$

3.2.2 *Inter-modality, Intra-modality and Cluster-based Similarities in Joint Matrix Factorization*

All matrices in Eq. (3) have to be jointly factorized to simultaneously compute the inter-modality and intra-modality similarities of the documents in the m modalities, and to capture the associations with the cross-modal cluster matrix. We formulate a joint matrix factorization process with the constraint that pushes the matrices $X^{(j)}$ of the m modalities and the cross-modal cluster matrix Z into a common consensus matrix $B^* \in \Re^{k \times n}$, with B^* corresponding to a shared k-dimensional latent space of the n internal documents. To consider the case of having the representation of an external document in modality j, we denote the projection of each modality j into the shared k-dimensional space as a projection matrix $P^{(j)} \in \Re^{k \times d_j}$ on condition that:

$$V^{(j)} = P^{(j)} X^{(j)}, \quad \text{with} \quad j = 1, \ldots, m \tag{4}$$

where $V^{(j)} \in \Re^{k \times n}$ and $X^{(j)} \in \Re^{d_j \times n}$. To calculate the m projection matrices $P^{(j)}$ and the consensus matrix B^*, we formulate the problem of joint matrix factorization as a minimization problem [3]. Based on Eqs. (3) and (4), we have to minimize the following loss function $\mathfrak{L}$ for the joint matrix factorization:

$$\mathfrak{L}(U^{(1)}, \ldots, U^{(m)}, P^{(1)}, \ldots, P^{(m)}, U_z, V_z, B^*) = \sum_{j=1}^{m} \left\{ ||X^{(j)} - U^{(j)} P^{(j)} X^{(j)}||_F^2 + \lambda_j ||P^{(j)} X^{(j)} - B^*||_F^2 \right\} + ||Z - U_z V_z||_F^2 + \lambda_z ||V_z - B^*||_F^2 \quad (5)$$

where $||\cdot||_F$ denotes the Frobenius norm. In the second line of Eq. (5), the term $||X^{(j)} - U^{(j)} P^{(j)} X^{(j)}||_F^2$ denotes the approximation error of each factorized matrix $X^{(j)}$, while the term $||P^{(j)} X^{(j)} - B^*||_F^2$ is the *disagreement measurement* between the product $P^{(j)} X^{(j)}$ and the consensus matrix B^*. Accordingly, in the third line of Eq. (5), the first term $||Z - U_z V_z||_F^2$ denotes the approximation error of the factorized cross-modal cluster matrix Z; and $||V_z - B^*||_F^2$ is the respective *disagreement measurement.* The product $P^{(j)} X^{(j)}$, matrix V_z and the consensus matrix B^* are comparable, as they have the same dimensionality $(k \times n)$. $\forall\, j = 1, \ldots, m$ each parameter λ_j tunes the weight of modality j over the joint factorization, and the respective disagreement term; accordingly, parameter λ_z for the cross-modal cluster matrix. For reasons of simplicity we set $\lambda_1 = \ldots = \lambda_m = \lambda_z = \lambda$. In our approach, we solve the minimization problem of $\mathfrak{L}$, using the "multiplicative rules" [3], an iterative update procedure, where in each iteration we fix B^* and minimize $\mathfrak{L}$ over the rest of matrices, and then we fix the rest of matrices and minimize $\mathfrak{L}$ over B^*; The outcome of the joint factorization when minimizing the loss function $\mathfrak{L}$ of Eq. (5) is computing matrices $U^{(1)}, \ldots, U^{(m)}, P^{(1)}, \ldots, P^{(m)}, U_z, V_z, B^*$.

3.3 Hash Codes

We generate the unified hash codes in $B \in \{0, 1\}^{k \times n}$ by binarizing the real values of the consensus matrix $B^* \in \Re^{k \times n}$, thus generating a binary vector $\mathbf{b}_i = [y_1, y_2, \ldots, y_k]$ for each internal document i. According to [8], efficient hash codes should also maximize the entropy; based on the maximum entropy principle, a binary bit that gives balanced partitioning of the whole data set should provide maximum information. Hence, given the code length k, then $\forall a = 1, \ldots, k$ we set a threshold $thres_a$ for binarizing the a-th bit, with $thres_a$ being the median[1] of the a-th row in B^*. If a bit $y_a > thres_a$, then we set $y_a = 1$ and 0 otherwise. In doing so, the binary code achieves the best balance. To generate the hash code of an external document i that does not belong to matrix B, we use the projection matrices, computed by the joint matrix factorization when minimizing the loss function in Eq (5). Given the feature vector $\mathbf{x}_i^{(j)} \in \Re^{1 \times d_j}$ of the external document i in the j-th modality, we use the respective projection matrix $P^{(j)} \in \Re^{k \times d_j}$ to calculate the following real-value vector:

$$\mathbf{b}_i = \mathbf{x}_i^{(j)} {P^{(j)}}^T \in \Re^{1 \times k} \quad (6)$$

[1]We use the median as a threshold, because mean values are sensitive to extremely high or low values in B^*.

which is then binarized as in the internal case, creating the hash code $\mathbf{b}_i$ for the external document i.

4. EXPERIMENTAL EVALUATION

4.1 Data Sets

We use two real-world data sets *Wiki*[2] and *NUS-WIDE*[3]. The *Wiki* data set consists of 2,866 Wikipedia documents, with each document containing a text and one corresponding relevant image. In addition, images are represented by 128-dimensional SIFT feature vectors [10] and text by 10-dimensional topics vectors. All documents (image-text pairs) are labeled by 10 semantic categories. We split the data set as follows, 20% as query set; 5% as cross-validation set to tune the parameters of each method; while the remaining 75% of the data set is considered as the database, from which the hash codes are learnt and the results are retrieved. *NUS-WIDE* consists of 269,648 image-tag pairs from Flickr, where we keep the image-tag pairs that belong to one of the 10 largest concepts [11, 14]. Images are represented by 500-dimensional SIFT vectors and text as 1000-dimensional vectors, by performing PCA on the original tag occurrences [14]. The query set consists of 1% of the dataset; 1% is used as cross-validation set; while the remaining data set is the database to retrieve the results. The hash codes are learned from 5K image-text pairs from the database [2].

4.2 Evaluation Protocol

As both data sets are bi-modal with images and texts, we evaluate our hashing method on the following cross-modal retrieval tasks: (i) image-query $\rightarrow$ text results and (ii) text-query $\rightarrow$ image results. Following the evaluation protocol of relevant studies [2, 11, 14], we measure the performance of cross-modal hashing in terms of mAP. Given a query and the top result set $\mathcal{R}$, Average Precision (AP) is defined as:

$$AP = \frac{1}{l} \sum_{r \in \mathcal{R}} P(r)\delta(r) \quad (7)$$

where l is the number of true neighbors in the retrieved set $\mathcal{R}$, that is, the results which belong to the same category with the query; $P(r)$ denotes the precision of the top retrieved results in set $\mathcal{R}$ and $\delta(r)$=1 if the r-th result is a true neighbor and 0 otherwise. In the experiments we set $|\mathcal{R}|$=50, and mAP is computed by averaging the AP values over all the queries. We repeated our experiments five times and we report mean mAP values and standard deviations over the runs.

4.3 Results

In the proposed **C**luster-based **J**oint **M**atrix **F**actorization **H**ashing method (**C-JMFH**), we varied the parameter λ in $[10^{-4}\ 10^{-1}]$, concluding in 10^{-2} and 10^{-3} for *Wiki* and *NUS-WIDE*, respectively. To evaluate the impact of the cross-modal cluster matrix when computing the consensus matrix B^* in Eq. (5), and consequently the binary codes in B, we use as baseline a variant of our method, namely **JMFH**, which does not consider the cross-modal cluster matrix in the joint factorization process. We use **IMH**[4] [12] as baseline, and we compare the proposed C-JMFH method

[2]http://www.svcl.ucsd.edu/projects/crossmodal/
[3]http://lms.comp.nus.edu.sg/research/NUS-WIDE.htm
[4]http://staff.itee.uq.edu.au/shenht/publications.htm

with **CMFH**[5] [2], a hashing method that also follows a joint matrix factorization strategy when generating the binary codes. The parameter values in the baselines were determined by cross-validation, using the publicly available implementations and we report the best results.

Figures 1 and 2 show the results for the cross-modal retrieval tasks in *Wiki* and *NUS-WIDE*, respectively. The baseline IMI method has poor performance, compared with the rest of cross-modal hashing methods, by not following a joint matrix factorization strategy and thus not computing the inter-modality and intra-modality similarities as well as CMFH, JMFH and C-JMFH do. As also observed in relevant studies [2, 6], the retrieval accuracy does not necessarily improve when increasing the number of bits in many baseline methods such as IMI, as it does not follow a joint matrix factorization strategy. Meanwhile, we observe that CMFH and JMFH achieve comparable performance, as both hashing methods jointly factorize the representations in the different modalities, with the retrieval accuracy increasing when a larger number of bits is selected. This happens because in these methods the hamming space corresponds to the latent space of the joint matrix factorization process, consequently encoding more information for a large number of bits. The proposed C-JMFH method boosts the *mAP* retrieval accuracy by incorporating the cross-modal cluster representations of the documents when learning the hash codes. Compared to the second best method, the proposed C-JMFH method achieves a relative improvement of 3.1-12.9% in all the cross-modal retrieval tasks, with the exceptional case of 1.9% relative improvement in the case of a low selection of number of bits, that is, the case of 16 bits in *NUS-WIDE* for the text → image cross-modal retrieval task. To verify the superiority of the proposed C-JMFH method, we used the paired t-test and we found that the differences between the reported results for C-JMFH against the competitive hashing methods were statistically significant for $p<0.05$.

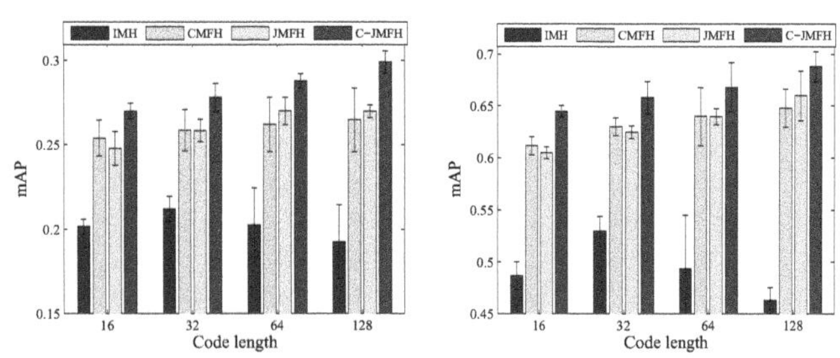

image → text   text → image

Figure 1: Performance evaluation on *Wiki* for the cross-modal retrieval tasks.

5. CONCLUSION

In this study, we presented a cross-modal hashing method using a cluster-based representation into a joint factorization process. In our experiments, we showed that the proposed method outperforms other state-of-the-art hashing methods in terms of cross-modal retrieval accuracy. Although we focused on the case of cross-modal retrieval, that is, given a query from one modality to retrieve results from another modality, an interesting future direction is to extend our method to multimodal retrieval, where given a query from one or more modalities to retrieve documents from all the different modalities [9].

[5]http://ise.thss.tsinghua.edu.cn/MIG/publications.jsp

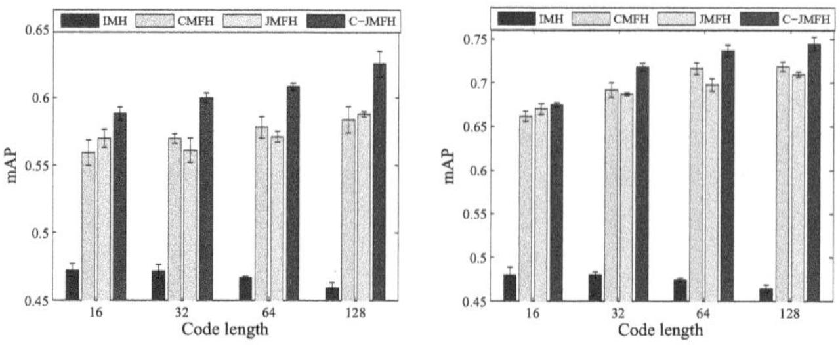

image → text   text → image

Figure 2: Performance evaluation on *NUS-WIDE*.

6. REFERENCES

[1] M. M. Bronstein, A. M. Bronstein, F. Michel, and N. Paragios. Data fusion through cross-modality metric learning using similarity-sensitive hashing. In *CVPR*, pages 3594–3601, 2010.

[2] G. Ding, Y. Guo, and J. Zhou. Collective matrix factorization hashing for multimodal data. In *CVPR*, pages 2083–2090, 2014.

[3] J. Gao, J. Han, J. Liu, and C. Wang. Multi-view clustering via joint nonnegative matrix factorization. In *SDM*, pages 252–260, 2013.

[4] A. Gionis, P. Indyk, and R. Motwani. Similarity search in high dimensions via hashing. In *VLDB*, pages 518–529, 1999.

[5] Y. Gong and S. Lazebnik. Iterative quantization: A procrustean approach to learning binary codes. In *CVPR*, pages 817–824, 2011.

[6] S. Kumar and R. Udupa. Learning hash functions for cross-view similarity search. In *IJCAI*, pages 1360–1365, 2011.

[7] F. Lin and W. W. Cohen. Power iteration clustering. In *ICML*, pages 655–662, 2010.

[8] R. Lin, D. A. Ross, and J. Yagnik. SPEC hashing: Similarity preserving algorithm for entropy-based coding. In *CVPR*, pages 848–854, 2010.

[9] X. Liu, Y. Mu, B. Lang, and S. Chang. Mixed image-keyword query adaptive hashing over multilabel images. *TOMCCAP*, 10(2):22, 2014.

[10] D. G. Lowe. Distinctive image features from scale-invariant keypoints. *IJCV*, 60(2):91–110, 2004.

[11] S. Moran and V. Lavrenko. Regularised cross-modal hashing. In *SIGIR*, pages 907–910, 2015.

[12] J. Song, Y. Yang, Y. Yang, Z. Huang, and H. T. Shen. Inter-media hashing for large-scale retrieval from heterogeneous data sources. In *SIGMOD*, pages 785–796, 2013.

[13] Y. Wang, X. Lin, L. Wu, W. Zhang, and Q. Zhang. Lbmch: Learning bridging mapping for cross-modal hashing. In *SIGIR*, pages 999–1002, 2015.

[14] Y. Zhen and D. Yeung. Co-regularized hashing for multimodal data. In *NIPS*, pages 1385–1393, 2012.

Collaborative Ranking with Social Relationships for Top-N Recommendations

Dimitrios Rafailidis
Department of Informatics
Aristotle University of Thessaloniki
Thessaloniki, Greece
draf@csd.auth.gr

Fabio Crestani
Faculty of Informatics
Università della Svizzera italiana (USI)
Lugano, Switzerland
fabio.crestani@usi.ch

ABSTRACT

Recommendation systems have gained a lot of attention because of their importance for handling the unprecedentedly large amount of available content on the Web, such as movies, music, books, etc. Although Collaborative Ranking (CR) models can produce accurate recommendation lists, in practice several real-world problems decrease their ranking performance, such as the sparsity and cold start problems. Here, to account for the fact that the selections of social friends can leverage the recommendation accuracy, we propose SCR, a Social CR model. Our model learns personalized ranking functions collaboratively, using the notion of Social Reverse Height, that is, considering how well the relevant items of users and their social friends have been ranked at the top of the list. The reason that we focus on the top of the list is that users mainly see the top-N recommendations, and not the whole ranked list. In our experiments with a benchmark data set from Epinions, we show that our SCR model performs better than state-of-the-art CR models that either consider social relationships or focus on the ranking performance at the top of the list.

CCS Concepts

•**Information systems → Collaborative and social computing systems and tools;**

Keywords

Recommendation systems; collaborative ranking; social relationships

1. INTRODUCTION

The collaborative filtering strategy has been widely followed in recommendation systems, where users with similar preferences tend to get similar recommendations [5]. User preferences are expressed explicitly in the form of ratings or implicitly in the form of number of views, clicks, purchases, etc. Relevant studies examine how to predict the rating of a user on an unseen item, also known as the rating prediction problem [8]. Instead of focusing on the accuracy of rating prediction, ranking-based models try to produce accurate ranked lists for the top-N recommendation problem [9]. In relevant studies [2, 13], it has been shown that ranking-based models achieve higher recommendation accuracy than rating prediction-based approaches in the top-N recommendation problem.

Collaborative Ranking (CR) models learn a personalized scoring/ranking function to rank the recommended items for each individual, while all functions are constructed collaboratively across all the users [9, 10]. In [2], authors introduce CR models that perform push at the top of the recommendation list, by considering that what matters in a recommendation system is the ranking performance at the top of the list, that is, the items the user will actually see. In doing so, the CR models that focus on the ranking performance at the top of the list achieve high ranking accuracy in the top-N recommendation problem.

Although CR models can generate accurate recommendation lists, in practice several real-world problems decrease the recommendation accuracy, such as the sparsity and the cold-start problems [5]. Several approaches have been proposed for handling them in the rating prediction problem, assuming that users tend to trust the recommendations of their social friends [1]. However, a little effort has been made to exploit social relationships in CR models, such as the studies in [6, 14]. Nonetheless, the CR models in [6, 14] do not focus on the ranking performance at the top of the list, when learning the ranking functions.

Therefore, a pressing challenge resides on generating accurate recommendations able to exploit the social relationships that simultaneously focus on the top of the list. In this paper, we propose a Social CR model, namely SCR. Our CR model learns the personalized ranking function of each individual in a collaborative manner using the notion of Social Reverse Height. When learning the ranking functions, SCR attempts to push up users' relevant items above the irrelevant ones at the top of the list, by considering the ranking positions that the relevant items of their friends have. We formulate the objective function of the proposed SCR model as a minimization problem, and we provide an efficient optimization algorithm based on alternating minimization [4] and gradient descent. Our experiments on a data set from Epinions[1] demonstrate the superiority of our SCR model over state-of-the-art CR models.

[1] http://www.epinions.com/

SIGIR '16, July 17-21, 2016, Pisa, Italy

DOI: http://dx.doi.org/10.1145/2911451.2914711

2. RELATED WORK

Learning to rank methods have been widely studied in Information Retrieval and in recommendation systems. The goal is to define a ranking function on each item, and then learn toward some loss functions. Liu et al. [7] categorize learning to rank methods into point-wise, list-wise and pair-wise. In short, point-wise approaches predict ranking scores for individual items. List-wise approaches consider an individual training example as an entire list of items and use loss functions to express the distance between the reference list and the output list from the ranking model. Representative list-wise approaches in recommendation systems are `CofiRank` [12] and `CLiMF` [10], which use loss functions based on Normalized Discounted Cumulative Gain and Reciprocal Rank, respectively. Pair-wise approaches make a prediction for every pair of items concerning their relative ordering in the final list. A pair-wise recommendation approach is the Bayesian Personalized Ranking framework (`BPR`) [9], a CR model that learns the personalized ranking functions collaboratively. To account for the fact that users focus on recommendations at the top of the list, in [2] authors introduce optimization algorithms for three CR models `P-Push`, `Inf-Push` and `RH-Push`, which follow different strategies when learning the personalized ranking functions. `P-Push` tries to push irrelevant items in the top-N list below those that have been selected as relevant; `Inf-Push` attempts to move the most irrelevant item in the list below all the relevant ones; while `RH-Push` tries to move the relevant items above the irrelevant ones. However, all the aforementioned models do not exploit the social relationships in the learning process.

Although several approaches incorporate social relationships in the rating prediction problem, e.g. [8], a few attempts have been made in the top-N recommendation problem. Rendle et al. [6] present the `MR-BPR` model, where they combine Multi-Relational matrix factorization with the `BPR` framework [9] to model both users' feedback on items and on social relationships. Zhao et al. [14] propose `SBRP`, a Social Bayesian Personalized Ranking model that incorporates social relationships into a pair-wise ranking model, assuming that users tend to assign higher ranks to items that their friends prefer. However, `MR-BPR` and `SBRP` do not focus on the ranking performance at the top of the list.

3. PROBLEM FORMULATION

Let $\mathcal{U}$ and $\mathcal{I}$ be the sets of users and items, respectively. We assume that users express their preferences over the items by marking them as relevant or irrelevant (either via explicit or implicit feedback), stored in a $(|\mathcal{U}| \times |\mathcal{I}|)$ matrix R, with $[R]_{ij}$=1 if user i has selected item j as relevant, -1 as irrelevant, and 0 if user i has not expressed her preference over item j. For each user i the sets of relevant and irrelevant items are denoted as $\mathcal{I}_i^+$ and $\mathcal{I}_i^-$, with $x_i^+ \in \mathcal{I}_i^+$, $x_i^- \in \mathcal{I}_i^-$ and $n_i = |\mathcal{I}_i^+ \cup \mathcal{I}_i^-|$ being the total number of marked items by user i. For each user $i \in \mathcal{U}$, we define the Reverse Height of a relevant item x_i^+ as follows [2]:

DEFINITION 1. *The **Reverse Height** $RH_i(x_i^+)$ of a relevant item x_i^+ in the recommendation list of user i is the number of irrelevant items ranked above x_i^+.*

In our setting, we assume that each user i has a set $\mathcal{F}_i$ of friends with trusted social relationships. Given $x_i^+ \in \mathcal{I}_i^+$, $x_i^- \in \mathcal{I}_i^-$ and $x_w^+ \in \mathcal{I}_w^+$, with $w \in \mathcal{F}_i$, we define the Social Reverse Height of a relevant item x_i^+ as follows:

DEFINITION 2. *The **Social Reverse Height** $SRH_i(x_i^+)$ of a relevant item x_i^+ in the recommendation list of user i is the sum of (1) the number of irrelevant items x_i^- ranked above x_i^+; and (2) the number of the irrelevant items x_i^- ranked above the relevant items x_w^+ of all her $|\mathcal{F}_i|$ friends.*

DEFINITION 3. *The **goal of the proposed*** `SCR` ***model** is to learn the personalized ranking functions collaboratively by trying to minimize $SRH_i(x_i^+)$, that is, pushing up the relevant items x_i^+ of user i above the irrelevant items x_i^-, by considering the ranking positions of the relevant items x_w^+ of her $|\mathcal{F}_i|$ friends.*

4. SOCIAL COLLABORATIVE RANKING

4.1 Social Reverse Height

A trusted friend $w \in \mathcal{F}_i$ might point to an interesting item that does not match the preferences of user i [1]. Hence, to measure the social influence between user i and her friend w we define the *social regularization term* $s_{iw} = |\mathcal{I}_i^+ \cap \mathcal{I}_w^+|$, which is the intersection of the sets of relevant items of user i and her friend w. For each user i we normalize s_{iw} in $[0,1]$, by dividing each s_{iw} value with the maximum value of all the $|\mathcal{F}_i|$ friends.

Given a personalized ranking function $r_i(x)$, with $i \in \mathcal{U}$ and $x \in \mathcal{I}$, according to Definition 2 we have:

$$SRH_i(x_i^+) = \sum_{x_i^- \in \mathcal{I}_i^-} \Big\{ \mathbb{1}[r_i(x_i^+) \leq r_i(x_i^-)] + \frac{1}{|\mathcal{F}_i|} \sum_{w \in \mathcal{F}_i} \frac{1}{|\mathcal{I}_w^+|} \sum_{x_w \in \mathcal{I}_w^+} s_{iw} \mathbb{1}[r_i(x_w^+) \leq r_i(x_i^-)] \Big\} \quad (1)$$

where $\mathbb{1}$ is the indicator function and s_{iw} the social regularization term. Note that $r_i(x_w^+)$ expresses the ranking of the relevant item x_w^+ of friend w using the ranking function of user i. The above optimization problem in Eq. (1) is intractable due to the non-convex indicator function $\mathbb{1}$. Thus, we take a surrogate $g_i(\cdot)$ as follows:

$$g_i(x_i^+, x_i^-) = r_i(x_i^+) - r_i(x_i^-) + \frac{1}{|\mathcal{F}_i|} \sum_{w \in \mathcal{F}_i} \frac{1}{|\mathcal{I}_w^+|} \sum_{x_w \in \mathcal{I}_w^+} s_{iw} \big(r_i(x_w^+) - r_i(x_i^-) \big) \quad (2)$$

4.2 Objective Function

In the proposed `SCR` model we follow a collaborative strategy, instead of learning a ranking function $r_i(\cdot)$ for each individual i. Given the low-rank d decomposition $\hat{R} \approx U^T V$ of the initial matrix R, with U and V being $(d \times |\mathcal{U}|)$ and $(d \times |\mathcal{I}|)$ matrices, we consider $\mathbf{u}_i$ and $\mathbf{v}_j$ as the $(d \times 1)$ latent vectors of user i and item j respectively, that is, the i-th and j-th columns of U and V, respectively. For readability, we denote the relevant item of user i as $a = x_i^+$, the irrelevant item of user i as $b = x_i^-$, and the relevant item of a friend $w \in \mathcal{F}_i$ as $c = x_w^+$. Using the representation of the latent factors $\mathbf{u}_i$ and $\mathbf{v}_j$, Eq. (2) can be rewritten as:

$$g_i(a,b) = \mathbf{u}_i^T(\mathbf{v}_a - \mathbf{v}_b) + \frac{1}{|\mathcal{F}_i|} \sum_{w \in \mathcal{F}_i} \frac{1}{|\mathcal{I}_w^+|} \sum_{c \in \mathcal{I}_w^+} s_{iw} (\mathbf{u}_w^T(\mathbf{v}_c - \mathbf{v}_b)) \quad (3)$$

where $a \in \mathcal{I}_i^+$, $b \in \mathcal{I}_i^-$ and $c \in \mathcal{I}_w^+$. As the logistic loss function is a convex upper bound to the indicator function $\mathbb{1}$, based on Eq. (3) we can reformulate Eq. (1) as:

$$SRH_i(a) = \sum_{b \in \mathcal{I}_i^-} \left(\log\left(1 + \exp\left(-g_i(a,b)\right)\right) \right) \quad (4)$$

According to Definition 3, for all the relevant items $a \in \mathcal{I}_i^+$ we have to minimize the $SRH_i(a)$ value of Eq. (4). Hence, $\forall$ $i \in \mathcal{U}$ the goal is to minimize the following objective function (log-log loss function [2]) with respect to matrices U and V:

$$\mathfrak{L}(U,V) = \sum_{i=1}^{|\mathcal{U}|} \left\{ \frac{1}{n_i} \sum_{a \in \mathcal{I}_i^+} \log(1 + SRH_i(a)) \right\} + \frac{\lambda}{2} \left(||U||^2 + ||V||^2 \right) \quad (5)$$

where the last term, called regularization term, is used to avoid model overfitting, and λ is the regularization parameter.

4.3 Model Learning

The goal is to learn (compute) matrices U and V to minimize the loss function $\mathfrak{L}(U,V)$ in Eq. (5). We follow the alternating minimization strategy [4] using the gradient descent optimization algorithm, where we update U keeping V fixed, and then, update V keeping the updated U fixed. Based on the (sub)gradients of objective function $\mathfrak{L}(U,V)$ with respect to $\mathbf{u}_i$ and $\mathbf{v}_j$, the update rules for each iteration $t+1$ are:

$$\mathbf{u}_i^{t+1} \leftarrow \mathbf{u}_i^t - \eta \nabla_{\mathbf{u}_i} \mathfrak{L}(U^t, V^t), \quad i = 1 \dots |\mathcal{U}| \quad (6)$$

$$\mathbf{v}_j^{t+1} \leftarrow \mathbf{v}_j^t - \eta \nabla_{\mathbf{v}_j} \mathfrak{L}(U^{t+1}, V^t), \quad j = 1 \dots |\mathcal{I}| \quad (7)$$

where η controls the learning rate.

4.3.1 *Computing the Gradient* $\nabla_{\mathbf{u}_i} \mathfrak{L}(U,V)$

We apply the chain rule to Eq. (5) to take the gradient of $\mathfrak{L}$ with respect to $\mathbf{u}_i$, that is, the composition of gradients $\nabla_{\mathbf{u}_i} g_i(a,b)$ and $\nabla_{g_i(a,b)} SRH_i(a)$ with respect to $\mathbf{u}_i$ in Eq. (3) and $g_i(a,b)$ in Eq. (4), respectively. Note that the gradient of the regularization term in Eq. (5) with respect to $\mathbf{u}_i$ equals $\lambda \mathbf{u}_i$. Thus, provided that $i \neq w$, we have:

$$\nabla_{\mathbf{u}_i} g_i(a,b) = \mathbf{v}_a - \mathbf{v}_b \quad (8)$$

$$\nabla_{g_i(a,b)} SRH_i(a) = \frac{-1}{1 + \exp(g_i(a,b))} \quad (9)$$

the gradient of $\mathfrak{L}$ with respect to $\mathbf{u}_i$ in Eq. (5) equals:

$$\nabla_{\mathbf{u}_i} \mathfrak{L}(U,V) = \frac{1}{n_i} \sum_{a \in \mathcal{I}_i^+} \left\{ \frac{1}{1 + SRH_i(a)} \sum_{b \in \mathcal{I}_i^-} \frac{1}{1 + \exp(g_i(a,b))} (\mathbf{v}_b - \mathbf{v}_a) \right\} + \lambda \mathbf{u}_i \quad (10)$$

4.3.2 *Computing the Gradient* $\nabla_{\mathbf{v}_j} \mathfrak{L}(U,V)$

When calculating the gradient of $g_i(a,b)$ with respect to $\mathbf{v}_j$ in Eq. (3), there are the following two cases:

$$\nabla_{\mathbf{v}_j} g_i(a,b) = \begin{cases} \mathbf{u}_i, & \text{if } j{=}a. \\ -\left[\mathbf{u}_i + \frac{1}{|\mathcal{F}_i|} \sum_{w \in \mathcal{F}_i} \frac{1}{|\mathcal{I}_w^+|} \sum_{c \in \mathcal{I}_w^+} s_{iw} \mathbf{u}_w \right], & \text{if } j{=}b. \end{cases} \quad (11)$$

Similarly, we apply the chain rule to Eq. (5), to compute the gradient of $\mathfrak{L}$ with respect to $\mathbf{v}_j$, that is, the composition of the gradient $\nabla_{\mathbf{v}_j} g_i(a,b)$ based on the two cases in Eq. (11), and the gradient $\nabla_{g_i(a,b)} SRH_i(a)$, as presented in Eq. (9). The gradient of the regularization term in Eq. (5) with respect to $\mathbf{v}_j$ equals $\lambda \mathbf{v}_j$. Let $\mathcal{U}_j^+$ and $\mathcal{U}_j^-$ be the sets of users who selected item j as relevant and irrelevant, respectively. We can divide the sum over all users into sums over $\mathcal{U}_j^-$ and $\mathcal{U}_j^+$ [2], in order to calculate the gradient of $\mathfrak{L}$ with respect to $\mathbf{v}_j$ as follows:

$$\begin{aligned} \nabla_{\mathbf{v}_j} \mathfrak{L}(U,V) = & \sum_{i \in \mathcal{U}_j^-} \frac{1}{n_i} \sum_{j \in \mathcal{I}_i^-} \left\{ \frac{1}{1 + SRH_i(a)} \right. \\ & \left. \sum_{a \in \mathcal{I}_i^+} \frac{1}{1 + \exp(g_i(a,b))} \left[\mathbf{u}_i + \frac{1}{|\mathcal{F}_i|} \sum_{w \in \mathcal{F}_i} \frac{1}{|\mathcal{I}_w^+|} \sum_{c \in \mathcal{I}_w^+} s_{iw} \mathbf{u}_w \right] \right\} \\ & - \sum_{i \in \mathcal{U}_j^+} \frac{1}{n_i} \sum_{j \in \mathcal{I}_i^-} \left\{ \frac{1}{1 + SRH_i(a)} \sum_{a \in \mathcal{I}_i^+} \frac{1}{1 + \exp(g_i(a,b))} \mathbf{u}_i \right\} + \lambda \mathbf{v}_j \end{aligned} \quad (12)$$

Having computed U and V based on Eqs. (6) and (7) with the respective gradients in Eqs. (10) and (12), we calculate the low-rank d approximation $\hat{R} \approx U^T V$ of the initial $(|\mathcal{U}| \times |\mathcal{I}|)$ matrix R, and we generate a recommendation list by sorting the items in the respective i-th row of $\hat{R}$ in descending order, for each user i.

5. EXPERIMENTAL EVALUATION

5.1 Data Set & Evaluation Protocol

In our experiments we used a publicly available data set[2] from Epinions, which consists of 71,002 users and 104,356 items. The total number of ratings is 571,235 at a 5-star scale, where we considered 4-5 star ratings as relevant to a user and 1-3 as irrelevant. The total number of trusted social relationships is 508,960. The data set is divided into two sub-sets: the training set and the test set. Following the evaluation protocol of similar studies [13, 14], for users with less than five ratings, one randomly selected rating is inserted into the test set. For users with five ratings or more, 10% of the randomly selected ratings are moved to the test set. The training set is further split into two subsets: the cross-validation training set and the cross-validation test set, which are used to determine the tuning parameters of each examined ranking model. We repeated our experiment ten times, and we report mean values and standard deviations on the (actual) test set over the runs.

We evaluated the performance of the examined ranking models in terms of Recall ($R@N$), which is defined as the ratio of the relevant items in the top-N ranked list over all the relevant items for each user. In addition, we used the Normalized Discounted Cumulative Gain ($NDCG@N$) metric, which considers the ranking of the relevant items in the top-N list. For each user the Discounted Cumulative Gain is defined as:

$$DCG@N = \sum_{j=1}^{N} \frac{2^{rel_j} - 1}{\log_2 j + 1} \quad (13)$$

where rel_j represents the relevance score of the item j, binary relevance in our case, that is, relevant or irrelevant to the user. $NDCG@N$ is the ratio of $DCG@N$ over the ideal $iDCG@N$ value for each user, that is, the $DCG@N$ value given the ratings in the test set. In our experiments we averaged $R@N$ and $NDCG@N$ over all users.

[2] http://alchemy.cs.washington.edu/data/epinions/

5.2 Results

To evaluate the parameter sensitivity in SCR, we varied the learning rate η in the range of $[10^{-5}\ 10^{-2}]$ and we concluded in $\eta=10^{-4}$. This means that a more conservative learning strategy is required, as higher values of η decreased the performance of SCR, by falling in local optima when minimizing the loss function in Eq. (5). In Figure 1, we vary the number of latent factors d and the regularization parameter λ, while keeping $\eta=10^{-4}$ fixed. For presentation purposes, we plot $R@$ as a percentage (%). Figures 1(a)-(b) show that there is a slight increase on $R@$ after $d \geq 40$, while there is a drop on $R@$ when λ is in the range of 0.01-1, and we select d=40 and λ=0.001.

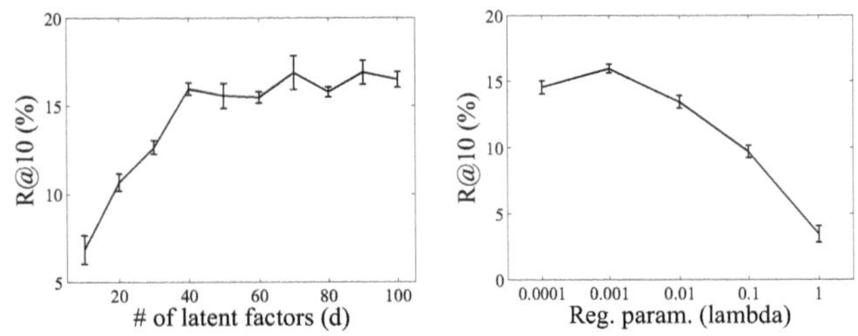

Figure 1: Effect of (a) # of latent factors d and (b) regularization parameter λ on $R@10$ (%).

We use CofiRank[3] [12] as baseline, and we compare the proposed SCR method with P-Push, Inf-Push and RH-Push using the optimization algorithms[4] of [2]. In addition, we compare SCR with MR-BPR[5] [6], a state-of-the-art method for ranking with social relationships in the recommendation problem. We also evaluate the performance of SCR against SBRP [14], a ranking model that also considers social relationships in the learning process, assuming that users tend to assign higher ranks to items that their friends prefer. In all ranking models, we followed the same cross-validation strategy to select the optimal parameters as in SCR. In Table 1 we compare the examined ranking models, where we observe that P-Push, Inf-Push and RH-Push outperform CofiRank, as these models focus on the ranking performance at the top of the list; while MR-BPR, SBPR and SCR achieve better performance than the models that do not exploit social relationships. The proposed SCR model beats the competitors by exploiting social relationships and focusing on the top of the ranking list. Using the paired t-test, we found that the differences between the reported results for SCR against the competitive approaches were statistically significant for $p<0.05$.

6. CONCLUSION AND FUTURE WORK

In this study, we presented SCR, a CR model that focuses on the ranking accuracy at the top of the list by also considering users' trusted social relationships. Our learning strategy uses the notion of Social Reverse Height to consider the ranking positions of friends' relevant items, while our SCR method outperforms other state-of-the-art ranking models.

An interesting future direction is to exploit both the trust and distrust social relationships in the proposed SCR model, accounting for the fact that users with distrust relationships usually do not have similar preferences [3]. In addition, we plan to evaluate the performance of SCR in terms of diversity, that is, how well we can generate diversified recommendations in SCR to capture the interest range of the target user [11].

[3]https://github.com/markusweimer/cofirank
[4]http://www-users.cs.umn.edu/~christa/
[5]http://www.ismll.uni-hildesheim.de/software

Table 1: Methods comparison in terms of $NDCG@$ and $R@$, with bold values denoting the best scores ($^*p<0.05$ in paired t-test). MR-BPR, SBPR and SCR exploit social relationships.

	$NDCG@10$	$R@10$	$R@100$
CofiRank	.1423 ± .0043	.0698 ± .0075	.2398 ± .0047
P-Push	.1671 ± .0058	.1134 ± .0044	.2977 ± .0054
Inf-Push	.1563 ± .0091	.1073 ± .0053	.2789 ± .0035
RH-Push	.1574 ± .0079	.1266 ± .0062	.2980 ± .0028
MR-BPR	.1798 ± .0084	.1401 ± .0089	.3081 ± .0051
SBPR	.1886 ± .0076	.1490 ± .0055	.3296 ± .0042
SCR	**.2065 ± .0064***	**.1596 ± .0043***	**.3654 ± .0035***

7. REFERENCES

[1] A. J. Chaney, D. M. Blei, and T. Eliassi-Rad. A probabilistic model for using social networks in personalized item recommendation. In *RecSys*, pages 43–50, 2015.
[2] K. Christakopoulou and A. Banerjee. Collaborative ranking with a push at the top. In *WWW*, pages 205–215, 2015.
[3] R. Forsati, M. Mahdavi, M. Shamsfard, and M. Sarwat. Matrix factorization with explicit trust and distrust side information for improved social recommendation. *TOIS*, 32(4):17:1–17:38, 2014.
[4] P. Jain, P. Netrapalli, and S. Sanghavi. Low-rank matrix completion using alternating minimization. In *STOC*, pages 665–674, 2013.
[5] Y. Koren, R. M. Bell, and C. Volinsky. Matrix factorization techniques for recommender systems. *IEEE Computer*, 42(8):30–37, 2009.
[6] A. Krohn-Grimberghe, L. Drumond, C. Freudenthaler, and L. Schmidt-Thieme. Multi-relational matrix factorization using bayesian personalized ranking for social network data. In *WSDM*, pages 173–182, 2012.
[7] T.-Y. Liu. Learning to rank for information retrieval. *Found. Trends Inf. Retr.*, 3(3):225–331.
[8] H. Ma, H. Yang, M. R. Lyu, and I. King. Sorec: social recommendation using probabilistic matrix factorization. In *CIKM*, pages 931–940, 2008.
[9] S. Rendle, C. Freudenthaler, Z. Gantner, and L. Schmidt-Thieme. Bpr: Bayesian personalized ranking from implicit feedback. In *UAI*, pages 452–461, 2009.
[10] Y. Shi, A. Karatzoglou, L. Baltrunas, M. Larson, N. Oliver, and A. Hanjalic. Climf: Learning to maximize reciprocal rank with collaborative less-is-more filtering. In *RecSys*, pages 139–146, 2012.
[11] Y. Shi, X. Zhao, J. Wang, M. Larson, and A. Hanjalic. Adaptive diversification of recommendation results via latent factor portfolio. In *SIGIR*, pages 175–184, 2012.
[12] M. Weimer, A. Karatzoglou, Q. V. Le, and A. J. Smola. COFI RANK - maximum margin matrix factorization for collaborative ranking. In *NIPS*, pages 1593–1600, 2007.
[13] X. Yang, H. Steck, Y. Guo, and Y. Liu. On top-k recommendation using social networks. In *RecSys*, pages 67–74, 2012.
[14] T. Zhao, J. McAuley, and I. King. Leveraging social connections to improve personalized ranking for collaborative filtering. In *CIKM*, pages 261–270, 2014.

Community-based Cyberreading for Information Understanding

Zhuoren Jiang
Institute of Computer Science and Technology
Peking University
Beijing, China, 100871
jiangzr@pku.edu.cn

Xiaozhong Liu*
School of Informatics and Computing
Indiana University Bloomington
Bloomington, IN, USA, 47405
liu237@indiana.edu

Liangcai Gao*
Institute of Computer Science and Technology
Peking University
Beijing, China, 100871
glc@pku.edu.cn

Zhi Tang
Institute of Computer Science and Technology
Peking University
Beijing, China, 100871
tangzhi@pku.edu.cn

ABSTRACT

Although the content in scientific publications is increasingly challenging, it is necessary to investigate another important problem, that of scientific information understanding. For this proposed problem, we investigate novel methods to assist scholars (readers) to better understand scientific publications by enabling physical and virtual collaboration. For physical collaboration, an algorithm will group readers together based on their profiles and reading behavior, and will enable the cyberreading collaboration within a online reading group. For virtual collaboration, instead of pushing readers to communicate with others, we cluster readers based on their estimated information needs. For each cluster, a learning to rank model will be generated to recommend readers' communitized resources (i.e., videos, slides, and wikis) to help them understand the target publication.

Keywords

Information Understanding, Cyberreading, Education, User Study

1. INTRODUCTION AND MOTIVATION

STEM (Science, Technology, Engineering, and Mathematics) publications, for various reasons, generally do not place a premium on writing for readability, and young scholars struggle to understand the scholarly literature available to them. Unfortunately, few efforts have been made to help graduate students and other junior scholars understand and consume the essence of those scientific readings. In other words, while scholarly search and recommendation algorithms are well-documented, few studies address a critical problem – scientific information understanding. Compared to search and recommendation, information understanding can be more challenging. It can be more difficult to characterize user (implicit and explicit) information needs when a user is reading a paper, and it can be even more challenging to address the personalization problem. For example, one can assume that when a user is reading a paper, he/she may require different kinds of assistance to understand the specific sentences/paragraphs/sections/formulas in the paper. Meanwhile, given the same piece of text/formula in a paper, other users may need different types of help, such as personalized information understanding.

In this study, we propose two different kinds of information understanding scenarios: **information understanding via reader-reader collaboration** and **information understanding via Open Education Resources (OER) recommendation**. The former scenario is based on prior studies in collaborative scaffolding (a.k.a. peer support) studies in education domain [9, 10]. Despite some criticism, evidence shows that the benefits of this type of peer support exceed its limitations, and that readers can learn from each other for information understanding (physical collaboration). The latter type is based on the pilot-evidence that accessing multi-modal OER about a scholarly publication, including presentation videos, slides, source code or Wikipedia pages, in a collaborative framework will enhance a student's ability to understand the paper itself [6]. However, different kinds of readers, given the same publication content, may prefer different kinds of OERs for information understanding. A reader community (sharing the similar information needs) may prefer similar OERs, and when we don't have reader statistics, (virtual) 'community' can be a latent variable.

In this paper, we propose a novel collaborative cyberreading environment, OER-based Collaborative PDF Reader (OCPR), which enables reader collaboration and community-based OER recommendation for information understanding.

The contribution of this paper is threefold. First, we propose a novel method to group readers into a number of physical communities, and readers from the same groups are more likely to collaborate while reading. Second, when readers don't want to collaborate, we propose the new algorithm to group similar users into virtual communities for information need estimation and OER recommendation. Last but not least, an experiment (with 60 participants) is employed to validate the usefulness of the proposed methods. Experiment results show our methods can significantly improve OER recommendation performance for information understanding.

2. RELATED WORK

From an educational viewpoint, scaffolding has been widely used in educational research [10]. In particular, a collaborative scaffolding study [3] finds that students achieved better reading comprehension and metacognitive skills when reading within the context of small team collaboration, e.g., comment on part of a document, share ideas, and provide feedback among a group of users [11].

*Xiaozhong Liu and Liangcai Gao are the corresponding authors

SIGIR'16, July 17-21, 2016, Pisa, Italy.

DOI: http://dx.doi.org/10.1145/2911451.2914744.

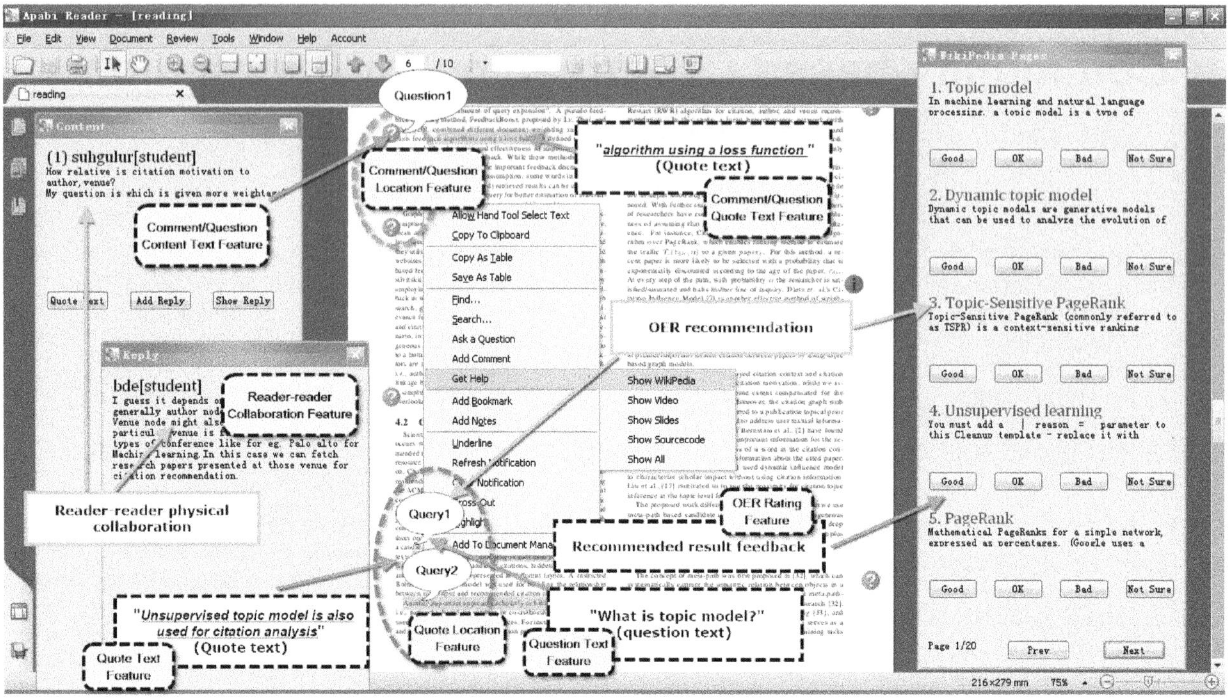

Figure 1: OER-based Collaborative PDF Reader System.

However, prior studies also found collaborative scaffolding approaches can be quite limited [9], and readers may not have enough incentives to collaborate while reading. Not until recently did researchers begin to focus on the usefulness of OER. For instance, Dennis, et al. [1] found that video presentations had significantly positive impacts on students' learning based on quiz scores. More recently, Liu [4, 5] found OERs, such as YouTube video, technology slides, and Wikipedia pages, can help students better understand scientific readings. Meanwhile, information retrieval and text mining methods, i.e., language model and BM25, had been proven to be useful for building OER index for a large number of publications automatically [4]. However, this approach cannot accurately address students' emerging information need while reading a paper, especially for personalized or communitized reader information need estimation.

3. RESEARCH METHODS

3.1 Reader Profile and Reading Behavior

To generate physical and virtual communities and assist readers in understanding publications, we need to generate a number of features for reader clustering. There are two kinds of features: reader profile features (RPF) and reading behavior features (RBF). Note that RPF can be important but can be missing in some cases (e.g., online journal or proceeding paper readers). Compared to RPF, RBF can be more reliable.

To capture RBF and implement information understanding, we designed OCPR, which is depicted in Figure 1. OCPR enables two types of scaffoldings:

Collaborative Scaffolding: enabling readers to asynchronously annotate PDF publications or provide feedback and comments to existing information needs from other readers. By using the OCPR, any reader can view other readers' information needs, such as highlighted (quoted) parts of PDFs or specific questions/comments (as shown in Figure 1, the question or exclamation marks on the side of PDF). These readers also can provide their own replies and feedbacks to the existing or proposed information needs (reader collaboration).

OER-based Scaffolding: capturing evidence of students' emerging implicit or explicit information needs when reading a scientific paper and recommending high quality OERs to address their information needs. As Figure 1 shows, by using OCPR, readers can ask a specific question given a piece of text which serves as evidence of an explicit information need or highlight (quote) part of a text in the paper as evidence of an implicit information need. In either case, the OCPR is able to recommend OERs given the textual content and the target paper, i.e., $P(OER|text, paper)$.

The detailed RPF and RBF features are listed in Table 1.

3.2 To Enable Physical Collaboration

For any publication, a large number of readers could potentially access and read it. For this approach, the proposed task is to predict reader physical collaboration. In other words, by using the features presented in Table 1 (except for 'reader-reader collaboration'), we will cluster users together, and inner cluster users are more likely to collaborate with each other. This information can be important for online cyberreading environment, e.g., OCPR. For instance, when a large number of readers are reading a paper, $user_x$'s question(s) will be broadcast to the target reader group ($user_x$ belongs to) for potential collaboration. Compared to most existing clustering problems, reader cluster copes with a smaller number of instances, so we chose the K-medoids clustering algorithm [2]. Compared to K-means and EM clustering, K-medoids is more efficient with small dataset. For evaluation, we use "reader-reader collaboration" data extracted by OCPR system.

However, incentive can be a challenge for physical collaboration. Prior studies in scaffolding show that even though reader collaboration may be potentially useful, not all the readers would like to participate the online reading collaboration (e.g., reply to communicate with other readers).

3.3 To Enable Virtual Collaboration

To address the limitations of the physical collaboration, we propose a two-step method for OER-based scaffolding. First, by using the features in Table 1, we group the readers based on RPF and/or RBF. The readers from the same group are more likely to share

Table 1: All features for information understanding

Feature Group	Feature Name	Feature Description
RPF	Reader Profile	*Feature for explicit reader characterization, i.e., reader research topics/expertises (for scholars) or reader course taking history (for students). This kind of features is not always available.*
RBF	Quote Location	*Feature for location of reader's quote text, we assume that if readers share the similar information needs, they will launch queries at the similar place of the reading. To generate this kind of feature, we first cluster all of the readers' queries by their quote text location coordinates, then we use the query count of each reader in each cluster as the feature value.*
	Quote Text	*Feature for quote text, we assume that if readers share the similar information needs, their quote texts(implicit information need) will have a higher text similarity. We use term frequency of reader's quote text as this kind of feature.*
	Question Text	*Feature for question text, we assume that if readers share the similar information needs, their question texts(explicit information need) will have a higher text similarity. We use term frequency of reader's question text as this kind of feature.*
	OER Rating	*Feature for reader's OER ratings, we assume that if readers share the similar information needs, their preference of OER will be similar. We use OER ratings of readers as this kind of feature.*
	Comment/Question Location	*Feature for location of reader's quote text of comment/question, we assume that if readers share the similar information needs, they will comment or have a question at the similar place of the reading. To generate this kind of feature, we first cluster all the readers' comments/questions by their quote text location coordinates, then we use the comment/question count of each reader in each cluster as the feature value.*
	Comment/Question Quote Text	*Feature for quote text of reader's comment/question, we assume that if readers share the similar information needs, their quote texts of comments/questions will have a higher text similarity. We use term frequency of reader's quote text of comments/questions as this kind of feature.*
	Comment/Question Content Text	*Feature for content text of reader's comment/question, we assume that if readers share the similar information needs, their content texts of comments/questions will have a higher text similarity. We use term frequency of reader's content text of comment/question as this kind of feature.*
	Reader-reader Collaboration	*Feature for reader's communication behavior, we assume that if readers share the similar information needs, they will communicate more frequently. We use reader's reply relation as this kind of feature.*

the similar information needs. Second, for each group, we train an OER-recommendation (ranking) model, and the communitized recommendation model can recommend the optimized OERs, which could highly likely help readers (from the same group) to understand the target publication. Note that by using this method, readers from the same group don't necessarily know each other or need to physically collaborate with others. Instead, the group information can be used to train the OER-recommendation models. For instance, given the same piece of text in a paper, some CS students may prefer to access the source code for information understanding, while another group (e.g., information science students) may like to watch a video or presentation slides.

As mentioned earlier, RPF quality can be higher than RBF (as RBF can be noisy), but RPF is not always available. Motivated by these observations, we propose a new method to optimize the clustering performance: (1) select the readers whose RPF are available; (2) cluster this part of readers using K-medoids algorithm based on RPF; (3) use the clustering result for a reader as his/her community label and train a Maximum Entropy classifier [8] based on readers' RBF; (4) use trained classifier to predict the community of the reader who only has RBF. Unlike clustering, the proposed method can enhance the informative RBF while punishing noisy RBF.

The Maximum Entropy classifier is a discriminative classifier commonly used in NLP and IR problems. Unlike the other similar probabilistic classifiers, the Max Entropy does not assume that the features are conditionally independent of each other. This is particularly true in this study where our features are usually not independent (i.e., readers with same background tend to have similar reading behavior).

In this study, by using the meta-search algorithm presented in [4], we indexed four kinds of OERs for information understanding, such as Wikipedia pages, presentation slides, presentation videos, and source code, from various sites (e.g., Videolecture, and GitHub).

As shown in Figure 1, readers can get OER recommendation from the system when they are reading a scientific paper and highlighting a piece of text in the paper. Readers can also provide judgments for the recommended OERs, e.g., rated as 'Good,' 'OK,' and 'Bad.' We then accumulate all the OER judgments from the same reader group to train a learning to rank model for OER recommendation. For learning to rank model generation, we employed 56 text- and graph-based ranking features[1]. For text ranking method, we recommend OER based on the language model between the query text (in the paper) and OER content. For graph-based features, we created a heterogeneous graph, and the OER recommendation is conceptualized as a random walk problem on a heterogeneous graph. Three kinds of vertices – paper, topic and OER – are interconnected by using different kinds of edges. We created different kinds of meta-paths to address different ranking hypotheses, and each meta-path carries one or more types of ranking information [12]. For instance, $K^* \xrightarrow{s} R \xleftarrow{r} R^?_{video}$ is a meta-path function, and it means the candidate OER should relate to the important topic's related OER and candidate OER's type is video. We use the random walk probability from starting (query) vertices to the target OER vertices following a meta-path: $r(v_i^{(1)}, v_j^{(l+1)}) = \sum_{t=v_i^{(1)} \rightsquigarrow v_j^{(l+1)}} RW(t)$, where t is a tour from $v_i^{(1)}$ to $v_j^{(l+1)}$ following the meta-path, and $RW(t)$ is the simulated random walk probability of the tour t.

As this study is not focusing on learning to rank, we used a relative simple algorithm (Coordinate Ascent [7], which iteratively optimizes a multivariate objective ranking function) for OER ranking feature integration and algorithm evaluation.

4. EXPERIMENT

4.1 Data

We tested our collaboration algorithms in a real learning environment. A graduate-level information retrieval course at Indiana University is used for this experiment. Sixty students (masters and PhDs) voluntarily participated in this experiment, and they were required to use the OCPR system for a semester [2]. They could use OCPR functions to read scientific readings, ask questions, write comments and receive access to the system-recommended OERs. Meanwhile, we asked each participant to provide OER relevance judgments for the top five system-recommended OERs. There are a total of 39 valid users (who launched requests in more than six different readings and has made more than eight OER ratings) for this experiment. Meanwhile, there are total 626 OER recommendation requests with 3,551 valid OER usefulness judgments. For reader collaboration, there are total 568 messages sent among 39 users.

In this experiment, we collect two kinds of RPF: 1. students' course taking history ('RPF-C' boolean features), e.g., if student has taken *'machine learning'* and *'statistics'* courses. 2. students'

[1]The detailed feature list is available in the project website: http://59.108.48.32:8086/CCIU/algorithm.html

[2]The dataset can be download in the project website: http://59.108.48.32:8086/CCIU

Table 2: Virtual collaboration performance with clustering result (* means the best result)

Feature Name	MAP@3	MAP@5	MAP@all	nDCG@3	nDCG@5	nDCG@all	MRR
Globe Learning-to-rank(baseline)	0.5582	0.6677	0.7012	0.6346	0.6667	0.6822	0.7340
RPF-C	0.5643	0.6545	0.6958	0.6247	0.6546	0.6781	0.7257
RPF-TB	0.5699	0.6800	0.7070	0.6356	0.6708	0.6843	0.7357
RPF-all	**0.5849***	**0.6960**	**0.7148**	**0.6490***	**0.6837**	**0.6938**	**0.7399**
RBF	0.5523	0.6632	0.6938	0.6270	0.6625	0.6755	0.7209
RPF-all+RBF	0.5547	0.6561	0.6868	0.6168	0.6491	0.6648	0.7147
RBF with Max Entropy	**0.5818**	**0.6985***	**0.7155***	**0.6481**	**0.6881***	**0.6966***	**0.7401***

technical background survey ('RPF-TB' ordinal features from 1 to 4), e.g., if they have expertise in *'R'* and *'NoSQL'*.

At the backend of OCPR, we created text and graph indexes for OER recommendation. For paper, we used 41,370 publications from 1,553 venues (mainly from the ACM digital library). The paper vertices are connected to 9,263 keyword labeled topics. By using meta-search, we collected a total of 1,112,718 OERs.

4.2 Experiment results

As Table 3 shows, we use different kinds of feature sets to cluster the students, and the evaluation metrics are precision, recall, and F1. In the experiment, we set the cluster number as 3 (for total 39 participants). The ground truth is student-student communication data via OCPR. For instance, if $student_1$ and $student_2$ communicate via OCPR, they should belong to the same cluster. Otherwise, they should belong to different clusters. Evaluation results shows that **RPF-all** achieves the best recall, while **RPF-TB** optimizes the precision. When RPF features are not available, RBF features achieve 0.3862 F1, which is lower than RPF.

Table 3: Physical collaboration performance

Feature Name	Precision	Recall	F1-measure
RPF-C	0.3536	**0.4502***	0.3961
RPF-TB	**0.4479***	0.4280	**0.4377***
RPF-all	0.3567	**0.4502***	0.3980
RBF	0.3625	0.4133	0.3862
RPF-all+RBF	0.3569	0.3358	0.3460

1. * means the best result; 2. RBF doesn't include reply information

For OER recommendation task, participants rated 19.8% of the recommended OERs as *"Good"*, 23.9% as *"OK"*, 49.3% as *"Bad"*, and 6.9% as *"Not Sure"*. For this experiment, we use the globe learning-to-rank as baseline [6] (without student clusters). From an nDCG viewpoint, we score $Good = 2, OK = 1$, and $Bad = 0$. The OER recommendation performance can be found in Table 2. We use nDCG@3 as the indicator to train the learning to rank models. For evaluation, 10-fold cross-validation was utilized.

In experiment, all valid readers have RPF, we use 4-fold Cross-validation to simulate the reality situation(randomly choose 25% students, assume they have no RPF, use the other 75% readers to train a Max entropy classifier to predict this 25% readers' communities).

As Table 2 shows, the recommendation based on RPF (*p<0.001*) and RBF with Max Entropy training (*p<0.05*) outperforms globe learning-to-rank (baseline) OER-recommendation method for all the metrics. The recommendation based on RPF achieved the best MAP@3 and nDCG@3, while RBF with Max Entropy training achieved MAP@5, MAP@all, nDCG@5, nDCG@all and MRR (mean reciprocal rank).

5. ANALYSIS AND CONCLUSION

In this study, we propose a novel task to assist readers to better understand scientific publications by enabling their physical or virtual collaboration. For reader community detection, we employed two kinds of features, RPF and RBF. The former one's quality is high, but not always available. The latter one can be noisy.

Experiment results show that: first, for physical collaboration, RPF-based clusters are more useful to predict the user physical collaboration. When RPF is not available, we can use RBF, but the performance will be compromised. Second, for virtual collaboration, the proposed two-step method can significantly improve the OER-scaffolding performance, i.e., recommend communitized OERs to help the readers from each community to better understand the scientific publications given their information needs. When RPF are partially missing, Max Entropy algorithm can be used to infer the community labels by combining partial RPF plus RBF. One limitation of this study is the lack of collaboration between different clusters. We will address this problem in the future work by exploring a soft or overlapping clustering algorithm.

6. ACKNOWLEDGMENTS

This work is supported by the Projects of National Natural Science Foundation of China (No. 61573028 and No. 61472014).

7. REFERENCES

[1] Alan R Dennis, Kelly O McNamara, Stacy Morrone, and Joshua Plaskoff. Improving learning with etextbooks. In *Proceedings of the 48th Hawaii International Conference on System Sciences*, pages 5253–5259, 2015.

[2] Francesco Gullo, Giovanni Ponti, and Andrea Tagarelli. Clustering uncertain data via k-medoids. In *Scalable Uncertainty Management*, pages 229–242. Springer, 2008.

[3] Tristan E Johnson, Thomas N Archibald, and Gershon Tenenbaum. Individual and team annotation effects on students' reading comprehension, critical thinking, and meta-cognitive skills. *Computers in human behavior*, 26(6):1496–1507, 2010.

[4] Xiaozhong Liu. Generating metadata for cyberlearning resources through information retrieval and meta-search. *Journal of the American Society for Information Science and Technology*, 64(4):771–786, 2013.

[5] Xiaozhong Liu and Han Jia. Answering academic questions for education by recommending cyberlearning resources. *Journal of the American Society for Information Science and Technology*, 64(8):1707–1722, 2013.

[6] Xiaozhong Liu, Zhuoren Jiang, and Liangcai Gao. Scientific information understanding via open educational resources (OER). In *Proceedings of the 38th International ACM SIGIR Conference on Research and Development in Information Retrieval*, pages 645–654. ACM, 2015.

[7] Donald Metzler and W Bruce Croft. Linear feature-based models for information retrieval. *Information Retrieval*, 10(3):257–274, 2007.

[8] Kamal Nigam, John Lafferty, and Andrew McCallum. Using maximum entropy for text classification. In *IJCAI-99 workshop on machine learning for information filtering*, volume 1, pages 61–67, 1999.

[9] Elena Novak, Rim Razzouk, and Tristan E Johnson. The educational use of social annotation tools in higher education: A literature review. *The Internet and Higher Education*, 15(1):39–49, 2012.

[10] Roy D Pea. The social and technological dimensions of scaffolding and related theoretical concepts for learning, education, and human activity. *The journal of the learning sciences*, 13(3):423–451, 2004.

[11] Addison Su, Stephen JH Yang, Wu-Yuin Hwang, and Jia Zhang. A web 2.0-based collaborative annotation system for enhancing knowledge sharing in collaborative learning environments. *Computers & Education*, 55(2):752–766, 2010.

[12] Y. Sun, J. Han, X. Yan, P. S. Yu, and T. Wu. PathSim: Meta path-based top-k similarity search in heterogeneous information networks. In *Proc. 2011 Int. Conf. Very Large Data Bases (VLDB'11)*, Seattle, WA, 2011.

Computational Creativity Based Video Recommendation

Wei Lu
Department of Computing
Hong Kong Polytechnic University
Kowloon, Hong Kong
cswlu@comp.polyu.edu.hk

Fu-lai Chung
Department of Computing
Hong Kong Polytechnic University
Kowloon, Hong Kong
korris.chung@polyu.edu.hk

ABSTRACT

Computational creativity, as an emerging domain of application, emphasizes the use of big data to automatically design new knowledge. Based on the availability of complex multi-relational data, one aspect of computational creativity is to infer unexplored regions of feature space and novel learning paradigm, which is particularly useful for online recommendation. Tensor models offer effective approaches for complex multi-relational data learning and missing element completion. Targeting at constructing a recommender system that can compromise between accuracy and creativity for users, a deep Bayesian probabilistic tensor framework for tag and item recommending is adopted. Empirical results demonstrate the superiority of the proposed method and indicate that it can better capture latent patterns of interaction relationships and generate interesting recommendations based on creative tag combinations.

Keywords

recommendation; serendipity; Bayesian tensor factorization

1. INTRODUCTION

Computational creativity, a study on algorithms for computer to generate artifacts that humans perceive to be creative, is a newly emerging field in today's e-commerce operations. Colton et al. [4] provide a definition for computational creativity research as: *"The philosophy, science and engineering of computational systems exhibit impersonally creative behaviors by taking on particular responsibilities."* Based on this definition, attempts including automatic culinary recipe generating system [9] have been made through cognitive flavor assessment. For recommendation, diversity also has become an important aspect for evaluation [11], where content-based systems usually suffer from over-specialization, since only items similar to those rated by users will be more likely recommended. Computational creativity is also related to serendipity, as defined in [6], a user-oriented measurement balancing between surprise and accuracy. Serendipitous recommendations by definition are also novel. Consider a recommender system that simply recommends movies directed by the user's favorite director, comparing to recommend a movie of the same director that the user was not aware of, a movie by a new director catering to the user's taste, is more likely to be not only novel but also serendipitous.

SIGIR '16, July 17-21, 2016, Pisa, Italy

DOI: http://dx.doi.org/10.1145/2911451.2914707

This whole idea of calculating computational creativity for recommender system from the automated processing of mass collection of item tags requires us to address several problems. First, we face the issue of effective user profiling. A two-dimensional collaborative filtering approach cannot be directly employed to build a tag-based recommender system, since it cannot efficiently capture the multi-dimensional characteristic and hence, will result in poorer recommendation performance. Second, creativity of new ideas built upon domain knowledge are difficult to be measured quantitatively. Besides traditional performance measurements, e.g. precision, recall, F-1, new evaluation metrics are required. Past approaches use historical viewing frequency based distance measurement, but as user preference is a complicated topic combination, pure frequencies would hardly express their real interest.

Fortunately, comparing to traditional user-item based recommender system, meta-data such as tags, which are reusable and shareable, play significant roles in helping manage online resources. As an additional source for item recognition, tags help in revealing user and improving user profiles that can be used in recommendation [5]. Hence, in this paper, we explore the following challenges: *given the inordinate amount of candidate items and their corresponding textual tag information now accessible online, is it possible to automatically generate serendipitous tag combinations for users via machine learning?* For example, given an online video recommender system, if a user has watched two videos with tag "Romance, Comedy" and "Thrilling, Horror", how would he react to a video tagged by "Comedy, Horror"? Will he find it creative or just as expected?

We assume that the historical behavior of users is a sound source for preference estimation, the high-level semantic topics of video tags can be regarded as a comprehensive representation of user features. There are some work on incorporating user features (e.g. age, gender, geographic information) and their social relationships (e.g. community groups) into a multi-way data analysis [10]. However, for video recommendation, users are more accurately clustered based on their overlapping of preferences, which can be represented by semantic relations among video tags. Integrating such multi-facet information, user profiles can be naturally modeled with higher-order data mining models. Tensor modeling is a well-known approach for representing latent relationships inherent in the multi-dimensional data.

There are typically three steps for tensor-based recommendation: (1) tensorial construction for multi-relational data; (2) tensor decomposition for latent feature (topic) representation; and (3) tensor reconstruction for interaction regeneration. Traditional multi-way factor models suffer from the drawback of failing to capture

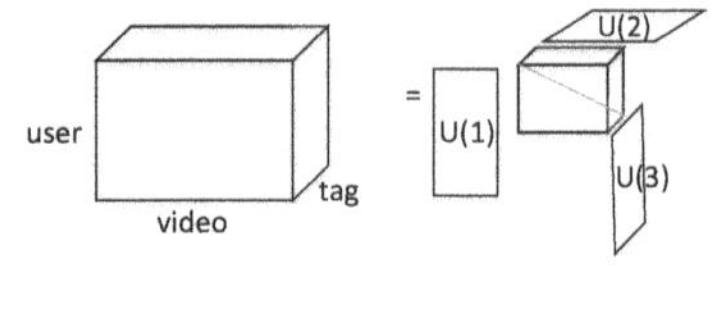

Figure 1: CP decomposition: a three mode user-video-tag relational dataset example. The tensor can be expressed in a matrix format: $\mathcal{X} = \{\lambda, U^{(1)}, U^{(2)}, \ldots, U^{(k)}\}$

coupled and nonlinear interactions between entities [13]. Also, they are not robust to datasets containing noisy and missing values. Through proper generative model, nonparametric Bayesian multi-way analysis algorithms are especially appealing, since they provide efficient ways to deal with distinct data types as well as data with missing values and noises. Moreover, since we are expected to recommend items not only considering the accuracy but also the creativity and serendipity, the posterior likelihood of Bayesian model can also be leveraged as a probabilistic ranking generating mechanism. Meanwhile, deep networks prove great empirical success in various domains [2]. They are capable of providing more compact nonlinear representations for feature learning. It would be interesting to adopt deep learning in one or more of the tensor modes and assess its effectiveness on tensor completion.

In this paper we address the aforementioned challenges through a novel Deep Tensor for Probabilistic Recommendation (DTPR) method. It breaks the task at hand into the following components: 1. a tensor construction stage of building user-item-tag correlation; 2. a tensor decomposition stage learning factors for each component mode; 3. a stage of tensor completion, which computes the creativity value of tag pairs; and 4. a recommender stage that ranks the candidate items according to both precision and creative consideration. This approach is evaluated using a real world video recommender system, with large amount of users, videos and corresponding video description tags.

2. PROPOSED METHODS

2.1 Frame of the Method

For a typical online video recommender system, the first step is to construct a third-order tensor from the video clicking logs; secondly, factoring the tensor using a decomposition method; and then reconstructing the decomposed elements. Following these steps, a three-way tensor, Tag $\times$ User $\times$ Video, is then constructed populated with the times of video being clicked by a user (Figure 1). For the factorization part, a Deep Canonical PARAFAC Factorization (DCPF) Model [8] is applied.

Accordingly, the next step is ranking the candidate items for recommendation. To encourage creative recommendation, it includes the consideration of tag pair preferences from the reconstructed tensor through introducing Bayesian surprise, which will be further elaborated in the following subsections. The preferences of users to rank the top-N list of item candidates are then probabilistically calculated.

2.2 Model Description

We briefly review the DCPF model discussed in [8]. Let $\mathcal{Y}$ denote an observed incomplete K-order tensor. For different types of observation, a noise function f can be applied on, depending on the data type being modeled [14] (e.g. Gaussian for real-valued data). The parameters of CP decomposition, $\{U^{(k)}\}_{k=1}^{K}$, are further represented by lower rank component factor score $V^{(k)}$ and factor loading $D^{(k)}$. $B^{(k)}$ is an indicator of which factors are actually used. Since it is fully conjugate, the sampler cycling steps are presented in Algorithm 1. In the algorithm, R is a positive integer indicating the rank of the core tensor. λ_r is the weight associated with the rth rank component. a and b are hyper-parameters for δ_r. All the parameters with "^" in the updating steps are the posterior expectation and precision. Details about the distributions are elaborated in [8].

Algorithm 1 Gibbs sampler steps

Begin
Initialize $U^{(k)}$, $B^{(k)}$, $V^{(k)}$, $D^{(k)}$
for iteration i **do**
  for each diagonal element r of the core tensor Λ, which is independently drawn from a normal distribution **do**
    1. Sample its independent conditionally conjugate posteriors from $\lambda_r \sim \mathcal{N}(\hat{\mu_r}, \hat{\tau_r}^{-1})$
    2. Update $\delta_r \sim Ga(a + \frac{1}{2}(R - r + 1), b + \frac{1}{2}\sum_r \tau_r^2 \delta_r)$
  end for
  for each mode factor matrix $U^{(k)}$ **do**
    1. Update binary indicator matrix $B^{(k)}$, factor loading matrix $V^{(k)}$ and factor score matrix $D^{(k)}$
    2. Sample column vector conditionally conjugate posteriors from $U_{i_k}^{(k)} \sim \mathcal{N}(\hat{\mu}_{i_k}^{(k)}, \hat{\Sigma}_{i_k}^{(k)-1})$
    3. Update hyper-parameters
  end for
end for

2.3 Calculation of Computational Creativity

In dynamic situations, surprise is an important indicator of the belief changing significance [1]. It can be also calculated as a quantization for creativity measure. According to Bayesian theorem, for an observer with prior distribution $P(X)$, the collection of data D leads to a re-evaluation of beliefs $P(X|D)$, the posterior distribution. Surprise is to define the distance between the prior and posterior distributions, specifically as:

$$S(D, X) = d[P(X), P(X|D)] \tag{1}$$

where d is a distance measure function. For example, if we use the relative entropy or Kullback-Liebler [7] divergence, which is a common practice for many well-know dissimilarity measures, the surprise S can be calculated as:

$$S(D, X) = logP(D) - \int_X P(X)logP(D|X)\,\mathrm{d}X \tag{2}$$

Since we can regard the novel tag generation process as a tensor completion problem, based on the posterior distribution of factor matrix $U^{(1)}$, the posterior distribution for co-occurring tags t_1, t_2 for user u can be written as:

$$p(y_{i_1=\{t_1,t_2\}, i_2=u, i_3}) = \prod_{i_3=1}^{n_3} \prod_{i_1} \mathcal{N}(y_{\mathbf{i}}|\hat{x}_{\mathbf{i}}, \hat{\tau}_e^{-1}) \tag{3}$$

where $\hat{x}_{\mathbf{i}} = \hat{p}_{i_k r}^{(k)} U_{i_k r}^{(k)} + \hat{q}_{i_k r}^{(k)}$, $\hat{p}_{i_k r}$ and $\hat{q}_{i_k r}^{(k)}$ are the posterior values calculated from the conditional posterior of $U_{i_k r}^{(k)}$.

2.4 Probabilistic Ranking Incorporated with Bayesian Surprise

Most existing tensor-based recommendation approaches rank the recommendations based on the values of reconstructed tensor. For example, Zheng et al. [15] utilize the linear add-up of the ith row of each mode factor matrix. The higher weight it is, the more relevant user i is related to the topic. Since the goal of our task is not only providing accurate but also creative recommendations, instead of solely using the final reconstructed tensor from the model, we propose to rank the result of tensor modeling incorporating the Bayesian surprise value for generating the top-N list of candidate items to the users.

Using the reconstructed tensor $\hat{\mathcal{Y}}$, for each user u, two candidate lists can be created: (1) a list of items that the user might be interested in based on the posterior add-up values of user and item factor matrices; and (2) a list of tag preference pairs based on the normalized maximum values of Bayesian surprise metric. Assume the number of candidate item is n, and the number of tag pairs is J. J can be adjusted depending on how much compromise on creativity the system wishes to make. The score for ranking user-item pair is calculated as follows:

$$Score_{u,v} = w_{u,v} \sum_{i=1}^{N_j \in v} \frac{S_{u,i}}{\sum_j^J S_{u,j}} \quad (4)$$

Where $\mathbf{w} = \sum_{r=1}^{R} \lambda_r \mathbf{u}_r^{(1)} \mathbf{u}_r^{(2)T}$ is the weight matrix obtained from reconstructed tensor, N_j is the number of tag pairs belonging to video v, in the top-J surprising list to user u. $\mathbf{S}$ is the surprise degree matrix of users to tag pairs. Each row vector of the final score matrix is then ranked in descending order, indicating the top-N weighted items as recommendation candidates.

3. EXPERIMENTAL RESULTS

3.1 Datasets

We perform experiments on a large-scale real-word dataset to verify the performance of the DTPR model on expressing high-level semantic features of user behavior and incorporating creativity consideration into recommendation. The real-world records were collected in three consecutive weeks at the same time slot from Tencent QQ browser (http://video.browser.qq.com) in August, 2014. The database stores historical clicking logs of active users extracted from the Hadoop distributed file system, with each record referring to one video clicked. Besides the time slot, user id, video id, number of clicks by this particular user and the total number of clicks in history, there are four categories of information provided as video description tag (in Chinese): (1) type (e.g. action, mystery); (2) region (e.g. US, main land China); (3) director; and (4) actor. Based on these information, a three-way User$\times$ Video $\times$ Tag tensor is constructed. There are $4,071,811$ samples in total with $137,465$ unique users, and $9,393$ unique videos they clicked. The rank of the tensor equals to 140.

3.2 Tag Completion Evaluation

Recall that our goal is to automatically generate serendipitous tag combinations for users, it is important to, analyze the tag completion performance part of the proposed method first. If we regard each type of tags as semantic words from different domains, this problem can also be regarded as multi-task clustering. We would like to evaluate how well the system ranks the correct items for each user based on single category and multiple categories of tags. Two metrics are employed for this: (1) the Mean Reciprocal Rank (MRR) and (2) Precision at 1 (P@1). MRR computes the inverse rank of the correct item and averages the score across the whole data. P at 1 computes the percentage of times the ground truth item are ranked as the top one.

From Table 1, although having high frequency of occurrence, tags from category II "Region" have the lowest MRR and P@1 due to its low differentiable vocabulary. For single layer DTPR, comparing to use purely actor tags, combining information from all these four categories increases the MRR by 1.7% (from 0.3662 to 0.3726). The 2-layer DTPR, in comparison, increases the MRR from 0.4110 to 0.3744, which is a 9% relative increase. Comparing to single layer DTPR, the increase in P@1 is also more obvious (36%) comparing to 1-layer implementation. This encouraging results indicate that a deep decomposition utilizing information from multiple aspects for factor matrix can better capture the semantic representation of user behavior.

Table 1: Results for 1-layer and 2-layer DTPR on different categories of tags.

	1-layer DTPR		2-layer DTPR	
	MRR	P@1	MRR	P@1
I	0.1867	0.0093	0.1974	0.0099
II	0.0009	0.0013	0.0009	0.0012
III	0.2900	0.2500	0.2990	0.2541
IV	0.3662	0.2233	0.3744	0.2350
ALL	0.3726	0.2249	0.4110	0.3197

3.3 Bayesian Surprise Assessment

For a subset of 3-way tensor, since Bayesian surprise is user dependent, the surprise value for each pair-wise combination of tags is presented in Figure 3. To make the figure clear, only the first $4,000$ pairs from a total $22,155$ are shown. A higher value indicates a more diverse posterior belief. In other words, if the semantic themes from the pair of tags co-occur in the same video, a higher Bayesian surprise would indicate that the user regard it as more creative. As indicated from the figure, the response of users to these $4,000$ tag pairs can generally be grouped into five folds. Within each fold, the surprise degree of each user varies according to the past video preference. The clustering of tag pairs also illustrates that the user preference has its probabilistic topic features. Hence comparing to traditional serendipity measurements, which are based on fixed distance of observed records, the posterior likelihoods are more suitable for creativity evaluation, as they incorporate the uncertainty and the cluster characteristics of user preference.

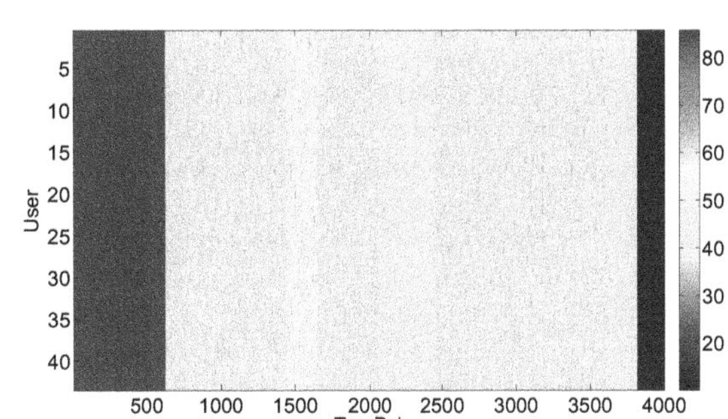

Figure 3: The surprise value for each user in the subset if the two tags occur together. X-axis indicates 4000 distinct tag combinations. Y-axis is 43 users

3.4 Performance Comparison

In this sub-section, we compare the recommendation performances with and without incorporating Bayesian surprise, using common evaluation metrics, including precision, recall and averaged hit rate.

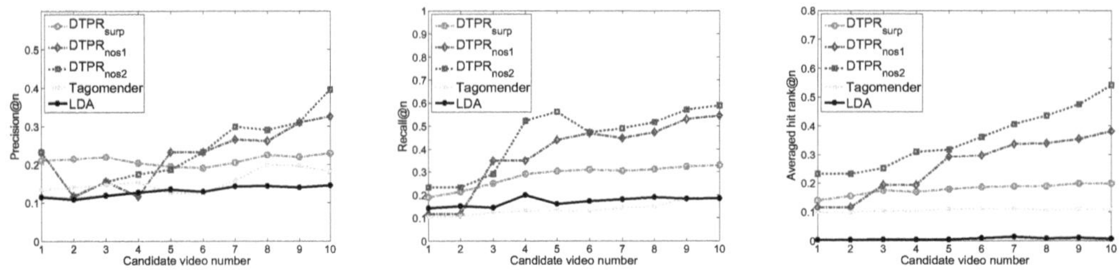

(a) Precision@N (b) Recall@N (c) Averaged hit rate

Figure 2: Video recommendation performance comparison for single layer DTPR incorporated with Bayesian surprise (DTPR$_{surp}$), 1-layer (DTPR$_{nos1}$) and 2-layer (DTPR$_{nos2}$) DTPR without Bayesian surprise, Latent Dirichlet Allocation [3], and Tag matching method [12], with varying candidates number n ranging from 1-10.

The measures are defined as: $Precision = \frac{N_r}{N}$, $Recall = \frac{N_r}{N_t}$, $Averaged\ hit\ rate = \frac{\sum_{i=1}^{N_r} \frac{1}{r_i}}{N_t}$ where N_r is the number of relevant videos in top-N item candidates, N_t is the ground truth of relevant videos that user has watched, r_i is the rank of each relevant video in the recommender pool. The pair number J is fixed at 5.

As shown in Figure 2, we compare the proposed model in single layer and 2-layer version with and without incorporating Bayesian surprise for item ranking. The increase of pool number will enhance the probability to recommend the favored video. Thus, the three metrics have the trend of gradually growing. Although single layer and 2-layer DTPR have similar precision for predicting, a multi-layer implementation allows an obvious higher hit rate, which indicates that it can pick the correct choice of users at an earlier stage of recommendation. Through incorporating Bayesian surprise, the performance does degrade due to the additional uncertainty it introduces to the item ranking. However, it still outperforms both LDA and Tagommender [12] method. Considering the surprise it brings to the users, which will in return enhance user experience, this kind of recommending has its merits in practice.

4. CONCLUSION

Given the increasing growth in large-scale multi-relational data, we study the computational creativity problem in video recommendation domain. To effectively learn user-item-tag correlations, we utilize deep Bayesian tensor model, which provides an effective way for joint analysis of user and video features. Through a scalable framework for tensor decomposition and completion, and through introducing Bayesian surprise into probabilistic ranking, we are able to recommend personalized items taking creativity as a consideration. Our model can perform fully conjugate Bayesian inference via Gibbs sampling inference. The quantization index, Bayesian surprise, for computational creativity is assessed. Currently the creativity is valuated based on generating new combination of existent items. Creative construction for data from previously unexplored domain based on current knowledge are also appealing for future targets.

5. ACKNOWLEDGMENTS

This research was supported by project B-Q43W, B-Q49B, and G-UA3W. We would also like to thank Kunfeng Lai and the Mobile Internet group at Tencent Shenzhen for providing the data.

6. REFERENCES

[1] P. Baldi and L. Itti. Of bits and wows: a bayesian theory of surprise with applications to attention. *Neural Networks*, 23(5):649–666, 2010.

[2] Y. Bengio. Learning deep architectures for ai. *Foundations and trends® in Machine Learning*, 2(1):1–127, 2009.

[3] D. M. Blei, A. Y. Ng, and M. I. Jordan. Latent dirichlet allocation. *the Journal of machine Learning research*, 3:993–1022, 2003.

[4] S. Colton, G. A. Wiggins, et al. Computational creativity: the final frontier? 2012.

[5] N. Ifada. A tag-based personalized item recommendation system using tensor modeling and topic model approaches. In *Proceedings of the 37th international ACM SIGIR conference on Research & development in information retrieval*, pages 1280–1280. ACM, 2014.

[6] P. B. Kantor, L. Rokach, F. Ricci, and B. Shapira. *Recommender systems handbook*. Springer, 2011.

[7] S. Kullback. *Information theory and statistics*. Courier Corporation, 1997.

[8] W. Lu and F.-l. Chung. Deep bayesian tensor for recommender system. In *Proceedings of the ECMLPKDD 2015 Doctoral Consortium*, pages 135–144, 2015.

[9] F. Pinel and L. R. Varshney. Computational creativity for culinary recipes. In *CHI'14 Extended Abstracts on Human Factors in Computing Systems*, pages 439–442. ACM, 2014.

[10] P. Rai, Y. Wang, and L. Carin. Leveraging features and networks for probabilistic tensor decomposition. 2015.

[11] F. Ricci, L. Rokach, and B. Shapira. *Introduction to recommender systems handbook*. Springer, 2011.

[12] S. Sen, J. Vig, and J. Riedl. Tagommenders: connecting users to items through tags. In *Proceedings of the 18th international conference on World wide web*, pages 671–680. ACM, 2009.

[13] Z. Xu, F. Yan, et al. Infinite tucker decomposition: Nonparametric bayesian models for multiway data analysis. *arXiv preprint arXiv:1108.6296*, 2011.

[14] Z. Xu, F. Yan, and Y. Qi. Bayesian nonparametric models for multiway data analysis. 2013.

[15] N. Zheng, Q. Li, S. Liao, and L. Zhang. Flickr group recommendation based on tensor decomposition. In *Proceedings of the 33rd international ACM SIGIR conference on Research and development in information retrieval*, pages 737–738. ACM, 2010.

Controversy Detection in Wikipedia Using Collective Classification

Shiri Dori-Hacohen*, David Jensen†, James Allan*

*Center for Intelligent Information Retrieval, †Knowledge Discovery Laboratory
College of Information and Computer Sciences
University of Massachusetts Amherst
{shiri,jensen,allan}@cs.umass.edu

ABSTRACT

Concerns over personalization in IR have sparked an interest in detection and analysis of controversial topics. Accurate detection would enable many beneficial applications, such as alerting search users to controversy. Wikipedia's broad coverage and rich metadata offer a valuable resource for this problem. We hypothesize that intensities of controversy among related pages are not independent. Thus, we propose a stacked model which exploits the dependencies among related pages. Our approach improves classification of controversial web pages when compared to a model that examines each page in isolation, demonstrating that controversial topics exhibit homophily. Using notions of similarity to construct a subnetwork for collective classification, rather than using the default network present in the relational data, leads to improved classification with wider applications for semi-structured datasets, with the effects most pronounced when a small set of neighbors is used.

1. INTRODUCTION

Critical literacy, civic discourse and trustworthy information are not immediate results of effective information retrieval. Controversies proliferate online, but the "filter bubble" effect encourages confirmation bias by offering users the answers they want to hear [11]. Exposure to diverse opinions can potentially improve civic discourse, but these benefits will only be available to users who can detect controversial topics. Automated tools performing such detection can support users in their browsing and search experience [6].

Prior work on controversy detection focused on Wikipedia (cf. [9, 12]), analyzing each page in isolation or studying its editors. We hypothesize that controversies occur in neighborhoods of related topics. Thus, advanced ML techniques that take relational data into account, such as *collective* and *stacked* inference [7, 10], can improve controversy detection by exploiting the dependencies among related pages. In a departure from most work on collective inference, we also hypothesize that a definition of "relatedness" that incorporates textual or topical similarity will hold more predictive power than pre-existing relationships such as hyperlinks. If so, using a constructed network based on similarity will outperform collective models based on explicit relations. Our research questions are: What is the relative performance of intrinsic versus collective classification for detecting controversy in Wikipedia? And, what types of page relationships most improve the classification? We hypothesize that collective models will substantially outperform intrinsic models, and particularly when related pages are defined in terms of their textual or topical similarity to the classified page.

SIGIR '16, July 17 - 21, 2016, Pisa, Italy

ISBN 978-1-4503-4069-4/16/07...$15.00

DOI: http://dx.doi.org/10.1145/2911451.2914745

2. RELATED WORK

The related work falls broadly under three themes: the need for controversy detection, methods for controversy detection, and collective and stacked inference.

The Need for Controversy Detection. Increasing personalization reduces exposure to diverse opinions, which is a serious risk for the tenets of deliberative democracy. Search engines and social media use personalization to tailor results to the users' opinions, creating a "Filter Bubble" [11] which can further exacerbate confirmation bias. It is increasingly evident that digesting material about controversies is a challenging task for end users. These concerns have sparked controversy analysis and detection, a research area of growing interest (for a survey of prior work, challenges and important implications, see Dori-Hacohen et al.[6]). Accurately and automatically distinguishing between controversial and noncontroversial topics is one such challenge which is currently within technical reach, yet far from a solved problem. Our paper focuses on automatically detecting controversial topics in Wikipedia, a task proposed by Kittur et al. [9], which can also serve as a crucial step in other algorithms (cf. [4]).

Methods for Controversy Detection in Wikipedia. Of the relatively sparse prior work on automatically detecting controversy, most focuses on Wikipedia, since its rich user-generated content base offers a wealth of semi-structured data (for a survey and comparative study, see

Table 1: Data set size and annotations (Wikipedia Articles)

Set	Articles	Controversial
DHA [5]	1926	293 (15.2%)
SRMRB [12]	480	240 (50%)

Algorithm 1 Cross-validation stacked training procedure

for fold $i = 1..k$, $Set_i = A \setminus \text{fold}_i$ **do**
  Train IM_i, an intrinsic model on Set_i
  Select $subneighbors(Set_i) \subseteq neighbors(Set_i)$
  Apply IM_i on $subneighbors(Set_i)$
  Aggregate predictions of $subneighbors(Set_i)$ to create an extended feature set, Set'_i
  Train SM_i, a stacked collective model on Set'_i
end for

Algorithm 2 Cross-validation stacked inference procedure

for fold $i = 1..k$ **do**
  Select $subneighbors(fold_i) \subseteq neighbors(fold_i)$
  Apply IM_i (trained above) on $subneighbors(fold_i)$
  Aggregate predictions of $subneighbors(fold_i)$ to create an extended feature set, $fold'_i$
  Apply SM_i (trained above) on $fold'_i$
end for

[12]). Most of this work has used an approach that classifies each page in isolation [9, 14]. In contrast, this paper examines networks of pages that are topically related, and argues that controversy detection can be improved by considering a page in the context of its neighbors. While some recent work has alluded to the possibility that controversies occur in neighborhoods of related topics [4] or demonstrated such clusters anecdotally [8], this potential connection has yet to be tested or used to improve controversy detection.

Web-page Classification and General Collective Classification Approaches. Collective and relational inference are ML techniques that can be applied to relational data, which have been successful on many complex problems such as hyperlink categorization [3], by exploiting homophily between related objects [7]. Stacked models are a type of collective classification that avoids the need for computationally intensive inference procedures, and is particularly useful in situations where there is a lack of extensive ground truth data for the neighborhood of a page [10]. In stacked models, an *intrinsic classifier*, relying only on the features of the data instance being evaluated, is trained first, and then applied to generate predictions for the neighbors of every instance in the set. These predictions are then aggregated into an extended dataset and used as features of the instance. Finally, a *stacked model* is trained by using this extended dataset, as in regular collective inference. In other words, the collective inference classifier is "stacked" over the intrinsic classifier (see e.g. Algorithms 1 and 2 below). Instead of using known truth labels of neighbors, a stacked model uses the outputs of an intrinsic classifier. Stacked models have been demonstrated to be effective at collective classification due to a reduction in bias [7].

When stacked models are used in semistructured datasets, they are usually applied in a relational manner: relatedness is defined directly in the structured data. In several domains, however, a relational link between two objects does not imply a strong connection between them. Inspired by the needs of our task, we propose *explicitly constructing* a subnetwork of relationships for the purpose of improving stacked classification. Using features of the semi-structured dataset, such as relation directionality and object similarity, we construct a more useful notion of relationship; we thus depart from most stacked classification approaches that assume that the dataset contains a fixed relational schema (cf. [7, 10]). Our work is distinct from Probabilistic Similarity Logic [2], which reasons about similarity for inference purposes; we propose to construct an induced subgraph of relationships based directly on similarity measures.

Table 2: Intrinsic and Stacked features

Type	Description
Intrinsic	# of Revisions; # of Minor Revisions; # of Editors; # of Anonymous Editors; # of Anonymous Revisions; % of Anonymous Editors; % of Anonymous Revisions; Max Edits Per Editor; Avg Edits Per Editor; Std Dev of Edits Per Editor
Stacked	Proportion of neighbors above X% probability, where X = {10%, 30%, 50%, 70%, 90%}. This represents a discretized version of the probability distribution of controversy among the neighbors; Max Controversy probability among neighbors; Avg Controversy probability among neighbors

3. APPROACH

We will classify Wikipedia pages as controversial or not, using a combination of intrinsic features of a page, as well as predictions of controversy from pages related to it. There are two novel parts to our approach (described below): first, we construct a subnetwork of relations based on similarity, and then proceed to use a stacked model on top of this constructed network. The training procedure for the intrinsic model is the standard fashion. Following Kou and Cohen [10], our stacked training procedure creates neighbor predictions in a cross-validated manner with 10 folds. The main difference from their approach is the use of a subset of the neighbors, rather than all neighbors. The training procedure is applied to the i-th fold, as seen in Algorithm 1. At inference time, the stacked model pipeline is applied to the i-th fold in an analogous manner, as seen in Algorithm 2.

Constructing a Subnetwork. We examine the neighborhood of each Wikipedia page, for stacked classification and to evaluate whether homophily exists for controversial topics. The effectiveness of collective inference relies on homophily between related instances. Presumably, if a page is controversial, then the pages related to it are likely to be controversial. The controversy level of related pages, therefore, can be used as a feature to the collective model. However, links in Wikipedia are noisy, and not necessarily the best indication of relatedness. We expect stacked classification to be more useful when applied specifically to more relevant links. We thus do not consider every hyperlink to be an equally valid neighbor, but instead apply a similarity function to generate a relative ranking among all neighbors. Additionally, we argue that links pointing into, and out of, an article, should be viewed as separate types of relationships. Incoming links consist of a zipfian-like distribution which grows on a logarithmic scale, while outgoing links exhibit a more linear relationship. Specifically, we construct a subnetwork by applying a TF-IDF-based pairwise cosine similarity function on the text of the page, and then selecting the top-scoring neighbors (taken as two separate lists, for in-links and out-links) as most "related" to the center page.

Creating a Stacked Model. To evaluate our hypotheses, we create intrinsic and collective models of controversy.

Table 3: Compared Systems

Name	Description
Stacked-Ranked-k	Proposed stacked inference system with a similarity-based subnetwork
Intrinsic	A classifier using only intrinsic features
Stacked-All	A stacked inference system, as above, but which uses all Wikipedia neighbors
Stacked-Random-k	A stacked inference system which uses k randomly selected neighbors
Neighbors-Only-k	A classifier based only on the neighbor predictions (as in a regular stacked model), without using the intrinsic features of the center page
Prior work	See Sepehri Rad & Barbosa [12] for details

We compare an *intrinsic classifier* that classifies each page independently, and a **collective inference classifier** that assumes dependence between controversy values of related pages.

4. DATASET AND EXPERIMENTAL SETUP

We would like to examine the following hypotheses: (1) using a subset of chosen neighbors, based on a similarity ranking, represents an improvement upon using all neighbors; (2) using this subset also represents an improvement upon using the same amount of random neighbors. We will describe the datasets used, the model features and setup, and finally the alternative systems we created in order to examine our hypotheses.

4.1 Data Sets

We use two datasets for this work, as described in Table 1, which were created by two independent groups. The first dataset is the publicly available[1] Wikipedia Web Controversy dataset (denoted DHA [5]). The second is a collection provided on request (denoted SRMRB [12]). The incidence of controversy is different in the two sets (about 15% in DHA and exactly 50% in SRMRB). While it is quite challenging to estimate the precise incidence of controversy in the wild, we believe that an unbalanced setting is more realistic - in general, noncontroversial topics far outnumber controversial topics. In order to partially mitigate the challenges of training on an imbalanced set (DHA), we applied weights to all the instances in the training folds, such that the sum of weights of all controversial pages was equal to the sum of weights for the noncontroversial pages.

4.2 Model Features and Setup

For both the intrinsic and the stacked models, we use the Random Forest classifier provided by Weka, set to use 100 trees, and the default behavior for all other settings. For training and inference, we used 10-fold cross-validation, as described in Section 3.

Similarity for Subnetwork Construction. In order to generate the collective model, we observed all Wikipedia pages linking into, and out of, the center page. We ranked all these pages by pairwise, TF-IDF based cosine similarity (ignoring stop words), then chose the top k in-links and the top k out-links of the central page. We considered several alternatives for thresholding the similarity. In the experiments described below, we simply pick the top k ranked neighbors for incoming links, as well as the top k for outgoing links, where k is either 10 or 300.

[1] ciir.cs.umass.edu/downloads/

Table 4: Results for compared models with $k = [10, 300]$

Dataset	Model	AUC	F1	Acc
DHA	Intrinsic	0.692	0.322	0.788
	NbrOnly-10	0.694	0.244	0.813
	Random-10	0.718	0.289	0.775
	Stacked-10	0.762	0.303	0.823
	NbrOnly-300	0.788	0.348	0.833
	Random-300	0.790	0.367	0.838
	Stacked-300	**0.800**	0.372	**0.844**
	AllNeighbors	0.793	**0.399**	**0.844**
SRMRB	Intrinsic	0.778	0.704	0.696
	NbrOnly-10	0.655	0.620	0.617
	Random-10	0.705	0.697	0.658
	Stacked-10	0.783	0.684	0.670
	NbrOnly-300	0.794	0.704	0.707
	Random-300	0.838	0.736	0.735
	Stacked-300	**0.840**	0.730	0.738
	AllNeighbors	0.828	**0.744**	**0.744**

Features. The features of both of the intrinsic and stacked models are displayed in Table 2. *Intrinsic Features* follow prior work that used metadata features of the Wikipedia pages [9, 12]. All intrinsic features are extracted from the May 2014 Wikipedia dump [2]. A subset of the features were extracted using JWPL[3]. We use the intrinsic model to generate predictions (probabilities of controversy) for each neighbor in the subnetwork described above. Collective inference requires that the relevant features of pages be aggregated in order to use them: we use the aggregate functions in Table 2, applied separately to in-links and out-links. In total, 14 *Stacked Features* were added (7 aggregates each, which were applied to the top k in-links and out-links separately).

4.3 Alternative Systems

Our proposed system described above, which we denote *Stacked-Ranked-k*, uses a similarity function to induce a subnetwork for the purpose of stacked inference. In order to test our hypotheses, we construct several alternative systems (see Table 3). In each case, we train the model on the same intrinsic and stacked features described above (as appropriate for that system). Where possible, we compare our results to several baselines from prior work [1, 9, 13, 14], as reported in a recent comparative study [12].

5. RESULTS

We discuss some differences in data imbalance between the two datasets and our choice of metrics, and our findings: using similar neighbors improve stacked inference, neighbors can provide good inference even without intrinsic features, and a stacked model outperforms existing classifiers.

Data Imbalance and Metrics. The results of our experiments are displayed in Table 4. Due to the unbalanced

[2] https://dumps.wikimedia.org/

[3] https://github.com/dkpro/dkpro-jwpl

nature of the DHA dataset, neither F1 nor accuracy are representative metrics for classification. Thus, we focus most of our subsequent discussion on Area under ROC (AUC), a metric commonly used to evaluate unbalanced sets, as it is insensitive to dataset imbalance. We report F1 and accuracy results for comparison with prior work.

Similar Neighbors Improve Results, particularly for the first few neighbors. The predictive power of the stacked model grows with the number of neighbors. Results increase substantially within the first 25 neighbors, with diminishing returns afterwards. The Stacked classifier outperforms both the Intrinsic and Neighbor-only models, for both datasets and all metrics presented (see Table 4). For most values of k, our proposed system (which chooses neighbors according to a similarity metric), outperforms a random selection of the same number of neighbors, with the difference clearest when a small number of neighbors is used (figure omitted due to lack of space). As the number of neighbors increase and approach all neighbors of the page, the subnetwork approach converges to a "regular" stacked approach.

Neighbors Provide Quality Inference Without Intrinsic Features. As expected, each stacked model outperforms its equivalent Neighbors-only version, which ignores the intrinsic features of the page. Interestingly, in some cases the Neighbors-only model outperforms an intrinsic classifier (see Table 4), despite not receiving any features of the page itself. Further work is needed to examine this phenomenon.

Stacked Models Outperform Prior Work. There are some challenges in comparing our results to prior work on controversy detection in the SRMRB dataset, chief of which is that our results are reported on a more up-to-date Wikipedia dump (see [12] for comprehensive comparative analysis of controversy classification). Unfortunately, these results were reported only in terms of accuracy (percent correct) with no AUC or other metrics reported. With these constraints in mind, our result of 74.4% accuracy outperforms the Basic method (60%, [13]), the bipolarity method (56%, [1]), and the Mutual Reverts method (67%, [14]) - all results as reported in [12][4]. Our result of 74.4% is slightly lower than the Meta classifier [9] (75%)[5]. Notably, stacked models are ensemble methods and agnostic to the choice of intrinsic classifier for the problem, so any intrinsic classifier can be enhanced by applying our stacked classifier on top of it.

6. CONCLUSIONS AND FUTURE WORK

We present a novel stacked collective inference approach to detecting controversy in Wikipedia. By demonstrating that collective inference improves classification for this problem, we show that controversial articles exist in topical neighborhoods of controversy (i.e. exhibit homophily). Additionaly, we demonstrate that a subnetwork constructed based on similarity can yield better classification results than the default relationship in the dataset or randomly selected neighbors, particularly when a small subset of neighbors is used. This subnetwork approach can be generalized to other problem domains and is an effective way of incorporating similarity in collective and stacked inference. Depending on the degree of nodes and the tradeoffs between the computational cost of calculating pairwise similarity and those of running inference on all the neighbors, using similar neighbors may be preferable to all neighbors; we leave analysis of such tradeoffs to future work. The resulting stacked model improved over models using randomly selected neighbors, as well as over prior work. Future improvements in intrinsic classification of controversy can translate to additional improvements in the stacked model. Future work in collective classification could explore other similarity constructions. Automated detection of controversy holds promise for increased civic participation and a better informed public, by raising awareness and encouraging search users to consider alternative perspectives.

[4]We do not compare to the Editor Collaboration classifier [12], since it has intractable running time complexity (Sepehri Rad, personal communication) and cannot be reliably reproduced.

[5]Our Intrinsic classifier at 69.6% accuracy is the Meta classifier [9] without Talk Page features. While these features may be useful, Talk pages are infrequently used in non-English Wikipedias [14]. Using those features would likely improve the stacked model.

Acknowledgments

This work was supported in part by the Center for Intelligent Information Retrieval and in part by NSF grant number IIS-1217281. Any opinions, findings and conclusions or recommendations expressed in this material are the authors' and do not necessarily reflect those of the sponsor.

The authors thank Hosein Azarbonyad, Laura Dietz, Cibele Freire, Myungha Jang, Sandeep Kalra, Ariel Levavi, Raelen Recto, and Randy West for their comments on various drafts. Special thanks also go to Laura Dietz and Katerina Marazopoulou for fruitful discussions and to Hoda Sepehri Rad and Taha Yasseri for providing valuable resources.

7. REFERENCES

[1] U. Brandes, P. Kenis, J. Lerner, and D. van Raaij. Network analysis of collaboration structure in Wikipedia. *WWW*, 2009.

[2] M. Bröcheler, L. Mihalkova, and L. Getoor. Probabilistic Similarity Logic. *CoRR*, 2012.

[3] S. Chakrabarti, B. Dom, and P. Indyk. Enhanced hypertext categorization using hyperlinks. 1998.

[4] S. Das, A. Lavoie, and M. Magdon-Ismail. Manipulation Among the Arbiters of Collective Intelligence. *CIKM*, 2013.

[5] S. Dori-Hacohen and J. Allan. Detecting controversy on the web. In *CIKM*, 2013.

[6] S. Dori-Hacohen, E. Yom-Tov, and J. Allan. Navigating Controversy as a Complex Search Task. In *Supporting Complex Search Tasks*, 2015.

[7] A. Fast and D. Jensen. Why stacked models perform effective collective classification. In *ICDM*, 2008.

[8] R. Jesus, M. Schwartz, and S. Lehmann. Bipartite networks of Wikipedia's articles and authors - a meso-level approach. *WikiSym*, 2009.

[9] A. Kittur, B. Suh, B. A. Pendleton, E. H. Chi, L. Angeles, and P. Alto. He Says, She Says: Conflict and Coordination in Wikipedia. In *CHI*, 2007.

[10] Z. Kou and W. W. Cohen. Stacked Graphical Models for Efficient Inference in Markov Random Fields. *SDM*, 2007.

[11] E. Pariser. *The Filter Bubble: What the Internet is hiding from you.* Penguin Press HC, 2011.

[12] H. Sepehri Rad and D. Barbosa. Identifying controversial articles in Wikipedia. *WikiSym*, 2012.

[13] B.-q. Vuong, E.-p. Lim, A. Sun, M.-T. Le, H. W. Lauw, and K. Chang. On ranking controversies in Wikipedia: models and evaluation. In *WSDM*, 2008.

[14] T. Yasseri, R. Sumi, A. Rung, A. Kornai, and J. Kertész. Dynamics of conflicts in Wikipedia. *PloS one*, 2012.

Discovering Author Interest Evolution in Topic Modeling

Min Yang
University of Hong Kong
Pokfulam Road, Hong Kong
myang@cs.hku.hk

Jincheng Mei
University of Alberta
Edmonton, AB, Canada
ljmei2@ualberta.ca

Fei Xu*
Chinese Academy of Sciences
Haidian District, Beijing, China
xufei@iie.ac.cn

Wenting Tu
University of Hong Kong
Pokfulam Road, Hong Kong
wttu@cs.hku.hk

Ziyu Lu
University of Hong Kong
Pokfulam Road, Hong Kong
zylu@cs.hku.hk

ABSTRACT

Discovering the author's interest over time from documents has important applications in recommendation systems, authorship identification and opinion extraction. In this paper, we propose an interest drift model (IDM), which monitors the evolution of author interests in time-stamped documents. The model further uses the discovered author interest information to help finding better topics. Unlike traditional topic models, our model is sensitive to the ordering of words, thus it extracts more information from the semantic meaning of the context. The experiment results show that the IDM model learns better topics than state-of-the-art topic models.

1. INTRODUCTION

Author interests play a crucial role in a variety of natural language processing (NLP) application. Motivated by the demand of understanding people's preferences and behavioral pattern, a flurry of researches devote to discovering author interests. The common approach is to build a generative model that represents the author's interests as a latent variable (see Section 2). Most of these models (LDA-style models) make the bag-of-word assumption, which states that the meaning of the document is fully characterized by the unigram statistics of words. The bag-of-word assumption neglects the ordering of words, sentences and paragraphs, though these factors are important in defining the semantics meaning of the context.

We propose a Interest Drift Model (IDM) for modeling the dynamic evolution of individual author's interest. The IDM learns the representation of words, sentences and document as vectors. It also learns the interests of authors as vectors. Since the interests of authors may change over time, each author's interests is represented by a sequence of vectors, where the speed of the interest drifting is controlled by the similarity of consecutive vectors. The IDM model also captures the fact that co-authors usually share common interests, by making their interest vectors positively correlated. The parameters of the model are learnt through a prediction task: given vectors associated with the context, the goal is to predict each word in the document. This scheme has been proven effective in discovering topics from documents [7, 6, 11].

Our model is conceptually related to the work of [11] that incorporates the ordering of words and the semantic meaning of sentences into topic modeling. However, [11] does not consider the authorship and temporal information of the text. In contrast, the goal of this paper is to address the challenges of modeling author interest evolution. Our model has three advantages over the traditional LDA model. First, given the document's authors, the document's topic is determined by the authors' interests, which may change over time. Second, our model provides a natural way to measure the similarity of interest, which helps controlling the speed of interest drift, as well as measuring the similarity between authors. Third, our model takes the ordering of words, sentences and paragraphs into account, so that the topics reflect the semantics of the context.

2. RELATED WORK

The Author-Topic model [8] is the first generative model that simultaneously models the content of documents and the interests of authors. There are also some variants of Author-Topic models such as [5]. These models are devoted to discovering static latent topics and author's interests, without considering temporal information.

To characterize topics and their evolution over time, [2] propose a dynamic topic model (DTM) which jointly models word co-occurrence and time. [9] propose a non-Markov continuous-time model (ToT). These models capture the evolution of topics, but they completely ignore the authorship information.

There are recent works taking both timestamp and authorship information into account, including the Temporal-Author-Topic (TAT) model [4], the Author-topic over time (AToT) model [10]. Nevertheless, these models do not characterize the drift of the individual author's interests.

All of the aforementioned topic models employ the bag-of-words assumption, which is rarely true in practice. [11]

*Fei Xu is the corresponding author.

SIGIR '16, July 17 - 21, 2016, Pisa, Italy

ISBN 978-1-4503-4069-4/16/07...$15.00

DOI: http://dx.doi.org/10.1145/2911451.2914723

propose a generative topic model that represent each topic as a cluster of multi-dimensional vectors. Nevertheless, this model doesn't use temporal information or models the interest of authors.

3. INTEREST DRIFT MODEL

In this section, we describe the IDM model as a generative model. Then we illustrate the inference algorithm for estimating the model parameters.

3.1 Model description

We assume that there are W different words in the vocabulary and there are D documents in corpus. In addition, these documents belong to T topics, where T is a hyper-parameter specified by the user. For a specific document d, suppose that it has m authors a_1,..., a_m. We use an interest vector $\text{vec}(a_i, d) \in \mathbb{R}^p$ to represent the interests of author a_i when he/she writes document d. Two authors have similar interests if the distance between their interest vectors is small. Our goal is to learn these interest vectors from the content of the corpus. It is clear that the interests of co-authors should be correlated. The interests of the same author in writing different documents should consistent.

3.1.1 Author interests

We now specify the generative model for vectors $\text{vec}(a_i, d) \in \mathbb{R}^p$ $(i = 1, \ldots, m)$, conditioning on the interest vectors of all earlier documents. This defines a valid model, since interest vectors can be generated sequentially from the earliest document to the latest document. Let t be the time that document d was written. Let d_i' be the last document that author a_i has written before she writes the current document, and let the timestamps for d_i' be t_i'. We have $t_i' \leq t$ for all $i = 1, ..., m$. We define a joint distribution on the vectors $\text{vec}(a, d) := (\text{vec}(a_1, d), ..., \text{vec}(a_m, d))$. It is a multivariate normal distribution on $\mathbb{R}^{mp}$ taking the form $N(\mu_d, \Sigma_d)$. Firstly, we specify the mean μ_d. Let

$$\mu_d := (\text{vec}(a_1,d_1'), ..., \text{vec}(a_m,d_m')), \quad (1)$$

where $\text{vec}(a_i; d_i')$ is the interest vector for author a_i when she wrote document d_i'. This definition implies that the new interests of authors have connections to the history.

Second, we define the covariance matrix Σ_d. Note that Σ_d is an $mp \times mp$ matrix, so that it can be partitioned into m^2 sub-matrices, each with dimension $p \times p$. Let $\Sigma_{ij} \in \mathbb{R}^{p\times p}$ be the sub-matrix of Σ_d on the i-th row and j-th column. If $i = j$, then the sub-matrix characterize the covariance of the author i's interest. Let

$$\Sigma_{ii} := (\sigma(t - t_i'))^2 I, \quad (2)$$

where $\sigma(x)$ is an increasing function of x. It means that as time passing, the covariance matrix entries get bigger, indicating that the interest of author i is less likely to concentrate on its mean – the interest vector when she wrote the earlier document d'. More concretely, we adapt a linear function $\sigma(x) = \alpha + \beta x$ with hyper-parameters $\alpha > 0$ and $\beta > 0$. The values of α and β are chosen by cross-validation.

If $i \neq j$, then the sub-matrix Σ_{ij} characterizes the correlation between the interest of the author i and the author j. Let

$$\Sigma_{ij} := \rho\sigma(t - t_i')\sigma(t - t_j')I, \quad (3)$$

where $\rho \in [0, 1]$ is another hyper-parameter measuring the correlation of the interest of co-authors. if $\rho = 0$, then $\text{vec}(a_1, d)$,...,$\text{vec}(a_m, d)$ are mutually independent, meaning that there is no correlation between co-authors. If $\rho = 1$, then the drift vectors $\text{vec}(a_i, d) - \text{vec}(a_i, d_i')$ are in the same direction for all co-authors, meaning that the interest drift is perfectly correlated. In summary, the density function of vector $\text{vec}(a, d)$ is defined by

$$p(\text{vec}(a, d) = v) \propto \exp\Big(- \frac{(v - \mu_d)^T \Sigma_d^{-1}(v - \mu_d)}{2}\Big) \quad (4)$$

The vector μ_d and the matrix Σ_d follow the definition above.

3.1.2 Words, sentences and documents

The words, sentences and documents are represented by vectors so that their semantic representations are naturally connected with that of the author interests. For each word $w \in \{1, \ldots, W\}$, there is a p-dimensional vector representation $\text{vec}(w) \in \mathcal{R}^p$. Each document with index $d \in \{1, \ldots, D\}$ has a vector representation $\text{vec}(d) \in \mathcal{R}^p$. There are S sentences in the corpus, each sentence indexed by $s \in \{1, \ldots, S\}$. The sentence with index s is associated with a vector representation $\text{vec}(s) \in \mathcal{R}^p$.

We assume that all these vectors are generated from a multi-variate normal distribution conditioning on the topic. Given the a topic k, the conditional distribution of vectors are defined by $\text{vec}(w) \sim N(\mu_k^{\text{word}}, \Sigma_k^{\text{word}})$, $\text{vec}(s) \sim N(\mu_k^{\text{sen}}, \Sigma_k^{\text{sen}})$ and $\text{vec}(d) \sim N(\mu_k^{\text{doc}}, \Sigma_k^{\text{doc}})$ where μ_k and Σ_k represent the mean and the covariance matrix. We assume that the topic k is chosen with probability π_k such that $\sum_{k=1}^{T} \pi_k = 1$. Thus, the vectors are generated from a Gaussian mixture model with unknown mixture weights and unknown Gaussian parameters. We use Ψ to collectively represent these parameters.

3.1.3 Word tokens

Given the vectors representing author interests, words, sentences and documents, we describe how the word tokens are generated. Let V be the collection of all latent vectors:

$$V := \{\text{vec}(w)\} \cup \{\text{vec}(d)\} \cup \{\text{vec}(s)\} \cup \{\text{vec}(a, d)\} \quad (5)$$

For the i-th word in the sentence, we represent its word realization by w_i, which is generated by

$$p(w_i = w|d, a, s, w_{i-n}, \ldots, w_{i-1}) \propto \exp(a^w_{\text{author}} + a^w_{\text{doc}} + a^w_{\text{sen}} + \sum_{t=1}^{n} a^w_t) \quad (6)$$

where a^w_{author}, a^w_{doc}, a^w_{sen} and a^w_t are linear transformations of the vectors of the author interest, the document, the sentence and the previous n words. These linear transformations are defined by

$$a^w_{\text{author}} = \langle u^w_{\text{author}}, \text{vec}(a, d)\rangle \quad (7)$$

$$a^w_{\text{doc}} = \langle u^w_{\text{doc}}, \text{vec}(d)\rangle \quad (8)$$

$$a^w_{\text{sen}} = \langle u^w_{\text{sen}}, \text{vec}(s)\rangle \quad (9)$$

$$a^w_t = \langle u^w_t, \text{vec}(w_{i-t})\rangle \quad (10)$$

where $u^w_{author}, u^w_{\text{doc}}, u^w_{\text{sen}}, u^w_t \in \mathcal{R}^p$ are transformation coefficient. These coefficients are unknown parameters of the model. They are shared across all word slots in the corpus. We use U to represent this collection of these coefficients.

Finally, we summarize the set of unknown parameters to be learned: the set V containing the vector of author interests, words, sentences and documents, the set U containing the unknown linear transformation coefficients, and the set Ψ containing parameters that defines the Gaussian mixture model. We will see that given arbitrary two of these sets, the remaining set of parameters can be solved by efficient algorithms.

3.2 Topic Inference

Given the model parameters U, Ψ and the vectors V, we can infer the posterior probability distribution of topics. In particular, for a word w with vector representation vec(w), the posterior distribution of its topic, namely $q(z(w))$, is easy to derive given the generative model. For any topic $z \in 1, 2, \ldots, T$, we have

$$q(z(w) = z) = \frac{\pi_z \mathcal{N}(\text{vec}(w)|\mu_z, \Sigma_z)}{\sum_{k=1}^{T} \pi_k \mathcal{N}(\text{vec}(w)|\mu_k, \Sigma_k)}. \quad (11)$$

The topics of sentences, documents and author interest can be inferred in the same way. Similarly, we can use the same formula for inferring the author interest vectors' associated topics, i.e.

$$q(z(a,d) = z) = \frac{\pi_z \mathcal{N}(\text{vec}(a,d)|\mu_z, \Sigma_z)}{\sum_{k=1}^{T} \pi_k \mathcal{N}(\text{vec}(a,d)|\mu_k, \Sigma_k)}. \quad (12)$$

The term $q(z(a,d) = z)$ reflects the ratio of the author a's interests in topic z when she writes document d. In the experiments, we demonstrate that such a scheme yields reasonable representation for the author's interests.

3.3 Estimating model parameters

We estimate the model parameters and latent vectors λ, U and Ψ by maximizing the likelihood of the generative model. The parameter estimation consists of two stages. In Stage I, we maximize the likelihood of the model with respect to λ. Since λ characterizes a Gaussian mixture model, this procedure can be implemented by the Expectation Maximization (EM) algorithm. In Stage II, we maximize the model likelihood with respect to U and Ψ, this procedure can be implemented by stochastic gradient descent. We alternatively execute Stage I and Stage II until the parameters converge.

3.3.1 *Stage I: Estimating λ*

In this stage, the latent vector of words, sentences and documents are fixed. We estimate the parameters of the Gaussian mixture model $\lambda = \{\pi_k, \mu_k, \Sigma_k\}$. This is a classical statistical estimation problem which can be solved by running the EM algorithm. The reader can refer to the book [1] for the implementation details.

3.3.2 *Stage II: estimating U and Ψ*

When λ is known and fixed, we estimate the model parameters U and the latent vectors Ψ by maximizing the log-likelihood of the generative model. In particular, we iteratively sample a location in the corpus, and consider the log-likelihood of the observed word at this location. Let the word realization at location i be represented by w. The log-likelihood of this location is equal to

$$J_i(U,\Psi) = \log(p(\Psi|\lambda)) + a^w_{\text{author}} + a^w_{\text{doc}} + a^w_{\text{sen}} + \sum_{t=1}^{m} a^w_t + b$$
$$- \log\Big(\sum_w \exp(a^w_{\text{author}} + a^w_{\text{doc}} + a^w_{\text{sen}} + \sum_{t=1}^{m} a^w_t + b)\Big),$$

where $\log(p(\Psi|\lambda))$ is the log-prior of parameters Ψ. The quantities a^w_{doc}, a^w_{sen}, a^w_a and a^w_t are defined in equations (7)-(10). Using stochastic gradient descent, we update

$$\text{vec}(w_i) \leftarrow \text{vec}(w_i) + \alpha \frac{\partial J_i(U,\Psi)}{\partial \text{vec}(w_i)} \quad (13)$$

$$u^{w_i}_t \leftarrow u^{w_i}_t + \alpha \frac{\partial J_i(U,\Psi)}{\partial u^{w_i}_t} \quad (14)$$

Data Set	LDA	AT	DTM	GMNTM	AToT	IDM
NIPS	2820	2766	2685	2490	2580	2442
Enron	1208	1134	1095	1049	1066	1016

Table 1: Comparison of test perplexity per word

for the word vector vec(w_i) and the associated weight $u^{w_i}_t$. Similarly, we update vec(s), vec(d), vec(a,d) and u^w_{doc}, u^w_{sen}, u^w_{author} using the same gradient step. Once the gradient update is complete, we randomly sample another location to continue the update. The procedure terminates when there are sufficient number of updates performed, so that both U and Ψ converge to stationary values.

4. EXPERIMENTS

In this section, we test the IDM model on two publicly available datasets. We compare our model with state-of-the-art topic models with both quantitative and qualitative evaluations.

4.1 Datasets

We use the NIPS paper data and the Enron emails data in our experiment. Data preprocessing is executed before training the models. We remove non-alphabet characters, numbers, pronoun, punctuation and stop words from the text. Then, stemming is applied to reduce the vocabulary size and settle the issue of data spareness. The detailed properties of the datasets are described as follow.

NIPS papers (NIPS): This dataset is a collection of papers from the NIPS conference between 1987 and 1999[1]. After data preprocessing, the data set contains 1,740 research papers with 2,037 authors. Each timestamp is determined by the year of the proceedings. Following the preprocessing in [8, 12], the 1,740 papers are further divided into a training set of 1,557 papers and a test set of 183 papers of which 102 are single-authored papers.

Enron emails (Enron): This data was originally published by the FERC during its investigations[2]. We further clean the corpus by removing computer generated files from each user and remove "quoted original messages" in replies. Finally, there are 75,686 messages in our Enron data set. We further divide the data into a training set of 65,686 messages and a test set of 10,000 messages. Each author has at least one document in the training set.

4.2 Baseline methods

In the experiments, the proposed IDM model is compared with several baseline methods, including Latent Dirichlet Allocation (LDA) model[3], Author-Topic (AT) model [8], Dynamic Topic model (DTM) [2], Gaussian Mixture Neural Topic Model (GMNTM) [11] and Author-Topic over Time (AToT) model [10]. We use the same settings for all hyper parameters as in their original papers.

4.3 Implementation details

In our model, the learning rate α is set to 0.05 and gradually reduced to 0.0001. For each word, the previous six words in the same sentence are included in the context. For easy comparison with other models, the word vector size is set to $p = 100$. Increasing the word vector size further

[1] Available at http://www.cs.nyu.edu/~roweis/data.html
[2] http://www.cs.cmu.edu/~enron/

Time	Neural networks
1995	Bengio_Y, Sejnowski_T, LeCun_Y, Giles_C, Ruppin_E
1996	Giles_C, Horn_D, Bengio_Y, LeCun_Y, Giles_C
1997	Bengio_Y, Tresp_V, Niranjan_M, LeCun_Y, Giles_C
1998	LeCun_Y, Spence_C, Niranjan _M, Bengio_Y, Tresp_V
1999	Bengio_Y, Tresp_V, Bengio_S, Doucet_A, LeCun_Y

Table 2: Top 5 most likely authors

Time	M. I. Jordan
1995	Mixtures model, HMM, Probabilistic model
1996	Belief networks, Graphical models, Mixture model
1997	Belief networks, Graphical models, EM
1998	EM, Mixture model, Unsupervised learning
1999	Bayesian learning, Graphical models, Probabilistic model

Table 3: Top 5 most likely topics

improves the quality of the topics. To perform comparable experiments with restricted vocabulary, words outside of the vocabulary is replaced by a special token and doesn't count into the word perplexity calculation.

4.4 Quantitative evaluation

To evaluate the predictive power of the proposed model, we compare test-set perplexity of our model with that of the baselines on both NIPS and Enron data sets. Following the same evaluation as in [8], for the NIPS corpus we calculate the perplexity for the 102 single-authored test document. Whereas, for the Enron corpus, we calculate the perplexity for the 1000 held-out documents that are sampled from the test sets. After running the algorithm that estimates the vector representation of words, sentences, documents and author interests, the averaged test perplexity is defined as

$$\exp\left(-\frac{1}{N_{test}}\sum_{w}\log p(w_d|a_d, D_{train})\right),$$

where N_{test} are the total number of words in the held-out test documents and $p(w_d|a_d, D_{train})$ is the probability assigned to the words w_d in the test document, conditioned on the known authors a_d of the test document and training data D_{train}.

Table 1 shows the results of the perplexity comparison on both data sets, with $T = 100$ topics. The IDM model is clearly better than the other models, as illustrated by its relatively low perplexity score on both data sets. This is because that the IDM model take the authorship information and the timestamps information into consideration. In addition, it also use the ordering of the words.

4.5 Author interest evolution analysis

An interesting feature of our model is the capability of discovering those authors who have drifting interests. This interest-tracking feature is crucial in recommender systems and in assisting investigators finding criminal activities such as insider threats. Due to the limited space, in this experiment, we test our model on the NIPS dataset between 1995-1999. We take Neural Networks topic as an example. For the selected topic, we choose the top 5 most likely authors according to equation (12). The results are illustrated in Table 2. By examining the author's homepage, our results are consistent with the truth. For example, Bengio was interested in neural network over the whole period, while Sejnowski shown great interest in neural network only in the early phase.

We can also extract individual author's interests over time. In this paper, we report M. I. Jordan, who has published a sufficient number of paper on the NIPS conference. We show the top 3 most likely topics of the corresponding author (by equation (12)). The research interest evolution for the selected authors between 1995 and 1999 are reported in Table 3. As shown by Table 3, the most likely topics of the author are varying during the experimental period. For instance, Jordan's research interest is mainly focused on "expert networks" and "dynamical model" in the early years, then it expanded to Reinforcement learning and Graphical models. This can be verified from his homepage.

5. CONCLUSION

In this paper, we have proposed a interest drift model (IDM) for topic modeling. The IDM model achieves significantly lower perplexity compared to the state-of-the-art methods, indicating that our model finds high-quality topics.

6. REFERENCES

[1] C. M. Bishop. *Pattern recognition and machine learning*, volume 1. springer New York, 2006.

[2] D. M. Blei and J. D. Lafferty. Dynamic topic models. In *Proceedings of the 23rd ICML*, pages 113–120. ACM, 2006.

[3] D. M. Blei, A. Y. Ng, and M. I. Jordan. Latent dirichlet allocation. *the Journal of machine Learning research*, 3:993–1022, 2003.

[4] A. Daud. Using time topic modeling for semantics-based dynamic research interest finding. *Knowledge-Based Systems*, 26:154–163, 2012.

[5] N. Kawamae. Author interest topic model. In *Proceedings of the 33rd international ACM SIGIR*, pages 887–888. ACM, 2010.

[6] Q. V. Le and T. Mikolov. Distributed representations of sentences and documents. *arXiv preprint arXiv:1405.4053*, 2014.

[7] T. Mikolov, I. Sutskever, K. Chen, G. S. Corrado, and J. Dean. Distributed representations of words and phrases and their compositionality. In *Advances in Neural Information Processing Systems*, pages 3111–3119, 2013.

[8] M. Rosen-Zvi, T. Griffiths, M. Steyvers, and P. Smyth. The author-topic model for authors and documents. In *Proceedings of the 20th conference on Uncertainty in artificial intelligence*, pages 487–494. AUAI Press, 2004.

[9] X. Wang and A. McCallum. Topics over time: a non-markov continuous-time model of topical trends. In *Proceedings of the 12th ACM SIGKDD*, pages 424–433. ACM, 2006.

[10] S. Xu, Q. Shi, X. Qiao, L. Zhu, H. Jung, S. Lee, and S.-P. Choi. Author-topic over time (atot) a dynamic users interest model. In *Mobile, Ubiquitous, and Intelligent Computing*, pages 239–245. Springer, 2014.

[11] M. Yang, T. Cui, and W. Tu. Ordering-sensitive and semantic-aware topic modeling. In *Proceedings of the 28th AAAI*, 2015.

[12] M. Yang, D. Zhu, and K.-P. Chow. A topic model for building fine-grained domain-specific emotion lexicon. In *ACL (2)*, pages 421–426, 2014.

Distributional Random Oversampling for Imbalanced Text Classification

Alejandro Moreo, Andrea Esuli
Istituto di Scienza e Tecnologie dell'Informazione
Consiglio Nazionale delle Ricerche
56124 Pisa, Italy
E-mail: {firstname.lastname}@isti.cnr.it

Fabrizio Sebastiani
Qatar Computing Research Institute
Hamad bin Khalifa University
Doha, Qatar
E-mail: fsebastiani@qf.org.qa

ABSTRACT

The accuracy of many classification algorithms is known to suffer when the data are imbalanced (i.e., when the distribution of the examples across the classes is severely skewed). Many applications of binary text classification are of this type, with the positive examples of the class of interest far outnumbered by the negative examples. Oversampling (i.e., generating synthetic training examples of the minority class) is an often used strategy to counter this problem. We present a new oversampling method specifically designed for classifying data (such as text) for which the *distributional hypothesis* holds, according to which the meaning of a feature is somehow determined by its distribution in large corpora of data. Our *Distributional Random Oversampling* method generates new random minority-class synthetic documents by exploiting the distributional properties of the terms in the collection. We discuss results we have obtained on the Reuters-21578, OHSUMED-S, and RCV1-v2 datasets.

1. INTRODUCTION

Many applications of binary text classification exhibit severe data *imbalance*, i.e., are characterized by sets of data in which the examples of one class are far outnumbered by the examples of the other. Such cases are especially frequent in information retrieval and related tasks, where the binary distinction to be captured is between a class of interest and "the rest", i.e., between the (typically few) documents relevant to a certain concept (e.g., as expressed by a query) and the (typically many) documents unrelated to it. This phenomenon is exacerbated in applications of multi-label multi-class (MLMC) text classification, i.e., applications where, given a set $\mathcal{C} = \{c_1, ..., c_{|\mathcal{C}|}\}$ of classes, each document may be labelled by several classes at the same time[1]. In these applications the average prevalence (i.e., relative frequency) of a class is low, since $\mathcal{C}$ typically exhibits a power-law behaviour, with few classes having high prevalence and very many classes having low or very low prevalence.

[1]MLMC classification is typically solved by training $|\mathcal{C}|$ independent binary classifiers, one for each class of interest.

SIGIR '16, July 17-21, 2016, Pisa, Italy
© 2016 ACM. ISBN 978-1-4503-4069-4/16/07...$15.00
DOI: http://dx.doi.org/10.1145/2911451.2914722

Severe imbalance is known to degrade the performance of a number of inductive learning algorithms, such as decision trees, neural networks, or support vector machines [8]. The main approaches previously proposed for solving this problem may be grouped into the following classes: [7, 9]: (i) data-level approaches, which perform a random resampling of the dataset in order to rebalance class prevalences (ii) algorithmic approaches, which focus on adapting traditional classification methods to scenarios where data are imbalanced; and (iii) cost-sensitive learning approaches, that combine the data-level and algorithmic approaches by imposing a higher cost on the misclassification of examples from the minority class. We here focus on approaches of type (i), most of which rely on oversampling the minority class (i.e., adding new minority-class training examples, typically duplicates or quasi-duplicates of the existing ones) and/or undersampling the majority class (i.e., removing some majority-class examples from the training set), with the goal of rebalancing the class distribution in the training set.

We propose a novel method based on oversampling the minority class, and specifically designed to deal with types of data (such as text) where the *distributional hypothesis* (according to which the meaning of a feature is somehow determined by its distribution in large corpora of data – see [6]) may be assumed to hold. Our method, dubbed *Distributional Random Oversampling* (DRO), consists of extending the standard vector representation (based on the bag-of-words model) with random latent dimensions based on distributional properties of the observed features. We assign to each document a discrete probabilistic function that operates in a latent space and is queried as many times as desired in order to oversample a given document (i.e., to produce distributionally similar versions of it). Since this generative function is based on the distributional hypothesis, the expectation is that the variability introduced in the newly generated examples reflects semantic properties of the terms that occur in the document being oversampled. We present the results of experiments conducted on popular text classification benchmarks such as Reuters-21578, OHSUMED-S, and RCV1-v2.

Our method is presented in Section 2; Section 3 discusses our empirical results, while Section 4 concludes.

2. THE LATENT SPACE OVERSAMPLING FRAMEWORK

We assume a binary classification context, with classes $\mathcal{C} = \{c, \overline{c}\}$. Let $Tr = \{d_1, \ldots, d_{|Tr|}\}$ be a set of training documents and $F = \{t_1, \ldots, t_{|F|}\}$ its vocabulary. We use $W_{|Tr| \times |F|}$ to denote the document-term matrix, where $w_{ij} \in \mathbb{R}$ is the weight of term t_j in document d_i as computed by a weighting function. By $\vec{d}_i \in \mathbb{R}^{|F|}$ we denote the vectorial representation of document d_i.

We present a general framework for oversampling, that we dub *Latent Space Oversampling* (LSO); our Distributional Random Oversampling method will be a specific instantiation of it. In LSO we oversample minority-class documents by extending the original feature space F with an additional latent space L. Each new synthetic example o_k for a document d_i will be expressed as $\vec{o}_k = [\vec{d}_i; \vec{v}_k] \in \mathbb{R}^{|F|+|L|}$, where $\vec{d}_i \in \mathbb{R}^{|F|}$ is the (fixed) observed part in the original feature space (i.e., a copy of the i-th row of W), and $\vec{v}_k \in \mathbb{R}^{|L|}$ is the variable part in the latent space L, which is generated by some stochastic function.

The vector expansion involves a two-step process for each document d_i, i.e., (i) the estimation of model parameters Θ_i for d_i via a *parameter estimation criterion* $\Psi(W, d_i)$, such that $\Theta_i \leftarrow \Psi(W, d_i)$ is calculated only once for each example d_i; and (ii) the generation of the variable part $\vec{v}_k \leftarrow \mathcal{G}(\Theta_i)$, obtained by means of a *generation function* $\mathcal{G}$. This function is called several times for each minority-class example until the desired level of balance is reached, and exactly once for each majority-class example, since we neither oversample nor undersample majority-class examples. The oversampled matrix is then re-weighted (e.g., in order to bring to bear updated *idf* values, and in order to perform correct length normalization) before training the classifier. Each test document d_t is also expanded to the enlarged vector space before being fed to the classifier; the only difference with the expansion process we carry out for training documents is that any global knowledge involved in the estimation of parameters Θ_t comes from the training data.

Different oversampling strategies could thus be defined by considering different parameter estimation criteria Ψ and different generation functions $\mathcal{G}$. In the following sections we first illustrate one possible such strategy, based on probabilistic topic models (Section 2.1); we then present our DRO method based on the distributional hypothesis (Section 2.2).

2.1 Latent Dirichlet Oversampling

One possible instantiation of the LSO framework is what we will here call *Latent Dirichlet Oversampling* (LDO). LDO relies on *Latent Dirichlet Allocation* (LDA – [1]), a probabilistic topic model that assumes, in order to define the model parameters and the generative function, that each (observed) document in a collection is generated by a mixture of (unobserved) topics. As the weight w_{ij} we here take the raw number of occurrences of term t_j in document d_i.

As the parameter estimation criterion Ψ_{LDO} we may choose any Bayesian inference method (such as Variational Bayes or Gibbs Sampling). The document-specific model parameters are $\Theta_i = [\theta_i; \varphi]$, where θ_i is the topic distribution of d_i and φ is the per-topic word distribution obtained from Tr.

We will choose a generation function $\mathcal{G}_{LDO}$ that returns a vectorial representation of a bag of n words, each of which is drawn by first choosing a topic $z_k \sim \textit{Multinomial}(\theta_i)$, and then choosing a term $t_j \sim \textit{Multinomial}(\varphi_{z_k})$. We set $n = \textit{length}(d_i)$ (i.e., to the total number of word occurrences in d_i) so that the synthetic bag of words will allocate the same number of term occurrences as the original document (thus preserving sparsity in the new space). Note that, in this case, the latent space is mirroring the original feature space, with a dedicated latent dimension for each term in the vocabulary, i.e., $|L| = |F|$. LDO assumes each minority-class document to be governed by similar topic distributions, causing the variable part of oversampled documents to exhibit topically similar patterns.

2.2 Distributional Random Oversampling

We propose *Distributional Random Oversampling* (DRO), a different instantiation of LSO. DRO is based on the hypothesis that related documents (such as, e.g., the minority-class documents) may be expected to contain semantically similar words, and relies on a direct application of the distributional hypothesis, by virtue of which the meaning of feature t_j is embedded in column $\vec{t}_j^T \in \mathbb{R}^{|Tr|}$ of matrix W. Unlike in LDO, we here take weight w_{ij} to be generated by a real-valued weighting function such as, e.g., tfidf or BM25.

As the parameter estimation criterion we take a function Ψ_{DRO} that returns $\Theta_i = (p_1^i, \ldots, p_{|Tr|}^i)$, where p_k^i will be used as parameters of a multinomial distribution for document d_i. Parameter p_k^i is computed as

$$p_k^i = \frac{\sum_{t_j \in d_i} \vec{t}_j^T[k] \cdot w_{ij} \cdot s(t_j)}{\sum_{k=1}^{|Tr|} \sum_{t_j \in d_i} \vec{t}_j^T[k] \cdot w_{ij} \cdot s(t_j)} \quad (1)$$

i.e., by (i) summing together the k-th components $\vec{t}_j^T[k]$ of the (length-normalized) feature vectors $\vec{t}_j^T$ (i.e., the columns of the W matrix) corresponding to all unique terms $t_j \in d_i$, weighted by (a) their relative importance with respect to the document (the w_{ij} component) and by (b) their relative importance with respect to the classification task (the $s(t_j)$ component)[2], and (ii) normalizing to satisfy $\sum_{k=1}^{|Tr|} p_k^i = 1$.

We will choose a generation function $\mathcal{G}_{DRO}$ that returns a vectorial representation of a bag of n (latent) words, each of which is drawn from $l_k \sim \textit{Multinomial}(\Theta_i)$. Note that in this case $|L| = |Tr|$. Similarly to the case of LDO we set $n = \textit{length}(d_i)$, so that sparsity is preserved in the enlarged feature space. In contrast to LDO, the multinomial distribution of DRO is deterministically obtained from the training collection, thus avoiding the need for computationally expensive statistical inference methods.

Each test document is also expanded to the enlarged vector space before being fed to the classifier. In this case note that, in Equation 1, $\vec{t}_j^T$ – which encodes the distributional knowledge – and $s(t_j)$ are the supervised components, i.e., they are obtained from Tr. Instead, w_{ij} is computed partly from the document itself (e.g., the tf component) and partly from the training set (e.g., the *idf* component).

In sum, the rationale of our method is to generate synthetic minority-class vectors where the part corresponding to the latent space is the result of a generative process that brings to bear the distributional properties of the words contained in the document being oversampled.

3. EXPERIMENTS

As the datasets for our experiments we use REUTERS-21578, OHSUMED-S, and RCV1-v2. All these collections are multi-label, i.e., each document may be labelled by zero, one, or

[2]In this paper we compute s as the mutual information between the feature and $\mathcal{C} = \{c, \overline{c}\}$.

several classes at the same time, which gives rise to $|\mathcal{C}|$ binary classification problems, with $\mathcal{C}$ the set of classes in the dataset. For REUTERS-21578[3] we use the standard ("ModApté") split, which identifies 9,603 training documents and 3,299 test documents. We restrict our attention to the 115 classes with at least one positive training example. OHSUMED-S [4] consists instead of 12,358 training and 3,652 test MEDLINE textual records from 1987 to 1991, classified according to 97 MeSH index terms. RCV1-v2[4] comprises 804,414 news stories generated by Reuters from Aug 20, 1996, to Aug 19, 1997. In our experiments we use the entire training set, containing all 23,149 news stories written in Aug 1996; for the test set we pick the 60,074 news stories written during Sep 1996. We restrict our attention to the 101 classes with at least one positive training example.

As the evaluation measures we use microaveraged F_1 (F_1^μ) and macroaveraged F_1 (F_1^M).

We compare the performance of LDO[5] and DRO with the following baselines: (i) *Random Oversampling* (RO), a method that performs oversampling by simply duplicating random minority-class examples; (ii) *Synthetic Minority Oversampling Technique* (SMOTE – [2]), a method that generates new synthetic minority-class examples as convex linear combinations of the document d_i being sampled and a document randomly picked among the k minority-class nearest neighbours of d_i (typically using $k = 5$); (iii) *Borderline-SMOTE* (BSMOTE – [5]), a more recent version of SMOTE that only oversamples those borderline minority-class examples that would be misclassified as negatives by a k-NN classifier; (iv) DECOM [3], a probabilistic topic model that assumes all documents belonging to the same class to follow the same topic distribution that, once determined, is used to oversample minority-class examples following the LDA generation procedure[6]; (v) a bag-of-words model (BoW) where no oversampling is performed. For LDA-based methods we follow the related literature and set the number of topics to 30; in order to favour convergence, i.e., to allow the system to find a stationary point for the distribution parameters Θ that maximize the posterior probability of the corpus, we set the number of iterations to 3,000 and perform 10 passes over the corpus in each iteration.

As the learner of our experiments we adopt linear-kernel SVMs (in the popular SVM-light implementation[7]); in all our experiments we use the default SVM-light parameters. All methods are fed with the same preprocessed version of the datasets where, for each distinct binary decision problem, the top 10% most informative words have been selected, using mutual information as the selection function and tfidf as the weighting function. We perform oversampling of the minority class until a desired prevalence α for the minority-class is reached; we let α range on $\{0.05, 0.10, 0.15, 0.20\}$. We do not consider undersampling in this paper, i.e., all negative examples are picked exactly once. The results we present are all averages across 5 random trials we have run for each setting. For each dataset we partition the classes into (i) *HighPrevalence* (HP), the classes with a prevalence higher than 0.050; (ii) *LowPrevalence* (LP), the classes with a prevalence in the range [0.015, 0.050]; and (iii) *VeryLowPrevalence* (VLP), the classes with a prevalence smaller than 0.015. The reason for partitioning the classes according to prevalence is to allow the results to provide insights as to which classes benefit from oversampling and which do not.

Dataset	Training	Test	Features	Classes	HP	LP	VLP
Reuters-21578	9,603	3,299	23,563	115	3	50	62
Ohsumed-S	12,358	3,652	26,382	97	9	60	28
RCV1-v2	23,149	60,074	37,211	101	16	73	12

Table 1: Details on the 3 datasets used.

	Prev.	α	BoW	RO	SMOTE	BSMOTE	DECOM	LDO	DRO
F_1^M	HP	.05	.907	.907	.907	.907	.907	.907	.907
		.10	.907	.907	.911	.904	**.912**	.909	.897
		.15	.907	.910	**.911**	.902	**.911**	.908	.905
		.20	.907	.909	**.911**	.899	**.911**	**.911**	.899
	LP	.05	.633	.700	.754	.678	.650	.706	**.761**
		.10	.633	.682	.718	.678	.639	.690	**.766**†
		.15	.633	.662	.684	.678	.629	.679	**.759**†
		.20	.633	.648	.654	.678	.629	.664	**.764**†
	VLP	.05	.426	.485	.478	.426	.441	.484	**.568**†
		.10	.426	.456	.416	.426	.418	.482	**.568**†
		.15	.426	.473	.395	.426	.398	.476	**.567**†
		.20	.426	.473	.387	.426	.398	.474	**.570**†
F_1^μ	HP	.05	.954	.954	.954	.954	.954	.954	.954
		.10	**.954**	.952	.953	.952	**.954**	.953	.950
		.15	**.954**	.953	.953	.951	.953	.952	.951
		.20	.954	.953	.953	.950	**.955**	.952	.947
	LP	.05	.767	.788	.809	.782	.773	.790	**.810**
		.10	.767	.778	.784	.783	.762	.786	**.812**†
		.15	.767	.770	.756	.783	.750	.777	**.807**†
		.20	.767	.764	.731	.782	.738	.774	**.805**†
	VLP	.05	.132	.319	.428	.212	.315	.310	**.509**†
		.10	.132	.272	.357	.212	.280	.308	**.515**†
		.15	.132	.269	.302	.212	.250	.289	**.519**†
		.20	.132	.269	.277	.212	.240	.287	**.507**†

Table 2: Results on Reuters-21578.

Table 1 shows some details of the document collections used in the experiments. Tables 2 to 4 report the results of our experiments in terms of F_1^M and F_1^μ, for REUTERS-21578, OHSUMED-S, and RCV1-v2, respectively. Results are reported at different levels α of oversampling; we use boldface to highlight the best performing method, while symbol "†" indicates that the method outperforms all others in a statistically significant sense[8]. Note that, for each block of 4 rows identifying a certain set of classes (HP, LP, VLP), the results for BoW are always the same; this is obvious since there is no oversampling in BoW, which thus does not depend on the value of α. Note also that, in all three tables, the first row of the HP results for $\alpha = 0.05$ always contains identical values, since the HP classes have a prevalence ≥ 0.05.

Overall, the results of these experiments indicate that DRO is superior to the other six methods presented (including LDO). In the low-prevalence groups (LP and VLP) DRO is superior in most cases, across the different datasets and the different degrees α of oversampling, and especially so in terms of F_1^M; when DRO is not superior, the differences in performance with the top-performing method are

[3]Available from http://bit.ly/1F8AFcO

[4]Available from http://1.usa.gov/1mp7RGr

[5]For LDO we used the Gensim implementation of LDA (see http://bit.ly/1Rl7pFV) which also allows estimating the document-topic distribution of test examples.

[6]For this method, as suggested in [3], we used the MATLAB implementation of Gibbs sampling available at http://bit.ly/1Rl7DNl

[7]http://svmlight.joachims.org/

[8]Two-tailed t-test on paired examples at 0.05 confidence level.

	Prev.	α	BoW	RO	SMOTE	BSMOTE	DECOM	LDO	DRO
F_1^M	HP	.05	.753	.753	.753	.753	.753	.753	.753
		.10	.753	**.758**	.756	.754	.755	.757	.752
		.15	.753	.764	**.767**	.763	.760	.765	.753
		.20	.753	.769	**.771**	.767	.763	.769	.756
	LP	.05	.479	.557	**.603**	.571	.538	.569	.588
		.10	.479	.552	.578	.570	.532	.565	**.588**†
		.15	.479	.526	.550	.569	.525	.555	**.578**
		.20	.479	.514	.524	.568	.523	.542	**.576**
	VLP	.05	.354	.385	.455	**.458**	.354	.396	.451
		.10	.354	.372	.433	.448	.352	.378	**.469**
		.15	.354	.363	.440	.448	.330	.373	**.455**
		.20	.354	.364	.427	.448	.314	.376	**.476**
F_1^μ	HP	.05	.801	.801	.801	.801	.801	.801	.801
		.10	.801	**.803**	**.803**	.802	.802	**.803**	.798
		.15	.801	.804	**.806**	.805	.804	.804	.795
		.20	.801	.805	**.807**	.806	.805	.805	.795
	LP	.05	.616	.662	.672	.666	.647	**.668**	.647
		.10	.616	.657	.654	**.669**	.644	.665	.640
		.15	.616	.645	.625	**.666**†	.640	.658	.626
		.20	.616	.642	.595	**.666**†	.633	.652	.620
	VLP	.05	.282	.299	.518	.437	.365	.313	**.552**†
		.10	.282	.241	.484	.416	.328	.262	**.570**†
		.15	.282	.198	.446	.416	.311	.243	**.553**†
		.20	.282	.200	.415	.416	.291	.251	**.553**†

Table 3: Results on OHSUMED-S.

	Prev.	α	BoW	RO	SMOTE	BSMOTE	DECOM	LDO	DRO
F_1^M	HP	.05	.843	.843	.843	.843	.843	.843	.843
		.10	.843	**.848**	**.848**	.846	.845	.847	.839
		.15	.843	**.848**	**.848**	**.848**	.845	.847	.838
		.20	.843	.846	.845	**.848**†	.844	.846	.838
	LP	.05	.489	.600	.616	.573	.577	.613	**.617**
		.10	.489	.602	.603	.582	.587	.619	**.631**†
		.15	.489	.597	.584	.583	.591	.617	**.632**†
		.20	.489	.594	.563	.584	.593	.614	**.629**†
	VLP	.05	.048	.249	.257	.148	.263	.269	**.295**
		.10	.048	.237	.210	.148	.271	.261	**.294**†
		.15	.048	.228	.186	.148	.265	.252	**.297**†
		.20	.048	.220	.172	.148	.267	.245	**.295**†
F_1^μ	HP	.05	.877	.877	.877	.877	.877	.877	.877
		.10	.877	**.878**	**.878**	**.878**	.877	.877	.873
		.15	.877	.877	.877	**.878**	.877	.876	.871
		.20	.877	.876	.875	**.878**	.876	.875	.869
	LP	.05	.638	.676	.674	.666	.663	**.677**	.664
		.10	.638	.685	.672	.678	.673	**.691**†	.683
		.15	.638	.680	.656	.680	.675	**.688**†	.680
		.20	.638	.676	.637	.680	.675	**.683**†	.674
	VLP	.05	.106	.408	.408	.268	.426	.446	**.489**†
		.10	.106	.391	.343	.268	.431	.437	**.489**†
		.15	.106	.379	.303	.268	.429	.424	**.497**†
		.20	.106	.367	.283	.268	.430	.415	**.493**†

Table 4: Results on RCV1-v2.

fairly small. This superiority is more pronounced for the VLP classes, where DRO obtained 23 out of 24 best results, almost always with very large margins. In the HP classes, instead, our results do not reveal any clear winner, since the best results are haphazardly distributed among all of the baselines. Moreover, the best system is not substantially better to BoW in the vast majority of cases, which makes the idea of oversampling such classes questionable.

In sum, the results seem to indicate that the smaller the prevalence of the minority class is, the higher is the gain that can be obtained due to the use of DRO. This is an appealing feature for an oversampling method. We attribute this behaviour to DRO's distributional nature, which enables the information of the entire collection to contribute in the generation of each synthetic example (whereas RO and SMOTE-based methods are limited to local information provided by one or two examples, respectively). This could be advantageous for ill-defined classes (as those belonging to LP and VLP). It may instead introduce noise, or even some redundancy, for well-defined ones (i.e., those in HP); this suggests that the best policy may be that of applying DRO to low- or very-low prevalence classes only, while leaving high-prevalence classes untouched.

4. CONCLUSIONS

We have presented a new oversampling method for imbalanced text classification, based on the idea of assigning a probabilistic generative function to each minority-class document in the training set, a function that can be iteratively queried until the desired level of balance is reached. This probabilistic function is built upon distributional representations of the words contained in the document being oversampled, which allows the model to introduce some random variability in the new examples while preserving the underlying semantic properties motivated by the distributional hypothesis.

5. REFERENCES

[1] David M. Blei, Andrew Y. Ng, and Michael I. Jordan. Latent Dirichlet allocation. *Journal of Machine Learning Research*, 3:993–1022, 2003.

[2] Nitesh V. Chawla, Kevin W. Bowyer, Lawrence O. Hall, and W. Philip Kegelmeyer. SMOTE: Synthetic minority over-sampling technique. *Journal of Artificial Intelligence Research*, 16(1):321–357, 2002.

[3] Enhong Chen, Yanggang Lin, Hui Xiong, Qiming Luo, and Haiping Ma. Exploiting probabilistic topic models to improve text categorization under class imbalance. *Information Processing & Management*, 47(2):202–214, 2011.

[4] Andrea Esuli and Fabrizio Sebastiani. Improving text classification accuracy by training label cleaning. *ACM Transactions on Information Systems*, 31(4):Article 19, 2013.

[5] Hui Han, Wen-Yuan Wang, and Bing-Huan Mao. Borderline-SMOTE: A new over-sampling method in imbalanced data sets learning. In *Proceedings of the 1st International Conference on Intelligent Computing (ICIC 2005)*, pages 878–887, Hefei, CN, 2005.

[6] Zellig S. Harris. Distributional structure. *Word*, 10(23):146–162, 1954.

[7] Haibo He and Edwardo A. Garcia. Learning from imbalanced data. *IEEE Transactions on Knowledge and Data Engineering*, 21(9):1263–1284, 2009.

[8] Nathalie Japkowicz and Shaju Stephen. The class imbalance problem: A systematic study. *Intelligent Data Analysis*, 6(5):429–449, 2002.

[9] Yanmin Sun, Andrew K. Wong, and Mohamed S. Kamel. Classification of imbalanced data: A review. *International Journal of Pattern Recognition and Artificial Intelligence*, 23(4):687–719, 2009.

Doc2Sent2Vec: A Novel Two-Phase Approach for Learning Document Representation

Ganesh J
IIIT, Hyderabad, India
ganesh.j@research.iiit.ac.in

Manish Gupta
Microsoft, India
gmanish@microsoft.com

Vasudeva Varma
IIIT, Hyderabad, India
vv@iiit.ac.in

ABSTRACT

Doc2Sent2Vec is an unsupervised approach to learn low-dimensional feature vector (or embedding) for a document. This embedding captures the semantics of the document and can be fed as input to machine learning algorithms to solve a myriad number of applications in the field of data mining and information retrieval. Some of these applications include document classification, retrieval, and ranking.

The proposed approach is two-phased. In the first phase, the model learns a vector for each sentence in the document using a standard word-level language model. In the next phase, it learns the document representation from the sentence sequence using a novel sentence-level language model. Intuitively, the first phase captures the word-level coherence to learn sentence embeddings, while the second phase captures the sentence-level coherence to learn document embeddings. Compared to the state-of-the-art models that learn document vectors directly from the word sequences, we hypothesize that the proposed decoupled strategy of learning sentence embeddings followed by document embeddings helps the model learn accurate and rich document representations.

We evaluate the learned document embeddings by considering two classification tasks: scientific article classification and Wikipedia page classification. Our model outperforms the current state-of-the-art models in the scientific article classification task by ~12.07% and the Wikipedia page classification task by ~6.93%, both in terms of F_1 score. These results highlight the superior quality of document embeddings learned by the Doc2Sent2Vec approach.

1. INTRODUCION

Document representations plays a vital role in the performance of several downstream IR applications such as document classification (or tagging), retrieval, ranking and so on. The most commonly used document representation is bag-of-words (BOW) or bag-of-n-grams [1]. Despite its simplicity and efficiency, it fails to capture the semantics of the documents as it suffers from data sparsity and curse of high dimensionality. Latent Dirichlet Allocation (LDA) [2] is another widely adopted distributed document representation.

In an attempt to harness the power of neural networks for document representations, Le et al. [3] propose a simple approach to learn document embedding from the word sequence using a standard word-level language model. The representations learned capture the ordering of words (unlike BOW) and also the semantics of the words in an efficient way (unlike LDA). In their follow-up work [4], the authors proposed an incremental model by jointly learning the word embeddings along with its document embedding. This change leads to learning rich and accurate representation compared to the previous model, which freezes the word vectors while learning the document vectors.

Inspired by the superior results obtained by the neural language models, we present a two-phase approach, Doc2Sent2Vec, to learn document embedding. In the first phase, we learn the sentence embedding using the word sequence generated from the sentence. Intuitively, the sentence representation is computed by modeling word-level coherence. In the next phase, we propose a novel model that learns the document representation from the sentence sequence generated from the document. Intuitively, the document embedding is computed by modeling sentence-level coherence. We argue in this work that the proposed decoupled strategy allows our model to compute accurate and rich document representations.

We validate the learned document embeddings using two classification tasks. In the first task, we aim at classifying a research article (or paper) among one of the eight different fields of computer science domain. In the second task, we predict the tag of a Wikipedia page. Doc2Sent2Vec outperforms the existing state-of-the-art model in scientific article classification task by ~12.07% and Wikipedia page classification task by ~6.93%, both in terms of F_1 score.

Our main contributions are summarized below.

- We present a novel two-phase approach, Doc2Sent2Vec, to learn document embeddings. To this end, we introduce a novel sentence-level language model which effectively constructs document representations by explicitly modeling sentence-level coherence.
- Experiments on Citation Network and Wikipedia datasets show that Doc2Sent2Vec learns high quality document embeddings outperforming the competitive baselines in both the classification tasks.

SIGIR '16, July 17-21, 2016, Pisa, Italy

DOI: http://dx.doi.org/10.1145/2911451.2914717

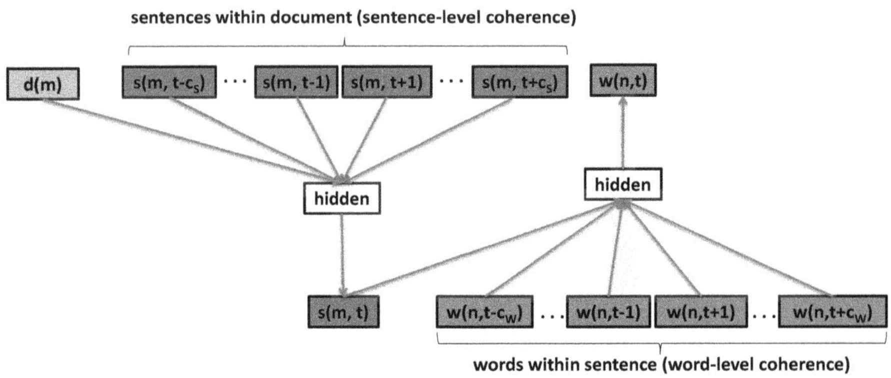

Figure 1: Architecture diagram of the Doc2Sent2Vec approach. Sentence embedding weights are shared between the two tiers.

2. THE DOC2SENT2VEC APPROACH

Our hierarchical framework as shown in Figure 1 consists of two tiers; one learning the sentence representation from the word context, another learning the document representation from the sentence context.

Problem Formulation: Formally, let us denote a set D of M documents, $D = \{d_1, d_2, \cdots, d_M\}$, where each document d_m is a sequence of T_m sentences, $d_m = \{s_{(m,1)}, s_{(m,2)}, \cdots, s_{(m,T_m)}\}$. Each sentence is a sequence of T_n words, $s_{(m,n)} = \{w_{(m,n,1)}, w_{(m,n,2)}, \cdots, w_{(m,n,T_n)}\}$. For brevity, we drop the sentence index m when it is obvious in the context. The goal of the Doc2Sent2Vec approach is to jointly learn low-dimensional representations of words, sentences and documents as a continuous feature vector of dimensionality D_w, D_s and D_d respectively. We will realize this goal in two phases, as discussed in the following.

Modeling word-level coherence: In the first phase, the model aims to learn sentence representation from the word sequence within the sentence. We add the sentence vector to the standard language model that predicts the next word given its context word. This sentence vector must capture the topics of the sentence in a compact form. Each word is mapped to a unique vector, denoted by a column in the matrix V_{word}, whose size is given by $D_w \times |V_w|$ (where $|V_w|$ is the vocabulary size). Similarly, each sentence in a document is mapped to a unique vector denoted by a column in the matrix V_{sent} with size $D_s \times |V_s|$, where $|V_s|$ is the number of unique sentences. The model uses the concatenation of word vectors of context words along with the sentence vector as features to predict the given word in a sentence.

Formally, consider $w_{(n,t-c_w)}, \cdots, w_{(n,t-1)}, w_{(n,t+1)}, \cdots, w_{(n,t+c_w)}$ as the context words for the target word $w_{(n,t)}$, appearing in the sentence $s_{(m,n)}$. The objective of the word-level language model is to maximize the log likelihood probability.

$$\mathcal{L}_{word} = \sum_{d_m \in D} [\sum_{s_{(m,n)} \in d_m} \log \mathbb{P}(s_{(m,n)} | w_{(n,1)}, \cdots, w_{(n,T_n)}) + \sum_{s_{(m,n)} \in d_m} \sum_{w_{(n,t)} \in s_{(m,n)}} \log \mathbb{P}(w_{(n,t)} | w_{(n,t-c_w)}, \cdots, w_{(n,t-1)}, w_{(n,t+1)}, \cdots, w_{(n,t+c_w)}, s_{(m,n)})] \quad (1)$$

Here $2 \times c_w$ denotes the length of the context for the word sequence. The probability of observing the central word $w_{(n,t)}$ given the context words and the sentence is defined using the following softmax function.

$$\mathbb{P}(w_{(n,t)} | w_{(n,t-c_w)}, \cdots, w_{(n,t-1)}, w_{(n,t+1)}, \cdots, w_{(n,t+c_w)}, s_{(m,n)}) = \frac{exp\left(\bar{\mathbf{v}}^{1T}_{word} \mathbf{v}'_{w_{(n,t)}}\right)}{\sum_{w=1}^{|V_w|} exp\left(\bar{\mathbf{v}}^{1T}_{word} \mathbf{v}'_{w}\right)} \quad (2)$$

where $\mathbf{v}'_{w_{(n,t)}}$ is the output representation of $w_{(n,t)}$ and $\bar{\mathbf{v}}^1_{word}$ is the concatenation of the input embeddings (ignoring the central term $w_{(n,t)}$), with dimensionality $2 \times c_w \times D_w + D_s$.

$$\bar{\mathbf{v}}^1_{word} = [\mathbf{v}_{s_{(m,n)}}; \mathbf{v}_{w_{(n,t-c_w)}}; \cdots; \mathbf{v}_{w_{(n,t-1)}}; \mathbf{v}_{w_{(n,t+1)}}; \cdots; \mathbf{v}_{w_{(n,t+c_w)}};] \quad (3)$$

Similarly, we define the probability of observing the sentence $s_{(m,n)}$, given the words present in it as follows.

$$\mathbb{P}(s_{(m,n)} | w_{(n,1)}, \cdots, w_{(n,T_n)}) = \frac{exp(\bar{\mathbf{v}}^{2T}_{word} \mathbf{v}'_{s_{(m,n)}})}{\sum_{s=1}^{|V_s|} exp(\bar{\mathbf{v}}^{2T}_{word} \mathbf{v}'_s)} \quad (4)$$

where $\mathbf{v}'_{s_{(m,n)}}$ is the output representation of $s_{m,n}$ and $\bar{\mathbf{v}}^2_{word}$ is the concatenation of the input embedding of all the words present in the sentence $s_{m,n}$, with dimensionality $T_n \times D_w$.

$$\bar{\mathbf{v}}^2_{word} = [\mathbf{v}_{w_{(n,1)}}; \cdots; \mathbf{v}_{w_{(n,T_n)}};] \quad (5)$$

Modeling sentence-level coherence: In the next phase, we propose a novel language model which constructs the document representations from the sentence sequence present in the document. The novel task is to predict the current sentence using the embeddings of the surrounding sentences and the document embedding as features. We add the document vector in the input layer of this model, that captures the topics of the entire document in a compact form. Each document is mapped to a unique vector denoted by a column in the matrix V_{doc}, whose size is given by $D_d \times |V_d|$ (where $|V_d|$ is the number of unique documents).

Formally, consider $s_{(m,t-c_s)}, \cdots, s_{(m,t-1)}, s_{(m,t+1)}, \cdots, s_{(m,t+c_s)}$ as the context sentences for the target sentence $s_{(m,t)}$, appearing in the document d_m. The objective of our novel sentence-level language model is to maximize the following log likelihood probability.

Dataset	# Docs	Labels
CND	8000	information retrieval, data mining, artificial intelligence, machine learning and pattern recognition, natural language and speech, computer vision, distributed and parallel computing, human-computer interaction
Wiki10+	19740	wiki, art, reference, people, culture, books, design, politics, technology, psychology, interesting, wikipedia, research, religion, music, math, development, theory, philosophy, article, language, science, programming, history, software

Table 1: Dataset Details

$$\mathcal{L}_{sent} = \sum_{d_m \in D} [\log \mathbb{P}(d_m | s_{(m,1)}, \cdots, s_{(m,T_m)}) + \sum_{s_{(m,t)} \in d_m} \log \mathbb{P}(s_{(m,t)} | s_{(m,t-c_s)}, \cdots, s_{(m,t-1)}, s_{(m,t+1)}, \cdots, s_{(m,t+c_s)}, d_m)] \quad (6)$$

Here $2 \times c_s$ denotes the length of the context for the sentence sequence. The probability of observing the central sentence $s_{(m,t)}$ given the context sentences and the document is defined using the softmax function as given below.

$$\mathbb{P}(s_{(m,t)} | s_{(m,t-c_s)}, \cdots, s_{(m,t-1)}, s_{(m,t+1)}, \cdots, s_{(m,t+c_s)}, d_m) = \frac{exp(\bar{\mathbf{v}}_{sent}^{1T} \mathbf{v}'_{s_{(m,t)}})}{\sum_{s=1}^{|V_s|} exp(\bar{\mathbf{v}}_{sent}^{T} \mathbf{v}'_s)} \quad (7)$$

where $\mathbf{v}'_{s_{(m,t)}}$ is the output representation of $s_{(m,t)}$ and $\bar{\mathbf{v}}_{sent}^1$ is the concatenation of the input embeddings (ignoring the central term $s_{(m,t)}$), with dimensionality $2 \times c_s \times D_s + D_d$.

$$\bar{\mathbf{v}}_{sent}^1 = [\mathbf{v}_{d_m}; \mathbf{v}_{s_{(m,t-c_s)}}; \cdots; \mathbf{v}_{s_{(m,t-1)}}; \mathbf{v}_{s_{(m,t+1)}}; \cdots; \mathbf{v}_{s_{(m,t+c_s)}};] \quad (8)$$

Similarly, we define the probability of observing the document d_m given the sentences present in it as follows.

$$\mathbb{P}(d_m | s_{(m,1)}, \cdots, s_{(m,T_m)}) = \frac{exp(\bar{\mathbf{v}}_{sent}^{2T} \mathbf{v}'_{d_m})}{\sum_{d=1}^{|V_d|} exp(\bar{\mathbf{v}}_{sent}^{2T} \mathbf{v}'_d)} \quad (9)$$

where $\mathbf{v}'_{d_m}$ is the output representation of d_m and $\bar{\mathbf{v}}_{sent}^2$ is the concatenation of the input embedding of all the sentences present in the document d_m, with dimensionality $T_m \times D_s$.

$$\bar{\mathbf{v}}_{sent}^2 = [\mathbf{v}_{s_{(m,1)}}; \cdots; \mathbf{v}_{s_{(m,T_m)}};] \quad (10)$$

Training details: The overall objective function of Doc2Sent2Vec is to maximize the log likelihood probability as follows.

$$\mathcal{L} = \mathcal{L}_{word} + \mathcal{L}_{sent} \quad (11)$$

We employ stochastic gradient descent to learn the parameters, where the gradients are obtained via backpropagation [12], with fixed learning rate of 0.1. However, it takes $O(V_w)$, $O(V_s)$, $O(V_s)$ and $O(V_d)$ to compute $\nabla \log \mathbb{P}$ from Equations 2, 4, 7 and 9, which is undesirable in practice. Hence, we use hierarchical softmax [6], to facilitate faster training. The testing phase was excluded as the embeddings for all the documents in the dataset are estimated during the training phase.

3. EXPERIMENTS

In this section, we present the experimental results to show the effectiveness of the learned document embeddings by considering two classification tasks.

Model	F_1
Paragraph2Vec w/o WT [3]	0.1275
Paragraph2Vec [4]	0.135
Doc2Sent2Vec w/o WT	0.1288
Doc2Sent2Vec	**0.1513**

Table 2: Classification Performance on CND Dataset

Dataset Description: The dataset details are displayed in Table 1. Citation Network Dataset (CND) [5] consists of a collection of research papers (along with abstracts) from different fields of computer science domain. Inspired by the recent work [13], we use only a sample of the original dataset to speed up the training process. We construct a dataset of 8000 papers by randomly sampling 1000 research papers from 8 different fields, as mentioned in Table 1. In the second task where we perform Wikipedia page classification, we make use of Wiki10+ dataset [14], which contains one or more social tags (along with the number of users who have annotated this tag) for each Wikipedia page retrieved from delicious.com. We find the most frequent 25 social tags and only keep those documents that contain any of these tags. It results in a collection of 19740 documents as shown in Table 1, with each document associated with the most voted social tag. For simplicity, we consider only the first paragraph of the Wikipedia article for learning the embeddings.
Experimental Setup: In all our experiments, we consider the following four models.

- Paragraph2Vec w/o WT [3]: Paragraph2Vec algorithm without **W**ord **T**raining (i.e. the word embedding matrix V_w is freezed during training).
- Paragraph2Vec [4]: Extension of [3] which allows joint training of both word and document vectors.
- Doc2Sent2Vec w/o WT: Model discussed in Section 2 without word training.
- Doc2Sent2Vec: Model discussed in Section 2.

To ensure fair comparison, we empirically set C_w, C_s, D_w, D_s, D_d to 5, 1, 100, 100, 100 respectively, for all the models. We lowercase all the words, remove those which occur less than 10 (15) times in the CND (Wiki10+) corpus. We use pre-trained Glove [11] word vectors trained successively on Wikipedia 2014[1] and Gigaword 5[2] corpus, to initialize the word embeddings (V_w). It is important to notice that we use a linear classifier (one-vs-rest logistic regression[3]) to do prediction. It can be argued that the model performance can be improved using non-linear models, but this falls out of scope of our goal. We use 5-fold cross-validation to report the model performance for both the tasks.

[1]http://dumps.wikimedia.org/enwiki/20140102/
[2]https://catalog.ldc.upenn.edu/LDC2011T07
[3]http://scikit-learn.org/stable/modules/generated/sklearn.linear_model.LogisticRegression.html

Model	F_1
Paragraph2Vec w/o WT [3]	0.0476
Paragraph2Vec [4]	0.0445
Doc2Sent2Vec w/o WT	0.0401
Doc2Sent2Vec	**0.0509**

Table 3: Classification Performance on Wiki10+ Dataset

Analysis on CND: Scientific article classification results are shown in Table 2. We observe that it is beneficial to learn word vectors too while training instead of merely using pre-initialised word vectors. On incorporating the learning of word vectors, the improvement of ~5.88% and ~17.47% in F_1 score for Paragraph2Vec and Doc2Sent2Vec respectively, justifies this claim. Moreover, we see that our model outperforms the state-of-the-art model by a significant margin of ~12.07%. This is mainly because our model is able to exploit both word-level and sentence-level coherence to enrich the embeddings.

Analysis on Wiki10+: We present the Wikipedia page classification results in Table 3. It is interesting to see that learning the word vectors has a negative impact for Paragraph2Vec algorithm. This is shown by a decline in the F_1 score by ~6.5%. We believe that the word vectors before training are semantically accurate as they are learned from the complete Wikipedia corpus. While training them again, the vectors tend to get distorted leading to poor results. It can be argued that the same trend should follow for our model when we learn the word vectors. However, the Doc2Sent2Vec results indicate that the F_1 improves by ~26.93% on learning word vectors. This illustrates that the proposed strategy of jointly exploiting sentence level and word level coherence is insensitive to the distortions generated by word vectors, resulting in robust embeddings of the Wikipedia pages. The performance improvement of ~6.93% over the best baselines in terms of F_1 score, highlights the superiority of the Doc2Sent2Vec approach.

4. RELATED WORK

Our work is inspired by the outburst of representation learning works using neural networks [6, 8, 9] to solve many natural language processing tasks. In this work, we focus on the important problem of capturing the semantics of the document in a machine-understandable format (or representation).

A recent work Paragraph2Vec [3] provides a simple solution to this problem by extending the popular algorithm 'Word2Vec' [6]. Their strategy of adding a memory vector to the input layer of the neural network exhibits significantly better results than commonly used representations such as LDA, BOW and so on. In the original work the authors freeze the word vectors, while in the extension [4] they let the gradients update the word vectors too, along with document vectors. This trick further improves the results in understanding longer documents such as research articles and Wikipedia pages. Our work is inspired by the superior results of these neural language models.

Similar to the spirit of Doc2Sent2Vec, Djuric et al. [7] propose a Hierarchical Document Vector (HDV) model to learn representations from a document stream. In the first phase, the model learns document representation from the word sequence (similar to [3]). In the next phase, the model enriches the representations further by exploiting the document sequence in the stream. The Doc2Sent2Vec approach is different from HDV because our model does not assume the existence of a document stream and HDV does not model sentences.

5. CONCLUSION

We proposed a novel two-phase approach Doc2Sent2Vec to learn document representations in an unsupervised fashion. To this end, we introduced a novel sentence-level language model which exploits the sentence sequence present in the document. We validated the document embeddings by considering two classification tasks. Our classification results indicate the superiority of the proposed approach, thereby constituting a step towards learning accurate and rich document representations.

In the future, we plan to extend the current approach to a general multi-phase approach where every phase corresponds to a logical sub-division of a document like words, sentences, paragraphs, subsections, sections and documents. Also, it will be interesting to investigate how the document embeddings that are learned through the Doc2Sent2Vec approach can be enhanced by considering the document sequence in a stream such as news click-through streams [7].

Acknowledgement

This work is supported by SIGIR Donald B. Crouch Travel Grant. The authors would like to thank NVIDIA for donating one Tesla K40 GPU card.

6. REFERENCES

[1] Harris, Z.: Distributional structure. Word, 10(23). (1954) 146–162
[2] Blei, D., Ng, A.Y., Jordan, M.I.: Latent Dirichlet Allocation. In: JMLR. (2013)
[3] Le, Q., Mikolov, T.: Distributed Representations of Sentences and Documents. In: ICML. (2014) 1188–1196
[4] Dai, A.M., Olah, C., Le, Q.V., Corrado, G.S.: Document embedding with paragraph vectors. In: NIPS Deep Learning Workshop. (2014)
[5] Chakraborty, T., Sikdar, S., Tammana, V., Ganguly, N., Mukherjee, A.: Computer Science Fields as Ground-truth Communities: Their Impact, Rise and Fall. In: ASONAM. (2013) 426–433
[6] Mikolov, T., Chen, K., Corrado, G., Dean, J.: Efficient Estimation of Word Representations in Vector Space. In: ICLR Workshop. (2013) vol. abs/1301.3781
[7] Djuric, N., Wu, H., Radosavljevic, V., Grbovic, M., Bhamidipati, N.: Hierarchical Neural Language Models for Joint Representation of Streaming Documents and their Content. In: WWW. (2015) 248–255
[8] Bengio, Y., Ducharme, R., Vincent, P., Jauvin, C.: A Neural Probabilistic Language Model. In: JMLR. (2003) 1137–1155
[9] Collobert, R., Weston, J., Bottou, L., Karlen, M., Kavukcuoglu, K., Kuksa, P.: Natural Language Processing (Almost) from Scratch. In: JMLR. (2011) 2493–2537
[10] Morin, F., Bengio, Y.: Hierarchical Probabilistic Neural Network Language Model. In: AISTATS. (2005) 246–252
[11] Pennington, J., Socher, R., Manning, C.D.: GloVe: Global Vectors for Word Representation. In: EMNLP. (2014) 1532–1543
[12] Rumelhart, D., Hinton, G., Williams, R.: Learning Representations by Back-propagating Errors. In: Nature. (1986) 533–536
[13] Dos Santos, C.N., Gatti, M.: Deep convolutional neural networks for sentiment analysis of short texts. In: COLING. (2014) 69–78
[14] Zubiaga, A.: Enhancing navigation on wikipedia with social tags. In: arxiv. (2012) vol. abs/1202.5469

Dynamically Integrating Item Exposure with Rating Prediction in Collaborative Filtering

Ting-Yi Shih, Ting-Chang Hou, Jian-De Jiang, Yen-Chieh Lien, Chia-Rui Lin, and Pu-Jen Cheng

Department of Computer Science and Information Engineering
National Taiwan University, Taiwan

{r02922038, r03922041, r03922057, r03922056, r03944009, pjcheng}@csie.ntu.edu.tw

ABSTRACT

The paper proposes a novel approach to appropriately promote those items with few ratings in collaborative filtering. Different from previous works, we force the items with few ratings to be promoted to the users who would potentially be able to give ratings, and then leverage the gathered user preference to punish the promoted items with low quality intrinsically. By slightly sacrificing the benefit of recommending the best items in terms of user satisfaction, our approach seeks to provide all of the items with a chance to be visible equally. The results of the experiments conducted on MovieLens and Netflix data demonstrate its feasibility.

CCS Concepts

•**Information systems** → **Recommender systems;**

Keywords

Item Exposure; Novelty; Collaborative Filtering

1. INTRODUCTION

Collaborative Filtering (CF) is a well-known technique to predict user preference by identifying similar preferences shared by collaborating users (user-based CF) or similar items of interest to the same users (item-based CF). As only popular items are able to collect sufficient rating data and then be recommended more frequently, CF-based solutions often face the problem of *monopoly*: popular items will become more popular while unknown items (those coming with few ratings) will have less and less chance to get noticed.

Numerous studies on CF have investigated the effect of item popularity on user preference [7]. Oh et al. [4] found the phenomenon of personal popularity tendency. Their solution tended not to promote popular items to those who preferred relatively obscure items. Liu et al. [3] showed that pushing new items to inactive users could statistically increase the chance of new items to be recommended. Some studies concerned about items with less training data and attempted to save such items. In [8, 9], Steck managed to fix recommendation biases against unpopular items, where items with less training ratings were treated as a result of non-randomly missing data. Park et al. [5] clustered unknown items and recommended them based on their clusters. There have also been studies trying to solve the cold-start problem by considering additional content-based features [6] and latent aspects [1].

Although various methods have been developed to recommend unknown items, less investigations paid attention to the integration of item exposure with user preference as a critical determinant of recommendation and balanced the trade-off between them in CF. Here *item exposure* is defined as the number of ratings an item gets. Unknown items are the items with low exposure. More exposure does not always lead to higher popularity. But more exposure does help us to determine the true quality of unknown items. It motivates us to investigate the possibility of forcing unknown items in the user's recommended pool in the beginning as a fair treatment. If the promoted unknown item is potentially good enough, it will become popular soon. Our risk is to promote the unknown items that have low quality intrinsically. In this case, the users would rate them low and prevent them from popularity. Promoting bad unknown items can then be balanced by leveraging user preference.

The goal of this paper is to appropriately promote unknown items by carefully integrating item exposure with user preference in CF. To put user preference and item exposure together, we define *Recommendation Value* (RV) to be how much a system would like to recommend an item to a user. A novel approach is proposed. First, the RVs are moved towards user preference (similar to conventional CF). Secondly, the RVs are appropriately elevated for unknown items, where two main challenges will be encountered: (1) how to balance the trade-off between recommending preferable items and unknown items, and (2) how to determine to which users to promote a given unknown item (not all of the users would agree to provide ratings for any items requested by the system). The approach is designed to promote an unknown item to appropriate users until it gets sufficient reliable ratings. We have conducted the experiments on MovieLens and Netflix data. The result demonstrates that the proposed approach outperforms state-of-the-art CF solutions in maximizing the exposure-stratified recall.

SIGIR '16, July 17-21, 2016, Pisa, Italy

DOI: http://dx.doi.org/10.1145/2911451.2914769

2. THE PROPOSED APPROACH

The task of a recommendation system is to provide a user with a ranking list of items. Given a set of users $U = \{u_1, u_2, ..., u_{|U|}\}$ and items $I = \{i_1, i_2, ..., i_{|I|}\}$, an *observed* rating of user u for item i, denoted $r_{u,i}^{obs}$, is an actual rating collected from training data. Unrated user-item pairs are called *unobserved.* For each of the unobserved user-item pairs, the system generates a RV, denoted $RV(u,i) \in [0,1]$, to indicate how much the system would like to recommend item i to user u. For each user u, the system sorts the RVs of all items unobserved by u, denoted $I_u^* \subseteq I$, and recommends the top-k highest RVs, denoted $I_u^{*,k} \subseteq I_u^*$.

The RV of an unobserved user-item pair is defined as:

$$RV(u,i) = P_p(i|u) + \alpha(i)P_r(i|u)\Big(1 - P_p(i|u)\Big), \quad (1)$$

where $P_p(i|u)$ is **preference probability** indicating the probability that user u prefers item i. $P_r(i|u)$ is **rating probability** indicating the probability that user u would rate item i. $\alpha(i)$ is the coefficient indicating the condition of being unknown. It varies from 0 to 1. A larger $\alpha(i)$ value means the lower exposure for item i. That is, $\alpha(i) = 1$ if item i is totally unknown. Initially, the RV moves towards user preference $P_p(i|u)$, i.e., the first term. For unknown items, the RV is appropriately elevated. The remainder $1 - P_p(i|u)$ is added according to how likely user u will provide a rating for item i, i.e., $P_r(i|u)$. In other words, the RV is augmented only when the unknown item (big $\alpha(i)$) has a low predicted preference (small $P_p(i|u)$) and user u has more chance to rate item i (high $P_r(i|u)$). If it is not the case, the second term approaches to 0.

$P_p(i|u)$ is computed based on user preference as follows:

$$P_p(i|u) = \frac{(r_{u,i})^\gamma}{\sum_{i'} (r_{u,i'})^\gamma}, \quad (2)$$

where we learn to predict user preference with Matrix Factorization (MF). $r_{u,i}$ for unobserved (u,i) is computed as the dot product of corresponding user and item vectors. $\gamma \in \mathbb{R}$ is the exponent that controls the discrimination between high and low ratings. For $\gamma > 1$, the distance between high and low ratings is strengthened. By this transformation, the preference probability is restricted to the range $[0,1]$. The MF-based method proposed in [2] only uses the observed data for predicting the preference probability (called MF-preference). Except the MF, we also consider AllRank (AR) [8], which uses the observed data and models the unobserved data, to predict the preference probability (called AF-preference) as an alternative.

To calculate $P_r(i|u)$, we extend the probability model presented in [1]. The probability of user u to rate item i can be factorized as:

$$P(u,i) = \sum_z P(z)P(u|z)P(i|z), \quad (3)$$

where z is the random variable for a latent topic or aspect. The parameters are learned by the EM algorithm as follows.

E-step:

$$P(z|u,i) = \frac{P(z)P(u|z)P(i|z)}{\sum_z P(z)P(u|z)P(i|z)}. \quad (4)$$

M-step:

$$P(u|z) = \frac{\sum_i P(z|u,i)\mathbf{1}(u,i)}{\sum_{u'} \sum_i P(z|u',i)\mathbf{1}(u',i)}, \quad (5)$$

$$P(i|z) = \frac{\sum_u P(z|u,i)\mathbf{1}(u,i)}{\sum_{i'} \sum_u P(z|u,i')\mathbf{1}(u,i')}, \quad (6)$$

$$P(z) = \frac{\sum_u \sum_i P(z|u,i)\mathbf{1}(u,i)}{\sum_z \sum_u \sum_i P(z|u,i)\mathbf{1}(u,i)}, \quad (7)$$

where $\mathbf{1}(.)$ is the indicator function outputting 1 if user u rates item i and 0 otherwise. To this end, given user u, the rating probability $P_r(i|u)$ for item i is computed as:

$$P_r(i|u) = \frac{P(u,i)}{\sum_{i'} P(u,i')}. \quad (8)$$

There is an explicit drawback due to the nature of EM. The EM process learns the probability from the observed data so that the probability of unknown items would be underestimated owing to the lack of observed ratings. To solve this issue, we assign a prior to each item when updating $P(i|z)$ in Eq.(6) as follows:

$$P(i|z) = \frac{\sum_u P(z|u,i)s(u,i)}{\sum_{i'} \sum_u P(z|u,i')s(u,i')}, \quad (9)$$

where $s(.)$ is a *weighted* indicator function and defined as:

$$s(u,i) = \begin{cases} (\frac{1}{N_i^{obs}})^{\beta_s} & \text{, if } u \text{ rates } i \\ 0 & \text{, otherwise,} \end{cases} \quad (10)$$

where N_i^{obs} denotes the number of users rating item i in the training data. β_s determines the discriminative power of the weight ($\beta_s = 0$ leads to identical weight of each rated item).

Alternatively, there are also other choices able to form the rating probability such as the preference probabilities obtained from Eq.(2) using MF-preference and AR-preference. The underlying assumption is that a user tends to rate her preferable items. All the choices will be evaluated in the experiments.

In some sense, given an unknown item whose rating probability is equal to the preference probability for a well-known item, the unknown item generally has higher priority to be recommended. The details of the proof are omitted here.

To identify whether an item is unknown, we define **exposure** as the number of users rating this item. In this paper, function $\alpha(i)$ is simply estimated by a sigmoid function as follows:

$$\alpha(i) = Sigmoid(N_{unk} - N_i^{obs}), \quad (11)$$

where N_{unk} is the exposure threshold of unknownness.

To avoid that the recommended pool is full of unknown items, we limit the number of unknown items for each user to a predefined value. Overall, as an unknown item i comes in, no matter how the predicted preference for item i is, the preference predicted based on unreliable, few ratings of item i is regarded as untrusted. The RV of item i can, therefore, be updated due to its low exposure (i.e., big $\alpha(i)$), especially for users who may rate it (i.e., high $P_r(i|u)$). There may be a great number of unknown items competing. If item i fails to be promoted, it waits for the next round. If its RV is enriched by update enough, item i will be promoted and earn more exposure. As the exposure grows, its priority of promotion is eventually removed (i.e., small $\alpha(i)$). Other unknown items which failed previously will have more chance to get promoted in the next iteration.

Table 1: $AUC_{Recall(\beta)}$ of the proposed (with label -RV) and competitive methods.

method / data	MF	MF-RV	AR	AR-RV	AR-pop	AR-pop-RV	PR	UF	RAND
MovieLens	0.23024	**0.23146**	0.22525	**0.22541**	0.28419	**0.28446**	0.27038	0.10874	0.09251
Netflix	0.24732	**0.31874**	0.21512	**0.31378**	0.20044	**0.29529**	0.20162	0.10759	0.10383

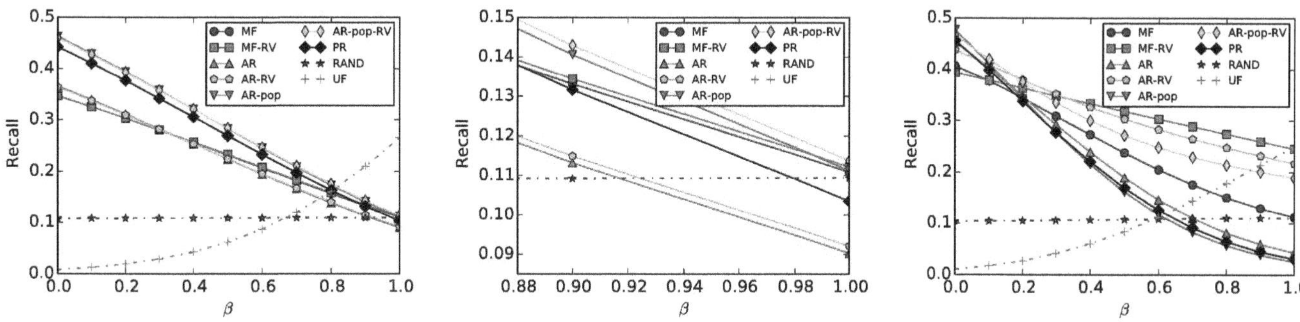

(a) MovieLens data.
(b) MovieLens (zoomed in at $\beta \to 1$).
(c) Netflix data.

Figure 1: Comparison of $Recall(\beta)$ over different approaches.

3. EXPERIMENTS

3.1 Datasets and Comparative Approaches

MovieLens[1] and Netflix[2] datasets are adopted in the experiments. Each rating of a user for an item takes an integer value from 1 (worst) to 5 (best) with a timestamp. For MovieLens, we sort the timestamps to form a timeline, which is divided into 1:1. Ratings with timestamps in the former timeline are for training and the later for testing. Users and items whose ratings appear only in the testing set but not in the training set are carefully removed. After preprocessing, there are 505,021 training ratings, 48,467 testing ratings, 3,287 users and 3,551 items. We randomly sample 200 items as the candidate set $\hat{I}$ for evaluation. The candidate set is sampled for 5 times. The experiments are performed on each of the sampled set to average the results. For the sampled candidate item set, each user rates 0.8 items on average. The standard deviation is 3.2.

For Netflix, the ratings are sorted by the timestamps and only the former $\frac{1}{5}$ ratings are kept to scale down the data size. The rest preprocessing is the same with what we do for MovieLens data. After preprocessing, there are 500,676 training ratings, 269,284 testing ratings, 5,643 users and 3,511 items. We randomly sample 200 items as the recommendation set $\hat{I}$ for 5 times. For the sampled candidate item set, each user rates 2.5 items on average. The standard deviation is 4.4.

We choose MF that optimizes RMSE to be the preference model. It's also one of the baselines. AllRank (AR) [8] and AllRank-pop (AR-pop) [9] both try to handle missing ratings. Different from AR, AR-pop further emphasizes the prediction of items with few *relevant* ratings (e.g., 5-star) and is one of the state-of-the-art competitive approaches. MF, AR, and AR-pop incorporated with RV are respectively denoted by MF-RV, AR-RV, and AR-pop-RV, where AR-pop and AR-RV can both be treated as the advanced versions of AR. Personalized Ranking (PR) [1], which models personalized rating probability for solving the cold-start problem, is also adopted as one of the competitive approaches. The heuristic unknown-item-first (UF) approach that greedily recommends the mostly unknown items and the random (RAND) approach that recommends randomly are included in our experiments as well.

[1]MovieLens dataset. http://datahub.io/dataset/movielens
[2]Netflix dataset. https://www.netflix.com/

3.2 Experimental Results

The parameters for our approach are set as follows. $\gamma = 2$ (the exponent for preference probability in Eq.(2)). $\beta_s = 0.3$ (the discriminative power of the weight in Eq.(10)). As 80% of the items in MovieLens data have exposure lower than 200 while 150 in Netflix data, we let this exposure be the unknownness threshold in Eq.(11), i.e., N_{unk}.

Let a *hit* be a recommended item to a user for which the user provides a rating in the testing data, i.e., the user rates it. In the experiments, we propose a metric called **exposure-stratified recall**, which is defined as:

$$Recall@K = \frac{\sum_u \sum_{i \in \hat{I}_u^{*,k}} \mathbf{1}(u,i)\, w_i}{\sum_u \sum_{i \in \hat{I}_u^{*}} \mathbf{1}(u,i)\, w_i}, \quad (12)$$

where $\mathbf{1}(.)$ is the indicator function; w_i is the item weight. The metic is similar to the popularity-stratified recall in [9], where the ordinary recall measure is extended by a weight, which is proportional to an inverse response probability. We replace the weight in [9] with a new one w_i, which is inversely proportional to the item exposure and defined as follows:

$$w_i = \frac{1}{(N_i^{obs})^{\beta}}, \quad (13)$$

where $\beta \in [0, 1]$ is the exponent deciding the effect of the exposure. The exposure-stratified recall measures two things: (1) how many *unknown* items are *hit*, and (2) hitting unknown items with lower exposure would contribute more to recall. Note that $\beta = 0$ if we care about how many items are hit regardless of exposure, i.e., ordinary recall. Ordinary recall is proportional to the hit ratio in the top-k list. To

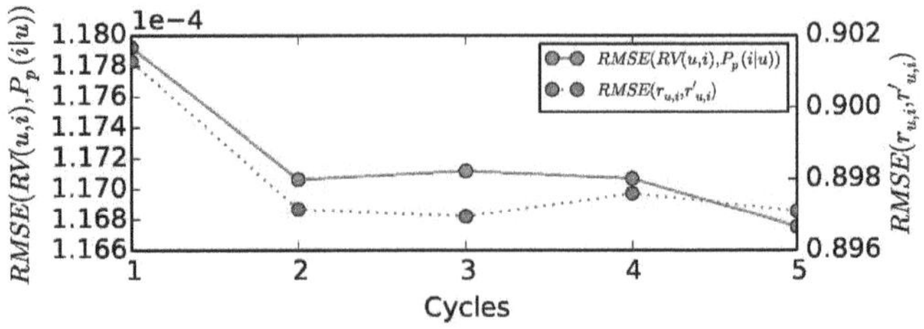

Figure 2: RMSE between RVs and preference probabilities (the red solid line) and RMSE between actual ratings and predicted ratings (the green dotted line) on MovieLens data.

tell which of item exposure and recommendation precision affects more in a single recall ($\beta > 0$), the **Area Under the Recall-β Curve** is given as follows:

$$AUC_{Recall(\beta)} = \int_0^1 Recall(\beta)@K \, d\beta. \qquad (14)$$

Table 1 compares the $AUC_{Recall(\beta)}$ of the proposed and competitive methods. The proposed methods (with label - RV) outperform the original (preference) models, especially in Netflix data, saying our methods are superior to the original methods over potentially ratable unknown items. The shapes of *Recall-β* curves, shown in Fig. 1, reveal the item exposure of the recommended items. UF recommends the mostly unknown items and gains a surprisingly high recall as $\beta \to 1$ but becomes low as $\beta \to 0$; namely, blindly recommending unknown items leads to very low hit ratio. If we zoom in both of the curves at $\beta \to 1$ (as shown in Fig. 1b), the recall of our methods is higher than the original ones, implying that more unknown items are recommended and hit. The recall at $\beta \to 0$ is sightly lowered for our methods due to the lower hit ratio of unknown items. As unknown items grow their exposure, our methods are expected to lean back towards the original methods and recommend preferable items.

One of the properties of RV is that RV is updated only when the item is unknown; otherwise, RV stays close to preference probability. To demonstrate this property, we sample 200 users, denoted $U_s \subseteq U$ (all users), with their ratings in the testing data for evaluation; these users are hold not to be recommended any items. The other users, i.e., $U - U_s$, are recommended 20 out of all items in a recommendation cycle. After a recommendation cycle, the ratings of hit items are *shifted* from testing data to training data. That is to say, the ratings of hit items are removed from the testing data and added to the training data of the *next* recommendation cycle. The training data in each cycle depends on the recommendation result of the previous cycle. In the first cycle, there are no previously recommended items. By shifting the ratings along the cycles, the item exposure in the training data is expected to grow. The ratings of the sampled users will not be shifted as they are not recommended any items. The above experiment is run for 5 cycles.

For each recommendation cycle, we compute the RMSE of the RVs and preference probabilities for the 200 sampled users. As the exposure of items grows along the recommendation cycles, some of the unknownness coefficient $\alpha(i)'s$ approach to 0 and their RVs start to lean towards the preference probability. The RMSE will decrease along the cycles as shown in Fig. 2 (the solid red line). In the meanwhile, the RMSE between the actual ratings and the predicted ratings, which are produced by the preference model, generally shrinks as well along the cycles (the dotted green line) – the preference model would be trained better as more ratings for unknown items are added to the training data. That is, the red line decreases because of the property of RV; the green line decreases because of the property of the model training.

4. CONCLUSIONS

We have proposed a novel approach to integration of item exposure with rating prediction. Its major benefits include: (1) The growth of item exposure for unknown items is sped up to get sufficient reliable ratings; it encourages item providers to get responses from the market as soon as possible. (2) Unknown items are promoted only to the users who may be interested in them; we pursue effective recommendations. (3) We not only leverage the information to unknown items, but also target collecting ratings from users to balance the trade-off between user preference and item exposure. (4) Our approach is flexible and can be combined with any available models that are able to precisely predict the user preference and user rating behavior. Besides, a new metric, the exposure-stratified recall, is proposed to measure how many unknown items are hit. All the experiments are conducted on real datasets, i.e., MovieLens and Netflix, to demonstrate the feasibility of the proposed approach. We plan to address the starving problem for the promotion of unknown items in the future.

5. REFERENCES

[1] A. S. Harpale and Y. Yang, "Personalized active learning for collaborative filtering," in *Proc. of ACM SIGIR Conference*, pp. 91–98, 2008.

[2] Y. Koren, R. Bell, and C. Volinsky, "Matrix factorization techniques for recommender systems," *Computer 42(8)*, pp. 30–37, 2009.

[3] J.-H. Liu, T. Zhou, Z.-K. Zhang, Z. Yang, C. Liu, and W.-M. Li, "Promoting cold-start items in recommender systems," *PLoS ONE 9(12)*, pp. 1–13, 2014.

[4] J. Oh, S. Park, H. Yu, M. Song, and S. T. Park, "Novel recommendation based on personal popularity tendency," in *Proc. of IEEE International Conference on Data Mining*, pp. 507–516, 2011.

[5] Y.-J. Park and A. Tuzhilin, "The long tail of recommender systems and how to leverage it," in *Proc. of ACM Conference on Recommender Systems*, pp. 11–18, 2008.

[6] A. I. Schein, A. Popescul, L. H. Ungar, and D. M. Pennock, "Methods and metrics for cold-start recommendations," in *Proc. of ACM SIGIR Conference*, pp. 253–260, 2002.

[7] Y. Shi, M. Larson, and A. Hanjalic, "Collaborative filtering beyond the user-item matrix: A survey of the state of the art and future challenges," *ACM Comput. Surv. 47(1)*, pp. 3:1–3:45, 2014.

[8] H. Steck, "Training and testing of recommender systems on data missing not at random," in *Proc. of ACM SIGKDD Conference*, pp. 713–722, 2010.

[9] H. Steck, "Item popularity and recommendation accuracy," in *Proc. of ACM Conference on Recommender Systems*, pp. 125–132, 2011.

Effective Trend Detection within a Dynamic Search Context

Anat Hashavit
IBM Haifa Research Lab
Haifa, Israel
anath@il.ibm.com

Roy Levin
IBM Haifa Research Lab
Haifa, Israel
levin.royl@gmail.com

Ido Guy
Ben Gurion University of the Negev, Israel
Yahoo Research, Israel
idoguy@acm.org

Gilad Kutiel
Department of Computer Science
Technion, Haifa, Israel
gkutiel@cs.technion.ac.il

ABSTRACT

In recent years, studies about trend detection in online social media streams have begun to emerge. Since not all users are likely to always be interested in the same set of trends, some of the research also focused on personalizing the trends by using some predefined personalized context.

In this paper, we take this problem further to a setting in which the user's context is not predefined, but rather determined as the user issues a query. This presents a new challenge since trends cannot be computed ahead of time using high latency algorithms. We present RT-Trend, an online trend detection algorithm that promptly finds relevant in-context trends as users issue search queries over a dataset of documents.

We evaluate our approach using real data from an online social network by assessing its ability to predict actual activity increase of social network entities in the context of a search result. Since we implemented this feature into an existing tool with an active pool of users, we also report click data, which suggests positive feedback.

Keywords: Trends, Analytics, Tag Cloud, Word Cloud,Trend Cloud

1. INTRODUCTION

Nowadays, large social media sites such as Twitter, Facebook and LinkedIn generate huge amounts of information. These social networks expose activity streams which are composed of actions generated by hundreds of millions of users over time. As such, some characteristics are likely to change over time. In recent years, many research papers have focused specifically on the problem of detecting trends over such data [2,3,5]. In addition, since not all trends may warrant the same level of attention from all users. Some research effort was directed at detecting trends within some predefined context such as regional [2] or a predefined user profile [9]. Yet, such approaches require a context to be provided in advance.

In contrast to such predefined contexts, users have traditionally relied on keyword search to explore textual content. However getting a list of relevant documents is only a partial solution. As an extension, Faceted search [8] allows users to explore these results by applying multiple filters. For example, in a social network settings such as Twitter, documents can be defined as microblogs and their authors can be added as facets. Using faceted search, the top-k users that appear in the microblogs of the search results can also be displayed. Other examples of facets can also be categories, topics, or when the social network contains structured data [1], entities such as the communities that the search results belong to.

In this paper we present a framework that utilizes faceted search along with a novel realtime algorithm called RT-Trends which calculates trending facets related to the search results. This approach employs a two phase solution. First, during indexing, we associate, as facets, to each document the trending candidate entities along with their corresponding information. Then, when a search query is issued, we collect and aggregate, in real time, trend scores for each candidate trend. We then rank them, and select the top-k to be displayed.

We implemented the feature of detecting trending entities within a search context into the Streamz [4] application. In our experiments we examine how well the RT-Trends algorithm can actually predict which entities exhibit increased activity levels. As further validation we analyze the Streamz query log and report on some encouraging results.

SIGIR '16, July 17-21, 2016, Pisa, Italy

DOI: http://dx.doi.org/10.1145/2911451.2914705

2. TREND SCORING

In this section, we describe the method for calculating trend scores for a stream of events.

2.1 Intuition

We begin by describing the intuition behind our trend scoring algorithm. Consider a community in a social network (a trend candidate in the example), which for the past month has had a relatively stable volume of activity within it. As such, predicting future activity volumes can be based on previous activity levels, even when they are not very recent. Note that the term stability here implies relatively small changes in daily frequencies. However, if a sudden trend appears in the amount of activity then we except our predicted value to significantly deviate from the actual volume of activity. This is due to the fact that our prediction does not give high significance to recent activity volumes. The idea is therefore to use this *predicated error* to derive a trend score.

2.2 Computing an Entity's Trend Score

Let $C = c_i, .., c_n$ denote the time series representing the occurrences of a trending entity candidate e in a sequence of time intervals $T = t_1, .., t_n$. We begin by assuming that the dataset behaves in a predictable manner (as described in the intuition above) and we predict its volume based on an Exponential Moving Average [6] as follows:

$$\chi_{i+1}(e) = \alpha \cdot \chi_i(e) + (1 - \alpha) \cdot c_{i+1}(e) \quad (1)$$

We define the starting condition for the recursion to be $\chi_0(e) = 0$. Note that $\alpha \in (0, 1)$ is a smoothing parameter, which controls the weights of older versus newer values. As stated before, when an entity is trending there is a sudden and abrupt change in it's arrival rate (volume per time interval) which can not be predicted based on its previous behavior. In practice we set a high value to α. This captures the underlying assumption that the rate of change is predictable. If there is a trend then this calculation will result in an error. By aggregating these errors we get a quantitative measure of how much the new behavior deviates from the predicted one. The trend score can thus be based on this aggregated error by the recursive formula bellow:

$$TS_{i+1}(e) = TS_i(e) + (c_{i+1}(e) - \chi_i(e)) \quad (2)$$

The starting condition for the recursive formula is set to be $TS_0(e) = 0$. Note that not every time series that is not predicted well by this Exponential Moving Average will produce a high aggregated error. For example, white noise will constantly exhibit prediction errors, yet when summing these errors, since there are likely to be an equal number of under predictions and over predictions, the aggregated error will be close to zero. This is good since we would not like such cases to be determined as being trendy.

2.2.1 Optimizing the Recursion

Since an entity is not necessarily active at each time interval in the series it is possible to optimize Equation (2) such that $TS_{i+1}(e)$ will be dependent solely on the values of $TS_j(e)$ $(j \le i)$ for which $c_j(e) \neq 0$. This is an important optimization since indeed the volumes in each time interval yield a sparse vector. As a result, the trend score of an entity can be updated only for time slots in which it actually occurs. Let j be an index such that for every index $j < k < i$ it follows that $c_k(e) = 0$ and $c_j(e) \neq 0$. First, note that based on Equation (1) as $c_k(e) = 0$ it follows that $\chi_{k+1} = \alpha \cdot \chi_k(e)$ and therefore:

$$\chi_{i+1}(e) = \alpha^{i-j} \cdot \chi_j(e) + (1 - \alpha) \cdot c_j(e) \quad (3)$$

We can now develop Equation (2) as follows: (Note that we use a shorthand notation here in which $*_i$ denotes $*_i(e)$).

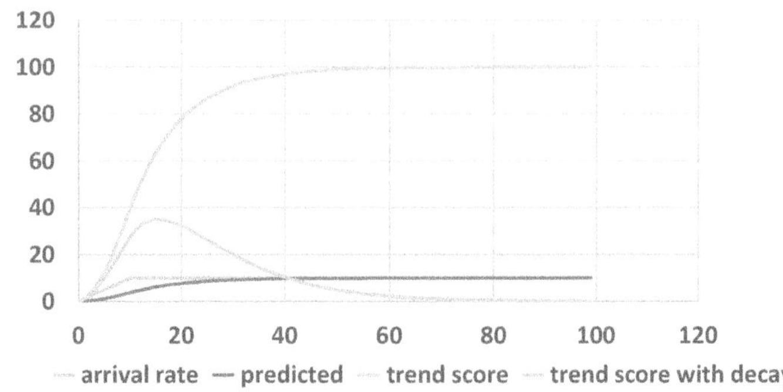

Figure 1: The trend score is based on the difference between the actual and predicted arrival rate. The actual arrival rates in this Figure have been synthetically generated for the purpose of illustration.

$$\begin{array}{lll}
(a) & TS_i = & TS_{i-1} + (c_i - \chi_{i-1}) = \\
(b) & & c_i + TS_{i-2} - \chi_{i-2} - \chi_{i-1} = (\text{since } c_{i-1} = 0) \\
(c) & & c_i + TS_{i-3} - \chi_{i-3} - \chi_{i-2} - \chi_{i-1} = \\
\vdots & \vdots & \vdots \\
(*) & & c_i + TS_j - \chi_j \cdot \sum_{k=0}^{i-j-1} \alpha^k
\end{array}$$

We can now rewrite Equation (2) based on previous values that have been calculated only when the entity e occurs within the corresponding time window.

$$TS_i(e) = c_i(e) + TS_j(e) - \chi_j(e) \cdot \sum_{k=0}^{i-j-1} \alpha^k \quad (4)$$

2.3 Trend Decay Factor

In Figure 1, we see an example of the gap between the predicted arrival rate, based on the exponential smoothing method proposed above and actual arrival rate of an entity as it becomes a trend. The figure also shows the trend score as calculated by Equation (4). Note that the trend score increases as the difference between the actual and predicted rate grows and levels when the entity's arrival rate convergence to a new constant value. The problem is however, that this new constant value is high and is the result of mispredictions (errors) that have occurred for older values. In fact, note that for values of around $i = 30$ (in the x-axis) the predictions become very accurate, i.e., the arrival rate no longer deviates from its predicted value yet the trend score remains high due to the fact that the entity "was" trending in the past. We therefore need to add a decay factor to "forget" past trends. Therefore, we introduce a slight modification to Equation (4) by multiplying it by a *Decay Factor* $\beta \in (0, 1)$.

$$TS_i(e) = \beta \cdot (c_i(e) + TS_j(e) - \chi_j(e) \cdot \sum_{k=0}^{i-j-1} \alpha^k) \quad (5)$$

The "trends with decay" line in bright green now shows the new trend score with the decay for the example of the trending entity presented in Figure 1. We now see that once the entity's rate is correctly predicted the trends score starts to slowly decrease, as would be expected.

3. ALGORITHM AND EVALUATION

In this section we describe our dataset and the algorithm that calculates trend scores based on the description in Section 2 over our data and within a faceted search context. We also present our experimental evaluation of the results.

3.1 The Dataset and Environment

To construct the dataset for our experiments we used social data from the activity stream of an enterprise social network called IBM-Connections [1]. This data consists of more than 800,000 individuals including employees, contractors and ex-employees. The activities consist of generating and modifying several types of web entities, such as Blogs, Wikis, Files and Discussion Forums. Another web entity form is a Community [7] which groups together Blogs, Wikis, Files and Forums pertaining to a certain topic.

To keep things simple, we defined our documents as Blogs, Wikis, Files and Forums and, since each of them is contained within a community, we define the communities as our trending candidates (which are added as facets).

In addition, we implemented the "in-context trending communities" feature into a web application called Streamz [4] which is deployed in our organization and has more than a thousand internal users. This allowed us to track click rates for each trending community shown based on its rank in the top-5 trends results (1-5) including the overall clicks ratio of the trends feature in general.

3.2 Application in Search Context

We next describe how we implemented our trends score within a search context using the Apache Lucene Open Source search framework. During the indexing phase a document is created for social entities (in our case Blogs, Wikis, Files and Forums) and the unique id of the containing community is associated to that document as a facet [1]. Note that we could similarly add other associations like categories, topics, users and others using the same method. The document along with its facets are then indexed. In addition, during indexing we also calculate our time intervals span denoted $T = \{t_1, t_2, \ldots, t_n\}$.

The next phase occurs during search. Given a search query q we retrieve the matching documents D_q along with their associated facets denoted $F(D_q)$. For a given facet $f \in F(D_q)$, let $VT_f = \{VT_{i_1}, VT_{i_2}, \ldots, VT_{i_{fn}}\}$ denote the set of non-zero volumes per time intervals in T, i.e., VT_j represents the number of times facet f appears in $F(D_q)$ within time interval $T_j \in T$. Note that zeros are not needed due to the trend score calculation optimization described in Section 2. We next compute the facet's trend scores. This can be done efficiently, in memory, by using Lucene's facets mechanism as next described. We start by mapping each facet to its time interval in T and then aggregate the counts to find VT_f for each facet. This represents the volume within the corresponding time interval. Each VT_f is maintained in ascending order and is therefore a time series which we can apply our trend score algorithm over. The trend score algorithm of each VT_f is calculated in parallel. As the trend scores are updated we also maintain a top-k list of the 5 trends with the highest trend scores. Based on trial and error we selected the values for the trend scoring to be α , β which we report in the subsections below.

3.3 Evaluation Based on Prediction

In order to evaluate the RT-Trends algorithm we examined its ability to identify trending communities that contain documents (Blogs, Wikis, Files and Forums) from the search results of a given search query. We evaluate this by checking to see if, in retrospect, these exhibit an actual increase in their activity volume. Specifically, we examined the algorithm's ability to predict a volume increase within a predefined time span Δ, called the *Query Activity Time Span*, from the moment the search query is issued. Given a community c and a search query at time t, we compare the volume of activity in the community c during the time window before the query, $[t - \Delta, t)$, namely the *Prequery Activity* to that after the query, $[t, t + \Delta)$, herein the *Postquery Activity.* If for a community c the postquery activity is greater than the prequery activity we consider c to be an *Accurate Prediction* with respect to the query and the activity time span. To make sure the trends are meaningful, we also report the average factor by which the postquery activity actually increases.

In our experiments, we distinguish between short and long-term trends. The former represent current and immediate topics of interests in the organization. Announcements about new appointments, annual report publishing and internal conferences are just a few examples of events that can trigger short term trends. These events are classified as short term since they need to be quickly detected and their effect usually subsides within a few days. Long term trends, on the other hand, suggest slower but often more significant changes that affect the organization. Examples include adopting new technologies, releasing new products, and starting a new line of business. Oftentimes, such trends tend to exhibit slow and gradual changes but are nevertheless quite meaningful. Taking this into account, we separately examined how well the algorithm can predict both types of trends.

We began by selecting a random sample of user queries from the query log of the Streamz application. Note that these queries are typically more than just a set of keywords. They commonly also contain constraints on employees or departments as well as combinations of all the above. For short term trends, we then picked the date and time d_s of each day within a time period of one month (the month was selected arbitrarily) and set the query activity time span Δ_s to be twelve hours. The queries above were then issued while limiting them to return results before the date d_s. For each retrieved community, the prequery activity was compared to the postquery activity. Similarly, for long term trends we picked a date and time d_l at the beginning of every forth day in a time period of three months. We then applied the RT-Trends algorithm as well as two baseline algorithms to retrieve the trending communities relevant to the given query. The first baseline algorithm, called *Random*, merely selects ten communities relevant to the query by random (in fact this is not really an algorithm, its merely

[1]https://lucene.apache.org/core/4_0_0/facet/org/apache/lucene/facet/doc-files/userguide.html

Trend Type	Random	Volume	RT-Trends
Short Term (Δ_s = day)	17.6%	39.0%	42.4% ($\alpha = 0.999, \beta = 0.999$), |t|=minute
Long Term (Δ_s = month)	22.2%	25.8%	54.2% ($\alpha = 0.7, \beta = 0.765$), |t|=day

Table 1: Average percentage of accurate predictions for each algorithm for short and long term trends.

the ratio of communities whose postquery activity is greater than its prequery activity). The second baseline algorithm called *Volume* selects ten communities from all the relevant communities such that their volume of activity in a given time window is the highest. For short term trends this time window is defined to be the day prior to the query date and for long term trends it is defined as the prior month. We summarize the average percentage of accurate predictions made by each algorithm for short and long term trends in Table 1. The table also includes the activity time span and values of α and β, and the time interval size denoted $|t|$ used for the RT-Trends algorithm.

3.3.1 *Results Analysis*

We start by looking at the, more important, long term trends. Note that the volume of activity in the previous month is a very weak indicator for long term trends whereas the RT-Trend algorithm, which examines a finer granularity, is able to significantly outperform both Random and Volume by almost a factor of 2.5. Intuitively, the key difference lies in the fact that the RT-Trends algorithm is based on a weighted moving average which gives more weight to recent activities.

For short term trends, the Volume algorithm performs much better than Random. This means that the activity volume of the previous day is a significant indicator for the activity volume of the next day. RT-Trends does not significantly outperform Volume in detecting short term trends since looking at levels of activities of smaller time units than a single day is not that significant. The reason is that in our data the amount of activity in a single community per one day is not high enough to merit such a fine-grained granularity. In addition, short-term trends are somewhat noisier and thus more difficult to predict than long-term trends.

We also report that the average factor by which the activity in communities found trendy by RT-Trends is 2.354 for short term trends and 3.057 for long term trends. That is, the algorithm finds communities that exhibit a significant increase in their activity.

3.4 Analysis of User Log Data from Streamz

When displaying search results Streamz also depicts what we refer to as a **Search Analytics Box**. This box contains information about the search results such as the most active people, topics, and the new addition of trending communities. Since the launch of the trends feature in Streamz we tracked user activity and found that in 19.8% of the searches, the search analytics box was clicked. Out of these clicks, 80% were on the trends feature, indicating that users found this feature to be interesting. As the ranking of the trending communities in the search context is based on the trend score, we expect that the number of user clicks should correlate with the rank. Table 2 depicts the percentage of clicks on the trending communities by users based on their rank in the results. The main point of this is to show that there is no evidence of mis-ranked communities by the RT-Trends algorithm.

Rank	1	2	3	4	5
Clicks	38.5%	25.7%	15.6%	11.0%	9.2%

Table 2: Percentage of user clicks on trending communities based on their rank in the results.

4. CONCLUSION

In this paper, we introduce a new problem, namely finding trending entities, in real time and within a dynamic search context which is not known in advance. We devise a novel framework and an algorithm called RT-Trends, which retrieves scores, ranks, and selects the top-k trending items that are relevant to the search results. We implement the algorithm using Apach Lucene's Faceted Search and deployed it into a web application used within the organization to track its usage. The tool is used by thousands of users in our organization and enables search and analytics capabilities over streaming social media data.

In our experiments, we analyze the algorithm's ability to predict trends. We show that it predicts an actual growth in the level of activity within communities relevant to answers of user queries. Moreover, we show that the average factor by which the activity increases is also significant. Analysis of the Streamz query log shows that a high percentage of users that use the Search Analytics Box click specifically on the trends feature. Finally, we also show that a correlation exists between how we rank trending communities and the number of clicks they receive in the analytics box by users.

5. REFERENCES

[1] IBM-Connections. www-03.ibm.com/software/products/en/conn, 2007.

[2] Z. Al Bawab, G. H. Mills, and J.-F. Crespo. Finding trending local topics in search queries for personalization of a recommendation system. In *SIGKDD 2012*.

[3] N. G. Golbandi, L. K. Katzir, Y. K. Koren, and R. L. Lempel. Expediting search trend detection via prediction of query counts. In *WSDM 2013*.

[4] I. Guy, T. Steier, M. Barnea, I. Ronen, and T. Daniel. Swimming against the streamz: search and analytics over the enterprise activity stream. In *CIKM 2012*.

[5] J. Kleinberg. Bursty and hierarchical structure in streams. In *SIGKDD 2002*.

[6] S. Roberts. Control chart tests based on geometric moving averages. *Technometrics*, 1(3):239–250, 1959.

[7] I. Ronen, I. Guy, E. Kravi, and M. Barnea. Recommending social media content to community owners. Proc. SIGIR '14, pages 243–252. ACM, 2014.

[8] D. Tunkelang. aceted search (synthesis lectures on information concepts, retrieval, and services). *Claypool: Morgan*, 2009.

[9] X. Zhou, S. Wu, C. Chen, G. Chen, and S. Ying. Real-time recommendation for microblogs. *Information Sciences*, 2014.

Enhancing First Story Detection using Word Embeddings

Sean Moran, Richard McCreadie, Craig Macdonald, Iadh Ounis
{firstname.secondname}@glasgow.ac.uk
University of Glasgow, UK

ABSTRACT

In this paper we show how word embeddings can be used to increase the effectiveness of a state-of-the art Locality Sensitive Hashing (LSH) based first story detection (FSD) system over a standard tweet corpus. Vocabulary mismatch, in which related tweets use different words, is a serious hindrance to the effectiveness of a modern FSD system. In this case, a tweet could be flagged as a first story even if a related tweet, which uses different but synonymous words, was already returned as a first story. In this work, we propose a novel approach to mitigate this problem of lexical variation, based on tweet expansion. In particular, we propose to expand tweets with semantically related paraphrases identified via automatically mined word embeddings over a background tweet corpus. Through experimentation on a large data stream comprised of 50 million tweets, we show that FSD effectiveness can be improved by 9.5% over a state-of-the-art FSD system.

1. INTRODUCTION

First Story Detection (FSD) is the task of identifying the first document that is related to a particular topic in a voluminous stream of documents. FSD has wide applicability across many disciplines ranging from the security industry to news reporting [11]. For example, a financial analyst may want the system to immediately flag up the first story that day relating to a stock of interest, so that they can make an informed buy/sell decision before the market shifts. The task of FSD was initially popularised by the Topic Detection and Tracking (TDT) initiative, which examined FSD over low volume newswire streams [2]. However, FSD has recently garnered considerable renewed attention with the availability of large-scale social media streams such as Twitter.

The most effective approaches to FSD have generally involved nearest neighbour search. Under this strategy, the most recent document in the stream is compared to a set of previous documents. If the nearest neighbour is sufficiently dissimilar to the current document, it is flagged as a first story. However, nearest neighbour search can often fail when working with social media data due to lexical variation. Indeed, consider the tweets 'Imogen lashing parts of England and Wales #bbc' and 'Storm hits Cornish Coast, waves of up to 19.1m (63ft) reported'. These tweets discuss the same event, but do not share any terms, hence both of these tweets would be emitted as first stories, causing the same event to be reported multiple times. Prior work [11] has proposed the use of paraphrases as a means to expand short social media posts with related terms from knowledge-bases such as WordNet [6]. However, while this improves FSD performance, the gain is much smaller than that observed when the same technique is applied to newswire data, likely due to lexical mismatch between the knowledge bases and social media [11]. Hence, an alternative paraphrase expansion approach would be advantageous.

Word embeddings have been proposed as a method for producing more effective word representations. In the Word2-vec model [9], a shallow neural network learns dense real-valued vectors for each word in the vocabulary by attempting to maximise the probability of seeing that word within a fixed context window. Word embeddings have shown to be an effective means to improve a variety of tasks that involve the representation of text items in a vector space, such as text classification [7]. In this paper, we propose to leverage word embeddings to enhance the representation of social media posts for the purposes of FSD. In our method, we use a background corpus of tweets to learn a set of word embeddings. These word embeddings are then used to find semantically related terms with which to expand each tweet. We conjecture that by expanding posts in this manner, we will be able to reduce cases where textually distinct posts about a single event are erroneously reported as first stories.

The primary contribution of this paper is a simple and effective method for using word embeddings (WE) to automatically compute good paraphrase pairs for the purposes of mitigating the problem of vocabulary mismatch in FSD. We show that our approach can enhance FSD effectiveness by approximately 9.5% over a state-of-the-art FSD model without expansion [11].

2. RELATED WORK

The task that we examine in this paper is *first story detection* (FSD). FSD is an application of nearest neighbour search as a means to identify novel textual documents. Each new document in the stream is compared to a set of previously observed documents. If the nearest neighbour to the

SIGIR '16, July 17-21, 2016, Pisa, Italy

DOI: http://dx.doi.org/10.1145/2911451.2914719

current document is sufficiently dissimilar then the current document is considered novel and hence emitted as a first story for a new topic. FSD was initially examined over low volume news article streams [2], but has recently been extended for use over high volume social media streams [10]. In particular, traditional implementations of nearest neighbour search are too computationally expensive to apply to high volume streams [10]. Hence, recent works have focused on making the nearest neighbour search process scalable while minimising the loss in effectiveness [5, 10]. For instance, Petrovic *et al.* [10] proposed the use of a locality sensitive hashing (LSH) algorithm [4, 8] to perform FSD in bounded time and memory.

Lexical variation is a significant barrier to achieving effective FSD performance over social media streams, as it can result in the same event being reported multiple times. State-of-the-art FSD approaches use paraphrase expansion to overcome this issue [11]. A paraphrase expresses the meaning of a written piece of text using different words. There are three common levels of paraphrasing: lexical paraphrases (single word paraphrases); phrasal paraphrases (multi-word paraphrases); and sentential paraphrases (sentence-length paraphrases). Petrovic *et al.* [11] used lexical paraphrases extracted from WordNet [6], Microsoft Research (MSR) paraphrase tables [12] and syntactically constrained paraphrases [3] for document expansion. They showed that text expansion using these paraphrases were effective over newswire, but performance improvements were much smaller when applied over tweets. We propose an alternative approach based on learning word embeddings directly from Twitter data.

3. IMPROVING FSD WITH PARAPHRASES

An FSD system must produce a novelty score for each tweet $\mathbf{x}_i$ indicating the likelihood that the tweet describes a first story, i.e. a topic not previously described by an earlier tweet observed within the stream. High novelty scores indicate a greater likelihood that the tweet is reporting a first story. We propose a novel approach to improve the estimation of these novelty scores by expanding each tweet $\mathbf{x}_i$ using lexical paraphrases mined via word embeddings from a background corpus of tweets. We aim to answer the following research question:

RQ-1: Can word embeddings be used to automatically mine lexical paraphrases that are effective at mitigating the problem of lexical mismatch for FSD in Twitter?

3.1 Expanding tweets using paraphrases

To explore **RQ-1** we build upon the Locality Sensitive Hashing (LSH)-based FSD model of [11]. Their model computes the cosine similarity between tweets, and uses that score as a measure of novelty. To drastically reduce the number of required comparisons from $\mathcal{O}(N)$ to $\mathcal{O}(1)$, LSH-FSD applies LSH to bucket the tweets into the buckets of L hashtables. The cosine similarity is only computed between tweets that collide in the same bucket as the current tweet in the stream. To compute the hashcodes that index into the hashtable buckets, LSH fractures the input feature-space with a set of K randomly sampled hyperplanes with normal vectors $\{\mathbf{u}_k \in \Re^V\}_{k=1}^{K}$, where V is the vocabulary size. The K-bit binary hashcodes $\mathbf{b}_i$ for each tweet $\mathbf{x}_i$ can be computed simply by determining on which side of the hyperplanes the tweet feature vector falls. This operation reduces into K dot products, followed by sign thresholding, as illustrated in Equation (1):

$$\mathbf{b}_i = F(\mathbf{x}_i) = sgn\left[\mathbf{u}_1^{\intercal}\mathbf{x}_i \dots \mathbf{u}_K^{\intercal}\mathbf{x}_i\right] \quad (1)$$

where sgn denotes the sign function, $sgn(x) = 1$ if $x > 0$, and 0 otherwise. It has been shown that this procedure causes the Hamming distance between the binary hashcodes to correlate with the cosine similarity computed on the tweet TF-IDF feature vectors [8]. This means that tweets colliding in the same hashtable bucket are most likely to have a high cosine similarity, and therefore to be nearest neighbours. In our work we are interested in the modified cosine similarity given by Equation (2):

$$cos_Q(\mathbf{x}_i, \mathbf{x}_j) = \frac{\mathbf{x}_i \mathbf{Q} \mathbf{x}_j}{\sqrt{\mathbf{x}_i^{\intercal}\mathbf{Q}\mathbf{x}_i}\sqrt{\mathbf{x}_j^{\intercal}\mathbf{Q}\mathbf{x}_j}} \quad (2)$$

where $\mathbf{Q} \in \{0,1\}^{V\times V}$ is a binary paraphrase indicator matrix. In this matrix, $Q_{ij} = 1$ if words w_i, w_j are considered paraphrases (e.g. blast $\leftrightarrow$ explosion, source $\leftrightarrow$ informant), and $Q_{ij} = 0$, otherwise. In comparison to using unmodified cosine similarity, Equation (2) will assign higher similarity scores between tweets that share paraphrases from $\mathbf{Q}$. Petrović et al. [11] show that LSH can be adapted to preserve this modified cosine similarity in the resulting binary hashcodes simply by pre-multiplying the tweets with the square root of $\mathbf{Q}$ (Equation (3)):

$$\mathbf{b}_i = F(\mathbf{x}_i) = sgn\left[\mathbf{u}_1^{\intercal}(\mathbf{Q}^{1/2})\mathbf{x}_i \dots \mathbf{u}_K^{\intercal}(\mathbf{Q}^{1/2})\mathbf{x}_i\right] \quad (3)$$

The term $\mathbf{Q}^{1/2}\mathbf{x}_i$ can be interpreted as mapping the tweet $\mathbf{x}_i$ into a new inner product space defined by the paraphrase matrix $\mathbf{Q}$ [11]. The hashcodes resulting from Equation (3) can be used to index the tweets into hashtable buckets. Tweets colliding in the same bucket should have a high likelihood of being similar, i.e. discussing the same event.

3.2 Automatically mining lexical paraphrases

Our primary contribution in this paper is a new way of automatically computing the lexical paraphrase matrix $\mathbf{Q}$ using word embeddings. There has been an extensive amount of prior research that has shown that the cosine similarity between word embeddings is correlated with the semantic relatedness between the corresponding words [9]. In our work we make use of this property by deeming two words to be lexical paraphrases if the cosine similarity between their word embeddings is sufficiently high. More concretely, to automatically construct the lexical paraphrase matrix we follow a simple three-step procedure:

Learn Word Embeddings: Learn a set of word embedding vectors using Word2vec [9] on a background corpus containing the same type of documents that are to be expanded. In our case, we use a random sample of tweets crawled from a different time period to train our word embedding vectors.

Word Filtering: Note that the majority of the words within the background corpus will not be useful for expansion, since they are either too general to make effective expansion terms (e.g. words like 'about' or 'news') or are specific Twitter terminology from the period of that corpus (e.g. '#eusew15'). Hence, we filter the words considered within the word embedding corpus to only words that are likely to be informative based on a series of public word lists (see Section 4).

Word Similarity Computation: Finally, we compute the cosine similarity $s_{ij} \in \Re$ between the embeddings of every word $\mathbf{w}_i \in \Re^D, \mathbf{w}_j \in \Re^D$, where D is the word embedding dimensionality, and threshold the resulting similarities using a threshold $\theta \in \Re$. Similarities are only computed between words in the same word list. Note that the cosine similarity we use here is the standard cosine similarity, not that given in Equation (2).

Words pairs with a similarity above θ are retained and used to construct the paraphrase matrix $\mathbf{Q}$. We use a binary matrix and set element Q_{ij} to 1 if the corresponding similarity $s_{ij} \geq \theta$, and $Q_{ij} = 0$ otherwise. We note that our method only relies on word embeddings and the availability of word lists to construct the paraphrase matrix. Given the wide availability of standard word embedding software and word lists for most languages, both resources are significantly easier to obtain than manually curating lexical paraphrases, for example by creating WordNet synsets. WordNet is an expensive resource that was relied upon by the LSH-FSD system of [11] to obtain high FSD effectiveness.

4. EXPERIMENTAL SETUP

Datasets: Our experimental testbed is the collection of over 50 million tweets introduced by [11]. The tweets in the dataset were sampled from July to September 2011, with a subset of the tweets manually labeled as being on-topic for one of 27 events (e.g. 'Amy Winehouse dies' or 'Earthquake in Virginia'). To learn the word embeddings that we use to calculate the semantic distance between terms (which we then use to select terms with which to expand each tweet), we use a background set of tweets from a different time period. In particular, we use a random sample of 451 million tweets crawled using Twitter Streaming API from the period of the 1 January 2015 to 30 June 2015.

Tweet text pre-processing: When working with Twitter data, pre-processing applied to the terms can have a marked impact on overall effectiveness. To this end, we explore the effect of the term processing techniques used by [10]. Specifically we explore Porter and Krovetz stemming in addition to *Twitter specific text pre-processing* that was reported to be effective in [11], namely ignoring links, @-mentions and treating hashtags as normal words (i.e. removing the leading # character).

Word Dictionaries: Given that our evaluation dataset is largely US-centric, we experiment with a set of freely available English term word lists. These word lists can be downloaded from http://icon.shef.ac.uk/Moby/. In particular, we experiment with five word lists representing different types of information, namely: common male names (denoted by M) (3,897 words), common female names (F) (4,946 words); place names in the United States (P) (10,196 words); commonly misspelt words (S) (366 words); and common dictionary words (W) (74,550 words).

Metrics: We use the widely accepted normalised Topic Weighted Minimum Cost (C_{min}) [2, 5, 10, 11]. C_{min} is a linear combination of miss and false alarm probabilities and is computed across all possible threshold values on the first story confidence score. This allows a comparison of different methods based on a single value metric. For C_{min} a smaller number is better. We compare the significance of the results by performing a paired t-test over the 27 per topic C_{min} scores.

Training and Parameters: We use the popular Word2Vec tool[1] to train our word embeddings with dimensionality D= 200. The threshold θ on the cosine similarity between Word2-vec embeddings is a tunable parameter of our model. In practice we use a different value θ_1 for the four smaller word dictionaries (M,F,P,S) and a separate value of θ_2 for the much larger common dictionary words list (W). We optimise thresholds $\{\theta_1, \theta_2\}$ jointly by conducting a parameter sweep over $\theta \in \{0.0, 0.1, \ldots, 0.9, 1.0\}$ on a *held-out training dataset*, minimising for C_{min}. The training dataset for parameter tuning was entirely independent of our test dataset, and consisted of 806,342 tweets in total. 7,512 of these tweets were manually labelled as on-topic for one of 10 events. The training dataset events occurred in 2011 and include, amongst others, the death of Steve Jobs, the Seoul floods, and the Indiana State Fair stage collapse[2]. We use the same LSH-FSD system parameters as [10, 11], namely K=13 hashcode bits and L=70 hashtables, the hashing trick is used with a pool of size 2^{18} and we select 2000 tweets and a back-off threshold of b_t=0.6 for the variance reduction step.

Baselines: We compare our method to two state-of-the-art FSD models as follows. First, UMass [2], is a system that produced state-of-the-art performance in the TDT2 and TDT3 competitions [1] and which has since formed the de-facto baseline for comparison in subsequent research on first story detection [5, 10, 11]. UMass uses k-nearest neighbour clustering and an inverted index to identify first stories in the tweet stream. Second, LSH-FSD [10] is a streaming FSD model that was shown to be both more effective and more efficient than UMass. LSH-FSD employs Locality Sensitive Hashing (LSH) to hash tweets into buckets. Tweets colliding in the same bucket are tested for similarity using the cosine similarity. If the similarity is low enough a tweet is deemed to report a first story (Section 3.1).

5. RESULTS

In this section we present a series of results designed to answer **RQ-1**. Table 1 reports C_{min} FSD effectiveness for the baseline FSD systems and our proposed approach that uses paraphrases obtained from word embeddings. In particular, the first column highlights the FSD strategy - from inverted indexing (UMass) to hashing (LSH). The second column indicates the pre-processing applied to each tweet in terms of stemming or Twitter specific text processing [11]. The third column denotes any tweet expansion with various paraphrase sources. Importantly, it is not possible to reproduce all approaches from the literature due to efficiency constraints (UMass) and lack of access to the paraphrase resources used in [11]. Hence, we provide C_{min} scores that have been reported in the literature (column 4) and, where possible, our re-implementation of the approach (column 5). The bottom row of Table 1 reports the performance of our approach using the five word lists to filter the word embeddings.

From Table 1, we observe the following: firstly, comparing the reported performance of LSH using Twitter specific pre-processing to our implementation of this approach we see that performances are very similar (reported: 0.694 vs. implemented: 0.705). Furthermore, we see almost identical performance between the LSH-FSD systems using Porter

[1]https://code.google.com/archive/p/word2vec/

[2]Annotations provided by [5, 10] and available on request.

Approach	Pre-Processing	Paraphrase Expansion	Reported C_{min}	Implemented C_{min}
UMass	Twitter (Krovetz)	None	0.798	-
LSH	None	None	-	0.890
LSH	Twitter	None	0.694	0.705
LSH	Twitter (Porter)	None	0.756	0.745
LSH	Twitter	MSR	0.739	-
LSH	Twitter	Syntactic	0.729	-
LSH	Twitter	WordNet	0.679	-
LSH	Twitter	Word Embeddings	-	**0.638▲**

Table 1: C_{min} results over the Twitter testing dataset that have either been reported in the literature (Reported) or implemented by the authors (Implemented). Lower C_{min} scores are better. Statistically significant improvements (paired t-test signed rank test $p < 0.05$) over the (Implemented) LSH baseline (with Twitter pre-processing) are denoted ▲.

stemming (reported: 0.756 vs. implemented: 0.745). We therefore confirm the finding of [11] that stemming hurts FSD performance in Twitter. Overall, since our implemented results are similar to the reported results it is reasonable to compare results between the reported column and implemented column of Table 1.

Next, we present the FSD results arising from using our proposed data-driven method for generating lexical paraphrases. As explained in Section 4, we first tune the model parameters (i.e. thresholds on the cosine similarity scores) θ_1, θ_2 on the training dataset, obtaining a minimum C_{min}= 0.458 with θ_1=0.2, θ_2=0.8 (Figure 1). We then fix these parameters at the optimal values found on the training dataset and run our model once on the testing dataset, reporting the result. Comparing our proposed approach with the LSH-FSD baseline we observe that FSD performance can be improved by a statistically significant margin of 9.5% (baseline: 0.705, WE: 0.638). To answer our research question (**RQ-1**), we can conclude that using word embeddings to obtain lexical paraphrases can improve FSD effectiveness on Twitter data.

Finally, comparing the performance of our proposed approach to the LSH-FSD system of [11] using the MSR, syntactic and WordNet curated paraphrases, we make two findings. Firstly, our automatic means of computing paraphrases using word embeddings markedly improves FSD performance, whereas the automatically curated MSR and syntactic paraphrases of [11] actually were found to hurt FSD performance (e.g. MSR: 0.739 vs. WE: 0.638). Secondly, we observe a relative 6.0% gain in performance over tweet expansion using WordNet (WordNet: 0.679 vs. WE: 0.638), a particularly encouraging finding given that WordNet is manually curated whereas our paraphrases are automatically generated.

6. CONCLUSIONS

In this paper we showed how the similarity between dense real-valued word embeddings could be used to mine effective lexical paraphrases in an entirely automatic manner. We used the obtained paraphrase pairs to mitigate the problem of lexical variation on the task of first story detection (FSD) over Twitter data. Tweets were expanded with related terms, allowing the FSD system to ignore related tweets that were seen earlier in the stream but used different, related words. Through evaluation on a standard Twitter FSD dataset, we showed that FSD effectiveness can be improved by a statistically significant margin over a state-of-the-art FSD system. Furthermore, this approach is more

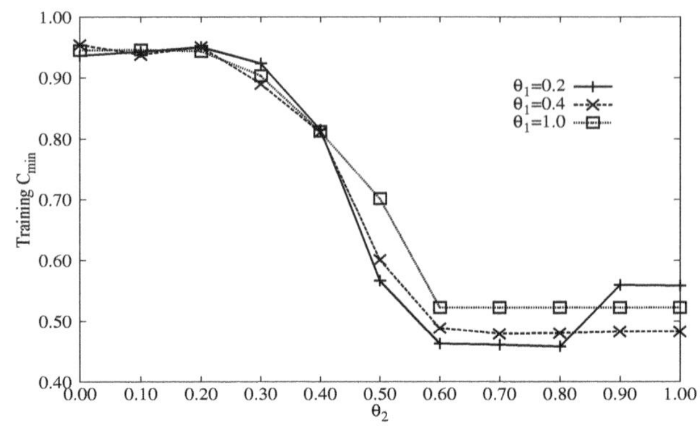

Figure 1: Tuning the θ_1, θ_2 threshold parameters on the training dataset. Filtering embeddings using all five word lists leads to the lowest C_{min}=0.458 at $\theta_1 = 0.2, \theta_2 = 0.8$.

effective than an approach that expands tweets using paraphrases obtained from WordNet, a linguistic resource that is very expensive to construct. For future work, we are interested in extending our approach to harvest paraphrases in other languages, such as Arabic, for use in a multilingual streaming FSD system.

7. ACKNOWLEDGMENTS

We acknowledge support from both the integrated Multimedia City Data (iMCD) project within the ESRC-funded Urban Big Data Centre (ES/L011921/1) and the EC co-funded SUPER (FP7-606853) project.

8. REFERENCES

[1] J. Fiscus Overview of of the TDT 2001 evaluation and results. In *Proc. TDT*, 2001.

[2] J. Allan. Introduction to topic detection and tracking. In *Proc. TDT*, 2002.

[3] C. Callison-Burch Syntactic constraints on paraphrases extracted from parallel corpora. In *Proc. EMNLP*, 2008.

[4] P. Indyk and R. Motwani. Approximate nearest neighbors: Towards removing the curse of dimensionality. In *Proc. STOC*, 1998.

[5] D. Wurzer, V. Lavrenko, M. Osborne Twitter-scale New Event Detection via K-term Hashing. In *Proc. EMNLP*, 2015.

[6] G. Miller. WordNet: a lexical database for English. Communications of the ACM, 38 (11), 1995.

[7] R. Lebret, and R. Collobert. N-gram-Based Low-Dimensional Representation for Document Classification. In *Proc. ICLP*, 2015.

[8] M. Charikar. Similarity Estimation Techniques from Rounding Algorithms. In *Proc. STOC*, 2002.

[9] T. Mikolov, K. Chen, G. Corrado and J. Dean. Efficient estimation of word representations in vector space. In *Proc. ICLR*, 2013.

[10] S. Petrović, M. Osborne, and V. Lavrenko. Streaming first story detection with application to Twitter. In *Proc. NAACL*, 2010.

[11] S. Petrović, M. Osborne and V. Lavrenko. Using paraphrases for improving first story detection in news and Twitter. In *Proc. NAACL*, 2012.

[12] C. Quirk, C. Brockett, and W. Dola. Monolingual machine translation for paraphrase generation. In *Proc. EMNLP*, 2004.

Examining the Coherence of the Top Ranked Tweet Topics

Anjie Fang[1], Craig Macdonald[2], Iadh Ounis[2], Philip Habel[2]
[1]a.fang.1@research.gla.ac.uk, [2]{firstname.secondname}@glasgow.ac.uk
University of Glasgow, UK

ABSTRACT

Topic modelling approaches help scholars to examine the topics discussed in a corpus. Due to the popularity of Twitter, two distinct methods have been proposed to accommodate the brevity of tweets: the *tweet pooling method* and *Twitter LDA*. Both of these methods demonstrate a higher performance in producing more interpretable topics than the standard Latent Dirichlet Allocation (LDA) when applied on tweets. However, while various metrics have been proposed to estimate the coherence of the generated topics from tweets, the coherence of the top ranked topics, those that are most likely to be examined by users, has not been investigated. In addition, the effect of the number of generated topics K on the topic coherence scores has not been studied. In this paper, we conduct large-scale experiments using three topic modelling approaches over two Twitter datasets, and apply a state-of-the-art coherence metric to study the coherence of the top ranked topics and how K affects such coherence. Inspired by ranking metrics such as *precision at n*, we use *coherence at n* to assess the coherence of a topic model. To verify our results, we conduct a pairwise user study to obtain human preferences over topics. Our findings are threefold: we find evidence that *Twitter LDA* outperforms both LDA and the *tweet pooling method* because the top ranked topics it generates have more coherence; we demonstrate that a larger number of topics (K) helps to generate topics with more coherence; and finally, we show that *coherence at n* is more effective when evaluating the coherence of a topic model than the average coherence score.

1. INTRODUCTION

Topic modelling approaches – e.g. Latent Dirichlet Allocation (LDA) [1] – are widely used to discover latent topics within a corpus [4, 5]. As Twitter has gained in popularity, scholars have sought out ways to understand and model discussions on the forum. However tweet corpora are unlike other corpora (e.g. news articles and books), namely because they are short (limited to 140 characters), and they contain colloquial phrases and snippet text such as hashtags. Two well-known topic modelling applications for Twitter data are *Twitter LDA* (TLDA) [12] and LDA applied alongside the *tweet pooling method* (PLDA) [7]. Both methods have been shown to produce more interpretable topics than LDA on Twitter corpora [7, 12]. On the other hand, several metrics have been proposed in the literature to automatically estimate the coherence of the generated topic models. For example, Newman et al. [8] proposed a Pointwise Mutual Information(PMI)-based metric using Wikipedia as a background dataset to evaluate the coherence of a topic from news articles and books. More recently, a new coherence PMI-based metric using a Twitter background has been proposed for tweet corpora, and was found to be the closest to human judgements [2].

However, the coherence of the top ranked topics from tweets, those most likely to be examined by users, has not been previously investigated, nor has the effect of the number of generated topics K on the topic coherence scores. In this paper, we conduct large-scale experiments on two Twitter datasets to investigate the coherence of ranked topics generated by three topic modelling approaches (LDA, TLDA and PLDA). Inspired by the *precision at n* evaluation metric, we also explore the *coherence at n* scores of the generated topic models by using the state-of-the-art Twitter PMI-based coherence metric [2], which we describe in Section 3. The contributions of this paper are as follows: 1) we examine which of the three existing topic modelling approaches for Twitter data generates more coherent topics, 2) we analyse the relationship between the coherence of a topic model and the number of topics (K), and 3) we evaluate the utility of the *coherence at n* coherence metric for a topic model. To validate our findings, we perform a pairwise preference user study conducted on a crowdsourcing platform, where the workers are asked to choose the more coherent topic in a topic pair. The obtained human judgements are then compared with the coherence score of the generated topic models. We show, first, that TLDA performs better than LDA and PLDA; second, that a higher topic number K helps to produce topics with higher coherence; and finally, that the *coherence at n* scores are more effective than the commonly used averages in evaluating the coherence of a topic model.

2. BACKGROUND & RELATED WORK

LDA [1] models latent *topics* across *terms* and *documents*, where a topic is described as a probability distribution over terms Φ, and a document has its own probability distribution over topics. LDA has been used extensively to extract latent topics in standard corpora such as news articles and books [5]. Because tweets can be of lower quality due to the brevity of their content [6, 12], topics generated by using LDA are likely to be both mixed [11] and harder to interpret by the associated terms. In order to improve the performance of LDA for Twitter data, Mehrotra et al. [7] have proposed the *tweet pooling method*, which groups tweets into virtual documents (e.g. sharing the same author or the same hashtag). We refer to the application of LDA alongside the *tweet pooling method* as PLDA. TLDA is another approach

SIGIR '16, July 17-21, 2016, Pisa, Italy

DOI: http://dx.doi.org/10.1145/2911451.2914731

from Zhao et al. [12], where a background term distribution is used to distinguish "real" topic terms from background terms, with the assumption that a single tweet contains a single topic. Indeed both PLDA and TLDA have outperformed LDA in producing more coherent topics [7, 12].

Newman et al. [8] conducted a user study to evaluate several proposed coherence metrics based on capturing the semantic similarity of the topics using external sources, e.g. Wikipedia and WordNet. They found that the most suitable coherence metric was based on estimating the Pointwise Mutual Information (PMI) of word pairs in a topic for corpora such as news articles. Stevens et al. [9] used the same Wikipedia PMI-based metric to analyse the coherence of the generated topic models from news articles.

Recently, a large-scale user study in [2] evaluated several coherence metrics including the Wikipedia PMI-based and WordNet-based metrics on tweets. Fang et al. [2] showed that a newly proposed coherence metric leveraging a Twitter background dataset, called the *Twitter PMI-based metric* (hereafter, T-PMI), has a markablely high agreement with human judgements on tweet corpora. In the following, we use the T-PMI metric to evaluate the coherence of the topics generated by using three topic modelling approaches: LDA, TLDA, and PLDA. We further study the coherence of the top ranked topics likely to be examined by users, and the effect of the number of generated topics K on the topic coherence scores. To the best of our knowledge, this paper contributes the first study of the coherence of the top ranked topics and how K affects such coherence on tweets.

3. METRICS

We now describe the T-PMI coherence metric, which analyses the coherence of topics and topic models. In the T-PMI metric [2], a topic t is first represented by the 10 most frequent words $\{w_1, w_2, ..., w_{10}\}$ selected by the topic term probabilities in Φ. Any two words among the 10 words in a topic make a word pair, e.g. Pair(w_i,w_j). The coherence C of a topic is measured by averaging the PMI score of all its word pairs using Equation (1), where we use the top 10 words representing a topic, i.e. $n = 10$. The PMI score of a word pair is pre-calculated using Equation (2) from a Twitter background dataset. We describe how we set up this metric in Section 4.

$$C(t) = \frac{1}{\sum_{m=1}^{n-1} m} \sum_{i=1}^{n} \sum_{j=i+1}^{n} PMI(w_i, w_j) \quad (1)$$

$$PMI(w_i, w_j) = log \frac{p(w_i, w_j)}{p(w_i) \times p(w_j)} \quad (2)$$

We use the three aforementioned topic modelling approaches to obtain the topic models from tweets, varying the topic number K. We use the T-PMI coherence metric to calculate the average coherence of a topic model, i.e. the coherence score across all K topics. Intuitively, the average coherence of a topic model reflects the quality of the entire topic model (containing K topics). However, end-users typically are only interested in the most coherent topics in a topic model, rather than the whole model. Inspired by ranking metrics such as the *precision at n* metric, we use *coherence at n* to evaluate the coherence of a topic model. In particular, *coherence at n* (coherence@n) indicates the average coherence score of the top n most coherent topics, where a topic is ranked by its coherence score. We argue that *coherence at n* can more effectively capture the coherence of a Twitter topic model.

Table 1: Two used Twitter datasets.

Name	Time Period	Users#	Tweets#
(1) MAY	1 to 31 May 2015	2,452	334,922
(2) TVD	8 to 10pm, 02 Apr 2015	121,594	343,511

4. DATASETS & EXPERIMENTAL SETUP

We use two datasets in our experiments. The first[1] is comprised of the tweets of 2,452 newspaper journalists in New York posted from 01/05/2015 to 31/05/2015, denoted here as MAY. We can reasonably assume that journalists discussed a large number of topics over this one-month period. The second dataset[1] consists of tweets related to the first TV debate among political party leaders during the UK General Election of 2015, denoted here as TVD. We expect that the number of topics covered over this short time period to be more limited, as conversations on Twitter tended to focus around the issues introduced during the two-hour debate. Details of these two datasets are shown in Table 1.

We use a Twitter background dataset from [2, 3], which contains 1%-5% random tweets posted from 01/01/ 2015 to 30/06/2015. Following [2, 3], we remove stopwords, terms occurring in less than 20 tweets and the retweets from this background dataset. The remaining tweets (30,151,847) are used to calculate the prior PMI score of the occurring word pairs in order to implement the T-PMI metric.

We use the Mallet[2] and Twitter LDA[3] toolkits to apply the three topic modelling approaches. For PLDA, we group the tweets posted by the same user in a given time interval into a virtual document[4]. The time interval is set to 10 minutes for TVD, and 6 hours for MAY, given the narrow time period of the TVD dataset and the more expansive one for the MAY dataset. The LDA parameters α and β are set to $50/K$ and 0.01 following [10], and the TLDA parameter γ is set to 20 following [12]. Since the TVD dataset contains just two hours of tweets, we set the maximum topic number K to 100, and then use 46 different K values between 10 and 100 (step = 2). We set K to a maximum of 500 for MAY, and use 49 different K values ranging from 10 to 500 (step = 10). Each topic modelling approach is run 5 times for each K. Thus, we obtain 5 topic models for each K. In the next section, we analyse the coherence of these 1,425 topic models ($46 \times 5 \times 3 + 49 \times 5 \times 3$).

5. COHERENCE OF TOPIC MODELS

Figure 1 shows the T-PMI coherence of three types of topic models (LDA, TLDA, and PLDA) for MAY and TVD, varying K. Each point in Figure 1 represents the average coherence or coherence@n score of 5 topics models, for $n = \{5, 10, 20, 30, 40\}$. For instance, the point (20, 0.0020) on the red line in Figure 1(a) shows that the average coherence score of the top 5 topics (coherence@5) in the 5 topic models where K=20 is 0.0020. Higher scores indicate better coherence.

First, it is clear that the average coherence (the solid black line) of all topics in a model decreases as K increases across the three topic modelling approaches. These results are similar to what Stevens et al. [9] observed. However, the coherence@n score (represented by coloured lines with distinguishing symbols) of all topic models increases as K grows. This finding tells us that setting a higher number of topics,

[1] Collected using the Twitter API. [2] mallet.cs.umass.edu
[3] github.com/minghui/Twitter-LDA [4] We do not group tweets by hashtags since there are not many hashtags in our datasets.

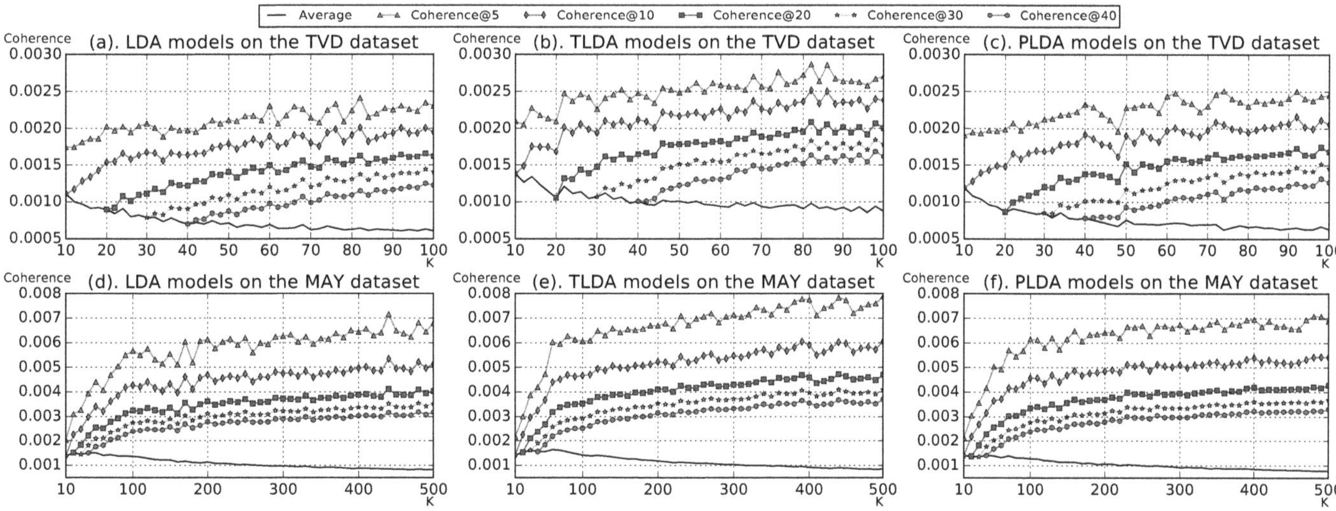

Figure 1: The coherence of three types of topic models with varying K over two datasets.

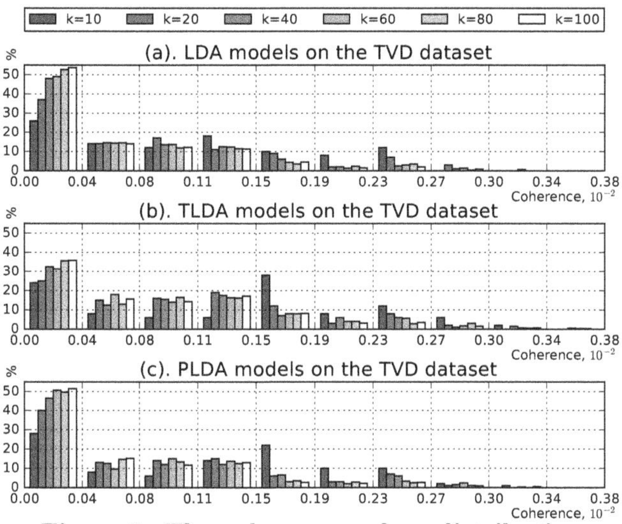

Figure 2: The coherence values distribution.

K, increases the coherence of the n most coherent topics. Second, the coherence@n score is higher for TLDA across the two datasets, which suggests that the top n topics in the TLDA models have a higher coherence. We also see that PLDA generates slightly more coherent topics than LDA, although the performance of PLDA is closer to LDA than to TLDA. Third, we observe that the average coherence and coherence@n score of the LDA & PLDA topic models on the TVD dataset become stable around K=80, while the coherence of the TLDA topic models on the MAY dataset has a local peak around K=390. It should be noted that the average coherence score cannot adequately capture the performance differences of the 3 topic modelling approaches on the MAY dataset (see Figure 1(d), (e) and (f)), and so coherence@n is preferred. Since a larger K leads to a higher computational cost, a K should be selected when the coherence of the topic model begins to stabilise or when it reaches a local peak.

Next, in Figure 2, we show the distribution of the topics' coherence scores for topic models with varying K on the TVD dataset. The coherence scores are distributed across 10 bins, to show the number of topics exhibiting different levels of coherence. First, the volume of topics with coherence $[0, 0.4^{-3})$ is highest across all topic models in the TVD dataset. As K increases, the topic models include more topics with less coherence. This is why the average coherence of the topic models declines as K increases, shown in Figure 1 by the solid black lines. Second, the volume of topics with coherence $[0, 0.4^{-3})$ is lowest in the TLDA models. This result further indicates that TLDA outperforms PLDA and LDA, as it generates fewer meaningless topics. We also observe the same pattern for the MAY dataset[5].

To verify that a larger K helps generate topics with higher coherence, and to examine the utility of the coherence@n metric, we conduct a user study in Section 6 where we compare human preferences with the topics' coherence scores from the T-PMI metric.

6. USER STUDY

Because it is challenging for humans to give a graded coherence score for topics, we conduct a pairwise preference user study. Similar studies have been conducted previously in [2, 3]. We recruited workers from CrowdFlower[6] and asked them to select the more coherent topic from two provided topics (a topic pair). We describe here how we generate the topic pairs, the CrowdFlower job, how we control the job quality, and the crowdsourcing results.

Generating Topic Pairs For a given approach (e.g. TLDA), we choose two K = {a,b} ($a < b$) values representing different topic model outcomes with difference coherences (recall that each approach is repeated 5 times, hence 10 models in total). From each selected topic model, we select the top n most coherent topics. Thus, we have two topic pools: $P_{k=a}$ & $P_{k=b}$, and each pool has $5 \times n$ topics[7]. To make the preference task easier for workers, we show two similar topics in a topic pair. First, we sample a number of topics from $P_{k=a}$ randomly. For each sampled topic ($t_j^{P_{k=a}}$), we use Equation (3) to identify its closest topic in $P_{k=b}$, where V_t is a vector representation using the term distribution of topic t. We denote the selected pairs of topics as Pairs($P_{k=a} \rightarrow P_{k=b}$). Likewise, we also generate the same number of Pairs($P_{k=b} \rightarrow P_{k=a}$). In our user study, we use TLDA topic models on the MAY dataset with K={50,100,300,390}, since its K range is set wider than that of the TVD dataset. We compare the coherence of models with K=50 vs. K=300 (denoted as comparison

[5] The figure is not shown due to space limitations.
[6] crowdflower.com [7] Each experiment is repeated 5 times.

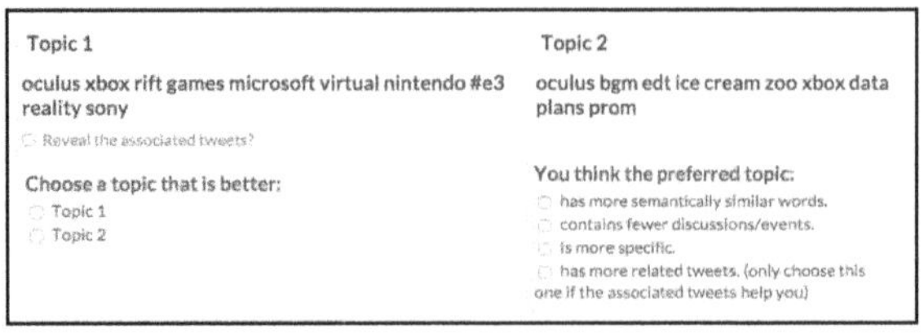

Figure 3: The CrowdFlower user interface.

Unit(50,300)) and topic models with K=100 vs. K=390 (comparison Unit(100,390)). Therefore, we can examine whether topic models with a larger K (300/390) have more coherent topics than the models with smaller K (50/100). For the comparisons Unit(50,300)/Unit(100,390), we select the top 30/20[8] topics for the topic pools ($P_{k=\{50,100,300,390\}}$). We generate 40 topic pairs for each comparison unit. Note that we ignore the topic pairs where two topics in the pair share the same top 10 words or share less than 3 mutual words among the top 10 words. Hence this ensures that the two selected topics in a topic pair are similar enough for humans.

$$closest(t_j^{P_{k=a}}) = argmax_{i<K}\ (cosine(V_{t_j^{P_{k=a}}}, V_{t_i^{P_{k=b}}})) \quad (3)$$

Job Description We present each CrowdFlower worker with the top 10 words (ranked by their probabilities in a topic) from two topics in a topic pair, labelled Topic 1 and Topic 2, along with their 3 most retweeted tweets[9]. Based on these 10 words, we ask the workers to select the more coherent topic among the two shown. We tell the worker that a more coherent topic is one that is less mixed and that can be interpreted. The workers are instructed to take into account: 1) the number of semantically similar words (e.g. President & Obama) among the 10 shown words, 2) whether the words shown suggest a mixed topic (i.e. more than one discussion), and 3) whether the words shown are more specific. A worker can also consider two associated tweets for the two topics if he/she cannot make a decision. We also offer guidance for using these tweets: 1) whether the 10 shown words are reflected by their tweets and 2) whether these tweets are related with the two topics. Figure 3 captures the user interface on CrowdFlower, along with an example of a topic pair. We collect a total of 5 judgements from 5 different workers for each topic pair. For each judgement, we paid workers $0.05.

Quality Control We used test questions for worker quality control. To set these test questions, we began by choosing a number of topic pairs, where the topic preference was manually verified in advance. Only those workers who passed the test were allowed to enter the task. The worker must have maintained more than 70% accuracy on the test questions throughout the whole task, otherwise their judgements were not used. We limited the workers' country to the United States as the MAY tweets were written by New York journalists. Our user study engaged 52 trusted workers.

Crowdsourcing Results Table 2 lists the human judgement results compared with the coherence scores from the T-PMI metric. For comparison unit (50,300) - Table 2(a) - the 40 topics we select from topic models with K=300 are significantly more coherent than those from topic models with K=50 according to both the human vote[10] fraction

[8] The top 20 topics in Unit(100,390) are more distinguishable than the top 30. [9] These tweets help workers understand the topic. [10] A topic in a topic pair receives one vote when it is preferred by a human.

Table 2: The comparison of coherence scores.

(a). TLDA topic models with K=50 vs. K=300, Unit(50,300)

K	Human vote fraction	T-PMI
50	0.311	2.06^{-3}
300	**0.689**$^{(*)}$	$\mathbf{3.15^{-3}}$$^{(*)}$

(b). TLDA topic models with K=100 vs. K=390, Unit(100,390)

K	Human vote fraction	T-PMI
100	0.411	3.54^{-3}
390	**0.589**$^{(**)}$	$\mathbf{4.00^{-3}}$$^{(**)}$

*/(**) denote $p < 0.01$ ($p < 0.05$) according to the Wilcoxon signed-rank test, compared to the smaller K.

and the T-PMI coherence scores. We observe the same results for comparison unit (100,390), c.f. Table 2(b). This finding shows again that a larger K helps to obtain topics with more coherence. However, if one uses only the average coherence score to evaluate the topic model, then these models are indistinguishable. This finding suggests that the coherence@n metric should be used to measure the coherence quality of a topic model.

7. CONCLUSIONS

This paper studied the coherence of Twitter topic models through a large scale experiment varying both the topic modelling approach and K, and thereafter verified conclusions using a pairwise user study. To summarise, we first found that *Twitter LDA* (TLDA) outperformed PLDA and LDA, as it generated topics with a higher coherence and also less meaningless topics. Second, we showed that increasing the number of topics (K) helped to generate topics with a higher coherence. Third, *coherence at n* is more effective in evaluating a topic model than the average coherence. Our paper has two implications for researchers implementing topic modelling on tweets: first, larger K values result in the top n topics being the most coherent ($n < K$); second, when evaluating the coherence of a topic model, scholars should use the *coherence at n* metric.

8. REFERENCES

[1] D. M. Blei, A. Y. Ng, and M. I. Jordan. Latent dirichlet allocation. *the Journal of machine Learning research*, 3:993–1022, 2003.

[2] A. Fang, C. Macdonald, I. Ounis, and P. Habel. Topics in tweets: A user study of topic coherence metrics for Twitter data. In *Proc. of ECIR*, 2016.

[3] A. Fang, C. Macdonald, I. Ounis, and P. Habel. Using word embedding to evaluate the coherence of topics from Twitter data. In *Proc. of SIGIR*, 2016.

[4] A. Fang, I. Ounis, P. Habel, C. Macdonald, and N. Limsopatham. Topic-centric classification of Twitter user's political orientation. In *Proc. of SIGIR*, 2015.

[5] T. L. Griffiths and M. Steyvers. Finding scientific topics. In *Proc. of NAS*, 2004.

[6] L. Hong and B. D. Davison. Empirical study of topic modeling in Twitter. In *Proc. of SOMA*, 2010.

[7] R. Mehrotra, S. Sanner, W. Buntine, and L. Xie. Improving LDA topic models for microblogs via tweet pooling and automatic labeling. In *Proc. of SIGIR*, 2013.

[8] D. Newman, J. H. Lau, K. Grieser, and T. Baldwin. Automatic evaluation of topic coherence. In *Proc. of NAACL*, 2010.

[9] K. Stevens, P. Kegelmeyer, D. Andrzejewski, and D. Buttler. Exploring topic coherence over many models and many topics. In *Proc. of EMNLP-CoNLL*, 2012.

[10] M. Steyvers and T. Griffiths. Probabilistic topic models. *Handbook of latent semantic analysis*, 427:424–440, 2007.

[11] J. Tang, Z. Meng, X. Nguyen, Q. Mei, and M. Zhang. Understanding the limiting factors of topic modeling via posterior contraction analysis. In *Proc. of ICML*, 2014.

[12] W. X. Zhao, J. Jiang, J. Weng, J. He, E.-P. Lim, H. Yan, and X. Li. Comparing Twitter and traditional media using topic models. In *Proc. of ECIR*, 2011.

Explicit In Situ User Feedback for Web Search Results

Jin Young Kim
Microsoft
Redmond, WA USA
jink@microsoft.com

Jaime Teevan
Microsoft Research
Redmond, WA USA
teevan@microsoft.com

Nick Craswell
Microsoft
Redmond, WA USA
nickcr@microsoft.com

ABSTRACT
Gathering evidence about whether a search result is relevant is a core concern in the evaluation and improvement of information retrieval systems. Two common sources of evidence for establishing relevance are judgements from trained assessors and logs of online user behavior. However, both are limited; it is hard for a trained assessor to know exactly what users want to find, and user behavior only provides an implicit and ambiguous signal. In this paper, we aim to address these limitations by collecting explicit feedback on web search results from users in situ as they search. When users return to the search result page via the browser back button after having clicked on a result, we ask them to provide a binary thumbs up or thumbs down judgment and text feedback. We collect in situ feedback from a large commercial search engine, and compare this feedback with the judgments provided by trained assessors. We find that in situ feedback differs significantly from traditional relevance judgments, and that it suggests a different interpretation of behavior signals, with the dwell time threshold between negative and positive in situ feedback being 87 seconds, longer than the more common heuristic of 30 seconds. Using text feedback from users, we discuss why user feedback may differ from editorial judgments.

CCS Concepts
• **Information systems→Evaluation of retrieval results**

Keywords
IR evaluation, explicit user feedback, web search

1. INTRODUCTION & RELATED WORK
Web search engines are able to collect large scale behavioral log data as users search. This has enabled significant advances in search engine's ability to identify relevant content and evaluate various approaches. Because logs are collected in situ, they provide a rich picture of real people performing self-motivated searches. However, logs are not a direct source of relevance judgments. Instead they provide some implicit evidence of relevance, which must be interpreted with care.

One common way that search engines use log data is to try to determine if a search result is relevant. The most obvious approach is to assume that any search result that a user clicks after issuing a query is relevant, but it quickly becomes clear that users sometimes click on irrelevant results. To refine this measure, researchers began using the amount of time that a user spends engaging with the clicked result before performing their next action, referred to as their *dwell time* on a result, as a signal of relevance. A popular heuristic for this is to consider search results with a dwell time equaling to or exceeding 30 seconds as relevant [3, 6]. While experimental results suggest that dwell time can serve as a proxy for relevance or interest [2, 3, 5], researchers have shown that it can be impacted by characteristics of the query [8], task [1, 5], or search result page [6, 8].

To better understand a user's intent behind observed web search log data, it is useful to correlate the implicit data with some sort of explicit ground truth. A number of early studies [2, 3, 5] did this by instrumenting people's browsers to actively request feedback from real users in situ as they performed real self-motivated tasks. For example, Claypool et al. [2] developed a custom browser that was used by 75 students during undirected web browsing in a lab setting. Over the course of several days, these students provided feedback by answering the question, "How interesting is this page?" each time they left a page. Other researchers [3, 5] collected in situ feedback in the context of web search. Kelly & Belkin [5] provided seven graduate students with laptops installed with custom logging software to collect feedback related to their search task and the usefulness of the content they found over the course of 14 weeks. Fox et al. [3] provided a web browser plug-in to 146 Microsoft employees that popped up a dialog box requesting explicit feedback whenever a participant searched. A general finding across this research is that users dwell longer on web content they find relevant or interesting. We take a similar approach to collect explicit feedback from search engine users, updating these findings with insight from a more recent search system, as web search has changed a lot in the past 10 years. Additionally, because we collect feedback within the context of an existing search system we are able to capture a much broader array of users, versus just students or employees at a single institution.

Of course, there are drawbacks to collecting explicit feedback from users in situ. The feedback request may be missed or ignored by many users. Giving feedback may be inconvenient and disruptive to the search process, possibly impacting the logged user behavior. One way to address the challenges with collecting user feedback or interpreting log data is to instead collect explicit relevance judgments from expert raters. For example, Kim et al. [6] develop a rich model of dwell time by collecting relevance judgments from trained assessors for thousands of queries. However, we know that personal context (task [5], individual preferences [9], etc.) matters a lot, making it hard to provide external judgments. For this reason, we look at the difference between external relevance judgments from trained assessors and in-situ feedback from the actual user.

This paper presents an illustration of the different ways to understand large scale behavioral data via in situ relevance feedback and judge ratings, using dwell time as an example. We begin by describing our approach to collecting data – including implicit log data, explicit in-situ user feedback, and relevance judgments from trained assessors – and show that there are significant differences between a user's explicit feedback and that of trained assessors. We look at both data in terms of dwell time,

SIGIR'16, July 17–21, 2016, Pisa, Italy .
© 2016 ACM. ISBN 978-1-4503-4069-4/16/07…$15.00.
DOI: http://dx.doi.org/10.1145/2911451.2914754

Figure 1. The user experience for collecting in situ feedback.

and suggest based on the data we collect that the current dwell time cut-off for satisfaction in search should be extended to 87 seconds.

2. METHODOLOGY

Here we describe the data collection method for our analysis. We focus on the in-situ feedback collection, which a novel aspect of our work. To explore dwell time from many different perspectives, we collected data for the same set of query-URL pairs from three different sources: search engine logs, in situ user feedback, and relevance judgments from external trained assessors.

2.1 Search Engine Log Data

We analyze the behavioral logs collected by a major internet search engine. We sampled five days of log data from September 2015 for users in the United States English language locale, collecting data for 4,738,204 total search result page views (see Table 1). The sample was filtered to remove bots, spam, and outliers. The logs contain anonymous user ID, time stamp, query, and results clicked. To determine how long a user dwelt on a search result page from the logs, we use the time stamp of the result click and the timestamp of any subsequent behavior the user has with the search within 30 minutes. Note that this means we are only able to identify the dwell time for results where the user has a subsequent interaction with the search engine.

2.2 In Situ User Feedback

In addition to collecting implicit behavioral information from users, the search engine was also instrumented to solicit in situ explicit feedback from users.

Table 1. Statistics of the Feedback Data

Statistics	Count	Ratio
# Overall	4,738,204	N/A
# Request	370,126	7.81%
# Response	1,044	0.28%
# Comments	18	1.7%

2.2.1 Feedback User Experience

Figure 1 shows how this was feedback was collected. As is the case with dwell time, it is only possible for a search engine to collect feedback from a user after having visited a search result is the user returns to the search engine to interact with it. For this reason, we created a feedback experience for users following a back button click. A user first clicks on a web search result (step 1) and visits that result. When the user returns to the search engine results page (step 2), the result they clicked is augmented with the question, "Was this result helpful?" along with a thumbs up and thumbs down button. To draw the user's attention to the feedback request, the result is outlined with a blue bounding box. Users are free to ignore the request, but if they click thumbs up or down (step 3), we request additional comments with the prompt, "Give more feedback." Again, users can ignore this additional request, but if they click it (step 4), we show a comment box in the bottom right corner of the screen.

The feedback experience is designed to be lightweight and unobtrusive. For example, while previous studies have offered between 3 [3] and 7 [5] options for feedback, we limit the interface to a simple binary to make it familiar and easy for users. It is only visible when users return after clicking, and only on the clicked result. We also stop showing feedback requests for the rest of the session after the user responds.

2.2.2 Feedback Data Collection

We collected feedback from a fraction of real users of a large commercial search engine. As summarized in Table 1, we displayed 370,126 feedback requests out of a sample of more than 4.7 million, touching 7.8% of the traffic in this sample. Among the feedback requests we made, we received 1,044 responses, which translates into 0.28% response rate. All of the results for which a user provides a thumbs up feedback we consider "satisfactory," and all results that receive a thumbs down are considered "unsatisfactory." Among the thumbs up/down feedback responses, we further received textual comments in 18 cases (1.7%). While the response rate is low, it is consistent with the fact that collecting in situ feedback from people is challenging. For example, the search engine displays a generic "Send Feedback" button at the bottom of each search result page, and receives feedback on less than 0.00001% of all pages displayed.

2.2.3 Limitations to the Feedback Collected

While the collected feedback represents real people's experiences on real search tasks, there are some limitations of data collected in this manner. Of particular note are potential query and user biases.

Potential query and result biases: Because the search engine can only instrument the results page, feedback is limited to cases where the user returns to the search engine after clicking. While over half of all queries involve a return [7], many queries (including most navigational queries) do not. Previous work (e.g., [3]) has addressed this issue by requiring people to install software. This

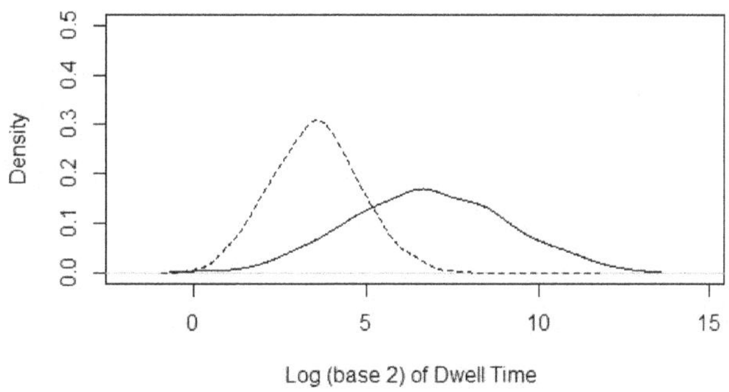

Figure 2. Density estimation for dwell time (in log scale) on web results for satisfactory results (solid line) vs. unsatisfactory results (dotted line)

enables feedback to be captured for all queries, but limits the set of users from whom feedback can be captured.

Potential user biases: Because users are able to decide whether or not to provide feedback, there is a selection bias among users. As shown in Table 2, We see that the subset of users who provided feedback tended to interact more with the results, with much higher chances to click on SERP. However, their dwell time behavior is similar (median dwell time of users who did not provided the feedback: 59 second, who provided any feedback: 62 second), and that is the area of focus for this paper.

Table 2. Comparing the aggregate behavior of user groups

Response to Feedback	% of pages with any click on SERP	Median dwell time on web results
Yes	88.4%	62 seconds
No	55.2%	59 seconds

2.3 External Assessor Relevance Judgments

To compare in situ user feedback with relevance judgments provided by trained assessors, we also collected external relevance judgments for the 1,044 query-URL pairs for which we received in situ user feedback. The assessors were trained for this kind of labeling, receiving instructions to rate the relevance of the URL for given query in 5-point scale representing: Perfect, Excellent, Good, Fair, and Bad. In doing so, judges are asked to imagine a population of possible users who issued the query, considering multiple possible intents behind the query and their relative likelihood.

3. DATA ANALYSIS

We correlate the in situ feedback we collected with user behavior observed in the logs, focusing on dwell time, and then look at the dwell time threshold suggested using external assessor relevance judgments. We see that the ideal dwell time to separate satisfied and unsatisfied clicks is different depending on the type of judgment used, and show that the reason for this is that the in situ feedback looks very different from external relevance judgments.

3.1 Dwell Time Using In Situ Feedback

Online user behavior may be used to understand various aspects of the search service. Here we focus on dwell time as an indicator of the user's satisfaction with the page. We know that users can spend a long time and still be dissatisfied, or vice versa. Our goal is to determine how accurate dwell time is as the measure of user satisfaction using our in situ user feedback.

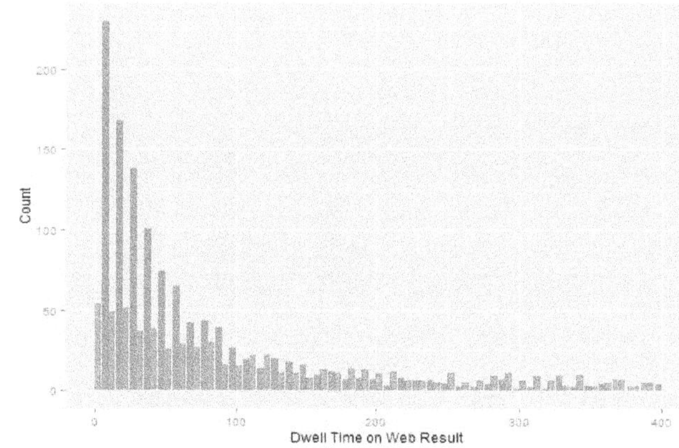

Figure 3. Histogram of dwell time distribution for satisfactory (green) vs. unsatisfactory results (red)

We refer to the thumbs up case as a satisfied (SAT) user and the thumbs down case as a dissatisfied (DSAT) user. Figure 2 shows dwell time density estimates (in log scale) for the two cases, with SAT as a solid line and DSAT as a dotted line. It is clear that the dwell time distribution is skewed toward right for SAT results. The median dwell time for SAT results is 110 seconds, 34 seconds for DSAT results.

But can the dwell time alone clearly separate between satisfactory vs. unsatisfactory results? In Figure 3 we plotted the histogram of dwell time distribution for SAT results (green) vs. DSAT results (red). Here, while there is clear trend of satisfactory results having relatively longer dwell time, there are some fraction of results where users are satisfied with less than 30 seconds of visit, and dissatisfied after spending quite a long time. This confirms the

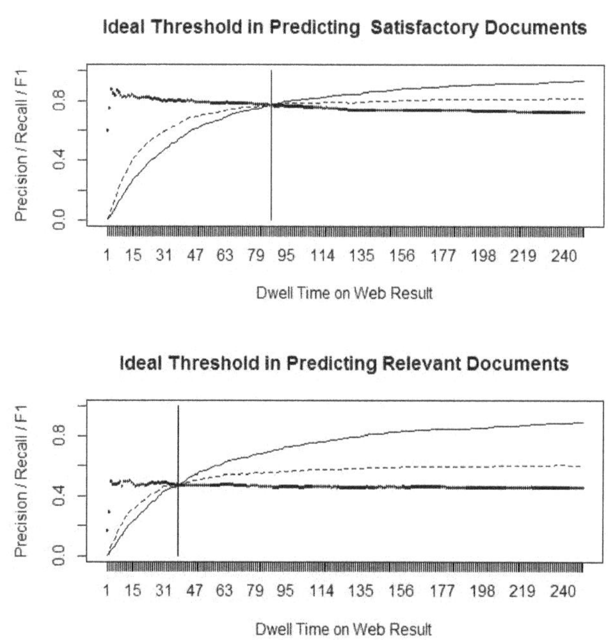

Figure 4. The precision-recall curve when using dwell time threshold to predict in situ user feedback (top) or external judgments by trained assessors (bottom).

Figure 5. Comparison of in situ user feedback with external judgments from trained assessors.

conjecture that time is an important, but not a sufficient indicator of user satisfaction.

One way to find the ideal threshold is to consider the dwell time threshold as the classification boundary between SAT vs. DSAT cases, where we consider any impression with dwell time above the threshold as SAT, and vice versa. When we try to predict user satisfaction, we found that the threshold which gives the best F1 score is 87 seconds as shown in a dashed lines in Figure 4 (top).

3.2 Dwell Time Using External Judgments

Using the same analysis we used to extract the ideal dwell time based on the in situe feedback we collected, we also look at the ideal dwell time that can be calculated using the external assessor relevance judgments. To map 5-scale label to SAT and DSAT, we binarized the judgments to consider Perfert, Excellent, Good and Fair labels as SAT, and Bad as DSAT. Here we find that the threshold was 38 seconds, which roughly agrees with the threshold known in literature [3] yet is significantly shorter than the 87 seconds based on user feedback as shown in Figure 4 (bottom).

3.3 In Situ Feedback vs. External Judgments

To understand why the dwell time differs so significantly as a function of the data we use, we look more closely at the data we collected via in situ feedback and judgments from trained assessors. Figure 5 shows how SAT / DSAT labels from in situ user feedback compares with 5-scale labels from trained assessors. Overall, we can see the increase in DSAT labels as we move into lower scale in relevance judgment. However, there are considerable fraction of DSAT feedback in Perfect judgment, and vice versa for Bad judgment.

As was the case for user behavior, the results indicate a reasonable correlation with user satisfaction, yet the degree of disagreement is nontrivial. Among many possible explanations, the most plausible one is that the nature of human judgment where judges are asked to target the satisfaction of user population. For instance, we found several instances where user expressed dissatisfaction when we returned the right result for queries with clear navigational intent. (e.g., www.facebook.com for query 'facebook'). This illustrates that users in situ have idiosyncratic search intents which are not easy to be predicted by external judges.

Some of text comments we received following feedback reveal insights for why user feedback may not match the external judgments. There was a user who left a negative feedback on a page about a nurse practitioner after typing the name of the nurse. The comment said, "No phone number listed," implying that the user was looking for phone number. (Judge rating: Fair.) Also, there was a query {what is a connection string} which resulted in a click on a page with reasonable explanation of the concept. But the textual user feedback said, "No example to go with your instruction." (Judge rating: Good.) Examples like this show that user feedback can reveal varied nuances on users' intent which would not have been clear from the query.

4. CONCLUSIONS

We discussed the limitations to the use of human judgement or online user behavior for improving information retrieval systems, and addressed these limitations by collecting explicit feedback for web search results from searchers in situ as they search. When users return to the search result page after having clicked on a result, they are given an opportunity to provide a binary thumbs up or thumbs down judgment and text feedback. Our experiment with large commercial search engine reveals that this high-quality in situ feedback differs significantly from relevance judgments inferred using human judgment or online behavior. Using search result dwell time as an example, we show that the best possible cutoff to identify relevant documents is 87 seconds, while the 30 second limit that is commonly used in the literature risks accidentally identifying irrelevant documents as relevant. Based on users' comments, we also find that individual user's feedback can be different from labels from trained judges who aim to predict the satisfaction of user population as a whole.

5. REFERENCES

[1] Chilton, L. and Teevan, J. (2011). Addressing information needs directly in the search result page. In *Proceedings of WWW 2011.*

[2] Claypool, M., Le, P., Wased, M. and Brown, D. (2001). Implicit interest indicators. In *Proceedings of IUI 2001.*

[3] Fox, S., K. Karnawat, M. Mydland, S. Dumais, and T. White. Evaluating implicit measures to improve Web search. TOIS, 23(2), 2005, 147-168.

[4] Joachims, T., L. Granka, B. Pan, H. Hembrooke, F. Radlinski, and G. Gay. Evaluating the accuracy of implicit feedback from clicks and query reformulations in Web search. TOIS 25(2), 2007.

[5] Kelly, D. and Belkin, N. (2004). Display time as implicit feedback: Understanding task effects. In *Proceedings of SIGIR 2004.*

[6] Kim, Y., Hassan, A., White, R.W. and Zitouni, I. (2014). Modeling dwell time to predict click-level satisfaction. In *Proceedings of WSDM 2014.*

[7] Lee, C.J., Teevan, J. and de la Chica, S. (2014). Characterizing multi-click behavior and the risks and opportunities of changing results during use. In *Proceedings of SIGIR 2014.*

[8] Liu, C., White, R.W. and Dumais, S.T. (2010). Understanding web browsing behaviors through Weibull analysis of dwell time. In *Proceedings of SIGIR 2010.*

[9] Teevan, J., Dumais, S.T. and Horvitz, E. (2010). Potential for Personalization. TOCHI, 17(1).

Exploiting CPU SIMD Extensions to Speed-up Document Scoring with Tree Ensembles

Claudio Lucchese
ISTI–CNR, Italy and Istella Srl
c.lucchese@isti.cnr.it

Franco Maria Nardini
ISTI–CNR, Italy and Istella Srl
f.nardini@isti.cnr.it

Salvatore Orlando
U. of Venice, Italy
orlando@unive.it

Raffaele Perego
ISTI–CNR, Italy and Istella Srl
r.perego@isti.cnr.it

Nicola Tonellotto
ISTI–CNR, Italy and Istella Srl
n.tonellotto@isti.cnr.it

Rossano Venturini
U. of Pisa, Italy and Istella Srl
rossano@di.unipi.it

ABSTRACT

Scoring documents with *learning-to-rank* (LtR) models based on large ensembles of regression trees is currently deemed one of the best solutions to effectively rank query results to be returned by large scale Information Retrieval systems.

This paper investigates the opportunities given by SIMD capabilities of modern CPUs to the end of efficiently evaluating regression trees ensembles. We propose V-QuickScorer (vQS), which exploits SIMD extensions to vectorize the document scoring, i.e., to perform the ensemble traversal by evaluating multiple documents simultaneously. We provide a comprehensive evaluation of vQS against the state of the art on three publicly available datasets. Experiments show that vQS provides speed-ups up to a factor of 3.2x.

1. INTRODUCTION

Additive ensembles of regression trees, such as GBRT [3] and λ-MART [6], are nowadays considered among the most advanced LtR models for ranking documents in IR systems, although these require very efficient scoring algorithms for processing queries by strict time budgets [1]. The state-of-the-art algorithm for efficient scoring via additive ensemble of regression trees is QuickScorer (QS) [4]. The main novelty of QS is given by the novel traversal strategy of a tree ensemble $\mathcal{T}$: QS does not traverse $\mathcal{T}$ one tree at a time, but rather evaluates the branching nodes of the trees in a feature-wise order. This strategy was proven to be very efficient for a number of reasons: *(i)* a very small number of nodes is actually visited, *(ii)* the exploited data structures have a cache-friendly access pattern, and *(iii)* fast bitwise operations with few and predictable branch instructions are performed.

In this paper we discuss how QS can be parallelized by exploiting the advanced SIMD capabilities of mainstream CPUs [5]. Streaming SIMD Extensions (SSE) and Advanced Vector Extensions (AVX) are sets of instructions exploiting wide registers of 128 and 256 bits. A single SIMD instruction performs parallel operations on simple data types, e.g., a 128 bit register can manage four single precision or two double precision floats simultaneously. We use in the following a notation similar to the one of Intel Intrinsics[1], where a SIMD instruction codes in its name: (i) a prefix _mm or _mm256 stating if 128 or 256 bits registers are used; (ii) the name of actual operation; (iii) a suffix indicating the types of the operands, e.g., _ps or _pd for 32 and 64 bit floats, respectively. For instance,

$$\overrightarrow{c} = \text{\_mm\_cmpgt\_ps}(\overrightarrow{a}, \overrightarrow{b})$$

is a SIMD instruction that works on two registers $\overrightarrow{a}$ and $\overrightarrow{b}$ of 128 bits, each storing a sequence of four single precision floats, and performing four *greater than* comparisons in parallel. The result is stored in a 128-bit register $\overrightarrow{c}$, which will contain four 32-bits sequences of 1s or 0s, depending on the test outcome of the four comparisons. In the following, we will use the notation $\overrightarrow{c} \equiv \langle c_3, c_2, c_1, c_0 \rangle$ to refer to the four elements of a SIMD register.

In this work we propose V-QuickScorer (vQS)[2], a version of QS that exploits CPU vector extensions to boost the efficient traversing of additive ensembles of regression trees. Since exploiting SIMD instructions requires to identify data parallelism opportunities in the code, in QS the most natural source of data parallelism derives from the need of scoring multiple documents for a given query. In particular, we discuss the use of both SSE-4.2 and AVX-2, providing different register widths as well as different SIMD instruction sets, to score up to 8 documents in parallel. Experiments show that vQS provides up to 3.2x speedup compared to the state-of-the-art sequential QS algorithm.

2. QUICKSCORER

Given a query-document pair (q, d_i), represented by a feature vector $\mathbf{x}$, a LtR model based on an additive ensemble of regression trees predicts a relevance score $s(\mathbf{x})$ used for ranking a set of documents. Typically, a tree ensemble encompasses several binary decision trees, denoted by $\mathcal{T} = \{T_0, T_1, \ldots\}$. Each interal (or branching) node $n \in T_h$ is associated with a Boolean test over a specific feature $f_\phi \in \mathcal{F}$, and a constant threshold $\gamma \in \mathbb{R}$. Tests are of the form $\mathbf{x}[\phi] \leq \gamma$, and, during the visit, the left branch is taken

[1] `https://software.intel.com/sites/landingpage/IntrinsicsGuide`

[2] Source code: `https://github.com/hpclab/vectorized-quickscorer`

SIGIR '16, July 17 - 21, 2016, Pisa, Italy

ISBN 978-1-4503-4069-4/16/07...$15.00

DOI: `http://dx.doi.org/10.1145/2911451.2914758`

Algorithm 1: The QuickScorer Algorithm

```
QuickScorer(x,T):
  foreach T_h ∈ T do
    leafindexes[h] ← 11...11
  foreach f_φ ∈ F do                    // Mask Computation Step
    foreach (γ, h, n) ∈ N_φ in ascending order do
      if x[φ] > γ then
        leafindexes[h] ← leafindexes[h] ∧ nodemasks[n]
      else
        break
  score ← 0
  foreach T_h ∈ T do                    // Score Computation Step
    j ← index of leftmost bit set to 1 of leafindexes[h]
    l ← h · Λ + j
    score ← score + leafvalues[l]
  return score
```

iff the test succeeds. Each leaf node stores the tree prediction, representing the potential contribution of the tree to the final document score. The scoring of $\mathbf{x}$ requires the traversal of all the ensemble's trees and it is computed as a *weighted sum* of tree predictions.

Algorithm 1 illustrates QS [4]. One important result of QS is that to compute $s(\mathbf{x})$ it needs to identify only the branching nodes whose tests evaluate to false, called *false nodes*. To do so, QS maintains for each tree $T_h \in \mathcal{T}$ a bitvector `leafindexes[h]`, made of Λ bits, one per leaf. Initially, every bit in `leafindexes[h]` is set to 1. Moreover, each branching node n is associated with a binary mask `nodemasks[n]` idendifying the set of unreachable leaves in case the corresponding test evaluates to false. Whenever a false node is visited, the set of unreachable leaves `leafindexes[h]` is updated through a *logical and* with `nodemasks[n]`. Eventually, the leftmost bit set in `leafindexes[h]` identifies the leaf corresponding to the score contribution of T_h, stored in the lookup table `leafvalues`.

To efficiently identify all the *false nodes* in the ensemble, QS processes the branching nodes of all the trees *feature by feature* and in ascending order of their predicate thresholds. Specifically, for each feature f_ϕ, QS builds a list $\mathcal{N}_\phi$ of tuples (γ, h, n), where γ is the predicate threshold of node n occurring in tree T_h. When processing $\mathcal{N}_\phi$ in ascending order by γ, as soon as a test evaluates to true, i.e., $\mathbf{x}[\phi] \leq \gamma$, the remaining occurrences surely evaluate to true as well, and their evaluation is thus safely skipped.

We call *mask computation* the first step of the algorithm during which all the bitvectors `leafindexes[h]` are updated, and *score computation* the second step where such bitvectors are used to retrieve tree predictions.

3. VECTORIZED QUICKSCORER

SIMD extension of modern CPUs provide powerful fine-grained parallelism which can be exploited to score multiple documents simultaneously. Note that the QS paper [4] already investigated multiple documents scoring as a strategy to improve cache performance. In this work, we propose V-QuickScorer (vQS), a SIMD-based algorithm exploiting the natural *data parallelism* deriving from this strategy.

Both the *mask computation* and *score computation* steps of QS can be engineered to take advantage of SIMD registers. During the first step, multiple documents can be tested against a given node predicate and their `leafindexes[h]` updated in parallel. Similarly, the score of multiple documents can be computed simultaneously during the second step. The data structure `leafindexes` used to encode the exit leaves must be replicated to accomodate the documents scored simultaneously.

Algorithm 2: The vQS Algorithm (SSE-4.2, $\Lambda = 32$)

```
    V-QuickScorer( {x_i}_{i=0,1,2,3}, T, scores_{3:0} ):
1     foreach T_h ∈ T do
2       leafindexes[h] ← 11...11
3     foreach f_φ ∈ F do                    // Mask Computation Step
4       foreach (γ, h, n) ∈ N_φ in ascending order do
5         →γ ← _mm_set1_ps(γ)
6         →x ← _mm_set_ps(x3[φ], x2[φ], x1[φ], x0[φ])
7         →c ← _mm_cmpgt_ps(→x, →γ)
8         if ¬(_mm_test_all_zeros(→c, →c)) then
9           →b ← _mm_load_ps(leafindexes_{3:0}[h])
10          →m ← _mm_set1_ps(nodemask[n])
11          →y ← _mm_andnot_ps(→m, →c)
12          →y ← _mm_andnot_ps(→y, →b)
13          _mm_store_ps(leafindex_{3:0}[h], →y)
          else
14          break
15    →s_{1:0} ← _mm_set1_pd(0)             // Score Computation Step
16    →s_{3:2} ← _mm_set1_pd(0)
17    foreach T_h ∈ T do
18      ∀i = 3:0 :  j_i ← index leftmost 1 bit of leafindex_i[h]
19      ∀i = 3:0 :  l_i ← h · Λ + j_i
20      →v_{1:0} ← _mm_set_pd(leafvalues[l_1], leafvalues[l_0])
21      →v_{3:2} ← _mm_set_pd(leafvalues[l_3], leafvalues[l_2])
22      →s_{1:0} ← _mm_add_pd(→s_{1:0}, →v_{1:0})
23      →s_{3:2} ← _mm_add_pd(→s_{3:2}, →v_{3:2})
24    _mm_store_pd(→s_{1:0}, scores_{1:0})
25    _mm_store_pd(→s_{3:2}, scores_{3:2})
```

The specific optimizations used by vQS depend on the SIMD register width available and on the maximum number of leaves Λ in the ensemble. We first discuss how vQS exploits SSE-4.2 or AVX-2 instructions when $\Lambda = 32$, then we highlight the differences when $\Lambda = 64$.

V-QuickScorer with $\Lambda = 32$ and SSE-4.2

SSE-4.2 registers are 128 bits wide, and permit processing 4 documents simultaneously during the *mask computation* step. Therefore, as shown in Alg. 2, vQS is given in input a set of four instances $\{\mathbf{x}_i\}_{i=0,1,2,3}$, and a vector $\texttt{scores}_{3:0}$ of four double precision floats where the scores are stored upon completion.

During the *mask computation* step, one 128-bit SIMD register $\overrightarrow{\gamma}$ is used to store 4 copies of the same test threshold γ, and another register $\overrightarrow{x}$ to store the feature $\mathbf{x}_i[\phi]$, $i = 0, ..., 3$ of the 4 input instances (lines 5-6). A single instruction is used to compare the feature values of these four documents against γ (line 7). If all tests evaluate to true, i.e., we do not have any *false node*, then the next feature is processed, otherwise `leafindexes` is updated. Note that unlike the QS sequential implementation, the need of verifying the true condition for all 4 documents rather than for a single one, may lead to some overheads in the strategy aimed at identifying false nodes only in the tree ensemble.

The update of **leafindexes** involves potentially four documents and should occur only for those where $\mathbf{x}_i[\phi] > \gamma$. Since SSE-4.2 does not support masked/predicated SIMD instructions, to avoid conditional branches vQS implements the update with two bitwise operations. Let $\texttt{leafindexes}_i[h]$ be a 32-bit vector ($\Lambda = 32$), relative to tree T_h and associated with document $\mathbf{x}_i$. Let variable c_i store a string of 32 bits of 1s or 0s, depending on the outcome of the test $\mathbf{x}_i[\phi] > \gamma$. We can rewrite the update as:

$$\texttt{leafindexes}_i[h] \leftarrow (\texttt{nodemask}[n] \vee \neg c_i) \wedge \texttt{leafindexes}_i[h]$$

where the *bitwise logical or* has the effect of leaving $\texttt{nodemask}[n]$ unaltered when $\mathbf{x}_i[\phi] > \gamma$, or making it useless otherwise. We can re-write the expression as follows by applying the De Morgan law:

$$\texttt{leafindexes}_i[h] \leftarrow \neg(\neg\, \texttt{nodemask}[n] \wedge c_i) \wedge \texttt{leafindexes}_i[h]$$

which we can straightforwardly implement by a repeated application of the SIMD function $\text{andnot}(x, y) = \neg x \wedge y$.

The layout of **leafindexes** is tree-wise, i.e., given a tree T_h the bitvectors $\texttt{leafindexes}_i[h]$ of the four $\mathbf{x}_i$ are stored contiguously in memory. As shown in Alg. 2 (lines 9–13), this allows loading the four bitvectors with a single 128-bit load instruction, and to apply them the two SIMD andnot instructions. Indeed, first the four $\texttt{leafindexes}_{3:0}[h]$ are loaded into the register $\overrightarrow{b}$ and $\texttt{nodemask}[n]$ is replicated into $\overrightarrow{m}$. After composing $\overrightarrow{m}$, $\overrightarrow{c}$ and $\overrightarrow{b}$, the resulting mask is finally copied back to memory.

The *score computation* is also parallelized (see Alg. 2, from line 15). To provide the required precision, tree predictions are stored as double precision float values (64 bits), which means that only 2 document scores can be processed simultaneously using 128-bit registers. Thus, vQS uses two (pd) SIMD variables, namely $\overrightarrow{s_{1:0}}$ and $\overrightarrow{s_{3:2}}$, to maintain the score of our 4 documents. For each tree, the predicted partial scores related to the 4 input instances are similarly stored in $\overrightarrow{v_{1:0}}$ and $\overrightarrow{v_{3:2}}$, and added up to update the final document scores. Eventually, the computed scores for the 4 documents are copied to vector $\texttt{scores}_{3:0}$.

V-QuickScorer with $\Lambda = 32$ and AVX-2

When AVX-2 is supported, it is possible to increase the parallelism degree of vQS. Trivially, 8 document features tests can be performed simultaneously instead of 4, and 4 document scores updated instead of 2. In this case, vQS scores 8 documents at each invocation. We do not discuss the pseudocode for the document feature testing and document scores calculation, as it simply requires to adopt the 256-bit versions of the respective instructions illustrated above.

More interestingly, AVX-2 also provides additional instructions, such as _mm256_maskstore_ps: this copies a 256-bit register to memory according to a given mask enabling/disabling sub-groups of 32-bits. This makes it possible to *conditionally* update each of the 8 elements of $\texttt{leafindexes}_{7:0}$ (or to leave it unchanged) depending on the output of the 8 node predicates, which is stored in $\overrightarrow{c}$. Lines 11–13 of Alg. 2 are replaced as follows, where the vector variables involved are now 256 bit registers:

$$\overrightarrow{y} \leftarrow \text{\_mm256\_and\_ps}(\overrightarrow{m}, \overrightarrow{b})$$
$$\text{\_mm256\_maskstore\_ps}(\texttt{leafindexs}_{7:0}[h], \overrightarrow{c}, \overrightarrow{y})$$

V-QuickScorer with $\Lambda = 64$

Increasing Λ (the maximum number of tree leaves) impacts on the size of the bitwise structures **leafindexes** and **nodemask**, as each bitvector they store is Λ bits wide. As a consequence, the number of bitvectors (either **leafindexes** or **nodemask**) that can be processed simultaneously in a SIMD register decreases. Recall that, when $\Lambda = 32$, the number of tests and the number of bitvectors fitting in a SIMD register are the same, either 4 or 8 for SSE-4.2 or AVX-2, respectively. Therefore, the variables $\overrightarrow{m}$, $\overrightarrow{c}$ and $\overrightarrow{b}$ are seamlessly processed together. When $\Lambda = 64$, there is a mismatch between the 32 bits returned by each predicate test, and the 64 bits of the **leafindexes** and **nodemask** bitvectors.

For 128-bits registers, let $\overrightarrow{c} \equiv \langle c_3, c_2, c_1, c_0 \rangle$ be the outcome of the four comparisons against a threshold γ. For the subsequent update of the 64-bits masks, vQS requires to process $\overrightarrow{c}$ in order to obtain two variables, storing only two comparison outcomes of 64 bits each. To this end, we use the following two instructions, working on the low and high half of $\overrightarrow{c}$, respectively.

$$\langle c_1, c_1, c_0, c_0 \rangle \equiv \texttt{\_mm\_unpacklo\_ps}(\overrightarrow{c}, \overrightarrow{c})$$
$$\langle c_3, c_3, c_2, c_2 \rangle \equiv \texttt{\_mm\_unpacklhi\_ps}(\overrightarrow{c}, \overrightarrow{c})$$

Once prepared these two result variables, they are used in the subsequent andnot operations, similarly to Alg. 2. The only difference is that the code from line 11 to 13 must be repeated twice, one for updating the two copies of leafindexes associated with the first pair of documents, and the other for the second pair.

By using 256-bits registers on AVX-2, vQS performs 8 tests in parallel, while we update the 8 copies of leafindexes by exploiting two blocks of SIMD instruction, each performing 4 operations in parallel on the 64-bit bitwise data structures. As before, from $\overrightarrow{c} \equiv \langle c_7, c_6, \ldots, c_0 \rangle$, we would like to extract two vectors with the following layout $\langle c_3, c_3, c_2, c_2, c_1, c_1, c_0, c_0 \rangle$ and $\langle c_7, c_7, c_6, c_6, c_5, c_5, c_4, c_4 \rangle$. Unfortunately, the AVX-2 instructions for unpacking these bitmasks, namely _mm256_unpacklo_ps and _mm256_unpackhi_ps, work by considering each 256-bits registers as two 128-bit lanes, and thus pick the least/most significant 64 bits from each of these lanes. The solution adopted by vQS is to set a different layout for $\overrightarrow{c}$ in order to be able to apply the above unpacking instructions. To this end, we load the 8 features of $\overrightarrow{x}$, to be compared with the threshold γ, in the following suitable order:

$$\overrightarrow{x} \leftarrow \text{\_mm256\_set\_ps}(\,\mathbf{x}_7[\phi], \mathbf{x}_6[\phi], \mathbf{x}_3[\phi], \mathbf{x}_2[\phi], \mathbf{x}_5[\phi], \mathbf{x}_4[\phi], \mathbf{x}_1[\phi], \mathbf{x}_0[\phi]\,)$$

This new 256 bit instruction replaces line 6 of Alg. 2.

4. EXPERIMENTS

Datasets. We used three publicly available datasets: Microsoft LETOR (MSN-1[3]) and Yahoo LETOR (Y!S1[4]), commonly used in the scientific community for LtR experiments, and a new larger one called Istella LETOR (istella[5]). istella is composed of 33,018 queries and 10,454,629 query-document pairs, where each pair is represented by a vector of 220 features. This is split in training and test sets with a 70%-30%

[3] http://research.microsoft.com/en-us/projects/mslr/
[4] http://learningtorankchallenge.yahoo.com
[5] http://blog.istella.it/istella-learning-to-rank-dataset/

Table 1: Per-document scoring time in μs of QS, vQS (SSE 4.2), vQS (AVX-2) on MSN-1, Y!S1, and istella datasets. Speedups over the baseline QS are reported in parentheses.

Λ	Method	Number of trees/dataset					
		1,000			10,000		
		MSN-1	Y!S1	istella	MSN-1	Y!S1	istella
32	QS	6.3 (–)	12.5 (–)	8.9 (–)	73.7 (–)	88.7 (–)	69.9 (–)
	vQS (SSE 4.2)	3.2 (2.0x)	5.2 (2.4x)	4.2 (2.1x)	46.2 (1.6x)	53.7 (1.7x)	38.6 (1.8x)
	vQS (AVX-2)	**2.6 (2.4x)**	**3.9 (3.2x)**	**3.1 (2.9x)**	**39.6 (1.9x)**	**43.7 (2.0x)**	**30.7 (2.3x)**
64	QS	11.9 (-)	18.8 (-)	14.3 (-)	183.7 (-)	182.7 (-)	162.2 (-)
	vQS (SSE 4.2)	10.2 (1.2x)	13.9 (1.4x)	11.0 (1.3x)	173.1 (1.1x)	164.3 (1.1x)	132.2 (1.2x)
	vQS (AVX-2)	**7.9 (1.5x)**	**10.5 (1.8x)**	**8.0 (1.8x)**	**138.2 (1.3x)**	**140.0 (1.3x)**	**104.2 (1.6x)**

partitioning. To the best of our knowledge, this is the largest publicly available LtR dataset, particularly useful for large-scale experiments on the efficiency and scalability of LtR solutions. In all the three datasets, feature vectors are labeled with judgments ranging from 0 (irrelevant) to 4 (perfectly relevant).

Experimental methodology. We trained λ-MART [6] models optimizing NDCG@10 on the three datasets, and generated models with $\Lambda = 32$ or $\Lambda = 64$ leaves and with $|\mathcal{T}|$=1,000 or $|\mathcal{T}|$=10,000 trees. We used the open source implementation of λ-MART by [2], however it is worth noting that the results reported in this work are independent of the training algorithm implementation. To provide a fair comparison, vQS was implemented by engineering the source code of QS. In the following we reported the average per-document scoring time averaged over 10 runs. The tests were performed on a machine equipped with an Intel Xeon CPU E5-2630 v3 clocked at 2.40GHz with 20 MB of cache L3 and 64GB RAM.

Efficiency evaluation. Table 1 reports the average time (in μs) for scoring a single document across the three datasets, when varying both the number of trees and leaves in the ensemble. The best improvements are achived with $\Lambda = 32$, as vQS can use either 4- or 8-way parallelism for both feature predicate testing and bitvectors updating. When using AVX-2, speed-ups range from 1.9x (for MSN-1 with 10,000 trees) to 3.2x (for Y!S1 with 1,000 trees). These are greatly reduced woth SSE 4.2, with a maximum speedup of 2.4x for the 1,000 trees model over Y!S1. As expected, performance worsen with $\Lambda = 64$, with a maximum speed-up of 1.8x. The lower improvement is due to inefficiencies deriving from additional processing required to align the 4-/8-way comparisons to the 2-/4-way conditional mask updates.

A final note regards the overheads of the vectorized code during the scan of the ordered list of feature thresholds $\mathcal{N}_\phi$. While QS stops as soon as the single document feature is greater of the current threshold, vQS must continue as long as at least one among the 4 or 8 documents evaluated simultaneously does not match the exit criterion. We instrumented the code to measure this difference. The tests conducted on MSN-1, with 10K trees and $\Lambda = 64$, confirmed the hypothesis: to score a single document QS executes in average 15.76 tests per tree, while this number increases to 22.80 and 26.68 for the SSE 4.2 and AVX-2 versions of vQS, respectively. In fact, we observed that while the *score computation* step benefits significantly of the increased parallelism provided by AVX-2, the *mask computation* step exhibits only a limited improvement, due to the additional comparison costs mentioned above.

5. CONCLUSION

We discussed in depth the vectorization of QS, the state-of-the-art algorithm for scoring documents with LtR tree ensembles. Using SIMD capabilities of mainstream CPUs, namely SSE 4.2 and AVX 2, vQS can process up to 8 documents in parallel, although there is a tradeoff due to the possible increase in the number of operations carried out. We also highlighted some features of these SIMD coprocessors, which force to re-design algorithms in non trivial ways.

The upcoming AVX-512 extension, due to wider registers, would allow to further increase the parallelism degree up to 16 documents. Wider registers are not the only benefit, since many new instructions will be available. One example is _mm512_lzcnt_epi32, which counts the number of leading zeros, i.e., the index of the first bit set to 1, in each of the 16 sub-groups of 32 bits. This would allow to parallelize the code at lines 18-19 of Alg. 2, where the indexes of 16 exit leaves in `leafvalues` would be computed simultaneously. Moreover, masked/predicated instructions would allow to more easily pipeline comparision, update and store operations.

Acknowledgements. This work was partially supported by the EC H2020 Program INFRAIA-1-2014-2015 SoBigData: Social Mining & Big Data Ecosystem (654024).

6. REFERENCES

[1] N. Asadi, J. Lin, and A. P. de Vries. Runtime optimizations for tree-based machine learning models. *IEEE Transactions on Knowledge and Data Engineering*, 26(9):2281–2292, 2014.

[2] G. Capannini, C. Lucchese, F. M. Nardini, S. Orlando, R. Perego, and N. Tonellotto. Quality versus Efficiency in Document Scoring with Learning-to-Rank Models. *Information Processing and Management*, 2016.

[3] J. H. Friedman. Greedy function approximation: a gradient boosting machine. *Annals of Statistics*, 2001.

[4] C. Lucchese, F. M. Nardini, S. Orlando, R. Perego, N. Tonellotto, and R. Venturini. Quickscorer: A fast algorithm to rank documents with additive ensembles of regression trees. In *Proc. of the 38th ACM SIGIR Conference*, pages 73–82, 2015.

[5] O. Polychroniou, A. Raghavan, and K. A. Ross. Rethinking simd vectorization for in-memory databases. In *Proc. of the 2015 ACM SIGMOD Conference*, pages 1493–1508, New York, NY, USA, 2015.

[6] Q. Wu, C. J. Burges, K. M. Svore, and J. Gao. Adapting boosting for information retrieval measures. *Information Retrieval*, 2010.

Exploiting Semantic Coherence Features for Information Retrieval

Xinhui Tu[1] Jimmy Xiangji Huang[1,2] Jing Luo[3] Tingting He[1]
[1]School of Computer Science, Central China Normal University, Wuhan, China
[2]School of Information Technology, York University, Toronto, Canada
[3]School of Computer Science, Wuhan University of Science and Technology, Wuhan, China
tuxinhui@mail.ccnu.edu.cn jhuang@yorku.ca luojing@wust.edu.cn tthe@mail.ccnu.edu.cn

ABSTRACT
Most of the existing information retrieval models assume that the terms of a text document are independent of each other. These retrieval models integrate three major variables to determine the degree of importance of a term for a document: within document term frequency, document length and the specificity of the term in the collection. Intuitively, the importance of a term for a document is not only dependent on the three aspects mentioned above, but also dependent on the degree of semantic coherence between the term and the document. In this paper, we propose a heuristic approach, in which the degree of semantic coherence of the query terms with a document is adopted to improve the information retrieval performance. Experimental results on standard TREC collections show the proposed models consistently outperform the state-of-the-art models.

Keywords
Document ranking; Retrieval model; Term weighting

1. INTRODUCTION AND MOTIVATION
Most of the existing information retrieval (IR) models assume that the terms of a text document are independent of each other. Generally, these retrieval models integrate three major variables to determine the degree of importance of a term for a document: within document term frequency, document length and the specificity of the term in the collection [4]. Though these approaches are reasonably simple and easy-to-use, the coherence aspect of a term's saliency in a document cannot be taken into account by the term independence assumption.

The terms in a document can generally be classified into two groups: topical term and non-topical term. The topical terms will be highly associated with each other, while the non-topical terms will have very low association with the other terms within the document. Let us consider two arbitrary documents d_1 and d_2 as follows:

d_1*: So let's say you're out for a walk in the woods, with your* ***iPhone*** *handy, and you run into a grizzly bear ……*

d_2*: Currently, Apple company has had to allocate massive resources to its iTunes and* ***iPhone*** *......*

The first document is concerned about "*grizzly bear*" and the second document is related to "*Apple Company*". Suppose that the two documents are equal in length. When we use "*iPhone*" as query, all the retrieval models mentioned above will give approximately the same score for the two documents. However, the word "*iPhone*" is a topical term in document d_2 and a non-topical term in document d_1. Apparently, the document d_2 is more relevant to the query than document d_1. As we can see from the example, the degree of importance of a term for a document is dependent not only on the three aspects mentioned before, but also dependent on the degree of semantic coherence between the term and the document.

Humans can easily identify the topical terms and the non-topical terms of a document, because they have the knowledge of the "word association". In d_2, the term "*iPhone*" appears with many other terms such as "*Apple*", "*iTunes*", which are associated with the term "*iPhone*". In d_2, however, the term "*iPhone*" seems to be irrelevant to the other terms such as "*woods*"*and* "*bear*"". For computational purposes, this knowledge can be discovered by analyzing the corpus. Semantic association measures based on corpus analysis have served this purpose for many applications related to natural language processing and IR [6].

In this paper, we study how to efficiently use semantic coherence features to improve the information retrieval performance. We propose an approach to use the degree of semantic coherence between term and document for document ranking. First, each document is represented as a graph-of-word that corresponds to a weighted directed graph whose vertices represent unique terms, whose edges represent the translation probability between two terms. Then, a graph-based algorithm is adopted to calculate coherence-based weighting score of a term within a document. The coherence-based weight score of a term for a document is determined by the degree of semantic relatedness between the term and the other terms within the document. Finally, the coherence-based document score and the frequency-based score obtained by the existing retrieval function are integrated into a linear feature-based model for document ranking. Experimental results on standard TREC collections show the proposed model consistently outperform the state-of-the-art models.

2. RELATED WORK
Over the decades, many different retrieval models have been proposed and studied, including the vector space model [16, 17], the classic probabilistic model [7, 13, 14] and the language modeling approach [12, 19]. Most of the existing retrieval models assume a "bag-of-words" representation of both documents and queries. A typical effective retrieval function involves a TF part, an IDF part, and a document length normalization part [4]. The TF part intents to give a higher score to a document that has more occurrences of a query term, while the IDF part is to penalize words that are popular in the whole collection. The document length normalization is to avoid favoring long documents.

SIGIR '16, July 17–21, 2016, Pisa, Italy.
© 2016 ACM. ISBN 978-1-4503-4069-4/16/07…$15.00.
DOI: http://dx.doi.org/10.1145/2911451.2914691

Most of the traditional retrieval models employ a single term frequency normalization mechanism that does not take into account various aspects of a term saliency in a document [11, 18]. Paik [11] proposes a novel TF-IDF term weighting schema (MATF) that employs two different within document term frequency normalizations to capture two different aspects of term saliency. The experimental results show that MATF achieves significantly better precision than the start-of-the-art models, such as BM25 [14] and LMDir (the language modeling approach with Dirichlet prior smoothing) [19].

Intuitively, the degree of semantic coherence between a term and a document is an important factor to determine the importance of the term in the document. However, little work has been done around coherent-based term weighting. To the best of our knowledge, the model proposed in [6] is the only work closely related to ours. In the paper, the authors propose a neighborhood based document smoothing model by exploiting lexical association between terms. Different from their work, we adopt a linear feature-based model for final document ranking instead of modifying the traditional retrieval functions.

Inspired by the success of graph-based ranking algorithms like TextRank [9], some researches attempt to adopt graph-based document representation for improving information retrieval performance [1, 15]. Generally, a graph based ranking algorithm is a way of deciding on the importance of a vertex within a graph, by taking into account global information recursively computed from the entire graph rather than relying only on local vertex-specific information. Our work is different from the existing graph-based retrieval methods in two aspects: (1) Each edge is weighted by the mutual information between the two terms, instead of by the number of co-occurrences of the two term in sliding windows; (2) The final ranking score of a document is determined by the combination of the graph-based term weighting score and the frequency-based score instead of by the graph-based term weighting score alone.

3. PROPOSED APPROACH

In this section, we introduce a graph-based model to calculate weighting score for terms and then use these score for final document ranking.

3.1 Coherence-based Term Weighting

The coherence-based weight score of a term for a document is determined by the degree of semantic relatedness between the term and the other terms within the document. Let us consider the example mentioned in section 1 again. Once the semantic relatedness has been calculated, "*iPhone*" will have a higher relatedness with the terms such as "*Apple, iTunes, company*" than the terms such as "*bear, woods, walk*". Therefore, "*iPhone*" will get a higher coherence-based weight score in document d_2 than in document d_1. When we use *iPhone* as query, document d_2 will get a higher coherence-based score.

In this paper, we adopt a graph-based ranking algorithm to calculate the coherence-based weight score of a term within a document. Each textual document is represented as a graph-of-word that corresponds to a weighted directed graph whose vertices represent unique terms, whose edges represent the translation probability between two terms. We prefer to use term rather than word because tokenization and feature selection algorithms (such as stop word removal) have already been applied. The coherence-based weight score of a term within a document is determined by the votes that are casting for it and the weight of the terms casting that votes. The weight of term t_j within document d is initially set to 1 and the following PageRank function is run for several iterations

$$S(t_j) = (1-k) + k * \sum_{t_i \in d, j \neq i} S(t_i) * tran(t_i, t_j) \quad (1)$$

where k is a damping factor that can be set between 0 and 1, which has the role of integrating into the model the probability of jumping from a given vertex to another random vertex in the graph. In the context of the Web, this graph based ranking algorithm implements a random walk model, where a user clicks on links at random with a probability d, and jumps to a completely new page with probability $(1-k)$ [10]. We set the damping factor to 0.85, the convergence threshold to 0.0001, following [9, 10]. Our experiments showed that only a small number of iterations (< 50) is required to obtain convergence.

In formula (1), $tran(t_i, t_j)$ is the translation probability from term t_i to term t_j in the graph of document d. A simple way to estimate $tran(t_i, t_j)$ is as follows:

$$tran(t_i, t_j) = \frac{sim(t_i, t_j)}{\sum_{t' \in d} sim(t_i, t')} \quad (2)$$

where $sim(t_i, t_j)$ is the strength of association between two term t_i and t_j.

To calculate $sim(t_i, t_j)$ in formula (2), we adopted a pairwise term similarity score, which is a combination of mutual information and a distance factor. The distance factor exponentially decreased as the distance between terms increased. The assumption behind this work is that semantically related words are usually located in proximity, and the distance between two words could indicate the strength of their association. The pairwise term similarity score of terms t_i and t_j can be calculate as follows:

$$sim(t_i, t_j) = MI(t_i, t_j) * df(t_i, t_j) \quad (3)$$

$$df(t_i, t_j) = e^{-\alpha * (dist(t_i, t_j) - 1)} \quad (4)$$

where $dist(t_i, t_j)$ is the average distance between terms t_i and t_j in all the documents in the collection; α is the decaying rate for the exponential function. In our experiments, the decaying rate α is set to 0.8, following [5].

In formula (3), $MI(t_i, t_j)$ denotes the mutual information between term t_i and t_j , which can be calculated as follows:

$$MI(t_i, t_j) = \sum_{X_i = 0,1} \sum_{X_j = 0,1} P(X_i, X_j) \log \frac{P(X_i, X_j)}{P(X_i)P(X_j)} \quad (5)$$

where X_i and X_j are binary variables indicating whether term t_i or t_j is present or absent. The probabilities are estimated as follows:

$$P(X_i = 1) = \frac{c(X_i = 1)}{N}$$

$$P(X_i = 0) = 1 - P(X_i = 1)$$

$$P(X_j = 1) = \frac{c(X_j = 1)}{N}$$

$$P(X_j = 0) = 1 - P(X_j = 1)$$

$$P(X_i = 1, X_j = 1) = \frac{c(X_i = 1, X_j = 1)}{N}$$

$$P(X_i = 1, X_j = 0) = \frac{c(X_i = 1) - c(X_i = 1, X_j = 1)}{N}$$

$$P(X_i = 1, X_j = 0) = \frac{c(X_j = 1) - c(X_i = 1, X_j = 1)}{N}$$

$$P(X_i = 0, X_j = 0) = 1 - P(X_i = 1, X_j = 1) - P(X_i = 0, X_j = 1) - P(X_i = 1, X_j = 0)$$

where $c(X_i = 1)$ and $c(X_j = 1)$ are the numbers of documents containing term t_i or t_j, respectively, $c(X_i = 1, X_j = 1)$ is the number of documents that contain both t_i or t_j, and N in the total number of documents in the collection.

3.2 Retrieval Function

Coherence-based term weighting score itself may be not effective to be used as the only scoring function for retrieval. It's a potential way to incorporate coherence-based term weighting score into the traditional retrieval functions for document ranking. However, it is not always possible to easily incorporate new feature into the traditional retrieval functions, which are built upon some underlying theoretical framework [8]. For example, it proved non-trivial to include query independent features such as PageRank into BM25 ranking formula [2]. Therefore we adopt a linear feature-based model for final document ranking, instead of modifying the traditional retrieval functions. The linear feature-based model has been proven to be an effective way to incorporate different features into a united retrieval model [8]. The final retrieval function can be described as follows:

$$ConRank(q,d) = \lambda * \frac{Con(q,d)}{1 + Con(q,d)} + (1 - \lambda) * \frac{R(q,d)}{1 + R(q,d)} \quad (6)$$

where $R(q,d)$ is the document score calculate by the existing retrieval functions, such as BM25, LMDir, and MATF; $Con(q,d)$ is the coherence-based weight scores of all query's term within a document, which can be calculate as follows:

$$Con(q,d) = \sum_{t_j \in q} S(t_j) * IDF(t_j) \quad (7)$$

where $S(t_j)$ can be calculated by formula (1); $IDF(t_j)$ is the inverse document frequency of term t_j。

4. EXPERIMENTS

4.1 Test Collections and Baseline Models

Table 1 summarizes that statistics on test collections used in our experiments. These collections are different in size and genre. Each document is processed in a standard way for indexing. Words are stemmed (using porter-stemmer), and stop words are removed. In the experiments, we only use title of the queries. In order to evaluate our model and compare it to other models, we use the MAP and P@10 measure, which are widely accepted measure for evaluating effectiveness of ranked retrieval systems. The methods used in our experiments are as listed in Table 2.

4.2 Parameter Sensitivity Study

An important issue that may affect the robustness of the proposed models is the sensitivity of their parameter λ (in Equation 6). The parameter λ controls weight of coherence-based weighting score in the final ranking function. In this section, we study how sensitive the parameter is to MAP measure. At the current stage of our work, the parameter is selected through grid search.

In order to find the optimal value of parameter λ, we sweep the values from 0 to 1 with an interval of 0.1. When λ equals to 0, we reach the baseline. When λ equals to 1, the retrieval model use coherence-based weighting score only. The value of λ controls the influence of coherence-based weighting score. Figure 1 shows the sensitivity of the value of parameter λ according to MAP measure. The experimental results show that parameter λ can greatly impact the performance of the proposed models. Generally, the performance of all models increases at the beginning when the value of λ grows up. The performance of each model starts to continually drop after a peak. However, this is no unique optimal

Table 1. Test collection statistics

Collection	# of Docs	Topics	# of Topics
AP88-89	164,597	51-100	50
TREC8	528,155	301-450	50
WT2G	247,491	401-450	50
WT10G	1,692,096	451-550	100

Table 2. The retrieval models used in the experiments

Model	Description
BM25	The classical probabilistic model [14]
LMDir	The language modeling approach with Dirichlet prior smoothing [19]
MATF	A novel TF-IDF model with excellent retrieval performance [11].
ConRank-BM25	The proposed model using BM25 function to calculate $R(q,d)$
ConRank-LMDir	The proposed model using LMDir function to calculate $R(q,d)$.
ConRank-MATF	The proposed model using MATF function to calculate $R(q,d)$

value of λ for all of them. For example, the best λ values on collection AP88-89 are 0.3, 0.4, and 0.3 for ConRank-BM25, ConRank-LMDir, and ConRank-MATF, respectively. For all models on all datasets, we can gain the best retrieval performance when $0.2 \leqslant \lambda \leqslant 0.4$. The proposed models constantly perform better than the corresponding baseline while λ range from 0.1 to 0.6. When the value of λ is too large in the linear feature-based model, the performance is downward and even worse than that of the baseline.

4.3 Comparing with the State-of-the-art Models

In order to make the comparison fair, we need to carefully choose suitable values for the parameters in all the models. To build strong baselines, we adopt a method proposed in [3] to find the optimal parameter settings for BM25 and LMDir. All parameters in BM25 and LMDir are respectively set to the optimal values in our experiments. As a parameter free model, MATF does not need parameter tuning. In the proposed models, parameter α and k are respectively set to 0.8 and 0.85 following [5, 10]. The previous research work [20] has demonstrated that when a new feature is integrated into a traditional retrieval function under linear interpolation, the best retrieval performance can be obtained by assigning a relatively small weight (0.1-0.2) to the new feature. As we can see from the experiments presented in section 4.2, good performance can be archived with parameter λ are set to 0.3. Therefore, the parameter λ in the proposed models is set to 0.3 in the following experiments.

Table 3 present the retrieval results of the six retrieval models on the four collections respectively. The results indicate that the proposed models constantly outperform the corresponding baseline on all collections. In most of the cases, the improvement of MAP and P@10 was statistically significant. The maximum average improvement is as high as 7.81% and 7.32% in terms of MAP and P@10, respectively. It is worth noting that MATF has obtained significant improvements over BM25 and LMDir, and is therefore a strong baseline. The significant performance improvements from such a strong baseline are very encouraging. The results confirm that semantic coherent features can be used to improve the retrieval performance.

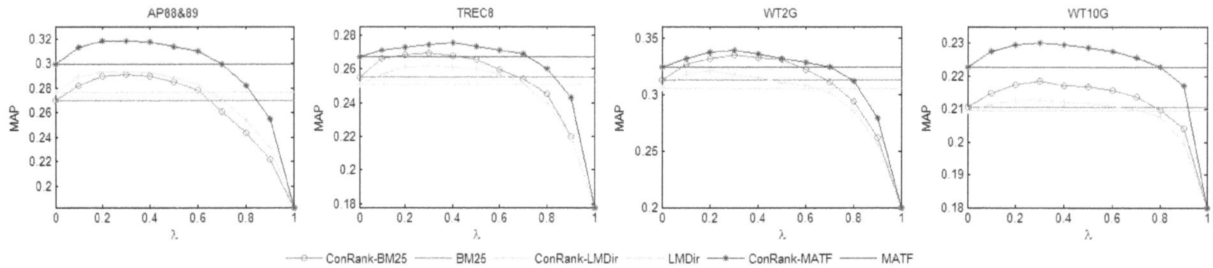

Figure 1. Sensitivity of parameter λ to MAP measure

Table 3. Comparison of the performance of the six models in terms of MAP and P@10

*(The values in the parentheses are the improvement over the model in the previous row in the table; * indicates a statistically improvements over the model in the previous row according to the Wilcoxon signed-rank test at the 0.05 level)*

Model	AP88-89		TREC8		WT2G		WT10G	
	P@10	MAP	P@10	MAP	P@10	MAP	P@10	MAP
BM25	0.4216	0.2702	0.4645	0.2552	0.4957	0.3128	0.3626	0.2107
ConRank-BM25	0.4489* (+6.48%)	0.2913* (+7.81%)	0.4853* (+4.48%)	0.2693* (+5.53%)	0.5320* (+7.32%)	0.3349* (+7.07%)	0.3747* (+3.34%)	0.2184* (+3.65%)
LMDir	0.4416	0.2768	0.4753	0.2509	0.5063	0.3057	0.3108	0.2094
ConRank-LMDir	0.4595* (+4.05%)	0.2936* (+6.07%)	0.4918* (+3.47%)	0.2615* (+4.22%)	0.5409* (+6.83%)	0.3211* (+5.04%)	0.3154 (+1.48%)	0.2128 (+1.62%)
MATF	0.4679	0.2994	0.4905	0.2671	0.5481	0.3241	0.3283	0.2226
ConRank-MATF	0.4872* (+4.12%)	0.3186* (+6.41%)	0.5097* (+3.91%)	0.2752* (+3.03%)	0.5594* (+2.06%)	0.3392* (+4.66%)	0.3327 (+1.34%)	0.2301* (+3.37%)

5. CONCLUSIONS AND FUTURE WORK

In this paper, a new term weighting approach is proposed to calculate the degree of semantic coherence of the query terms with a document. The coherence-based term weighting score can further be used in combined with the existing retrieval functions for document ranking. Experimental results on standard TREC collections show the proposed retrieval methods consistently outperform the corresponding strong baselines. The results confirm that semantic coherent features can be used to improve the retrieval performance. At the current stage of our work, only one type of distance measure is adopted to calculate semantic similarity between terms, and the values of the parameters in the proposed models are chosen empirically. For future work, we will investigate the effectiveness of other distance measures and study how to find the optimal parameter setting for further improving the retrieval performance.

6. ACKNOWLEDGMENTS

This work was partially supported by the National Science Foundation of China under the grant number 61572223, a Discovery grant from the Natural Sciences & Engineering Research Council (NSERC) of Canada and an NSERC CREATE award. We thank anonymous reviewers for their thorough review comments.

7. REFERENCES

[1] Blanco R. and Lioma C. Graph-based term weighting for information retrieval. *Information Retrieval*, 15(1), 54–92, 2012.

[2] Craswell N., Robertson S. and Zaragoza H. Relevance weighting for query independent evidence. *ACM SIGIR*, 416-423, 2005.

[3] Diaz, F. and Metzler, D. Improving the estimation of relevance models using large external corpora. *ACM SIGIR*, 154-161, 2006.

[4] Fang, H., Tao, T. and Zhai, C. A formal study of information retrieval heuristics. *ACM SIGIR*, 49–56, 2004.

[5] Gao, J., Zhou, M., Nie, J. Y., He, H., and Chen, W. Resolving query translation ambiguity using a decaying co-occurrence model and syntactic dependence relations. *ACM SIGIR*, 183-190, 2002.

[6] Goyal, P., Behera, L. and McGinnity, T. M. A novel neighborhood based document smoothing model for information retrieval. *Information retrieval*, 16(3), 391-425, 2013

[7] Jones, K. S., Walker, S. and Robertson, S. E. A probabilistic model of information retrieval: development and comparative experiments - part 1. *Information Processing Management*, 36(6), 779–808, 2000.

[8] Metzler, D. and Croft, W. B. Linear feature-based models for information retrieval. *Information Retrieval*, 10(3), 257-274, 2007.

[9] Mihalcea, R. and Tarau, P. TextRank: bringing order into texts. *EMNLP*, 2004.

[10] Page, L., Brin, S., Motwani, R. and Winograd, T. The PageRank citation ranking: bringing order to the Web. Technical report, Stanford Digital Library Technologies Project, 1998.

[11] Paik, J. H. A novel TF-IDF weighting scheme for effective ranking. *ACM SIGIR*, 343-352, 2013.

[12] Ponte, J. M. and Croft, W. B. A language modeling approach to information retrieval. *ACM SIGIR*, 275–281, 1998.

[13] Robertson, S. E. Readings in information retrieval. Chapter The probability ranking principle in IR, pages 281–286. Morgan Kaufmann Publishers Inc., 1997.

[14] Robertson, S. and Zaragoza, H. The probabilistic relevance framework: BM25 and beyond. *Foundations and Trends in Information Retrieval*, 3(4), 333–389, 2009.

[15] Rousseau, F. and Vazirgiannis, M. Graph-of-word and TW-IDF: new approach to ad hoc IR. *ACM CIKM*, 59-68, 2013.

[16] Salton, G., Wong, A., and Yang. C. S. A vector space model for automatic indexing. *Communications of the ACM*, 18(11), 613–620, 1975.

[17] Salton, G. McGill, M. J. *Introduction to modern information retrieval.* McGraw-Hill, Inc., 1986.

[18] Ye, Z. and Huang, J. X. A simple term frequency transformation model for effective pseudo relevance feedback. *ACM SIGIR*, 323-332, 2014.

[19] Zhai, C. and Lafferty, J. A study of smoothing methods for language models applied to information retrieval. *ACM Transaction on Information System*, 22(2), 179–214, 2004.

[20] Zhao, J., Huang, J. X., and Ye, Z. Modeling term associations for probabilistic information retrieval. *ACM Transactions on Information Systems*, 32(2), 7, 2014.

Extracting Information Seeking Intentions for Web Search Sessions

Matthew Mitsui
Department of Computer Science
Rutgers University
New Brunswick, NJ, USA, 08901
mmitsui@cs.rutgers.edu

Chirag Shah, Nicholas J. Belkin
School of Communication and Information
Rutgers University
New Brunswick, NJ, USA, 08901
{chirags,belkin}@rutgers.edu

ABSTRACT

We present a method for extracting the self-reported intentions of users engaged in an information seeking episode. We recruited participants to conduct search sessions and subsequently asked them to self-report their intentions. A total of 27 users participated in a lab study, during which they worked on two search tasks. After each search session, participants indicated their intentions during that session while viewing a video replay. Results indicate that the set of search intentions provided to participants was sufficient to account for intentions in four journalism-related information seeking tasks: a copy editing task, interview preparation task, relationships task, and story pitch task. The results also suggest regular patterns in intentions that can be exploited for identification of task type as well as potential applications to personalization and recommendation during a search episode.

CCS Concepts

•**Information systems → Query intent; Task models;**

Keywords

search intentions; information seeking intentions; motivating task; information seeking episode; search session analysis

1. INTRODUCTION

It is becoming increasingly recognized that in general, information retrieval (IR) system performance cannot be evaluated in single query-single response format. Contrary to the Cranfield paradigm that has been presupposed in decades of IR system evaluation, performance must be measured over information seeking episodes - entire sessions of related queries, search results, clicks, and other interactions with IR systems. Moreover, these episodes are understood to be motivated by an external goal.

Therefore, it seems IR systems should directly support the accomplishment of user goals, whether it is the motivating task/goal for the entire session or the various goals throughout the course of the session. We must hence be able to extract these goals - or an indicator of the goals - from patterns in interaction data, to gain a better understanding of the relationship between goals and behavioral patterns. Recent work has attempted to articulate and define searchers' *intentions* at various parts of a session [11], though little work has been done to extract such intentions for a fixed set of tasks. In this paper, we present a novel framework for extracting information seeking intentions from session data. The work reported here represents preliminary results of a project which aims to predict search intentions during a search session, on the basis of observable searcher behaviors.

2. BACKGROUND

Early proposals of why people engage in information seeking addressed the fundamental "why", discussing the motivating task to some extent (e.g. [1]; [10]). Later work has followed to characterize these motivating tasks. Much of this work focused on categorizing tasks into broad categories. Byström and Järvelin, for instance, characterize tasks by complexity [2]. Freund, Toms & Clarke relate task type to document genre and differences in usefulness and relevance [5]. Li classified motivating and search tasks into various facets, such as the product of the task, its complexity, and its degree of specificity [7].

Other work segmented information seeking into various levels of actions. Marchionini, for instance, differentiated between patterns, strategies, tactics, and moves, which are hierarchically related in increasing order of specificity [8]. In a later hierarchy proposed by Xie, the motivating search task eventually leads to more concrete "interactive search intentions", actual behaviors that are executed as steps in the search session [11]. Xie defined a concrete list of these intentions, identified through coding of empirical data, and found consistent patterns between the intentions and the information seeking strategies that were applied for these intentions. Literature exists in extracting intentions in a different sense, such as topical intent [6]. Teevan, Dumais & Horvitz also allowed users to give free form answers for intentions for search sessions as a whole, and related that to whether a query was worthwhile for personalization [9]. To our knowledge, though, little of the previous literature except Xie gives a fixed list of intentions that can serve as concrete, general steps in a query segment. In the work we present here, we choose a subset of the intentions of Xie to study. Rather than asking independent assessors to annotate query segments, we ask lab participants to annotate

SIGIR '16, July 17-21, 2016, Pisa, Italy

DOI: http://dx.doi.org/10.1145/2911451.2914746

their own segments. In additional contrast to Xie, rather than studying library users who bring their own library-related task, we study lab participants with a controlled set of topics and tasks, for the purpose of understanding the relationships between task, topic, and intentions.

Table 1: Search Tasks (Descriptions are on the coelacanths topic. Equivalent tasks were set for the topic of methane clathrates and global warming).

Assignment 1. Copy Editing **Your Assignment:** You are a copy editor at a newspaper and you have only 20 minutes to check the accuracy of the six italicized statements in the excerpt of a piece of news story below. **Your Task:** Please find and save an authoritative page that either confirms or disconfirms each statement.
Assignment 2. Story Pitch **Your Assignment:** You are planning to pitch a science story to your editor and need to identify interesting facts about the coelacanth ("see-la-kanth"), a fish that dates from the time of dinosaurs and was thought to be extinct. **Your Task:** Find and save web pages that contain the six most interesting facts about coelacanths and/or research about coelacanths and their preservation.
Assignment 3. Relationships **Your Assignment:** You are writing an article about coelacanths and conservation efforts. You have found an interesting article about coelacanths but in order to develop your article you need to be able to explain the relationship between key facts you have learned. **Your Task:** In the following there are five italicized passages, find an authoritative web page that explains the relationship between two of the italicized facts.
Assignment 4. Interview Preparation **Your Assignment:** You are writing an article that profiles a scientist and their research work. You are preparing to interview Mark Erdmann, a marine biologist, about coelacanths and conservation programs. **Your Task:** Identify and save authoritative web pages for the following: Identify two (living) people who likely can provide some personal stories about Dr. Erdmann and his work. Find the three most interesting facts about Dr. Erdmann's research. Find an interesting potential impact of Dr. Erdmann's work.

3. TASK AND DATASET

Our user data was collected in a lab setting. Participants were undergraduate students from one university, recruited from undergraduate journalism courses. To register, students were required to have completed at least one course in news writing. Each study session consisted of 2 search tasks, each followed by an annotation task, and several interspersed questionnaires, with a verbal exit interview at the end. All activity except for the exit interview was conducted at a desktop computer, with search activity recorded in Firefox by a browser plugin, eye-fixation behavior by GazePoint[1], and annotatable video of the search by Morae[2].

Participants began by answering a demographic questionnaire and watching a tutorial video on how to use our system before beginning the search task. Then, participants read the task description and answered a short questionnaire on their familiarity with the topic and task as well as the anticipated difficulty. They then had 20 minutes to complete the search task; this was shown to be a sufficient amount of time in pilot tests, and the time limit needed to be constant among task types. They could finish before 20 minutes if they felt they completed their task early. Afterwards, participants answered a post questionnaire on the actual difficulty of the task. They then read a handout of the intention annotation task and watched a video demonstrating how to conduct the task. Users were also given a handout of a short description of each intention (see the Appendix for intention definitions). This was for further clarification and to also reduce variability in our data from differing interpretations of the intentions. They then completed the intention annotation task with no time limit. They then repeated the process with more questionnaires, another search task, and then another intention annotation task before the exit interview. The entire experimental session lasted about two hours.

For the intention annotation task, participants were asked to select which intentions applied to each *query segment* (all that occurred from one query to the next) in the search session. This was accomplished by playing the video of the search, segment by segment. They could select, from a displayed list, any number of intentions for a segment. For instance, if a participant knew nothing about coelacanths and issued the query "coelacanths" as the first query in a session, that person might mark "identify something to get started" and "learn domain knowledge". The participant was then asked to mark whether each of these checked intentions was satisfied. Our example participant may mark "yes" for "identify something to get started" but "no" for "learn domain knowledge". If a participant marks "no", she must then state why that intention was not satisfied. For example, while she found some new keywords to search, she may not have learned any knowledge that was required by the task description. If the participant had some other intention in addition to the 20 we listed, the participant may also check "other", give a short description of that additional intention, and also mark whether it was satisfied. They repeated this annotation process for each query segment separately. For the entire process, participants were incentivized with additional reward for being among the best performers. This provided incentive to issue good searches, instead of meeting the minimum requirements. Participants were told that "good performance" also included marking intentions well - i.e. marking all and only those that applied.

Table 2: Task characteristics (F=Factual, I=Intellectual, S=Specific, A=Amorphous).

Task	Product	Level	Goal	Named
CPE	F	Segment	S	True
STP	F	Segment	A	False
REL	I	Document	A	True
INT	I	Document	A	False

There were 4 possible tasks and 2 topics per task. Two of our task types are a copy editing task (CPE) and interview preparation task (INT), as specified in Cole et al [3]. Our other tasks - Relationships (REL) and Story Pitch (STP) task - were novel to this study. One topic was "coelacanths", and another was "methane clathrates and global warming".

[1]http://www.gazept.com/
[2]https://www.techsmith.com/morae.html

We give descriptions of each task for the coelacanth topic in Table 1. The chosen topics were familiar enough to generate participant interest yet unfamiliar enough so participants would likely not know the requested information before arrival. We further give a faceted classification of each task in Table 2, according to a subset of facets in Li [7]. For definitions of each facet, see [3, 7]. Each user completed 2 search tasks and hence 2 annotation tasks. Task types were paired into 4 groups, based on differences in facet values. Each participant searched for 2 tasks in one of these 4 groups, each task on a different topic. Order of the 2 tasks and 2 topics in each group was flipped, yielding a total possible $4 \times 2 \times 2 = 16$ configurations. In our current dataset, we have 27 users. For analyzing intentions, we filtered out 3 users for misinterpreting instructions; they marked every intention for every query, thus skewing our data. This results in 24 searchers, conducting a total of 48 search sessions, and having assigned a total of 434 sets of intentions (i.e. 434 queries).

4. ANALYSIS

In defining our list of intentions, we took a subset of those from Xie [11], eliminating those that did not apply to our situation. While this may raise concerns that we may have missed some possibly valuable intentions, we found that the intentions were both necessary and sufficient. Intentions that were rarely selected in some task types were more frequently chosen in others. Good coverage was also demonstrated in our exit interviews. We asked participants if there were some missing intentions, to which no users gave a possible intention. We also found that users listed an "Other" intention in the task 19 out of 434 times. None of the "other" intentions that participants provided were repeated; they ranged from "I just wanted to see what the fish looked like" to "I found that Dr. Gerald Allen worked with Dr. Erdmann so I looked for Dr. Allen." With more data, we will attempt to categorize "other" intentions. Their answers suggest that while other intentions may be possible, this list of intentions gives a very good coverage of the possible intentions for these task types.

In Figure 1, we present the total counts of all selected intentions across all task types - i.e. the number of intentions that users marked as present in their query segments. We also show the number of users and queries per task. Because the number of search sessions is small, we provide only descriptive - and not inferential - statistics, but consistent patterns can still be drawn from the data. Two intentions consistently ranked among the 4 most common intentions in the query segments: "find specific information" and "obtain specific information". We can say this is due to the episodic nature of query segments. Since users break up information needs into succinct queries, each query almost always involves finding or obtaining specific information. More important is the obvious difference in relative occurrence of intentions in different task types. For instance, "evaluate correctness" is the third most frequently checked intention in CPE by a large margin, a pattern not exhibited by any other task type. "Identify something more to search" was common overall but also the most frequent intention in REL. In REL, users are more likely to "access items with common characteristics" (AC). Other differences suggest that some intentions can serve as distinguishing features for task facets. AC is much more common in Document tasks than Segment tasks, while "evaluate duplication of an item" is lowest in the Document tasks. Lastly, the relative ordering of most to least frequent intention differs greatly between task types, suggesting that such differences may be useful for distinguishing task type.

5. CONCLUSION AND FUTURE WORK

Despite the relatively small data set, the results suggest the potential strength of our approach in identifying searchers' intentions during information seeking episodes. Our findings suggest that, at least in the four types of task we have studied, our chosen intentions provide sufficient coverage for characterizing search intentions. They also suggest that there may be regular patterns of intentions throughout a search session that differ from task to task. Similarly, Cole, et al. [4] identified a small number of clusters of sequences of eye-fixation behaviors, whose frequency of occurrence differs between tasks similar to those in our research. We therefore are continuing to collect search session data using these tasks and methods, in preparation for the next step in this line of research, which is to attempt to discover relationships between logged behaviors during search, and corresponding search intentions. The ultimate goal of the research of which this milestone is a part, is to be able to identify different search intentions during the course of an information seeking episode, in order to provide support specific to each different type of intention throughout.

6. ACKNOWLEDGMENTS

This work was supported through the National Science Foundation, grant #IIS-1423239.

7. REFERENCES

[1] N. J. Belkin. Anomalous states of knowledge as a basis for information-retrieval. *Canadian Journal of Information Science-Revue Canadienne Des Sciences De L Information*, 5:133–143, 1980.

[2] K. Byström and K. Järvelin. Task complexity affects information seeking and use. *Inf. Process. Manage.*, 31(2):191–213, Mar. 1995.

[3] M. J. Cole, J. Gwizdka, C. Liu, R. Bierig, N. J. Belkin, and X. Zhang. Task and user effects on reading patterns in information search. *Interacting with Computers*, 23(4):346 – 362, 2011. Cognitive Ergonomics for Situated Human-Automation Collaboration.

[4] M. J. Cole, C. Hendahewa, N. J. Belkin, and C. Shah. User activity patterns during information search. *ACM Trans. Inf. Syst.*, 33(1):1:1–1:39, Mar. 2015.

[5] L. Freund, E. G. Toms, and C. L. Clarke. Modeling task-genre relationships for ir in the workplace. In *Proceedings of the 28th Annual International ACM SIGIR Conference on Research and Development in Information Retrieval*, SIGIR '05, pages 441–448, New York, NY, USA, 2005. ACM.

[6] D. Kelly. *New Directions in Cognitive Information Retrieval*, chapter Implicit Feedback: Using Behavior to Infer Relevance, pages 169–186. Springer Netherlands, Dordrecht, 2005.

[7] Y. Li. *Relationships among work tasks, search tasks, and interactive information searching behavior.* ProQuest, 2008.

[8] G. Marchionini. *Information seeking in electronic environments.* Number 9. Cambridge university press, 1997.

[9] J. Teevan, S. T. Dumais, and E. Horvitz. Potential for personalization. *ACM Trans. Comput.-Hum. Interact.*, 17(1):4:1–4:31, Apr. 2010.

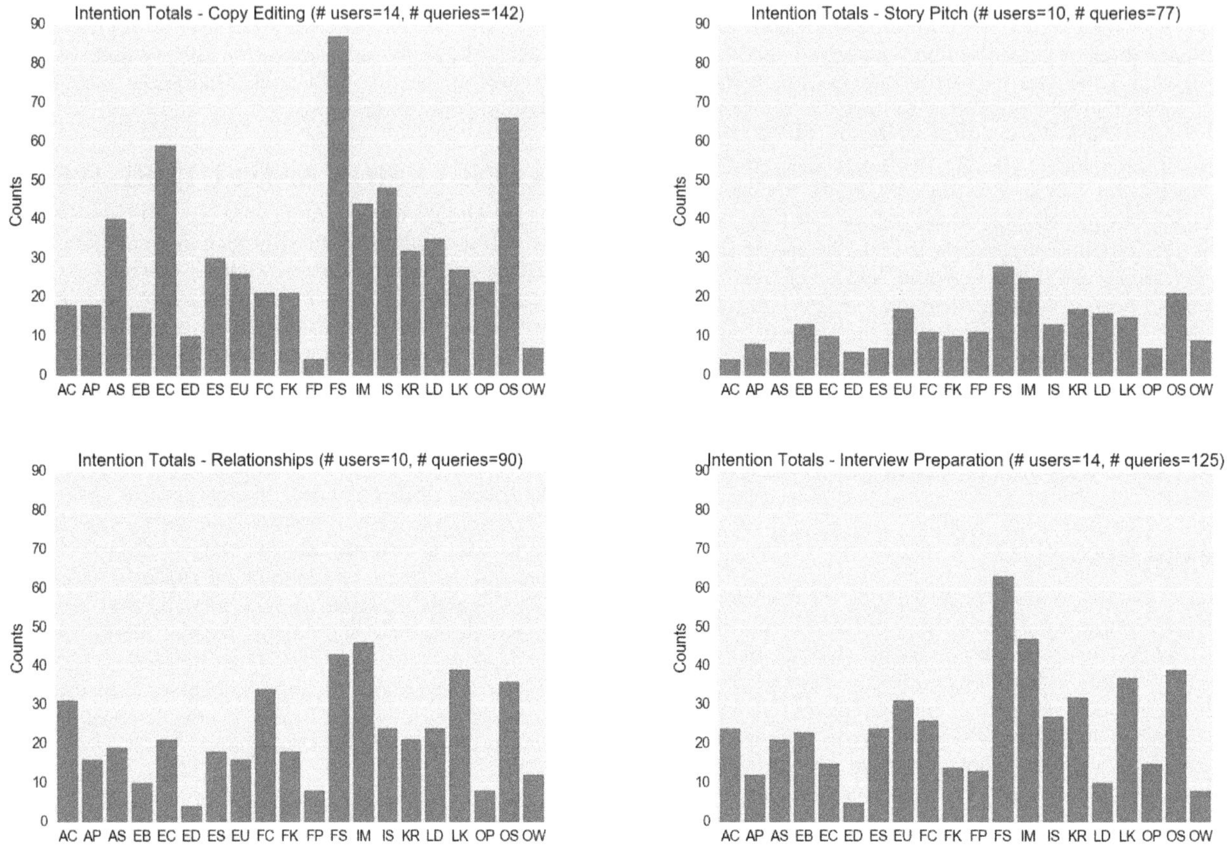

Figure 1: Total number of checked intentions for each task type.

[10] T. D. Wilson. On user studies and information needs. *Journal of documentation*, 31(1):3–15, 1981.

[11] H. I. Xie. Patterns between interactive intentions and information-seeking strategies. *Information Processing & Management*, 38(1):55 – 77, 2002.

APPENDIX

A. INTENTION DESCRIPTIONS

At walk-in, users were given two handouts: a description of the intention annotation task and a short bulleted list of each possible intention and a clarifying description. Here is the bulleted list they were given for the 20 intentions. Intentions were listed in this order on the handout, grouped by first word (e.g., "Identifying" and "finding").

- **Identify something to get started (IS)** - For instance, find good query terms.
- **Identify something more to search (IM)** - Explore a topic more broadly.
- **Learn domain knowledge (LK)** - Learn about the topic of a search.
- **Learn database content (LD)** - Learn the type of information/resources available at a particular website - e.g., a government database.
- **Find a known item (FK)** - Searching for an item that you were familiar with in advance.
- **Find specific information (FS)** - Finding a predetermined piece of information.
- **Find items sharing a named characteristic (FC)** - Finding items with something in common.
- **Find items without predefined criteria (FP)** - Finding items that will be useful for a task, but which haven't been specified in advance.
- **Keep record of a link (KR)** - Saving a good item or an item to look at later
- **Access a specific item (AS)** - Go to some item that you already know about.
- **Access items with common characteristics (AC)** - Go to some set of items with common characteristics.
- **Access a web site/home page or similar (AP)** - Relocating or going to a website.
- **Evaluate correctness of an item (EC)** - Determine whether an item is factually correct.
- **Evaluate usefulness of an item (EU)** - Determine whether an item is useful.
- **Pick best item(s) from all the useful ones (EB)** - Determine the best item among a set of items.
- **Evaluate specificity of an item (ES)** - Determine whether an item is specific or general enough.
- **Evaluate duplication of an item (ED)** - Determine whether the information in one item is the same as in another or others.
- **Obtain specific information (OS)** - Finding specific information to bookmark, highlight, or copy.
- **Obtain part of the item (OP)** - Finding part of an item to bookmark, highlight, or copy.
- **Obtain a whole item(s) (OW)** - Finding a whole item to bookmark, highlight, or copy.

First Story Detection using Multiple Nearest Neighbors

Jeroen B. P. Vuurens
The Hague University of Applied Science
Delft University of Technology, The Netherlands
j.b.p.vuurens@tudelft.nl

Arjen P. de Vries
Radboud University Nijmegen
Institute for Computing and Information Sciences, Nijmegen, The Netherlands
arjen@acm.org

ABSTRACT

First Story Detection (FSD) systems aim to identify those news articles that discuss an event that was not reported before. Recent work on FSD has focussed almost exclusively on efficiently detecting documents that are dissimilar from their nearest neighbor. We propose a novel FSD approach that is more effective, by adapting a recently proposed method for news summarization based on 3-nearest neighbor clustering. We show that this approach is more effective than a baseline that uses dissimilarity of an individual document from its nearest neighbor.

1. INTRODUCTION

Internet users are turning more frequently to online news as a replacement for traditional media sources such as newspapers or television. For the user, the news stream is a source to both track topics of interest and to become informed about important new events the user was not yet aware of. Automated detection of new events can save to user a great deal of time, for instance by notifying users about new events, which is especially interesting to users and organizations for whom the information is time-critical and who need to act on that information.

FSD systems aim to identify those news articles that discuss an event that was not reported before in earlier stories, without knowledge of what events will happen in the news [2]. Recently, FSD has been suggested as a useful tool to monitor the Twitter feed [7], and while previous work has addressed the efficiency that is required for this purpose, there has been little work on improving the effectiveness in over a decade [7, 8].

In this study, we propose a novel approach that is more effective that the widely used function proposed by Allen et al. that declares a story new if it is dissimilar to its nearest neighbor [1].

2. RELATED WORK

The task of detecting events can be automated using information about the events published online. For this purpose, the Topic Detection and Tracking (TDT) program was initiated to discuss applications and techniques to organize broadcast news stories by the real world events that they discuss in real-time. News stories are gathered from several sources in parallel to create a single stream of constantly arriving news. The problem of first story detection is to identify the stories in a stream of news that contain discussion of a new topic, i.e. whose event has not been previously reported [6].

FSD has been recognized as the most difficult task in the research area of TDT [11]. In early work, Allen et al. detect first stories as news articles whose cosine similarity over tf-idf vectors to its nearest neighbor is less than a threshold, an effective approach that outperforms complex language model approaches in most cases [1]. This baseline is still used for FSD in recent work, in which more focus is put on efficiency than to improve effectiveness [3, 5, 4].

Papka and Allen, argue that a side-effect of the timely nature of broadcast news is that stories closer together on the news stream are more likely to discuss related topics than stories farther apart on the stream. When a significant new event occurs, there are usually several stories per day discussing it; over time, coverage of old events is displaced by more recent events. They use temporal proximity as a distinguishing feature to incorporate the salient properties of broadcast news [2, 6].

In recent work, Vuurens et al. proposed a novel 3-nearest neighbor clustering (3NN) approach to retrieve sentences from news articles that contain novel and useful news facts. In this approach every text is linked to its three nearest neighbors that must be from a different domain [10]. The so-called '2-degenerate cores' constructed by the algorithm correspond to highly similar texts from three different sources. Their existence indicates the importance or salience of the information contained. Temporal proximity is incorporated in the model by weighting the time between news articles in the similarity function used. In [9] normalized information gain is shown to be more effective than cosine similarity for the task of clustering news articles that are topically related.

3. METHOD

In this work, we adapt the 3NN clustering approach to First Story Detection, by clustering news articles rather than sentences, and using a similarity function based on normalized information gain to promote the clustering of news articles that are likely to be topically related.

3.1 Single Linkage

We compare our efforts to the approach described by Allen et al. [1], which is considered a state-of-the-art approach in recent studies on First Story Detection, e.g. [7, 4]. In this approach, documents are represented as tf-idf weighted vectors, and the novelty of a document d is estimated by the cosine similarity to its nearest neighbor n in the collection C [1]:

SIGIR '16, July 17 - 21, 2016, Pisa, Italy

ISBN 978-1-4503-4069-4/16/07...$15.00

DOI: http://dx.doi.org/10.1145/2911451.2914761

$$novelty(d) = 1 - \max_{n \in C} cos(d,n) \quad (1)$$

Then, a news article is marked as a first story when its novelty is below a threshold $\alpha \in [0,1]$.

3.2 3NN First Story Detection

In this study, we propose a novel approach that is based on 3-nearest neighbor clustering (3NN), using the existing open source implementation [10]. In 3NN clustering, every node is assigned to its three nearest neighbors, not allowing links between nodes from the same news domain, and based on temporal proximity between publication dates which allows the clustering to be continuously updated in near real-time. 2-generate cluster cores are formed when three nodes each link to the other two as a one of its 3 nearest neighbors. These clusters contain information that is locally most central and therefore likely to be salient information [10]. The key idea for First Story Detection, is that acting on formed 3NN clusters rather than individual documents is less likely to return false positives. However, instead of truly detecting the first story as was the objective in the TDT program, here we aim to improve detection performance at the expense of slightly delayed detection. It may also be that the story detected as the first of a new event is more central to the information, and therefore more suitable as a seed to start tracking a topic, however, this hypothesis is outside the scope of this study and left for future work.

In [9], news sentences were fitted into a hierarchy that distinguishes between different events and topics by forming clusters of topically related the news articles, for which normalized information gain was shown to be more effective than cosine similarity. Therefore, to promote 3NN clusters to be formed around topically related news articles we use a similarity function based on normalized information gain. In Equation 2, the normalized information gain between two documents d and d' results in a score of 0 between identical documents and a score of 1 between disjoint documents, by dividing the information gain IG between the documents by an upper bound of the information gain IG_{max} that would be obtained if these documents have the same internal distributions over terms but are completely disjoint. For the remainder of this paper we use IG_{sim} as defined in Equation 3 as a similarity function between two documents d, d' based on IG_{norm}.

$$IG_{norm}(d,d') = \frac{IG(d,d')}{IG_{max}(d,d')} \quad (2)$$

$$IG_{sim}(d,d') = 1 - IG_{norm}(d,d') \quad (3)$$

From the obtained 3NN clustering, the newly formed 2-degenerate cores are inspected for first stories. Similar to the Single Linkage baseline, first stories are detected when a newly formed cluster core is dissimilar from news articles seen recently. In 3NN every news article is linked to its three nearest neighbors, therefore the members of a newly formed 2-degenerate core that contains a first story each have two links to the other core members and the third link links to a dissimilar news article. The most similar non-core news article that a core member links to, is then used to estimate the novelty of that cluster core. Formally, in Equation 4 a cluster core A is declared novel when the similarity between a news article $d \in A$ and a news article n in the remainder of the collection C is below a threshold $\phi_{novelty}$.

$$novelty(A) = \max_{d \in A, n \in C-A} IG_{sim}(d,n) < \phi_{novelty} \quad (4)$$

Lastly, we add a threshold to filter out newly formed clusters that are less likely to be topically related to each other. Vuurens et al. show that news articles that have a high normalized information gain are rarely topically related [9]. Following their findings, we filter out clusters that fail the coherence criterium in Equation 5, that enforces that the similarity between all nodes d, d' that are members of the same 2-degenerate core A exceeds a threshold $\phi_{coherence}$, for which different settings are tried to examine the sensitivity and impact on effectiveness.

$$coherence(A) = \min_{d \in A, d' \in A-\{d\}} IGsim(d,d') > \phi coherence \quad (5)$$

3.3 Test set

For the evaluation, we use the TREC Temporal Summarization test sets of 2013 and 2014. The corpus for these test sets is the 2013 TREC KBA Streaming corpus, which contains approx. 150M news articles that are processed in a strict online setting. Table 1 shows the topics from the test sets, which are all types of a crisis that received continuous updates in the media over time. Arguably, the news regarding a single topic could be considered to be all part of the same story, or in some cases be regarded as separate stories within a topic. Here we regard all news articles that are matched to the same topic as part of one news story, for which ideally only the first article should be returned. TREC assessors annotated the sentences that TREC participants retrieved as relevant if they contain a news fact relevant to the topic.

The basis for the evaluation of the FSD systems is a list per topic of all documents that contain relevant news facts according to the TREC ground truth or the online published extended lists that contain duplicate sentences found in the collection. For the combined 23 topics, there are 65,358 documents that were annotated as containing relevant information. For this task, a returned news article is considered as a first for a topic when it is the first relevant article returned by the system, and a false alarm when another relevant article for the same topic was returned earlier. News articles that are not marked as relevant to the topic are ignored in the evaluation.

3.4 Experiment setup and evaluation metrics

The effectiveness of First Story Detection systems is measured by the miss rate, false alarm rate, recall and precision, which we explain using the contingencies in Table 2. For any topic, we only consider articles that are annotated as relevant for the topic, thus if T is the number of documents annotated as relevant for the topic, then $TP + FN + FP + TN = T$. Since there can only be one first story per topic per system, $TP + FN = 1$ and $FP + TN = T - 1$. A miss occurs when the system fails to detect a new event, i.e. $miss\ rate = \frac{FN}{TP+FN}$. A false alarm occurs when the system emits a news article when a first story was already emitted for that topic, i.e. $false\ alarm\ rate = \frac{FP}{FP+TN}$. Recall is the fraction of topics for which a first story was detected $Recall = \frac{TP}{TP+FN}$, and Precision is the fraction of retrieved news articles that is a fist story $Precision = \frac{TP}{TP+FP}$, which here only considers the news articles that are relevant to the topic.

Table 2: Contingency table for evaluation metrics

	Retrieved	Not retrieved
First story	TP	FN
Not first story	FP	TN

Table 1: Topics for the 2013 and 2014 TREC TS track

Topic	Title
1	2012 Buenos Aires Rail Disaster
2	2012 Pakistan garment factory fires
3	2012 Aurora shooting
4	Wisconsin Sikh temple shooting
5	Hurricane Isaac (2012)
6	Hurricane Sandy
8	Typhoon Bopha
9	2012 Guatemala earthquake
10	2012 Tel Aviv bus bombing
12	Early 2012 European cold wave
13	2013 Eastern Australia floods
14	Boston Marathon bombings
15	Port Said Stadium riot
16	2012 Afghanistan Quran burning protests
17	In Amenas hostage crisis
18	2011-13 Russian protests
19	2012 Romanian protests
20	2012-13 Egyptian protests
21	Chelyabinsk meteor
22	2013 Bulgarian protests against the Borisov cabinet
23	2013 Shahbag protests
24	February 2013 nor'easter
25	Christopher Dorner shootings and manhunt

4. RESULTS

In this Section, we compare the effectiveness of first story detection using Single Linkage (SL) to FSD using 3NN.

4.1 Effectiveness

In Figure 1, a DET curve shows the relationship between miss rate and false alarm rates. Overall, the 3NN runs perform better than SL, regardless of the setting used for $\phi_{coherence}$. In Figure 2, we show a tradeoff between recall and precision, which further supports that 3NN is consistently more effective than Single Linkage. Table 3 gives the precision and false alarm rate when the novelty thresholds for both systems are set to the highest precision that can be obtained at recall = 1. When $\alpha = 0.48$ and $\phi_{novelty} = 0.6$ are set to allow for the lowest false alarm rate at a missed rate of 0 (i.e. recall=1), precision is respectively 0.0149 for SL and 0.0618 for 3NN, meaning that SL more redundantly retrieves 4 times more news articles for the same event.

Table 3: Optimal effectiveness at recall=1.

	Precision	false alarm rate
Single Linkage $\alpha = 0.48$	0.0149	0.0195
3NN $\phi_{novelty} = 0.60$	0.0618	0.0053

4.2 Timeliness

In Figure 3, the y-axis shows the aggregated number of relevant news articles per hour over time on the x-axis. In this Figure, we can visually compare the moment a first story was detected against the volume of published news articles. We can see that the systems occasionally missed early detection, e.g. 3NN for topic 3, and Single Linkage for topic 9. On topic 12, detection may be late for 3NN, but there is a difficult tradeoff between early detection and a lower false alarm rate.

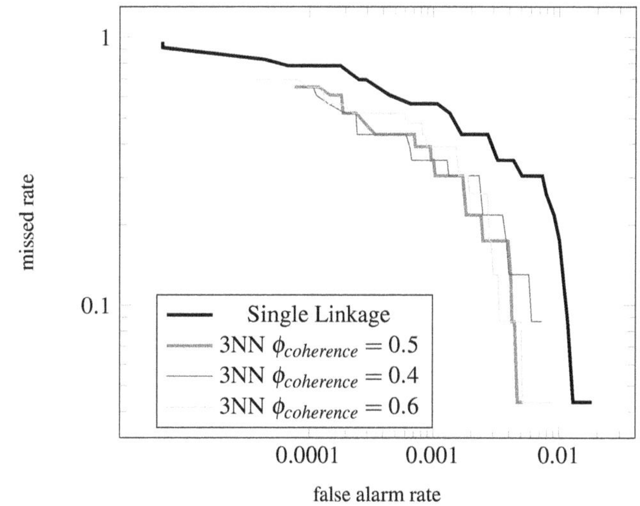

Figure 1: Detection Error Tradeoff curve, closer to the origin is better.

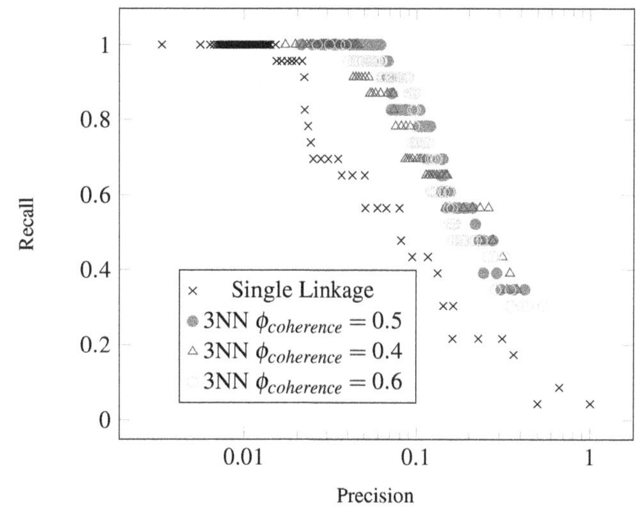

Figure 2: Plotted point show the Recall/Precision that correspond to the systems' effectiveness at the given threshold.

Some topics are related to an incident that is followed by a quick burst (e.g. topic 1), while other topics initially have a phase of little media attention and have intervals of increased interest later in time (e.g. topic 16). An interesting case is topic 18, which concerns the demonstrations that followed the Russian elections. For this topic, the news slowly shifted over the cause of days from a focus on the election itself to the steadily increasing demonstrations. This gradual shift towards a new topic is relatively difficult to detect for the approaches used in this study. The effective detection of these types of event may require a novel FSD approach that is not solely based on dissimilarity.

An inspection on the timeliness of the first stories detected reveals weaknesses in both approaches, and potentially an important aspect that should be taken into consideration in attempts to improve FSD. Timeliness of the detection is currently not addressed by the traditional evaluations that use a DET-curve and the tradeoff between recall and precision. To evaluate future work that addresses this issue, an additional metric to compare the timeliness of FSD approaches is required.

5. CONCLUSION

In this study, we propose a novel approach for the task of First Story Detection based on clustering news articles that are likely to be topically related, and estimating the novelty of newly formed clusters by comparison to previously seen news articles. We compared this approach to a baseline that estimates the novelty of a single news article by the cosine similarity to its nearest neighbor. The evaluation shows that the proposed model outperforms the existing baseline both in tradeoff between missed first stories and false positives, and in tradeoff between recall and precision. An analysis of the timeliness of the first story detections revealed that both systems missed early detection on some cases, and that there are specific cases such as evolving events that are particularly hard to detect.

Acknowledgment

This work was carried out with the support of SURF Foundation.

References

[1] J. Allan, V. Lavrenko, D. Malin, and R. Swan. Detections, bounds, and timelines: Umass and TDT-3. In *Proceedings of TDT-3 Workshop*, pages 167–174, 2000.

[2] J. Allan, R. Papka, and V. Lavrenko. On-line new event detection and tracking. In *Proceedings of SIGIR 1998*, pages 37–45. ACM, 1998.

[3] M. Karkali, F. Rousseau, A. Ntoulas, and M. Vazirgiannis. Efficient online novelty detection in news streams. In *WISE 2013*, pages 57–71. Springer, 2013.

[4] R. McCreadie, C. Macdonald, I. Ounis, M. Osborne, and S. Petrovic. Scalable distributed event detection for Twitter. In *IEEE Big Data*, pages 543–549. IEEE, 2013.

[5] M. Osborne, S. Petrovic, R. McCreadie, C. Macdonald, and I. Ounis. Bieber no more: First story detection using twitter and wikipedia. In *SIGIR 2012 TAIA Workshop*, 2012.

[6] R. Papka and J. Allan. Topic detection and tracking: Event clustering as a basis for first story detection. In *Advances in Information Retrieval*, pages 97–126. Springer, 2002.

[7] S. Petrović, M. Osborne, and V. Lavrenko. Streaming first story detection with application to twitter. In *Proceedings of NAACL 2010*, pages 181–189. ACL, 2010.

[8] S. Petrović, M. Osborne, and V. Lavrenko. Using paraphrases for improving first story detection in news and twitter. In *Proceedings of NAACL 2012*, pages 338–346, 2012.

[9] J. B. Vuurens, A. P. de Vries, R. Blanco, and P. Mika. Hierarchy construction for news summarizations. In *Proceedings of SIGIR 2015 TAIA Workshop*, 2015.

[10] J. B. Vuurens, A. P. de Vries, R. Blanco, and P. Mika. Online news tracking for ad-hoc information needs. In *Proceedings of ICTIR 2015*, pages 221–230. ACM, 2015.

[11] Y. Yang, J. Zhang, J. Carbonell, and C. Jin. Topic-conditioned novelty detection. In *Proceedings of SIGKDD 2002*, pages 688–693. ACM, 2002.

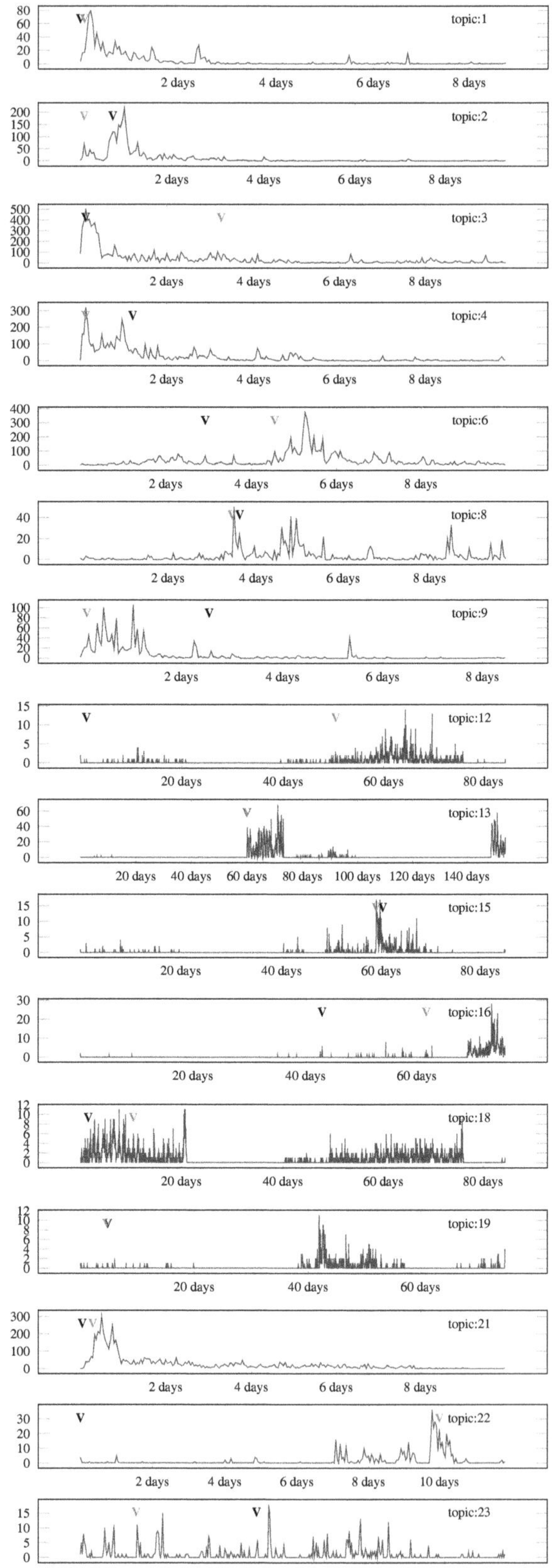

Figure 3: On the y-axis is the number of relevant news articles for the topic per hour, over time on the x-axis. A red V indicates when a fist story is detected by 3NN $\phi_{coherence} = 0.5$, and a black V indicates when a first story is detected by Single Linkage, both at the 'optimal' novelty threshold that obtained recall=1 and the highest precision.

Health Monitoring on Social Media over Time

Sumit Sidana, Shashwat Mishra, Sihem Amer-Yahia,
Marianne Clausel, Massih-Reza Amini
Univ. Grenoble Alps/CNRS
Grenoble, France
firstname.lastname@imag.fr

ABSTRACT

Social media has become a major source for analyzing all aspects of daily life. Thanks to dedicated latent topic analysis methods such as the Ailment Topic Aspect Model (ATAM), public health can now be observed on Twitter. In this work, we are interested in monitoring people's health over time. Recently, Temporal-LDA (TM–LDA) was proposed for efficiently modeling general-purpose topic transitions over time. In this paper, we propose Temporal Ailment Topic Aspect (TM–ATAM), a new latent model dedicated to capturing transitions that involve health-related topics. TM–ATAM learns topic transition parameters by minimizing the prediction error on topic distributions between consecutive posts at different time and geographic granularities. Our experiments on an 8-month corpus of tweets show that it largely outperforms its predecessors.

Keywords

public health; ailments; social media; topic models

1. INTRODUCTION

Social media has become a major source of information for analyzing many aspects of daily life. In particular, public health monitoring can be conducted on Twitter to measure the well-being of different geographic populations [5]. The ability to model transitions for ailments and detect statements such as "people talk about smoking and cigarettes before talking about respiratory problems", or "people talk about headaches and stomach ache in any order", has a range of applications in syndromic surveillance such as measuring behavioral risk factors and triggering public health campaigns.

Popular probabilistic topic modeling methods such as Latent Dirichlet Allocation [2] and pLSA [4] have a long history of successful application to news articles and academic abstracts. However, the short length of social media posts such as tweets poses serious challenges to the efficacy of such methods [9]. Dedicated methods, such as the Ailment Topic Aspect Model (ATAM), have thus been proposed to discover ailments from tweets [5].

While the primary goal of probabilistic topic modeling is to learn topic models, an equally interesting objective is to examine *topic transitions*. A temporal extention to LDA (TM–LDA) was hence developed for discovering the evolution of general-purpose topics in tweets [8]. In this paper, we examine the feasibility of measuring and predicting ailment transitions in Twitter, by combining ATAM and TM-LDA into a new model, coined TM–ATAM. Our model is different from dynamic topic models such as [1,7], as it is designed to learn topic transition patterns from temporally-ordered posts, while dynamic topic models focus on changing word distributions of topics over time. TM–ATAM learns transition parameters by minimizing the prediction error on ailment distributions of consecutive periods at different temporal and geographic granularities.

The effectiveness of TM–ATAM requires to carefully model two key granularities, temporal and geographic. A temporal granularity that is too-fine may result in sparse and spurious transitions whereas a too-coarse one could miss valuable ailment transitions. Similarly, a too-fine geographic granularity may produce false positives and a too coarse one may cover a user population that is exposed to different weather conditions and miss meaningful transitions. Our experiments on a corpus of more than $500K$ health-related and geo-localized tweets collected over a period of 8 months, show that TM–ATAM outperforms ATAM, TM–LDA and LDA in estimating temporal health-related topic transitions of different geographic populations. The health-related topic transitions we unveiled can be broadly classified in 2 kinds: *stable-topics* are those where a health-related topic is mentioned continuously. *One-way-transitions* cover the case where some topics are discussed after others. For example, our study of tweets from Arizona revealed many self-transitions such as headaches and body pain. On the other hand, tweets about smoking, drugs and cigarettes in California, are followed by respiratory ailments.

2. MODEL, PROBLEM AND APPROACH

Table 1 summarizes the terminology we use throughout this paper. By using suitable geographic granularity g (country, state, county) and temporal granularity t (week, fortnight and months), we build our document sets D_g^t. While LDA is successful at uncovering generic topics, its limitations at discovering infrequent and specific topics such as health has already been shown [5]. The probabilistic *Ailment Topic Aspect Model* (ATAM) was designed specifically

SIGIR '16, July 17 - 21, 2016, Pisa, Italy

ISBN 978-1-4503-4069-4/16/07...$15.00

DOI: http://dx.doi.org/10.1145/2911451.2914697

Table 1: Mapping tweets to documents

Term	Description
$\mathcal{P}$	set of (tweet) posts
$\mathcal{G}$	set of regions
$\mathcal{T}$	set of time periods
$\mathcal{P}_g^t$	posts from region g during time t
D_g^t	document-set built by mapping the content of each post $p \in \mathcal{P}_g^t$ to a document
Θ_g^t	ailment distribution vector for document-set D_g^t of region g during time t
m	distance measure between distributions

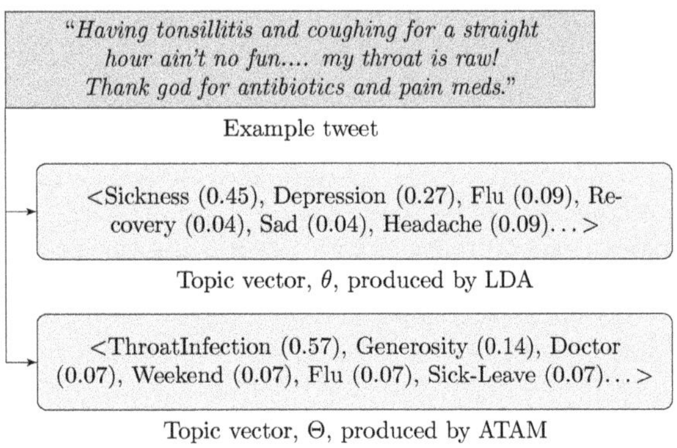

Figure 1: LDA vs ATAM: Comparison of topic distributions for an example tweet.

to uncover latent health-related topics present in a collection of tweets [5]. ATAM achieves remarkable improvement over LDA in discovering topics that correspond to ailments (in addition to discovering general topics). The topic distribution vector generated by ATAM for a sample tweet is shown in Figure 1. Note the stronger relevance to health-related matters in this vector than in the topic distribution vector generated by LDA for the same tweet. While ATAM is effective at modeling health-related topics, it is not designed to model topic transitions over time.

2.1 Ailment prediction problem

In [8], TM–LDA was introduced to extend LDA with modeling topic evolution over time. However, While being quite elegant in modeling general-purpose topics TM–LDA is not specialized to capture ***health*** transitions over time.

Let Θ_g^t be a ailment distribution vector where the weight of each ailment is representative of the discourse density of ailment in the tweets originating from region g during period t. For a region g, the interval of time spanning a set of consecutive time periods $\{t_i, t_{i+1}, \ldots\}$ during which discovered ailment distributions $\{\Theta_g^{t_i}, \Theta_g^{t_{i+1}}, \ldots\}$ do not change appreciably forms a ***homogenous time period*** w.r.t. ailments. By definition, a ***homogenous time period*** is (nearly) homogeneous in terms of ailments. In other words, the ailments evolve in a smooth fashion within a ***homogenous-time period*** and change abruptly across ***homogenous time-period*** boundary. We posit that such ***homogenous time periods*** exist after which they encounter ***change-points*** in ailment topic discussions. These ***change-points*** in ailment topic discussions may be caused by onset of the disease or some other external factors. Nevertheless, they are the interesting points for analyzing purposes. As an example, in Figure 2, we show the difference between ailment distributions of consecutive months for 3 different regions Kuala Lumpur (a city in Indonesia), Oklahoma (a state in the USA), and Bristol (a city in the UK). The sharp peaks obtained validate the existence of time intervals that are homogeneous w.r.t. ailments.

Algorithm 1 TM-ATAM: ***change-point*** Detection and Training Ailment Distribution Predictor

for all $g \in G$ **do**
  Run ATAM on D_g
  for all $t \in \mathcal{T}$ **do**:
    for all $z \in \mathcal{Z}$ **do**:
      $\Theta_g^t[z] \leftarrow 0$
    end for
    for all $d \in D_g^t$ **do**:
      for all $w \in d$ **do**:
        $z \leftarrow topic(w)$
        $\Theta_g^t[z] \leftarrow \Theta_g^t[z] + \frac{1}{|d| \times |D_g^t|}$
      end for
    end for
  end for
  $t_c = \underset{t}{\operatorname{argmax}}\ m(\Theta_g^{t-1}, \Theta_g^t)$
  $pre = [t_1 , t_{c-1}]$
  $post = [t_c , t_{|\mathcal{T}|}]$
  for all $s \in \{pre, post\}$ **do**:
    $A_g^t \approx A_g^{t-1}.M$
    $M = (A_g^{t-1\intercal} A_g^{t-1})^{-1} A_g^{t-1\intercal} A_g^t$
  end for
end for

Our problem: Given a set of documents $D_g^{t_{i-1}}$ formed by tweets originating from a region $g \in G$ during time period t_{i-1}, predict $\Theta_g^{t_i}$, the ailment distribution of documents in $D_g^{t_i}$, corresponding to posts from g in period t_i from $\Theta_g^{t_{i-1}}$, the ailment distribution of document $D_g^{t_{i-1}}$ corresponding to posts from g during period t_{i-1}.

2.2 Modeling Health Topics over Time with TM–ATAM

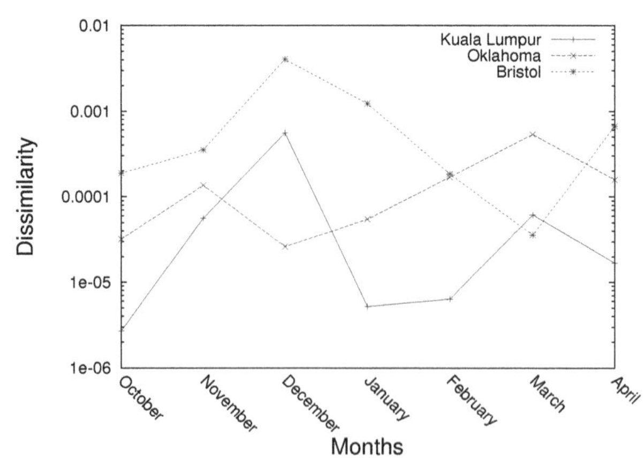

Figure 2: Topic transitions over time.

To solve our problem, we propose TM–ATAM that builds on top of ATAM and TM–LDA. We first convert inferences of ATAM over a single document to associate with a given set of documents D_g^t, an ailment distribution, Θ_g^t. We then go on to find *homogenous time periods*. We model ailment transitions within each *homogenous time period* and when a *change-point* is encountered we update these transitions. This is a fresh departure from existing solutions that operate in a *homogenous time period*-agnostic fashion [8]. TM–ATAM, at its heart, solves the following equation.

$$A_g^t \approx A_g^{t-1}.M^* \quad (1)$$

where

$$A_g^{t-1} = \begin{pmatrix} \Theta_g^1 \\ \vdots \\ \Theta_g^t \end{pmatrix}, A_g^t = \begin{pmatrix} \Theta_g^2 \\ \vdots \\ \Theta_g^{t+1} \end{pmatrix} \quad (2)$$

M^* is an unknown transition matrix which is obtained by solving the following least squares problem.

$$M^* = \underset{M}{argmin} \, \|A_g^t - A_g^{t-1}.M\|_F$$

Algorithm 1 contains the steps of our solution. It has two parts: *change-point detection* and *ailment prediction*.

Change Point Detection.

We use $\mathcal{Z}$ to refer to the set of all health-related and non-health related topics. For each region $g \in \mathcal{G}$ (Line 1) we first run ATAM over the full time period D_g (Line 2). Next for each period $t \in \mathcal{T}$ (Line 3), we use the output of ATAM over D_g to generate a topic distribution Θ_g^t (Lines 4– 12). We then examine the *Bhattacharyya Distance* between consecutive distributions Θ_g^{t-1} and Θ_g^t of the region g to identify the most significant *change-point*, t_c, for region g (Line 14). The time periods preceding and succeding *change-point* are termed as *homogenous time periods*.

Ailment Prediction.

In the second module of TM–ATAM algorithm, we predict distribution of ailments in twitter discourse ahead of time for each *homogenous time period*. Lines 17–20 of Algorithm 1 outline the steps undertaken to identify the detection of ailments for intra-homogeneous periods.

3. EXPERIMENTS

We conducted experiments to evaluate the performance of TM–ATAM and to compare with the state of the art.

3.1 Experimental setup

We employ Twitter's Streaming API to collect tweets between 2014-Oct-8 and 2015-May-31. Collected tweets were subjected to two pre-processing steps as follows.

Identifying health-related tweets: We filter the tweets returned by the *Decahose Stream* to obtain *health-related* tweets. We say that a tweet is health-related if it contains a health keyword and passes our classification criteria. We used 20,000 health-related keywords crawled from wrongdiagnosis.com to first filter the tweets. The process is then automated with the help of an SVM classifier [3]. To this end, 5128 tweets were annotated through crowdsourcing efforts. The precision and recall of the classifier are 0.85 and 0.44. Table 2 shows that out of the 1.36B tweets we collected, 698K were health-related.

Table 2: Dataset Statistics

collection period (days)	235
#tweets	1,360,705,803
#tweets (health-related)	698,212
#tweets (health-related+geolocated)	569,408

Identifying geolocalized tweets: The ability to operate seamlessly at varying geographic resolutions mandates that the exact location of each tweet be known to TM–ATAM. Twitter affords its users the option to share their geolocation. In our case, over half a million tweets are retained ($569K$ as indicated in Table 2).

We examine various choices for the geographic granularities, temporal granularities and distance measures. TM–ATAM performs better on smaller regions. We attribute this result to the fact that tweets from smaller regions show less diversity in topics. We also found weekly ailment distributions to be very sparse. We also used 2 distance measures to measure distribution difference namely, cosine similarity and Bhattacharyya distance. We observed that number of tweets at a given time granularity t may affect the performance of Cosine Similarity. Finally, we chose to work with geographic granularity of *states*, temporal granularity of *months* and distance measure of *Bhattacharyya*.

Test-bench and measures: We run our experiments on a 32 core Intel Xeon @ 2.6Ghz CPU (with 20MB cache per core) system with 128 Gig RAM running Debian GNU/Linux 7.9 (wheezy) operating system. All subsequently discussed components were implemented in Java 1.8.0_60. We used *perplexity* to compare between models [6].

3.2 Experimental Results

Recall that the terms *change-point* and *homogenous-time period* refer to the point in time at which discourse density of ailments changes substantially, and the time period before and after that point, respectively. We divide each *homogenous time period* into training and test sets. ATAM is then *re-run* over the training set of each *homogenous-time period*. We then model a *transition matrix* M_{tmatam}^* on the training set of each *homogenous time period* as described in Section 2.2. We compute the probability of "health topic" z for each tweet p of the first month ($|\mathcal{T}| - 1$) in the test set using the following formulas:

$$P(z|t_{|\mathcal{T}|-1}) = \frac{\sum_{p \, \in t_{|\mathcal{T}|-1}} P(z|p \; for \; t_{|\mathcal{T}|-1})}{\#tweets \; for \; t_{|\mathcal{T}|-1}} \quad (3)$$

$$P(z|p) = \sum_w P(z|w)P(w|p) = \sum_w \frac{n(z,w)}{n(w)} P(w|p) \quad (4)$$

Here, values for $n(z,w)$,$n(w)$ are taken from ATAM run on the training months. P(w|p) is simply the number of times word w occurs in the tweet p divided by the total number of words in p. We then predict the future probability of each topic in the second month of the test data using the corresponding *transition matrix* M_{tmatam}^*. Probability of word $p_l(w_i)$ for any document set is calculated as follows:

$$p_l(w_i) = \sum_z P(w|z)P(z) = \sum_z \frac{n(z,w)}{n(z)} P(z) \quad (5)$$

Having computed $P(w)$, we can compute perplexity against the words of the tweets of second test month.

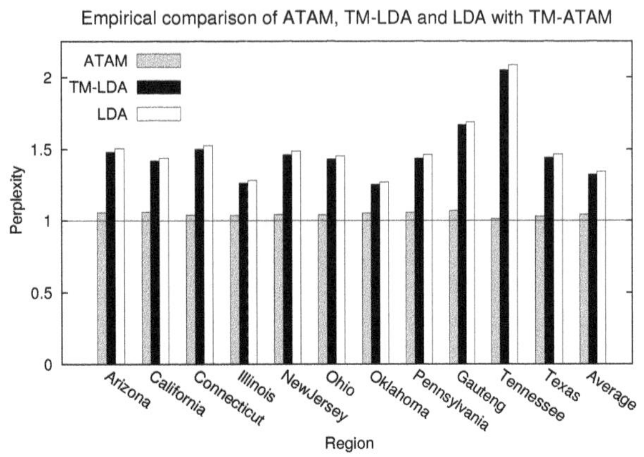

Figure 3: Comparison for top 10 active regions. Histograms denote ratio of perplexities. TM–ATAM is always at 1.0.

Figure 4: Top-2 Monthly *homogenous time period* for top active regions.

Table 3: One-Way Transitions for California (threshold: 0.815)

From Topic	To Topic	Weight
smoking/junkies /drugs/cigarettes	respiratory diseases	2.70
depression/complaining /cursing/slangs/self-pity	joint pains/body pains	3.25

3.2.1 TM–ATAM vs ATAM, TM–LDA vs LDA

Figure 3 shows the perplexity ratio of TM–ATAM with state-of-the art models. If ratio computes to be less than "1" for *competitor topic model*, TM–ATAM is performing worse. If ratio is more than "1" for *competitor topic model*, TM–ATAM is performing better. In order to assert the fact that health topics transit from one to another, we compute the perplexity of ATAM on words of the *first month* of the test set and not predicting any topic distribution using any *transition matrix*. Hence, this denotes the case where health topics stay *static*. As shown in Figure 3, TM–ATAM beats ATAM in all social media active regions (an active region is a region where the proportion of tweets if high enough). For training TM–LDA, we merge the training data (same as TM–ATAM) of each *homogenous time period* in each region and train a *transition matrix* of TM–LDA by solving least squares problem. For each tweet p of the first month of the test set, we compute the probability of topics using LDA trained on merged training data (Formula 3). We then predict the future probability of each topic in the following month using M^*_{tmlda}. We can then compute the perplexity of TM–LDA against words of actual tweets in the test set. Figure 3 shows that TM–ATAM consistently beats TM–LDA and LDA in predicting future health topics on the test month. Perplexity is indeed lower for all words of the test month in all active states.

3.2.2 Homogenous Time Periods

In Figure 4 we show the top-2 sharpest *change-points* for the top regions. Those points can be explained with weather changes in those regions. Texas can be explained with a drop in temperature while Jervis Bay can be explained by an increase in rainfall. Dublin sees its lowest temperature in November. Singapore and Manila have very similar weather conditions and exhibit the same change point.

3.2.3 Topic Transitions

Entry m_{ij} in the *transition matrix* M produced by TM–ATAM, shows the degree that topic z_i will contribute to topic z_j in the subsequent *homogenous time period*. We adapt the threshold used in [8] to our settings: Threshold $= \mu + 2 \times \sigma_{non-diagonal}$. We identify two kinds of interesting transitions based on the above threshold: *selftransitions*: popular topics and *one way transitions*: i^{th} topic is discussed before j^{th} topic. As an example, one-way-transitions of California are summarized in Table 3.

4. CONCLUSION

We studied how to uncover ailment distributions over time in social media. We proposed a granularity-based model to conduct region-specific analysis that leads to the identification of time intervals characterizing homogeneous ailment discourse, per region. We modeled disease evolution within each homogeneous region and attempted to predict ailments. The fine-grained nature of our model results in significant improvements over state of the art methods.

5. REFERENCES

[1] D. M. Blei and J. D. Lafferty. Dynamic Topic Models. In *ICML*, pages 113–120, 2006.

[2] D. M. Blei, A. Y. Ng, and M. I. Jordan. Latent Dirichlet Allocation. *JMLR*, 3:993–1022, 2003.

[3] C. Cortes and V. Vapnik. Support-vector networks. *Machine Learning*, 20(3):273–297, 1995.

[4] T. Hofmann. Probabilistic Latent Semantic Indexing. In *SIGIR*, pages 50–57, 1999.

[5] M. J. Paul and M. Dredze. You Are What You Tweet: Analyzing Twitter for Public Health. In *ICWSM*, 2011.

[6] H. M. Wallach, I. Murray, R. Salakhutdinov, and D. Mimno. Evaluation methods for topic models. In *ICML*, pages 1105–1112, 2009.

[7] X. Wang and A. McCallum. Topics Over Time: A Non-Markov Continuous-time Model of Topical Trends. In *KDD*, pages 424–433, 2006.

[8] Y. Wang, E. Agichtein, and M. Benzi. TM-LDA: Efficient Online Modeling of Latent Topic Transitions in Social Media. In *KDD*, pages 123–131, 2012.

[9] W. X. Zhao, J. Jiang, J. Weng, J. He, E. Lim, H. Yan, and X. Li. Comparing Twitter and Traditional Media Using Topic Models. In *ECIR*, pages 338–349, 2011.

How Informative is a Term? Dispersion as a measure of Term Specificity

Rodney McDonell
Department of Computing and Information Systems
University of Melbourne
Parkville, Australia
r.mcdonell@student.unimelb.edu.au

Justin Zobel
Department of Computing and Information Systems
University of Melbourne
Parkville, Australia
jzobel@unimelb.edu.au

Bodo Billerbeck*
Department of Computing and Information Systems
University of Melbourne
Parkville, Australia
bodob@microsoft.com

ABSTRACT

Similarity functions assign scores to documents in response to queries. These functions require as input statistics about the terms in the queries and documents, where the intention is that the statistics are estimates of the relative informativeness of the terms. Common measures of informativeness use the number of documents containing each term (the document frequency) as a key measure. We argue in this paper that the distribution of within-document frequencies across a collection is also pertinent to informativeness, a measure that has not been considered in prior work: the most informative words tend to be those whose frequency of occurrence has high variance. We propose use of *relative standard deviation* (RSD) as a measure of variability incorporating within-document frequencies, and show that RSD compares favourably with *inverse document frequency* (IDF), in both in-principle analysis and in practice in retrieval, with small but consistent gains.

1. INTRODUCTION

The effectiveness of a retrieval system hinges on its ability to retrieve relevant documents in response to a query. The core of retrieval methods are similarity functions, whose scores are used to construct document rankings and are, in effect, proxies for statistical estimates of the likelihood of document relevance. Term weighting schemes are input to these functions; these are used to allocate values to terms that represent their significance within the collection and each document. That is, they represent the informativeness of words. A common approach to calculation of the informativeness of a term is measurement of the *term specificity.*

In their development of the Robertson–Spärck Jones relevance weight (RSJ) [10], the authors argued that, if any information in a distribution 'has any bearing on the probability of relevance, then we should make use of it'. Typical similarity functions have both a collection-wide measure and a document-specific measure. The *inverse document frequency* (IDF) is arguably the best-known collection-wide measure, and is a straightforward function of the number of documents containing a specific term; other measures, such as language models, use the total frequency of the term in the collection. Within-document frequency, also known as *term frequency* (TF), is a well-known document-specific measure. RSJ is used in probabilistic retrieval weighting schemes such as BM25 [7].

In other work from the same year, Salton and Wong [11] observed that:

> the most useful content indicators are terms whose overall occurrence frequencies are neither too large nor too small, and whose frequency distributions across the documents of a collection are skewed: they occur with high frequencies in some documents and with much lower frequencies in others.

We argue that a 'content indicator' based on variance in frequency can indeed make a useful contribution to informativeness. In this paper, we propose a measure based on statistical dispersion as an estimate of informativeness. This measure, *relative standard deviation* (RSD), increases the weight of terms whose within-document frequency has high variance. As an intuition, consider a term that is part of the vocabulary of a particular community; it may only occur in a small number of documents – and thus have high IDF – but would be expected to have consistent density of use in those documents, and not be particularly informative. Variability in density, in contrast, would suggest that the term relates to a specific topic.

We have directly compared the behaviour of IDF and RSD, and also explored them in the context of retrieval experiments. These investigations illustrate that RSD is richer than IDF, and can yield improvements in retrieval effectiveness. With a direct basis in statistical principles, in particular entropy, our work suggests that RSD should be used as a replacement for simple document frequency.

2. DISPERSIONAL TERM SPECIFICITY

Shannon [13] defined the value of information as proportional to the uncertainty of the information; uncertainty is

*This work was conducted while the author was employed by Microsoft, Melbourne, Australia.

SIGIR '16, July 17-21, 2016, Pisa, Italy

DOI: http://dx.doi.org/10.1145/2911451.2914687

proportional to the variability. In the context of document retrieval, the theory implies that the words that exhibit the most uncertainty carry the most information and thus should be the most informative. In information retrieval, entropy has previously been investigated for term weighting, feature selection, and the building of probabilistic models of information retrieval [2, 4, 6, 8]. We explore statistical dispersion as a novel method of calculating variability for use in information retrieval.

Dispersion as used in this paper is the median or mean of the deviations of the random variable $X_t = \{x_1, x_2, \ldots, x_n\}$ from the the expected value $\mathbb{E}[X_t]$ for some term t with term frequencies x_i over n documents. Here x_i are $f_{t,d}$, the frequency of term t in document d, or the relative term frequency $rf_{t,d} = \frac{f_{t,d}}{|d|}$, where $|d|$ is the length of d. Equation (1) is thus a measure of the extent to which the actual distribution differs from the expected (normal) distribution.

$$DTS\left(t, X_t, \alpha, \beta, \gamma\right) = \frac{\mathbb{E}\left[\left\{\left(x - \mathbb{E}\left[X_t\right]\right)^{\alpha} | x \in X_t\right\}\right]^{\beta}}{\gamma} \tag{1}$$

where $\mathbb{E}$ is the median or mean and α, β and γ together determine the statistical deviation being calculated.

The difference between the predictor (expected value) and an observed value is an observation of the predictors uncertainty: the error in the prediction. The mean error of the predictor is thus a measure of the predictor's uncertainty.

The uncertainty inherent in dispersion suggests a connection with probability theory and Shannon's theory of information. Shannon's entropy determines the value of information by calculating the average self-information of a term t; the self-information of an item k is the log of the inverse probability $1/P(k)$ or the non-likelihood of item k.

As the inverse probability of an event is proportional to the uncertainty of the event, we may define $1/P(k)$ as the uncertainty of an event U_t. Thus Equation (2) gives the formulation of a slightly different method of self-information, based on uncertainty:

$$\mathtt{I}'(U_t) = \log\left(U_t\right) \tag{2}$$

Equation (3) defines the informativeness of IDF as the self-information of the uncertainty of the terms frequency distribution $U_t = {}^{N}/_{n_t} + 1$.

$$IDF\left(t\right) = \mathtt{I}'\left(\frac{N}{n_t} + 1\right) \tag{3}$$

$$TF\text{-}IDF\left(t\right) = \log\left(rf_{t,d}\right) + IDF(t) \tag{4}$$

Here, N is the total number of documents and n_t is the number of documents containing t. Similarly RSD is a measure of informativeness calculated from the self-information of the uncertainty of the terms distribution as given by Equation (1).

$$RSD\left(t, X_t\right) = \mathtt{I}'\left(DTS\left(t, X_t, 2, {}^{1}/_{2}, \bar{X}_t\right)\right) \tag{5}$$

Here, $\bar{X}_t$ is the mean of the distribution of term frequencies X_t. We now examine the potential for RSD to act as a measure of term specificity and compare to IDF.

3. QUALITATIVE EXPERIMENTS

Our investigation of RSD is in two parts. The second part is its value as a component of similarity measures; our experiments with retrieval are reported in the next section. The first part, reported in this section, is to examine how it relates to IDF as a description of the set of terms in a collection.

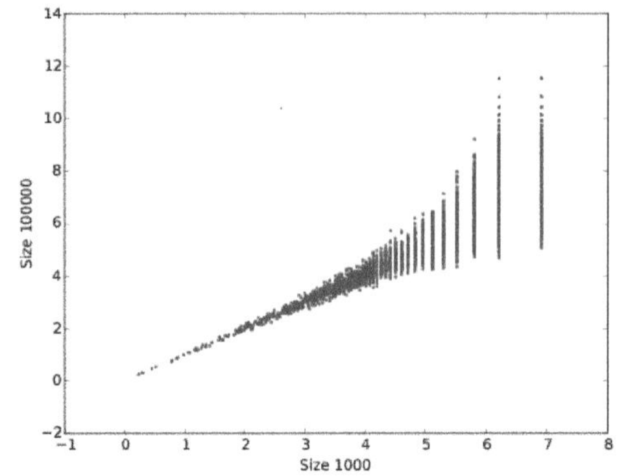

Figure 1: IDF sample size comparison

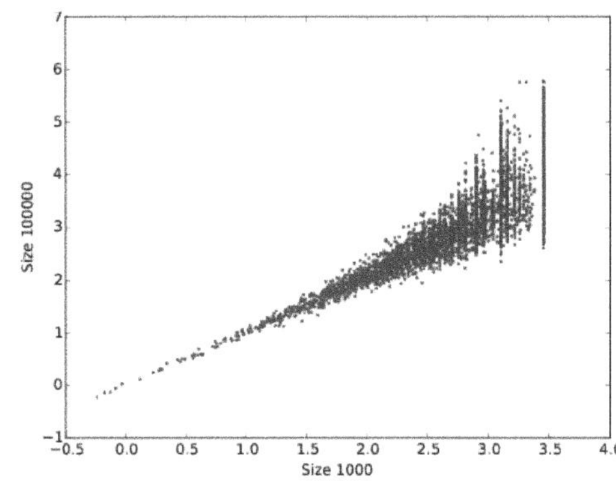

Figure 2: RSD sample size comparison

These qualitative experiments use the weighting methods in Equation (3) and Equation (5). RSD makes use of Equation (1) where parameters α, β and γ are 2, $^1/_2$, and $\bar{X}_t$ respectively. In the experiments and results in this section, we used the OHSUMED text collection [5], and where applicable the text category used was `ohsu30`. This collection, although old, provides a framework for examining the behaviour of terms in the context of classes, and illustrates the discriminative power of IDF and RSD.

Sample size correlation. We constructed scattergrams to investigate the estimated informativeness of the terms in two samples of documents, as determined by IDF and RSD. We constructed a set of 100,000 documents from the OHSUMED text collection, and a smaller sample of 1000 documents was selected from the larger sample. The scattergrams for each measure of informativeness was constructed by applying the function to each sample and then plotting the values on the opposite axis. Thus each scattergram shows the extent to which a value (IDF or RSD) estimated from 1000 documents is predictive of the observed value in 100,000 documents.

The behaviour of IDF is well known [12, 14]. If RSD is an accurate measure of informativeness, a similar difference in weights, for a given sample size, should be observed.

The two figures show similar overall correlation, with, therefore, similar levels of predictivity from one sample size to the other. Figure 1 demonstrates the gaps in the range of

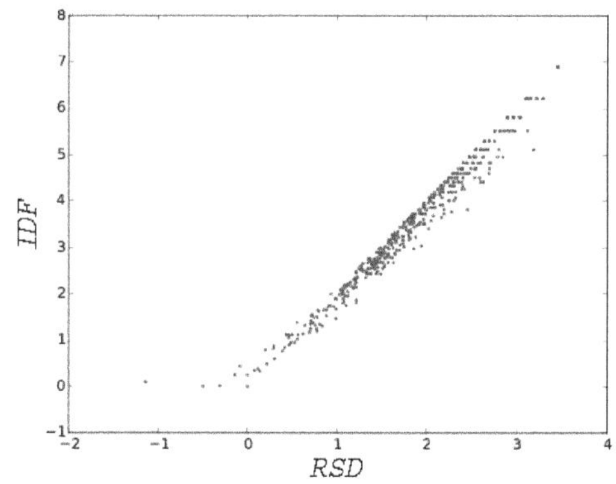

Figure 3: IDF vs Relative SD

values as generated by IDF that are one of the motivations for use of within-document term frequency. RSD compares favourably, showing a lack of gaps in the range of values for the same sample size, suggesting a finer-grained measure of informativeness.

The shape of the RSD scattergram is strongly similar to that of IDF. Both exhibit a similar growth in values, particularly at the right-hand side. For Figures 1 and 2, these values from approximately 4 to 12 and 2 to 6 within a total value range of 0 to 12 and 0 to 6 respectively. This represents 66% of the total value range of both IDF and RSD, further demonstrating the similarity between the two.

IDF weighting correlation. Measures of term specificity that produce weights similar to IDF are likely to also be useful measures of informativeness.

Figure 3 was produced plotting the weights as determined by the IDF and RSD weighting functions. Then comparative analysis determined the similarities in the visual properties between IDF and RSD plot values. Each graph is generated from a random sample of 1000 documents of the OHSUMED text collection.

The IDF weighting scattergrams clearly show that RSD correlates strongly with IDF, supporting results from Section 3. The strong correlation supports the hypothesis that RSD, like IDF, is a measure of term specificity. This further supports the hypothesis that IDF and RSD are similar measures of uncertainty, and that these measures can be used interchangeably.

Term rank comparison. Salton et al. showed that a decrease in the space between like documents in the vector space and a corresponding increase in the space between unlike documents increases the precision of a retrieval system [12, p. 617-619].

We define the 'discriminating power of a function' as the distance between term weights of two opposing classes of documents as generated by a given function. Figures 4 and 5 depict the term weights as determined by IDF and RSD respectively, of two samples of opposing classes. Then for IDF and RSD the discriminating power of the weighting function is determined by analysing the differences between the weights of the document sample for each class.

Figure 4 depicts the differences between the weights of the rarest terms for the positive set relative to the same terms in the negative set. The average difference between

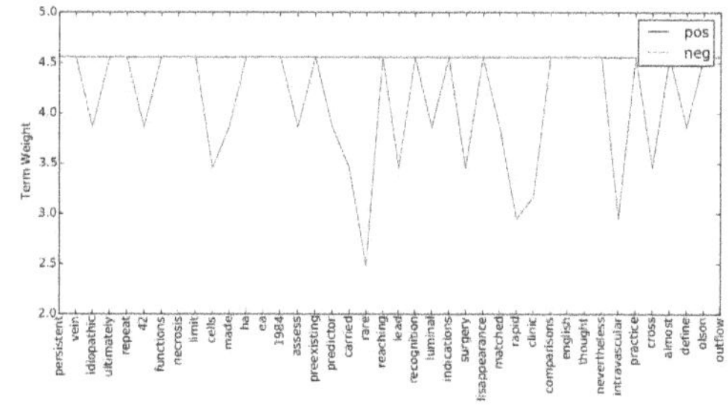

Figure 4: Top 40 IDF Terms

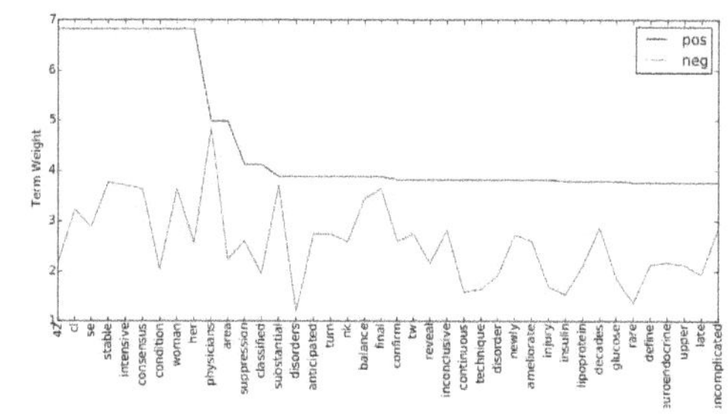

Figure 5: Top 40 Relative SD Terms

the term weights for the top 40 words of the positive classes (Figures 4 and 5), relative to the negative classes for IDF and RSD is approximately 20% and 57% respectively. Similar observations were made by Church and Gale [1], who explored another form of variance: the relationship between number of documents and total frequency of occurrence.

The differences alone are not the determining factor in the measurements. RSD could be weighting terms incorrectly, but still separating them more so than IDF; but this seems unlikely given the strong correlations. Thus RSD is likely to have a higher discriminating value than IDF.

4. RETRIEVAL EXPERIMENTS

A term weighting scheme based on RSD was developed for use in ad hoc information retrieval experiments and compared to TF-IDF.

$$\mathit{TF\text{-}RSD} = \log\left(rf_{t,d}\right) \times \mathit{RSD}\left(t, X\right) \tag{6}$$

Tables 1 and 2 present the results for ad hoc retrieval for MAP over 1000 retrieved documents and the precision at 10 retrieved documents (P@10). Results of FBIS+FR94 are presented first, followed by WT10G [15]. Each table compares the output of `trec_eval` for TF-IDF and TF-RSD where RSD takes term frequency distributions of raw frequencies or relative frequencies denoted by TF-RSD(raw) or TF-RSD(rel) respectively.

TF-RSD calculated from TF-RSD(raw) shows improved MAP figures for all experiments except the stopped (wordnet stopword list [3]) and stemmed [9] description-only test. TF-RSD calculated from TF-RSD(rel) retrieved more relevant documents than TF-IDF and also resulted in higher MAP scores. For P@10, TF-RSD outperformed TF-IDF in all experiments, often by a relatively large margin.

Title queries on the WT10G data set for TF-RSD achieve a significant improvement over TF-IDF. In comparison, description-only queries for TF-RSD rank the top 1000 documents less effectively than TF-IDF. However the top 10 doc-

		MAP			P@10		
Config	#Queries	TF-IDF	TF-RSD(raw)	TF-RSD(rel)	TF-IDF	TF-RSD(raw))	TF-RSD(rel)
raw title	247	0.1743	**0.1823**	0.1818†	0.1834	0.1842	**0.1883**†
raw desc	249	0.1798	**0.1856**	0.1845†	0.1779	**0.1904**†	0.1871‡
ss title	248	0.1973	**0.2038**†	0.2001†	0.1980	**0.2032**	0.2024
ss desc	249	0.2118	0.2065	**0.2156**	0.2072	0.2076	**0.2120**

Table 1: FBIS+FR94 TF-IDF vs. TF-RSD. Best results in each category are bolded and statistical significance at the 0.05 and 0.01 levels are indicated by † and ‡, respectively.

		MAP			P@10		
Config	#Queries	TF-IDF	TF-RSD(raw)	TF-RSD(rel)	TF-IDF	TF-RSD(raw)	TF-RSD(rel)
raw title	98	0.1158	**0.1248**‡	0.1224†	0.1939	0.2041	**0.2051**
raw desc	100	**0.1504**	0.1401	0.1464	0.2630	0.2610	**0.2690**
ss title	97	0.1296	0.1339	**0.1341**	0.1938	0.2031	**0.2082**
ss desc	100	0.1676	0.1667	**0.1688**	**0.2900**	**0.2900**	0.2820

Table 2: WT10G TF-IDF vs. TF-RSD. Best results and statistical significance indicated as above.

ument rankings are not as impacted and thus this is likely not to affect the user. TF-RSD calculated from relative term frequencies also shows significant improvement in the MAP for title-only queries, relative to description-only queries.

These results support the claims that RSD is a useful measure of term specificity, and show that TF-RSD is more effective than TF-IDF for the data sets and queries used.

5. CONCLUSIONS

We have proposed that the informativeness of a word is proportional to the self-information of the uncertainty of the word's occurrence in a set of documents, and defined new measures of informativeness and corresponding term weighting schemes, by calculating the self–information of the statistical dispersion (variability) of a terms frequency across a set of documents.

We have shown that RSD, a new measure of informativeness, correlates strongly with IDF on essential qualitative properties of measures of informativeness. We then demonstrated that TF-RSD, a new term weighting scheme for information retrieval, achieves improved results compared to TF-IDF in 12 of 16 retrieval experiments, seven of which were statistically significant. The retrieval results for the top 10 ranked documents were equally impressive – where only two of the 16 experiments failed to perform better than TF-IDF. Thus TF-RSD is an effective term weighting scheme that is a plausible replacement for TF-IDF.

References

[1] Church, K. and Gale, W. [1999], Inverse document frequency (IDF): A measure of deviations from Poisson, *in* 'Natural language processing using very large corpora', Springer, pp. 283–295.

[2] Cooper, W. S. and Huizinga, P. [1982], 'The maximum entropy principle and its application to the design of probabilistic retrieval systems.', *Information Technology, Research and Development* **1**, 99–112.

[3] Fellbaum, C. [1998], *WordNet: An Electronic Lexical Database*, Bradford Books.

[4] Greiff, W. R. and Ponte, J. M. [2000], 'The maximum entropy approach and probabilistic IR models', *ACM Trans. Inf. Syst.* **18**(3), 246–287.

[5] Hersh, W., Buckley, C., Leone, T. and Hickam, D. [1994], Ohsumed: An interactive retrieval evaluation and new large test collection for research, *in* 'SIGIR94', Springer, pp. 192–201.

[6] Jiao, Y., Cornec, M. and Jakubowicz., J. [2015], An entropy-based term weighting scheme and its application in e-commerce search engines, *in* 'Proceedings of the first International Symposium on Web Algorithms', International Symposium on Web Algorithms.

[7] Jones, K. S., Walker, S. and Robertson, S. E. [2000], 'A probabilistic model of information retrieval: Development and comparative experiments, Parts 1 and 2', *Inf. Process. Manage.* **36**(6), 779–840.

[8] Ke, W. [2013], Information-theoretic term weighting schemes for document clustering, *in* 'Proceedings of the 13th ACM/IEEE-CS joint conference on Digital libraries', ACM, pp. 143–152.

[9] Porter, M. [1980], 'An algorithm for suffix stripping', *Program* **14**(3), 130–137.

[10] Robertson, S. and Spärk Jones, K. [1976], 'Relevance weighting of search terms', *Journal of the American Society for Information Science* **27**(3), 129–146.

[11] Salton, G. and Wong, A. [1976], 'On the role of words and phrases in automatic text analysis', *Computers and the Humanities* **10**, 291–391.

[12] Salton, G., Wong, A. and Yang, C. [1975], 'A vector space model for automatic indexing', *Communications of the ACM* **18**(11), 613–620.

[13] Shannon, C. [1948], 'A mathematical theory of communication', *Bell System Technical Journal* **27**, 379–423.

[14] Spärk Jones, K. [1972], 'A statistical interpretation of term specificity and its application in retrieval', *Journal of Docmentation* **28**(1), 11–21.

[15] Voorhees, E. M., Harman, D. K. et al. [2005], *TREC: Experiment and evaluation in information retrieval*, Vol. 1, MIT press Cambridge.

Identifying Careless Workers in Crowdsourcing Platforms: A Game Theory Approach

Yashar Moshfeghi
School of Computing Science
University of Glasgow
Glasgow, UK
Yashar.Moshfeghi@glasgow.ac.uk

Alvaro F. Huertas-Rosero
School of Computing Science
University of Glasgow
Glasgow, UK
Alvaro.Huertas@glasgow.ac.uk

Joemon M. Jose
School of Computing Science
University of Glasgow
Glasgow, UK
Joemon.Jose@glasgow.ac.uk

ABSTRACT

In this paper we introduce a game scenario for crowdsourcing (CS) using incentives as a bait for careless (gambler) workers, who respond to them in a characteristic way. We hypothesise that careless workers are risk-inclined and can be detected in the game scenario by their use of time, and test this hypothesis in two steps: first, we formulate and prove a theorem stating that a risk-inclined worker will react to competition with shorter Task Completion Time (TCT) than a risk-neutral or risk-averse worker. Second, we check if the game scenario introduces a link between TCT and performance, by performing a crowdsourced evaluation using 35 topics from the TREC-8 collection. Experimental evidence confirms our hypothesis, showing that TCT can be used as a powerful discrimination factor to detect careless workers. This is a valuable result in the quest for quality assurance in CS-based micro tasks such as relevance assessment.

Keywords: Game Theory, Crowdsourcing, Relevance Assessment, Chicken Game

1. INTRODUCTION

Crowdsourcing (CS) platforms offer new ways of collecting relevance assessments for IR evaluation and are already used widely [4]. The advantages associated with this platform, i.e. low monetary cost and high task completion speed are, however, entangled with a mixed output quality, making the effective use of CS a non-trivial problem. Past studies have shown the importance of careful quality assurance [8], particularly when the task is 'micro', such as relevance assessment (RA), and involves financial incentives [6].

Research in quality assurance for CS has been largely heuristic and non-generalisable. Zhao reports in 2012 that only 9 out of 55 studies of crowdsourcing include any kind of theoretical bases [14]. Quality is usually assured with the use of "gold standard" data, multiple answers [5], qualification tests, honey pots (i.e. questions whose answers are known in advance) or a combination of the above. Such quality assurance techniques can potentially increase the general experiment cost, task completion time, and experimenters' intervention [2].

We propose a systematic approach to the problem based on spotting workers who undertake the task as gambling. A worker taking insufficient time to complete a task is knowingly taking the risk of getting a wrong result [9], so we will assume that careless workers (gamblers) are risk-inclined [10]. Therefore we formulate our research question as: **"Is workers' inclination towards risk, reflected in low Task Completion Times (TCT) in a competition scenario, a good predictor of poor performance?"**

We propose a competitive game where we motivate workers to finish their RA task correctly (pushing towards longer time) and fast (pushing towards shorter time). As a result of these two opposing forces, TCTs will become sensitive to the worker's attitudes towards risk and their perceptions of the task and payoff, i.e. workers adjust the time they take to perform a task to be longer or shorter according to whether they perceive the risk of not taking enough time as more or less important than being fast.

The rest of the paper is organised as follows: our game theoretical model is described in section 2, the theorem linking risk inclination with TCT is stated and proved in Section 3. Section 4 describes the empirical experiment where we link TCT and performance, results and discussion are in Section 5. Finally we conclude in Section 6.

2. THEORETICAL MODEL

We start from a theoretical model based on Game Theory, which builds on a few assumptions and leads us to our first result, linking TCT with inclination to risk. This result motivates a CS experiment where we check the correlation between TCT and performance, completing our argument for detecting careless workers by their TCT under competition conditions.

Best scenarios, worst scenarios and risk: Attitudes towards risk can be viewed as ways of perceiving utility [10], relative to the probabilistic average. A *risk-inclined* player perceives uncertain utility as higher than the average, a *risk-neutral* player perceives it exactly like the average, and a *risk-averse* player perceives it as lower than the average. Fig. 1 illustrates these pessimistic and optimistic views.

SIGIR '16, July 17-21, 2016, Pisa, Italy

DOI: http://dx.doi.org/10.1145/2911451.2914756

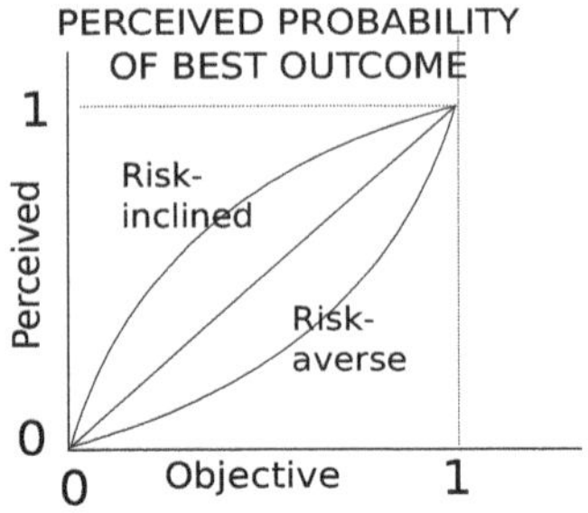

Figure 1: Perceived probability of getting the highest utility for different attitudes towards risk. Risk-inclined players will perceive a higher probability in uncertain situations (convex, upper curve), risk-neutral players will perceive a probabilistic mean utility (linear, middle curve) and risk-averse players will perceive a lower probability in uncertain situations (concave, lower curve).

Risk inclined workers are more sensitive to incentives to compete, because they perceive an uncertain outcome as more profitable. Risk averse workers, on the other hand, are more interested in certain aspects of the game, e.g. non-competitive incentives that do not depend on other workers.

The Mathematical Concept of Game: A game, in the context of mathematical game theory, consists of three components: (i) several agents (players), (ii) a set of decisions (actions) they take based on a set of strategies, and (iii) an outcome (payoff) which is aimed to be maximised by considering their own and other players' strategies.

It is important to note that a mathematically defined game differs from *gamification* scenarios, even though it shares common elements. Gamification involve managing affective incentives, as is the case of image labeling games (called ESP) or *Games With a Purpose* [12]. These are not necessarily game-theoretical approaches, but they do involve quantifying and managing entertainment rewards in order to improve the work obtained from volunteers. Gamification has been used for RA tasks in [3], where individuals were persuaded to assess relevance as entertainment. Our approach relies entirely on monetary rewards, and models the motivation of workers as a simple rational principle of maximising monetary gain.

Chicken Game for RA: The Chicken game, also known as Hawk-Dove game [11] is a particular game setting based on time choices, whose characteristics are determined mostly by competition. In the n-player version, a group of teenagers compete with each other for the prestige of being the bravest. They engage in a racing game towards a cliff in their cars as fast as they can, and the player who jumps out of the car the last without falling off the cliff is the winner. Each player chooses the time for an action, and the outcome depends on the times other players chose. A rational player will aim to an optimal trade-off between the two opposing forces of the game, i.e. one preventing them from jumping too quick (competition) and the other pushing them to jump before it is too late (survival). When each player is uncertain about the choices of the other players (i.e. imperfect information), the chicken game can present a Bayesian Nash Equilibrium (BE), which is an important solution concept in game theory. In a BE the strategy of a player is optimal according to their available private knowledge about what the other players would do. Their expected payoff cannot increase by changing their strategy.

We propose a game in which an assessor is paid only if he or she produces a correct RA result. If no other assessor produced a correct result quicker, he or she also gets an extra bonus. This is a similar but inverse version of the Chicken game: in our setting a player needs to choose a time longer than the minimum, but shorter than the other players, while in the Chicken game a player needs to choose a time shorter than a limit (i.e. when they reach the cliff), but longer than the other players.

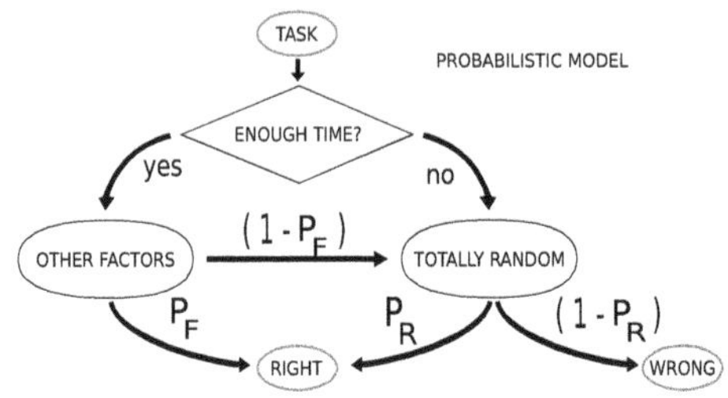

Figure 2: Graph representation of a probabilistic model of an assessment. The rhomboid represents the condition of taking enough time, and ellipses represent random processes: left for hidden but deterministic factors, and right for randomness. The arrows with their probabilities, represent the possible outcomes of each subprocess.

In our model, time is related to payoff through the probability of a correct assessment. If a worker takes an insufficient time, their result will be completely random. In Fig. 2 we represent our model as a probability graph: the condition of taking enough time determines whether the result is random (with probability P_R of being correct). If the worker takes enough time to complete an assessment, then other processes involving knowledge, difficulty, etc. determine whether the worker gets the correct result (with probability P_F).

The minimum time is uncertain, with a probability distribution $D(t_{min})$. The probability of getting the answer right when taking time t will be a monotonically increasing function:

$$P_{correct}(t) = P_R + (P_F - P_R) \int_0^t D(t_{min}) dt_{min} \quad (1)$$

Similarly, given a distribution of times when the quickest worker will finish the task $Q(t)$:

$$P_{quickest}(t) = 1 - \int_0^t Q(t') dt' \quad (2)$$

Expected utility is then:

$$U(t) = K_R P_{correct}(t) P_{quickest}(t) - K_P (1 - P_{correct}(t)) \quad (3)$$

where K_R is the value of the quickness reward and K_P the incorrectness punishment. Note that the term with K_P is monotonically increasing, while that with K_R has a maximum. This means that the position of the maximum will only change notably with these paremeters when $K_P > K_R$ (small incentive for competing).

3. TCT AND INCLINATION TOWARDS RISK

The following theorem links risk inclination to short TCTs in the game scenario, assuming rationality and condition of BE:

THEOREM 1. *In the BE of our game, optimal times for risk-inclined players will be shorter than those for risk-neutral or risk-averse players.*

PROOF. A situation of BE is defined by maximal values of $U(t)$, i.e. $dU(t)/dt = 0$. From Eq. 3:

$$K_R(P_{quick}(dP_{correct}/dt) + P_{correct}(dP_{quick}/dt)) + K_P(dP_{correct}/dt) = 0 \quad (4)$$

From explicit expressions for $P_{correct}(t)$ and P_{quick} we obtain the condition for an optimal time t_{op}:

$$K_R(P_{quick}D(t_{op}) - P_{correct}Q(t_{op})) + K_P D(t_{op}) = 0 \quad (5)$$

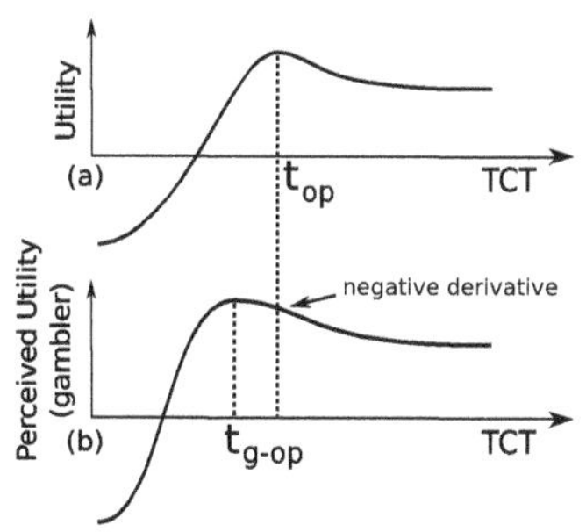

Figure 3: Utility as a function of TCT with objective probabilities (a) and perceived by a risk-inclined player (b). Optimal time t_{op} and gambler's perceived optimal time t_{g-op} are marked with dotted lines.

A gambler over-estimates propitious probabilities, which we represent with a convex function $P' = F_\cap(P)$ and underestimate adverse probabilities, which we represent as a concave function $P' = F_\cup(P)$. which we represented as a concave function $P' = F_\cup(P)$. These are the monotonic transforms depicted in Fig. 1. Optimal time for gamblers t_{g-op} is calculated wit These monotonic transforms are depicted in Fig. 1. Using the chain formula $dF(P)/dt = (dF/dP)(dP/dt)$ we obtain a gambler's optimal time:

$$\begin{aligned} &K_R(dF_\cap/dP_{correct})P_{quick}D(t_{g-op}) \\ &-K_R(dF_\cup/dP_{quick})P_{correct}Q(t_{g-op}) \\ &+K_P(dF_\cap/dP_{correct}D(t_{g-op})) \quad = 0 \end{aligned} \quad (6)$$

Since Eq 6 correspond to the maximal gambler utility $U(t_{g-op})$, the derivative will be positive for shorter times $t < t_{g-op}$ and negative for longer times $t > t_{g-op}$.

We know that both $F_\cap$ and $F_\cup$ are monotonously increasing, so their derivatives are always positive. We also know that in the region of high probabilities of being correct and quickest (where we expect optimal times) a convex function will have a lower derivative than a concave function, so $dF_\cap/dP < dF_\cup/dP$.

This means that the negative term in Eq 6 has become larger than that in Eq 5

$$K_R(dF_\cup/dP_{quick})P_{correct}Q(t_{op}) < K_R P_{correct}Q(t_{op}) \quad (7)$$

The positive term in Eq 6, on the contrary, has become smaller than that in Eq 5

$$(dF_\cap/dP_{correct})(K_R P_{quick}D(t_{op}) + K_P D(t_{op})) < (K_R P_{quick}D(t_{op}) + K_P D(t_{op})) \quad (8)$$

This means that overall, the derivative will be negative, and therefore $t_{op} > t_{g-op}$. (this argument is depicted in Fig. 3) □

4. EXPERIMENTAL METHODOLOGY

In Section 3 we proved that a risk-averse worker would tend to take shorter TCT than others in the game scenario, because of their perception of the competition incentive. In this section, we devise an between-group study to investigate the relation between TCT and precision in the competitive scenario where the independent variable to be competition setting (with two levels: "Base" and "Game"), differing in the description and pay conditions given to the participants. The dependent variables are the accuracy of gathered labels and corresponding TCTs. We make use of Amazon's Mechanical Turk (M-Turk), as our crowdsourcing platform. It provides a convenient participant pool to draw upon to carry out many tasks, especially relevance assessment labelling.

Data Collection: We used TREC-8, in particular the LA Times, FT, FR94 and FBIS sub-collections as our test collection. We randomly selected 35 out of 50 topics in the TREC-8 test set and used the judged articles as a gold standard set, following previous research in the domain, e.g. [1].

Task: We define two tasks, i.e. Base and Game. In both tasks the participants were asked to evaluate the relevance of a set of document-topic pairs. We used plain text to indicate the task rather than the original TREC instructions, according to the suggestions given in [7] for M-Turk crowds. We adopt the concept of relevance used in [13] which has been used in previous work in this domain [1]. We followed the guidelines provided in [1] to instruct our workers, e.g. asking for their consistency with their judgement, etc.

Base Task: We asked participants to perform the relevance judgment task for ten document-topic pairs. In order to ensure quality we highlighted that random assessment will not work, because we know the answer of a few of the pairs. If they fail to assess them correctly, their HIT will not be approved. We also highlighted that presence of topic terms in the document does not necessary mean that the document is relevant to the given topic. They need to make a decision by considering more than solely this criteria.

Game Task: For the game task, in addition to above, we instructed the worker that they would be competing with a few other M-Turk workers in completing the task. In order to create the conditions of the game, we highlighted that they need to complete the assessment correctly and quicker than the other workers. We also mentioned that the winner will be with rewarded with a $2.0 additional bonus.

Relevance Assessment System: For the completion of the tasks we used a custom-made relevance assessment environment designed to gather the workers' judgement, while retaining a minimum of graphical elements and distractions. The back-end layer of the system created a set of random ten topic-document pairs from the QRel file and fetched the associated document and topic information from collections and topic files, respectively. It also ensured that workers judge a topic-document pair only once, while each topic-document pair is judged by no fewer than three workers and no more than five. The documents were presented without their title in order to avoid it being used as the only criterion. The user Interface (UI) contained a topic, document and closed question (binary relevance; yes/no). Workers were required to log in to the system in order to capture their Worker ID. After workers log in, the UI layer gets a set of ten topic-document pairs from the back-end layer and presents them, one at a time, in the same exact order as they were obtained. The interface also prevents them from skipping difficult assessments.

Workers' actions were monitored and logged by the search interface, including the log-in and log-out time to the system, workers' as well as their judgement of each document-topic pair. The length of time workers spent to judge a pair was calculated on client side to avoid interference from network delay: it is computed as the time difference between the moment a topic-document pair was shown until the assessment was submitted.

Procedure: At the beginning of the experiment, participants were instructed that the experiment would take approximately 10 minutes to complete, though they would be given 30 minutes between the time they accepted and submitted the HIT assignment. They were informed that they could participate in each task more than once.Workers could only accept the HIT if they agreed to a consent form. Subsequently, participants were assigned to one of two external surveys ("base" or "game"). At the beginning of the survey, we describe that all the collected data will be treated as confidential and anonymous. Payment for HIT completion was \$1.0. The total cost of the evaluation was \$270, including the cost of the pilot studies and some of the rejected participants, which we consider to be cost-effective.

5. RESULTS AND DISCUSSION

This section presents the experimental findings of our study. To fulfil the conditions of a between-group study, we eliminated participants whom we found had taken part in the experiment under different conditions (e.g. taken part in the Game task after taking part in the Base task, or vice versa). Out of 235 workers who started the tasks, 200 workers completed them successfully (100 workers per group).

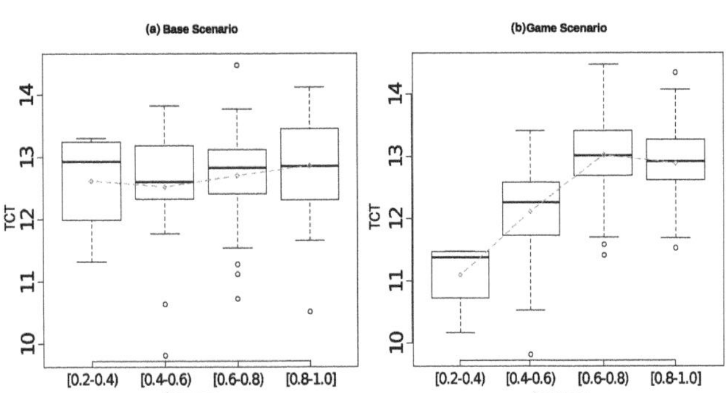

Figure 4: Distributions of TCT (in minutes) for four ranges of precision, in a non-competitive base scenario (a) and game scenario (b). Bars represent the quartiles of the distribution, and the red line connects the mean values.

Figure 4 shows the box plot corresponding to the TCTs of each of four categories according to their fraction of correct results (precision): 0.2 to 0.4, 0.4 to 0.6, 0.6 to 0.8 and 0.8 to 1.0, and show the distribution of TCT in each category by their minimum, first, second (median) third and maximum quartiles. across data collections and tasks. We found that distributions of task completion time changed notably between the Base and Game tasks. As shown in Fig. 4 (b), we can see that there is a clear tendency of the lowest performance categories to low values of TCT in the game (competitive) scenario. In the base task scenario, however, the values of task completion time did not seem to bear any relation to performance, as shown in Fig. 4 (a). Therefore, we confirmed that lower performing players react to our game competing scenario by lowering their TCT and hence turning TCT into a powerful discriminative factor.

Normally in settings like the base task, extra information about users (previous performance, background, etc.) or hints about their current performances (previously known judgments, test questions) are used to detect untrustworthy workers. These strategies, however, require settings that are potentially more expensive and/or discouraging for workers.

6. CONCLUSION

In this paper we hypothesised that it is possible to design a mechanism based on a game theory model that makes task-completion time an effective discriminative factor between careless (i.e. risk-inclined) and other (i.e. risk-neutral or risk-averse) workers. We therefore designed a CS relevance assessment task scenario inspired by an n-player Chicken game model, where there are two opposing forces: one pushing towards quickness and another pushing towards correctness. We tested our hypotheses with a crowdsourced evaluation using 35 topics from TREC-8 collection. Our findings show that the proposed framework allows to use task completion time as a powerful discriminative factor to identify different types of workers. An obvious direction to continue the research on this promising approach is to explore post-filtering methodologies based in risk attitudes inferred from TCT and other indirect data.

7. REFERENCES

[1] O. Alonso. Implementing crowdsourcing-based relevance experimentation: an industrial perspective. *Inf. Retr.*, pages 1–20, 2013.

[2] B. Carterette and I. Soboroff. The Effect of Assessor Error on IR System Evaluation. In *SIGIR '10*, pages 539–546, 2010.

[3] C. Eickhoff, C. G. Harris, A. P. de Vries, and P. Srinivasan. Quality through flow and immersion: gamifying crowdsourced relevance assessments. In *SIGIR '12*, pages 871–880, 2012.

[4] C. Grady and M. Lease. Crowdsourcing document relevance assessment with Mechanical Turk. In *CSLDAMT '10*, pages 172–179, 2010.

[5] P. G. Ipeirotis, F. Provost, and J. Wang.

[6] G. Kazai, J. Kamps, and N. Milic-Frayling. The face of quality in crowdsourcing relevance labels: Demographics, personality and labeling accuracy. In *CIKM '12*, pages 2583–2586, 2012.

[7] G. Kazai, J. Kamps, and N. Milic-Frayling. An Analysis of Human Factors and Label Accuracy in Crowdsourcing Relevance Judgments. *Inf. Retr.*, 16(2):138–178, Apr. 2013.

[8] J. Le, A. Edmonds, V. Hester, and L. Biewald. Ensuring quality in crowdsourced search relevance evaluation: The effects of training question distribution. In *SIGIR 2010 workshop on crowdsourcing for search evaluation*, pages 21–26, 2010.

[9] Y. Moshfeghi, A. F. H. Rosero, and J. M. Jose. A Game-Theory Approach for Effective Crowdsource-Based Relevance Assessment. *ACM Trans. Intell. Syst. Technol.*, 7(4):55:1–55:25, Mar. 2016.

[10] T. Straub, H. Gimpel, and F. Teschner. The negative effect of feedback on performance in crowd labor tournaments. *Collective Intelligence 2014*, 2014.

[11] M. Szilagyi. Agent-Based Simulation of the N-Person Chicken Game. In *Advances in Dynamic Game Theory*, volume 9, pages 696–703. Birkhäuser Boston, 2007.

[12] L. Von Ahn and L. Dabbish. Designing games with a purpose. *Communications of the ACM*, 51(8):58–67, 2008.

[13] E. Voorhees, D. Harman, N. I. of Standards, and T. (US). *TREC: Experiment and evaluation in information retrieval*, volume 63. MIT press Cambridge, 2005.

[14] Y. Zhao and Q. Zhu. Evaluation on crowdsourcing research: Current status and future direction. *Information Systems Frontiers*, pages 1–18, 2012.

Impact of Review-Set Selection on Human Assessment for Text Classification

Adam Roegiest
University of Waterloo

Gordon V. Cormack
University of Waterloo

ABSTRACT

In a laboratory study, human assessors were significantly more likely to judge the same documents as relevant when they were presented for assessment within the context of documents selected using random or uncertainty sampling, as compared to relevance sampling. The effect is substantial and significant [0.54 vs. 0.42, $p<0.0002$] across a population of documents including both relevant and non-relevant documents, for several definitions of ground truth. This result is in accord with Smucker and Jethani's SIGIR 2010 finding that documents were more likely to be judged relevant when assessed within low-precision versus high-precision ranked lists. Our study supports the notion that relevance is malleable, and that one should take care in assuming any labeling to be ground truth, whether for training, tuning, or evaluating text classifiers.

1. INTRODUCTION

In supervised learning for text classification, each of a set of training documents is labeled as relevant or non-relevant by a human assessor. The training documents and their labels are used to induce a classifier to predict the relevance or non-relevance of the remaining documents in the population from which the training documents were drawn. Training documents may be selected using random sampling, or using active learning methods such as uncertainty sampling or relevance sampling [8, 7]. Simulation studies comparing these approaches typically rely on the assumption that the sampling strategy does not influence how the assessor will label a particular document. We show, in a study involving 36 paid assessors recruited from a university community, that the same documents are much more likely to be judged relevant when embedded in a set selected by random sampling or uncertainty sampling, than one selected by relevance sampling.

The influence of sampling strategy on labeling has impact beyond the selection of training sets for inducing classifiers. In technology-assisted review, where every document with a positive classification is assessed and labeled, a superior (higher precision) classifier might yield fewer labeled-relevant documents than an inferior (lower precision) classifier. In the Cranfield approach to IR evaluation (*see* [13]), a set of relevance assessments based on a pool of likely relevant documents might yield substantially different results from one based a sample of the whole. Our result calls into question the common practice of estimating measures like recall and precision from statistical samples, especially those employing non-uniform inclusion probabilities.

A number of studies [11, 12, 6, 10, 5] have shown that the proportion, as well as the order of presentation of relevant and non-relevant documents, can affect user assessment behaviour. Taken together, the results suggest that assessors are less likely to label documents relevant once they have seen a number of relevant documents, either due to presentation order or due to the overall proportion of relevant documents. This observation forms the basis of the question we addressed: Since relevance sampling produces a higher proportion of relevant documents than uncertainty sampling or random sampling, does it suppress the assessor's propensity to judge a document relevant? We further addressed the question of whether this effect was conditioned on ground truth, for several definitions of ground truth.

2. EXPERIMENTAL DESIGN

Our design specified that assessors would review batches of 100 documents for relevance to several topics, where the batches for each topic contained the same 12 known documents, and 88 documents selected by one of random sampling, uncertainty sampling, or relevance sampling.[1] There were 9 topics, and hence 36 batches in total; each batch was assessed by three different assessors.

Table 1 provides a glossary of terms specific to our experimental design.

2.1 Documents and Labels

Documents were selected from the TREC-6 Ad Hoc collection, which has been the subject of previous relevance assessment studies [14, 9, 4], and has two independent sets of relevance assessments: the official NIST binary relevance assessments ("relevant," and "not relevant") created using the pooling method, and a set of graded relevance assess-

[1]Due to an error in our setup that went undetected until the assessments were complete, for some topics, the batches contained only 10 or 11 of the same known documents. The corresponding shortfall reduced the statistical power of our experiment, but does not affect its validity.

SIGIR '16 July 17-21, 2016, Pisa, Italy

ACM ISBN 978-1-4503-4069-4/16/07.

DOI: http://dx.doi.org/10.1145/2911451.2914709

Batch	100 documents presented to assessors for review, consisting of known documents, and context documents
Known documents	12 common documents presented for assessment with different contexts
Context	The manner in which the documents other than the known documents in a batch are selected
NIST assessments	Relevance assessments rendered by NIST for TREC 6
Waterloo assessments	Relevance assessments rendered by the University of Waterloo at TREC 6
Rel	The relevance class of a document, as determined by some combination NIST and/or Waterloo assessments
CAL	Context in which documents are selected iteratively using relevance sampling [2]
SAL	Context in which documents are selected iteratively using uncertainty sampling [2]
SPL	Context in which documents are selected at random [2]

Table 1: Glossary of terms used throughout this work.

ments ("relevant," "iffy," and "not relevant") constructed by the University of Waterloo using interactive search and judging [1]. We augmented each set of assessments with an additional category "unjudged" for documents that were excluded from the pool. The net effect is that each document has one of 12 combinations of three NIST and four Waterloo assessment categories. We chose at random one document with each combination of assessments as the 12 known documents for each of 9 topics.

Our selection of topics was predicated on the fact that, of the 50 topics in the collection, only the nine we chose had at least one document labeled with each of the 12 combinations of assessment categories. Using each sampling method, as discussed below, we selected a list of 90 documents as detailed below, and inserted the known documents at fixed positions, chosen at random. Surplus documents (at positions beyond 100) were discarded.

For random sampling, the list of 100 documents was a uniform random sample of the 560,000-document TREC corpus, in random order. Following Cormack and Grossman [2], we label this protocol, simple passive learning ("SPL"). For uncertainty sampling and relevance sampling, we employed the simple active learning ("SAL") and continuous active learning ("CAL") methods [2, 3], training a classifier to retrieve 10 documents, adding those documents to the training set, and repeating the process nine times. `Sofia-ML` was used as the base classifier, configured to minimize logistic loss, and applied to a tf-idf representation of the documents. The initial training set consisted of a positively labeled pseudo-document consisting of the topic description, plus 100 negatively labeled documents selected at random without regard to their relevance. The training set was used to train the classifier, which was used to compute the likelihood of relevance for each document in the collection. For SAL, the 10 documents with likelihood closest to 0.5 were selected and added to the training set; for CAL, the 10 documents with greatest likelihood were selected. Training labels were derived from the Waterloo assessments: "relevant" and "iffy" were labeled positive; "non-relevant" and "unjudged" were labeled negative.

Our list of 90 context documents consisted of the documents retrieved by these nine iterations, in the order retrieved. Table 2 depicts the prevalence of positive (Waterloo "relevant" or "iffy") documents in the corpus, as well as the number in each batch, including known documents.

Topic	Corpus Prevalence (%)	Context Count		
		CAL	SAL	SPL
301	0.24	40	6	5
304	0.13	26	4	4
306	0.11	41	6	6
307	0.14	65	5	5
319	0.17	63	6	4
324	0.09	74	5	5
332	0.08	41	5	5
337	0.11	83	6	6
343	0.12	33	5	6

Table 2: Corpus prevalence and number of positive documents for each context, where Waterloo "relevant" and "iffy" assessments are considered positive. The counts for each batch include known documents.

2.2 Assessment Protocol

Following approval from the ethics review panel, we recruited 36 participants at large from University of Waterloo, including undergraduate students, graduate students, and faculty. At the outset, a participant was assigned one of the methods and topics at random, and was told that they would be remunerated \$20 for reviewing all 100 documents. If the participant took 2 hours or less to judge the documents and achieved at least 25% recall and 25% precision with respect to the NIST assessments for the 100 documents, they were paid a bonus of \$10 and offered the opportunity to assess up to two additional batches. For each subsequent batch, a new context and topic were selected at random, such that no participant saw the same context or the same topic more than once. Participants whose assessments did not meet the criteria were paid \$20 and not invited to continue. The criteria and bonus were used to encourage participants to perform to the best of their ability. The recall and precision cutoffs were chosen with the intention of ensuring quality but not forcing users to be NIST-quality. 19 participants assessed 3 batches, 7 participants completed 2 batches, and 10 participants completed 1 batch. In total, three batches representing each context and each topic were assessed. The the continuation criterion was intended to limit the impact of poor assessments, while the random context and topic assignment without repetition was intended to mitigate learning effects.

2.3 User Interface

Participants conducted their assessments using a full-screen HTML interface, that displayed panels containing:

- The topic title and description.
- The document, with topic title words highlighted.

- Progress information, including the number of documents reviewed, elapsed time for the current document, cumulative time per document, and target time per document.
- Single-click action buttons to render an assessment and proceed to the next document.

2.4 Evaluation

The outcome of general interest is the probability Pr[User$^+$] that an assessor will render a positive judgement. The primary predictor variable is the context within which the document is assessed. Accordingly, we wish to measure the conditional probability Pr[User$^+$|Context] in order to test the hypothesis that Pr[User$^+$|CAL] < Pr[User$^+$|SAL$\vee$SPL]. Assuming this hypothesis to be supported, we wish to test whether, individually, Pr[User$^+$|CAL] < Pr[User$^+$|SAL] and Pr[User$^+$|CAL] < Pr[User$^+$|SPL].

A second predictor variable is the relevance class *Rel* of the document, as determined by some combination of Waterloo and NIST assessments. To preserve the statistical power of our experiment, we restrict our consideration to the class W-RI, and its complement W-NU, where W-RI denotes any combination of assessments for which the Waterloo assessment is either "relevant" or "iffy." We assumed that the hypothesis Pr[User$^+$|W-RI] > Pr[User$^+$|W-NU] was extremely unlikely to be rejected, and concerned ourselves instead with the two hypotheses:

(1)Pr[User$^+$|CAL$\wedge$W-RI] < Pr[User$^+$|(SAL$\vee$SPL)$\wedge$W-RI]

(2)Pr[User$^+$|CAL$\wedge$W-NU] < Pr[User$^+$|(SAL$\vee$SPL)$\wedge$W-NU]

To estimate the conditional probabilities, we computed the fraction of positive assessments for documents satisfying the specified predictors. To evaluate the significance of hypothesized differences, we applied a paired binomial test, where possible, to corresponding batches. There are an equal number of batches for each context, and for each of the relevance classes W-RI and W-NU. Across these sets, batches may be matched by topic and by the specific combination of relevance assessments, leaving us to match within corresponding triples of batches, each reviewed by a different assessor. We matched the members of these triples by the assessor's experience: As far as possible, the first batch reviewed by one assessor was matched to the first batch reviewed by another assessor; the second batch reviewed by one assessor was matched to the second match reviewed by another assessor; and so on.

Predictor	Pr[User$^+$|Predictor]	p-value
Context: CAL	0.42 (0.36,0.48)	-
Context: SAL	0.54 (0.48,0.59)	0.0002
Context: SPL	0.54 (0.48,0.60)	0.0002
Rel: W-RI	0.63 (0.58,0.68)	< 0.0001
Rel: W-NU	0.39 (0.34,0.43)	

Table 3: Probability of a study participant making a positive assessment, with 95% confidence intervals, for the primary predictors. For context, p-values were computed using a two-tailed paired binomial test; for relevance, p-values were computed using a z-test for difference in proportions. the CAL context.

Predictor	Pr[User$^+$|Predictor]	p-value
CAL and W-RI	0.52 (0.43,0.61)	-
SAL and W-RI	0.67 (0.58,0.75)	0.0037
SPL and W-RI	0.70 (0.62,0.78)	0.0005
CAL and W-NU	0.33 (0.26,0.41)	-
SAL and W-NU	0.42 (0.34,0.50)	0.0288
SPL and W-NU	0.40 (0.32,0.48)	0.1214

Table 4: Probability of a study participant making a positive assessment, with 95% confidence intervals, for combined predictors. p-values were computed relative to CAL, using a two-tailed paired binomial test.

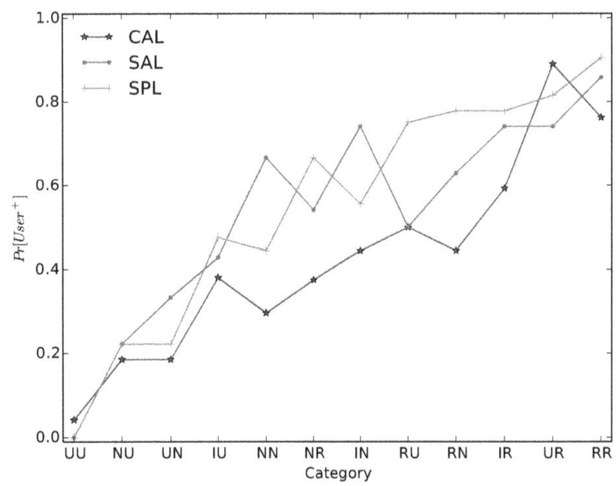

Figure 1: Probability of positive assessment given a context and elementary relevance class. Relevance classes are denoted xy where $x \in R, I, N, U$ denotes Waterloo relevant, iffy, non-relevant and unjudged, and $x \in R, N, U$ denotes NIST relevant, non-relevant, and unjudged.

3. RESULTS

Table 3 shows the results of our primary hypotheses, that context and relevance class separately influence the probability of a positive assessment. Separately, SAL and SPL both yield a substantially and significantly higher probability of positive assessment than CAL; W-RI yields a substantially and significantly higher probability of positive assessment than W-NU.

Table 4 shows the combined effect of context and relevance class. With respect to the W-NU relevance class, SAL and SPL separately yield a substantially and significantly higher probability of positive assessment than CAL. With respect to W-RI, the difference appears to be substantive, but only the difference between CAL and SAL appears to be significant, and even so would not be significant under Bonferroni correction for multiple hypothesis testing. The difference Pr[User$^+$|CAL$\wedge$W-RI] − Pr[User$^+$|(SAL$\vee$SPL)$\wedge$ $W - R$)] is significant ($p \ll 0.0288$), by the following argument: for the null hypothesis to be true, it would be necessary that Pr[User$^+$|CAL$\wedge$W-RI] $\geq$ Pr[User$^+$|SAL$\wedge$W-RI)] *and* Pr[User$^+$|CAL$\wedge$W-RI] $\geq$ Pr[User$^+$|SPL$\wedge$W-RI)]. The probability of both of these occurring by chance cannot exceed the probability of either one, which implies

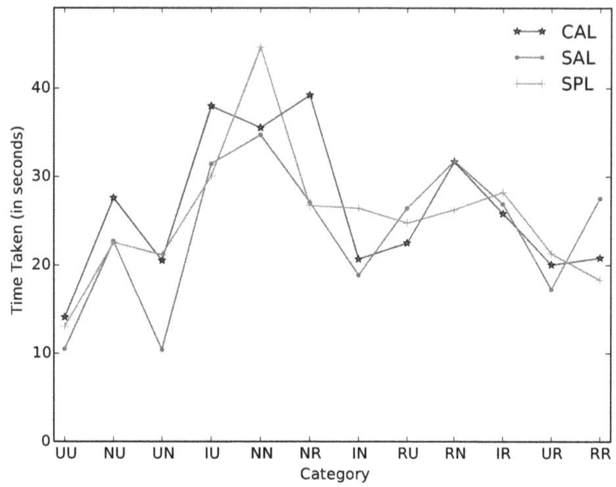

Figure 2: Average time for assessment given a context and elementary relevance class. Relevance classes are denoted xy where $x \in R, I, N, U$ denotes Waterloo relevant, iffy, non-relevant and unjudged, and $x \in R, N, U$ denotes NIST relevant, non-relevant, and unjudged

$p < \min(0.0288, 0.1214) = 0.0288$. For each combination of Waterloo and NIST assessments, Figure 1 plots the probability of a positive user assessment. Consistent with our statistical findings, the curves for SAL and SPL are generally superior to the curve for CAL. It appears that for cases where one of the Waterloo or NIST assessments is "relevant" and is not discordant with the other (*i.e.*, the other is "relevant" or "unjudged") there may be an insubstantial difference between CAL and the other contexts. Whether this observation reflects chance or an effect is a subject for future research.

4. ASSESSMENT TIME

We collected timing information in the course of implementing our participant retention criteria. Table 5 indicates that neither the context nor the relevance class has a substantial or significant effect on the time taken by participants to review documents. Figure 2, which plots assessment time taken against elementary relevance classes, suggests that non-relevant documents that were included in both the Waterloo and NIST judging pools may take longer to review. An interesting avenue of research would be to investigate whether this observation is a manifestation of the observation by Smucker and Jethani [12], who found that assessors took longer to make incorrect assessments. Namely, we are interested in answering the following question: Are the long prediction times observed for the NN relevance class the result of false positives?

5. CONCLUSIONS

Our results show clearly that assessors are less likely to judge documents relevant when they are presented within the context of documents selected using relevance sampling, than when they are presented within the context of documents selected using uncertainty sampling or random sampling. The effect holds for both relevant and non-relevant documents, as determined by archived assessments rendered by the University of Waterloo. Whether this effect applies to all relevant documents, or only to marginally relevant documents, remains an open question.

Our results call into question the practice of deeming the assessments of one individual to be authoritative [15], or of assuming that validation based on sampling is equivalent to validation using the pooling method.

Predictor	Time Taken Per Doc	p-value
Rel: W-RI	26.56 (23.86,29.27)	0.1775
Rel: W-NU	23.92 (21.19,26.64)	
Context: CAL	26.44 (22.69, 30.19)	-
Context: SAL	23.53 (20.58, 26.48)	0.1984
Context: SPL	25.46 (22.21, 28.72)	0.6781

Table 5: Average time, in seconds, taken to assess documents under each condition with 95% confidence intervals for both all documents and known documents only. For context, p-values are with respect to a paired two-tailed t-test against the CAL predictor. For relevance, p-values are from Welch's t-test.

6. REFERENCES

[1] G. V. Cormack, C. L. A. Clarke, C. R. Palmer, and S. S. L. To. Passage-Based Refinement (MultiText Experiments for TREC-6). In *Proc. TREC-6*, 1997.

[2] G. V. Cormack and M. R. Grossman. Evaluation of Machine-learning Protocols for Technology-assisted Review in Electronic Discovery. In *Proc. SIGIR 2014*, 2014.

[3] G. V. Cormack and M. R. Grossman. Autonomy and reliability of continuous active learning for technology-assisted review. *arXiv Preprint*, 2015.

[4] G. V. Cormack, C. R. Palmer, and C. L. A. Clarke. Efficient construction of large test collections. In *Proc. SIGIR 1998*, 1998.

[5] M. Eisenberg and C. Barry. Order effects: A study of the possible influence of presentation order on user judgments of document relevance. *J. Amer. Soc. Info. Sci.*, 1988.

[6] M.-h. Huang and H.-y. Wang. The influence of document presentation order and number of documents judged on users' judgments of relevance. *J. Amer. Soc. Info. Sci.*, 55(11), 2004.

[7] D. D. Lewis. A sequential algorithm for training text classifiers: Corrigendum and additional data. *SIGIR Forum*, 29(2), Sept. 1995.

[8] D. D. Lewis and W. A. Gale. A sequential algorithm for training text classifiers. In *Proc. SIGIR 1994*, 1994.

[9] A. Roegiest, G. V. Cormack, C. L. A. Clarke, and M. R. Grossman. Impact of surrogate assessments on high-recall retrieval. In *Proc. SIGIR 2015*, 2015.

[10] F. Scholer, D. Kelly, W.-C. Wu, H. S. Lee, and W. Webber. The effect of threshold priming and need for cognition on relevance calibration and assessment. In *Proc. SIGIR 2013*, 2013.

[11] M. D. Smucker and C. P. Jethani. Human performance and retrieval precision revisited. In *Proc. SIGIR 2010*, 2010.

[12] M. D. Smucker and C. P. Jethani. Time to judge relevance as an indicator of assessor error. In *Proc. SIGIR 2012*, 2012.

[13] E. M. Voorhees. The philosophy of information retrieval evaluation. In *Proc. CLEF 2001*.

[14] E. M. Voorhees. Variations in relevance judgments and the measurement of retrieval effectiveness. *J. Info. Proc. & Man.*, 36(5), 2000.

[15] W. Webber, D. W. Oard, F. Scholer, and B. Hedin. Assessor error in stratified evaluation. In *Proc. CIKM 2010*.

Improving Automated Controversy Detection on the Web

Myungha Jang and James Allan
Center for Intelligent Information Retrieval
College of Information and Computer Sciences
University of Massachusetts Amherst
{mhjang, allan}@cs.umass.edu

ABSTRACT

Automatically detecting controversy on the Web is a useful capability for a search engine to help users review web content with a more balanced and critical view. The current state-of-the art approach is to find K-Nearest- Neighbors in Wikipedia to the document query, and to aggregate their controversy scores that are automatically computed from the Wikipedia edit-history features. In this paper, we discover two major weakness in the prior work and propose modifications. First, the generated single query from document to find KNN Wikipages easily becomes ambiguous. Thus, we propose to generate multiple queries from smaller but more topically coherent paragraph of the document. Second, the automatically computed controversy scores of Wikipedia articles that depend on "edit war" features have a drawback that without an edit history, there can be no edit wars. To infer more reliable controversy scores for articles with little edit history, we smooth the original score from the scores of the neighbors with more established edit history. We show that the modified framework is improved by up to 5% for binary controversy classification in a publicly available dataset.

1. INTRODUCTION

The Web is an excellent source for obtaining accurate and useful information for a huge number of topics, but it is also an excellent source for obtaining misguided, untrustworthy and biased information. To help users review webpage contents with a more balanced and critical view, alerting users that the topic of a webpage is controversial will be a useful feature for a search engine.

Dori-Hacohen and Allan [4] proposed a framework for making binary classification on general webpage, whether the webpage presents a perspective on a controversial topic or not. Their framework consists of four steps:

1. **Matching k-NN Wikipages:** When a webpage is given as an input, they find k nearest-neighbor Wikipages by generating a query from the 10 most frequent terms in the document.
2. **Computing Controversy Score on Wikipages:** From each of the k Wikipage, they automatically extracted three controversy scores: C score [2], M score [10], and D score [4].
3. **Aggregate:** They aggregated the three types of k scores using average or max operators.
4. **Vote and Classify:** They apply a voting scheme to turn the aggregated scores into a final binary decision, controversial or non-controversial.

While examining the performance of the current framework, we identified two major weaknesses. First, generating a single query from a document in Step 1 has issues. As documents almost always contain multiple sub-topics, the generated query contains an unknown mixture of different sub-topics. This makes the query's intent less clear, as it targets many sub-topics at the same time and in unknown balance. It is also unlikely that all sub-topics are covered in the query – or covered appropriately – because keywords are extracted from a bag-of-words, which does not model the existence of sub-topics as it is. As an alternative, we propose a text-segmentation based query generation approach named TILEQUERY. We first segment the document into multiple tiles, where each tile contains fewer sub-topics than the document, ideally one sub-topic per tile. We generate a query from each tile and then aggregate the ranked lists obtained from the tiles' queries. This can be viewed as a "divide-and-conquer" approach for document query generation.

Another issue is that the Wikipedia controversy scores depend on "edit-war" features, evidence of multiple editors exchanging opposing opinions. However, the controversy level is naturally underestimated on specific and sub-topical Wikipages whose topical disputes have often been delegated to other Wikipages of the broader topic. In other words, not having the "edit-war" does not necessarily mean that there was no war in this topic, but that the war has been happening somewhere else instead. This phenomenon causes the algorithm to easily make false negative errors (i.e., classifying "controversial" as "non-controversial").

We next provide details of the modified query generation approach and how we address the problem of missing or underestimated controversy scores using smoothing from neighbors. We then carry out an evaluation using 303 non-Wikipages as starting points and show the impact of our modifications to the framework on classification accuracy. We show that gains come from both changes but that correcting controversy scores has a greater impact, yielding 5% improvements in classification accuracy over the state-of-the art performance.

SIGIR '16, July 17 - 21, 2016, Pisa, Italy

ISBN 978-1-4503-4069-4/16/07...$15.00
DOI: http://dx.doi.org/10.1145/2911451.2914764

2. RELATED WORK

To the best of our knowledge, Dori-Hacohen and Allan were the first team to extend controversy detection to general open-domain web-pages [4]. However, many efforts have been made to understand and estimate controversy in Wikipedia. As Wikipedia contains manually tagged controversial articles by editors, machine-learning based methods approaches were trained to learn them. To estimate the level of controversy in Wikipages, information extracted from the edit-history, such as revision count, number of unique editors, number of reverts, the number of editors participating in the edit-war, and their reputations have been exploited [6, 10]. Sepehri Rad and Barbosa surveyed five established controversy detection algorithms on Wikipedia and compared their performances [8].

Outside of Wikipedia, controversy detection has also been studied within Twitter [7] or news corpus [1], focusing on political domain. Wang and Cardie recently studied online dispute detection using sentiment-analysis based method trained from controversial corpus in Wikiepdia [9]. However, as in Wikipedia, this method requires evidence of explicit disputes between two people, which is not applicable to general web-pages.

3. MODIFIED FRAMEWORK

Here we provide details of the two modifications that we propose to the existing framework.

3.1 TileQuery Generation

Document Segmentation We first use the block comparison algorithm described by the TextTiling technique [5]. The block comparison method defines as block with a few sentences, and computes a lexical similarity score for every gap between two blocks. When the similarity score dramatically changes at a gap, we assume that is where a sub-topic shift occurs and create a tile of blocks.

Query Generation Once we create tiles from a document using TextTiling, we generate a query from each tile. There are often some tiles that are hard to understand its meaning without the context of the full text. Therefore, adding the global context helps clarify the topic of each tile, anchoring the tile's query to the containing document's topic. We hence generate a query by using the g (global) most frequent terms from the document,and the l (local) most frequent terms from the tile. We empirically found that $g = 3, l = 7$ gives the best performance when using 10 terms.

Aggregating the Ranked Lists Each TILEQUERY returns a ranked list. We compute the relevance score for each retrieved Wikipage w_i by aggregating the reversed ranking order:

$$Relevance(w_i) = \sum_{t_i \in T} (k - rank_{t_i}(w_i)) \qquad (1)$$

where T is the set of tiles generated from the document. This scoring prioritizes Wikipages that appear high in some tile or at reasonable ranks in many tiles, or preferably both.

3.2 Smoothing Controversy Score of Wikipages

Wikipedia Controversy Scores Previous work studied algorithms for automatically computing scores that estimate the level of controversy. They use features available in Wikipages, meta-data, talk pages, and edit-history. We briefly explain the three scores that the previous framework adopted.

C Score This is a regression-based method that estimates the revision count of Wikipages with {controversial} tags. The features include information from the edit-history, such as number of unique editors and number of reverts, as well as some metadata of Wikipages [6].

M Score Yasseri et al. investigated edit-wars based on statistical features of edits [10]. This score is theoretically unbounded ranging from 0 to a few billions.

D Score This is a Boolean value indicating whether a Wikipage contains a dispute tag in it, which is assigned by the page's contributors This dataset is extremely sparse, covering only 0.03% of the articles [4].

Unfortunately, these approaches are limited for the same reason that many Wikipages with controversial topics do not have sufficient edit-history or explicit edit-wars. There is a tendency that the heat of the edit-wars are focused on one Wikipage of a general and broad topic, leaving other related but sub-topical pages less attended. After all, there is simply no point of having the same "war" on all similar Wikipages. Table 1 shows an example of a few "abortion" related topics and their M and C Score. While the "Abortion" page received a lot of attention, other pages with more specific topics such as *Abortion in certain countries* and *Abortion Act* had virtually no edit-wars. Unless there is a specific issue or event specifically tied to the page, all general disputes on abortion have been delegated to the "Abortion" page.

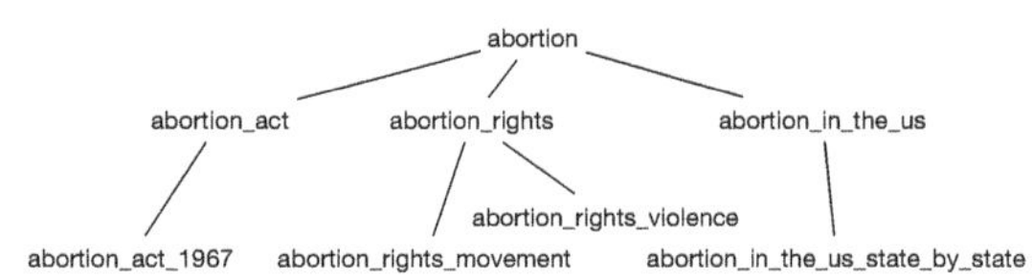

Figure 1: An example of the constructed network for *Abortion*

Due to this phenomenon, even if we generate a better query to find more relevant k pages, the framework still would not be able to fully take advantage of that due to the underestimated scores. Hence, it is necessary to revise these scores to reflect controversy better. If the purpose of the M or C score was to measure the controversy level presented in the Wikipage *per se*, we need newly revised scores that accurately signify controversiality of the topic in general. To do this, we will construct a network that links topically related neighbors within the Wikipedia. We then revise the controversy score by "smoothing" using the scores of neighbors with more edit history, whose scores were computed with more confidence.

Constructing Wikipages' Graph We construct a tree-structured graph to identify topically related neighbors of a Wikipage. Let $G = (V, E)$ be a directed graph with nodes V (Wikipages) and edges E (sub-topical relations). An edge $e(u, v)$ represents that node v is a sub-topic of u.

As a simple and straightforward method to construct the edges, we look at their titles. If a Wikipage u's title is used as a prefix of other v's title, we assume that v is sub-topic of u. While we use nodes' titles to construct edges, we assume there is a mapping between a title and a node and will use them interchangeably.

Let a Wikititle T be a ordered list $[t_1, t_2, ..., t_n]$, where t_i is an i-th space-delimited token. The parent node set

P(T) (i.e., Wikipages whose titles that have T as a child) is obtained by:

$$P(T) = \{P_T^i | P_T^i \in W_T, i \in \{1..n\}\}, P_T^i = concatenate[t_1, ..., t_i]$$

where W_T is a set of all Wikipedia titles. The graph also contains many noisy relations when the prefix is an ambiguous entity, or a simply too general word, such as "American". To filter out the noisy relations, we remove the edges if two pages are not linked in any direction. Using this graph, we finally revise the controversy score using smoothing.

Network-based Smoothing When Wikipage is given as a query, we extract a sub-graph around the node from the constructed graph using one of the two methods:

Pair-based: A sub-graph around the query node including its children at all depth and its parents. The resultant graph only consists of nodes that have a direct prefix-contain relation with the query node.

Clique-based: Pair-based sub-graph + sibling nodes that share the same parents with the query node. Although siblings may not be topically related to the query node especially if the parent (i.e., prefix) is a general term, this allows broader coverage of potentially related pages.

Once we obtain the sub-graph, we treat all nodes in the sub-graph as topically related neighbors of the query node. We want to fix the query node's controversy score by smoothing from neighbors that have more reliable scores. For that we assume that the controversy score of a Wikipage with more revision history is more reliable. Hence we convert this graph into a weighted, directed network whose direction represents which way influence should extend to (i.e., the one with higher revision count to the other with lower count), and whose edge weight represents the confidence of the influence relation, which is the revision count of the source (Figure 2). From the graph, the new controversy score of Wikipage W_i is computed as:

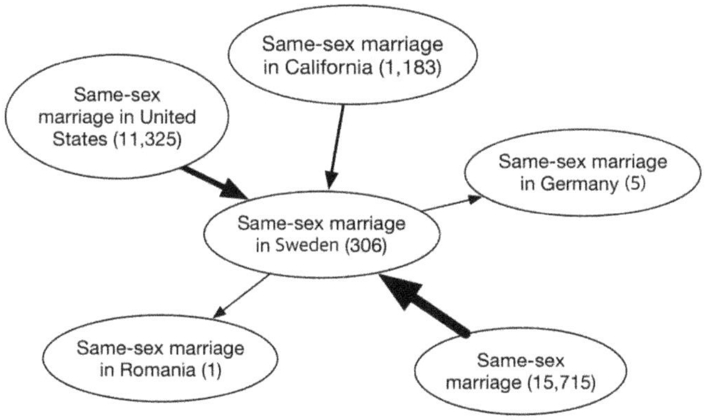

Figure 2: A network constructed around the query "Same-sex marriage in Sweden". The scores are borrowed from three neighbors that have more revision counts than the query page by weighted smoothing.

$$C'(W_i) = \sum_{W_j \in inLinks(W_i)} \frac{C(W_j) * r_j}{\sum r_k} \quad (2)$$

where r_i is a revision count of W_i.

Table 1: An example of two controversy scores on several Wikipages on "Abortion", before and after score smoothing

	Original scores		Revised scores	
	M	C	M	C
Abortion	4,102,593	0.300	4,102,593	0.300
Abortion_Act	0	0	0	0
Abortion_in_China	0	0	2,062,156	0.166
Abortion_in_England	0	0	2,128,909	0.172
Abortion_in_the_US	0	0.002	2,983,300	0.218

3.3 Aggregation and Voting

We summarize the aggregation and voting schemes introduced by previous work. Once the controversy scores are obtained for k Wikipages, we aggregate the k scores by taking average or max of them. Since we use three different scores, M, C, and D, three aggregated scores, M_{agg}, C_{agg}, and D_{agg} are computed. We turn these scores into binary label indicating controversial (1) or non-controversial (0), using corresponding thresholds. $M_{label} = 1$ if $M_{agg} \geq Threshold_M$, and 0 otherwise. Using the three generated labels, we use a voting scheme to make a final decision. We test 6 voting schemes as parameters in our experiments.

The webpage is controversial if:

— **C/M/D**: $\{C_{label}, M_{label}, D_{label}\}$ is 1, respectively.

— **Majority**: the majority (i.e., at least two) of $\{C_{label}, M_{label}, D_{label}\}$ is 1.

— **Or/And**: $C_{label}\{\vee/\wedge\}M_{label}\ \{\vee/\wedge\}D_{label}$ is 1.

4. EXPERIMENTS

4.1 Dataset

We use the publicly available controversy dataset released by Dori-Hacohen et al. [3]. We used 303 clueweb documents whose controversy level was annotated with four scales: 1 - "clearly controversial", 2 - "possibly controversial", 3 - "possibly non-controversial", and 4 - "clearly non-controversial". To convert the annotations to binary judgments, we treated the documents with average ratings among annotators of less than 2.5 as controversial, and otherwise non-controversial. Of 303 documents, 42% of them are controversial.

To test the effectiveness of the proposed query method, we consider two other query baselines. One is TF10, the 10 most frequent terms, as in the prior work. As taking only k terms as in a query might miss information, we consider another baseline, ALL query that uses all terms in a document as a query to observe the extreme case of TFN.

We consider 9 settings from all possible combinations of three query methods and three scoring schemes (Table 2). Run 4 is the setting proposed in the prior work [4]. In each setting, we varied the four sets of parameters, the number of neighbors K (1, 5, 10, 15, 20), aggregation method (avg, max), voting methods (C, M, D, Majority, Or, And, D∨(C ∧ M)), and thresholds for C and M as tested in [4]. We found the best parameter setting for each run using 5-fold cross validation with the target metric accuracy. Thus, for 9 settings, there are 5 sets of parameters learned for each fold. We used McNemar's Test[1] for statistical significance test.

[1]https://en.wikipedia.org/wiki/McNemar%27s_test

Table 2: Accuracy, F1, and the best parameters in 5-fold runs for different query and inferred score settings.

Run	Query	Inferred Score	K	C Threshold	M Threshold	Aggregation	Acc.	F1
1		N/A	{5, 20}	$\{0.17, 4.18 \cdot 10^{-2}\}$	{40000,20000}	{M, Maj.}	0.72	0.50
2	ALL	Clique	15	$\{0.17, 4.18 \cdot 10^{-2}\}$	{40000,20000}	{M, Maj.}	0.78	0.68
3		Pair	{5, 20}	$\{0.17, 4.18 \cdot 10^{-2}\}$	{40000,20000}	{M, Maj.}	0.73	0.53
4		N/A	20	$4.18 \cdot 10^{-2}$	{20000, 40000, 84930}	{M, Maj.}	0.75	0.57
5	TF10	Clique	20	$4.18 \cdot 10^{-2}$	84930	Maj.	0.79	0.68
6		Pair	{10, 20}	$4.18 \cdot 10^{-2}$	{20000, 84930}	Maj.	0.75	0.57
7		N/A	{10,15,20}	$4.18 \cdot 10^{-2}$	{40000,20000}	{M, Maj.}	0.75	0.59
8	TILE	Clique	20	0.17	40000	M	0.80	0.71
9		Pair	{10,15,20}	$4.18 \cdot 10^{-2}$	{40000,20000}	{M, Maj.}	0.75	0.61

Table 3: Improvements of accuracy and F1 Score between runs (bold: statistically significant)

Row #	Runs	$\lvert Acc_1\text{-}Acc_2 \rvert$	$\lvert F1_1\text{-}F1_2 \rvert$	p value
1	1 vs 2	**6%**	**2%**	$0.01 \cdot 10^{-2}$
2	1 vs 4	3%	7%	0.61
3	1 vs 7	**3%**	**9%**	0.08
4	4 vs 5	**4%**	**11%**	$0.17 \cdot 10^{-2}$
5	4 vs 7	0%	2%	0.18
6	5 vs 8	**1%**	**3%**	$0.06 \cdot 10^{-2}$
7	6 vs 9	**0%**	**4%**	$0.01 \cdot 10^{-2}$
8	7 vs 8	**5%**	**12%**	$0.01 \cdot 10^{-2}$

4.2 Results

Impact of Query Methods Our statistical significant tests suggest that the difference of accuracies between the three query methods in runs 1, 4, and 7 are not significant (Row 2 & 5 in Table 3), which suggest that the three methods mostly made similar classifications.

However, once we apply neighbor-based smoothing on controversy scores, query methods cause classification to work differently. The accuracy gain of TileQuery over TF10 was 1%, and 4% of F1-score with smoothing. Although the accuracy gain was small, the query set that each method performed well was different as the significance test implies (Row 6 & 7 in Table 3).

Impact of Neighbor-based Smoothing In all settings, using controversy score smoothing significantly improved the classification accuracy and F1-score. As row 1, 4, and 8 in Table 3 show, the accuracy was improved by 4-6% and the F1-score was improved by 2-12% in all three query methods. Clique-based neighbor selection consistently outperformed pair-based selection.

5. CONCLUSION AND FUTURE WORK

We revisited the prior work for automatically detecting controversy from the general open-domain webpages. We identified two major weakness in the framework and proposed two modifications to fix the issues. The controversy score smoothing consistently improved the controversy classification accuracies by 4-6% compared to those without smoothing. Overall, the run with our two modifications of TILEQUERY and controversy score smoothing gave the best accuracy improving the previous framework by 5%. In the future, we plan to further investigate different scenarios when TF10 and TileQuery works well. As we were only able to find topically related neighbors for 5% of the Wikipages with prefix-relation, we will explore more sophisticated methods to increase this coverage.

Acknowledgement

This work was supported in part by the Center for Intelligent Information Retrieval, in part by NSF grant #IIS-0910884, and in part by NSF grant #IIS-1217281. Any opinions, findings and conclusions or recommendations expressed in this material are those of the authors and do not necessarily reflect those of the sponsor. The authors thank Shiri Dori-Hacohen for providing valuable resources.

6. REFERENCES

[1] Y. Choi, Y. Jung, and S.-H. Myaeng. Identifying controversial issues and their sub-topics in news articles. In *PAISI*, volume 6122 of *Lecture Notes in Computer Science*, pages 140–153. Springer, 2010.

[2] S. Das, A. Lavoie, and M. Magdon-Ismail. Manipulation among the arbiters of collective intelligence: how wikipedia administrators mold public opinion. CIKM '13, pages 1097–1106, New York, NY, USA, 2013. ACM.

[3] S. Dori-Hacohen and J. Allan. Detecting controversy on the web. In *CIKM*, pages 1845–1848. ACM, 2013.

[4] S. Dori-Hacohen and J. Allan. Automated controversy detection on the web. ECIR '15, pages 423–434, 2015.

[5] M. A. Hearst. Texttiling: Segmenting text into multi-paragraph subtopic passages. *Comput. Linguist.*, 23(1):33–64, Mar. 1997.

[6] A. Kittur, B. Suh, B. A. Pendleton, and E. H. Chi. He says, she says: Conflict and coordination in wikipedia. CHI '07, pages 453–462, New York, NY, USA, 2007. ACM.

[7] A.-M. Popescu and M. Pennacchiotti. Detecting controversial events from twitter. CIKM '10, pages 1873–1876. ACM, 2010.

[8] H. S. Rad and D. Barbosa. Identifying controversial articles in wikipedia: A comparative study. WikiSym '12, pages 7:1–7:10. ACM, 2012.

[9] L. Wang and C. Cardie. A piece of my mind: A sentiment analysis approach for online dispute detection. ACL '14, pages 693–699, 2014.

[10] T. Yasseri, R. Sumi, A. Rung, A. Kornai, and J. Kertész. Dynamics of conflicts in wikipedia. *PLoS One*, 7(6):e38869, June 2012.

Improving Language Estimation with the Paragraph Vector Model for Ad-hoc Retrieval

Qingyao Ai[1], Liu Yang[1], Jiafeng Guo[2], W. Bruce Croft[1]
[1]College of Information and Computer Sciences,
University of Massachusetts Amherst, Amherst, MA, USA
{aiqy, lyang, croft}@cs.umass.edu
[2]CAS Key Lab of Network Data Science and Technology, Institute of Computing Technology,
Chinese Academy of Sciences, China
guojiafeng@ict.ac.cn

ABSTRACT

Incorporating topic level estimation into language models has been shown to be beneficial for information retrieval (IR) models such as cluster-based retrieval and LDA-based document representation. Neural embedding models, such as paragraph vector (PV) models, on the other hand have shown their effectiveness and efficiency in learning semantic representations of documents and words in multiple Natural Language Processing (NLP) tasks. However, their effectiveness in information retrieval is mostly unknown. In this paper, we study how to effectively use the PV model to improve ad-hoc retrieval. We propose three major improvements over the original PV model to adapt it for the IR scenario: (1) we use a document frequency-based rather than the corpus frequency-based negative sampling strategy so that the importance of frequent words will not be suppressed excessively; (2) we introduce regularization over the document representation to prevent the model overfitting short documents along with the learning iterations; and (3) we employ a joint learning objective which considers both the document-word and word-context associations to produce better word probability estimation. By incorporating this enhanced PV model into the language modeling framework, we show that it can significantly outperform the state-of-the-art topic enhanced language models.

Keywords

Retrieval Model; Language Model; Paragraph Vector

1. INTRODUCTION

Language models have been successfully applied to IR tasks[8, 14]. The core of this approach is to estimate a language model for each document and rank documents according to the likelihood of observing a query given the estimated model. The simple language model approach represents documents and queries under the bag-of-words assumption. This approach fails when query words are not observed in a document. A typical solution to this issue is to apply smoothing techniques by incorporating a corpus language model for "unseen" words, such as the Jelinek-Mercer method, absolute discounting, and Bayesian smoothing using Dirichlet priors [14]. However, smoothing every document with the *same* corpus language model is intuitively not optimal since we essentially assume that all the unseen words in different documents would have similar probabilities [13].

One way to improve the smoothing techniques is to introduce document dependent smoothing that can reflect the content of the document, for example by representing documents and queries in a latent topic space and estimating the generation probability accordingly. By incorporating topic level estimation into language model approaches, previous work such as the cluster-based retrieval model [6] and the LDA-based retrieval model [12] obtained consistent improvements over the basic language models. Nonetheless, the existing topic model based approaches have several drawbacks. Firstly, the model estimation relies on the predefined number of topics. Secondly, the topic models typically assign high probabilities to frequent words. Finally, the learning cost (of the LDA model) is expensive on a large corpus.

Recent advances in Natural Language Processing (NLP) have shown that semantically meaningful representations of words and documents can be efficiently acquired by neural embedding models. In particular, a paragraph vector (PV) model [4] has been proposed to jointly learn word and document embeddings by directly optimizing the generative probabilities of each word given the document. In contrast to existing topic models, PV can automatically cluster topic related words and documents without explicitly defining the number of topics a priori. The negative sampling based optimization strategy makes PV assign high probabilities to discriminative words rather than frequent words. Moreover, the online learning algorithm enables PV to learn over a large-scale corpus efficiently. Existing work has shown that PV can outperform the LDA model on several linguistic tasks [1], but its effectiveness for IR remains mostly unknown.

In this paper, we study how to effectively use the PV model in the language model framework to improve ad-hoc retrieval. Specifically, we use the Distributed Bag of Words version of PV (PV-DBOW) because it naturally constructs a

SIGIR '16, July 17-21, 2016, Pisa, Italy

DOI: http://dx.doi.org/10.1145/2911451.2914688

document language model that fits the framework of the language modeling approach. However, the original PV-DBOW model is not designed for IR, and we find there are three inherent problems make the original PV-DBOW less effective for ad-hoc retrieval. Firstly, the learning objective of PV-DBOW makes it suppress the importance of frequent words excessively. Secondly, PV-DBOW is prone to over-fit short documents during the training iterations. Finally, PV-DBOW does not model word-context associations, making it difficult to capture word substitution relationships that are important in IR. To address these problems, we proposed three modifications to enhance PV-DBOW model for ad-hoc retrieval, including document-frequency based negative sampling, document regularization and a joint learning objective. Empirical results show that consistent and significant improvements over baselines can be obtained with our enhanced PV model.

2. RELATED WORK

Previous work has shown that generative topic models are beneficial for language model estimation. For example, Liu and Croft [6] showed that document clustering can significantly improve retrieval effectiveness when incorporated in language smoothing. The cluster model, also known as the mixture of unigrams model, groups documents into a finite set of clusters (topics) and associates each cluster with a multinomial distribution over the vocabulary. Later, Wei and Croft [12] proposed an LDA-based retrieval model by combining language estimation based on LDA with query likelihood model. Their results showed that the LDA-based retrieval model can consistently outperform the clustering based model.

Recently, there have been several studies exploring the application of word embeddings in the IR scenario. For example, Vulić and Moens [11] construct dense representations for queries and documents by aggregating word vectors and rank results based on the fusion of cosine similarities and query likelihood scores. Ganguly et al. [2] proposed a generalized language model based on word embeddings by considering three term transformation processes. In contract to these studies that construct retrieval models based on bag of word embeddings, our work mainly focuses on how to effectively use the paragraph vector model to improve estimation in the language model approach.

3. ENHANCED PARAGRAPH VECTOR

In this section, we describe the details of how we enhance the PV model for language estimation in ad-hoc retrieval.

3.1 PV-DBOW

PV-DBOW maps words and documents into low-dimension dense vectors. Each document vector is trained to predict the words it contains. Under the bag-of-words assumption, the generative probability of word w in document d is obtained through a softmax function over the vocabulary:

$$P_{PV}(w|d) = \frac{exp(\vec{w} \cdot \vec{d})}{\sum_{w' \in V_w} exp(\vec{w'} \cdot \vec{d})} \quad (1)$$

where $\vec{w}$ and $\vec{d}$ are vector representations for w and d; and V_w is the vocabulary of the training collections.

In training, negative sampling is used to approximate the softmax function in Equation (1). Formally, the local objective function for each (w, d) pair in PV-DBOW with negative sampling is

$$\ell = \log(\sigma(\vec{w} \cdot \vec{d})) + k \cdot E_{w_N \sim P_n}[\log \sigma(-\vec{w_N} \cdot \vec{d})] \quad (2)$$

where $\sigma(x) = 1/(1 + exp(-x))$, k denotes the number of negative samples, w_N denotes the sampled word, and $P_n(w)$ denotes the distribution of negative samples. In [7], $P_n(w)$ is defined as the unigram distribution raised to the power 0.75:

$$P_n(w) = \frac{\#(w)^{0.75}}{|C|} \quad (3)$$

where $\#(w)$ denotes the corpus frequency of w and $|C| = \sum_{w' \in V_w} \#(w')^{0.75}$.

3.2 PV-DBOW based Retrieval Model

From the learning objective of PV-DBOW, we can see that it can be naturally applied in the probabilistic language model framework for IR. With the learned word and document embeddings, we can directly estimate the generative probability of each word given the document in a latent semantic space. Therefore, we can incorporate the language estimation of PV-DBOW into the query likelihood model as a document dependent smoothing technique:

$$P(w|d) = (1 - \lambda)P_{QL}(w|d) + \lambda P_{PV}(w|d) \quad (4)$$

where $P_{QL}(w|d)$ and $P_{PV}(w|d)$ represent the word probability estimated with QL and PV-DBOW respectively. λ is the parameter that controls the weights of QL and PV-DBOW.

3.3 Adaptation for IR

Now we describe in detail the major problems of the original PV-DBOW model that makes it less effective for IR, as well as the techniques we employ to solve these issues.

Document Frequency Based Negative Sampling. Following the idea in [5], we can see that PV-DBOW with negative sampling is implicitly factorizing a shifted matrix of point-wise mutual information between words and documents:

$$\vec{w} \cdot \vec{d} = \log(\frac{\#(w,d)}{\#(d)} \cdot \frac{|C|}{\#(w)}) - \log(k) \quad (5)$$

where $\#(w, d)$ is the term frequency of w in d; $\#(d)$ is the length of d and k is the number of negative instances. From Equation (5), we can see that the original PV-DBOW model implicitly weights words according to inverse corpus frequencies (ICF). However, previous studies have shown that term weighting with ICF may over-penalize frequent words, and often performs worse than term weighting with inverse document frequency (IDF) [9]. Inspired by this, we propose a novel document-frequency based negative sampling strategy for PV-DBOW to better fit the IR scenario. More formally, we replace $P_n(w)$ with a new sample distribution:

$$P_n(w) = \frac{\#D(w)}{\sum_{w' \in V_w} \#D(w')} \quad (6)$$

where $\#D(w)$ represents the document frequency of w. We can find that the new learning objective of PV-DBOW with document-frequency based negative sampling is equal to the following factorization:

$$\vec{w} \cdot \vec{d} = \log(\frac{\#(w,d)}{\#(d)} \cdot \frac{\sum_{w' \in V_w} \#D(w')}{\#D(w)}) - \log(k) \quad (7)$$

Since k and $\sum_{w' \in V_w} \#D(w')$ are constants, the training process of PV-DBOW with document-frequency based negative sampling is actually factorizing a shifted tf-idf matrix.

In practice, the exact value of the inverse document frequency is too aggressive for tf-idf weighting and its logarithmic version is more widely used. To achieve similar effects, we adapt a power version of document frequency that uses $\#D(w)^\eta$ ($\eta \leq 1$) instead of $\#D(w)$.

Document Regularization. The original PV-DBOW does not handle the varied lengths of documents, making it prone to over-fit short documents during the training iterations. Specifically, through the training process of PV-DBOW, vector norms of long documents remain roughly the same while vector norms of short documents keep growing. Increasing vector norms affect the dot product value in Equation (1) and make the language estimation concentrate on the observed words. This in turn significantly decreases the smoothing power of the PV-DBOW model on short documents. To solve this problem, we propose to introduce document regularization into the learning objective to avoid the ever-growing norm of short documents. Specifically, we add an L2 constraint on the document norm to the learning objective of PV-DBOW:

$$\ell = \log(\sigma(\vec{w} \cdot \vec{d})) + k \cdot E_{w_N \sim P_n}[\log \sigma(-\vec{w_N} \cdot \vec{d})] - \frac{\gamma}{\#(d)} ||\vec{d}||^2 \quad (8)$$

where $\#(d)$ is the number of words in d, $||\vec{d}||$ is the norm of vector $\vec{d}$ and γ is a hyper-parameter that control the strength of regularization. Each iteration of the stochastic gradient descent in PV-DBOW goes through each word exactly once, so we use the document length $1/\#(d)$ to ensure equal regularizations over long and short documents.

Joint Objective. The original PV-DBOW model learns over the word-document co-occurrence information as shown in Equation (2), making it focus on capturing syntagmatic relations between words (i.e., words that frequently co-occur in same documents). It lacks the modeling of paradigmatic relations between words (e.g. "car" and "vehicle") since no word-context information is leveraged in its learning process. As suggested by [1, 10], by modeling both word-document and word-context information, one can usually obtain better word and document vectors for NLP tasks. Following the same idea as [10], we introduce a joint learning objective to the PV-DBOW model. Specifically, we apply a two-layer structure that first uses the document to predict the target word and then uses the target word to predict its context. The new objective function is as follows:

$$\begin{aligned} \ell = & \log(\sigma(\vec{w_i} \cdot \vec{d})) + k \cdot E_{w_N \sim P_n}[\log \sigma(-\vec{w_N} \cdot \vec{d})] \\ & + \sum_{\substack{j=i-L \\ j \neq i}}^{i+L} \log(\sigma(\vec{w_i} \cdot \vec{c_j})) + k \cdot E_{c_N \sim P_n}[\log \sigma(-\vec{w_i} \cdot \vec{c_N})] \quad (9) \end{aligned}$$

where $\vec{c_j}$ is the context vector for word w_j, c_N denotes the sampled context and L represents the context window size.

4. EXPERIMENTS

Experimental Setup. We evaluate three baselines: query likelihood model (QL), LDA-based retrieval model (LDA-LM) and original PV-DBOW model (PV-LM). We add document frequency based negative sampling (D), document regularization (R), and joint objective (J) to PV-DBOW one by one, and refer to the enhanced PV based retrieval model as EPV-D-LM, EPV-DR-LM, and EPV-DRJ-LM respectively. We use two TREC collections, Robust04 and GOV2. We report the results of different versions of enhanced PV based retrieval models on Robust04, but only the full model (EPV-DRJ-LM) on GOV2 due to the space limitation. We use the Galago search engine[1] to index the corpus and report results for both the title and description of each TREC topic (stop words removed). Queries and documents are stemmed with the Krovetz stemmer. For test efficiency, we adopt a re-ranking strategy. An initial retrieval is performed with QL to obtain 2,000 candidate documents, and then a re-ranking is performed with both LDA-LM and EPV based retrieval models. The final evaluation is based on the top 1,000 results. We use a 5-fold cross validation in the same way as [3]: 4 folds are used to tune λ in smoothing process and 1 fold is used to test retrieval performance. We includes three evaluation metrics: mean average precision (MAP), normalized discounted cumulative gain at 20 (nDCG@20) and precision at 20 (P@20).

Parameter Settings. We train both LDA and EPV on the whole Robust04 collection. However, for the GOV2 collection, due to the prohibitive training time, we train both LDA and EPV on a randomly sampled subset with 500k documents for fair comparison. The topic number (K) in LDA and the vector dimension in PV-DBOW/EPV are empirically set as 300. For LDA, we set the hyper-parameters α and β to $50/K$ and 0.01 as described in [12]. For EPV, we tuned γ from 1 to 100 (1, 10 and 100), and η from 0.1 to 0.9 (0.1 per step). The final value for γ is 10 (Robust04/GOV2), for η is 0.1 (Robust04) and 0.2 (GOV2).

Results. The results on Robust04 are shown in the top part of Table 1. As we can see, by incorporating topic level estimation, LDA-LM can outperform the QL model on both topic titles and descriptions. Meanwhile, by estimating the language model using the original PV-DBOW model, PV-LM obtains very similar results as LDA-LM. By adding the proposed techniques one by one to enhance the PV-DBOW model for IR, we obtain better and better retrieval performance. The results indicate the effectiveness of the proposed techniques for the PV based retrieval model. Finally, the full enhanced model EPV-DRJ-LM can outperform both QL and LDA-LM significantly on both topic titles and descriptions. For example, the relative MAP improvement of EPV-DRJ-LM over QL and LDA-LM in Robust04 is 5.5% and 3.5% on titles, 2.5% and 2.4% on descriptions, respectively.

From the results on GOV2, however, we find that the incorporation of the LDA model may even hurt the retrieval performance in most cases. A major reason is that GOV2 is a large Web collection with many diverse and noisy topics. By using only 300 topics, the learned topics in LDA might be too coarse and noisy, which can hurt the language model estimation. Therefore, one may observe better performance with LDA-LM by increasing the number of topics (with correspondingly lower efficiency). On the other hand, although the vector dimension of our enhanced PV model is also 300, the potential number of topics is not limited to that number. Therefore, EPV-DRJ-LM can capture much finer topic relations between words and documents, and produce better language estimation in the latent semantic space. We

[1] http://www.lemurproject.org/galago.php

Table 1: **Comparison of different models over Robust04 and GOV2 collection. ∗, + means significant difference over QL, LDA-LM respectively at 0.05 significance level measured by Fisher randomization test.**

	Robust04 collection					
	Topic titles			Topic descriptions		
Method	MAP	nDCG@20	P@20	MAP	nDCG@20	P@20
QL	0.253	0.415	0.369	0.246	0.391	0.334
LDA-LM	0.258*	0.421	0.374*	0.247	0.392	0.336
PV-LM	0.259*	0.418	0.371	0.247	0.392	0.335
EPV-D-LM	0.260*	0.417	0.371	0.251*	0.397*	0.340*
EPV-DR-LM	0.262*	0.418	0.368	0.252*+	0.397*	0.338*
EPV-DRJ-LM	**0.267*+**	**0.425***	**0.376***	**0.253*+**	**0.404*+**	**0.347*+**
	GOV2 collection					
	Topic titles			Topic descriptions		
Method	MAP	nDCG@20	P@20	MAP	nDCG@20	P@20
QL	0.295	0.409	0.510	0.249	0.371	0.470
LDA-LM	0.292	0.405	0.504	0.244	**0.375**	0.467
EPV-DRJ-LM	**0.297+**	**0.415*+**	**0.519*+**	**0.252*+**	0.371	**0.472**

observe much better performance with EPV-DRJ-LM compared with both QL and LDA-LM.

The results in Table 1 also show that the topic level smoothing is more effective on short queries (topic titles) than long queries (topic descriptions). For example, the relative improvement of LDA-LM over QL is 2.0% on titles and 0.4% on descriptions in terms of MAP respectively; while the relative improvement of EPV-DRJ-LM over QL is 5.5% on titles and 2.5% on descriptions in terms of MAP. With fewer words in a query, the language model estimation would be more difficult based on exact matching. Therefore, by involving topic level estimation, the smoothing technique can bring larger benefits by alleviating the vocabulary mismatch problem.

5. CONCLUSION

In this paper, we study how to effectively use the PV model to improve ad-hoc retrieval. We identify several problems that make the original PV-DBOW model less effective for the IR scenario. To solve these issues, we proposed three techniques to enhance the original PV model. The experimental results demonstrate the effectiveness of our enhanced PV based retrieval model compared with the state-of-the-art topic enhanced language models. This is also the first study to show that a PV model can work better than a topic model on language model estimation for IR.

6. ACKNOWLEDGMENTS

This work was supported in part by the Center for Intelligent Information Retrieval, in part by NSF IIS-1160894, and in part by NSF grant IIS-1419693. Any opinions, findings and conclusions or recommendations expressed in this material are those of the authors and do not necessarily reflect those of the sponsor.

7. REFERENCES

[1] A. M. Dai, C. Olah, Q. V. Le, and G. S. Corrado. Document embedding with paragraph vectors. In *NIPS Deep Learning Workshop*, 2014.

[2] D. Ganguly, D. Roy, M. Mitra, and G. J. Jones. Word embedding based generalized language model for information retrieval. In *Proceedings of the 38th International ACM SIGIR Conference on Research and Development in Information Retrieval*, pages 795–798. ACM, 2015.

[3] S. Huston and W. B. Croft. A comparison of retrieval models using term dependencies. In *Proceedings of the 23rd ACM International Conference on Conference on Information and Knowledge Management*, pages 111–120. ACM, 2014.

[4] Q. Le and T. Mikolov. Distributed representations of sentences and documents. In *Proceedings of the 31st International Conference on Machine Learning (ICML-14)*, pages 1188–1196, 2014.

[5] O. Levy and Y. Goldberg. Neural word embedding as implicit matrix factorization. In Z. Ghahramani, M. Welling, C. Cortes, N. Lawrence, and K. Weinberger, editors, *Advances in Neural Information Processing Systems 27*, pages 2177–2185. Curran Associates, Inc., 2014.

[6] X. Liu and W. B. Croft. Cluster-based retrieval using language models. In *Proceedings of the 27th annual international ACM SIGIR conference on Research and development in information retrieval*, pages 186–193. ACM, 2004.

[7] T. Mikolov, I. Sutskever, K. Chen, G. S. CJorrado, and M. I. Dean, Jeffdan. Distributed representations of words and phrases and their compositionality. In *Advances in neural information processing systems*, pages 3111–3119, 2013.

[8] J. M. Ponte and W. B. Croft. A language modeling approach to information retrieval. In *Proceedings of the 21st annual international ACM SIGIR conference on Research and development in information retrieval*, pages 275–281. ACM, 1998.

[9] S. Robertson. Understanding inverse document frequency: on theoretical arguments for idf. *Journal of Documentation*, 60(5):503–520, 2004.

[10] F. Sun, J. Guo, Y. Lan, J. Xu, and X. Cheng. Learning word representations by jointly modeling syntagmatic and paradigmatic relations. In *Proceedings of the 53rd Annual Meeting of the Association for Computational Linguistics*, pages 136–145, Beijing, China, 2015.

[11] I. Vulić and M.-F. Moens. Monolingual and cross-lingual information retrieval models based on (bilingual) word embeddings. In *Proceedings of the 38th International ACM SIGIR Conference on Research and Development in Information Retrieval*, pages 363–372. ACM, 2015.

[12] X. Wei and W. B. Croft. LDA-based document models for ad-hoc retrieval. In *Proceedings of the 29th Annual International ACM SIGIR Conference on Research and Development in Information Retrieval*, SIGIR '06, pages 178–185, New York, NY, USA, 2006. ACM.

[13] C. Zhai. Statistical language models for information retrieval. *Synthesis Lectures on Human Language Technologies*, 1(1):1–141, 2008.

[14] C. Zhai and J. Lafferty. A study of smoothing methods for language models applied to ad hoc information retrieval. In *Proceedings of the 24th annual international ACM SIGIR conference on Research and development in information retrieval*, pages 334–342. ACM, 2001.

Improving Retrieval Quality Using Pseudo Relevance Feedback in Content-Based Image Retrieval

Dinesha Chathurani Nanayakkara Wasam Uluwitige, Timothy Chappell, Shlomo Geva, Vinod Chandran
School of Electrical Engineering and Computer Science
Queensland University of Technology
Brisbane, Australia
(d.nanayakkara@hdr.qut.edu.au, t.chappell@connect.qut.edu.au, s.geva@qut.edu.au, v.chandran@qut.edu.au)

ABSTRACT

The increased availability of image capturing devices has enabled collections of digital images to rapidly expand in both size and diversity. This has created a constantly growing need for efficient and effective image browsing, searching, and retrieval tools. Pseudo-relevance feedback (PRF) has proven to be an effective mechanism for improving retrieval accuracy. An original, simple yet effective rank-based PRF mechanism (RB-PRF) that takes into account the initial rank order of each image to improve retrieval accuracy is proposed. This RB-PRF mechanism innovates by making use of binary image signatures to improve retrieval precision by promoting images similar to highly ranked images and demoting images similar to lower ranked images. Empirical evaluations based on standard benchmarks, namely Wang, Oliva & Torralba, and Corel datasets demonstrate the effectiveness of the proposed RB-PRF mechanism in image retrieval.

General Terms

Performance, Measure.

Keywords

CBIR, Content based image retrieval, Image signature, Pseudo relevance feedback, Scaling factor.

1. INTRODUCTION

The development of the Internet created an ever-growing need for efficient and effective image browsing, searching, and retrieval tools. Retrieving relevant images accurately to satisfy an information need from a large, diversified collection using visual queries is a challenging task in information retrieval. Despite many years of research in content-based image retrieval (CBIR), an effective general solution - in terms of speed, precision and scalability still eludes researchers.

Relevance feedback (RF) [1] is an approach that seeks to improve the precision of search results through the incorporation of user feedback in response to an initial results list. When interacting with a RF interface, the user informs the search engine as to whether the results that have already been inspected are useful or not. With this feedback the system can attempt to improve upon the initial query results, usually by reformulating the original query or by re-ranking the initial result list on the basis of available feedback, at the cost of requiring additional input from the user.

SIGIR '16, July 17-21, 2016, Pisa, Italy.
© 2016 ACM. ISBN 978-1-4503-4069-4/16/07…$15.00
DOI: http://dx.doi.org/10.1145/2911451.2914747

Even in cases where explicit user feedback is not available, some aspects of the relevance feedback approach can be used by making the often reasonable assumption that the first pass results returned by the search engine will include a sufficiently large number of images that match the user's information need. The system then makes use of that set of top ranked initial results as if it were actual positive feedback provided by the user. This technique is often referred to as pseudo-relevance feedback (PRF). The assumption is that despite being noisy feedback, it will still help to promote relevant documents in the initial retrieval list.

Motivated by the concept of PRF, the RB-PRF approach is proposed to improve retrieval performance by applying PRF on binary image signatures. While PRF is not a new concept, two original contributions are made - the first is the original use of document signatures directly in feedback processing - as opposed to traditional approaches, which return to the original images (or documents). The second is the incorporation of the rank order of the initial results in utilising feedback to re-rank the results - rather than assume equal importance as traditionally done.

Image representation is derived through sub-image decomposition, and a full image signature is generated by the combination of sub-image features. Sub image signatures are generated from low-level features of each sub image. Image signatures are fixed length binary strings derived through a form of locality sensitive hashing [2]. The derivation of an image signature from image features is described in more detail in section 2.

A retrieved image list of length K, (much smaller than the collection size) which is small enough to be practical, is re-ranked through RB-PRF by using the top N image signatures as relevant image signature examples and the bottom N as non-relevant examples, where $N << K$. K is selected to be large enough that it can be assumed that the bottom N results are unlikely to be relevant, yet small enough to ensure that the bottom N results are still similar to the query signature, albeit irrelevant. The entire feedback-based re-ranking is performed in signature space. There is no need to return to the original image representation, as is

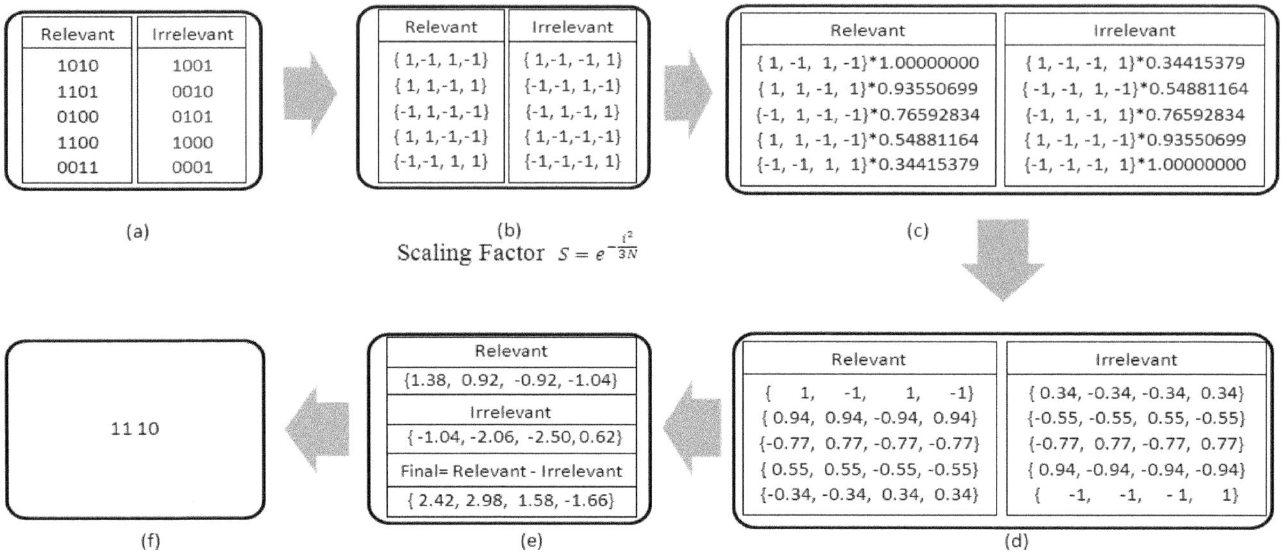

Figure. 1. Toy example to show the process of PRF using a toy dataset with signature size four bits and sample size (N) five (which are considered as relevant).

done with conventional PRF. Here we re-rank only the retrieved list of first K binary image vectors against the generated FB signature. Results presented here show that RB-PRF achieves effective and efficient relevance feedback in CBIR and a considerable improvement in retrieval performance over earlier approaches.

The rest of the paper is organized as follows: Section 2 provides an overview of the proposed PRF method. Section 3 provides a detailed explanation of the experiment and the results obtained relative to published baselines. Conclusions drawn from these findings are included in section 4.

2. PROPOSED RANK BASED PSEUDO RELEVANCE FEEDBACK TECHNIQUE

Our approach divides each image into a 3x3 non-overlapping grid and extracts visual features from each sub-image using global feature descriptors such as colour, texture, and shape. Each feature set is clustered using the k-means algorithm; with similar feature vectors placed together and independent visual vocabularies per feature generated. Then each sub-image is represented by those visual words from these vocabularies through codebook lookup of each raw image feature and finally the full image feature set is constructed. This representation is finally translated into a binary image signature using random indexing for efficient retrieval. This process is performed by producing text files to be parsed by the TopSig signature based search system (www.topsig.org).

Initially the search produces a list of images with signatures ranked from the most similar to least similar. The top-ranked K signatures are then used in RB-PRF process. The RB-PRF process considers the binary vectors of the top N (size of the PRF list) and the bottom N form the list of K binary vectors as relevant and irrelevant respectively, to generate FB signature. Each selected signature is represented by values of {-1, 1} with 1-bits being interpreted as 1 and 0-bits interpreted as -1. The binary signatures are transformed into real valued vectors as a weighted linear combination of the feedback signatures, weighted by rank (with negative feedback ranked in reverse order.) The feedback vectors are then added together independently and two vectors are generated - one from the pseudo-relevant signatures and one from the pseudo-irrelevant signatures. The vector generated from irrelevant signatures is then subtracted from the vector generated by relevant signatures. Finally the vector is 'squashed' back to a binary representation {1,0} simply taking the sign bit. The resulting binary signature is the feedback (FB) signature. The signatures in the result list that are to be re-ranked are then sorted according to the Hamming distance from the new FB signature. Note that the entire re-ranking process takes place in signature space without ever going back to the original image features. Furthermore, the initial list of signatures that is being re-ranked is already in memory following the initial search so the process is computationally efficient.

Figure 1 gives detailed description of the RB-PRF process for an example problem with 4-bit signatures and N=5 (Figure 1a). These are converted to real valued vectors as shown in Figure 1b, and multiplied by the scaling factor S (with N = 5 and i ranging from 0 to 4 for this example). The scaling formula used here ensures a smooth decay of feedback with increased rank position and was chosen after experiments with cross-validation. Scaling performs significantly better than without scaling. Moreover, it is not very sensitive and it is easy to tune. Figure 1c shows the process of scaling and Figure 1d shows the results. Vectors are added and subtracted as shown in Figure 1e. Finally a binary image signature is generated as shown in Figure 1f. This is then used to re-rank the initial search results.

3. EVALUATION

The RB-PRF approach is evaluated on different datasets using different evaluation measures to confirm the effectiveness in terms of precision.

3.1 CBIR System

In the CBIR system, global features such as colour, texture, and shape are used to represent images. Colour is often the most cognitively informative feature and it is relatively robust and simple to represent. Texture is also an important feature and it is very helpful in describing real world images. Shape features are vital for describing the shape of an object. Three colour descriptors are used in the CBIR system. The color histogram [3] is generated with 64 bins. First order, second order, and third order moments are calculated. Colour coherence vectors [4] are used with 16 buckets. For texture, Gabor wavelets [5] are used with five scales and eight orientations. GIST features are used with eight orientations and three scales as they describe the spatial envelope of the image. The Edge histogram descriptors are using five filters which represent shape features as well as texture. Seven invariant moments are used to further describe the shapes. YCbCr, HSV and RGB color spaces are used in these descriptors. Image representation and searching are described in section 2.

3.2 Datasets

The Wang dataset [6] of 1000 images is used for evaluation of the system and for comparisons with earlier work. It is a subset of manually selected images from the standard Corel image database and consists of 10 classes with 100 images each. For further validation the Oliva and Torralba dataset [7] is also used. It includes 2688 images classified into eight categories. As these datasets are well classified, it was possible to quantitatively evaluate and compare the performance.

In order to compare our PRF method with existing baselines that use PRF we conducted another set of experiments on subset of images from the Corel Photo Gallery [8] for which we have results for three earlier systems [8,9,10]. That data set is larger and it consists of about 12K images which are classified into 83 semantic concepts with about 100 images in each. These images are JPEG files with a resolution of 120 x 80 or 80 x 120. Even though many images containing the same semantic content are distributed across different Corel categories we use the same set as it provides consistent comparison with the PRF systems from the literature.

3.3 Evaluation Measures

Precision is used to evaluate the proposed RB-PRF approach. Precision is defined as the fraction of retrieved images in a result list that are relevant to a given query. Specifically the average precision (AP) at *n*, where *n* is the length of the result list is used. Images are considered to be correct matches if they are in the same class as the query image.

3.4 Approaches and Settings

AP@*n* is calculated for both datasets. AP@20, AP@50 and AP@100 are calculated for each class to compare with existing systems. RB-PRF is compared with the baseline signature based system (CBIR-ISIG) [11], and with existing systems from the literature. It may be noted that we do use proxies for both positive FB and negative FB in our approach as described in section 2.

3.5 Results

Tables 1 and 2 show how the baseline signature-based CBIR (CBIR-ISIG) system performs. Table 2 shows the results of CBIR-ISIG compared with other baseline systems for AP@20 and it shows that the CBIR-ISIG system generates slightly better results [11] using the signature-based approach. The differences are not statistically significant at 95% significance level but are significant at the 90% significance level. CBIR-ISIG with RB-PRF is statistically significantly better at 95% significance level. In addition Table 2 shows the results of CBIR-ISIG system compared with other systems for AP@100. They are not statistically significantly better but averages are higher. Table 3 shows the results of comparing our CBIR-ISIG system with another baseline [12] on the Oliva and Torralba dataset. In tables 1-3 bold values signify the highest AP for each class among the compared systems. The underlined values signify that CBIR-ISIG system [11], our underlying signature retrieval system, outperforms the compared system without any FB. Furthermore italic values signify cases where RB-PRF is higher when using both positive and negative FB than using only positive FB. We observe that the underlying CBIR-ISIG system outperforms the baseline systems on the Wang, and Oliva and Torralba datasets and the proposed additional RB-PRF mechanism works well having further considerable performance improvement.

Table 4 shows the results of CBIR-ISIG system with PRF compared with other systems for AP@20, using a sample size of

Table 1. AP@20 of Wang with the performance in the literature

Category	2005 [13]	2007 [14]	2011 [15]	2011 [16]	2013 [17]	2015 [11]	+VE PRF	+&- PRF
1	0.23	0.48	0.57	**0.90**	0.7	0.75	0.82	*0.83*
2	0.23	0.34	0.58	0.38	0.28	0.68	0.74	***0.76***
3	0.23	0.36	0.43	**0.72**	0.56	0.53	0.56	*0.60*
4	0.23	0.61	**0.93**	0.49	0.84	0.86	0.90	***0.93***
5	0.23	0.95	0.98	**1.00**	0.81	**1.00**	**1.00**	***1.00***
6	0.23	0.48	0.58	0.39	0.58	0.86	**0.89**	0.87
7	0.23	0.61	0.83	0.56	0.55	0.98	0.99	***1.00***
8	0.23	0.74	0.68	0.87	0.87	0.98	1.00	***1.00***
9	0.23	0.42	0.46	0.45	0.48	0.77	**0.77**	0.74
10	0.23	0.50	0.53	0.87	0.66	0.86	0.88	***0.91***
AP	0.23	0.55	0.66	0.66	0.63	0.83	0.86	0.87

Table 2. AP@100 of Wang with the performance in the literature

Category	2000 [18]	2002 [19]	2008 [20]	2009 [21]	2011 [22]	2015 [11]	+VE PRF	+&- PRF
1	0.48	0.47	0.48	0.45	0.49	0.52	**0.62**	0.60
2	0.33	0.33	0.34	0.35	0.40	0.46	0.55	***0.56***
3	0.33	0.33	0.33	0.35	0.39	0.38	0.39	***0.40***
4	0.36	0.60	0.52	0.60	0.58	0.63	0.69	***0.74***
5	0.98	0.95	0.95	0.95	0.96	0.95	0.98	***0.99***
6	0.40	0.25	0.40	0.6	0.50	0.57	0.67	***0.68***
7	0.40	0.63	0.60	0.65	0.75	0.84	**0.95**	***0.95***
8	0.72	0.63	0.70	0.70	0.80	0.76	0.87	***0.89***
9	0.34	0.25	0.36	0.40	0.40	0.47	**0.51**	0.48
10	0.34	0.49	0.46	0.40	0.51	0.60	**0.67**	***0.67***
AP	0.47	0.49	0.51	0.55	0.55	0.62	0.69	***0.70***

Table 3. AP@50 of Oliva & Torralba

Category	2007 [12]	2015 [11]	+VE PRF	+&-PRF
1	0.84	0.63	0.72	***0.79***
2	0.50	0.50	0.48	***0.50***
3	0.76	0.85	0.96	***0.97***
4	0.80	0.73	**0.75**	0.72
5	0.62	0.75	0.81	***0.81***
6	0.44	0.94	0.95	***0.96***
7	0.38	0.67	0.76	***0.80***
8		0.73	**0.75**	0.73
AP	0.62	0.73	0.77	0.79

Table 4. AP@20 of Corel with the performance in the literature

Evaluation Criteria	No FB	+&- PRF	Simulated RF
MTSVM [8] (2006)	0.28		0.37
KBMCM [9] (2007)	0.28		0.44
BDEE [10] (2010)	0.28		0.37
CBIR-ISIG	0.29	0.31	0.44

500 random images and 15-fold cross-validation. Here images are considered as positive FB (relevant) if and only if they are in the same class as the query image. All others are considered as negative FB (non-relevant).

Finally, on the time efficiency of retrieval; the use of signature-based methods, which are designed to make efficient retrieval of high-dimensionality data feasible, allows our approach to work quickly and achieve retrieval times in the milliseconds through the use of scalable signature search approaches [23]. The PRF process can also be performed efficiently due to the fact that the signatures for the retrieved images remain resident in memory after the initial search and performing the requisite re-ranking only requires the calculation of a small number of Hamming distances and a sort.

4. CONCLUSIONS

In this paper a RB-PRF approach is described for the application of pseudo relevance feedback in CBIR. The original contribution is in the first application of PRF to signatures and in taking into account the initial rank order of results to weight the feedback from each image. This approach has balance of retrieval speed and quality. The proposed RB-PRF approach performs well and outperforms several systems with previously published results on the same data sets. Our experiments demonstrate that the RB-PRF approach is effective and efficient on signature-based representation for image retrieval.

5. REFERENCES

[1] D. Harman," Relevance feedback revisited," *in Proc. of the Fifteenth Annual International ACM Special Interest Group on Information Retrieval Conference on Research and Development in Information Retrieval*, pp. 110,1992.

[2] S. Geva, and C. M. De Vries, "TOPSIG: Topology Preserving Document Signatures." Proceedings of the 20th ACM international conference on information and knowledge management. CIKM, 2011.

[3] G. Qiu, "Indexing chromatic and achromatic patterns for content-based image retrieval," *Journal of pattern recognition,* pp. 1675-1686, 2002.

[4] G. Pass, R. Zabih, and J. Miller, "Comparing images using color coherence vectors." *Proceedings of the fourth ACM international conference on Multimedia.* ACM, 1997.

[5] M. H. Rahmana, M. R. Pickering, and M.R. Frater, "Scale and Rotation Invariant Gabor Features for Texture Retrieval," in *Proc. DICTA International Conference on Digital Image Computing Techniques and Applications*, pp. 602-607, 2011.

[6] J. Li, and J. W. Wang, "Automatic linguistic indexing of pictures by a statistical modeling approach," *IEEE transaction on Pattern Analysis and Machine Intelligence*, vol. 25, no. 9, pp. 1075-1087, 2003.

[7] A. Oliva, and A. Torralba, "Modeling the shape of the scene: A Holistic representation of the spatial envelope," *International Journal of Computer Vision*, vol. 42, no. 3, pp. 145-175, 2001.

[8] J. Li, N. Allinson, D. Tao, and X. Li, "Multitraining Support Vector Machine for Image Retrieval," *IEEE Transaction on Image Processing*, vol. 15, no. 11, pp. 3597-3601, 2006.

[9] D. Tao, X. Li, and J. M. Stephen, "Negative Samples Analysis in Relevance Feedback," *IEEE Transaction on Knowledge and Data Engineering*, vol. 19, no. 4, pp. 568-580, 2007.

[10] W. Bian, and D. Tao, "Biased Discriminant Euclidean Embedding for Content-Based Image Retrieval," *IEEE Transaction on Image Processing*, vol. 19, no. 2, pp. 545-553, 2010.

[11] N. W. U. D. Chathurani, S. Geva, and V. Chandran, "Conversion of an Image to a Document Using Grid-based Decomposition For Efficient Content-Based Image Retrieval." *International Journal of Information Science and Intelligent Systems*, vol.4, no 3, 2015.

[12] G. Demir, and A. Selim, "Scene Classification Using Bag-of Region Representations," *IEEE Conference on Computer Vision and Pattern Recognition*, pp. 1-8, 2007.

[13] V. Takala, T. Ahoen, and M. Pietikainen, "Block-based methods for image retrieval using local binary patterns," *in Proc. of the 14th Scandinavian Conference on Image Analysis*, pp. 882-891, 2005.

[14] P. S. Hiremath, and J. Pujari, "Content based image retrieval based on color, texture and shape features," *in Proc. 15th International Conference on Advance Computing and Communications*, pp. 780-784, 2007.

[15] X. Yuan, J. Yu, Z. Qin, and T. Wan, "A SIFT-LBP image retrieval model based on bag-of-features," *in Proc. IEEE ICIP 18th International Conference on Image Processing*, pp. 1061-1064, 2011.

[16] M. H. Saad, H. I. Saleh, H. Konbor, and M. Ashour, "Image retrieval based on integration between YCbCr color histogram and shape feature," *in Proc. ICENCO 7th International Computer Engineering Conference*, pp. 97-102, 2011.

[17] N. S. Mansoori, M. Nejati, P. Razzaghi, and S. Samavi, "Bag of visual words approach for image retrieval using color information," *in Proc. ICEE 21st Iranian Conference on Electrical Engineering*, pp. 1-6, 2013.

[18] J. Li, J. Z. Wang, and G. Wiederhold, "IRM: Integrated Region Matching for Image Retrieval," *in Proc. ACM Multimedia 00'*, pp. 147-156, 2000.

[19] Y. Chen, and J. Wang, "A region-based fuzzy feature matching approach to content-based image retrieval," *IEEE Transactions on Pattern Analysis and Machine Intelligence*, pp. 1252-1267, 2002.

[20] P. S. Hiremath, and J. Pujari, "Content Based Image Retrieval Using Color Boosted Salient Points and Shape Features of an Image," i*n Proc. International Journal of Image Processing*, pp. 10- 17, 2008.

[21] M. Banerjee, M. Kundu, and P. Maji, "Content-based image retrieval using visually significant point features," *Journal of Fuzzy Sets and Systems,* vol. 160, no. 23, 2009.

[22] M. Chowdhury, S. Das, and M. Kundu, "Interactive content based image retrieval using Ripplet transform and fuzzy relevance feedback," *in Proc. 1st Indo-Japan Conference*, pp. 243-251, 2012.

[23] T. Chappell, S. Geva, and G. Zuccon, "Approximate Nearest-Neighbour Search with Inverted Signature Slice Lists," in: Pro. of the 37th European Conference on IR Research, 2015.

Ingrams – A Neuropsychological Explanation for Why People Search

Peter Bailey
Microsoft
pbailey@microsoft.com

Nick Craswell
Microsoft
nickcr@microsoft.com

ABSTRACT

Why do people start a search? Why do they stop? Why do they do what they do in-between? Our goal in this paper is to provide a simple yet general explanation for these acts that has its basis in neuropsychology and observed user behavior. We coin the term "ingram", as an information counterpart to Richard Semon's "engram" or "memory trace". People search to create ingrams. People stop searching because they have created sufficient ingrams, or given up. We describe these acts through a pair of user models and use it to explain various user behaviors in search activity. Understanding people's search acts in terms of ingrams may help us predict or model the interaction of people's information needs, the queries they issue, and the information they consume. If we could observe certain decision-making acts within these activities, we might also gain new insight into the relationships between textual information and knowledge representation.

1. INTRODUCTION

To build better interactive information seeking systems, we need to understand more clearly *why* people search, *how* they formulate search queries, and *what* activities lead them to be satisfied (or not) with the information they choose to consume. It is very challenging to build a comprehensive model of what a person knows, or of what they do not know. However, by observing users directly or indirectly through their long-term and short-term interactions with information seeking systems, we can propose a model for *changes* in knowledge that occur. The model should be consistent with the observed search behavior. By focusing solely on knowledge state changes, our model, while less comprehensive or accurate than more contextually situated models, may prove more amenable to extraction of significant events that can be used as data for machine learning algorithms building text-to-knowledge relationships.

For example, a query such as [olives] provides us relatively little information about the motivation and information need of a searcher. If instead we observe a sequence of queries: [olives]; [when to harvest olives]; [olive picking technique], interspersed by various examined document summaries on the corresponding search results pages and also specific clicked documents, we have a much richer set of data from which to infer the changes in the searcher's knowledge. In Section 3, we name and describe concepts for specific neuropsychological knowledge states that arise throughout the search process.

SIGIR '16, July 17–21, 2016, Pisa, Italy.

ACM 978-1-4503-4069-4/16/07…$15.00
DOI: http://dx.doi.org/10.1145/2911451.2914712

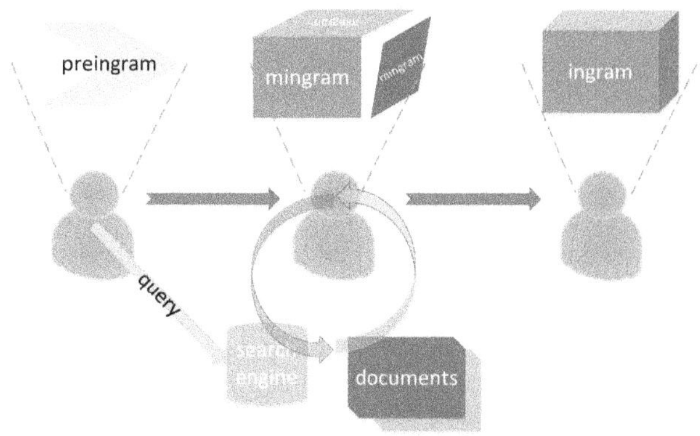

Figure 1 – A successful search process, moving from a preingram via mingrams to an ingram

There are several theories of why or how people search – some of the more influential ones include [2][9][16]. In recent years, the mass availability of effective information retrieval systems coupled with enormous information resources has exploded the amount of information system log data available to researchers in modeling user behavior when searching. Yet because the motivations for any individual search reside within people's minds, it has proven challenging to model these directly from the observable log traces of behavior alone. While user studies have become increasingly sophisticated, with mouse-tracking, gaze-tracking, and physio-logical monitoring, these often place searchers in artificial environments and typically involve carefully curated information seeking tasks. These experimental settings are optimized for gathering data, but do not address the original motivations for search in situ. Alternative ethnographic research studies are more closely aligned with our work, seeking to understand why searchers carry out information search and exploration, e.g. [11]. In Section 4 we consider how our knowledge state changes correspond to a subset of published user behavior models for generalized information search, and the implications for future experiments.

Our contributions in this paper are: (1) provide a simple yet general hypothesis for what neuropsychological *changes* occur in people's minds throughout the course of a search process; (2) align these changes with observed interaction with information seeking systems; and (3) describe decision points and acts of the searcher that could illuminate the relationship between text and knowledge representation as these changes occur, for use by other researchers.

2. RELATED WORK

Taylor's original work on information need is foundational in describing four different levels of cognitive awareness between inception and action within a search process [18]. Taylor's work is more complex than our own in characterizing different levels, but does not proceed to describe subsequent knowledge changes. Like Taylor, Nordlie conducted a comparative study within a library information seeking environment, which suggests dialogue-based interaction might help improve search processes [15]. Nordlie's observations also suggest that the human intermediary must construct (through their dialog with the searcher) their own mental model of the desired goal so they can assist the searcher, a process he describes as "revealment". Belkin et al developed an influential theory of anomalous states of knowledge ASK (that a user comprehends an anomaly in their current state of understanding), akin to the visceral need level of Taylor, and applied it to the task of improving information retrieval systems [2]. Our explanation aligns with this visceral need or anomalous state as a starting neurophysiological frame. Kuhlthau's Information Search Process framework is also influential, describing a 6-stage series of tasks, with associated thoughts, feelings, actions and strategies [9]; we seek a simpler explanation. Pirolli et al developed an Information Foraging model, inspired from anthropological theories of food seeking behavior to describe information seeking [16]; again, this has been influential in our explanation of partially attained states in completion of an information seeking task. Recently Azzopardi proposed an economic theory of user behavior to describe the choices made during searching, hypothesizing that users seek to minimize cognitive load [1]. We see this as primarily an operational explanation of search activity, rather than our focus which is more on changes in information and knowledge acquisition.

3. CONCEPTS

3.1 Ingram

We coin the term "ingram", as an information counterpart to Richard Semon's hypothetical "engram" [17]. In neuropsychology, the engram is a memory trace that has been physically encoded in the brain. Though science lacks a comprehensive understanding of this, it is still useful to hypothesize that there must be some biophysical or biochemical change in the brain to support the encoding and retrieval of a memory.

Just as an engram is an encoding of memory there must be some changes in the brain that occur during information seeking. We propose the ingram as the change in the brain, comprising one or more engrams, that occur during a given information seeking process. The main outcome and motivation for search is a change in knowledge [9][16], and that change as encoded in the brain is an ingram. In programmatic terms we might denote this as:

SearchProcess(Person) → Person', s.t. Person' = Person+Ingram

That is, on successfully completing a search process, a person has now incorporated an ingram within their knowledge memory.

For example, suppose we have an olive tree in our garden, and wish to know when and how best to harvest the olive fruits, yet have never done so previously. Without a lot of trial and error, the olives may go unharvested, or be harvested at the wrong time, or be harvested but damaged. Instead, given access to appropriate search engine technology and assuming that our search process is successful, we subsequently know what months to pick olives and how to avoid bruising them, without ever having picked an olive still. These engrams, as encodings in the brain, constitute the ingram of the olive harvesting search process.

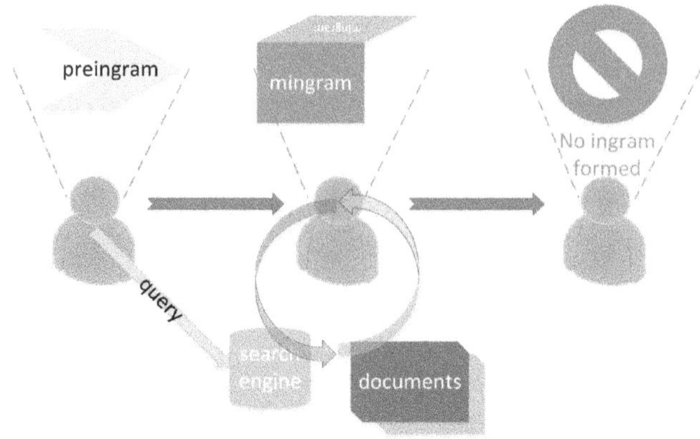

Figure 2 – A partially successful search process, but does not involve creation of an ingram on completion.

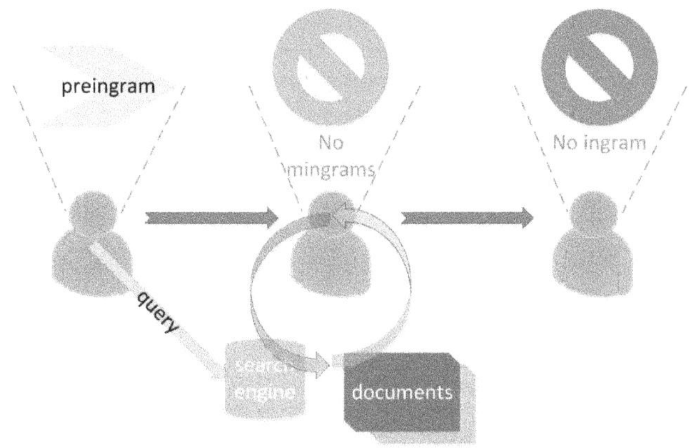

Figure 3 – A completely unsuccessful search process.

3.2 Preingram

If the goal of searching is the ingram, which is a change in the state of knowledge, then prior to searching, people must in some sense be aware of the *need* for an ingram. The awareness of the absence, and the formulation of key characteristics of what the ingram might consist of, must also be present in the mind's knowledge substrate. We term this awareness and formulation of key characteristics of the future ingram a "preingram" (like a premonition of an ingram). Taylor's concept of "information need" [18] and Belkin's concept of an "anomalous state of knowledge" [2] are obviously influential precursors to our preingram.

We propose that people formulate search queries by mapping the key characteristics of a preingram to (typically) a linguistic surface form, in a similar way to how people translate their ideas to language. The precise mapping chosen is conditioned on many different factors, including the person's mental model of how search engines work, the query construction tools provided by the search engines (e.g. query suggestions interfaces), and most importantly, the key characteristics of the ingram that are understood in the preingram.

Returning to our olive tree example, the awareness of needing to know about when the best time to harvest olives, and generalized concepts like "olives", "fruit", "ripeness" "picking", "harvesting" form the corresponding preingram. A natural language expression might be "when is the best time to harvest olives and how should I do it". However, since few search engines are optimally suited to natural language queries, we are more likely to construct a search query similar to [olive picking time] or [when to harvest olives].

3.3 Mingram

While simple search intents (for example, navigational search [3] or refinding activities [19]) may be satisfied by a single query-document pair, many are not. As described by Cole et al [5] while investigating the practical application of Belkin's ASK model for information retrieval [2], there may be an "issue of unknown item information need and the non-specifiability of this sort of need". In fact, it is perhaps even more complex – there are the "known unknowns" that we seek and can partially name when our search process commences, and there are the "unknown unknowns" that we only discover during the process of seeking itself. We believe that a common example of these "unknown unknowns" occurs when searchers acquire vocabulary while reading documents, such that they subsequently employ some of these words as query terms that lead to satisfied search activity. Overall, what we see is that many search sessions require multiple queries and entail extended information discovery and progressive learning [7].

To characterize the partial information accumulation aspect of search processes, we need one additional concept – the "mingram" (like a micro or minimal or most of an ingram). A mingram arises in the searcher's knowledge memory when some useful piece of content is comprehended as part of the information seeking process in order to form the final ingram. Once a sufficient set of mingrams have been assembled, the searcher may determine that the ingram is complete, and cease their search task. Conversely a searcher may be able to assemble a number of mingrams, but still be unable to complete their ingram. At this point, they may either abandon their search altogether, or continue their search process with new queries, browsing, or re-queries. Mingrams have an analog in the relevance measurement domain, being the "information nugget" concept described by Voorhees in the TREC Question Answering track [21], and Clarke et al's work on novelty and diversity [4].

Returning to the olive example, one mingram may represent a document passage stating that that olives are best harvested in the fall or autumn season. Another mingram may be an illustrated document showing that the olives change color progressively, and these colors correspond to levels of acid in the fruit. A final mingram may be a video showing that harvesting needs to be careful, as the fruit will easily bruise, and suggest containers and receptacles that can limit bruising of the fruit. Collectively, these three mingrams then lead to the ingram that was sufficient for the user to conclude the information seeking session.

The three primary search process patterns (success, partial success, and no success) can thus be represented by state diagrams which show the sequencing of preingram to ingram via mingrams, with interactions to a search engine and documents. A successful search process is shown in Figure 1, a partially successful search process is shown in Figure 2, and an unsuccessful search process is shown in Figure 3. Note that these are all relatively simple models, and make no account of interrupted search processes (where they extend beyond a single session) or parallel search processes (where multiple goals are pursued within a single session). Arguably, both of these more complex behaviors can be captured by reducing the activities involved to aggregates of these simple forms.

4. USER BEHAVIOR MODELING

We now turn our attention to how our neuropsychological explanation of why people search corresponds to a couple of search user behavior models. These models have been developed to explain observed user behavior from log-based analysis and gaze-tracking user studies. The decision points described by the models may help us focus on where preingram, mingram and ingrams arise.

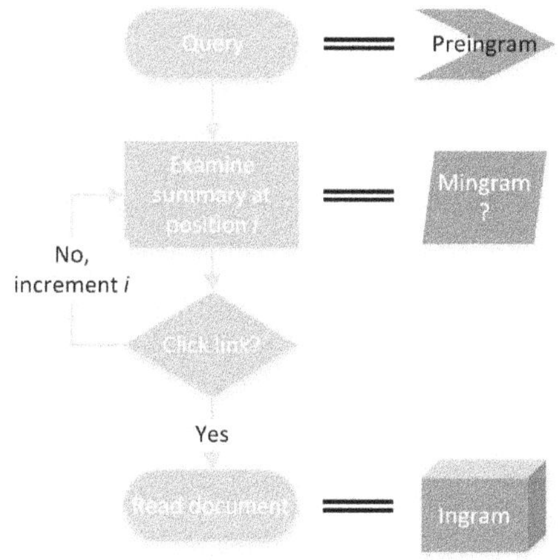

Figure 4 – Cascade model actions and decisions

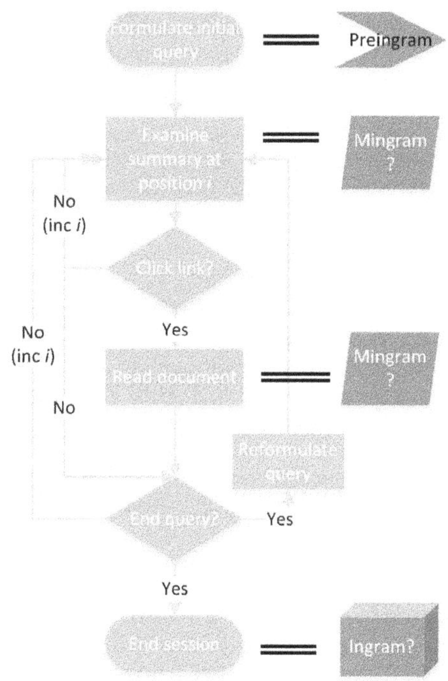

Figure 5 – Behavior model actions and decisions

4.1 Cascade model

The "cascade" model developed by Craswell et al [6] is a simple and influential model that attempts to explain the phenomenon of position bias – that is, that users click on relevant documents nearer the top of a ranked list of results. The model is elegant in its simplicity, suggesting that users traverse a list from top to bottom, examining each document summary, and clicking with a probability proportional to the underlying document's relevance. Once a document is clicked, the searcher does not return, and they are assumed to have found relevant material. The model was the best of four they considered in explaining click patterns in a commercial search engine log. The model does not attempt to describe query reformulation.

In Figure 4, we illustrate the equivalence stages between the simplest cascade model and the ingram explanations. The query is assumed in the cascade model, and the equivalence is a preingram. As the searcher examines each summary, a mingram may (or may not) be created, depending on the content of the summary. Then, after clicking the document, the searcher reads it (and does not return), which corresponds to the creation of the ingram. Ignoring "good abandonment" scenarios [10], we can make a simplifying assumption that the summaries of skipped documents (ones which are not clicked) do not create mingrams at all. The decision to click becomes the critical factor in this model. Deciding not to click means we can ignore these documents. Deciding to click means we need to examine the summary as a candidate for mingram creation, and the full document for both mingram and ingram creation.

4.2 A user behavior-based model

There have been several enhancements to the cascade model. In one of the most comprehensive, recent efforts by Moffat, Thomas and Scholer have focused on using gaze tracking from user studies to understand actual summary examination behavior, document reading behavior, and query reformulations. These observations were used to describe new user models and metrics that may be more aligned to real behavior than some existing relevance metrics [14][20]. In particular, their user model specifically encompasses query reformulations, and also query abandonment independent of having found relevant material.

In Figure 5, we illustrate the equivalence stages between their combined user behavior model (Fig.s 6 and 7 from [14]) and the ingram explanations. We note that this user model is still not quite in alignment with the observed user behavior reported in [20], where the authors found examination of multiple summaries in a "window" of attention prior to clicking. In contrast to Figure 4, we place a question-mark after Ingram, as the user model acknowledges that users may abandon at any time, without being successful, and we align it with the "End session" termination point in the process, rather than the "Read document" activity. We do this in part as it helps us identify the critical decisions in the model. Again, for simplicity we assume that a summary that is skipped does not contribute to creation of a mingram. Summaries that are clicked may create a mingram, as may the clicked document itself. Query reformulation is now seen as a significant act, as it indicates that an ingram has not yet been created. It is only when the search session ends that an ingram may (or may not) have been created; this is a less deterministic outcome than with the cascade model.

5. CONCLUSION

In both the cascade model and the user behavior-based model, the mapping of preingram, mingrams and ingram to the user actions and decisions being made (examining summaries, clicking links and reading documents, reformulating queries) are consistent with the three search processes we described in Section 3. The observable acts of users, and the decisions we can infer are being made by them, in conjunction with our hypothesized neuropsychological changes, provide us with an opportunity to focus future experiments on these critical points within a searcher's information seeking process. Future advances in detecting and understanding brain activities (e.g. [12]) may also enable us to observe these transitions, from preingram to mingram, and from mingrams to ingram. Similarly, characterizing the neuro-physiological changes occurring in searchers' brains throughout a search process may help us more effectively focus the selection and mapping of specific text fragments (queries, result page summaries, document fragments) from user behavior logs for the modeling of knowledge representation via new machine learning approaches involving distributed representations (e.g. [13]). In these approaches, our model's simple but general characterizations for identifying transition points in knowledge acquisition change are preferred to more complex ones.

6. REFERENCES

[1] Azzopardi, L. (2011). The economics in interactive information retrieval. *Proc. SIGIR* (pp. 15-24).

[2] Belkin, N. J., Oddy, R. N., & Brooks, H. M. (1982). ASK for information retrieval: Part I. Background and theory. *Journal of Documentation*, 38(2), 61-71.

[3] Broder, A. (2002). A taxonomy of web search. In *ACM SIGIR Forum* (Vol. 36, No. 2, pp. 3-10).

[4] Clarke, C. L., Kolla, M., Cormack, G. V., Vechtomova, O., Ashkan, A., Büttcher, S., & MacKinnon, I. (2008). Novelty and diversity in information retrieval evaluation. *Proc. SIGIR* (pp. 659-666).

[5] Cole, C., Leide, J., Beheshti, J., Large, A., & Brooks, M. (2005). Investigating the Anomalous States of Knowledge hypothesis in a real-life problem situation: A study of history and psychology undergraduates seeking information for a course essay. *JASIST*, 56(14), 1544-1554.

[6] Craswell, N., Zoeter, O., Taylor, M., & Ramsey, B. (2008). An experimental comparison of click position-bias models. *Proc. WSDM* (pp. 87-94).

[7] Eickhoff, C., Teevan, J., White, R., & Dumais, S. (2014). Lessons from the Journey: A Query Log Analysis of Within-Session Learning. *Proc. WSDM.*

[8] Hassan, A., Shi, X., Craswell, N., & Ramsey, B. (2013). Beyond clicks: query reformulation as a predictor of search satisfaction. *Proc CIKM* (pp. 2019-2028).

[9] Kuhlthau, C. C. (1991). Inside the search process: Information seeking from the user's perspective. *JASIS*, 42(5), 361-371.

[10] Li, J., Huffman, S., & Tokuda, A. (2009). Good abandonment in mobile and PC internet search. *Proc. SIGIR* (pp. 43-50).

[11] Lindley, S. E., Meek, S., Sellen, A., & Harper, R. (2012). It's simply integral to what I do: enquiries into how the web is weaved into everyday life. *Proc. WWW* (pp. 1067-1076).

[12] Mitchell, T. M., Shinkareva, S. V., Carlson, A., Chang, K. M., Malave, V. L., Mason, R. A., & Just, M. A. (2008). Predicting human brain activity associated with the meanings of nouns. *Science*, 320(5880), 1191-1195.

[13] Mitra, B. (2015) Exploring Session Context using Distributed Representations of Queries and Reformulations. *Proc. SIGIR* (pp. 3-12).

[14] Moffat, A., Thomas, P., & Scholer, F. (2013). Users versus models: What observation tells us about effectiveness metrics. *Proc. CIKM* (pp. 659-668).

[15] Nordlie, R. (1999). "User revealment"—a comparison of initial queries and ensuing question development in online searching and in human reference interactions. *Proc. SIGIR* (pp. 11-18).

[16] Pirolli, P., & Card, S. (1999). Information foraging. *Psychological Review*, 106(4), 643.

[17] Semon, R. W. (1911). *Die Mneme: als erhaltendes Prinzip im Wechsel des organischen Geschehens*. Engelmann.

[18] Taylor, R. S. (1967). *Question-Negotiation and Information-Seeking in Libraries* (No. 3). Lehigh University, Bethlehem PA Center for Information Science.

[19] Teevan, J., Adar, E., Jones, R., & Potts, M. (2006). History repeats itself: repeat queries in Yahoo's logs. *Proc. SIGIR* (pp. 703-704).

[20] Thomas, P., Scholer, F., & Moffat, A. (2013). What users do: The eyes have it. *Information Retrieval Technology* (pp. 416-427). Springer Berlin Heidelberg.

[21] Voorhees, E. M. (2003). Overview of the TREC 2003 Question Answering Track. In TREC (pp. 54-66).

Investment Recommendation using Investor Opinions in Social Media

Wenting Tu, David W. Cheung, Nikos Mamoulis, Min Yang, Ziyu Lu
Department of Computer Science, The University of Hong Kong
Pokfulam, Hong Kong
{wttu, dcheung, nikos, myang, zylu}@cs.hku.hk

ABSTRACT

Investor social media, such as StockTwist, are gaining increasing popularity. These sites allow users to post their investing opinions and suggestions in the form of microblogs. Given the growth of the posted data, a significant and challenging research problem is how to utilize the personal wisdom and different viewpoints in these opinions to help investment. Previous work aggregates sentiments related to stocks and generates buy or hold recommendations for stocks obtaining favorable votes while suggesting sell or short actions for stocks with negative votes. However, considering the fact that there always exist unreasonable or misleading posts, sentiment aggregation should be improved to be robust to noise. In this paper, we improve investment recommendation by modeling and using the quality of each investment opinion. To model the quality of an opinion, we use multiple categories of features generated from the author information, opinion content and the characteristics of stocks to which the opinion refers. Then, we discuss how to perform investment recommendation (including opinion recommendation and portfolio recommendation) with predicted qualities of investor opinions. Experimental results on real datasets demonstrate effectiveness of our work in recommending high-quality opinions and generating profitable investment decisions.

1. INTRODUCTION

In the past few years, social-media sites (e.g., Twitter) have emerged as one of prime platforms where people share their ideas and opinions. Some social media sites attract special categories of users, who exchange specialized information. For instance, StockTwits (www.stocktwits.com) is Twitter-like platform for users who share their investing and trading opinions.

Given the availability of platforms such as Twitter or Stocktwits, an interesting question is how to exploit the opinions of investors posted there in order to properly invest in stock markets. Previous work on the subject extracts [7] and aggregates [3, 8, 5, 4] the sentiments of users in the posted messages into a representative investment opinion about a stock. However, few of them explicitly consider the problem that there could be posts with misleading opinions either by non-experts or by malicious users. Our work explicitly considers filtering out such noisy posts by evaluating the quality of each single investing opinion. Among previous work, only [1] noticed that different users post opinions of different quality and propose a framework to identify experts by considering the performance of users' past opinions. The main difference between our work and [1] is that [1] identifies the quality of users rather than that of specific opinions. However it is possible that different posts by the same user may have different quality (e.g., the user is expert only for a subset of the investment products). On the other hand in our work, we explicitly predict the quality of specific opinions and use additional information (e.g., content) for this purpose. Moreover, [1] only uses the opinions posted by authors in the past to derive the characteristics of authors, while we consider more features (e.g., social popularity) of authors.

Our work deals with the problem of predicting the quality of investing opinions and employs this knowledge to recommend to users high-quality opinions and portfolios to invest in. We first formulate the opinion quality prediction problem. Then, we propose multiple categories of features related to opinion author, opinion content and stocks that the opinion talks about. We also discuss how to construct a prediction function upon the proposed features using regression theory. After that, we show how to perform investment recommendation based on the predicted opinion qualities. Finally, we conduct experiments for evaluating the performance of investment recommendation using our methodology and competitor approaches to verify the effectiveness of our work.

2. PROBLEM DEFINITION

Consider a collection of opinions $\mathcal{O}$. For each opinion $o \in \mathcal{O}$, we denote by a^o the author of o, by c^o the content of o, and by $\mathcal{E}^o$ the set of stocks o talks about. Moreover, we formulate a set $\mathcal{V}^o$ of *investment views* in o, which consists of (e, l) pairs, where e is a stock discussed in o and l is the corresponding sentiment label: *bullish* (positive) or *bearish* (negative). For example, Figure 1 shows two investment opinions posted in Stocktwits. The investment views of the first opinion are {(GE, bearish)} and those of the second opinion are {(BBUX, bullish)}.

Next we define the quality of an investing opinion o, denoted as $\mathcal{Q}(o)$. In our work we regard o to be of high-quality if the investment views $\mathcal{V}^o$ *could help readers to perform profitable trading*. Specifically, suppose $\mathcal{E}^o_{bu}$ ($\mathcal{E}^o_{be}$) includes the stocks corresponding to bullish (bearish) sentiment labels in $\mathcal{V}^o$. If o is of high-quality, the prices of stocks in $\mathcal{E}^o_{bu}$ ($\mathcal{E}^o_{be}$) should significantly rise (fall) in the future. Then, if a reader of o *longs* the stocks in $\mathcal{E}^o_{bu}$ (i.e., buys the stocks in $\mathcal{E}^o_{bu}$ and sells them in the future) and *shorts* the stocks in $\mathcal{E}^o_{be}$ (i.e., borrows the stocks in $\mathcal{E}_{be}$ to sell them and buys them back in the future), the reader could obtain high profit. According

SIGIR '16, July 17–21, 2016, Pisa, Italy.

DOI: http://dx.doi.org/10.1145/2911451.2914699

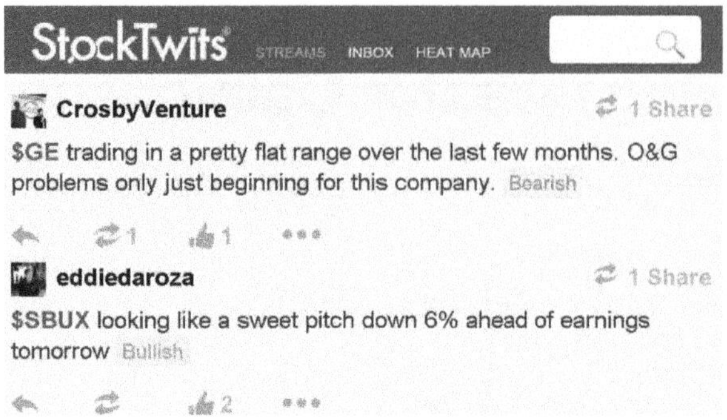

Figure 1: Stocktwits platform.

to the above discussion, $\mathcal{Q}(o)$ can be defined as

$$\frac{1}{|\mathcal{E}^o|}\left(\sum_{e\in\mathcal{E}^o_{bu}}\frac{p^f(e)-p^c(e)}{p^c(e)}+\sum_{e\in\mathcal{E}^o_{be}}\frac{p^c(e)-p^f(e)}{p^c(e)}\right), \quad (1)$$

where $p^c(e)$ and $p^f(e)$ are current price and future price of stock e (in this paper, we set as future price the price after a week). In this formula, $\frac{p^f(e)-p^c(e)}{p^c(e)}\left(\frac{p^c(e)-p^f(e)}{p^c(e)}\right)$ is the increase (decrease) rate of e's price in the future, which actually equals to the return rate corresponding to the investment view (e, l), where l is bullish (bearish).

The main goal of our work is to correctly predict the qualities of investment opinions and then use them for investment recommendation. We focus on two recommendation tasks. One is suggesting a set of high-quality investor opinions to users (i.e., *opinion recommendation*). The other is recommending a portfolio consisting of a set of stocks to long or short (i.e., *portfolio recommendation*).

3. QUALITY ESTIMATION FOR INVESTING OPINIONS

3.1 Features

We start by exploring how well different categories of features capture the quality of investing opinions. We consider features related to the opinion author, opinion content and the stocks the opinion talks about. Below we describe each of them in detail.

The author of an opinion is one of the main factors determining its quality; if the author is an expert in the domain, the opinions posted by him/her are more likely to be high quality. The most intuitive information reflecting author expertise is the performance of opinions posted by the author in the past. Suppose we are predicting the quality of opinion o. We first extract the opinions posted by a^o (i.e., the author of o) in the past. Then, we take the average quality of opinions written by a^o in the past as the first feature describing author expertise. This feature is denoted by *A_avgqual*. Moreover, we also take the percentage of high-quality opinions in all opinions posted by a^o in the past as the second feature. Specifically, we regard an opinion to be of high-quality if its quality value is larger than a threshold (e.g., 0.1). Then, the percentage of high-quality opinions in $\mathcal{O}_u$ is used as another feature (denoted by *A_perchigh*) in our model. Besides measuring author expertise from his/her past opinions, we also explore additional information. In investor-based social media, a user typically *follows* other users if he/she values their opinions. Thus, we use social popularity of authors (denoted by *A_social*) as a third author expertise feature. We model *A_social* as the PageRank score [2] of the author (i.e., a commonly used measurement for evaluating social popularity of users). The fourth feature of author expertise is the number of opinions the author posted in the past (denoted as *A_onum*); i.e., we assume that if a user actively posts opinions, he/she has higher expertise.

The content of an opinion is also potentially related to its quality since it may explain why the authors post their particular view. Sentiment strength in an opinion can also be extracted from the content. Thus, we believe content features may play an important role in predicting opinion quality. In our work, we consider word-level content features. Specifically, for a given opinion, we analyze the words it contains. For each word w, we calculate *w_avgqual* and *w_perchigh*: the average quality of opinions containing w and the percentage of high-quality opinions in all opinions posted containing w, respectively (similar to *A_avgqual* and *A_perchigh*). Let $v^a(w)$ and $v^p(w)$ be the *w_avgqual* and *w_perchigh* values of word w, respectively. Then, assuming that the content of opinion o consists of words $\{w_1, w_2, \cdots, w_n\}$, we define two opinion content features *C_avgqual* and *C_perchigh*, denoted by $\mathbb{E}(v^a)$ and $\mathbb{E}(v^f)$, as the mean of discrete values $\{v^a(w_i)\}_{i=1}^n$ and $\{v^p(w_i)\}_{i=1}^n$, respectively.

Besides features related to opinion author and content, we also define features for stocks. Similar to *C_avgqual* and *C_perchigh*, for a given opinion, we examine the stocks it talks about. For each stock e mentioned in o, *e_avgqual* and *e_perchigh* are the average quality of opinions talking about e and the percentage of high-quality opinions in all opinions talking about e, respectively. Then, assuming that o mentions stocks $\{e_1, e_2, \cdots, e_n\}$, we employ the mean of *e_avgqual* and *e_perchigh* values of $\{e_i\}_{i=1}^n$ as two features (denoted as *S_avgqual* and *S_perchigh*) to describe the stocks mentioned in o.

3.2 Regression-based Quality Prediction

For a new opinion o_i, we extract the values of features *A_avgqual, A_prechigh, A_social, A_onum, C_avgqual, C_prechigh, S_avgqual, S_prechigh*, as defined in Section 3.1. Suppose the features of o_i are $[x_1^i, x_2^i, \cdots, x_n^i]$. The predicted quality of o_i (denoted as $\hat{\mathcal{Q}}(o_i)$) can be obtained by a function f (i.e., $\hat{\mathcal{Q}}(o_i) = f([x_1^i, x_2^i, \cdots, x_n^i])$). We can choose regression models [9] for defining f. For this purpose, we can use as training set all $\{o_j, \hat{Q}(o_j)\}$ pairs, where o_j is an opinion posted in the past and $\hat{Q}(o_j)$ is the real quality of o_j. After f is trained, we can use it to estimate the quality of o_i.

4. INVESTMENT RECOMMENDATION WITH PREDICTED OPINION QUALITIES

In our work, we utilize the predicted opinion qualities for two investment-recommendation tasks: recommending high-quality opinions and recommending portfolios. The high-quality opinions are selected as those with the highest predicted qualities. For generating portfolios, we use the predicted qualities of opinions to weigh them and then aggregate the sentiment about stocks in the opinions to generate scores for the stocks. This way, we can create daily investment recommendations based on the posted opinions.

4.1 Quality Sensitive Sentiment Aggregation for Recommending Portfolios

In previous work on constructing portfolios based on investor opinions, stocks are selected according to their aggregate sentiment indexes. One of the most popular aggregate bullish and bearish sentiment indexes [3, 8, 5] are:

$$\delta_i^{bu} = \ln\left[\frac{1+|\mathcal{O}_i^{bu}|}{1+|\mathcal{O}_i^{be}|}\right], \quad \delta_i^{be} = \ln\left[\frac{1+|\mathcal{O}_i^{be}|}{1+|\mathcal{O}_i^{bu}|}\right], \quad (2)$$

where δ_i^{bu} (δ_i^{be}) denotes bullish (bearish) sentiment index for stock

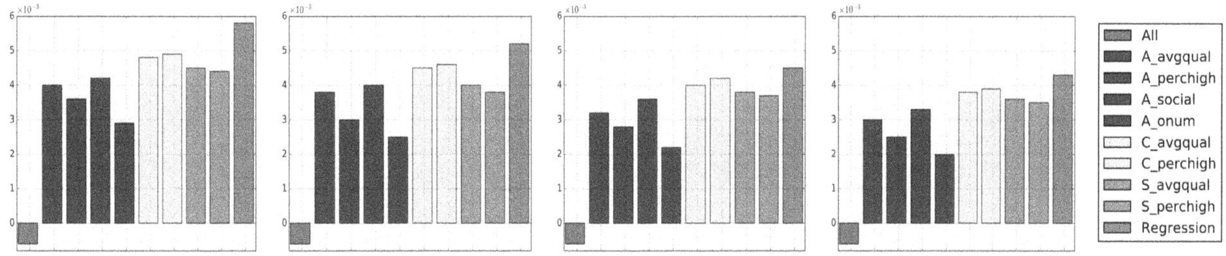

(a) k=5 (b) k=10 (c) k=20 (d) k=50 (e) labels

Figure 2: Performance comparison of recommended opinions. From left to right in order, the bars correspond to the average quality of all opinions in $\mathcal{O}_d$ (*All*), the average quality of $\mathcal{O}_d^{rec}$ by feature *A_avgqual*, *A_prechigh*, *A_social*, *A_onum*, *C_avgqual*, *C_prechigh*, *S_avgqual*, *S_prechigh*, and the average quality of $\mathcal{O}_d^{rec}$ by our regression model based on multiple features (*Regression*). The y-axis shows the average value of recommended opinions' performances (i.e., equation 4)

.

e_i while $\mathcal{O}_i^{be}$ ($\mathcal{O}_i^{be}$) is the set of opinions containing bullish (bearish) views on e_i. In other words, for each o in $\mathcal{O}_i^{bu}$ ($\mathcal{O}_i^{be}$), the investment views $\mathcal{V}^o$ should contain (e_i, l_i) and l_i is bullish (bearish). Obviously, if δ_i^{bu} is larger than δ_i^{be} (i.e., $|\mathcal{O}_i^{bu}| > |\mathcal{O}_i^{be}|$), we should consider to long e_i while if the δ_i^{be} is larger than δ_i^{bu} (i.e., $|\mathcal{O}_i^{be}| > |\mathcal{O}_i^{bu}|$), we should consider to short e_i. Moreover, if the difference between δ_i^{bu} and δ_i^{be} (i.e., $|\delta_i^{bu} - \delta_i^{be}|$) is larger, the views are more consistent and the rising (if $\delta_i^{bu} > \delta_i^{be}$) or falling (if $\delta_i^{be} > \delta_i^{bu}$) probability should also be large. Thus, for generating a portfolio, we could sort stocks in decreasing order of $|\delta_i^{bu} - \delta_i^{be}|$ and take the top k' ones as the portfolio suggestion. Finally, we long (short) the stocks if their bullish indexes are larger (smaller) than their bearish indexes.

In our work, we attempt to utilize the predicted qualities in portfolio recommendation by giving higher weights to views in high-quality opinions when we aggregate sentiment labels in opinions' investment views. We call this *quality-sensitive* portfolio recommendation. Note that in Equation (2), $|\mathcal{O}_i^{bu}|$ actually equals $\sum_{o\in\mathcal{O}_i^{bu}} 1$. Thus, by weighting views in o with $\hat{\mathcal{Q}}(o)$, the quality-sensitive aggregation for sentiment indexes should be

$$\delta_i^{bu} = \ln\left[\frac{1+\sum_{o\in\mathcal{O}_i^{bu}}\hat{\mathcal{Q}}(o)}{1+\sum_{o\in\mathcal{O}_i^{be}}\hat{\mathcal{Q}}(o)}\right],\ \delta_i^{be} = \ln\left[\frac{1+\sum_{o\in\mathcal{O}_i^{be}}\hat{\mathcal{Q}}(o)}{1+\sum_{o\in\mathcal{O}_i^{bu}}\hat{\mathcal{Q}}(o)}\right]. \tag{3}$$

4.2 Daily Investment Recommendation

Now, we discuss in detail how to perform opinion recommendation and portfolio recommendation on each tradable day. Thus, our framework recommends a set of high-quality opinions before the stock market opening time, in order for these opinions to help users determine their trading strategy. In addition, we recommend a set of stocks to users to trade. As a test case, in our work, we focus on the stocks traded at New York Stock Exchange (NYSE) and Nasdaq stock markets. The opening time of the stock markets is 9:30 am (Eastern Standard Time). We set the time to generate recommendations at 8:00 am. The recommendation procedure for k opinions and k'-stock portfolios is summarized by Algorithm 1 (assuming the recommendation is performed on day d).

Algorithm 1 Daily Investment Recommendation

Input:
  $\mathcal{E}_d$ = tradable stocks on day d
  $\mathcal{O}_d$ = opinions mentioning stocks in $\mathcal{E}_d$ and posted during from 8am on day $d-1$ to 8:00 am on day d
Output:
  k recommended opinions $\mathcal{O}_d^{rec}$
  a portfolio $\mathcal{E}_d^{rec} \subseteq \mathcal{E}_d$ consisting of k stocks

```
for all o_i ∈ O_d do
    calculate the features [x_1^i, x_2^i, ··· , x_n^i]
    estimate predicted quality Q̂(o_i) = f([x_1^i, x_2^i, ··· , x_n^i])
end for
O_d^rec = k opinions in O_d according to k highest Q̂(o_i) values
for all e_i ∈ E_d do
    calculate sentiment indexes δ_i^bu and δ_i^be
    calculate stock score s(e_i) = |δ_i^bu − δ_i^be|
end for
E_d^rec = k' stocks in E_d according to k' highest stock scores
```

5. EXPERIMENTS

5.1 Data

For experiments, we collect all messages posted in 2014 from the investor-based social media StockTwits. StockTwits users post short messages (limited to 140 characters) that include ideas or opinions on specific investments. Stock symbols in messages are preceded by a "CashTag" ($) (as Figure 1 shows). Here, we only use of StockTwits messages have at least one CashTag. Finally, the dataset we used contains 1,630,914 messages posted by 29,804 users and related to 5,541 stocks traded at NYSE and Nasdaq. Finally, we used the Yahoo! Finance API to crawl historical prices of stocks, used in Equation (1) and for evaluating effectiveness.

5.2 Experiments on Recommending Opinions

To generate $\mathcal{O}_d^{rec}$, we first predict qualities in $\mathcal{E}_d$. Specifically, we train a linear regression model [6] with {opinion, quality} pairs corresponding to the opinions posted on other days. After the regression model is trained and the qualities of opinions in $\mathcal{E}_d$ are predicted, $\mathcal{O}_d^{rec}$ is set as the opinions with the top k predicted qualities.

For each $\mathcal{O}_d^{rec}$, we evaluate its performance as the average quality of opinions in it:

$$\frac{1}{|\mathcal{O}_d^{rec}|}\sum_{o\in\mathcal{O}_d^{rec}} \mathcal{Q}(o). \tag{4}$$

Figure 2 presents the average performance of all $\mathcal{O}_d^{rec}$s generated on all tradable days in 2014. Besides the results corresponding to our model (multiple features + regression, denoted by *Regression*, we also show the average quality of all opinions in $\mathcal{E}_d$ (to see if the average quality of $\mathcal{O}_d^{rec}$ is larger than it) and the results of using

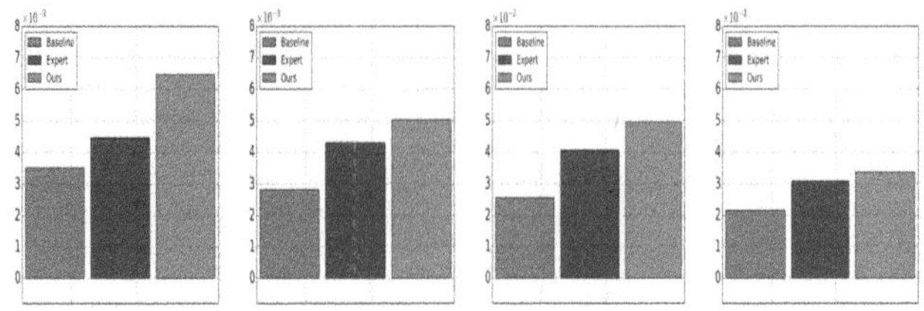

(a) k'=5 (b) k'=10 (c) k'=20 (d) k'=50

Figure 3: Comparison of recommended portfolios obtained by *Baseline* and *Expert* and our method (*Ours*). The y-axis shows the average value of recommended portfolios' performances (i.e., equation 5).

each of the features alone. To test each feature alone, we generate $\mathcal{O}_d^{rec}$ as opinions corresponding to k highest values based on each single feature. As Figure 2 shows, each of the proposed features could be used retrieve high-quality opinions to a different extent, since the average quality of opinions in $\mathcal{O}_d^{rec}$ corresponding to all features are larger than the average quality of all opinions. The best performance is achieved by our model (multiple features + regression).

5.3 Experiments on Recommending Portfolios

To generate $\mathcal{E}_d^{rec}$, we use conventional sentiment indexes (denoted as *Baseline*) used in previous work [3, 8, 5] (see Equation (2)) and our (quality-sensitive) sentiment indexes (denoted as *Ours*) corresponding to Equation (3) to construct portfolios (see Section 4.1 and Algorithm 1 for details). Moreover, as another baseline, we employ the author expertise model proposed in [1] to to generate expert-sensitive sentiment indexes (denoted as *Expert*, see [1] for details).

For evaluating $\mathcal{E}_d^{rec}$, we calculate the return rate obtained if we long the stocks for which opinions in $\mathcal{E}_d^{rec}$ give bullish recommendations and short the stocks for which opinions in $\mathcal{E}_d^{rec}$ give bearish suggestions. Specifically, let $\mathcal{E}_{d_{bu}}^{rec}$ ($\mathcal{E}_{d_{be}}^{rec}$) be the stocks that attract bullish (bearish) ballots from opinions in $\mathcal{E}_d^{rec}$. The performance of $\mathcal{E}_d^{rec}$ can be evaluated as

$$\frac{1}{|\mathcal{E}_d^{rec}|}\left(\sum_{e\in\mathcal{E}_{d_{bu}}^{rec}}\frac{p^f(e)-p^c(e)}{p^c(e)}+\sum_{e\in\mathcal{E}_{d_{be}}^{rec}}\frac{p^c(e)-p^f(e)}{p^c(e)}\right), \quad (5)$$

Figure 3 shows the average performance of all $\mathcal{E}_d^{rec}$s generated on all tradable days in 2014. We compare the performances corresponding to our method and other competitors (i.e., *Baseline* and *Expert*). The results show that our quality-sensitive method suggests the most profitable portfolios.

Besides, we also study the cumulative return obtained if we just trade stocks in portfolios recommended by our method and perform continuous trading from the beginning to the end of 2014. Specifically, from the first tradable day in 2014, we repeat the following procedure: Suppose money for trading is available on day d. Firstly, we long stocks in $\mathcal{E}_{d_{bu}}^{rec}$ and short stocks in $\mathcal{E}_{d_{be}}^{rec}$ for a week. After a week passes since day d, we sell stocks in $\mathcal{E}_{d_{bu}}^{rec}$ and buy back the borrowed stocks in $\mathcal{E}_{d_{be}}^{rec}$. Thus, money for trading will be available again on day $d+7$. In the next iteration of trading, d becomes $d+7$ and we perform trading again according to $\mathcal{E}_{d+7}^{rec}$. Figure 4 shows the cumulative gain after 39 such trading sessions. Here, we also include the cumulative return obtained if we trade on Dow Jones Industrial Average (DJIA) index, which simulates a portfolio of 30 significant stocks traded at NYSE and Nasdaq. We can see that, the return rates obtained by our portfolios are much higher than those

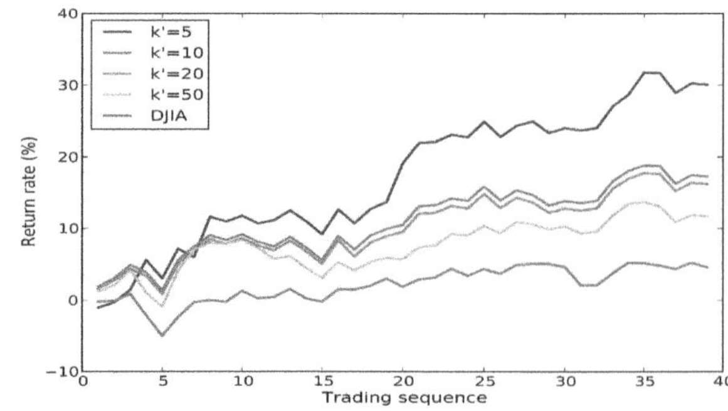

Figure 4: Cumulative return with recommended portfolios (in 2014).

by the DJIA index, proving that our portfolios consisted from stocks performing better than average. Also note that the return rate increases and that smaller values of k' give higher return. Specifically, for $k' = 5$, at the end of 2014, we could obtain a revenue of around 30%.

6. CONCLUSIONS

In this paper, we studied the problem of analyzing the qualities of investor opinions posted on social media. Moreover, we explore the use of predicted opinion qualities for opinion recommendation and portfolio recommendation. Experiments on a real-world dataset verify the effectiveness of our work in recommending high-quality investment opinions and profitable portfolios.

7. REFERENCES

[1] R. Bar-Haim, E. Dinur, R. Feldman, M. Fresko, and G. Goldstein. Identifying and following expert investors in stock microblogs. In *Proceedings of the Conference on Empirical Methods in Natural Language Processing (EMNLP)*, 2011.

[2] J. Heidemann, M. Klier, and F. Probst. Identifying key users in online social networks: A pagerank based approach. In *Proceedings of the International Conference on Information Systems (ICIS)*, 2010.

[3] C. Oh and O. Sheng. Investigating predictive power of stock micro blog sentiment in forecasting future stock price directional movement. In *Proceedings of the International Conference on Information Systems (ICIS)*, 2011.

[4] N. Oliveira, P. Cortez, and N. Areal. On the predictability of stock market behavior using stocktwits sentiment and posting volume. In *Progress in Artificial Intelligence*, pages 355–365. Springer, 2013.

[5] T. Rao and S. Srivastava. Analyzing stock market movements using twitter sentiment analysis. In *Proceedings of the International Conference on Advances in Social Networks Analysis and Mining (ASONAM)*, 2012.

[6] G. A. Seber and A. J. Lee. *Linear regression analysis*, volume 936. John Wiley & Sons, 2012.

[7] W. Tu, D. Cheung, and N. Mamoulis. Improving microblog rtrieval from exterior corpus by automatically constructing microblogging corpus. In *Proceedings of the AAAI Conference on Artificial Intelligence (AAAI)*, 2015.

[8] W. Tu, D. Cheung, and N. Mamoulis. Time-sensitive opinion mining for prediction. In *Proceedings of the AAAI Conference on Artificial Intelligence (AAAI)*, 2015.

[9] V. Vapnik. *The nature of statistical learning theory*. Springer Science & Business Media, 2013.

"Is Sven Seven?": A Search Intent Module for Children

Nevena Dragovic
Computer Science Dept.
Boise State University
Boise, Idaho, USA

Ion Madrazo Azpiazu
Computer Science Dept.
Boise State University
Boise, Idaho, USA

Maria Soledad Pera
Computer Science Dept.
Boise State University
Boise, Idaho, USA

{nevenadragovic, ionmadrazo, solepera}@boisestate.edu

ABSTRACT

The Internet is the biggest data-sharing platform, comprised of an immeasurable quantity of resources covering diverse topics appealing to users of all ages. Children shape tomorrow's society, so it is essential that this audience becomes agile with searching information. Although young users prefer well-known search engines, their lack of skill in formulating adequate queries and the fact that search tools were not designed explicitly with children in mind, can result in poor outcomes. The reasons for this include children's limited vocabulary, which makes it challenging to articulate information needs using short queries, or their tendency to create queries that are too long, which translates to few or irrelevant retrieved results. To enhance web search environments in response to children's behaviors and expectations, in this paper we discuss an initial effort to verify well-known issues, and identify yet to be explored ones, that affect children in formulating (natural language or keyword) queries. We also present a novel search intent module developed in response to these issues, which can seamlessly be integrated with existing search engines favored by children. The proposed module interprets a child's query and creates a shorter and more concise query to submit to a search engine, which can lead to a more successful search session. Initial experiments conducted using a sample of children queries validate the correctness of the proposed search intent module.

CCS Concepts

•**Information systems** → **Query intent;** *Web search engines;* •**Social and professional topics** → **Children;**

Keywords

Query Intent; Children; Search engines;

1. INTRODUCTION

The Web is an essential forum for gathering information for different purposes. To assist end users in locating materials from the Web, different tools have been developed. Among these tools, general-purpose search engines, such as Bing, Google, and Yahoo!, are the most prominent ones, as users of all ages turn to them on a daily basis to retrieve desired information. As one of the largest communities that search for online resources, children are introduced to the Web at increasingly young ages. Trends in the U.S. indicate that by age 5, *half* of all children will turn to the Web on the daily basis, a number that increases to *two-thirds* by age 8 [9]. While early exposure can help them build foundational skills vital in a knowledge-rich society, search tools were not designed with children in mind nor do retrieved results explicitly target children, which causes many of them to fail to complete successful searches [8]. Most engines do not explicitly support, or offer weak support, for children's inquiry approaches. This is important to address given that early experiences can affect attitudes in using the Web, skill development in making adequate use of resources for personal and educational interests, and the ability to leverage information and use it to make contributions into adulthood [14].

As described in the 2013 book, Search Engine Society, "Children growing up in the 21st century have only ever known a world in which search engines could be queried, and almost always provide some kind of an answer, even if it may not be the best one" [10]. However, like most adults, children struggle with describing their information needs in a concise query [6]. Moreover, they are known to sometimes use long natural language queries that can often lead to retrieving irrelevant resources [4]. To facilitate the search task, search engines offer query suggestions. Unfortunately, children often bypass suggested queries altogether, which could eliminate possible misspellings or better reflect their information needs. Even if children, as inexperienced users, struggle with stating the right queries to initiate successful searches, search engines are expected to retrieve relevant information in response to their requirements. While search intent modules have been developed to automatically generate queries that capture users' needs [11, 12], none of these specifically target children's queries. With that in mind, in this paper we introduce $QuIK$ (Query Intended for Kids), a simple, yet effective, search intent module tailored towards children ages 6-15. Its goal is to transform an initial children query Q into Q', a query that captures the intended meaning of Q. In accomplishing this task, we analyze the terms in Q to: (1) distinguish misspelled terms from the ones used by children that are not included in traditional dictionaries, (2) identify cultural references transmitted via mass media (children trendy terms), and (3) alter terms that

SIGIR '16, July 17-21, 2016, Pisa, Italy
© 2016 ACM. ISBN 978-1-4503-4069-4/16/07...$15.00
DOI: http://dx.doi.org/10.1145/2911451.2914738

could diminish the probability of a successful search session. Thereafter, *QuIK* identifies representative (updated) terms to be included in *Q*' which is submitted to Google, the preferred search engine for children [1].

The novelty of the proposed module is highlighted in its ability to modify children queries to initiate the retrieval of kid-related materials, which can lead to improving search engines' performance. The design of the proposed module explicitly considers different patterns kids use while searching the Web to adequately capture the intended meaning of their original queries. Furthermore, the proposed module has the ability to distinguish misspellings from terms commonly used by kids, as is the case of terms that refer to children trendy terms to which they are exposed on a daily basis (e.g., *Xbox*), emphasized terms (e.g., *aammaazziinngg* can indicate that something is very amazing), or diminutives (e.g., *daddy*). *QuIK* also handles long queries or questions, which is a must, given that children between 10 and 15 years old represent the largest group of users who tend to create natural language queries, some of which are in the form of a question [7]. Furthermore, by replacing an original query without imposing the burden on the child of analyzing the suggestions provided by search engines' "did you mean" feature (that eliminates misspellings from originally-submitted queries), *QuIK* considers children's habit to scroll pass the provided suggestions, due to the lack of visual cues [4]. To the best of our knowledge, no module that can be coupled with existing search engines can capture search intent exclusively from children's queries and regenerate queries on-the-fly to foster the retrieval of child-friendly results.

2. RELATED WORK

As described by Bilal et al. [2], to adequately serve children, search engines must address the fact that children are seldom successful in formulating succinct queries. In fact, researchers have observed that children tend to use long (natural language) queries, as opposed to keyword queries, when performing a web search [4]. Unfortunately, the longer the query, the less likely a web search engine can retrieve relevant resources in response [4] to it, which can be very frustrated for them. Search intent can help capture users' information needs by understanding the purpose behind the used words, which is important not only for children, but for all groups of users with a web search issue.

A number of studies [11, 12, 15] address the issue of search intent. Their strategies focus on: creating a hierarchical taxonomy using a tree to find representations of generic intents from user queries [15], examining bias between users' search intent and the query generated in each search session [11], or investigating query intent when users search for cognitive characteristics in documents [12]. Mentioned strategies, however, fail to specifically consider issues pertaining directly to children, which demonstrates a clear need for new modules that automatically create queries on their behalf. *QuIK* simultaneously addresses misspellings, queries with terms that children use but that are harder to match by search engines, purposely emphasized terms, and trendy topics that are more popular among children than among adults. Such topics are yet to be addressed in the literature.

3. QUIK, A SEARCH INTENT MODULE

To understand children's writing patterns along with the manner in which they search the Web, it is imperative to examine children query logs. Unfortunately, the Yahoo dataset used in [7] is not publically available, while other query logs available through Webscope[1] contain only the most popular queries among users, which do not give a real representation of child-formulated queries. Consequently, we consider children's search sessions extracted from the AOL query log following the strategy in [5]. These sessions (6471 queries), however, are outdated and lack references to trendy terms. Knowing this limitation, we also consider an alternative to query logs that captures recent content of interest to children and treat content (i.e., sentences) written by children as queries. In doing so, we identify common information needs, writing styles and issues that may influence the manner in which queries are formulated by kids. We relied on reviews (275004 sentences) written by elementary school-aged children archived at Spaghetti Book Club[2].

Based on the analysis of AOL and Spaghetti, we observed that 76% and 54% of the queries contained one or more terms[3] not recognized by WordNet[4], a large lexical database of English words. Deeper analysis allowed us to identify a number of patterns related to the way in which children express their information needs (see Figure 1). Children are not always proficient typists, and many look at the keyboard as they type. Unfortunately, looking down instead of up at the screen causes them to miss search engine query suggestions [4]. Given that *misspellings* negatively impact a search session and children tend to make more spelling mistakes than adults, correction is a must [4]. However, it is an imperative to differentiate misspelled words from words favored by children, including *diminutives* and *exaggerated* words. As described in [3], "diminutives are a characteristic of child-directed speech and diminutive suffixes are among the first morphemes that a child acquires and uses in his/her speech". Exaggerated words refer to intentionally misspelled terms to provide emphasis. Another characteristic of children search, is explicitly referencing *trendy* terms among their peers. Some of those terms can be treated as misspellings by search engines (e.g., Google suggests "*seven*" instead of "*Sven*" a character in Frozen, a popular Disney movie) which causes poor retrieval of desired resources.

To better understand children's information needs, *QuIK* infers the search intent from a child's query Q and automatically replaces it with a shorter, more concise query Q' that can lead to better search outcomes. To do so, *QuIK* analyzes every non-stop term t in Q to determine if it is a good candidate to capture the intended meaning of Q and thus should be included in Q'. To verify if t is misspelled, *QuIK* uses the popular Apache Lucene SpellChecker[5]. However, not all $t's$ (not recognized by WordNet) are treated as misspellings, if t ends with a common diminutive suffix, we retrieve the root form of t by eliminates last two letters of t. If t is an exaggerated term, then its true meaning is determined by eliminating multiple repeating characters, which generates a new, normalized version of t. Furthermore, it is

[1]https://webscope.sandbox.yahoo.com/

[2]https://wordnet.princeton.edu/

[3]For practical reasons, stopwords in AOL and Spaghetti were removed, terms were lemmatized and URLs were ignored, since search engines adequately handle queries including the names of popular sites.

[4]http://www.spaghettibookclub.org/

[5]https://lucene.apache.org/

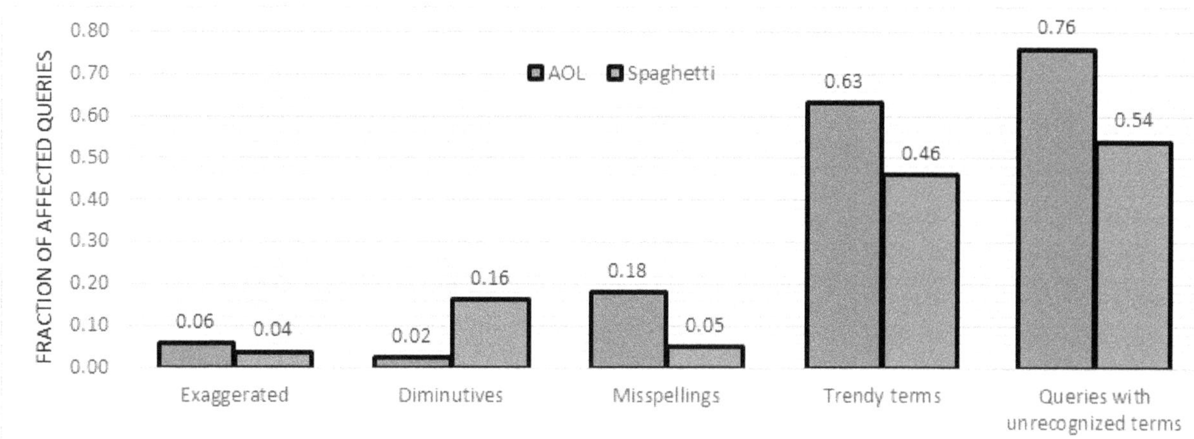

Figure 1: Writing patterns observed on AOL and Spaghetti data sources

very important to capture trendy terms and enable $QuIK$ to understand their significance and provide relevant results for children. Hence, $QuIK$ considers existing categories on well-known websites with children content (e.g., Amazon[6] and Common Sense Media[7]) to determine if a t is misspelled or if it is in fact a trendy, child-related term. We cannot assume that kids will use only child-friendly vocabulary in formulating Q. To address this issue, we study term associations and consider terms related to the ones in Q that can steer the search towards retrieving child-related resources. For example, a query that uses the term *doctor* instead of *surgeon* is better tailored towards the retrieval of suitable children content, since the former is a simpler term. To precisely understand the complexity of terms used in queries, we created a children's dictionary CD. CD includes close to 100,000 lemmatized, non-stop words, extracted from texts retrieved from a sample of various children-related websites (where content is written for and by children), such as Long Long Time Ago, KidPub and Teenreads. If t is contained in CD, then $QuIK$ treats it as child-related, otherwise it turns to WordNet to find a more suitable term by selecting one of t' hypernyms and use it instead of t[8].

After each t in Q has been updated based on the identified patterns, if needed, or recognized as a trendy term, $QuIK$ proceeds to create a new, "cleaner" version of Q. Given the results from previous studies, we know that general audiences use just 2.3 words on average for a query generation [13], while the number increases to 3.8 when considering children [5]. For this reason, $QuIK$ uses the 3 most representative terms to correctly capture the information need expressed in Q. To quantify the degree to which each non-trendy term t in Q expresses children's information need, we calculate a score for t using the content retrieved from children-related sites (used in the creation of the children dictionary), as shown in Equation 1.

$$RepScore(t) = \frac{\sum_{d \in C} \frac{freq_{t,d}}{|d|}}{|C|} \quad (1)$$

[6]http://www.amazon.com/

[7]https://www.commonsensemedia.org/

[8]If the returned term does not belong to CD, then t remains unchanged.

where C represents a collection of documents of size $|C|$, d is a document in C, $|d|$ is the number of words in d, and $freq_{t,d}$ represents frequency of occurrence of t in d.

In creating Q', $QuIK$ gives priority to children trendy terms in order to better understand the search intent. The rest of the terms to be included in Q' are the terms in Q that yield the highest *RepScore*(t). Lastly, Q' is submitted to Google to initiate a search on behalf of a child for Q.

4. QUIK IN ACTION

We applied $QuIK$ on 55000 queries from Spaghetti (created as discussed in Section 3 and disjoint from the set of queries used for development purposes) and observed that the number of queries with one or more words non-recognized by WordNet decreased from 16% to 2.3%. At the same time, we submitted sampled children queries to Google that included a number of the aforementioned identified patterns. We observed that when submitting queries including exaggerated and trendy terms, Google retrieves no results (see Figure 2). Furthermore, after submitting "sven movie", Google provided suggestions such as "seven movie online", "seven movie ending", "seven movie deaths" and "seven movie trailer". As we can see, none of these suggestions is kid-related, and obviously does not pertain to the popular Disney movie Frozen. These examples provide further evidence on the need for modules such as $QuIK$, which are tailored towards satisfying children's needs.

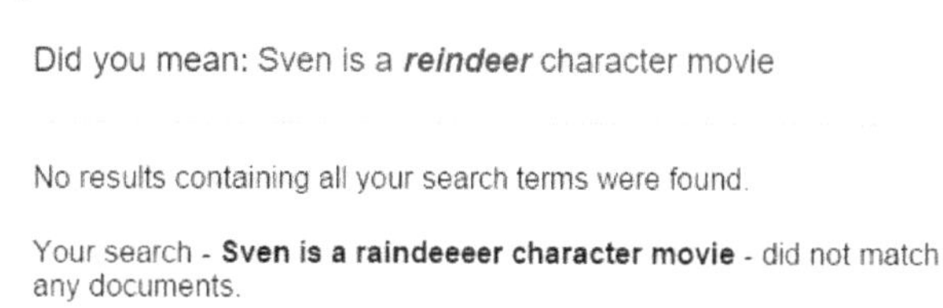

Figure 2: Screen capture of Google in response to the query "Sven is a raindeeeer character movie"

5. INITIAL ASSESSMENT

We conducted an initial assessment to evaluate both (i) the quality of the updated queries generated by $QuIK$ given an initial child-formulated query and (ii) the degree to which

QuIK-generated queries influence the retrieval of documents relevant to children. Due to the lack of benchmark datasets, we created a survey in which, for a given child-generated query *CQ*, we asked appraisers to (1) choose the query reformulation that best captures the intended meaning of *CQ* and (2) choose the document that is the most relevant given *CQ*. Among the provided query reformulations, we included (in random order) the *QuIK*-generated query for *CQ* as well as two query suggestions provided by Google[9] for *CQ*. Similarly, among the provided results, we included (in random order) the top-two ones retrieved using *CQ* as well as the top-retrieved one using *QuIK*-generated query for *CQ*. We asked 25 elementary-school educators to complete the surveys using a small sample of children queries (including "Sven is a reindeer character in a movie" and "how does the baby kengaroos stay inside the pouch"[10]).

Based on the collected evaluations (the results of which are summarized in Table 1), we observed that in 59% of the responses, queries generated by *QuiK* were selected as the ones that best capture the intended meaning of a given children query. Moreover, 88% of the responses indicated that *QuIK*-generated queries lead to the retrieval of relevant resources, as opposed to resources retrieved by Google in response to the original given query.

	QuIK	Google
Favored search intent	0.59	0.41
Favored relevant resources	0.88	0.12

Table 1: Initial assessment of *QuIK*

6. CONCLUSION AND FUTURE WORK

We discussed an initial analysis conducted to identify common struggles children face when expressing information needs while searching the Web. Knowing that children represent a large group of online users, and the importance that search outcomes have on their development, it is crucial to provide more attention to this task. While a number of studies identify issues and flaws of search engines while interacting with young users, very few research works explicitly focus on solving these problem, which is why research pertaining towards search intent modules tailored for this group is a must. *QuIK* simultaneously considers newly discovered and well-known patterns identified in queries created by children, and creates queries that capture the information needs meant to be expressed by children.

Our discussed efforts represent the groundwork of an in-depth research. We plan to extend initial work by analyzing children query logs, and simultaneously addressing new (and already identified) issues pertaining to children querying to further enhance the design of proposed search intent module. A limitation of *QuIK* is not considering extremely short queries often generated by young users. This is sometimes insufficient to retrieve needed information and as such creates more opportunity for improvement for *QuIK*. Another opportunity for *QuIK's* enhancement is understanding the ambiguity of users' search intent during a session. This is important given that the same query may target different information for different users. As mentioned in Section 5, further assessment is a must. We plan on conducting online evaluations with a greater number of appraisers (including teachers and children) complemented with measuring the effect of performance of search engines coupled with *QuIK* to enhance Web search environment.

[9]We consider Google for comparison purposes, since, as previously stated, is the search engine of choice for children.

[10]Any misspelled terms included in the queries provided in the survey were reproduced as per the original children queries.

7. REFERENCES

[1] D. Bilal. Ranking, relevance judgment, and precision of information retrieval on children's queries: Evaluation of google, yahoo!, bing, yahoo! kids, and ask kids. *JASIST*, 63(9):1879–1896, 2012.

[2] D. Bilal and R. Ellis. Evaluating leading web search engines on children's queries. In *Human-Computer Interaction. Users and Applications*, pages 549–558. Springer, 2011.

[3] I. Dabasinškienž. Intimacy, familiarity and formality: Diminutives in modern lithuanian. *Lituanus*, 55(1), 2009.

[4] A. Druin, E. Foss, L. Hatley, E. Golub, M. L. Guha, J. Fails, and H. Hutchinson. How children search the internet with keyword interfaces. In *IDC*, pages 89–96, 2009.

[5] S. Duarte Torres, D. Hiemstra, and P. Serdyukov. Query log analysis in the context of information retrieval for children. In *ACM SIGIR*, pages 847–848, 2010.

[6] S. Duarte Torres, D. Hiemstra, I. Weber, and P. Serdyukov. Query recommendation for children. In *ACM CIKM*, pages 2010–2014, 2012.

[7] S. Duarte Torres, I. Weber, and D. Hiemstra. Analysis of search and browsing behavior of young users on the web. *ACM TWEB*, 8(2):7, 2014.

[8] E. Foss, A. Druin, R. Brewer, P. Lo, L. Sanchez, E. Golub, and H. Hutchinson. Children's search roles at home: Implications for designers, researchers, educators, and parents. *JASIST*, 63(3):558–573, 2012.

[9] A. L. Gutnick, M. Robb, L. Takeuchi, J. Kotler, L. Bernstein, and M. Levine. Always connected: The new digital media habits of young children. Joan Ganz Cooney Center at Sesame Workshop, 2011.

[10] A. Halavais. *Search engine society*. John Wiley & Sons, 2013.

[11] B. Hu, Y. Zhang, W. Chen, G. Wang, and Q. Yang. Characterizing search intent diversity into click models. In *WWW*, pages 17–26, 2011.

[12] M. P. Kato, T. Yamamoto, H. Ohshima, and K. Tanaka. Investigating users' query formulations for cognitive search intents. In *ACM SIGIR*, pages 577–586, 2014.

[13] T. Lau and E. Horvitz. *Patterns of search: analyzing and modeling web query refinement*. Springer, 1999.

[14] N. Vanderschantz, A. Hinze, and S. J. Cunningham. "sometimes the internet reads the question wrong": Children's search strategies & difficulties. *Am. Soc. Info. Sci. Tech.*, 51(1):1–10, 2014.

[15] X. Yin and S. Shah. Building taxonomy of web search intents for name entity queries. In *WWW*, pages 1001–1010, 2010.

Is This Your Final Answer? Evaluating the Effect of Answers on Good Abandonment in Mobile Search

Kyle Williams[†], Julia Kiseleva[‡], Aidan C. Crook[Γ], Imed Zitouni[Γ],
Ahmed Hassan Awadallah[Γ], Madian Khabsa[Γ]
[†]The Pennsylvania State University, University Park, PA 16802, USA
[‡]Eindhoven University of Technology, Eindhoven, NL
[Γ]Microsoft, One Microsoft Way, Redmond, WA 98052, USA
kwilliams@psu.edu, j.kiseleva@tue.nl,
{aidan.crook, izitouni, hassanam, madian.khabsa}@microsoft.com

ABSTRACT

Answers on mobile search result pages have become a common way to attempt to satisfy users without them needing to click on search results. Many different types of answers exist, such as weather, flight and currency answers. Understanding the effect that these different answer types have on mobile user behavior and how they contribute to satisfaction is important for search engine evaluation. We study these two aspects by analyzing the logs of a commercial search engine and through a user study. Our results show that user click, abandonment and engagement behavior differs depending on the answer types present on a page. Furthermore, we find that satisfaction rates differ in the presence of different answer types with simple answer types, such as time zone answers, leading to more satisfaction than more complex answers, such as news answers. Our findings have implications for the study and application of user satisfaction for search systems.

1. INTRODUCTION

Mobile search has seen explosive growth in recent years. For instance, in 2013 it was estimated that 63% of Americans used their mobile phones to go online in comparison to only 31% in 2009 [5]. With this growth in mobile use, search engines have had to adapt to better suit user needs and behavior, which have been shown to be different on mobile devices [8, 10]. For instance, previous research has shown that mobile users may formulate queries in such a way so as to increase the likelihood of them being directly satisfied by the SERP [10] and that mobile queries differ from traditional desktop queries in being shorter and in their intents [8].

Search engines have had to adapt in order to accommodate these differences and one way they have done this is by showing answers on the Search Engine Results Page (SERP), such as answers about weather, the time, and sports scores. These answers typically appear in small boxes that appear on the SERP and contain factual information. For instance, Figure 1 shows a mobile answer for the query *$134 in pounds*. This mobile answer has the ability to satisfy a user who is interested in performing a currency conversion without having to click on, say, the first search result, which would take them to a currency conversion webpage. Thus, one of the effects of including these answers on a SERP is that users may no longer need to click on search results in order to satisfy their information need. However, most approaches to modeling and measuring user satisfaction have been based on user click behavior [6, 7] and, traditionally, a lack of clicks on a SERP has been seen as a negative indication of search result quality and the phenomenon has been labeled query abandonment [11]. However, recently there has been increasing awareness that query abandonment can be good [1, 3, 10, 11] in what is referred to as "good abandonment." In these cases, the user abandoned the query not because they were dissatisfied with the results but because the SERP satisfied the user without them needing to click on any search results. Previous research has estimated an upper bound for good abandonment on mobile devices of 54.8%, compared to only 31.8% on PC devices [10].

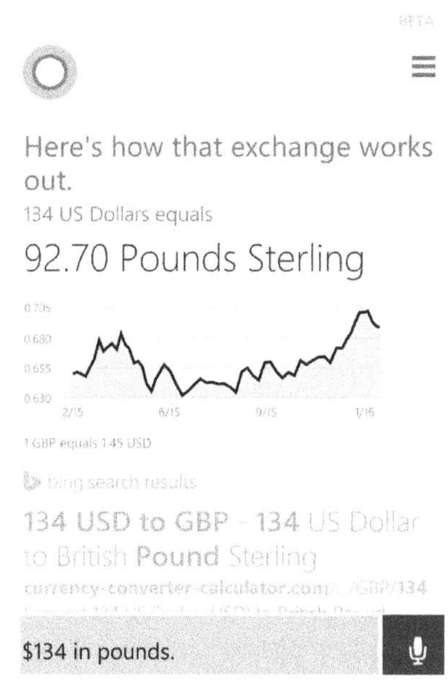

Figure 1: An example of a mobile SERP, showing an answer triggered in response to a currency conversion query.

SIGIR '16, July 17-21, 2016, Pisa, Italy
 ISBN 978-1-4503-4069-4/16/07...$15.00
DOI: http://dx.doi.org/10.1145/2911451.2914736

Furthermore, previous research has also shown that factual answers on a SERP were responsible for 56% of the satisfaction from abandoned queries in mobile search [12]. Thus, it is clear that a relationship exists between mobile answers, abandonment, and satisfaction. However, to date, most research investigating answers on mobile devices have not differentiated among answer types and investigated how the answer type affects abandonment behavior. We hypothesize that it may be useful to take the answer type into consideration when developing a metric to assess abandonment in the presence of answers on a mobile SERP based on the belief that not all answer types contribute equally to good abandonment. Thus, in this study, we choose to empirically investigate the relationship between answer types and abandonment behavior. In doing so, we seek to answer the following two research questions:

> **RQ1:** *How does the presence of different answer types affect user click behavior and abandonment?*

> **RQ2:** *How do different answer types affect satisfaction in abandoned queries?*

To answer our research questions, we conduct a large scale analysis of the logs of a commercial search engine and also analyze satisfaction ratings gathered in a controlled user study. To our knowledge, this is the first work to investigate the relationship between answer types and good abandonment in mobile search.

2. RELATED WORK

This paper extends a long line of work investigating satisfaction in search [1, 3, 7, 11]. Previous work has shown how gesture features can be used to differentiate between good and bad abandonment in mobile search [12]. However, while the cited work showed that answers were a large driver of good abandonment, it did not investigate the effect that different answers types have on satisfaction as we do in this study. Chilton and Teevan [2] show how users interact with different types of answers in desktop search, where interaction specifically focused on click behavior. It was found that, as expected, answers reduced interaction with the rest of the SERP, which the authors refer to as *cannibalization*. Our work is similar to the cited work in that it seeks to understand the relationship between answers and user interactions. However, whereas the cited work focuses on the desktop, we focus on mobile search. Furthermore, we go further than the cited work in that we empirically evaluate the relationship between answer types and satisfaction. In [10] it was shown how mobile users often construct queries in such a way so as to be directly satisfied by the SERP. Furthermore, in [4] it was shown that high quality SERPs lead to increased satisfaction and good abandonment and answers are one way of potentially increasing the quality of SERPs and thus good abandonment. Lagun et al. [9] use viewport and eye-tracking to measure user engagement in mobile search and studied the effect of having relevant/irrelevant answers on a mobile SERP. Our work is similar in studying the effect of answers on a mobile SERP; however, it differs in that we attempt to understand how different answer types affect satisfaction and abandonment behavior.

3. ANSWERS AND BEHAVIOR METRICS

As previously mentioned, we hypothesize that the answer type, such as weather, time, etc., has an effect on abandonment and satisfaction. Thus, we begin by describing the answer types that we investigate in this study and also describe the metrics that we use.

3.1 Answer Types

Answers are triggered by the search engine in response to certain query intents and query types. In this study, we consider the following set of answer types, which were selected due to their frequency in search impressions, their variety and their use in previous studies evaluating answers on non-mobile SERPs [2].

1. **Math** An answer to a math question, such as 2×4
2. **Currency** A currency conversion answer
3. **Dictionary** A dictionary definition
4. **Finance** Financial information about a company
5. **Flight Status** The status of a flight
6. **News** News related to the query
7. **Package Tracking** Tracking information for the query
8. **Phonebook** Contact information
9. **Reference** An inline reference fact
10. **Show Times** Show times related to the query, e.g., movie show times
11. **Sports** Information about sports teams, such as scores
12. **Timezone** The time in a specified time zone
13. **Twitter** Posts from Twitter
14. **Translation** A translation of the query
15. **Weather** The weather forecast in the specified region

3.2 Metrics

We define three metrics that we use to describe user behavior on the SERP in the presence of answers. We are specifically interested in how answers affect good abandonment and thus we define metrics that focus on user click behavior or lack thereof. We denote the set of answer types as A. For each answer type, $a \in A$, we define the click rate (CR) for answer type a as as:

$$CR_a = \frac{\sum_s^S \mathbf{1}_{S_a}(s)click(s)}{\sum_s^S \mathbf{1}_{S_a}(i)}, \tag{1}$$

where S is the set of SERP impressions sampled from the log, S_a is the set of SERPs containing answer type a, $\mathbf{1}_{S_a}(s)$ is an indicator function indicating membership of s in $\boldsymbol{S_a}$, and $click(s)$ is equal to 1 if SERP s received a click and 0 otherwise. This metric captures the rate that users click on SERPs containing answer type a. From this, we define the abandonment rate (AR) for answer type a as:

$$AR_a = 1 - CR_a. \tag{2}$$

This metric captures the rate at which users abandon SERPs containing answer type a.

We also define an engagement rate (ER) for answer type a as the rate at which the actual answer on the SERP is clicked on. First, we calculate the average number of clicks that SERPs with answer type a receive as:

$$AvgClicks_{S_a} = \frac{\sum_s^S \mathbf{1}_{S_a}(s)TotalClicks(s)}{\sum_s^S \mathbf{1}_{S_a}(s)}, \tag{3}$$

where $TotalClicks(s)$ is the number of clicks on SERP s. We also calculate the average number of direct clicks that answer type a receives on the answer itself as:

$$AvgClicks_a = \frac{\sum_s^S \mathbf{1}_{\mathbf{S}_a}(s) TotalAnswerClicks(s)}{\sum_s^S \mathbf{1}_{\mathbf{S}_a}(s)}, \quad (4)$$

where $TotalAnswerClicks(s)$ is the number of clicks on the clickable components of the answer box in SERP s. We then define the ER for answer type a as:

$$ER_a = \frac{AvgClicks_a}{AvgClicks_{\mathbf{S}_a}}. \quad (5)$$

Thus the engagement rate captures the extent to which page clicks are engagements with the answer.

4. ANSWER EFFECT ON BEHAVIOR

The previous section described the answer types that we consider in this study when evaluating abandonment and also defined the metrics that we consider. In this section, we use these metrics to assess how user behavior in terms of clicks, abandonment, and engagement differs in the presence of different answer types.

4.1 Large Scale Log Sample

We perform our analysis on a large scale sample of mobile search logs from a commercial search engine. We sample over 20 million mobile impressions from a week during June 2015. These impressions come from about 9 million sessions and 1 million users. Each impression is associated with anonymized information about the query and session, information about the SERP elements that were visible, such as answers and organic search results, and information about the click behavior of the user. We use this dataset to perform a large-scale analysis of behavior for different answer types.

4.2 Results

Figure 2 shows the click rate (CR) and abandonment rate (AR) for different types of answers on the mobile SERP. In the figure we observe different click and abandonment behavior depending on the answer type. For instance, we notice from Figure 2 that pages that contain answers, such as *package tracking*, *phonebook*, *news*, *math*, and *show times* have relatively high click rates ranging from 59% to 93%, meaning that people often click on pages containing these types of answers. This is perhaps not surprising since information needs related to news, package tracking, and show times, often require the user to perform additional navigation in order to fully satisfy their information need. By contrast, it can also be seen from Figure 2 that pages containing answers related to *currency*, *finance*, *dictionary*, and *time zones* experience relatively low click rates ranging from 14% to 32% implying high abandonment rates from 68% to 86%. As was the case with answer types that led to high click rates, the fact that pages with these types of answers experience relatively high abandonment rates is not surprising since the answers satisfy simple and straightforward information needs. The evidence here suggests that, when evaluating abandonment, it is useful to take into consideration the type of information present on the SERP. For instance, when abandonment happens on a SERP that usually has a high click rate, that may suggest that the user was not satisfied. By contrast, abandonment on a SERP that usually has a high abandonment rate may not indicate dissatisfaction.

Engagement rates for different answer types are shown in Figure 3. As can be seen from the figure, some answer types dominate the SERP page clicks or, to use the language of [2], the answers

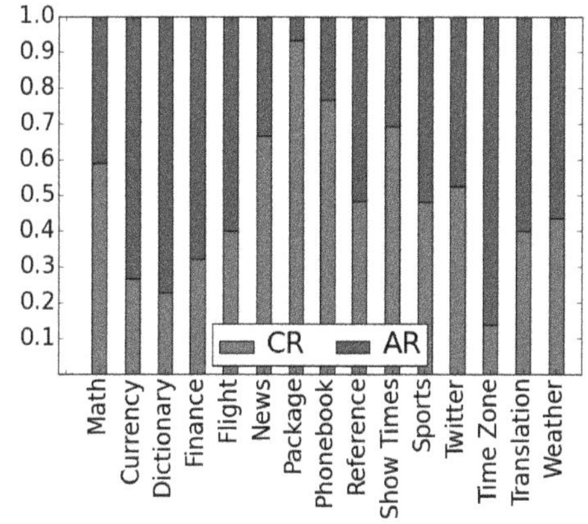

Figure 2: Click rate (CR) and abandonment rate (AR) for different answers on mobile SERPs.

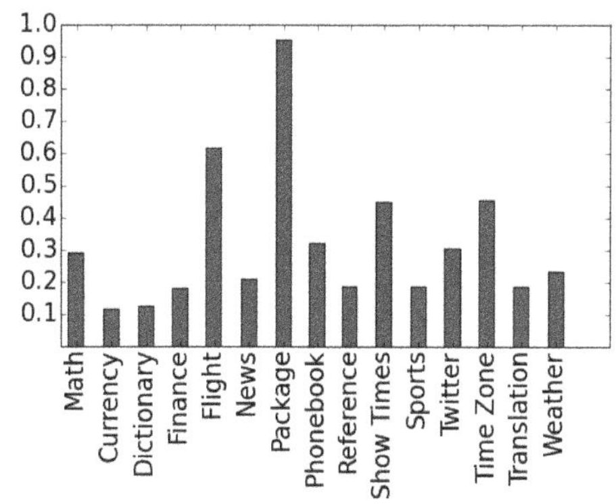

Figure 3: Engagement Rate (ER) for different answers on mobile SERPs.

cannibalize the clicks from the rest of the SERP. For instance, the answer engagement rate on pages containing a *package tracking* answer is 95%, indicating that users likely had to engage with the answer to satisfy their information needs. By contrast, for answer types that had high abandonment rates, the engagement rates are relatively low indicating that not much information is gained by engaging with the answer. Thus we have an answer to **RQ1:** *How does the presence of different answer types affect user click behavior and abandonment?* The data shows that user behavior differs depending on answer types and suggests that it is worth further investigating the relationship between answer presence and satisfaction since some answers require clicks for satisfaction, whereas other answers are able to satisfy a user without them needing to click. We investigate this further in the next section.

5. ANSWER EFFECT ON ABANDONMENT

The previous section showed how different answer types on the SERP lead to different abandonment behavior. However, are these abandonment differences good or bad? In this section, we analyze labeled data in order to try and answer this question.

5.1 Dataset

We perform our analysis on a dataset gathered through a controlled user study. We briefly describe the dataset in this section with a more complete description presented in [12]. 60 participants were recruited from the United States of which 25% were female and the remainder male. The mean age of participants was

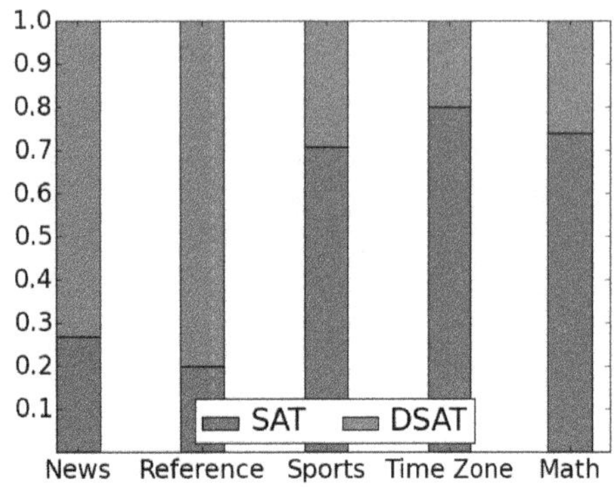

Figure 4: SAT and DSAT rating associated with the different answer types gathered in the user study.

25.5 ($\pm$5.4) years and the user study included 5 information seeking tasks, which were designed to increase the likelihood of good abandonment [12]. At the end of the tasks, the users were asked to provide a satisfaction ratings. The dataset contains a total of 607 queries of which 576 were classified as abandoned since they received no clicks. Since this dataset involved a controlled user study experiment, not all of the answer types described in Section 3.1 were present. Thus, we only focus on the following subset of answer types: *news, reference, time zone, sports, math* with frequencies of 62, 5, 5, 14, and 19, respectively. After filtering out queries that did not trigger these answer types, we retained 105 queries.

5.2 Results

For each answer type that appeared for the queries in the data described above, we measure the SAT and DSAT rates. As can be seen in Figure 4, we observe different SAT and DSAT rates for different answer types. For instance, the presence of *time zone, sports*, and *math* answer types are all associated with relatively high SAT rates in the data, with all being above 70%. By contrast, the SAT rates in the presence of news and reference answers are both below 30%. Thus, there is evidence that the presence of different answer types may affect satisfaction. Though the data are drawn from different sources and under different circumstances, it is also interesting to observe the relationship between the SAT rates in Figure 4 and the abandonment rate in Figure 2. For instance, mobile SERPs containing *sports* and *reference* answers both have abandonment rates of 52%, but very different SAT rates of 71% and 20%, respectively. Similarly, mobile SERPs containing *math* and *news* answers have somewhat similar abandonment rates of 41% and 33%, but very different SAT rates of 74% and 27%, respectively. This is in contrast to, say, SERPs containing *timezone* and *math* answers, which have very different abandonment rates of 86% and 41%, but similar SAT rates of 80% and 74%, respectively. As an example of bad abandonment, SERPs with *reference* answers experience an abandonment rate of 52% in Figure 2 and a satisfaction rate of only 20%. Thus most of the abandonment is bad. The findings in this section allow us to begin answering **RQ2:** *How do different answer types affect satisfaction in abandoned queries?* It is clear that user behavior and whether it indicates good or bad abandonment is influenced by the answer types seen by users. The reason for this is that, as shown in Figures 2 and 3, different answers lead to different user behavior and some answers require clicks, whereas others do not. Thus, we argue that any evaluation of satisfaction and abandonment in the presence of mobile answers should take the answer type and its properties into consideration.

6. CONCLUSIONS AND FUTURE WORK

We investigated the effect that different types of mobile answers have on good abandonment. Similar to the desktop case [2], it was shown how user behavior differs in the presence of different answer types in terms of clicks and answer engagement. Furthermore, it was shown how the rates of satisfaction differ for answer types that have similar abandonment rates, thereby showing that the answer type influences whether abandonment is good or bad.

It is interesting to hypothesize why this may be the case; we propose two areas for further investigation. (1) Ambiguity in query intent – if the query intent is unambiguous (as is the case in a math or time zone queries) then an informational answer is more likely to satisfy the user than if the query intent is ambiguous, such as a query about a place or celebrity, where the intent could vary from factual information to topical news. (2) The ability of an answer to fully address the interpreted intent - e.g., answering an inquiry on the height of Mount Everest can be more succinctly presented than a query for the latest news on the election. Modeling the likelihood of good abandonment in terms of properties of the query intent, as opposed to the rendered answer types, will be important in enabling future experimentation and improvement of answers that attempt to satisfy the underlying intent without necessitating a click.

Our study does have some limitations. For instance, user behavior in response to an answer is largely related to answer design in terms of display, ranking, etc. By considering answer type we effectively seek to capture some of these properties but acknowledge the limitation. Also, the frequency of the reference and time zone answers was relatively low in the dataset presented in Section 5.1.

In summary, this paper has shown that answer types are relevant in SAT measurement and we believe it will be useful to account for the underlying reason that different answer types appear to influence SAT on abandoned pages. However, answers should be considered alongside other features, such as gestures and features from the query and session. This is especially the case for answer types that achieve relatively equal levels of clicks and abandonment.

References

[1] M. S. Bernstein, J. Teevan, S. Dumais, D. Liebling, and E. Horvitz. Direct answers for search queries in the long tail. In *CHI*, pages 237–246, 2012.

[2] L. B. Chilton and J. Teevan. Addressing people's information needs directly in a web search result page. In *WWW*, pages 27–36, 2011.

[3] A. Chuklin and P. Serdyukov. Potential good abandonment prediction. In *WWW*, pages 485–486, 2012.

[4] A. Chuklin and P. Serdyukov. Good abandonments in factoid queries. In *WWW*, pages 483–484, 2012.

[5] M. Duggan and A. Smith. Cell Internet Use 2013, 2013. URL http://www.pewinternet.org/2013/09/16/cell-internet-use-2013/.

[6] S. Fox, K. Karnawat, M. Mydland, S. Dumais, and T. White. Evaluating implicit measures to improve web search. *ACM Transactions on Information Systems*, 23(2):147–168, 2005.

[7] A. Hassan, R. Jones, and K. L. Klinkner. Beyond dcg: User behavior as a predictor of successful search. *WSDM*, pages 221–230, 2010.

[8] M. Kamvar, M. Kellar, R. Patel, and Y. Xu. Computers and iphones and mobile phones, oh my! In *WWW*, pages 801–810, 2009.

[9] D. Lagun, C.-H. Hsieh, D. Webster, and V. Navalpakkam. Towards better measurement of attention and satisfaction in mobile search. *SIGIR*, pages 113–122, 2014.

[10] J. Li, S. Huffman, and A. Tokuda. Good abandonment in mobile and pc internet search. In *SIGIR*, pages 43–50, 2009.

[11] Y. Song, X. Shi, R. White, and A. H. Awadallah. Context-aware web search abandonment prediction. In *SIGIR*, pages 93–102, 2014.

[12] K. Williams, J. Kiseleva, I. Zitouni, A. C. Crook, A. H. Awadallah, and M. Khabsa. Detecting good abandonment in mobile search. In *WWW*, pages 495–505, 2016.

Jointly Modeling Review Content and Aspect Ratings for Review Rating Prediction

Zhipeng Jin[1,2], Qiudan Li[1], Daniel D. Zeng[1,2,3], YongCheng Zhan[3], Ruoran Liu[1,2], Lei Wang[1], Hongyuan Ma[4]
[1] The State Key Laboratory of Management and Control for Complex Systems,
Institute of Automation, Chinese Academy of Sciences, Beijing 100190, China
[2] University of Chinese Academy of Sciences, Beijing, China
[3] Department of Management Information Systems, University of Arizona, Tucson, Arizona, USA
[4] CNCERT/CC, Beijing, China
{jinzhipeng2013, qiudan.li, dajun.zeng, liuruoran2016, l.wang}@ia.ac.cn,
yongchengzhan@email.arizona.edu, mahongyuan@foxmail.com

ABSTRACT
Review rating prediction is of much importance for sentiment analysis and business intelligence. Existing methods work well when aspect-opinion pairs can be accurately extracted from review texts and aspect ratings are complete. The challenges of improving prediction accuracy are how to capture the semantics of review content and how to fill in the missing values of aspect ratings. In this paper, we propose a novel review rating prediction method, which improves the prediction accuracy by capturing deep semantics of review content and alleviating data missing problem of aspect ratings. The method firstly learns the latent vector representation of review content using skip-thought vectors, a state-of-the-art deep learning method, then, the missing values of aspect ratings are filled in based on users' history reviewing behaviors, finally, a novel optimization framework is proposed to predict the review rating. Experimental results on two real-world datasets demonstrate the efficacy of the proposed method.

General Terms
Algorithms, Design, Experimentation

Keywords
Review Rating Prediction; Skip-thought Vectors; Aspect Rating; Data Missing

1. INTRODUCTION
With the rapid development of e-commerce, abundant product reviews available on the Web have become a valuable source for consumers and organizations. Given a dataset of customer reviews, rating predictors can learn and predict the rating of a target product by a customer[1]. Horrigan[2] pointed out that consumers are willing to pay from 20% to 99% more to buy a product whose rating is 5-star than 4-star. Companies have more fine-grained requirements for keeping track of product quality. Therefore, review rating prediction is of much importance for sentiment analysis and business intelligence, because it enables the market to estimate how satisfied a customer will be with a product.

SIGIR '16, July 17-21, 2016, Pisa, Italy.

DOI: http://dx.doi.org/10.1145/2911451.2914692

Review content and aspect rating play important roles in predicting review ratings[3,4], where the former includes the semantics and users' opinion and sentiment, and the latter reflects users' feelings on more specific aspects of a product. [5] used a linear regression to learn the user's specific aspect preference extracted from the review content, and predicted the overall review rating. [1] improved the accuracy of rating prediction using feature words extracted from customer reviews to reduce the dimension of the feature vector. These methods work well when aspect-opinion pairs can be accurately extracted from review texts and aspect ratings are complete. However, this is often difficult to implement by relying only on natural language processing techniques or other corpora such as WordNet[1]. Furthermore, in a real scenario, aspect ratings are optional for users, the incomplete aspect ratings will reduce prediction accuracy. To solve these problems, in this paper we propose a novel method for review rating prediction.

Recently, deep learning has been a hot research topic and successfully applied to sentiment analysis and natural language processing. The key aspect of deep learning is that it automatically learns features from raw data using a general-purpose learning procedure, instead of designing features by human engineers[6] . The characteristics of requiring very little engineering by hand makes it easily discover interesting patterns from large-scale social media data. [7] proposed a model, called skip-thought vectors, for learning high-quality sentence vectors without a particular supervised task in mind. The model abstracts the skip-gram model of words to the sentence level, and encodes a sentence to predict the sentences around it. Inspired by the good idea, our key idea is to adopt skip-thought vectors to learn the representation of review content, where review contents with similar semantics and sentiment will have similar vector representations. The novel vector representation of review encodes deep semantics and sentiment, thus will help improve the prediction accuracy. Then, we hypothesize that users' history reviewing behaviors of aspect rating can be explored and propose a novel model to alleviate data missing of aspect ratings. Finally, the obtained vector representation of review content and the dense aspect ratings are integrated into a unified optimization framework to predict the overall review rating.

2. METHOD
Figure 1 depicts the proposed method of review rating prediction. It consists of three modules: learning latent vector representation for review content, alleviating the missing values of aspect ratings with users' rating preference and predicting the overall rating in an optimization framework.

Learning latent vector representation for review content

The skip-thoughts [7] is adopted to learn the representation of

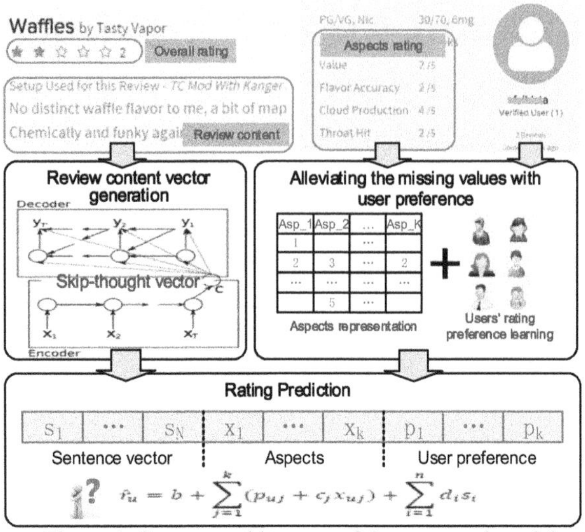

Figure 1. System architecture of the proposed model

review content. The model uses an RNN(Recurrent Neural Network) encoder to map words sequence to a sentence vector and an RNN decoder to generate the surrounding sentences. Given a sentence tuple (y_{i-1}, y_i, y_{i+1}), let w_i^t denote the *t*-th word in sentence y_i, h_i denote the encoder output of y_i. Then, the model aims to maximize the following objective function:

$$\sum_t logP(w_{i+1}^t | w_{i+1}^{<t}, h_i) + \sum_t logP(w_{i-1}^t | w_{i-1}^{<t}, h_i)$$

Where $P(w_{i+1}^t | w_{i+1}^{<t}, h_i)$, $P(w_{i-1}^t | w_{i-1}^{<t}, h_i)$ denote the probabilities of the *t*-th word for forward and backward sentences y_{i+1} , y_{i-1} given the previous *t*-1 words and the encoder representation h_i. The RNN structure can take any length of sentence as input, we thus employ the learnt encoder in [7] as a feature extractor to encode the review contents, then each review content is represented as a *n*-dimension vector $s \in R^n$.

Filling in the missing values of aspect ratings The aspect ratings are important features for overall rating. For aspects set $[a_1, a_2, \dots, a_k]$, the normalized aspect ratings of user v_i are represented as$[x_{i1}, x_{i2}, \dots, x_{ik}]$, where k is the number of aspects and x_{i*} is set to be 0 if the aspect rating is missing. The missing values of aspect ratings will result in prediction bias. Generally, random value or mean constant cannot accurately predict the missing values[8]. As shown in[5], users have different preferences on different aspects. Some users are harsh on specific aspect thus give lower ratings while others tend to be tolerant with minor flaws and give relatively higher ratings. Therefore, we propose to learn user's aspect rating preference based on his/her history reviewing behavior to handle the missing values problem. A user preference matrix $P \in R^{m \times k}$ is constructed, where m is the number of users, each element p_{ij} denotes the user v_i's preference on aspect a_j. The element of the matrix is automatically learnt during the process of predicting the overall ratings, which is explained in detail in the next step.

Predicting the overall rating Based on the above analysis, the overall rating is highly related to three key factors: semantics of review content , aspect ratings with missing values and user preference, therefore, the overall rating of user v_u for one product is predicted as follows:

$$\hat{r}_u = b + \sum_{j=1}^{k} (p_{uj} + c_j x_{uj}) + \sum_{i=1}^{n} d_i s_i$$

To optimize the model parameters b, p_{uj}, c_j and d_i , we minimize the L2-regularized square error with SGD:

$$\min_{b, p_{uj}, c_j, d_i} \sum (r_u - \hat{r}_u)^2 + \lambda_1 (b^2 + \sum_{j=1}^{k} c_j^2 + \sum_{i=1}^{n} d_j^2) + \lambda_2 \sum_{j=1}^{k} p_{uj}^2$$

For each given rating r_u, prediction error is denoted as $e_u = r_u - \hat{r}_u$, then the parameters are updated as follows:

- $b \leftarrow b + \gamma(e_u - \lambda_1 b)$
- $p_{uj} \leftarrow p_{uj} + \gamma(e_u - \lambda_2 p_{uj})$ iff $x_{uj} > 0$
- $c_j \leftarrow c_j + \gamma(e_u x_{uj} - \lambda_1 c_j)$
- $d_i \leftarrow d_i + \gamma(e_u s_i - \lambda_1 d_i)$

Where γ is the learning rate , λ_1, λ_2 are regularization parameters. It should be noted that the second rule explains the learning process of user preference matrix. $x_{uj} > 0$ indicates that the specific aspect rating is valid, thus we update p_{uj} to mine the underlying preference.

3. EXPERIMENTS

3.1 Dataset and Baseline Methods

To validate the performance of our review rating prediction model, we build two datasets from product review website JuiceDB[1] and service review website TripAdvisor[2] respectively.

JuiceDB: this website provides a very interesting review service for e-cigarettes, we use API to collect e-liquid reviews from June 2013 to November 2015. The dataset contains 14737 reviews for 4813 e-liquid products, each review is accompanied by an overall rating and a set of four aspect ratings of an e-liquid, each on a scale of 1-5: flavor accuracy, throat hit, value and cloud production. 25% of the reviews have incomplete aspect ratings.

TripAdvisor: this website provides reviews of travel-related content such as tourist attractions, hotels and restaurants. We use API to collect reviews about restaurants in New York from January 2015 to December 2015. The dataset contains 14524 reviews for 117 restaurants. Besides the overall rating, each review has three aspect ratings on a scale of 1-5: food, service, value. 38.3% of the reviews have incomplete aspect ratings.

We randomly partition the data into 75% for training and 25% for testing, repeat this process 5 times and present the averages. For the vector representation of review content, we use a 4800 dimensional vector, according to [7], it is formed by a unidirectional encoder with 2400 dimensions and a bidirectional encoder with another 2400 dimensions.

We compare our method against the following four baselines:

- **PredictMean**: This method simply uses the mean value of the ratings in the training set to predict rating.
- **BoW**(Bag-of-words): This method is a traditional representation method for documents, where unigrams and bigrams are used to represent a document.
- **ParagraphVector[9]**: This method learns the paragraph representations by predicting the surrounding words in contexts sampled from the paragraph. We utilize this unsupervised learning algorithm to represent each review content by a dense vector.
- **Aspects**: this method takes normalized aspect ratings as features to predict the overall rating directly.

The methods of BoW, ParagraphVector and Aspects map each review to different feature spaces. We then predict the

[1] https://www.juicedb.com/

[2] https://www.tripadvisor.com/

review ratings in a unified regression framework with these different feature representations.

3.2 Results and Discussions

To evaluate the accuracy of the method, we adopt mean absolute error (*MAE*) measure and coefficient of determination (R^2) measure:

$$\mathrm{MAE} = \frac{1}{M}\sum_{i=1}^{M}|r_u - \hat{r}_u|$$

$$R^2 = 1 - \frac{\sum_{i=1}^{M}(r_u - \hat{r}_u)^2}{\sum_{i=1}^{M}(r_u - \bar{r}_u)^2}$$

Where M is the number of samples, $\bar{r}_u$ denotes the average value of true ratings. MAE reflects the average difference between the predicted rating and the true rating, R^2reflects how much of the total variance is captured by the model. The comparison results of different methods on two datasets are shown below in Table 1 and Table 2 respectively in which Skip is short for Skip-thoughts , Aspects* refers to aspect ratings with user preference.

3.2.1 Review Rating Prediction in JuiceDB

Table 1 shows the performance comparison of different methods in JuiceDB. We empirically set $\gamma, \lambda_1, \lambda_2$ to 0.001, 0.0005, 0.01in this experiment.

Table 1. The comparison results in JuiceDB

	Method	MAE	R^2
Part 1	PredictMean	0.778	0.000
	BoW	0.645	0.322
	ParagraphVector	0.696	0.190
	Aspects	0.659	0.291
	Skip	**0.597**	**0.416**
Part 2	BoW +Aspects	0.616	0.386
	ParagraphVector +Aspects	0.603	0.412
	Skip +Aspects	**0.548**	**0.512**
Part 3	**Skip +Aspects***	**0.517**	**0.555**

- Rate Prediction using only review content or aspect ratings

We first study the prediction effects of different methods using only review content or aspect ratings. It can be observed from part 1 that all these methods perform better than PredictMean which indicates the importance of both review content and aspect ratings. Skip-thoughts model achieves the best performance in terms of both MAE and R^2. Results of Aspects is relatively poor due to the high percentage(25%) of incomplete aspect ratings. Compared with Aspects, better results of Skip-thoughts indicate that accurate semantic representation of review content has more impact than aspect ratings in overall rating prediction.

- Rate Prediction using both review content and aspect ratings

The above experimental results enlighten us to combine both of aspect ratings and review content for overall rating prediction. Results in Part 2 of Table1 demonstrate the effectiveness of the combination and "Skip+Aspects" achieves better performance than the other two. Furthermore, by filling in the missing values of aspect ratings using the learnt user preference matrix, the proposed "Skip+Aspects*" in Part3 that integrates vector representation of review content by skip-thought vectors and aspect ratings achieves the best performance. Our final model can predict a user's review rating of a product with MAE 0.517 on average. This implies that the deep semantics of review content can be captured by skip-thought vectors, moreover, the learnt user preference matrix based on the users' history reviewing behaviors is more reliable, thus solving the missing data problem of aspect ratings and improving the performance of overall rating prediction.

3.2.2 Review Rating Prediction in TripAdvisor

Table 2 shows the comparison results of different methods in TripAdvisor. We set $\gamma, \lambda_1, \lambda_2$ to 0.001, 0.0005, 0.01 in this experiment empirically.

- Rate Prediction using only review content or aspect ratings

From Part 1, it can be observed that compared with PredictMean, all the other learning methods achieve significant improvements and Skip still has the best performance in both MAE and R^2. The good performance in both two datasets further indicates that Skip-thoughts model is robust to mine the semantic representations of review contents and predict the ratings.

Table 2. The comparison results in TripAdvisor

	Method	MAE	R^2
Part 1	PredictMean	0.614	0.000
	BoW	0.535	0.165
	ParagraphVector	0.535	0.153
	Aspects	0.588	0.043
	Skip	**0.477**	**0.322**
Part 2	BoW +Aspects	0.531	0.187
	Paragraph Vector +Aspects	0.522	0.191
	Skip +Aspects	**0.473**	**0.344**
Part 3	Skip +Aspects*	0.476	0.308

- Rate Prediction using both review content and aspect ratings

We further combine the review content representation and the aspect ratings to predict the overall rating. From Part 2 and Part 3 in Table 2, we can observe that the three combination ways all achieve better results than methods considering only one factor in Part 1. "Skip+Aspects" obtains the best results in both measures. This further implies that deep semantics of review content and aspects ratings do play important roles in review rating prediction. It can be seen from the results in JuiceDB and TripAdvisor that "Skip+Aspects*" works better than "Skip+Aspects" in the former data set, which has less incomplete aspect ratings. The reason may be that a larger percentage of missing aspect ratings on TripAdvisor makes it difficult for Skip+Aspects* to learn user preference from users' history reviewing behaviors.

3.2.3 Case Study

The above experiments in JuiceDB and TripAdvisor have demonstrated the effectiveness of our proposed model. Specially, learning semantic representations of review content using skip-thought vectors and filling in missing values of aspect ratings show advantages on improving the accuracy of rating prediction. To give deep insights into the proposed model, we illustrate these two aspects by using intuitive examples in detail.

Firstly, we select some seed reviews and calculate their similar reviews using cosine similarity based on the skip-thought vectors. The results are shown in Table 3 and Table 4. For each seed review, we represent two similar reviews along with their similarities.

In Table 3, we represent one seed review with negative sentiment from JuiceDB. Both the similar reviews are negative and contain negative words like "horrible", "bad", "nauseous" which are synonyms to "awful" in the seed. Table 4 presents one positive seed review from TripAdvisor. The similar reviews include similar expressions such as "would definitely return","will definitely return". Besides, the similar reviews contain some positive words like "great", "good", "excellent", "helpful" to express compliments about the experience. The above examples show that without feature engineering, the skip-thought vector is capable of mapping reviews with similar sentiment and semantics into similar vector representations successfully. This verifies the advantage of skip-thought vectors over other representation methods.

Secondly, aspects features are also of importance to the overall review rating prediction. By observing the weights of the aspect features from the trained model, we can have a fine-grained analysis of the aspects. In JuiceDB, aspects are ranked in terms of weights: flavor accuracy, value, throat hit, cloud production. Flavor accuracy and value are the two most important factors when users evaluate one e-liquid product. In TripAdvisor, we rank the aspects in the same way: value, food, service. We can observe that value and food are two factors people care most when they choose a restaurant. Moreover, by incorporating users' aspect rating preferences, our final model predicts the overall rating more accurately. For example, in the test stage in JuiceDB, a user rates one e-liquid with 3 stars. The "Skip+Aspects" method can predict it with a score of 2.86. But by utilizing the user's learnt preference vector [0.387 0.305 -1.44 0.385], our final model "Skip+Aspects*" can predict the rating with a score of 2.95 which further illustrate the effectiveness of the preference matrix.

Take JuiceDB for an example, it could serve as an early warning on the use patterns of e-liquid. Policy makers of FDA (Food and Drug Administration) could make use of the predicted ratings and similar sentiments to identify e-liquids that are potentially harmful and addicting. For example, e-liquids that are found to hurt users' throat, make users feel bad in some way or significantly make users want to use more, could in turn inform the development and implementation of new regulations or laws.

Table 3. The similar reviews mined by Skip-thought vectors in JuiceDB

	review content	similarity
seed review 1	**Awful. Just awful.**	
similar reviews	**horrible**. imagine an ashtray with cloves...**just bad**.	0.746
	Pretty **bad**. Can't even vape it without feeling **nauseous**.	0.714

Table 4. The similar reviews mined by Skip-thought vectors in TripAdvisor

	review content	similarity
seed review 2	Really enjoyed our pizza, which was huge. The service was **quick**, **efficient** and really **friendly**. Was very **good** value for money, **will definitely return**.	
similar reviews	We went here for the prix fixe lunch which was very **reasonable** - all the food was **great** and really **good** service - **would definitely return**.	0.839
	A special restaurant for celebrations. Portions are very ample. Quality of food **excellent**. We split an appetizer and salad and thought it was a full order. The staff was **attentive** and extremely **helpful**. **Would definitely return**.	0.832

4. CONCLUSIONS AND FUTURE WORK

In this paper, we proposed a novel review rating prediction method. Experimental results show that high-quality representation of review content and complete aspect ratings play important roles in improving prediction accuracy. This work is a first step towards learning deep semantics of review content using skip-thought vectors in review rating prediction. The framework can integrate other information such as reviewer's information, product information, etc. in the future. It will also be very interesting to apply the method to analyze users' detail experience and how producers and marketers use social media to promote and sell various products or service, which could provide valuable information for regulatory decision-makers.

5. ACKNOWLEDGMENTS

This research is supported by the NNSFC projects (No. 61172106, 91224008, 61402123, 71472175) and Important National Science & Technology Specific Project (No. 2013ZX10004218).

6. REFERENCES

[1] Ochi, M., Okabe, M., and Onai, R., 2011. Rating prediction using feature words extracted from customer reviews. In *Proceedings of the 34th international ACM SIGIR conference on Research and development in Information Retrieval*. ACM, 1205-1206.

[2] Horrigan, J.A., 2008. Online shopping. *Pew Internet & American Life Project Report.*

[3] Ganu, G., Elhadad, N., and Marian, A., 2009. Beyond the Stars: Improving Rating Predictions using Review Text Content. In *WebDB*. Citeseer, 1-6.

[4] Diao, Q., Qiu, M., Wu, C.-Y., Smola, A.J., Jiang, J., and Wang, C., 2014. Jointly modeling aspects, ratings and sentiments for movie recommendation (JMARS). In *Proceedings of the 20th ACM SIGKDD international conference on Knowledge discovery and data mining*. ACM, 193-202.

[5] Mukherjee, S., Basu, G., and Joshi, S., 2013. Incorporating author preference in sentiment rating prediction of reviews. In *Proceedings of the 22nd international conference on World Wide Web companion*. International World Wide Web Conferences Steering Committee, 47-48.

[6] Lecun, Y., Bengio, Y., and Hinton, G., 2015. Deep learning. *Nature*. 521, 7553, 436-444. DOI= http://dx.doi.org/10.1038/nature14539.

[7] Kiros, R., Zhu, Y., Salakhutdinov, R.R., Zemel, R., Urtasun, R., Torralba, A., and Fidler, S., 2015. Skip-thought vectors. In *Advances in neural information processing systems*, 3276-3284.

[8] Soley-Bori, M., 2013. *Dealing with missing data: Key assumptions and methods for applied analysis.* Boston University.

[9] Le, Q.V. and Mikolov, T., 2014. Distributed representations of sentences and documents. In *Proceedings of the international conference on machine learning(ICML).*

Learning to Project and Binarise for Hashing Based Approximate Nearest Neighbour Search

Sean Moran
sean.moran@glasgow.ac.uk
University of Glasgow, UK

ABSTRACT

In this paper we focus on improving the effectiveness of hashing-based approximate nearest neighbour search. Generating similarity preserving hashcodes for images has been shown to be an effective and efficient method for searching through large datasets. Hashcode generation generally involves two steps: bucketing the input feature space with a set of hyperplanes, followed by quantising the projection of the data-points onto the normal vectors to those hyperplanes. This procedure results in the makeup of the hashcodes depending on the positions of the data-points with respect to the hyperplanes in the feature space, allowing a degree of locality to be encoded into the hashcodes. In this paper we study the effect of learning both the hyperplanes and the thresholds as part of the same model. Most previous research either learn the hyperplanes assuming a fixed set of thresholds, or vice-versa. In our experiments over two standard image datasets we find statistically significant increases in retrieval effectiveness versus a host of state-of-the-art data-dependent and independent hashing models.

1. INTRODUCTION

Nearest neighbour search is the problem of finding the most similar data-points to a query in a database, and is a fundamental operation that has found wide applicability in many fields of study, ranging from Information Retrieval (IR) to Bioinformatics. Hashing-based approximate nearest neighbour (ANN) search methods permit the nearest neighbours to a query data-point to be retrieved in constant time [5]. Hashing permits constant time search per query by condensing both the database and the query into fixed-length compact binary hashcodes or fingerprints. The hashcodes exhibit the neighbourhood preserving property that similar data-points will be assigned similar (low Hamming distance) hashcodes. To compute these hashcodes, many hashing models partition the input feature space into disjoint regions with hyperplanes [1, 6, 9]. In the case of hyperplanes the polytope-shaped regions formed by the intersecting hyperplanes constitute the hashtable buckets. The hashtable key for a data-point is generated by simply determining which side of the hyperplanes the data-point lies. Depending on which side it falls a '0' or a '1' is appended to the hashcode for that data-point. By repeating this procedure for each hyperplane we can build up a hashcode for each data-point that is the same length as the number of hyperplanes partitioning the space.

Algorithmically this hashcode generation procedure can be accomplished in two separate steps performed in a pipeline: *projection* followed by *quantisation*. Projection involves a dot product of the feature vector representation of a data-point (e.g. bag of visual words) onto the hyperplane normal vectors positioned either randomly or in data-aware positions in the data-space. The hyperplanes should ideally partition the space in a manner that gives a higher likelihood that similar data points will fall within the same region, and therefore assigned the same hashcode. In the second step the real-valued projections are quantised into binary ('0' or '1') by thresholding the corresponding projected dimensions[1] typically with a single threshold placed at zero for mean centered data.

In our contribution we depart from most previous work and study the effect of learning both of the hyperplanes and the quantisation thresholds as part of the same hashing model. On image retrieval experiments over standard collections we demonstrate that learning both parameters can achieve a significant increase in retrieval effectiveness versus models that learn either parameter in isolation.

2. RELATED WORK

In the most closely related past research authors have generally focused on either learning the hashing hyperplanes [1, 4, 6] or the quantisation thresholds [2, 3, 7, 8] based on the distribution of the data. Seminal approaches for data-dependent hyperplane learning either solving an eigenvalue problem to generate a set of orthogonal hyperplanes, for example using Principal Components Analysis (PCA) [9], or frame a custom objective functions that uses pairwise labels to appropriately position the hyperplanes within the feature space [1]. Many of these models for hyperplane learning use a single threshold placed directly at zero (for mean centered data) to quantise the projections into binary. This approach is commonly known as Single Bit Quantisation (SBQ). Recently there has been significant interest in improving on

[1]We define a projected dimension as the collection of the real-valued projections (dot products) of all data-points onto the normal vector to a hyperplane.

SIGIR '16, July 17 - 21, 2016, Pisa, Italy

ISBN 978-1-4503-4069-4/16/07...$15.00
DOI: http://dx.doi.org/10.1145/2911451.2914766

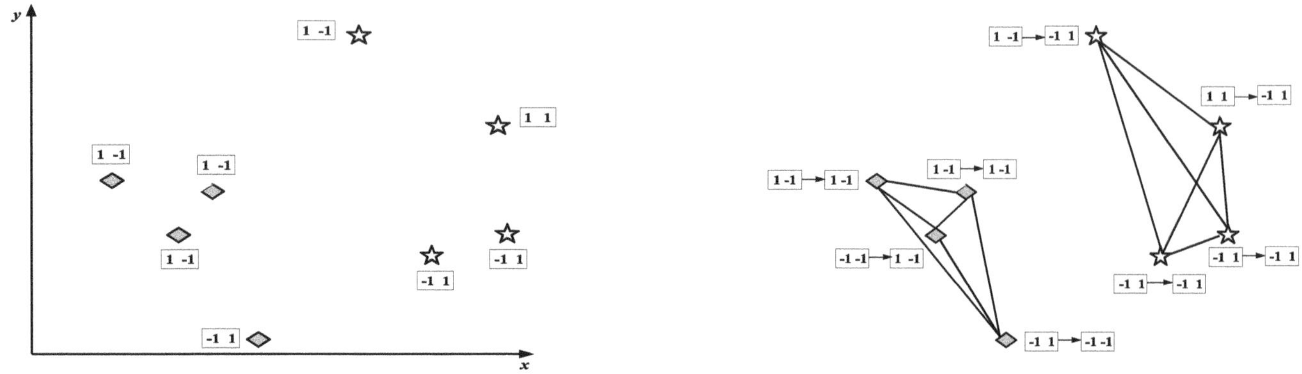

(a) **Initialisation** (b) **Regularisation**

Figure 1: **Initialisation**: 2-bit hashcodes initialised by LSH. Coloured shapes indicated data-points, and those with the same shape and colour are 1-NNs. **Regularisation** (Step 1): The hashcodes are regularised over the adjacency matrix. Lines between points indicate a nearest neighbour relationship. The hashcodes are updated as shown by the directed arrows.

SBQ by learning one or more thresholds to quantise projections [2, 3, 8, 7]. These quantisation models use either an unsupervised objective such as k-means or squared error minimisation to learn a good set of thresholds for each projected dimension [7, 8], or propose a semi-supervised objective that takes into consideration the neighbourhood structure between the data-points in the input feature space [2, 3].

3. LEARNING TO PROJECT AND BINARISE

3.1 Overview of the Approach

We couple the graph regularised projection model (GRH) of [1] and the semi-supervised quantisation model (NPQ) of [2]. The hyperplanes are learnt using GRH and the projections quantised using NPQ. We aim to answer the following research question:

RQ-1: Can learning the hashing hyperplanes and *multiple* quantisation thresholds as part of the same model give a higher retrieval effectiveness than a model which learns either the hyperplanes or thresholds?

Initially, the model is first run for M iterations, in which the following three steps (1-3) are applied per iteration:

- **1) Regularisation:** Regularise the hashcodes using Equation (1):

$$\mathbf{B}_m \leftarrow \operatorname{sgn}\left(\alpha\, \mathbf{S}\mathbf{D}^{-1}\mathbf{B}_{m-1} + (1-\alpha)\mathbf{B}_0\right) \quad (1)$$

  $\mathbf{B}_m \in \{-1,1\}^{N_{trd}\times K}$ are the hashcodes for the N_{trd} training data-points ($N_{trd} \ll N$) at iteration m, $\alpha \in [0,1]$ is the GRH interpolation parameter, $\mathbf{S}$ is the $N_{trd} \times N_{trd}$ adjacency matrix, which has S_{ij}=1 if $\mathbf{x}_i$ $\mathbf{x}_j$ are true nearest neighbours and 0 otherwise, $\mathbf{D}$ is a diagonal matrix containing the degree of each node in the graph. $\mathbf{B}_0$ is initialised using any existing projection function e.g. PCA.

- **2) Partitioning:** Solve K constrained optimisation problems in Equation (2), where K is the length of the hashcodes:

$$\text{for } k = 1..K: \quad \min\ ||\mathbf{w}_k||^2 + C\textstyle\sum_{i=1}^{N_{trd}} \xi_{ik}$$
$$s.t.\ B_{ik}(\mathbf{w}_k^{\intercal}\mathbf{x}_i) \geq 1 - \xi_{ik} \quad \text{for} \quad i = 1..N_{trd} \quad (2)$$

  $\mathbf{w}_k \in \mathbb{R}^D$ is the hyperplane normal vector, $\xi_{ik} \in \mathbb{R}_+$ are slack variables that allow points $\mathbf{x}_i$ to fall on the wrong side of hyperplane $\mathbf{h}_k$ and $C \in \mathbb{R}_+$ is the flexibility of margin. We use `liblinear` [10] as our solver.

- **3) Prediction:** Compute the N_{trd} dot products in Equation (3):

$$y_i^k = \mathbf{w}_k^{\intercal}\mathbf{x}_i \ \text{ for } i=\{1\ldots N_{trd}\} \text{ and } k=\{1\ldots K\} \quad (3)$$

  SBQ is applied to generate the updated hashcode matrix $\mathbf{B}_m$. We repeat steps 1-3 for M iterations. This is the GRH model of [1].

Having learnt the projections of our data-points in steps 1-3, we then quantise the learnt projections using NPQ [2]:

- **4) Quantisation:** Quantise $\mathbf{y}^k$ with thresholds $\mathbf{t}_k = [t_{k1}, t_{k2}, \ldots, t_{kT}]$ learnt by optimising $\mathcal{J}_{npq}(\mathbf{t}_k)$ in Equation (4):

$$\mathcal{J}_{npq}(\mathbf{t}_k) = F_1(\mathbf{t}_k) \quad (4)$$

  Here $T \in [1,3,7,15]$ is the number of thresholds per projected dimension and $F_1(\mathbf{t}_k)$ is a supervised term that leverages the neighbourhood structure encoded in $\mathbf{S}$. For a fixed set of thresholds $\mathbf{t}_k = [t_{k1}\ldots t_{kT}]$ we define a per-projected dimension indicator matrix $\mathbf{P}^k \in \{0,1\}^{N_{trd}\times N_{trd}}$ with the property given in Equation (5):

$$P_{ij}^k = \begin{cases} 1, & \text{if } \ \exists_\gamma \ \ s.t. \ \ t_{k\gamma} \leq (y_i^k, y_j^k) < t_{k(\gamma+1)} \\ 0, & \text{otherwise.} \end{cases} \quad (5)$$

  The index $\gamma \in \mathbb{Z}$ spans the range: $0 \leq \gamma \leq T$, where the scalar quantity T denotes the total number of thresholds for a projected dimension. Intuitively, matrix $\mathbf{P}^k$ indicates whether or not the projections (y_i^k, y_j^k) of any pair of data-points $(\mathbf{x}_i, \mathbf{x}_j)$ fall within the same thresholded region of the projected dimension $\mathbf{y}^k \in \mathbb{R}^{N_{trd}}$. Given thresholds $[t_{k1}\ldots t_{kT}]$, the algorithm counts *true positives* (TP), *false negatives* (FN) and *false positives* (FP) (Equations (6)-(8)).

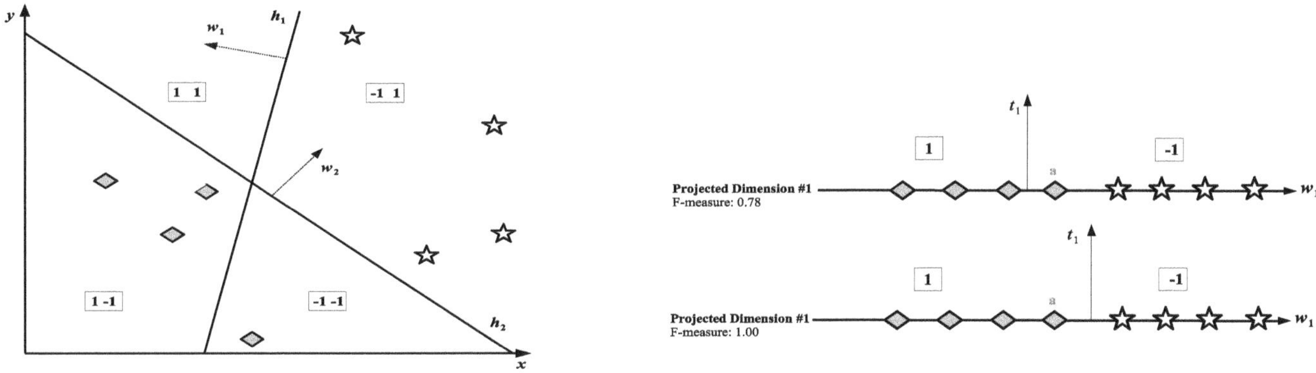

(a) **Partitioning** (b) **Quantisation**

Figure 2: **Partitioning step** (Step 2): hyperplanes are positioned to separate opposing bits (-1,1) with maximum margin. **Quantisation step** (Step 4) using the projections for hyperplane $\mathbf{h}_1$ as an example. The top-most diagram shows the quantisation obtained with a threshold placed at zero. Point a is on the wrong side of the threshold. The bottom diagram shows the result obtained by optimising the threshold t_1 to maximise pairwise F_1. In this case the threshold is shifted so that point a receives the same bits as its neighbours.

$$TP = \frac{1}{2}\sum_{ij} P_{ij}S_{ij} = \frac{1}{2}\|\mathbf{P}\circ\mathbf{S}\|_1 \tag{6}$$

$$FN = \frac{1}{2}\sum_{ij} S_{ij} - TP = \frac{1}{2}\|\mathbf{S}\|_1 - TP \tag{7}$$

$$FP = \frac{1}{2}\sum_{ij} P_{ij} - TP = \frac{1}{2}\|\mathbf{P}\|_1 - TP \tag{8}$$

where $\circ$ denotes the Hadamard product and $\|.\|_1$ is the L_1 matrix norm defined as $\|\mathbf{X}\|_1 = \sum_{ij}|X_{ij}|$. TP is the number of positive pairs that are found within the same thresholded region, FP is the negative pairs found within the same region, and FN are the positive pairs found in different regions. The counts are combined using the familiar F_1-measure (Equation (9)):

$$F_1(\mathbf{t}_k) = \frac{2\|\mathbf{P}\circ\mathbf{S}\|_1}{\|\mathbf{S}\|_1 + \|\mathbf{P}\|_1} \tag{9}$$

Equation (9) is directly maximised using Evolutionary Algorithms [2], and encourages a clustering of the projected dimension that respects the constraints in $\mathbf{S}$.

Figures 1-2 provide an intuitive overview of steps 1,2 and 4.

4. EXPERIMENTAL EVALUATION

4.1 Experimental Setup

Groundtruth: We define the groundtruth nearest neighbours using the ϵ-NN paradigm[2], that is if a data-point is within a radius of ϵ to the query then it is deemed to be true nearest neighbour for the purposes of evaluation ([2, 6, 8, 7]). To evaluate the quality of the hashcodes, database images are ranked based on the Hamming distance to the hashcodes of the queries. The resulting ranked lists are used to compute the area under the precision recall curve (AUPRC). The higher the AUPRC, the better the quality of the hashcodes.

Parameter Optimisation: We use three thresholds ($T = 3$) per projected dimension for NPQ and use the Manhattan hashing codebook and ranking strategy [8]. This corresponds to a 2-bit per projected dimension encoding, which means that $K/2$ hyperplanes are learnt for a K-bit hashcode. For GRH we use a held out validation dataset to find the number of iterations $M \in \mathbb{Z}_{+}$, the interpolation parameter $\alpha \in [0, 1]$ and the flexibility of margin $C \in \mathbb{R}_{+}$ for the linear SVM. Our parameter tuning strategy for the GRH model is as follows: firstly, we set $C = 1$ and perform a grid search over $M \in \{1 \dots 20\}$ and $\alpha \in \{0.1, \dots, 0.9, 1.0\}$, selecting the setting that gives the highest validation AUPRC. To find M we stop the sweep when the validation dataset AUPRC falls for the first time, and set M to be the number of the penultimate iteration. Finally, we then find the optimal value for the flexibility of margin $C \in \{0.01, 0.1, 1.0, 10, 100\}$.

Datasets: CIFAR-10[3] and Tiny 100K image [8] datasets both encoded with GIST features. To define the test queries we randomly sample N_{teq}=1,000 data points with the remaining points forming the database for retrieval and the training dataset for learning the hyperplanes and quantisation thresholds. We set N_{trd}=2,000 for learning. Reported AUPRC figures are the average over 10 independent runs.

Initialisation Methods: LSH [5], Shift-invariant Kernel-based Locality-Sensitive Hashing (SIKH) [6], PCA Hashing (PCAH) [4] and Spectral Hashing (SH) [9].

[2] ϵ is set to be the average L_2 distance to the 50th nearest neighbour. This parameter setting follows previous work [7, 8].

[3] https://www.cs.toronto.edu/~kriz/cifar.html

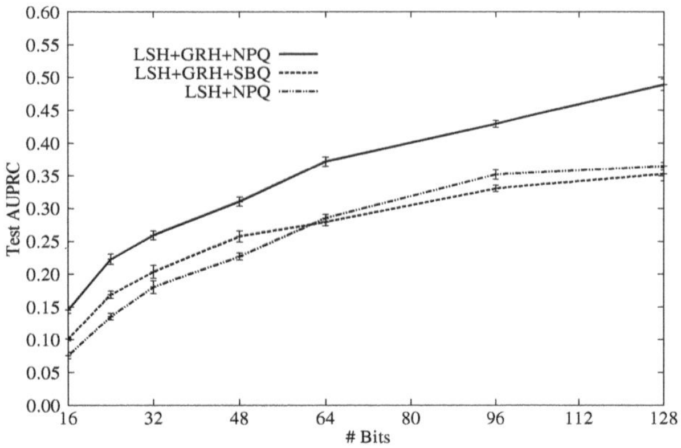

(a) **LSH projections**

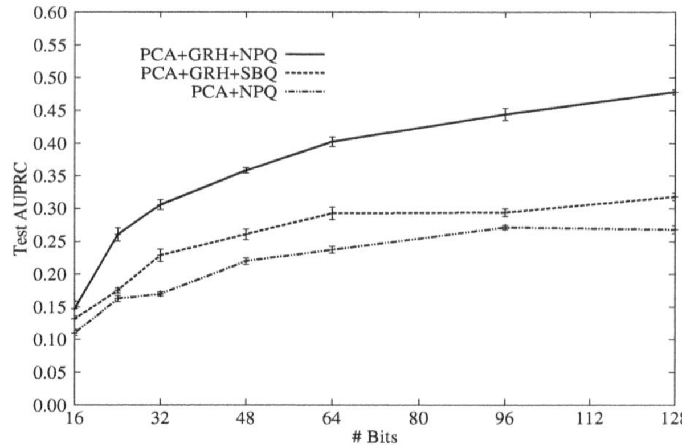

(b) **PCA projections**

Figure 3: The effect of learning the hashing hyperplanes and quantisation thresholds as part of the same model **(GRH+NPQ)** versus independently **(GRH+SBQ, SBQ)** over a haschode length of 16-128 bits on the CIFAR-10 dataset for LSH and PCA. Bars show standard error of the mean.

	Tiny 100K				
	SBQ	**NPQ**	**GRH**	**VBQ**	**GRH+NPQ**
LSH	0.3623	0.4970	0.4791	0.4796	**0.5680▲▲**
SH	0.1431	0.4519	0.4837	0.5014	**0.5827▲▲**
PCA	0.0439	0.3785	0.4749	0.5116	**0.5791▲▲**
SKLSH	0.1585	0.4357	0.4337	0.5198	**0.5309**

Table 1: AUPRC on the **Tiny 100K** dataset with a hashcode length of 32 bits. ▲▲ indicates statistical significance (Wilcoxon signed rank test, $p < 0.01$) when comparing **GRH+NPQ** to the next best model.

	CIFAR-10				
	SBQ	**NPQ**	**GRH**	**VBQ**	**GRH+NPQ**
LSH	0.0954	0.1621	0.2023	0.2035	**0.2593▲▲**
SH	0.0626	0.1834	0.2147	0.2380	**0.2958▲▲**
PCA	0.0387	0.1660	0.2186	0.2579	**0.2791▲▲**
SKLSH	0.0513	0.1063	0.1652	0.2122	**0.2566▲▲**

Table 2: AUPRC on the **CIFAR-10** dataset with a hashcode length of 32 bits.

4.2 Experimental Results

The Hamming ranking retrieval results are shown in Tables 1-2 and Figures 3(a)-(b). We observe in Tables 1-2 that learning the hyperplanes and thresholds as part of the same combined model (GRH+NPQ) yields the highest retrieval effectiveness compared to learning the hyperplanes (GRH) or the thresholds (NPQ, VBQ) independently. For example, for LSH projections GRH+NPQ gains a relative increase in AUPRC of 60% over NPQ and 28% over GRH on CIFAR-10. Furthermore, the combination of GRH+NPQ outperforms the adaptive thresholds allocation model (VBQ) of [3] by a relative margin of 27%. Each of these increases are found to be statistically significant using a Wilcoxon signed rank test (p-value < 0.01). We find that the superior retrieval effectiveness of GRH+NPQ is maintained when the hashcode length is varied between 16-128 bits for both LSH and PCA projections (Figure 3(a)-(b)) on CIFAR-10. In most cases, significant increases in effectiveness are found for other popular projection functions including SH and SKLSH across both datasets (Tables 1-2). Based on these experimental results we can answer **RQ-1** in the affirmative.

5. CONCLUSIONS

In this paper we have explored the benefits of learning the hashing hyperplanes and multiple quantisation thresholds as part of the same hashing model. We introduce a simple coupling of two state-of-the-art models for projection function and quantisation threshold learning [1, 2] and find statistically significant increases in retrieval effectiveness. Future research will explore a tighter coupling between the learning of the hyperplanes and quantisation thresholds by creating a unified objective function encompassing both parameters that could be jointly learnt using gradient-based optimisers.

6. ACKNOWLEDGEMENTS

The author would like to thank Victor Lavrenko for his valuable feedback on this research.

7. REFERENCES

[1] S. Moran and V. Lavrenko. Graph Regularised Hashing. In *Proc. ECIR*, 2015.

[2] S. Moran, V. Lavrenko, and M. Osborne. Neighbourhood Preserving Quantisation for LSH. In *Proc. SIGIR*, 2013.

[3] S. Moran, V. Lavrenko, and M. Osborne. Variable Bit Quantisation for LSH. In *Proc. ACL*, 2013.

[4] J. Wang, S. Kumar, and SF. Chang. Semi-Supervised Hashing for Large-Scale Search. In *Proc. PAMI*, 2012.

[5] P. Indyk and R. Motwani. Approximate nearest neighbors: towards removing the curse of dimensionality. In *Proc. STOC*, 1998.

[6] M. Raginsky and S. Lazebnik. Locality-sensitive binary codes from shift-invariant kernels. In *Proc. NIPS*, 2009.

[7] W. Kong and W. Li. Double-Bit Quantisation for Hashing. In *Proc. AAAI*, 2012.

[8] W. Kong, W. Li, and M. Guo. Manhattan hashing for large-scale image retrieval. In *Proc. SIGIR*, 2012.

[9] Y. Weiss, A. Torralba, and R. Fergus. Spectral Hashing. In *Proc. NIPS*, 2008.

[10] Rong-En Fan et al. LIBLINEAR: A Library for Large Linear Classification. In *JMLR, 9*, 2008.

Linking Organizational Social Network Profiles

Jerome Cheng[1] Kazunari Sugiyama[1] Min-Yen Kan[1,2]

[1]School of Computing, National University of Singapore, Singapore

[2]Interactive and Digital Media Institute, National University of Singapore, Singapore

jerome@ayulin.net

{sugiyama,kanmy}@comp.nus.edu.sg

ABSTRACT

Many organizations possess social media accounts on different social networks, but these profiles are not always linked. End applications, users, as well as the organization themselves, can benefit when the profiles are appropriately identified and linked. Most existing works on social network entity linking focus on linking individuals, and do not model features specific for organizational linking. We address this gap not only to link official social media accounts but also to discover and solve the identification and linking of associated *affiliate* accounts – such as geographical divisions and brands – which are important to distinguish.

We instantiate our method for classifying profiles on social network services for Twitter and Facebook, which major organizations use. We classify profiles as to whether they belong to an organization or its affiliates. Our best classifier achieves an accuracy of 0.976 on average in both datasets, significantly improving baselines that exploit the features used in state-of-the-art comparable user linkage strategies.

CCS Concepts

•**Information systems → Web and social media search;** *Entity resolution;* •**Human-centered computing →** *Social networking sites;*

Keywords

Organizational social profiles, Organization entity profiling, Record linkage, Social networks

1. INTRODUCTION

With the pervasiveness of social network services (SNSs), organizations also leverage them to reach out to and keep tabs on their fans and potential customers. However, unlike individual users, organizations usually maintain multiple profiles, even within a single SNS, to distribute targeted messages. This kind of intra-network profiles often represent *affiliates* – entities such as brands or geographical divisions which are part of the organization but is not the whole organization. An important task for both users and organizations is to automatically identify such profiles and link them to get a holistic social media profile of an organization, but to the best of our knowledge, up to now, this problem has been completely ignored by the community.

Figure 1: Google's manual organization profile linkage for "Boeing" in search results (captured May 2015).

Individual users do follow organizations through these profiles to stay informed of their products, events and developments. However, they do not have ways to easily identify all such profiles that belong to these organizations. Search engines of most SNSs currently do not distinguish between individual user profiles and organizational ones. While some Web search engines do provide links to profiles in their search results, these links still rely on manual effort by the organization (*i.e.*, Google requires organizations to include specific markup in their Web page[1]; Figure 1). As such, one may think that the organization itself should be responsible to link their SNS account on their websites. Our experience shows that this is not always the case, possibly due to challenges in organizational knowledge management or ignorance. Finally, to the best of our knowledge, services that aggregate locations where we can find such comprehensive links do not currently exist: we can identify only an organization's main profile on the most popular SNS, but not identify its affiliate profiles.

Organizations would benefit from automatic profile linkage to help monitor their competitors' profiles and activities – a fact that has been proven by the existence of nascent start-ups[2]. In addition, organizations also face the problem of tracking and policing attempts by others to impersonate them or infringe upon their trademarks. For instance, *Jetstar Airways* fell victim to impersonation, with a "Jetstar Australia" profile created on Facebook. This is used to insult customers who mistakenly provided malicious feedback through it[3].

SIGIR '16, July 17–21, 2016, Pisa, Italy.

© 2016 ACM. ISBN 978-1-4503-4069-4/16/07. . . $15.00

DOI: http://dx.doi.org/10.1145/2911451.2914698

[1] "Specify your social profiles to Google" in Google Developers. Accessed: Feb 12th, 2016, from https://developers.google.com/structured-data/customize/social-profiles

[2] e.g., http://nexgate.com

[3] http://bit.ly/1Eyruke

To solve these problems, it is important to identify an organization's social networking profiles on a specific network. We address this task by defining three categories of profiles related to a given organization:

Official. Profiles that represent the organization as a whole. For instance, Microsoft Corporation's official profile on Twitter is `@Microsoft`.

Affiliate. Profiles that represent one of the organization's brands, or a division. For example, Microsoft has several divisional profiles such as `@MicrosoftDesign`, `@MicrosoftAsia`, and so on.

Unrelated. These profiles are not run by the organization in question, belonging to an individual or other organization. We note that a profile unrelated to one organization may be an official or affiliate profile for another.

The contributions in our work are: 1) An implemented, automated system to perform organization profile linkage on social networks – given an organization's name as a query, it first searches for profile candidates from the target social networks, then constructs a model by using supervised learning to classify each candidate into **Official**, **Affiliate**, or **Unrelated** for the query; 2) The creation of a publicly available dataset that consists of 6,784 profiles from about 220 real-world organizations across Twitter and Facebook, where the profiles are manually classified into the above three categories.

2. RELATED WORK

The name fields of a profile have been shown to be of high importance in linking users. Two kinds of proposed linkage methods rely on usernames: either through generating candidate usernames to match with [7], or by examining behavioural patterns that influence the way usernames are created [8]. Another study found that the user and display names are the "most discriminative features" [3] when disambiguating profiles.

Several works have examined user activities to identify a profile's holder. These focused on using profile data and the content created by the user [1], or combining the information with other metadata (*e.g.,* location or time [2]). Their findings are helpful for our work as organizations often "cross-post" the same (or similar) material across different social networks.

Works have addressed social network profiles in the context of security – re-identification for anonymized social networks [4], spam bot detection [6], malicious profile detection [5] – but these are beyond the scope of our current review due to space considerations.

The aforementioned studies have identified profiles on social networks, to the best of our knowledge, they have all focused on profiles belonging to individual users and do not consider the specific properties of organization profiles, and are thus insufficient for linking organizations. For example, organizations often use an abbreviated form of their names online (*e.g.,* General Motors uses just "GM"), and their names often contain some common words such as "Company" or "Corporation." To accurately link organization profiles, it is necessary to take these properties into account.

3. FEATURES FOR CLASSIFIERS

We adopt supervised learning to classify organization names into the three categories previously defined. We extract 14 features that belong to the following four broad feature sets, annotating novel, specific features we introduce for this organization linkage problem with an asterisk (*):

Baseline Features (BL). These features examine the relationship between the target organization's name (hereafter, "query"), and the two name fields on a profile: the handle and the display names. The handle name is sometimes known as a username, and is a unique identifier that represents the profile on the social network. On the other hand, the display name is a free-text string that provides a more user-friendly name, but is not unique. For example, on *General Motors'* Twitter profile[4], the username is **GM** while the display name is **General Motors**. We adopt the following as baseline features:

- NED between the query and target handle name*
- NED between the query and target display name*

Normalized edit distance (NED) gives a relative measure of similarity accounting for their lengths. Let $ED(s_1, s_2)$ be edit distance between two strings s_1 and s_2. Then, normalized edit distance $NED(s_1, s_2)$ between them is defined as follows:

$$NED(s_1, s_2) = 1 - \frac{ED(s_1, s_2)}{\max(len(s_1), len(s_2))},$$

where $len(s_i)$ denotes the length of string s_i $(i = 1, 2)$.

In these features, we first process the query to generate a simple abbreviation and remove stop words (*e.g.,* "Company," "Corporation," and so on) defined for this task before calculating the edit distances between both the processed string and the original query. These features best simulate how a human would approach this problem.

Name-based Features (N). Name string lengths are also useful. We term these as name-based features:

- Length of the query
- Length of the target display name*
- Length of the target handle name*

Description-based Features (D). These features are based on the description field of the organization's profile. Besides the relationship between the description and query, we further searched for the organization's description from DuckDuckGo[5], a search engine that provides the results from sources such as Wikipedia.

- Cosine similarity between the target profile's description and the query
- Number of occurrences of the query in the target profile's description*
- Cosine similarity between the target profile's description and DuckDuckGo description*

The first two features give measures of the extent to which the profile's description is relevant to the organization's name. The third yields a similarity score between the profile's description and organization descriptions provided by the DuckDuckGo general search engine, which we deem as a more general, third-party description. Note that this feature requires an external API call.

Content-based Features (C). Posted content is also evidence for linkage. We construct two bigram language models for each category's training data (Official, Affiliate, or Unrelated): one from the profile descriptions in the target class, and the other from the textual content of recent 20 posts by the target profiles. We use add-one smoothing as a simple mechanism to address zero occurring bigrams in the query. This process yields six models in total that capture writing style differences:

- Probability that the query appears in bigram models constructed from official/affiliate/unrelated description*
- Probability that the query appears in bigram models constructed from official/affiliate/unrelated posted content*

[4]https://www.twitter.com/GM

[5]https://api.duckduckgo.com

Table 1: Statistics on our Twitter and Facebook dataset.

SNS	Organizations	Official	Affiliate	Unrelated	Total
Twitter	228	232	675	2,474	3,381
Facebook	216	145	491	2,767	3,403

4. EXPERIMENTS

We first construct the dataset for our experiments. We search for organization names which are listed on Freebase[6] as having at least one social network presence, and then submit the each organization name as a query to Twitter and Facebook. Finally, we manually label the profiles that Twitter and Facebook return. We obtain 3,381 profiles from 228 organizations and 3,403 profiles from 216 organizations on Twitter and Facebook, respectively (Table 1 shows relevant statistics). Note that the number of organizations included in each dataset differs from the number of official profiles that we found, as some organizations either lack an official profile or have more than one. To encourage the community to work on this important and understudied research work on social networks, we have made our entire dataset publicly available[7].

To study linkage performance across classification methods, we employ several different classifiers, namely: Bernoulli naïve Bayes (BNB), Gaussian naïve Bayes (GNB), decision tree (DT), logistic regression (LR), random forest (RF), support vector machine (SVM), and maximum entropy (ME), all which are implemented in *scikit-learn*[8]. We perform 10-fold cross validation, evaluating each classifier with their accuracy on the official and affiliate classes.

We compare the accuracies of classifiers constructed by combining "Baseline (BL)," "Name-based (N)," "Description-based (D)," and "Content-based (C)" features described earlier (Table 2) . In user identification works across SNSs, Iofciu *et al.* [1] reported that longest common subsequence-based distance is an effective feature in their "user maching based on username" experiments. In a related vein, Zafarani and Liu [8] disclosed their top 10 most important features, most of which are length-based ones. We also compare our classifiers with those constructed using the features from both [1] and [8].

5. DISCUSSION

In this section, we refer to "Twitter (Official)," "Twitter (Affiliate)," "Facebook (Official)," "Facebook (Affiliate)" as "TW-Off," "TW-Aff," "FB-Off," "FB-Aff," respectively.

Classification Accuracies. In both Twitter and Facebook datasets, DT, LR, RF, SVM, and ME achieve accuracies over 0.7 in almost all feature sets (Table 2). Naïve Bayes in both forms (BNB and GNB) yields lower accuracies (only about 0.2 to 0.7), especially in the Affiliate category, even when adding more features.

Among the classifiers, Random Forest (RF) achieves the best in both Twitter and Facebook datasets (0.983, 0.973, 0.972, 0.977 in TW-Off, TW-Aff, FB-Off, FB-Aff, respectively). RF is an ensemble approach, taking an average of multiple decision trees' decisions, which are separately trained on different parts of the same training set, to reduce overfitting. While this step slightly increases the bias of the forest, it decreases its variance. This framework of RF works well for our task as each of our features tends to have large variance.

With respect to features, we observe that using all features yields the best accuracy in each classifier, and also outperforms the accuracies obtained by the features used in [1] and [8] with statistical significance. This indicates that our ALL feature set is more effective than longest common subsequence-based distance in [1] and length-based features in [8].

With respect to individual feature contributions, we further study the improvement when adding N, D, or C feature set to the baseline (Table 3). We observe higher improvement rate on affiliate profiles in both Twitter and Facebook datasets (N: 15.02%, D: 7.57%, C:16.49% in TW-Aff and N: 7.61%, D: 4.54%, C:22.88% in FB-Aff). Among the feature sets, C is the most effective feature set to distinguish official and affiliate profiles (9.56%, 16.49%, 7.49%, 22.88% in TW-Off, TW-Aff, FB-Off, and FB-Aff, respectively). This indicates that content information extracted from profile description and recent posts do contain useful signal that can help distinguish organizational names. Although acquiring such data can be expensive, our experiments validates its significant impact on the linkage accuracy.

Linking Affiliates. The existence of affiliate profiles is a distinguishing characteristic of our problem, differentiating it from general linkage of individual profiles, or even linking official profiles alone. Both individuals and official profiles have names which are generally close to that of their holder, and as such linkage of affiliates would be expected to be more difficult. However, RF, ME, and SVM classifiers all prove to be good and equally adept at detecting both official and affiliate profiles, countering this intuition. Investigating this more fully reveals that this actually does not hold with certain subclasses of affiliate profiles – while geographic affiliates do tend to contain their parent company's name with a location as a suffix as their profile name (*e.g.,* "Microsoft Asia"), brand names often have little in common (*e.g.,* "Lenovo" and "ThinkPad"). Hence, the use of the parent company name for these brand profiles is insufficient to identify them as belonging to the organization; additional information is required. These classifiers, with the equipped features from our study, still significantly outperform the baseline and comparative methods.

Network Idiosyncrasies. On Twitter, all users are given the same type of profiles regardless of whether they are a person or an organization. On the other hand, Facebook has multiple profile types including *Pages*, which are designed for "artists, public figures, businesses, brands, organizations, and non-profits[9]."

We considered only Pages here, effectively resulting in a level of filtering provided by Facebook which Twitter does not have. Pages with handle and display names similar to those of an organization name are likely to belong to the organization.

However, this observation is not the case with affiliate profiles on Facebook. Facebook does not require pages that specify a unique handle name; in this scenario, we instead treat the page's numerical ID as its handle name. This substitution greatly impacts on the normalized edit distance scores in BL. It is sometimes the case that an affiliate profile does not have a specific handle name – for instance, *Netflix* uses "Netflix" as its official profile's handle name[10], but does not provide one for its Latin American affiliate[11].

In addition, Facebook also generates "topic pages" from Wikipedia articles, giving them a display name from the title of that article but no handle name. For example, a page exists for *Samsung* which has just "Samsung" as its display name[12]. We consider these pages to

[6] http://www.freebase.com

[7] http://wing.comp.nus.edu.sg/downloads/corpsearch/OrgSocialNetworkData.html

[8] http://www.scikit-learn.org (Version 0.15.0)

[9] "Products" in Facebook Newsroom. Accessed Feb 12th, 2016, from https://newsroom.fb.com/products/

[10] https://www.facebook.com/netflix

[11] https://www.facebook.com/pages/Netflix-Latinoam\%C3\%A9rica/553454298124413

[12] https://www.facebook.com/pages/Samsung/114938905184804

Table 2: Accuracies obtained by several classifiers constructed using various feature sets on Twitter ((a-1) Official, (a-2) Affiliate)) and Facebook ((b-1) Official, (b-2) Affiliate)) datasets. The best accuracy in each category is denoted with bold font. "" and "*" denote the difference between the best results obtained by the most effective feature set in [1] or [8] (underlined scores) and the best result obtained by each classifier (italic or bold scores) in our approach is significant for $p < 0.01$ and $p < 0.05$, respectively.**

(a-1) Twitter (Official)

Feature set	BNB	GNB	DT	LR	RF	SVM	ME
Baseline (BL)	0.787	0.405	0.870	0.720	0.801	0.893	0.904
BL+N	0.911	0.410	0.919	0.842	0.923	0.921	0.943
BL+D	0.891	0.437	0.918	0.785	0.940	0.851	0.908
BL+C	0.894	0.461	0.929	0.820	0.961	0.944	0.914
BL+N+D	0.916	0.407	0.926	0.846	0.972	0.845	0.945
BL+N+C	0.931	0.578	0.942	0.951	0.976	0.956	0.949
BL+D+C	0.878	0.498	0.932	0.842	0.972	0.936	0.945
ALL (BL+N+D+C)	*0.934**	*0.645***	*0.952**	*0.955**	**0.983***	*0.963**	*0.954**
Iofcia et al. [1]	0.853	0.386	0.919	0.774	0.940	0.901	0.938
Zafarani and Liu [8]	0.846	0.414	0.929	0.863	0.967	0.869	0.926

(a-2) Twitter (Affiliate)

Feature set	BNB	GNB	DT	LR	RF	SVM	ME
Baseline (BL)	0.235	0.413	0.788	0.681	0.740	0.828	0.878
BL+N	0.325	0.511	0.924	0.521	0.931	0.835	0.872
BL+D	0.140	0.501	0.922	0.531	0.935	0.798	0.846
BL+C	0.327	0.432	0.502	0.837	0.944	0.878	0.914
BL+N+D	0.324	0.468	0.917	0.528	0.932	0.805	0.870
BL+N+C	0.330	0.556	0.928	0.953	0.949	0.963	0.933
BL+D+C	0.322	0.515	0.919	0.831	0.937	0.848	0.898
ALL (BL+N+D+C)	*0.339**	*0.639**	*0.934**	*0.971**	**0.973***	*0.967**	*0.947**
Iofcia et al. [1]	0.321	0.499	0.927	0.535	0.931	0.824	0.873
Zafarani and Liu [8]	0.327	0.536	0.917	0.543	0.926	0.815	0.865

(b-1) Facebook (Official)

Feature set	BNB	GNB	DT	LR	RF	SVM	ME
Baseline (BL)	0.802	0.502	0.827	0.816	0.794	0.816	0.959
BL+N	0.815	0.414	0.874	0.839	0.913	0.930	0.956
BL+D	0.738	0.401	0.905	0.739	0.937	0.939	0.963
BL+C	0.740	0.462	0.874	0.830	0.945	0.913	0.960
BL+N+D	0.755	0.344	0.901	0.860	0.951	0.948	0.955
BL+N+C	0.831	0.564	0.913	0.866	0.957	0.950	0.967
BL+D+C	0.699	0.412	0.897	0.821	0.946	0.921	0.958
ALL (BL+N+D+C)	*0.897**	*0.684***	*0.919**	*0.878**	**0.972***	*0.960**	*0.970**
Iofcia et al. [1]	0.815	0.460	0.881	0.797	0.917	0.948	0.955
Zafarani and Liu [8]	0.743	0.467	0.893	0.814	0.929	0.949	0.966

(b-2) Facebook (Affiliate)

Feature set	BNB	GNB	DT	LR	RF	SVM	ME
Baseline (BL)	0.283	0.317	0.560	0.289	0.790	0.836	0.903
BL+N	0.309	0.327	0.685	0.385	0.859	0.847	0.911
BL+D	0.397	0.266	0.689	0.486	0.847	0.750	0.858
BL+C	0.359	0.308	0.699	0.703	0.962	0.796	0.942
BL+N+D	0.305	0.272	0.692	0.470	0.952	0.743	0.910
BL+N+C	0.404	0.360	0.704	0.712	0.966	0.927	0.953
BL+D+C	0.331	0.304	0.687	0.693	0.932	0.898	0.949
ALL (BL+N+D+C)	*0.443**	*0.399**	*0.727**	*0.734***	**0.977***	*0.964**	*0.968**
Iofcia et al. [1]	0.355	0.342	0.665	0.424	0.762	0.806	0.874
Zafarani and Liu [8]	0.359	0.314	0.684	0.439	0.743	0.802	0.869

Table 3: Improvement rate by adding N, D, or C feature set to baseline features (BL).

	Twitter (Official)	Twitter (Affiliate)	Facebook (Official)	Facebook (Affiliate)
N	6.56%	15.02%	6.72%	7.61%
D	2.39%	7.57%	0.46%	4.54%
C	**9.56%**	**16.49%**	**7.49%**	**22.88%**

be unrelated. However, they have a similar edit distance as legitimate affiliate profiles. This makes it difficult to distinguish an affiliate profile on Facebook using just the handle and display names.

As we go forward, it is likely that other social networks will exhibit their own unique set of quirks, which will similarly pose challenges to linking profiles on them. We recommend that the reader be mindful of these idiosyncrasies when adapting our work for linkage with other SNSs.

6. CONCLUSION

We have proposed an approach to organizational social profile linkage. To the best of our knowledge, this problem has not been tackled before in the literature, but is a problem of growing importance given the amount of influence that social media plays in lives today. A key difference in organization linkage is the presence of affiliates – both geographic and brand – that change the nature of the problem.

While previous efforts have done linkage through manual means, our automated approach finds that profile description and posted content are the most effective features for detecting linkage. In future work, we plan to leverage unique characteristics of the different types of affiliate accounts to achieve better classification accuracy. This will allow us to infer affiliate structure (with respect to the parent company), as well as to expand our work to include other social networks.

7. REFERENCES

[1] T. Iofciu, P. Fankhauser, F. Abel, and K. Bischoff. Identifying Users Across Social Tagging Systems. In *Proc. of the 5th International AAAI Conference on Weblogs and Social Media (ICWSM-11)*, pages 522–525, 2011.

[2] X. Kong, J. Zhang, and P. S. Yu. Inferring Anchor Links across Multiple Heterogeneous Social Networks. In *Proc. of the 22nd ACM International Conference on Information and Knowledge Management (CIKM'13)*, pages 179–188, 2013.

[3] A. Malhotra, L. C. Totti, W. Meira Jr, P. Kumaraguru, and V. Almeida. Studying User Footprints in Different Online Social Networks. In *Proc. of the 2012 International Conference on Advances in Social Networks Analysis and Mining (ASONAM 2012)*, pages 1065–1070, 2012.

[4] A. Narayanan and V. Shamatikov. De-anonymizing Social Networks. In *Proc. of the 30th IEEE Symposium on Security and Privacy (SP 2009)*, pages 173–187, 2009.

[5] M. Singh, D. Bansal, and S. Sofat. Detecting Malicious Users in Twitter using Classifiers. In *Proc. of the 7th International Conference on Security of Information and Networks (SIN'14)*, pages 247–253, 2014.

[6] A. H. Wang. Detecting Spam Bots in Online Social Networking Sites: A Machine Learning Approach. In *Proc. of the 24th Annual IFIP WG 11.3 Working Conference on Data and Applications Security and Privacy (DBSec'10)*, pages 335–342, 2010.

[7] R. Zafarani and H. Liu. Connecting Corresponding Identities across Communities. In *Proc. of the 3rd International AAAI Conference on Weblogs and Social Media (ICWSM-09)*, pages 354–357, 2009.

[8] R. Zafarani and H. Liu. Connecting Users across Social Media Sites: A Behavioral-Modeling Approach. In *Proc. of the 19th ACM SIGKDD International Conference on Knowledge Discovery and Data Mining (KDD'13)*, pages 41–49, 2013.

Load-Balancing in Distributed Selective Search

Yubin Kim Jamie Callan
Carnegie Mellon University
USA

J. Shane Culpepper
RMIT University
Australia

Alistair Moffat
The University of Melbourne
Australia

ABSTRACT

Simulation and analysis have shown that *selective search* can reduce the cost of large-scale distributed information retrieval. By partitioning the collection into small *topical shards*, and then using a resource ranking algorithm to choose a subset of shards to search for each query, fewer postings are evaluated. Here we extend the study of selective search using a fine-grained simulation investigating: selective search efficiency in a parallel query processing environment; the difference in efficiency when term-based and sample-based resource selection algorithms are used; and the effect of two policies for assigning index shards to machines. Results obtained for two large datasets and four large query logs confirm that selective search is significantly more efficient than conventional distributed search. In particular, we show that selective search is capable of both higher throughput and lower latency in a parallel environment than is exhaustive search.

1. INTRODUCTION

A *selective search* architecture divides a document corpus or corpus tier into P topic-based partitions (*shards*), and assigns them to M processing *machines*, typically with $P \gg M \geq 1$. When a query arrives, a resource ranking algorithm (also known as "resource selection" or "shard ranking") selects a small number of shards to be interrogated for that query, and passes the query to the machines hosting those shards. The per-shard search results are then combined to produce an answer list [9]. If only a few shards are searched for each query, costs are reduced compared to searching all of the shards for every query. Selective search provides similar effectiveness to exhaustive search when measured by metrics such as P@10, NDCG@100, and Average Precision [1, 5, 6].

Previous work estimated efficiency by summing the length of the postings lists processed for each query, and compared selective search to exhaustive search using those counts as a surrogate for total workload. But this approach does not consider how effort is divided across processors, or interactions between queries resulting from parallelism. In particular, traditional distributed search architecture that use a random assignment of documents to shards and then search within all shards tend spread the workload evenly, and are relatively immune to bottlenecks. Selective search deliberately concentrates similar documents into index shards and might be vulnerable to uneven workloads that restrict overall query throughput, a consequence that cannot be identified by counting postings.

We use an event-based simulator to provide a more refined evaluation of selective search, and in doing so lay a foundation on which a full operational implementation can be built. That is, we define a more realistic experimental methodology for studying the efficiency of sharded search. Simulation makes it possible to investigate a wider range of machine configurations than would be practical in a live system; in our case, we provide realistic estimated measurements of query latency, system throughput, and hardware utilization, for several different hardware arrangements. These measurements lead to an improved shard allocation policy that provides better load balancing across machines.

In doing so, we have extended previous evaluations, and are able to provide answers to three key questions: (1) does selective search provide higher query throughput than exhaustive search in parallel environments; (2) does the choice of resource selection algorithm affect throughput and load distribution in selective search; and (3) do different methods of allocating shards to machines affect overall query throughput.

SIGIR '16, July 17–21, 2016, Pisa, Italy

ISBN 978-1-4503-4069-4/16/07. . . $15.00

DOI: http://dx.doi.org/10.1145/2911451.2914689

2. SIMULATION MODEL

Resource Selection We make use of the *Taily* and *Rank-S* resource selection mechanisms. In *Rank-S*, the query is used to rank documents in a centralized sample index (CSI); document scores are then decayed exponentially and treated as votes for the shards the documents were sampled from [7]. *Taily* assumes that the distribution of document scores for a single query term is approximated by a Gamma distribution. Taily's resource selection database stores the two parameters describing each term's distribution; then, at query time, they are used to estimate the number of documents from each resource that will have a score above a certain threshold. In most situations Taily is faster to compute than Rank-S [1].

Simulation Design The simulator is based on the DESMO-J (http://desmoj.sourceforge.net/) framework. It models a selective search system that incorporates a cluster of multi-core machines and parallel query execution across those machines. Figure 1 describes the flows embedded in the simulator; Table 1 lists the quantities that are manipulated; and Algorithm 1 describes the actions that take place at each machine. The hardware is assumed to consist of M machines, with the i th of those, machine m_i, providing c_i CPU cores ($c_i = 8$ throughout the paper).

Each *broker* holds a copy of the resource selection database and performs two tasks: resource selection, and result merging. For resource selection, it accesses a shared *central query queue*, from

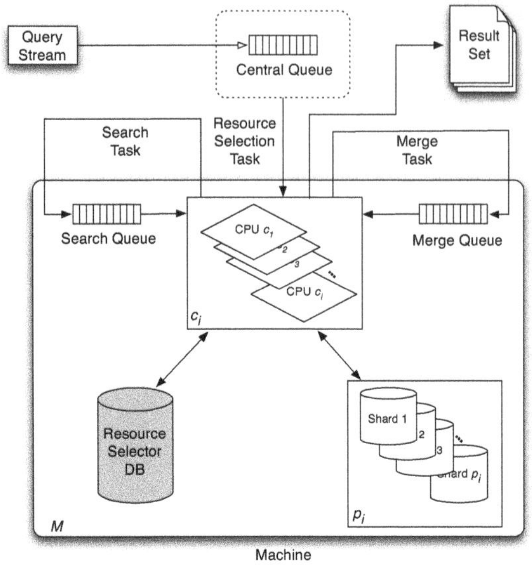

Figure 1: Distributed selective search. The i th of the M machines has c_i cores used for shard search across the p_i shards allocated to it, and (if allowed) for resource selection and result merging.

M	Number of machines; m_i is the i th of these.
c_i	Number of cores on m_i; the default is $c_i = 8$.
C	Total number of cores, $\sum_{i=1}^{M} c_i$.
p_i	Number of shards assigned to m_i.
P	Total number of shards. When each shard is assigned to just one machine, $P = \sum_{i=1}^{M} p_i$.
B	Number of broker machines.
S	Number of searcher machines.
T	Query arrival rate described by an exponential distribution with mean $1/\lambda, T = \lambda$.
t_s	Seek plus latency access time, ms/postings list, $t_s = 4$ throughout.
t_p	Processing cost, ms/posting, $t_p = 9 \times 10^{-4}$ throughout.
t_m	Merging cost, ms/item, $t_m = 5 \times 10^{-5}$ throughout.

Table 1: Simulation parameters.

which it extracts queries, determines which shards will be searched, and assigns search tasks to other machines. Each broker also has a job queue for pending *result merge* processes, containing results returned by the searcher machines, waiting to be combined. A machine m_i is a *searcher* if it is allocated $p_i > 0$ search shards. It also has a job queue that holds *shard search* requests. Each of the available cores on the machine can access any of the shards assigned to the machine, and can respond to any request in that machine's search queue. When a search job is finished, the result is returned to the result merge queue of the originating broker.

The assignment of shards and copies of the resource selection database to machines is assumed to be fixed at indexing time, and machines cannot access shards that are not hosted locally. A key factor for success is thus the manner in which the P shards are partitioned across the M machines.

Simulation Parameters Queries are assumed to arrive at the central queue at random intervals determined by an exponential distribution with a mean query arrival rate T. Query processing costs are computed based on the number of postings processed, plus an overhead cost to account for initial latency for a disk seek, taking $t_s + \ell \cdot t_p$ milliseconds, where ℓ is the number of postings. The processing rate is based on measurement of the cost of handling posting lists in the open source Indri search engine (http://lemurproject.org/) on a machine with a 2.44 GHz CPU, and includes I/O and similarity calculation costs. In the case of in-memory or SSD-based execution, t_s can be set to zero.

Algorithm 1 – Processing loop for each core on machine m_i.

while forever **do**
  if *isBroker*(m_i) and $|mergequeue_i| > 0$ and all shard responses have been received for q **then**
    remove those responses from *mergequeue*$_i$
    finalize the output for query q and construct a document ranking
  else if *isSearcher*(m_i) and $|searchqueue_i| > 0$ **then**
    remove a query request (q, p, b) from *searchqueue*$_i$
    perform a shard search for query q against shard p
    append the results of the search to *mergequeue*$_b$
  else if *isBroker*(m_i) and $|centralqueue| > 0$ **then**
    remove a query q from *centralqueue*
    perform resource selection for q
    for each partition p to be searched for q **do**
      determine the machine m_h that is host for p
      append (q, p, i) as a search request to *searchqueue*$_h$
endwhile

For the sample-based Rank-S algorithm, the same computational model is used for resource selection as for shard search. For Taily, the cost is computed for a nominal postings list of $2P$ parameters. Result merging requires transferring of up to k $\langle$*doc-id*, *score*$\rangle$ results from each shard searched, where k is either fixed or is determined as part of resource selection. The cost of network communication over a Gigabit switched network was modeled as described by Cacheda et al. [2], and an allocation of t_m milliseconds per document added to the cost. The processing model assumed that all postings were processed for every query; in recent work, Kim et al. [3] have shown that the use of WAND pruning does not affect the *relative* efficiency relationship of selective vs. exhaustive search.

Simulation Input and Output All systems were configured to return the top-ranked 1,000 documents, meaning that the selective search required 1,000 documents to be returned from each of the (typically) 3–5 shards that processed the query, but that less than 10% of that number was required from each shard in the exhaustive search baseline because of the random allocation process used to form them [2]. Overall, the simulator takes as input a list of queries, the resource selection cost for each query, the shards to be searched for the query, and the search cost for each shard. The simulator converts these posting list costs into "milliseconds" on a per-shard basis, and from them computes an overall elapsed time for each query, taking into account contention for processor and disk, and including queuing times. The primary variable in the simulator is the query arrival rate, which determines the system load, and hence the extent to which query response is affected by queuing delays.

3. EXPERIMENTS AND RESULTS

Document Collections and Query Streams Gov2 (25 M documents, 24 B words, split into 50 shards) and ClueWeb09-A English (ClueWeb09, 500 M documents and 381 B words, split into 884 shards) are used in our experiments. The shard definitions were generated by Kulkarni [4] and the resource selection parameters are from Kulkarni [4] and Aly et al. [1]; preliminary trials con-

Queries	Res. sel.	Gov2		ClueWeb09	
		avg.	sddev.	avg.	sddev.
MQT	Taily	2.5	1.4	3.6	2.9
	Rank-S	4.2	1.8	4.4	1.7
AOL	Taily	2.9	1.6	11.9	31.3
	Rank-S	4.6	1.9	4.2	1.7

Table 2: Average number of shards selected by Taily and Rank-S for the two query logs, for the system configurations in Figure 2. Parameters for Taily, $n = 400$, $v = 50$; for Rank-S, sample rate $= 1\%$, base $= 3$ (Gov2), base$= 5$ (ClueWeb09).

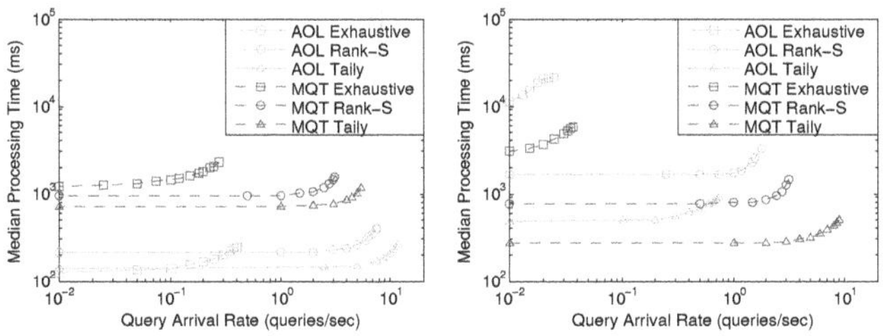

(a) Gov2 (b) ClueWeb09

Figure 2: Exhaustive search and selective search using random shard assignment, two query sets, and $M = S = 2$ and $B = 1$.

firmed that we were able to match their effectiveness results. We make use of the AOL query log and the TREC Million Query Track queries. The AOL log was sorted by timestamp, and deduplicated to simulate a system with a large answer cache. For ClueWeb09, the first 1,000 queries were used as training, to set parameters; the next 10,000 queries were used for testing. For Gov2, we used only queries that had at least one .gov-domain result click recorded, and then 1,000 and 10,000 queries used for training and testing. Similar test sets were extracted from the TREC Million Query Track (MQT), taking queries in the supplied order. Two further test query sets were also extracted from the AOL log: 10,000 queries starting one week after the main query stream; and another 10,000 queries commencing one month after the main query stream.

Query Throughput We compare selective and exhaustive search in an environment similar to that examined by Kulkarni [4, 5]. In both cases the shards are randomly distributed across all machines, with each machine receiving the same number of shards; exhaustive search shards were constructed by placing $1/c_i$ of the collection in to each of c_i shards, with $c_i = 8$. In both configurations, only one machine ($B = 1$) accepted broker tasks, to mimic the previous experimentation. Table 2 summarizes the average number of shards selected by the resource selection algorithms.

Figure 2 shows the simulated throughput of two selective search variants, compared to exhaustive search. The vertical axis shows the median time to process a single query, plotted as a function of the query arrival rate on the horizontal axis. (Alternative summary metrics such as the mean or the 95% percentile processing times produced similar patterns of behavior.) Each curve represents one combination of query set and processing regime, and the right-hand end of each curve is truncated at a point at which the system configuration reaches saturation, defined as when the median processing time exceeds twice the median processing time for queries in the corresponding unloaded system (at the left-hand end of the curve). Configurations in which the curve is lower have superior latency under light load; configurations with elbows that are further to the right require fewer resources per query, and attain higher throughput rates when the system is under heavy load.

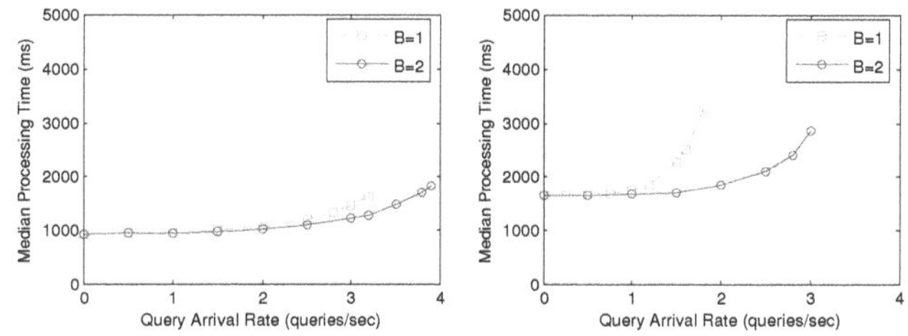

(a) Rank-S, Gov2 (b) Rank-S, ClueWeb09

Figure 3: Effect of number of brokers, using Rank-S, $M = 2$ machines (16 cores in total), and random shard assignment.

Selective search outperforms exhaustive search by a factor of more than ten on the ClueWeb09 dataset because only a small fraction of the 884 shards are searched for each query. Importantly, query latency is also lower, despite the two-step process that is involved – topical shards are smaller than random shards, and can be searched more quickly. A larger fraction of the shards are searched in Gov2, and the performance improvement is not as great. Even so, selective search of Gov2 handles four to five times the query load of exhaustive search. As expected, Taily has better throughput and latency than Rank-S for the majority of combinations tested.

That is, Figure 2 extends the findings of Kulkarni [4] to show that total workload is lower in selective search than in exhaustive search in a parallel query environment; and in addition also shows that over a broad range of query loads, selective search improves per-query response times as well, a win-win outcome.

Broker Load Balancing The difference between Rank-S and Taily is a consequence of their approaches to resource selection [1]. In Figure 2 only one machine acted as broker, and the shards were evenly distributed across the two machines ($B = 1, S = 2$), matching the configuration explored by Kulkarni [4]. However, this configuration is not optimal for selective search, and in experiments not reported here, we observed that an uneven machine load arises, especially when using Rank-S.

The situation can be improved by employing more broker processes. Figure 3 compares the previous $B = 1$ outcomes to $B = 2$, that is, a configuration in which both machines perform resource selection. The change results in a moderate gain in throughput on Gov2, and a marked improvement in throughput on ClueWeb09. The difference is due to the size of the corresponding CSIs. Rank-S uses an approximately 1% sample of the corpus in the CSI, or about half the size of the average Gov2 shard. But for ClueWeb09, the CSI is eight times the average shard size, and a much greater fraction of the search time is spent on shard selection. Taily requires much less computation than does Rank-S, and the best setting was $B = 1$. With $M = 2$ and $B = 1$, resource selection for Taily accounted for less than 2% of m_1's processing capability. On the other hand, sample-based algorithms have other advantages, including the ability to run structured queries.

Shard Assignment With two machines ($M = 2$), random assignment of shards to machines tends to distribute query traffic evenly across machines, since there are many more shards than machines ($P \gg M$). That balance erodes as M increases, because selective search deliberately creates shards that have skewed term distributions. In exploratory experiments, we observed that Rank-S applied to Gov2 and the AOL queries results in the five most popular shards accounting for 29% of all shards selected. The MQT query set displays a similar, but more moderate, skew.

The next experiment compares the *Random* shard assignment with an alternative *Log-based* mechanism that uses training queries

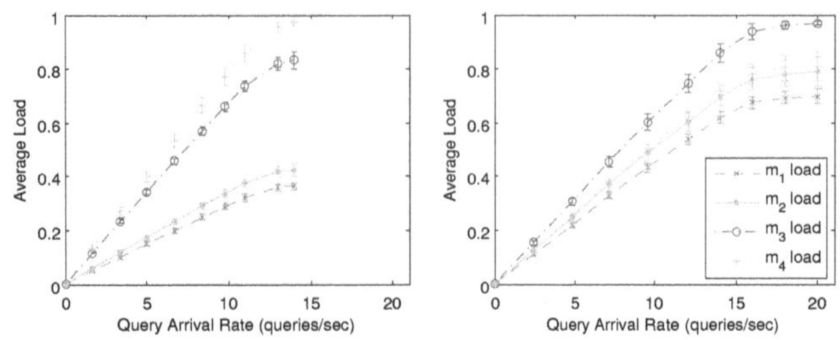

(a) Random assignment (b) Log-based assignment

Figure 4: Machine workload fractions for Taily on Gov2, the MQT test queries, and $M = S = 4$ and $B = 1$. Each point is the mean over 10 sequences of 1,000 queries; error bars represent 95% confidence intervals. The broker is on m_1 in both configurations.

to estimate and balance the average load across machines [8]. The training queries are evaluated via the resource selection process, and for each shard, the sum of the postings costs computed and used as an estimate of its workload. Shards are then ordered from most to least loaded, and assigned to machines one by one, in each case choosing the machine that currently has the lowest total estimated load. Any remaining shards that were not accessed by the training queries are assigned similarly, based on their size. In these experiments a set of 1,000 training queries was employed. Using Taily shard selection, Gov2 had no unaccessed shards for either query set, and for the ClueWeb09 collection, 7% and 4% of shards were unaccessed by the AOL and MQT training sets respectively.

Figure 4 shows the effect of shard assignment policy on the per-host workload for $M = 4$ hosts using Gov2, with the vertical axis showing machine utilization in the range 0.0–1.0. The wide spread of loads in the left pane shows that the Random policy produces an uneven utilization of machines, with m_4 becoming a bottleneck. In comparison, the Log-based policy (right pane) markedly reduces the load variance, and allows higher query throughput rates to be attained. When compared to ten other randomly generated shard assignments, the Log-based policy remained the best performer. Results for Rank-S are similar, and are omitted.

The risk of using Log-based allocations is that the learned attributes may become dated as a result of query drift. Table 3 investigates this potential shortcoming by showing machine usage (denoted as $load_i$ for machine m_i) for three time-separated query sets each containing 10,000 queries: one from immediately after the training queries; a second from one week after the training queries; and a third from one month after the training queries. Average utilization is similar in each case, and variance increases marginally as the query stream evolves, but the changes are generally small. Results for Gov2 one month after assignment have a markedly lower utilization due to a burst of shorter queries that occurred at this time (2.18 words on average versus 2.44 for the "straight after" query stream), meaning that at any given arrival rate less total work is required. Shard assignments should be periodically revised to maximize throughput, but it is not necessary to do it frequently, and the cost of refreshing shard assignments can be amortized.

4. CONCLUSION

Selective search is known to be more efficient than exhaustive search in a single-query-at-a-time environment [4, 5]. We have reproduced and extended those earlier findings using a simulator that models realistic parallel processing environments. Our results demonstrate that for some hardware configurations the selective search architecture – resource selection followed by shard access – delivers both greater total throughput (number of queries processed per time interval) and lower latency (faster response time) than conventional approaches to distribution. We also investigated the effects of the resource selection algorithm, and found that Rank-S usually resulted in higher latency and lower throughput than Taily.

Selective search uses topical shards that are likely to differ in access rate. Typical random assignments of shards produce imbalances in machine load, even when as few as four machines are in use. We introduced a Log-based assignment policy using training queries that provides higher throughput and more consistent query processing times than random assignments. The Log-based assignment is also resilient to temporal changes, and throughput degradation was slight, even after delays of a month.

Test	Average $load_i$ and range of $load_i$					
	avg.	rnge.	avg.	rnge.	avg.	rnge.
Gov2	30 qry/s		40 qry/s		50 qry/s	
immediate	0.59	0.20	0.73	0.25	0.78	0.26
one week	0.56	0.19	0.71	0.24	0.76	0.25
one month	0.47	0.20	0.62	0.26	0.72	0.30
ClueWeb09	2.0 qry/s		2.5 qry/s		3.0 qry/s	
immediate	0.52	0.02	0.65	0.02	0.77	0.03
one week	0.51	0.02	0.63	0.02	0.75	0.02
one month	0.53	0.02	0.66	0.02	0.77	0.03

Table 3: Average $load_i$ and range ($\max load_i - \min load_i$) as the training data ages, using the Log-based shard allocation policy. The query sets begin immediately after the training queries; one week after the training queries; and one month after the training queries.

Acknowledgment This work is supported by the National Science Foundation (IIS-1302206); and by the Australian Research Council (DP140101587 and DP140103256). Shane Culpepper is the recipient of an Australian Research Council DECRA Research Fellowship (DE140100275). Yubin Kim is the recipient of the Natural Sciences and Engineering Research Council of Canada PGS-D3 (438411). Any opinions, findings, conclusions or recommendations expressed in this paper are those of the authors, and do not necessarily reflect those of the sponsors.

References

[1] R. Aly, D. Hiemstra, and T. Demeester. Taily: Shard Selection Using the Tail of Score Distributions. In *Proc. SIGIR*, pages 673–682, 2013.

[2] F. Cacheda, V. Carneiro, V. Plachouras, and I. Ounis. Performance analysis of distributed information retrieval architectures using an improved network simulation model. *Inf. Proc. Man.*, 43:204–224, 2007.

[3] Y. Kim, J. Callan, J. S. Culpepper, and A. Moffat. Does selective search benefit from WAND optimization? In *Proc. ECIR*, pages 145–158, 2016.

[4] A. Kulkarni. *Efficient and Effective Large-Scale Search.* PhD thesis, Carnegie Mellon University, 2013.

[5] A. Kulkarni and J. Callan. Document allocation policies for selective searching of distributed indexes. In *Proc. CIKM*, pages 449–458, 2010.

[6] A. Kulkarni and J. Callan. Selective search: Efficient and effective search of large textual collections. *ACM Trans. Inf. Sys.*, 33(4):17:1–17:33, 2015.

[7] A. Kulkarni, A. Tigelaar, D. Hiemstra, and J. Callan. Shard ranking and cutoff estimation for topically partitioned collections. In *Proc. CIKM*, pages 555–564, 2012.

[8] A. Moffat, W. Webber, and J. Zobel. Load balancing for term-distributed parallel retrieval. In *Proc. SIGIR*, pages 348–355, 2006.

[9] A. L. Powell, J. C. French, J. Callan, M. Connell, and C. L. Viles. The impact of database selection on distributed searching. In *Proc. SIGIR*, pages 232–239, 2000.

Multi-Rate Deep Learning for Temporal Recommendation

Yang Song
Microsoft Research Redmond
yangsong@microsoft.com

Ali Mamdouh Elkahky
Columbia University
ame2154@columbia.edu

Xiaodong He
Microsoft Research Redmond
xiaohe@microsoft.com

ABSTRACT

Modeling temporal behavior in recommendation systems is an important and challenging problem. Its challenges come from the fact that temporal modeling increases the cost of parameter estimation and inference, while requiring large amount of data to reliably learn the model with the additional time dimensions. Therefore, it is often difficult to model temporal behavior in large-scale real-world recommendation systems. In this work, we propose a novel deep neural network based architecture that models the combination of long-term static and short-term temporal user preferences to improve the recommendation performance. To train the model efficiently for large-scale applications, we propose a novel pre-train method to reduce the number of free parameters significantly. The resulted model is applied to a real-world data set from a commercial News recommendation system. We compare to a set of established baselines and the experimental results show that our method outperforms the state-of-the-art significantly.

1. INTRODUCTION

Recommendation systems are core components of many of the modern Internet services including News, E-commerce, online movie sites and more. Each recommendation scenario has its unique attributes which creates needs for different approaches in building recommendation systems. For example, News recommendation is more focused on the freshness of the content, while movie recommendation may put more emphasis on the content relatedness. In addition, user interests constantly evolve over time. While many existing techniques assume the user preferences to be static, this seems to be unrealistic assumption in many scenarios, particularly in News or shopping related scenarios. For example, In a previous work [6], the authors showed that users who visited *spligle.de*, a popular German news portal, are likely to be interested in football-related news, the reason being that the data was collected around the dates of world cup 2014. While the trained model may work very well for a period of time, eventually after the event the model's performance will degrade significantly and therefore needs to be retrained.

One way to handle temporal changes in user's interests is to use only the recent interactions from the users in order to provide the most timely recommendation. While this may work for users of who have rich interactions with the systems, it will fail in the cold-start scenario. In addition, this approach needs constantly re-train the model, which is both expensive and difficult for performance evaluation.

A better approach is therefore to make use of both long-term user history as well as their short-term temporal interests. In this case, we assume that user's preferences are composed of two components: the long-term preference which reflects the *fairly stable* interests of the users based on their online activities; and the temporal interests which represents the users' current immanent need/interests.

Specifically, in this work, we propose a *multi-rate* temporal deep learning model that jointly optimizes long-term and short-term user interests to improve the recommendation quality. The model consists of several components: a Deep Semantic Structured Model (DSSM) [11] to model user static interests; two LSTM-based temporal models to capture daily and weekly user temporal patterns; and an LSTM temporal model to capture global user interests. The term multi-rate indicates the capability of our model which is able to capture user interests at different granularity, so that temporal dynamics at different rates can be effectively and jointly optimized.

2. RELATED WORK

In recommendation systems, temporal modeling of data is an important element in many tasks such as news recommendation [16, 15], movie recommendation [14, 23], and recently, music recommendation [12]. It has been shown to improve results over non-temporal model significantly. In this section, we will survey some of the recent approaches and refer readers to a more extensive review on temporal recommendation in [5].

In [14], the matrix factorization model is extended to allow each user to have a base latent vector and another set of time dependent vectors. A regularization term to enforce each time-dependent vector to be similar to the one in the previous time step is added to maintain the smoothness over time. A Bayesian extension to this work was introduced in [23] where regularization is replaced by prior distributions. By treating matrix factorization as an autoregressive model, the authors introduced a temporal matrix factorization approach [24] which aims at predicting next

SIGIR '16, July 17-21, 2016, Pisa, Italy

DOI: http://dx.doi.org/10.1145/2911451.2914726

steps from historical data. A simple and scalable Bayesian approach for News recommendations was proposed in [16]. The authors used a probability distribution of user's topic preferences at the current time which have priors that depends on both the user's historical preferences as well as the preferences of other users sharing the same geographic location. In [25], the authors used collaborative filtering technique to compute explicit user similarity function and extends the similarity function to incorporate temporal pattern similarities between users. Another approach presented in [2] divided user interaction with the system into discrete partitions, each of which represents the user interests in a particular time range. A similar approach that mines temporal sequential patterns from usage data was presented in [23] where the authors modeled the transition between (user, item, time) nodes and then used certain rules to mine meaningful temporal patterns and fused them with long term user interests. In [15], long-term user history was leveraged to provide coarse grain news recommendation for certain news groups. The short-term history of the user was then used to recommend specific news articles within the selected groups.

Using deep learning approaches for recommendation systems has recently received many attentions [20, 21, 22]. However, using deep learning for temporal recommendation has not yet been extensively studied. In [8], the authors proposed to use Recurrent Neural Networks (RNN) for recommending shopping items to users based on the user's current session history. A similar idea of session-based recommendation was proposed for music recommendation in [1] by modeling music playlist as sessions.

3. TEMPORAL DEEP SEMANTIC STRUCTURED MODEL (TDSSM)

The Deep Semantic Structured Models (DSSM) was proposed in [11] for ranking purpose and was later on extended to the recommendation scenarios in [6]. We briefly review DSSM here. Essentially, DSSM can be viewed as a multi-view learning model that often composes of two or more neural networks for each individual view. In the original two-view DSSM model, the left network represents the query view and the right network represents the document view. The input of each neural network can be arbitrary types of features, e.g., letter-tri-gram used in the original paper [11], or bag of unigram features used in [6]. Each input feature vector goes through non-linear transformations in the feedforward network to output an embedding vector, which is often much smaller than the original input space. The learning objective of DSSM is to maximize the cosine similarity between the two output vectors. During training, a set of positive examples and randomly sampled negative examples are generated in each minibatch to minimize the cosine loss on the positive examples. In [6], the authors used DSSM for recommendation where the first neural network contains user's query history (and thus referred to as user view) and the second neural network contains implicit feedback of items (e.g., News clicks, App downloads). The resulting model is named multi-view DNN (MV-DNN) since it can incorporate item information from more than one domains and jointly optimize all of them using the same loss function in DSSM.

In the MV-DNN model (and DSSM as well), both the user view and item view are *static* in the sense that the input

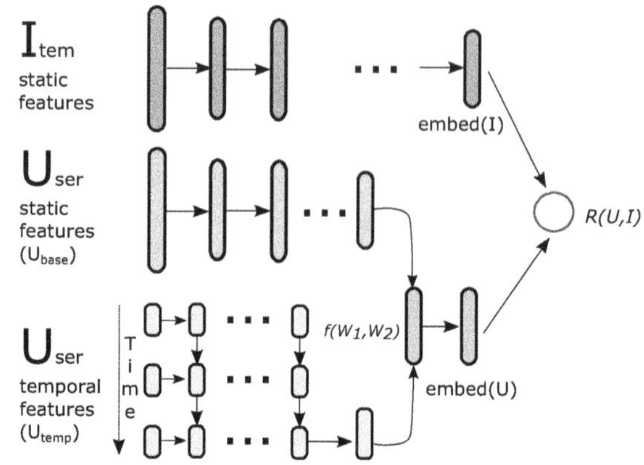

Figure 1: The temporal DSSM (TDSSM) model for temporal user modeling.

features represent a holistic view of users interests during a certain period of time. The model thus lacks the ability of responding promptly to some scenarios where freshness and the temporal dynamics of the items is sometimes more important than the content relevance itself, e.g., News recommendation. Therefore, we propose to extend DSSM to include temporal information by incorporating recurrent neural networks (RNN) into the user-view of the model. Instead of modeling the entire user history using RNN which is difficult to train, our model combines the long-term user preferences which remains relatively stable over time, with the short-term temporal user interests using feedforward neural network as follows:

$$E(U, t_i) = f_{U,t_i}(E_{base}(U), E_{t_i}(U)) \tag{1}$$

where $E(U, t_i)$ is the output embedding of the user U at time t_i, which is a combination of the baseline user preferences $E_{base}(U)$ and the temporal user preference $E_{t_i}(U)$. Here f is a aggregation function which can take one of the three forms:

$$f(W_1, W_2) = \begin{cases} W_1 \odot W_2 & \text{elem-wise multiplication} \\ W_1 \odot A \odot W_2 & \text{weighted elem-wise multiplication} \\ [W_1; W_2] & \text{concatenation} \end{cases}$$

On the other hand, the content of the items often remain unchanged. This implies that we can use the same embedding for the items over different time period and thus makes the training tractable. The objective function can then be written as:

$$\min_{W_{user} W_{item}} -\log \prod_{user,item^+,t_i} p(item^+|user, t_i) \tag{2}$$

where $p(item^+|user, t_i)$ is defined as:

$$p(item^+|user, t_i) = \frac{e^{cos(E(user,t_i),E_{item^+})}}{\sum_{\forall item} e^{cos(E(user,t_i),E_{item})}} \tag{3}$$

Figure 1 shows the architecture of the proposed model, namely the temporal DSSM (TDSSM). The key difference to the previous model is the introduction of the user temporal features network, where we use RNN to model user interests at different time spots. One design decision in this model is how we choose the granularity of each input time spot t_i. While modeling using smaller time spans (say hourly) can capture more fine-grained interest changes, it will make the feature space very sparse and thus make the learning difficult. On the other hand, having time large spans may lead to less sparse feature spaces but also makes the model less adaptive and efficient for capturing temporal dynamics. The next section addresses this issue by extending the current TDSSM.

3.1 Mutli-Rate TDSSM

Instead of having temporal embedding $E(user, t_i)$ computed on a single granularity, we propose a new model to that aggregate temporal information at different rates, each of which is modeled using a separate RNN. *Fast-rate* RNNs are used to adapt to very recent user interests, while *slow-rate* RNNs are designed to model seasonal user interest shift. RNNs at different rates are combined using fully-connected feedfoward network. This design allows for the independence of each RNN in terms of feature aggregation, while also in principle jointly optimizes the parameters from all RNNs and the baseline model effectively. The resulted model is named multi-rate TDSSDM, or MR-TDSSM. One drawback of such model is the large number of model parameters from the RNNs. In the next section, we discuss how to use a technique called pre-train to reduce the free parameters and speed up the training process.

4. TRAINING SPEED-UP USING PRE-TRAIN

Pre-train is a known approach to make neural network training faster and more effective [9, 4]. Previously, pre-train was used to train deep networks in incremental fashion where training of the first layer is done separately then its output is taken as input to the next layer. Recently, it becomes popular to use pre-train of word embedding for NLP applications [17], by first training on a large unlabeled data set, then use the trained embedding in the target supervised task.

In this work, we use a similar idea as word embedding to initialize the embedding of user and item feature vectors via additional training data. To be concrete, we started by training a DSSM model in the same way as proposed in [6]. The resulted DSSM is then used to generate embedding for MR-TDSSM inputs.

The use of pre-train reduces the size of input feature space by a factor proportional to the ratio between the size of the original feature space (i.e. $\|X_{user}\| = D_{user}$ and $\|X_{item}\| = D_{item}$) to the size of the embedding space(i.e. $\|E_{user}\| = \|E_{item}\| = d$). In addition, it no longer requires the item view to go through another multi-layer neural networks. The reduction of the parameters in the input layers comes with the cost of converting those inputs from sparse vectors to dense ones during initialization. However, this operation actually improves the training efficiency since implementing efficient operations for sparse vectors is still a challenging task[3].

5. EXPERIMENTAL SETUP AND RESULTS

The data set used in our experiment comes from a commercial news portal which serves millions of daily users in a variety of countries and languages. The dataset consists of user's news click history between 04/01/2014 and 09/30/2014. The first four months are used for training the model while the last two months are used for testing. In order to get enough signal for the temporal model, we filtered out users who have less than 20 news clicks during those six months. This resulted in 64,669 users, 26.5 million training pairs of $(user, news)$ clicks for training and 13.3 million pairs for testing. For each test triplet $(user, news, time)$, we generate 9 random news from the same time span for evaluation. The evaluation objective is to see how well the model can rank the clicked news on top of those randomly sampled news. Therefore, we employee five popular metrics for evaluation: precision at position 1 (P@1) and 5 (P@5), Area Under Curve (AUC), Mean Average Precision (MAP) and Mean Reciprocal Rank (MRR).

To make the result more convincing, we also compare with several state-of-the-art recommendation algorithms. Those include SVD++ and RegSVD [18], WRMF [10], CF-KNN [13] and AoBPR [19]. Note that matrix factorization techniques including SVD++, RegSVD, WRMF and CF-KNN cannot deal with out-of-matrix predictions thus during evaluation novel users are removed from these algorithms. We also added the popularity-based baseline by ranking news based on the number of clicks they received. For those baseline algorithms we used the implementation of LibRec from [7].

For DSSM implementation, we used the implementation of Sent2Vec from [11]. The output embedding is set to 300. To implement the TDSSM and MR-TDSSM, we used Theano [1] and Keras[2]. The RNNs in the models are implemented using LSTM in Keras. We also tried GRU but the results seem to be worse than LSTM. To verify whether the RNN model itself can achieve good performance for evaluation, we also trained an LSTM-only model that uses only recent user embedding. In addition, a variant of the LSTM-only model which adds the user static input as the input in the beginning of the model is also evaluated. Additionally, to verify the recency effect, we implemented a baseline which leverages the embedding from the immediate previous time spot to test the performance of the news on the current time spot.

For TDSSM we used previous two-week clicks as short-term history, with each day as a time spot. Therefore, the length of the LSTM for TDSSDM is 14. For MR-TDSSM, we implemented two LSTMs in different rates, where the fast-rate LSTM uses daily signals and the slow-rate LSTM uses weekly signals.

Table 1 summarizes the results. We first observe that the most-popular baseline performs no better than random guess, indicating that popularity does not necessarily correlates with user interests. Secondly, we can observe that most matrix factorization-based techniques performed quite poorly, with the only exception of WRMF [10] which takes implicit feedback as additional signals and thus performed well (0.195 P@1) on this data set. Now let's examine the performance of models that take short-term user interests into consideration. We first observe that by only using the immediate previous day's news click, the model (prev-day click) already shows better performance (0.211 P@1) than all MF-based methods, with competitive results against the DSSM baseline (0.229 P@1) which only leverages user long-term static features. On the other hand, LSTM-based methods (LSTM-only and LSTM-DSSM) failed to outperform

[1]https://github.com/Theano/Theano
[2]http://keras.io

Table 1: Performance comparison of our models vs. state-of-the-art methods.

Method	P@1	P@5	AUC	MAP	MRR
Most Popular	0.105	0.053	0.504	0.042	0.284
SVD++ [13]	0.157	0.072	0.647	0.056	0.296
RegSVD [18]	0.156	0.072	0.638	0.052	0.294
AoBPR [19]	0.168	0.076	0.659	0.064	0.315
UserKNN (k=80)	0.174	0.093	0.684	0.068	0.323
WRMF [10]	0.195	0.114	0.692	0.071	0.347
Prev-day Click	0.2109	0.119	0.727	0.074	0.358
DSSM [11]	0.229	0.126	0.763	0.085	0.379
LSTM-Only	0.189	0.102	0.688	0.07	0.329
LSTM-DSSM	0.196	0.116	0.691	0.073	0.349
TDSSM	0.231	0.134	0.779	0.091	0.381
MR-TDSSM	0.245	0.147	0.814	0.099	0.397

the DSSM model, which indicates that ignoring the long-term user interests may not lead to optimal performance. Since the short-term user history is often quite sparse, models like LSTM that has many training parameters cannot learn enough evidence from the sparse inputs. Finally, by combining long-term and short-term user interests, our proposed models TDSSM and MR-TDSSM successfully outperformed all the methods significantly. We can notice that by adding a slow-rate LSTM (weekly-based features) to the MR-TDSSM, it leads to great performance improvement over TDSSM with only one fast-rate LSTM component.

6. CONCLUSION

In this work we explored the use of deep learning for temporal news recommendation. We showed that deep learning can be effective in learning temporal recommendation models by combining traditional feedforward networks (DSSM) with recurrent networks (LSTM). To address the issue of different granularity, we also introduced the MR-TDSSM which had the ability to model sequence of data at multiple levels of rate. In addition, we showed that pre-train can significantly decrease the number of parameters in the model and make it efficiently trainable. Comparisons with several state-of-the-art methods indicated that both of models can significantly improve the recommendation performance.

Future work includes applying this model to different recommendation scenarios. One obvious domain is shopping recommendation where user's history of recently purchased items can be good indicators of their immediate purchasing interests. For the models, we also want to explore the attention-based memory network to further improve the performance of LSTM models.

7. REFERENCES

[1] Recurrent neural networks for collaborative filtering. http://erikbern.com/2014/06/28/recurrent-neural-networks-for-collaborative-filtering/. Accessed: 2016-01-18.

[2] L. Baltrunas and X. Amatriain. Towards time-dependant recommendation based on implicit feedback. In *Workshop on (CARS09)*, 2009.

[3] N. Bell and M. Garland. Implementing sparse matrix-vector multiplication on throughput-oriented processors. In *Proceedings of the Conference on High Performance Computing Networking, Storage and Analysis*, page 18. ACM, 2009.

[4] Y. Bengio, P. Lamblin, D. Popovici, H. Larochelle, et al. Greedy layer-wise training of deep networks. 2007.

[5] P. G. Campos, F. Díez, and I. Cantador. Time-aware recommender systems: a comprehensive survey and analysis of existing evaluation protocols. *User Modeling and User-Adapted Interaction*, 24(1-2):67–119, 2014.

[6] A. M. Elkahky, Y. Song, and X. He. A multi-view deep learning approach for cross domain user modeling in recommendation systems. In *Proceedings of WWW2015*, pages 278–288, 2015.

[7] G. Guo, J. Zhang, Z. Sun, and N. Yorke-Smith. Librec: A java library for recommender systems.

[8] B. Hidasi, A. Karatzoglou, L. Baltrunas, and D. Tikk. Session-based recommendations with recurrent neural networks. *CoRR*, abs/1511.06939, 2015.

[9] G. E. Hinton and R. R. Salakhutdinov. Reducing the dimensionality of data with neural networks. *Science*, 313(5786):504–507, 2006.

[10] Y. Hu, Y. Koren, and C. Volinsky. Collaborative filtering for implicit feedback datasets. In *ICDM'08*.

[11] P.-S. Huang, X. He, J. Gao, L. Deng, A. Acero, and L. Heck. Learning deep structured semantic models for web search using clickthrough data. In *CIKM'13*.

[12] N. Koenigstein, G. Dror, and Y. Koren. Yahoo! music recommendations: modeling music ratings with temporal dynamics and item taxonomy. In *Recsys'11*.

[13] Y. Koren. Factorization meets the neighborhood: a multifaceted collaborative filtering model. In *KDD'08*.

[14] Y. Koren. Collaborative filtering with temporal dynamics. *Communications of the ACM*, 53(4):89–97, 2010.

[15] L. Li, L. Zheng, F. Yang, and T. Li. Modeling and broadening temporal user interest in personalized news recommendation. *Expert Systems with Applications*, 41(7):3168–3177, 2014.

[16] J. Liu, P. Dolan, and E. R. Pedersen. Personalized news recommendation based on click behavior. In *Proceedings of the 15th international conference on Intelligent user interfaces*, pages 31–40. ACM, 2010.

[17] T. Mikolov, I. Sutskever, K. Chen, G. S. Corrado, and J. Dean. Distributed representations of words and phrases and their compositionality. In *Advances in neural information processing systems*, pages 3111–3119, 2013.

[18] A. Paterek. Improving regularized singular value decomposition for collaborative filtering. 2007.

[19] S. Rendle and C. Freudenthaler. Improving pairwise learning for item recommendation from implicit feedback. In *WSDM'14*.

[20] R. Salakhutdinov, A. Mnih, and G. Hinton. Restricted boltzmann machines for collaborative filtering. In *Proceedings of the 24th international conference on Machine learning*, pages 791–798. ACM, 2007.

[21] A. Van den Oord, S. Dieleman, and B. Schrauwen. Deep content-based music recommendation. In *NIPS'13*.

[22] H. Wang, N. Wang, and D.-Y. Yeung. Collaborative deep learning for recommender systems. *arXiv preprint arXiv:1409.2944*, 2014.

[23] L. Xiong, X. Chen, T.-K. Huang, J. G. Schneider, and J. G. Carbonell. Temporal collaborative filtering with bayesian probabilistic tensor factorization. SIAM.

[24] H. Yu, N. Rao, and I. S. Dhillon. Temporal regularized matrix factorization. *CoRR*, abs/1509.08333, 2015.

[25] Q. Yuan, G. Cong, Z. Ma, A. Sun, and N. M. Thalmann. Time-aware point-of-interest recommendation. In *SIGIR'13*.

Network-Aware Recommendations of Novel Tweets *

Noor Aldeen Alawad
Sapienza University of Rome
Rome, Italy
alawad@dis.uniroma1.it

Aris Anagnostopoulos
Sapienza University of Rome
Rome, Italy
aris@dis.uniroma1.it

Stefano Leonardi
Sapienza University of Rome
Rome, Italy
leonardi@dis.uniroma1.it

Ida Mele
Università della Svizzera Italiana
Lugano, Switzerland
ida.mele@usi.ch

Fabrizio Silvestri
Yahoo
London, UK
silvestr@yahoo-inc.com

ABSTRACT

With the rapid proliferation of microblogging services such as Twitter, a large number of tweets is published everyday often making users feel overwhelmed with information. Helping these users to discover potentially interesting tweets is an important task for such services. In this paper, we present a novel tweet-recommendation approach, which exploits network, content, and retweet analyses for making recommendations of tweets. The idea is to recommend tweets that are not visible to the user (i.e., they do not appear in the user timeline) because nobody in her social circles published or retweeted them. To do that, we create the user's ego-network up to depth two and apply the transitivity property of the *friends-of-friends* relationship to determine interesting recommendations, which are then ranked to best match the user's interests. Experimental results demonstrate that our approach improves the state-of-the-art technique.

Keywords

Tweet Recommendation, Content and Network Analysis.

1. INTRODUCTION

Online social networks allow people to connect to one another and to share information, opinions, and ideas. Twitter is a popular micro-blogging system where users can post short messages, called tweets, whose length is at maximum 140 characters. Tweets typically consist of personal information, status updates, news, or links to webpages or other web content (e.g., images and videos). Twitter users, by following one another, define a social graph, where nodes are users, and a direct edge (u, v) represents the fact that the user u follows the user v.

The tweets posted or retweeted by a user are shown on the user's profile page as well as on the timeline of her followers. These users can reply to the author of the tweet, or they can retweet the original message, so that it is made visible to their followers, too. Retweets are very frequent, allowing the propagation of interesting information into the Twitter community, and, for this reason, the users follow news channels, favorite celebrities, or friends to obtain new information as soon as possible. However, the huge number of tweets posted everyday causes the problem of information overload, and recommendation systems can play a key role in solving this problem. In Twitter most of these systems are based on recommending users to follow [7], webpages to visit [17], or they consist in reranking the tweets appearing in the user's timeline [16]. A new line of research is based on recommending concealed tweets, by which we mean, tweets that are not posted or retweeted by anybody in the user's social circles. As a result, users have access to additional tweets that may be of interest. Consider, for example, the following scenario: A user is interested in computer science and everyday she checks the tweets of the computer scientists she is following. Some of these tweets are originally posted by them, whereas others are just the result of a retweet. When nobody has retweeted a message that is potentially interesting for the user, such message remains concealed from the user's eyes, because it does not appear in her timeline. Pennacchiotti et al. [10] tackled this problem by proposing tweets whose content matches the user's interests. We follow and extend their idea of recommending hidden tweets that are potentially interesting to the user, but instead of using only the content analysis, we propose to exploit the structure of the network around the user as well as the analysis of mutual retweets; we demonstrate that this yields an improvement in the quality of the recommendations.

*This research was partially supported by the Google Focused Research Award "Algorithms for Large-Scale Data Analysis" and by the EU FET project MULTIPLEX 317532.

SIGIR '16, July 17–21, 2016, Pisa, Italy.
© 2016 ACM. ISBN 978-1-4503-4069-4/16/07...$15.00
DOI: http://dx.doi.org/10.1145/2911451.2914760

2. RELATED WORK

Recommendation systems help the users to find products and services, music and videos as well as blogs and news articles, and they have been widely studied in the past [11]. With the rapid growth of Twitter, a lot of research has been focusing on analyzing Twitter data and the activities of its users for improving personalization and recommendations [8]. Depending on the type of recommendations, we can divide the recommendation tasks into three categories:

Followee recommendations: In [1], the authors proposed an approach which recommends the people to follow by analyzing the topology of the network around the user. Other studies have based their followee recommendations on the popularity and activity of Twitter users [3, 6]. Twittomender [7] is a famous system, which recommends followees based on the users' tweets and their relationships in the social graph. Although our system does not recommend people to follow but novel interesting tweets, there are some similarities with these approaches, because we also exploit the network structure of the social graph.

Tweet-based content recommendations: Due to the lack of user-profiling information, recommending web content is often challenging, and Twitter has demonstrated to be a rich source from which is possible to obtain more information about web users. In particular, it has been proven that using Twitter data (e.g., tweets, retweets, hashtags of the user and of her friends) it is possible to improve the URL recommendations [4, 17]. Differently from these works, we do not recommend web content but focus on recommendations of tweets.

Tweet recommendations: Most of these approaches offer a ranking of tweets based on a query or they re-rank the tweets appearing in the user's timeline. Yan et al. [16] rank tweets and their authors using hybrid networks, and Uysal and Croft [15] proposed to rank the incoming tweets based on their probability to be retweeted by the users. Our approach differs from these, because it aims at making recommendations of concealed tweets, which are tweets that do not appear in the user timeline, because they have not been posted or retweeted by anybody in the user's social circles. Moreover, our approach is user-centric in the sense that the recommendations do not depend on a specific query but they rather match the user's interests inferred from previous user's (re)tweets. In this way, our recommendation algorithm is similar to [10] where the authors recommend unseen tweets based on the content similarity. Differently from them, we exploit not only the analysis of tweet content but also the structure of the network around the users (ego-network) and the users' interest similarity which is mined from their common retweets. As we will explain in Section 3, we define a set of candidate tweets to recommend by creating the user's ego-network with depth two and exploiting the transitivity property of the following–follower relationships among users. These candidate tweets are then ranked by using content-similarity measures plus the users' interest similarity to best match the user's interests.

3. METHODOLOGY

Our recommendation approach is based on recommending tweets that cannot be seen by the user, for example, because nobody in her circles wrote or retweeted them. Twitter users who subscribe to our system receive recommendations of novel tweets, which do not appear in their timeline but which are of potential interest.

For making recommendations we applied network, content, and retweet analyses. The idea is to use the network structure around the user as a pre-filtering step to find candidate tweets to recommend. Then, these tweets are ranked by using the content-similarity features and the number of common retweets, which is an indication of how much the users' interests are similar.

To explore our method more deeply, when a user u subscribes to the service, the system uses the Twitter API to retrieve u's friends, friends of friends, and timeline (i.e., tweets and retweets). Given u's ego-network up to depth two, the recommendation algorithm exploits the transitivity property of the following–follower relationships. For example, assume that user u follows a set of users v_i who follow user z, and that u does not follow z, the (re)tweets of z are not visible to u, unless some v_i retweeted them. The idea is to use z's (re)tweets, which do not appear in u's timeline, as possible candidates for the recommendations. To weigh the importance of the tweets of z, we count the number of users v_i that are in between.

Network Analysis. The scenario described in the end of the previous paragraph can be mapped to the problem of finding open triangles in the ego-network of a user. Inspired by the MapReduce approach of Suri et al. [13] for counting triangles, we designed and implemented a MapReduce algorithm to find open triangles, so that when user u follows v, and v follows z, the predicted link would be (u, z), and recommendations would go from z to u as if u is actually one of z's followers. We also count the missing edges that close triangles so as to rank the nodes at distance two from the ego based on how many incoming links they have. Specifically, given the ego node u, let $\Gamma(u)$ be the set of u's friends (followees) and $\Gamma(\Gamma(u)) \setminus \Gamma(u)$ the set of u's friends of friends who are not friends of u. We define as the weight of user $z \in \Gamma(\Gamma(u)) \setminus \Gamma(u)$ to be the number of in-links $weight(z) = |(\Gamma(u), z)|$ as described in Algorithm 1. Nodes are then ranked based on decreasing values of their weights.

Algorithm 1 MR-Counting-Open-Triangles(V, E)

/* Let $G = (V, E)$ be the graph and $(u, v) \in E$ the edge from u to v. Let *ego* be the id of the ego node and let $\Gamma(v)$ be v's neighborhood */
Map 1: Input: $key, (u, v)$; ego
  if $u = ego$ **then**
    emit $key, (u, v)$ // *key* is the default input key
Reduce 1: Input: $key, [(u, v1), (u, v2), \ldots]$
// for each node at distance 2 from the ego, check cycles.
  for $(u, v) \in values$ **do**
    for $z \in \Gamma(v)$ **do**:
      if $u \neq z$ **then**:
        emit $(v, (u, z))$
Map 2: Input: $v, (u, z)$
/* check if the edge (u, z) that closes a triangle is open. If so, then u doesn't follow z and cannot see z's tweets. */
  if $(u, z) \notin E$ **then**:
    emit $((u, z), 1)$
Reduce 2: Input: $(u, z), [1, 1, \ldots]$
/* sum the counts for each missing edge and emit a single key/value with the edge (u, z) and sum. */
  $sum \leftarrow 0$
  for $i \in values$ **do**
    $sum = sum + i$
  emit $(u, z), sum$

The first mapper identifies the set $\Gamma(ego)$. The first reducer identifies the nodes in $\Gamma(\Gamma(ego)) \setminus ego$. The second mapper identifies the set $\Gamma(\Gamma(ego)) \setminus (\Gamma(ego) \cup ego)$ and the final reducer counts for each node $z \in \Gamma(\Gamma(ego)) \setminus (\Gamma(ego) \cup ego)$ how many nodes v_i such that $ego \rightarrow v_i \rightarrow z$ exist.

Content Analysis. Tweets that best match the user's interests can be discovered by applying the content similarity between a candidate tweet and the ego's (re)tweets as well as the similarity between ego's and candidate users' timelines.

As content-similarity measures we used the *cosine similarity* and *Jaccard distance*, which are typically employed for making recommendations of tweets [2], news articles [12], and research papers [9]. Before applying the similarity measures, tweets were preprocessed to eliminate non-English content, stopwords, punctuations, and so on. We computed the similarity of tweets by using single terms and bi-grams. Moreover, one type of similarity is computed between the timelines of u and of $z \in \Gamma(\Gamma(u))$ and another similarity is between the candidate tweet originated from z and u's (re)tweets. This gives us an overall number of six content-similarity features: both cosine similarity and Jaccard distance for the tweets, the timelines, and the timelines using bigrams.

Retweet Analysis. We include another feature based on the number of common retweets, which provides an indication of the similarity between the interests of the user u and her neighbors at distance two. Indeed, we noticed that users share on average 15 retweets, so we can use the number of mutual retweets to infer how close the users' interests are [5].

Ranking of Recommendations. We obtained the ranked list of tweets to recommend by using the pairwise comparison [14]. In more detail, we create a matrix of tweets and features (we assume that all the features have the same importance). We consider all pairwise combinations of candidate tweets and we compare them with respect to the features. A tweet beats another one if it has a better value for more features. At the end each tweet has a number of wins against the rest of the tweets, which induces a ranking among all the tweets. Tweets with higher number of wins are more likely to be relevant to the user's interests and are shown on the top of the ranked list of recommendations.

4. EXPERIMENTAL RESULTS

In this section, we present the experiment that we performed to validate our methodology and its results. As our approach does not recommend (re)tweets that are visible to the user, because it aims at recommending concealed tweets, we could not use retweets to assess if the recommendations are interesting or not. Therefore, we conducted a user study, where we proposed to real Twitter users our recommended tweets and collected their feedback.

4.1 User Study Evaluation

In the user study we involved 42 active Twitter users. The users could participate to our experiment by registering to our system using their screen name and email. Optional information, such as real name, gender, age range, Twitter and Internet usage, could be also provided. Participants of our user study were recruited from the list of the authors' followers. Most of them are young (between 20 and 30 years old) researchers, coming from different countries, affiliations, and research areas. The selected users are very active online (all of them use Internet everyday and 81% access Twitter on a daily basis). After the registration, the system retrieved the user's information needed to make the recommendations, and once these were ready, the user was notified by an email and could rate the list of recommended tweets. A total of 420 tweets from Oct. 7 to Nov. 17, 2015 were rated by our users. We compare the precision of our recommendations against a baseline approach for recommending concealed tweets. Since our aim is to recommend not visible tweets, we cannot compare our performance against algorithms that re-rank tweets appearing in the user's timeline. As a baseline, we used the approach presented by Pennacchiotti et al. [10], which exploits the content similarity among tweets, and, to the best of our knowledge, is the only work on recommendation of unseen tweets. We adopted their approach based on the cosine similarity, and for the evaluation we proposed the top-5 recommended tweets from our approach and the top-5 recommendations from the baseline. The two rankings were presented to the users, in a way that the user could not identify what system was used for creating the corresponding ranking. Following the same experiment of [10], our users could rate the proposed recommendations using a four-grade scale: *Excellent* (the tweet is very interesting/informative w.r.t. her interests), *Good* (the tweet is interesting/informative w.r.t. her interests), *Fair* (the tweet is somehow interesting/informative w.r.t. her interests), *Bad* (the tweet is not interesting/informative at all).

4.2 Assessing the Performance of the Recommendation System

For assessing the performance of our recommendation algorithm, we computed the following measures:

Precision@k (p@k): It is the percentage of relevant tweets found in the top-k ranked tweets. To apply this measure, we casted the four-grade scale to a binary score (1 for interesting and 0 for uninteresting). In particular user's answers *Excellent*, *Good*, and *Fair* correspond to 1 and *Bad* to 0. We obtain similar results if we map *Excellent* and *Good* to 1 and *Fair* and *Bad* to 0.

Normalized Discounted Cumulative Gain (nDCG): It measures the performance of a recommendation system based on the graded relevance of the recommendations. We used this metric to asses the effectiveness of our recommendation algorithm using the actual nonbinary rates. It compares the ranking of tweets based on the recommendation scores and the ranking based on the user grades.

We calculated the average of these metrics over all the users who subscribed to the system. In Table 1 we show a comparison of our approach and the baseline for the average precision and nDCG of the top-k tweets (with $k = 1, ..., 5$). Compared to the baseline we could observe an average improvement of 12.4% for Precision@k and of 1.6% for nDCG. We run t-test and could observe that the results were statistically significant at $p < 0.1$ for $p@1$ and at $p < 0.05$ for the other precisions.

Table 1: Comparison between our approach and the baseline.

	Precision				
	p@1	p@2	p@3	p@4	p@5
Our Approach	**0.85**	**0.82**	**0.80**	**0.79**	**0.80**
Baseline	0.73	0.67	0.67	0.68	0.69
	nDCG				
	@1	@2	@3	@4	@5
Our Approach	**0.75**	**0.79**	**0.84**	**0.88**	**0.92**
Baseline	0.74	0.77	0.82	0.86	0.91

We also computed the Reciprocal Rank (RR), which is the inverse of the ranking position of the first relevant tweet (i.e., the tweet which has been rated as *Excellent*, *Good*, or *Fair* by the user). The average RR over all users is of 91% for our approach and 83% for the baseline.

We report in Figure 1 the summary statistics with respect to the Likert scale judgements for both methods. We can observe that there is a larger number of tweets rated as *Excellent* and *Good*, while the number of tweets rated as *Bad* is lower compared to the baseline.

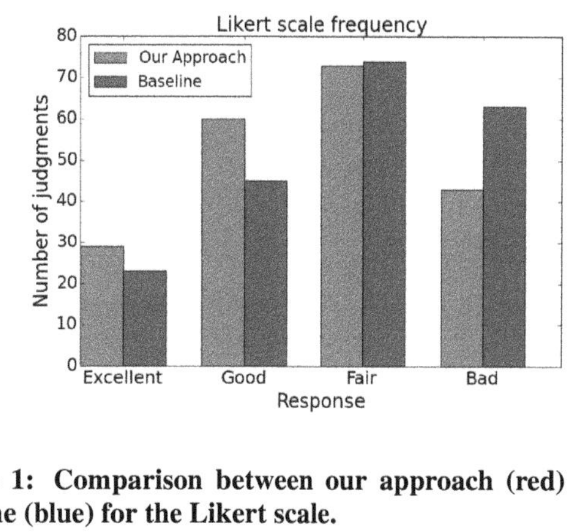

Figure 1: Comparison between our approach (red) and the baseline (blue) for the Likert scale.

Finally, in Figure 2 there are the percentages of tweets rated as *Excellent*, *Good*, *Fair*, and *Bad*, respectively. From these figures, it is clear that our method outperforms the baseline with higher percentage value.

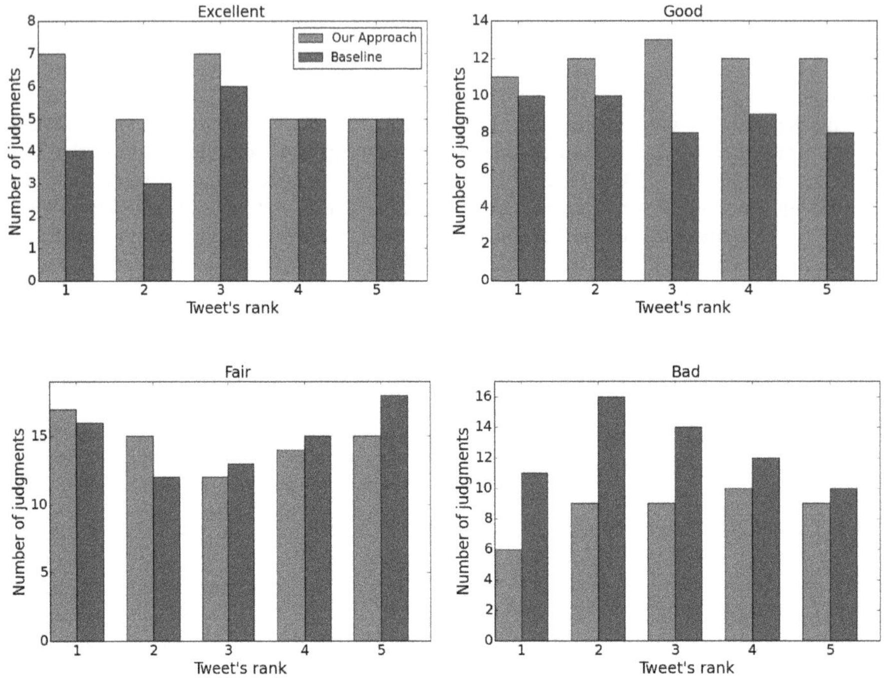

Figure 2: Comparison between our approach (red) and the baseline (blue) for each value of the Likert scale.

5. CONCLUSIONS

In this paper we have presented a novel approach for recommending concealed tweets. Our methodology uses the structure of a network with two-hop distance from the user, the content similarity, and the analysis of shared retweets in order to propose interesting tweets that otherwise would remain hidden from the user.

Experimental results corroborated that our recommendation system overcomes the existing approach for recommending unseen tweets with an improvement of 12.4% in the precision.

For future work, we would like to extend our study in order to consider also the feedback from the users. Finally, here we considered only a particular graph property, but we plan to try other approaches to find potential tweets (e.g., from the followers) and for weighting these tweets.

Acknowledgement

We would like to thank the authors of [10] for having provided the code of their recommendation algorithm.

6. REFERENCES

[1] M. G. Armentano, D. L. Godoy, and A. A. Amandi. A topology-based approach for followees recommendation in Twitter. In *ITWP'11*.

[2] S. Benzarti and R. Faiz. EgoTR: Personalized tweets recommendation approach. In *CSOC'15*.

[3] H. Chen, X. Cui, and H. Jin. Top-k followee recommendation over microblogging systems by exploiting diverse information sources. *Future Generation Computer Systems*, 55, 2016.

[4] J. Chen, R. Nairn, L. Nelson, M. Bernstein, and E. Chi. Short and tweet: experiments on recommending content from information streams. In *CHI'10*.

[5] K. Chen, T. Chen, G. Zheng, O. Jin, E. Yao, and Y. Yu. Collaborative personalized tweet recommendation. In *SIGIR'12*.

[6] R. Garcia and X. Amatriain. Weighted content based methods for recommending connections in online social networks. In *RSWeb'10*.

[7] J. Hannon, K. McCarthy, and B. Smyth. Finding useful users on Twitter: Twittomender the followee recommender. In *ECIR'11*.

[8] S. M. Kywe, E.-P. Lim, and F. Zhu. A survey of recommender systems in Twitter. In *SocInfo'12*.

[9] A. B. Patel, N. B. Suthar, and J. S. Dhobi. Recommending top-n research papers (based on with, without and boolean items preferences: An user base collaborative filtering approach in mahout). In *ICCCIT'12*.

[10] M. Pennacchiotti, F. Silvestri, H. Vahabi, and R. Venturini. Making your interests follow you on Twitter. In *CIKM'12*.

[11] P. Resnick and H. R. Varian. Recommender systems. *Commun. ACM*, 40(3), 1997.

[12] A. Sotsenko, M. Jansen, and M. Milrad. Using a rich context model for a news recommender system for mobile users. In *NRA'14*.

[13] S. Suri and S. Vassilvitskii. Counting triangles and the curse of the last reducer. In *WWW'11*.

[14] P. Tannenbaum and R. Arnold. *Excursions in modern mathematics*. Prentice Hall, 1995.

[15] I. Uysal and W. B. Croft. User oriented tweet ranking: a filtering approach to microblogs. In *CIKM'11*.

[16] R. Yan, M. Lapata, and X. Li. Tweet recommendation with graph co-ranking. In *ACL'12*.

[17] N. Yazdanfar and A. Thomo. Link recommender: Collaborative-filtering for recommending urls to Twitter users. *ANT'13*.

Not All Links Are Created Equal: An Adaptive Embedding Approach for Social Personalized Ranking

Qing Zhang, Houfeng Wang*
Key Laboratory of Computational Linguistics (Peking University) Ministry of Education, China
{zqicl,wanghf}@pku.edu.cn

ABSTRACT

With a large amount of complex network data available, most existing recommendation models consider exploiting rich user social relations for better interest targeting. In these approaches, the underlying assumption is that similar users in social networks would prefer similar items. However, in practical scenarios, social link may not be formed by common interest. For example, one general collected social network might be used for various specific recommendation scenarios. The problem of noisy social relations without interest relevance will arise to hurt the performance. Moreover, the sparsity problem of social network makes it much more challenging, due to the two-fold problem needed to be solved simultaneously, for effectively incorporating social information to benefit recommendation. To address this challenge, we propose an adaptive embedding approach to solve the both jointly for better recommendation in real world setting. Experiments conducted on real world datasets show that our approach outperforms current methods.

1. INTRODUCTION

With a large amount of complex network data available, how to effectively incorporate rich social information for recommendation is an important research topic [1]. Collaborative Filtering (CF) with implicit feedback [7] which is also called personalized ranking [7] is the consideration in this paper, since in most real applications, the collected data of user behaviors, e.g., assigning tags, purchasing products and watching videos, are usually implicit [5] without explicit feedback. To incorporate rich social information, existing approaches utilize social connections in different ways, but all of those hold the same underlying assumption [1] that given social networks, *similar users would prefer similar items*. In this paper, we argue that this assumption is too strong, and even not reasonable in many real applications, because social link may not be formed by common interest. For example, one general collected social network might be used for various specific recommendation scenarios. To investigate the issue, we first show the following two problems observed from the widely used real-world datasets.

*Corresponding author.

SIGIR '16, July 17-21, 2016, Pisa, Italy
© 2016 ACM. ISBN 978-1-4503-4069-4/16/07...$15.00
DOI: http://dx.doi.org/10.1145/2911451.2914740

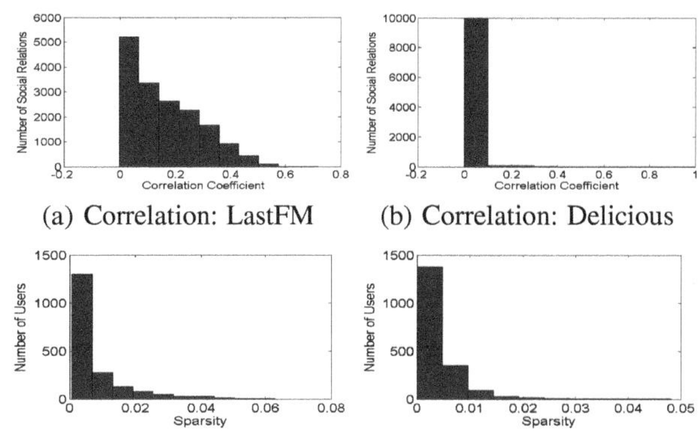

(a) Correlation: LastFM (b) Correlation: Delicious

(c) Sparsity: LastFM (d) Sparsity: Delicious

Figure 1: Subfigure(a,b): The distribution of interest correlation for links. Subfigure(c,d): The distribution of link sparsity.

Problem 1: **Noisy Social Link.** From Figure (1.a,1.b), we can see that the interest correlation, calculated by Pearson's correlation coefficient, is not high enough to support the assumption in the conventional social regularization based approaches, that the similar user in social networks leads to similar interest. In fact, this is the fundamental reason why social regularization based approach may lead to inconsistent results for different datasets, due to the noisy social patterns, violating the model assumption.

Problem 2: **Sparse Social Link.** From Figure (1.c,1.d), we can see that the sparsity of the social relation is quite low. A large number of users have only a small fraction of social connections in the entire network. Thus, directly using the social information is hard to achieve the best performance, and even may hurt the performance, due to the underlying noisy links in real applications.

Intuitively, to solve the problem 1, we would like to eliminate the noisy social links, but this will cause the sparse social link problem. Likewise, to solve the problem 2, we would like to create more links, which may also incorporate extra noisy social links causing the problem 1, even though the underlying noisy patterns that may have existed in the sparse links as shown in Figure 1, are not considered. Thus, we are in a dilemma, while only considering one specific problem of the two. In fact, the two tasks are mutually beneficial. If we can incorporate interest information to control social link selection, the noisy link problem could be alleviated, and if we can utilize more clean and higher order social relations, the sparsity problem could be alleviated for benefiting interest targeting. Thus, joint considering the two problems is an intuitive solution.

However, in previous widely adopted Matrix Factorization (MF) framework, the matrix factorizing process is a global process with

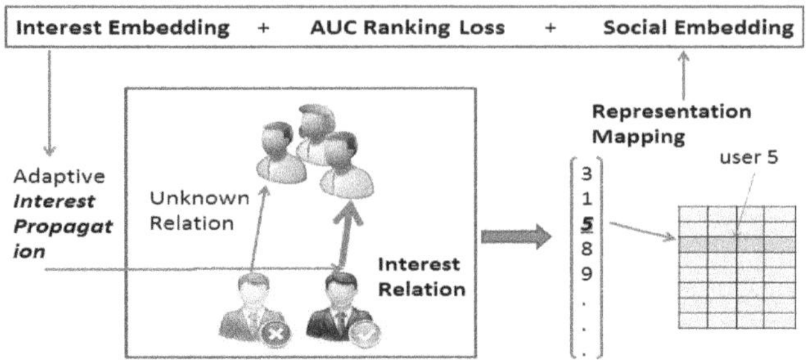

Figure 2: Model Framework. Joint learning interest and social embeddings with adaptive interest propagation.

low-rank constraint. It is hard to incorporate local interest information to control the global factorization process. To solve this challenge, inspired by the recent revealed equivalency [2] between word embedding (word2vec) [3] and matrix factorization, we propose a novel solution from an embedding perspective instead of the original matrix factorization view, as illustrated in Fig.(2), which allows a more flexible way to model user interest with complex social interactions.

2. A UNIFIED EMBEDDING APPROACH

The goal of the joint embedding is to learn user interest embedding e_u^i, user social embedding e_u^s and item embedding e'_i, by maximizing a posterior of AUC ranking based criterion [7] for interest embedding, and maximizing a criterion for social embedding,

$$\begin{aligned}\mathcal{L} &= \ln p(\Theta| >_u, G) \propto \ln(p(>_u, G|\Theta)\cdot p(\Theta)),\\ &= \ln(\underbrace{p(>_u|\Theta)}_{Interest\ Embedding} \cdot \underbrace{p(G|\Theta)}_{Social\ Embedding} \cdot \underbrace{p(\Theta)}_{Prior})\end{aligned} \quad (1)$$

where Θ the model parameters, G the user social information, and $>_u$ the ranking-based user interest information.

2.1 Interest Embedding

BPR-opt Criterion. For personalized ranking, a widely employed optimization criterion is Bayesian Personalized Ranking criterion denoted as BPR-opt as shown in Eq.(2). It has a strong theoretical underpinning as a surrogate objective, for optimizing the ranking-based AUC loss [7].

$$\begin{aligned}BPR-opt &:= \ln p(\Theta| >_u) = \ln p(>_u|\Theta)p(\Theta),\\ &= \ln \prod_{(u,i,j)} \sigma(\widehat{x}_{uij})p(\Theta)\end{aligned} \quad (2)$$

where σ is a sigmoid function $\sigma(x) = \frac{1}{1+exp(-x)}$, $p(\Theta)$ is a normal distribution $N(0, \Sigma_\Theta)$ with zero mean and a diagonal covariance matrix $\Sigma_\Theta = (1/\sigma)I$, I identity matrix, x_{uij} suggests that user *u* is assumed to prefer item *i* over item *j*. In the following, we show how to formulate the ranking score $\widehat{x}_{uij}$ as a function of the model parameters Θ. In Eq.(2), we define the ranking score as

$$\widehat{x}_{uij} = e_u {e'}_i^T - e_u {e'}_j^T \quad (3)$$

where e_u is the user *u* embedding; e'_i and e'_j are the item *i* and item *j* embeddings. All these embeddings are the model parameters which can be learned by our model.

Interest Embedding. We model item *i* embedding e'_i in Eq.(3) as a vector representation with real values. We model user *u* embedding e_u in Eq.(3) as a linear combination of e_u^i and e_u^s, $\lambda_s \in [0, 1]$,

$$e_u = (1 - \lambda_s)e_u^i + \lambda_s e_u^s \quad (4)$$

where e_u^i is the user *i* interest-specific embedding, and e_u^s is the corresponding social-specific embedding as a structured bias, which will be discussed in the next section.

2.2 Social Embedding

The goal of social embedding is to maximize the likelihood of a specific sequence of vertexes appearing in a user neighbour context, with the fundamental assumption that *similar context leads to similar representation.* To achieve the goal, formally, given a sequence of vertexes $V^n = (v_0, v_1, \cdots, v_n)$, where $v \in V$ the vertex set in a social network, in general, we would like to maximize the Eq.(5) over all the training corpus with the window size w,

$$\sum_i logP(e_i^s|e_{i-w}^s, ..., e_{i+w}^s \setminus e_i^s) \quad (5)$$

where $\setminus e_i^s$ excluding e_i^s. For our $p(G|\Theta)$, we present a novel so-

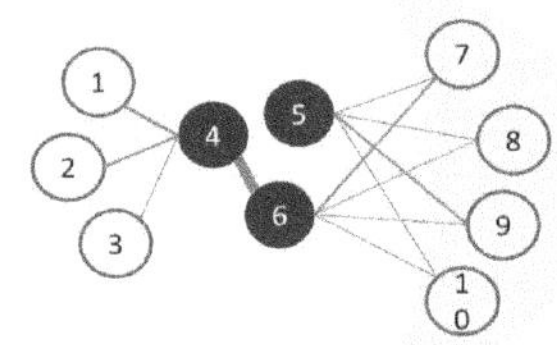

Figure 3: A toy example of social network.

lution as a variant of Deep-walk (Perozzi et al. 2014) [6] and LINE (Tang et al. 2015) [9], the state-of-the-art network embedding models, to incorporate both first-order and second-order proximities simultaneously in a unified framework with interest propagation.

Incorporating First-order Proximity. Many existing graph embedding algorithms, have the objective to preserve the first-order proximity [9] directly. However, in real world, the links observed are only a small proportion, and even with much noise. To solve the problem, we do not directly enforce the pairwise constraint on the two connected users. Instead, we add a virtual common node, representing the neighbourhood relation, for each user and its adjacent neighbours. The effectiveness of this modeling approach with the similar idea has been proved in NLP community [8].

DEFINITION 1 (LOCAL: FIRST-ORDER PROXIMITY). *The first-order proximity in a network is the local pairwise proximity between two vertices,* ***such as nodes 4,6 in Fig.(3).*** *For each pair of vertices linked by an edge (u, v), the weight on that edge, w_{uv}, indicates the first-order proximity between u and v. If no edge is observed between u and v, their first-order proximity is 0.*

The objective function of the first-order modeling is the log likelihood of all users,

$$l_1 = \sum_{n=1}^{N} \sum_{u_i \in A_n} log(P(e_{u_i}^s|e_{A_n}^s)) \quad (6)$$

where A_n denotes the neighbour set of user n as user context; $e_{u_i}^s$ denote the user i embedding in context A_n, and $e_{A_n}^s$ denotes the user context embedding $e_{A_n}^s$. We use a softmax function to define the probability, e_U^s denotes the entire set of user social embeddings,

$$P(e_{u_i}^s|e_{A_n}^s) = \frac{exp(e_{u_i}^s \cdot e_{A_n}^s)}{\sum_{e_u^s \in e_{U \setminus A_n + u_i}^s} exp(e_u^s \cdot e_{A_n}^s)}. \quad (7)$$

Incorporating Second-order Proximity. Following previous study [6], we assume nodes occurring in similar contexts tend to have similar meanings. This assumption leads to a more robust way of measuring the similarity between two users, compared with the direct pair-wise link assumption, which may cause overfitting due to the link sparsity and noise problems.

DEFINITION 2 (GLOBAL: SECOND-ORDER PROXIMITY). *The second-order proximity between two vertices (u, v) in a network is the similarity between their neighborhood network structures,* ***such as nodes 5,6 in Fig.(3).*** *Let $p_u = (w_{u,1}, ..., w_{u,|V|})$ denote the first-order proximity of u with all other vertices, then the second-order proximity between u and v is determined by the similarity between p_u and p_v. If no vertex is linked from/to both u and v, the second-order proximity between u and v is 0.*

The objective function of the second-order modeling is as follows,

$$l_2 = \sum_{i=1}^{N} log(P(e^s_{u_i}|e^s_{c_i})) \tag{8}$$

where $P(e^s_{u_i}|e^s_{c_i})$ is similarly defined by using a softmax function as in the first-order. We define the user 2-order context embedding,

$$e^s_{c_i} = f(c^s_{u_{i_1} \in A(u_i)}, ..., c^s_{u_{i_k} \in A(u_i)}), \tag{9}$$

where $f()$ can be sum, average, concatenate or max pooling of context user vectors $c^s_{u_{i_k}}$ in set $A(u_i)$. In this paper, we use ***weighted average*** on user social neighbour set $A(u_i)$ (SCHEME-1), which is different from that of [3] and [6]. The weights here are learnt from data automatically for adaptive interest propagation. We define the weight $p(u_{i_k \in A(u_i)}|u_i)$ for $e^s_{u_{i_k}}$ in Eq.(10), a random-walk like transition probability for each user to propagate interest,

$$p(u_{i_k \in A(u_i)}|u_i) = \frac{1}{Z} \cdot \frac{e_{i_k} e_i^T}{||e_{i_k}|| ||e_i||}, \tag{10}$$

where e_u, e_j are defined in Eq.(4); $p(u_{i_k \in A(u_i)}|u_i)$ is calculated by the percentage of weights, i.e., the interest embedding based cosine similarity by this edge against the total edge weight Z of a user. Note that in the above objective, the interest strength is naturally incorporated for different users by Eq.(10) adaptively.

Moreover, we also introduce ***an alternative scheme*** to generate $e^s_{c_i}$ (SCHEME-2), which is similar to DeepWalk. The difference is that we adaptively generate the *higher order* user specific context set $A'(u_i)$ by an interest-aware random walk process [6] using Eq.(10). Then we use an average $f()$ for those generated vectors in $A'(u_i)$, instead of using the social neighbour set $A(u_i)$ for Eq.(9).

Combination: First-order and Second-order Proximities. To embed the networks by preserving both the first-order and second-order proximities with interest propagation, we linearly combine the two objectives for joint learning as $ln(p(G|\Theta))$ in Eq.(1),

$$l = \alpha l_1 + (1 - \alpha) l_2 \tag{11}$$

where $\alpha \in [0, 1]$ is the strength weight; l_1 and l_2 are the first-order objective and second-order objective respectively. The social regularization parameter λ_l can be added $\lambda_l * l$ for controlling the overall social network strength, as in the traditional MF approaches.

2.3 Parameter Learning

We employ the widely used Stochastic Gradient Descent (SGD) algorithm to optimize the objective function in Eq.(1). The main process of SGD is to randomly select a pair of positive and negative feedbacks, and iteratively update model parameters. Specifically, for each training instance (user,positive-item,negative-item), we calculate the derivative and update the corresponding parameters by walking along the ascending gradient direction,

$$\Theta^{t+1} = \Theta^t + \eta \frac{\partial \mathcal{L}}{\partial \Theta}. \tag{12}$$

where the model parameters Θ are user interest and user social embeddings e^i_u, e^s_u; item embedding e'_i and user context embeddings $e^s_{A_n}, c^s_{u_{i_k}}$. In the above process, to optimize Eq.(11), we adopt the negative sampling technique (Mikolov et al., 2013) [3] for efficient learning since it is generally intractable for direct optimization.

3. RELATED WORK

Social recommendation methods focus on using the social network to improve the recommendation performance. Most existing methods are based on Matrix Factorization (MF) with regularization approaches. The social information is typically used as two ways. The first way is to directly use the ***first-order proximity*** to construct Laplacian matrix for regularizing the latent user. The limitation is that it only works well if the social is dense and noiseless. To overcome the limitation, recent approaches [1] employ the twice matrix factorization approach, i.e., not only factorizing the original rating matrix but also the social adjacent matrix, and then employ the latent social representation as regularization for users. This approach can be seen as a way of utilizing the ***second-order proximity*** due to the equivalency between the word2vec objective [3] and matrix factorization as shown in [2]. While the sparse social link problem may be solved, the noisy link problem is seldom addressed in previous work successfully. The most similar work to this paper is [10], which proposed a model with joint friendship and interest propagation in social network. However, it mainly focus on modeling the explicit feedback using regression-based modeling approach, and did not consider social representation modeling with ranking-based optimization criterion. Different from the above approaches, this work can incorporate *both first-order and second-order proximities* simultaneously in a unified embedding framework jointly *with local interest propagation.*

4. EXPERIMENTS

4.1 Experiment Setup

Dataset and Evaluation Metrics. We evaluate our method on two public real-world datasets[1], LastFM and Delicious as shown in Table 1. We use three popular metrics [5], Recall@K (R@K), NDCG@K (Normalized Discounted Cumulative Gain@K) and Area Under the Curve (AUC), to measure the recommendation quality of our proposed approach in comparison to baseline methods. $Recall@k = \frac{\#relevant\ in\ TopK}{\#total\ relevant}$, $NDCG@k = \frac{\sum_{i=1}^{k} \frac{2^{rel_i}-1}{log_2(1+i)}}{IDCG}$, where rel_i denotes the relevant degree which is binary in our task, i.e., 1 denotes it is relevant, 0 denotes it is not relevant and IDCG is the optimal score computed using the same form in numerator but with optimal ranking result known in advance. $AUC = \frac{1}{|U|} \sum_u \frac{1}{|E(u)|} \sum_{(i,j) \in E(u)} \delta(\widehat{x}_{ui} > \widehat{x}_{uj})$, where U user set; the evaluation pairs per user u are $E(u) := \{(u, i) \in S_{test} \wedge (u, j) \notin (S_{test} \cup S_{train})\}$, S denotes observed Set.

Dataset	#User	#Item	Sparsity	#Ratings	#Avg.R
LastFM	1892	18745	0.28%	92834	49
Delicious	1867	69223	0.08%	104799	56

Table 1: Datasets Statistics. R denotes the #rated per user. The statistics of social relations can be found in Fig.(1).

Settings. We conducted experiments on one validation set and one test set, by randomly drawing new train/test (90%/10%) splits of the observed data, for users with more than 20 items. Our

[1]Data available at http://grouplens.org/datasets/hetrec-2011/

Dataset	Metric	WRMF	BPR-MF	GBPR	GBPR-1	MR-BPR	EBPR-U	EBPR
	R@30	0.2221	0.2383	0.2418	0.2497	0.2501	0.2545	**0.2636**
	NDCG@30	0.1312	0.1472	0.1518	0.1515	0.1597	0.1613	**0.1694**
LastFM $\lambda_s = 0.2, \alpha = 0.7$	R@100	0.4414	0.4622	0.4791	0.4742	0.5036	0.5247	**0.5428**
	NDCG@100	0.2008	0.2119	0.2292	0.2286	0.2353	0.2416	**0.2494**
	AUC	0.9772	0.9848	0.9866	0.9855	0.9886	0.9902	**0.9924**
	R@30	0.1533	0.1622	0.1815	0.1785	0.1933	0.2047	**0.2280**
	NDCG@30	0.1031	0.1119	0.1342	0.1304	0.1419	0.1531	**0.1814**
Delicious $\lambda_s = 0.5, \alpha = 0.4$	R@100	0.2215	0.2303	0.2441	0.2432	0.2520	0.2597	**0.2789**
	NDCG@100	0.1212	0.1329	0.1519	0.1441	0.1604	0.1701	**0.1974**
	AUC	0.6813	0.6962	0.7091	0.7041	0.7101	0.7106	**0.7143**

Table 2: Model Comparison. Our best results are achieved while adopting the Scheme-2 on LastFM dataset, and the Scheme-1 on Delicious dataset respectively, for modeling $e^s_{c_i}$ as shown in Eq.(9). For simplicity, we do not consider item bias fairly for all methods.

datasets are more challenging than [5], since we have a much larger number of item candidates for each user while predicting. The hyperparameters for baseline methods are optimized via grid search following the original works in the validation set, and afterwards are kept constant in the test set. For the optimization, we iteratively update the parameters until the likelihood does not increase by 0.01 or the maximum iteration limit is reached, i.e., 250 on LastFM; 400 on Delicious. In each iteration, we randomly select instances $2{*}|U|$ for training. The latent dimension is fixed as 100. For our method, the parameters are randomly initialized within $[0, 1]$. The learning rate η for SGD is set to 0.01. The optimal parameters σ in $p(\Theta)$ for user embedding e_u and item embedding e_i are 0.1, 0.1 on LastFM, and 0.01, 0.1 on Delicious respectively. The best social strength parameters λ_l are 1 on LastFM, and 0.001 on Delicious respectively.

Baselines. We compare the following popular and the state-of-the-art social regularization based models for personalized ranking. **WRMF** [4] is a weighted matrix factorization method, which uses a point-wise strategy for one-class recommendation. **BPR-MF** [7] is a well known BPR method with pairwise assumption for item ranking. **GBPR** [5] is a state-of-the-art BPR method which relaxes BPR's assumption to a group pairwise preference assumption. Here we also introduce additional first-order social connection to construct groups, denoted as **GBPR-1**. **MR-BPR** [1] is a state-of-the-art social regularization based BPR method, as a second-order regularization approach which combines BPR-MF with social matrix factorization. **EBPR** is our proposed method. In addition, we also test a variant, EBPR-U. **EBPR-U** denotes using a uniform distribution instead of the weighting in Eq.(10).

4.2 Result and Analysis

From Table 2, we can see that the proposed method consistently performs batter than other baselines in different datasets. It shows the increased recommendation performance in the presence of link sparsity and noise, getting improvements of Recall, NDCG and AUC, with strong baselines. It could be explained that the adaptive interest propagation for social link modeling is important for achieving the good results in real applications. In addition, we show that an appropriate linear combination in Eq.(4) with λ_s can benefit the performance for different datasets while using different second order proximities. In fact, different social networks may have different properties. Empirically, in the process of finding the optimal α in Eq.(11), to balance the strength of different order proximities, we found that our model is more relaying on the first-order proximity on LastFM, and slightly more relaying the second-order proximity on Delicious, but adding the complementary one is also a necessary which can improve the performance. In contrast, purely using one specific of the two did not achieve the best results, which verifies our joint proximity modeling is a necessity.

5. CONCLUSION

In this paper, we studied the social personalized ranking problem. To relax the conventional assumption, in practical scenarios we argue that not all links are created equal, and we consider to do automatic social link selection jointly with learning user interest representation for social recommendation. The challenge is that solving the noisy social link problem solely may aggravate the sparsity problem and vice versa. To tackle this challenge, we developed a unified embedding framework to present a new viewpoint of social network regularization, which provides an avenue to allow a more flexible way of incorporating user social information with complex interactions. Experiment results demonstrate the superiority of the proposed method for real world applications.

6. ACKNOWLEDGMENTS

Our work is supported by National High Technology Research and Development Program of China(863 Program)(No.2015AA015402), National Natural Science Foundation of China(No.61370117) and Major National Social Science Fund of China(No.12&ZD227).

7. REFERENCES

[1] A. Krohn-Grimberghe, L. Drumond, C. Freudenthaler, and L. Schmidt-Thieme. Multi-relational matrix factorization using bayesian personalized ranking for social network data. In *Proceedings of WSDM*, pages 173–182, 2012.

[2] Y. Li, L. Xu, F. Tian, L. Jiang, X. Zhong, and E. Chen. Word embedding revisited: A new representation learning and explicit matrix factorization perspective. In *Proceedings of IJCAI*, pages 3650–3656, 2015.

[3] T. Mikolov, K. Chen, G. Corrado, and J. Dean. Efficient estimation of word representations in vector space. *CoRR*, abs/1301.3781, 2013.

[4] R. Pan, Y. Zhou, B. Cao, N. N. Liu, R. M. Lukose, M. Scholz, and Q. Yang. One-class collaborative filtering. In *Proceedings of ICDM*, pages 502–511, 2008.

[5] W. Pan and L. Chen. GBPR: group preference based bayesian personalized ranking for one-class collaborative filtering. In *Proceedings of IJCAI*, 2013.

[6] B. Perozzi, R. Al-Rfou, and S. Skiena. Deepwalk: online learning of social representations. In *Proceedings of KDD*, pages 701–710, 2014.

[7] S. Rendle, C. Freudenthaler, Z. Gantner, and L. Schmidt-Thieme. BPR: bayesian personalized ranking from implicit feedback. In *Proceedings of UAI*, pages 452–461, 2009.

[8] F. Sun, J. Guo, Y. Lan, J. Xu, and X. Cheng. Learning word representations by jointly modeling syntagmatic and paradigmatic relations. In *Proceedings of ACL*, pages 136–145, 2015.

[9] J. Tang, M. Qu, M. Wang, M. Zhang, J. Yan, and Q. Mei. LINE: large-scale information network embedding. In *Proceedings of WWW*, pages 1067–1077, 2015.

[10] S. Yang, B. Long, A. J. Smola, N. Sadagopan, Z. Zheng, and H. Zha. Like like alike: joint friendship and interest propagation in social networks. In *Proceedings of WWW*, pages 537–546, 2011.

On a Topic Model for Sentences

Georgios Balikas,[†*] Massih-Reza Amini[†] and Marianne Clausel[‡]
University of Grenoble Alpes
[†]Computer Science Laboratory (LIG), [‡]Applied Mathematics Laboratory (LJK)
Grenoble, France
{FirstName.LastName}@imag.fr

ABSTRACT

Probabilistic topic models are generative models that describe the content of documents by discovering the latent topics underlying them. However, the structure of the textual input, and for instance the grouping of words in coherent text spans such as sentences, contains much information which is generally lost with these models. In this paper, we propose *sentenceLDA*, an extension of LDA whose goal is to overcome this limitation by incorporating the structure of the text in the generative and inference processes. We illustrate the advantages of *sentenceLDA* by comparing it with LDA using both intrinsic (perplexity) and extrinsic (text classification) evaluation tasks on different text collections.

Keywords

Text Mining; Topic Modeling; Unsupervised Learning

1. INTRODUCTION

Statistical topic models are generative unsupervised models that describe the content of documents in large textual collections. Prior research has investigated the application of topic models such as Latent Dirichlet Allocation (LDA) [2] in a variety of domains ranging from image analysis to political science. Most of the work on topic models assumes exchangeability between words and treats documents in a bag-of-words fashion. As a result, the words' grouping in coherent text segments, such as sentences or phrases, is lost.

However, the inner structure of documents is generally useful, when identifying topics. For instance, one would expect that in each sentence, after standard pre-processing steps such as stop-word removal, only a very limited number of latent topics would appear. Thus, we argue that coherent text segments should pose "constraints" on the amount of topics that appear inside those segments.

In this paper, we propose *sentenceLDA* (*senLDA*), whose purpose is to incorporate part of the text structure in the topic model. Motivated by the argument that coherent text spans should be produced by only a handful of topics, we propose to modify the generative process of LDA. Hence, we argue that the latent topics of short text spans should be consistent across the units of those spans. In our approach, such text spans can vary from paragraphs to sentences and phrases depending on the task's purpose. Also, note that in the extreme case where words are the coherent text segments, the standard LDA model becomes a special case of *senLDA*.

In the remainder of the paper we present the *senLDA* and we derive its collapsed Gibbs sampler in Section 2, we illustrate its advantages by comparing it with LDA on intrinsic (*in vitro*) and extrinsic (*ex vivo*) evaluation experiments using collections of Wikipedia and PubMed articles in Section 3, and we conclude in Section 4.

*Also affiliated with: Coffreo, Clermont Ferrand, France

SIGIR '16, July 17-21, 2016, Pisa, Italy

DOI: http://dx.doi.org/10.1145/2911451.2914714

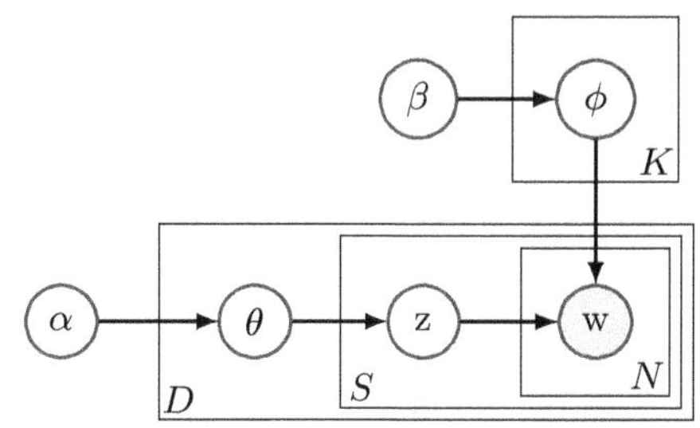

Figure 1: The *senLDA* model. The words w of a sentence share the same topic z.

2. THE PROPOSED MODEL

A statistical topic model represents the words in a collection of D documents as mixtures of K "topics", which are multinomials over a vocabulary of size V. In the case of LDA, for each document d_i a multinomial over topics is sampled from a Dirichlet prior with parameters $\boldsymbol{\alpha}$. The probability $p(w|z=k)$ of a term w, given the topic k, is represented by $\phi_{k,t}$. We refer to the complete $K \times V$ matrix of word-topic probabilities as Φ. The multinomial parameters ϕ_k are again drawn from a Dirichlet prior parametrized by $\boldsymbol{\beta}$. Each observed term w in the collection is drawn from a multinomial for the topic represented by a discrete hidden indicator variable z_i. For simplicity in the mathematical development and notation, we assume symmetric Dirichlet priors but the extension to the asymmetric case is straightforward. Hence, the values of α and β are model hyper-parameters.

We extend LDA by adding an extra plate denoting the coherent text segments of a document. In the rest, without loss of generality we use sentences as coherent segments. A finer level of granularity can be achieved though, by analysing the structure of sentences and using phrases as such segments. The graphical representation of the *senLDA* model is shown in Figure 1 and the generative process of a document collection using *senLDA* is described in Algorithm 1. For inference, we use a collapsed Gibbs sampling method [5]. We now derive the Gibbs sampler equations by estimating the hidden topic variables.

In *senLDA* the joint distribution can be factored:

$$p(w, z|\alpha, \beta) = p(w|z, \beta)p(z|\alpha) \tag{1}$$

because the first term is independent of α and the second from β. After standard manipulations as in the paradigm of [6] one arrives at:

$$p(\vec{z}, \vec{w}|\alpha, \beta) = \prod_{z=1}^{K} \frac{\Delta(\vec{n}_z + \beta)}{\Delta(\beta)} \prod_{m=1}^{D} \frac{\Delta(\vec{n}_m + \alpha)}{\Delta(\alpha)} \tag{2}$$

where $\Delta(\vec{x}) = Beta(x_1, \ldots, x_m) = \frac{\prod_{k=1}^{dim \vec{x}} \Gamma(x_k)}{\Gamma(\sum_{k=1}^{dim \vec{x}} x_k)}$ is a multidimensional extension of the beta function used for notation convenience, and $\vec{n}_m$, $\vec{n}_z$ refer to the occurrences of topics with documents and topics with terms respectively. To calculate the full conditional we take into account the structure of the document d and the fact that $\vec{w_d} = \{\vec{w}_{d\neg s}, \vec{w}_{\neg s}\}$, $\vec{z} = \{\vec{z}_{d\neg s}, \vec{z}_{\neg s}\}$. The subscript s in $\vec{w}_s, \vec{z}_s$ denotes the words and the topic respectively of sentence s. For the full conditional of topic k we have:

$$\begin{aligned} p(z_s = k|\vec{z}_{\neg s}, \vec{w}) &= \frac{p(\vec{w}, \vec{z})}{p(\vec{w}, \vec{z}_{\neg s})} = \frac{p(\vec{w}|\vec{z})}{p(\vec{w}_{\neg s}|\vec{z}_{\neg s})p(w_s)} \frac{p(\vec{z})}{p(\vec{z}_{\neg s})} = \\ &= \frac{p(\vec{w}, \vec{z})}{p(\vec{w}_{\neg s}, \vec{z}_{\neg s})} \propto \frac{\Delta(\vec{n}_z + \beta)}{\Delta(\vec{n}_{z,\neg s} + \beta)} \frac{\Delta(\vec{n}_m + \alpha)}{\Delta(\vec{n}_{m,\neg s} + \alpha)} \end{aligned} \tag{3}$$

For the first term of equation Eq. (3) we have:

$$\begin{aligned} \frac{\Delta(\vec{n}_z + \beta)}{\Delta(\vec{n}_{z,\neg s} + \beta)} &= \frac{\frac{\prod_{w \in s} \Gamma(\vec{n}_z + \beta)}{\Gamma(\sum_{w \in s}(\vec{n}_z + \beta))}}{\frac{\prod_{w \in s} \Gamma(\vec{n}_{z,\neg s} + \beta)}{\Gamma(\sum_{w \in s}(\vec{n}_{z,\neg s} + \beta))}} = \\ &= \prod_{w \in s} (\frac{\Gamma(\vec{n}_z + \beta)}{\Gamma(\vec{n}_{z,\neg s} + \beta)}) \frac{\Gamma(\sum_{w \in s}(n_{z,\neg s} + \beta))}{\Gamma(\sum_{w \in s}(n_z + \beta))} = \\ &= \frac{\overbrace{\prod_{w \in s} (n_{k,\neg s}^{(w)} + \beta) \cdots (n_{k,\neg s}^{(w)} + \beta + (n_{k,s}^{(w)} - 1))}^{A}}{\underbrace{(\sum_{w \in V}(n_{k,\neg s}^{(w)} + \beta)) \cdots (\sum_{w \in V} n_{k,\neg s}^{(w)} + \beta + (N_{k,s}^{(w)} - 1))}_{B}} \end{aligned} \tag{4}$$

Here, for the generation of A and B we used the recursive property of the Γ function: $\Gamma(x+m) = (x+m-1)(x+m-2) \cdots (x+1)x\Gamma(x)$; w is a term that can occur many times in a sentence and $n_{k,s}^{(w)}$ denotes w's frequency in sentence s given that the sentence s belongs to topic k; $N_{k,s}^{(w)}$ denotes how many words of sentence s belong to topic t.

The development of the second factor in the final step of Eq. (3) is similar to the LDA calculations with the difference that the counts of topics per document are calculated given

Algorithm 1: Text collection generation with *senLDA*

for document $d \in [1, \ldots, D]$ **do**
  sample mixture of topics $\theta_m \sim$ Dirichlet(a)
  sample sentence number $S_d \sim Poisson(\xi)$
  //Sentence plate
  for sentence $s \in [1, S_d]$ **do**
    sample number of words $W_s \sim Poisson(\xi_d)$
    sample topic $z_{d,s} \sim Multinomial(\theta_m)$
    //Word plate in each language
    for words $w \in [1, W_{d,s}]$ in sentence s **do**
      sample term for $w \sim Multinomial(\phi_{z_{d,s}})$
    end
  end
end

the allocation of sentences to topics and not the allocation of words to topics. This yields:

$$\begin{aligned} p(z_s = k|\vec{z}_{\neg s}, \vec{w}) &= (n_{m,\neg s}^{(k)} + \alpha) \times \\ &\times \frac{\prod_{w \in s}(n_{k,\neg s}^{(w)} + \beta) \cdots (n_{k,\neg s}^{(w)} + \beta + (n_{k,s}^{(w)} - 1))}{(\sum_{w \in V}(n_{k,\neg s}^{(w)} + \beta)) \cdots (\sum_{w \in V} n_{k,\neg s}^{(w)} + \beta + (N_{k,s}^{(w)} - 1))} \end{aligned} \tag{5}$$

where $n_{m,\neg s}^{(w)}$ denotes the number of times that topic k has been observed with a sentence from document d, excluding the sentence currently sampled. Note that Eq. (5) reduces to the standard LDA collapsed Gibbs sampling inference equations if the coherent text spans are reduced to words.

The idea of integrating the sentence limits in the LDA model has been previously investigated. For instance, in [9] in the context of summarization the authors combine the unigram language model with topic models over sentences so that the latent topics are represented by sentences instead of terms. In [4] the notion of *sentence topics* is introduced and they are sampled from separate topic distributions and co-exist with the word topics. Also, Boyd et al. [3] propose an adaptation of topic models to the text structure obtained by the parsing tree of a document. Our method resembles these works in that it integrates the notion of sentences to extend LDA. In our case though, we directly extend LDA maintaining the association of words to topics, we retain its simplicity without adding extra hyper-parameters thus allowing a fast, gibbs sampling inference, and we do not require any language-dependent tools such as parsers.

3. EMPIRICAL RESULTS

We conduct experiments to verify the applicability and evaluate the performance of *senLDA* compared to LDA. The process is divided into two steps: (i) the training phase, where the topic models are trained to learn the their parameters, and (ii) the inference phase that is for new, unseen documents their topic distributions are estimated. We use the Gibbs sampling inference approach given by Eq. (5). The hyper-parameters α and β are set to $\frac{1}{K}$, with K being the number of topics. Table 1 shows the datasets we used. They come from the publicly available collections of Wikipedia [7] and PubMed [8]. The first four datasets (WikiTrain* and PubMedTrain*) were used for learning the topic model parameters; they differ in their respective size. Also, the vocabulary of the PubMed datasets is significantly larger due to the medical terms that appear. During preprocessing

	Documents	$\|V\|$	Classes	Timing (sec)
WikiTrain1	10,000	46,051	-	182|271
WikiTrain2	30,000	65,820	-	332|434
PubMedTrain1	10,000	55,115	-	304|433
PubMedTrain2	60,000	150,440	-	1830|2799
Wiki37	2,459	23,559	37	-
Wiki46	3,657	27,914	46	-
PubMed25	7,248	40,173	25	-
PubMed50	9,035	47,199	50	-

Table 1: Description of the data used after preprocessing. "Timing" refers to the 25 first training iterations with the left (resp. right) values corresponding to *senLDA* (resp. LDA).

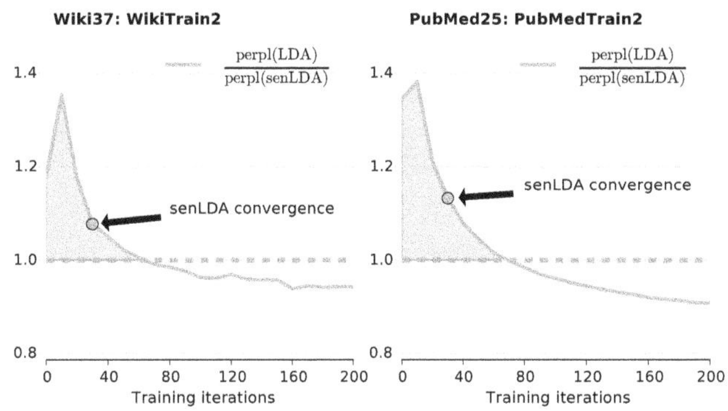

Figure 2: The ratio of perplexities of *senLDA* and LDA calculated on Wiki37 and PubMed25.

we only applied lower-casing, stop-word removal and lemmatization using the WordNet Lemmatizer.[1] The rest of the document collections of Table 1 are used for classification purposes and are discussed later in the section.

Intrinsic evaluation Topic model evaluation has been the subject of intense research. For intrinsic evaluation we report here perplexity [1], which is probably the dominant measure for topic models evaluation in the bibliography. The perplexity of d held out documents given the model parameters $\vec{\vartheta}$ is defined as the reciprocal geometric mean of the token likelihoods of those data, given the parameters of the model:

$$p(w_{\text{heldOut}}) = \exp - \frac{\sum_{i=1}^{d} \sum_{j=1}^{w_i} \log p(w_{i,j}|\vec{\vartheta})}{\sum_{i=1}^{d} \sum_{j=1}^{w_i} 1} \quad (6)$$

Note that *senLDA* samples per sentence and thus results in less flexibility at the word level where perplexity is calculated. Even though, the comparison between *senLDA* and LDA, at word level using perplexity, gives insights in the relative merits of the the proposed model.

Figure 2 depicts the ratio of the perplexity values between *senLDA* and LDA. We set $K = 125$ after grid searching $K \in \{25, 75, 125, 175\}$ for perplexity with 5-fold cross-validation on the training data. Values higher (resp. lower) than one signify that *senLDA* achieves lower (resp. higher) perplexity than LDA. The figure demonstrates that in the first iterations before convergence of both models, *senLDA* performs better. What is more, *senLDA* converges after only around 30 iterations, whereas LDA converges after 160 iterations on Wikipedia and 200 iterations on the PubMed datasets respectively. We define convergence as the situation where the model's perplexity does not any more decrease over training iterations. The shaded area in the figure highlights the period while *senLDA* performs better. It is to be noted, that although competitive, *senLDA* does not outperform LDA given unlimited time resources. However, that was expected since for *senLDA* the training instances are sentences, thus the model's flexibility is restricted when evaluated against a word-based measure.

An important difference between the models however, lies in the way they converge. From Figure 2 it is clear that *senLDA* converges faster. We highlight this by providing exact timings for the first 25 iterations of the models (column "Timing" of Table 1) on a machine using an Intel Xeon CPU E5-2643 v3 at 3.40GHz. For both models we use our own Python implementations with the same speed optimisations. Using "WikiTrain2" and 125 topics, for 25 iterations the *senLDA* needs 332 secs, whereas LDA needs 434 sec., an improvement of 30%. Furthermore, comparing the convergence, *senLDA* needs 332 secs (25 iterations) whereas LDA needs more than 2770 secs (more than 160 iterations) making *senLDA* more than 8 times faster. Similarly for the "PubMedTrain2" dataset which is more complex due to its larger vocabulary size, *senLDA* converges around 12 times (an order of magnitude) faster. Note that *senLDA*'s fast convergence is a strong advantage and can be highly appreciated in different application scenarios where unlimited time resources are not available.

Extrinsic evaluation Previous studies have shown that perplexity does not always agree with human evaluations of topic models [1] and it is recommended to evaluate topic models on real tasks. To better support our development for *senLDA* applicability we also evaluate it using text classification as the evaluation task. For text classification, each document is represented by its topic distribution, which is the vectorial input to Support Vector Machines (SVMs). The classification collections are split on train/test (75%/25%) parts. The SVM regularization hyper-parameter λ is selected from $\lambda \in [10^{-4}, \ldots, 10^{4}]$ using 5-fold cross-validation on the training part of the classification data. The PubMed testsets are multilabel, that is each instance is associated with several classes, 1.4 in average in the sets of Table 1. For the multilabel problem with the SVMs we used a binary relevance approach. To assess the classification performance, we report the F_1 evaluation measure, which is the harmonic mean of precision and recall.

The classification performance on F_1 measure for the different classification datasets is shown in Figure 3. First note that in the majority of the classification scenarios, *senLDA* outperforms LDA. In most cases, the performance difference increases when the larger train sets ("WikiTrain2" and "PubMedTrain2") are used. For instance, in the second line of figures with the PubMed classification experiments, increasing the topic models' training data benefits both LDA and *senLDA* , but *senLDA* still performs better. More importantly though and in consistence with the perplexity experiments, the advantage of *senLDA* remains: the faster *senLDA* convergence benefits the classification performance. The *senLDA* curves are steeper in the first training iterations and stabilize after roughly 30 iterations when the model converges. We believe that assigning the latent topics to coher-

[1]The code and the data are publicly available at https://github.com/balikasg/topicModelling/

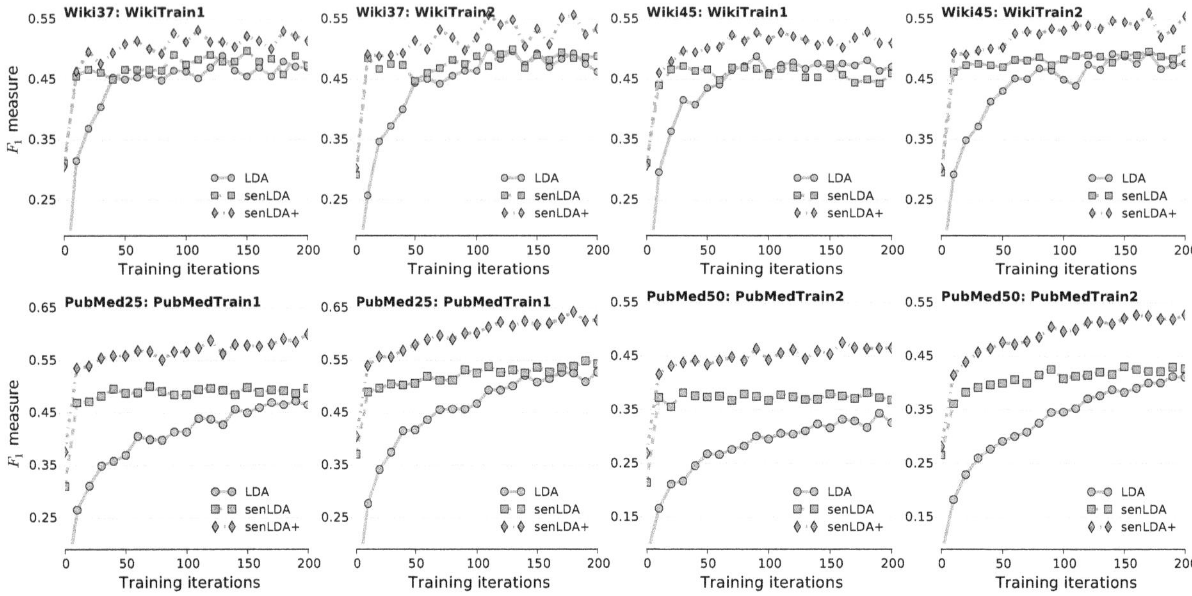

Figure 3: Classification performance on PubMed and Wikipedia text collections using F_1 measure.

ent groups of words such as sentences results in document representations of finer level. In this sense, spans larger than single words can capture and express the document's content more efficiently for discriminative tasks like classification.

To investigate the correlation of topic model representations learned on different levels of text, we report the classification performance using as document representations the concatenation of a document's topic distributions output by LDA and *senLDA* . For instance, the concatenated vectorial representation of a document when $K = 125$ for each model is a vector of 250 dimensions. The resulting concatenated representations are denoted by "senLDA+" in Figure 3. As it can be seen, "senLDA+" performs better compared to both LDA and *senLDA* . Its performance combines the advantages of both models: during the first iterations it is as steep as the *senLDA* representations and in the later iterations benefits by the LDA convergence to outperform the simple *senLDA* representation. Hence, the concatenation of the two distributions creates a richer representation where the two models contribute complementary information that achieves the best classification performance. Achieving the optimal performance using those representations suggests that the relaxation of the independence assumptions between the text structural units can be beneficial; this is also among the contributions of this work.

4. CONCLUSION

We proposed *senLDA*, an extension of LDA where topics are sampled per coherent text spans. This resulted in very fast convergence and good classification and perplexity performance. LDA and *senLDA* differ in that the second assumes a very strong dependence of the latent topics between the words of sentences, whereas the first assumes independence between the words of documents in general. In our future research, our goal is to investigate this dependence and further adapt the sampling process of topic models to cope with the rich text structure.

5. ACKNOWLEDGEMENTS

This work is partially supported by the CIFRE N 28/2015.

6. REFERENCES

[1] L. Azzopardi, M. Girolami, and K. van Risjbergen. Investigating the relationship between language model perplexity and IR precision-recall measures. In *SIGIR*, pages 369–370, 2003.

[2] D. M. Blei, A. Y. Ng, and M. I. Jordan. Latent dirichlet allocation. *the Journal of machine Learning research*, 3:993–1022, 2003.

[3] J. L. Boyd-Graber and D. M. Blei. Syntactic topic models. In *Advances in neural information processing systems*, pages 185–192, 2009.

[4] R.-C. Chen, R. Swanson, and A. S. Gordon. An adaptation of topic modeling to sentences. 2010.

[5] T. L. Griffiths and M. Steyvers. Finding scientific topics. *Proceedings of the National Academy of Sciences*, 101(suppl 1):5228–5235, 2004.

[6] G. Heinrich. Parameter estimation for text analysis. Technical report, Technical report, 2005.

[7] I. Partalas, A. Kosmopoulos, N. Baskiotis, T. Artieres, G. Paliouras, E. Gaussier, I. Androutsopoulos, M.-R. Amini, and P. Galinari. LSHTC: A benchmark for large-scale text classification. *CoRR*, abs/1503.08581, march 2015.

[8] G. Tsatsaronis, G. Balikas, P. Malakasiotis, I. Partalas, M. Zschunke, M. R. Alvers, D. Weissenborn, et al. An overview of the BIOASQ large-scale biomedical semantic indexing and question answering competition. *BMC bioinformatics*, 16(1):1, 2015.

[9] D. Wang, S. Zhu, T. Li, and Y. Gong. Multi-document summarization using sentence-based topic models. In *Proceedings of the ACL-IJCNLP 2009 Conference Short Papers*, pages 297–300. Association for Computational Linguistics, 2009.

On Information-Theoretic Document-Person Associations for Expert Search in Academia

Vitor Mangaravite
mangaravite@dcc.ufmg.br

Rodrygo L. T. Santos
rodrygo@dcc.ufmg.br

Department of Computer Science
Universidade Federal de Minas Gerais
Belo Horizonte, MG, Brazil

ABSTRACT

State-of-the-art expert search approaches rely on document-person associations to infer the expertise of a candidate person for a given query. Such associations have traditionally been modeled as boolean variables, indicating whether or not a candidate authored a document, and further normalized to penalize prolific authorships. In this paper, we address expert search in academia, where the authorship of a document can be determined with reasonable certainty. In contrast to traditional approaches, we propose to model associations as non-boolean variables, reflecting the probability that a document is *informative* of the expertise of a candidate. Moreover, we introduce an alternative normalization scheme that measures how *discriminative* a particular document-person association is in light of all associations involving either the document or the person. Through a large-scale user study with academic experts from several areas of knowledge, we demonstrate the suitability of the proposed association and normalization schemes to improve the effectiveness of a state-of-the-art expert search approach.

CCS Concepts

•**Information systems** → **Expert search;**

Keywords

Academic search; expertise retrieval

1. INTRODUCTION

Users search for an expert whenever they need proficient knowledge on a given topic [7]. For instance, an expert on "*information retrieval*" could be searched for providing consultancy or for being recruited by a search company. Expert search has received considerable attention from the information retrieval community over the past decade, with a particular focus on finding experts within an enterprise organization [2, 8, 10, 19]. Several expert search approaches have been proposed that attempt to model the expertise of candidate persons and their relevance given a user's query (e.g., [3, 12, 15]). In common, all of these approaches rely on some form of association between people and documents in order to model the expertise profile of each candidate [7].

Document-person associations are commonly modeled as boolean variables, indicating whether or not a person has authored or is mentioned in a document. Given the ambiguous nature of such associations in typical enterprise collections [1, 10], attempts to model non-boolean associations have been made that reflect the confidence that the right person has been identified (e.g., based upon the frequency of occurrence of the person's name in the document [6] or its occurrence in proximity to the query terms [20]). In addition, to limit the impact of false positives, the inferred associations are typically normalized to penalize prolific authorships. In contrast, many other expert search scenarios provide unambiguous associations, such as email-sender in email corpora [5] and paper-author in academic corpora [4, 11], which preclude the need for authorship inference.

In this paper, we address expert search in academia. In this scenario, the authorship of a document can be determined with reasonable certainty, by leveraging metadata associated with individual publication records. As a result, rather than attempting to infer the authorship of a document, we propose to model associations as non-boolean variables reflecting the probability that the document is *informative* of the expertise of a candidate. Moreover, because authorships in this scenario are unambiguous, penalizing documents with many associated authors or authors with many associated documents becomes arguably counterintuitive. Therefore, we further introduce an alternative normalization scheme that measures how *discriminative* a particular document-person association is in light of all associations involving either the document or the person. Through a large-scale user study with academic experts from several areas of knowledge, we demonstrate the suitability of the proposed association and normalization models to improve the effectiveness of a state-of-the-art expert search approach. To the best of our knowledge, this is the first attempt to infer the strength of document-person associations beyond authorship attribution for expert search in academia.

In the remainder of this paper, Section 2 discusses related work on expert search and association models. Section 3 introduces our information-theoretic models for weighting document-person associations. Section 4 describes the setup and the results of the empirical evaluation of our proposed models. Finally, Section 5 presents our conclusions.

SIGIR '16, July 17–21, 2016, Pisa, Italy.
© 2016 ACM. ISBN 978-1-4503-4069-4/16/07...$15.00
DOI: http://dx.doi.org/10.1145/2911451.2914751

2. RELATED WORK

Expert search has been the subject of intense research over the past decade, particularly with the introduction of an expert search task at the TREC 2005 Enterprise track [10]. For instance, Balog et al. [3] introduced two alternative generative probabilistic approaches for expert search, which estimate the likelihood that a given query is generated by each candidate expert. Their Model 1 performs this estimation directly, by relying on the candidate's language model built from his or her associated documents. In turn, their Model 2 assumes a generative process in which candidates generate documents, which themselves generate the query. Discriminative probabilistic models have also been proposed, which attempt to estimate the relevance of a given query-candidate pair directly from training data [12]. Other prominent approaches include graph-based models [18], which perform inference on an expertise graph built from document-person associations, and voting models [15], which aggregate the query-biased document relevance estimates into relevance estimates for the associated candidate experts.

A common characteristic of most existing expert search approaches is their reliance on document-person associations. In particular, almost all approaches consider boolean associations, indicating whether or not a candidate has authored a particular document. However, in a typical enterprise setting, document-person associations can be ambiguous. For instance, candidate names may be mentioned in different parts of a meeting minute without any explicit authorship indication. To overcome such an ambiguity, non-boolean association models have been proposed to estimate the confidence that the correct candidate has been identified. For instance, Balog and de Rijke [6] proposed to weight document-person associations based on the Kullback-Leibler divergence between the document and the candidate's language models built using only the candidate's name. Other association models also estimated the distance between the candidate's name and the query terms to improve the identification of authorships related to the query topic [20].

In contrast to the aforementioned approaches, we tackle expert search in academia, a domain where authorships can be determined with reasonable certainty via publication metadata records uniquely associated with each candidate. As a result, we propose to model associations as non-boolean variables aimed to convey the *informativeness* of each document for the expertise profile of a candidate. In a similar spirit, Macdonald and Ounis [14] proposed to estimate the extent to which a document is related to the core interests of each candidate associated with it. To this end, they clustered each candidate's profile and ranked the resulting clusters in decreasing order of their size, weighting a document-person association by the inverse of the rank of the cluster that contained the document. Our proposed approach is simpler, and relies on a standard information-theoretic measure of the informativeness of the document for the candidate's expertise. The cluster-based approach of Macdonald and Ounis [14] is included as a baseline in our experiments.

Another aspect of document-person associations that is relevant to our proposal is normalization. For instance, both generative models proposed by Balog et al. [3] rely on a normalization component to estimate the probability $p(d|e)$ that document d is associated with candidate e. This estimation can be either document- or candidate-centric, depending on whether the association weight is normalized by the sum of the weights of all associations related to the document or the candidate, respectively. Normalizing associations may be useful even for non-probabilistic approaches, to counter the noise introduced by spurious associations resulting from false-positive authorship attributions. With this in mind, Macdonald and Ounis [16] proposed to normalize associations by the length of the candidate's profile, measured in either number of terms or number of documents. Given the absence of spurious associations in our scenario, we propose a normalization scheme that does not penalize prolific candidates, but instead measures how discriminative each association is for each document or candidate. The normalization schemes of Balog et al. [3] and Macdonald and Ounis [16] are used as baselines in our investigation.

3. INFORMATION-THEORETIC DOCUMENT-PERSON ASSOCIATIONS

A key element of any expert search approach is its ability to represent the expertise of each candidate expert. As discussed in the previous sections, most expert search approaches in the literature rely on explicit document-person associations to model a candidate's expertise profile. Without loss of generality, we can formalize the association $f(d, e)$ between document d and candidate e according to:

$$f(d, e) = \psi(\rho(d, e)), \tag{1}$$

where $\rho(d, e)$ and $\psi(\bullet)$ denote *association* and *normalization* schemes for the association between document d and candidate e, respectively. The majority of the expert search approaches in the literature rely on a boolean association scheme, which assigns a constant value $\rho(d, e) = 1$ for all existing associations. In turn, the most straightforward normalization scheme simply divides the association $\rho(d, e)$ by the sum of all document or candidate associations, such that $\psi(\bullet) \equiv \bullet/\sum_{e'} \rho(d, e')$ or $\psi(\bullet) \equiv \bullet/\sum_{d'} \rho(d', e)$ [3].

In the following, we introduce novel information-theoretic association and normalization schemes for expert search in academia. The proposed schemes exploit the unambiguous nature of document-person associations leveraged from publication records in order to better quantify the informativeness of each association for a candidate's expertise.

3.1 Association Scheme

Our proposed association scheme aims to weight a given document-person association based on how informative the document is of the expertise of the candidate. To this end, we rely on an information-theoretic measure of the distance between the language use in the document and in the entire profile of the candidate. Precisely, our proposed association scheme $\rho_H(d, e)$ can be instantiated as follows:

$$\begin{aligned} \rho_H(d, e) &= H(\theta_e, \theta_d) \\ &= -\sum_t p(t|\theta_e) \log p(t|\theta_d), \end{aligned} \tag{2}$$

where $H(\theta_e, \theta_d)$ is the cross-entropy between the candidate language model θ_e—built by concatenating all documents associated with candidate e—and the document language model θ_d. It can be shown that this formulation is equivalent to estimating the likelihood of generating the candidate language model θ_e given the document language model θ_d [13]. It is also equivalent to the standard Kullback-Leibler divergence between the two models minus the entropy $H(\theta_e)$

of the candidate model θ_e, which is discarded here as it is the same for all documents d. Based upon the latter observation, our proposed formulation can also be seen as a generalization of the association scheme proposed by Balog et al. [6] and discussed in Section 2. While their approach is based on language models built from candidates' names, we evaluate our approach using multiple textual representations for the document and candidate models. Finally, while alternative formulations (e.g., based on non-textual features) are possible, we leave their investigation for future research.

3.2 Normalization Schemes

Existing expert search approaches linearly normalize association weights either by the sum of all related association weights [3] or by the length of the candidate's profile [16]. As discussed in Section 2, these approaches have been shown to be effective, particularly in the enterprise domain, where ambiguous associations may spuriously compromise the estimation of a candidate's expertise. In the academic domain, where associations are generally unambiguous, such linear normalization approaches may harshly penalize prolific candidates. To counter this limitation, we propose two alternative normalization schemes aimed to measure the discriminativeness of each association. In particular, our soft document-centric (SDC) normalization scheme is given by:

$$\psi_{SDC}(\bullet) \equiv \log \frac{\left(\sum_{e'} \rho(d,e')\right)^{\alpha}}{\bullet}, \tag{3}$$

where the summation in the numerator comprises the weights of all other associations related to target document d. Our soft candidate-centric (SCC) normalization scheme can be defined analogously with respect to target candidate e:

$$\psi_{SCC}(\bullet) \equiv \log \frac{\left(\sum_{d'} \rho(d',e)\right)^{\alpha}}{\bullet}. \tag{4}$$

In both the SDC and SCC schemes, the logarithm provides for a softer normalization compared to existing approaches from the literature, with parameter α in the numerators controlling the intensity of the normalization—the larger α, the softer the normalization. With $\alpha = 1$, both normalization schemes reduce to the information-theoretic concept of self-information [9], which quantifies the improbability of occurrence of a particular association given all other associations related to the same document or candidate.

4. EXPERIMENTAL EVALUATION

In this section, we evaluate our information-theoretic association models for expert search in academia. In particular, we aim to answer two research questions:

Q1. How effective is our proposed association scheme?

Q2. How effective are our proposed normalization schemes?

In the following, we describe the setup and discuss the results of our empirical investigations.

4.1 Experimental Setup

Our evaluation is based on the Lattes Expertise Retrieval (LExR) test collection [17], a publicly available test collection built on top of the Lattes platform,[1] an internationally renowned initiative for managing information about science, technology, and innovation for individual researchers and research institutions in Brazil. The LExR test collection comprises metadata records for 11,942,014 scientific publications associated with 206,697 candidate experts from all areas of knowledge working in multiple Brazilian research institutions spread all over the country. Moreover, it includes 235 queries suggested by real experts who judged one another on a graded scale. Grades 0, 1, 2, and 3 indicate an unknowledgeable, somewhat knowledgeable, very knowledgeable, and expert person on the query topic, respectively.

As baseline association schemes, we consider a standard boolean scheme (B), as well as non-boolean schemes based on the divergence (KL) of document and candidate language models built from each candidate's name [6] and on a clustering (CL) of each candidate's profile [14]. As baseline normalization schemes, we consider the standard document-centric (DC) and candidate-centric (CC) schemes [3] as well as schemes aimed at profile length normalization based on terms (Nt) and documents (Nd). All association and normalization schemes are deployed on top of Model 2 [3] as a representative of state-of-the-art expert search approaches. Model 2 is set to operate with the top 1,000 documents retrieved by a standard language model with Dirichlet smoothing with parameter $\mu = 2,000$. We index the title, keywords, abstract, and author names as separate document fields after removing stop words and applying no stemming. All indexing and retrieval operations use Apache Lucene 5.3.[2]

Our proposed association scheme in Equation (2) is deployed with document and candidate language models built using the abstract and author name fields of each document. Other textual representations showed similar effectiveness. In turn, our normalization schemes in Equations (3) and (4) are deployed with $\alpha = 2$, which showed marginal improvements compared to the standard setting of $\alpha = 1$. A full parameter sensitivity analysis is left for future research.

4.2 Experimental Results

Table 1 shows the retrieval effectiveness of several association (ρ) and normalization (ψ) schemes in terms of normalized discounted cumulative gain (nDCG@10), precision (P@10), and mean reciprocal rank (MRR). Our proposed association (ρ_H, Equation (2)) and normalization (ψ_{SDC} and ψ_{SCC}, Equations (3)-(4)) schemes are highlighted in gray. Statistical significance is verified using a paired t-test with $p < 0.01$. Superscript and subscript triangles (▲) denote significant improvements against the boolean association scheme (ρ_B) and the standard document- (ψ_{DC}) or candidate-centric (ψ_{CC}) normalization schemes, respectively.

From Table 1, in order to address research question Q1, we first analyze the effectiveness of our proposed association scheme. In particular, when using a standard document-centric normalization scheme (ψ_{DC}), our association scheme ρ_H consistently outperforms all other association schemes (ρ_B, ρ_{CL}, and ρ_{KL}) with respect to all evaluation metrics, with significant improvements compared to the strongest boolean association baseline (ρ_B). On the other hand, when using the standard candidate-centric normalization (ψ_{CC}), both the boolean association baseline as well as our proposed association scheme underperform, probably because of the harsh penalization applied to prolific candidates. Recalling research question Q1, these results attest the effectiveness

[1] http://lattes.cnpq.br/

[2] http://lucene.apache.org/

	nDCG	P@10	MRR	nDCG	P@10	MRR
ρ_{CL}	0.022	0.014	0.060	–	–	–
ρ_{KL}	0.135	0.082	0.240	–	–	–
	ψ_{Nt}			ψ_{Nd}		
ρ_B	0.012	0.009	0.039	0.061	0.008	0.028
	ψ_{DC}			ψ_{CC}		
ρ_B	0.133	0.079	0.254	0.004	0.004	0.018
ρ_H	$0.146^{\blacktriangle}$	$0.088^{\blacktriangle}$	$0.279^{\blacktriangle}$	0.005	0.004	0.020
	ψ_{SDC}			ψ_{SCC}		
ρ_B	$0.164_{\blacktriangle}$	$0.096_{\blacktriangle}$	$0.294_{\blacktriangle}$	$0.167_{\blacktriangle}$	$0.102_{\blacktriangle}$	$0.295_{\blacktriangle}$
ρ_H	$0.164_{\blacktriangle}$	$0.099_{\blacktriangle}$	$0.291_{\blacktriangle}$	$0.168_{\blacktriangle}$	$0.103_{\blacktriangle}$	$0.293_{\blacktriangle}$

Table 1: Retrieval effectiveness of several association (ρ) and normalization (ψ) schemes. Our proposed weighting schemes are highlighted in gray.

of our proposed information-theoretic association scheme, particularly under a document-centric normalization.

To address research question Q2, we contrast our soft normalization schemes (ψ_{SDC} and ψ_{SCC}) to their standard counterparts (ψ_{DC} and ψ_{CC}) and the two profile length normalization baselines (ψ_{Nt} and ψ_{Nd}). From Table 1, we observe that both of our proposed normalization schemes substantially outperform all baselines, with significant improvements compared to the standard document- and candidate-centric baselines with respect to all metrics. Recalling question Q2, these observations confirm the effectiveness of our proposed soft normalization schemes. Indeed, substantial improvements can be observed even when normalizations are candidate-centric, which further emphasizes the benefits of avoiding a harsh penalization of prolific candidates. On the other hand, the benefits of our improved association scheme ρ_H over boolean associations seem to be offset, which suggests further investigations towards an improved combination of association and normalization schemes.

5. CONCLUSIONS

We have proposed novel information-theoretic models to weight document-person associations for expert search in academia. Unlike existing approaches, which attempt to ascertain the authorship of a document, we proposed an association scheme aimed to estimate the extent to which the document is informative of the expertise of each candidate associated with it. Likewise, rather than penalizing prolific documents or candidates to avoid noisy estimations of expertise, we proposed soft normalization schemes that seek to infer how discriminative each association is. We evaluated our proposed association and normalization schemes using a publicly available test collection for expertise retrieval in academia encompassing candidate experts from multiple organizations and with expertise in a range of diverse knowledge areas. Our results demonstrated the effectiveness of the proposed weighting schemes, with substantial and statistically significant improvements over several baselines from the literature. As a direction for future research, we plan to extend our current investigation to non-textual association schemes, exploiting temporal and social signals of expertise.

Acknowledgments

This work was partially funded by projects InWeb (MCT/CNPq 573871/2008-6) and MASWeb (FAPEMIG/PRONEX APQ-01400-14), and by the authors' individual grants from CNPq and FAPEMIG.

6. REFERENCES

[1] P. Bailey, N. Craswell, I. Soboroff, and A. P. de Vries. The CSIRO enterprise search test collection. *SIGIR Forum*, 41(2):42–45, 2007.

[2] P. Bailey, A. P. de Vries, N. Craswell, and I. Soboroff. Overview of the TREC 2007 Enterprise track. In *Proc. of TREC*, 2007.

[3] K. Balog, L. Azzopardi, and M. de Rijke. Formal models for expert finding in enterprise corpora. In *Proc. of SIGIR*, pages 43–50, 2006.

[4] K. Balog, T. Bogers, L. Azzopardi, M. de Rijke, and A. van den Bosch. Broad expertise retrieval in sparse data environments. In *Proc. of SIGIR*, pages 551–558, 2007.

[5] K. Balog and M. de Rijke. Finding experts and their details in e-mail corpora. In *Proc. of WWW*, pages 1035–1036, 2006.

[6] K. Balog and M. De Rijke. Associating people and documents. In *Proc. of ECIR*, pages 296–308, 2008.

[7] K. Balog, Y. Fang, M. de Rijke, P. Serdyukov, and L. Si. Expertise retrieval. *Found. Trends Inf. Retr.*, 6(2–3):127–256, 2012.

[8] K. Balog, I. Soboroff, P. Thomas, N. Craswell, A. P. de Vries, and P. Bailey. Overview of the TREC 2008 Enterprise track. In *Proc. of TREC*, 2008.

[9] T. M. Cover and J. A. Thomas. *Elements of information theory.* John Wiley & Sons, 2012.

[10] N. Craswell, A. P. de Vries, and I. Soboroff. Overview of the TREC 2005 Enterprise track. In *Proc. of TREC*, 2005.

[11] H. Deng, I. King, and M. R. Lyu. Formal models for expert finding on DBLP bibliography data. In *Proc. of ICDM*, pages 163–172, 2008.

[12] Y. Fang, L. Si, and A. P. Mathur. Discriminative models of integrating document evidence and document-candidate associations for expert search. In *Proc. of SIGIR*, pages 683–690, 2010.

[13] V. Lavrenko and W. B. Croft. *Relevance Models in Information Retrieval*, chapter 2. 2003.

[14] C. Macdonald, D. Hannah, and I. Ounis. High quality expertise evidence for expert search. In *Proc. of ECIR*, pages 283–295, 2008.

[15] C. Macdonald and I. Ounis. Voting for candidates: adapting data fusion techniques for an expert search task. In *Proc. of CIKM*, pages 387–396, 2006.

[16] C. Macdonald and I. Ounis. Searching for expertise: experiments with the Voting Model. *Comput. J.*, 52(7):729–748, 2009.

[17] V. Mangaravite, R. L. T. Santos, I. S. Ribeiro, M. A. Gonçalves, and A. H. F. Laender. The LExR collection for expertise retrieval in academia. In *Proc. of SIGIR*, 2016.

[18] P. Serdyukov, H. Rode, and D. Hiemstra. Modeling multi-step relevance propagation for expert finding. In *Proc. of CIKM*, pages 1133–1142, 2008.

[19] I. Soboroff, A. P. de Vries, and N. Craswell. Overview of the TREC 2006 Enterprise track. In *Proc. of TREC*, 2006.

[20] J. Zhu, D. Song, and S. Rüger. Integrating multiple windows and document features for expert finding. *J. Am. Soc. Inf. Sci. Technol.*, 60(4):694–715, 2009.

On the Applicability of Delicious for Temporal Search on Web Archives*

Helge Holzmann, Wolfgang Nejdl, Avishek Anand
L3S Research Center
Appelstr. 9a
30167 Hanover, Germany
{holzmann, nejdl, anand}@L3S.de

ABSTRACT

Web archives are large longitudinal collections that store webpages from the past, which might be missing on the current live Web. Consequently, temporal search over such collections is essential for finding prominent missing webpages and tasks like historical analysis. However, this has been challenging due to the lack of popularity information and proper ground truth to evaluate temporal retrieval models. In this paper we investigate the applicability of external longitudinal resources to identify important and popular websites in the past and analyze the social bookmarking service Delicious for this purpose.

The timestamped bookmarks on Delicious provide explicit cues about popular time periods in the past along with relevant descriptors. These are valuable to identify important documents in the past for a given temporal query. Focusing purely on recall, we analyzed more than 12,000 queries and find that using Delicious yields average recall values from 46% up to 100%, when limiting ourselves to the best represented queries in the considered dataset. This constitutes an attractive and low-overhead approach for quick access into Web archives by not dealing with the actual contents.

1. INTRODUCTION

Most of the information and published content is either online or has been moving to the Web. Consequently, there has been a surge of collection, curation and preservation efforts to archive the live and ephemeral Web. While some institutions, such as the Internet Archive[1], attempt to archive the Web comprehensively, more and more national organizations and libraries target the Web under their own top-level domains. The growing number of such endeavors all around the world make Web archives a valuable resource for social scientists, historians, computer scientists as well as for the average user.

Web archives can provide access to historical information that is absent on the current Web, like previous companies, products, events, entities etc. However, even after a long time of existence, Web archives are still lacking *search capabilities* that make them truly accessible and usable as temporal resources. Available access methods include lookup services, such as the Wayback Machine [2], or indexing methods for efficient temporal queries [1, 2], but retrieval models to rank versions of webpages are limited to relevance cues from document content [3]. This is primarily due to the inability of the models to determine which page was important at a given instant or interval of time. Furthermore, as there are often multiple versions of a page, it is difficult to identify which version among them is the most relevant and different versions of the same page may be relevant at different points in time. To make matters worse, it is even more difficult to identify the variations of a page that are the most interesting for users in a given time period only by analyzing *internal* properties of a page, like its content, as detailed in [5].

While determining authority of pages in an archive independent of a query has been attempted [8], popularity cues from external sources have not been considered. By incorporating *external* data, such as explicit temporal information about a website's popularity, this can be simplified and lead to a better retrieval performance. Sources for this can be any websites reporting about other websites, such as social networks, where users post their favorite or most controversial websites at a specific time of interest. Besides the explicit time information, another advantage of searching *external* data instead of websites itself is the more focused descriptions of only relevant pages. Users typically post the essence instead of the often verbose contents found on the websites, including layouts, comments, etc. Finally, this also allows for a much more clean and compact index, a critical factor for ever growing Web archive collections with sizes of hundreds of terabytes.

One of those resources is the social bookmarking service Delicious[3], where users post popular links and describe them with a concise set of tags as succinct descriptors. These tags carry temporal information that can be exploited for search: While the tag *commuity* is frequently assigned to *facebook.com* today, other communities, such as *myspace.com* were tagged with the term before. The idea to base search on tags has been previously explored, but never in a temporal dimension [4, 6].

*This work is partly funded by the European Research Council under ALEXANDRIA (ERC 339233)

[1]http://archive.org

[2]https://github.com/iipc/openwayback

[3]https://del.icio.us

SIGIR '16, July 17-21, 2016, Pisa, Italy
© 2016 ACM. ISBN 978-1-4503-4069-4/16/07...$15.00
DOI: http://dx.doi.org/10.1145/2911451.2914724

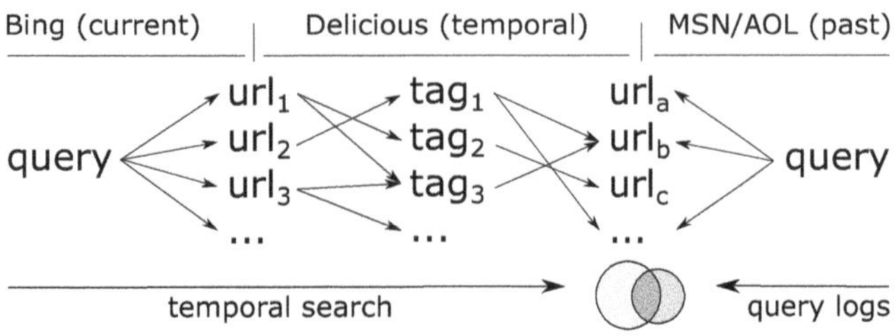

Figure 1: The analysis workflow from query-tag mapping using Bing and Delicious to querying Delicious and comparing against MSN/AOL query logs.

With *Tempas (Temporal archive search)* we have created a prototype to search webpages based on a Delicious dataset over nine years[4]. Tempas links directly into a Web archive to show the versions described by the users in their posts [7]. We exploit the frequencies of posts as well as mutual information of tags attached to a page as indicator of their relevance to a certain topic. Tempas is a fully functional system to search Web archives in a temporal manner on a relatively small and concise index. However, before we can continue to tune this system to a high precision it is essential to understand what is available in the used dataset and which of the websites that really mattered to users of search engines in the past can be found with it. It is crucial to keep in mind the inherent bias of the dataset used for this task.

In this paper we analyze the applicability of Delicious for searching documents published in the past based on the following research questions:

(**R1**) *What fraction of websites clicked by users on a search engine in the past are included in Delicious as well?*
(**R2**) *What topics or entities are covered by Delicious?*
(**R3**) *What are the natural limitations of Delicious as a dataset for temporal Web archive search?*
(**R4**) *How do posting times on Delicious and query times in search engines relate to each other?*

2. ANALYSIS

The Delicious dataset spans nine years from 2003 to 2011 and contains about 340 mio. bookmarks, 119 mio. unique URLs, 15 mio. tags and 2 mio. users [9]. Each bookmarked URL is time stamped and tagged with descriptors. The methodology of our analysis is shown in Figure 1.

We begin with a query workload and identify the associated tags for each query in Delicious. This is done by using Bing search results as a proxy and selecting tags attached to the returned URLs. We then compute the overlap of clicked search results in two query logs, from AOL and MSN, and the URLs tagged with the query or its expanded tags to compute the *recall* of Delicious for temporal search. This is done for overlapping time intervals of both datasets, query logs and Delicious, which are May 2006 for MSN and March to May 2006 for AOL.

As an example scenario consider the clothing brand `American Apparel`. Using the approach as described below, we map this query to the tags `americanapparel` and `apparel` as well as `t-shirts`, which appears to be used quite synonymously on Delicious. In the next step, we retrieve all URLs that were tagged with any of these tags during a given time, here May 2006. This results in 227 URLs. As a ground truth we compare against query logs from MSN and AOL from the same time. These contain two and four URLs that users clicked on for the query `american apparel`: `americanapparel.net` and `americanapparelstore.com` on MSN as well as `allonlinecoupons.com` and `usawear.org` additionally on AOL. As only the first two are contained in the set of URLs from Delicious, it reaches a full recall of 100% (1.0) with respect to MSN and 50% (0.5) w.r.t. AOL. Analyzing the precision remains for future work as it will require an appropriate retrieval model to rank the relevant links up to the top. A high recall, however, is a crucial prerequisite to make the system usable in practice.

2.1 Query-Tag Mapping

Our query workload comprises article titles from the German Wikipedia, which we consider as entities in the following. In principle, the approach is applicable to any type of queries, but the mapping of entity names to tags is more straightforward than arbitrary multi-keyword queries, which would usually refer to a set of tags instead of single representatives. The used Wikipedia collection consists of 1.8 million articles from the main namespace without disambiguation and list pages. The focus on German aligns with the Web archive available to us and also narrows down the vast number of articles on Wikipedia. The titles were issued as queries to Bing between August 7 and 13, 2015 and we stored the top 100 results for each query.

To map the queries to tags that best represent the corresponding entity, we collected all tags from Delicious that were attached to the retrieved URLs from Bing and used by at least 10 users. From these we kept only those tags that were used by at least 10% of the users who posted one of the URLs for that query. In addition, we selected a reference tag w_{ref} tag that exactly matches the query after down-casing and removing special characters. E.g., w_{ref}(Barack Obama) = `barackobama`. For the remaining tags we computed an adaption of *IDF* (inverse document frequency) based on the total number of considered queries and relative to the reference tag for normalization:

$$\text{idf}(w) = \frac{\log(|\text{queries}|)}{|\{q \in \text{queries} \mid w \in \text{tags}(q)\}|}$$

$$\text{rel.idf}(w) = \frac{\text{idf}(w)}{\text{idf}(w_{\text{ref}})}$$

This number indicates the generality of the tag, i.e., how specific it is to the assigned query. Additionally, we computed what we call *exclusiveness*. A high exclusiveness indicates that the tag does not often co-occur with the reference tag, which would be uncommon if both tags represent the same entity:

$$\text{excl}(w) = 1 - \frac{\#\text{posts}(w, w_{\text{ref}})}{\min(\#\text{posts}(w),\ \#\text{posts}(w_{\text{ref}}))}$$

$\#\text{posts}(w_1, w_2, ...)$ defines the number of posts on Delicious with all specified tags $w_1, w_2, ...$ as unique pairs of user and posted URL to filter spammers with a large number of posts of the same URL.

To combine the numbers we computed the average score of each tag w as $0.5 \cdot (\text{rel.idf}(w) + \text{excl}(w))$ for every query with reference tag w_{ref}. The resulting score indicates how specific a tag is to its considered query and at the same time how complementary or exchangeable it is to the reference

[4]http://tempas.L3S.de

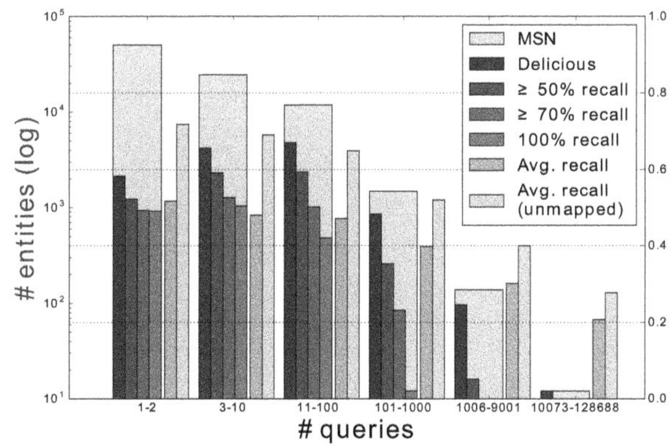

Figure 2: Comparison of the numbers of entities in the MSN query log vs. Declicious with different recalls and the average recall considering entity-tag mapping or not, partitioned by the popularity of entities according to number of queries in the logs.

tag, which we consider a representation of the corresponding entity. Experiments have shown that a threshold of 0.7 reliably identifies true representative tags for a query. Thus, we took all tags with a score equal or greater as well as w_{ref}.

Examples are shown in Table 1. Although this simple approach is not accurate in all cases, it is good enough for an experiment like ours. While it worked well for entities like `Wikipedia`, it sometimes yields too general tags, like `popular` in case of `Craigslist`. For other entities, some tags seem too generic at the first glance, but appear to be used almost synonymously on Delicious, such as the format `flv` for `YouTube`. However, the quality is acceptable and a better mapping would have only resulted in even higher recall values as we will show in the following.

2.2 Querying

To assess the recall of the considered Delicious dataset, we *queried* it for the identified tags and at the same time selected records for the corresponding entity from the MSN and AOL query logs. We matched queries with exact name as extracted from the Wikipedia titles, ignoring case. The clicked URLs for a given query served as ground truth in the experiment and we measured recall by counting how many of those could be also found in Delicious. Each URL annotated with one of the considered tags was selected. We operated under the assumption that tags identified by us were also used back in the past, which we believe is valid, as most tags relate to entity names or variations. In total, 12,106 entities could be successfully mapped to tags as well as corresponding queries in the MSN query logs and 12,170 in the AOL logs.

From Table 1, which shows the top 10 entities with highest frequency in the MSN logs and a recall of greater than 0.5 on Delicious, a certain bias towards rather technical and Internet related entities can be observed (**R2**). A bias to a certain, less popular type of entities could also be affirmed by counting numbers and recall values for entities of different popularities as shown in Figure 2: Even though all of the most popular entities could be mapped to tags in Delicious, their recall is relatively low. However, the highest presence in Delicious was not among the least popular entities either, but among those that were queried by up to 100 search sessions in the MSN logs. Also, the highest recall values were reached for the long-tail as well, rather than for the more popular entities (**R3**).

Table 1: Top 10 entities according to MSN query logs from May 2006 with a recall value of greater than 0.5.

Entity	Tags	#Q	Recall
ESPN	`espn`	7492	0.60
Gmail	`gmail`	5285	0.92
Craigslist	`classifieds, popular, imported, craigslist`	4943	0.80
Wikipedia	`wiki, encyclopedia, wikipedia`	3063	0.60
Imdb	`cinema, imdb`	2626	0.92
AIM	`aim`	2180	0.57
YouTube	`flv, converter, youtube`	1965	0.75
Sudoku	`sudoku`	1739	0.75
PayPal	`paypal`	1710	0.60

To ensure the observed recalls are not due to a poor mapping (s. Sec. 2.1), we computed the recall values of the same entities also by considering the entire Delicious dataset, not only results retrieved by the mapped tags (*unmapped*). This suggests the upper bound, which could potentially be reached given a better entity-tag mapping. However, as presented in the figure, these recall values are only slightly higher than the ones achieved with our mapping.

Overall, the average recall values of the entire experiment resulted in 48% w.r.t. MSN and 46% w.r.t. AOL. Although this is already a good result, it gets even better by looking at those entities, which are strongly represented on Delicious and reached the highest recalls in the experiment. As presented in Figure 3, for the top 2000 entities we achieve a full recall w.r.t. both query logs. The top 6000, which is about 50%, still exhibit a recall of almost 0.8 with even slightly higher values w.r.t. AOL (**R1**).

This shows, about half of the URLs that users clicked in a search engine can be found by using Delicious as an external data source to search Web archives. Even more intriguing, if used with the queries that are best represented by the dataset, we can even reach much higher values up to a recall of 100%.

3. TEMPORAL SEARCH

So far, none of the presented analyses has taken into account the temporal aspect, although our ultimate goal was to evaluate the applicability of Delicious as external data source for temporal Web archive search. Thus we wanted to know,

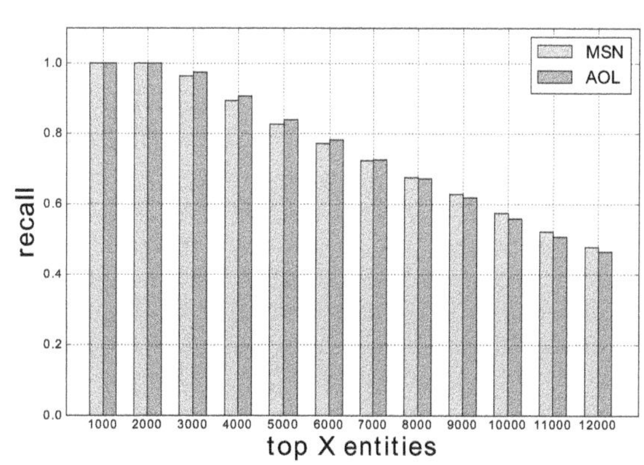

Figure 3: Top X entities according to their Delicious recall with respect to MSN and AOL query logs.

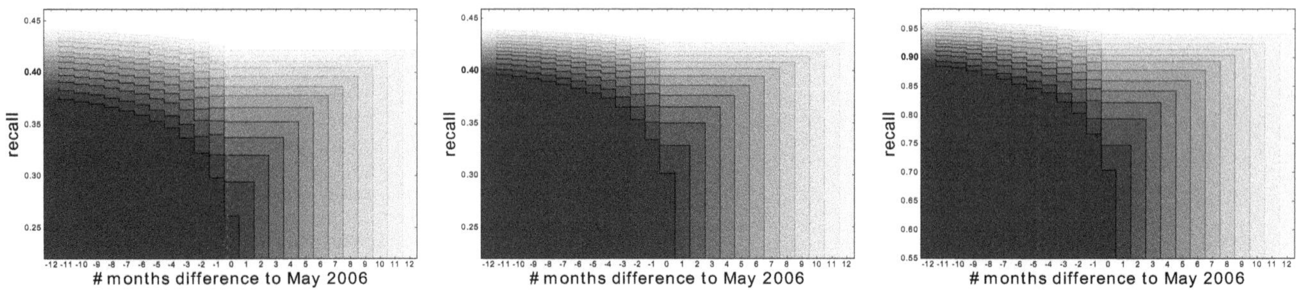

(a) all entities (MSN) (b) all entities (AOL) (c) top 2000 entities (AOL)

Figure 4: Recall w.r.t. MSN query logs from May 2006 (0) and AOL query logs from March 2006 (-2) to May 2006 (0).

given the fairly good recalls achieved before, are the URLs spread across the entire dataset or focused around the query times of the available logs. Figure 4 presents these temporal recall results. To get comparable values, we queried Delicious with the same approach as before just only around the time spans of the logs, i.e., May 2006 for MSN (0) and March (-2) to May 2006 (0) for AOL. The x-axis in the figures denotes the time difference in months up to one year in the future and the past.

Notable is that in all plots, up to a difference of around three months, the recall grows faster by relaxing the search interval to the past. However, from the third month on the recall gain is higher by expanding the search interval to the future. This suggests posts on Delicious are lagging slightly behind the queries in the considered search engines. Overall the results are a slightly higher w.r.t. the AOL query logs, which, however, may be due to the fact that it spans three months instead of one, covered by MSN. Hence, in May Delicious is already two months ahead of AOL. This corresponds to the observation that the recall w.r.t. MSN for three months from 0 to 2 approximately matches the recall w.r.t. AOL in month 0. Overall, the recall results come very close to what we observed in Figure 3. While we achieved a full recall for the top 2,000 entities from the entire dataset, already a search span of two years, 12 month in the future and 12 in the past, is sufficient to retrieve 95% w.r.t. MSN and even more than 95% w.r.t. AOL, as presented in Figure 4c. Even more intriguing, we only lose about 10% of recall by searching as little as two months in the past and three months in the future (**R4**). However, in favor of Delicious was the fact that the platform was relatively popular during the analyzed time. Thus, the results might be lower today and call for alternative datasets.

4. CONCLUSION AND OUTLOOK

In this work we introduced the idea of using external data sources with explicit temporal information for Web archive search. We investigated the applicability of the social bookmarking service Delicious as a resource for this task and have shown that it indeed serves as a suitable dataset for a certain kind of entity queries. It is crucial to keep in mind the bias of any dataset used with the presented approach, as obviously only queries supported by the dataset can lead to satisfying results. It turns out, the best represented entities among the most popular ones on Delicious are from the technical or Internet domain. Nevertheless, even overall we reached a promising recall of 46% to 48% w.r.t. the analyzed query logs from MSN and AOL. By focusing on the top queries, which exhibit the best recall results, a full recall of 100% could be retained up to the top 2000 of all of the about 12,100 analyzed entities. The top 50%, approx. 6000 entities, still result in a recall of almost 80% on average.

As a second analysis of the paper, we investigated temporal recall values with respect to the time spans of the query logs around May 2006. It has shown that most of the websites of interest w.r.t. the query logs also appeared on Delicious around one year before and after the query times. Already five months around the query time result only in a little loss of recall. This indicates that Delicious is applicable for temporal search as it appears to resemble query logs of the past. The next step in this endeavor will be to create an appropriate retrieval model that ranks the URLs according to their relevance as derived by the query logs. Eventually, our goal is to incorporate different sources, such as different social networks as well as external websites from the Web archive itself, that cover the missing entities over time for a more complete Web archive search.

References

[1] A. Anand, S. Bedathur, K. Berberich, and R. Schenkel. Temporal index sharding for space-time efficiency in archive search. *SIGIR*, 2011.

[2] A. Anand, S. Bedathur, K. Berberich, and R. Schenkel. Index maintenance for time-travel text search. *SIGIR*, 2012.

[3] K. Berberich, S. Bedathur, O. Alonso, and G. Weikum. *A language modeling approach for temporal information needs. ECIR*, 2010.

[4] K. Bischoff, C. S. Firan, W. Nejdl, and R. Paiu. Can all tags be used for search? *CIKM*, 2008.

[5] R. Campos, G. Dias, A. M. Jorge, and A. Jatowt. Survey of temporal information retrieval and related applications. *ACM Computing Surveys (CSUR)*, 47(2):15, 2015.

[6] P. Heymann, G. Koutrika, and H. Garcia-Molina. Can social bookmarking improve web search? *WSDM*, 2008.

[7] H. Holzmann and A. Anand. Tempas: Temporal archive search based on tags. *WWW [Demo]*, 2016.

[8] T. N. Nguyen, N. Kanhabua, C. Niederée, and X. Zhu. A time-aware random walk model for finding important documents in web archives. *SIGIR*, 2015.

[9] A. Zubiaga, V. Fresno, R. Martinez, and A. P. Garcia-Plaza. Harnessing folksonomies to produce a social classification of resources. *IEEE Transactions on Knowledge and Data Engineering*, 25(8):1801–1813, 2013.

On the Effectiveness of Contextualisation Techniques in Spoken Query Spoken Content Retrieval

David N. Racca
ADAPT Centre
School of Computing
Dublin City University
Dublin 9, Ireland
dracca@computing.dcu.ie

Gareth J.F. Jones
ADAPT Centre
School of Computing
Dublin City University
Dublin 9, Ireland
gjones@computing.dcu.ie

ABSTRACT

In passage and XML retrieval, contextualisation techniques seek to improve the rank of a relevant element by considering information from its surrounding elements and its container document. Recent research has demonstrated that some of these techniques are also particularly effective in spoken content retrieval tasks (SCR). However, no previous research has directly compared contextualisation techniques in an SCR setting, nor has it studied their potential to provide robustness to speech recognition errors. In this paper, we evaluate different contextualisation techniques, including a recently proposed technique based on positional language models (PLM) on the task of retrieving relevant spoken passages in response to a spoken query. We study the benefits of these techniques when queries and documents are transcribed with increasingly higher error rates. Experimental results over the Japanese NTCIR SpokenQuery&Doc collection show that combining global and local context is beneficial for SCR and that models usually benefit from using larger amounts of context in highly noisy conditions.

1. INTRODUCTION

Recent advances in mobile and network technologies have led to an exponential increase in the amount of spoken material that is produced and stored. Effective spoken content retrieval [9] (SCR) techniques are needed to enable information access from these type of collections. SCR has been traditionally framed as an ad-hoc retrieval task: given some information need represented by a text or spoken query, one must produce a ranked-list of spoken documents or passages in order of relevance to the query to be presented to the user for further assessment. A standard approach for SCR uses an automatic speech recognition (ASR) system to obtain a 1-best recognition transcription of the collection and standard text-based IR techniques to index the transcripts and to perform document or passage retrieval. Passage retrieval is normally preferred over full-document retrieval in cases where documents are long and multi-topical and in applications that seek to minimise audio playback time [1]. This typically requires a mechanism to identify topically coherent units of information in the speech recordings that could be treated as retrieval elements and returned in response to a query. When the spoken content is known to be delivered in a structured fashion and when structural cues are available to the SCR system, retrieval elements can be defined accordingly. Otherwise, suitable elements may be obtained by using a topic segmentation algorithm.

Although the quality of ASR systems has improved significantly over the past few years, ASR errors still pose a challenge to traditional text retrieval techniques. This occurs in domains where speech is informal, conversational, or spontaneous [9] or when the elements to be retrieved are short in length or lack sufficient contextual information and verbosity to be retrieved effectively [2]. Context and verbosity are desirable properties of an element because they can increase its chances of matching query terms, even when many of its terms are misrecognised by ASR. In general, the more repetitions of important terms used to convey the topic and the more exhaustively this topic is covered by the terms in the element to be retrieved, the more robust will be its matching process against ASR errors.

The context of an element, that is, the information that is present in its document, has been shown to be valuable for improving element-retrieval effectiveness [3]. The process of taking context into account when computing the relevance score of an element is known as contextualisation [3]. Various contextualisation techniques have been proven effective in XML retrieval [3], passage retrieval [6, 8], and SCR [12, 15] tasks. In these techniques, elements are scored depending not only on the query terms occurring within the element itself but also on those occurring in other positions within the document. Two simple and widely adopted approaches are interpolating the scores of an element with those of its document to consider global context [12], or with those from a fixed number of surrounding elements to consider local context [15]. In contrast, techniques based on positional models (PM) [6, 8] allow consideration of longer-spans of context ignoring element boundaries.

In this paper, we study the impact of incorporating context into the task of retrieving short spoken passages given a spoken query from a collection of long spoken documents. Our hypothesis is that context becomes increasingly valuable for improving retrieval effectiveness as ASR errors increase in the transcripts of the spoken queries and documents. We

SIGIR '16, July 17-21, 2016, Pisa, Italy

DOI: http://dx.doi.org/10.1145/2911451.2914730

Table 1: List of manual and ASR transcript types.

SpokenQuery&Doc ID	Short ID
MANUAL	M
K-REF-WORD-MATCH	A0
REF-WORD-MATCH	A1
REF-WORD-UNMATCHLM	A2
REF-WORD-UNMATCHAMLM	A3

validate this empirically by comparing the performance of various contextualisation techniques in a SCR task.

The remainder of the paper is organised as follows. Section 2 describes the spoken test collection. Section 3 presents our baseline retrieval approach which we extend with the contextualisation techniques presented in Section 4. Section 5 describes experiments and results obtained. Finally, Section 6 concludes and discusses future work.

2. SPOKEN TEST COLLECTION

The SDPWS dataset has been used at recent editions of the NTCIR SpokenQuery&Doc (SQD) tasks [1]. This corpus contains speech recordings of 98 oral presentations in Japanese totalling approximately 27 hours. The task organisers provided automatic transcripts of the recordings of varying quality. These were generated using an ASR system with different combinations of acoustic and language models. Furthermore, human transcripts are provided which are manually annotated with the times when slide transitions were made by the presenters, as well as groups of consecutive slides used to present a single topic or idea. These slide groups define a list of topical segments within a presentation, used in the task as pre-defined passages to be retrieved in response to a query. In our experiments, we similarly use these segments as retrieval passages. Table 1 lists the different transcript types. The first column shows the ID of each type as mentioned in the task overview [1], while the second shows short IDs used throughout this paper.

Since no characters are placed between words in written Japanese, we process text transcripts with the morphological analyser MeCab[1] to obtain tokens that can be used as indexing features. For this purpose, we configure MeCab to output the base form of the identified words along with their part-of-speech tags. As lemmas of nouns and verbs are effective indexing features for Japanese SCR [12], we remove all tokens not tagged as verbs or nouns. Further, we remove function words that are misclassified as nouns or verbs with a stop word list containing 44 of the most frequent prepositions and determiners. After processing the text, we use the Terrier platform v4.0[2] to generate an index with positional information for each transcription type. Table 2 shows term statistics of post-processed documents and passages. In total, the collection comprises 98 documents which are split into 2330 passages. For each transcript, we report word error rates (WER) averaged across utterances and term error rates (TER) [7] averaged across passages.

The spoken queries used in the SQD-1 and SQD-2 tasks are available for the SDPWS collection. These sets contain 35 and 80 queries respectively. Also, organisers generated human and ASR transcripts for the queries by using the same ASR models used to transcribe the presentations. Table 3 summarises term statistics and ASR error rates for the spoken queries. Relevance judgements for these query sets were created by the task organisers from a pool of results submitted for the SQD tasks. Three relevance levels were annotated: full, partial, and no relevance. In our experiments, we treat partially relevant passages as fully relevant.

[1]http://mecab.sourceforge.net/

[2]http://terrier.org

Table 2: Collection statistics of documents and passages.

ID	WER	TER	#Terms	Documents		Passages	
				Ave.len.	S.D.len.	Ave.len.	S.D.len.
M	0%	0%	6230	1769.17	276.15	74.48	67.61
A0	22.0%	39.3%	6350	1763.09	274.01	74.19	67.42
A1	43.7%	70.0%	6131	1752.15	262.81	73.62	67.56
A2	67.5%	121.9%	11219	1922.76	285.21	80.73	74.77
A3	70.5%	120.6%	14190	1594.50	247.70	67.06	62.55

Table 3: Error rates and statistics of query transcripts.

Queries	ID	WER	TER	#Terms	Ave.len.	S.D.len.
SQD-1	M	0%	0%	373	24.13	11.61
	A1	51.6%	80.6%	490	29.64	15.14
	A2	77.7%	125.5%	871	39.10	23.34
	A3	69.1%	109.6%	754	32.89	19.64
SQD-2	M	0%	0%	714	30.77	12.06
	A0	33.7%	45.3%	766	30.32	13.67
	A1	49.2%	68.3%	961	36.85	16.65
	A2	75.4%	111.8%	1763	50.81	28.37
	A3	66.1%	98.9%	1615	42.41	21.09

3. BASIC RETRIEVAL MODEL

In our simplest retrieval set-up, we treat passages as retrieval elements and use standard document retrieval to rank them in order of their relevance to the query. Our ranking function is based on the Okapi BM25 function of probabilistic retrieval [14]. Besides the well known k_1, b, and k_3 parameters, we include a fourth parameter, namely $d \geq 1$, as the exponent of the IDF weight [16]. This parameter can be adjusted to increase the relative difference between weights assigned to frequent and rare terms. In our experiments, setting $d > 1$ results in improved effectiveness as this may provide better estimates of IDF weights for small collections. Similar effects can be obtained with the modification proposed in [11], although this results in lower retrieval effectiveness in our task. The resulting function calculates the weight of a term t occurring in element e and query Q as:

$$w_e(t) = \frac{(k_1+1)tf(t)}{tf(t)+k_1(1-b+b\frac{\text{docl}}{\text{avel}})}\frac{(k_3+1)qf(t)}{qf(t)+k_3}w_1(t)^d \quad (1)$$

where $tf(t)$ and $qf(t)$ denote the number of occurrences of t in e and Q respectively, *docl* is the length of e, *avel* is the average length of all the elements of the same type in the collection, n_t is the number of elements containing term t, N is the number of elements in the collection, $w_1(t)$ is $\log(N - n_t + 0.5) - \log(n_t + 0.5)$ and b, k_1, k_3, and d are tuning parameters. Given this term scoring function, we rank elements according to their relevance score with respect to Q given by $S_{BM25}(Q,e) = \sum_{t \in Q \cap e} w_e(t)$.

4. CONTEXTUALISATION TECHNIQUES

In this section, we present the contextualisation techniques that are investigated in our study.

4.1 Document Score Interpolation

A simple and popular contextualisation approach consists of combining a passage relevance score with the score of its document. Firstly, passages and documents are scored independently to form two separate ranked-lists of results. Secondly, initially retrieved passages are re-ranked according to the combination of their document scores. For score combination, we adopt a simple weighted linear sum of scores or CombSUM [5]. The relevance score of passage p within document D is given by:

$$S_{DSI}(Q,p) = \lambda S_{BM25}(Q,D) + (1-\lambda)S_{BM25}(Q,p) \quad (2)$$

where the interpolation parameter λ adjusts the influence of the document score over the combined score.

4.2 Positional Models

Positional models (PM) seek to improve IR effectiveness by exploiting information about the positions where query terms occur in a document. A representative example of these models are positional language models (PLM) [10] which were introduced in IR as a mechanism to integrate evidence from term proximity features and passages into the language modelling framework. A PLM estimates the probability $P(t|i,D)$ that term t is generated at position i in document D. In this estimation, the so-called pseudo-frequency of the term is used which is calculated by means of a kernel decay function that propagates occurrences of the term to distant positions in the document. This probability can possibly be influenced by all occurrences of t in D depending on their distance to i. The kernel function is commonly parametrised by a propagation parameter σ which adjusts the influence that a term occurrence has over distant positions. Among these, the Gaussian kernel $\exp(-(j-i)^2/2\sigma^2)$ has been shown effective in previous studies [10, 6, 8].

In recent work, PMs were proposed as a contextualisation technique for passage retrieval [6]. In this work, a standard TFIDF approach was used to compute the relevance score of a passage p within document D where the frequency of term t in p is given by its pseudo-frequency estimate:

$$tf_{PM}(t) = \sum_{i \in pos(t,D)} \sum_{j=p_1}^{p_n} kernel(j,i) \quad (3)$$

where $pos(t,D)$ is the set of positions where t occurs in D, $p_1,\ldots,p_n$ are the spanning positions of p in D, and *kernel* is the symmetric Gaussian kernel. To avoid longer passages from receiving unmerited pseudo-frequency counts, the summation over the kernel function is applied across a fixed number of positions independent of p's length.

In our experiments with PMs, we incorporate the pseudo-frequencies into the TF factor within the Okapi BM25 model. This is performed by replacing the raw term frequency $tf(t)$ by $tf_{PM}(t)$ in Equation 1 to obtain a modified weight w'_e. The resulting passage scoring function is then defined as:

$$S_{PM}(Q,p) = \sum_{t \in Q \cap D} w'_p(t) \quad (4)$$

To reduce the execution time of our scoring algorithm, we evaluate the kernel only at the position within the passage that gives its maximum value. That is, we evaluate the kernel at $j = p_1$ or $j = p_n$ if $i < p_1$ or $i > p_n$ respectively, or at $j = i$ otherwise. Finally, we also experiment with a model that combines passage scores obtained with S_{PM} and document scores obtained with S_{BM25}, this is:

$$S_{DSI\text{-}PM}(Q,p) = \lambda S_{BM25}(Q,D) + (1-\lambda)S_{PM}(Q,p) \quad (5)$$

5. RETRIEVAL EXPERIMENTS

To study the value of context for improving passage ranking in noisy conditions, we evaluate the effectiveness of the models presented in Sections 3 and 4 on various combinations of query and document transcripts. In all experiments, retrieval effectiveness is measured in terms of mean average precision (MAP) at depth 1000. Each combination of transcripts imposes a different evaluation condition with varying level of noise, each of which may require adjusting model parameters differently in order to achieve optimal performance. Further, in order to validate our hypothesis, we would like to find values for the contextualisation parameters σ and λ that provide the best performance in each case. Consequently, we optimise parameters for each model by seeking to maximise retrieval effectiveness in each evaluation condition. The optimisation method we use is a greedy iterative approach called "Promising Directions" [13] which performs multiple line searches over decreasing trusted regions in the parameter search space. Since MAP is not a smooth nor a convex function [13] this method is not guaranteed to find a global maximum. Nevertheless, it can still find configurations that perform significantly better in our task than if using default BM25 parameters[3].

To obtain a fair estimate of the relative performance of the models, we optimise parameters on the SQD-1 queries and evaluate on the SQD-2 queries. Table 4 reports MAP scores obtained by the BM25, DSI, PM, and DSI-PM models on the SQD-2 queries for different combinations of transcript types. The percentages next to the MAP scores show relative differences with respect to BM25. In each row, bold values and markers *, †, and ◇ indicate statistically significant differences with respect to BM25, DIS, PM, and DIS-PM respectively based on a *MaxT* permutation test ($B = 100,000$, $\alpha = 0.05$) that corrects for multiple hypothesis testing [4]. Also, we report query-averaged TERs for each transcript combination calculated by restricting terms to only those occurring in the queries. Overall, results indicate that using global (DSI) and local (PM) context either in isolation or in combination (DSI-PM) provide gains in retrieval effectiveness across all evaluation conditions. Furthermore, the relative gains of using context in highly noisy conditions (TER > 55%) are greater on average than in less noisy conditions.

Finally, we study the effects of varying the contextualisation parameter σ in the PM scoring function. Figure 1 shows how MAP scores vary as we increase the values of σ in six representative evaluation conditions. Data points were generated considering optimal parameter values for the SQD-2 queries. For perfect or quasi-perfect transcripts (M-M and A0-A0), the model achieves maximum performance at $\sigma = 76$ and $\sigma = 111$ respectively, while for moderately noisy transcripts (A1-A1 and M-A3) it does so at $\sigma = 296$ and $\sigma = 341$ respectively. Finally, in extremely noisy conditions (A2-A2 and A2-A3), the maximum points are located at $\sigma = 530$ and $\sigma = 682$ respectively. These observations provide supporting evidence for our claim that longer spans

[3]Due to space limitations, we do not report here the full set of optimal parameter values which generally vary across models and transcripts. These are available at: github.com/dracca/context.

Table 4: MAP scores for test queries.

TER	Transcripts		Models						
	Query	Doc.	BM25	PM		DSI		DSI-PM	
0%	M	M	.272	.291	+6%	**.305**	+12%	.314	+15%
20%	M	A0	.261	.294	+12%	.260	0%	.299	+14%
43%	M	A1	.228	.267	+16%	**.272**	+19%	.278	+21%
51%	A0	A0	.261	.292	+11%	.261	0%	.293	+12%
58%	M	A2	.085	**.178**	+108%	**.160**	+87%	**.174**	+103%
62%	A0	A1	.236	.267	+13%	**.271**	+14%	.274	+15%
71%	A0	A2	.091	**.177**	+94%	**.166**	+82%	**.172**	+88%
78%	M	A3	.119	**.209**	+75%	**.214**	+80%	**.192**	+60%
82%	A1	A1	.186	**.239**	+28%	**.249**	+34%	**.277**	+49%
87%	A1	A2	.097	.124	+27%	**.126**	+29%	.139	+43%
88%	A0	A3	.111	**.173**	+55%	**.191**	+72%	**.167**	+50%
100%	A2	A2	.117	.096	-21%	.112	-4%	.155†	+33%
106%	A1	A3	.048	**.144***	+200%	**.142**◇	+196%	**.134**	+178%
108%	A2	A3	.066	.100	+52%	**.122**	+86%	.126	+91%
115%	A3	A3	.095	.145	+52%	**.146**	+53%	**.168**	+76%

Figure 1: MAP scores versus σ for the PM model.

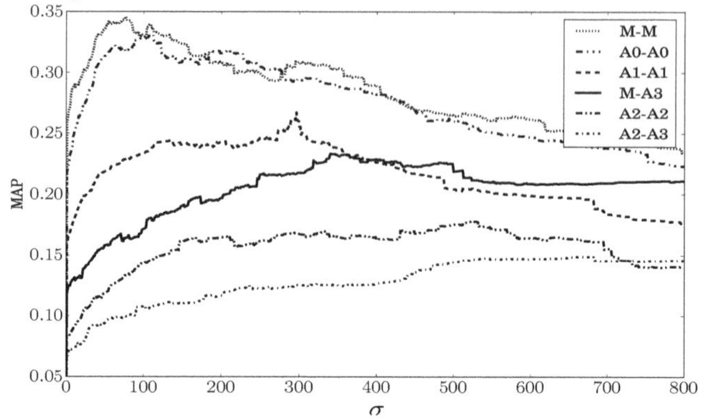

of context become increasingly useful for retrieval as ASR errors increase in the transcripts.

6. CONCLUSIONS

This paper has investigated the benefits of using context for improving the ranking of spoken passages given a spoken query. Three contextualisation techniques have been evaluated and compared against a well-tuned state-of-the-art retrieval model: a document score interpolation, a positional model, and their combination. Results of retrieval experiments with transcripts of varying quality validate previous findings that highlight the importance of using context in element-retrieval and SCR tasks and indicate that a combination of local and global context performs best for SCR. Further analysis reveals that considering greater extents of local context can improve IR effectiveness as ASR errors increase in the transcripts. In future work, we will evaluate models on an unsegmented spoken collection where we could fully exploit the "soft" characterisation of passage boundaries provided by PMs. Since recognition quality may vary greatly across utterances, we also plan to develop new techniques that could re-adjust context-incidence parameters according to ASR confidence estimates.

7. ACKNOWLEDGEMENT

This work is supported by Science Foundation Ireland through the CNGL Programme (Grant No: 12/CE/I2267) in the ADAPT Centre at Dublin City University.

8. REFERENCES

[1] T. Akiba, H. Nishizaki, H. Nanjo, and G. J. F. Jones. Overview of the NTCIR-12 SpokenQuery&Doc-2 task. In *Proceedings of NTCIR-12*, Tokyo, Japan, 2016.

[2] J. Allan. Perspectives on information retrieval and speech. In *Information Retrieval Techniques for Speech Applications*, pages 323–326. 2002.

[3] P. Arvola, J. Kekäläinen, and M. Junkkari. Contextualization models for XML retrieval. *Information Processing & Management*, 47(5):762–776, 2011.

[4] L. Boytsov, A. Belova, and P. Westfall. Deciding on an adjustment for multiplicity in IR experiments. In *Proceedings of SIGIR'13*, pages 403–412, Dublin, Ireland, 2013.

[5] J. P. Callan. Passage-level evidence in document retrieval. In *Proceedings of SIGIR'94*, pages 302–310, Dublin, Ireland, 1994.

[6] D. Carmel, A. Shtok, and O. Kurland. Position-based contextualization for passage retrieval. In *Proceedings of CIKM'13*, pages 1241–1244, San Francisco, CA, USA, 2013.

[7] S. E. Johnson, P. Jourlin, K. S. Jones, and P. C. Woodland. Spoken document retrieval for TREC-7 at Cambridge University. In *Proceedings of TREC-7*, pages 191–200, 1999.

[8] M. Keikha, J. H. Park, W. B. Croft, and M. Sanderson. Retrieving passages and finding answers. In *Proceedings of ADCS'14*, pages 81–84, Melbourne, Australia, 2014.

[9] M. Larson and G. J. F. Jones. Spoken content retrieval: A survey of techniques and technologies. *Foundations and Trends in Information Retrieval*, 5(4—5):235–422, 2012.

[10] Y. Lv and C. Zhai. Positional language models for information retrieval. In *Proceedings of SIGIR'09*, pages 299–306, Boston, MA, USA, 2009.

[11] M. Murata, H. Nagano, R. Mukai, K. Kashino, and S. Satoh. BM25 with exponential IDF for instance search. *IEEE Transactions on Multimedia*, 16(6):1690–1699, 2014.

[12] H. Nanjo, T. Yoshimi, S. Maeda, and T. Nishio. Spoken document retrieval experiments for SpokenQuery&Doc at Ryukoku University (RYSDT). In *Proceedings of NTCIR-11*, pages 365–370, Tokyo, Japan, 2014.

[13] S. Robertson and H. Zaragoza. The probabilistic relevance framework: BM25 and beyond. *Foundations and Trends in Information Retrieval*, 3(4):333–389, 2009.

[14] S. E. Robertson, S. Walker, S. Jones, M. M. Hancock-Beaulieu, and M. Gatford. Okapi at TREC-3. In *Proceedings of TREC-3*, pages 109–126, 1995.

[15] S.-R. Shiang, P.-W. Chou, and L.-C. Yu. Spoken term detection and spoken content retrieval: Evaluations on NTCIR 11 SpokenQuery&Doc task. In *Proceedings of NTCIR-11*, pages 371–375, Tokyo, Japan, 2014.

[16] C. Zhai. Notes on the Lemur TFIDF model. Technical report, Carnegie Mellon University, 2001.

Ordinal Text Quantification

Giovanni Da San Martino
Qatar Computing Research Institute
Hamad bin Khalifa University
Doha, Qatar
gmartino@qf.org.qa

Wei Gao
Qatar Computing Research Institute
Hamad bin Khalifa University
Doha, Qatar
wgao@qf.org.qa

Fabrizio Sebastiani*
Qatar Computing Research Institute
Hamad bin Khalifa University
Doha, Qatar
fsebastiani@qf.org.qa

ABSTRACT

In recent years there has been a growing interest in text quantification, a supervised learning task where the goal is to accurately estimate, in an unlabelled set of items, the prevalence (or "relative frequency") of each class c in a predefined set $\mathcal{C}$. Text quantification has several applications, and is a dominant concern in fields such as market research, the social sciences, political science, and epidemiology. In this paper we tackle, for the first time, the problem of *ordinal text quantification*, defined as the task of performing text quantification when a total order is defined on the set of classes; estimating the prevalence of "five stars" reviews in a set of reviews of a given product, and monitoring this prevalence across time, is an example application. We present OQT, a novel tree-based OQ algorithm, and discuss experimental results obtained on a dataset of tweets classified according to sentiment strength.

Keywords

Ordinal Quantification; Quantification; Sentiment Analysis;

1. INTRODUCTION

Ordinal classification (OC – also known as *ordinal regression*, or *rating inference*) is the problem of automatically labelling data items $\mathbf{x} \in X$ according to a set of classes $\mathcal{C} = \{c_1, ..., c_{|\mathcal{C}|}\}$ such that $|\mathcal{C}| > 2$ and there is a total order $\prec$ defined on the classes in $\mathcal{C}$. OC is usually viewed as a supervised learning problem, whereby the classifier $h : X \rightarrow \mathcal{C}$ needs to be generated from training data. OC is different from standard *single-label multi-class* (SLMC) classification, since in SLMC there is no order defined on $\mathcal{C}$.

OC is receiving increasing attention from the sentiment analysis and opinion mining community, due to the importance of managing increasing amounts of product reviews (and opinion-laden data in general) in digital form. An example of a totally ordered set of classes {VeryNegative, Negative, Fair, Positive, VeryPositive}, according to which customers may be asked to evaluate a product or service; the case of product reviews evaluated on a scale of 1 to 5 stars is another such example. More generally, OC is of key importance in the social sciences, since it is well-known that humans find it cognitively easier to express their judgments and evaluations on ordinal (i.e., discrete) scales.

In this paper we do not deal with ordinal classification, but with *ordinal quantification* (OQ). *Quantification* [6] is defined as the task of estimating the prevalence (i.e., relative frequency) $p_{Te}(c_i)$ of the classes $c_i \in \mathcal{C}$ in an unlabelled set Te, given a set Tr of labelled training items. Quantification finds its natural application in contexts characterized by *distribution drift*, i.e., contexts where the unlabelled data may not exhibit the same class prevalences as the test data. Distribution drift may be due to different reasons, including the inherent non-stationary character of the context, or class bias that affected the selection of the training data.

A naïve way to tackle quantification is via the "classify and count" (CC) approach, i.e., classify each unlabelled item independently and compute the fraction of the unlabelled items that have been attributed the class. However, a good classifier is not necessarily a good quantifier: assuming the binary case, even if $(FP + FN)$ is comparatively small, bad quantification accuracy might result if FP and FN are significantly different (since perfect quantification coincides with the case $FP = FN$). This has led researchers to study quantification as a task on its own right [1, 4, 6], rather than as a byproduct of classification.

However, while quantification has been studied both for the binary case and the SLMC case, no paper has tackled OQ yet. We do so for the first time by presenting an algorithm for OQ (dubbed OQT) based on "OQ-trees".

In §2 we describe OQT, while in §3 we discuss experiments we have run on a tweet sentiment analysis dataset.

2. OQ-TREES

In tackling OC our goal has been to design an algorithm that (a) leverages the information inherent in the class ordering $\prec$, and (b) performs quantification in the style of the *Probabilistic Classify and Count* (PCC) method [1], since this is the method that has proven the best performer in our SLMC text quantification experiments of [7]. We first introduce PCC, since OQT uses it as a subroutine; we will then move on to presenting OQT itself.

*Fabrizio Sebastiani is currently on leave from Consiglio Nazionale delle Ricerche, Italy.

SIGIR '16, July 17 - 21, 2016, Pisa, Italy

ISBN 978-1-4503-4069-4/16/07...$15.00

DOI: http://dx.doi.org/10.1145/2911451.2914749

1 **Function** GenerateTree $(\mathcal{C}, Tr, Va)$;
`/* Generates the OQ-tree */`
Input : Ordered set $\mathcal{C} = \{c_1, ..., c_{|\mathcal{C}|}\}$;
Set Tr of labelled items;
Set Va of labelled items;
Output: OQ-tree $T_{\mathcal{C}}$.
2 **for** $j \in \{1, ..., (|\mathcal{C}| - 1)\}$ **do**
3 | Train classifier h_j from $\underline{Tr}_j$ and $\overline{Tr}_j$;
4 **end**
5 $T_{\mathcal{C}} \leftarrow$ Tree$(\mathcal{C}, \{h_j\}, Va)$;
6 **return** $T_{\mathcal{C}}$;

7 **Function** Tree $(\mathcal{C}, \mathcal{H}_{\mathcal{C}}, Va)$;
`/* Recursive subroutine for generating the OQ-tree */`
Input : Ordered set $\mathcal{C} = \{c_1, ..., c_{|\mathcal{C}|}\}$ of classes;
Set of classifiers $\mathcal{H}_{\mathcal{C}} = \{h_1, ..., h_{(|\mathcal{C}|-1)}\}$;
Output: OQ-tree $T_{\mathcal{C}}$.
8 **if** $\mathcal{C} = \{c\}$ **then**
9 | Generate a leaf node T_c;
10 | **return** T_c;
11 **else**
12 | $h_t \leftarrow \arg\min_{h_j \in \mathcal{H}_{\mathcal{C}}} KLD(p, \hat{p}, h_j, Va)$;
13 | Generate a node $T_{\mathcal{C}}$ and associate h_t to it;
14 | $\mathcal{H}'_{\mathcal{C}} \leftarrow \{h_1, ..., h_{(t-1)}\}$;
15 | $\mathcal{H}''_{\mathcal{C}} \leftarrow \{h_{(t+1)}, ..., h_{(|\mathcal{C}|-1)}\}$;
16 | $LChild(T_{\mathcal{C}}) \leftarrow$ Tree$(\underline{\mathcal{C}}_t, \mathcal{H}'_{\mathcal{C}}, Va)$;
17 | $RChild(T_{\mathcal{C}}) \leftarrow$ Tree$(\overline{\mathcal{C}}_t, \mathcal{H}''_{\mathcal{C}}, Va)$;
18 | **return** $T_{\mathcal{C}}$;
19 **end**

Algorithm 1: Function GenerateTree for generating an OQ-tree.

2.1 Probabilistic Classify and Count (PCC)

PCC, originally proposed in [1], consists of generating a classifier from Tr, classifying the items in Te, and estimating $p_{Te}(c)$ as the *expected* fraction of items predicted to belong to c. If (i) by $p(c|\mathbf{x})$ we indicate the posterior probability, i.e., the probability (as estimated by the classifier) of membership in c of the unlabelled item $\mathbf{x}$, (ii) by $p_{Te}(\hat{c})$ we indicate the fraction of items in Te predicted to be in c, and (iii) by $E[x]$ we indicate the expected value of x, this corresponds to computing

$$\hat{p}_{Te}(c) = E[p_{Te}(\hat{c})] = \frac{1}{|Te|} \sum_{\mathbf{x} \in Te} p(c|\mathbf{x}) \tag{1}$$

where the "hat" symbol indicates estimation. The rationale of PCC is that posterior probabilities contain richer information than binary decisions, which are usually obtained from posterior probabilities by thresholding.

2.2 Generating an OQ-tree

We will tackle OQ by arranging the classes in $\mathcal{C}$ into an *OQ-tree*; we thus dub our algorithm OQT. Given any $j \in \{1, \ldots, (|\mathcal{C}| - 1)\}$, $\underline{\mathcal{C}}_j = \{c_1, \ldots, c_j\}$ will be called a *prefix* of $\mathcal{C}$, and $\overline{\mathcal{C}}_j = \{c_{j+1}, \ldots, c_{|\mathcal{C}|}\}$ will be called a *suffix* of $\mathcal{C}$. Given any $j \in \{1, \ldots, (|\mathcal{C}| - 1)\}$ and a set S of items labelled according to $\mathcal{C}$, by $\underline{S}_j$ we denote the set of items in S whose class is in $\underline{\mathcal{C}}_j$, and by $\overline{S}_j$ we denote the set of items in S whose class is in $\overline{\mathcal{C}}_j$. Our algorithm for training such a tree is described in concise form as Algorithm 1, and goes as follows.

Assume we have a training set Tr and a held-out validation set Va of items labelled according to $\mathcal{C}$. The first step (Line 3) consists of training $(|\mathcal{C}| - 1)$ binary classifiers h_j, for $j \in \{1, \ldots, (|\mathcal{C}| - 1)\}$. Each of these classifiers must separate $\underline{\mathcal{C}}_j$ and $\overline{\mathcal{C}}_j$; for training h_j we will take the items in $\underline{Tr}_j$ as the negative training examples and the items in $\overline{Tr}_j$ as the positive training examples. We require that these classifiers, aside from taking binary decisions (i.e., predicting if a test item is in $\underline{\mathcal{C}}_j$ or in $\overline{\mathcal{C}}_j$), also output posterior probabilities, i.e., probabilities $p(\underline{\mathcal{C}}_j|\mathbf{x})$ and $p(\overline{\mathcal{C}}_j|\mathbf{x}) = (1 - p(\underline{\mathcal{C}}_j|\mathbf{x}))$.

The second step (Line 5) is building the OQ (binary) tree. In order to do this, among the classifiers h_j we pick the one (let us call it h_t) that displays the highest quantification accuracy (Line 12) on Va, and we place it at the root of the binary tree. Here, quantification is performed according to the PCC method described in §2.1. We measure the quantification accuracy of h_j via the standard measure for evaluating SLMC quantification, i.e., *Kullback-Leibler Divergence* (KLD)[1], defined as

$$KLD(p, \hat{p}) = \sum_{c_j \in \mathcal{C}} p(c_j) \log \frac{p(c_j)}{\hat{p}(c_j)} \tag{3}$$

where $\hat{p}$ is the distribution estimated via PCC using the posterior probabilities generated by h_j. We then repeat the process recursively on the left and on the right branches of the binary tree (Lines 14 to 17), thus building a fully grown quantification tree.

2.3 Estimating class prevalences via OQT

The algorithm for estimating class prevalences by using an OQ-tree is described in concise form as Algorithm 2, and goes as follows. Essentially, for each item $\mathbf{x} \in Te$ and for each class $c \in \mathcal{C}$, we compute (Line 6) $p(c|\mathbf{x})$; the estimate $\hat{p}_{Te}(c)$ is computed as the average, across all $\mathbf{x} \in Te$, of $p(c|\mathbf{x})$. The posterior probability $p(c|\mathbf{x})$ is computed in a recursive, hierarchical way (Lines 13 to 18), i.e., as the probability that, in a SLMC setting, the binary classifiers that lie on the path from the root to leaf c, would classify item $\mathbf{x}$ exactly in leaf c (i.e., that they would route $\mathbf{x}$ exactly to leaf c). This probability is computed as the product of all the posterior probabilities returned by the classifiers that lie on the path from the root to leaf c.

An example quantification tree for a set of $|\mathcal{C}| = 6$ classes is displayed in Figure 1; for brevity, classes are represented by natural numbers, the total order defined on them is the

[1]Note that KLD is a measure of error, and not of accuracy; i.e., lower values are better. Note also that KLD is undefined when one of the $\hat{p}(c_j)$ is 0. To solve this problem, in computing KLD we smooth both $p(c_j)$ and $\hat{p}(c_j)$ via additive smoothing, i.e., we compute

$$p^s(c_j) = \frac{p(c_j) + \epsilon}{(\sum_{c_j \in \mathcal{C}} p(c_j)) + \epsilon \cdot |\mathcal{C}|} \tag{2}$$

where $p^s(c_j)$ denotes the smoothed version of $p(c_j)$ and the denominator is just a normalizing factor (same for the $\hat{p}^s(c_j)$'s); the quantity $\epsilon = \frac{1}{2 \cdot |Te|}$ is used as a smoothing factor. The smoothed versions of $p(c_j)$ and $\hat{p}(c_j)$ are then used in place of the non-smoothed versions in Equation 3; as a result, KLD is always defined.

```
Function QuantifyViaHierarchicalPCC (Te, T_C);
  /* Estimates class prevalences on Te using
     the quantification tree */
  Input  : Unlabelled set Te;
           Quantification tree T_C;
  Output: Estimates p̂(c) for all c ∈ C;
for c ∈ C do
| p̂(c) ← 0
end
for x ∈ Te do
|  CPost(x, T_C, 1); /* Compute the {p(c|x)} */
|  for c ∈ C do
|  |  p̂(c) ← p̂(c) + p(c|x) / |Te|;
|  end
end
return {p̂(c)}

Procedure CPost (x, T_C, SubP);
  /* Recursive subroutine for computing all the
     posteriors {p(c|x)} */
  Input  : Unlabelled item x;
           Quantification tree T_C;
           Probability SubP of current subtree;
  Output: Posteriors {p(c|x)};
if T_C = {c} then
|  /* T_C is a leaf, labelled by class c */
|  p(c|x) ← SubP;
else
|  CPost(x, LChild(T_C), p(C_t|x) · SubP);
|  CPost(x, RChild(T_C), p(C̄_t|x) · SubP);
|  /* p(C_t|x) and p(C̄_t|x) are the posteriors
|     returned by the classifier associated
|     with the root of T_C   */
end
```

Algorithm 2: Function QuantifyViaHierarchicalPCC for estimating prevalences via an OQ-tree.

order defined on the natural numbers, and sets of classes are represented by sequences of natural numbers. Note that, as exemplified in Figure 1, OQT generates trees for which (a) there is a 1-to-1 correspondence between classes and leaves of the tree, (b) leaves are ordered left to right in the same order as the classes in $\mathcal{C}$, and (c) each internal node represents a decision between a suffix and a prefix of $\mathcal{C}$.

Point (c) is interesting, and deserves some discussion. In Figure 1, internal node "1234 vs. 56" is trained by using items labelled as 1, or 2, or 3, or 4, as negative examples and items labelled as 5, or 6, as positive examples; however, by looking at Figure 1, it would seem intuitive that items labelled as 6 should *not* be used, since the node is root to a subtree where class 6 is not an option anymore. The reason why we do use items labelled as 6 (which is the reason why the node is labelled "1234 vs. 56" and not "1234 vs. 5") is that, during the classification stage, the classifier associated with the node might be asked to classify an item whose true label is 6, and which has thus been misclassified high up in the tree. In this case, it would be important that this item be classified as 5, since this minimizes the contribution of this item to misclassification error; and the likelihood that this happens is increased if the classifier is trained to choose between 1234 and 56, rather than between 1234 and 5. Note also that this is one aspect for which OQT is a true *ordinal*

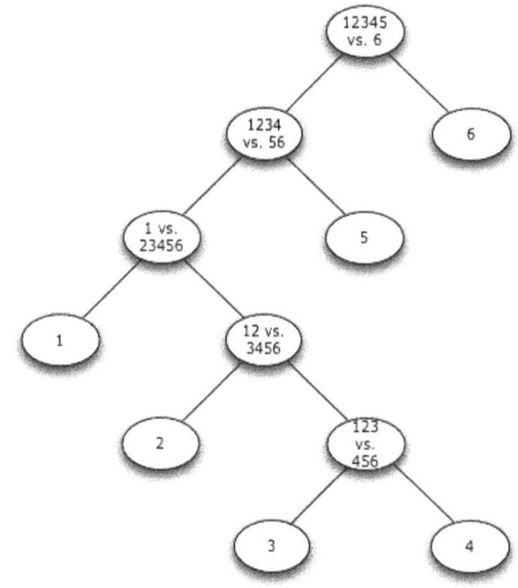

Figure 1: An example OQ-tree.

quantification algorithm: if there were no order defined on the classes this policy would make no sense.

A second reason why OQT is a truly OQ algorithm is that the groups of classes (such as 1234 and 56) between which a binary classifier needs to discriminate are groups of *contiguous* classes. It is because of this contiguity that the trees we generate makes sense: if, say, our classes represent degrees of positivity of product reviews, with 1 indicating most negative and 6 indicating most positive, group 56 may be taken to represent the positive reviews (to different degrees), while 1234 may be taken to represent the reviews that are not positive; a group such as, say, 256, would instead be very hard to interpret, since it is formed of non-contiguous classes that have little in common with each other[2].

3. EXPERIMENTS

The evaluation measure we adopt for our experiments is the only one known for OQ, i.e., the *Earth Mover's Distance* (*EMD*) [9], a measure well known in the field of computer vision and whose use in OQ was proposed in [4]. When there is a total order on the classes in $\mathcal{C}$, EMD is defined as

$$EMD(\hat{p},p) = \sum_{j=1}^{|\mathcal{C}|-1} |\sum_{i=1}^{j} \hat{p}(c_i) - \sum_{i=1}^{j} p(c_i)| \quad (4)$$

and can be computed in $|\mathcal{C}|$ steps from the estimated and true class prevalences. Like KLD in Equation 3, EMD is a measure of error, so lower values are better; EMD ranges between 0 (best) and $|\mathcal{C}|-1$ (worst).

The dataset we use is the one released within SemEval 2016 Task 4 "Sentiment Analysis in Twitter" [8], and consists of tweets labelled according to five degrees of sentiment, from VeryNegative to VeryPositive. The dataset comes broken down into subsets TRAIN (6000 tweets), DEV (2000 tweets), and DEVTEST (2000 tweets); we use them for training, parameter optimization, and testing, respectively.

[2]The code that implements our method is available from http://alt.qcri.org/tools/quantification/

Table 1: ***EMD*** **values obtained by the six methods (lower is better) and percentage of deterioration with respect to the best performer.**

PCC(SVM)	CC(SVORIM)	ACC(SVORIM)	CC(ϵ-SVR)	ACC(ϵ-SVR)	OQT(SVM)
0.222	0.337	0.653	0.325	0.675	**0.210**
+5.71%	+60.48%	+210.95%	+54.76%	+221.43%	

Each of these three sets is broken down into "topics" consisting of 100 tweets each; i.e., the task is to quantify the prevalence of a certain class (say, VeryPositive) among the comments *about a certain topic*. One thus needs to compute EMD separately on each topic, and then average the results.

For lack of space (and because it is not the main focus of this paper) we do not describe the preprocessing steps we adopt to generate the vectorial representations for our tweets; the details are given in [7, §4.1].

We evaluate OQT against the following baselines. The 1st is a PCC SLMC quantifier; it does not take order $\prec$ into account but, as shown in [7] it is a very strong SLMC classifier anyway. The 2nd is a CC quantifier (see §1) that uses the SVORIM OC learning algorithm [2]. The 3rd is an ACC ("Adjusted Classify and Count" – see [6, §2]) quantifier that also relies on SVORIM. The 4th and 5th are again a CC quantifier and an ACC quantifier, this time using an adaptation to ordinal regression of the ϵ-SVR metric regression algorithm [3]. While OQT and PCC are not inherently SVM-based, we choose SVMs as their base learner, also for better experimental uniformity with the other four methods, which are inherently SVM-based; from now on the two former methods will thus be called OQT(SVM) and PCC(SVM). We use the implementations of (i) standard SVMs, (ii) SVORIM, and (iii) ϵ-SVR, as available in the LIBSVM suite[3]. For each learning algorithm we have optimized the C parameter (which sets the tradeoff between the training error and the margin) on the DEV set, performing a grid search on all values of type 10^x with $x \in \{-6, ..., 7\}$. Note that both PCC(SVM) and OQT(SVM) (which depends on PCC(SVM)) require as input not the classifier's binary decisions but its posterior probabilities. Since SVMs do not natively generate posterior probabilities, we use the `-b` option of LIBSVM, which converts the scores originally generated by SVMs into posterior probabilities according to the algorithm of [10].

The results of our experiments are given in Table 1. Our OQT(SVM) method is the best performer, with PCC(SVM) the second best, with a +5.71% deterioration with respect to OQT(SVM). Two aspects are interesting to discuss here.

The first is that the two best methods are the ones that make use of posterior probabilities, i.e., where class prevalences are computed as *expected values* of the binary class assignments; the other 4 methods are based on CC and ACC, which do not make use of posterior probabilities and use the binary class assignments instead. This seems a further (albeit indirect) confirmation of the results of [7], where PCC(SVM) emerged as the best of 8 methods in SLMC tweet quantification. The good result of PCC(SVM) is even more striking if we consider that the other 4 methods, which PCC(SVM) beats by a wide margin, leverage the $\prec$ class order while PCC(SVM) does not; this seems further evidence of the value of posterior probabilities in quantification.

A second observation is that ACC, a quantification method that has been consistently reported to perform better than CC [1, 5, 7, 6], here performs much worse than CC, in the context of both SVORIM and ϵ-SVR. This is an aspect that will deserve further investigation.

In Subtask E of the SemEval 2016 Task 4 shared task (a subtask which deals with ordinal tweet quantification by sentiment – see [8]), the system described in this paper obtained an EMD score of 0.243, ranking 1st in a set of 10 participating systems, with a high margin over the other ones (systems from rank 2 to rank 8 obtained EMD scores between 0.316 and 0.366). Overall, these results are encouraging and preliminary at the same time. For the future we plan to run more experiments, using more datasets (e.g., product review datasets) and more baseline systems from the world of ordinal classification and SLMC quantification.

[3]LIBSVM is available from http://www.csie.ntu.edu.tw/~cjlin/libsvm/

4. REFERENCES

[1] A. Bella, C. Ferri, J. Hernández-Orallo, and M. J. Ramírez-Quintana. Quantification via probability estimators. In *Proceedings of the 11th IEEE International Conference on Data Mining (ICDM 2010)*, pages 737–742, Sydney, AU, 2010.

[2] W. Chu and S. S. Keerthi. Support vector ordinal regression. *Neural Computation*, 19(3):145–152, 2007.

[3] H. Drucker, C. J. Burges, L. Kaufman, A. Smola, and V. Vapnik. Support vector regression machines. In *Proceedings of the 11th Annual Conference on Neural Information Processing Systems (NIPS 1997)*, pages 155–161, Denver, US, 1997.

[4] A. Esuli and F. Sebastiani. Sentiment quantification. *IEEE Intelligent Systems*, 25(4):72–75, 2010.

[5] A. Esuli and F. Sebastiani. Optimizing text quantifiers for multivariate loss functions. *ACM Transactions on Knowledge Discovery and Data*, 9(4):Article 27, 2015.

[6] G. Forman. Quantifying counts and costs via classification. *Data Mining and Knowledge Discovery*, 17(2):164–206, 2008.

[7] W. Gao and F. Sebastiani. From classification to quantification in tweet sentiment analysis. *Social Network Analysis and Mining*, 2016. Forthcoming.

[8] P. Nakov, A. Ritter, S. Rosenthal, F. Sebastiani, and V. Stoyanov. SemEval-2016 Task 4: Sentiment analysis in Twitter. In *Proceedings of the 10th International Workshop on Semantic Evaluation (SemEval 2016)*, San Diego, US, 2016. Forthcoming.

[9] Y. Rubner, C. Tomasi, and L. J. Guibas. The Earth Mover's Distance as a metric for image retrieval. *International Journal of Computer Vision*, 40(2):99–121, 2000.

[10] T.-F. Wu, C.-J. Lin, and R. C. Weng. Probability estimates for multi-class classification by pairwise coupling. *Journal of Machine Learning Research*, 5:975–1005, 2004.

Pearson Rank: A Head-Weighted Gap-Sensitive Score-Based Correlation Coefficient

Ning Gao, Mossaab Bagdouri, and Douglas W. Oard
University of Maryland, College Park
{ninggao, mossaab, oard}@umd.edu

ABSTRACT

One way of evaluating the reusability of a test collection is to determine whether removing the unique contributions of some system would alter the preference order between that system and others. Rank correlation measures such as Kendall's τ are often used for this purpose. Rank correlation measures are appropriate for *ordinal* measures in which only preference order is important, but many evaluation measures produce system scores in which both the preference order and the magnitude of the score difference are important. Such measures are referred to as *interval*. Pearson's ρ offers one way in which correlation can be computed over results from an interval measure such that smaller errors in the gap size are preferred. When seeking to improve over existing systems, we care the most about comparisons among the best systems. For that purpose we prefer head-weighed measures such as τ_{AP}, which is designed for ordinal data. No present head weighted measure fully leverages the information present in interval effectiveness measures. This paper introduces such a measure, referred to as Pearson Rank.

Keywords

Evaluation Metric; Correlation Coefficient

1. INTRODUCTION

In information retrieval evaluation, we often wish to compare the effectiveness of alternative systems by using some single-valued evaluation metric (e.g., F_1 or Mean Average Precision) on some publicly available collections. Judgments of all the items in the collections are required to get the ground-truth evaluation of the systems, which is often infeasible. Hence, sampling or pooling techniques are used in shared tasks (e.g., TREC, CLEF) to choose the documents that will be assessed. Naturally, we want to quantify the adequacy of test collections created this way for assessing the effectiveness of different systems, especially systems that did not participate to the creation of the pool [5]. We might also want to know whether we can approximate the effectiveness of these systems by reducing the number of relevance judgments [1]. We can attempt to answer these questions by measuring the correlation between two ranked lists of system scores (e.g., the reference and the approximated).

When making comparisons in the aforementioned cases, we focus on two considerations. First, we prefer the comparison to be on an interval rather than ordinal scale. In shared tasks, the systems are ranked according to their measured effectiveness on a test collection. In addition to system ranks, it is important to know whether some systems are substantially better than the others. Moreover, for formative evaluation it can be useful to characterize small incremental improvements, even when the new evaluation scores do not alter a system's rank with regard to other systems. For this reason, we prefer a correlation coefficient that is sensitive to the size of the gaps between system scores. Second, we care more about comparisons among the best systems, so we prefer a correlation coefficient that is influenced more by differences near the top of a ranked list of systems. We call such measures head-weighted.

Several statistics have been proposed to quantify the correlation between two ranked lists of scores. Pearson's ρ [4] assumes that the scores are on an *interval* scale (i.e., one in which all score differences of the same size have the same meaning). Mean Average Precision can properly be treated as being on an interval scale because precision is *interval* and expected values computed on *interval* scales are *interval*. Kendall's τ [3] and Yilmaz et al.'s τ_{AP} [6], by contrast, make the weaker assumption of an *ordinal* scale in which score differences are not necessarily informative, but the relative ordering of systems by those scores is informative.

Gao and Oard suggest a head-weighted gap-sensitive correlation coefficient called τ_{GAP} [2], giving greater penalty to larger gaps when a swap occurs, but assigning no penalty for misestimating the gap size if no swap occurs. Consider, for example, the situation depicted in Figure 1, which occurred in an unpublished system-ablation study in which we were studying the reuse of a test collection by systems that did not contribute to a judgment pool. The x-axis is the reference system score (measured in this case as mean precision at rank one) obtained using relevance judgments for the unique contributions of every system, while the y-axis is the score that we estimated for that same system without using any relevance judgments for documents uniquely contributed by that system. As Pearson's $\rho = 0.89$ shows, the estimates exhibit a strong linear correlation with the reference scores. Note, however, the substantial gap in the reference scores between the best and second-best systems; the estimate does not preserve that gap. Pearson's correlation coefficient is dominated by the many other well approximated gaps, however, and does not emphasize the problem. Kendall's $\tau = 0.74$ is affected by several swaps in the preference order, but as the high value of ρ indicates, most of these swaps are among systems with small gaps that should not trouble us much. There are several reversals near the top of the ranked list that affect $\tau_{AP} = 0.64$, although

SIGIR '16, July 17 - 21, 2016, Pisa, Italy

ISBN 978-1-4503-4069-4/16/07...$15.00

DOI: http://dx.doi.org/10.1145/2911451.2914728

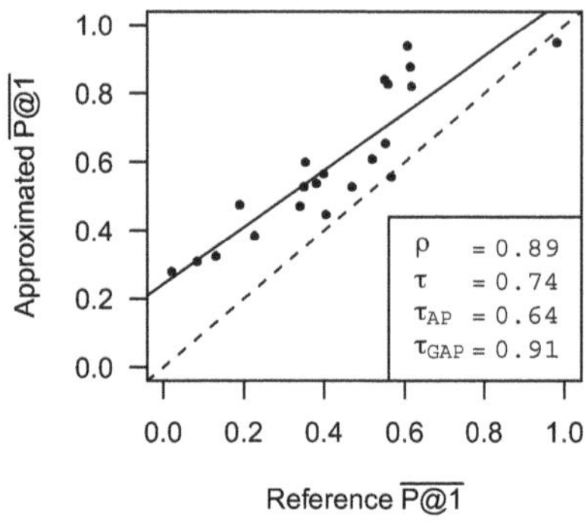

Figure 1: Different correlation coefficient values when the gap between the best system and a lower one is mischaracterized.

as $\tau_{GAP} = 0.91$ shows, these reversals are among systems that had very small differences in the reference condition.

Intuitively, this seems like the wrong answer, since if we were to make a system that was considerably better than the second-best one, we have no reason to believe that the effectiveness score estimates on the y-axis would reflect that. None of the standard measures capture the fact that the difference we should care the most about—the large gap in the reference system scores between the best two systems, is completely mischaracterized by the approximated scores as being of only negligible gap size. Pearson's ρ misses this because it is not head-weighted, τ_{AP} misses this because it is not gap-sensitive, and τ_{GAP} misses it because it is gap-sensitive only when a swap occurs. None of these measures focus on what we care about the most when we have an evaluation measure that is *interval*, which is that the size of the gaps among the best systems be correctly estimated.

This example illustrates the need for a new correlation coefficient that is at the same time head weighted and sensitive to both swapped and unswapped gaps. Section 2 introduces Pearson Rank (ρ_r), our novel correlation coefficient, and shows that it has several desirable properties. Through extensive simulation, Section 3 contrasts some behaviors of ρ_r with those of rank-based correlation coefficients. We conclude in Section 4.

2. PEARSON RANK

This section defines Pearson Rank, demonstrates its satisfaction of desired properties, and contrasts it with other correlations.

2.1 Definition

Let $S = \{s_1, \cdots, s_m\}$ be a list of m items ranked in descending order by their reference scores $X = \{x_1, \cdots, x_m\}$; and $Y = \{y_1, \cdots, y_m\}$ be their approximated scores, after scaling all of the scores so that $x_i, y_i \in [0, 1]$. We define the new (asymmetric) Pearson Rank correlation coefficient (ρ_r) X and Y as:

$$\rho_r(Y|X) = \frac{1}{\sum_{i=2}^{m} x_i} \cdot \sum_{i=2}^{m} x_i \cdot \frac{\sum_{j=1}^{i-1}(x_j - x_i)\cdot(y_j - y_i)}{\sqrt{\sum_{j=1}^{i-1}(x_j - x_i)^2 \sum_{j=1}^{i-1}(y_j - y_i)^2}}. \quad (1)$$

Figure 2 is a toy example for calculating ρ_r of two lists, where $X = \{x_1, x_2, x_3\}$ and $Y = \{y_1, y_2, y_3\}$. The solid arrows show the score differences between item pairs considered when calculating ρ_r at x_2. The value of ρ_r at x_2 is:

$$\rho_{r,2} = \frac{x_2}{x_2 + x_3} \cdot \frac{(x_1 - x_2)(y_1 - y_2)}{\sqrt{(x_1 - x_2)^2 (y_1 - y_2)^2}}.$$

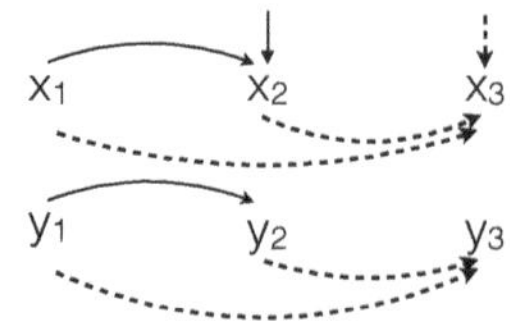

Figure 2: Example for calculating ρ_r correlation coefficient.

The dotted arrows show the score differences between item pairs considered for ρ_r at x_3. The value of ρ_r at x_3 is:

$$\rho_{r,3} = \frac{x_3}{x_2 + x_3} \cdot \frac{(x_1 - x_3)(y_1 - y_3) + (x_2 - x_3)(y_2 - y_3)}{\sqrt{(x_1 - x_3)^2 + (x_2 - x_3)^2}\sqrt{(y_1 - y_3)^2 + (y_2 - y_3)^2}}.$$

The value of ρ_r is the sum of $\rho_{r,i}$ at items from 2 to m = 3.

2.2 Properties

THEOREM 1. *The value of ρ_r is always between -1 and 1. $\rho_r = 1$ if and only if $Y = X$; and $\rho_r = -1$ if and only if $Y = 1 - X$.*

PROOF. Due to the Cauchy-Schwarz inequality, we have:

$$\left(\sum_{j=1}^{i-1}(x_j - x_i)\cdot(y_j - y_i)\right)^2 \le \sum_{j=1}^{i-1}(x_j - x_i)^2 \sum_{j=1}^{i-1}(y_j - y_i)^2, \quad (2)$$

where the two sides are equal if and only if X and Y are linearly dependent (or, in a geometrical sense, they are parallel). Since the scores are scaled $x_i, y_i \in [0, 1]$, we have

$$-1 \le \frac{\sum_{j=1}^{i-1}(x_j - x_i)\cdot(y_j - y_i)}{\sqrt{\sum_{j=1}^{i-1}(x_j - x_i)^2 \sum_{j=1}^{i-1}(y_j - y_i)^2}} \le 1, \quad (3)$$

where the upper bound 1 is reached when $Y = X$, and lower bound -1 is reached when $Y = 1 - X$. Therefore,

$$-1 = \sum_{i=2}^{m} \frac{-x_i}{\sum_{i=2}^{m} x_i} \le \rho_r \le \sum_{i=2}^{m} \frac{x_i}{\sum_{i=2}^{m} x_i} = 1. \quad (4)$$

□

THEOREM 2. *Let $X = \{x_1, \cdots, x_{i-1}, x_i, \cdots, x_{p-1}, x_p, \cdots, x_m\}$ be a reference score list; $Y^1 = \{x_1, \cdots, x_i, x_{i-1}, \cdots, x_{p-1}, x_p, \cdots, x_m\}$ and $Y^2 = \{x_1, \cdots, x_{i-1}, x_i, \cdots, x_p, x_{p-1}, \cdots, x_m\}$ be two lists of approximated scores, where Y^1 has only one swapped adjacent item pair s_{i-1} and s_i near the head of the lists; Y^2 has only one swapped adjacent item pair s_{p-1} and s_p near the end of the list. If the score difference between the swapped pairs are identical $(x_{i-1} - x_i) = (x_{p-1} - x_p)$, the ρ_r score for Y^1 with error near the head will be lower than Y^2 with error near the end.*

PROOF. Let $\varepsilon = 1 - \rho_r$ be the loss of a list of approximated scores, therefore, $\varepsilon = \sum_{i=2}^{m} \varepsilon_i$ where ε_i is the loss for each position from 2 to m. For Y^1, we have $\varepsilon_2 = \cdots = \varepsilon_{i-2} = 0$;

$$\begin{aligned}\varepsilon_{i-1} &= \frac{x_{i-1}}{\sum_{i=2}^{m} x_i} \cdot \left(1 - \frac{\sum_{j=1}^{i-2}(x_j - x_{i-1})(y_j - y_{i-1})}{\sqrt{\sum_{j=1}^{i-2}(x_j - x_{i-1})^2 \sum_{j=1}^{i-2}(y_j - y_{i-1})^2}}\right) \\ &= \frac{x_{i-1}}{\sum_{i=2}^{m} x_i} \cdot \left(1 - \frac{\sum_{j=1}^{i-2}(x_j - x_{i-1})(x_j - x_i)}{\sqrt{\sum_{j=1}^{i-2}(x_j - x_{i-1})^2 \sum_{j=1}^{i-2}(x_j - x_i)^2}}\right).\end{aligned} \quad (5)$$

Let $n = x_j - x_{i-1}$ and $c = x_{i-1} - x_i$, the derivative of

$$\frac{\sum_{j=1}^{i-2}(x_j - x_{i-1})(x_j - x_i)}{\sqrt{\sum_{j=1}^{i-2}(x_j - x_{i-1})^2 \sum_{j=1}^{i-2}(x_j - x_i)^2}} \tag{6}$$

could be represented in an alternative form of

$$\frac{\partial\left(\frac{\sum n(n+c)}{\sqrt{\sum n^2 \sum (n+c)^2}}\right)}{\partial n} = \frac{3((1+2n)(1+2n(2+n)) + c(3-4n^2(2+n)))}{(\sqrt{n}((2+n)(1+2n)(3+2n))^{3/2})}, \tag{7}$$

which is positive when both n and c are positive. Therefore, the value of equation (6) increases with increasing i; and thus the value of ε_{i-1} decreases with increasing i. Similarly,

$$\begin{aligned} \varepsilon_i &= \frac{x_i}{\sum_{i=2}^m x_i} \cdot \left(1 - \frac{\sum_{j=1}^{i-1}(x_j - x_i)(y_j - y_i)}{\sqrt{\sum_{j=1}^{i-1}(x_j - x_i)^2 \sum_{j=1}^{i-1}(y_j - y_i)^2}}\right) \\ &= \frac{x_i}{\sum_{i=2}^m x_i} \cdot \frac{2(x_{i-1} - x_i)^2}{\sqrt{\sum_{j=1}^{i-1}(x_j - x_i)^2 \sum_{j=1}^{i-1}(x_j - x_{i-1})^2}}. \end{aligned} \tag{8}$$

As can be seen, the value of ε_i decreases with increasing i. The penalty for $\varepsilon_{t \in [i+1,m]}$

$$\begin{aligned} \varepsilon_{t \in [i+1,m]} &= \frac{x_t}{\sum_{i=2}^m x_i} \cdot \left(1 - \frac{\sum_{j=1}^{t-1}(x_j - x_t)(y_j - y_t)}{\sqrt{\sum_{j=1}^{t-1}(x_j - x_t)^2 \sum_{j=1}^{t-1}(y_j - y_t)^2}}\right) \\ &= \frac{x_t}{\sum_{i=2}^m x_i} \cdot \left(1 - \frac{\sum_{j \in [1,n], j \neq (i-1,i)}(x_j - x_t)^2 + 2(x_{i-1} - x_t)(x_i - x_t)}{\sqrt{\sum_{j=1}^{t-1}(x_j - x_t)^2 \sum_{j=1}^{t-1}(x_j - x_t)^2}}\right) \\ &= \frac{x_t}{\sum_{i=2}^m x_i} \cdot \frac{(x_{i-1} - x_i)^2}{\sum_{j=1}^{t-1}(x_j - x_t)^2} \end{aligned} \tag{9}$$

depends only t. Therefore, the value of $\varepsilon = \varepsilon_{i-1} + \varepsilon_i + \sum_{i+1}^m \varepsilon_t$ is larger when the swapped error appears in the head of the list. □

THEOREM 3. *Let $X = \{x_1, \cdots, x_{i-1}, x_i, \cdots, x_m\}$ be a reference score vector, and $Y = \{x_1, \cdots, x_i, x_{i-1}, \cdots, x_m\}$ be an approximation list with one adjacent swapped pair x_{i-1} and x_i, then the value of ρ_r is inversely related to the score difference between the swapped pair $(x_{i-1} - x_i)$.*

PROOF. The derivative of $\frac{\sum n(n+c)}{\sqrt{\sum n^2 \sum (n+c)^2}}$ with respect to c

$$\frac{\partial\left(\frac{\sum n(n+c)}{\sqrt{\sum n^2 \sum (n+c)^2}}\right)}{\partial c} = \frac{3c(1+n)(1+2n)(1-n^2)}{((1+n)(1+2n)(1+6c+6c^2+3n+6cn+2n^2))^{1.5}} \tag{10}$$

is negative. Therefore, from equations (5) and (7), we can conclude that the value of ε_{i-1} is positively related to the value of $c = x_{i-1} - x_i$. The derivative of $\frac{2c^2}{\sqrt{\sum n^2 \sum (n+c)^2}}$ with respect to c

$$\frac{\partial\left(\frac{2c^2}{\sqrt{\sum n^2 \sum (n+c)^2}}\right)}{\partial c} = \frac{12cn^2(n+1)(2n+1)(6c^2+9cn+9c+4n^2+6n+2)}{[n^2(2n^2+3n+1)(6c^2+6cn+6c+2n^2+3n+1)]^{1.5}} \tag{11}$$

is positive. Therefore, from equation (8) and (11) we can conclude that ε_i is positively related to $c = x_{i-1} - x_i$. Similarly, equation (9) also shows that the value of ε_t is positively related to $c = x_{i-1} - x_i$. As a conclusion, when excluding the effect of item weights $(x_i / \sum_{i=2}^m x_i)$, the approximation list is penalized more when swapping item pairs with larger score differences. □

Table 1: Property comparisons.

	Ordinal	Interval	Head Weighted	Symmetric
ρ	yes	yes	no	yes
τ	yes	no	no	yes
τ_{AP}	yes	no	yes	no
τ_{GAP}	yes	yes	yes	no
ρ_r	yes	yes	yes	no

2.3 Analysis

Table 1 shows the properties of our proposed ρ_r and the other correlation measures. As can be seen, all the measures can be applied with *ordinal* effectiveness measures, but only τ_{GAP}, ρ and ρ_r leverage the fact that typical information retrieval effectiveness measures are *interval*. τ_{GAP}, however, is a hybrid that treats the reference scores as *interval* but the approximated scores as *ordinal*. τ_{AP}, τ_{GAP} and ρ_r are head-weighted measures giving more weights to the items at the head of the list. As a result, all the head-weighted measures are asymmetric, yielding different results if the roles of the reference and the approximation are swapped. If a symmetric measure is desired, the results in both directions could be averaged. For example, we could define $\rho_r(X,Y) = (\rho_r(X|Y) + \rho_r(Y|X))/2$.

3. SIMULATION EXPERIMENTS

In Section 2.2 we proved some properties of ρ_r when a swap occurs between two items. Another aspect we explore next is its reaction to score changes that maintain the ranking of the systems.

One way of characterizing the behavior of ρ_r is to simulate cases in which the rank of each system is held invariant but the gap sizes are allowed to differ in some systematic way. When we do this, the rank correlation coefficients we have considered (τ, τ_{AP}, τ_{GAP}) show a perfect correlation of 1. Some approximations are better than others, however, and we can use simulation to characterize the behavior of ρ_r in such cases. We assume that the reference and approximated scores follow some distributions. To implement this condition, we sample N systems from the distribution of the reference scores $\mathscr{X}$, and sort them in a descending order of scores. We scale these scores to the interval $[0,1]$ by subtracting the minimum score before dividing by the difference between the maximum and minimum scores, yielding a vector X. In a similar manner, we generate a vector of the ranked scaled approximated scores Y, from a distribution $\mathscr{Y}$. We compute the ρ_r for this pair of vectors, and repeat this process 100,000 times.

We study three different distributions, but others could have been considered as well. In the uniform distribution ($\mathscr{U}_{[0,1]}$), the gaps between different systems are equal (in expectation). In the normal distribution ($\mathscr{N}_{(0.5,1)}$), a few systems would have a score close to each end of the ranked list, while the majority of the systems would be located around the middle of the score distribution. With Zipf's distribution ($\mathscr{Z}_{(2^{31}-1,2)}$), a few systems would have a score close to the head of the ranked list, while most of the systems would be clustered towards its tail. Each scatter plot in Figure 3 corresponds to the median ρ_r, for a pair of distributions, out of the 100,000 pairs of score vectors corresponding to 50 simulated systems. We also indicate in that figure the different quartiles of the values of ρ_r.

We first observe that ρ_r is more likely to have a high value when both of the reference and approximated scores follow the uniform distribution (Figure 3(a)). In fact, the differences between the scores are equal in expectation. The next highest ρ_r values appear to be those of the normal distribution (Figure 3(b)). The gaps there are bigger (in expectation) closer to either end. Thus, the penalty (which is weighted towards the head of the list) is expected to be

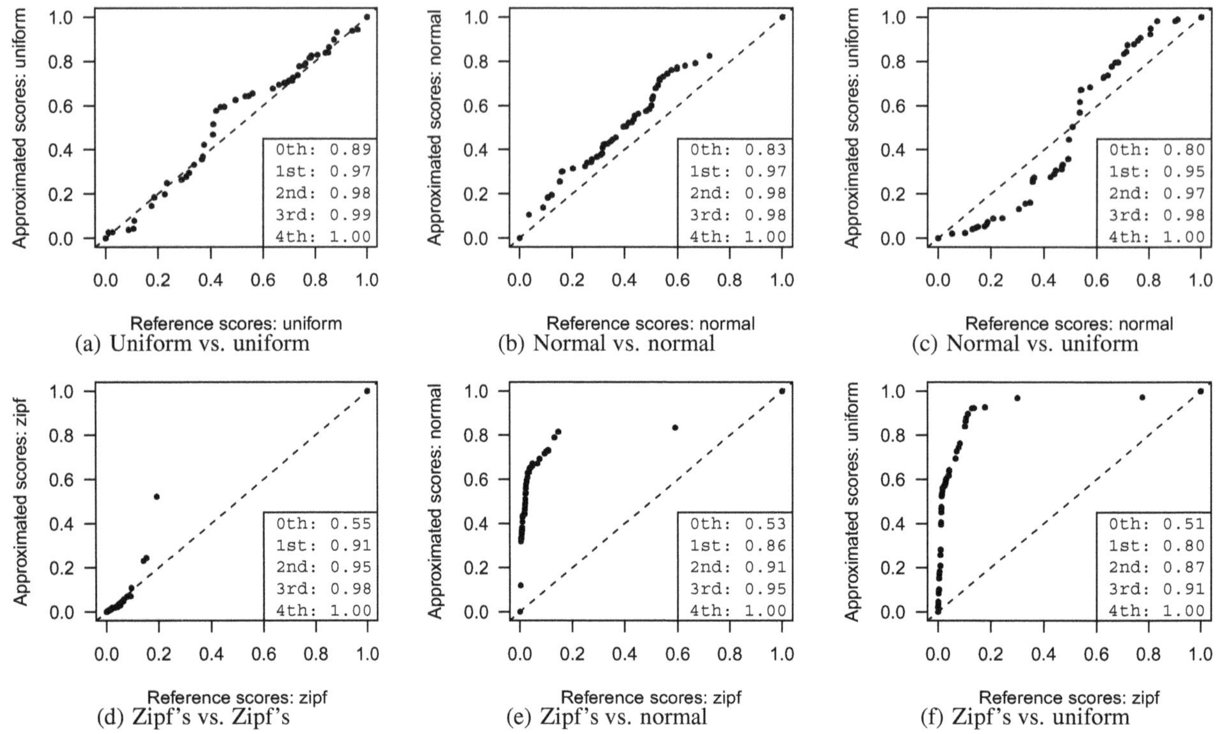

(a) Uniform vs. uniform
(b) Normal vs. normal
(c) Normal vs. uniform
(d) Zipf's vs. Zipf's
(e) Zipf's vs. normal
(f) Zipf's vs. uniform

Figure 3: Pearson Rank quartile values for simulated scores of 50 systems, and actual simulated scores for the median case.

larger than that of the uniform distribution. Figure 3(c) shows lower values of Pearson Rank. In this case, the reference scores are drawn from the normal distribution, which means there is (in expectation) a high gap towards either end of the reference scores. However, these gaps are lost in the approximated scoring space, as successive scores are expected to be equally distant.

We now turn to the bottom row of Figure 3, where at least one of the axes follows Zipf's distribution. In this distribution, we expect that large gaps would appear only close to the head of the ranked list. Figure 3(d) shows that ρ_r can have a low value of 0.55 and a median of 0.95, even when both the reference and approximated scores are drawn from an identical distribution. This can be explained by the high variance of the gaps near the head of the scores. In Figure 3(e) we observe even lower ρ_r scores (e.g., the median value is 0.91). Although, both of the normal and Zipf's distributions have a tendency for high gaps close to the head of the score list, those of the Zipf's are (in expectation) much larger. Thus, the gaps appear to get lost when the Zipf's scores are "converted" into normal ones. Finally, the worst ρ_r values are shown in Figure 3(f), when very large gaps are expected to appear at the head of the reference scores, while those of the approximated scores are expected to be much smaller. In this case, we observe the lowest ρ_r value of 0.51, and a median of 0.87.

4. CONCLUSION

We have proposed a novel head-weighted gap-sensitive score-based correlation coefficient ρ_r. By construction, ρ_r gives more weight to the items with higher reference scores. We have also shown that ρ_r more severely penalizes the swaps occurring near the head of the list, and those with larger reference score gaps. Simulation experiments illustrate the sensitivity of ρ_r to score values, even when (as happened by construction in our simulation) rank-based metrics fail to detect any difference between reference and approximated scores due to the consistent ranking of all systems.

ACKNOWLEDGMENT

This work was made possible by NSF award 1065250, and NPRP grant # NPRP 6-1377-1-257 from the Qatar National Research Fund (a member of Qatar Foundation). The statements made herein are solely the responsibility of the authors.

References

[1] B. Carterette. Robust test collections for retrieval evaluation. In *SIGIR*, pages 55–62, 2007.

[2] N. Gao and D. Oard. A head-weighted gap-sensitive correlation coefficient. In *SIGIR*, pages 799–802, 2015.

[3] M. G. Kendall. A new measure of rank correlation. *Biometrika*, pages 81–93, 1938.

[4] K. Pearson. Note on regression and inheritance in the case of two parents. *Proceedings of the Royal Society of London*, 58(347-352):240–242, 1895.

[5] E. M. Voorhees. Variations in relevance judgments and the measurement of retrieval effectiveness. *Information processing & management*, 36(5):697–716, 2000.

[6] E. Yilmaz et al. A new rank correlation coefficient for information retrieval. In *SIGIR*, pages 587–594, 2008.

Polarized User and Topic Tracking in Twitter

Mauro Coletto
IMT Lucca, ISTI–CNR Pisa
mauro.coletto@isti.cnr.it

Claudio Lucchese
ISTI–CNR Pisa
claudio.lucchese@isti.cnr.it

Salvatore Orlando
DAIS–University of Venice
orlando@unive.it

Raffaele Perego
ISTI–CNR Pisa
raffaele.perego@isti.cnr.it

ABSTRACT

Digital traces of conversations in micro-blogging platforms and OSNs provide information about user opinion with a high degree of resolution. These information sources can be exploited to understand and monitor collective behaviors. In this work, we focus on *polarization classes*, i.e., those topics that require the user to side exclusively with one position. The proposed method provides an iterative classification of users and keywords: first, *polarized users* are identified, then *polarized keywords* are discovered by monitoring the activities of previously classified users. This method thus allows tracking users and topics over time. We report several experiments conducted on two Twitter datasets during political election time-frames. We measure the user classification accuracy on a golden set of users, and analyze the relevance of the extracted keywords for the ongoing political discussion.

1. INTRODUCTION

Recently, the analysis of blogging platforms and streaming information sources (e.g., Twitter) has received great attention in the Information Retrieval and in the Data Mining communities. We focus on the frequent scenario where users interact and produce contents according to a set of *polarization classes*. By polarization classes we mean subjects that require the user to side exclusively with one part. Political parties are typical examples of these classes. Other examples include brand analysis, products comparison, and opinion mining in general. In these scenarios the polarization classes are known, and some limited information may also be available, e.g., a set of relevant keywords. This limited knowledge allows us to restrict the scope of the analysis, but several challenging tasks are left open. The first is how to identify the users being polarized (or not) according to those classes. The second task concerns the identification of the most relevant sub-topics being discussed among such users. The third is how to monitor the evolution of such user communities and their on-line discussions over time. Those tasks are all very challenging as the available knowledge may be approximate or insufficient, and it may also become obsolete over time. Therefore, the classification into polarization classes should be able to self-update continuously by catching upcoming relevant users and discussion topics. The present work is related to the Topic Detection and Tracking (TDT) subject [2], which has been widely explored within the scope of news stream analysis [11]. We focus on content and user tracking for polarized users. This notion is connected with the concept of controversy in Social Media, which have been studied, mostly in political contexts, using data coming from different sources [1,4,6,8]. Another related research area is trending topics analysis. Various trend detection models are proposed in [7,9]. Our approach is different in several regards from current literature, since we rather focus on the identification of polarized communities. In our experiments we use electoral data from Twitter. In this case, the polarization classes are political parties and candidates. Several works analyzed the opportunities and limitations in using Twitter as a predictor of an election's outcome [3,5,10]. Our goal is completely different, as we do not draw any conclusion about the expected share of votes for the given parties or candidates. We use this specific kind of data, as it is a typical example of polarized users. We show that the proposed algorithm is able to identify polarized users, by also analyzing the ongoing discussions among the respective communities.

The main contribution of this work is a new iterative algorithm, named PTR (Polarization TRacker), for the discovery of *polarized users* in a Twitter stream, and a temporal version TPTR (Temporal PTR), able to track users and topics over time. While there exist several works about community detection and trending topic tracking, we propose a novel setting where the number of communities is known, but very little information is provided (a keyword per class only), and those communities are competing with each other. We conduct an objective evaluation of the proposed algorithms by measuring their classification accuracy on a *golden* set of users.

SIGIR '16, July 17 - 21, 2016, Pisa, Italy

ISBN 978-1-4503-4069-4/16/07...$15.00

DOI: http://dx.doi.org/10.1145/2911451.2914716

2. USER AND TOPIC TRACKING

Let $\mathcal{T} = \{t_1, t_2, \ldots\}$ be the stream of tweets generated by the set of users $\mathcal{U} = \{u_1, u_2, \ldots\}$. We focus on the analysis of user behavior with respect to a set of *polarization classes* $\mathcal{C}$. The goal of this work is thus to build a *partitional clustering* of the Twitter users, where each of the clusters is associated by construction with a single polarization class (or unassigned). Our method can be seen as a *semi-supervised clustering* one, although, unlike classic methods, we do not provide any class representative around which the final clustering is induced. Indeed, the proposed method is only *loosely* supervised as the only knowledge available is the number of classes, and a short class description (a keyword).

An important issue is the evaluation of our algorithm. To this end, we exploit a *golden set* of polarized users, each unequivocally associated with a class $c \in \mathcal{C}$. Note that such knowledge is not exploited to train a classifier, but only for evaluation purpose.

Algorithm 1 User Classification Algorithm

Require: The set of polarized hashtags H_c and the previously found set of polarized users U_c^* for each class $c \in \mathcal{C}$
Ensure: New set of polarized users $\{U_c\}_{c\in\mathcal{C}}$

1: **procedure** USERSCLASS($\{H_c\}_{c\in\mathcal{C}}, \{U_c^*\}_{c\in\mathcal{C}}$)
2: **for** $u \in \mathcal{U}, c \in \mathcal{C}$ **do** ▷ Find polarized tweets
3: $T_{u,c} = \{t \in \mathcal{T}_u \mid \mathcal{H}_t \cap H_c \neq \emptyset \wedge \mathcal{H}_t \cap H_{c' \neq c} = \emptyset\}$
4: **for** $c \in \mathcal{C}$ **do**
5: $U_c \leftarrow \emptyset$
6: **for** $u \in \mathcal{U}$ **do** ▷ Check user's polarization
7: **if** $\exists c \in \mathcal{C} \mid \forall c' \in \mathcal{C}, c' \neq c \quad |T_{u,c}| > \alpha \cdot |T_{u,c'}|$ **then**
8: $U_c \leftarrow U_c \cup u$
9: **else if** $\exists c \in \mathcal{C} \mid u \in U_c^*$ **then**
10: $U_c \leftarrow U_c \cup u$
11: **return** $\{U_c\}_{c\in\mathcal{C}}$

Algorithm 2 Hashtag Classification Algorithm

Require: The set of polarized users U_c for each class $c \in \mathcal{C}$
Ensure: Polarized hashtags H_c

1: **procedure** HASHTAGSCLASS($\{U_c\}_{c\in\mathcal{C}}$)
2: **for** $c \in \mathcal{C}$ **do**
3: $H_c \leftarrow \emptyset$
4: $H_c^* \leftarrow \bigcup_{u\in U_c} \mathcal{H}_u$
5: **for** $h \in \bigcup_{c\in\mathcal{C}} H_c^*$ **do**
6: **if** $\exists c \mid \forall c' \neq c \quad S_c(h) > \beta \cdot S_{c'}(h)$ **then**
7: $H_c \leftarrow H_c \cup h$
8: **return** $\{H_c\}_{c\in\mathcal{C}}$

2.1 The PTR algorithm

The Polarization TRacker (PTR) algorithm requires some initial *seed topics* that identify the classes of interests. We propose to identify them with a single textual keyword for each class $c \in \mathcal{C}$. Although each keyword identifies a topic, e.g., a political party, it is not sufficient to correctly classify users, as all these seed topics are likely to be mentioned in many users' tweets, e.g., to contrast the achievements of a given party with the deficiencies of the others. Without loss of generality, we limit our keyword selection to Twitter *hashtags*. Therefore, the single textual keyword we initially choose for each class c is a single hashtag appearing in the user tweets, and around them we start identifying the user clusters. The final goal is to extract the best discriminating hashtags that are able to identify the actual clusters of polarized users, who belong with high probability to one of the classes $c \in \mathcal{C}$.

We denote the representative hashtags, one for each $c \in \mathcal{C}$, called *seed hashtags*, by $H_c^{\tau=0}$, where τ is the algorithm's iteration number. Note that each initial set $H_c^{\tau=0}$, one for each c, is not necessarily composed of a discriminating hashtag. This set $H_c^{\tau=0}$ is then used to classify polarized users on the basis of their use of the seed hashtags. We denote by $U_c^{\tau+1}$ the clusters of users in $\mathcal{U}$ that are identified as belonging to class c, according to their tweets and to the given hashtags H_c^τ. Similarly, the new hashtags $H_c^{\tau+1}$ are generated by finding those that best discriminate the users in $U_c^{\tau+1}$. This refinement process is iterated for all $c \in \mathcal{C}$: from hashtags $\{H_c^\tau\}_{c\in\mathcal{C}}$ to users $\{U_c^{\tau+1}\}_{c\in\mathcal{C}}$, and finally to hashtags $\{H_c^{\tau+1}\}_{c\in\mathcal{C}}$. The algorithm terminates when H_c^τ converges.

Specifically, PTR iterates the two classification steps USERCLASS and HASHTAGSCLASS. Algorithm 1 illustrates the former step of the iterative process[1]. The goal of this step is to identify polarized users on the basis of the given hashtags. First, we identify polarized tweets, which mention hashtags in H_c. We consider the classification of each single tweet t by considering all the mentioned hashtags $\mathcal{H}_t$, as we believe each tweet is a very relevant expression of a user's thought on a specific topic. Since we are interested in polarized users, with the goal of achieving high precision we discard all the tweets which contain hashtags belonging to more than one set $\{H_c\}_{c\in\mathcal{C}}$. For each user $u \in \mathcal{U}$ and for each class $c \in \mathcal{C}$ we denote the set of polarized tweets by $T_{u,c}$. We thus measure the user polarization: if for some classes c, the number of tweets in $T_{u,c}$ is significantly larger than for any other class (parameter α), then the user is labeled with the class c and added to the set of polarized users U_c (see line 7). Note that the user classification is intended to be an update of the classification conducted during the previous step. The goal the second step is to process all the hashtags adopted by classified users U_c in order to discover a new set of discriminating hashtags H_c, as illustrated in Alg. 2. In order to detect $\{H_c\}_{c\in\mathcal{C}}$, we take into considerations all the hashtags $\mathcal{H}_u$ used by any user $u \in U_c$, and not only those occurring in the polarized tweets $T_{u,c}$ (line 4). This allows to extend our analysis to the full set of topics discussed by the users, even if they were not captured in the early iterations of the algorithm. First, for each $c \in C$ we retrieve the set of hashtags used by the users in U_c, considering all their tweets, denoted by $\mathcal{T}_c$, independent of the classification of the single tweets in the previous iteration. In our experiments we consider the top frequent 500 hashtags in $\mathcal{T}_c$. Given the resulting set of candidate hashtags for each $c \in \mathcal{C}$, namely H_c^*, we extract from them the new hashtags that highly discriminate each class c, and these are eventually added to the new set H_c (line 7). Specifically, the discriminating hashtags are those highly used by the current set of users U_c, and partially used by any other user in $U_{c'}$, $c' \neq c$. We define a function $S_c(h)$ to measure the goodness of hashtag h for each community of polarized users U_c. Let $\mathcal{T}_h$ be the set of tweets in $\mathcal{T}$ mentioning hashtag h, independent of the users who posted these tweets. Moreover, let $\mathcal{T}_{H_c^*}$ be the set of tweets in $\mathcal{T}$ containing at least one hashtag in the set H_c^*. We score the goodness of a hashtag for a polarization class as follows:

$$S_c(h) = \frac{|\mathcal{T}_h \cap \mathcal{T}_{H_c^*}|}{|\mathcal{T}_{H_c^*}|} \cdot \prod_{c'\in\mathcal{C}, c'\neq c} \left(1 - \frac{|\mathcal{T}_h \cap \mathcal{T}_{H_{c'}^*}|}{|\mathcal{T}_{H_{c'}^*}|}\right)$$

where we consider the naive hypothesis of independent occurrence of the hashtags in the various sets. In practice, $S_c(h)$ is the probability of seeing h only in H_c^*, whereas h is not present in all the other sets of hashtags $H_{c'\neq c}^*$. Given a hashtag h, the score $S_c(h)$ is used to rank the various classes, thus assigning h to class with the highest score. Since we aim at promoting high discriminating hashtags, not only we assign the hashtag h having the highest $S_c(h)$ to the new set H_c, but only if $S_c(h) > \beta \cdot S_{c'}(h), \forall c' \neq c$, where $\beta \geq 1$. Note that if a tie exists between the to 2-top scores classes, the hashtag h is not assigned to any H_c, since it is considered not discriminating enough.

3. EXPERIMENTAL EVALUATION

3.1 Data collection and cleansing

We use two Twitter datasets related to political elections that recently took place in Italy. **Dataset IT13**: data about primary election for largest social democratic political party in Italy (PD), which took place in December 2013 with 3 candidates: Mr. Renzi, Mr. Cuperlo, and Mr. Civati. **Dataset EU14**: data about European Parliament election held in Italy in May 2014[2]. The data are collected through Twitter API by querying a list of keywords related to the topic and the candidates, large enough to guarantee a good coverage

[1]Note that we omitted the superscript τ for the sake of simplifying the notation.

[2]The main national parties connected to different European political groups were: *Partito Democratico* (PD), *Movimento 5 Stelle* (M5S), *Forza Italia* (FI), *Lega Nord* (LN), *Tsipras* (AET). We ignore smaller parties and NCD-UDC for its limited presence in Twitter.

Table 1: Data Statistics

(a) Full dataset

Dataset	IT13	EU14
tweets in original raw data	1.7 M.	2.3 M.
pre-electoral tweets $\mathcal{T}$	95,627	364,132
users with $\|\mathcal{H}_u\| > 0$	11,368 (65%)	28,340 (56%)

(b) Golden dataset

Dataset IT13			Dataset EU14		
$\mathcal{C}$	Tweets	Users	$\mathcal{C}$	Tweets	Users
Renzi	330	109	PD	262	129
Cuperlo	4759	243	M5S	146	95
Civati	2925	700	FI	1263	199
			LN	480	226
			AET	757	328
total	8014	1052	*total*	2908	977

of the elections. Both final datasets cover 9 days before the election day. We discard partial data and potentially irrelevant tweets, considering only tweets being geo-located and in Italian language. Table 1b reports some information about the two datasets.

3.2 Evaluation of the PTR algorithm

We build an evaluation dataset by identifying those users whose opinion can be inferred with high confidence. During elections, as for other events, very specific hashtags are used over Twitter to express a strong intention of vote or an explicit membership in a group. We assume that users that frequently use one of such hashtags are strongly sided with one of the competing parties and they will not change idea in the short term. Such hashtags, named *golden hashtags*, are handpicked among the 500 most frequent in the data. The used golden hashtags are of the kind `#IVoteParty`. We identify one/two golden hashtags per class $c \in \mathcal{C}$ both in the EU14 (e.g. `#IVoteTsipras` for AET) and in the IT13 (e.g. `#prefeRenzi` for Renzi) dataset. The set of reference users were identified by applying Algorithm 1 with the above *golden* hashtags as input. This guarantees that a user is safely considered as polarized to a party $c \in \mathcal{C}$ if her tweets contain only one of the golden hashtags associated with the various classes $c \in \mathcal{C}$. We denote with $\mathcal{Z} = \{z_1, z_2, \ldots\}$ this set of polarized users, and with $Z_c \subseteq \mathcal{Z}$ those supporting a specific formation c (Z_c is a partitioning of $\mathcal{Z}$). The composition of resulting *golden dataset* is reported in Table 1a. The golden dataset is thus a small fraction of the full dataset. A global analysis of the Twitter stream cannot be based on a few very polarized hashtags. Note that the relative popularity of the parties is not simply proportional to the number of votes received, but it depends on the efficacy of the hashtag promoted. We remark that, for the sake of fairness, we remove the *golden* hashtags from the datasets before the application of any algorithm. The set of users $\mathcal{Z}$ in the golden dataset, is used to evaluate the users classification accuracy of the proposed method. Given the users classification U_c provided by some given algorithm, precision, recall and F-Measure are restricted to the set $\mathcal{Z}$. Formally, for any given class $c \in \mathcal{C}$, precision and recall are defined as:

$$P_c(U_c) = \frac{|U_c \cap Z_c|}{|U_c \cap \mathcal{Z}|} \qquad R_c(U_c) = \frac{|U_c \cap Z_c|}{|Z_c|}$$

The F-measure F_c is the harmonic means of P_c and R_c. The macro F-measure average over the classes $c \in \mathcal{C}$ is denoted with F. In addition, as the proposed algorithm may not be able to classify all of the users in $\mathcal{Z}$, we report also the user coverage γ and Γ on both the golden set and the overall dataset respectively:

$$\gamma(U = \cup_{c \in \mathcal{C}} U_c) = \frac{|U \cap \mathcal{Z}|}{|\mathcal{Z}|} \qquad \Gamma(U = \cup_{c \in \mathcal{C}} U_c) = \frac{|U|}{|\mathcal{U}|}$$

As a baseline we use the k-means clustering algorithm. Each user u is represented by a vector of 500 features, corresponding to the 500 most frequent hashtags in the dataset. The user feature vector stores the frequency of a hashtag in the stream of tweets $\mathcal{T}_u$ published by the user. We discard users who do not use any hashtag in their tweets. We normalize the feature vectors for each user to unit L^2 norm. We impose the number of the clusters k equal to the number of classes $|\mathcal{C}|$ and, to simulate the same starting condition of our method, we built the initial centroids so as to encode the *seed* hashtags. The centroid for a class c is thus a vector with a single 1 in the position of the seed hashtag, and 0 otherwise. The result of the k-means baseline is thus a clustering of users based on the *seed* hashtags provided. Table 2a reports the results of the k-means baseline. F-measure values are low for the IT13 dataset. For instance, k-means provides low accuracy and recall for the first class. This is mainly due to the fact that the hashtags corresponding to popular parties or candidates are very often used by different users, regardless of their orientation. In other cases (e.g., LN and AET), the hashtags are used mostly within the respective communities.

In the following, we analyze in detail the iteration-by-iteration behavior of the proposed PTR algorithm. We test our algorithm by setting $\alpha = 2$ and $\beta = 1$, after a tuning step. During the first iteration, PTR is fed with the *seed* hashtags. Algorithm 1 uses those hashtags to find a subset of polarized users in $\mathcal{U}$. This step is similar to other works, where mentions of a party or candidate are used to estimate their popularity or to classify users [3, 10]. Unlike other approaches, PTR aims at discovering a subset of polarized users, thus requiring,that a user mentions a party at least twice any other. The results of such user classification are evaluated over the *golden dataset*, as reported in the first line of Table 3a. Regarding average precision, PTR is already significantly superior to the k-means baseline for IT13 dataset. This is already surprising, as the seed hashtags are very generic. On the other hand, the k-means baseline might be negatively affected by the sparsity of the data. The results are different on the two datasets in terms of average recall. PTR has similar performance to k-means on the IT13 dataset, while the recall is significantly lower on the EU14 dataset. This is

Table 2: Comparison with the Baseline.

(a) k-means baseline performance

Dataset IT13				Dataset EU14			
$\mathcal{C}$	P_c	R_c	F_c	$\mathcal{C}$	P_c	R_c	F_c
Renzi	0.144	0.257	0.185	PD	0.536	0.457	0.493
Cuperlo	0.252	0.543	0.344	M5S	0.359	0.895	0.512
Civati	0.766	0.366	0.495	FI	0.495	0.734	0.591
				LN	0.995	0.916	0.954
				AET	1.000	0.387	0.558
avg.	0.387	0.389	0.341	*avg.*	0.677	0.678	0.622
$\gamma = 1.0$		$\Gamma = 0.653$		$\gamma = 1.0$		$\Gamma = 0.557$	

(b) PTR Iteration-2 performance

Dataset IT13				Dataset EU14			
$\mathcal{C}$	P_c	R_c	F_c	$\mathcal{C}$	P_c	R_c	F_c
Renzi	0.350	0.752	0.478	PD	0.733	0.488	0.586
Cuperlo	0.869	0.300	0.446	M5S	0.325	0.842	0.469
Civati	0.916	0.747	0.823	FI	0.955	0.533	0.684
				LN	0.981	0.938	0.959
				AET	0.974	0.451	0.617
avg.	0.712	0.600	0.582	*avg.*	0.794	0.650	0.663
$\gamma = 0.845$		$\Gamma = 0.532$		$\gamma = 0.830$		$\Gamma = 0.367$	

Table 3: Algorithm Performance.

(a) PTR iteration by iteration performance

Iter	Dataset IT13 F	Dataset IT13 γ	Dataset IT13 Γ	Dataset EU14 F	Dataset EU14 γ	Dataset EU14 Γ
1	0.358	0.490	0.218	0.514	0.670	0.163
2	0.582	0.845	0.522	0.663	0.830	0.367
3	0.588	0.853	0.532	0.662	0.831	0.386
4	0.588	0.853	0.534	0.661	0.834	0.390

(b) TPTR day-by-day performance

Day	Dataset IT13 F	Dataset IT13 γ	Dataset IT13 Γ	Dataset EU14 F	Dataset EU14 γ	Dataset EU14 Γ
1	0.177	0.199	0.045	0.155	0.164	0.025
2	0.225	0.348	0.114	0.464	0.465	0.079
3	0.304	0.457	0.166	0.529	0.570	0.116
4	0.333	0.563	0.234	0.585	0.671	0.180
5	0.368	0.606	0.261	0.588	0.726	0.235
6	0.397	0.671	0.315	0.574	0.762	0.269
7	0.387	0.721	0.363	0.596	0.794	0.302
8	0.387	0.765	0.408	0.637	0.846	0.334
9	0.391	0.811	0.461	0.635	0.876	0.349

confirmed by the coverage values γ and Γ. In comparison with the baseline, the performance of PTR in terms of macro F-measure is satisfactory on the IT13 dataset, but not on the EU14 dataset yet. The output of the first iteration is a new set of hashtags which is exploited in the next iteration. By looking at the best scoring hashtag, we can already observe an interesting behavior of the algorithm for some $c \in \mathcal{C}$. In dataset EU14, the best tags for FI and LN are the leaders of the respective parties, detecting that the original *seed* hashtags are not discriminating in this case. In Table 2b we report in detail the results after the second iteration of PTR. The first interesting result is that the average recall is significantly higher on both datasets. This is due to the new hashtags discovered in addition to the *seed* ones during the previous iteration, which, in turn, lead to the identification of a larger set of users: the coverage γ is now beyond 80% on the *golden* set, and Γ has doubled in this iteration. Also the average precision is higher w.r.t. the previous iteration scoring more than 0.7. This is both because of the increased number of classified users, and of the updated user classification. As a result, the F-measure has an overall improvement w.r.t. the k-means baseline of +71% and +7% on datasets IT13 and EU14 respectively. As shown in Table 3a PTR becomes stable very early. The largest improvement is achieved with the second iterations. This means that the most relevant hashtags are discovered early, and only slight changes occur afterwards. The subsequent iterations marginally increase the number of classified users. Note that the algorithm is classifying the polarized users found in the whole set $\mathcal{U}$. PTR found about 6.7 and 27 thousands polarized users on the dataset IT13 and EU14 respectively. We conclude that in most cases, two iterations of the algorithm provide sufficient classification quality. For the lack of space we can not report a exhaustive qualitative analysis of the outcome, but we observe that the procedure is able to extract relevant keywords: namely prominent politicians, the party itself and political mottoes characterizing each c in the political scene.

We finally propose a variant of PTR, that is TPTR (temporal PTR), to perform the tracking of topics and users in time. In our case we consider the evolution day by day. The procedure follows Algorithm 1 and Algorithm 2 with the difference that at iteration τ only the tweets $\mathcal{T}_u$ written in the τ-th day are considered. We perform TPTR on IT13 and on EU14 datasets. In Table 3b the evaluation of the temporal iterative procedure is shown. The macro F-measure is increasing day by day both for the effect of a better classification and for the presence of new users. Note that we evaluate the time iterative method day by day on the entire *golden set* of users. F-measure values are low because not all users in the *golden set* were active every day.

4. CONCLUSION

We propose a novel algorithm for the simultaneous tracking of *polarized users* and *discriminating topics* in OSNs. Specifically, it iteratively detects polarized users, and from their contents the discussed discriminating topics. We also introduce a temporal variant, where the information extracted during one day of analysis is exploited for the next day. Indeed, the classification of users makes the algorithm more robust in terms of concept drifts, as new trends may be detected as early as they pop up. At the same time, the identification of discriminating topics helps in detecting users moving from one class to another. The algorithm is tested on two Twitter data samples. We evaluate the quality of user classification on a *golden set* of users, showing significant improvements over the baseline. The proposed methodology is general and it can be applied to different scenarios. We believe that this methodology based on *polarization* may also impact on broad area of social network analysis, e.g., by complementing the proposed classification with community detection and information diffusion over time. As a future work, we aim to improve the temporal analysis dealing with streaming data.

Supported by EC H2020 Program INFRAIA-1-2014-2015 (654024).

5. REFERENCES

[1] L. A. Adamic and N. Glance. The political blogosphere and the 2004 us election: divided they blog. In *Proc. of the 3rd Workshop on Link discovery*, pages 36–43. ACM, 2005.

[2] J. Allan. *Topic detection and tracking: event-based information organization*, volume 12. Springer Science & Business Media, 2012.

[3] M. Coletto, C. Lucchese, S. Orlando, and R. Perego. Electoral predictions with twitter: a machine-learning approach. *IIR*, 2015.

[4] K. Garimella, G. De Francisci Morales, A. Gionis, and M. Mathioudakis. Quantifying controversy in social media. In *ACM WSDM*, pages 33–42, 2016.

[5] D. Gayo-Avello, P. T. Metaxas, and E. Mustafaraj. Limits of electoral predictions using twitter. In *ICWSM*, 2011.

[6] C. V. Gysel, B. Goethals, and M. de Rijke. Determining the presence of political parties in social circles. In *AAAI ICWSM*, 2015.

[7] J. Lin, R. Snow, and W. Morgan. Smoothing techniques for adaptive online language models: topic tracking in tweet streams. In *ACM SIGKDD*, pages 422–429. ACM, 2011.

[8] A. Makazhanov, D. Rafiei, and M. Waqar. Predicting political preference of twitter users. *Social Network Analysis and Mining*, 4(1):1–15, 2014.

[9] M. Mathioudakis and N. Koudas. Twittermonitor: trend detection over the twitter stream. In *Proc. of the 2010 ACM SIGMOD*, pages 1155–1158. ACM, 2010.

[10] A. Tumasjan, T. O. Sprenger, P. G. Sandner, and I. M. Welpe. Predicting elections with twitter: What 140 characters reveal about political sentiment. *ICWSM*, 10:178–185, 2010.

[11] F. Walls, H. Jin, S. Sista, and R. Schwartz. Topic detection in broadcast news. In *Proceedings of the DARPA broadcast news workshop*, pages 193–198, 1999.

Post-Learning Optimization of Tree Ensembles for Efficient Ranking

Claudio Lucchese
ISTI–CNR, Italy and Istella Srl
c.lucchese@isti.cnr.it

Franco Maria Nardini
ISTI–CNR, Italy and Istella Srl
f.nardini@isti.cnr.it

Salvatore Orlando
Università Ca' Foscari
Venezia, Italy
orlando@unive.it

Raffaele Perego
ISTI–CNR, Italy and Istella Srl
r.perego@isti.cnr.it

Fabrizio Silvestri
Yahoo Labs, London
silvestr@yahoo-inc.com

Salvatore Trani
ISTI–CNR, Italy
s.trani@isti.cnr.it

ABSTRACT

Learning to Rank (LtR) is the machine learning method of choice for producing high quality document ranking functions from a ground-truth of training examples. In practice, efficiency and effectiveness are intertwined concepts and trading off effectiveness for meeting efficiency constraints typically existing in large-scale systems is one of the most urgent issues. In this paper we propose a new framework, named CLEAVER, for optimizing machine-learned ranking models based on ensembles of regression trees. The goal is to improve efficiency at document scoring time without affecting quality. Since the cost of an ensemble is linear in its size, CLEAVER first removes a subset of the trees in the ensemble, and then fine-tunes the weights of the remaining trees according to any given quality measure. Experiments conducted on two publicly available LtR datasets show that CLEAVER is able to prune up to 80% of the trees and provides an efficiency speed-up up to 2.6x without affecting the effectiveness of the model.

Keywords

Learning to Rank; Efficiency; Pruning

1. INTRODUCTION

The problem of ranking objects in response to a user query is of general interest as it is of paramount importance for all kinds of information systems. In Web Search, for example, the problem of ranking documents is particularly challenging due to the large amount of data to manage. Modern Web search engines are expected to return highly relevant results in a fractions of seconds to satisfy hard back-end latency requirements. Nowadays, Learning-to-Rank (LtR) [6] methodologies are pervasively used as effective solutions to the most difficult ranking problems. LtR methods, which *score* a set of candidate documents according to their relevance to a given user query, use machine learning models trained on *ground truth* datasets providing an ideal rankings compiled either using human-based or automatic methods. Typically these approaches do not directly take into account efficiency concerns resulting in models that cannot be used in production environments because they do not meet their strict efficiency requirements.

In this paper, we tackle the problem of improving efficiency in (LtR). We present a framework, named CLEAVER, for the optimization of tree ensemble ranking models *after* the learning phase has completed. The cost of predicting the relevance for a document by using a tree ensemble model is linear in the number of trees. Larger ensembles, despite being more accurate, come with larger costs thus being very expensive. We study the following novel problem: given a tree ensemble model is it possible to improve its efficiency without affecting its quality? We show that the answer is positive, and we solve the problem by pruning some of the trees in the ensemble and re-weighting the remaining ones.

CLEAVER integrates in a novel way a number of tree pruning strategies with a local optimization method aimed at re-weighing the trees in the pruned ensemble. We analyze several pruning strategies for the identification of the less relevant trees in a given ensemble, and we conduct a comprehensive evaluation of the various strategies on two publicly available datasets. The CLEAVER framework is able to improve the efficiency of a given ranking ensemble up to a 2.6x speed-up without affecting the effectiveness of original the model.

Related Work. Efficiency in Learning to Rank has been investigated in the past from two different research directions. The first includes proposals that trade efficiency off for effectiveness in the learning algorithm. Asadi and Lin observe that compact, shallow, and balanced trees yield faster predictions [1]. They incorporate a notion of execution cost during training to encourage trees with these topological characteristics. Authors propose two strategies for accomplishing this: i) by directly modifying the node splitting criterion during tree induction, and ii) by stage-wise tree pruning. Experiments on a standard learning-to-rank datasets show that the pruning approach is the best. Wang *et al.* present a unified framework for jointly optimizing effectiveness and efficiency [10]. Authors propose new metrics that capture the trade-off between these two competing forces and devise a

SIGIR '16, July 17 - 21, 2016, Pisa, Italy

ISBN 978-1-4503-4069-4/16/07...$15.00

DOI: http://dx.doi.org/10.1145/2911451.2914763

strategy for automatically learning models that directly optimize the trade-off metrics. Experiments show that models learned in this way provide a good balance between retrieval effectiveness and efficiency. Authors also show that their approach naturally leads to a reduction in the variance of query execution times, which is important for query load balancing and user satisfaction.

The second research line considers low-level optimizations to the inference phase by speeding-up the traversal of a given tree ensemble. Asadi *et al.* [2] propose to rearrange the code visiting the ensemble by transforming *control hazards* into less expensive *data hazards*, i.e., data dependencies introduced when one instruction requires the result of another. Lucchese *et al.* [7] propose QuickScorer a scoring algorithm, which adopts a new representation of the tree ensemble based on bit-vectors. The tree traversal, aimed to detect the leaves contributing to the final scoring of a document, is performed feature by feature, over the whole tree ensemble, through efficient logical bitwise operations.

To the best of our knowledge this is the first work focusing on post-learning optimization of tree-based LtR models. The two research directions above are orthogonal to ours as we aim at producing a faster model that does not lose its effectiveness and that can by integrated in any scoring algorithm. Moreover, our methodology is totally agnostic w.r.t. both the LtR algorithm. It can be applied to all LtR algorithms producing ensemble models.

2. OPTIMIZATION OF TREE ENSEMBLES

Let $\mathcal{F} = \{t_1, \ldots, t_n\}$ be an additive ensemble of regression trees, composed of n decision trees. Let $s_i(q, d)$ be the score returned by decision tree t_i to document d in response to query q. Moreover, we denote with $S(q, d)$ the final score predicted by forest $\mathcal{F}$ for query-document pair (q, d), obtained as a linear combination of tree predictions:

$$S(q, d) = \sum_{i=1}^{n} \lambda_i \cdot s_i(q, d)$$

where λ_i is the weight associated with tree t_i.

We make no assumption on the learning algorithm used to train $\mathcal{F}$ and on the loss function optimized during the training. Independently of the algorithm or the loss function adopted, we observe that the cost for computing score $S(q, d)$ is linear in the size n of the forest. As it is desirable to keep this cost as low as possible, either to comply with time budget constraints or to improve the overall effectiveness of query processing by ranking larger amount of candidate documents returned for a given query [4], we aim at reducing the complexity of a tree-based model by pruning trees. Specifically, given an input forest $\mathcal{F}$ providing the desired quality, CLEAVER produces a smaller forest $\mathcal{F}_p$ with at least the same effectiveness as $\mathcal{F}$ but with higher efficiency. Our solution consists in a combination of *pruning strategies* and *tree weighting* optimization. The CLEAVER framework encompasses the two following steps:

1. prune $\mathcal{F}$ to select a subset $\mathcal{F}_p$ of $p, p < n$ trees. We propose and assess different strategies to choose the trees to be removed from $\mathcal{F}$. These strategies estimate differently the impact of each tree in order to devise the less relevant ones;

2. assign new weights to the trees in $\mathcal{F}_p$ so as to optimize a given loss function. We use a greedy line search algorithm to optimize the weights λ_i by minimizing a given loss function.

The resulting forest $\mathcal{F}_p$ therefore contains a subset of the trees in $\mathcal{F}$ but with a different weighting scheme. Since our goal is to produce a more efficient model without affecting its effectiveness, CLEAVER evaluates different pruned model sizes p, and then returns the smallest forest $\mathcal{F}_p$ providing at least the same quality as $\mathcal{F}$ according to the user-defined loss function.

In the following, we first discuss the pruning strategies integrated in CLEAVER, and then discuss how line search is used to improve weights λ_i.

Ensemble Pruning Strategies. Let $p < n$ be the number of trees in the pruned forest $\mathcal{F}_p$. The goal of CLEAVER is to remove $n-p$ trees without affecting the predictive power of the initial forest $\mathcal{F}$. To this end, we propose the following strategies:

- LAST: the last $n-p$ trees in the forest are pruned. The rationale is that forests are usually build sequentially by progressively adding trees optimizing a given loss function. The last trees learned generally provide limited changes in the predicted scores and ranking. The resulting model is equivalent to a model trained with p trees.

- RANDOM: selects uniformly at random $n-p$ trees from the forest and removes them.

- SKIP: keeps p equidistant trees from the forest. The rationale is that close trees are quite similar and potentially redundant. The distance between the selected trees is computed as $\lceil \frac{n}{p} \rceil$.

- LOW-WEIGHTS: removes the $n-p$ trees with the lowest weights λ_i. The assumption is that they are less relevant for the final document scoring. When the learning algorithm used associates uniform weights to all the trees, a preliminary line search process is applied to $\mathcal{F}$ in order to obtain the initial vector Λ to which this strategy is applied.

- SCORE-LOSS: considers the contribution given by each tree to the final score of a document. The normalized contribution for each tree is measured as $s_i(q, d)/S(q, d)$ and used to select the $n-p$ trees that contribute less.

- QUALITY-LOSS: is based on the impact of each tree to the optimization of a given loss function L. For a given tree t_i, the average quality loss over the training dataset is computed by scoring the document with $S(q, d) - s_i(q, d)$. The $n-p$ trees that generate the smallest quality drop can be considered less important and thus removed from the forest.

All the pruning strategies are followed by the line search optimization aimed at tuning the weights of the trees in the pruned forest $\mathcal{F}_p$.

Tree Weighting with Line Search. Let $L\colon \mathbb{R}^p \to \mathbb{R}$ be a given loss function, and let $\Lambda = \{\lambda_1, \lambda_2, \ldots, \lambda_p\}$ be the current weighting schema for forest $\mathcal{F}_p$. Optimizing the tree weighting means finding:

$$\overline{\Lambda} = \operatorname*{argmin}_{\Lambda \in \mathbb{R}^p} L(\Lambda).$$

Due to the large dimensionality involved and the non differentiability of most loss functions, finding $\overline{\Lambda}$ is not possible. We thus adopt a heuristic approach to improve the weighting schema Λ obtained after pruning: *i)* find a descent direction $D \in \mathbb{R}^p$ along which L decreases, and *ii)* compute a step length α so as to minimize $L(\Lambda + \alpha \cdot D)$. This procedure is iterated as long as the solution improves beyond a given tolerance. The descent direction D can be chosen with various methods, *e.g.*, by computing gradient, and the step length α can be computed either exactly or approximately. The strategy we use to find α is referred to as *line search*. It is worth noting that the above process performs a local exploration of the solution space, without making any assumption on the loss function employed.

In our LtR scenario, we are interested in ranking loss functions such as *NDCG*, for which it is not possible to directly compute the gradient. Therefore, we adopt a greedy variant of the above procedure as in [9]. Given the current solution Λ^k at iteration k, we perform a line search along each axis of the weight vector independently, *i.e.*, find the value $d_i = \delta_i + \lambda_i^k$ that optimizes the loss function while keeping fixed all the other directions. The value of δ_i is found by choosing it among σ equi-spaced samples in an interval $[-\omega, +\omega]$ around λ_i^k, excluding negative values. The resulting vector D defines a promising descent direction along which to perform line search. The new weight vector Λ^{k+1} is chosen by optimizing $L(\Lambda^k + \alpha \cdot D)$. In this case, the best value for α is chosen among σ equi-spaced samples in the same interval $[0, 1]$. The above procedure is iterated until no improvement is measured on a separate validation set.

In order to make faster the above search process, at each iteration the search interval $[-\omega, +\omega]$ is reduced by a shrinking factor η. In addition, thread-level parallelism is used in order to evaluate different directions d_i and different σ samples in parallel. Finally, we avoid to visit the whole forest at each step. The ensemble of trees is in fact visited only once and tree predictions $s_i(q, d)$ for all the documents of the training dataset are stored in a memory data structure.

3. EXPERIMENTS

Experiments were conducted with two publicly available datasets: the MSN-1[1] (Fold 1) dataset and a new dataset provided by Istella[2] (Small) we make publicly available with this work. The MSN-1 dataset consists of 31,351 queries and 136 features extracted from 3,771,125 query-document pairs, while the Istella dataset is composed of 33,018 queries and 220 features extracted from 3,408,630 query-document pairs. The query-document pairs in both the datasets are labeled with relevance judgments ranging from 0 (irrelevant) to 4 (perfectly relevant). Each dataset is split in train, validation and test sets according to a 60%-20%-20% scheme.

Training and validation data were used to learn a *full reference* model, to which we applied CLEAVER[3] by testing different pruning levels in the range 0%-90% with steps of 10%. Eventually, we selected the smallest (and thus most efficient) model generated by CLEAVER still providing greater or equal performance on the validation set w.r.t. the *reference un-pruned* model, measured in terms of *NDCG*@10. The parameters adopted for the greedy line search are $\sigma = 20$ equi-spaced samples taken from an interval of radius $\omega = 2$ and adopting a shrinking factor $\eta = 0.95$.

For the sake of fairness, we aimed at building a *full reference* model that is the best performing state-of-the-art ranking ensemble. On both datasets, we trained two different algorithms: *i)* the Gradient Boosting Regression Tree (GBRT, a.k.a., MART), a *point-wise* algorithm that uses the root mean squared error as loss function, resulting in a predictor of relevance labels [5], and *ii)* λ-MART, a *list-wise* algorithm that is capable of using *NDCG* in its loss function, resulting in a predictor of the ranking [11]. We used the open-source implementation of these algorithms provided by [3]. Both were fine-tuned by sweeping their parameters aiming at maximizing *NDCG*@10. The maximum number of leaves was tested in the set $\{5, 10, 25, 50\}$, while the learning rate in $\{0.05, 0.1, 0.5, 1.0\}$. To avoid overfitting, we allowed the algorithm to train up to 1,500 trees unless the relative improvement in *NDCG*@10 on the validation set during the last 50 iterations was smaller than 0.5‰. The resulting forests include 737 and 736 trees for MSN-1 and Istella, respectively, with unitary weighting schema (*i.e.*, $\lambda_i = 1, 1 \le i \le n$). To assess the validity of the pruning strategies also for smaller forests, we build two more *reference* models consisting of the first 100 and 500 trees of the *full reference*. *NDCG*@10 values for the RANDOM strategy were averaged over 10 runs. We also performed randomization test [8] to assess if the differences in effectiveness between the reference models and the pruned ones are statistically significant.

We found that the largest number of leaves and the smaller learning rate always provide the best results with both LtR algorithms. We highlight that it was not possible, by varying the training parameters, to build more efficient rankers (e.g., with smaller total number of nodes) providing the same level of quality of the *reference* models. MART resulted the best performing on MSN-1, and λ-MART on Istella.

Results. Table 1 reports the performance of CLEAVER on MSN-1 and Istella datasets. In bold the best performance in terms of number of trees composing the pruned forest. Interestingly, both RANDOM and SKIP perform quite well, meaning that trees are somehow redundant by construction. Strategy LAST is the worst performing, suggesting that the last trees built by the model still provide a relevant contribution. The LOW-WEIGHTS pruning performs worse than expected, especially with the largest models. We deduce the tree weight cannot be evaluated in isolation from the actual predictions at the tree leaves. The pruning based on SCORE-LOSS exhibits good performance on average, especially on the Istella dataset. We highlight that this strategy approximates well the final document score, but small score variations may generate large rank variations, thus resulting in a negative impact on the *NDCG* metric. Finally, QUALITY-LOSS is quite consistently the best pruning strategy on both the datasets and for all the model sizes, except for the full λ-MART model on Istella dataset where SKIP and SCORE-LOSS are able to prune 10% more trees. Indeed, QUALITY-LOSS is the only strategy that takes into consideration the target quality function *NDCG*@10.

Pruning the reference models allows to significantly reduce the number of trees from 50% to 70% thus obtaining a scoring speed-up from 1.6x to 2.6x while preserving the effectiveness of the original *reference* model.

We run statistical significance tests, with significance level $p = 0.05$, obtaining a two-fold result. On the one hand, they

[1]http://research.microsoft.com/en-us/projects/mslr/

[2]http://blog.istella.it/istella-learning-to-rank-dataset/

[3]CLEAVER is available here: http://quickrank.isti.cnr.it.

Table 1: Comparison of CLEAVER pruning strategies against the *reference* models. Pruned forest size, document scoring time (μs), and *NDCG*@10 are reported for each of the pruned models.

MART on MSN-1

Strategy	100 Trees				500 Trees				737 Trees			
	Trees	Time	Speed-up	*NDCG*@10	Trees	Time	Speed-up	*NDCG*@10	Trees	Time	Speed-up	*NDCG*@10
Reference	100	5.55	–	0.4590	500	19.36	–	0.4749	737	27.46	–	0.4766
RANDOM	40	3.28	1.7x	0.4603	350	14.27	1.4x	0.4756	516	19.64	1.4x	0.4768
LAST	60	3.93	1.4x	0.4601	400	16.17	1.2x	0.4755	590	22.76	1.2x	0.4771
SKIP	**30**	**2.84**	**2.0x**	0.4593	300	12.98	1.5x	0.4749	442	17.25	1.6x	0.4766
LOW-WEIGHTS	40	3.26	1.7x	0.4609	400	15.75	1.2x	0.4753	663	25.28	1.1x	0.4779
QUALITY-LOSS	**30**	**2.89**	**1.9x**	0.4618	**150**	**7.35**	**2.6x**	0.4752	**369**	**14.42**	**1.9x**	0.4771
SCORE-LOSS	50	3.50	1.6x	0.4591	250	11.16	1.7x	0.4751	442	17.47	1.6x	0.4766

λ-MART on Istella

Strategy	100 Trees				500 Trees				736 Trees			
	Trees	Time	Speed-up	*NDCG*@10	Trees	Time	Speed-up	*NDCG*@10	Trees	Time	Speed-up	*NDCG*@10
Reference	100	5.37	–	0.6923	500	15.74	–	0.7397	736	20.40	–	0.7432
RANDOM	30	2.65	2.0x	0.7003	250	9.10	1.7x	0.7424	515	14.81	1.4x	0.7449
LAST	70	4.22	1.3x	0.6969	400	13.55	1.2x	0.7418	442	14.09	1.4x	0.7437
SKIP	**20**	**2.36**	**2.3x**	0.6976	250	9.09	1.7x	0.7416	**368**	**11.42**	**1.8x**	0.7438
LOW-WEIGHTS	30	2.85	1.9x	0.6986	350	11.07	1.4x	0.7418	589	15.55	1.3x	0.7437
QUALITY-LOSS	**20**	**2.29**	**2.3x**	0.6989	**200**	**7.83**	**2.0x**	0.7412	442	13.22	1.5x	0.7438
SCORE-LOSS	**20**	**2.13**	**2.5x**	0.6976	300	10.68	1.5x	0.7407	**368**	**12.39**	**1.6x**	0.7433

show a statistical equivalence when dealing with forests of 500 or more trees. On the other hand, they prove that the improvement of the pruned model w.r.t. the reference one when dealing with 100-tree models is statistically significant. Smaller models, whose quality is still far from optimal, can greatly benefit from the line search optimization, which can also better deal with a low-dimensional search space.

To confirm the effectiveness of CLEAVER we also performed the following experiment. We allowed pruning as long as no statistically significance difference w.r.t. the *reference* model is observed. In this setting, CLEAVER provides an even further improvement on the largest models: 70% pruning (221 trees) with QUALITY-LOSS on MSN-1 and 60% (294 trees) with SKIP on Istella, corresponding to a scoring speed-up of 2.9x and 2.1x respectively.

An important outcome of this work is that, in order to build a model with a given number of trees, we found to be best performing to use CLEAVER to prune a large model than to exploit line search optimization only. As an example, a λ-MART model with 100 trees on Istella dataset provides an *NDCG*@10 of 0.6923 and of 0.7085 after line search re-weighting. Instead, by pruning a larger model of 500 trees with the QUALITY-LOSS strategy, CLEAVER produces a model providing an outstanding *NDCG*@10 of 0.7329.

4. CONCLUSION AND FUTURE WORK

We proposed a novel algorithm, named CLEAVER, which is able to improve the efficiency of a given ensemble-based model. CLEAVER, first removes the less relevant elements in the ensemble according to their expected impact, then fine-tunes the weights of the remaining ones through line search. Eventually, CLEAVER provides a smaller and more efficient model with at least the same quality as the original one. In our experiments, CLEAVER allowed to built models being more than twice as fast. As future work we intend to integrate CLEAVER in several ensemble learning algorithms to systematically prune and improve the models while being generated. We also believe CLEAVER can be successfully extended to non tree-based ensembles and applied to other tasks than document ranking.

Acknowledgments. This work was partially supported by the EC H2020 Program INFRAIA-1-2014-2015 SoBigData: Social Mining & Big Data Ecosystem (654024).

5. REFERENCES

[1] N. Asadi and J. Lin. Training efficient tree-based models for document ranking. In *Advances in Information Retrieval*, pages 146–157. Springer, 2013.

[2] N. Asadi, J. Lin, and A. P. de Vries. Runtime optimizations for tree-based machine learning models. *IEEE TKDE*, 2014.

[3] G. Capannini, C. Lucchese, F. M. Nardini, S. Orlando, R. Perego, and N. Tonellotto. Quality versus Efficiency in Document Scoring with Learning-to-Rank Models. *Information Processing and Management*, 2016.

[4] V. Dang, M. Bendersky, and W. B. Croft. Two-stage learning to rank for information retrieval. In *Advances in Information Retrieval*, pages 423–434. 2013.

[5] J. H. Friedman. Greedy function approximation: a gradient boosting machine. *Annals of Statistics*, 2001.

[6] T.-Y. Liu. Learning to rank for information retrieval. *Foundations and Trends in IR*, 3(3):225–331, 2009.

[7] C. Lucchese, F. M. Nardini, S. Orlando, R. Perego, N. Tonellotto, and R. Venturini. QuickScorer: A fast algorithm to rank documents with additive ensembles of regression trees. In *ACM SIGIR*, pages 73–82. 2015.

[8] M. D. Smucker, J. Allan, and B. Carterette. A comparison of statistical significance tests for information retrieval evaluation. In *ACM CIKM*, 2007.

[9] M. Taylor, H. Zaragoza, N. Craswell, S. Robertson, C. Burges. Optimisation methods for ranking functions with multiple parameters. In *CIKM*, 2006.

[10] L. Wang, J. Lin, and D. Metzler. Learning to efficiently rank. In *ACM SIGIR*, 2010.

[11] Q. Wu, C. Burges, K. Svore, and J. Gao. Adapting boosting for information retrieval measures. *Information Retrieval*, 2010.

Quit While Ahead: Evaluating Truncated Rankings

Fei Liu, Alistair Moffat, Timothy Baldwin
The University of Melbourne
Melbourne, Australia
fliu3@student.unimelb.edu.au,
ammoffat@unimelb.edu.au, tb@ldwin.net

Xiuzhen Zhang
RMIT University
Melbourne, Australia
xiuzhen.zhang@rmit.edu.au

ABSTRACT

Many types of search tasks are answered through the computation of a ranked list of suggested answers. We re-examine the usual assumption that answer lists should be as long as possible, and suggest that when the number of matching items is potentially small – perhaps even zero – it may be more helpful to "quit while ahead", that is, to truncate the answer ranking earlier rather than later. To capture this effect, metrics are required which are attuned to the length of the ranking, and can handle cases in which there are no relevant documents. In this work we explore a generalized approach for representing truncated result sets, and propose modifications to a number of popular evaluation metrics.

1. INTRODUCTION AND BACKGROUND

Ranked answer lists are a staple of search; and mechanisms for generating and evaluating them are widely known [1]. In most experimentation, ranked lists are taken to be of arbitrary length, that is, potentially spanning every item in the underlying collection; or to be of some fixed but large length, perhaps to depth $d = 1{,}000$. But there are also situations in which there is only a small number of relevant answers ("find the home page of ...") or no relevant answers to date ("how do I get LaTeX to ..."), for which generating a long list of unhelpful results is counter-productive. When confronted with such questions, an effective retrieval system might truncate its ranking after just a few suggestions, or even offer no answers at all, choosing to "quit while ahead"; assuming, of course, that the user understands the message being conveyed when a truncated ranking is generated by a system. Here we consider how to compute an effectiveness score for rankings that are of variable – and possibly zero – length, based on which we propose modifications to a range of popular evaluation metrics.

Effectiveness Metrics for Extended Rankings A large number of effectiveness metrics for ranked lists have been described, covering both binary relevance (the gain r_i associated with position i in the ranking is either zero or one), and graded relevance (r_i may take on arbitrary non-negative values). These include precision-focused metrics such as Precision@k and Reciprocal Rank (RR), which is the precision at the first relevant document in the ranking. Other metrics add a recall component, such as Average Precision (AP).

Järvelin and Kekäläinen [2] describe a top-weighted evaluation metric they call *discounted cumulative gain* (DCG). A key development in this metric is that items near the top of the ranking are explicitly given a greater influence on the final score than are items later in the ranking. The formulation usually used is given by DCG@$d = \sum_{i=1}^{d}(r_i/\log_2(1+i))$, where d is the chosen evaluation depth. An issue with DCG is that the values generated are unbounded; to address this, Järvelin and Kekäläinen also introduce a normalized version (NDCG), defined as the DCG score at that depth divided by the DCG of a permuted ideal ranking in which all relevant documents are returned at the head of the answer list: NDCG@d = DCG@d / DCG$_I$@d. An NDCG@d score of 1.0 indicates that, down to depth d, the ranking is as good as would have been attained by an omniscient system. Note, however, that the DCG score of a ranking in which there are no relevant answers is zero; and hence that NDCG is undefined on nil-answer queries. Other recall-based metrics, including Average Precision and the Q-measure [5], face the same challenge.

Moffat and Zobel [3] proposed an alternative top-weighted approach that avoids the need for the normalizing step. Their *Rank-Biased Precision* (RBP) metric is based on a simple user model, assuming that the user always looks at the first returned document, and then continues from one depth i in the ranking to the next depth $i + 1$ with a fixed probability p, their *persistence*. The expected per-document rate at which gain is accrued is then given by RBP $= (1 - p) \cdot \sum_{i=1}^{\infty} r_i \cdot p^{i-1}$. Rank-biased precision assigns a score of zero to an empty ranking list, regardless of whether the query that led to the ranking has answers or not.

Effectiveness Metrics for Truncated Rankings Peñas and Rodrigo [4] note that in some question-answering (QA) scenarios, not responding is preferable to responding incorrectly, and propose a metric they denote c@1. Scores are based on having correct answers at the head of the ranked list, together with a component that is extrapolated for empty lists: $c@1 = n_{ac}/n + (n_{ac}/n) \cdot (n_u/n)$, where n_{ac} is the number of correctly answers across a set of n questions, and n_u is the number of unanswered questions. However, c@1 is only applicable in cases where each question has a single correct answer, such as reading comprehension tests.

Another option for adding nil-answer assessment to an evaluation is to treat questions for which there are no answers differently from the *has-answer* queries. This may be appropriate if the distribution for the two classes of questions is imbalanced and nil-answer questions account for a small fraction of queries; the evaluation can then be one of correct classification between the two classes, followed by a standard evaluation within the has-answer class. For example, in the TREC 2001 QA track, there are 49 nil-answer ques-

SIGIR '16, July 17–21, 2016, Pisa, Italy

ISBN 978-1-4503-4069-4/16/07...$15.00
DOI: http://dx.doi.org/10.1145/2911451.2914737

tions, out of 492 test questions. Similar statistics arise in the TREC 2002–2007 QA tracks. But note also that there are cases where nil-answer queries dominate. For example, in duplicate question detection for community question answering, the expectation is that most new questions will not have previously been asked.

Sakai [5] proposed that NIL be regarded as a valid answer list of length one with positive gain, and showed that under this interpretation the Q-Measure (and other recall-based approaches) can be used to evaluate nil-answer questions. A similar approach was also used in the 2001 TREC QA track [6], where systems were permitted to return NIL in their answer lists. Any NIL's that appeared were assigned a gain of $r_i = 1.0$ if and only if there were no "actual" answers to that query, and a gain of $r_i = 0$ otherwise. Systems were free to continue listing documents after the NIL, meaning that a simple hedging strategy is to prefix NIL to every returned list; another, to insert NIL part way through every answer list. We explore the implications of this approach in more detail in Section 3.

2. EVALUATING ARBITRARY RANKINGS

All Rankings Are Different We propose that a system always be viewed as returning a ranking of documents, and that the length of that ranking always be regarded as having been determined by the system in response to the query. We then require that the evaluation process employed should be applicable to all rankings, including those of zero length.

As a motivating example, consider the case of a query for which there are known to be $R = 3$ relevant answers. For this query the five-document ranking (reading r_i values from left to right, with "1" representing relevant, and "0" denoting non-relevant) "10100" is almost certainly superior to the ranking "01001", a relativity supported by all of RR, AP, NDCG, and RBP. Now consider the three-element ranking "101". It seems clear that "101" must be regarded as superior (or, at the very least, not inferior) to "10100", since it has the relevant documents in the same positions, and fewer non-relevant documents. Next, consider the ranking "011". Where does it fit in relation to the other three rankings? Most metrics would assess it as being inferior to "101" and better than "01001", but what about in comparison to "10100"? That is, is: "101" > "10100" > "011" > "01001" the preferred ordering from a user's point of view, where > is used as an abbreviation for numeric order, based on score? Or is: "101" > "011" > "10100" > "01001" the preferred relationship? And, what about the ranking "1" – is one correct answer and no non-relevant answers better, or worse, than the rankings shown, all of which contain two correct answers? Finally, do any of these relativities change if instead of $R = 3$ relevant documents, there are known to be $R = 5$, or $R = 10$?

In the proposed new framework, in which ranking length is also regarded as being a factor that affects the score, dealing with nil-answer queries becomes a natural extension. If a query has no answers, then we would expect the evaluation metric to tell us that "" > "0" > "00" > "000", and so on. Indeed, if a query has no answers, and a system returns a ranking containing no documents, would we not wish the score of that ranking to be 1.0, representing "fully correct system response, and cannot be improved on"?

Depth-Sensitive Evaluation To allow ranking length to influence assessed effectiveness, we modify every ranking to add a nominal *terminal document* at the first rank position after the last one supplied by the retrieval system. For example the ranking "011" is extended to make a new ranking "011t", where "t" represents the terminal document, and reflects that the system declined to provide an answer document in that or any subsequent position. Provided that a corresponding gain value r_t is also assumed, any weighted-precision effectiveness metric, such as RR, Precision@k, or RBP, can then be used to score the ranking.

The key to making this approach work is selecting a value for r_t, the gain value associated with the terminal document. In the 2001 TREC QA Track, and in the example presented by Sakai [5], $r_t = 1.0$ iff the question is a nil-answer one, and $r_t = 0.0$ if not. We propose a more gradual approach. Suppose that the total gain pool for the query is $R \geq 0$. Then at depth $d \geq 0$ in any given ranking the fraction of the available gain that has been accrued is given by $\sum_{i=1}^{d} r_i/R$. On this basis, we define:

$$r_t = \begin{cases} 1 & \text{if } R = 0 \\ \sum_{i=1}^{d} r_i/R & \text{if } R > 0\,. \end{cases} \quad (1)$$

To understand the implications of this definition, consider the metric RR, defined for binary gain values as the reciprocal of the first rank at which a relevant document appears. If a ranking of length d contains a relevant answer, then RR has the same value as it always does, since the terminal document at depth $d+1$ has no bearing. If a ranking of length d does not contain a relevant answer, and if $R > 0$, then $r_t = 0$ and hence the value of RR is zero, as it should be – the system failed to return an answer that exists. But if $R = 0$, then $r_t = 1$, and the value of RR is given by $1/(d+1)$. That is, an empty ranking will be given a score of 1.0 if there are no relevant documents in the collection; the ranking "0" will be given a score of 0.5 when $R = 0$, and so on. Overall, the adjusted RR$'$ computation that takes the terminal document into account smoothly adapts its score on nil-answer queries, as required; and has its previous behavior on has-answer queries.

In the case of RBP, r_t is used in a slightly different way. Since RBP computes an infinite weighted sum over a geometric sequence of weights, it is appropriate to presume an arbitrary number of answers past the dth one, all with gain r_t. That is, the finite truncated gain vector $\langle r_1, r_2, \cdots, r_d \rangle$ is treated as an infinite one, $\langle r_1, r_2, \cdots, r_d, r_t, r_t, r_t, \cdots \rangle$, and the RBP score computed as normal. This has the same effect as taking the RBP residual at depth d, which is given by p^d, and multiplying it by r_t. That is, we define the adjusted RBP as

$$\text{RBP}' = \text{RBP}'@d = (1-p) \cdot \sum_{i=1}^{d} r_i \cdot p^{i-1} + r_t \cdot p^d\,. \quad (2)$$

As a third example, consider NDCG. To adjust this metric to handle truncated lists, we add r_t as a $(d+1)$ th gain value, as for RR, and then use the usual scoring approach to depth $d+1$ rather than to depth d:

$$\text{NDCG}' = \text{NDCG}'@d = \frac{\text{DCG}@(d+1)\langle r_1, r_2, \cdots, r_d, r_t \rangle}{\text{DCG}_I@(d+1)}\,. \quad (3)$$

Note that this approach also means that d is no longer a parameter of the metric and is instead the length of the ranking supplied by the system; note also that the ideal $(d+1)$-element ranking used in the denominator includes an extra gain of 1.0 in the first zero-gain position only if there are fewer than $d+1$ full- or part-gain answers for the query. For example, if $R = 3$, and all gain values are binary, then the ranking "101" leads to $r_t = 2/3$, and is scored as:

$$\text{NDCG}' = \frac{1/\log 2 + 1/\log 4 + (2/3)/\log 5}{1/\log 2 + 1/\log 3 + 1/\log 4 + 1/\log 5} = 0.698\,,$$

where the final term in the denominator arises because in an ideal ranking of $d = 3$ documents, the corresponding ideal r_t value placed in the fourth position of the ranking would be 1.0.

Ranking	R	r_{t}	RR′	RBP′	NDCG′	AP′
"00"	$R=0$	1.000	0.333	0.250	0.500	0.333
"000"	$R=0$	1.000	0.250	0.125	0.431	0.250
"111"	$R=3$	1.000	1.000	1.000	1.000	1.000
"11"	$R=3$	0.667	1.000	0.917	0.922	0.648
"11100"	$R=3$	1.000	1.000	0.906	0.971	0.917
"101"	$R=3$	0.667	1.000	0.708	0.698	0.528
"1"	$R=3$	0.333	1.000	0.667	0.742	0.306
"10100"	$R=3$	0.667	1.000	0.646	0.678	0.491
"011"	$R=3$	0.667	0.500	0.458	0.554	0.403
"01001"	$R=3$	0.667	0.500	0.302	0.490	0.299

Table 1: Example truncated answer rankings and their modified scores, for two different queries, one with $R = 0$ and one with $R = 3$. The parameter $p = 0.5$ is assumed for the RBP computation. Within each group, the results are sorted by RBP′, which (by chance, for these examples) also corresponds to RR′-order.

Average precision (AP) is handled similarly, by defining $r_{d+1} = r_{\text{t}}$, and then scoring the resulting extended-by-one ranking:

$$\text{AP}' = \frac{1}{R+1} \sum_{i=1}^{d+1} r_i \frac{\sum_{j=1}^{i} r_j}{i} . \quad (4)$$

As is also the case with NDCG′, the reference ranking used by AP′ contains R instances of $r_i = 1$, followed by a nominal terminating document with a gain of 1.0, that is, $R + 1$ values in total.

Table 1 shows scores computed for a range of rankings using the modified versions of RR, RBP, NDCG, and AP. The different adjusted metrics place different emphases on the tradeoff between recall and precision. All of the metrics respect the strict pairwise orderings noted earlier, for example, that "101" $\geq$ "10100"; but they vary in their response to other relativities, such as the question as to whether "1" is better or worse than "101". Note how the different metrics place different emphases on the rankings, resulting in variations in their score orderings.

3. EXPERIMENTS AND RESULTS

Tasks and Test Collections To explore the ramifications of the proposed approach, we employ the runs submitted to the main task of the TREC 2001 QA track. Participants were invited to submit a ranked list of *[doc-id, answer-str]* pairs of length up to five for each question; and for questions deemed to have no answer, were permitted to return "NIL" rather than one of the pairs. Overall, 36 groups contributed a total of 67 submissions to the QA main task; 47 of them are available for download.[1] The question set consists of 492 queries, 49 of which are nil-answer queries. The 443 has-answer questions have on average 25.7 relevant answers each.

Interpretation of Truncation To evaluate the proposed approach, we transform each individual run using the rules shown in Table 2, so that we accurately capture any evidence of deliberate truncation. The first two rules, covering cases where fewer than five results are provided, or where an explicit "NIL" is provided, are evidence of system-initiated truncation, and are processed as such in our comparison; in the third case we cannot infer truncation, and those runs are retained intact and scored in the original manner by the unmodified metrics throughout our experimentation.

[1]http://trec.nist.gov/results/trec10/qa_main_input.html

a_{NIL}	n	modified run
i	≤ 5	$a_1, \cdots, a_{i-1}, \text{t}$
-1	< 5	$a_1, \cdots, a_n, \text{t}$
-1	$= 5$	$a_1, \cdots, a_5$

Table 2: Transformation of a run $\langle a_1, \cdots, a_{\text{NIL}}, \cdots, a_n \rangle$, where a_{NIL} is the rank of an explicit NIL document (either rank $i \in [1, n]$, or -1 indicating not present) to a new ranked list.

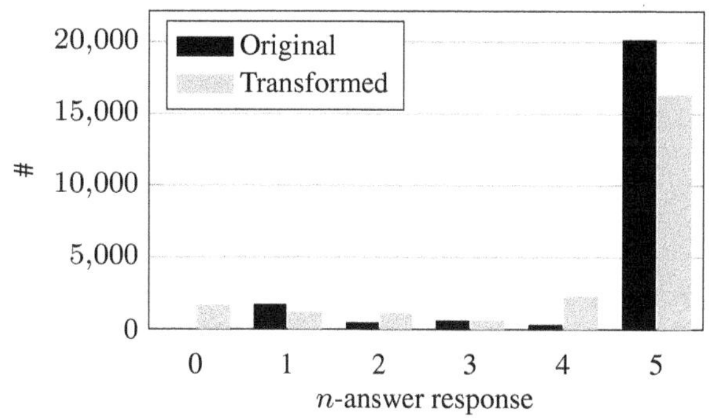

Figure 1: Distribution of lengths of 23,124 query responses.

Figure 1 shows the distribution before and after transformation of the 23,124 runs submitted for the 492 queries by the 47 participants. The number of five-answer lists is reduced from around 20k to 16k, generating a total of approximately 7k truncated answer lists post-transformation. The number of zero-answer lists is zero before the transformation, because even when a system believes a query is a nil-answer question, it must return a "NIL" to indicate so. This also accounts for the decline in the number of single-answer responses post-transformation.

Results and Analysis We first compare the TREC QA systems against each other using the TREC methodology (that is, with NIL in runs given a gain of 1.0 iff a query is nil-answer and otherwise given a gain of 0.0, and with metrics then applied in their standard form), and using our proposed modified approach applied to the transformed version of each run. Four different effectiveness metrics were explored, with the goal of determining the extent to which systems are affected by the proposed alteration in methodology. Each run for each system was scored using the two different approaches, and then system averages computed. In all of these evaluations, a *[doc-id, answer-str]* pair is considered correct iff the *answer-str* contains an answer to the question and is supported by the document specified by the *doc-id*.

Table 3 compares the system orderings generated by the four pairs of original/modified metrics using Kendall's τ, which computes a correlation coefficient between pairs of ordered lists over the same domain. Three evaluation metric pairs give rise to τ scores greater than 0.9, indicating strong agreement between the system ordering induced by the original metric and the system ordering generated by its modified version. The strong agreement between RR and RR′ was expected, because scores are primarily derived from just one relevant document, and because only a minority of the runs had explicit NIL markers. The similarly strong agreement between NDCG and NDCG′ was more surprising. At the other end of the scale, the pair AP/AP′ has the lowest τ among the four metrics, but they are still strongly correlated.

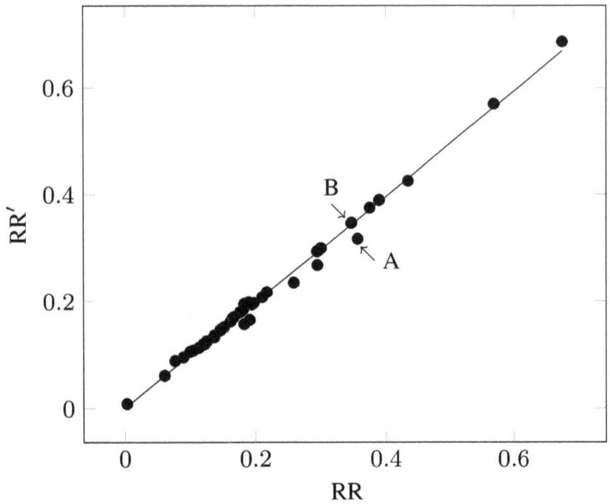

Figure 2: Relationship between RR and RR′ scores for 47 systems, with each system's score the mean over 492 queries.

Metric Pair	Kendall's τ
RR/RR′	0.960
NDCG/NDCG′	0.958
RBP@0.5/RBP′@0.5	0.916
AP/AP′	0.870

Table 3: Kendall's τ correlation coefficient calculated from the system orderings generated by pairs of original and modified metrics.

Figure 2 provides details of the relationship between the RR and RR′ scores for the set of systems. Overall, RR and RR′ are in high agreement in regard to both system ordering (Table 3) and in terms of the actual scores assigned. However, there are also inverted pairs, where a system is ranked higher by the original metric but has inferior score in the modified. For example, the system marked with "A" has a slightly higher score than does "B" for RR, but is ranked lower than "B" by RR′ because of "B"s aggressive (and effective) truncation strategy.

We also investigated the impact of truncation on performance of individual systems. The horizontal axis in Figure 3 (% truncation) is the fraction of answer lists of length less than five, including NIL, but excluding terminal documents. Both of the top two systems receive a boost in score when truncation is taken into consideration. In the $[0.15, 0.3]$ score range, despite the aggressive truncation, there are systems that obtain little improvement, in part due to their placement of a NIL at the end of every run. In addition, much of the truncation is a consequence of the system's inability to find a correct answer, rather than intentionally terminating the answer list. In such cases, even though there is explicit truncation, the system is not rewarded as there is no relevant document in the truncated answer list. Some systems sometimes prematurely truncate an answer list by placing a NIL before relevant documents. This causes the performance to drop when the modified metrics are employed. Two of the systems generated a NIL in the fifth position of all of their answer lists.

4. CONCLUSIONS AND FUTURE WORK

We have identified an opportunity to refine the way in which truncated rankings are evaluated, and at the same time deal seamlessly with a well-known shortcoming of recall-based evaluation metrics, namely, their inability to cope with queries with no relevant documents. By providing modified effectiveness approaches that provide subtle differentiation between runs of different lengths (for example, because "110" $<$ "11" in our mechanism, but not in previous approaches to the problem) we are better able to nuance system evaluations. The approach we employ – the appending of a terminal document to every ranking, to indicate the truncation point, and modifications to a range of standard evaluation metrics including RR, RBP, NDCG and AP – is both intuitive, and also easy to implement and apply. In retrieval experiments over a large QA dataset, containing a non-trivial fraction of nil-answer queries, we illustrated the effectiveness of the modified metrics, and demonstrated that a refined evaluation of truncated document rankings can help differentiate system orderings.

The obvious next step in our project is the development of methods for taking long document rankings and identifying, relative to the truncation-sensitive metrics, the point in each at which truncation is appropriate. One possible way of approaching this problem would be through analysis of the distribution of document scores in the ranking, in both relative and absolute terms. Query analysis could also be performed to predict the R value for a given query, for incorporation into the truncation process. We leave this exploration to future work.

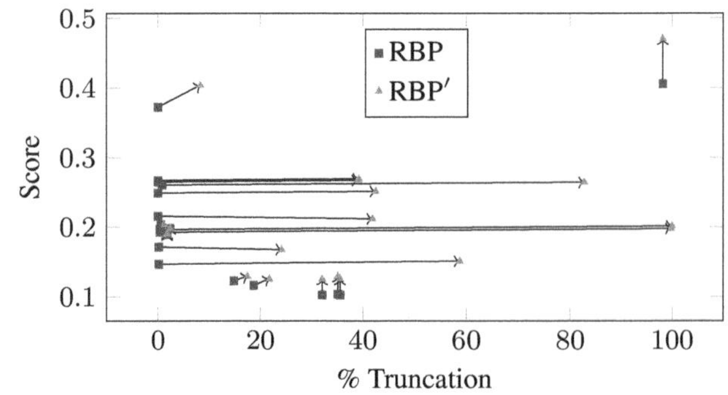

Figure 3: Impact of proposed methodology on effectiveness scores of the top 20 systems. Percentage truncation (horizontal axis) is the fraction of truncated answers (length of answer list < 5, excluding the terminal document), with the two points marking pre- and post transformation scores. The RBP parameter is 0.5 throughout.

Acknowledgments The authors thank MACE Engineering Group for their early support of this work. The third author was supported by ARC grant FT120100658.

References

[1] C. Buckley and E. M. Voorhees. Retrieval system evaluation. In E. M. Voorhees and D. K. Harman, editors, *TREC: Experiment and Evaluation in Information Retrieval*, chapter 3, pages 53–75. MIT Press, 2005.

[2] K. Järvelin and J. Kekäläinen. Cumulated gain-based evaluation of IR techniques. *ACM Trans. Inf. Sys.*, 20(4):422–446, 2002.

[3] A. Moffat and J. Zobel. Rank-biased precision for measurement of retrieval effectiveness. *ACM Trans. Inf. Sys.*, 27(1):2:1–2:27, 2008.

[4] A. Peñas and A. Rodrigo. A simple measure to assess non-response. In *Proc. ACL/HLT*, pages 1415–1424, 2011.

[5] T. Sakai. New performance metrics based on multigrade relevance: Their application to question answering. In *Proc. NTCIR*, 2004.

[6] E. M. Voorhees. Overview of the TREC 2001 question answering track. In *Proc. TREC*, pages 42–51, 2002.

Quote Recommendation in Dialogue using Deep Neural Network

Hanbit Lee*, Yeonchan Ahn*, Haejun Lee**, Seungdo Ha*, Sang-goo Lee*
*School of Computer Science and Engineering, Seoul National University, Seoul, Korea
**Artificial Intelligence Team, Samsung Electronics, Seoul, Korea
*{skcheon, acha21, seungtto, sglee}@europa.snu.ac.kr, **haejun82.lee@samsung.com

ABSTRACT

Quotes, or quotations, are well known phrases or sentences that we use for various purposes such as emphasis, elaboration, and humor. In this paper, we introduce a task of recommending quotes which are suitable for given dialogue context and we present a deep learning recommender system which combines recurrent neural network and convolutional neural network in order to learn semantic representation of each utterance and construct a sequence model for the dialog thread. We collected a large set of twitter dialogues with quote occurrences in order to evaluate proposed recommender system. Experimental results show that our approach outperforms not only the other state-of-the-art algorithms in quote recommendation task, but also other neural network based methods built for similar tasks.

Categories and Subject Descriptors

I.2.7.7 [**Artificial Intelligence**]: Natural Language Processing—*Text Analysis*

Keywords

Quote recommendation, Dialogue model, Deep neural network

1. INTRODUCTION

Quotes, or quotations, are well known phrases or sentences that we use in our writings and conversations for various purposes such as emphasis, elaboration, and humor. However, it is not always easy to promptly come up with an adequate quote that fits the situation at hand. We can try to find one on search engines, but it is also hard to figure out the right search keywords because in most cases the quotes are metaphorical so the words in those quotes do not always match the words expressing our intentions. A quote recommender can be quite useful in these situations.

Meanwhile, as we rely more and more on mobile devices in written communications including text messages, tweets, emails and blogs, convenience in text entry has become a very important feature for these devices. It is more so for wearable devices like Apple Watch and Samsung Galaxy Gear where the input/output spaces are constrained even further. An effective quote recommender, after monitoring an ongoing discourse, could recommend a few useful quotations from which the user can select instead of having to (laboriously) type in the entire sentence. Moreover, the system can be extended to recommend not only quotes but also other frequently-used responses as well.

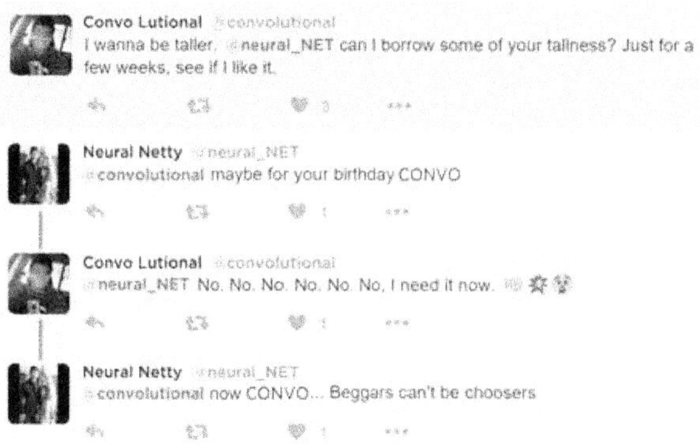

Figure 1: The example of tweet thread that includes the quote, "Beggars can't be choosers."

Quote recommendation for writing (composition) has been introduced in Tan, et al., [10]. In this paper, we extend the task to dialogs. Dialogs differ from plain composition in that they consist of sequences of utterances, each of which forms a semantic unit. Thus, it is important to construct a recommendation model that is capable of capturing such sequential structure of dialogs.

We propose a deep neural network based quote recommendation system, which combines recurrent neural network (*RNN*) and convolutional neural network (*ConvNetwork*) in order to learn semantic representation of each utterance and construct a sequence model for the dialog thread.

As a dialog database, we use twitter dialog threads (threads where only two users are exchanging tweets). A twitter thread, or tweet thread, is a sequence of linked tweets, composed of an initial tweet and subsequent reply tweets. Figure 1 shows an example of a tweet thread that contains the quote, "Beggars can't be choosers". We use a large set of such threads with quote occurrences as the training set for the recommendation task.

Experimental results show that our approach outperforms

SIGIR '16, July 17-21, 2016, Pisa, Italy

DOI: http://dx.doi.org/10.1145/2911451.2914734

not only the other state-of-the-art algorithms for quote recommendation task, but also other neural network based methods built for similar tasks.

2. RELATED WORK

Quote recommendation can be viewed as a task of searching quote that fits in the given query texts. Tan et al., 2015 [10] apply learning-to-rank framework using cosine similarity-based features between query and quote context to recommend ranked list of quotes relevant to query. He et al., 2010 [2] also exploit similarity features between candidate paper and current writing context. Huang et al., 2012 [4] proposes to use translation model to connect the context of writing and the cited paper. These approaches use the traditional bag-of-words model which have a clear drawback: the loss of semantics. The bag-of-words model performs especially worse when it comes to dialogues because utterances in dialogues are in short and irregular colloquial forms.

With recent success of distributional word representation which overcomes such drawback, there are several approaches trying to learn distributional representation of sentences or paragraphs. One of the most prominent and recently emerging method is convolutional neural network. [5] Convolutional network based approaches are resulting in state-of-the-art performance for the tasks like sentence classification [6] and relevant short text matching [9]. We also take advantages of convolutional network to learn intermediate representation of each tweet.

Our work is related to dialogue models which have been studied for the purpose of building automatic dialogue systems. [13, 1] Recently with the significant advances in training of neural network, deep neural networks based dialogue models are actively being proposed. Most of them take recurrent neural network based approaches to model the utterance sequence. [12, 8] Their purpose is to generate natural language sentences, but our task focuses on recommending a ranked list of quotes among candidate quotes.

3. OUR DEEP NEURAL NETWORK MODEL

In this section we describe our deep neural network model for quote recommendation. Our architecture is a combination of the convolutional neural network (*ConvNetwork*) and the recurrent neural network (*RNN*) as shown in Figure 2. *ConvNetwork* maps tweets in the thread to their distributional vectors. And then the sequence of tweet distributional vectors are fed to *RNN* so as to compute the relevance of target quotes to the given tweet dialogue. In the following, we briefly explain main components of our network.

3.1 Recurrent Neural Network for tweet sequence modeling

Since use of a quote in a dialogue highly depends on temporal history of previous utterances, it is important to model a dialogue as a sequence of utterances. Recurrent neural network is a neural network which is widely used in modeling sequence, because it effectively learns significant patterns of sequential data. So we exploit recurrent neural network to recommend quotes suitable for given context of dialogue.

3.1.1 Long short-term memory unit

We use long short-term memory unit (LSTM) [3] which is a recurrent neural network with several gates which allow networks to learn long-term dependencies without loss of information. LSTM retains latent vectors and updates those vectors by several gated functions with input vector for each time step. In our model we recurrently feed LSTM with distributional vector that represent each tweet in the tweet thread as shown in Figure 2. Formally, the input of LSTM is a tweet thread which is a sequence of tweet vectors: $[\mathbf{v}_1, \mathbf{v}_2, \ldots, \mathbf{v}_n]$ where n is length of the tweet thread.

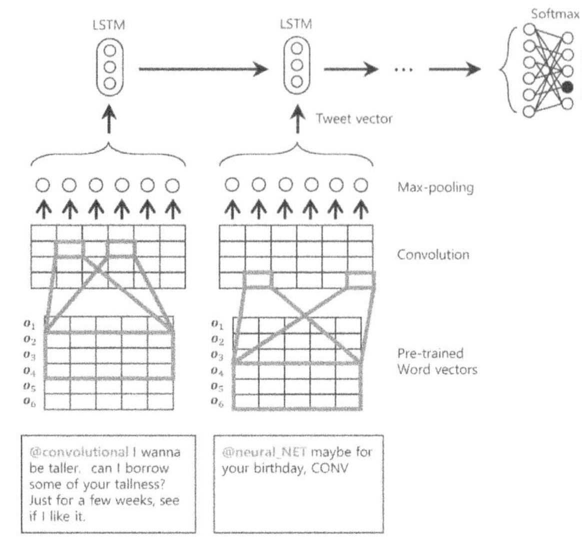

Figure 2: Overall architecture of our deep neural network model for quote recommendation

3.1.2 Softmax

The output of LSTM layer is passed to fully connected layer with softmax activation in order to compute the probability of candidate quotes to be recommended. It computes probability of recommending quote j as follows:

$$p(y = j|\boldsymbol{x}) = \frac{e^{\boldsymbol{x}\cdot\boldsymbol{w}_j}}{\sum_{k=1}^{K} e^{\boldsymbol{x}\cdot\boldsymbol{w}_k}}$$

where $\boldsymbol{x}$ is the output vector of LSTM, $\boldsymbol{w}_j$ is the weight vector of class j in fully-connected networks, and K is the number of class, in this case, the number of target quotes.

3.2 Convolutional Neural Networks for mapping tweets to intermediate vectors

We use convolutional neural networks to map tweets to their intermediate vectors. Convolution operation captures the significant local semantics, i.e., n-grams, of a tweet, so convolutional neural network can learn the optimal tweet representation for our quote recommendation task. Our *ConvNetwork* is composed of a single convolution layer and a max pooling layer.

3.2.1 Convolution

The input to *ConvNetwork* is a tweet matrix $\mathbf{t} \in \mathbb{R}^{d\times m}$ where m is the number of words in the tweet and d is the dimensionality of word vectors. i-th column of $\mathbf{t}$ is d-dimensional word vector $\mathbf{o}_i \in \mathbb{R}^d$ corresponding to the i-th word in the tweet. Convolution layer captures the local patterns in tweet by convolving a filter matrix of weights $\mathbf{w} \in \mathbb{R}^{d\times h}$ with the input tweet matrix $\mathbf{t} \in \mathbb{R}^{d\times m}$, where h is the filter width which is a hyper parameter. A feature map $\mathbf{c} \in \mathbb{R}^{m-h+1}$ is produced by convolution where each component is computed as follows:

$$c_i = f(\sum_{k,j} \mathbf{w} \circ \mathbf{t}_{[:,i:i+h-1]} + b_i)$$

where $\circ$ is element-wise multiplication, $\mathbf{t}_{[:,i:i+h-1]}$ is matrix slice of size h, b_i is the bias value, and f is non-linear activation function. Generally, more than one filter is applied to convolution layer to yield richer information, so we use multiple filters $\mathbf{w}^{(1)}, \mathbf{w}^{(2)}, \ldots, \mathbf{w}^{(p)}$ where p is another hyper parameter which indicates the number of filters. With multiple filters, we get multiple feature maps $\mathbf{c}^{(1)}, \mathbf{c}^{(2)}, \ldots, \mathbf{c}^{(p)}$.

3.2.2 Max-pooling

After obtaining feature maps, we apply max-pooling operation which take the maximum value $\hat{c}^{(i)}$ from each of feature map $\mathbf{c}^{(i)}$ and form a p-length feature vector:

$$\mathbf{v} =< \hat{c}^{(1)}, \hat{c}^{(2)}, \ldots, \hat{c}^{(p)} >$$

Eventually m tweet matrices in tweet thread are mapped to sequence of m tweet representation vectors.

$$[\mathbf{t}_1, \mathbf{t}_2, \ldots, \mathbf{t}_m] \xrightarrow{ConvNetwork} [\mathbf{v}_1, \mathbf{v}_2, \ldots, \mathbf{v}_m]$$

3.3 Training of the networks

We initialize the word vectors in our network with those trained from unsupervised neural language model and keep them static. It is a popular method to improve performance in case supervised training data is not sufficient. We use publicly available pre-trained word vectors, which were trained on 27 billion words of 2 billion tweets from Twitter. [7]

The entire networks are trained to minimize the cross-entropy of the predicted and true distributions. The objective function includes an L_2 regularization term over the parameters to prevent overfitting. RMSProp [11] is used to optimize stochastic gradient decent with a learning rate of 10^{-3} and a decay rate of 0.9. Dropout is adapted on max-pool layer in *ConvNetwork* and fully-connected layer in *RNN*. We set other hyper-parameters as follows: 3 for filter width (h), 500 for the number of feature maps (p), and dropout rate as 0.5. And we use ReLU activation function.

4. EXPERIMENTS

4.1 Data Construction

We collected the quotes to be recommended from two sources of quotes: one is the Wikiquote[1] website, and the other is Oxford Concise Dictionary of Proverbs[2]. For each quote, we collected tweet dialogues that contain at least one occurrence of the quote.

From each tweet dialogue thread, we only use the tweets up to the quote occurrence as *context*. For the tweet that contains the quote, only the part from the first word to the last word before the quote is used as *context*.

We started out with top 100 quotes in order of quantity of relevant tweet threads and then expanded to top 200, 300, and 400. Table 1 shows the statistics of datasets. q is total number of quotes, N is total number of tweet threads, t is average number of collected tweet threads per quote,

Table 1: Statistics of our dataset

Dataset	q	N	t	n	m
ALL	412	222,645	540.4	3.85	13.9
Top100	100	159,302	1593.0	3.94	13.4
Top200	200	202,920	1014.6	3.90	13.6
Top300	300	218,132	727.1	3.89	13.7
Top400	400	222,408	556.0	3.89	13.7

n is average number of tweets in a tweet thread, and m is average number of words in a tweet. We use 10% of dataset as validation set, another 10% as test set and rest of dataset as training set.

Originally there is only one gold quote for each query context in test data, but there are many cases in which more than one quote can be used. For example, the quote "Great minds think alike." can be substituted with the quote "Birds of a feather flock together." in the situation when two people share an idea. We sampled test queries from the top100 dataset and manually tagged the appropriate quotes that can be used in each query context. (*MultipleGold*)

4.2 Baselines and Evaluation Metrics

4.2.1 Baselines

We compare our approach with three state-of-the-art content based recommendation approaches [2, 4, 10]. Context-aware relevance model (CRM) recommends a quote based on similarity between the query and the contexts of the quote using bag-of-words representation. Citatioin translation model (CTM) applies a translation model to quote recommendation by using the probability that the query context would be translated into the quote. Learning-to-recommend quote (LRQ) is most recent approaches that use learning-to-rank framework with quote-based features, quote-context similarity features, and context similarity features. We also experiment with CNN and RNN separately to compare with our combined networks. Since these simple neural models cannot accept tweet sequence as input, so we concatenate all tweets in a tweet thread into one long context tweet and use it as the input for the particular thread.

4.2.2 Evaluation Metrics

MRR: Mean reciprocal rank (MRR) is the average score of inverse rank of the gold quote in recommendation list.

$$MRR = \frac{1}{|test|} \sum \frac{1}{rank(gold_quote)}$$

Recall@*k*: Since there is only one gold quote for each query in original test set, Recall@k is the number of cases that the gold quote is recommended in top-k result divided by total test cases.

NDCG@*k*: Normalized discounted cumulative gain (NDCG) is a widely used evaluation metric in various IR tasks. It takes into account the ranking position of gold quotes in recommendation list.

Hit@*k*: For MultipleGold test set, we use Hit@k which is the number of cases that any of gold quotes are recommended in top-k result divided by total test cases.

4.3 Results and Discussion

The comparison results of different methods for the top100 dataset are shown in table 2. As we can see, CRM and LRQ

[1]http://en.wikiquote.org

[2]Oxford University Press, 1998

Table 2: **Recommendation performance of different methods for top100 dataset**

Method	MRR	Recall@5	NDCG@5	Hit@5
CRM	0.207	0.279	0.198	0.470
CTM	0.274	0.359	0.269	0.579
LRQ	0.221	0.308	0.214	0.523
CNN	0.378	0.486	0.385	0.668
RNN	0.375	0.489	0.389	0.661
CNNRNN	**0.416**	**0.532**	**0.422**	**0.698**

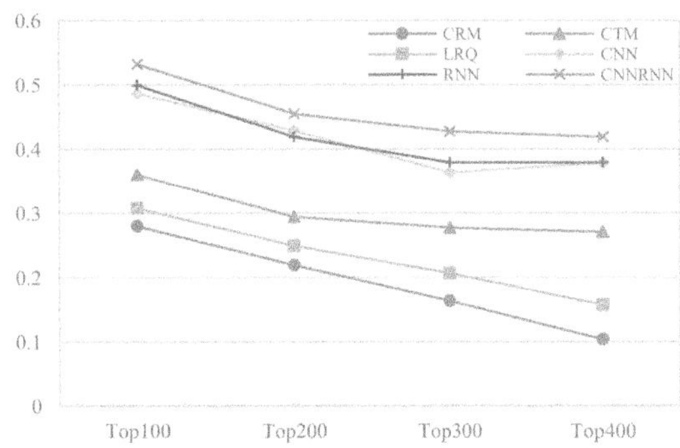

Figure 3: Results of recall@5 of different methods when increasing # of target quotes

which search for quotes based on similarity features between query and quote contexts, do not result in successful performance. That is because they cannot find out contexts which are semantically similar to the query but expressed in different words. CTM which use translation model performs slightly better. Deep neural network based approaches achieve higher scores than the non-neural methods, which shows that the distributed word representation helps semantic word matching and the deep neural network automatically extract meaningful representation of tweet context in respect to the quote recommendation. CNN captures significant local semantic features, i.e., n-grams, while RNN captures the overall ordering of words in context. Our approach outperforms both separate CNN and RNN models showing that per-tweet feature extraction captures structural context of dialogue while simple concatenation of tweets cannot. Figure 3 shows the results of recall@5 when increasing the number of target quotes. Although overall accuracy decreases as the number of target quotes increases, our approach consistently outperforms other methods.

Hit@5 evaluation of our model reaches almost 0.7 for top100 dataset which means that our recommendation system recommends at least one relevant quote in top 5 list in seven out of ten times. This proves that our recommendation model is practically useful. Figure 4 shows the example of recommendation results for a query context in the test set. As we can see, our system recommends quotes comforting the user named "convolution" and it is quite appropriate to the situation.

5. CONCLUSION

In this work, we present a task of quote recommendation in a dialogue. We propose a deep neural network model which efficiently extracts meaningful local semantic features from each tweet using convolutional network and learns each tweet features in sequence. We evaluate the proposed model

Query context	Results
@convolution Ahh! I'm so excited now looking forward to September! **@neural_NET** yay me too!!! I didn't think u would still be in Orlando in September!!! **@convolution** yea...things are taking longer than expected **@neural_NET** hey don't worry! [Quote]	1.**Slow and steady wins the race** 2.Business before pleasure 3.Patience is a virtue 4.**All good things must come to an end** 5.Better safe than sorry

Figure 4: An example results of quote recommendation

on real twitter dialogue data to show that our approach is effective for quote recommendation. In the future, we plan to investigate several useful dialogue features that may not be captured via neural networks.

6. ACKNOWLEDGEMENT

This paper was supported by Samsung Electronics.

7. REFERENCES

[1] M. Gasic, C. Breslin, M. Henderson, D. Kim, M. Szummer, B. Thomson, P. Tsiakoulis, and S. Young. On-line policy optimisation of bayesian spoken dialogue systems via human interaction. In *ICASSP*, 2013.

[2] Q. He, J. Pei, D. Kifer, P. Mitra, and C. L. Giles. Context-aware citation recommendation. In *WWW*, 2010.

[3] S. Hochreiter and J. Schmidhuber. Long short-term memory. *Neural Computation*, 9(8):1735–1780, 1997.

[4] W. Huang, S. Kataria, C. Caragea, P. Mitra, C. L. Giles, and L. Rokach. Recommending citations: Translating papers into references. In *CIKM*, 2012.

[5] N. Kalchbrenner, E. Grefenstette, and P. Blunsom. A convolutional neural network for modelling sentences. In *ACL*, 2014.

[6] Y. Kim. Convolutional neural networks for sentence classification. In *EMNLP*, 2014.

[7] J. Pennington, R. Socher, and C. D. Manning. Glove: Global vectors for word representation. In *EMNLP*, 2014.

[8] I. V. Serban, A. Sordoni, Y. Bengio, A. Courville, and J. Pineau. Building end-to-end dialogue systems using generative hierarchical neural network models. In *ICASSP*, 2013.

[9] A. Severyn and A. Moschitti. Learning to rank short text pairs with convolutional deep neural networks. In *SIGIR*, 2015.

[10] J. Tan, X. Wan, and J. Xiao. Learning to recommend quotes for writing. In *AAAI*, 2015.

[11] T. Tieleman and G. Hinton. Lecture 6.5 - rmsprop, coursera: Neural networks for machine learning. In *Technical report*, 2012.

[12] O. Vinyals and Q. V. Le. A neural conversational model. In *arXiv*, 2015.

[13] S. Young, M. Gasic, B. Thomson, and J. D. Williams. Pomdp-based statistical spoken dialog systems: A review. *IEEE*, 101(5):1160–1179, 2013.

Ranking Documents Through Stochastic Sampling on Bayesian Network-based Models: A Pilot Study

Xing Tan[1], Jimmy Xiangji Huang[1] and Aijun An[2]
Information Retrieval and Knowledge Management Research Lab
[1]School of Information Technology, [2]Department of Computer Science & Engineering
York University, Toronto, Canada
{xtan, jhuang}@yorku.ca, aan@cse.yorku.ca

ABSTRACT

Using approximate inference techniques, we investigate in this paper the applicability of Bayesian Networks to the problem of ranking a large set of documents. Topology of the network is a bipartite. Network parameters (conditional probability distributions) are determined through an adoption of the weighting scheme tf-idf. Rank of a document with respect to a given query is defined as the corresponding posterior probability, which is estimated through performing Rejection Sampling. Experimental results suggest that performance of the model is *at least* comparable to the baseline ones such as $BM25$. The framework of this model potentially offers new and novel ways in weighting documents. Integrating the model with other ranking algorithms, meanwhile, is expected to bring in performance improvement in document ranking.

Keywords

Info. Retrieval; Bayesian Networks; Stochastic Sampling

1. INTRODUCTION

Probabilistic Graphical Models [10] in the form of Bayesian Networks (BN) [6] are widely used to represent knowledge with uncertainties. In the recent years, computational technologies and tools for BN-based models are becoming increasingly powerful. That being the case, modeling problems in Information Retrieval (IR), in particular for document ranking, as probabilistic inference problems in BN-based models has achieved only limited success to date. Major reasons for such relatively small progress in BN-based approaches for document ranking are, for one, conceptually it is challenging to appropriately identify causalities in document ranking (i.e., deciding network topology) and then to accurately capture the uncertainties (i.e., deciding network parameters) in order to construct a BN model for IR; and two, computationally exact inference algorithms associated with the model is bound to be intractable as practically the size of the BN model in terms of nodes representing both the number of documents and vocabulary size in words, can be easily in a few millions.

SIGIR '16, July 17-21, 2016, Pisa, Italy

DOI: http://dx.doi.org/10.1145/2911451.2914750

In this paper, we investigate the applicability of BNs to the problem of ranking a large set of documents. We propose a model, which specifically takes into considerations both the appropriateness in the semantics of causalities, and the computational tractability of probabilistic inferences. Topology of the network is a bipartite. Conditional probability distributions are determined through adopting the weighting scheme tf-idf. Experimental results, obtained from working on both computer-generated and standard document sets suggest that performance of the model is *at least* comparable to the baseline ones such as $BM25$ ([2, 11]).

The remainder of this paper is organized as follows. Section 2 presents the background and preliminaries. Section 3 introduces the model. Experimental results are reported and analyzed in Section 4. Section 5 concludes the paper.

2. PRELIMINARIES

In this section, document ranking in IR, and BN, are briefly reviewed.

2.1 Document Ranking in IR

One of the fundamental tasks in IR is document-ranking: Given a set of documents $\mathcal{D}$ such that $\mathcal{D} = \{d_1, \ldots, d_M\}$ and $|\mathcal{D}| = M$, a set of terms $\mathcal{T} = \{t_1, \ldots, t_N\}$ and $|\mathcal{T}| = N$, and a collection of query terms $\vec{q}$ such that $\vec{q} \subset \mathcal{T}$, documents in $\mathcal{D}$ need to be ranked in a complete order according to their respective relevance to $\vec{q}$ (other criteria such as "diversity" might also be considered for ranking). To do this, a typical approach is to define a score function $score(\vec{q}, d_i)$ that returns a numeric score for each document $d_i \in \mathcal{D}$ with respect to $\vec{q}$. Documents can then be ranked on their scores in descending order. The top S elements will be selected to construct the set $\mathcal{S}$, where $|\mathcal{S}| = S$.

Let $tf_{t,d}$ denote *term frequency*, the number of occurrences of term t in document d; df_t denotes *document frequency*, the number of documents in $\mathcal{D}$ that contain the term t; and $idf_t = \log(M/df_t)$ denotes *inverse document frequency*. Summing up on $tf_{t,d} \times idf_t$ for each term $t \in \vec{q}$ with respect to d defines a baseline score function for document ranking: $score(\vec{q}, d) = \sum_{t \in \vec{q}}(tf_{t,d} \times idf_t)$. Definitions for variant score functions of tf-idf such as BM25, can be found in [11]. In addition, *collection frequency* in $\mathcal{D}$ and its subset $\mathcal{S}$, are defined as the total number of occurrences of t in $\mathcal{D}$ and in $\mathcal{S}$, and denoted by cf_t and sf_t, respectively.

2.2 Bayesian Networks

A Bayesian Network is a directed acyclic graph where nodes correspond to random variables [6]. Pairs of nodes in the graph might be connected by a directed edge. For example, given two nodes X and Y in the graph, if X enters Y, it is said that X is a parent of Y. Effect of the parents of a node X in the graph is quantified by a conditional probability distribution $P(X|Parents(X))$.

BNs are often used to carry out probabilistic inference: computing posterior distribution of a set of variables given a set of *evidence variables* – variables whose values are observed or assigned. Consider a simple example of *Baby World*, which consists of four random variables H, T, C, and R, corresponding to the variable facts that the baby is *Hungary*, *Tired*, *Crying*, and *scReaming*, respectively. A BN for this world is shown in Figure 1. After all four conditional probability distributions as listed in the figure are specified, we could compute, for example, the probability that the baby is hungry if we observe that it is crying but not screaming: $P(H \text{ is true} \mid C \text{ is true, and } R \text{ is false})$.

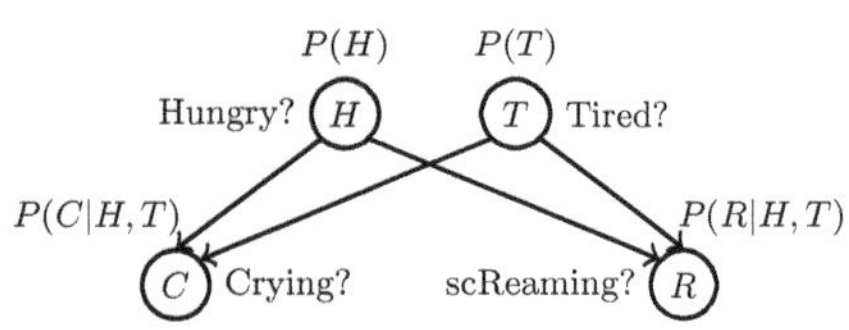

Figure 1: A Bayesian Network: *Baby World*.

3. MODEL

This section presents the model, explains how samplings are performed, and justifies the merits of our model.

3.1 Network Topology and Conditional Probabilities

Suppose a user specifies a set of terms as a query $\vec{q}$ for a set of documents $\mathcal{D}$, a subset $\mathcal{S} \subset \mathcal{D}$ of documents need to be retrieved and ranked in a complete order. To be explained in this section, we formulate this problem into the problems of calculating posterior probability values in a BN-based model where the original query is treated as the observed evidence.

In our model, the probability space is induced accordingly by two sets of random variables $\mathcal{D}$ (document random variables) and $\mathcal{T}$ (term random variables), where $D_i \in \mathcal{D}$ for $1 \leq i \leq M$, and $T_j \in \mathcal{T}$ for $1 \leq j \leq N$. Each document D_i takes two values: $Val(D_i) = \{d_i^1, d_i^0\}$, which represents the values of "D_i selected with respect to a query" (d_i^1) or not (d_i^0); Similarly, $Val(T_j) = \{t_j^1, t_j^0\}$, which represents the values of term "T_j is a query term" (t_j^1) or not (t_j^0). The BN, as shown in Figure 2, is a two-layer directed graph, which contains a node in the top layer for each document variable D_i and a node in the bottom layer for each term variable T_j. In the graph, an edge from D_i to T_j represents that term T_j appears in the document D_i. We assume no edges between document variables in $\mathcal{D}$, and no edges between term variables in $\mathcal{T}$. In addition to the graph, two types of

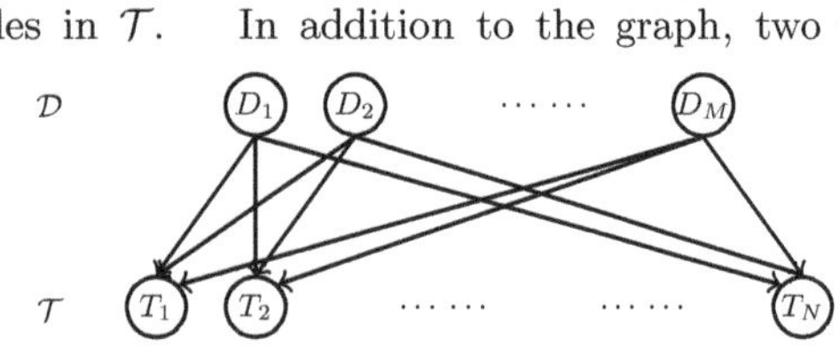

Figure 2: A BN graph for document ranking.

probabilities need to be specified to capture the nature of the dependence of variables: $P(D_i)$, the prior distribution over a document D_i, and $P(T_j|D1, \ldots, D_M)$, the conditional probability distribution of T_j given D_1, D_2, ..., and D_M. In our model, $P(D_i)$ represents the distribution that D_i is selected in $\mathcal{S}$ or not, hence it is reasonable to define, for any document D_i in $\mathcal{D}$, the probability that D_i is eventually selected into S equals the ratio of the size of $\mathcal{S}$ to the size of $\mathcal{D}$, i.e., $P(d_i^1) = S/M$.

The conditional distribution $P(T_j|D1, \ldots, D_M)$ specifies the distribution over the term T_j, which depends on the actual content of $\mathcal{S}$, the set of documents selected. That is to say, specifically, for each subset of $\mathcal{D}$ (totally 2^M of them), we need to specify a distribution for t_j^1, the event that t_j is actually a query term. Since the number of parents of a term in the network is not bounded by a constant, we know that exact inference here has exponential time complexity in worst cases. Nevertheless what we really need is to calculate, for any document variable D_i where $1 \leq i \leq M$, the relevance of D_i to evidence $\tilde{\mathbf{q}}$, i.e., the posterior probability of $P(d_i^1|\tilde{\mathbf{q}})$, the value of which can be estimated through stochastic sampling. For simplicity in explanation, we assume that $\tilde{\mathbf{q}}$ contains only one term $\mathbf{t}$, without loss of generality.

3.2 Estimating Posteriors Through Sampling

General reasoning problems of probabilistic inference in BNs, and even their corresponding approximate versions, are NP-hard ([4], [5]). Due to this computational intractability, one often turns to randomized sampling methods (e.g., Rejection Sampling [12], which is used in our current research) to approximate posterior probabilities. Asymptotically accuracy of these sampling methods would usually be improved as the number of samples increases.

Given a BN and its specified prior distributions for all n variables $\{X_1, X_2, \ldots, X_n\}$, where $X_i \in \mathcal{X}$ for $1 \leq i \leq n$, *forward sampling* samples all nodes in $\mathcal{X}$ in an order consistent with the topological structure of the BN, and the probability of a specific event, written as $(x_1, \ldots, x_n)$[1], generated from forward sampling equals to $\prod_{i=1}^{n} P(x_i|\ parents(X_i))$, which in turn equals to the joint distribution $P(x_1, \ldots, x_n)$. Suppose totally N samples are taken, and the number of occurrences of an event $(x_1, \ldots, x_n)$ equals to $N_{(x_1,\ldots,x_n)}$, then the ratio $N_{(x_1,\ldots,x_n)}/N$ is an approximation to $P(x_1, \ldots, x_n)$. With observation of evidence $\mathbf{e}$ for $\mathcal{E}$, where $\mathcal{E} \subset \mathcal{X}$, the conditional probability $P(X = x|\mathbf{e})$ can be further estimated through *Rejection*: first, all samples that do not match $\mathbf{e}$ are rejected in N, to obtain N_1; second, all samples in N_1 and compatible with $X = x$ are put into N_2; third, N_2/N_1 is an estimate to $P(X = x|\mathbf{e})$.

Consider our model again and suppose there are $\mathcal{P}$ samples where $|\mathcal{P}| = P$. During sampling, we dynamically maintain a vector of counters C, where $|C| = M$. All counters in C are initialized to zero. Our sampling strategy say for the jth sample P^j where $1 \leq j \leq P$: Step 1, each document variable is sampled according to the distribution S/M; Those selected document variables are put into $\mathcal{S}^j$, thus the expected value of $|\mathcal{S}^j|$ is S. Step 2, we accept this sample if and only if the collection frequency of $\mathcal{S}^j$ with respect to term t proportionally exceeds the one of $\mathcal{D}$. Formally, the sample is accepted iff $\frac{sf_t^j}{cf_t} > \frac{S}{M}$. If sample P^j is accepted and $D_i \in \mathcal{S}^j$, $c_i \in C$, which is the corresponding counter for D_i, would be increased by one.

After completion of sampling, the set $\mathcal{P}$ would be mutual-exclusively partitioned into two sets, the set of accepted samples $\mathcal{P}^{accepted}$, and the set of rejected ones $\mathcal{P}^{rejected}$. The vector C would be updated for $|\mathcal{P}^{accepted}|$ times. Values

[1]The term $(x_1, \ldots, x_n)$ is an abbreviation for $(X_1 = x_1, \ldots, X_n = x_n)$.

stored in the counters of C, are actually scores for their corresponding documents with respect to the query term t. The documents can thus be ranked according to their scores.

3.3 Justification of Methodology

In the literature, considerable research in investigating potential linkages between BNs and IR in general, has been reported (most notably [1], [7], [13], [14]). The originality and value of our research contribution lies in the following facts.

Model Semantics. The model defines $2^{(M+N)}$ different states, for different combinations of truth assignments to all random variables in $\mathcal{D} \cup \mathcal{T}$. A state specifies an instance of which random variables are true and which are false. For each state, its joint probability distribution theoretically can be calculated (although computationally it might be impractical). We are only interested in those states where statistically S out of D variables are true, since we only concern about the problem of selecting $\mathcal{S}$ out of $\mathcal{D}$ documents related to a given query.

Causality. In the model, document variables in $\mathcal{D}$ are designed, in consistence with common perceptions, to have direct causal influence on term in $\mathcal{T}$. For example, causal relation "$D_i \rightarrow T_j$" is interpreted as: If D_i is selected to be a member of $\mathcal{S}$ (i.e., $D_i \in \mathcal{S}$) then the term T_i should be of interest to the user.

Scalability. The size of the problem of document ranking in practise is often in the magnitude of a few millions, if not more. A network built-up from these problems is large in size and multiply connected, making it dauntingly challenging to perform exact probabilistic inference. Consequently, it can be seen from the literature that experiments in earlier work (e.g., [7] and [1]), are restricted to cases with maximal a few thousand documents only. The development of BNs however has reached the point where approximate inference algorithms, such as randomized sampling, loopy propagation, or variational approximation, can make a practical difference. We adopt a direct sampling method in this research.

Bipartite Network Structure. The underlying undirected graph of the network is a bipartite: nodes are grouped into two types, only connections between nodes from two different types are allowed. Recently, Bayesian models on bipartite graphs have found their ways to modeling real-world applications in social networks, with appealing properties demonstrated [3]. It remains to be investigated how these results can be utilized into our own framework of BN for IR. Nevertheless, due to this simplicity of topological structure, additional features (e.g., ontological/relational/logical representation and reasoning: see [8] for a mosaic of such proposals) can be incorporated into the current model.

4. EXPERIMENTAL RESULTS

In this section we compare the performance of our proposed model with the ones of *tf-idf*, *BM*25 and *Golden* (to be explained in Section 4.1). We first work on a set of computer-generated random documents ($\mathcal{D}_R^1$, $\mathcal{D}_R^2$, $\mathcal{D}_R^3$ and $\mathcal{D}_R^4$) and then on $\mathcal{D}_1$ and $\mathcal{D}_2$, which are two subsets of WT2G, a standard TREC test collection.

4.1 Documents Generation

To simplify matters, we assume that all generated documents in $\mathcal{D}_R$ are with same document length, which equals to the size of the vocabulary $\mathcal{T}_R$. For any document $D_r \in \mathcal{D}_R$, occurrences of terms in D_r follow a Normal Distribution $N(\mu, \sigma)$, where the values of mean μ and the standard deviation σ can be adjusted. However all documents in $\mathcal{D}_R$ share the same μ and σ. Note that the smaller the value of σ, the terms cluster more closely to μ. The center of a given document is shifted to a random center before being stored into a vector. To illustrate the idea, an example document with $\mu = 50$, $\sigma = 17$, $|\mathcal{D}_R| = 10000$, and $|\mathcal{T}_R| = 100$, and its variant with shifted center (now, $\mu = 18$) is respectively shown in the left subplot (and the right one) of Figure 3.

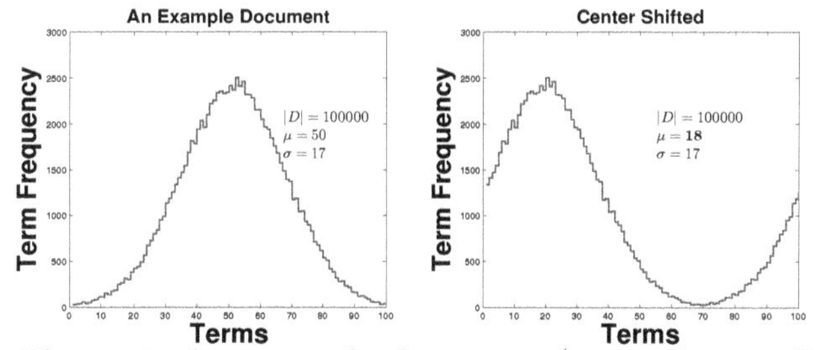

Figure 3: An example document (created according to a Normal Distribution with $\mu = 50$ and $\sigma = 17$), and its variant with the center shifted to 18 ($\mu = 18$).

Accordingly we introduce the baseline ranking method *Golden*. That is, given an input query q and a document d, the *score*(q, d) is defined as the difference between the center of d, and q. When the value of *score*(q, d) is smaller (greater), it means document d is more (less) related to the term q. *Golden* is used as one of the three methods for comparisons in Figure 4.

4.2 Experiments

We first work on four sets of randomly generated documents: $\mathcal{D}_R^1$, where $\sigma = 1250$, $\mathcal{D}_R^2$, $\sigma = 1000$, $\mathcal{D}_R^3$, $\sigma = 833$, $\mathcal{D}_R^4$, $\sigma = 416$. Between these sets from $\mathcal{D}_R^1$ up to $\mathcal{D}_R^4$, documents are more closely clustered around their means, thus intuitively more reliable in the sense of IR. Collection size, document length, and vocabulary size, are set to be all equal: $|\mathcal{D}_R| = |\mathcal{T}_R| = 10000$. Experiments related to a specific set is pictorially summarized in the corresponding sub-figure in Figure 4.

Consider Figure 4.a, for example, a term is queried against $\mathcal{D}_R^1$, three different ranking methods, i.e., Golden, BM25, and Rejection, return three different completely ordered sequences of 500 elements (the number 500 is obtained from $|\mathcal{D}_R| \times 0.05$, where 0.05 is the pre-specified ratio, i.e., portion of all documents in $\mathcal{D}_R^1$ need to be ranked). Results of pair-wise comparisons between these three methods are reported in Figure 4.a, where x-axis values indicate sample sizes and y-axis values indicate how many documents out of the 500 ranked ones are actually agreed between two given methods. For example, the red dot pointed by the arrow in Figure 4.a refers to the fact that totally 336 documents are shared by the 500 documents retrieved from applying BM25 on $\mathcal{D}_R^1$, and the 500 elements obtained from performing Rejection Sampling on $\mathcal{D}_R^1$ (with the sample size equaling to 0.1 Million).

Documents in both $\mathcal{D}_1$ and $\mathcal{D}_2$ (Figure 5) are drawn from dataset collection WT2G where $|\mathcal{D}_1| = |\mathcal{D}_2| = 2500$, $|\mathcal{T}_1| = 50961$ and $|\mathcal{T}_2| = 127487$. First 100 elements obtained from three different ranking methods, *tf-idf*, *BM*25, and *Rejection* are pair-wise compared in Figure 5.

4.3 Brief Discussion

This section draws the major observations from the present experimental study, and discusses some implications.

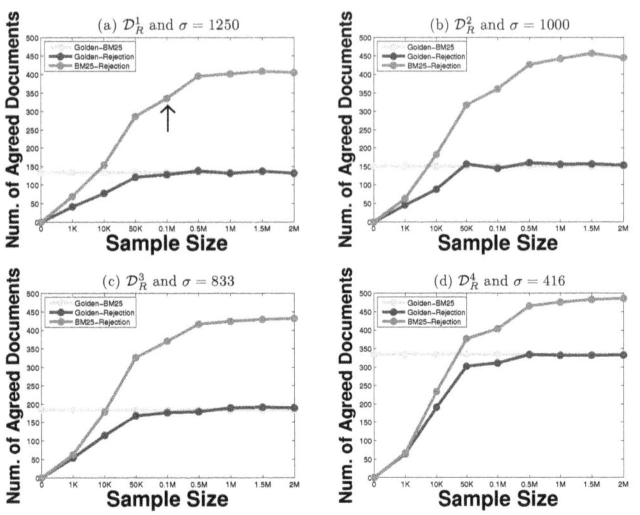

Figure 4: Pair-wise comparisons among the ranking methods Golden, BM25, and Rejection on data-sets with different standard deviations.

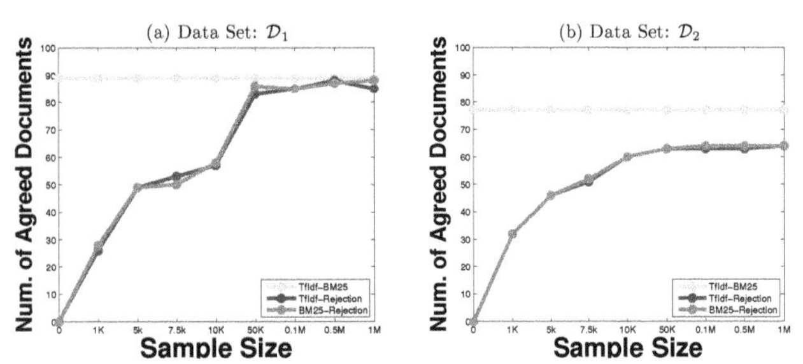

Figure 5: Pair-wise comparisons among the ranking methods tf-idf, BM25, and Rejection on two data-sets (2500 documents each) from WT2G.

For more closely clustered documents, in essence all methods agree more on their rankings (as shown in Figure 4, they agree most on the set $\mathcal{D}_R^4$, but least on $\mathcal{D}_R^1$); Following the same argument, we should claim that $\mathcal{D}_1$ is more clustered than $\mathcal{D}_2$.

In our experimental settings, increasing sample size initially improves the performance sharply, but it tends to be leveling off after sample size is greater than certain value (e.g., 0.5M in the subplots of Figure 4). As the sample size increases, asymptotically the *Rejection* method agrees at least 80% with BM25 for almost all sets except for $\mathcal{D}_2$ (around 60% only). It seems that we should conclude that the proposed BN-based model can achieve competitive performance levels at relatively low cost in sampling.

Since in *Rejection*, estimating posterior probabilities are based on the *tf-idf* ranking scheme, *Rejection* is a stochastic variant to the *tf-idf* ranking method. $BM25$, meanwhile, can be deemed as a refinement to *tf-idf*. Hence, it is not a surprise that $BM25$ agrees largely with *Rejection*. The more intriguing observation is that, with standard data-sets, the two methods disagree at least on 20% of their rankings. The reason as we speculate is either *Rejection* behaves somewhat differently from $BM25$ in practise, or sampling with the current settings can get trapped and do not converge. In order to unravel this intricacy, a further investigation is necessary and desirable.

5. SUMMARY & FUTURE WORK

In this paper, document ranking in IR is transformed into the problems of estimating posterior probabilities through stochastic sampling on a BN designed for IR. Experimental results from this pilot study is quite encouraging in the sense that, with moderate sampling efforts, the model demonstrates its ranking capability comparable to $BM25$. Additionally, graph-based structure and probability-based parameters of the model, together with other considerations in the model, suggest that new and novel weighing schemes for document ranking are conjecturally within a reach.

Among many possible avenues, our direct future research includes 1) further evaluating performance of the model on WT2G, WT10G, and other standard dataset collections; 2) testing on parametric settings other than the current one that is based on term-frequency; 3) testing other sampling strategies (e.g., Gibbs Sampling [10], and the most recent ones [9]) to improve sampling efficiency and performance.

Feedback to this work we have received encourages us to investigate in a broader context the relationships between the proposed BN model and other term weighting models ([15, 16]). With ease, most existing probability theory-based models in IR can actually be derived in this BN-based framework. It is thus rather promising to exploit this framework for a deeper understanding of existing term weighting models, and for the developments of new and better models in Information Retrieval.

6. ACKNOWLEDGEMENTS

We gratefully acknowledge the anonymous reviewers for their insightful comments and suggestions. This research is supported by a Discovery grant from the Natural Sciences and Engineering Research Council of Canada (NSERC), an NSERC CREATE award in ADERSIM[2] and an ORF-RE (Ontario Research Fund - Research Excellence) award in BRAIN Alliance[3].

7. REFERENCES

[1] S. Acid, L. M. de Campos, J. M. Fernández-Luna, and J. F. Huete. An information retrieval model based on simple Bayesian networks. *Int. J. Intell. Syst.*, 18(2):251–265, 2003.

[2] M. Beaulieu, M. Gatford, X. Huang, S. Robertson, S. Walker, and P. Williams. Okapi at TREC-5. In *Proc. of TREC*, pages 143–166, 1996.

[3] F. Caron. Bayesian nonparametric models for bipartite graphs. In *Advances in Neural Information Processing Systems 25*, pages 2051–2059. Curran Associates, Inc., 2012.

[4] G. F. Cooper. The computational complexity of probabilistic inference using Bayesian belief networks. *Artificial Intelligence*, 42(2):393 – 405, 1990.

[5] P. Dagum and M. Luby. Approximating probabilistic inference in Bayesian belief networks is NP-hard. *Artificial Intelligence*, 60(1):141 – 153, 1993.

[6] P. A. Darwiche. *Modeling and Reasoning with Bayesian Networks*. Cambridge University Press, New York, NY, USA, 1st edition, 2009.

[7] R. Fung and B. Del Favero. Applying Bayesian networks to information retrieval. *Commun. ACM*, 38(3):42–ff., Mar. 1995.

[8] L. Getoor and B. Taskar. *Introduction to Statistical Relational Learning (Adaptive Computation and Machine Learning)*. The MIT Press, 2007.

[9] K. Kandasamy, J. G. Schneider, and B. Póczos. Bayesian active learning for posterior estimation - IJCAI-15 distinguished paper. In *Proc. of the 24th IJCAI*, pages 3605–3611, 2015.

[10] D. Koller and N. Friedman. *Probabilistic Graphical Models: Principles and Techniques - Adaptive Computation and Machine Learning*. The MIT Press, 2009.

[11] C. D. Manning, P. Raghavan, and H. Schütze. *Introduction to Information Retrieval*. Cambridge University Press, New York, NY, USA, 2008.

[12] S. Russell and P. Norvig. *Artificial Intelligence: A Modern Approach*. Prentice Hall Press, Upper Saddle River, NJ, USA, 3rd edition, 2009.

[13] H. Turtle and W. B. Croft. Inference networks for document retrieval. In *Proc. of the 13th ACM SIGIR*, pages 1–24, New York, NY, USA, 1990.

[14] H. Turtle and W. B. Croft. Evaluation of an inference network-based retrieval model. *ACM Trans. Inf. Syst.*, 9(3):187–222, July 1991.

[15] J. Zhao, J. X. Huang, and B. He. CRTER: Using Cross Terms to Enhance Probabilistic IR. In *Proc. of the 34th ACM SIGIR*, pages 155–164, 2011.

[16] J. Zhao, J. X. Huang, and Z. Ye. Modeling Term Associations for Probabilistic Information Retrieval. *ACM Trans. Inf. Syst.*, 32(2):1–47, 2014.

[2] `http://www.yorku.ca/adersim`

[3] `http://brainalliance.ca`

Ranking Health Web Pages with Relevance and Understandability

Joao Palotti
Vienna University of Technology, Austria
palotti@ifs.tuwien.ac.at

Lorraine Goeuriot
Université Grenoble Alpes, France
lorraine.goeuriot@imag.fr

Guido Zuccon
Queensland University of Technology, Australia
g.zuccon@qut.edu.au

Allan Hanbury
Vienna University of Technology, Austria
hanbury@ifs.tuwien.ac.at

ABSTRACT

We propose a method that integrates relevance and understandability to rank health web documents. We use a learning to rank approach with standard retrieval features to determine topical relevance and additional features based on readability measures and medical lexical aspects to determine understandability. Our experiments measured the effectiveness of the learning to rank approach integrating understandability on a consumer health benchmark. The findings suggest that this approach promotes documents that are at the same time topically relevant and understandable.

1. INTRODUCTION

An increasing number of people rely on online health information to understand and manage their health; this information is commonly accessed through search engines [4]. The retrieval of incorrect or unclear health information poses potential risks as people may dismiss serious symptoms, use inappropriate treatments or unfoundedly escalate their health concerns about common symptomatology [1, 10]. However, an extensive number of studies has shown that the average user experiences difficulty in understanding the content of a large portion of the results retrieved by current search engine technology, e.g., see [11].

In the context of consumer health information seeking, search engines should not only retrieve relevant information, but they should also promote information that is understandable by the user and that is reliable and verified [10]. This paper tackles one aspect of this problem by investigating the effectiveness of a learning to rank approach aimed at retrieving documents that are at the same time topically relevant and understandable by the user. Specifically, we employ a range of standard *retrieval features* to capture information about relevance, and exploit a number of *readability features* comprising of readability measures and medical lexical aspects to determine document understandability.

Through experiments on a consumer health search collection, we show that our approach improves health search results, demonstrating that the combination of retrieval features and readability features within a learning to rank approach best promotes search results that are relevant and understandable for the user.

SIGIR '16, July 17 - 21, 2016, Pisa, Italy

ISBN 978-1-4503-4069-4/16/07...$15.00

DOI: http://dx.doi.org/10.1145/2911451.2914741

2. RELATED WORK

Our work tackles the problem of retrieving health information in answer to queries issued by laypeople. This problem has been largely investigated in the context of the CLEF eHealth Evaluation Lab[1], from which we take the data to evaluate the proposed approach. Specifically, the 2015 task provides a test collection to evaluate the effectiveness of search engines in answering self-diagnosing queries [6]. The evaluation framework explicitly accounts for both the topical relevance of the search results and their understandability, interpreted as how easy it is for a layperson to understand the content of a specific search result. This is done using understandability-biased evaluation measures, where gains obtained from relevant information are weighted by how hard it is for a layperson to understand that information [15, 16]. In this paper we use the CLEF eHealth 2015 test collection along with the explicit understandability assessments distributed and the understandability-biased RBP measure (see [6, 15, 16]). In addition, we further expand the understandability-biased evaluation framework by modifying the Bpref measure in the same spirit of understandability-biased RBP (see Section 4.4).

Our approach exploits a number of readability measures as features for the learning to rank approach. The measures we employ are based on surface-level characteristics of text, such as characters, syllables and word counts [3]. For example, the Dale-Chall readability formula is based on a corpus of words that can be understood by fourth-grade students; the Flesch-Kincaid measure instead computes a readability score based on a weighted combination of the number of words and the number of syllables in a sentence. The Gunning-Fog index combines the intuitions of these two approaches using sentence length and frequency of "complex" words. Previous work that has explored the under-

[1] http://sites.google.com/site/clefehealth/

standability of the health content retrieved by search engines extensively relied on these measures (along with other surface-level measures we also use to compute readability features) [12]. Readability measures specific to the health domain have been proposed, e.g. [13]. These however rely on the mapping of the text content of documents to health terminologies and the assessment of readability based on hierarchy and relationships encoded in it: a computationally intensive and error prone process. We defer the use of these techniques to compute readability features in the context of learning to rank to future work. We do however use clinical terminologies (Mesh, ICD) and dictionaries (Drugbank, CHV) to compute readability by testing whether a word is present in such resources.

We are not the first to explore the use of readability features to improve search engine results. Collins-Thompson et al. have shown the benefits of personalising search results to the reading levels of individual users [2]. Similarly, Tan et al. have modelled both the comprehensibility of texts and the users reading proficiency to improve content ranking [9]. The understandability issue is crucial in consumer health search, and the application of readability measures has not been well explored yet. Zuccon et al. have encoded readability measures as language modelling priors but have found no improvements in search results [17]. In this paper, we investigate the application of new approaches to effectively include understandability in consumer health search.

3. FEATURES FOR LEARNING TO RANK

In this work we study the effectiveness of a learning to rank approach that exploits retrieval features and readability features. The hypothesis is that the combined use of these feature sets not only improves results in terms of topical relevance, but promotes search engine results that are more understandable by the general public. Here, readability measures (and other features) are used as a proxy for document understandability. To validate this hypothesis, we investigated a number of retrieval and readability features, which we then alternated and combined to verify the contribution of each feature type to the improvement of search engine results.

The features used in our investigation are summarised in Table 1. As retrieval features, we used the matching scores provided by a number of common retrieval models, along with query independent features and document score modifiers. To compute these features, we indexed two fields: the document titles only; and the entire document bodies.

As readability features, we used a large number of existing readability measures, as well as lexical and morphological measures. Readability features fall into four main categories:

Traditional formulas: these are the existing well known readability formulas for general text. A thorough description of these formulas can be found in [3].

Surface measures: these are basic syntactic and lexical features, based on document statistics. Examples of this type of feature are the number of characters, syllables, words, and sentences present in a document. This category also includes the word length distribution in documents, e.g., #(|Word|>6) is the number of words in a document with more than 6 characters.

General vocabulary related measures: these are common lexical features used to assess text difficulty, e.g. proportion of numbers, stopwords, and common words in documents.

Medical vocabulary related measures: these are lexical and morphological features specifically adapted to the scientific domain, such as acronyms, or greco-latin affixes; or adapted to the medical domain, such as the number of terms present in lexicons such as Drugbank, Mesh or the ICD. We also compute the number of terms from the Consumer Health Vocabulary (CHV) contained in documents, as well as the sum of the terms' difficulty scores from CHV and the document mean score.

For features in the last three categories, we computed their raw values, as well as their average values per sentence and per word, i.e., we divided the value of the feature by the number of words and sentences in the document.

<table>
<tr><th>Feature Type</th><th>Feature Category</th><th>Feature Name</th></tr>
<tr><td rowspan="3">IR Features (18)</td><td>Common IR Models (14)</td><td>BM25 $\star$
PL2 $\star$
DirichletLM $\star$
LemurTF_IDF $\star$
TF_IDF $\star$
DFRee $\star$
Hiemstra_LM $\star$</td></tr>
<tr><td>Query Independ. (2)</td><td>Document Length $\star$</td></tr>
<tr><td>Doc. Score Modifier (2)</td><td>Divergence from Randomness
Markov Random Field</td></tr>
<tr><td rowspan="4">Readability Features (72)</td><td>Traditional Formulas (8)</td><td>ARI Index
Coleman Liau Index
Dale-Chall Score
Flesch Kincaid Grade
Flesch Reading Ease
Gunning Fog Index
LIX Index
SMOG Index</td></tr>
<tr><td>Surface Measures (25)</td><td># Characters $^{\diamond\dagger}$
Sentences $^{\diamond}$
Syllables $^{\diamond\dagger}$
Words †
(| Syllables(Word) | > 3) $^{\diamond\dagger}$
(| Word | > 4) $^{\diamond\dagger}$
(| Word | > 6) $^{\diamond\dagger}$
(| Word | > 10) $^{\diamond\dagger}$
(| Word | > 13) $^{\diamond\dagger}$</td></tr>
<tr><td>General Vocabulary Related Features (12)</td><td>Numbers $^{\diamond\dagger}$
English Dictionary $^{\diamond\dagger}$
Dale-Chall List $^{\diamond\dagger}$
stopwords $^{\diamond\dagger}$</td></tr>
<tr><td>Medical Vocabulary Related Features (27)</td><td>Acronyms $^{\diamond\dagger}$
Mesh $^{\diamond\dagger}$
DrugBank $^{\diamond\dagger}$
ICD10 (International classification of Diseases) $^{\diamond\dagger}$
Medical Prefixes $^{\diamond\dagger}$
Medical Suffixes $^{\diamond\dagger}$
Consumer Health Vocabulary $^{\diamond\dagger}$
Sum(chv Score) $^{\diamond\dagger}$
Mean(chv Score) $^{\diamond\dagger}$</td></tr>
</table>

Table 1: Features used in the learning to rank process; the number of features for each group is reported in parenthesis. $\star$: scores from both titles and document bodies are used (thus doubling the number of features). $\diamond$: raw feature values and values normalised by number of words in a documents are used. $\dagger$: raw feature values and values normalised by number of sentences in a document are used.

4. EXPERIMENTS AND ANALYSIS

4.1 Dataset

To investigate methods that provide users with search results that are both topical and understandable in answer to health queries, we use the CLEF 2015 eHealth Evaluation Lab collection [6]. This collection contains approximately 1 million web pages and 66 queries from people seeking self-diagnosing information. A key aspect of this collection is that it contains explicit graded assessments of both the topical relevance of documents to queries and the understandability of documents, which indicates whether a document

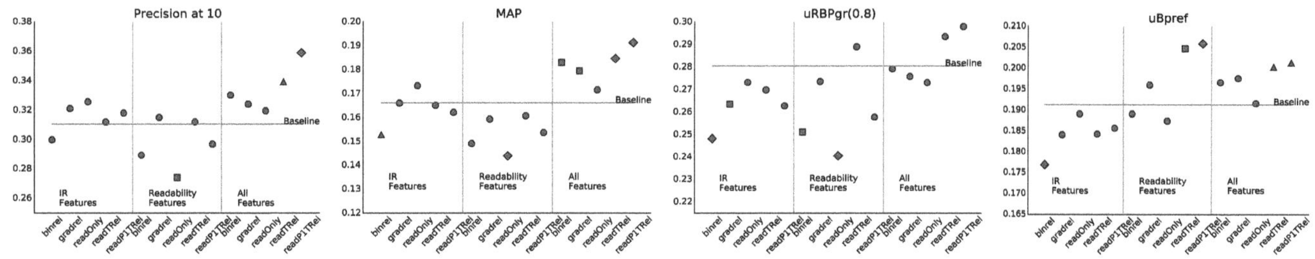

Figure 1: Comparison of different combinations of feature sets and relevance functions (x-axis). The score of the baseline system (BM25) for each metric is shown using the horizontal line. Diamond (square/triangle) markers are for experiments when $p < 0.05$ ($p < 0.1$ / $p < 0.15$) for a paired t-test w.r.t the baseline system.

is hard to read (label 0), somewhat hard to read (1), somewhat easy to read (2), and easy to read (3). Almost 70% of the documents are judged as easy or somewhat easy to read, and just 2% are both highly relevant and easy to read.

4.2 Experiment Settings

We used the learning to rank framework provided in Terrier 4.0 with Jforest and LambdaMART [5]. To extract readability features, we preprocessed the documents using *boilerplate* following the methods by Palotti et al. [7]. To learn and evaluate the learning to rank models, we used a leave-one-out approach where we train models using 60 topics, validate them using 5 topics to optimise the number of iterations and finally test with the learned model using a single topic; this process is repeated to test on all 66 topics. We set nDCG as the metric to optimize as it considers different grades of relevance, and we explored five functions $f(d)$ for the relevance label assigned to each document d in the training and validation steps (listed in Table 2). *ReadTRel* is the direct product combination of topical relevance and understandability, which would assign label 0 (i.e., not relevant) to documents that have understandability of 0 (i.e., very hard to read). As this renders irrelevant those relevant documents with an understandability score of 0, we designed the function *readP1TRel* in which the relevance of very hard to understand documents has a not null contribution to the score of the documents.

4.3 Retrieval evaluation

We first tested retrieval and readability features[2] separately; we then evaluated the effectiveness of their combination. The two left-most plots of Figure 1 report the values of P@10 and MAP obtained by the learning to rank approaches. A baseline system based on BM25 with parameters set to their default values in Terrier is also shown as a horizontal line. Note that P@10 was the primary measure used in CLEF 2015. As would be expected, the results show that retrieval features contributed more than readability ones to increase the relevance of document ranking. However, the best P@10 and MAP were obtained when both feature types were combined, suggesting that (1) learning to rank using both feature types improves the general result ranking, and (2) readability features improve relevance-based ranking.

[2]In these experiments, we included in the readability features also the raw retrieval score of the baseline (BM25), but not all other retrieval features.

Function Name	Description
binrel	binary relevance only
gradrel	graded relevance only
readOnly	graded readability only
readTRel	graded readability × graded relevance
readP1TRel	(graded readability + 1) × graded relevance

Table 2: The five variants used for document labels for the learning to rank approach.

4.4 Understandability-biased evaluation

In this section, we study effectiveness according to the understandability-biased evaluation. Figure 1 reports the value of uRBPgr, a graded version of RBP where the gain of a document is a joint function of the relevance label and the understandability label [15, 16]. The persistency parameter of RBP (ρ) was set to 0.8 (as in previous work [15, 16]). The results show that retrieval features alone did not improve uRBPgr; neither did the readability features alone. Their combination however improved uRBPgr, but not consistently across different label functions.

Further analysis of the results revealed that rankings obtained by the learning to rank models trained with readability only features contained many unassessed documents (on average only $\sim$ 79% of top 10 documents were assessed); while most of the documents obtained with retrieval features only or combination were assessed ones ($\sim$ 94% of the top 10 documents were assessed). Thus, results for readability only features may be affected by the lower coverage of the assessments. To overcome this limitation, we adopted a version of Bpref modified in the spirit of the understandability-biased evaluation framework (uBpref). Bpref considers only documents that have been explicitly assessed with respect to their relevance. uBpref also considers only assessed documents (for relevance and for readability); the (binary) gain from the relevance status of an assessed document (0: irrelevant, 1: relevant) is multiplied by the graded gain from the understandability assessment (with weights as in uRBPgr).

Figure 1 reports the results evaluated with uBpref. The results suggest that the effectiveness of learning to rank with readability only features was underestimated because of the many unassessed documents. Readability only features, in fact, led to increased uBpref over the baseline; often higher than the combination. While using all features did not lead to the highest uBpref, they provided consistent gains over the baseline across different label functions.

4.5 Feature analysis

We performed a feature ablation study to analyse the impact of features on the effectiveness of systems. We experimented with the best two models from our previous experiment (Figure 1), using all features (combining retrieval and readability features) and using as document labels the prod-

Funct.	System	P@10	uRBPgr	uBPref
-	**Baseline**	0.3106	0.2805	0.1913
readTRel	**All Features**	0.3394 △	0.2935	0.2003 △
	All - Formulas	0.3409 ◇	0.2915	0.1970
	All - Surface	**0.3606** ◇	**0.2999**	**0.2009** △
	All - General Voc.	0.3348	0.2948	0.1974
	All - Medical Voc.	0.3379 △	0.2879	0.1983
readP1TRel	**All Features**	**0.3591** ◇	**0.2980**	**0.2013** △
	All - Formulas	0.3258	0.2820	0.1951
	All - Surface	0.3485 ◇	0.2797	0.1951
	All - General Voc.	0.3439 □	0.2773	0.1916
	All - Medical Voc.	0.3303	0.2899	0.1994

Table 3: Feature ablation study based on the two best methods in Figure 1. The best results are in bold. Diamonds, squares, triangles markers indicate statistical significance (paired t-test w.r.t. baseline) with $p < 0.05$, $p < 0.1$, $p < 0.15$, respectively.

System	BPREF	τ_{AP}
BM25 w.o. learning	0.4432	0.4628
Readability	0.4682	0.4994
ReadTRel	0.4451	0.4459
ReadP1TRel	0.4443	0.4483

Table 4: Effectiveness comparison of different system variations with respect to the rank obtained using understandability assessments.

uct of topical relevance and readability scores (*readTRel* and *readP1TRel*). At each ablation step, we removed a feature group from the readability features, and then learned and evaluated a new model. Retrieval results are shown in Table 3. When document labels were assigned using *readTRel* as a function, the removal of some feature groups improved results over the model that used all features. For example, removing surface features improved the results of P@10 from 0.3394 to 0.3606.

4.6 Is Understandability Learnt?

We analysed whether learning to rank did learn to prefer more understandable documents. We trained a model using only readability features, not including the raw retrieval score of the baseline, and experimented with a different function for document labels. We report Bpref for each system variation with respect to understandability assessments only, as we are only interested to know if the assessed documents were correctly ranked. Additionally, we compared the ranking generated by each system with the perfect order of documents according to their understandability; for that, we used τ_{AP} [14], as it is based on average precision and assigns more weight to differences in the top rankings[3].

The learning to rank model learned how to better rank documents according to understandability when it was exclusively trained with functions based on understandability labels (see Table 4, second row). In this case, baseline effectiveness was improved by 5% for Bpref (where understandability assessments are used in place of relevance ones) and 7% for τ_{AP}. On the other hand, when the model was trained combining readability and retrieval features, document understandability did not appear to be learnt.

5. CONCLUSIONS

We describe a method that integrates understandability in the ranking of search results for consumer health search. This method is based on a learning to rank approach that combines features capturing topical relevance and features measuring the readability of health documents. We found that the combination of retrieval features and readability features indeed did improve search engine results, both for relevance and understandability retrieval measures. The provision of documents that are both relevant and understandable in answer to health related queries is an important requirement for next generation search engines [8]. Source code, all data analysed in this paper, and results (including other baseline models and evaluation measures) are available online at http://github.com/ielab/sigir2016-ranking-relevance-understandability.

As future work, we want to perform a wider feature analysis and evaluation. The results in Section 4.5, in fact, indicate that feature selection may improve system effectiveness.

[3]Usually τ_{AP} is used to compare systems rankings; here we used it to compare documents rankings.

Acknowledgement

JP and AH were supported by Horizon 2020 program (H2020-ICT-2014-1) n°644753 (KCONNECT). JP has also been supported by the ESF project ELIAS.

6. REFERENCES

[1] M. Benigeri and P. Pluye. Shortcomings of health information on the internet. *Health Prom. Inter.*, 2003.

[2] K. Collins-Thompson, P. N. Bennett, R. W. White, S. de la Chica, and D. Sontag. Personalizing web search results by reading level. In *Proc. of CIKM*, 2011.

[3] W. H. Dubay. The principles of readability. *Costa Mesa, CA: Impact Information*, 2004.

[4] S. Fox and M. Duggan. Health online. Technical report, Pew Research, 2013.

[5] C. Macdonald, R. L. Santos, I. Ounis, and B. He. About learning models with multiple query-dependent features. *ACM Trans. Inf. Syst.*, 2013.

[6] J. Palotti, G. Zuccon, L. Goeuriot, L. Kelly, A. Hanbury, G. Jones, M. Lupu, and P. Pecina. CLEF eHealth Evaluation Lab 2015, Task2: Retrieving Information About Medical Symptoms. In *Proc. of CLEF*, 2015.

[7] J. Palotti, G. Zuccon, and A. Hanbury. The Influence of Pre-processing on the Estimation of Readability of Web Documents. In *Proc. of CIKM*, 2015.

[8] N. Pletneva, A. Vargas, and C. Boyer. D8.1.1. requirements for the general public health search. Technical report, Khresmoi Project, 2011.

[9] C. Tan, E. Gabrilovich, and B. Pang. To each his own: personalized content selection based on text comprehensibility. In *Proc. of WSDM*, 2012.

[10] R. White and E. Horvitz. Cyberchondria: Studies of the escalation of medical concerns in web search. In *ACM Trans. on Inf. Sys*, 2008.

[11] R. C. Wiener and R. Wiener-Pla. Literacy, Pregnancy and Potential Oral Health Changes: The Internet and Readability Levels. *Maternal and child health journal*, 2013.

[12] D. Wu, D. Hanauer, Q. Mei, P. Clark, L. An, J. Lei, J. Proulx, Q. Zheng-Treitler, and K. Zheng. Applying multiple methods to assess the readability of a large corpus of medical documents. In *Proc. of MEDINFO*, 2013.

[13] X. Yan, D. Song, and X. Li. Concept-based Document Readability in Domain Specific Information Retrieval. In *Proc. of CIKM*, 2006.

[14] E. Yilmaz, J. A. Aslam, and S. Robertson. A New Rank Correlation Coefficient for Information Retrieval. In *Proc. of SIGIR*, 2008.

[15] G. Zuccon. Understandability biased evaluation for information retrieval. In *Proc. of ECIR*, 2016.

[16] G. Zuccon and B. Koopman. Integrating Understandability in the Evaluation of Consumer Health Search Engines. In *MedIR Workshop at SIGIR*, 2014.

[17] G. Zuccon, B. Koopman, and A. Nguyen. Retrieval of Health Advice on the Web: AEHRC at ShARe/CLEF eHealth Evaluation Lab Task 3. In *CLEF eHealth*, 2013.

Rethinking the Cost of Information Search Behavior

Yinglong Zhang
School of Information and Library Science
University of North Carolina at Chapel Hill
216 Lenoir Dr, Chapel Hill, NC 27599
yinglongz@unc.edu

Jacek Gwizdka
School of Information
University of Texas, Austin
1616 Guadalupe St. Austin, TX 78703 USA
sigir2016@gwizdka.com

ABSTRACT

In this paper, we present a cognitive-economic approach to examining the cost in information search. Unlike previous studies on economic models, we calculated the cost in information search based on participants' eye-tracking data as well as their behavioral data, such as query formulation, search task duration, SERP and web page visits. Using Principal Component Analysis (PCA), we explored a possible latent factor structure of variables representing the cost in information search. Our results indicated that the cost of information seeking could be associated with two distinct aspects of search, exploratory and validation processes.

Keywords

Information seeking stopping behavior, eye tracking.

1. INTRODUCTION

An extensive review of prior research on information search has been made into how people define information needs, generate queries, examine documents, refine queries, and make sense of the information they find (for a review see [1]). It has been found that terminating search too early or too late can bring harmful effects to its outcomes [2, 3]. In previous studies, information search stopping behavior has been investigated from different perspectives. Based on the economic principle as well as the findings reported by Azzopardi and his collegues [4-6], the cost of information search is one of the most important factors contributing to stopping behavior. Inspired by theories and methods from cognitive science, we report on a cognitive-economic approach to calculating the cost in information searching behavior.

2. RELATED WORK

Economic principle is one of the well-developed theories for understanding stopping behavior in information search. This principle was first proposed by Varian [7]. In his SIGIR 1999 keynote, he addressed the relation between economics and search, and pointed out the feasibility of applying economics to solve several questions in Information Retrieval (IR), such as how to examine the economic value of information based on consumer theory, how to better estimate the probability of relevance, and how to apply Stigler's theory [8] on Optimal Search Behavior to IR.

An integral part of the economic perspective is to estimate the gain and the cost in information search. In previous studies, the cost has been mainly considered to result from a sequence of interactions. For instance, Azzopardi and his colleagues [4-6] simulated the cost of search in terms of a number of queries posted (*Q*), a number of search result pages examined per query (*V*), a number of snippets inspected per query (*S*), and a number of documents assessed per query (*A*) with some probability P_a. The total of interaction was modeled as shown in **Eq 1**:

$$c(Q,V,S,A) = c_q.Q + c_v.V.Q + c_s.S.Q + c_a.A.Q \quad (1)$$

Where c_q is the cost of a query, c_v is the cost of viewing a page, c_s is the cost of inspecting a snippet, and c_a is the cost of assessing a document.

In contrast to the models proposed in [4-6], Smucker proposed that the gain and the cost can be expressed in terms of time [1]. Specifically, if users invest time ***t*** in assessing a result list, they will have a total benefit of ***G(t)*** - the cumulative gain experienced by the users at time ***t***. Assuming a decay function ***D(t)***, in this time-based model, users will stop searching information when ***D(t)*** decreases to 0. The time-based model is shown in **Eq 2**:

$$\frac{1}{N}\sum_{k=1}^{\infty} g_k D(T(k)) \quad (2)$$

Where *T(k)* refers to the expected time it would take for a user to reach result rank *k* and begin to judge the document.

Although the aforementioned studies investigated the cost of search based on varying perspectives, all of them essentially considered information search as one-stage process. However, a number of well established information search models include multiple stages [9, 10]. Thus, it is possible that some costs are only associated with a specific stage of information search and that the cost associated with different stages can have varying effects on information search behavior. In addition, the impact of individual differences on information search was neglected by most of these studies. For instance, when reading the same irrelevant document, participant A may invest more cognitive effort than participant B due to the differences in their working memory capacity. Lastly, in Azzopardi's models, all of the queries were regarded as the cost. However, it has been found that generating queries of high quality also brings benefit to information search process [11-13], though all queries carry a cost associated with them as it takes effort to generate and type them. In this regard, it could be more proper to only include queries with low quality in the estimation of the cost in information search.

3. PROPOSED MEASURE OF THE COST OF INFORMATION SEARCH

In our research, we have developed a method that includes both economic and cognitive aspects of information searching behavior. Specifically, we add eye fixations to the assessment of the cost in information search. Previous research has demonstrated that the internal cognitive activity is reflected, to some extent, in the change of the number of fixations [14, 15]. In our study, the number of fixations was used to reflect the

SIGIR'16, July 17–21, 2016, Pisa, Italy.
© 2016 ACM. ISBN 978-1-4503-4069-4/16/07…$15.00
DOI: http://dx.doi.org/10.1145/2911451.2914742

cognitive effort that each participant invested when they examine documents and search engine result pages (SERPs). We consider the cost of information search results from query generation, document examination, search engine result pages (SERPs) and task description examinations.

3.1 Cost in Query Generation

Recall that generating queries of high quality can bring benefit to information search process [11-13], though all queries carry a cost with them as it takes effort to generate and type them. In our work, only *not useful* queries were considered in assessing the cost associated with query generation; their cost was reflected in two variables:

- The number of words used in all *not useful* queries $W_{notUseful}$
- Total time taken to enter *not useful* queries $T_{notUseful}$

***Not useful* queries** were defined here as the queries that were used only once and did not return relevant documents (as judged by participants). For the queries that returned no relevant documents, but were used more once, we made an assumption that participants re-typed them on purpose. That is, these queries are not treated here as cost because they likely provided information that aided the participants in information search, for example, in reformulating existing or creating new queries. Queries that returned relevant documents are not treated as cost, because they directly facilitated discovery of the relevant documents.

3.2 Cost in Document Examination

In information search, users might invest time and effort in reading some documents that are not useful for meeting their search goals. Examining such *not useful* documents could be regarded as a kind of a cost. This cost was reflected in the variable:

- The number of fixations on visited *not useful* documents $D_{notUseful}$

***Not useful* documents** were defined as the examined documents that were located through *not useful* queries. This definition was based on an assumption that the documents returned by a query were less likely to be located by another completely different query (word stems of terms in both queries were different) in our experiment. That is to say, all of the assessed documents, located by *not useful* queries, were considered not useful, since useful documents could either be saved by participants as a relevant document (the interfaces in our experiment supported this functionality) or be found again by re-typing certain queries and then be re-examined. In contrast to *not useful* documents, all of the other documents that participants examined in the tasks were considered *useful* documents. The documents that were not examined were not considered as a cost since participants did not invest any effort reading them.

3.3 Cost in SERP and Task Description Examinations

The costs of examining SERPs were estimated based on the variable:

- The number of fixations on all SERPs F_{SERP}.

Task descriptions were available to participants during their searches in our study. We assume that participants opened task description, when they forgot or were not confident about information they were asked to find and needed to confirm it. In our study, opening tasks descriptions was regarded as a cost in the information search process. The cost of description examination was modeled, as follows:

- Total time of visiting task descriptions $T_{taskDescription}$
- The number of fixations on visited task descriptions $F_{taskDescription}$

4. METHOD

We conducted a controlled, lab-based experiment to investigate Web searches on Wikipedia. Each experiment session was held in Information eXperience lab at the School of Information, University of Texas at Austin .

4.1 Participants

32 university students (15 females), aged 18 to 37, participated in this experiment. To control the influence of language on reading as well as the impact of diversity in human vision on eye tracking, we pre-screened participants and recruited native English speakers who had normal to corrected-to normal vision. Upon completing the experiment session, each participant received $30.

4.2 Experiment Design

Experiment had a within-subject design. Each participant completed four search tasks in an experiment session that lasted up to 1.5 hours. The tasks were designed based on prior work [16] to be at two complexity levels: simple and complex, shown in Table 2. Two types of search user interfaces were designed based on a commercial test search engine developed by Search Technologies Corp[1][17]. To control the order effect, we created 32 rotations of task complexity levels and user interface types with a constraint that UI is switched after two tasks. A rotation was assigned to each participant in a random order. In each search task, participants were required to read task description, complete pre- and post- questionnaires, and search information on Wikipedia using either of the two user interfaces. Participants were asked to bookmark and save the documents they judged relevant. There were no time limits set for search tasks. Before completing their experiment session, participants were asked to fill out exit questionnaires. Data analysis presented in this paper does not include user interface factor.

5. Data Analysis and Results

5.1 Data Preprocessing

Table 1 shows descriptive statistics for queries, documents examined and task descriptions visited.

	Median	Mean	SD
Not useful queries	9	7.81	4.81
Useful queries	6	6.00	2.17
Not useful documents	6	7.69	6.69
Useful documents	10	11.00	4.70
Task descriptions	18	17.53	9.66

Table 1. Descriptive statistics for queries, documents examined, and task descriptions visited per participants.

Before performing data analysis, we removed bad fixation data (marked by Tobii as validity=4) and standardized all predictors: each predictor variable was divided by its standard deviation.

[1] http://www.searchtechnologies.com/

5.2 Principal Component Analysis (PCA)

We used principal component analysis **[18]** to explore a possible factor structure of variables representing the cost in information search, such as $W_{notUseful}$, $T_{notUseful}$, F_{SERP}, $D_{notUseful}$, $F_{taskDescription}$, *and* $T_{taskDescription}$. Prior to PCA, we performed Kaiser-Mayer-Olkin (KMO) Measure of Sampling Adequacy and Bartlett's Test of Sphericity to ensure our sample supports valid PCA [19]. The result of KMO was 0.64, with Bartlett's Test yielding 600.46 ($p < 0.001$). Both values indicate that our own sample could satisfy the requisite assumptions for proceeding with PCA.

Type	Task scenario
Simple 1	You love history and, in particular, you are interested in the Teutonic Order (Teutonic Knights). You have read about their period of power, and now you want to learn more about their decline. You want to find out: What year was the Order defeated in a famous battle? And you also want to find out which army (or armies) defeated the Order?
Simple 2	You recently attended an outdoor music festival and heard a band called Wolf Parade. You really enjoyed the band and want to purchase their latest album. What is the name of their latest (full- length) album? And you also want to know when this band resumed their work together?
Complex 1	A local water conversation group requests ideas to expand their efforts. Currently, they pick up debris from local waterways and try to raise awareness about water pollution. In an effort to help out, you volunteer for the group but also, you want to expand their efforts. What other forms of land use are impacting waterways? Which forms of land use have are the highest impact to the environment?
Complex 2	A debate is underway after an international logging and mining corporation submitted a bid to buy a local nature reserve. The city needs more jobs but many residents are upset because they find selling a nature reserve as short sighted. And many people actively use the nature reserve for recreation and educational field trips. In an effort to be balanced with support for the community and to be fair to economic development, you decide to investigate both sides further. What are the small and large scale impacts of logging and mining? What are some economic considerations for land preservation? What are your recommendations to the city if the corporation's bid is successful?

Table 2. Task Descriptions

To determine the number of components to keep, we used parallel analysis [20]. Specifically, a random dataset was generated with the same number of rows and variables as that in our sample data. Based on the generated dataset, we then created a correction matrix and computed eigenvalues. The results of parallel analysis are shown in Figure 1 with red line. According to the results, we kept only two components that appeared above the red line.

Given the number of the components determined in parallel analysis, we ran PCA gain with oblique (Promax) rotation and the number of factors fixed to 2. The factor loadings for manifest variables were shown in **Table 3**. The standardized loadings of these manifest variables (highlighted in **Table 3**) ranged from 0.70 to 0.98. The value of h^2 indicates the final communality estimate: the proportion of variance accounted for by retained components. A value of $h^2 < 0.40$ indicates that an item is less strongly correlated with its corresponding components [21]. Based on this criterion, all of the six variables in our research were correlated with their corresponding components.

Analyzing the results of PCA, we named the two factors *exploratory* process and *validation* process (shown in **Table 3**). The exploratory process was reflected in 3 variables: total time taken to enter *not useful* queries ($T_{notUseful}$), number of words used in all *not useful* queries ($W_{notUseful}$), and number of fixations on all SERPs (F_{SERP}). The validation process was reflected in three other variables: number of fixations on visited task descriptions ($F_{taskDescription}$), Total time of visiting task descriptions ($T_{taskDescription}$), and number of fixations on visited *not useful* documents ($D_{notUseful}$).

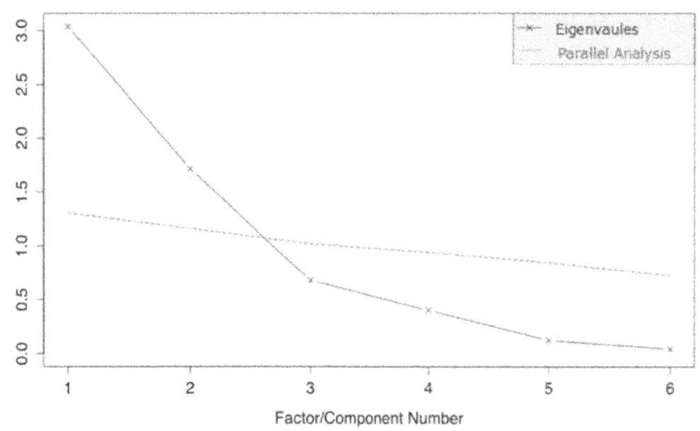

Figure 1. Revised scree plot showing parallel analysis results

In the exploratory process, people first define their goals and express their information problem by generating queries that are expected to retrieve the relevant materials. The results of executing different queries are then explored by examining search engine result pages (SERPs). In the validation process people confirm whether the collected information satisfies task goals [10] by examining documents and task descriptions.

Each of these two processes could span several stages of information search and that searchers can move back and forth between these processes. Roughly, the exploratory process takes place during Initiation, Selection and Exploration stages in Kuhlthau's ISP model; it corresponds to Define Problem, Select Source, Formulate and Execute Query stages in Marchionini's information seeking-process [9, 10]. The validation process takes place during Formulation and Collection stages in Kuhlthau's model, and it corresponds to Examine Results stage in Marchionini's information seeking-process.

	Exploratory Process	Validation Process	h^2
$T_{notUseful}$	**0.98**	-0.09	0.91
$W_{notUseful}$	**0.94**	-0.07	0.85
F_{SERP}	**0.75**	0.17	0.68
$F_{taskDescription}$	-0.08	**0.98**	0.92
$T_{taskDescription}$	0	**0.94**	0.88
$D_{notUseful}$	0.04	**0.7**	0.51

Table 3: Factor loadings for each manifest variable

6. DISCUSSION AND CONCLUSION

Using PCA, we attempted to identify a possible factor structure of variables that represented different costs in information search. Our results demonstrated that these variables load onto two very well separated factors. This enables us to suggest that these two factors correspond to the two different processes in information search. We observe that they correspond quite well to exploratory process and validation process.

To the best of our knowledge, this point has not been considered in previous studies. As mentioned before, in exploration process, people try to issue as many useful queries as they can to maximize the likelihood of finding information that satisfies their information needs; during the validation process people confirm whether useful information has been found. In particular, validation process involves high level cognitive activities, during which people need to be aware what information has been gained from information seeking and whether the information meets their information needs. The evaluation of the cost in validation process possibly enabled people to monitor and control when to modify or enter new queries so that they can lower their cost and maximize gain in search.

Our findings can inform further studies on the cost of information search. For instance, in the previous studies, the different kinds of costs were linearly combined. Based on our findings, in the future study, we can examine relationships between the costs coming from the exploratory process and validation process and ask for example, *are they linearly correlated with each other? Do they have different effect size on the information searching stopping behavior*?

Moreover, in our study, we have attempted to consider cognitive factor in the estimation of the cost in information search. For instance, we used the number of eye fixations to reflect people's cognitive efforts in reading. In the future study, we plan to examine how participants' working memory (WM) ability affects their performance and subjective perception of the cost of information search. It has been found that WM has a significant correlation with reading comprehension ability [22]. Thus individuals with low WM capacity are expected to exert more cognitive effort and suffer higher costs when examining documents, as compared to those with high WM capacity.

Limitations of our study include, firstly, PCA was used to find a possible underlying factor structure of a set of variables; it cannot be used to confirm the factor structure. Our study focused on the exploration of possible relations between the variables representing different costs in information search. In a future study, we intend to utilize confirmatory factor analysis (CFA) [20] to verify the factor structure that have been found in this paper. In addition, we made several simplifying assumptions about the *not useful* queries and documents. Lastly, owing to the limitation of our data sample, we had no additional dataset to the examine the gain of information search. We will try to address these limitations in our follow up studies.

7. ACKNOWLEDGMENTS

This research was supported, in part, by IMLS Career award to Jacek Gwizdka # RE-04-11-0062-11.

8. REFERENCES

[1] Smucker, M. D. and Clarke, C. L. A. 2011. Time-based calibration of effectiveness measures. In *Proceedings of SIGIR'2011*. ACM, New York, NY. 95-104.

[2] Hemmer, E. 2013. *Information Seeking Stopping Behavior in Online Scenarios*. Peter Lang Pub Inc.

[3] Speier, C. and Morris, M. G. 2003. The influence of query interface design on decision-making performance. *Mis Quart*, 27, 3, 397-423.

[4] Azzopardi, L. 2011. The economics in interactive information retrieval. In *Proceedings of SIGIR'2011*. ACM, New York, NY. 15-24.

[5] Azzopardi, L. 2014. Modelling interaction with economic models of search. In *Proceedings of SIGIR'2014*. ACM, New York, NY. 3-12.

[6] Azzopardi, L., Kelly, D. and Brennan, K. 2013. How query cost affects search behavior. In *Proceedings of SIGIR'2013*. ACM, New York, NY. 23-32.

[7] Varian, H. R. 1999. Economics and search. In *Proceedings of ACM SIGIR Forum*. ACM. 1-5.

[8] Stigler, G. J. 1961. The economics of information. *The journal of political economy*, 213-225.

[9] Kuhlthau, C. C. 1991. Inside the search process: Information seeking from the user's perspective. *Journal of the American Society for Information Science*.

[10] Marchionini, G. 1997. *Information seeking in electronic environments*. Cambridge university press.

[11] Hauff, C., de Jong, F., Kelly, D. and Azzopardi, L. 2010. Query quality: user ratings and system predictions. In *Proceedings of SIGIR'2010*. ACM. 743-744.

[12] Kelly, D., Cushing, A., Dostert, M., Niu, X. and Gyllstrom, K. 2010. Effects of popularity and quality on the usage of query suggestions during information search. In *Proceedings of SIGCHI' 2010*. ACM, New York, NY. 45-54.

[13] Wu, W.-C., Kelly, D. and Huang, K. 2012. User evaluation of query quality. In *Proceedings of SIGIR'2012*. ACM, New York, NY. 215-224.

[14] Cole, M. J., Gwizdka, J., Liu, C., Bierig, R., Belkin, N. J. and Zhang, X. M. 2011. Task and user effects on reading patterns in information search. *Interact Comput*, 23, 4, 346-362.

[15] Gwizdka, J. and Cole, M. 2010. Eye Movement Patterns and Interaction for High Level Information Seeking.

[16] Kelly, D., Arguello, J., Edwards, A. and Wu, W.-c. 2015. *Development and evaluation of search tasks for IIR experiments using a cognitive complexity framework*. ACM, City.

[17] Zhang, Y. and Gwizdka, J. 2014. Effects of tasks at similar and different complexity levels. *Proceedings of the American Society for Information Science and Technology*, 51, 1, 1-4.

[18] Jolliffe, I. 2014. *Principal Component Analysis*. John Wiley & Sons, Ltd.

[19] Worthington, R. L. and Whittaker, T. A. 2006. Scale development research - A content analysis and recommendations for best practices. *Couns Psychol*, 34, 6, 806-838.

[20] Zhang, Y., Zhang, J., Lease, M. and Gwizdka, J. 2014. Multidimensional relevance modeling via psychometrics and crowdsourcing. In *Proceedings of SIGIR'2014*. ACM, New York, NY. 435-444.

[21] Norris, M. and Lecavalier, L. 2010. Evaluating the Use of Exploratory Factor Analysis in Developmental Disability Psychological Research. *Journal of Autism and Developmental Disorders*, 40, 1, 8-20.

[22] Daneman, M. and Carpenter, P. A. 1980. Individual differences in working memory and reading. *Journal of verbal learning and verbal behavior*, 19, 4, 450-466.

Retrievability of Code Mixed Microblogs

Debasis Ganguly
ADAPT Centre, School of Computing
Dublin City University
Dublin, Ireland
dganguly@computing.dcu.ie

Ayan Bandyopadhyay
CVPR Unit
Indian Statistical Institute
Kolkata, India
bandyopadhyay.ayan@gmail.com

Mandar Mitra
CVPR Unit
Indian Statistical Institute
Kolkata, India
mandar@isical.ac.in

Gareth J.F. Jones
ADAPT Centre, School of Computing
Dublin City University
Dublin, Ireland
gjones@computing.dcu.ie

ABSTRACT

Mixing multiple languages within the same document, a phenomenon called (linguistic) code mixing or code switching, is a frequent trend among multilingual users of social media. In the context of information retrieval (IR), code mixing may affect retrieval effectiveness due to the mixing of different vocabularies with different collection statistics within a single collection of documents. In this paper, we investigate the indexing and retrieval strategies for a mixed collection of documents, comprising of code-mixed and the monolingual documents. In particular, we address three alternative modes of indexing, namely (a) a single index for the two sub-collections; (b) a separate index for each sub-collection; and (c) a clustered index with two individual sub-collection statistics coupled with the overall one. We make use of the expected *retrievability* scores of the two classes of documents to empirically show that indexing strategies (a) and (b) mostly retrieve the monolingual documents at top ranks with standard retrieval approaches. Our experiments show that, by contrast, the clustered index (c) is able to alleviate this problem by improving the retrievability of the code-mixed documents.

CCS Concepts

•**Information systems** → **Content analysis and feature selection;**

Keywords

Microblog Retrieval; Code Mixing; Retrievability; Fusion

1. INTRODUCTION

Mixing multiple languages within the same document, a phenomenon called (linguistic) code mixing or code switching, is a popular trend among multilingual social media users [11]. Although, code mixing can involve a switch between languages within a document, sentence or even a word [3], and hence can be classified into further fine-grained categories, in our study we treat all these cases equivalently. As an example of code mixing from Twitter[1], consider the following tweet, where for illustration purposes, we have annotated each word with its source language, namely EN (English), BN (Bengali), and NE (a named entity), along with a candidate English translation.

> **Tweet:** Not/EN so/EN soon/EN re/BN arko/NE dayitto/BN nebe/BN I/EN guess/EN
>
> **English translation:** Hey, not so soon. Arko will take responsibility, I guess.

We see that Bengali words, such as 'dayitto' (responsibility) and 'nebe' (will take), appear in transliterated form interspersed within a primarily English sentence. The prevalence of code mixed content in social media, such as Twitter, has spurred considerable natural language processing (NLP) research activity, such as language identification [10] and part-of-speech (POS) tagging [13]. To the best of our knowledge, no previous research has investigated the effect of code mixed content on information retrieval (IR).

In the context of IR, the code mixing effect can change retrieval effectiveness due to the introduction of a different/diverse vocabulary which can lead to different collection statistics (e.g. document frequency of terms), which in turn can lead to different similarity scores between code-mixed and mono-lingual documents with respect to a given query. Another research challenge arises from the fact that although a significant amount of code mixing can be seen on Twitter, the search queries executed on Twitter are usually not code mixed, i.e., searchers typically do not use code mixing when formulating their queries. This in turn leads to the difficulty of retrieving relevant code mixed tweets at the top ranks due to word mismatch issues. For example, the sample code mixed tweet shown above is less likely to appear within top ranks for a query such as 'Arko responsibility', due to the presence of the Bengali word 'dayitto' in the tweet instead of its English counterpart.

To investigate the effects of code mixing in IR, we seek to address the following research questions:

RQ-1: How frequently can a code mixed document be retrieved within top ranks for a *monolingual* query?

RQ-2: How can the average retrieval rank of relevant code mixed documents be improved?

[1]https://twitter.com/

SIGIR '16, July 17-21, 2016, Pisa, Italy

DOI: http://dx.doi.org/10.1145/2911451.2914727

2. EXPERIMENT SETUP

In this section, we describe the construction process for our experimental dataset of code-mixed and monolingual tweets. This is followed by a description of three alternative indexing approaches on which we execute queries. We then compare the retrievability values [4] of tweets obtained for each of these approaches.

2.1 Dataset Construction

In order to investigate retrievability of code-mixed documents, a document collection comprising of a mixture of monolingual and code mixed documents needs to be constructed. This section elaborates the data collection process.

Geo-tagged Twitter Streaming. Since social media is a prevalent source of code mixed content, we use Twitter as our source of code mixed documents. Since it is more likely to find instances of code mixing in multilingual language dense areas [11], we collected data from India which is predominantly a multi-lingual country with a majority of the population being trilingual. We therefore collected tweets with two types of code mixing, one for Hindi and the other for Bengali.

We used the streaming API of Twitter to collect tweets from three geo-tagged locations referring to three major cities of India, namely Delhi, Mumbai and Kolkata. The streaming API collects all tweets from a given region. Since we are only interested in a mixture of code mixed content and monolingual English content, we filtered out tweets which do not use the Roman script, because such tweets are likely to be written in one of the official languages of India (including Hindi) and hence is less likely to be code mixed. The streaming API was executed for a period of about 6 months, after which a total of about 2.68 million tweets had been accumulated.

Dictionary based Classification. To conduct retrievability experiments, the next step is to determine which documents from this collection are code mixed and which ones are monolingual. Note that we do not need to identify the language of each constituent word to detect the exact code switching points for which supervised approaches such as SVM (bag-of-words based) and CRF (word sequence based) have been reported to work well [5]. Instead, we rather need to detect whether any code mixing exists in a tweet, which is rather a simpler problem. Since the effectiveness of code mixing detection is not the core focus of this paper, we employ a simple dictionary based classification approach to classify the tweets of our collection into one of the two classes, i.e. code mixed or monolingual.

The dictionary that we use for classification is comprised of a list of 154 commonly used words in Hindi and Bengali in the transliterated form. If a tweet contains any of these 154 words, it is classified as a code mixed tweet. We use keywords from these two languages for two reasons. Firstly, these two are the most spoken among Indian languages (Hindi ranks 4th in the world with 310M speakers whereas Bengali ranks 7th with 205M speakers [1]). The second reason is due to the location of the tweets themselves. Bengali is the native language of Kolkata and there are a vast majority of Bengali speaking people in both Delhi and Mumbai, whereas Hindi is spoken with almost native fluency in all the three cities. Consequently, it is more likely that the tweets from these locations will borrow words from the vocabulary of one or both of these languages.

We evaluated the accuracy of code mixing detection on a subset of 100 tweets drawn randomly from each of the two classes, i.e. monolingual and code mixed. We found out that 89 and 95 out of the 100 in each class were truly code mixed and mono-lingual respectively. This shows that the dictionary based method works satisfactorily in the context of our experiments.

Dataset Statistics. Table 1 summarizes the dataset characteristics, from which we can make the following observations. Firstly, it can be seen that about 7.25% of the tweets are code-mixed, i.e. contains a transliterated Bengali or Hindi function word. The percentage of code-mixed tweets is thus significant, and hence the very question on the retrievability of this type of documents is a relevant one. Secondly, the vocabulary of the code mixed documents is more diverse in comparison to the monolingual one. Although the absolute value of the vocabulary size for the code mixed documents is smaller, the average document frequency (DF), computed as the ratio of the number of unique terms to the number of documents, is higher for the code mixed type. Another measure which indicates vocabulary diversity is the TTR (Type-token ratio), which is also higher for the code mixed documents. This indicates that the collection statistics, e.g. DF, of the non-English terms, e.g. hashtags, named entities or transliterated Bengali (BN) or Hindi (HN) words of the code mixed documents, can be significantly different in comparison to monolingual English (EN) documents.

Document type	#Docs	#Vocab	Av len	Av DF	TTR
Monolingual (EN)	2,502,343	8,335,003	10.69	3.30	0.311
Code mixed (BN/HN)	181,282	1,330,727	10.78	7.34	0.681

Table 1: Characteristics of the dataset constructed by streaming tweets from 3 major cities of India.

Query set construction. To execute large scale retrievability experiments, one needs to construct a set of sample queries. To compute average retrievability of documents, [4] uses frequently occurring unigrams and bigrams from the collection vocabulary as as sample queries. In contrast to [4] of selecting all word unigrams and bigrams as the set of queries, in our experiments we restrict this set of queries to all unigrams and bigrams belonging to the set of intersection between the two vocabularies, the query terms thus comprising hashtags, named entities and English words. This is because code mixing, being a linguistic phenomenon, is likely to be present in well-formed English (or non-English) sentences and usually absent in keyword-based user queries.

This way of selecting sample queries ensures that no Bengali or Hindi words can appear as a part of the query set because these words do not belong to the monolingual (EN) sub-collection. Note that English words exist in the query samples since due to the code mixing property, these words are a part of the code mixed documents vocabulary. A similar argument also applies for neutral words such as named entities and hashtags because they are a part of both monolingual EN and code-mixed vocabulary.

From the intersection set of the vocabularies of the two sub-collections of Table 1, we selected all unigrams and bigrams having document frequencies higher than 20 (similar to the settings of [4]) as the set of queries. In total, the number of queries used for our retrievability experiments is 36,422. Similar to [4], we set the prior likelihood factor of a query to the value of 1.

2.2 Indexing and Retrieval

In order to explore the retrievability of a code mixed document, from among a collection of monolingual and other code mixed documents, we compare three different approaches to indexing and retrieval of the mixed dataset described in Section 2.1.

A standard IR model uses collection statistics, e.g. the DF of a term, to estimate the relative importance of a match between a document word with a given query term [6]. Since collection statistics can play an important role in scoring documents against a query, we investigate three different indexing approaches that use the collection statistics in three different ways, described as follows.

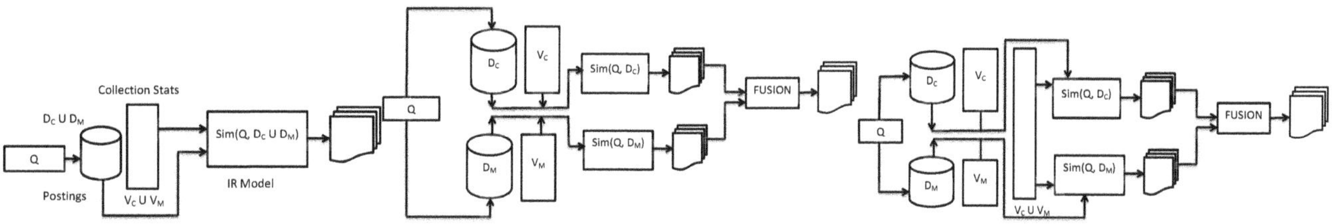

(a) Combined Index. (b) Separate Indexes. (c) Clustered Index.

Figure 1: Three different indexing and retrieval strategies for the mixture collection of monolingual and code-mixed documents.

Single Index. This indexing scheme does not require a code-mixing detection classifier. Both types of documents, namely the monolingual and the code-mixed, are stored in a single index without any distinction. Obviously, there is a single collection statistics table for both the vocabulary types, say V_M (monolingual) and V_C (code-mixed). A schematic diagram is shown in Figure 1a. The similarity score between a query Q and a document D is given by a function of the term frequency of a query term t in D, $tf(t, D)$, and the collection statistics of t computed over the set $V_M \cup V_C$, which we denote by $df_{M\cup C}(t)$ in Equation 1.

$$sim(Q, D) = f(tf(t, D), df_{M\cup C}(t)) \quad (1)$$

Split Index. In this indexing scheme, a code-mixing detection approach, e.g. a dictionary based approach, is required to construct separate indexes for each type of document, i.e. EN or code-mixed. Each index maintains its own collection statistics. A query is executed separately on these two indexes and the final result-list can be obtained with a standard fusion technique, e.g. COMBSUM [7]. The schematic diagram of this approach is shown in Figure 1b. The similarity score between a query Q and a document D is given by Equation 2, where t is a query term, D is a document which is either monolingual or code-mixed, i.e., $D \in \{D_M, D_C\}$, and g is a fusion function.

$$sim(Q, D) = g\Big(f\big(tf(t, D_M), df_M(t)\big), f\big(tf(t, D_C), df_C(t)\big)\Big) \quad (2)$$

Clustered Index. In this indexing scheme, schematically shown in Figure 1c, separate indexes are maintained for the two different document classes, similar to the *split index* approach. However, in addition to the local collection statistics, the similarity score also depends on the global collection statistics, $df_{M\cup C}(t)$, similar to the *single index* approach. This is shown in Equation 3, where it can be seen that the similarity score additionally depends on a linear combination of the local (per document type) and the overall collection statistics, parameterized by a number $\alpha \in [0, 1]$.

$$\begin{aligned} sim(Q, D) = g\Big(&f\big(tf(t, D_M), \alpha \cdot df_{M\cup C}(t) + (1-\alpha)\cdot df_M(t)\big), \\ &f\big(tf(t, D_C), \alpha \cdot df_{M\cup C}(t) + (1-\alpha)\cdot df_C(t)\big)\Big) \end{aligned} \quad (3)$$

Equation 3 is similar in principle to the clustered language model [9]. However, any other retrieval model can be applied in the general scheme of Equation 3 and Figure 1c.

Retrieval Models. In our experiments, for the abstract function f shown in Equations 1, 2 and 3, we apply standard retrieval models, namely, a) BM25 with $k = 1.2$ and $b = 0.75$ [12]; b) LM with $\lambda = 0.4$ [8]; c) DFR with Bose-Einstein model and H_1 normalization [2]); and d) a COMBSUM [7] fusion of all these models.

Evaluation Measures. To measure the average ranks at which monolingual documents are retrieved in comparison to code-mixed ones, we compute the retrievability score of each class of documents as defined in Equation 4, where c is a rank threshold parameter, set to 10 and 20 in our experiments, as suggested in [4].

$$r(d) = \sum_{q\in Q} \mathbb{I}[rank(d, q) \leq c] \quad (4)$$

The expected retrievability, $\hat{r}$, for a particular class of document, i.e. M or C, is then computed by averaging over the computed $r(d)$ values for documents of that class. The Gini coefficient of the $r(d)$ values measures the inequality of the $r(d)$ score distribution, i.e., lower the value, the more uniform the distribution is. In the context of our experiments, higher Gini scores would give the code mixed documents more chance to be retrieved at top ranks.

3. RESULTS

The retrievability scores, $\hat{r}$ values for the two document classes along with the Gini coefficients, G, are reported in Table 2. The highest expected retrievability values for each document class in each index type are shown with bold face, e.g., the DFR model results in highest retrievability of the monolingual documents with the combined indexing approach (Equation 1).

It can be seen that the combined indexing approach results in lower retrievability of the code-mixed documents. On assuming uniform likelihood of a document to be retrieved from any class, the number of possible ways of selecting the top c documents for the monolingual case is much higher than the code-mixed case (from Table 1 it can be seen that the number of monolingual English documents is more than 10 times that of the number of code-mixed ones), which means that a code-mixed document is likely to lose the 'competition' of getting a berth into the top ranks to its monolingual counterpart. With respect to the research question **RQ-1**, it can be commented that standard IR models (and their fusion) with a combined index of monolingual and code-mixed documents is not prone to retrieving the code-mixed documents at top ranks.

It can also be observed from Table 2 that the retrievability scores of the code-mixed documents increase with the use of separate indexes and fusing the results. The best results are obtained with BM25. However, the retrievability scores of the code-mixed documents are still lower compared to the mono-lingual documents. This shows that late fusion alone does not suffice to alleviate the bias towards retrieving more number of monolingual documents at top ranks.

Table 2 shows that with the clustered index and the use of a combination of collection statistics (Equation 3 with α set to 0.4), the retrievability scores of the code-mixed documents can be increased significantly by the LM retrieval model and the fusion approach. The expected retrievability of the code-mixed documents obtained with LM is in fact higher than that of monolingual documents. However, the BM25 and DFR models continue to favour

Index	Model	Type	c = 10 $\hat{r}$	c = 10 Gini	c = 20 $\hat{r}$	c = 20 Gini
Single	BM25	M	1.2298	0.1649	1.3258	0.2048
		C	1.1790	0.1399	1.2354	0.1656
	LM	M	1.2259	0.1620	1.3150	0.2001
		C	**1.1975**	0.1510	**1.2521**	0.1785
	DFR	M	**1.2484**	0.1732	1.3545	0.2159
		C	1.1758	0.1357	1.2342	0.1633
	FUSION	M	1.2305	0.1645	**1.3944**	0.2352
		C	1.1873	0.1437	1.2482	0.1723
Split	BM25	M	1.2456	0.1725	1.3385	0.2105
		C	**1.2036**	0.1574	**1.2604**	0.1822
	LM	M	1.2493	0.1735	1.3423	0.2112
		C	1.1829	0.1454	1.2455	0.1779
	DFR	M	**1.2559**	0.1768	**1.3527**	0.2150
		C	1.1766	0.1410	1.2416	0.1721
	FUSION	M	1.2431	0.1710	1.3355	0.2089
		C	1.1810	0.1451	1.2477	0.1762
Cluster	BM25	M	1.2796	0.1940	1.3804	0.2319
		C	1.2345	0.2002	1.1450	0.1345
	LM	M	1.2680	0.1878	1.3578	0.2232
		C	**1.4105**	0.2480	**1.5101**	0.2801
	DFR	M	**1.2974**	0.2016	**1.4063**	0.2415
		C	1.1960	0.1739	1.1252	0.1119
	FUSION	M	1.2798	0.1933	1.3769	0.2298
		C	1.3021	0.2319	1.1867	0.1610

Table 2: Expected Retrievability scores of the monolingual (M) and the code-mixed (C) documents along with the Gini coefficients. Cluster results were obtained with $\alpha = 0.4$ (Eqn. 3).

the monolingual documents, which shows that these models do not naturally extended to the clustered case as is the case with clustered LM [9]. A bias-variance trade-off is achieved with a fusion of the respective models on the clustered index, where we observe that bias towards any particular class of documents decreases. Going back to research question **RQ-2**, i.e. how can the retrievability of code-mixed documents be improved, it can be commented that the clustered mode of indexing and retrieval seems to be the best choice for retrieval of code-mixed content from within a collection of both code-mixed and monolingual documents.

Figure 2 shows how α, the linear combination parameter of Equation 3, affects the expected retrievability scores of the code-mixed documents. An interesting observation is that the average retrievability scores obtained with LM increase when more importance is given to the collection statistics obtained from the individual clusters ($1 - \alpha = 0.8$) than the global collection statistics ($\alpha = 0.2$).

4. CONCLUSIONS AND FUTURE WORK

In this paper, we studied how code-mixing can affect IR effectiveness. To conduct this study, we constructed a collection of about 2.68M tweets (written using the Roman script), out of which about 181K are code-mixed and the rest are English tweets without code-mixing. We investigated three alternative strategies to index and retrieve content from this collection, a) a single index which combines both types of documents; b) separate indexes for each type with the ranked lists obtained from each being fused; and c) a clustered index (each cluster having its own local collection statistics) coupled with a combined collection statistics table and a fusion of

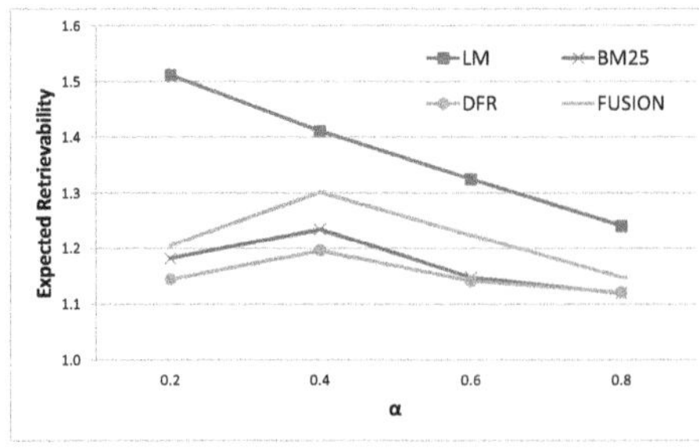

Figure 2: α vs retrievability of code-mixed documents for the clustered index.

the result-lists. We found that the clustered index leads to maximum information access for the code-mixed content with the LM retrieval model. A fusion of LM with BM25 and DFR on the clustered index results in a balanced information access for the two information types, namely monolingual and code-mixed.

In future, we would like to develop query sets with depth pooled relevance judgements on this collection of code-mixed tweets. We would also like to conduct user studies on task driven code-mixed content search to better understand user search behaviour.

Acknowledgements

This research is supported by Science Foundation Ireland (SFI) as a part of the ADAPT Centre at DCU (Grant No: 13/RC/2106) and by a grant under the SFI ISCA India consortium.

5. REFERENCES

[1] List of languages by number of native speakers. https://en.wikipedia.org/wiki/List_of_languages_by_number_of_native_speakers. Accessed: 2016-02-09.

[2] G. Amati and C. J. Van Rijsbergen. Probabilistic models of information retrieval based on measuring the divergence from randomness. *ACM Trans. Inf. Syst.*, 20(4):357–389, 2002.

[3] P. Auer. *Code-switching in conversation: language, interaction and identity.* Taylor and Francis, 2002.

[4] L. Azzopardi and V. Vinay. Retrievability: an evaluation measure for higher order information access tasks. In *Proceedings of CIKM*, pages 561–570, 2008.

[5] U. Barman, A. Das, J. Wagner, and J. Foster. Code mixing: A challenge for language identification in the language of social media. In *Proceedings of First Workshop on Computational Approaches to Code Switching*, pages 13–23, 2014.

[6] H. Fang and C. Zhai. An exploration of axiomatic approaches to information retrieval. In *Proceedings of SIGIR '05*, pages 480–487, 2005.

[7] E. A. Fox and J. A. Shaw. Combination of multiple searches. In *Proc of TREC-2*, pages 243–252, 1994.

[8] D. Hiemstra. *Using Language Models for Information Retrieval.* PhD thesis, Center of Telematics and Information Technology, AE Enschede, 2000.

[9] X. Liu and W. B. Croft. Cluster-based retrieval using language models. In *Proc of SIGIR '04*, pages 186–193, 2004.

[10] D. Nguyen and A. S. Dogruöz. Word level language identification in online multilingual communication. In *Proceedings of EMNLP '13*, pages 857–862, 2013.

[11] C. J. Paolillo. "conversational" codeswitching on usenet and internet relay chat. *Language@Internet*, 8(3), 2011.

[12] S. E. Robertson, S. Walker, S. Jones, and M. Hancock-Beaulieu. Okapi at TREC-3. In *Proceedings of the Third Text REtrieval Conference (TREC 1994)*. NIST, 1994.

[13] Y. Vyas, S. Gella, J. Sharma, K. Bali, and M. Choudhury. POS tagging of english-hindi code-mixed social media content. In *Proceedings of EMNLP '14*, pages 974–979, 2014.

Retweeting Behavior Prediction Based on One-Class Collaborative Filtering in Social Networks

Bo Jiang[†], Jiguang Liang[†], Ying Sha[†], Rui Li[†], Wei Liu[§], Hongyuan Ma[§], Lihong Wang[§]
[†] Institute of Information Engineering, Chinese Academy of Sciences, Beijing 100093, China
{jiangbo, liangjiguang, shaying, lirui}@iie.ac.cn
[§] National Computer Network Emergency Response Technical Team/Coordination Center of China, Beijing 100029, China
mahongyuan@foxmail.com, {liuwei, wlh}@isc.org.cn

ABSTRACT

Social behaviors such as retweetings, comments or likes are valuable information for human activities analysis. We focus here on user's retweeting behavior which has been considered as a key mechanism of information diffusion in social networks. Since we can only observe on which messages user retweet. It is a typically one-class setting which only positive examples or implicit feedback can be observed. However, few research works on retweeting prediction consider one-class setting. In this paper, we analyze and study the fundamental factors that might affect retweetability of a tweet, and then employ one-class collaborative filtering method by quantitatively measure the user personal preference and social influence between users and messages to predict user's retweeting behavior. Experimental results on a real-world dataset from social network show that the proposed method is effective and can improve the performance of retweeting behavior prediction over baseline methods through leveraging weighted negative examples information.

CCS Concepts

•**Information Systems** → Data Mining; •**Applied computing** → Social and Behavioral Sciences;

Keywords

Retweeting Prediction; One-Class Collaborative Filtering; User Preference; Social Influence; Weighted Negative

1. INTRODUCTION

In recent years, social network platforms, such as Twitter and Facebook, have been emerged as a popular platform for users to publish their messages, share their opinions and engage in interesting activities. Social user can follow any other users and receive the messages published by the followed users. As a consequence, social networks provide a powerful platform for the spread of information among users. The process of information diffusion consists of user's retweeting behavior which has been considered as a key mechanism of information diffusion in Twitter [6]. However, unlike the traditional recommendation systems such as Netflix, Amazon, large amounts of social information is implicit data which can be generated by user's behaviors such as following, like, retweeting, etc. In this paper, we focus primarily on user's retweeting behavior in which we can only observe explicit retweeting information. This is a typically implicit feedback setting referred to as one-class collaborative filtering (OC-CF) problems [5].

Considerable work has been conducted for studying the prediction of user's retweeting behavior. For example, some research work considers the retweeting behavior prediction as a classification problem [3, 8]. These methods predict whether a message will be retweeted or not by using defined features as evidence. Besides, there are also some models proposed to handle this problem in matrix factorization setting [2, 7]. They treat the prediction as a matrix completion task by integrating different social factors simultaneously from few observed entries. A common property of all the above mentioned models is that all the missing data (namely non-retweeting) is treated as negative examples. The drawback is that this biases the retweeting results because some of the missing data might be positive. On the other hand, these methods ignore all the missing examples and utilize the positive examples only and then feed it into prediction algorithms that only model non-missing data cause all the predictions on missing values are positive examples. Meanwhile, as the retweeting positive examples are very sparse, the prediction performance is less than satisfactory.

In this paper, we propose a strategy of incorporating user personal preference and social influence information into a one-class collaborative filtering model to predict user's retweeting behavior. More specifically, we argue that user's retweeting behavior not only indicates user interest preference in a message, but also reflects social influence from the publisher. Therefore, we quantitatively measure the user personal preference and social influence, and then combine them using a linearly ensemble. Finally, we assign the linearly combine score for each negative example into collaborative filtering baseline model for user's retweeting behavior prediction. Experiments on a large-scale dataset from a real-world social network show that the proposed method can obtain better performance of retweeting prediction than state-of-the-art methods.

SIGIR '16, July 17-21, 2016, Pisa, Italy
© 2016 ACM. ISBN 978-1-4503-4069-4/16/07...$15.00
DOI: http://dx.doi.org/10.1145/2911451.2914713

2. OCCF RETWEETING PREDICITON

2.1 Problem Formulation

The one-class collaborative filtering problem can be formalized as follows. Suppose that we have M users with the ith user denoted as u_i, and N messages with the jth message denoted as m_j. The user's retweeting behavior for the messages can be represented by an $M \times N$ user-message retweeting matrix $\mathbf{R} = [\mathbf{r}_1, \cdots, \mathbf{r}_N]$, in which each row corresponds to a user and each column corresponds to a message. Here, the $(i,j)^{th}$ entry with $\mathbf{R} \in \mathbb{R}^{M \times N}$ can be represented as

$$R_{ij} = \begin{cases} 1 & \text{if } u_i \text{ retweeted } m_j \\ 0 & \text{otherwise} \end{cases} \tag{1}$$

Note that $R_{ij} = 1$ represents user u_i favorited message m_j and $R_{ij} = 0$ means user u_i not seen or not liked message m_j. Our goal is to predict the missing retweeting examples based on partially observed entities in $\mathbf{R}$. Therefore we will hide for evaluation a certain proportion of '1' values per user and measure how well we predict them.

2.2 Measuring User's Retweeting Confidence

The most common method for information diffusion in social network platforms is retweeting, which allows user to repost others' tweets in their own content stream. Although a number of features that might affect retweetability of tweets, such as user profile, content freshness and temporal informaion, have been analyzed by [6], the user survey results recently have been indicated that user's personal preferences and social influence from target user are the two most important factors when users consider whether or not to retweet a given message [1, 4]. Therefore, we will quantify two strength metrics: interest similarity between user and message, and social influence between two users.

2.2.1 Quantifying Interest Similarity

Much research has pointed out that personal interest in a message is the primary reason for retweeting. Moreover, user's interests can be profiled in the content of user's messages, and users who repost similar kinds of messages may share common interests. Therefore, we can mine user's interests directly from their personal messages and extract topics from a specific message by topic model. Then we calculate the similarity between user's interest set and a specific message's topic set by using the cosine similarity as follows:

$$S_{interest}(u,m) = \frac{I(u)I(m)}{\|I(u)\| \, \|I(m)\|} \tag{2}$$

where u and m denote a user and a message, respectively. $I(i) = \frac{1}{|D(i)|}\sum_{a \in D(i)} T_a$, $D(i)$ is the set of messages posted by user u, T_a is the vector representations for message a.

2.2.2 Quantifying Social Influence

Since social influence is meant to come from both two users of interactive activities, a metric which can quantitatively measure the influence strength is crucial to deeply understand user's social actions. Related work has proved the existence of social influence locality for user's retweeting behavior [8]. Specifically, we argue that social influence can be reflected from spreading capacity and activity among users. Hence, we propose a new method that can make more accurate measurement the strength of social influence between two users. More precisely, the spreading capacity can be represented the transition probability of message from user u to user v.

$$P(u,v) = \frac{|\tau_{u \to v}|}{|\tau_v|} \times S_{interest}(u,v) \tag{3}$$

where $|\tau_{u \to v}|$ represents the number of interactive messages sent from u to v, $|\tau_v|$ represents the number of messages posted by v, $S_{interest}(u,v)$ represents the interest similarity between users u and v which can be computed by Eq. (2).

The user's activity means interaction frequency between two users. More precisely, the activity can be measured as follows:

$$H(u,v) = \frac{n(u,v)}{t_m - t_f} \tag{4}$$

where $n(u,v)$ is the interaction frequency from u to v, t_m represents the posting timestamp of message m, t_f denotes the timestamp of the first interaction from u to v.

The social influence from u to v is measured as

$$S_{influence}(u,v) = wP(u,v) + (1-w)H(u,v) \tag{5}$$

where w is employed to control the contribution of each factor and we set $w = 0.5$ in this paper.

2.2.3 Retweeting Probability Score

Based on the above descriptions, we define the score of retweeting probability that user u retweets message m published by user v by using an linearly ensemble from user's preference and social influence as follows:

$$S(u,m) = \eta \times S_{interest}(u,m) + (1-\eta) \times S_{influence}(u,v) \tag{6}$$

where η is employed to control the contribution of each factor and we set $\eta = 0.5$ in this paper.

2.3 OCCF Retweeting Prediction Model

Now we will formulate the retweeting behavior prediction problem mathematically. Let $\mathbf{U} \in \mathbb{R}^{M \times K}$ be the latent user feature matrix, and $\mathbf{V} \in \mathbb{R}^{K \times N}$ be the latent message feature matrix, where K ($K \ll M, N$) is the number of the latent features. In the OCCF setting, there are several general strategies to tackle the one-class problem. The first strategy is to simply treat all missing values in R as negative examples, which corresponds to the AMAN. However, this strategy doesn't fully consider the missing examples where some of the missing data might be positive. A better method proposed in [5] is to treat all missing values as negative by using low weights on the loss function (wAMAN):

$$\mathcal{L}(U,V) = \sum_{ij} W_{ij}((R_{ij} - U_i V_j)^2 + \lambda(\|U\|_F^2 + \|V\|_F^2)) \tag{7}$$

where $\|\cdot\|_F$ denotes the Frobenius norm fitting constraint, λ is the regularization parameter. $\mathbf{W} \in \mathbb{R}^{M \times N}$ is a non-negative weighted matrix in which W_{ij} reflects the contribution of minimizing the term to the objective $\mathcal{L}(U,V)$. The last two regularization terms are added to avoid overfitting.

In wAMAN, they treat all missing examples as negative examples by using a global weighting scheme. This assumption cannot be precisely represented the relationship between user and message. In many realistic scenarios, whether a user retweets a message in social networks is determined by the two most important factors: (1) how does the user interest on the message content; and (2) who are the publishers. Therefore, we compute the user-message retweeting probability matrix $\mathbf{S} \in \mathbb{R}^{M \times N}$ by Eq. (6) as following:

$$S_{ij} = S(u_i, m_j) \quad (8)$$

where, similar to wAMAN, we only assign the weights to the negative examples, and remaining the weights for positive examples to be 1. Then given the user-message retweeting probability matrix $\mathbf{S}$, the previous optimization problem can be rewritten as follows:

$$\mathcal{L}(U,V) = \sum_{ij} S_{ij}((R_{ij} - U_i V_j)^2 + \lambda(\|U\|_F^2 + \|V\|_F^2)) \quad (9)$$

We represent the proposed method as OCCFRP. We can adopt a weighted alternating least squares scheme to solve the problem. That is, starting from some random initialization on U (or V), we solve each of them alternatively with the another matrix fixed and proceed step by step until convergence. More specifically, holding V fixed, the update of U amounts to the following optimization problem by taking derivatives of $\mathcal{L}(U,V)$ with respect to each entry of U,

$$\frac{1}{2}\frac{\partial \mathcal{L}(U,V)}{\partial U_{ik}} = \sum_j S_{ij}(U_i V_j - R_{ij})V_{jk} + \lambda(\sum_j S_{ij})U_{ik} \quad (10)$$

for $\forall 1 \le i \le M, 1 \le k \le K$. Then we have

$$\begin{aligned}\frac{1}{2}\frac{\partial \mathcal{L}(U,V)}{\partial U_i} &= \frac{1}{2}(\frac{\partial \mathcal{L}(U,V)}{\partial U_{i1}}, \ldots, \frac{\partial \mathcal{L}(U,V)}{\partial U_{iK}}) \\ &= U_i(V^T \tilde{S}_i V + \lambda(\sum_j S_{ij})I) - R_i \tilde{S}_i V\end{aligned} \quad (11)$$

where $\tilde{S}_i \in \mathbb{R}^{N \times N}$ is a diagonal matrix with the elements of ith row in S_i on the diagonal, and I is a $K \times K$ identity matrix.

Fixing V and solving $\frac{\partial \mathcal{L}(U,V)}{\partial U_i} = 0$, we have

$$U_i = R_i \tilde{S}_i V(V^T \tilde{S}_i V + \lambda(\sum_j S_{ij})I)^{-1}, \forall 1 \le i \le M \quad (12)$$

Similarly, The update of V with fixed U by taking derivative of $\mathcal{L}(U,V)$ with respect to each entry of V, we have

$$V_j = R_j^T \tilde{S}_j U(U^T \tilde{S}_j U + \lambda(\sum_i S_{ij})I)^{-1}, \forall 1 \le j \le N \quad (13)$$

where $\tilde{S}_j \in \mathbb{R}^{M \times M}$ is a diagonal matrix with the elements of jth column in S_j on the diagonal. Thus, we apply the following iterative algorithm on our retweeting prediction model in Algorithm 1.

Complexity Analysis Assume that the number of iterations is T. The complexity of one-class collaborative filtering model for retweeting behavior prediction is analyzed as follows. For the runtime performance, since in each iteration it takes time O(K^2MN) to update the U (or V), the computational complexity of running Algorithm 1 is O(TK^2MN).

Algorithm 1 OCCF for Retweeting Prediction.

Require: retweeting matrix R_{ij}, weight matrix S;
Ensure: predicted retweeting matrix: R'_{ij};
Initialize V
Initialize S, $\forall 1 \le i \le M, 1 \le j \le N$
if $R_{ij} = 0$ **then**
  $S_{ij} = S(u_i, m_j)$
else
  $S_{ij} = 1$
end if
repeat
  $U_i := R_i \tilde{S}_i V(V^T \tilde{S}_i V + \lambda(\sum_j S_{ij})I)^{-1}, \forall 1 \le i \le M$
  $V_j := R_j^T \tilde{S}_j U(U^T \tilde{S}_j U + \lambda(\sum_i S_{ij})I)^{-1}, \forall 1 \le j \le N$
until $R^{(t)} \leftarrow \mathcal{L}(U^{(t)}, V^{(t)})$ reaches to convergence
return $R'_{ij} = U_i V_j$

3. EXPERIMENTS

In this section, we conduct several experiments to compare the prediction performance of our OCCFRP approach with other state-of-the-art retweeting prediction methods.

3.1 Dataset and Experimental Settings

We evaluate our proposed method on a large-scale publicly available dataset released by [8]. The dataset was crawled from Sina Weibo which allows users to follow other users and receive the messages from the followed users similar to Twitter. Specifically, in this paper, we randomly sample 10,000 messages retweeted by 690,787 users from the above dataset. The total number of retweetings are 1,435,720. To validate the proposed method, we randomly sample 80% of the retweetings from user-message retweeting matrix as the training data to predict the remaining 20% of retweetings. The corresponding entries in R of positive instances for testing data are set to 0. Calculated with number of users, number of messages and number of retweetings, the density of conducted dataset is 0.02%. The sparsity problem is very serious in the retweeting matrix.

3.2 Baselines and Evaluation Metrics

We implement the following baselines for comparison with our proposed model.

- **Naive Bayes**: The retweeting prediction can be considered as a binary classification task, where each message is labelled either positive or negative instance to represent whether it will be retweeted or not.
- **LRC-BQ**: The method proposes a notion of social influence locality based on pairwise influence and structural diversity, and then uses a logistic regression classifier to predict user's retweeting behavior [8].
- **MNMFRP**: This method utilizes nonnegative matrix factorization to predict retweeting behavior from user and content dimensions by using strength of social relationship to constrain objective function [7].
- **CRPM & IRPM**: The two methods use the clustering relationships of messages to predict retweeting behavior based on matrix factorization [2].
- **AMAN**: The method treats all missing as negative example. We can directly apply traditional collaborative filtering algorithm to solve the problem.
- **wAMAN**: The method considers all missing data as negative examples by assigning a uniform weighting scheme [5].

To quantitatively evaluate the performance of the proposed model, we employ four metrics to evaluate the performance of retweeting prediction in terms of Precision (Prec.), Recall (Rec.), F_1-score (F_1), and Accuracy (Acc.).

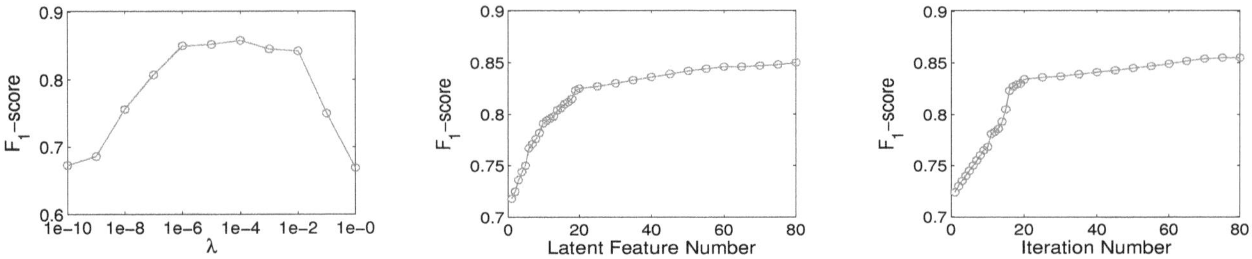

(a) F_1-score v.s. λ (b) F_1-score v.s. #Feature (c) F_1-score v.s. #Iteration

Figure 1: F_1-score vs. (a) λ and (b) Latent Feature Number and (c) Iteration Number on Weibo Dataset

3.3 Parameter Settings

Parameter λ: The parameter λ plays the role of adjusting the strengths of different terms in the objective function. Taking the scales of U and V into account, we scan orders of magnitude and try a number of different parameters as shown in Figure 1(a). The results show that the parameter set $\lambda = 10^{-4}$ produce the best performance. In our following experiments, we just use this parameter setting.

Number of Latent Features: To find a K-dimensional joint latent space for users and messages, we train U and V using gradient descent method. Specifically, we conduct extensive experiments with K from 2 to 80 on the dataset as shown in Figure 1(b). From the figure, we can see conclude that the proposed model can converge at around 30 features. Hence, we use $K = 30$ as the latent space dimension.

Number of Iterations: We preset the number of updating iterations to get a good performance while avoid overfitting. Figure 1(c) shows the impacts of the number of iterations on F_1-score. Considering the trade-off between the computational efficiency and the accuracy of prediction, we conduct 30 iterations for the solution in our experiments.

3.4 Prediction Performance

Our goal is to find who will be retweeted based on partially observed retweeting instances. Therefore, we will demonstrate the prediction performance of the proposed method, and compare it with other methods. Specifically, we set the optimal parameters when running the baselines. Then all experiments are performed 5 runs. We list the average results of each method in Table 1. From these results, we can see the following conclusions: (1) The proposed OCCFRP model significantly outperforms the baseline methods in our experimental results; (2) The OCCFRP can obtain better performance than CRPM & IRPM using message clustering information, which demonstrates that social influence can impact the performance of the prediction; (3) The prediction performance of OCCFRP is better than AMAN and wAMAN, which reveals that the weight for each negative example is effectiveness of factor for retweeting prediction.

4. CONCLUSIONS

In this paper we cast the problem of retweeting prediction as the one-class collaborative filtering task. We propose a new weighting strategy which measure retweeting probability score between user and message to improve the OCCF performance. Empirical study on real world dataset demonstrates that our proposed approach can achieve better performance than state-of-the-art methods.

Table 1: Performance of retweeting prediction.

Method	Prec.	Rec.	F_1	Acc.
Naive Bayes	0.562	0.555	0.558	0.555
LRC-BQ	0.698	0.770	0.733	0.719
MNMFRP	0.796	0.791	0.793	N/A
CRPM	0.814	0.833	0.823	0.821
IRPM	0.817	0.833	0.825	0.823
AMAN	0.524	0.546	0.535	0.546
wAMAN	0.785	0.692	0.736	0.692
OCCFRP	**0.853**	**0.842**	**0.847**	**0.845**

5. ACKNOWLEDGMENTS

This work is supported by National Key Technology R&D Program (No.2012BAH46B00), Strategic Leading Science and Technology Projects of CAS (No.XDA06030200), Natural Science Foundation of China (No.61402123, No.61170230).

6. REFERENCES

[1] N. A. Abdullah, D. Nishioka, Y. Tanaka, and Y. Murayama. User's action and decision making of retweet messages towards reducing misinformation spread during disaster. *Journal of Information Processing*, 23(1):31–40, 2015.

[2] B. Jiang, J. Liang, Y. Sha, and L. Wang. Message clustering based matrix factorization model for retweeting behavior prediction. In *CIKM*, pages 1843–1846. ACM, 2015.

[3] Z. Luo, M. Osborne, J. Tang, and T. Wang. Who will retweet me?: finding retweeters in twitter. In *SIGIR*, pages 869–872. ACM, 2013.

[4] P. Metaxas, E. Mustafaraj, K. Wong, L. Zeng, M. O'Keefe, and S. Finn. What do retweets indicate? results from user survey and meta-review of research. In *ICWSM*, pages 658–661. AAAI Press, 2015.

[5] R. Pan, Y. Zhou, B. Cao, N. N. Liu, R. Lukose, M. Scholz, and Q. Yang. One-class collaborative filtering. In *ICDM*, pages 502–511. IEEE, 2008.

[6] B. Suh, L. Hong, P. Pirolli, and E. H. Chi. Want to be retweeted? large scale analytics on factors impacting retweet in twitter network. In *Socialcom*, pages 177–184. IEEE, 2010.

[7] M. Wang, W. Zuo, and Y. Wang. A multidimensional nonnegative matrix factorization model for retweeting behavior prediction. *Mathematical Problems in Engineering*, 2015:1–10, 2015.

[8] J. Zhang, J. Tang, J. Li, Y. Liu, and C. Xing. Who influenced you? predicting retweet via social influence locality. *ACM TKDD*, 9(3):25, 2015.

Sampling Strategies and Active Learning for Volume Estimation

Haotian Zhang, Jimmy Lin, Gordon V. Cormack, and Mark D. Smucker
University of Waterloo, Ontario, Canada
{haotian.zhang, jimmylin, gvcormac, mark.smucker}@uwaterloo.ca

ABSTRACT

This paper tackles the challenge of accurately and efficiently estimating the number of relevant documents in a collection for a particular topic. One real-world application is estimating the volume of social media posts (e.g., tweets) pertaining to a topic, which is fundamental to tracking the popularity of politicians and brands, the potential sales of a product, etc. Our insight is to leverage active learning techniques to find all the "easy" documents, and then to use sampling techniques to infer the number of relevant documents in the residual collection. We propose a simple yet effective technique for determining this "switchover" point, which intuitively can be understood as the "knee" in an effort vs. recall gain curve, as well as alternative sampling strategies beyond the knee. We show on several TREC datasets and a collection of tweets that our best technique yields more accurate estimates (with the same effort) than several alternatives.

1. INTRODUCTION

Suppose we would like to estimate the number of relevant documents in a collection for a particular topic. We refer to this as the volume estimation problem. How would we go about doing this both *accurately*, such that our estimate is as close as possible to the actual value, and *efficiently*, with as little effort as possible? This problem presents an interesting twist on the problem of high-recall retrieval. For example, in electronic discovery [6], the litigants are interested in the *actual* documents, whereas we just want the *volume* of the relevant documents. Of course, if we can find all the relevant documents, we can just count them—so existing active learning techniques for high-recall retrieval provide a baseline. Alternatively, we could just randomly sample from the collection to estimate the prevalence and infer the volume. The question is: can we do better than either approach?

Even assuming we can, who cares? Under what circumstances would we like to know the number of relevant documents without identifying the actual relevant documents? The concrete instantiation of our problem is estimating the volume of social media posts (e.g., tweets) pertaining to a topic. Volume estimation in this case is fundamental to several real-world applications: tracking the popularity of politicians and brands, the box-office appeal of movies, the audience for a sporting event, the potential sales of a product, and so on. The number of tweets pertaining to unfolding events is an often-quoted statistic in media coverage. Thus, volume estimation is not only academically interesting, but has significant real-world value.

The contribution of this paper is the development and evaluation of a technique for volume estimation based on active learning and sampling. Consider an active learning approach that can be characterized by a gain curve. The "knee" of that curve corresponds to the point where all the "easy" documents have been found. Our idea is to take advantage of active learning until the knee, and then use sampling techniques to extrapolate on the remainder of the collection. We present a simple technique for finding the knee that works well in practice and explore three different sampling approaches past the knee. On several TREC datasets and a collection of tweets, we show that our stratified sampling technique yields the most accurate estimates compared to other techniques with the same amount of effort.

2. BACKGROUND AND RELATED WORK

The volume estimation problem is related to retrieval techniques that focus on achieving very high recall—motivating application domains include legal eDiscovery, systematic reviews in evidence-based medicine, and locating prior art in patent search. The starting point of our work is the so-called baseline model implementation (BMI) that was provided to participants of the TREC 2015 Total Recall track, whose principal purpose was to evaluate, through a controlled simulation, methods to achieve very high recall—as close as practicable to 100%—with a human assessor in the loop. BMI is based on the "AutoTAR" technique of Cormack and Grossman [3]. Starting with a query, AutoTAR applies continuous active learning using relevance feedback to prioritize documents for human assessment. As in standard active learning, relevance judgments incrementally refine an underlying relevance model—but unlike the standard formulation of active learning, the point of AutoTAR is not to arrive at the best decision boundary between relevant and non-relevant documents, but rather to find all the relevant documents within a finite collection.

The effectiveness of techniques for high-recall retrieval is typically characterized by gain curves plotting effort (x-axis) vs. recall (y-axis). Most techniques, including the BMI and

SIGIR '16, July 17 - 21, 2016, Pisa, Italy

ISBN 978-1-4503-4069-4/16/07...$15.00
DOI: http://dx.doi.org/10.1145/2911451.2914685

even manual approaches, exhibit gain curves that begin with a "ramp up" phase, followed by a period where gain rises steadily, indicating the continuous discovery of "easy to find" relevant documents, and end with a region where the gain curves level off as the remaining relevant documents become more difficult to find. The "knee" is where the gain curve levels off, and this is a feature we exploit in our solution. In this work, we use the BMI from the TREC 2015 Total Recall track as-is, with the enhancement of a stopping criterion.

3. APPROACH

Suppose we would like to estimate the number of relevant documents in a particular collection consisting of D documents. How might we go about doing this?

A naïve approach might be to randomly sample (without replacement) documents from the collection and assess them for relevance. We can approximate this as a Bernoulli process, for which the volume estimate R_T is $D \cdot R_E/E$, where we find R_E relevant documents after examining a total of E documents. Note that this does not form a complete algorithm because we still need to know how many samples to draw. We return to this issue later when explaining our paired experimental methodology.

An alternative starting point might be to leverage an existing high-recall retrieval technique such as the BMI (Section 2). That is, we simply *find* all the relevant documents, which is a trivial way to determine the count. The problem, however, is that the BMI also does not come with a stopping criterion. Although various researchers have tackled this and related issues [7, 1], it is by no means solved.

Regardless, let's say we apply BMI to judge A documents. During this process, we will have explored some fraction of the collection that is more likely to contain relevant documents, and say we discover R_A documents. This value, of course, provides a lower bound on the number of relevant documents in the collection. But the problem is that we don't know how many relevant documents there are in the documents we didn't look at (what we refer to as the residual collection). Nevertheless, we can estimate an upper bound using the rate at which we're finding relevant documents just before we stopped, and extrapolate to the remainder of the collection. However, this makes a terrible assumption because any active learning technique will prioritize documents more likely to be relevant before documents less likely to be relevant, and so such an extrapolation would yield an unrealistically large overestimate.

One solution is to sample the residual collection. This requires answering two questions: First, how do we find the knee (i.e., the value of A)? Second, how do we sample after the knee? We tackle these two questions in turn.

3.1 Find the Knee

In our approach, we employ the BMI augmented by the following the knee-finding method proposed by Cormack and Grossman [4]. In each iteration, the BMI selects exponentially larger batches of documents for human judgment. After receiving feedback for each batch, we can trace the gain curve described in Section 2; to be precise, the y axis is now the number of relevant documents found and not recall.

At the end of each iteration, we have a point that corresponds to the total number of relevant documents found and the total number of documents judged thus far. We propose a candidate knee point as follows: find a point on the gain curve with maximum perpendicular distance from a line between the origin and the current (i.e., last) point of the curve. Let p_0 be the slope of the line from the origin to the candidate knee, p_1 be the slope of the line from the candidate knee to the last point, and the slope ratio $\rho = \frac{p_0}{p_1}$. We accept the candidate knee (and terminate) if: (1) the number of documents examined exceeds 1000 (to ensure that the active learning process has gotten beyond the "ramp up" phase), and (2) $\rho > 6$, if at least 150 relevant documents have been retrieved, or $\rho > 156 - r$, if $r < 150$ relevant documents have been retrieved. The second clause in (2) is a special case for handling topics with few relevant documents. The parameters for this technique were tuned on a private dataset.

Note that to be precise, this technique doesn't actually discover the knee until we've "passed" the knee, but the intuition nevertheless holds. The actual switchover point where we stop active learning and begin sampling corresponds to the point where we discovered the knee. However, for expository convenience we still refer to "stopping at the knee".

3.2 Sampling Strategies

Based on the knee-finding algorithm described in the previous section, we apply the BMI until the stopping criterion is met. At that point, we have judged A documents and found R_A relevant documents. The next question is: what do we do with the residual collection that we have not yet examined? We present three sampling strategies:

Negative Binomial Sampling. In this approach, we sample from the residual collection until we encounter M relevant documents; let's say this process requires us to examine S documents. Each sample can be modeled as a Bernoulli trial, and thus the sampling process can be characterized by a negative binomial distribution. Under this interpretation, the minimum variance unbiased estimator for $\hat{p}$, the probability of success (i.e., probability of a document being relevant) is given as $\hat{p} = (r-1)/(r+k-1)$, where r is the number of successes (relevant documents, which we set to M) and k is the number of failures (non-relevant documents) in our sequence of observations [5].

From this, our estimate of the total number of relevant documents, R_T, is as follows (note $S = r + k$):

$$R_T = R_A + (D - A)\frac{(M-1)}{(S-1)}, \text{ for } M > 1. \quad (1)$$

In our experiments, we tried setting $M \in \{2, 4, 8\}$. Naturally, higher values of M reduce the variance, but at the cost of requiring more assessment effort. The total effort required with this approach is $A + S$, where S is the number of documents we must assess to find M relevant documents.

The Horvitz-Thompson Estimator. The downside of the negative binomial sampling strategy is that for cases where the prevalence of relevant documents in the residual collection is low, it might require a lot of effort to find M relevant documents. An alternative is to use the BMI to score all documents in the residual collection at the point when it terminates, thus ordering all remaining documents in decreasing probability of relevance.

From here, we can apply a standard sampling technique called the Horvitz-Thompson Estimator (HT estimator) [8]: we compute a distribution over all documents in the residual collection such that its probability of being sampled is proportional to its probability of relevance (as estimated by the BMI). This renormalized distribution is referred to as the inclusion probability, i.e., π_i refers to the probability that document i will be sampled. The Horvitz-Thompson estimate of the number of relevant documents is:

$$R_T = R_A + \sum_{i=1}^{n} \pi_i^{-1} Y_i \tag{2}$$

where Y_i is an indicator variable for relevance in each of the n sampled documents. Note that this does not form a complete algorithm because we are missing a stopping criterion. Once again, we address this issue in our paired experimental methodology below.

Stratified Sampling. We propose a novel stratified sampling strategy, also based on a relevance ranking of the residual collection at the point when the BMI terminates. This approach proceeds in iterations: at the i-th iteration, we randomly sample K^S documents ($= 1000$) from the next top ranking K documents ($= 10000$) and judge those documents. Suppose we find R_i relevant documents: we can then estimate that there are $K \cdot (R_i/K^S)$ in the top K hits. We then proceed to the next iteration and sample K^S documents from the *next* K top ranking documents, repeating as long as we find at least one relevant document. The total number of relevant documents can then be computed as:

$$R_T = R_A + \sum_{i=1}^{n} K \cdot (R_i/K^S) \tag{3}$$

where n is the number of iterations. The total effort expended is $A + n \cdot K^S$.

4. EXPERIMENTAL SETUP

To evaluate our volume estimation techniques, we used test collections from the TREC 2015 Total Recall Track [7]. In particular, we used three collections: the (redacted) Jeb Bush Emails (called "Athome1"), consisting of 290k emails from Jeb Bush's eight-year tenure as the governor of Florida (10 topics); the *Illicit Goods* dataset (called "Athome2") collected for the TREC 2015 Dynamic Domain Track, consisting of 465k documents from a web crawl (10 topics); and the *Local Politics* dataset (called "Athome3") collected for the TREC 2015 Dynamic Domain Track, consisting of 902k documents from various news sources (10 topics). The relevance assessment process is described in the track overview paper [7], but for the purposes of our study, it suffices to say that the evaluation methodology has been sufficiently validated for assessing the effectiveness of high-recall tasks (and thus these collections are suitable for our volume estimation problem). Finally, as a validation set, we evaluated our techniques on the Twitter collection described in Bommannavar et al. [2], who *exhaustively* annotated approximately 800k tweets from one day in August 2012 with respect to four topics: Apple (the technology company), Mars (the planet), Obama, and the Olympics. This dataset exactly matches our motivating application: how much "buzz" is there on social media about a particular topic?

Note that random sampling and the HT estimator approaches are not complete estimation algorithms since they lack a stopping criterion. Therefore, they are compared to negative binomial sampling and stratified sampling in a paired setup, where we evaluate how the techniques compare at the same level of effort. This models an A/B testing scenario where we have two parallel efforts proceeding at exactly the same pace assessing documents. When one technique terminates, we also stop the other. At that point, we ask: how do the two estimates compare?

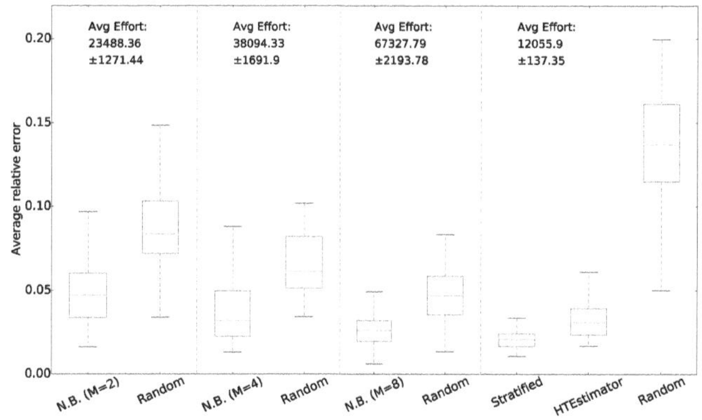

Figure 1: Box-and-whiskers plot characterizing 50 trials of each of our techniques on the Athome1 collection.

Our experimental procedure is as follows: for each topic in a collection, we ran our estimation technique (either negative binomial sampling or stratified sampling) and recorded the total effort. We then ran a paired experiment with either random sampling or the HT estimator (or both) using exactly the same level of effort. We recorded the estimated volume for all techniques. For each collection, we report the average (relative) error across all topics and the root mean square error. The Athome1 collection was used as our training set, on which we ran 50 trials of the above procedure to characterize the variability of estimates. The Athome2, Athome3, and Twitter collections were used as held-out test sets—we report the results of a single trial.

5. RESULTS

The results of 50 trials of our experimental procedure are shown in Figure 1, where the average relative error across the trials is characterized by a standard box-and-whiskers plot. We compared negative binomial sampling, $M = \{2, 4, 8\}$, with random sampling using the paired approach described above. We compared stratified sampling with the HT estimator and random sampling using exactly the same procedure. Each of these comparisons is shown by grouped bars (separated by dashed lines) in the figure.

As expected, the negative binomial sampling approach becomes more accurate with increasing values of M (but requires correspondingly more effort). For reference, the entire collection contains 290k documents, so with $M = 8$, on average we must examine nearly a quarter of the collection. However, we see that negative binomial sampling is more accurate than random sampling at the same level of effort. It is clear that our stratified sampling approach is superior to all other techniques. On average, stratified sampling requires about half as much effort as negative binomial sampling with $M = 2$ but gives much more accurate estimates. In fact, stratified sampling provides more accurate estimates than negative binomial sampling with $M = 8$, at about a fifth of the effort. Stratified sampling also beats both the HT estimator and random sampling at the same level of effort.

Results for Athome2 and Athome3 are shown in Table 1.

Measure	Avg Effort	Avg Relative Error	Root Mean Square Error
Athome2			
Neg. Binomial ($M = 2$)	80925	0.016	0.021
= sample	80925	0.094	0.122
Neg. Binomial ($M = 4$)	122527	0.014	0.023
= sample	122527	0.052	0.062
Neg. Binomial ($M = 8$)	181407	0.015	0.020
= sample	181407	0.045	0.060
Stratified	8363	0.026	0.042
= HTEstimator	8363	0.051	0.070
= sample	8363	0.410	0.621
Athome3			
Neg. Binomial ($M = 2$)	482237	0.041	0.105
= sample	482237	0.045	0.079
Neg. Binomial ($M = 4$)	546379	0.011	0.030
= sample	546379	0.042	0.073
Neg. Binomial ($M = 8$)	597489	0.023	0.058
= sample	597489	0.032	0.064
Stratified	3168	0.053	0.113
= HTEstimator	3168	0.100	0.200
= sample	3168	0.867	1.119
Twitter			
Neg. Binomial ($M = 2$)	24160	0.261	0.233
= sample	24160	0.222	0.240
Neg. Binomial ($M = 4$)	39162	0.106	0.090
= sample	39162	0.046	0.041
Neg. Binomial ($M = 8$)	40295	0.007	0.036
= sample	40295	0.179	0.181
Stratified	22687	0.047	0.048
= HTEstimator	22687	0.093	0.092
= sample	22687	0.170	0.218

Table 1: Results of various volume estimation techniques on the Athome2, Athome3, and Twitter collections.

Since these comprise our held-out test data, we only report the results of a single trial. In the table, rows are grouped in terms of different techniques at the same level of effort, e.g., the rows marked "= sample" denote accuracy with the same number of judged documents as the corresponding negative binomial or stratified condition. Due to the variability inherent in our sampling strategies, in our particular trial we observe greater error with $M = 8$ than with $M = 4$ using negative binomial sampling. This, however, is not inconsistent with the results in Figure 1.

Overall, the results on Athome2 (465k documents) are consistent with the results from Athome1, our training set. Negative binomial sampling becomes more accurate with increasing M and is more accurate than random sampling with the same level of effort. However, our stratified sampling technique provides comparable error at far less cost, beating both the HT estimator and random sampling.

Results on the Athome3 collection, which contains 902k documents, are quite poor. Table 2 shows why: for each topic in that collection, we list the total number of relevant documents, the effort expended in the active learning portion of our procedure, and the number of relevant documents found at that point. For five of the topics (those in bold), with active learning we've found either all or all but one of the relevant documents, which means that our termination condition for negative binomial sampling (e.g., with $M = 2$) is never met and hence the procedure forces us to examine *the entire collection*. In contrast, with stratified sampling we examine 1000 of the top 10000 documents, find zero relevant, and terminate.

The bottom of Table 1 shows our results for the Twitter collection. Once again, we report results from a single trial. Overall, the findings are consistent with the other collections: our stratified sampling technique clearly yields more accurate estimates than all other techniques. This gives us some degree of confidence that our algorithms, developed on email (Athome1), generalize to entirely different collections (tweets). We have no explanation as to why negative binomial sampling with $M = 4$ gives worse estimates than comparable random sampling, or why comparable random sampling with $M = 8$ gives such poor results. We purposely decided against error analysis in order to preserve the sanctity of this validation set.

Topic	Rel Docs	Knee Stop Effort	RelAtKnee
athome3089	**255**	1105	**254**
athome3133	**113**	1105	**112**
athome3226	2094	3478	2022
athome3290	**26**	2316	**26**
athome3357	629	1526	599
athome3378	**66**	1105	**66**
athome3423	76	1232	40
athome3431	1111	1232	1106
athome3481	2036	3478	1924
athome3484	**23**	1105	**23**

Table 2: Relevant documents identified and effort when BMI terminates for Athome3.

6. CONCLUSION

Estimating the number of relevant documents in a collection presents an interesting twist to the high-recall retrieval problem. Our results show that actually *finding* the relevant documents is a good approach to *counting* the total volume. However, we develop and verify the insight that we should first identify the "easy to find" documents and then extrapolate via sampling on the rest. Our approach establishes a baseline for future work on an important real-world application, particularly in the social media space.

Acknowledgments. This work was supported in part by the U.S. National Science Foundation under awards IIS-1218043 and CNS-1405688, the Natural Sciences and Engineering Research Council of Canada (NSERC), Google, and the University of Waterloo. Any opinions, findings, conclusions, or recommendations expressed are those of the authors and do not necessarily reflect the views of the sponsors.

7. REFERENCES

[1] M. Bagdouri, W. Webber, D. Lewis, and D. Oard. Towards minimizing the annotation cost of certified text classification. *CIKM*, 2013.

[2] P. Bommannavar, J. Lin, and A. Rajaraman. Estimating topical volume in social media streams. *SAC*, 2016.

[3] G. Cormack and M. Grossman. Autonomy and reliability of continuous active learning for technology-assisted review. *arXiv:1504.06868v1*, 2015.

[4] G. Cormack and M. Grossman. Engineering quality and reliability in technology-assisted review. *SIGIR*, 2016.

[5] N. Johnson, A. Kemp, and S. Kotz. *Univariate Discrete Distributions, 3rd Edition.* Wiley, 2006.

[6] D. Oard and W. Webber. Information retrieval for e-discovery. *FnTIR*, 7(2–3):99–237, 2013.

[7] A. Roegiest, G. Cormack, M. Grossman, and C. Clarke. TREC 2015 Total Recall track overview. *TREC*, 2015.

[8] Y. Tillé. *Sampling Algorithms.* Springer Series in Statistics. Springer, 2006.

Search-based Evaluation from Truth Transcripts for Voice Search Applications

François Mairesse
Amazon.com
101 Main street, Suite 900
Cambridge, MA 02142, USA
mairessf@amazon.com

Paul Raccuglia
Amazon.com
101 Main street, Suite 900
Cambridge, MA 02142, USA
praccu@gmail.com

Shiv Vitaladevuni
Amazon.com
101 Main street, Suite 900
Cambridge, MA 02142, USA
shivnaga@amazon.com

ABSTRACT

Voice search applications are typically evaluated by comparing the predicted query to a reference human transcript, regardless of the search results returned by the query. While we find that an exact transcript match is highly indicative of user satisfaction, a transcript which does not match the reference still produces satisfactory search results a significant fraction of the time. This paper therefore proposes an evaluation method that compares the search results of the speech recognition hypotheses with the search results produced by a human transcript. Compared with a strict sentence match, a human evaluation shows that search result overlap is a better predictor of (a) user satisfaction and (b) search result click-through. Finally, we propose a model predicting the Expected Search Satisfaction Rate (ESSR), conditioned on search overlap outcomes. On a held out set of 1036 voice search queries, our model predicted an ESSR within 0.9% (relative) of the ground truth satisfaction averaged over 3 human judges.

Keywords

Evaluation, voice search, automatic speech recognition, search engines, entity resolution

1. INTRODUCTION

Voice search applications are typically evaluated by comparing the automated speech recognition (ASR) output to a single human reference transcript, and measuring either the Word Error Rate (WER) or the ratio of exact string matches (Sentence Error Rate or SER) [4, 1]. We find that while an exact sentence match is highly indicative of user satisfaction, a sentence error is a poor indicator of user dissatisfaction (see Sections 3 and 4). Sentence errors are not predictive of user satisfaction because transcribers produce a single transcript per audio sample, while many other transcription variants could produce satisfactory search results. Table 1 shows how a normalization variant between *t-shirts* and *t shirts* affects search results in a product search engine.

SIGIR '16, July 17 - 21, 2016, Pisa, Italy

ACM 978-1-4503-4069-4/16/07...$15.00
DOI: http://dx.doi.org/10.1145/2911451.2914735

An error analysis reveals that 37% of the SER is due to arbitrary normalization choices (e.g. *tooth brush* vs *toothbrush*), function word deletion (e.g. *a*, *the*), possessives, plurals, or transcription errors. This is partly due to the fact that the language model is trained on search queries, hence the system is likely to output search-like utterances. A first solution is to handcraft normalization rules, however those do not scale and can mask errors that impact search (e.g., ignoring white-space mismatches could artificially increase accuracy). Another solution would be to ask transcribers to provide an exhaustive set of transcripts for each audio sample, however it is not cost effective.

In contrast, information retrieval systems are evaluated by asking human judges to estimate the relevance of individual results, and then compute the Mean Average Precision or Normalized Discounted Cumulative Gain (NDCG) [3]. Such metrics are costly when used for evaluating voice search systems, since the human judgments must be collected for new queries resulting from ASR model updates. While previous work has focused on jointly optimizing ASR and information retrieval systems [2], it assumes the existence of search relevance judgments for every test query. Our goal is to remove the need for collecting large amounts of search evaluation data for offline testing, by building a user satisfaction model from a small set of judgments.

In order to evaluate the effect of voice recognition errors more accurately without requiring additional transcription resources, in Section 2 we propose an evaluation method that compares the search results of the speech recognition hypotheses with the search results produced by a human transcript. This is related to the Google WebScore, which is defined as the number of times the first result of the ASR output matches the first result of the human transcript [5]. However, we find that using search results beyond the first one produces metrics that correlate better with human judgment. Section 3 reports experiments showing that partial overlap metrics outperform SER as a predictor of human search result ratings and user clicks. Finally, Section 4 proposes a model of user satisfaction conditioned on search overlap outcomes. Experiments on a held out test set of 1036 utterances predicted an Expected Search Satisfaction Rate (ESSR) within 0.9% relative to the ground truth satisfaction averaged over 3 human judges.

2. SEARCH-BASED EVALUATION

An ideal search-based evaluation would compare the returned search results with the set of satisfactory results that the user intended to find. Labeling search results is costly

Table 1: Search results for the queries *t-shirts* and *t shirts*. Results that occur in both searches within the first 10 results are in bold.

Search query: *t-shirts*	Search query: *t shirts*
1) **Hanes Men's 4 Pack Short Sleeve Comfortsoft Tee**	1) **Fruit of the Loom Men's 4-Pack Pocket T-Shirt - Colors May Vary**
2) Hanes Men's 5 Pack Comfort Soft Crew Neck Tee, White, Large	2) **Russell Athletic Men's Basic Cotton Tee**
3) **Fruit of the Loom Men's 4-Pack Pocket T-Shirt - Colors May Vary**	3) **Problem Solved T-shirt Funny Shirts**
4) **Russell Athletic Men's Basic Cotton Tee**	4) **Hanes Men's 4 Pack Short Sleeve Comfortsoft Tee**
5) **Problem Solved T-shirt Funny Shirts**	5) Soffe Men's Men'S Long Sleeve Cotton T-Shirt
6) **Fruit of the Loom Men's 4-Pack Crew Neck T-Shirt**	6) Original Penguin Men's Bold Stripe Print Tee
7) Next Level Mens Premium Fitted Short-Sleeve Crew	7) California Republic Men's T-Shirt
8) **Mens Funny Sayings Slogans T Shirts-I May Be Wrong tshirt-Ideal Gift Ideas**	8) **Fruit of the Loom Men's 4-Pack Crew Neck T-Shirt**
9) Hanes Men's Classics 6 Pack Crew Neck Tee	9) Fruit of the Loom Men's Short Sleeve Crew Tee
10) Hanes Women's Relax Fit Jersey V-Neck Tee	10) **Mens Funny Sayings Slogans T Shirts-I May Be Wrong tshirt-Ideal Gift Ideas**

and prone to ambiguities, since the annotator does not know what the user had in mind. However, human transcripts can be used to estimate the intended search results. Let us define $R_{ref}^{1:N}$ as the set of the first N results returned by sending the *reference* transcript to search, and $R_{asr,1}^{1:N}$ the first N results returned by sending the *1-best ASR hypothesis* to search.

Since the true user intent is unknown, we rely on R_{ref} as an approximation to the search results the user is looking for. Table 1 shows that search engines sometime fail to return consistent results between equivalent surface forms. As a result, the next section shows that a strict ordered result match correlates poorly with human judgments of search accuracy ($r = 0.65$), i.e., it over-penalizes the system. This paper therefore investigates a family of *search overlap* metrics characterizing the minimum number of results in common N_{min} between the two sets of N search results:

$$o(R_{asr}, R_{ref}, N_{min}, N) =$$
$$\begin{cases} \text{undefined} & \text{if } |R_{ref}| = 0 \\ 1 & \text{if } |R_{asr,1}^{1:N} \cap R_{ref}^{1:N}| \geq min(N_{min}, |R_{ref}|) \\ 0 & \text{otherwise} \end{cases}$$

Let us abbreviate $o(R_{asr}, R_{ref}, N_{min}, N)$ as $o(N_{min}, N)$. The search results in Table 1 have 6 results in common. Since the first 2 results do not overlap we can measure that $o(1,2) = o(2,2) = 0$. The first 4 results have exactly 3 items in common, hence $o(1,4) = o(2,4) = o(3,4) = 1$ and $o(4,4) = 0$. Note that the Google WebScore corresponds to $o(1,1)$ since it only takes the first result into account [5].

3. CORRELATION WITH HUMAN JUDGMENTS AND USER CLICKS

In order to identify the most suitable metric for evaluating ASR systems, we asked human judges to evaluate 3500 search results produced by the 1-best hypothesis of a mobile shopping voice recognition application, based on the corresponding human reference transcript. See instructions in Figure 1. Human judges associated each ASR hypothesis with a search quality rating, and discarded any non-shopping utterances. Additionally, we asked human judges to evaluate the search results produced by the reference transcript. Note that in a first experiment 2 judges rates 500 voice searches, and in a follow up experiment 6 groups of 3 judges each rated additional slices of 500 voice searches, for a total of 3500 utterances.

1. Press play to listen to the audio
2. Evaluate the search results on a scale from 1-3:
    - 1: I am not satisfied by the search results
    - 2: I am partially satisfied by the search results
    - 3: I am satisfied by the search results
    - N/A: not a shopping query, or I cannot make sense of what is being said after looking at the results page

Figure 1: Search evaluation instructions.

Each voice search with a rating of 3 is labeled as *satisfactory* while ratings below 3 are labeled as *unsatisfactory*. The *Rating* column of Table 2 shows the Pearson's correlations between the satisfaction ratings and the evaluation metrics mentioned in the previous section (for various values of N_{min} and N), as well as sentence error rate (SER). In order to focus on the effect of ASR errors, these were obtained after removing non-shopping utterances (e.g., navigation queries, phatic utterances) and utterances for which the search results of the reference transcript were labeled as unsatisfactory. Out of the remaining 2462 utterances, a training set of 1426 utterances was used in Table 2, while 1036 utterances from distinct groups of annotators were held out for testing.

Results show that whether or not the reference results and the ASR results have one result in common (i.e., *o(1,10)*) is the best predictor of human ratings ($r = .82$). All proposed search-based metrics are better predictors of search ratings than sentence match ($r = .60$). We find that the Google WebScore (i.e., *o(1,1)*) does not predict satisfaction as well as metrics that go beyond the first search result ($r = .71$).

Additionally, we investigated whether overlap metrics can predict user clicks following a voice search. The *Click* column in Table 2 shows the correlations between the result overlap and click events over 63,000 live voice queries. A query is associated with a click event only if the user clicks

Table 2: Pearson's correlation coefficient between overlap and SER metrics with (1) human search rating and (2) whether or not a user clicked on a search result. Largest correlations are in bold.

Metric	Correlation with rating	Correlation with click
o(1,10)	**0.82**	**0.22**
o(1,5)	0.81	0.21
o(1,3)	0.78	0.20
o(3,5)	0.72	0.16
o(1,1)	0.71	0.15
o(10,10)	0.62	0.04
Ordered result match	0.61	0.02
Sentence match	0.60	0.14
Word error rate	0.58	0.16
# utterances	1,426	63,000

on a product on the first page returned by the voice search. The results confirm that low result overlap metrics are better predictors than sentence match ($r = .22$ vs $r = .14$, respectively), however the correlations are weaker. This could be partly due to users not clicking on a result even though the result is relevant. Additionally, the reference search results were retrieved one month after the live results, hence the variation of the search results over time is likely to weaken the correlations too.

4. USER SATISFACTION PREDICTION

This section focuses on estimating a user satisfaction model based on the features investigated in the previous sections. Since the satisfaction model will be used to evaluate production ASR systems, it is important to (1) avoid any overfitting and (2) be able to inspect the learned model. For these reasons, we estimate a discrete conditional probability table based on rating counts of the training data detailed in Section 3. Table 3 shows the estimated probability distribution of user satisfaction conditioned on the search overlap. Given such a table, one can compute the expected probability of satisfaction over a set on unseen utterances by taking the average of the probability that the search results were rated as satisfactory, over all utterances in the test set.

In order to focus the attention on the effect of ASR on search accuracy, Table 3 only includes utterances for which the reference transcript's results are rated as satisfactory. Hence our approach provides an upper bound on user satisfaction. The method could trivially be extended to include utterances for which the search engine did not return relevant results to model the effect of search engine errors.

While observing an overlap is not more indicative than observing a sentence match, the absence of overlap is a better indicator of poor rating than a sentence mismatch ((P(r=non-sat|¬ o(1,10))=.79) vs P(r=non-sat|¬ sentence match)=.46).

This table provide a model of the expected user satisfaction s resulting from an ASR output given that the reference transcript produces valid results, by marginalizing over all search overlap outcomes. Because we focus on voice queries for which the reference transcript is a valid search, the probability of satisfaction is 1 if the ASR output matches the reference transcript. Hence, the overlap metric comes into play only when the transcripts do not match. As a result

Table 3: Probability of satisfactory rating (r=*sat*) conditioned on various metric outcomes, computed over 1426 training utterances. Utterances for which the reference transcript results in a non-satisfactory search were removed.

Rating r	r = non-sat	r = sat
P(r|o(1,10))	0.02	0.98
P(r|¬o(1,10))	**0.79**	**0.21**
P(r|o(1,3))	0.01	0.99
P(r|¬o(1,3))	0.71	0.29
P(r|o(3,5))	0.01	0.99
P(r|¬o(3,5))	0.61	0.39
P(r| sentence match)	0.00	1.00
P(r|¬ sentence match)	**0.46**	**0.54**

Table 4: Probability of satisfactory rating (r=*sat*) given a sentence mismatch, computed over the 486 training utterances not matching the reference transcript.

Rating r	r = non-sat	r = sat
P(r|o(1,10),¬sentence match)	0.08	0.92
P(r|¬o(1,10),¬sentence match)	0.79	0.21
P(r|o(1,3),¬sentence match)	0.06	0.94
P(r|¬o(1,3),¬sentence match)	0.71	0.29
P(r|o(3,5),¬sentence match)	0.05	0.95
P(r|¬o(3,5),¬sentence match)	0.61	0.39

our final model relies on the estimated satisfaction distribution conditioned on a sentence error, as shown in Table 4. The estimates in this table are computed over the subset of 486 training utterances for which the ASR output did not match the reference transcript. This table is our final user satisfaction model.

Equation 1 illustrates how the expected user satisfaction is computed based on the conditional probability table.

$$P(sat) = \begin{cases} 1.0 & \text{if sentence match} \\ P(sat|o(N_{min}, N), \neg sent\ match) & \text{if } o(N_{min}, N) = 1 \\ P(sat|\neg o(N_{min}, N), \neg sent\ match) & \text{if } o(N_{min}, N) = 0 \end{cases} \quad (1)$$

This value can then be averaged over an arbitrary dataset, to produce the Expected Search Satisfaction Rate (ESSR). A more fine-grained model could be derived by conditioning on a combination of overlap outcomes, e.g., $P(sat|o(1,10), \neg o(3,5))$. However a larger data collection would be required to estimate each parameter correctly.

4.1 User satisfaction prediction on held out data

In order to validate the satisfaction model introduced in the last section, we held out 1500 voice search ratings, each labeled by 3 annotators who did not label any of the training utterances. As in Section 3, the reference rating is computed through majority voting. Table 5 compares the estimated satisfaction probability based on the model in (1) with the actual percentage of satisfactory search results. Results are computed on 1036 utterances, after removing utterances for which the reference human transcript produced unsatisfac-

Table 5: Relative user satisfaction error for sentence match and the ESSR models in Table 4, on a held out human evaluation set of 1036 utterances for which the reference transcript returned satisfactory search results. The relative error is computed as 1-predicted satisfaction/actual satisfaction.

sentence match	Predicted ESSR P(sat|o(1,10))	Predicted ESSR P(sat|o(1,3))	Predicted ESSR P(sat|o(3,5))
-21.8%	-0.9%	-1.3%	-1.1%

Table 6: Individual satisfaction variation and relative ESSR error based on ground truths derived from individual human judges, using the ESSR model in Table 4. Satisfaction variation is the difference between the mean ground truth satisfaction and the satisfaction reported by individual judges.

Human judge	Test slice	Voice searches	Satisfaction variation	ESSR P(s|o(1,10))
Judge 1	1	444	-1.8%	0.1%
Judge 2	1	470	0.4%	-2.3%
Judge 3	1	470	1.2%	-2.9%
Judge 4	2	548	2.8%	-4.7%
Judge 5	2	523	-1.6%	-0.7%
Judge 6	2	526	-1.3%	-0.6%

tory search results. Results show that the satisfaction models predict the true user satisfaction within $\pm1.3\%$ relative error, with the best model predicting an ESSR 0.9% lower than the ground truth satisfaction percentage. In contrast, the percentage of exact sentence match (1-SER) is 21.8% lower than the ground truth satisfaction.

4.2 Impact of individual differences

In order to assess the impact of individual judges on our evaluation method, we evaluated the percentage of satisfaction according to a single human judge, rather than taking the majority vote. Table 6 reports the satisfaction estimated on the two slices of the test data used in Section 4.1, which was annotated by different groups of 3 judges. We find that on the same set the perceived satisfaction varies by up to 4.1% absolute in the worst case scenario. Since we remove utterances for which the reference transcript is out of domain or producing unsatisfactory results, it's important to note that this variation results from two factors: (1) whether or not an utterance is in domain and intelligible, and (2) whether the results are satisfactory.

Regarding inter-rater agreement on the full set of 3000 searches, we find that the judges agree 90.0% of the time on whether or not an utterance is in domain and intelligible (vs 50% by chance), with an average inter-rater correlation of 0.38. Regarding satisfaction judgments (1, 2 or 3), judges agrees 67.1% of the time (vs 33.3% by chance), for an average correlation of 0.65. Results are averaged over 15 judge pairs.

5. LIMITATIONS

An issue with the proposed approach is that search engines are not static over time. This can affect our evaluation method in two ways: (1) the reference search results should be collected at the same time as the test search results for the comparison to be meaningful; and (2) the satisfaction model might need to be re-estimated over time. While query/result pairs can be cached to speed up offline model evaluations, the cache needs to be updated frequently to address issue (1). Given the small number of parameters in our satisfaction model, we believe that the risk of overfitting is limited. However, significant changes in either the ASR model or the search engine could make the predicted ESSR inaccurate over time.

A second limitation is that the learned parameters are only valid for the search engine on which they were estimated. However the cost of estimating new parameters is fixed and relatively small compared to the cost of evaluating the search results produced by any ASR model update. Note that this paper focuses on product search as an example, however the methodology is content agnostic. Hence future work will assess how the method scales to other domains (e.g., text document retrieval), as well as to search engines with different levels of performance.

6. CONCLUSION

This paper has presented a voice search evaluation method which is a better predictor of user satisfaction than an exact sentence match, with no additional human annotation cost. Our model can be seen as a data-driven extension of the Google Webscore beyond the 1-best search result, which is crucial given that search engines are sensitive to the tokenization produced by the ASR. The satisfaction model predicts the Expected Search Satisfaction Rate (ESSR) within $\pm0.9\%$ relative to the ground truth satisfaction on held out data, while an exact sentence match underestimates the true satisfaction by 21.8% relative. Those results suggest that ESSR is a better objective function for (a) tuning voice search models and (b) monitoring accuracy over time.

7. REFERENCES

[1] A. Franz and B. Milch. Searching the web by voice. In *Proceedings of the International Conference on Computational Linguistics*, 2002.

[2] X. He and L. Deng. Speech-centric information processing: An optimization-oriented approach. *Proceedings of the IEEE*, 101(5):1116–1135, 2013.

[3] K. Jarvelin and J. Kekalainen. IR evaluation methods for retrieving highly relevant documents. In *Proceedings of SIGIR*, pages 41–48, 2000.

[4] P. Jyothi, L. Johnson, C. Chelba, and B. Strope. Large-scale discriminative language model reranking for voice-search. In *Proceedings of NAACL HLT*, 2012.

[5] J. Schalkwyk, D. Beeferman, F. Beaufays, B. Byrne, C. Chelba, M. Cohen, M. Kamvar, , and B. Strope. Google search by voice: A case study. In A. Neustein, editor, *Visions of Speech: Exploring New Voice Apps in Mobile Environments, Call Centers and Clinics.* Springer, 2010.

Seeking Serendipity

A Living Lab Approach to Understanding Creative Retrieval in Broadcast Media Production

Sabrina Sauer
Department of Computer Science
VU University Amsterdam
s.c.sauer@vu.nl

Maarten de Rijke
Informatics Institute
University of Amsterdam
derijke@uva.nl

ABSTRACT

This paper presents a method to map user needs and integrate serendipitous search behaviors in search algorithm development: the living lab approach. This user-centered design approach involves technology users during technology development to catch unexpected insights and successfully innovate. This paper focuses on the preliminary findings of a living lab case study to answer the question how this methodology reveals fine-grained information about users' serendipitous search behaviors. The case study involves a specific user group, media professionals who work in broadcast television and use audiovisual archives to create audiovisual content, during the development of new search algorithms for a large audiovisual archive. Research insights are based on data gathered during one co-design workshop, and ten in-depth semi-structured interviews with media professionals.

Findings stipulate that these users balance socio-technical constraints and affordances during creative retrieval to (1) find exactly what is sought; and (2) increase the possibility of serendipitous, unforeseen search results. We conclude that modeling these search processes in terms of improvising with constraints and affordances enables an effective articulation and channeling of user-technology interaction insights into new technology development. The paper suggests next steps in the living lab approach to further understand serendipitous search and creative retrieval processes.

Keywords

Serendipity; Living labs; Creative retrieval

1. INTRODUCTION

The idea that technology users can be sources of innovation has led to organized efforts by technology developers and policymakers to include end users and user communities in innovation practices [19]. One of the ways in which end user inclusion in design is sought is through living labs. These labs are organizations that facilitate technology innovation in partnerships between public, private and civic actors. Living labs develop technologies by engaging in an open innovation, user-driven research approach set in real-life experimentation environments in order to embrace the uncontrollable dynamics of daily life. Figure 1 shows the placement of living labs compared to other innovation approaches. The approach uses a myriad of user-centred design methods [6] to map user needs and gain unforeseen user insights. Recent living lab studies stress that to achieve optimal results, users should be included as equal partners throughout technology development and that, to catch unforeseen user ideas and behaviors, attention ought to be paid to how users improvise with technologies-in-the-making [15].

SIGIR '16, July 17 - 21, 2016, Pisa, Italy

ISBN 978-1-4503-4069-4/16/07...$15.00

DOI: http://dx.doi.org/10.1145/2911451.2914721

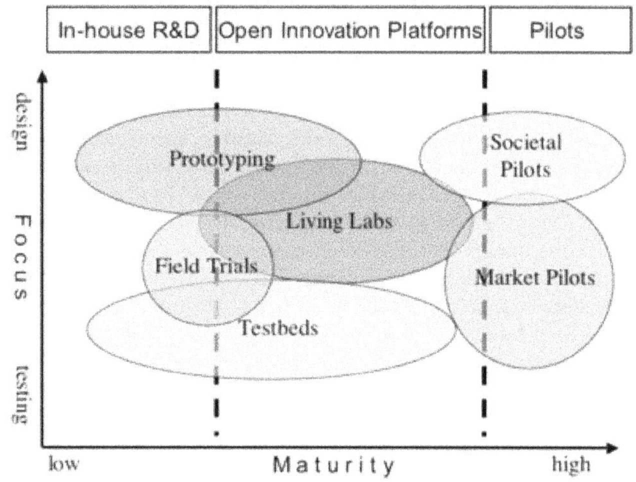

Figure 1: Position of Living Labs as an open innovation platform; included with permission from [4].

This paper presents ongoing research into the application of the living lab approach to develop new search algorithms for a large audiovisual archive. In particular, the paper seeks to unpack user contributions and insights into user needs and search behaviors during the first stage of the development process. The included users are media professionals who make daily use of the archive to create audiovisual stories. The paper investigates how the living lab's capacity to elucidate unforeseen user insights allows for a clear understanding of the role that serendipity plays when these users engage in creative retrieval; retrieving sources from the archive to create new audiovisual stories. The paper thus specifically aims to answer the question how the living lab approach facilitates and explicates the articulation of user-technology improvisation practices, which helps to understand the process of finding unexpected but useful search results and allows these to inform new search algorithm development. Our findings are useful for researchers who seek to implement a user-centered design approach that translates unforeseen user ideas and serendipitous user behaviors into technology development.

2. RELATED WORK

The living lab approach has been applied in Information Retrieval (IR) research to primarily involve users in IR evaluation [3, 16]. Instead of concentrating on IR evaluation with users, the present study focuses on one of the preceeding phases in technology development, namely ideation. In line with user-centered design cases in IR, which indicate that co-developing with users helps refine search goals, problems, and interface design [2, 20], this paper focuses on both identifying user needs as well as understanding factors that constrain user-technology interaction.

Related studies about the needs of audiovisual archive users, such as media scholars and news journalists, provide categorisations of information needs [10, 12] or more technologically-oriented needs such as ease of access especially in relation to time: searching is constrained by time pressures [1]. Bron et al. [5] map the (re)search cycle of media scholars into three phases to support the development of exploratory search systems: exploration, contextualization and presentation. During these phases, information needs change iteratively from vague, via initial search questions to a refined final research question. Search is thus about refinement, and the iterative search process itself contributes to the distillation of research questions.

It is fruitful to relate this interplay between search processes and search goals to McCay-Peet and Toms' research [13] into serendipitous search. They argue that serendipity should not be studied in terms of its triggers and instantaneity, but rather as a holistic process that takes place during active learning, specifically during exploratory search. In the IR literature, serendipity is seen as a paradoxical concept: valuable, yet elusive [8]. In this paper, the elusiveness of serendipity is connected to the living lab premise of harnessing unexpected, serendipitous user ideas and behaviors to innovate. To do so, we ground serendipity by theoretically relating it, as a process, to improvisation.

In organizational theory, the term improvisation is used to describe the unforeseen way in which people navigate with(in) structures. This activity takes the shape of a constant orientation, a mixture of making do and letting go "in response to an unexpected opportunity or challenge" [14]. There are several reasons why improvisation is a useful concept to study how media professionals search for and subsequently use audiovisual sources to create new audiovisual narratives. First, it allows for a description of the route that unfolds as users search in creative terms that move beyond what Hassan et al. [9] would characterize as struggling and exploring. Second, it anchors the unforeseen to (creative) retrieval practices, which shows how the unforeseen gains meaning during audiovisual narrative creation. Third, highlighting improvisations within the digital search environment makes it possible to understand the tacit knowledge these users have of said environment, which may then inform the development of new search algorithms.

3. METHODOLOGY

This research is based on a user-centered living lab methodology that seeks a close collaboration with the foreseen end users of the to-be-developed search algorithms. In the first stage of the research project, qualitative methods [7] are used to map the user context (Figure 2). A grounded theory approach is furthermore used to construct theoretical concepts from the collected data.

This first stage of research has taken the shape of 1 co-design session followed by 10 in-depth semi-structured interviews with me-

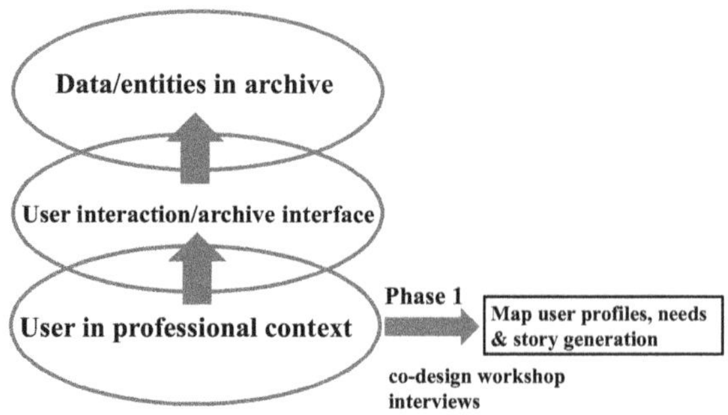

Figure 2: Phase 1 mapping the user context.

dia professionals who use the archive, such as news documentation specialists, television editors and digital storytelling practitioners. The co-design session involved 19 project partners: 11 representatives from private and public parties, and 8 representatives from the user group. Together, the partners discussed the project problem and objective: how to develop self-learning search algorithms that take into account professional user needs. During the session, three creative research methods were employed to map the user context and elicit user needs: empathic conversations and explorative play were facilitated and the users engaged in user profiling [18]. These methods were used in subsequent order, within a tight timeframe to ensure that the main problem was actively tackled by sharing ideas in different manners. The more abstract question to describe user needs was translated into one that asked the partners to describe what their ideal outcome of the project would be. They noted down or drew their ideas onto Post-it notes, after which they discussed their ideas within the larger group. The notes were collected and grouped, and reflected on by the group in terms of important themes and features. The second part of the session consisted of a user profiling session; the partners worked in two groups to draw overviews of the different media professionals within the media landscape. The produced drawings, together with the collected Post-its and a transcription of the group discussion, provide a user-generated reflection on and mapping of the characteristics of different (future) users of the to-be-developed search algorithms. The users created 6 user profiles:

- images researchers/curators,
- desk researchers who work for broadcast companies,
- more short-term employed researchers,
- documentations specialists, who aid editorial teams with retrieval activities and also archive and annotate material,
- media innovation specialists who primarily seek to manage projects, content, teams and cross-medial strategies, and
- mediacoaches who aid schools and develop educational concepts.

These user profiles formed the basis of the selection of interview respondents. During the interviews, users described their daily professional archive use and search behavior, elaborated on how they integrate found sources into audiovisual stories and reflected on ideas generated during the co-design session.

4. PRELIMINARY RESULTS

The co-design session allowed for a broad scoping of user needs and search behaviors. Users listed specific ideas to optimize their search processes, such as: the possibility to move beyond a text-based search engine to an image-based one, using keyframes to quickly identify similar images, or alternatively, using text-based search to find direct quotations within sources. In terms of enhancing search processes, users expressed the need to be able to upload annotations to the archive and view annotations of peers; user-generated annotation would allow for quick comparisons and decision-making ("what does my colleague use when compiling a news item, and how do I want to create an item about a similar news story?"). Users also suggested visualizing relations between found materials and the search query, to be able to quickly review the context of a specific topic or theme. The need to be agile was of utmost importance, due to extremely tight timelines associated with the profession. At the same time, the need to find the unexpected also came to the fore; materials need to be found quickly but should also be surprising (Table 1).

These insights formed the basis of the subsequent interviews. Taken together, preliminary results indicate that media professionals describe their search behavior as directly influenced by time constraints and by the type of materials sought (video, audio, photographs, found using keywords such as person, broadcaster or date). Their information needs are informed by profession type, professional contexts (work/team environment), and type of audiovisual product that needs to be created. The interviewed users perceive their search behavior as an iterative process during which they continuously consider whether a source aligns with the constraints and affordances of their foreseen end product (television show, news item or documentary). These are:

(1) time (for research as well as the duration of the final product, e.g., 30 seconds or 25 minutes);
(2) the format and genre of their product;
(3) the target audience;
(4) the budget; and,
(5) their personal interest.

Figure 3 summarizes these insights, of phases in the development of the audiovisual story, set against phases in their information-seeking behavior. It is an iterative process, and unfolds in the context of voiced constraints and affordances.

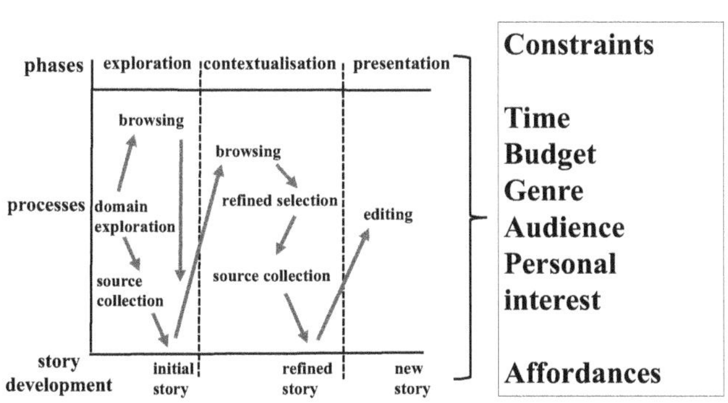

Figure 3: Overview of story development with associated search processes. Arrows show possible sequences (adaptation of Bron et al.'s model of the phases in media studies research).

The finding that users try to find sources that are directly relevant as well as surprising suggests that, in searching, users seek to elicit serendipity, or "the meaningful experience of chance encounters" [11]. These user expects that unforeseen and as-yet-unkown audiovisual sources will enrich their audiovisual products by allowing the telling of new stories. This expressed need to find both expected and unexpected sources can be translated into a user need for the digital search environment of the archive to afford serendipitous retrieval [17]; a fuzzy search approach, which supports user improvisation.

What is interesting is that users stress their craftiness in finding fitting sources by seeking, on the one hand, audiovisual materials that exactly fit their query, but also, on the other hand, sources that are on the margin of what would be exactly relevant. Users note a tension between finding "cliché" sources to, for instance, create a news report about sensitive subjects, and a need to use "fresh" material to keep audiences interested. This insight is not genre-specific: whether creating a news item, quiz question or documentary, users continuously explore the boundaries of what they term the collective memory of the viewer. It is within this exploration that users need serendipity, and seek in a "fuzzy" manner to find unforeseen sources.

This play with affordances and constraints, inviting serendipitous search results, is what we refer to as *creative retrieval*. Creative retrieval, finding sources by improvising with affordances and constraints of both the foreseen audiovisual end product and the search possibilities of archives, is an iterative process and geared at producing stories. The users' voiced reflections on this process explicate how they use their tacit knowledge to realize creative retrieval.

5. CONCLUSION AND NEXT STEPS

This paper explores what insights about users' serendipitous search behaviors can be gleaned from the first phase of a user-centered living lab approach, when the objective of the living lab is to involve media professionals during the development of new search algorithms. The living lab approach seeks to elicit unforeseen user ideas and behaviors to enhance product innovation. Likewise, our research objective is to analyze the role played by serendipity and unforeseen search result generation in order to develop search technology that complies with, and supports, media professionals' search needs and behaviors. Preliminary research outcomes suggest that users seek audiovisual materials in line with a number of affordances and constraints, which are informed by the to-be produced audiovisual product as well as by contextual socio-technical elements. This produces a search practice that can be characterized as improvisational: a play with structures, guided by processes of making do and letting go. It is within this improvisational practice that media professionals aim to find two types of search results: sources that exactly fit the search query as well as sources that are serendipitous, useful yet not foreseen.

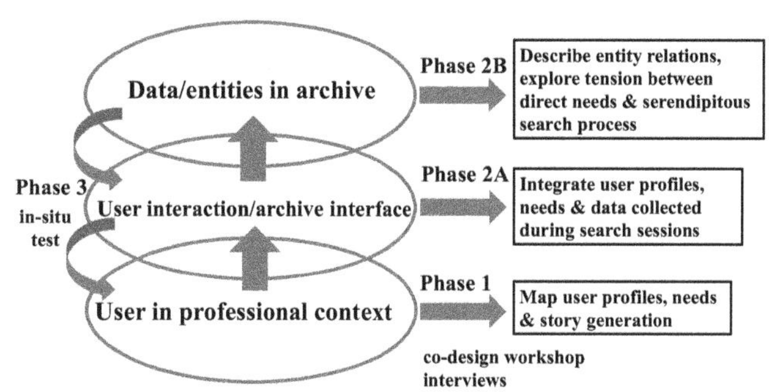

Figure 4: Next steps.

The next steps of the research aim to more fully grasp this improvisational search practice. In the next research phases (Phase 2A and 2B in Figure 4), data is collected about user-archive interactions via additional interviews, observations, and click-behavior analysis. In parallel with this, the archive data is studied to analyze how to technically translate user insights into algorithm development. In the final stage (Phase 3) an in-situ living lab is to be realized within

Table 1: Users' information needs and search behavior

User profile	Information need	Search behavior
Image researcher/curator	Content needs to fit topic, story, program genre and time limit. Needs an entertaining, surprising twist.	In accordance with an experience-based procedure that starts with a broad topic exploration; based on editorial team meetings and current events.
Documentation specialist	Content needs to correspond with very specific search queries of (news)editors.	Defined procedure (own archive first); sources found in text-based system; based on exact annotation.
(Desk) researcher	Content needs to be located fast; based on topic, program genre; surprising content needed for historical programs, less surprising for news broadcast.	Described as "mean and lean"; high time pressure; search based on entities, broadcaster, broadcast date.
Innovation specialist	Content needs to be found and presented it in a meaningful manner; draw viewers in via surprising stories/media use.	Find and coordinate editorial teams consisting of search experts to optimize processes.
Mediacoach	Content for media education needs to improve pupils' media skills.	Selecting appropriate material, in line with educational vision.

the audiovisual archive to test the new algorithms and elicit an even more fine-grained understanding of the iterative creative retrieval process. By combining these methods, the living lab approach will provide more definitive conclusions about the role that improvisation plays when media professionals engage in creative retrieval, as well as allow for an evaluation of the extent to which the living lab approach supports successful user-centered innovation practices.

Acknowledgements. This research was supported by Ahold, Amsterdam Data Science, the Bloomberg Research Grant program, the Dutch national program COMMIT, Elsevier, the European Community's Seventh Framework Programme (FP7/2007-2013) under grant agreement nr 312827 (VOX-Pol), the ESF Research Network Program ELIAS, the Royal Dutch Academy of Sciences (KNAW) under the Elite Network Shifts project, the Microsoft Research Ph.D. program, the Netherlands eScience Center under project number 027.012.105, the Netherlands Institute for Sound and Vision, the Netherlands Organisation for Scientific Research (NWO) under project nrs 727.011.005, 612.001.116, HOR-11-10, 640.006.013, 612.066.930, CI-14-25, SH-322-15, 652.002.001, 612.001.551, the Yahoo Faculty Research and Engagement Program, and Yandex. All content represents the opinion of the authors, which is not necessarily shared or endorsed by their respective employers and/or sponsors.

REFERENCES

[1] M. Anwar, H. Al-Ansari, and A. Abdullah. Information seeking behaviour of Kuwaiti journalists. *Libri*, 54:228–236, 2004.

[2] B. Aryana, T. Clemmensen, and C. Boks. Users' participation in requirements gathering for smart phones applications in emerging markets. *Universal Access in the Information Society*, 14:265–280, 2015.

[3] L. Azzopardi and K. Balog. Towards a living lab for information retrieval research and development. A proposal for a living lab for product search tasks. In *Multilingual and Multimodal Information Access Evaluation*, pages 26–37, Berlin, Heidelberg, 2011. Springer.

[4] P. Ballon, J. Pierson, and S. Delaere. Test and experimentation platforms for broadband innovation: Examining European practice. In *16th International Telecommunications Society Europe Conference*, pages 1–22, Porto, 2005.

[5] M. Bron, J. van Gorp, F. Nack, M. de Rijke, A. Vishneuski, and S. de Leeuw. A subjunctive exploratory search interface to support media studies researchers. In *SIGIR '12: 35th international ACM SIGIR conference on Research and development in information retrieval*. ACM, August 2012.

[6] K. Feurstein, A. Hesmer, K. Hribernik, K.-D. Thoben, and J. Schumacher. Living labs: A new development strategy. In *European Living Labs - A New Approach for Human Centric Regional Innovation*, pages 1–14, Berlin, Germany, 2009. Wissenschaftlicher Verlag Berlin.

[7] R. Fidel. Qualitative methods in information retrieval research. *LISR*, 15:219–247, 1993.

[8] A. Foster and N. Ford. Serendipity and information seeking: An empirical study. *Journal of Documentation*, 59(3):321–340, 2003.

[9] A. Hassan, R. White, S. Dumais, and Y. Wang. Struggling or exploring? Disambiguating long search sessions. In *SIGIR '14: 37th international ACM SIGIR conference on Research and development in information retrieval*. ACM, 2014.

[10] B. Huurnink, L. Hollink, W. van den Heuvel, and M. de Rijke. Search behavior of media professionals at an audiovisual archive: A transaction log analysis. *Journal of the American Society for Information Science and Technology*, 61(6):1180-1197, 2010.

[11] T. W. Leong, F. Vetere, and S. Howard. The serendipity shuffle. In *OZCHI 2005*, pages 25–28, Canberra, Australia, 2005.

[12] B. Lunn. User needs in television archive access: Acquiring knowledge necessary for system design. *Journal of Digital Information*, 10(6):1–15, 2009.

[13] L. McCay-Peet and E. G. Toms. The process of serendipity in knowledge work. In *Proceedings of the Third Symposium on Information Interaction in Context*, New Brunswick, New Jersey, 2010. ACM.

[14] W. Orlikowski. Using technology and constituting structures: A practice lens for studying technology in organizations. *Organization Science*, 11(4):404–428, 2000.

[15] S. Sauer. *User innovativeness in Living Laboratories – Everyday user improvisations with ICTs as a source of innovation*. PhD thesis, University of Twente, 2013.

[16] A. Schuth, K. Balog, and L. Kelly. Extended overview of the living labs for information retrieval evaluation (LL4IR) CLEF lab 2015. In *Experimental IR Meets Multilinguality, Multimodality, and Interaction*, pages 484–496. Springer, 2015.

[17] E. Toms. Serendipitous information retrieval. In *DELOS Workshop: Information Seeking, Searching and Querying in Digital Libraries*, 2000.

[18] D. van Dijk, F. Kresin, M. Reitenbach, E. Rennen, and S. Wildevuur. *Users as Designers – A hands-on approach to creative research*. Waag Society, Amsterdam, 2011.

[19] E. van Oost, S. Verhaegh, and N. Oudshoorn. From innovation community to community innovation: User-initiated innovation in Wireless Leiden. *Science Technology And Human Values*, 34(2): 182–205, 2008.

[20] S. M. Zabed Ahmed, C. McKnight, and C. Oppenheim. A user-centred design and evaluation of ir interfaces. *Journal of Librarianship and Information Science*, 38(3):157–172, 2006.

Selectively Personalizing Query Auto-Completion

Fei Cai[†‡]
f.cai@uva.nl

Maarten de Rijke[‡]
derijke@uva.nl

[†]Science and Technology on Information Systems Engineering Laboratory,
National University of Defense Technology, Hunan, China
[‡]Informatics Institute, University of Amsterdam, Amsterdam, The Netherlands

ABSTRACT

Query auto-completion (QAC) is being used by many of today's search engines. It helps searchers formulate queries by providing a list of query completions after entering an initial prefix of a query. To cater for a user's specific information needs, personalized QAC strategies use a searcher's search history and their profile. Is personalization consistently effective in different search contexts?

We study the QAC problem by selectively personalizing the query completion list. Based on a lenient personalized QAC strategy that encodes the ranking signal as a trade-off between query popularity and search context, we propose a model for selectively personalizing query auto-completion (SP-QAC) to study this trade-off. We predict effective trade-offs based on a regression model, where the typed query prefix, clicked documents and preceding queries in the same session are used to weigh personalization in QAC. Experiments on the AOL query log show the SP-QAC model can significantly outperform a state-of-the-art personalized QAC approach.

CCS Concepts

•**Information systems** → *Information retrieval query processing;*

Keywords

Personalization; Query auto completion; Web search

1. INTRODUCTION

Personalization techniques have been widely adopted by today's search engines [1, 3, 12]. Query auto-completion (QAC) is no exception [2]. In general, personalized lists of query completions produced by a generic QAC ranking approach are obtained by distinguishing individuals and their contexts, either based on their search history [1, 3, 7] or on their profiles [12]. Such personalization strategies have been proven to be effective as evidenced by a series of personalized query auto-completion approaches [1, 3, 7, 10, 12].

Generally, when ranking query completions in response to a prefix entered by a user, most existing personalized QAC approaches use an interpolation parameter λ that controls the trade-off between query popularity and the searcher's personal search context [1, 3]. This trade-off is uniformly applied to all typed prefixes [1, 3], so as to achieve a modest performance across all cases. It is unclear whether personalization will always boost the ranking performance over a generic QAC approach. As an aside, in web search and recommendation systems, it has been shown that not all queries should be personalized equally as personalization strategies occasionally harm the search accuracy [13, 14]. Similarly, we hypothesize that in QAC personalization of query prefixes should not be handled in a uniform manner because:

(1) a user's initial information needs may be addressed by previous interactions;
(2) users may change their search intent during a search session.

Such clues can be explicitly expressed by the clicks or directly revealed by the query flow in a session.

We propose a model for selectively personalizing query auto-completion (SP-QAC) to re-rank the top N query completions produced by the MPC (Most Popular Completion) model [1]. In particular, personalization in the proposed SP-QAC model is individually weighed when combined with ranking signals from search popularity. We study the following factors for weighing personalization: the typed prefix for which we recommend query completions, the clicked documents for inferring a user's satisfaction, and the topic changes of preceding queries in the same session for detecting search intent shifts. We use the description of each URL from the ODP data[1] to represent documents and queries based on the word2vec model [9] when inferring a user's satisfaction as well as shifts in query intent in a session. Finally, we test the improvements of our proposal over state-of-the-art QAC baselines on a publicly available query log dataset. We find that SP-QAC outperforms a traditional non-personalized QAC approach and a uniformly personalized QAC approach with a fixed trade-off controlling the contribution of search popularity and search context. Our contributions in this paper are summarized as:

(1) We propose a model for selectively personalizing query auto-completion (SP-QAC) that flexibly outweighs or depresses the contribution of personalization in QAC.
(2) We study the role of typed prefixes, clicked documents, and preceding queries in the same search session when estimating the weight of personalization in QAC.

2. APPROACH

A straightforward approach to ranking query completions is based on the popularity of queries. Bar-Yossef and Kraus [1] refer to this type of ranking as the Most Popular Completion (MPC) model:

$$MPC(p) = \underset{q \in S(p)}{\arg\max}\, w(q),\; w(q) = \frac{f(q)}{\sum_{q_i \in L} f(q_i)}, \quad (1)$$

where $f(q)$ denotes the number of occurrences of query q in search

[1]http://www.dmoz.org

SIGIR '16, July 17 - 21, 2016, Pisa, Italy

ACM ISBN 978-1-4503-4069-4/16/07... $15.00

DOI: http://dx.doi.org/10.1145/2911451.2914686

$\log L$, and $S(p)$ is a set of query completions matching prefix p.

To cater for a user's particular information need, personalization has been incorporated into the MPC model, as described in [1, 3]. A generic personalized QAC approach employs a fixed parameter λ to control the contribution of personal information to generate the final ranking of query completions. For instance, Bar-Yossef and Kraus [1] compute a hybrid score for each query candidate q_c, which is a convex combination of two scores, i.e., a query popularity score $MPCsco(q_c)$ and a personalization score $Psco(q_c)$:

$$hybsco(q_c) = \lambda \cdot MPCsco(q_c) + (1 - \lambda) \cdot Psco(q_c), \quad (2)$$

where $MPCsco(q_c)$ is estimated by candidate q_c's frequency in the query log and $Psco(q_c)$ is measured by q_c's similarity to the search context in session. This approach handles each prefix uniformly. However, users may modify their search intent during a session and personalization may harm the quality of the ranking of query completions if we continue to use the previous search context. Hence, we propose a model for selectively personalizing query auto-completion (SP-QAC) that varies the importance of personalization when generating the final hybrid score of a query completion:

$$hybsco(q_c) = \phi(\cdot) \cdot MPCsco(q_c) + (1 - \phi(\cdot)) \cdot Psco(q_c), \quad (3)$$

where $\phi(\cdot)$ outputs a trade-off in $[0, 1]$ and is parameterized by three arguments: the typed prefix, clicked documents and preceding queries in the same session; see below.

2.1 Signal from typed prefix

Most previous work on query auto-completion [1, 3, 7, 12] only considers the typed prefix for generating a list of query completions, ignoring the potential signal hidden in the typed prefix for personalization. However, the typed prefix normally reveals a strong clue for inferring a user's personal query activity, such as query expansion and query repetition, etc. We introduce a factor f_p to model the signal from the typed prefix p on weighing the personalization for query auto-completion as follows:

$$f_p = \frac{|\mathcal{W}(p)|}{|\mathcal{S}|} + c, \quad (4)$$

where $|\mathcal{W}(p)|$ and $|\mathcal{S}|$ indicate the number of words that start with p and that appear in the current session, respectively; c is a small constant used for smoothing. A larger value of f_p could imply a higher importance of personalization in the final ranking score in (3).

2.2 Inferring search satisfaction from clicked documents

User's clicks on documents retrieved in response to a query are a widely used behavioral signal for measuring search satisfaction [8]. Search satisfaction can be further approximated by the closeness between a submitted query and its clicked documents: the closer they are, the more satisfied the user could be [5]. The cosine similarity can be applied to model a factor f_d for measuring closeness as follows:

$$f_d = \begin{cases} c, & \text{no clicks} \\ \frac{1}{|\mathcal{Q}|} \sum_{q \in \mathcal{Q}} \frac{1}{|\mathcal{D}_q|} \sum_{d_c \in \mathcal{D}_q} \cos(q, d_c), & \text{otherwise,} \end{cases} \quad (5)$$

where $\mathcal{D}_q$ is a set of clicked documents corresponding to a submitted query q in a set $\mathcal{Q}$ of previous queries in the session. To each clicked document $d_c \in \mathcal{D}_q$ we assocaite a short description T extracted from the ODP. We vectorize this document description consisting of a sequence of words using the word2vec model [9], where each word is represented by a vector v_w. In doing so, a clicked document can be vectorized by averaging the words in T as $d_c = \frac{1}{|T|} \sum_{v_w \in T} v_w$. After that, a query q is then similarly represented by averaging its clicked documents $\mathcal{D}$ in the training log, i.e., $q = \frac{1}{|\mathcal{D}|} \sum_{d_c \in \mathcal{D}} d_c$. In practice, for a query q that has no clicked documents, the same representation of its most semantically similar query q_o, which is identified by the word2vec model [9] and has been vectorized in the training period, is assigned to it by

$$\begin{aligned} q_o &\leftarrow \arg\max_{q_l \in Q_L} \cos(q, q_l) \quad (6) \\ &= \arg\max_{q_l \in Q_L} \frac{1}{|q|} \times \frac{1}{|q_l|} \sum_{w_k \in q} \sum_{w_j \in q_l} \cos(w_k, w_j), \end{aligned}$$

where Q_L is a set of queries that have clicked documents in the training period.

Intuitively, a large score of f_d in (5) indicates a high probability that the user is satisfied with the results, thus resulting in a low weight of personalization in QAC. We assign a small constant c to f_d when no clicks are available, where personalization could make sense because the user's request has not been addressed and they may continue to submit similar queries.

2.3 Detecting topic shifts from preceding queries

A long session may contain queries on multiple topics [6]. We use this observation to infer signals for weighing personalization in QAC. A strong topical shift in the preceding queries implies a low-weight personalization in QAC because the user may have shifted topics. Hence, we model a factor f_q based on topic shifts in preceding queries in the session:

$$f_q = \begin{cases} c, & r = 1 \text{ or } 2 \\ \cos(q_1, q_2), & r = 3 \\ \cos(q_{r\text{-}1} - q_{r\text{-}2}, q_{r\text{-}2} - q_{r\text{-}3}), & r > 3, \end{cases} \quad (7)$$

where r is the query position in session and each query is vectorized by the scheme described in §2.2. For queries at the beginning of a session, i.e., $r = 1$ or 2, the topic shift from queries is unavailable, making no impact on personalization, and thus we assign a small constant c to f_q. Similarly, at query position $r = 3$, the relative topical shift of queries is still unavailable. Instead, we use the absolute query similarity between $q_{r\text{-}1}$ and $q_{r\text{-}2}$ as an indicator of query topical shift. For queries at position $r > 3$, we study the topic shift from their preceding queries, i.e., $q_{r\text{-}1}$, $q_{r\text{-}2}$ and $q_{r\text{-}3}$.

A large value of f_q is produced if the topical similarity of preceding queries is high, which, in turn, implies with high probability that the user's search intent has remained unchanged from previous queries in the current session. In this case, personalization should be emphasized in (3).

2.4 Weighing personalization

Taking these discussed factors into account, i.e., the typed prefix, clicked documents and preceding queries in the same session, we adopt logistic regression to model how likely each factor should affect the weight of personalization in a QAC task. In the training period, for each typed prefix, we manually change the value of λ in (3) from 0 to 1 (with steps of size 0.1) to guarantee that the final submitted query is ranked at the top position. By doing so, we obtain an optimal weight for personalization, which is used as a label in the regression model.

Regarding the inputs to the regression model, the factors discussed above, i.e., f_p, f_d and f_q, are involved. For the cases that no word appearing in the current session starts with the typed prefix, we perform the regression model based on the factors f_d and f_q; otherwise, we perform the regression model based on all three factors. Hence, the selective weight $\phi(\cdot)$ in (3) is determined as follows:

$$\phi(\cdot) = \begin{cases} Reg(f_d, f_q), & \text{if } f_p = c \\ Reg(f_p, f_d, f_q), & \text{otherwise.} \end{cases} \quad (8)$$

We use the personalization scenario proposed in [3] to compute the $Psco(q_c)$ score in (3) when generating the optimal personalization weights, i.e.,

$$Psco(q_c) = p(q_c \mid \mathcal{Q}) = \sum_{q_s \in \mathcal{Q}} Z_n \cdot p(q_c \mid q_s),$$

where $\mathcal{Q}$ is a set of preceding queries in the current session and Z_n is used for normalization; $p(q_c \mid q_s)$ is measured using the common strings of query terms in q_c and q_s.

3. EXPERIMENTS

We write SP-QAC for our proposed selectively personalized query auto completion model; it personalizes query completions based on a regression model considering the factors described in §2.1, §2.2 and §2.3, respectively. Our research questions are:

(**RQ1**) Does selective personalization help improve the accuracy of ranking query completions?

(**RQ2**) What is the performance of the proposed SP-QAC model under various inputs to the regression model for weighing the importance of personalization?

3.1 Experimental setup

We use the publicly available AOL query log dataset [11] in our experiments, which is split into three parts: a training set, a validation set and a test set consisting of the first 60%, the following 20% and the last 20% of the query log, respectively. A large volume of navigational queries containing URL substrings (.com, .net, .org, http, etc.) are removed. One-query and no-click sessions are both excluded in our experiments as not enough search context is available. In addition, we follow previous QAC work and adapt a commonly used evaluation methodology in QAC [3, 7, 12] by only keeping cases where the final submitted query is included in the top N query completions returned by the MPC approach,

For comparison, the following baselines are selected: (1) the most popular completion (MPC) method, which ranks query candidates by their frequency [1]; (2) a personalized QAC approach based on session context with a fixed tradeoff $\lambda = 0.5$ in (2), denoted as P-QAC [3].

We use Mean Reciprocal Rank (MRR) for evaluating the performance of QAC models. For a prefix p associated with a list of query completions $\mathcal{L}(p)$ and the user's finally submitted query q', the Reciprocal Rank (RR) is computed as:

$$RR = \begin{cases} \frac{1}{\text{rank of } q' \text{ in } \mathcal{L}(p)}, & \text{if } q' \in \mathcal{L}(p) \\ 0, & \text{otherwise.} \end{cases} \quad (9)$$

Then, MRR is computed as the mean of RR for all prefixes.

In addition, we set $N = 10$ in our experiments, which means the top ten query completions returned by the MPC approach are to be re-ranked. We randomly assign a small value 0.01 to the constant c in our experiments.

3.2 Results and discussions

To answer research question **RQ1**, we compare the results of our proposed model, i.e., SP-QAC, with those of the baselines. We report the results in Table 1. Clearly, as shown in Table 1, a generic

Table 1: Performance of QAC models in terms of MRR at a prefix length $\#p$ ranging from 1 to 5 characters. The best performance per row is highlighted. Statistical significance of pairwise differences of SP-QAC vs. MPC and SP-QAC vs. P-QAC are detected using a two-tailed t-test ($^\blacktriangle/^\blacktriangledown$ for α = .01, or $^\vartriangle/^\triangledown$ for α = .05) and marked in the upper left and upper right hand corners of SP-QAC scores, respectively.

$\#p$	MPC	P-QAC	SP-QAC
1	0.5368	0.5422	$^\vartriangle$**0.5535**$^\vartriangle$
2	0.5556	0.5628	$^\vartriangle$**0.5744**$^\vartriangle$
3	0.5944	0.6046	$^\vartriangle$**0.6165**
4	0.6294	0.6427	$^\blacktriangle$**0.6547**
5	0.6589	0.6646	$^\blacktriangle$**0.6762**

Table 2: Performance of QAC models in terms of MRR at various query positions. The best performer per row is highlighted. Statistical significance of pairwise differences of SP-QAC vs. MPC and SP-QAC vs. P-QAC are detected using a two-tailed t-test ($^\blacktriangle/^\blacktriangledown$ for α = .01, or $^\vartriangle/^\triangledown$ for α = .05) and marked in the upper left and upper right hand corners of SP-QAC scores, respectively.

Query position	MPC	P-QAC	SP-QAC
$\{1, 2, 3\}$	0.6283	0.6327	**0.6340**
$\{4, 5, 6\}$	0.6005	0.6113	$^\blacktriangle$**0.6257**$^\vartriangle$
$\{7, 8, 9, \cdots\}$	0.5737	0.5863	$^\blacktriangle$**0.6058**$^\vartriangle$

personalization scheme helps to improve the QAC performance in terms of MRR as the MRR scores of the P-QAC model are higher than that of the MPC approach at every prefix length. In addition, when a selective personalization strategy is embedded into the P-QAC model, the QAC performance is further boosted as the MRR scores of the SP-QAC model are higher than those of MPC and P-QAC. Compared to the MPC approach, significant MRR improvements of the SP-QAC approach are observed at level $\alpha = .05$ for the short prefixes, i.e., $\#p = 1, 2, 3$, and at level $\alpha = .01$ for the long prefixes, i.e., $\#p = 4, 5$. Compared to short prefixes, long prefixes are able to reveal a stronger signal for search personalization, like query repetition. However, compared to the results of the P-QAC model, significant MRR improvements of the SP-QAC model are only observed at short prefixes, i.e., $\#p = 1, 2$. This is due to the fact that, compared to short prefixes, long prefixes often return the correct query early in the list of query completions by both models.

To further examine the effectiveness of selective personalization for QAC, we examine the performance of QAC models at different query positions, i.e., at the beginning (1, 2 or 3), in the middle (4, 5 or 6) and in later (≥ 7) parts of a session. See Table 2. At the start of a session, these three models return competitive MRR scores as limited information from search context is available for the P-QAC and SP-QAC models. However, as the search context becomes richer, significant improvements in terms of MRR are achieved by both personalization models.

Next, we turn to research question **RQ2** and examine the performance of the SP-QAC model under different inputs to the regression model for generating the personalization weights for QAC. We manually remove one factor and keep the other two for the regression model, resulting in the SP-QAC-$f_d f_q$, SP-QAC-$f_p f_q$ and SP-QAC-$f_d f_p$ models, which corresponds to the SP-QAC model without considering the factors f_p, f_d and f_q for selectively personalizing QAC, respectively. We plot the results in Figure 1, including the model incorporating all three factors for selective personalization (i.e., SP-QAC).

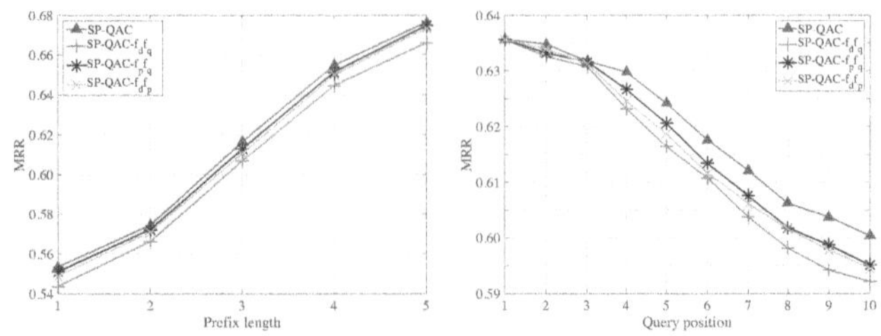

(a) QAC performance at varying prefix lengths. **(b) QAC performance at varying query positions.**

Figure 1: Performance in terms of MRR of the SP-QAC models under different schemes for weighing personalization, tested at varying prefix lengths (left) and varying query positions (right).

Generally, the SP-QAC model achieves the best performance in terms of MRR at any prefix length and any query position. As shown in Figure 1a, as the prefix length increases, the MRR scores monotonously go up because a long prefix can sharply cut down the space of possible completions matching the input prefix, resulting in increasing MRR scores. In contrast, as shown in Figure 1b, the MRR scores decrease when users continue to query in a session. In the latter part of a search session, users are inclined to submit uncommon queries, making it difficult for MPC to return a correct completion early, which our proposal depends on.

Next, we zoom in on the three factors considered in selective personalization for QAC. As shown in Figure 1a, the MRR scores of the SP-QAC-$f_p f_q$ and SP-QAC-$f_d f_p$ models approximate those of the SP-QAC model as the prefix length increases. The MRR scores of SP-QAC-$f_d f_q$ lag behind those of the SP-QAC model: the signal for personalization from the typed prefix becomes stronger as the prefix length increases, which benefits SP-QAC-$f_p f_q$ and SP-QAC-$f_d f_p$ (both consider the factor f_p). Regarding the QAC performance at varying query positions, Figure 1b shows that the models perform similarly at early positions of a session, as insufficient search context is available to tell them apart. In addition, SP-QAC-$f_p f_q$ outperforms SP-QAC-$f_d f_q$ and SP-QAC-$f_d f_p$ at most query positions. For later queries in a session, where a richer search context is available, information from the typed prefix and previous queries helps for QAC.

In essence, from the results in Figure 1, the SP-QAC model that does not consider the factor f_p works worst, from which we infer that f_p is the most important factor for selectively personalizing QAC. Similarly, we infer that f_q is more important than f_d.

4. CONCLUSION

We have proposed a selectively personalized approach for query auto-completion (QAC). Our model predicts whether a specific prefix prefers a personalized approach when ranking the query completions. We have explored several factors that influence the weight of personalization in a generic personalized QAC model, such as the typed prefix, the clicked documents and the preceding queries in the same session. The typed prefix yields the most benefits for weighing personalization in query completion re-ranking, and that the preceding queries contributes more than click information.

This work unifies prior work on personalized QAC by studying when and how to incorporate personalization in a QAC task. As to future work, other sources can be explored for investigating how to best personalize query auto-completion, e.g., a user's dwell time or their long-term search history. In addition, it is interesting to zoom in on individual users to determine whether they are likely to benefit from personalization in QAC and whether they stand to gain from diversifying query completions [4].

Acknowledgments. This research was supported by Ahold, Amsterdam Data Science, the Bloomberg Research Grant program, the Dutch national program COMMIT, Elsevier, the European Community's Seventh Framework Programme (FP7/2007-2013) under grant agreement nr 312827 (VOX-Pol), the ESF Research Network Program ELIAS, the Royal Dutch Academy of Sciences (KNAW) under the Elite Network Shifts project, the Microsoft Research Ph.D. program, the Netherlands eScience Center under project number 027.012.105, the Netherlands Institute for Sound and Vision, the Netherlands Organisation for Scientific Research (NWO) under project nrs 727.011.005, 612.001.116, HOR-11-10, 640.006.013, 612.-066.930, CI-14-25, SH-322-15, 652.002.001, 612.001.551, the Yahoo Faculty Research and Engagement Program, and Yandex. All content represents the opinion of the authors, which is not necessarily shared or endorsed by their respective employers and/or sponsors.

REFERENCES

[1] Z. Bar-Yossef and N. Kraus. Context-sensitive query auto-completion. In *WWW '11*, pages 107–116, 2011.

[2] F. Cai and M. de Rijke. Query auto completion in information retrieval. *Found. Trends in Inform. Retr.*, 2016. To appear.

[3] F. Cai, S. Liang, and M. de Rijke. Time-sensitive personalized query auto-completion. In *CIKM '14*, pages 1599–1608, 2014.

[4] F. Cai, R. Reinanda, and M. de Rijke. Diversifying query auto-completion. *ACM Trans. on Inform. Syst.*, 2016. To appear.

[5] S. Fox, K. Karnawat, M. Mydland, S. Dumais, and T. White. Evaluating implicit measures to improve web search. *ACM Trans. Inf. Syst.*, 23(2):147–168, 2005.

[6] J. Jiang, D. He, and J. Allan. Searching, browsing, and clicking in a search session: Changes in user behavior by task and over time. In *SIGIR '14*, pages 607–616, 2014.

[7] J.-Y. Jiang, Y.-Y. Ke, P.-Y. Chien, and P.-J. Cheng. Learning user reformulation behavior for query auto-completion. In *SIGIR '14*, pages 445–454, 2014.

[8] Y. Kim, A. Hassan, R. W. White, and I. Zitouni. Modeling dwell time to predict click-level satisfaction. In *WSDM '14*, pages 193–202, 2014.

[9] T. Mikolov, I. Sutskever, K. Chen, G. S. Corrado, and J. Dean. Distributed representations of words and phrases and their compositionality. In *NIPS 26*, pages 3111–3119, 2013.

[10] B. Mitra. Exploring session context using distributed representations of queries and reformulations. In *SIGIR '15*, pages 3–12, 2015.

[11] G. Pass, A. Chowdhury, and C. Torgeson. A picture of search. In *InfoScale '06*, pages 1–7, 2006.

[12] M. Shokouhi. Learning to personalize query auto-completion. In *SIGIR '13*, pages 103–112, 2013.

[13] J. Teevan, S. T. Dumais, and D. J. Liebling. To personalize or not to personalize: Modeling queries with variation in user intent. In *SIGIR '08*, pages 163–170, 2008.

[14] W. Zhang, J. Wang, B. Chen, and X. Zhao. To personalize or not: A risk management perspective. In *RecSys '13*, pages 229–236, 2013.

SG++: Word Representation with Sentiment and Negation for Twitter Sentiment Classification

Qinmin Hu, Yijun Pei, Qin Chen and Liang He
Shanghai Key Laboratory of Multidimensional Information Processing
Department of Computer Science & Technology
East China Normal University, Shanghai, 200241, China
qmhu@cs.ecnu.edu.cn, {yjpei, qchen}@ica.stc.sh.cn and lhe@cs.ecnu.edu.cn

ABSTRACT

Here we propose an advance Skip-gram model to incorporate both word sentiment and negation information. In particular, there is a a softmax layer for the word sentiment polarity upon the Skip-gram model. Then, two paralleled embedding layers are set up in the same embedding space, one for the affirmative context and the other for the negated context, followed by their loss functions. We evaluate our proposed model on the 2013 and 2014 SemEval data sets. The experimental results show that the proposed approach achieves better performance and learns higher dimensional word embedding informatively on the large-scale data.

Keywords

Twitter Sentiment Classification; Word Representation; Neural Network; Negation

1. INTRODUCTION

Twitter sentiment classification is to treat Tweets as positive, negative and neutral. This will help the stakeholders make proper decisions, when the public sentiment on topics, such as the newly released products or services, entertainment news and politics, can be obtained.

Nowadays, many approaches in Twitter sentiment classification, utilize a supervised classifier and rely on extensive feature engineering [3, 1, 10, 6, 9, 4, 8, 5]. However, there is an open problem for feather engineering is that it costs extensive labour work and specific domain knowledge. Therefore, feature learning is an alternative way to learn discriminative features automatically from data. The work presented by [12, 16] proves that the features of a sentence/document can be learnt through its word embedding. Current approaches of learning word embedding [2, 7, 15] focus on modeling the syntactic context. This situation does not take the sentiment information into account. [14] then proposed a complex neural network to learn sentiment-specific word embedding and language model simultaneously. However, it is very time-consuming to training a big neural network and the negation is not included in Tang's proposal as well.

SIGIR '16, July 17-21, 2016, Pisa, Italy
© 2016 ACM. ISBN 978-1-4503-4069-4/16/07...$15.00
DOI: http://dx.doi.org/10.1145/2911451.2914718

Hence, we are motivated to establish a novel approach, not only focusing on learning sentiment-specific word embedding efficiently, but also capturing the negation information. We propose an advanced Skip-gram model which incorporates word sentiment and negation into the basic Skip-gram model. First, the basic Skip-gram model is extended by inserting a softmax layer, in order to add the word sentiment polarity. Then, two paralleled embedding layers are set up in the same embedding space, one for the affirmative context and the other for the negated context, followed by their loss functions. After that, we design the experiments on the SemEval 2013 and 2014 data sets. The results show our advanced Skip-gram model is promising and superior. Further more, our proposal achieves better performance efficiently and can learn much higher dimensional word embedding informatively on the large-scale data.

2. THE PROPOSED APPROACH

Here we introduce the proposed approach, including the basic Skip-gram model and the advanced Skip-gram model.

2.1 The Basic Skip-gram Model

The basic Skip-gram model we adopt here is introduced by [7] to learn word embedding from text corpus. The training objective is to find word representations such that the surrounding words (the syntactic context) can be predicted in a sentence or a document. Mathematically, given a sequence of training words $w_1, w_2, ..., w_T$, the goal of Skip-gram model is to maximize the log probability

$$\frac{1}{T}\sum_{t=1}^{T}\sum_{-c\leq j\leq c, j\neq 0} logp(w_{t+j}|w_t) \tag{1}$$

where c is the size of the context window, $p(w_{t+j}|w_t)$ is defined using the softmax function:

$$p(w_O|w_I) = \frac{exp(\theta_{w_O}\cdot v_{w_I})}{\sum_{w=1}^{W} exp(\theta_w \cdot v_{w_I})} \tag{2}$$

where v_w is the vector representation of word w, θ_w is the parameter vector of word (or class) w, and W is the number of words in the vocabulary.

2.2 The Advanced Skip-gram Model

In order to learn better word embedding for Twitter sentiment classification, we develop two neural networks based on the Skip-gram model for word sentiment and negation.

Model 1 (SG+)..

The objective of our proposed SG+ is to incorporate word sentiment into the Skip-gram model. We then find word representa-

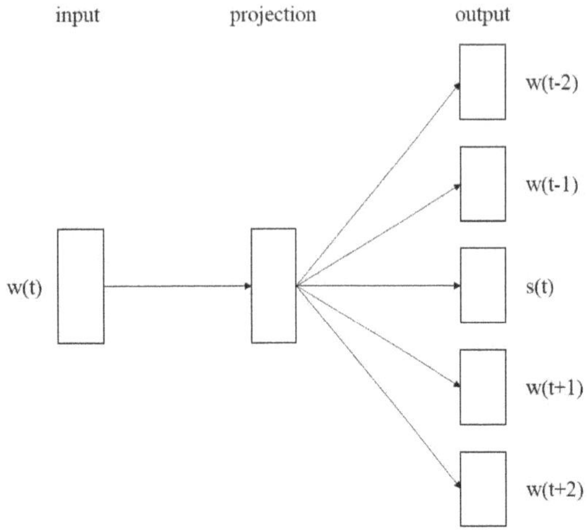

Figure 1: SG+

tions to predict both syntactic context and word sentiment. Figure 1 shows there layers, where the first one indicates the training word w_t, the second one is the projection and the third one includes the surrounding words $w_{t-2}, w_{t-1}, w_{t+1}, w_{t+2}$ and the sentiment information s_t . Correspondingly, given a sequence of training words $w_1, w_2, ..., w_T$, we modify Equation 1 and Equations 2 and then obtain the goal of SG+ to maximize the log probability

$$\frac{1}{T}\sum_{t=1}^{T}(\sum_{-c\leq j\leq c, j\neq 0}(1-\beta)logp(w_{t+j}|w_t)) + \beta logp(s_t|w_t) \tag{3}$$

where c is the size of the context window, s_t is the sentiment label of word w_t, and β is the hyper-parameter that weights the impact of word sentiment and syntactic context. Similar to $p(w_{t+j}|w_t)$, $p(s_t|w_t)$ is defined using the softmax function as well:

$$p(s_t|w_t) = \frac{exp(\theta_{s_t} \cdot v_{w_t})}{\sum_{s=1}^{S} exp(\theta_s \cdot v_{w_t})} \tag{4}$$

where v_w is the vector representation of w, θ_s is the parameter vector of sentiment label s, and S is the number of sentiment labels.

Model 2 (SG++)..

The objective of SG++ is to further incorporate negation. Here we propose to learn the affirmative and negated word embedding simultaneously. Intuitively, affirmative (negated) words are mapped to the affirmative (negated) representations, which can be used to predict the surrounding words and word sentiment in affirmative (negated) context. Figure 2 presents an example... Given a sequence of training words $w_1, w_2, ..., w_T$ where negation detection are already performed, the goal of NSSG+ is to maximize the log probability

$$\frac{1}{T}\sum_{t=1}^{T}\beta(n_t logp(sn_t|w_t) + (1-n_t)log(sa_t|w_t)) + (\sum_{-c\leq j\leq c, j\neq 0}(1-\beta)logp(w_{t+j}|w_t)) \tag{5}$$

where sa_t (sn_t) is the sentiment label in affirmative (negated) context, and n_t is the indicator whether w_t is negated or not. Technically, we set two paralleled embedding layers with the same initial values, one for affirmative context and the other for negated context. During the training process, they are updated for optimizing the training objective above.

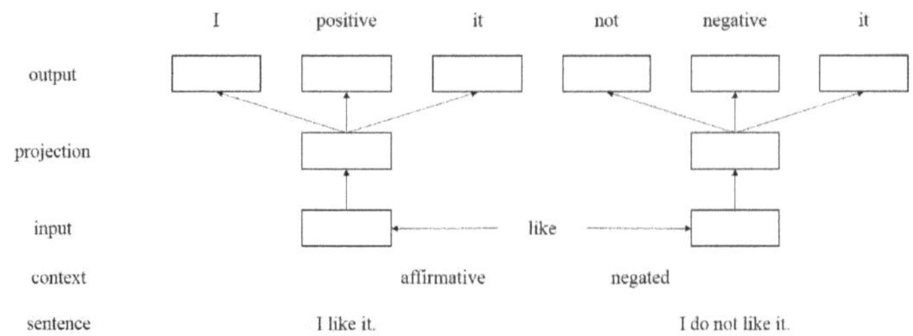

Figure 2: SG++

2.3 Tweet Representation

In order to obtain tweet representation, we adopt the *min*, *max*, and *average* convolutional layers for compositionality learning in vector-based semantics, similar to the work proposed by [14] . Figure 3 shows the compositionality of the input as "I don't wanna miss it" and the corresponding tweet representation.

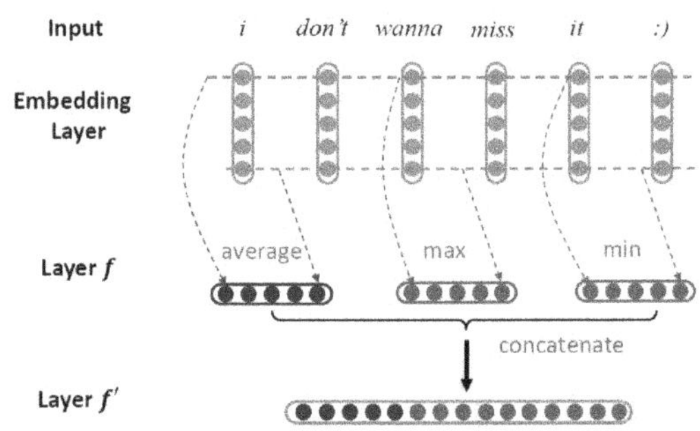

Figure 3: Tweet Representation

3. EXPERIMENTAL SETUP

In order to evaluate our proposed approach, we design the experiments on the SemEval 2013 and 2014 data sets.

3.1 Task Description

There are multiple subtasks in SemEval 2013 and 2014. Here we focus on Task B, which is a task of sentiment analysis in Twitter called "Message Polarity Classification". It is to classify whether a given message is of positive, negative, or neutral sentiment. The official evaluation metric is macro-F1 of positive and negative sentiment. Therefore, we remove the neutral tweets in the preprocessing.

3.2 Data Sets

Table 1 shows the statistics of the 2013 and 2014 SemEval datasets. Here the raining set contains annotated tweets, and the development set has a few of tweets and is intended to be used as a development-time evaluation dataset as the participants develop their systems. In particular, it's usually used for tuning parameters. These two datasets above are shared by SemEval 2013 and 2014.

The rest of the data sets are test sets. LiveJournal2014 contains sentences from LiveJournal in order to determine how systems trained on Twitter perform on other sources. SMS2013 obtains messages from NUS SMS corpus. Twitter2013 and 2014 are tweets, which express sentiment about popular topics in 2013 and 2014. Twitter2014Sarcasm is a small test set of tweets that contain the sarcasm hashtag to determine how sarcasm affects the tweet polarity.

Dataset	Pos	Neg	Total
Training set	3199	1258	4457
Development set	575	340	1654
LiveJournal2014	427	304	731
SMS2013	490	389	879
Twitter2013	1572	601	2173
Twitter2014	981	202	1183
Twitter2014Sarcasm	33	40	73

Table 1: Statistics of SemEval 2013 and 2014

4. EXPERIMENTAL RESULTS AND ANALYSIS

We present the experimental results on SemEval 2013 and 2014 in Table 2, where "SG++" is our proposed advanced Skip-gram model with sentiment and negation, "SG+" denotes the Skip-gram model with word sentiment and "SG" stands for the basic Skip-gram model. We can see that "SG++" outperforms "SG+" and "SG" on all the datasets besides of "Twitter2014Sarcasm".

Dataset	SG	SG+	SG++
LiveJournal2014	72.03	73.74	77.93
SMS2013	74.06	77.47	80.86
Twitter2013	76.16	78.91	82.21
Twitter2014	74.82	77.56	79.40
Twitter2014Sarcasm	52.21	54.79	52.21

Table 2: Results on SemEval 2013 and 2014

4.1 Influence of Sentiment and Negation

In Table 2, we design the experiments to evaluate the influence of sentiment by comparing the performance of "SG+" with "SG". At the same way, we investigate negation by testing "SG++" and "SG+" respectively. We can see that "SG+" outperforms "SG", and "SG++" is better than "SG+" on the first four data sets. Hence, we conclude that sentiment and negation play very important roles in Twitter sentiment classification. Furthermore, our experiments confirm our motivation and suggest the future work to consider sentiment and negation together.

The performance of Twitter2014Sarcasm is not stable in Table 2, since our proposed "SG++" deals with the normal tweets and the sarcasm ones equally.

4.2 Intuitive Insight of SG++

Here we present an example to show the intuitive insight of our proposed advanced Skip-gram model "SG++". Table 3 shows the neighbors of the target word "good" under "SG++" and "SG". We can see that the neighbor words found by "SG++" are more reasonable than those by "SG", considering the sentiment and negation. In particular, there are some negative words, such as *rough*, *testy* and *bad* in the list of "SG".

Note that the way to find the neighbors adopts the utility program *distance*. The *distance* program computes cosine similarity between two words in the embedding space, and returns the top 40 closest words.

	good
SG	nice, great, gr8, cool, rough, terrific, harmless blessed, interesting, **testy**, familiar, **bad**
SG++	nice, great, cool, :-), funny, special, interesting fantastic, lucky, :D, =), fair

Table 3: Top 40 neighbor words of *good*

4.3 Tuning of Parameter β

In the proposed advance Skip-gram model "SG++", parameter β indicates the importance of the sentiment label. When β equals 0, it means that only syntactic context is adopted. Otherwise if β is 1, negation dominates the label. Empirically, we draw the figure in Figure 4 to turn β. The results suggest that it is better to set β around 0.5. This also confirms our motivation to consider syntactic context and word sentiment at the same time in Twitter sentiment classification.

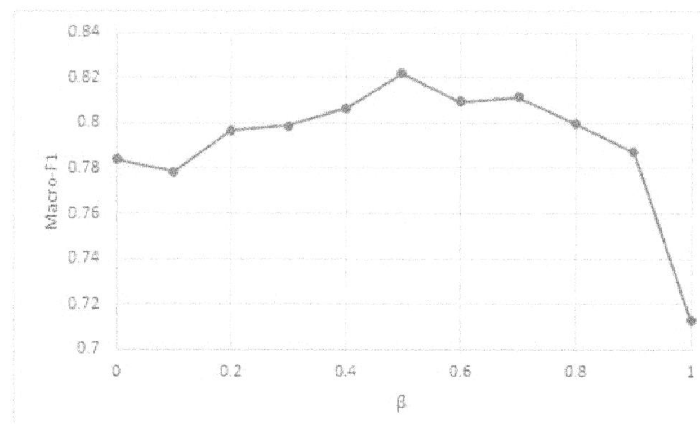

Figure 4: β Tuning of SG++ on SemEval 2013

4.4 Performance Comparisons

In order to evaluate the superiority of our proposed model, we conduct the experiments in Twitter2013 to compare the performance with the majority of the existing algorithms and models in the previous work, such as the work proposed by [14] and [13], the DistSuper algorithm [3] and SVM with unigram [11].

Approach	Macro-F1
DistSuper	68.70
SVM + unigram	74.50
MPQA (Append)	76.54
NRC-Emotion (Appended)	76.79
HL (Appended)	79.40
HashtagLex (Appended)	76.67
Sentiment140Lex (Appended)	80.68
TS-Lex (Appended)	**82.36**
RAE	75.12
$SSWE_u$ (unigram)	**82.93**
SG++	**82.21**

Table 4: Performance ComparisonsTwitter2013

Table 4 shows the performance with eleven algorithm/model configurations. The first two are based on unigram features. Then the following six are the work done by [14] and [13] with hand-crafted features. The last three are based on feature learning through neural networks. We observe that our proposed "SG++" achieves one of the best results.

Approach	Data Size	Data Quality	Sentiment	Syntactic
DistSuper	large	low	N/A	shallow
SVM + unigram	small	high	N/A	shallow
MPQA, NRC, HL	small	high	shallow	deep
HashtagLex, Sentiment140Lex	large	low	shallow	deep
TS-Lex	large	low	deep	deep
RAE	small	high	deep	deep
$SSWE_u$	high	low	deep	deep
SG++	large	low	deep	deep

Table 5: Advantage Analysis

In order to better understanding the advantages of "SG++", we summarize the characters of all the listed algorithms/models in Table 5. We draw the conclusions that: (1) the proposed "SG++" makes the best result with automatic feature learning; (2) although the quality of the hand-crafted labels is high, the amount is less and the coverage is low; (3) the deep model outperforms the shallow one, since the deep one can capture the latent connections and comprehensive linguistic phenomenon of words.

5. CONCLUSIONS AND FUTURE WORK

In this paper, we propose an advanced Skip-gram model (SG++) to learn better word embedding and negation for Twitter sentiment classification efficiently. Three layers are presented in SG++, namely the syntactic layer, the affirmative layer and the negation one. We also built an SG+ model to show the effectiveness of sentiment without negation. Our experiments on SemEval 2013 and 2014 indicate that both sentiment and negation play very important roles in Twitter sentiment classification. Furthermore, we conduct extensive performance comparisons with other similar algorithms/models. The proposed SG++ obtains the top 3 results with automatic feature learning.

Based on the analysis in Table 5, the deep neural network is able to achieve better tweet representation than the shallow one. In the future, we will focus on developing deep neural network to learn language models and other possibilities. This is also our ongoing work.

6. ACKNOWLEDGMENTS

This research is funded by the National High Technology Research and Development Program of China (No. 2015AA015801), and the Science and Technology Commission of Shanghai Municipality of China (No.15PJ1401700).

7. REFERENCES

[1] L. Barbosa and J. Feng. Robust sentiment detection on twitter from biased and noisy data. In *Proceedings of the 23rd International Conference on Computational Linguistics: Posters*, pages 36–44. Association for Computational Linguistics, 2010.

[2] R. Collobert, J. Weston, L. Bottou, M. Karlen, K. Kavukcuoglu, and P. Kuksa. Natural language processing (almost) from scratch. *The Journal of Machine Learning Research*, 12:2493–2537, 2011.

[3] A. Go, R. Bhayani, and L. Huang. Twitter sentiment classification using distant supervision. *CS224N Project Report, Stanford*, pages 1–12, 2009.

[4] H. Hamdan, F. Béchet, and P. Bellot. Experiments with dbpedia, wordnet and sentiwordnet as resources for sentiment analysis in micro-blogging. In *Second Joint Conference on Lexical and Computational Semantics (* SEM)*, volume 2, pages 455–459, 2013.

[5] Y. He, Q. Hu, Y. Song, and L. He. Estimating probability density of content types for promoting medical records search. In *Advances in Information Retrieval - 38th European Conference on IR Research, ECIR 2016, Padua, Italy, March 20-23, 2016. Proceedings*, pages 252–263, 2016.

[6] L. Jiang, M. Yu, M. Zhou, X. Liu, and T. Zhao. Target-dependent twitter sentiment classification. In *Proceedings of the 49th Annual Meeting of the Association for Computational Linguistics: Human Language Technologies-Volume 1*, pages 151–160. Association for Computational Linguistics, 2011.

[7] T. Mikolov, I. Sutskever, K. Chen, G. S. Corrado, and J. Dean. Distributed representations of words and phrases and their compositionality. In *Advances in Neural Information Processing Systems*, pages 3111–3119, 2013.

[8] S. M. Mohammad, S. Kiritchenko, and X. Zhu. Nrc-canada: Building the state-of-the-art in sentiment analysis of tweets. In *Proceedings of the Second Joint Conference on Lexical and Computational Semantics (SEMSTARÂąÂŕ13)*, 2013.

[9] S. Mukherjee, P. Bhattacharyya, et al. Sentiment analysis in twitter with lightweight discourse analysis. In *COLING*, pages 1847–1864, 2012.

[10] A. Pak and P. Paroubek. Twitter as a corpus for sentiment analysis and opinion mining. In *LREC*, volume 10, pages 1320–1326, 2010.

[11] B. Pang, L. Lee, and S. Vaithyanathan. Thumbs up?: sentiment classification using machine learning techniques. In *Proceedings of the ACL-02 conference on Empirical methods in natural language processing-Volume 10*, pages 79–86. Association for Computational Linguistics, 2002.

[12] R. Socher, A. Perelygin, J. Y. Wu, J. Chuang, C. D. Manning, A. Y. Ng, and C. Potts. Recursive deep models for semantic compositionality over a sentiment treebank. In *Proceedings of the conference on empirical methods in natural language processing (EMNLP)*, volume 1631, page 1642. Citeseer, 2013.

[13] D. Tang, F. Wei, B. Qin, M. Zhou, and T. Liu. Building large-scale twitter-specific sentiment lexicon: A representation learning approach. In *COLING 2014*, pages 172–182, 2014.

[14] D. Tang, F. Wei, N. Yang, M. Zhou, T. Liu, and B. Qin. Learning sentiment-specific word embedding for twitter sentiment classification. In *Proceedings of the 52nd Annual Meeting of the Association for Computational Linguistics*, pages 1555–1565, 2014.

[15] H. Yang, Q. Hu, and L. He. Learning topic-oriented word embedding for query classification. In *Advances in Knowledge Discovery and Data Mining - 19th Pacific-Asia Conference, PAKDD 2015, Ho Chi Minh City, Vietnam, May 19-22, 2015, Proceedings, Part I*, pages 188–198, 2015.

[16] A. Yessenalina and C. Cardie. Compositional matrix-space models for sentiment analysis. In *Proceedings of the Conference on Empirical Methods in Natural Language Processing*, pages 172–182. Association for Computational Linguistics, 2011.

SGT Framework: Social, Geographical and Temporal Relevance for Recreational Queries in Web Search

Stewart Whiting
School of Computing Science,
University of Glasgow,
Scotland, UK.
stewh@dcs.gla.ac.uk

Omar Alonso
Microsoft Corp.
Mountain View,
California, USA.
omalonso@microsoft.com

ABSTRACT

While location-based social networks (LBSNs) have become widely used for sharing and consuming location information, a large number of users turn to general web search engines for recreational activity ideas. In these cases, users typically express a query combining desired activity type, constraints and suitability, around an explicit location and time – for example, "parks for kids in NYC in winter", or "cheap bars for bachelor party in san francisco". In this work we characterize such queries as recreational queries, and propose a relevance framework for ranking points of interest (POIs) to present in the web search recreational vertical using signals from query logs and LBSNs. The first part of this framework is a taxonomy of recreational intents, which we derive from those previously seen in query logs and other behavioral data. Based on the most popular recreational intents, we proceed to outline a new relevance model combining social, geographical and temporal information. We implement a prototype and conduct a preliminary user-study evaluation. Results show the proposed relevance model and bundles greatly improve user satisfaction for recreational queries.

1. INTRODUCTION

LBSNs provide a platform for sharing and consuming local information during our every day lives through location check-ins and tips. When considered collectively, this user-generated information is very useful for understanding user mobility and preference at unprecedented scale.

Location is an essential part of web search, where a major percentage of queries have an explicit or implicit location intent [7, 8]. In this work, we focus on a specific segment of queries that have a recreational intent with a geographic preference. As an example, say that a family is planning an upcoming weekend city trip, and so are seeking suitable activity ideas. A query such as "`things to do in london with kids`" will trigger the recreational vertical to provide a short list of the most popular generic POIs such as tourist attractions and sightseeing spots. Real recreational queries are shown in Figure 1.

However, the recreational activity vertical does not contain specific suggestions tailored to the user's recreational intents, which

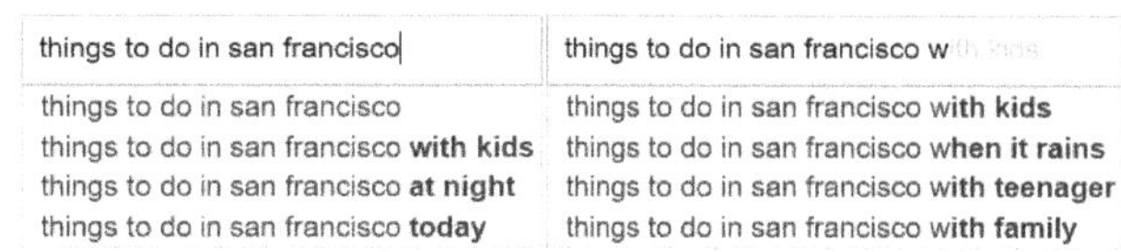

Figure 1: Recreational queries for "`things to do in san francisco...`" in the Bing query auto-suggest feature.

may comprise implicit and explicit expectations – such as *what* they want and *when* they want to do it (e.g., season, weekday/weekend, time of date, etc.), in addition to constraints and preferences such as being '*outside*', '*cheap*', '*romantic*', or '*with kids*', etc. As a result, the activity vertical POIs are often not relevant, so the user must resort to collectively reviewing the web search results for ideas. To address this issue, we aim to present to the user a number of suggestions – based on LBSN check-in and tip data – that summarize the activities relevant to their intent. Note that this scenario is distinguished from established venue recommendation techniques employed by LBSNs since we have no previous venue ratings provided. Hence, only the user's explicitly provided query and implicit context (e.g., their geo-location, or the current time) can be used to infer the user's intent and expectations in the relevance model.

In this paper we present SGT, a framework that combines social, geographical and temporal information for presenting results that address the user's explicit (i.e., query-specified) and implicit (i.e., assumed) search intent. A central part of our framework is a taxonomy that drives the modeling and user experience.

We are interested in connecting the relevant information provided by two, potentially, different crowds - the users who are looking for things to do in search engine, and the users who have performed an activity in a LBSN like Facebook or Foursquare. The goal is to use the data from LBSN to satisfy the user search query. To achieve this, we would like to understand the different types of recreational intents and queries and other user behavior, model the relevance of venues to different queries, combine them in bundles, and finally present the results to the user.

With this in mind, in this preliminary work we set out to answer the following three research questions: (1) What type of recreational queries are users issuing to a search engine, and what is their prevalence? (2) Can a retrieval model be built to offer relevant places for recreational queries, based on LBSN data? (3) Is a single linear list of relevant venues, or a set of intent-oriented bundles more effective for presenting results to users?

In answering these questions, we make the following contributions: (i) a taxonomy of common recreational queries, (ii) a relevance model incorporating LBSN data, (iii) an approach to generating result bundles for composing the results, and finally (iv) preliminary evaluation using a large-scale real-world data set.

SIGIR '16, July 17-21, 2016, Pisa, Italy

DOI: http://dx.doi.org/10.1145/2911451.2914743

2. RELATED WORK

The majority of work on LBSN data has concentrated on building context-aware venue recommender systems, where the context is typically the user's past preferences (expressed through check-ins) and any explicitly requested venue requirements and filtering. Because of the recent popularity of recommender systems, several evaluation tasks for optimising such systems have originated in the community. The recent TREC Contextual Suggestion (CS) Track [4] provided user rating data and user queries accompanied with context such as query submission time. While the recreational search scenario we outline in this paper has many similarities to this TREC CS task, we do not have past user preferences to consider in the POI relevance model since the majority of web search users are either anonymous, or do not frequently use an LBSN.

There has been considerable analysis of the social, geographical and temporal patterns and trends present in LBSN data from many perspectives. Check-ins have been found to contain many structural patterns, caused by geographic and social constraints of user's lives [3] – which must be incorporated into any relevance framework. Likewise, the preference for different activity types changes dramatically (e.g., going to the movie theatre on a Friday evening, versus going to the park in the morning at a weekend) [1]. Further, [5] models how check-in preferences change over different periods time – from hour-to-hour through to seasons of the year. In essence, in this work we integrate these findings in a retrieval model specifically for supporting recreational search in web search.

3. RECREATIONAL QUERY TAXONOMY

In this section, we present and discuss the SGT recreational query taxonomy as a structure of the constraints and preferences most commonly expressed in queries by users during recreational information seeking.

We study common recreational query patterns observed in a variety of user-generated content and behavioral logs. In particular, we mined a month of web and mobile search query logs and browser behavioral data from the Microsoft Bing search engine. In each source we looked for queries and links which contained to the substring seed text "things to", "places to" and "what to", and a city recognised by a disambiguating location entity tagger. Note we find the typical nature and expectations of recreational activity varies considerably from place to place, for instance, "romantic" queries are much more popular in Paris than in Chicago. In the following sections we elaborate the top-level taxonomy aspects.

3.1 Taxonomy Aspects

The taxonomy comprises the following high-level aspects: (i) geographical constraint, (ii) temporal constraint, (iii) activity preference, (iv) activity suitability, and (v) activity constraint.

Each aspect corresponds to the recreational activity requirements expressed in real user queries. In many cases the aspects are not independent, with a single query often containing many aspects (e.g., '`cheap things to do with kids in nyc in january`'). In the following subsections we describe each aspect along with illustrative query examples from a real query log.

Geographical Constraint. Most important is the place where the user is, or alternatively, is going. Locations expressed by a user include a country, state or city. City names must be disambiguated using established techniques [6]. Relative locations such as '*near*' and '*around*' must be resolved relative to specific location. In our experiments reported in Section 6, we use major world cities as the base geographical constraint.

Temporal Constraint. Time will define relevant POIs [3, 5, 1]. For example, eating will differ during the day as people desire breakfast, lunch, dinner or late night snacks. Similarly, it is unlikely a user will visit a park on a Sunday night in a cold city.

Time periods include seasons, months, weekday/weekends, day of the week and the time of day (e.g., morning, afternoon, evening and night). Alternatively, events such as Christmas, New Year, Thanksgiving and Memorial Day, etc., can be translated into an upcoming time anchor. Relative temporal constraints can be provided in the form of "now", "today", "tonight" and "this weekend" etc., can also be translated into temporal constraints. In this work we do not consider current or upcoming POI trendiness in ranking.

Activity Preference. Of course, many users will have a preference for the recreational activity they are seeking. They may wish to eat or drink, whether at a restaurant or in a lively outdoor area. Tourists are likely to want sightseeing areas and major POIs, in contrast to residents who may prefer cafes and parks to relax. Similarly, those looking for outdoor recreational activities will find parks and trails much more relevant.

Activity Suitability. In many cases, user's seek activities with certain characteristics to match an activity purpose. For instance, couples may wish to find a location that is romantic and therefore suitable for a date or anniversary. This could be a restaurant, or something to do, such as visiting a romantic sightseeing spot.

For different age groups, users may look for locations which are suitable for kids, such as babies, toddlers, teenagers, etc. Social group suitability may include friends, family and bachelor/bachelorette parties. Weather may also be a major factor in some locations and seasons.

Activity Constraint. Especially common are preferences for "free", "cheap", "unique" and "educational" activities. For nightlife recreational queries we often saw "lively" constraints, and likewise the "quiet" constraint for bars, cafes and restaurants where the objective was likely work-related. Disabled access and dog-friendly constraints were also commonly seen.

Together, these SGT taxonomy aspects can be used to represent complex recreational intents expressed in recreational queries, such as "`unique romantic things to do this weekend in new york`".

3.2 Query Classification & Aspect Popularity

For each taxonomy aspect we create a classifier incorporating related terms and phrases. We use this to classify and map user query and POI tip text (from the LBSN) to the aspects which they relate in the taxonomy. The query or tip keywords present to identify each aspect are intuitive, so we do not list them exhaustively here. For instance, the synonyms "for kids" or "for children" and "kid-friendly" are used for the "kids" age suitability aspect.

Since tips and queries are short text, term frequency is usually 1 so a simple binary term presence classifier is effective. Future work will explore more elaborate probabilistic and natural language classifiers which can better handle positive and negative sentiments expressed in more complex phrases, such as '*not* good for kids'and 'my kids loved this place' in tip text.

Taxonomy Aspect Popularity in Search Queries. With a long-tail distribution typical in search, we found the ten most common recreational aspects expressed in queries were for: (1) *tourism*, (2) *eating*, (3) *fun*, (4) *for kids*, (5) *weekend*, (6) *near*, (7) *free*, (8) *outside*, (9) *with dog*, and (10) *birthday*. Notably, we found the popularity of these aspects varies hugely between cities, and for the same city at different times. Accordingly, we propose activity bundles to better support this behaviour in Section 5. Based on this taxonomy, in the next section we outline the SGT relevance model to rank POIs for recreational queries.

4. MODELLING POI RELEVANCE

We extract a list of POIs for each major world city from LBSN data, and model various signals from the social data to quantify each location's relevance to a recreational query. For LBSN data, we use the full 2014 check-in and POI tip datasets from the popular Foursquare and Facebook LBSNs (a combined total of over 1B+ check-ins, with a considerable number including textual tips).

Check-in times tell us *when* places are popular. Likewise, tips tell us what people think about POIs, offering several clues such as whether they are good for kids, a romantic date, lively, or quiet etc. All these signals must be combined to filter and rank relevant POIs for queries spanning multiple aspects of our taxonomy.

In this work we use a very large dataset of LBSN data, and as we are most interested in major world cities with plenty of check-in data available (hence, sparsity is not a problem), at this stage we employ a basic maximum likelihood estimation (MLE) model to rank POIs based on the probability that the taxonomy aspects inferred from check-in and tip signals match the taxonomy-classified recreational query aspects. Accordingly, for a given recreational query q_{rec} relating to a specified city, we compute and rank the likelihood of a POI poi_i being relevant using the base MLE ranking formula as follows:

$$MLE(q_{rec}) = \arg\max_{poi_i \in poi_c} P(poi_i | q_t, q_a) \quad (1)$$

poi_c is set of all POIs in the desired city (future work will explore more fine-grained locations). q_t is the likelihood of the POI being relevant given any temporal activity constraints expressed in the recreational query. And finally, q_a is the POI relevance to any given SGT taxonomy aspects expressed in the recreational query. We elaborate on deriving the temporal and taxonomy aspect popularity components in the following two sections.

4.1 Temporal Ranking Component

From past check-ins, we observe the probability that a user will check-in at the POI during any given time period. We consider all permutations for parts of the day (morning/afternoon/evening/night), day of the week (Monday-Sunday), weekdays/weekends and season, similar to that presented in [5]. Thus, in the base MLE ranking equation (Equation 1), we define the temporal relevance q_t of poi_i probabilistically as $P(poi_i|q_t) = P(poi_i|City, PartOfDay, DayOfWeek, WeekdayWeekend, Season)$.

Recent trends such as new and trending POIs will not be observed in past data. We leave time series modelling to capture these more elaborate temporal trends to future work.

4.2 Aspect Ranking Component

To rank POIs for recreational queries, we must quantify the relevance of every POI to each aspect in the SGT taxonomy. We do this by examining the feedback in LBSN POI tips to determine which of those POIs, and POI categories, are most likely to satisfy a recreational query based. In essence, this means we higher rank POIs for a romantic recreational query when the POI is both in a typically romantic category (e.g., sightseeing spots, or French restaurants), and has tips mentioning that it is itself romantic.

Using the same keyword classifier detailed in Section 3.2, we classify all the POI tips into our taxonomy aspects. For example, the tip: "`my kids loved the great food here - and it was cheap`" would be classified with the aspects: "*for kids*", "*cheap*" and "*great*". In the first instance, this allows us to observe which local POIs have a propensity towards certain taxonomy aspects, based solely on their own tips. For example, major city parks with good play areas and open space have many tips mentioning fun, children and dogs. For the most popular POIs in major cities, this technique alone helps us quantify the relevance of the POI for the most common taxonomy aspects. However, the sparsity of tips for the majority of individual POIs and smaller cities means this approach quickly becomes ineffective.

To overcome this sparsity issue (especially for the long-tail) we rely on higher-level POI categories (e.g., "*bowling alley*", "*playground*", "*zoo*", "*theme bar*" and "*beach*", etc.) to determine the appropriateness of a POI to a given aspect via its category. This approach allows use to still present and effectively rank POIs with few or no tips relating to a given taxonomy aspect.

With this in mind, we organise aspect classified POI tips by their respective POI category – rather than their particular POI. From this, we compute a score that each POI category is relevant to each SGT taxonomy aspect. Henceforth, for each taxonomy aspect a_i, and POI category c_i we compute the category relevance score as:

$$categoryrelevance(a_i, c_i) = \frac{freq(a_i, c_i)}{freq(a_i)} \times log_{10}(freq(a_i)) \quad (2)$$

Where $freq(a_i, c_i)$ is the number of tips from the POI category c_i classified with the given aspect, and $freq(a_i)$ is the number of tips from any POI category classified with the given aspect. The final log term provides down-scaling for the overall most popular categories (e.g., bars), which tend to appear indiscriminately in all aspects, allowing more specific – yet, highly relevant – niche categories to rank highly.

The result of this scoring function provides intuitive ranking of categories for each taxonomy aspect. For example, this function ranks the POI categories "mini golf", "paintball field", "theme park ride", "go kart track" and "theme park" highest for the "fun" taxonomy aspect. Likewise, it ranks "playground", "science museum", "toy/game store", "theme park" and "zoo" as top for the "kids" taxonomy aspect.

To define aspect relevance for a POI to a recreational query, we combine POI-specific, if available, and POI category evidence together. Thus, we define the aspect relevance q_a for poi_i as $aspectrelevance(poi_i, q_a) = (1 + P(q_a|poi_i) \times$ $(categoryrelevance(q_i, poi_{category}))$. $P(q_a|poi_i)$ is the probability that the POI poi_i has a tip classified with the query aspect q_a. The preceding $1 + \ldots$ term is to smooth zero probabilities. Hence, in this model the POI-specific term can be seen as a boost for the typically more much more powerful POI category score term.

5. RESULT BUNDLES

Finally, we consider how to effectively present POI results to the user. When the user provides an ambiguous recreational query without any specific activity constraints, preferences or suitability (e.g., just "things to do in london"), we posit their need is exploratory – and so a more organised and diversified result presentation is required (as has been applied in web search scenarios [2]). Accordingly, we propose a simple POI result-bundling approach by activity aspect to maximise user understanding of all POI options, and thus overall satisfaction.

The prevailing approach used in the web search activity vertical is to simply present the top-*k* most relevant POIs in a linear list (accompanied by thumbnail) – as illustrated by (1) in Figure 2. This approach is limited since it offers unintuitive organisation of POI results, and little diversity. Hence, we look to group a small number of taxonomy aspect-related (e.g., "for kids", or "nightlife" etc.) POI results into bundles to present – illustrated by (2) in Figure 2.

Each bundle corresponds to set of most popular aspects we have observed for the city (or, from all cities in aggregate if no such ob-

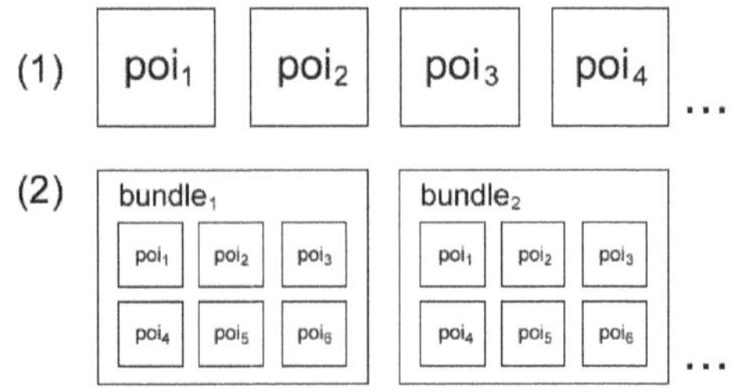

Figure 2: (1) linear list-based POI result presentation, and (2) bundle-based POI result list presentation.

servation is available, as is the case for smaller cities). These are the aspects we discussed in Section 3.2. Recall how we noted the aspect popularity varied from city-to-city, and indeed over time. For instance, Paris had far more recreational queries relating to romantic aspects. Likewise, for Santa Cruz (CA), recreational queries mainly related to beach, outdoor and leisure aspects were most popular, especially in summer.

For each city, we extracted the four most popular aspects as candidate result bundle aspects. As per the linear list, we rank the POIs using the SGT Framework presented in the previous section. However, we interleave the results into each bundle by selecting the top-k POI results by their category and relevance to the bundle taxonomy aspect. This means for San Francisco, one such bundle is "with kids" – so we present a bundle with a combination of top ranking POIs in the "playground", "science museum", "zoo", "theme park" and so forth categories.

6. EXPERIMENTAL PROCEDURE

We conducted a small user experiment to evaluate the effectiveness of the SGT framework for ranking POIs, and the presentation of POI results in linear lists versus bundles. 10 users were (5 males and 5 females, 20-40 years of age) with extensive web search experience. Participants were from 6 different countries, so tested the system for a wide range of major international cities.

After a brief training session, participants were asked to interact with two systems, and answer the same set of two questions for two tasks. System 1 is the linear list-based POI results, and System 2 is bundle-based POI presentation. The tasks and questions were as follows. **Task 1:** Choose a city you are very *familiar with*, but do not live in. This might be the city in which you grew up or attended school. **Task 2:** What is the major city you currently *live in*, or near? For each system, please type the name of the city and search for things to do. Based on your experiences, please answer the following questions: **(Q1)** Based your knowledge of the city, on a scale 1 to 5 (1=bad, 5=excellent), what is the quality of the POI suggestions? **(Q2)** On a scale 1 to 5 (1=bad, 5=excellent), how useful is this information for a user who is not familiar with your city but is looking for things to do?

7. RESULTS & DISCUSSION

Overall, questionnaire results presented in Figures 3 and 4 show that users in general like the POI results provided by the SGT framework for their recreational queries. In particular, we find that users much prefer bundle-based result presentation, especially for familiar cities – this is probably because they surface more unusual options beyond the typical top well-known POIs. We also note that they feel that tourists could benefit from them, demonstrating the potential for both major recreational query use cases. We note qualitative feedback which suggested we needed to introduce interaction to allow the user to specify the bundles they were presented.

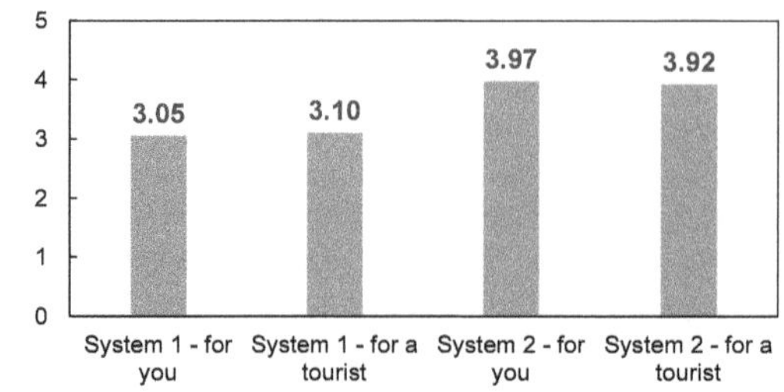

Figure 3: Average system rating for a city the user is familiar with, but does not live in (i.e., task 1).

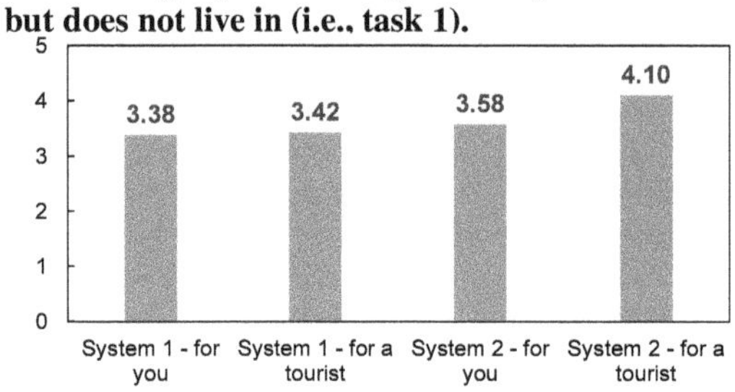

Figure 4: Average system rating for a city the user lives in, or near (i.e., task 2).

8. CONCLUSION

In this work, we investigated POI result ranking and presentation for the large number of recreational search queries posed to a web search engine. We outlined the Social, Geographical and Temporal (SGT) Framework as a first step for modelling POI relevance in this scenario. Further, recognising the issues of presenting POI results in a linear list in the activity search vertical, we proposed a POI result bundling to improve the user comprehension of results.

With respect to the research questions outlined in Section 1, we make several findings. A wide range of broand and specific recreational queries are posed to web search engines. We constructed a taxonomy of these, and report a long-tail frequency distribution. We outlined the SGT framework for modelling POI relevance based on the LBSN tip and check-in data. Preliminary evaluation indicated this first approach satisfied users. Finally, we found bundle-based result presentation is much preferred for familiar and tourist user scenarios. This work represents a first step; future work will better address city POI information sparsity, user personalisation, and bundling strategies along with more conclusive evaluation.

9. REFERENCES

[1] S. Bannur and O. Alonso. Analyzing temporal characteristics of check-in data. In *WWW '14*, pages 827–832.

[2] H. Bota, K. Zhou, J. M. Jose, and M. Lalmas. Composite retrieval of heterogeneous web search. In *WWW '14*, pages 119–130.

[3] E. Cho, S. A. Myers, and J. Leskovec. Friendship and mobility: user movement in location-based social networks. In *SIGKDD '11*, pages 1082–1090. ACM.

[4] A. Dean-Hall, C. L. Clarke, J. Kamps, P. Thomas, N. Simone, and E. Voorhees. Overview of the trec 2013 contextual suggestion track. In *TREC 2013*.

[5] H. Gao, J. Tang, X. Hu, and H. Liu. Modeling temporal effects of human mobile behavior on location-based social networks. In *CIKM '13*, pages 1673–1678.

[6] C. B. Jones and R. S. Purves. Geographical information retrieval. *International Journal of Geographical Information Science*, 22(3):219–228, 2008.

[7] M. Sanderson and J. Kohler. Analyzing geographic queries. In *Workshop on Geographic Information Retrieval, SIGIR '04*.

[8] L. Wang, C. Wang, X. Xie, J. Forman, Y. Lu, W.-Y. Ma, and Y. Li. Detecting dominant locations from search queries. In *SIGIR '05*.

SimCC-AT: A Method to Compute Similarity of Scientific Papers with Automatic Parameter Tuning

Masoud Reyhani Hamedani
Department of Computer and Software
Hanyang University, Seoul, Korea
masoud@agape.hanyang.ac.kr

Sang-Wook Kim
Department of Computer and Software
Hanyang University, Seoul, Korea
wook@agape.hanyang.ac.kr

ABSTRACT

In this paper, we propose SimCC-AT (similarity based on content and citations with automatic parameter tuning) to compute the similarity of scientific papers. As in SimCC, the state-of-the-art method, we exploit a notion of a *contribution score* in similarity computation. SimCC-AT utilizes an *automatic weighting scheme* based on SVM^{rank} and thus requires only a *smaller* number of experiments for parameter tuning than SimCC. Furthermore, our experimental results with a *real-world* dataset show that the accuracy of SimCC-AT is dramatically *higher* than that of other existing methods and is *comparable* to that of SimCC.

Keywords

Automatic Weighting, Citations, Content, Contribution Score, Similarity

1. INTRODUCTION

Scientific papers are one of primary sources to share information and knowledge among researchers. Recently, computing the similarity of scientific papers became an interesting topic in information retrieval and data mining [1][6][9]. SimCC [6] is state-of-the-art method that considers both content and citations in computing similarity of scientific papers. The philosophy of SimCC is that, when paper q cites paper p, it means p is a valuable paper on some topics discussed in q and *contributes* to q for *improving* the content of q. Based on this philosophy, SimCC introduces the notion of a *contribution score* as a key factor in similarity computation. SimCC *dramatically* outperforms text-based similarity measures such as Cosine [5], Dice coefficient [5], BM25 [5], and Kullback-Leibler Distance (KLD) [5], link-based similarity measures such as SimRank [3], rvs-simRank [11], and P-Rank [11], and also hybrid methods such as CEBC [1], Keyword-Extension [8], and WCO [7].

In spite of high accuracy, the parameter tuning is performed *manually* in SimCC, which is a *difficult* and *time-consuming* task. Consequently, it is *not* easy to adopt SimCC for practical applications. We *cannot* utilize automatic weighting schemes such as SVM^{rank} [4] *directly* for parameter tuning because SimCC applies a weighted linear combination to *two different feature scores* obtained from *single* paper p to get a single score as a new feature for p, which is later utilized in similarity computation. These two combined feature scores of a paper are *not* calculated in relating to other paper, thereby making SVM^{rank} *unable* to be applied to SimCC for indicating the importance of each feature in combination.

SIGIR '16, July 17-21, 2016, Pisa, Italy

DOI: http://dx.doi.org/10.1145/2911451.2914715

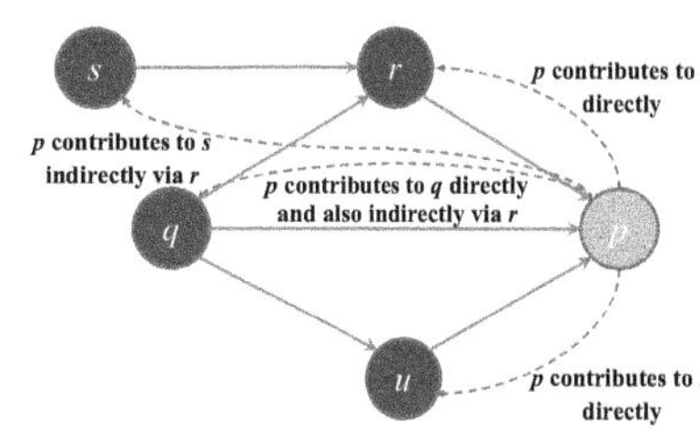

Figure 1: A sample citation graph.

In this paper, we propose a method, *SimCC-AT* (similarity based on content and citations with automatic parameter tuning), which performs parameter tuning *automatically*. In order to utilize automatic weighting schemes, we *reformulate* SimCC while *preserving* its philosophy in similarity computation. In SimCC-AT, only a *small* number of experiments are required for parameter tuning; therefore, it is *easily* adopted for practical applications. Our extensive experimental results show that the accuracy of SimCC-AT is dramatically *higher* than that of other existing methods and is *comparable* to that of SimCC.

The contributions of this paper are as follows. (1) We utilize *automatic parameter tuning* in similarity computation based on contribution scores; (2) we *simplify* the adoption of an accurate similarity computation based on contribution scores for *any* similarity measures applicable to vectors; (3) we evaluate the effectiveness of SimCC-AT extensively with a *real-world* dataset of scientific papers.

2. CONTRIBUTION SCORE

The contribution score measures how much a paper contributes to another *single paper* on a *specific term* via a *specific citation path*. Consider the sample citation graph in Figure 1 where nodes represent papers and edges do citation relationships among papers. As an example, p contributes to q directly (via citation path $q \rightarrow p$ where $\rightarrow$ denotes a direct citation) and indirectly (via citation paths $q \rightarrow r \rightarrow p$ and

$q \to u \to p$); p contributes to u only directly via citation path $u \to p$. Therefore, p has three contribution scores on a single term t to q via three distinct citation paths and has only one contribution score on t to u via a single citation path.

3. MOTIVATION

SimCC performs *both* feature extraction and similarity computation. For feature extraction, every paper p is represented as an n-dimensional vector. The weight of a term t in the vector of p is calculated as follows [6]:

$$w_t(p) = \lambda R_t(p) + (1 - \lambda) A_t(p) \tag{1}$$

where $R_t(p)$ is a *relevance score* of t to p calculated by applying any weighting factors such as TF, TF-IDF, and BM25. $A_t(p)$ is an *authority score* of p on t calculated by summing up *all* contribution scores of p on t to all other papers citing p. λ ($0 \leq \lambda \leq 1$) is a relative importance factor. For similarity computation, *any* similarity measures for vectors such as Cosine, Dice, BM25, and KLD can be employed.

The best value of λ is found *manually*, which is *difficult* and *time-consuming* since we have to conduct lots of experiments as follows. For *any* employed similarity measure, at least 55 distinct experiments are required [6] as five different path lengths from 1 to 5 are considered for computing the contribution scores, and the value of λ is set from 0.0 to 1.0 in steps of 0.1 for each path length. Consequently, it is *not* easy to adopt SimCC for practical applications.

We note that it is *not* possible to perform automatic parameter tuning in SimCC for the following reason. Automatic weighting schemes such as SVM^{rank} can be utilized to determine the importance (i.e., rank) of each feature in a set of features, each of which measures a *relatedness between* two objects based on its own criteria [4]. In SimCC, however, $R_t(p)$ and $A_t(p)$ are two features of *single* paper p; they do not measure any relatedness (e.g., similarity) between paper p and another paper.

4. PROPOSED METHOD

Our proposed method, *SimCC-AT*, has the goal of performing *automatic parameter tuning* with *preserving* the philosophy of SimCC in similarity computation. As in SimCC, the contribution score is a key factor in SimCC-AT which performs both feature extraction and similarity computation. However, there are *two major differences* between SimCC-AT and SimCC as follows.

In SimCC, $R_t(p)$ and $A_t(p)$ are combined into a single value, $w_t(p)$, for every paper p. The similarity score of a paper-pair (p, q), $S(p, q)$, is computed by employing a similarity measure on their corresponding vectors. On the contrary, in SimCC-AT, every paper p is represented by two separate vectors *R-vector* (relevance vector) and *A-vector* (authority vector) containing $R_t(p)$ and $A_t(p)$ for all terms t in p, respectively. For computing $S(p, q)$, *two distinct* similarity scores are computed based on their corresponding R-vectors, $SR(p, q)$, and their corresponding A-vectors, $SA(p, q)$. Then, the two scores $SR(p, q)$ and $SA(p, q)$ are combined into a *single score* by applying a *weighted* linear combination as $S(p, q)$. In this way, we reformulate SimCC while persevering its philosophy in similarity computation.

In SimCC, the parameter tuning is performed *manually*; however, in our method, the importance of $SR(p, q)$ and $SA(p, q)$ in the combination is determined *automatically* by utilizing an *automatic weighting scheme* based on SVM^{rank} [4]. We can utilize SVM^{rank} since, 1) for every paper p, we consider $R_t(p)$ and $A_t(p)$ as two separate features in similarity computation; 2) for both p and q, $SR(p, q)$ and $SA(p, q)$ measure a relatedness (i.e., similarity) between a pair of papers p and q. We *only* need to conduct 6 experiments as five different path lengths are considered for computing the contribution scores; then, SVM^{rank} is utilized to automatically determine the importance of $SR(p, q)$ and $SA(p, q)$ in the combination to obtain $S(p, q)$. Consequently, we can *easily* adopt SimCC-AT for *any* similarity measures applicable to vectors in practical applications.

4.1 Authority Score Calculation

$A_t(p)$ is calculated by the following formula:

$$A_t(p) = \sum_{i=1}^{d} \sum_{q \in D(p,i)} \sum_{\pi \in q \overset{i}{\rightsquigarrow} p} C_t(\pi) \tag{2}$$

where d denotes the maximum length of the path in the citation graph traversed to compute the contribution score, $D(p, i)$ does a set of papers that cite p via paths with length i ($1 \leq i \leq d$), and $q \overset{i}{\rightsquigarrow} p$ does a *set* of citation paths with length i from q to p. π denotes a *single* citation path $q \to r_1 \to \ldots \to r_{i-1} \to p$ with length i from q to p and $C_t(\pi)$ does the contribution score of p on t to q *via* π. For example, in Figure 1, $D(p, 1) = \{q, r, u\}$ and $D(p, 2) = \{q, s\}$.

Only for simplicity of presentation, we assume that there is *only* one citation path $q \overset{i}{\rightsquigarrow} p$ with length i from q to p. Equation (2) is rewritten as follows:

$$A_t(p) = \sum_{i=1}^{d} \sum_{q \in D(p,i)} C_t(q \overset{i}{\rightsquigarrow} p) \tag{3}$$

where $C_t(q \overset{i}{\rightsquigarrow} p)$ denotes the contribution score of p on t to q via the single path $q \overset{i}{\rightsquigarrow} p$ and is computed as follows:

$$C_t(q \overset{i}{\rightsquigarrow} p) = \varphi_t(q \overset{i}{\rightsquigarrow} p) R_t(q) \tag{4}$$

where $\varphi_t(q \overset{i}{\rightsquigarrow} p)$ denotes the contribution ratio of p on t to q via $q \overset{i}{\rightsquigarrow} p$. If q cites p directly (i.e., $i = 1$), the contribution ratio is calculated as follows:

$$\varphi_t(q \overset{1}{\rightsquigarrow} p) = \frac{R_t(p)}{R_t(q) + \sum_{r \in citations(q)} R_t(r)} \tag{5}$$

where *citations*(q) denotes a set of papers *directly* cited by q. If q cites p *indirectly* via other papers (i.e., $i \geq 2$), $\varphi_t(q \overset{i}{\rightsquigarrow} p)$ is determined by contribution ratios between *all* directly connected papers in the citation path. Let $q \to r_1 \to \ldots \to r_{i-1} \to p$ be a citation path with length i from q to p. Then, we have

$$\varphi_t(q \overset{i}{\rightsquigarrow} p) = \varphi_t(q \overset{1}{\rightsquigarrow} r_1) \cdot \Big(\prod_{j=1}^{i-2} \varphi_t(r_j \overset{1}{\rightsquigarrow} r_{j+1}) \Big) \cdot \varphi_t(r_{i-1} \overset{1}{\rightsquigarrow} p) \tag{6}$$

4.2 Similarity Computation

In our SimCC-AT, $S(p, q)$ is computed as follows:

$$S(p, q) = w_1 SR(p, q) + w_2 SA(p, q) \tag{7}$$

where w_1 and w_2 are weights for controlling the *degree of importance* of $SR(p, q)$ and $SA(p, q)$ in the combination since we do *not* consider them as equally significant in computing $S(p, q)$. We use SVM^{rank} [4] that is based on the support vector machine (SVM) to determine best values of w_1 and w_2 *automatically*.

SVM^{rank} solves a maximum-margin optimization problem by finding a hyperplane. In our case, the hyperplane is a vector of two weights represented as $V{=}{<}w_1, w_2{>}$ that provides an ideal *separation* between relevant and irrelevant papers in a training set by finding the best values of w_1 and w_2. The training set is used for the training process and contains training instances. The training instance represents a paper in regarding to a query paper as follows:

$$<r, qid, SR(p,q), SA(p,q)> \quad (8)$$

where r is set as 1 when p is relevant to the query paper q, and is set as 0 otherwise as described in Section 5.2. qid denotes a query number. SVM^{rank} indicates the hyperplane according to pairwise preference constraints, which are included for all pairs of training instances that have different r but the identical qid.

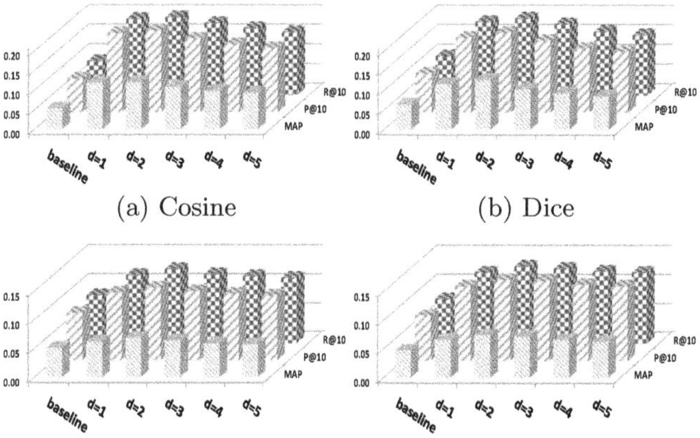

(a) Cosine (b) Dice

(c) BM25 (d) KLD

Figure 2: Accuracy with different values of *d*.

5. EVALUATION

In this section, we compare the effectiveness of SimCC-AT with those of Cosine, Dice, BM25, and KLD as text-based similarity measures, SimRank, P-Rank, and SimRank* [10] as link-based similarity measures, and CEBC, WCO, and Keyword-Extension as hybrid methods. Also, we compare the effectiveness of SimCC-AT with that of original SimCC.

5.1 Experimental Setup

We employed a real-world dataset of scientific papers by crawling information of 1,071,793 papers from DBLP[1] and their abstract and citation information from Microsoft Academic Search[2]. We do not have access to the body of papers due to the copyright issue. However, the combination of the title and abstract has been reported to show the better accuracy than the body in computing the similarity [8].

We constructed our ground truth sets based on a famous data mining textbook [2] where, as in *user studies*, relevant papers to research topics addressed in each chapter are categorized by experts (i.e., the authors of the book) in the bibliographic section of the chapter. We selected eleven research topics as our ground truth sets, each of which contains its related papers. Also, we utilize MAP, precision at top 10 results (P@10), and recall at top 10 results (R@10) [5] as evaluation measures.

As in SimCC, we employ Cosine, Dice, BM25, and KLD as *basic similarity measures* to be employed with R-vectors and A-vectors. To employ Cosine and Dice, we utilize the TF-IDF value as the relevance score. For BM25 and KLD, we utilize the BM25 weight and the TF value, respectively.

5.2 Results and Analysis

As described in Section 4.1, $A_t(p)$ depends on d, the maximum length of the path to compute contribution scores. Therefore, we investigate how the accuracy of a basic similarity measure changes with different values of d to find its best value for each measure. We set the value of d from 1 to 5 in Equation (2) and construct five distinct A-vectors for every paper in the dataset. Figure 2 represents the accuracy of Cosine, Dice, BM25, and KLD with different values of d in terms of MAP, P@10, and R@10. The *baseline* method denotes the similarity computation based on R-vectors (i.e., relevance scores).

For all basic similarity measures, we observe the following *common* results. The similarity computation based on authority scores significantly outperforms the baseline method *regardless* of the value of d. As a surprising result, the best value of d is 2 *regardless* of similarity measures. The accuracy decreases gradually for $d \geq 3$ since, when we go farther from each paper in the citation graph, contribution scores of the paper to other papers tend to be *noisier*.

For every basic similarity measure, we perform the automatic parameter tuning to determine best values of w_1 and w_2 in Equation (7) as follows. We construct the A-vector of all papers in the dataset based on d=2. Then, we compute $SR(p,q)$ and $SA(p,q)$ for all paper-pairs (p,q) where p and q belong to the dataset and ground truth sets, respectively. Finally, we construct the training set by defining training instances according to Equation (8) for 60% of papers in our dataset. If *both* p and q belong to the same ground truth set, r is set as 1, otherwise 0. SVM^{rank} is executed on the training set to determine values of w_1 and w_2.

Now, we compare the effectiveness of SimCC-AT with those of other existing methods in Figure 3. For example, Figure 3(a) represents the accuracy of CEBC, Keyword-Extension, WCO, and SimCC-AT, each of which is equipped by Cosine; also, this figure shows the accuracy of the baseline method (Cosine only with R-vectors) and SimRank*. For link-based similarity measures, we *only* represent the result of SimRank* because it is shown to outperform *both* SimRank and P-Rank with our dataset. The reason is that it considers those possible paths between papers in a citation graph, which are *neglected* by SimRank and P-Rank in similarity computation.

The following results are *commonly* observed with all the employed basic similarity measures. The baseline method and SimRank* show the *worst* accuracy since they consider *only* content and citations in similarity computation, respectively. However, the baseline method outperforms SimRank*. Hybrid methods significantly outperform the baseline method and SimRank* since they consider both content and citations in similarity computation. SimCC-AT *dramatically* outperforms all other methods. The reason is that SimCC-AT not only considers both content and citations in similarity computation but also, in contrary to other hybrid

[1]http://www.informatik.uni-trier.de
[2]http://academic.research.microsoft.com

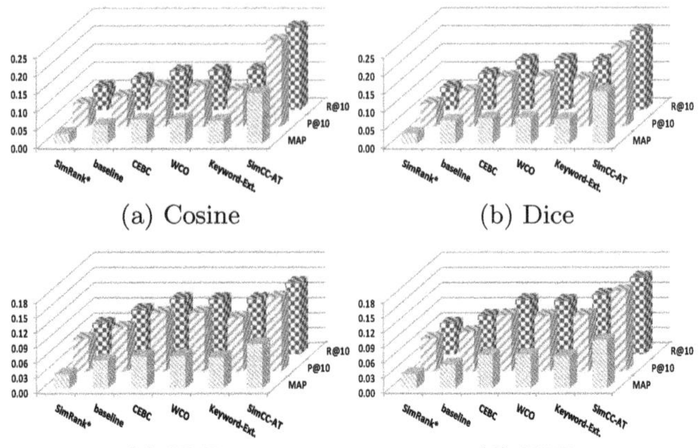

(a) Cosine (b) Dice

(c) BM25 (d) KLD

Figure 3: Accuracy of SimCC-AT and other methods.

methods, it does *not* simply combine the content of papers involved in a *direct* citation relationship; instead, SimCC-AT measures the amount of contribution between papers involved in a *direct or indirect* citation relationship as contribution scores to utilize them in similarity computation.

Now, we compare the accuracy of SimCC-AT with that of SimCC in terms of MAP, P@10, and R@10 in Figure 4. For all basic similarity measures, SimCC shows *slightly* (see Table 1) better accuracy than SimCC-AT. The reason is that, in SimCC, relevance and authority scores are combined into a single value as a *unique* feature for similarity computation. However, in SimCC-AT, these scores are considered as two *separate* features for similarity computation.

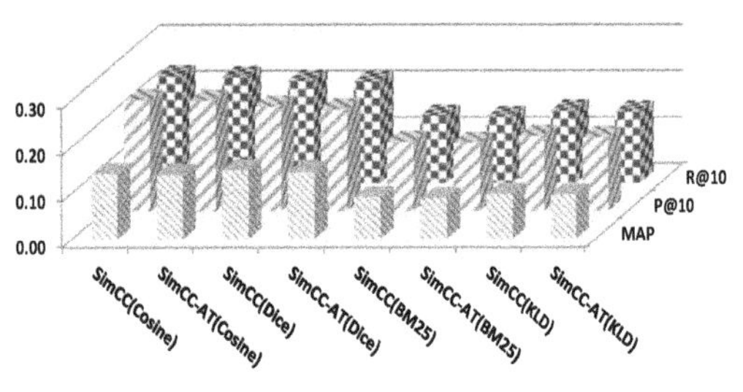

Figure 4: Accuracy of SimCC-AT and SimCC.

Despite the fact that SimCC-AT shows lower accuracy than SimCC, we claim that it is a *better* method than SimCC for similarity computation by the following aspects: 1) there is *no tangible* difference between the accuracy of SimCC-AT and that of SimCC as shown in Table 1; 2) compared with SimCC, SimCC-AT requires a much *smaller* number of experiments (i.e., 6) for parameter tuning; therefore, SimCC-AT can be *easily* adopted for practical applications; 3) the best value of d in SimCC-AT (i.e, 2) is less than that in SimCC (i.e, 3 [6]). Therefore, SimCC-AT has a smaller computational overhead in large citation graphs.

6. CONCLUSIONS

In this paper, we proposed SimCC-AT to compute the similarity of scientific papers by considering both content and citations, which utilizes SVM^{rank} for automatic parameter tuning. As in SimCC, the state-of-the-art method, the

Table 1: Relative accuracy (%) of SimCC-AT over SimCC.

	Cosine	Dice	BM25	KLD
MAP	98.48	96.85	97.22	98.29
P@10	99.40	97.05	98.82	98.36
R@10	98.86	98.85	98.26	98.70

contribution score is a key factor in SimCC-AT. However, to utilize SVM^{rank}, we reformulated SimCC while preserving its philosophy (i.e., contribution score) in similarity computation. As a result, it is *easy* to adopt SimCC-AT for practical applications since it requires a smaller number of experiments (i.e., 6) than SimCC (i.e., 55) for parameter tuning. SimCC-AT dramatically outperforms other existing methods, and its accuracy is comparable to that of SimCC.

Acknowledgment

This research was supported by (1) the Ministry of Science, ICT and Future Planning (MSIP), Korea, under the Information Technology Research Center (ITRC) support program (IITP-2016-H8501-16-1013) supervised by the Institute for Information & communication Technology Promotion (IITP) and (2) the National Research Foundation of Korea (NRF) grant funded by the Korea government (MSIP) (NRF-2014R1A2A1A10054151).

7. REFERENCES

[1] N. Chiki, B. Rothenburger, and N. Gilles. Combining Link and Content Information for Scientific Topics Discovery. In *ICTAI*, pages 211–214. 2008.

[2] J. Han, M. Kamber, and J. Pei. *Data Mining: Concepts and Techniques, Second Edition.* Morgan Kaufmann, San Francisco, 2006.

[3] J. Jeh and J. Widom. SimRank: A Measure of Structural-Context Similarity. In *SIGKDD*, pages 538–543. 2002.

[4] T. Joachims. Optimizing Search Engines using Clickthrough Data. In *SIGKDD*, pages 133–142. 2002.

[5] C. Manning, P. Raghavan, and H. Schutze. *Introduction to Information Retrieval.* Cambridge University Press, New York, 2008.

[6] M. Reyhani Hamedani, S. Kim, and D. Kim. SimCC: A Novel Method to Consider both Content and Citations for Computing Similarity of Scientific Papers. *Information Sciences*, 334-335:273–292, 2016.

[7] K. Sugiyama and M. Kan. Scholarly Paper Recommendation via User's Recent Research Interests. In *JCDL*, pages 29–38. 2010.

[8] S. Yoon, S. Kim, and J. Kim. On Computing Text-based Similarity in Scientific Literature. In *WWW*, pages 169–170. 2011.

[9] S. Yoon, S. Kim, and P. Sunju. C-Rank: A Link-based Similarity Measure for Scientific Literature Databases. *Information Sciences*, 326:25–40, 2016.

[10] W. Yu, X. Lin, W. Zhang, L. Chang, and J. Pei. More is Simpler: Effectively and Efficiently Assessing Node-pair Similarities Based on Hyperlinks. *PVLDB*, 7(1):2150–8097, 2013.

[11] P. Zhao, H. Han, and S. Yizhou. P-Rank: a Comprehensive Structural Similarity Measure over Information Networks. In *CIKM*, pages 553–562. 2009.

Simple Dynamic Emission Strategies for Microblog Filtering

Luchen Tan, Adam Roegiest, Charles L. A. Clarke, and Jimmy Lin
David R. Cheriton School of Computer Science
University of Waterloo, Ontario, Canada
{luchen.tan, aroegies, jimmylin}@uwaterloo.ca, claclark@gmail.com

ABSTRACT

Push notifications from social media provide a method to keep up-to-date on topics of personal interest. To be effective, notifications must achieve a balance between pushing too much and pushing too little. Push too little and the user misses important updates; push too much and the user is overwhelmed by unwanted information. Using data from the TREC 2015 Microblog track, we explore simple dynamic emission strategies for microblog push notifications. The key to effective notifications lies in establishing and maintaining appropriate thresholds for pushing updates. We explore and evaluate multiple threshold setting strategies, including purely static thresholds, dynamic thresholds without user feedback, and dynamic thresholds with daily feedback. Our best technique takes advantage of daily feedback in a simple yet effective manner, achieving the best known result reported in the literature to date.

1. INTRODUCTION

Filtering topical events from social media streams, such as Twitter, provides a means for users to keep up-to-date on topics of interest to them. If care is taken, these updates may even be pushed directly to the user through notifications on mobile devices or desktops. However, for push notifications to be successful, the user must be given means to control the frequency and volume of updates, avoiding indiscriminate and unwanted notifications. This frequency and volume depends both on the interests of the user, with topics of greater interest updated in greater volume, and on the topics themselves, with some topics naturally receiving updates more frequently than others.

We might update a user interested in polls for the 2016 U.S. presidential elections many times a day during the election cycle itself, but with updates stopping altogether after November 8. We might update a user interested in California residential water restrictions only when these restrictions change, perhaps a few times a year, but interest in the topic might persist for many years, as long as the user is a resident of the state. For causal sports and entertainment topics (cricket or the Kardashians), a user may not desire more than a few of the most significant updates per day, regardless of events taking place. For topics of great personal importance (a tornado warning or friend's wedding), we might push all updates.

SIGIR '16, July 17 - 21, 2016, Pisa, Italy

ISBN 978-1-4503-4069-4/16/07...$15.00
DOI: http://dx.doi.org/10.1145/2911451.2914704

The TREC Microblog tracks provide an experimental forum for research groups working in this area. In 2015, the track [4] required participating groups to monitor the live "spritzer" stream provided by Twitter over a period of ten days in July, selecting tweets relevant to 225 pre-defined interest profiles, each expressed through statements modeled after TREC *ad hoc* topics. Each tweet returned by participating systems was accompanied by the clock time at which the system would have pushed it to the user. This information was then used by the track organizers to compute various official evaluation measures for a subset of 51 interest profiles. The evaluation measures considered both the relevance of selected tweets and the time at which they were putatively pushed. In addition, the measures accounted for retweets, near-duplicate tweets, and other redundancies, reflecting an expectation that a user would not want to receive notifications about the same thing over and over again.

Along with this mobile notification scenario (called "scenario A") the evaluation supported a daily digest scenario (called "scenario B"). At the end of each of the ten days, participating systems returned a ranked list of tweets from that day, just as if a user was sent a summary of the day's events by email. Standard evaluation measures for ranked retrieval may be applied, provided that they also appropriately account for redundant content.

To achieve good results for scenario A, systems must successfully address three requirements implicit in the task:

1. A requirement to score individual tweets with respect to relevance. As a simplification, the evaluation focused on topical relevance. Social signals, such as the prominence of the source or its connection to the user, were not considered, so that the relevance of a tweet is primarily determined by its content.
2. A requirement for novelty, so that the system does not push redundant information. This requirement was operationalized by the assessors considering tweets chronologically: if two textually similar tweets arrive at different times, the later tweet is considered redundant if it does not contain substantive information beyond that found in the earlier tweet [9]. Again, only tweet content is considered, so that a duplicate tweet from a more prominent or authoritative source would still be considered redundant.

3. A requirement to avoid pushing non-relevant information altogether. The evaluation measures for scenario A explicitly rewarded systems that avoided pushing non-relevant information. Thus, appropriate selection of thresholds was critical to success. In some cases, the ideal response for a given day was to push nothing, and the "empty" strategy of never pushing anything formed a challenging baseline that many systems failed to beat.

Since the first two requirements are inherent in any ranking task, we focus on the third requirement. After demonstrating the impact of ignoring the third requirement, we consider various strategies for establishing and maintaining thresholds for pushing tweets. We examine strategies under two assumptions: with and without user feedback. When feedback is not available, thresholds are established from historical information. When feedback is provided, it is limited to once-per-day judgments based on the scenario B output. Of particular importance is the establishment of a global score threshold, applied across all topics in the absence of feedback. Our best technique takes advantage of daily feedback in a simple yet effective manner, achieving the best known result reported in the literature to date.

2. RELATED WORK

Filtering has been a longstanding subject for information retrieval research. Earlier work on Topic Detection and Tracking (TDT) investigated algorithms for the discovery of new topics and maintaining awareness when these topics reappear in newswire streams or broadcast news [2]. Experimental results from TREC from the mid-1990s to early-2000s indicated that simple IR techniques can achieve high quality results in TDT domains [1,3,10,11]. For example, Allan et al. [1] used the most common words from 1 to 16 training stories to generate short queries which were compared to documents using TF-IDF based similarity.

More recently, researchers have examined filtering and tracking problems in the context of social media. However, Twitter introduces several issues not present in previous topic tracking tasks, especially in relation to tweets. In particular, tweets have a maximum length of 140 characters and this length limitation implies that meaningful words rarely occur more than once, suggesting that TF-IDF weighting schemes may be less useful. Lin et al. [5] investigated the use of four language modeling smoothing techniques to filter tweets, mitigating issues with sparse terms, i.e., the zero-probability problem. Zhao and Tajima [12] framed a retweet recommendation problem as a multiple-choice secretary problem. They examined Twitter "portal accounts", which retweet selected tweets for their followers, and considered a number of strategies for tweet selection. They proposed and compared a number of online and near-online decision methods, including a history-based threshold algorithm, a stochastic threshold algorithm, a time-interval algorithm, and an "every k-tweets" algorithm.

3. TREC 2015 MICROBLOG TRACK

Topics (called "interest profiles") provided to participants in the TREC 2015 Microblog track included a short query-like description of the information need, called the "title" in TREC parlance. For example, topic MB235 has the title "California residential water restrictions". Other fields in a topic elaborate on the information need, providing a more complete indication of what is and is not relevant. While track participants were permitted to use these other fields for filtering purposes, we focused on the more realistic task in which the user provides only the short query.

Track participants filtered the so-called Twitter "spritzer" stream over ten days in July 2015, selecting those relevant to 225 pre-defined interest profiles and recording their tweet ids for submission. In addition to the tweet ids, the push time was recorded for each tweet, indicating the time the system decided to push the notification. After all experimental runs were submitted to the track organizers, 51 of the interest profiles were selected for judging. Tweets were pooled and judged on a three-point scale. In evaluating a run, a tweet was considered redundant, providing no gain, if it did not contain substantial new information not found in previously pushed tweets [9].

The primary evaluation measure for scenario A is expected latency-discounted gain:

$$\text{ELG} = \frac{1}{N}\sum_{i=1}^{N} G_i D_i \quad (1)$$

For N pushed tweets, G_i is the gain associated with tweet i based on the assigned relevance grade, after adjusting for redundancy. The temporal discount applied to tweet i is $D_i = \max(0, (100 - L_i)/100)$, where L_i is the latency in minutes between the time the tweet appears in the stream and the time the system decides to push it. ELG is computed on a daily basis, over the tweets pushed by a system that day, with the system's overall score averaged across all topics and all days.

ELG has an interesting discontinuity when a system decides not to push anything. For some topics on some days, when no relevant tweets appear in the stream, this is the correct action. On such days, a system pushing *any* tweet receives a score of zero (since none can possibly be relevant). To reward systems that push nothing on such days, the value of ELG is defined to be one. On the other hand, for systems that push nothing on days when relevant tweets appear in the stream, the value of ELG is defined to be zero. Since no relevant tweets appeared for many topics on many days, the "empty" strategy of never pushing anything receives a non-zero ELG score. Indeed, this strategy forms a challenging baseline which many participating systems failed to beat.

4. BASELINE SYSTEM

The system used for the experiments reported in this paper was deployed for the TREC 2015 Microblog track [7], with the design of the system based on substantial pilot experiments conducted prior to the actual evaluation. The system achieved the best ELG score across the 32 automatic runs submitted by 14 participating groups.

All experiments described in this paper are from *post hoc* runs using a replay mechanism over tweet data captured during the evaluation period. Following the TREC evaluation, we performed error analysis to understand the contributions of various system components, and have distilled our algorithm into simple strategies to address the three requirements listed in the introduction, detailed below.

Relevance. Although we recognize that social signals and other non-content features are important for relevance, as a first step we only consider tweet content. For pre-processing, we apply language detection tools to eliminate non-English tweets, tokenize the tweets using Twokenize,[1] and then apply some simple tweet quality heuristics, e.g., eliminating tweets containing less than five tokens.

For matching against the tweet stream, titles were tokenized by splitting on space and punctuation, and stopwords were removed. Since relevant tweets may not contain all, or even any, of the title terms, we employed a pseudo-relevance feedback step to expand the title terms with 5 hashtags and 10 other terms. This was accomplished by querying Twitter's own search engine with title terms at the beginning of each day and extracting the top terms using pointwise KL-divergence [6,8].

For relevance scoring, we applied a simple matching formula developed through pilot testing. Given the short length of tweets, many "standard" features such as query term frequency appear to have limited value. We found that (binary) query term occurrence appears to be the key feature, with the occurrence of title terms having greater importance than the occurrence of expansion terms. To achieve a balance, we score tweet relevance as follows:

$$(w_t \cdot N_t + w_e \cdot N_e) \cdot \frac{N_t}{|T|} \tag{2}$$

where N_t is the number of title terms that appear in the tweet, N_e is the number of expansion terms that appear in the tweet, and $|T|$ is the number of title terms. Based on pilot experiments, weights were set to $w_t = 3$ and $w_e = 1$.

Novelty. We de-duplicated tweets by computing unigram overlap between each new tweet and the tweets previously pushed for a given topic across all days. Tweets with 60% or more overlap were discarded and not further considered. As with the other parameters, we based this overlap setting on pilot experiments conducted prior to the actual TREC 2015 evaluation.

Thresholding. Thresholds for pushing tweets were based on the relevance score in Equation (2). Each day, a threshold is selected, and only tweets with scores greater than or equal to the threshold are considered for delivery. In addition, the evaluation placed a limit of $k = 10$ on the number of tweets that could be pushed each day. Once k tweets are pushed, all further system output is ignored.

Because of its simplicity, Equation (2) has the interesting property that reasonable thresholds are the same across all queries. Our simplest thresholding strategy is thus to select a single static global threshold (GT) across all queries and days. A simple dynamic strategy (without feedback) is to consider the top k from the previous day, selecting as a threshold the score of the kth tweet. However, under this strategy, we do not lower the threshold below a global minimum, selecting as a threshold max(GT, top-k yesterday).

For our TREC 2015 experiments, we used a global threshold of $GT = 5$ (determined based on previous pilot experiments). To better understand the impact of this threshold, Figure 1 shows the effectiveness of our system for these two strategies across a range of global threshold values. The baseline for this plot is the effectiveness of the empty strategy, i.e., never pushing anything, with low threshold values underperforming it. A global threshold of $GT = 6$ slightly outperforms our default threshold of $GT = 5$, which we retain for the remainder of this paper. We find that our simple strategy of dynamically adjusting the threshold without feedback is not effective—the difference compared to using a simple global threshold is negligible for most settings.

[1]http://www.ark.cs.cmu.edu/TweetNLP/

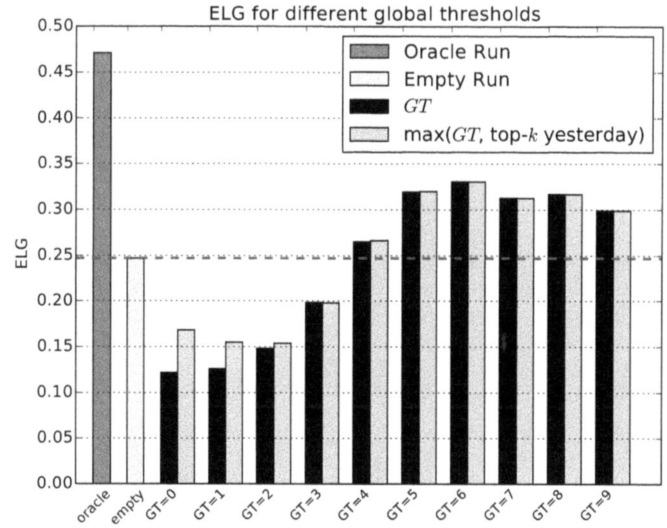

Figure 1: ELG for different global thresholds, the oracle run, and the empty run.

The oracle run in Figure 1 represents the ELG achievable if we made an ideal selection of the global threshold for each topic at the beginning of each day. Clearly, substantial improvements can be achieved through better threshold selection. In the next section, we explore a dynamic emission strategy that uses feedback from each day's digest (scenario B) to select the threshold for the following day.

5. FEEDBACK STRATEGIES

Under scenario B, participants submitted a ranked list of tweets for each topic for each day, providing a daily digest of events for the hypothetical user. Building on the baseline system described above, we use each day's digest to provide relevance feedback for determining thresholds for the following day. While in reality each system saved a ranked list during each day of the evaluation period for later submission, and thus system results were not judged until the evaluation concluded, here we assume that relevance information is provided at the end of each day and available for immediate use. We imagine a user interacting with the results once per day, providing feedback as a way of adjusting the filter for the next day. While in practice this daily interaction might be too onerous, the results provide a sense of what gains could be achieved with ongoing feedback.

For the feedback strategies described below, we used our official scenario B run submitted to TREC 2015 as the daily digest—this ensured that all tweets have relevance judgments. Our method of relevance scoring, Equation (2), often assigns the same score to several tweets. We use the term "score block" to denote a set of tweets with the same score. Accordingly, we say that for a score s_i, it has a corresponding score block SB_i. To determine a dynamic threshold using relevance feedback, we begin by combining all feedback received into a single list of score blocks. At the end of day one for a particular topic, we have 10 tweets worth of feedback, on day two, 20 tweets worth, and so on.

There are two edge cases to consider. In the first case, if there are no relevant tweets in any score block, we take

Baseline Strategies	ELG
$GT = 5$	0.3191
$GT = 6$	0.3303 ($p = 0.3819$)
Feedback Strategies	ELG
avg_gain	0.3257 ($p = 0.5664$)
weighted_avg_gain	0.3510 ($p = 0.0004$)
weighted_avg_gain+r_score	0.3678 ($p \sim 0.0000$)

Table 1: Effectiveness of various emission strategies; p-values are generated from a paired sign test with $GT = 5$.

the maximum of the global threshold (GT) and the highest score seen so far plus w_t, the weight assigned to a title term match. In the second case, if all tweets are relevant, we take the minimum score seen so far.

If we have a mix of relevant and non-relevant tweets, we first compute the average gain for each score as follows:

$$\text{avg\_gain}(s_i) = \frac{\sum_{s_j \geq s_i} \sum_{t \in SB_j} \text{gain}(t)}{\sum_{s_j \geq s_i} |SB_j|}$$

where gain(t) comes from the relevance judgments. We then weight each score's average gain by the proportion of relevant content provided by that score (i.e., the precision of that score):

$$\text{weight}(s_i) = \frac{|\{t | t \in SB_i \wedge \text{gain}(t) > 0\}|}{\sum_{s_j} |SB_j|}$$

$$\text{weighted\_avg\_gain}(s_i) = \text{avg\_gain}(s_i) \cdot \text{weight}(s_i)$$

While selecting a threshold that maximizes average gain doesn't perform particularly well, selecting a threshold that maximizes the weighted average gain significantly improves ELG (see Table 1). However, the weighted average gain method still returns too much non-relevant content. To further improve effectiveness, we use the relevance information to adjust the threshold based on the ratio between relevant and non-relevant content:

$$\text{r\_score}(s_i) = \frac{\sum_{s_j \geq s_i} |\{t | t \in SB_j \wedge \text{gain}(t) = 0\}|}{\sum_{s_j \geq s_i} |\{t | t \in SB_j \wedge \text{gain}(t) > 0\}|}$$

For use as a threshold, a score's r_score must be less than some cutoff, σ. We can vary σ to be more or less permissive of non-relevant tweets: via a coarse-grained parameter sweep, we find that $\sigma = 1.75$ achieves substantially improved results on ELG (see Table 1). Note that if no score achieves an r_score less than or equal to σ, we set the threshold for the next day to be the maximum of the global threshold (GT) and the highest score seen so far, across all days.

6. CONCLUSION

Simple techniques for content matching and novelty can achieve good effectiveness for microblog filtering, provided that care is taken to set appropriate thresholds to avoid pushing non-relevant information. Referring back to Figure 1, our most effective technique achieves an ELG of 0.3678, which is still substantially below what might be achieved if the optimal threshold could be determined for each topic at the beginning of each day, i.e., the oracle with an ELG of 0.4709. However, we significantly improve upon our already highly-effective baseline (already the best automatic run at TREC 2015). In fact, our technique achieves the best known result reported in the literature to date, including manual runs. Our experiments highlight the importance of proper threshold setting, and demonstrate that systems can automatically set appropriate thresholds using simple yet effective feedback techniques. While dynamic thresholds can be set from the tweets of previous days without feedback, such a strategy provides little value, at least with the simple technique we tried.

Our experiments show that dynamic thresholding using feedback has the potential to produce substantial and significant gains. While we have explored only one approach to this idea, through end-of-day relevance judgments, we can imagine more realistic interfaces, which might for example allow incremental judgments as tweets are pushed. In addition, we hope to incorporate social signals and other non-content features into the relevance and novelty components of our system, with the goal of retaining our simple approach to thresholding, while improving overall effectiveness.

Acknowledgments. This work was supported in part by the U.S. National Science Foundation under awards IIS-1218043 and CNS-1405688 and the Natural Sciences and Engineering Research Council of Canada (NSERC). Any opinions, findings, conclusions, or recommendations expressed are those of the authors and do not necessarily reflect the views of the sponsors.

7. REFERENCES

[1] J. Allan, R. Papka, and V. Lavrenko. On-line new event detection and tracking. *SIGIR*, 1998.

[2] J. G. Fiscus and G. R. Doddington. Topic detection and tracking evaluation overview. *Topic Detection and Tracking*. Kluwer, Norwell, MA, 2002.

[3] L. S. Larkey, F. Feng, M. Connell, and V. Lavrenko. Language-specific models in multilingual topic tracking. *SIGIR*, 2004.

[4] J. Lin, M. Efron, G. Sherman, Y. Wang, and E. M. Voorhees. Overview of the TREC-2015 Microblog track. *TREC*, 2015.

[5] J. Lin, R. Snow, and W. Morgan. Smoothing techniques for adaptive online language models: Topic tracking in tweet streams. *SIGKDD*, 2011.

[6] L. Tan and C. L. A. Clarke. Succinct queries for linking and tracking news in social media. *CIKM*, 2014.

[7] L. Tan, A. Roegiest, and C. L. A. Clarke. University of Waterloo at TREC 2015 Microblog Track. *TREC*, 2015.

[8] T. Tomokiyo and M. Hurst. A language model approach to keyphrase extraction. *ACL Workshop on Multiword Expressions*, 2003.

[9] Y. Wang, G. Sherman, J. Lin, and M. Efron. Assessor differences and user preferences in tweet timeline generation. *SIGIR*, 2015.

[10] J. Yamron, I. Carp, L. Gillick, S. Lowe, and P. Van Mulbregt. Topic tracking in a news stream. *DARPA Broadcast News Workshop*, 1999.

[11] Y. Yang, T. Ault, T. Pierce, and C. W. Lattimer. Improving text categorization methods for event tracking. *SIGIR*, 2000.

[12] X. Zhao and K. Tajima. Online retweet recommendation with item count limits. *Web Intelligence and Intelligent Agent Technologies*, 2014.

Subspace Clustering Based Tag Sharing for Inductive Tag Matrix Refinement with Complex Errors

Yuqing Hou† Zhouchen Lin*† Jin-ge Yao§
†Key Lab. of Machine Perception (MOE), School of EECS, Peking University, P. R. China
§Institute of Computer Science and Technology, Peking University, P. R. China
{yqh, zlin, yaojinge}@pku.edu.cn

ABSTRACT

Annotating images with tags is useful for indexing and retrieving images. However, many available annotation data include missing or inaccurate annotations. In this paper, we propose an image annotation framework which sequentially performs tag completion and refinement. We utilize the subspace property of data via sparse subspace clustering for tag completion. Then we propose a novel matrix completion model for tag refinement, integrating visual correlation, semantic correlation and the novelly studied property of complex errors. The proposed method outperforms the state-of-the-art approaches on multiple benchmark datasets even when they contain certain levels of annotation noise.

Keywords

image annotation; subspace clustering; matrix completion; complex errors

1. INTRODUCTION

It is useful to annotate images with textual tags for the purpose of image indexing and retrieval. To annotate proper tags, one need to bridge the gap between low level visual features of an image and corresponding high level semantic information [16]. Since manual annotation is labor intensive, automatic annotation has aroused much attention. Many machine learning based approaches have been developed.

Currently many image annotation data have been collected from crowdsourcing services [21, 12], providing large amount of data for training while being noisy due to annotation errors. Annotation errors are usually complex and mainly come in two forms: missing tags and inaccurate tags. Most image annotation approaches solely focus on one of those two, either trying to impute the missing tags (tag completion/tag assignment) [11] or correcting inaccurate tags (tag refinement) [22, 8, 16]. Other existing methods fail to model the complex errors properly. They either treat them in the same way [24], ignoring the complex property of the errors, or rigidly assign fixed weights to different kinds of errors [11], having no adaptability when working on different datasets with different levels of annotation errors.

In this paper, we propose a framework called Subspace clustering and Matrix completion with Complex errors (SMC). Since current tag refinement methods suffer from the extreme sparsity problem [20], SMC performs tag completion and refinement sequentially. During tag completion, SMC tries to introduce many additional proper tags to images via exploring subspace property in the image collection. We then adapt the inductive matrix completion [13] model to perform the following tag refinement procedure, utilizing side information such as the correlation between visual features and their corresponding tags (visual correlation), correlation between the semantic information of tags (semantic correlation) and the complex errors.

The main contributions of this paper include:

- We perform tag completion and tag refinement sequentially, showing that tag refinement benefits from tag completion.
- We formulate tag completion in a subspace clustering framework to tackle the extreme sparsity problem.
- We novelly adapt the inductive matrix completion model for tag refinement, taking visual correlation, semantic correlation and our novelly studied complex errors property into consideration.

2. THE PROPOSED FRAMEWORK

2.1 Overview

We denote the observed tag matrix as $\mathbf{O} \in \{0,1\}^{N_i \times N_t}$, where each row corresponds to one image, each column corresponds to one textual tag, and N_i and N_t denote the number of images and tags, respectively. $\mathbf{O}_{ij}$ takes value 1 only if image i is annotated with tag j and 0 otherwise.

We are targeting at modifying the values in matrix $\mathbf{O}$ by matrix completion methods to perform image annotation. After the matrix completion procedure, if the value of $\mathbf{O}_{ij}$ changes from nonzero (zero) to zero (nonzero), we say that the algorithm removes (adds) tag j from (to) image i. Methods based on matrix completion are robust and efficient since they only operate on the tag matrix, avoiding error propagation from image segmentation.

However, in many cases $\mathbf{O}$ is so sparse that some columns have at most one known entries and some rows have no known entries at all, making existing methods not applicable [20]. In order to overcome such extreme sparsity, we first

---

*Corresponding author.

SIGIR '16, July 17-21, 2016, Pisa, Italy
© 2016 ACM. ISBN 978-1-4503-4069-4/16/07...$15.00
DOI: http://dx.doi.org/10.1145/2911451.2914693

perform tag completion to make $\mathbf{O}$ denser, creating a better condition for the following tag refinement procedure. More specifically, we perform subspace clustering over images and share tags within subspaces.

For tag refinement, existing methods usually depends heavily on image segmentation and visual feature extraction accuracies [1]. However, image segmentation and feature extraction procedures always contain a lot of noises, which affect the following annotation procedure severely. Meanwhile, recent matrix completion based methods [10, 8, 9] stand out due to their robustness and efficiency, since these algorithms avoid the image segmentation procedure.

Our proposed framework is called Subspace clustering and Matrix completion with Complex errors (SMC), because it utilizes the subspace property of image collections (Section 2.2) and addresses the complex errors and side information in an inductive matrix completion model for tag refinement (Section 2.3).

2.2 Subspace Clustering for Tag Completion

2.2.1 Subspace Clustering

It is reasonable to assume that images belonging to different categories are approximately sampled from a mixture of several low-dimensional subspaces. The membership of the data points to the subspaces is unobserved, leading to the challenging problem of subspace clustering. Here the goal is to cluster data into k clusters with each cluster corresponding to a subspace.

One of the state-of-the-art method is the sparse subspace clustering (SSC) model [5]. The idea behind SSC is to express a data point as a linear (or affine) combination of neighboring data points. The neighbors can be any other points in the data set. While every point is a combination of all other data points, SSC seeks for the sparsest representation among all the candidates by minimizing the number of nonzero coefficients [6].

We denote the set of images, represented as visual feature vectors, as $\mathbf{V} = [\mathbf{v}_1, \mathbf{v}_2, \ldots, \mathbf{v}_n]$. Assuming that they are drawn from a union of k subspaces. Each column of $\mathbf{V}$ can be represented by a linear combination of the bases in a "dictionary". SSC uses the matrix $\mathbf{V}$ itself as the dictionary while explicitly considering noise:

$$\min_{\mathbf{Z},\mathbf{E}} \quad \|\mathbf{Z}\|_1 + \mu\|\mathbf{E}\|_F^2, \tag{1}$$

$$s.t. \quad \mathbf{V} = \mathbf{V}\mathbf{Z}^\top + \mathbf{E}, \mathrm{diag}(\mathbf{Z}) = \mathbf{0}, \mathbf{Z}\mathbf{1} = \mathbf{1}, \tag{2}$$

where $\mathbf{Z}^\top = [\mathbf{z}_1, \mathbf{z}_2, \ldots, \mathbf{z}_n]$ is the coefficient matrix with each $\mathbf{z}_i$ being the representation of $\mathbf{v}_i$ and $\mathbf{E}$ is the error matrix. This problem can be solved efficiently using modern sparse optimization algorithms, such as linearized alternating direction methods [17].

Given a sparse representation for each data point, we can define the affinity matrix as $\mathbf{A} = |\mathbf{Z}| + |\mathbf{Z}^\top|$. Subspaces are then obtained by applying spectral clustering to the Laplacian matrix of $\mathbf{A}$ [5].

2.2.2 Tag Sharing

We improve the search based neighbor voting algorithm proposed in [18] to share tags in each cluster separately. We rank all the tags for the cluster, taking tag frequency, tag co-occurrence and local frequency into consideration. The elements of tag matrix after tag sharing are no longer binary but take values in $[0, 1]$, representing the confidence level between each image-tag pair.

2.3 Matrix Completion for Tag Refinement

The tag completion procedure makes the tag matrix much denser and thus avoids the extreme sparsity problem. Then we can refine the tag matrix. In our framework we novelly adapt the inductive matrix completion model (IMC) [13] for tag refinement, due to its scalability and capability of incorporating various kinds of side information.

2.3.1 Inductive Matrix Completion

Let $\mathbf{v}_i \in \mathbb{R}^{f_i}$ denote the f_i-dimensional feature vector of image i and $\mathbf{t}_j \in \mathbb{R}^{f_t}$ denote the f_t-dimensional feature vector of tag j. Let $\mathbf{V} \in \mathbb{R}^{N_i \times f_i}$ denote the feature matrix of N_i images, where the i-th row is the image feature vector $\mathbf{v}_i^\top$, and $\mathbf{T} \in \mathbb{R}^{N_t \times f_t}$ denote the feature matrix of N_t tags, where the i-th row is the tag feature $\mathbf{t}_i^\top$.

For image annotation, we assume that the tag matrix can be approximated by applying visual feature vectors and tag feature vectors associated with its row and column entries onto an underlying low-rank matrix $\mathbf{M}$, i.e. $\mathbf{O} \approx \mathbf{V}\mathbf{M}\mathbf{T}^\top$, where $\mathbf{M} = \mathbf{P}\mathbf{Q}^\top$ [13] and $\mathbf{P} \in \mathbb{R}^{f_i \times r}$ and $\mathbf{Q} \in \mathbb{R}^{r \times f_t}$ are of rank $r \ll N_i, N_t$. The goal is to solve the following problem:

$$\min_{\mathbf{P},\mathbf{Q}} \quad \mathrm{loss}(\mathbf{O}, \mathbf{V}\mathbf{P}\mathbf{Q}^\top\mathbf{T}^\top) + \lambda_1(\mathrm{rank}(\mathbf{P}\mathbf{Q}^\top)). \tag{3}$$

A common choice for the loss function is the squared loss. The low-rank constraint on $\mathbf{P}\mathbf{Q}^\top$ makes (3) NP-hard. A standard relaxation is to use the trace norm, i.e. sum of singular values. Minimizing the trace-norm of $\mathbf{M} = \mathbf{P}\mathbf{Q}^\top$ is equivalent to minimizing $\frac{1}{2}(\|\mathbf{P}\|_F^2 + \|\mathbf{Q}\|_F^2)$ [13]. The relaxed optimization problem we use in this work is therefore:

$$\min_{\mathbf{P},\mathbf{Q}} \quad \|\mathbf{O} - \mathbf{V}\mathbf{P}\mathbf{Q}^\top\mathbf{T}^\top\|_F^2 + \frac{\lambda_1}{2}(\|\mathbf{P}\|_F^2 + \|\mathbf{Q}\|_F^2). \tag{4}$$

2.3.2 Visual Correlation

We want to get the refined tag matrix $\hat{\mathbf{O}} = \mathbf{V}\mathbf{P}\mathbf{Q}^\top\mathbf{T}^\top$ from the original tag matrix $\mathbf{O}$. Here we represent the ith row of $\hat{\mathbf{O}}$ as $\hat{\mathbf{O}}_i$, corresponding to the refined tag vector of image i. Thus we can measure the correlation between image i and image j in two ways: 1) similarity between image features $\mathbf{v}_i$ and $\mathbf{v}_j$, 2) similarity between refined tag vectors $\hat{\mathbf{O}}_i$ and $\hat{\mathbf{O}}_j$. Since visually similar images often belong to similar themes and thus are annotated with similar tags, these two kinds of similarities should be correlated.

Such visual correlation can be enforced by solving the following optimization

$$\min_{\mathbf{P},\mathbf{Q}} \quad \sum_{i=1}^{N_t}\sum_{j=1}^{N_t} \|\hat{\mathbf{O}}_i - \hat{\mathbf{O}}_j\|^2 g_{ij}, \tag{5}$$

where $\|\hat{\mathbf{O}}_i - \hat{\mathbf{O}}_j\|^2$ measures the similarity between tag vectors $\hat{\mathbf{O}}_i$ and $\hat{\mathbf{O}}_j$ and g_{ij} measures the similarity between visual features $\mathbf{v}_i$ and $\mathbf{v}_j$. In this work, we adopt cosine similarity, i.e. $g_{ij} = \cos(\mathbf{v}_i, \mathbf{v}_j)$. The formulation forces tag vectors with large similarities also have large similarity in their corresponding visual features and vice versa.

The formulation can be rewritten as

$$\min_{\mathbf{P},\mathbf{Q}} \mathrm{Tr}(\hat{\mathbf{O}}\mathbf{L}_\mathbf{v}\hat{\mathbf{O}}^\top) = \min_{\mathbf{P},\mathbf{Q}} \mathrm{Tr}(\mathbf{V}\mathbf{P}\mathbf{Q}^\top\mathbf{T}^\top\mathbf{L}_\mathbf{v}\mathbf{T}\mathbf{Q}\mathbf{P}^\top\mathbf{V}^\top), \tag{6}$$

where $\mathbf{L}_\mathbf{v} = \mathrm{diag}(\mathbf{G}\mathbf{1}) - \mathbf{G}$ is the Graph Laplacian [3] of the similarity matrix $\mathbf{G} = (g_{ij})$.

2.3.3 Semantic Correlation

Similarly, we can also enforce semantic correlation between tags. Since each column of the matrix $\hat{\mathbf{O}}$ represents the feature of a tag, we can measure the correlation between two tags using the similarity between their corresponding column vectors of $\hat{\mathbf{O}}$. Meanwhile, semantic similarity between two tags can be measured using word vectors. These two kinds of similarities should be correlated as well.

We can enforce the semantic correlation by solving the following optimization, in a similar form as (6):

$$\min_{\mathbf{P},\mathbf{Q}} \mathrm{Tr}(\hat{\mathbf{O}}^\top \mathbf{L_s} \hat{\mathbf{O}}) = \min_{\mathbf{P},\mathbf{Q}} \mathrm{Tr}(\mathbf{TQP}^\top \mathbf{V}^\top \mathbf{L_s} \mathbf{VPQ}^\top \mathbf{T}^\top), \quad (7)$$

where $\mathbf{L_s} = \mathrm{diag}(\mathbf{H1}) - \mathbf{H}$ is the Graph Laplacian of the similarity matrix $\mathbf{H} = (h_{ij})$, with each element $h_{ij} = \cos(\mathbf{t}_i, \mathbf{t}_j)$.

2.3.4 Features Vectors

We utilize DeCAF$_6$ [4] to extract 4,096-dimensional visual features for each image, which have high level information. Meanwhile, we adopt pre-trained word embedding vectors (word2vec) [19] to construct 300-dimensional features for each tag, trying to capture semantic information.

2.3.5 Complex Errors

As we have mentioned, annotation errors come in two forms: missing tags and inaccurate tags. Since human beings are relatively reasonable, the user-provided tags are reasonably accurate to certain level [24]. Users might miss one or several proper tags among the few related tags, but may become less probable to add one or several inaccurate tags from the massive unrelated tag sets [12]. In other words, if an image is not originally annotated with a tag, it is more likely that they really have no relation at all. Thus the errors are mainly composed of inaccurate tags rather than missing tags. And we should pay more attention to denoise the inaccurate tags rather than completing the missing ones.

To model the complex structure of errors, we improve the matrix completion model by putting less weights on the unannotated positions:

$$\min_{\mathbf{P},\mathbf{Q}} \|\mathbf{O} - \mathbf{VPQ}^\top \mathbf{T}^\top\|_F^2 - \mu \|\mathbf{U}_\Omega(\mathbf{O} - \mathbf{VPQ}^\top \mathbf{T}^\top)\|_F^2, \quad (8)$$

where $\mathbf{\Omega}$ represents the positions where the images are originally not annotated. $\mathbf{U}$ is a projection operator and μ acts as a weighting parameter which changes adaptively in different datasets according to their noise levels.

Existing methods never model these two kinds of errors separately. They simply model the errors as Laplacian noise [24] or Gaussian noise [22]. To our knowledge, our model is the first to model the missing errors and inaccurate errors separately. The model can further adapt to different datasets according to their noise levels.

3. FINAL MODEL

Based on the components regarding low-rankness, visual correlation, semantic correlation and complex errors, we formulate the objective function as follows:

$$\min_{\mathbf{P},\mathbf{Q}} \|\mathbf{O} - \mathbf{VPQ}^\top \mathbf{T}^\top\|_F^2 - \mu \|\mathbf{U}_\Omega(\mathbf{O} - \mathbf{VPQ}^\top \mathbf{T}^\top)\|_F^2$$
$$+ \frac{\lambda_1}{2}(\|\mathbf{P}\|_F^2 + \|\mathbf{Q}\|_F^2) +$$
$$\lambda_2[\mathrm{Tr}(\mathbf{VPQ}^\top \mathbf{T}^\top \mathbf{L_v} \mathbf{TQP}^\top \mathbf{V}^\top + \mathbf{TQP}^\top \mathbf{V}^\top \mathbf{L_s} \mathbf{VPQ}^\top \mathbf{T}^\top)].$$

By solving $\mathbf{P}$ and $\mathbf{Q}$ we can then construct the refined tag matrix $\hat{\mathbf{O}} = \mathbf{VPQ}^\top \mathbf{T}^\top$ and use it for refined annotation.

We set the regularization terms of visual correlation and semantic correlation with the same weight λ_2 for simplicity. This simplification does not harm performance, as we find during preliminary experiments.

This objective function is non-convex. To solve the optimization problem, we adapt the solver for low-rank empirical risk minimization for multi-label learning (LEML) [23], which naturally fits for the settings of large-scale multi-label learning with missing labels. The solver uses alternating minimization (fix $\mathbf{P}$ and solve for $\mathbf{Q}$ and vice versa) to update the variables. When either $\mathbf{P}$ or $\mathbf{Q}$ is fixed, the resulting subproblem in one variable ($\mathbf{Q}$ or $\mathbf{P}$) can be solved using iterative conjugate gradient procedure.

4. EXPERIMENTAL EVALUATION

4.1 Datasets and Experimental Setup

We evaluate our proposed SMC framework on two benchmark datasets: Labelme [21] and MIRFlickr-25K [12]. Table 1 demonstrates the detailed statistics. These two datasets, especially MIRFlickr-25K, are rather noisy, with a number of the tags being misspelled or meaningless. Hence, a preprocessing procedure is performed. We match each tag with entries in the Wikipedia thesaurus and only retain the tags in accordance with Wikipedia.

Table 1: Statistics of 2 Datasets

Statistics	Labelme	MIRFlickr-25K
No. of images	2,900	25,000
Vocabulary Size	495	1,386
Tags per Image (mean/max)	10.5/48	12.7/76
Images per Tag (mean/max)	67.1/379	416.5/76,890

We compare our method with the state-of-the-art methods, including matrix completion-based models (i.e. LRES [24], TCMR [8], RKML [9]), search-based models (i.e. JEC [18], TagProp [11], and TagRelevance [15]), mixture models (i.e. CMRM [14] and MBRM [7]) and co-regularized learning model (FastTag [2]). The tag refinement procedure by itself, denoted as SMC_IMC, is also compared to verify the benefit from the tag completion procedure. We tune the parameters on the validation set of the two datasets separately for every method in comparison. Note that the weighting parameter μ we tune changes from 0.4 (Labelme) to 0.7 (MIRFlickr-25K), confirming that as the data become more and more noisy, we should pay more attention to the noisy tags and less on missing tags.

We measure all the methods in terms of *average precision@N* (*AP@N*) and *average recall@N* (*AR@N*). In the top N completed tags, *precision@N* is to measure the ratio of correct tags and *recall@N* is to measure the ratio of missing ground-truth tags, both averaged over all test images.

4.2 Evaluation and Observation

Table 2 and Table 3 show performance comparisons on the two datasets, respectively.

We can observe that: 1) Generally, methods achieve better performance on Labelme, since tags in MIRFlickr-25K are more noisy. 2) Methods based on matrix completion, such as SMC, LRES and TCMR, usually achieve the best performances. 3) Our SMC framework shows increasing advantage to LRES as the data become more and more noisy, justifying our assumption and model on the noises. 4) SM-

Table 2: Performance Comparison on Labelme

	Labelme					
	N = 2		N = 5		N = 10	
	AP	**AR**	**AP**	**AR**	**AP**	**AR**
SMC	**0.51**	**0.36**	**0.46**	**0.50**	**0.35**	**0.62**
SMC_IMC	0.47	0.34	0.40	0.48	0.31	0.59
LRES [24]	0.42	0.32	0.35	0.45	0.27	0.56
TCMR [8]	0.44	0.32	0.37	0.45	0.29	0.55
RKML [9]	0.21	0.14	0.19	0.20	0.14	0.22
JEC [18]	0.33	0.29	0.27	0.38	0.20	0.48
TagProp [11]	0.39	0.31	0.33	0.45	0.25	0.56
TagRel [15]	0.43	0.32	0.34	0.45	0.27	0.55
CMRM [14]	0.20	0.14	0.18	0.19	0.12	0.22
MBRM [7]	0.23	0.14	0.18	0.20	0.12	0.27
FastTag [2]	0.43	0.34	0.37	0.44	0.28	0.57

Table 3: Performance Comparison on MIRFlickr-25K

	MIRFlickr-25K					
	N = 2		N = 5		N = 10	
	AP	**AR**	**AP**	**AR**	**AP**	**AR**
SMC	**0.53**	**0.39**	**0.40**	**0.47**	**0.33**	**0.61**
SMC_IMC	0.45	0.34	0.36	0.43	0.30	0.52
LRES [24]	0.43	0.35	0.32	0.40	0.26	0.45
TCMR [8]	0.45	0.35	0.35	0.41	0.28	0.48
RKML [9]	0.21	0.15	0.13	0.23	0.13	0.22
JEC [18]	0.33	0.30	0.25	0.34	0.19	0.35
TagProp [11]	0.39	0.35	0.28	0.37	0.20	0.41
TagRel [15]	0.42	0.34	0.30	0.37	0.20	0.40
CMRM [14]	0.20	0.15	0.13	0.18	0.11	0.20
MBRM [7]	0.22	0.16	0.13	0.18	0.10	0.22
FastTag [2]	0.43	0.35	0.30	0.41	0.27	0.42

C nearly outperforms all the other algorithms in all cases. 5) Performance comparison between SMC and SMC_IMC demonstrate the remarkable benefit of tag completion for tag refinement. 6) Performance on MIRFlickr-25K in some sense provides an evidence for the robustness of SMC.

5. CONCLUSION

In this work we present an effective framework for image annotation by performing tag completion and tag refinement sequentially. Our method first clusters images using sparse subspace clustering and shares tags using a neighbor voting algorithm, then refines tags by adapting inductive matrix completion while novelly utilizing visual and semantic information. Experiments show the effectiveness of our framework and suggest that tag refinement can benefit a lot from performing tag completion first.

Acknowledgments

Zhouchen Lin is supported by National Basic Research Program of China (973 Program) (grant no. 2015CB352502), National Natural Science Foundation (NSF) of China (grant nos. 61272341 and 61231002), and Microsoft Research Asia Collaborative Research Program.

6. REFERENCES

[1] G. Carneiro, A. Chan, P. Moreno, and N. Vasconcelos. Supervised learning of semantic classes for image annotation and retrieval. *TPAMI*, 2007.

[2] M. Chen, A. Zheng, and K. Weinberger. Fast image tagging. In *ICML*, 2013.

[3] F. Chung. *Spectral graph theory*. 1997.

[4] J. Donahue, Y. Jia, O. Vinyals, J. Hoffman, N. Zhang, E. Tzeng, and T. Darrell. Decaf: A deep convolutional activation feature for generic visual recognition. *arXiv preprint arXiv:1310.1531*, 2013.

[5] E. Elhamifar and R. Vidal. Sparse subspace clustering. In *CVPR*, 2009.

[6] E. Elhamifar and R. Vidal. Clustering disjoint subspaces via sparse representation. In *ICASSP*, 2010.

[7] S. Feng, R. Manmatha, and V. Lavrenko. Multiple Bernoulli relevance models for image and video annotation. In *CVPR*, 2004.

[8] Z. Feng, S. Feng, R. Jin, and A. Jain. Image tag completion by noisy matrix recovery. In *ECCV*. 2014.

[9] Z. Feng, R. Jin, and A. Jain. Large-scale image annotation by efficient and robust kernel metric learning. In *ICCV*, 2013.

[10] A. Goldberg, B. Recht, J. Xu, R. Nowak, and X. Zhu. Transduction with matrix completion: Three birds with one stone. In *NIPS*, 2010.

[11] M. Guillaumin, T. Mensink, J. Verbeek, and C. Schmid. Tagprop: Discriminative metric learning in nearest neighbor models for image auto-annotation. In *ICCV*, 2009.

[12] M. Huiskes and M. Lew. The MIR Flickr retrieval evaluation. In *ICMIR*, 2008.

[13] P. Jain and I. Dhillon. Provable inductive matrix completion. *arXiv preprint arXiv:1306.0626*, 2013.

[14] J. Jeon, V. Lavrenko, and R. Manmatha. Automatic image annotation and retrieval using cross-media relevance models. In *SIGIR*, 2003.

[15] X. Li, C. Snoek, and M. Worring. Learning social tag relevance by neighbor voting. *TM*, 2009.

[16] X. Li, T. Uricchio, L. Ballan, M. Bertini, C. G. Snoek, and A. Del Bimbo. Socializing the semantic gap: A comparative survey on image tag assignment, refinement and retrieval. *arXiv preprint arXiv:1503.08248*, 2015.

[17] Z. Lin, R. Liu, and Z. Su. Linearized alternating direction method with adaptive penalty for low-rank representation. In *NIPS*, 2011.

[18] A. Makadia, V. Pavlovic, and S. Kumar. A new baseline for image annotation. In *ECCV*. 2008.

[19] T. Mikolov, K. Chen, G. Corrado, and J. Dean. Efficient estimation of word representations in vector space. *arXiv preprint arXiv:1301.3781*, 2013.

[20] N. Natarajan and I. Dhillon. Inductive matrix completion for predicting gene–disease associations. *Bioinformatics*, 2014.

[21] B. Russell, A. Torralba, K. Murphy, and W. Freeman. Labelme: a database and web-based tool for image annotation. *IJCV*, 2008.

[22] L. Wu, R. Jin, and A. Jain. Tag completion for image retrieval. *TPAMI*, 2013.

[23] H. Yu, P. Jain, P. Kar, and I. Dhillon. Large-scale multi-label learning with missing labels. In *ICML*, 2014.

[24] G. Zhu, S. Yan, and Y. Ma. Image tag refinement towards low-rank, content-tag prior and error sparsity. In *ACM MM*, 2010.

Temporal Query Intent Disambiguation using Time-Series Data

Yue Zhao and Claudia Hauff
Web Information Systems, Delft University of Technology, The Netherlands
{y.zhao-1,c.hauff@tudelft.nl}

ABSTRACT

Understanding temporal intents behind users' queries is essential to meet users' time-related information needs. In order to classify queries according to their temporal intent (e.g. *Past* or *Future*), we explore the usage of time-series data derived from Wikipedia page views as a feature source. While existing works leverage either proprietary search engine query logs or highly processed and aggregated data (such as Google Trends) for this purpose, we investigate the utility of a freely available data source for this purpose. Our experiments on the NTCIR-12 Temporalia-2 dataset show, that Wikipedia pageview-based time-series data can significantly improve the disambiguation of temporal intents for specific types of queries, in particular those without temporal expressions present in the query string.

Categories and Subject Descriptors: H.3.3 Information Storage and Retrieval: Information Search and Retrieval
Keywords: temporal intents; disambiguation

1. INTRODUCTION

Understanding users' temporal query intents is an important step to meet their time-related information needs [8]. A query's temporal intent may be ambiguous though, as (in particular in Web search) queries often consist of 2-3 keywords only and users' information needs may be multifaceted.

This ambiguity can be analyzed on at least two levels, the *semantic* level and the *temporal* level. On the semantic level, the same query string may refer to different concepts with very different temporal intents. For example, a query "attack the movie" issued by a user in May 2013 may either refer to (i) a 1956 film named Attack (in this case the temporal intent would be *Past*), (ii) an — with respect to 2013 — upcoming and already announced 2015 film named Attack (*Future* intent) or, (iii) war movies in general (*Atemporal* intent). On the temporal level, ambiguity is often the result of queries referring to periodically occurring events. For example, the query "NBA playoff" issued on May 1, 2013 intuitively has two strong intents: *Recency* (the 2013 playoffs were running at the time and a user may be interested in this specific playoff instance) and *Atemporal* (a user may be interested in the concept of NBA playoffs in general).

Large-scale query logs offer a rich source of temporal signals that may be useful to determine temporal intent [12, 8, 11, 7]. They are however proprietary. Although search engines release highly-processed and aggregated temporal query signals to the public (e.g. Google Trends[1]) which are often employed in research [1], we believe that a *detailed* investigation into the impact of time-series features on temporal query intent disambiguation is only possible with an openly accessible and large-scale data log. To this end, in this paper we employ the Wikipedia page view logs (containing information on how often an article has been viewed during a time period) as a source of time-series based features. We propose a two-step temporal disambiguation approach which (1) extracts a set of concepts from a query string and expands this set with related concepts, and (2) derives time-series features of all concepts found in the previous step (based on the page views of that concept on Wikipedia) which are then fed into a machine learning framework. We explore the following research question:

RQ: Do features derived from an accessible time-series data source improve the disambiguation of users' temporal intents?

2. RELATED WORK

Jones and Diaz [6] introduced the use of time-series data for the analysis of query ambiguity, exploring three types of temporal ambiguity: atemporal, unambiguous and ambiguous. Their experiments centered around a news corpus (with all documents being timestamped according to their creation date) and they exploited the change in term frequencies over time to generate time-series data for queries. Similarly, Radinsky et al. [10] leveraged time-series data generated from the New York Times collection to measure the relatedness of text. While useful in some contexts, time-series data generated from document collections may not be suitable to disambiguate the temporal intents of the general Web search user.

Query logs are a more suitable resource to disambiguate Web users' queries and research in the temporality of query logs is ongoing: Kulkarni et al. [8] monitored one hundred queries over ten weeks to learn more about the dynamics of temporal queries, while Shokouhi [12] analyzed the monthly frequency of 259 queries (issued to the Bing search engine)

[1] `https://www.google.com/trends/`

SIGIR '16, July 17-21, 2016, Pisa, Italy
 ISBN 978-1-4503-4069-4/16/07 ...$15.00.
DOI: http://dx.doi.org/10.1145/2911451.2914767.

between 2006 to 2010. Although query logs would offer the most direct evidence of users' temporal intents, they are proprietary.

As a world-wide knowledge base which contains millions of concepts with well-defined explanations, Wikipedia[2] is a meaningful resource for understanding users' queries. Whiting et al. [13] use topics in Wikipedia disambiguation pages to represent ambiguous queries & various query intents and employed the time-series data from Wikipedia's page view statistics[3] to analyze their dynamics. We take inspirations from these works and employ this data source for the specific task of temporal intent disambiguation.

Lastly, it should be pointed out that most prior works that make use of time-series data to understand query intents [6, 8, 12, 13, 7] focus on the overview dynamics, while our work attempts to disambiguate the temporal intents of each query at their particular issue time.

3. APPROACH

3.1 Temporal Disambiguation

The approach we propose for temporal query intent disambiguation is depicted in Figure 1. We consider two levels: the semantic and the temporal level. On the semantic level, employing Wikipedia concepts (a concept is operationalized as a Wikipedia page) to represent the variate intents of queries is a common choice [10, 13]. On the temporal level, each Wikipedia concept is linked to the page view statistics of its corresponding Wikipedia page. Based on the time-series data of Wikipedia concepts, several temporal features can be extracted for the estimation of query temporal intents. Our model is similar to and inspired by the model proposed in [10], the main difference being that instead of relying on time-series data directly to compare entities, we extract features from the time-series data and incorporate the features into our machine learning framework. Based on features extracted from semantic level and temporal level of queries, machine learning models are trained and leveraged to predict the probabilities of temporal queries intents where queries may belong to.

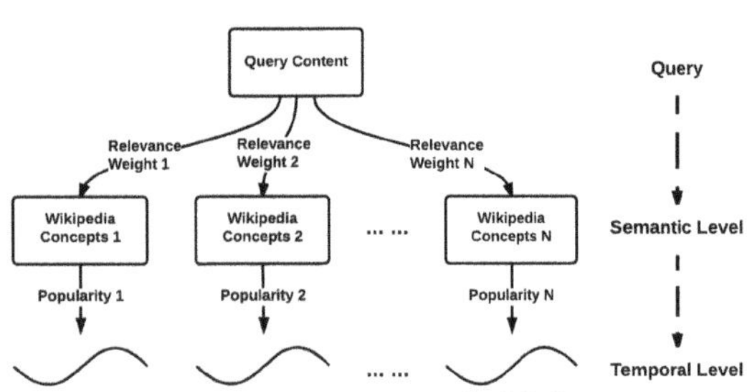

Figure 1: Conceptual overview of our approach.

3.2 Feature Extraction

We extract two types of features from the queries: (i) content features, and, (ii) time-series based features. We discuss them in turn.

[2]`https://www.wikipedia.org/`
[3]`http://dumps.wikimedia.org/other/pagecounts-raw/`

Our 209 **query-content features** (i.e. features that are not relying on any external data sources) are based on those proposed in [14]. We extract lemmas and named entities via the `Stanford CoreNLP` toolkit[4]. Since verb tenses can be good indicators of temporality, as [14] we represent the detected verbs in queries by their uppermost verb tense (*UVB_tense*) and verb tense with lemma (*tense_lemma*). For example, the query "when was television invented" has three verb features *UVB_VBD*, *VBD_be* and *VBD_invent*. Temporal expressions (TEs) are extracted with the `SUTime` module of `Stanford CoreNLP` and the relation of the detected TEs and the query issue time (assumed to be known) are encoded in five features:

- $\{ref_{past}, ref_{future}\}$: number of TEs referring to past/future times with respect to the query issue time;
- $\{same_Y, same_{YM}, same_{YMD}\}$: number of TEs referring to the same year, the same year & month, and the same year & month & day as the query issue time.

`SUTime` produces high quality temporal annotations, but is not able to detect all TEs, especially if the surrounding textual evidence is weak or misleading (e.g. in the query "When to File 2014 Taxes"[5] `SUTime` does not tag "2014" as TE; "2014" is though detected as numerical lemma by `Stanford CoreNLP`). The final three query-content features thus encode the relation between numerical lemmas[6] and query issue time:

- $\{lemY_{past}, lemY_{future}, lemY_{same}\}$: number of numerical lemmas referring to past/same/future years with respect to the query issue time.

As a concrete example, the query "NBA playoffs 2012 2013" issued May 1, 2012 will result in the following non-zero features: $\{ref_{future} = 1, same_Y = 1, lem_{future} = 1, lem_{same} = 1\}$.

The **time-series based features** and the evaluation of their impact on temporal query intent disambiguation are our main contribution in this work. We employ the `TAGME` toolkit [2] to detect Wikipedia concepts in our queries, as it has been shown to perform well for short texts. We derive 13 features per query, based on the Wikipedia concept most related to the query content[7] (i.e. having the highest relatedness score as computed by `TAGME`):

- *seasonality* [12]: represented by the cosine similarity between the time-series data and its seasonal component which is derived based on Holt-Winters additive method [3];
- *autocorrelation*: measures the periodicity of the time-series data by comparing the past 12 months of data to the same time period a year earlier;
- $\{ref_{view\_D}, ref_{view\_MD}\}$: difference between the query issue month (month/day combination) and the month (month/day combination) the concept had the most pageviews in our Wikipedia pageview traces;
- finally, the mean, standard deviation and median of the concept's time-series data are also computed.

Overall, for each query we generate 222 features based on query content and time-series data.

[4]`http://stanfordnlp.github.io/CoreNLP/`
[5]Query #199 in the Temporalia-2 dataset.
[6]To avoid noise, we only consider numerical lemmas within ±20 years of query issue time.
[7]We employ the most related concept only, as the combination of a variable number of time-series features is a non-trivial task considered in future work.

4. EXPERIMENTS

4.1 Experimental Setting

We utilize the benchmark dataset published at the NTCIR-12 Temporalia-2 task [5] for the temporal intent disambiguation (*TID*) subtask. It consists of *dry-run* (93 queries in total, 73 of those had their ground truth released for training purposes) and *formal-run* data (300 queries as test data). Each query has an assigned issue time. The ground truth for each query are the probabilities of the query falling into the four temporal intent classes: (*Past*, *Recency*, *Future*, *Atemporal*). For example, the query "'memorial day" (issue time May 1, 2013) has the following ground truth assignment: $(0.1, 0.0, 0.7, 0.2)$[8], i.e. the highest intent probability is assigned to the *Future* category.

In addition, for the exploratory analysis of temporal query intents, we also rely on the *formal-run* data (300 queries) released in the previous' year's (NTCIR-11) edition of the benchmark [4]. The task that year was slightly easier: queries had to be classified into a single temporal category, instead of deriving a probability distribution. The task was called temporal query intent classification (*TQIC*), a label we employ here as well to distinguish it from the *TID* task/data.

4.2 Data Exploration

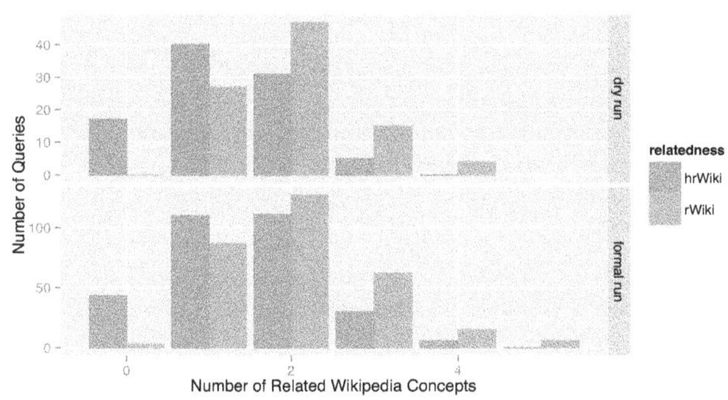

Figure 2: Overview of highly related Wikipedia concepts in the TID query set.

Concept detection: We first explored to what extent TAGME was able to detect concepts in our set of queries. All detected Wikipedia concepts are considered *related concepts* (*rWiKi*) while the concepts with relatedness scores ≥ 0.1 (suggested in [2]) are considered as *highly related concepts* (*hrWiki*). The number of *rWiKi* and *hrWiki* of queries in the dry-run dataset and the formal-run dataset of TID are shown in Figure 2. Almost every query contains at least *rWiki* concept and more than 60% of the queries contain at least two such concepts. Highly-related concepts appear considerably fewer, about 16% of queries do not contain any *hrWiki*.

Prevalence of Temporal Expressions (TEs): To verify the intuition that queries with higher temporal ambiguity have fewer TEs, we explore the prevalence of TEs in our query sets. The results are shown in Table 1. In the older TQIC query set, more than 40% of queries contained at least one TE (which in many cases makes it easier to classify temporal intent). In the newly released TID dataset however, less than 20% of the queries contain TEs, indicating the increased need for temporal features from other sources. It is also reported that the queries with explicit temporal expressions only represent about 1.5% of all queries [9]. Therefore, it is worth to generate temporal features from other sources.

[8]These intent distributions were derived by the benchmark organizers through crowdsourcing

	#Queries overall	#Queries with TEs	#Queries without TEs
TQIC formal-run	300	127	173
TID dry-run	93	15	78
TID formal-run	300	57	243

Table 1: Number of Queries with TEs

Page view sparsity: We explore Wikipedia page view data as one such source. If, however, the page views of our detected Wikipedia concepts were too low, no sensible time-series data features could be generated. We define those concepts whose average (maximum) daily page views are fewer than 22 (186) as queries without sufficient page views. The cutoff values were derived from the 5th percentiles of the average (maximum) daily page views across all detected concepts in our TID and TQIC datasets. In total, we find 7 queries in our datasets whose most related Wikipedia concepts (i.e. the concept to compute the time-series features from) has page views below these thresholds.

4.3 Temporal Query Intent Disambiguation

The TID taks is evaluated through: (i) the average cosine similarity between the ground truth temporal intent distribution and the predicted distribution, (ii) and the mean absolute error (MAE) which can be computed not only across all categories, but also separately for each temporal class.

Baseline: Our baseline [14] is the best performing approach for the *TQIC* task[9], relying on query content features alone (no time-series data). As the TQIC task differs from TID (instead of predicting class labels, we now predict probabilities), we employed Ridge regression instead of Logistic regression. The parameter settings are selected by 10-fold cross-validation on the TID training data.

In order to test the effectiveness of time-series features (our main research question in this work), we extract them as described in Section 3.2. In contrast to the baseline, our model (*BrTS*) contains the additional time-series features we hypothesize will improve the temporal intent disambiguation.

We incorporate the time-series data in two ways: (i) we train a single model across all TID training queries, and (ii) we train two separate models, by splitting the TID training queries into two sets, according to whether or not they contain TEs. The results of the TID formal-run data are shown in Tables 2 and 3. The results indicate that time-series features improve the temporal disambiguation results of those queries that do not contain TEs, in particular for the categories *Future* and *Atemporal*. In contrast, the time-series features hurt the predictions for queries that do already contain TEs, especially for the *Recency* category. Comparing the single vs. two-model setup indicates that the training of two separate models aids the accuracy of the prediction. Fi-

[9]Official results for the TID task are not yet available.

nally, we also computed an aggregate run (*Aggr* in Table 3), which employs the baseline approach for queries with TEs and the *BrTS* approach for those without (as this combination performs best on the training data). This combination yields a significant improvement over the baseline across all queries, not just those missing temporal expressions.

To open avenues for future work, we conducted a qualitative failure analysis on the queries where the baseline performed much worse than our *BrTS* approach. We found that the *BrTS* performs worse when (i) the detected Wikipedia concepts cannot capture the whole meaning of the query well, or (ii) the *Future* category has the highest intent probability and the page view log of the respective Wikipedia concepts contains multiple large irregular spikes (which lead to a larger probability of the *Past* category).

To summarize, these results suggest that 1) Time-series data can improve the disambiguation of queries with no TEs significantly, and 2) the disambiguation of users' temporal intent behind queries should be processed separately based on whether they have TEs, which is consistent with the classification of temporal queries in [7].

Method	CosSim	MAE	Per-Class MAE *Past*	*Rec.*	*Fut.*	*Atemp.*
+++ All queries +++						
Baseline	0.790	0.213	0.194	0.156	0.202	0.299
BrTS	0.791	0.211‡	0.198	0.158	0.188‡	0.299
+++ Queries with TEs +++						
Baseline	0.764	0.225	0.233	0.173	0.250	0.242
BrTS	0.761	0.224	0.224	0.174	0.251	0.246
+++ Queries without TEs +++						
Baseline	0.797	0.210	0.185	0.152	0.191	0.312
BrTS	0.799	0.208‡	0.192	0.154	0.174‡	0.312

Table 2: Overview of TID results (formal-run data). A single model was trained. ‡ indicates a significant improvement ($p < 0.05$).

Method	CosSim	MAE	Per-Class MAE *Past*	*Rec.*	*Fut.*	*Atemp.*
+++ All queries +++						
Baseline	0.790	0.212	0.193	0.161	0.207	0.287
Aggr	0.792	0.210‡	0.198	0.162	0.192‡	0.287
+++ Queries with TEs +++						
Baseline	0.717	0.243	0.251	0.243	0.257	0.223
BrTS	0.697	0.247	0.247	0.264	0.258	0.221
+++ Queries with no TEs +++						
Baseline	0.807	0.205	0.179	0.142	0.196	0.302
BrTS	0.809	0.202‡	0.186	0.143	0.177‡	0.302

Table 3: Overview of TID results (formal-run data). Two models were trained: one based on the training queries containing TEs, and one based on the training queries not containing TEs. ‡ indicates a significant improvement ($p < 0.05$).

5. CONCLUSIONS

In this work, we have presented our investigation into the use of time-series data, extracted from an openly accessible data source as an approximation and a proxy for large-scale query log data to predict the temporal intents of search queries.

We have provided an analysis of the NTCIR TID dataset within the context of our goal (deriving time-series data from Wikipedia page views) and found the data sparsity not to be a significant issue. Our experiments show that time-series features derived from Wikipedia page views can aid the temporal intent prediction, if sufficient care is taken to separate the easy queries (containing TAs) from the difficult ones during training.

Future work will explore additional mechanisms to incorporate the time-series features of a wider range of Wikipedia concepts (instead of the query's dominating one) and the eventual application of temporal intent prediction to the diversification and clustering of search results.

6. REFERENCES

[1] H. A. Carneiro and E. Mylonakis. Google trends: a web-based tool for real-time surveillance of disease outbreaks. *Clinical infectious diseases*, 49(10):1557–1564, 2009.

[2] P. Ferragina and U. Scaiella. Tagme: on-the-fly annotation of short text fragments. In *CIKM '10*, pages 1625–1628, 2010.

[3] C. C. Holt. Forecasting seasonals and trends by exponentially weighted moving averages. *International journal of forecasting*, 20(1):5–10, 2004.

[4] H. Joho, A. Jatowt, R. Blanco, H. Naka, and S. Yamamoto. Overview of NTCIR-11 temporal information access (temporalia) task. In *Proceedings of the 11th NTCIR Conference on Evaluation of Information Access Technologies*, 2014.

[5] H. Joho, A. Jatowt, R. Blanco, H. Yu, and S. Yamamoto. Overview of NTCIR-12 temporal information access (temporalia-2) task. In *Proceedings of the 12th NTCIR Conference on Evaluation of Information Access Technologies*, 2016.

[6] R. Jones and F. Diaz. Temporal profiles of queries. *ACM Transactions on Information Systems*, 25(3):14, 2007.

[7] N. Kanhabua, T. Ngoc Nguyen, and W. Nejdl. Learning to detect event-related queries for web search. In *WWW '15*, pages 1339–1344, 2015.

[8] A. Kulkarni, J. Teevan, K. M. Svore, and S. T. Dumais. Understanding temporal query dynamics. In *WSDM '11*, pages 167–176, 2011.

[9] S. Nunes, C. Ribeiro, and G. David. Use of temporal expressions in web search. In *Advances in Information Retrieval*, pages 580–584. Springer, 2008.

[10] K. Radinsky, E. Agichtein, E. Gabrilovich, and S. Markovitch. A word at a time: computing word relatedness using temporal semantic analysis. In *WWW '11*, pages 337–346, 2011.

[11] K. Radinsky, K. Svore, S. Dumais, J. Teevan, A. Bocharov, and E. Horvitz. Modeling and predicting behavioral dynamics on the web. In *WWW '12*, pages 599–608, 2012.

[12] M. Shokouhi. Detecting seasonal queries by time-series analysis. In *SIGIR '11*, pages 1171–1172, 2011.

[13] S. Whiting, J. M. Jose, and O. Alonso. Temporal dynamics of ambiguous queries. In *TAIA2015 Workshop*, volume 92, 2015.

[14] H. Yu, X. Kang, and F. Ren. Tuta1 at the ntcir-11 temporalia task. In *Proceedings of the 11th NTCIR Conference on Evaluation of Information Access Technologies*, 2014.

To Blend or Not to Blend? Perceptual Speed, Visual Memory and Aggregated Search

Lauren Turpin, Diane Kelly and Jaime Arguello
School of Information and Library Science
University of North Carolina at Chapel Hill
Chapel Hill, North Carolina, USA
lwturpin@gmail.com, dianek@email.unc.edu, jarguell@email.unc.edu

ABSTRACT
While aggregated search interfaces that present vertical results to searchers are fairly common in today's search environments, little is known about how searchers' cognitive abilities impact how they use and evaluate these interfaces. This study evaluates the relationship between two cognitive abilities – perceptual speed and visual memory – and searchers' behaviors and interface preferences when using two aggregated search interfaces: one that blends vertical results into the search results (blended) and one that does not (non-blended). Cognitive tests were administered to sixteen participants who subsequently performed four search tasks using the two interfaces. Participants' search interactions were logged and after searching, they rated the usability, engagement and effectiveness of each interface, as well as made comparative evaluations. Results showed that participants with low perceptual speed spent significantly more time completing tasks when using the blended interface, while those with high perceptual speed spent roughly equivalent amounts of time completing tasks with the two interfaces. Those with low perceptual speed also rated both interfaces as significantly less usable along many measures, and were less satisfied with their searches. There were also main effects for interface: participants rated the non-blended interface significantly more usable than the blended interface.

Keywords
Aggregated search interfaces, search behavior, cognitive ability

1. INTRODUCTION
The goal of *aggregated search* is to combine results from multiple search engines in a single presentation. Most commercial search portals such as Bing and Google provide access to a wide range of specialized search engines called *verticals*. Different verticals focus on different types of media (images, news) or help users perform different types of tasks (shopping, local). Vertical results can always be accessed using tabs at the top of the search results page (SERP). However, in certain cases, depending on the query, the search portal may also decide to showcase a particular vertical by blending a few of its top results somewhere above, within, or below the first page of web results. The idea is to inform users that the underlying vertical might have relevant content. For example, in response to the query "tiger", Bing mixes results from the news, video, and image verticals along with web results. A different mix of results might be generated for a different query.

SIGIR '16, July 17-21, 2016, Pisa, Italy

ACM 978-1-4503-4069-4/16/07...$15.00
DOI: http://dx.doi.org/10.1145/2911451.2914809

Recently, there have been a growing number of studies on aggregated search interfaces [3, 4, 6, 12, 14]. Some of this work suggests individual differences might play a role in users' evaluations of aggregated search interfaces. Both Arguello et al. [4] and Bron et al. [6] compared blended and non-blended interfaces for aggregated search and found no clear preference. In Arguello et al.'s study, participants who preferred the non-blended display stated the blended display was confusing and harder to navigate, and the vertical results distracting. Participants who preferred the blended display described it as helpful, visually pleasing and easier to use. The authors concluded, "people who are more visual thinkers might prefer the blended display and people who are novice users and/or have attention difficulties might prefer the non-blended display" (p. 443). Bron, et al. studied graduate students conducting multi-session searches and found most searchers moved between the blended and non-blended displays, suggesting the usefulness of the display might depend on the task or stage. However, there was no clear switching pattern: some started with blended then switched to non-blended, while others did the opposite. The authors noted these variations were likely a result of individual differences.

One way that individuals differ is according to cognitive abilities. A person's cognitive abilities are their capacities to perform various mental activities such as problem solving, reasoning, remembering, and decision-making [8]. Examples of cognitive abilities include perceptual speed, associative memory, and visualization ability. Variations in some cognitive abilities might make it more challenging for certain people to interact with vertical search interfaces. For example, someone who has low visual memory might have a more difficult time navigating around, or filtering out, visual verticals such as images and videos. Hiding these vertical results from view until the searcher is ready to use them might lead to a better search experience.

In this work, we focus on two cognitive abilities, *perceptual speed* and *visual memory*. The basic research question we address is: *How do users' perceptual speed and visual memory abilities impact their search behaviors and interface preferences in the context of aggregated search?* Perceptual speed is a person's "speed in comparing figures or symbols, scanning to find figures or symbols, or carrying out other very simple tasks involving visual perception" [9, p. 123]. Several recent studies have shown that people with lower perceptual speed experience greater workload during search and interact at slower rates than those with higher perceptual speed [1, 5]. Another study has shown that those with lower perceptual speed achieved lower precision and recall [2]. Thus, we choose this ability in part because existing evidence shows it plays a role in search interaction. In the context of aggregated search, perceptual speed may come into play as a person scans the search results to identify relevant bits of information. The inclusion of verticals might make this process more difficult for those with low perceptual speed since there are different types of information to parse.

Visual memory is "the ability to remember configuration, location and orientation of figural material" [9, p. 109]. Visualization ability, which is different from visual memory, has been studied frequently in search, although most studies have found little to no effects on visualization ability and search behavior and success. The one exception [5] found those with lower visualization ability issued fewer queries, made fewer SERP clicks and visited fewer URLs. Conversely, visual memory has not been investigated much in the context of search applications. In a study of email applications, it was found that people with low visual memory were slower carrying out certain tasks [10]. The authors observed that an interface that allows people with low visual memory to focus on the specific aspect of the interface that is most helpful to a particular task might be beneficial; this observation seems to have implications for aggregated search interfaces. When various verticals are blended into the SERP a person with low visual memory might have a more difficult time remembering the content of visual verticals and their locations on the SERP.

2. METHOD

A laboratory experiment was conducted using two aggregated search interfaces: one that blended vertical results into the Web results and one that only provided indirect access to the verticals through tabs. Figure 1 presents a screenshot of the blended interface. In both interfaces, vertical results could be accessed via tabs at the top and side of the interface. The blended interface also presented vertical results on the initial SERP, which were blocked in set positions for each vertical, if any were returned. They were blended in the same order: web results (1-3), images, video, web results (4-6), news, web results (7-10), and shopping The Bing API was used to generate Web results as well as results for the news, images and video verticals. The eBay API was used to generate results for the shopping vertical.

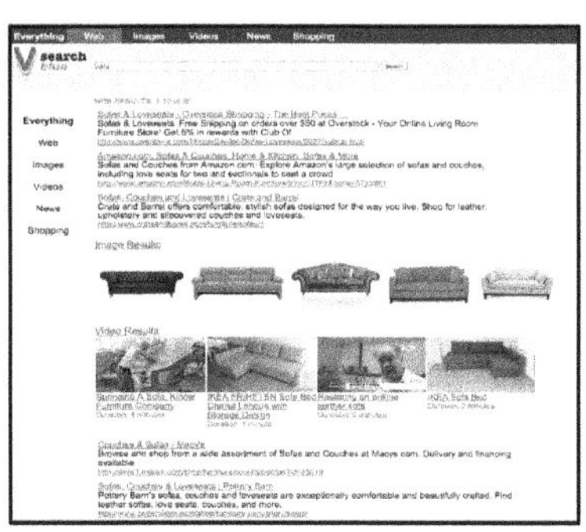

Figure 1. Screen shot of the blended search interface.

2.1 Participants

Participants were recruited through a mass email to the staff list at University of North Carolina. Sixteen participants were enrolled who had an average age of 36 (SD=11.81). Three participants were male and 13 female. Eleven participants had bachelor's degrees, three had master's degrees and two had doctorates. All participants had more than 10 years of computer experience. Participants were compensated with $15.00.

2.2 Cognitive Tests

Each participant completed two cognitive abilities tests from the Ekstrom Kit of Factor-Referenced Cognitive Test to assess perceptual speed and visual memory [9]. The *Finding A's* test was used to measure perceptual speed (PS) and the *Shape Memory* test was used to measure visual memory (VM). These are standardized tests that have been used in a large number of studies. Table 1 presents the descriptive statistics of the cognitive tests, which show our results were within one standard deviation of the reference score [9]. The median was used to divide participants equally into high/low PS and VM groups.

Table 1. Scores on cognitive abilities tests.

	Perceptual Speed	Visual Memory
Possible Range	0-200	-32 - +32
Mean (SD)	51.94 (10.41)	18 (8.69)
Median	51	20.5
Min, Max	34, 74	-2, 30
EKM Mean (SD) (Reference Scores)	Males: 47 (14.9) Females: 54 (14.9)	21.4 (4.3)

2.3 Search Tasks

Each participant completed four search tasks: two with each display. The order of the tasks and interfaces were counterbalanced, although participants always used one interface to complete two tasks before they moved to the next interface. The search tasks come from Kelly et al.'s [11] work; specifically, we used the four "Create" tasks. Create tasks require people to generate different things: a plan for constructing a soapbox derby car, an exercise program, a mascot for a sports team and a design for a living room. Kelly et al.'s [11] participants took about ten minutes completing these types of tasks, which is one reason we decided to use them. We also thought participants might need to use vertical results to address the tasks, or at least would issue queries that were likely to return vertical results. To limit the session to one hour, we gave participants a ten-minute task time limit; on average they spent about 6 minutes per task.

2.4 Interface Evaluation

Participants evaluated the interfaces and their search experiences using three types of questionnaires: post-task, post-system and exit questionnaires. The post-task questionnaire asked participants to rate how difficult it was to find relevant documents, their ability to find relevant documents, the system's ability at retrieving relevant documents, how many relevant documents they thought they found and search success. The post-system questionnaire contained the 10-item System Usability Scale (SUS) [7] and four subscales of the User Engagement Scale (UES) [13]: (1) focused attention, (2) felt involvement, (3) perceived usability and (4) endurability. All items were evaluated with 5-point scales, where higher values indicated more of the construct being measured or greater agreement. For both the SUS and UES, we followed the analyses guidelines put forward by the authors [6, 13]. Participants' responses to the 10-item SUS were averaged to arrive at an overall SUS score. Participants' responses to each of the four UES subscales were averaged to obtain overall scores for each subscale. These averages were then averaged to arrive at an overall engagement score.

The post-system questionnaire also contained five items about search effectiveness and four about ease of use, including items about the usefulness of the information returned and the presentation method. These items were evaluated with 5-point agreement scales. Reliability analysis was performed to determine if we could average items. The Cronbach's alpha for the search effectiveness items was 0.861 and 0.681 for the ease of use items. These values support combining responses for analyses.

3. RESULTS

Unless otherwise reported, mixed ANOVAs were used to analyze the data, with cognitive ability (high, low) as a between-subjects factor and interface (non-blended, blended) as a within-subjects factor. There were no significant main effects for visual memory for any of the user experience or search behavior measures, and there were no significant interaction effects between interface and either of cognitive abilities except for time. Because of space, we only present results related to perceptual speed and interface, and the interaction for time.

Figures 2, 3 and 4 display the post-task and post-system measures according to perceptual speed and interface. There were significant main effects for perceptual speed on four of the five post-task measures (Figure 2). High-PS participants rated their search skills higher ($F(1, 16)=4.42$, $p=0.04$) and system performance higher ($F(1, 16)=8.75$, $p=0.005$). They also rated their searches as more successful ($F(1, 16)=4.41$, $p=0.04$) and believed they had found more of the relevant documents ($F(1, 16)=9.58$, $p=0.003$). There were several significant main effects for perceptual speed on participants' post-system evaluations (Figures 3 and 4). High-PS participants rated the ease of use (Figure 2) and perceived usability (Figure 3) of *both* systems higher than low-PS participants [($F(1, 16)=5.20$, $p=0.04$) and ($F(1, 16)=5.60$, $p=0.03$), respectively. There were also several significant main effects for interface. The non-blended interface received significantly greater SUS scores ($F(1, 16)=5.48$, $p=0.03$) and ease of use scores ($F(1, 16)=6.09$, $p=0.03$) than the blended interface (Figure 2).

Figure 5 displays the mean number of queries and clicks made by participants according to perceptual speed and interface, and the amount of time taken to complete tasks. There were no significant main effects for perceptual speed or interface on any measure, but there was a significant interaction effect between perceptual speed and interface for time: Low-PS participants spent longer completing tasks with the blended interface, while High-PS participants spent similar amounts of time completing tasks regardless of interface ($F(1, 16)=6.33$, $p=0.015$).

Participants' clicks were further analyzed to determine if they selected any vertical results or navigated to another SERP display. Table 2 shows these frequencies according to perceptual speed. Overall, participants with high perceptual speed clicked on more vertical results (n=16) than those with low perceptual speed (n=6). An analysis of the mean number of clicks was not significant. Participants also clicked on more verticals when they were using the blended interface, which is not surprising since the vertical results were integrated into the default SERP. An analysis of the means showed a significant difference [nonblended: 0.06 (SD=0.35); blended: 0.63 (SD=0.91); $F(1, 16)=11.15$, $p=0.001$]. The last three columns of the table show how many clicks originated from different types of SERPs, some of which were only accessible via tabs. *Everything SERP* was only available in the blended display; this was also the default SERP for this interface, while in the non-blended interface *Web SERP* was the default. Table 2 shows that High-PS and Low-PS participants made similar numbers of clicks from the *Everything SERP*, but High-PS participants navigated more often to the vertical SERPs (images, videos, news or shopping) (7 vs. 0 clicks). Participants made more clicks on the *Web SERP* when using the non-blended display, which is not surprising since this was the default SERP. Of potential interest is that while there were 10 cases where High-PS participants made the effort to select the *Web SERP* over the default *Everything SERP* when using the blended interface, there were no instances of Low-PS participants doing this.

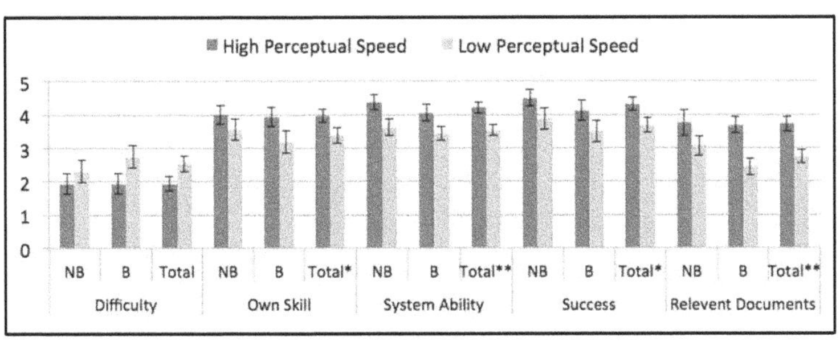

Figure 2. Post-task evaluations according to perceptual speed and interface (NB=Non-blended; B=Blended; *$p<0.05$; **$p<0.01$).

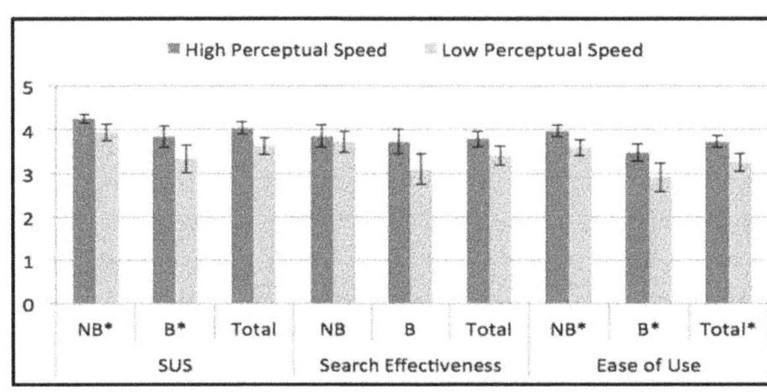

Figure 3. Post-system evaluations according to perceptual speed and interface (NB=Non-blended; B=Blended; *$p<0.05$).

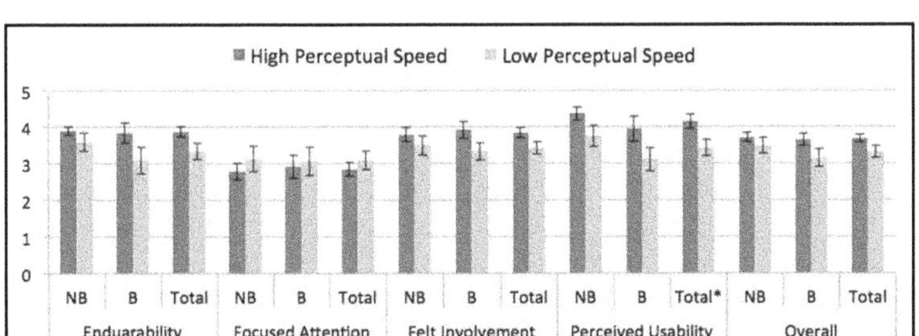

Figure 4. User Engagement post-system evaluations according to perceptual speed and interface (NB=Non-blended; B=Blended; *$p<0.05$).

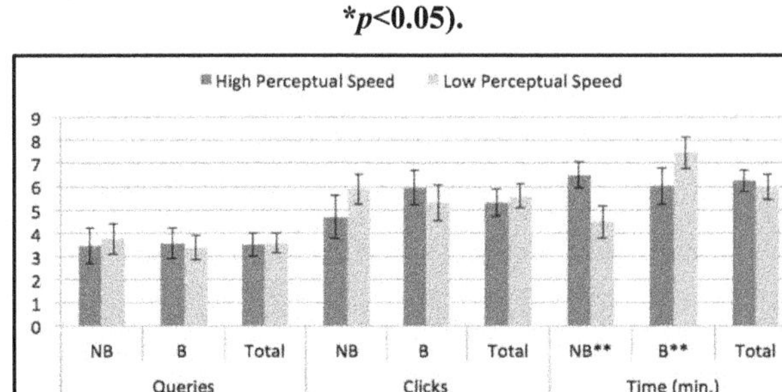

Figure 5. Search behaviors according to perceptual speed and interface (NB=Non-blended; B=Blended; **$p<0.01$).

Table 2. Number of clicks on vertical results and SERPs according to perceptual speed and interface.

		Vertical Results	Everything SERP	Web SERP	Vertical SERP
HPS	NB	2	-	73	2
	B	14	80	10	5
	Total	16	80	83	7
LPS	NB	0	-	94	0
	B	6	85	0	0
	Total	6	85	94	0
Total	NB	2	-	167	2
	B	20	165	10	5

4. DISCUSSION AND CONCLUSION

In this paper, we investigated the impact of two cognitive abilities, perceptual speed and visual memory, on searchers' behaviors and interface evaluations when using two aggregated search interfaces: one that blended vertical results into the search results and one that did not. Overall, we found no effects for visual memory ability, but a number of effects for perceptual speed, which is consistent with other studies (although none of these past studies have focused on aggregated search).

Perceptual speed (PS) had a significant effect on many of our user experience measures. High-PS participants rated the perceived usability and ease of use of both systems higher than Low-PS participants. These participants also rated their search skills higher, system performance higher, their searches as more successful and believed they had found a greater number of relevant documents. Overall, these results indicate that High-PS participants had more positive search experiences than Low-PS participants regardless of interface.

We also found a main effect for interface on usability and easy use. The non-blended interface received significantly higher usability and ease of use scores than the blended interface. An examination of participants' clicks showed that they did not select many vertical results. Thus, the difference in usability and easy or use measures might be because the verticals were not useful and therefore an unwelcome (and unusable) distraction on the blended interface. In this study, we controlled the type and placement of verticals and this finding might not apply to vertical displays that are generated dynamically in response to queries. Although participants could change the display of verticals by selecting *Web SERP*, there were few instances where this occurred and no instances of Low-PS participants clicking on *Web SERP*. Initially, we thought that Low-PS participants might be more inclined to do this so as to reduce the complexity of the perceptual space, but it might be that these participants did not notice or realize this was possible; indeed, Low-PS participants never changed the default SERP. Low-PS participants also spent significantly longer completing tasks with the blended interface, which might have contributed to its lower usability scores.

Overall, our results call into question the idea of one-size-fits-all search interfaces, especially when they involve aggregating different types of search results. Our results, combined with those of other researchers', highlight the importance of perceptual speed in search. Current search modalities place great demands on the perceptual system and future research might focus on developing interfaces that improve the search experience for people with Low-PS. Projecting even further into the future, researchers might also begin to consider the role of other cognitive abilities, such as those that emphasize auditory and memory skills, on voice-based search interactions.

5. ACKNOWLEDGEMENTS

This work was supported in part by NSF grant IIS-1451668. Any opinions, findings, conclusions, and recommendations expressed in this paper are the authors and do not necessarily reflect those of the sponsor.

6. REFERENCES

[1] Al-Maskari, A. & Sanderson, M. (2011). The effect of user characteristics on search effectiveness in information retrieval. *IP&M, 47*, 719-729.

[2] Allen, B. (1994). Perceptual speed, learning and information retrieval performance. *Proc. of SIGIR*, 71-80.

[3] Arguello, J. & Capra, R. (2012) The effect of aggregated search coherence on search behavior. *Proc. of SIGIR*, 1293-1302.

[4] Arguello, J., Wu, W.-C., Kelly, D., & Edwards, A. (2012). Task complexity, vertical display and user interaction in aggregated search. *Proc. of SIGIR*, 435-444.

[5] Brennan, K., Kelly, D. & Arguello, J. (2014). The effect of cognitive abilities on information search for tasks of varying levels of complexity. *Proc. of IIiX*, 165-174.

[6] Bron, M., van Gorp, J., Nack, F., Baltussen, L.B. & de Rijke, M. (2013). Aggregated search interface preferences in multi-session search tasks. *Proc. of SIGIR*, 123-132.

[7] Brooke, J. (1996). SUS: A "quick and dirty" usability scale. *Usability Evaluation in Industry*. Taylor & Francis.

[8] Carroll, J. B. (1993). *Human Cognitive Abilities: A Survey of Factor-analytic studies*. Cambridge University Press.

[9] Ekstrom, R.B., French, J.W., Harman, H.H. and Dermen, D. (1976). *Kit of Factor-Referenced Cognitive Tests*. Educational Testing Service, Princeton, NJ.

[10] Gwizdka, J. & Chignell, M. (2004). Individual differences and task-based user interface evaluation: A case study of pending tasks in email. *Interacting with Computers,* 769-797.

[11] Kelly, D., Arguello, J., Edwards, A. & Wu, W.-C. (2015). Development and evaluation of search tasks for IIR experiments using a cognitive complexity framework. *Proc. of ICTIR*, 101-110.

[12] Liu, Z., Liu, Y., Zhou, K., Zhang, M. & Ma, S. (2015). Influence of vertical result in Web search examination. *Proc. of SIGIR*, 193-202.

[13] O'Brien, H.L. & Toms, E.G. (2010). The development and evaluation of a survey to measure user engagement. *JASIST, 61*(1), 50-69.

[14] Sushmita, S., Joho, H., & Lalmas, M. (2009). A task-based evaluation of an aggregated search interface. *Proc. of SPIRE*, 322–333.

Topic Model based Privacy Protection in Personalized Web Search

Wasi Uddin Ahmad, Md Masudur Rahman, Hongning Wang
Department of Computer Science, University of Virginia, VA USA
{wua4nw, mr5ba, hw5x}@virginia.edu

ABSTRACT

Modern search engines utilize users' search history for personalization, which provides more effective, useful and relevant search results. However, it also has the potential risk of revealing users' privacy by identifying their underlying intention from their logged search behaviors. To address this privacy issue, we proposed a *Topic-based Privacy Protection* solution on client side. In our solution, each user query will be submitted with k additional cover queries, which will act as a proxy to disguise users' intent from a search engine. The set of cover queries are generated in a controlled way so that each query carries similar uncertainty to randomize a user's search history while still providing necessary utility for the search engine to perform personalization. We used statistical topic models to infer topics from the original user query and generated cover queries of similar entropy but from unrelated topics. Extensive experiments are performed on AOL search log and the promising results demonstrated the effectiveness of our solution.

Categories and Subject Descriptors

H.4 [**Information Systems Applications**]: Miscellaneous

Keywords

Privacy, Information Retrieval, Personalized Search

1. INTRODUCTION

Modern search engines, such as Google, Bing, Yahoo, exploit logged users' search behaviors to get insights of their search intents for personalization purpose. Although exploitation of search logs is helpful for improving search effectiveness, but the possibility of building individual user profile raises the concern of privacy breach. Anonymization of the search log data does not solve the problem. In 2006, AOL released an anonymized search query log of around 600,000 randomly selected users. The logs had been anonymized (at the server side) by removing individually identifying information such as IP address, username and any other personal information associated with that user. However, the actual queries and their corresponding query time, clicked URL and the anonymous ID were used to identify the gender, age and location of users [6]. Merely hiding a user's identity is not enough, but we need to hide a user's true search intent to ensure privacy. Obfuscate a user's true search intent to a search engine is very difficult: we need to first identify the search intent, properly embellish it before submitting to the search engine, such that the returned search results are still useful. As our preliminary attempt in this direction, we propose a *Topic-based Privacy Protection* (TPP) approach to enhance privacy in personalized web search. We have to admit that there are many different personalization techniques employed in commercial search engines; in this work, we assume personalization is achieved by server-side constructed user profiles [11].

Our proposed solution is client centered, and no facility is required on the search engine side. When a user submits a query to the search engine, we send k additional queries which act as a surrogate to randomize a user's profile. We refer to those additional queries as cover queries, since they cover or hide a user's true intent from the search engine. By adding noise through cover queries, we force search engine to have lower perception about the users. By varying the configuration of the generated cover queries, e.g., entropy, query length, topic proportion etc., we can affect the precision of the search engine constructed user profile as well as the level of personalization it can provide. The more cover queries are submitted with the original query, the less likely the user profile constructed on the search engine side will disclose a user's privacy (but it will be also less useful for personalization).

We use probabilistic topic models to infer users' search intent from their issued queries. In particular, we employed Latent Dirichlet Allocation (LDA) model [2] to infer topic proportion of the original query, and treat the inferred topics as a proxy of users' search intent. Then we create a set of cover queries by sampling queries from different topics. To ensure the plausibility of the automatically generated cover queries, we used entropy to measure the specificity of the cover queries and also varied their length with Poisson distribution. One advantage of our method is that the topic model can be trained on an isolated corpus, e.g., news archive, such that 1) the model can be readily deployed to new users without a requirement of pre-training; 2) the generated cover queries could be evenly distributed and sufficiently remote from a user's true intent.

2. RELATED WORKS

Complete privacy preservation is possible through *Private Information Retrieval* (PIR) [4], but its high complexity and inability to perform targeted personalized search prevent its practical adoption in commercial search engines. Server-controlled privacy is also assumed to protect user privacy; but after AOL search log release incident[1], several methods were proposed for improved query log anonymization. Researchers also proposed different user controlled or client-centered approach for privacy preservation. *Providing Privacy through Plausibly Deniable Search* (PDS) [7] is one of the client-centered privacy preserving approaches, and it is closely re-

SIGIR '16, July 17–21, 2016, Pisa, Italy.
© 2016 ACM. ISBN 978-1-4503-4069-4/16/07...$15.00
DOI: http://dx.doi.org/10.1145/2911451.2914753

lated to our proposed solution. In PDS, Latent Semantic Indexing is used to generate cover queries. PDS constructs a predefined set of all possible cover queries in an offline manner, while our method generates the cover queries on the fly. In addition, PDS does not consider generating standard varieties of cover queries in case of sequentially edited queries. One of the major bottleneck of PDS is that it cannot submit user query to the search engine if the query does not contain words in the predefined dictionary.

In [12, 3], better search results can be achieved with privacy guarantee if personalization is only performed based on a less sensitive or less specific part of the user profile, namely a generalized profile. The main idea is to build a hierarchical user profile and not to expose the sensitive part of the profile to the search engine by acquiring the level of privacy requirement from the user. [13] automatically builds a hierarchical user profile in the client side based on user specified privacy settings. In *Knowledge-based Scheme* [10] a similar approach is proposed to generate distorted user queries from a semantic point of view in order to preserve the utility of user profiles. In addition, linguistic analysis techniques are used to properly interpret complex queries submitted by users and generate new semantically-related queries accordingly. [8] proposed a different way to protect user privacy by embellishing the search queries with decoy terms that exhibit similar specificity spread as the genuine terms, but point to plausible alternative topics. [14] concentrated only on anonymizing user profiles by clustering them into user groups by taking into account the semantic relationships between query terms while satisfying the privacy constraints. Our proposed model is different from the aforementioned works as it concentrates on obfuscating users' true search intent at the topic level, which is constructed based on external data. And the balance between privacy protection and utility of search results is achieved at this topic-level obfuscation.

3. METHODOLOGY

Search engines track different type of user information, such as browsing history, clicked documents, amount of time spent in exploring a returned document, to build the user profile for personalizing the search results. Our proposed solution, *Topic-based Privacy Protection* (TPP), focuses on obfuscating the user profile by submitting cover queries along with the original query to the search engine. As a result, the user profiles constructed on the search engine side contain irrelevant information about the user such that it reduces the confidence of the search engine to predict users' specific information need (achieve privacy protection). By controlling noise injection from client side, TPP maintains the balance between privacy protection and search effectiveness. Figure 1 describes the work flow of our proposed solution. In our work, we inject k cover queries with the original query and submit them to the search engine. After getting the search results for all the submitted queries, we only keep the results of the original query and re-ranking them based on the user profile constructed and maintained on the client side. Finally, the re-ranked search results are provided to the user. In this way, we prevent the search engine to infer users' true information need with high fidelity.

3.1 Cover Query Generation

The amount of cover queries determines the strength of privacy protection. The more diverse those cover queries are, the more difficult it is for a search engine to distinguish individual user's information needs. But it will also result in degenerated search results. Therefore, balancing privacy preservation and search effectiveness is important. We generate cover queries based on the topics inferred by LDA topic model. We used a large collection of BBC news data set [5] for LDA model training and generate k cover queries randomly from the learned topics. Cover queries are generated on different topics with similar entropy to the original query's entropy e, e.g., $[e-\epsilon, e+\epsilon]$. Hence, if a user's query is highly concentrated in sports, less cover queries will be generated from the topic of sports but more will be generated from business, entertainment etc. If we failed to get a query within the required entropy range after n attempts, we will select the last generated cover query. To increase the plausibility of cover queries, we also randomize the length of cover queries by a Poisson distribution, where the rate parameter is set to the target user's average query length. We also generated random dummy clicks for the cover queries (with the same expectation of the number of clicks in true queries) so that search engines will not have explicit signal to recognize them. Therefore, our model disguises a user's true search intents through plausible cover queries such that search engines cannot easily recognize them.

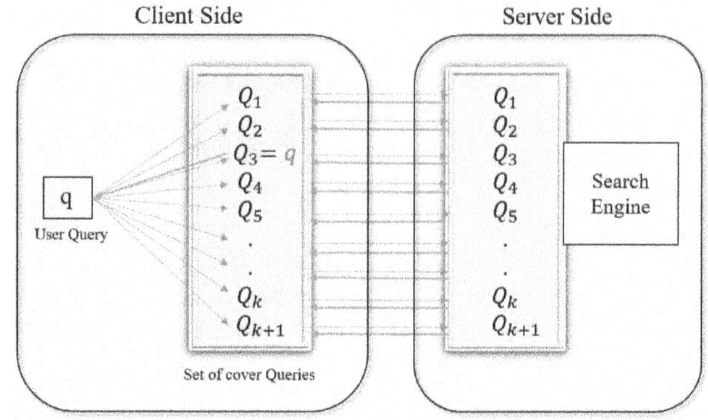

Figure 1: Workflow of Topic-based Privacy Protection solution.

3.2 Improving Search Effectiveness

To improve the utility of search results after cover query injection, we also build user profiles on client-side with a user's true queries and clicks for search result re-ranking. We assume a user's previous search queries and the corresponding clicked documents are good proxies of a user's search interests. Following the method proposed in [11], we use language models to build user profiles. In particular, we update the user profile immediately after each user query and result click. All the computation is performed at the client side, and no additional facility is required from search engine side. Once getting the search results, we only consider the results of the true user query, and re-rank the returned documents based on a linear combination of two scoring functions as shown in Eq (1).

$$\text{Score(d)} = \alpha \sum_t P(t) \times TF(t) + (1-\alpha)\frac{1}{\text{R}} \quad (1)$$

The first part is based on the true user profile constructed and maintained by the client side, where $P(t)$ is the probability of observing term t in user profile and $TF(t)$ is the term frequency of t in document d. The second part is based on the ranking R of the documents provided by the search engine. Because search engine is forced to use an obfuscated query log for personalization, client-side re-ranking will help to improve the utility of resulted ranking, given the client-side user profile is built on the users' true query history and result clicks.

4. EXPERIMENTS

We performed extensive experiments using AOL search log released in 2006 [9]. We built our own search engine based on Apache Lucene and compared our model with two other previous works [7, 10] for performance evaluation. To the best of our knowledge, no previous work has validated their solutions in terms of both search effectiveness and privacy preservation.

4.1 Dataset & Setup

The AOL search log contains 20M search queries from 0.65M users from March to May 2006. There are 1,632,797 unique clicked URLs. We crawled all those URLs using an open source web crawler, *crawler4j*. We found approximately 64.4% (1,051,483) of the URLs are alive and the rest are no longer active. We only collected the text content of each URL to build the index of our search engine using *Apache Lucene*, where *Okapi BM25* is employed for ranking. Just for simplicity purpose, our search engine always returns the top 100 documents and thus we calculated mean average precision (MAP) at 100 to evaluate ranking quality. To personalize the search results, our search engine re-ranks them using the server-side constructed user profiles before returning the results. In particular, the server-side user profiles are also constructed using each submitted user query and the corresponding clicked document content (with cover queries and dummy clicks). We have selected the top t words using tf-idf weight from clicked documents content to update user profile. In evaluation, we considered the top 250 users based on the size of their query history. We only used the unique queries from each user, and all the corresponding clicked URLs are considered as relevant when measuring the search effectiveness. This gives us 45,200 queries over 250 users. The reason to remove duplicated queries in each user is that both our method and baselines will generate different cover queries for repeated queries with high probability, and this makes it easy to recognize those generated cover queries.

To build the topic model, which is the core of our cover query generation procedure, we used BBC dataset [5]. This data set contains news articles of five major topics, namely, business, entertainment, politics, sports and technology. There are 2,225 news articles and 23,225 unique terms in this dataset. We evaluated our model by varying the number of cover queries from 1 to 5. We also experimented with 3 different entropy range (ϵ = 0.1/0.2/0.3). To evaluate whether the cover queries are disclosing any information about a user's original query, we computed mutual information (MI) defined in Eq (2) between them. On the other hand, we also used Kullback–Leibler divergence as in Eq (3) between the true user profile on client-side and the noisy user profile on server-side to measure the amount of privacy disclosure.

$$MI(X;Y) = \sum_{y \epsilon Y} \sum_{x \epsilon X} p(x,y) log(\frac{p(x,y)}{p(x)p(y)}) \quad (2)$$

$$D_{KL}(P \| Q) = \sum_{i} P(i) \log \frac{P(i)}{Q(i)} \quad (3)$$

4.2 Results

We compared our model with Plausible Deniable Search (PDS) [7] and Knowledge-based Scheme (KBS) [10], and the proposed TPP outperformed both of them in terms of search effectiveness and privacy preservation. The detailed comparison between our model and the baselines is presented in Table 1 under different number of cover queries.

We implemented the PDS model on BBC dataset and evaluated it in our search engine. The total number of seed queries was 13,668 and total number of canonical queries was 13,340. The number of PD query sets found at level 0 and level 1 was 6735 and 3367 respectively. Since PDS creates cover queries through hierarchical clustering, only 2^n number of cover queries can be generated and thus we cannot report the performance of it for $k = 1, 3, 5$ cases in Table 1. The major bottleneck of PDS is that it fails to generate any cover query if a query term can not be found in the predefined dictionary (no query will be submitted to search engine then). Another limitation of PDS is that the PD query sets do not cover all words in the predefined dictionary, and oftentimes the user query and the closest canonical queries does not have any similarity in their content which results in very poor retrieval performance. We improved their solution by submitting the original user query along with the cover queries generated. As a result, we got improved MAP but smaller KL divergence and higher mutual information which assert that our model is more effective than PDS.

Table 1: Comparison between TPP, PDS and KBS

Settings	Model Name	MAP	KL Divergence	MI
K = 1	TPP	0.1389	0.0496	0.7761
	PDS	NA	NA	NA
	KBS	0.0331	2.2723	0.6972
K = 2	TPP	0.1388	0.0981	0.8523
	PDS	0.1386	0.2281	1.0195
	KBS	0.0361	2.2658	1.0869
K = 3	TPP	0.1388	0.1473	0.9681
	PDS	NA	NA	NA
	KBS	0.0363	2.3525	1.1591
K = 4	TPP	0.1387	0.1894	1.0339
	PDS	0.1386	0.2414	1.0114
	KBS	0.0368	2.3965	1.2541
K = 5	TPP	0.1386	0.2292	1.1413
	PDS	NA	NA	NA
	KBS	0.0364	2.3923	1.3237

KBS relies on structured knowledge modeled in the form of ontology, and it focuses on nouns and noun phrases when analyzing user queries. We implemented this method based on WordNet and ODP categories [10], which are organized in hierarchical structures. According to KBS, a new query set is constructed from a semantic point of view using predefined hierarchical structure of topical categories. Since the original query is not submitted to search engine in KBS, it can only provide limited search quality to users. In its original paper, KBS model is not validated for search effectiveness but we evaluated its performance through our implemented search engine. It is important to note that, KBS only uses the category name in the predefined hierarchy as cover queries and as a result, the resulting retrieval performance is extremely bad. The generated cover queries in KBS are more specific compared to those from our model (since it is already a summary of users' search intents), which might give the search engine reasonable amount of information about user intents.

TPP has two parameters: the number of cover queries k, and the entropy range ϵ. Though the impact of entropy range is not evident in the average MAP across users, it is evident in individual user's MAP. Increase in entropy range (e.g., from 0.2 to 0.3) decreases MAP around 1% for some users as cover queries become more diverse. We have also evaluated TPP with different number of topics (e.g., 5, 7, 9) during topic model training and got very similar results (in terms of MAP), which indicates the robustness of TPP with respect to the specific topic model used. We also tested TPP for k=0 to verify how much TPP is affecting the search effectiveness, and found that the decrease in MAP is negligible. Moreover, We tested TPP without client side re-ranking and surprisingly we got better MAP in that scenario: with client side re-ranking, we got a MAP of 0.123 while the MAP without the client side re-ranking is 0.138. Though for some users, client side re-ranking greatly improved the MAP but for many users it has fallen short to ensure better MAP. One major reason for this degenerated retrieval performance after client-side re-ranking is due to our pre-processing, where we have removed the duplicated queries from each user but such profile-based personalization mostly improves repeated queries. In our future work, we will evaluate our model with larger number of users with their full search log.

We also computed the difference between Information Content (IC) [10] of true user query and a corresponding cover query generated in TPP, PDS and KBS. The degree of IC between original and cover query is evaluated as the ratio between the query with the highest hit count with respect to the other. We picked 1500 user queries randomly and their corresponding two cover queries, in total of 3000 query pairs from each model to calculate IC ratio which is depicted in Figure 2. We used Microsoft Bing API to find the hit counts of queries. As shown in Figure 2, information content ratio of our model is smaller compared to PDS and KBS, because in PDS cover queries are generated from frequent patterns and in KBS hierarchical category names from ODP is used to generate cover queries. Since higher IC ratio means the specificity of original query and cover queries are not similar, the cover queries generated in PDS and KBS may reveal user privacy which is handled in TPP.

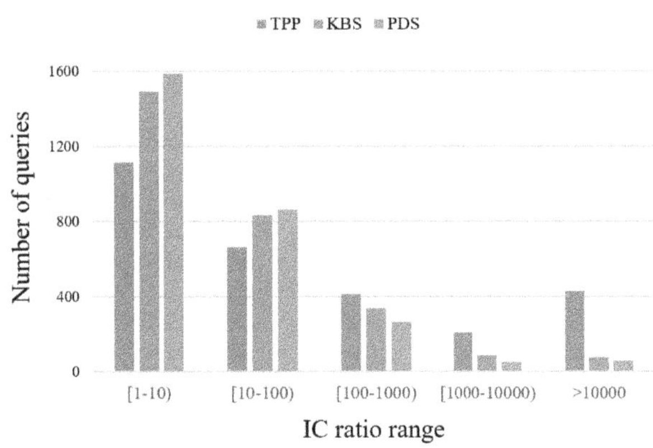

Figure 2: Information Content comparison between TPP, KBS and PDS

5. DISCUSSIONS

The number of generated cover queries are predefined in our model. But we should note that different users would need different level of privacy protection, and these trade-offs might also vary across different search tasks. We can rely on users to set their privacy level but it would be more useful if we can assess the level of protection required from a user's previous search history and behaviors. Moreover, we should be able to estimate the most feasible entropy range over a period of time to have more balanced personalization and privacy protection. We are learning the topic models only on news data set now, but increasing the diversity of training data sets, e.g., combining data from different sources (e.g., user reviews, social media, and forum discussions) would give us a more comprehensive topic model to generate cover queries.

6. CONCLUSIONS AND FUTURE WORKS

In this work, we developed a novel solution to protect user privacy based on their inferred search intent from topic models. The topic model, as a core component of our solution, can be estimated on an isolated document collection, which ensures protection of individual users' privacy and its general applicability. Both the specificity and length of the generated cover queries are carefully controlled to ensure the plausibility of cover queries. We experimented with 250 users over their 3 months' search history, in total of 45,200 queries from the AOL search log to prove the effectiveness of our model. The proposed method improved both search effectiveness and privacy protection against two state-of-the-art baselines.

Our current solution generates cover queries independently from the search context, e.g., queries in the same session and a user's previous clicks. This will inevitably hurt not only the plausibility of cover queries but also search effectiveness. As our future work, we will explicitly model a user's sequential search behaviors for generating better cover queries. In addition, we will also explore how to control the cover query generation dynamically such that the trade-off between personalization and privacy can be optimized for the long run. In addition, our current solution does not handle users' *ego-surfing* behaviors, such as searching for their own names or social security numbers. Classifiers can be built to recognize such queries and generate cover queries of the same type accordingly.

7. ACKNOWLEDGMENTS

We thank the anonymous reviewers for their insightful comments. This paper is based upon work supported in part by a Yahoo Academic Career Enhancement Award and the National Science Foundation under grants IIS-1553568.

8. REFERENCES

[1] M. Barbaro, T. Zeller, and S. Hansell. A face is exposed for aol searcher no. 4417749. *New York Times*, 9(2008):8For, 2006.

[2] D. M. Blei. Probabilistic topic models. *Communications of the ACM*, 55(4):77–84, 2012.

[3] G. Chen, H. Bai, L. Shou, K. Chen, and Y. Gao. Ups: efficient privacy protection in personalized web search. In *Proceedings of the 34th international ACM SIGIR conference on Research and development in Information Retrieval*, pages 615–624. ACM, 2011.

[4] B. Chor, E. Kushilevitz, O. Goldreich, and M. Sudan. Private information retrieval. *Journal of the ACM (JACM)*, 45(6):965–981, 1998.

[5] D. Greene and P. Cunningham. Practical solutions to the problem of diagonal dominance in kernel document clustering. In *Proc. 23rd International Conference on Machine learning (ICML'06)*, pages 377–384. ACM Press, 2006.

[6] D. Halse et al. I know what you did last summer. *Advocate: Newsletter of the National Tertiary Education Union*, 21(1):14, 2014.

[7] M. Murugesan and C. Clifton. Providing privacy through plausibly deniable search. In *SDM*, pages 768–779. SIAM, 2009.

[8] H. Pang, X. Ding, and X. Xiao. Embellishing text search queries to protect user privacy. *Proceedings of the VLDB Endowment*, 3(1-2):598–607, 2010.

[9] G. Pass, A. Chowdhury, and C. Torgeson. A picture of search. In *InfoScale*, volume 152, page 1, 2006.

[10] D. Sánchez, J. Castellà-Roca, and A. Viejo. Knowledge-based scheme to create privacy-preserving but semantically-related queries for web search engines. *Information Sciences*, 218:17–30, 2013.

[11] X. Shen, B. Tan, and C. Zhai. Implicit user modeling for personalized search. In *Proceedings of the 14th ACM international conference on Information and knowledge management*, pages 824–831. ACM, 2005.

[12] L. Shou, H. Bai, K. Chen, and G. Chen. Supporting privacy protection in personalized web search. *Knowledge and Data Engineering, IEEE Transactions on*, 26(2):453–467, 2014.

[13] Y. Xu, K. Wang, B. Zhang, and Z. Chen. Privacy-enhancing personalized web search. In *Proceedings of the 16th international conference on World Wide Web*, pages 591–600. ACM, 2007.

[14] Y. Zhu, L. Xiong, and C. Verdery. Anonymizing user profiles for personalized web search. In *Proceedings of the 19th international conference on World wide web*, pages 1225–1226. ACM, 2010.

Topic Quality Metrics Based on Distributed Word Representations

Sergey I. Nikolenko
Laboratory for Internet Studies,
National Research University Higher School of Economics, St. Petersburg,
Steklov Mathematical Institute at St. Petersburg
sergey@logic.pdmi.ras.ru

ABSTRACT

Automated evaluation of topic quality remains an important unsolved problem in topic modeling and represents a major obstacle for development and evaluation of new topic models. Previous attempts at the problem have been formulated as variations on the coherence and/or mutual information of top words in a topic. In this work, we propose several new metrics for evaluating topic quality with the help of distributed word representations; our experiments suggest that the new metrics are a better match for human judgement, which is the gold standard in this case, than previously developed approaches.

Keywords

topic quality; topic modeling; text mining

1. INTRODUCTION

Evaluating topic quality has been an important problem in topic modeling since its very inception. The problem here is that while it is usually immediately evident for a human whether a topic is "good" or not, i.e., whether it is easily interpretable and can serve to draw conclusions regarding the dataset, it is hard to evaluate it automatically. This problem is especially prominent in real-life applications of topic modeling to social sciences, where the goal is usually to get an overview of what the dataset is about and which documents to actually read, which is impossible without interpretable topics [5, 15]. However, it it still an open and interesting problem to devise metrics that would give good approximations to human interpretability; actual human evaluation remains the gold standard here.

In this work, we propose several candidate metrics based on distributed word representations. Word representations have been extensively used in natural language processing; the idea is to map words into some kind of semantic space where geometric relations between vectors will supposedly correspond to semantic relations between the original words.

SIGIR '16, July 17-21, 2016, Pisa, Italy

DOI: http://dx.doi.org/10.1145/2911451.2914720

In this work, we posit that such embeddings and the semantic information that they capture can be leveraged to evaluate topic models, with results significantly improving upon previously known techniques. We perform quantitative evaluation by comparing the ranking produced by automatic quality metrics with rankings produced by human experts asked specifically to evaluate topic interpretability. In other words, we measure interpretability directly by a consensus of human experts and try to approximate it by automated metrics. We show that even very simple metrics that measure how close top words in a topic are in the semantic space still significantly outperform previously used metrics.

The paper is organized as follows. In Section 2, we describe the problem setting in detail and survey related work, including previously known approaches to topic evaluation that we compare with. In Section 3, we describe the new metrics based on distributed representations. Section 4 describes our experimental setup and presents the results, and Section 5 concludes the paper.

2. RELATED WORK

2.1 Topic modeling

We begin by surveying (very briefly due to space constraints) the topic models whose results we try to evaluate. Let D be a finite set (collection) of texts and W a finite set (vocabulary) of all terms from these texts. Probabilistic topic models represent the text collection as a sequence of triples (d_i, w_i, z_i), where d_i is a document, w_i is a word, and z_i is the topic from which w_i has been drawn in this instance; d_i and w_i are observed from the data, while z_i are latent variables. Introducing the word-topic distributions Φ, $\phi_{wt} = p(w \mid t)$, and document-topic distributions Θ, $\theta_{td} = p(t \mid d)$, we get that $p(w \mid d) = \sum_{t \in T} p(w \mid t)\, p(t \mid d) = \sum_{t \in T} \phi_{wt}\theta_{td}$, and the generative process is similar in all topic models: for every word instance, we first sample the topic t_i from distribution $p(t \mid d)$ and then sample the word w_i from distribution $p(w \mid t_i)$.

In the basic *probabilistic latent semantic analysis* (pLSA) model [10], Φ and Θ matrices are learned by directly optimizing the log-likelihood of the training dataset $L(\Phi, \Theta) = \sum_{d \in D} \sum_{w \in d} n_{dw} \ln \sum_{t \in T} \phi_{wt}\theta_{td}$. In the recently developed approach known as *additive regularization of topic models* (ARTM) [19], the basic pLSA model is augmented with additive regularizers, and Φ and Θ matrices are learned by maximizing a linear combination of $L(\Phi, \Theta)$ and r regularizers $R_i(\Phi,\Theta)$, $i=1,\dots,r$ with *regularization coefficients* τ_i:

$$R(\Phi,\Theta)=\sum_{i=1}^{r}\tau_i R_i(\Phi,\Theta),\quad L(\Phi,\Theta)+R(\Phi,\Theta)\ \to\ \max_{\Phi,\Theta}.$$

This makes it easy to devise new regularizers, adding desired properties to the topic model [19, 20].

The latent Dirichlet allocation (LDA) model [3, 4, 8] introduces prior Dirichlet distributions for the vectors of term probabilities in topics $\phi_t\sim\mathrm{Dir}(\beta)$ as well as for the vectors of topic probabilities in documents $\theta_d\sim\mathrm{Dir}(\alpha)$ with parameters β and α respectively. Inference in LDA is usually done via either variational approximations or Gibbs sampling. Over the last decade, LDA has been subject to many extensions (too many to survey them here), each of them presenting either a variational of a Gibbs sampling algorithm for a model that builds upon LDA to incorporate some additional information or additional presumed dependencies.

In each case, the result of learning a topic model can be represented as the Φ and Θ matrices. In this work, we concentrate on evaluating the quality of the Φ word-topic distributions, usually presented to a user as an ordered list of top words for every topic, i.e., words with the largest $\phi_{wt}=p(w\,|\,t)$.

2.2 Distributed word representations for natural language processing

The modern neural network approaches to natural language processing can be roughly divided into two subproblems: constructing and training new models for individual words (this field is known as word embeddings or distributed word representations) and developing subsequent layers of deep architectures to find syntactic and semantic features while taking into account the context of a word in a sentence and specific problems that a system attempts to solve.

To train distributed word representations, one first constructs a vocabulary with one-hot representations of individual words (where each word is represented with a vector of size equal to vocabulary size with a single 1) and then trains representations for individual words starting from there, basically as a dimensionality reduction problem. For this purpose, researchers have usually employed a model with one hidden layer that attempts to predict the next word based on a window of several preceding words. Then representations learned at the hidden layer are taken to be the word's features; this approach has been applied, for instance in the Polyglot system developed in 2013 [1] and in other methods of learning distributed word representations [17]. A recent study on the performance of various vector space models for word semantic similarity evaluation [16] demostrates that compositions of models such as GloVe and Word2Vec as well as unsupervised one-model approaches show reasonable results for the Russian language (which we use in evaluations since we have expert evaluations available for Russian-language topics).

2.3 Topic quality metrics

Next, we survey the topic quality metrics that we build upon in this work. We begin with *coherence*, proposed as a topic quality metric in [7, 13]. For a topic t characterized by its set of top words W_t, coherence is defined as

$$c(t,W_t)=\sum_{w_1,w_2\in W_t}\log\frac{d(w_1,w_2)+\epsilon}{d(w_1)},$$

where $d(w_i)$ is the number of documents that contain w_i, $d(w_i,w_j)$ is the number of documents where w_i and w_j cooccur, and ϵ is a smoothing count usually set to either 1 or 0.01. Coherence and word cooccurrence statistics in general have also been used to initialize LDA parameters [18]. However, in a recent work [15] coherence was criticized for a number of shortcomings, primarily because it was found to be too heavily reliant on common words that cooccur often but do not define interpretable topics. To alleviate this, the work [15] proposed a modification of the coherence metric called tf-idf coherence defined as

$$c_{\mathrm{tfidf}}(t,W_t)=\sum_{w_1,w_2\in W_t}\log\frac{\sum_{d:w_1,w_2\in d}\mathrm{tfidf}(w_1,d)\mathrm{tfidf}(w_2,d)+\epsilon}{\sum_{d:w_1\in d}\mathrm{tfidf}(w_1,d)},$$

where the tfidf metric is computed with augmented frequency,

$$\mathrm{tfidf}(w,d)=\mathrm{tf}(w,d)\times\mathrm{idf}(w)=\left(\frac{1}{2}+\frac{f(w,d)}{\max_{w'\in d}f(w',d)}\right)\log\frac{|D|}{|\{d\in D:w\in d\}|},$$

where $f(w,d)$ is the number of occurrences of term w in document d. This skews the metric towards topics with high tfidf scores in top words, since the numerator of the coherence fraction has quadratic dependence on the tfidf scores and the denominator only linear.

Another class of topic quality metrics is based on the notion of *pairwise pointwise mutual information* (PMI) between the top words in a topic. Following a recent work [11], we compute three variations on this idea. For a given ordered set of top words $W_t=(w_1,\dots,w_N)$ in a topic,

(1) the basic *pairwise PMI* metric [14] is computed as

$$\mathrm{PMI}_t=\sum_{i<j}\log\frac{p(w_i,w_j)}{p(w_i)p(w_j)};$$

(2) the *normalized PMI* variation [6] is computed as

$$\mathrm{NPMI}_t=\sum_{i<j}\frac{\log\frac{p(w_i,w_j)}{p(w_i)p(w_j)}}{-\log p(w_i,w_j)};$$

(3) the *pairwise log conditional probability* (LCP) metric [13] is computed as

$$\mathrm{LCP}_t=\sum_{i<j}\log\frac{p(w_i,w_j)}{p(w_i)}.$$

3. TOPIC QUALITY METRICS BASED ON WORD VECTORS

In this section, we propose a number of metrics for evaluating topic quality based on distributed word representations. Suppose that a vector space model has been trained, and every vocabulary word $w\in W$ has been assigned with a vector $v_w\in\mathbb{R}^d$. The basic assumption in our metrics is that a good metric should be well localized in the semantic space: specifically, top words in a topic should be close to each other in the semantic space.

Hence, we use the following general scheme for topic quality metrics: given a set of top words W_t for a topic t with weights (word probabilities) ϕ_{wt}, $w \in W_t$, their distributed representations $c_w \in \mathbb{R}^d$, and a distance function $d : \mathbb{R}^d \times \mathbb{R}^d \to \mathbb{R}$, we define topic quality as the average distance between the top words in the topic:

$$Q_t = \frac{1}{|W_t|(|W_t|-1)} \sum_{w_1 \neq w_2 \in W_t} d(v_{w_1}, v_{w_2}).$$

If $d(w_1, w_2)$ is a distance function in the space $\mathbb{R}^d$, larger results correspond to, supposedly, worse topics (with words not as localized as in topics with smaller average distances). We have compared four different distance-like metrics:

(1) cosine distance $d_{\cos}(x, y) = 1 - x^\top y$ (no normalization here since we have used normalized word vectors);

(2) L_1-distance $d_{L_1}(x, y) = \sum_{i=1}^d |x_i - y_i|$;

(3) L_2-distance $d_{L_2}(x, y) = \sum_{i=1}^d (x_i - y_i)^2$;

(4) coordinate distance $d_{\text{coord}}(x, y) = \sum_{i=1}^d [x_i - y_i > \eta]$, where $[A] = 1$ if A holds and 0 otherwise; the intuition here was that different dimensions of the semantic space may represent different aspects of a word's semantics and may be incomparable directly, so it may make sense to simply count in how many coordinates the two vectors differ significantly; the threshold η was tuned by hand to give reasonable results.

4. EVALUATION

4.1 Datasets and experimental setup

The core of all proposed metrics are word vector representations. We used the skip-gram word2vec model of dimension 500 trained on a large Russian language corpus [2, 16]; the corpus consisted of:

- Russian Wikipedia: 1.15M documents, 238M tokens;
- web crawl data: 890K documents, 568M tokens;
- *lib.rus.ec* library: 234K documents, 12.9G tokens.

A large collection of general-purpose texts ensured good resulting distributed representations; for an in-depth description of the model we refer to [2, 16].

To evaluate the proposed approach, we have used a dataset with approximately 1.58 million lemmatized posts from the top *LiveJournal* bloggers, all in Russian; the Russian language was chosen since we had experts estimates available for topic interpretability only in Russian. The complete vocabulary amounted to 860K words, but after preprocessing it was reduced to 90K words; after dictionary reduction and filtering, there remained about 1.38 million nonempty documents. We have trained all models with $T = 400$ topics, a number chosen by training pLSA models with 100, 300, and 400 topics and evaluating the results.

We have evaluated the quality of six different topic models; since the human coding results were obtained as part of a case study for mining ethnic-related content, two models work specifically with ethnonyms, but in each case the assessors simply evaluated top words in every topic:

(1) probabilistic latent semantic analysis model (pLSA);

(2) latent Dirichlet allocation model (LDA);

(3) ARTM model with smoothing and sparsity regularizers;

(4) ARTM model with a decorrelation regularizer;

(5) ARTM model with a separate modality for ethnonyms, small dictionary of ethnonyms;

(6) ARTM model with a separate modality for ethnonyms, large dictionary of ethnonyms.

Human assessors were asked to interpret the topics based on 20 most probable words in every topic of each model. For each topic, assessors answered the following question: "Do you understand why these words are collected together in this topic?". They were also told that the idea was to see whether the topic was generally understandable and given three options: (a) absolutely not; (b) partially; (c) yes.

The "correct" (human-generated) ranking of topics was produced according to the total number of positive answers, counting (b) as 1 and (c) as 2. For comparison, we have computed five previously known metrics: coherence, tf-idf coherence, PMI, NPMI, and LPC[1], and four word2vec-based metrics with four different distances shown in Section 3.

To evaluate how well a metric matches this ranking, we have computed, for each subject and each metric, the *area-under-curve* (AUC) measure [9, 12]. AUC is a popular quality metric for classifiers that produce ranking results; by definition it represents the probability that for a uniformly selected pair consisting of a positive and a negative example the classifier ranks the positive one higher. Thus, the optimal AUC is 1 (all positive examples come before negative ones), the worst possible AUC is 0, and a random classifier would get an AUC of 0.5. In our case AUC is the perfect fit since the actual values of a metric are mostly irrelevant, and the users are interested in the ranking (to view the best topics from a dataset).

Results of our experiments are shown in Table 1. We see that the new word2vec-based metrics outperform, often significantly, previously known approaches. As expected, tf-idf coherence is better than regular coherence and NPMI is better than PMI, but all of them lose to vector space metrics in most cases. There is little difference between the new metrics themselves, but we can recommend to use L_1 and L_2 metrics.

5. CONCLUSION

In this work, we have proposed a number of simple metrics based on distributed word representations for the purpose of evaluating topic quality in topic modeling results. We have shown that the new metrics outperform previously used topic quality metrics in terms of agreeing with human interpretation. The metrics introduced in this work are rather straightforward; in further work we expect to significantly improve upon our results shown here by learning distributions in the semantic space that are better aligned with actual topics. For instance, it is perfectly plausible for a topic to have several clusters of closely matching words that describe the same issue from different sides; in this case, it would probably be beneficial to consider a clustering model. We expect new exciting developments along these lines, although even the basic metrics proposed here already outperform existing state of the art topic evaluation approaches.

[1]To compute PMI, NPMI, and LPC we have used the companion software for [11] available at https://github.com/jhlau/topic_interpretability.

Model	Quality metrics								
	Coherence		Mutual information			Word2vec metrics			
	regular	tf-idf	PMI	NPMI	LPC	cos	L_1	L_2	coord
1 (pLSA)	0.7720	0.8910	0.8675	0.8707	0.8811	0.8954	0.8957	**0.8965**	0.8832
2 (LDA)	0.7817	0.8748	0.8469	0.8372	0.8541	0.8786	0.8797	**0.8806**	0.8692
3 (ARTM smoothing + sparsity)	0.7513	0.8439	0.6637	0.6973	0.7738	0.8543	**0.8616**	0.8589	0.8597
4 (3 + decorrelation)	0.6783	0.8635	0.7571	0.7821	0.8408	0.8675	**0.8718**	0.8704	0.8605
5 (4 + ethnic modality, small vocab.)	0.7425	0.8924	0.8791	0.8865	0.8885	0.8889	**0.8920**	0.8906	0.8848
6 (5 + ethnic modality, large vocab.)	0.7857	0.8767	0.8526	0.8430	0.8672	0.8812	**0.8827**	0.8815	0.8588

Figure 1: Experimental comparison between LDA topic quality metrics: area under curve (AUC) comparison metrics between human-generated interpretability evaluation and automatic quality metrics.

Acknowledgements

This work was supported by the Russian Science Foundation grant no. 15-18-00091. I thank Olessia Koltsova and Sergei Koltcov for the experimental human coding data, Konstantin Vorontsov, Anna Potapenko, Murat Apishev, and Oleksander Frei for the topics themselves, and Alexander Panchenko and Nikolay Arefyev for the Russian-language training corpora used for the *word2vec* models.

6. REFERENCES

[1] R. Al-Rfou, B. Perozzi, and S. Skiena. Polyglot: Distributed word representations for multilingual NLP. In *Proc. 17th Conference on Computational Natural Language Learning*, pages 183–192, Sofia, Bulgaria, August 2013. Association for Computational Linguistics.

[2] N. Arefyev, A. Panchenko, A. Lukanin, O. Lesota, and P. Romanov. Evaluating three corpus-based semantic similarity systems for russian. In *Proc. International Conference on Computational Linguistics Dialogue*, 2015.

[3] D. M. Blei. Introduction to probabilistic topic models. *Communications of the ACM*, 2011.

[4] D. M. Blei, A. Y. Ng, and M. I. Jordan. Latent Dirichlet allocation. *Journal of Machine Learning Research*, 3(4–5):993–1022, 2003.

[5] S. Bodrunova, S. Koltsov, O. Koltsova, S. I. Nikolenko, and A. Shimorina. Interval semi-supervised LDA: Classifying needles in a haystack. In *Proc. 12th Mexican International Conference on Artificial Intelligence*, volume 8625 of *Lecture Notes in Computer Science*, pages 265–274. Springer, 2013.

[6] G. Bouma. Normalized (pointwise) mutual information in collocation extraction. In *Proc. Biennial GSCL Conference*, pages 31–40, 2013.

[7] J. Chang, J. Boyd-Graber, S. Gerrish, C. Wang, and D. M. Blei. Reading tea leaves: How humans interpret topic models. *Advances in Neural Information Processing Systems*, 20, 2009.

[8] T. Griffiths and M. Steyvers. Finding scientific topics. *Proceedings of the National Academy of Sciences*, 101 (Suppl. 1):5228–5335, 2004.

[9] D. J. Hand and R. J. Till. A simple generalisation of the area under the ROC curve for multiple class classification problems. *Machine Learning*, 45:171–186, 2001.

[10] T. Hoffmann. Unsupervised learning by probabilistic latent semantic analysis. *Machine Learning*, 42(1):177–196, 2001.

[11] J. H. Lau, D. Newman, and T. Baldwin. Machine reading tea leaves: Automatically evaluating topic coherence and topic model quality. In *EACL*, pages 530–539, 2014.

[12] C. X. Ling, J. Huang, and H. Zhang. AUC: a statistically consistent and more discriminating measure than accuracy. In *Proc. International Joint Conference on Artificial Intelligence 2003*, pages 519–526, 2003.

[13] D. Mimno, H. M. Wallach, E. Talley, M. Leenders, and A. McCallum. Optimizing semantic coherence in topic models. In *Proc. Conference on Empirical Methods in Natural Language Processing*, pages 262–272, Stroudsburg, PA, USA, 2011. Association for Computational Linguistics.

[14] D. Newman, J. H. Lau, K. Grieser, and T. Baldwin. Automatic evaluation of topic coherence. In *Human Language Technologies 2010*, HLT '10, pages 100–108, Stroudsburg, PA, USA, 2010. Association for Computational Linguistics.

[15] S. I. Nikolenko, O. Koltsova, and S. Koltsov. Topic modelling for qualitative studies. *Journal of Information Science*, 2015.

[16] A. Panchenko, N. Loukachevitch, D. Ustalov, D. Paperno, C. M. Meyer, and N. Konstantinova. Russe: The first workshop on Russian semantic similarity. In *Proc. International Conference on Computational Linguistics and Intellectual Technologies (Dialogue)*, pages 89–105, May 2015.

[17] J. Pennington, R. Socher, and C. Manning. GloVe: Global vectors for word representation. In *Proc. 2014 Conference on Empirical Methods in Natural Language Processing (EMNLP)*, pages 1532–1543, Doha, Qatar, October 2014. Association for Computational Linguistics.

[18] A. S. Rathore and D. Roy. Performance of LDA and DCT models. *Journal of Information Science*, 40(3):281–292, 2014.

[19] K. Vorontsov. Additive regularization for topic models of text collections. *Doklady Mathematics*, 89(3):301–304, 2014.

[20] K. V. Vorontsov and A. A. Potapenko. Additive regularization of topic models. *Machine Learning, Special Issue on Data Analysis and Intelligent Optimization with Applications*, 101(1):303–323, 2015.

Toward Estimating the Rank Correlation between the Test Collection Results and the True System Performance

Julián Urbano
Universitat Pompeu Fabra
Barcelona, Spain
urbano.julian@gmail.com

Mónica Marrero
National Supercomputing Center
Barcelona, Spain
monica.marrero@bsc.es

ABSTRACT

The Kendall τ and AP rank correlation coefficients have become mainstream in Information Retrieval research for comparing the rankings of systems produced by two different evaluation conditions, such as different effectiveness measures or pool depths. However, in this paper we focus on the *expected* rank correlation between the mean scores observed with a test collection and the *true*, unobservable means under the same conditions. In particular, we propose statistical estimators of τ and AP correlations following both parametric and non-parametric approaches, and with special emphasis on small topic sets. Through large scale simulation with TREC data, we study the error and bias of the estimators. In general, such estimates of expected correlation with the true ranking may accompany the results reported from an evaluation experiment, as an easy to understand figure of reliability. All the results in this paper are fully reproducible with data and code available online.

Keywords

Evaluation; Test Collection; Correlation; Kendall; Average Precision; Estimation

1. INTRODUCTION

The Kendall τ [3] and AP [8] rank correlation coefficients are widely used in Information Retrieval to compare rankings of systems produced by different evaluation conditions, such as different assessors [6], effectiveness measures [4] or topic sets [1]. One reason for this success is their simplicity: they provide a single score that is easy to understand.

In this paper we tackle the problem of estimating the correlation between the ranking of systems obtained with a test collection and the *true* ranking under the same conditions. Such estimates can make a nice companion to a set of evaluation results, as a single figure of the reliability of the experiment. Voorhees and Buckley [7] proposed to report a similar figure in terms of sensitivity, that is, the minimum difference required between two systems to ensure a maximum error rate in relative comparisons. Common practice nowadays is to report the p-value of a statistical significance test run either for each pair of systems (e.g. t-test) or for the whole set (e.g. ANOVA and F-test). They provide a sense of confidence about individual pairs of systems or about a swap somewhere in the ranking, but they do not give a general idea of how similar the observed ranking is to the truth.

We propose parametric and non-parametric approaches to estimate the τ and AP correlations. Through large scale simulation with TREC data, we show that they have very low bias and small error even for mid-sized collections.

SIGIR '16, July 17 - 21, 2016, Pisa, Italy

ISBN 978-1-4503-4069-4/16/07...$15.00
DOI: http://dx.doi.org/10.1145/2911451.2914752

2. CORRELATION BETWEEN TWO RANKINGS

Let $A = \langle a_1, \dots, a_m \rangle$ and $B = \langle b_1, \dots, b_m \rangle$ be the mean scores of the same set of m systems as observed under two different evaluation conditions, such that a_i and b_i refer to the i-th system. In many situations we are interested in the distance between the two rankings. Considering systems in pairs, a distance can be computed by counting how many pairs are concordant or discordant between the two rankings: a pair is concordant if their relative order is the same in both rankings, and discordant if it is the opposite. Kendall [3] followed this idea to define his τ correlation coefficient

$$\tau = \frac{\#concordants - \#discordants}{total} = 1 - 2\frac{\#discordants}{total}, \quad (1)$$

which evaluates to -1 when the rankings are reversed, $+1$ when they are the same, and 0 when there are as many concordant pairs as there are discordant. Note that the term *#discordants/total* can be interpreted as the expected value of a random experiment: pick two arbitrary systems and return 1 if they are discordant, or 0 if they are concordant. The Kendall τ coefficient can thus be interpreted in terms of the probability of discordance.

Yilmaz et al. [8] followed this idea to define a correlation coefficient with the same rationale as Average Precision. It is similar to Kendall τ, but it penalizes more if swaps occur between systems at the top of the ranking, much like AP penalizes more if the non-relevant documents appear at the top of the results. In particular, they considered that one of the rankings, say B, is the true ranking and the other one is an estimate of it. The random experiment is now as follows: pick one system at random from A and another one ranked above it, and return 1 if they are discordant, or 0 if they are concordant. Their AP correlation coefficient can then be defined just as in (1) as follows:

$$\tau_{AP} = 1 - \frac{2}{m-1}\sum_{i=2}^{m}\left(\frac{\#\text{discordants above } i}{i-1}\right). \quad (2)$$

Note that τ_{AP} also ranges between -1 and $+1$.

3. EXPECTED CORRELATION WITH THE TRUE RANKING

The previous section contemplated the case where we compute the correlation between two given rankings A and B. In this section we study the case where we are given a ranking A obtained with the sample of topics in the test collection, and want to estimate its correlation with the true ranking B over the population of topics, which is of course unknown. For simplicity, let us first assume that the systems are already sorted in descending order by their mean score. Let us further define D_{ij} as the random variable that equals 1 if systems i and j are discordant and 0 otherwise, that is, whether they are swapped in the true ranking. Both τ and τ_{AP} can be re-defined from (1) and (2) in terms of D_{ij} alone:

$$\tau = 1 - \frac{4}{m(m-1)}\sum_{i=1}^{m-1}\sum_{j=i+1}^{m} D_{ij}, \quad (3)$$

$$\tau_{AP} = 1 - \frac{2}{m-1}\sum_{i=1}^{m-1}\sum_{j=1}^{i-1}\frac{D_{ij}}{i-1}. \quad (4)$$

Since they are just a linear combination of random variables, their expectations are as in (3) and (4) but replacing D_{ij} with $\mathrm{E}[D_{ij}]$. Note that each D_{ij} is a Bernoulli random variable, so its expectation is just the probability of discordance $\mathrm{E}[D_{ij}] = P(\mu_i - \mu_j < 0) = p_{ij}$. The problem of estimating the correlation with the true ranking thus boils down to estimating the probability that any two systems are swapped. The next subsection presents four ways of achieving this.

3.1 Estimating the Probability of Discordance

Since each p_{ij} is estimated independently from the other systems, let us simplify notation here to just p. In addition, let $X_1, \dots, X_n$ be the differences in effectiveness between the two systems and for each of the n topics in the collection. The problem is therefore to estimate $p = P(\mu < 0)$ from these n observations. Recall that systems are assumed to be ranked by mean observed scores, so $\overline{X} > 0$.

In the following we present two parametric estimators based on the Central Limit Theorem (CLT) and then two non-parametric estimators based on resampling.

3.1.1 Maximum Likelihood (ML)

The CLT tells us that $\overline{X}$ is approximately normally distributed with mean μ and variance σ^2/n as $n \to \infty$. Using the *cdf* of the normal distribution we can therefore estimate the probability of discordance. However, our estimates are likely off with small samples (see Section 3.1.2), so we assume $X_i \sim N(\mu, \sigma^2)$ and employ the t distribution to account for the uncertainty in estimating σ^2. Standardizing, we have that $\sqrt{n}(\overline{X} - \mu)/\sigma \sim t(n-1)$, so

$$p = P(\mu < 0) \approx T_{n-1}\left(-\sqrt{n}\frac{\hat{\mu}}{\hat{\sigma}}\right), \quad (5)$$

where T_{n-1} is the *cdf* of the t distribution with $n-1$ degrees of freedom. The estimates $\hat{\mu}$ and $\hat{\sigma}$ are computed via Maximum Likelihood as

$$\hat{\mu} = \overline{X} = \frac{1}{n}\sum X_i, \quad (6)$$

$$\hat{\sigma} = s \cdot C_n, \quad (7)$$

$$s = \sqrt{\frac{1}{n-1}\sum (X_i - \overline{X})^2},$$

$$C_n = \sqrt{\frac{n-1}{2}}\frac{\Gamma((n-1)/2)}{\Gamma(n/2)},$$

where s is the sample standard deviation. The C_n factor [2] ensures that $\mathrm{E}[\hat{\sigma}] = \sigma$. This bias correction is applied because, even though s^2 is an unbiased estimator of σ^2, by Jensen's inequality s is *not* an unbiased estimator of σ.

3.1.2 Minimum Squared Quantile Deviation (MSQD)

The problem when estimating σ from a small sample is that the observations are likely to be concentrated around the mean and seldom occur near the tails. As a consequence, (7) is likely to underestimate the true dispersion in the population. If the sample contains a few dozen observations this is not expected to be a problem, but with very small samples of, say, just 10 topics, it might be.

We propose a new and generic estimator to avoid this problem. Let us consider a distribution function F with parameter θ. A random sample from this distribution is expected to uniformly cover the quantile space, that is, all quantiles are equally likely to appear in the sample. Thus, when we are given a sample we may force them to uniformly cover the quantile space and then select the θ that minimizes the observed deviations. For instance, if our sample contains only one observation, we force it to correspond to the quantile $1/2$; if we have two observations then we force them to be the quantiles $1/3$ and $2/3$. In general, if R_i is the rank of X_i within the sample, it will correspond to the $R_i/(n+1)$ quantile, which is $F^{-1}(\frac{R_i}{n+1}; \theta)$. The squared quantile deviation of an observation X_i is therefore

$$SQD(X_i; \theta) = \left(F^{-1}\left(\frac{R_i}{n+1}; \theta\right) - X_i\right)^2.$$

The Minimum Squared Quantile Deviation estimator is then the one that minimizes the sum of squared deviations:

$$\hat{\theta}_{MSQD} = \underset{\theta \in \Theta}{\arg\min} \sum SQD(X_i; \theta).$$

Let us assume again a normal distribution, so that

$$F^{-1}\left(\frac{R_i}{n+1}; \mu, \sigma\right) = \mu + \sigma\sqrt{2}e_i,$$

$$e_i = \mathrm{erf}^{-1}\left(2\frac{R_i}{n+1} - 1\right).$$

The sum of squared deviations is thus

$$\sum \mu^2 - \overset{\to 0}{\cancel{2\mu\sigma\sqrt{2}e_i}} + 2\sigma^2 e_i^2 - 2X_i\mu - 2X_i\sigma\sqrt{2}e_i + X_i^2,$$

and the second term cancels out because $\sum e_i = 0$. To find the μ and σ that minimize this expression, we simply differentiate, equal to 0, and solve. The partial derivatives are

$$\frac{\mathrm{d}SQD}{\mathrm{d}\mu} = \sum 2\mu - 2X_i = 2n\mu - 2\sum X_i \text{ and}$$

$$\frac{\mathrm{d}SQD}{\mathrm{d}\sigma} = \sum 4\sigma e_i^2 - 2\sqrt{2}X_i e_i,$$

and therefore, the estimators are

$$\hat{\mu} = \frac{1}{n}\sum X_i = \overline{X}, \tag{8}$$

$$\hat{\sigma} = \frac{\sqrt{2}\sum X_i \cdot \mathrm{erf}^{-1}\left(2\frac{R_i}{n+1} - 1\right)}{2\sum \mathrm{erf}^{-1}\left(2\frac{R_i}{n+1} - 1\right)^2}. \tag{9}$$

As above, the probability of discordance is estimated with the *cdf* of the t distribution as in (5), but using estimators (8) and (9) instead of (6) and (7).

3.1.3 Resampling (RES)

In both the ML and MSQD estimators above we assumed that scores are normally distributed, but this is clearly not strictly true. A non-parametric alternative is the use of resampling to estimate the sampling distribution of the mean and from there the probability of discordance.

Suppose we draw a random sample $X_1^*, \ldots, X_n^*$ with replacement from our original observations, and compute their sample mean $\overline{X}^*$. This experiment is replicated $T = 1,000$ times, yielding sample means $\overline{X}_1^*, \ldots, \overline{X}_T^*$. By the law of large numbers, the distribution of these sample means converges to the sampling distribution of $\overline{X}$ as $T \to \infty$. The probability of discordance can thus be estimated as the fraction of times that $\overline{X}_i^*$ is negative:

$$p = P(\mu < 0) \approx \frac{1}{T}\sum \mathrm{I}\left[\overline{X}_i^* < 0\right]. \tag{10}$$

3.1.4 Kernel Density (KD)

A potential problem with resampling from the original observations is again that estimates from very small samples are likely off. An alternative is to approximate the true *pdf* via Kernel Density Estimation, and use it to estimate the probability of discordance. The estimated *pdf* has the form

$$\hat{f}(x) = \frac{1}{nh}\sum k\left(\frac{x - X_i}{h}\right),$$

where k is the *pdf* of the kernel and h is the bandwidth. Next, we need to estimate the sampling distribution of the mean, which is basically the distribution of the sum of n variables drawn from $\hat{f}$. For $n = 2$ this requires the evaluation of the self-convolution of $\hat{f}$ as follows:

$$\hat{f}_{X+X}(x) = \frac{1}{n^2h^2}\sum_i\sum_j \int k\left(\frac{x-z-X_i}{h}\right)k\left(\frac{z-X_j}{h}\right)\mathrm{d}z,$$

which involves the sum of n^2 terms. In general, for n variables this requires the evaluation of n^n terms, which is clearly unfeasible even for small samples, so instead we resort to Monte Carlo methods. As with the RES estimator, we generate a random sample $X_1^*, \ldots, X_n^*$ from $\hat{f}$ and compute the mean $\overline{X}^*$. After T replications, the probability of discordance is estimated as the fraction of times that $\overline{X}_i^*$ is negative. We set $T = 1,000$ replications and use gaussian kernels.

4. EVALUATION

4.1 Criteria

There are two properties of the correlation estimators that we are interested in, namely error and bias. Error refers to the expected difference between the estimate and the truth. Here we measure absolute error, thus quantifying the expected magnitude of the error when estimating the correlation of a given collection:

$$error = \mathrm{E}\left[\left|\hat{\tau}(\mathbf{A}) - \tau(\mathbf{A}, \boldsymbol{\mu})\right|\right].$$

Even if the error is small, it could tend to be in the same direction, that is, over- or underestimating the correlation. Bias refers to this tendency, measured as the expected difference between the estimated and the true correlation:

$$bias = \mathrm{E}\left[\hat{\tau}(\mathbf{A}) - \tau(\mathbf{A}, \boldsymbol{\mu})\right].$$

If the bias is positive it means that the estimator tends to overestimate the correlations. In general, we seek estimators with small error and zero bias.

4.2 Methods, Data and Baselines

From the above definitions it is evident that we need to know the true ranking of systems $\boldsymbol{\mu}$, but this is of course unknown. To solve this problem we resort to the simulation method proposed by Urbano [5]. Given the topic-by-system matrix of scores $\mathbf{B}$ from an existing collection, it generates a new matrix $\mathbf{A}$ with the scores by the same set of systems over a new and random set of topics. There are two important characteristics of this method that are appealing for us. First, the simulated scores are realistic, as they maintain the same distributions and correlations among systems as in the original collection. Second, it is designed to ensure that the expected mean score of a system is equal to the mean score in the original collection, that is, $\mathrm{E}\left[\overline{A}_s\right] = \overline{B}_s$. For us, this means that the true mean scores are fixed to be the mean scores in the original collection, that is, $\mu_s := \overline{B}_s$. This allows us to analyze the error and bias of the estimators with a large number of simulated, yet realistic test collections.

We use the TREC 6, 7 and 8 ad hoc collections as evaluated with Average Precision. As is common practice, we first drop the bottom 25% of results to avoid effects of possibly buggy systems. From each original collection, we simulate 1,000 new collections of sizes $n = 10, 20, \ldots, 100$ topics, leading to a total of 30,000 simulated collections. For each of them, we estimate τ and τ_{AP} using each of the estimators defined above, and also compute the true correlations (recall that this is possible because the true system scores are fixed upfront when simulating new collections). Finally, for each correlation coefficient, original collection, topic set size and estimator, we compute expected error and bias.

Two baselines are used to compare our estimators to. They are based on a split-half method that randomly splits the available topic set in two subsets, and then computes the correlations as if one was the truth and the other one the estimate. This is replicated a number of times for different subset sizes, up to a maximum of $n/2$ topics. The observations are then used to fit a model and extrapolate the expected correlation with n topics. This simple estimator is found for instance in [7, 4]. Here we run 2,000 replicates to fit the model $y = a \cdot e^{b \cdot x}$, and sample topics with and without replacement, leading to baselines SH(w) and SH(w/o).

4.3 Results

Figure 1 shows that the error of the estimators is larger with small collections. This is somewhat expected, because collections with too few topics are unstable and the rankings of systems vary too much to begin with. The error seems to plateau at about 0.025 in all our estimators, though with small collections of just 10 topics they are expected to be off by about 0.065. With the usual 50 topics, the expected error is 0.035. We can finally observe that the typical SH

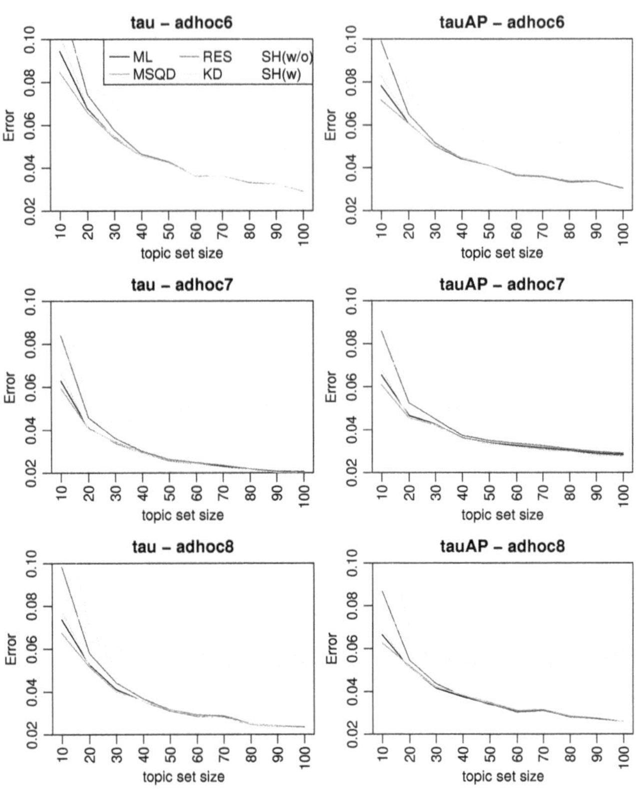

Figure 1: Error of the estimators of τ (left) and τ_{AP} (right) for each of the three original collections.

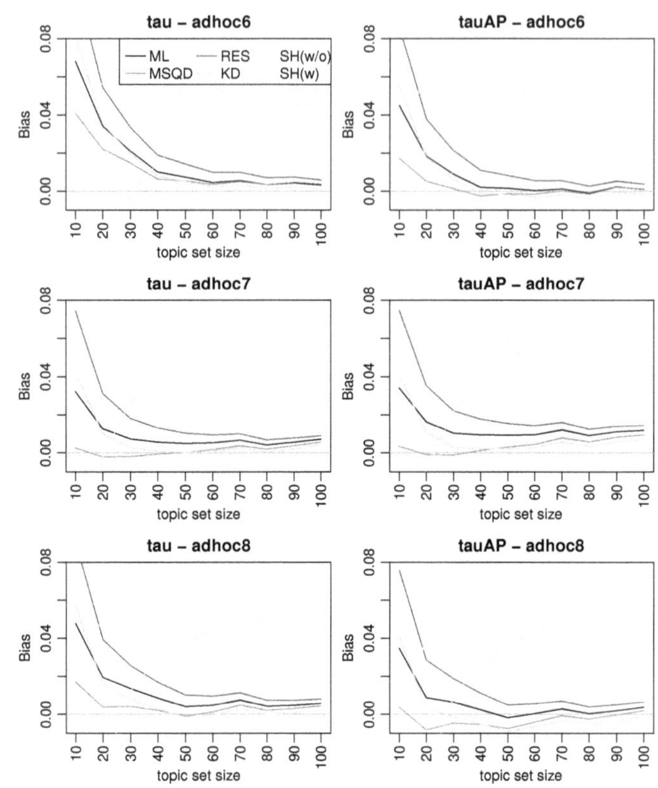

Figure 2: Bias of the estimators of τ (left) and τ_{AP} (right) for each of the three original collections.

estimators are clearly outperformed by all our proposed estimators. In general, with 30–40 topics they behave almost the same, but with small samples MSQD is slightly better.

Figure 2 shows that the correlations tend to be overestimated, especially with small collections, but this time we see clear differences among estimators. MSQD behaves much better than the others, especially with very small collections. With only 10 topics ML outperforms KD because there is just too little data to properly approximate the *pdf*, but with 20 or more topics it does a very good job at approximating the true distribution. ML, on the other hand, assumes a normal distribution and can therefore be less faithful to the data. Even at around 40–50 topics KD gets to slightly outperform MSQD for the same reason. Overall, they seem to plateau at about 0.004, and RES always performs worse than the others. Finally, the SH estimator with replacement has a roughly constant bias of about 0.055. The SH estimator without replacement shows a clearly biased behavior probably due to the choice of model.

5. CONCLUSION

In this paper we present two estimators of the Kendall τ and AP rank correlation coefficients between the mean system scores produced by a test collection and the true, unobservable means. We proposed parametric and non-parametric alternatives, and through large scale simulation with realistic collections we showed that even with small topic sets the estimators have little bias and the errors are generally small with collections of medium size. These estimators may prove useful as an easy to understand indicator of reliability in the results of an evaluation experiment.

In light of the expected error with individual collections, our future work will mainly focus on the development of interval estimates. We also plan to study other estimators of discordance as well as the application of a fully bayesian approach to estimate correlations. All the results in this paper are fully reproducible with data and code available online at `http://github.com/julian-urbano/sigir2016-correlation`.

Acknowledgments. Work supported by the Spanish Government: JdC postdoctoral fellowship, and projects TIN2015-70816-R and MDM-2015-0502. Florentino dimisión.

References

[1] B. Carterette, V. Pavlu, E. Kanoulas, J. A. Aslam, and J. Allan. If I Had a Million Queries. In *ECIR*, 2009.

[2] W. H. Holtzman. The Unbiased Estimate of the Population Variance and Standard Deviation. *Am. J. Psychology*, 1950.

[3] M. G. Kendall. A New Measure of Rank Correlation. *Biometrika*, 1938.

[4] T. Sakai. On the Reliability of Information Retrieval Metrics Based on Graded Relevance. *Inf. Proc. & Mngmnt*, 2007.

[5] J. Urbano. Test Collection Reliability: A Study of Bias and Robustness to Statistical Assumptions via Stochastic Simulation. *Information Retrieval*, 2016.

[6] E. M. Voorhees. Variations in Relevance Judgments and the Measurement of Retrieval Effectiveness. In *SIGIR*, 1998.

[7] E. M. Voorhees and C. Buckley. The Effect of Topic Set Size on Retrieval Experiment Error. In *SIGIR*, 2002.

[8] E. Yilmaz, J. Aslam, and S. Robertson. A New Rank Correlation Coefficient for Information Retrieval. In *SIGIR*, 2008.

Tracking Sentiment by Time Series Analysis

Anastasia Giachanou
Faculty of Informatics
Università della Svizzera italiana
Switzerland
anastasia.giachanou@usi.ch

Fabio Crestani
Faculty of Informatics
Università della Svizzera italiana
Switzerland
fabio.crestani@usi.ch

ABSTRACT

In recent years social media have emerged as popular platforms for people to share their thoughts and opinions on all kind of topics. Tracking opinion over time is a powerful tool that can be used for sentiment prediction or to detect the possible reasons of a sentiment change. Understanding topic and sentiment evolution allows enterprises or government to capture negative sentiment and act promptly. In this study, we explore conventional time series analysis methods and their applicability on topic and sentiment trend analysis. We use data collected from Twitter that span over nine months. Finally, we study the usability of outliers detection and different measures such as sentiment velocity and acceleration on the task of sentiment tracking.

CCS Concepts

•**Mathematics of computing** → **Time series analysis;**
•**Information systems** → **Sentiment analysis;**

Keywords

sentiment dynamics, sentiment change, time series analysis

1. INTRODUCTION

Recent years have seen the rapid growth of social media platforms that enable people to express their thoughts and perceptions on the web and share them with other users. Many people write their opinion about products, movies, people or events on microblogs, blogs, forums or review sites. The so-called User Generated Content (UGC) is a good source of user opinions and mining it can be very useful for a wide variety of applications that require understanding public opinion about a concept. For example, enterprises can capture negative or positive opinions of customers about products or about competitors and improve the quality of their services or products accordingly. It is also very important for government to understand the public opinion regarding different social issues and act promptly.

SIGIR '16, July 17-21, 2016, Pisa, Italy
 ISBN 978-1-4503-4069-4/16/07...$15.00
DOI: http://dx.doi.org/10.1145/2911451.2914702

Sentiment analysis focuses on developing methods that can classify a text as expressing positive or negative sentiment [7, 3]. However, public opinion towards a specific topic changes over time. Time series models seem to be an appropriate tool for sentiment tracking. Leveraging time series analysis on public opinions can be useful to understand data and identify patterns, trends and seasonality. In addition, time series is helpful in identifying outliers which are likely to be related with events that caused a sentiment change. Finally, they can be useful for sentiment prediction and intervention analysis that capture future sentiment and detect the effect of a single event on the public opinion respectively.

The development of models that focus on sentiment dynamics has recently attracted much research interest. Bollen et al. [2] performed a sentiment analysis of all public tweets posted from the 1st of August to the 20th of December, 2008 and mapped every day to a six dimensional mood vector. In another study, O'Connor et al. [6] investigated the relation between opinion expressed in tweets and public opinion obtained by polls. To this end, authors retrieved relevant tweets to some specific topics and then estimated the sentiment score of every day. An et al. [1] explored whether mining social media data can be used to yield insights on climate change sentiment whereas Nguyen et al. [4] tried to predict the sentiment change using a feature based method.

The aim of this preliminary study is to explore the usability of conventional time series methods on sentiment tracking and how they can be leveraged to address other challenging tasks such as detection of reasons of sentiment change. We first explore and decompose the data we collected from Twitter about different topics with the aim to identify patterns, trends and seasonality. In addition, we try to detect the outliers and investigate their usability in detecting important events or reasons of change. This is very important as it is possible to use the data that are around those peaks to automatically detect the sentiment change reasons.

2. DYNAMIC SENTIMENT TRACKING

In this initial study we explore conventional time series analysis methods on data collected from Twitter. The study mainly focuses on presenting the preliminary steps that are critical to track sentiment from social media.

Frequency Analysis. The initial step in time series analysis is to explore the data and observe how the frequencies change. Let $X = (x_1, x_2, .., x_n)$ be a set of data observed at consecutive and equal time partitions denoted as $\{t_1, t_2, ..., t_n\}$. Based on this, we can observe how the number of tweets about a topic z changes per day, denoted as $N_t(z)$. This time series is an indicator of the popularity of the topic independent from the sentiment that is expressed.

To explore sentiment trends we need to measure the frequencies of tweets that express a specific sentiment. For reasons of simplification, we only consider positive and negative sentiment. However, the approach can be also applied on sentiments that represent emotions such as love, anger, sadness etc. Let $N_t(z, s)$ be the number of tweets that express a sentiment s towards a specific topic z posted during a particular time period t and $N_t(z)$ the number of total tweets posted towards z at t. Then, we can define the ratio of tweets that share a common sentiment s as:

$$r_t(z, s) = \frac{N_t(z, s)}{N_t(z)}$$

Based on this, we can measure the *sentiment velocity* that represents the rate of sentiment change and is defined as: $Vel_t(z, s) = N_{t+1}(z, s) - N_t(z, s)$. Based on this we can measure *sentiment acceleration* that represents the rate of change of sentiment velocity at a particular time t. The sentiment acceleration of topic z and sentiment s is defined as: $Acc_t(z, s) = Vel_{t+1}(z, s) - Vel_t(z, s)$. Plotting sentiment velocity and acceleration is useful not only to observe how a specific sentiment changes but also to detect if there is any emerging sentiment. For example, a negative emerging sentiment about a specific topic means that the company should be alerted and act promptly.

Time Series Decomposition. To get better understanding of the data we further apply time series decomposition. According to decomposition that is of crucial importance for the subsequent analysis and modeling, time series data can be decomposed into three components: the trend (T_t), the seasonal (S_t) and the random (R_t). Based on this, we can define the time series X_t as a function of these components: $X_t = f(T_t, S_t, R_t)$.

The decomposition is such that the three components add up to the original time series. One well known decomposition method is the additive decomposition defined as: $y_t = T + S + R$. The trend component reflects the long-term increase or decrease in the data. Another way to find the trend is to smooth the data and remove any wide variation such as the seasonality. *Moving average* is one of the most well known smoothing techniques and can be very helpful to identify patterns and trends in time series because it evens out short term fluctuations and makes the trend more apparent. According to this approach, the value of data at time t is the unweighted mean of the data observed at the k previous time periods. This is defined as:

$$MA_t = \frac{x_{t-(k-1)} + \ldots + x_{t-1} + x_t}{k}$$

The seasonal component represents patterns that are repeated at fixed periods like days, weeks, months etc. *Seasonal adjustment* is a method for removing the seasonal component of a time series. This is useful to observe the data without the seasonal effects that may have an influence on them. One typical example is that users may tweet more at specific days or specific time. Seasonally adjusted data can be constructed as: $SeasAdj_t = X_t - S_t$. Finally, the random component represents noise in data and can be constructed by removing the trend and seasonal components as: $R_t = X_t - T_t - S_t$.

Outlier Detection. The last tool we explore is the detection of outliers and its usability on identifying the reasons of sentiment change. The outliers that are visually depicted as sudden peaks may be caused because of false measurements or because of some important events. We are mostly interested on those caused by some events. These important events not only influence the popularity of a topic but also the public sentiment towards the topic. Therefore, we believe that the data related with outliers may be useful in detecting possible reasons of a sentiment change.

In order to identify the outliers we use the following equation: $e_i = x_i - x'_i$ where x_i is the observation i and x'_i is the prediction of the observation i. In other words, this equation calculates the ordinary residuals for each observation. We use *LOESS* that is also known as locally weighted polynomial regression model and interquartile range to detect the residuals. Let Q_1 and Q_3 be the lower and upper quartiles respectively, then the outliers are the observations that are outside the following range:

$$[Q_1 - k * (Q_3 - Q_1), Q_3 + k * (Q_3 - Q_1)]$$

where k represents the span of the range and it is usually set between 1.5 and 3.0.

3. EXPERIMENTAL SETUP

A tweets' dataset that spans over several months was required for our study. However, due to the restriction in tweets' redistribution, a large part of tweets in existing collections is missing. Also, it is not possible to extend the existing collections and include data from additional months. Therefore, we started collecting data from Twitter since the 10th of April 2015. Due to the required preprocessing, in this study we use data[1] collected until the 31st of December 2015. To collect tweets we used a list of 70 topics from different domains including politics, TV series, cities, products etc. In our study, we focus on the following topics: *android lollipop* (346.714 tweets), *Michelle Obama* (1.076.732 tweets) and *Merkel* (1.369.756 tweets).

Preprocessing was performed on the data before the subsequent experiments which involved stop-word removal and stemming. For identifying the opinionated terms we use the AFINN Lexicon [5]. AFINN contains more than 2000 words each of which is assigned a valence from -5 to -1 for terms with a negative sentiment or from 1 to 5 for terms with a positive sentiment. The sentiment score of each tweet is a sum of the scores of its opinion words. We chose to use a simple approach to assign the sentiment score since our focus is not on sentiment analysis but on sentiment tracking. However, in future we plan to use a more complex method.

4. RESULTS

Figure 1 shows the number of total, positive and negative tweets published every day for the topic *android lollipop*. From this figure, we observe that the popularity of the topic is decreasing. It is also clear that there are some peaks that may be related to some important events. However, it may be also the case that these peaks are related to seasonal effects. To have better understanding of the data we need to isolate the different components.

Figure 2 shows the decomposition of the topic *android lollipop*. The decomposition confirms that the trend of the topic is decreasing. Also, there is a seasonal effect on the

[1] To get access to the collection, please contact the authors

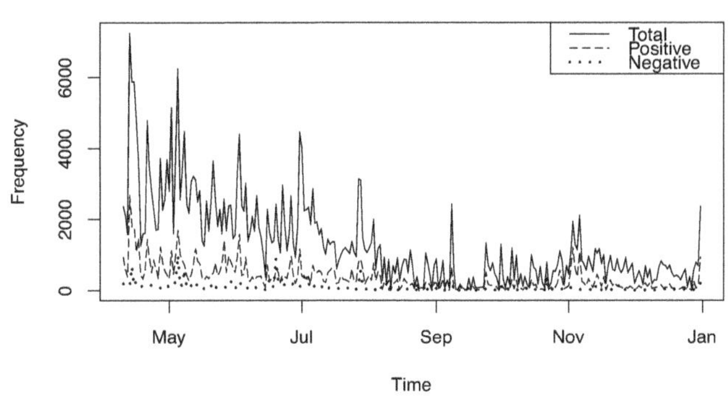

Figure 1: Number of total, positive and negative tweets of "android lollipop" topic per day

data. One possible explanation is that users tend to post more tweets on specific days of the week.

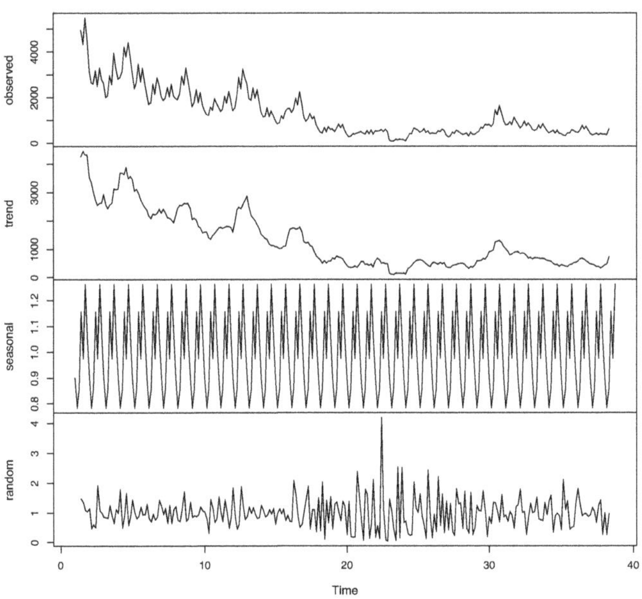

Figure 2: Decomposition of "android lollipop" topic

Another way to find the trend is to apply the moving average approach. Figure 3 shows the total, positive and negative number of tweets about the topic *Merkel* after applying the method of moving average using the past 10 days. In this case, we do not see any clear trend meaning that the popularity of this topic remains stable with a slight decreasing tendency. In its largest part, the positive and negative sentiment follow the trend of the topic's popularity. However, there are also cases that one sentiment seems to be stronger than the other. For example, in the end of November negative sentiment is stronger than positive. Looking through the collection and the news, we believe that this negative sentiment is related to the event mentioned in news as "Merkel under pressure from her own ahead of EU migration summit" that took place around the 27th of November.

The comparison between positive and negative tweets is better depicted on Figure 4 that shows the ratios of negative and positive over the total number of tweets collected for the topic *Merkel*. As expected, the sentiments tend to follow a contradictory behavior meaning that when positive sentiment trend is increasing the negative is decreasing and vice versa. For example, in the early of August the positive sentiment is clearly the dominant one whereas the negative has a very low ratio. This large difference implies that the positive sentiment was emerging at this specific time. Looking through the collection and the web, we discovered that on the 5th of August, "Merkel went to GlobalCitizen festival to show support for food security and nutrition for 500M people". We believe that this was the event that increased the positive sentiment. Knowing that this action was regarded positively by people is an important information for the press and information office of politicians.

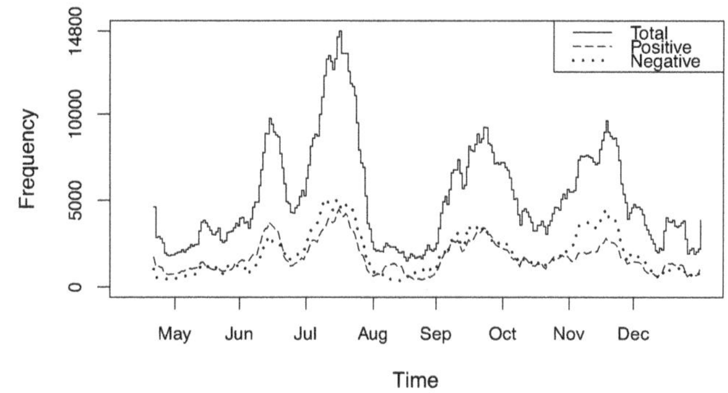

Figure 3: Smoothed data of "Merkel" topic

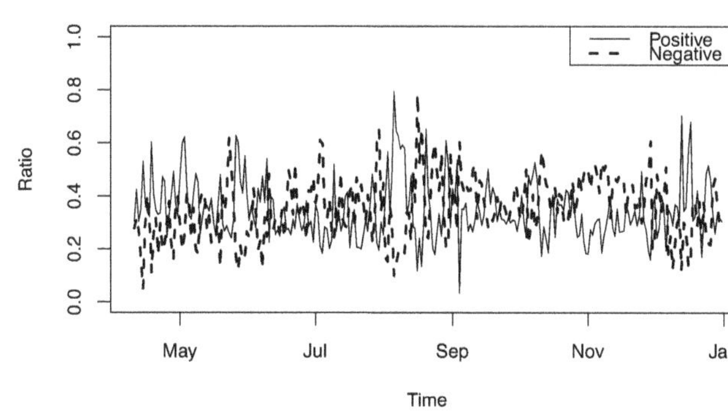

Figure 4: Ratio of positive and negative tweets about "Merkel" topic per day

Some important information is also reflected with sentiment velocity and acceleration that help us to understand how quickly a topic is gaining or losing preference. Figure 5 shows the positive and negative velocity and acceleration of the topic *Merkel*. Here, we observe that the negative sentiment grows faster in the middle of July whereas in August the positive sentiment has greater acceleration that lasts only few days.

Finally, we explore the usability of detecting outliers in finding reasons of sentiment change. Figure 6 shows the number of total, positive and negative tweets published every day for the topic *Michelle Obama* together with the detected peaks when retweets are considered and not. From

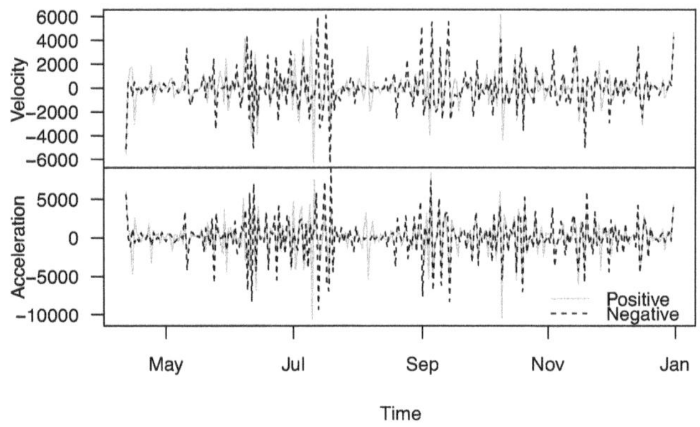

Figure 5: Velocity and acceleration of positive and negative tweets about "Merkel" topic per day

this figure we can observe the time when there was a sudden change in topic popularity or in sentiment towards the specific topic. Knowing the time of a potential peak is useful in identifying the events that caused those peaks. Apart from that, we observe that the peaks in topic's popularity, positive and negative peaks occur at different time periods. This implies that a sudden peak in a topic's popularity does not mean that there will be emerging sentiment. Another observation is that there are peaks that at different time points when we do and when we do not consider the retweets. This is an effect of the users's tendency to retweet some messages, an attitude that increases the popularity of the topic. Although retweets do not contain an explicit opinion, they can be seen as an endorsement of positive or negative sentiments. However, if few tweets are retweeted a lot, we may miss other events. Therefore, we believe that data should be explored in both scenarios. considering retweets and not.

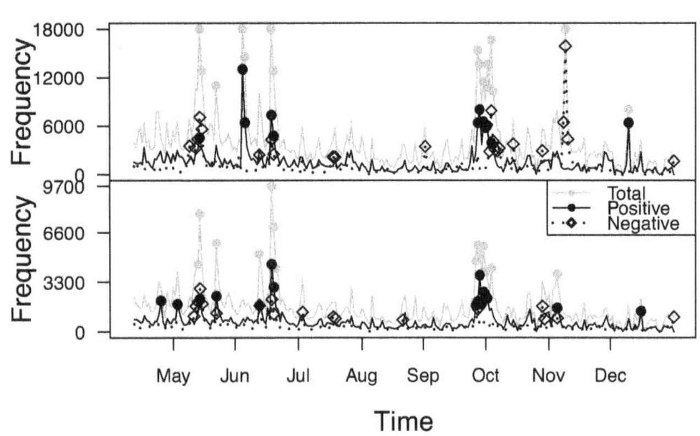

Figure 6: Number of total, positive and negative tweets about "Michelle Obama" when retweets are considered and when they are not per day

To understand the reasons of change on topic's sentiment, we need to look through the tweets that were published not only on the specific day but also a bit before and a bit after this day. Table 1 shows some manually detected tweets that we believe caused emerging sentiment. In some cases the tweets are not adequate to reveal the events but we need to look through the web. For example, on the 5th of May there was a great amount of tweets saying that "Michelle Obama ruined our lunch". Looking for more information on web, we found that this is related to the fact that Michele Obama changed schools' lunch program but students did not like the change. This example shows some of the challenges in addressing the task of detecting reasons of sentiment change.

Table 1: Dates and reason of emerging sentiment

Day	Emerging sentiment	Potential reason
5 May	negative	Michelle Obama ruined our lunch
12 May	negative	Michelle Obama gave a talk and mentions racism
2 June	positive	Michelle Obama responds to Kanye!
26 Sep	positive	Barack Obama & Michelle Obama shut the Internet down with class
16 June	negative and positive	First Lady Michelle Obama Meets With Prince Harry Over Tea
28 Oct	negative	Prince Harry and Michelle Obama to Meet With Wounded Vets

5. CONCLUSIONS AND FUTURE WORK

In this study we explored the usability of time series methods on sentiment tracking. We plotted frequencies and decomposed data from Twitter to identify patterns, trends and seasonality. Also, we tried to identify peaks in topic's popularity and in sentiment and we investigated their usability in detecting important events or the reasons of sentiment change. We believe that this is a good start for the development of methods that could automatically detect a sentiment change and the reasons that caused it. In future we plan to explore these problems more thoroughly.

Acknowledgments

This research was partially funded by the Swiss National Science Foundation (SNSF) under the project OpiTrack.

6. REFERENCES

[1] X. An, R. A. Ganguly, Y. Fang, B. S. Scyphers, M. A. Hunter, and G. J. Dy. Tracking Climate Change Opinions from Twitter Data. In *KDD '14*, 2014.

[2] J. Bollen and A. Pepe. Modeling Public Mood and Emotion: Twitter Sentiment and Socio-Economic Phenomena. In *ICWSM '11*, pages 450–453, 2011.

[3] A. Giachanou and F. Crestani. Like it or not: A survey of twitter sentiment analysis methods. *ACM Computing Surveys*, in press.

[4] L. T. Nguyen, P. Wu, W. Chan, W. Peng, and Y. Zhang. Predicting Collective Sentiment Dynamics from Time-series Social Media. In *WSDOM'12*, 2012.

[5] F. Å. Nielsen. A new ANEW: Evaluation of a word list for sentiment analysis of microblogs. In *ESWC'11 Workshop on 'Making Sense of Microposts': Big things come in small packages*, pages 93–98, 2011.

[6] B. O'Connor, R. Balasubramanyan, B. Routledge, and N. Smith. From tweets to polls: Linking text sentiment to public opinion time series. In *ICWSM '10*, 2010.

[7] B. Pang and L. Lee. Opinion mining and sentiment analysis. *Foundations and Trends in Information Retrieval*, 2(1-2):1–135, 2008.

Tweet2Vec: Learning Tweet Embeddings Using Character-level CNN-LSTM Encoder-Decoder

Soroush Vosoughi*
MIT Media Lab
soroush@mit.edu

Prashanth Vijayaraghavan*
MIT Media Lab
pralav@mit.edu

Deb Roy
MIT Media Lab
dkroy@media.mit.edu

ABSTRACT

We present *Tweet2Vec*, a novel method for generating general-purpose vector representation of tweets. The model learns tweet embeddings using character-level CNN-LSTM encoder-decoder. We trained our model on 3 million, randomly selected English-language tweets. The model was evaluated using two methods: tweet semantic similarity and tweet sentiment categorization, outperforming the previous state-of-the-art in both tasks. The evaluations demonstrate the power of the tweet embeddings generated by our model for various tweet categorization tasks. The vector representations generated by our model are generic, and hence can be applied to a variety of tasks. Though the model presented in this paper is trained on English-language tweets, the method presented can be used to learn tweet embeddings for different languages.

CCS Concepts

•**Information systems** → **Document representation;** •**Computing methodologies** → **Neural networks;** *Information extraction; Lexical semantics;*

Keywords

Twitter; Embedding; Tweet; Convolutional Neural Networks; CNN; LSTM; Tweet2Vec; Encoder-decoder

1. INTRODUCTION

In recent years, the micro-blogging site Twitter has become a major social media platform with hundreds of millions of users. The short (140 character limit), noisy and idiosyncratic nature of tweets make standard information retrieval and data mining methods ill-suited to Twitter. Consequently, there has been an ever growing body of IR and data mining literature focusing on Twitter. However, most of these works employ extensive feature engineering to create task-specific, hand-crafted features. This is time consuming and inefficient as new features need to be engineered for every task.

In this paper, we present *Tweet2Vec*, a method for generating general-purpose vector representation of tweets that can be used for any classification task. *Tweet2Vec* removes the need for expansive feature engineering and can be used to train any standard off-the-shelf classifier (e.g., logistic regression, svm, etc). *Tweet2Vec* uses a CNN-LSTM encoder-decoder model that operates at the character level to learn and generate vector representation of tweets. Our method is especially useful for natural language processing tasks on Twitter where it is particularly difficult to engineer features, such as speech-act classification and stance detection (as shown in our previous works on these topics [13, 12]).

There has been several works on generating embeddings for words, most famously *Word2Vec* by Mikolov et al. [9]). There has also been a number of different works that use encoder-decoder models based on long short-term memory (LSTM) [11], and gated recurrent neural networks (GRU) [1]. These methods have been used mostly in the context of machine translation. The encoder maps the sentence from the source language to a vector representation, while the decoder conditions on this encoded vector for translating it to the target language. Perhaps the work most related to ours is the work of Le and Mikolov [7], where they extended the *Word2Vec* model to generate representations for sentences (called *ParagraphVec*). However, these models all function at the word level, making them ill-suited to the extremely noisy and idiosyncratic nature of tweets. Our character-level model, on the other hand, can better deal with the noise and idiosyncrasies in tweets. We plan to make our model and the data used to train it publicly available to be used by other researchers that work with tweets.

2. CNN-LSTM ENCODER-DECODER

In this section, we describe the CNN-LSTM encoder-decoder model that operates at the character level and generates vector representation of tweets. The encoder consists of convolutional layers to extract features from the characters and an LSTM layer to encode the sequence of features to a vector representation, while the decoder consists of two LSTM layers which predict the character at each time step from the output of encoder.

2.1 Character-Level CNN Tweet Model

Character-level CNN (CharCNN) is a slight variant of the deep character-level convolutional neural network intro-

*The first two authors contributed equally to this work.

SIGIR '16, July 17 - 21, 2016, Pisa, Italy

ISBN 978-1-4503-4069-4/16/07...$15.00

DOI: http://dx.doi.org/10.1145/2911451.2914762

duced by Zhang et al [15]. In this model, we perform temporal convolutional and temporal max-pooling operations, which computes one-dimensional convolution and pooling functions, respectively, between input and output. Given a discrete input function $f(x) \in [1, l] \mapsto \mathbb{R}$, a discrete kernel function $k(x) \in [1, m] \mapsto \mathbb{R}$ and stride s, the convolution $g(y) \in [1, (l-m+1)/s] \mapsto \mathbb{R}$ between $k(x)$ and $f(x)$ and pooling operation $h(y) \in [1, (l-m+1)/s] \mapsto \mathbb{R}$ of $f(x)$ is calculated as:

$$g(y) = \sum_{x=1}^{m} k(x) \cdot f(y \cdot s - x + c) \tag{1}$$

$$h(y) = max_{x=1}^{m} f(y \cdot s - x + c) \tag{2}$$

where $c = m - s + 1$ is an offset constant.

We adapted this model, which employs temporal convolution and pooling operations, for tweets. The character set includes the English alphabets, numbers, special characters and unknown character. There are 70 characters in total, given below:

```
abcdefghijklmnopqrstuvwxyz0123456789
-,;.!?:'"/\|_#$%&^*~'+-=<>()[]{}
```

Each character in the tweets can be encoded using one-hot vector $x_i \in \{0,1\}^{70}$. Hence, the tweets are represented as a binary matrix $x_{1..150} \in \{0,1\}^{150x70}$ with padding wherever necessary, where 150 is the maximum number of characters in a tweet (140 tweet characters and padding) and 70 is the size of the character set.

Each tweet, in the form of a matrix, is now fed into a deep model consisting of four 1-d convolutional layers. A convolution operation employs a filter $w \in \mathbb{R}^l$, to extract n-gram character feature from a sliding window of l characters at the first layer and learns abstract textual features in the subsequent layers. The convolution in the first layer operates on sliding windows of character (size l), and the convolutions in deeper layers are defined in a similar way. Generally, for tweet s, a feature c_i at layer h is generated by:

$$c_i^{(h)}(s) = g(w^{(h)}.\hat{c}_i^{(h-1)} + b^{(h)}) \tag{3}$$

where $\hat{c}_i^{(0)} = x_{i...i+l-1}$, $b^{(h)} \in \mathbb{R}$ is the bias at layer h and g is a rectified linear unit.

This filter w is applied across all possible windows of characters in the tweet to produce a feature map. The output of the convolutional layer is followed by a 1-d max-overtime pooling operation [2] over the feature map and selects the maximum value as the prominent feature from the current filter. In this way, we apply n filters at each layer. Pooling size may vary at each layer (given by $p^{(h)}$ at layer h). The pooling operation shrinks the size of the feature representation and filters out trivial features like unnecessary combination of characters. The window length l, number of filters f, pooling size p at each layer are given in Table 1.

We define $CharCNN(T)$ to denote the character-level CNN operation on input tweet matrix T. The output from the last convolutional layer of CharCNN(T) (size: 10×512) is subsequently given as input to the LSTM layer. Since LSTM works on sequences (explained in Section 2.2 and 2.3), pooling operation is restricted to the first two layers of the model (as shown in Table 1).

Table 1: Layer Parameters of CharCNN

Layer (h)	*Window Size* (l)	*Filters* (f)	*Pool Size* (p)
1	7	512	3
2	7	512	3
3	3	512	N/A
4	3	512	N/A

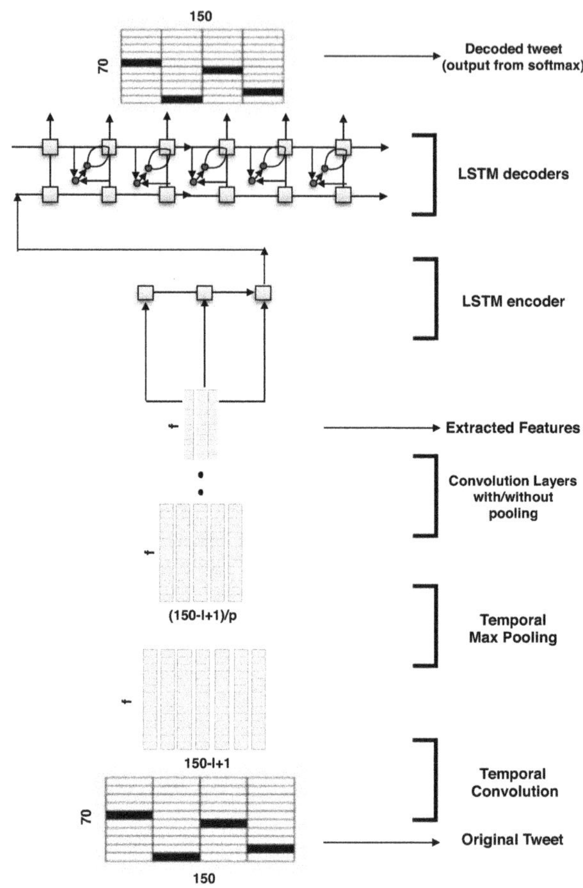

Figure 1: Illustration of the CNN-LSTM Encoder-Decoder Model

2.2 Long-Short Term Memory (LSTM)

In this section we briefly describe the LSTM model [4]. Given an input sequence $X = (x_1, x_2, ..., x_N)$, LSTM computes the hidden vector sequence $h = (h_1, h_2, ..., h_N)$ and and output vector sequence $Y = (y_1, y_2, ..., y_N)$. At each time step, the output of the module is controlled by a set of gates as a function of the previous hidden state h_{t1} and the input at the current time step x_t, the forget gate f_t, the input gate i_t, and the output gate o_t. These gates collectively decide the transitions of the current memory cell c_t and the current hidden state h_t. The LSTM transition functions are defined as follows:

$$\begin{aligned} i_t &= \sigma(W_i \cdot [h_{t-1}, x_t] + b_i) \\ f_t &= \sigma(W_f \cdot [h_{t-1}, x_t] + b_f) \\ l_t &= tanh(W_l \cdot [h_{t-1}, x_t] + b_l) \\ o_t &= \sigma(W_o[h_{t-1}, x_t] + b_o) \\ c_t &= f_t \odot c_{t-1} + i_t \odot l_t \\ h_t &= o_t \odot tanh(c_t) \end{aligned} \tag{4}$$

Here, σ is the *sigmoid* function that has an output in [0, 1], *tanh* denotes the hyperbolic tangent function that has an output in $[-1, 1]$, and $\odot$ denotes the component-wise multiplication. The extent to which the information in the old memory cell is discarded is controlled by f_t, while i_t controls the extent to which new information is stored in the current memory cell, and o_t is the output based on the memory cell c_t. LSTM is explicitly designed for learning long-term dependencies, and therefore we choose LSTM after the convolution layer to learn dependencies in the sequence of extracted features. In sequence-to-sequence generation tasks, an LSTM defines a distribution over outputs and sequentially predicts tokens using a softmax function.

$$P(Y|X) = \prod_{t\in[1,N]} \frac{exp(g(h_{t-1}, y_t))}{\sum_{y'} exp(g(h_{t1}, y'_t))} \tag{5}$$

where g is the activation function. For simplicity, we define $LSTM(x_t, h_{t-1})$ to denote the LSTM operation on input x at time-step t and the previous hidden state h_{t-1}.

2.3 The Combined Model

The CNN-LSTM encoder-decoder model draws on the intuition that the sequence of features (e.g. character and word n-grams) extracted from CNN can be encoded into a vector representation using LSTM that can embed the meaning of the whole tweet. Figure 1 illustrates the complete encoder-decoder model. The input and output to the model are the tweet represented as a matrix where each row is the one-hot vector representation of the characters. The procedure for encoding and decoding is explained in the following section.

2.3.1 Encoder

Given a tweet in the matrix form T (size: 150×70), the CNN (Section 2.1) extracts the features from the character representation. The one-dimensional convolution involves a filter vector sliding over a sequence and detecting features at different positions. The new successive higher-order window representations then are fed into LSTM (Section 2.2). Since LSTM extracts representation from sequence input, we will not apply pooling after convolution at the higher layers of Character-level CNN model. The encoding procedure can be summarized as:

$$H^{conv} = CharCNN(T) \tag{6}$$

$$h_t = LSTM(g_t, h_{t-1}) \tag{7}$$

where $g = H^{conv}$ is an extracted feature matrix where each row can be considered as a time-step for the LSTM and h_t is the hidden representation at time-step t. LSTM operates on each row of the H^{conv} along with the hidden vectors from previous time-step to produce embedding for the subsequent time-steps. The vector output at the final time-step, enc_N, is used to represent the entire tweet. In our case, the size of the enc_N is 256.

2.3.2 Decoder

The decoder operates on the encoded representation with two layers of LSTMs. In the initial time-step, the end-to-end output from the encoding procedure is used as the original input into first LSTM layer. The last LSTM decoder generates each character, C, sequentially and combines it with previously generated hidden vectors of size 128, h_{t-1}, for the next time-step prediction. The prediction of character at each time step is given by:

$$P(C_t|\cdot) = softmax(T_t, h_{t-1}) \tag{8}$$

where C_t refers to the character at time-step t, T_t represents the one-hot vector of the character at time-step t. The result from the softmax is a decoded tweet matrix T^{dec}, which is eventually compared with the actual tweet or a synonym-replaced version of the tweet (explained in Section 3) for learning the parameters of the model.

3. DATA AUGMENTATION & TRAINING

We trained the CNN-LSTM encoder-decoder model on 3 million randomly selected English-language tweets populated using data augmentation techniques, which are useful for controlling generalization error for deep learning models. Data augmentation, in our context, refers to replicating tweet and replacing some of the words in the replicated tweets with their synonyms. These synonyms are obtained from WordNet [3] which contains words grouped together on the basis of their meanings. This involves selection of replaceable words (example of non-replaceable words are stopwords, user names, hash tags, etc) from the tweet and the number of words n to be replaced. The probability of the number, n, is given by a geometric distribution with parameter l in which $P[n] \sim l^n$. Words generally have several synonyms, thus the synonym index m, of a given word is also determined by another geometric distribution in which $P[s] \sim r^m$. In our encoder-decoder model, we decode the encoded representation to the actual tweet or a synonym-replaced version of the tweet from the augmented data. We used $p = 0.5$, $r = 0.5$ for our training. We also make sure that the POS tags of the replaced words are not completely different from the actual words. For regularization, we apply a dropout mechanism after the penultimate layer. This prevents co-adaptation of hidden units by randomly setting a proportion ρ of the hidden units to zero (for our case, we set $\rho = 0.5$).

To learn the model parameters, we minimize the cross-entropy loss as the training objective using the Adam Optimization algorithm [5]. It is given by

$$CrossEnt(p, q) = -\sum p(x)\log(q(x)) \tag{9}$$

where p is the true distribution (one-hot vector representing characters in the tweet) and q is the output of the softmax. This, in turn, corresponds to computing the negative log-probability of the true class.

4. EXPERIMENTS

We evaluated our model using two classification tasks: *Tweet semantic relatedness* and *Tweet sentiment classification.*

4.1 Semantic Relatedness

The first evaluation is based on the SemEval 2015-Task 1: *Paraphrase and Semantic Similarity in Twitter* [14]. Given a pair of tweets, the goal is to predict their semantic equivalence (i.e., if they express the same or very similar meaning), through a binary yes/no judgement. The dataset provided for this task contains 18K tweet pairs for training and 1K pairs for testing, with 35% of these pairs being paraphrases, and 65% non-paraphrases.

We first extract the vector representation of all the tweets in the dataset using our *Tweet2Vec* model. We use two features to represent a tweet pair. Given two tweet vectors r and s, we compute their element-wise product $r \cdot s$ and their absolute difference $|r - s|$ and concatenate them together (Similar to [6]). We then train a logistic regression model on these features using the dataset. Cross-validation is used for tuning the threshold for classification. In contrast to our model, most of the methods used for this task were largely based on extensive use of feature engineering, or a combination of feature engineering with semantic spaces. Table 2 shows the performance of our model compared to the top four models in the SemEval 2015 competition, and also a model that was trained using *ParagraphVec*. Our model (*Tweet2Vec*) outperforms all these models, without resorting to extensive task-specific feature engineering.

Table 2: Results of the paraphrase and semantic similarity in Twitter task.

Model	*Precision*	*Recall*	$F1 - Score$
ParagraphVec	0.570	0.680	0.620
nnfeats	**0.767**	0.583	0.662
ikr	0.569	**0.806**	0.667
linearsvm	0.683	0.663	0.672
svckernel	0.680	0.669	0.674
Tweet2Vec	0.679	0.686	**0.677**

4.2 Sentiment Classification

The second evaluation is based on the SemEval 2015-Task 10B: *Twitter Message Polarity Classification* [10]. Given a tweet, the task is to classify it as either positive, negative or neutral in sentiment. The size of the training and test sets were 9,520 tweets and 2,380 tweets respectively (38% positive, 15% negative, and 47% neutral).

As with the last task, we first extract the vector representation of all the tweets in the dataset using *Tweet2Vec* and use that to train a logistic regression classifier using the vector representations. Even though there are three classes, the SemEval task is a binary task. The performance is measured as the average F1-score of the positive and the negative class. Table 3 shows the performance of our model compared to the top four models in the SemEval 2015 competition (note that only the F1-score is reported by SemEval for this task) and *ParagraphVec*. Our model outperforms all these models, again without resorting to any feature engineering.

Table 3: Results of Twitter sentiment classification task.

Model	*Precision*	*Recall*	$F1 - Score$
ParagraphVec	0.600	0.680	0.637
INESC-ID	N/A	N/A	0.642
lsislif	N/A	N/A	0.643
unitn	N/A	N/A	0.646
Webis	N/A	N/A	0.648
Tweet2Vec	0.675	0.719	**0.656**

5. CONCLUSION AND FUTURE WORK

In this paper, we presented *Tweet2Vec*, a novel method for generating general-purpose vector representation of tweets, using a character-level CNN-LSTM encoder-decoder architecture. To the best of our knowledge, ours is the first attempt at learning and applying character-level tweet embeddings. Our character-level model can deal with the noisy and peculiar nature of tweets better than methods that generate embeddings at the word level. Our model is also robust to synonyms with the help of our data augmentation technique using WordNet.

The vector representations generated by our model are generic, and thus can be applied to tasks of different nature. We evaluated our model using two different SemEval 2015 tasks: Twitter semantic relatedness, and sentiment classification. Simple, off-the-shelf logistic regression classifiers trained using the vector representations generated by our model outperformed the top-performing methods for both tasks, without the need for any extensive feature engineering. This was despite the fact that due to resource limitations, our *Tweet2Vec* model was trained on a relatively small set (3 million tweets). Also, our method outperformed *ParagraphVec*, which is an extension of *Word2Vec* to handle sentences. This is a small but noteworthy illustration of why our tweet embeddings are best-suited to deal with the noise and idiosyncrasies of tweets.

For future work, we plan to extend the method to include: 1) Augmentation of data through reordering the words in the tweets to make the model robust to word-order, 2) Exploiting attention mechanism [8] in our model to improve alignment of words in tweets during decoding, which could improve the overall performance.

6. REFERENCES

[1] J. Chung, C. Gulcehre, K. Cho, and Y. Bengio. Empirical evaluation of gated recurrent neural networks on sequence modeling. *arXiv preprint arXiv:1412.3555*, 2014.

[2] R. Collobert, J. Weston, L. Bottou, M. Karlen, K. Kavukcuoglu, and P. Kuksa. Natural language processing (almost) from scratch. *The Journal of Machine Learning Research*, 12:2493–2537, 2011.

[3] C. Fellbaum. *WordNet*. Wiley Online Library, 1998.

[4] S. Hochreiter and J. Schmidhuber. Long short-term memory. *Neural computation*, 9(8):1735–1780, 1997.

[5] D. Kingma and J. Ba. Adam: A method for stochastic optimization. *arXiv preprint arXiv:1412.6980*, 2014.

[6] R. Kiros, Y. Zhu, R. R. Salakhutdinov, R. Zemel, R. Urtasun, A. Torralba, and S. Fidler. Skip-thought vectors. In *Advances in Neural Information Processing Systems*, pages 3276–3284, 2015.

[7] Q. V. Le and T. Mikolov. Distributed representations of sentences and documents. *arXiv preprint arXiv:1405.4053*, 2014.

[8] J. Li, M.-T. Luong, and D. Jurafsky. A hierarchical neural autoencoder for paragraphs and documents. *arXiv preprint arXiv:1506.01057*, 2015.

[9] T. Mikolov, I. Sutskever, K. Chen, G. S. Corrado, and J. Dean. Distributed representations of words and phrases and their compositionality. In *Advances in neural information processing systems*, pages 3111–3119, 2013.

[10] S. Rosenthal, P. Nakov, S. Kiritchenko, S. Mohammad, A. Ritter, and V. Stoyanov. Semeval-2015 task 10: Sentiment analysis in twitter. In *SemEval*, 2015.

[11] I. Sutskever, O. Vinyals, and Q. V. Le. Sequence to sequence learning with neural networks. In *Advances in neural information processing systems*, pages 3104–3112, 2014.

[12] P. Vijayaraghavan, I. Sysoev, S. Vosoughi, and D. Roy. Deepstance at semeval-2016 task 6: Detecting stance in tweets using character and word-level cnns. 2016.

[13] S. Vosoughi and D. Roy. Tweet acts: A speech act classifier for twitter. In *proceedings of the 10th ICWSM*, 2016.

[14] W. Xu, C. Callison-Burch, and W. B. Dolan. Semeval-2015 task 1: Paraphrase and semantic similarity in twitter (pit). In *SemEval*, 2015.

[15] X. Zhang and Y. LeCun. Text understanding from scratch. *arXiv preprint arXiv:1502.01710*, 2015.

Two Sample T-tests for IR Evaluation: Student or Welch?

Tetsuya Sakai
Waseda University, Japan.
tetsuyasakai@acm.org

ABSTRACT

There are two well-known versions of the t-test for comparing means from unpaired data: Student's t-test and Welch's t-test. While Welch's t-test does not assume homoscedasticity (i.e., equal variances), it involves approximations. A classical textbook recommendation would be to use Student's t-test if either the two sample sizes are similar or the two sample variances are similar, and to use Welch's t-test only when both of the above conditions are violated. However, a more recent recommendation seems to be to use Welch's t-test unconditionally. Using past data from both TREC and NTCIR, the present study demonstrates that the latter advice should not be followed blindly in the context of IR system evaluation. More specifically, our results suggest that if the sample sizes differ substantially and if the larger sample has a substantially larger variance, Welch's t-test may not be reliable.

Keywords

statistical significance; test collections; topics; variances

1. INTRODUCTION

The present study concerns IR evaluation where two means from different samples need to be compared. The classical approach for this would be to employ a two-sample (i.e., unpaired) t-test to discuss whether, given the observed sample means, the population means may be different. There are two well-known versions of the two-sample t-test: Student's t-test and Welch's t-test. While Welch's t-test does not assume *homoscedasticity* (i.e., equal variances), it involves approximations. A classical textbook recommendation would be to use Student's t-test if either the two sample sizes n_1, n_2 are similar or the two sample variances V_1, V_2 are similar, and to use Welch's t-test only when both of the above conditions are violated [3]. However, a more recent recommendation seems to be to use Welch's t-test unconditionally. For example, Daniel Laken's blog posted on January 26, 2015 recommends researchers to "Always use Welch's t-test instead of Student's t-test," while demonstrating the superiority of Welch's t-test using simulated data[1]. The `t.test` function provided in the `stats` library of the R language uses Welch's t-test by default[2]; hence researchers who use this function as a black box may well be using Welch's t-test all the time. In fact, in as far back as 1981, Gans [1] recommended "the automatic use of the Welch test alone" as an option, based on simulations. The present study seeks to obtain the right recommendations for the purpose of IR system evaluation using real data from TREC and NTCIR.

SIGIR '16, July 17 - 21, 2016, Pisa, Italy

ISBN 978-1-4503-4069-4/16/07...$15.00
DOI: http://dx.doi.org/10.1145/2911451.2914684

2. PRIOR ART

In the IR evaluation literature, researchers have focussed mainly on the *paired data* setting, because the most basic method for comparing two IR systems is to use the same test collection with a single topic set to compare two systems. For example, Smucker *et al.* [7] compared the sign test, the Wilcoxon signed rank test, the paired t-test, the bootstrap test and the randomisation test from the viewpoint of how similar the p-values of different test types are to one another, and concluded that the use of the two nonparametric tests (sign and Wilcoxon) should be discontinued. Urbano *et al.* [8] conducted a follow-up study on the same set of paired significance tests, using repeated topic set splitting experiments in a way similar to earlier studies (e.g. [10]) to quantify the discrepancies across the pairs of topic sets for comparing two systems. Contrary to the recommendation by Smucker *et al.*, Urbano *et al.* report that "the permutation test is not optimal under any criterion."

In contrast to the aforementioned studies, the present study concerns *two-sample* t-tests for comparing two means, with sample sizes n_1, n_2. Possible applications of two-sample tests in IR include comparing sets of clicks from two different search engines, between-subject design user experiments, and comparing the "hardness" of two test collections using the same IR system. Sakai [4] used the two-sample bootstrap test (in addition to the paired bootstrap test) for the purpose of comparing different evaluation measures in terms of "discriminative power."

3. T-TEST: STUDENT'S AND WELCH'S

The common assumptions are as follows. We have scores $x_{11}, \ldots, x_{1n_1}$ that each obey $N(\mu_1, \sigma_1^2)$, as well as $x_{21}, \ldots, x_{2n_1}$ that each obey $N(\mu_2, \sigma_2^2)$. The population means and variances ($\mu_\bullet$'s and $\sigma_\bullet^2$'s) are unknown, and we want to test if $\mu_1 = \mu_2$, given sample means $\bar{x}_1 = \frac{1}{n_1}\sum_{j=1}^{n_1} x_{1j}$ and $\bar{x}_2 = \frac{1}{n_2}\sum_{j=1}^{n_2} x_{2j}$. Let $S_1 = \sum_{j=1}^{n_1}(x_{1j} - \bar{x}_1)^2, S_2 = \sum_{j=1}^{n_2}(x_{2j} - \bar{x}_2)^2$ for later purposes.

[1] http://daniellakens.blogspot.nl/2015/01/always-use-welchs-t-test-instead-of.html
[2] http://127.0.0.1:27533/library/stats/html/t.test.html

3.1 Student's t-test

Student's two-sample t-test further assumes homoscedasticity: $\sigma_1^2 = \sigma_2^2$. While this is a strong assumption, it is also known that this test is quite robust to assumption violations. For this test, we first define a pooled variance $V = (S_1 + S_2)/\phi$ where ϕ is the degree of freedom for V given by $\phi = \phi_1 + \phi_2, \phi_1 = n_1 - 1, \phi_2 = n_2 - 1$. The test statistic is:

$$t_0 = \frac{\bar{x}_1 - \bar{x}_2}{\sqrt{V(1/n_1 + 1/n_2)}} \tag{1}$$

which is compared against $t(\phi;\alpha)$, the critical t value for $\phi = n_1 + n_2 - 2$ degrees of freedom with the significance level of α.

3.2 Welch's t-test

The good news about Welch's t-test is that it does not assume homoscedasticity; the bad news is that it involves approximations [3], as briefly discussed below. Let $V_1 = S_1/\phi_1, V_2 = S_2/\phi_2$. For this test, the test statistic is

$$t_{w0} = \frac{\bar{x}_1 - \bar{x}_2}{\sqrt{V_1/n_1 + V_2/n_2}} \tag{2}$$

which is compared against $t(\phi^*;\alpha)$, where

$$\phi^* = (\frac{V_1}{n_1} + \frac{V_2}{n_2})^2 / \{\frac{(V_1/n_1)^2}{\phi_1} + \frac{(V_2/n_2)^2}{\phi_2}\} . \tag{3}$$

Welch's t-test approximates the distribution of the following statistic by a χ^2 distribution with ϕ_0 degrees of freedom:

$$W = \phi_0(\frac{V_1}{n_1} + \frac{V_2}{n_2})/(\frac{\sigma_1^2}{n_1} + \frac{\sigma_2^2}{n_2}) . \tag{4}$$

Furthermore, it estimates ϕ_0 as $\hat{\phi}_0 = \phi^*$ using Eq. 3. Do these approximations have any consequences for IR evaluation?

3.3 Analytical Relationships

Nagata [3] clarifies the relationship between the above two t-tests analytically. Let $a = n_2/n_1, b = V_2/V_1$. Then it is easy to derive that the ratio of the two test statictics t_{w0}/t_0 is given by:

$$\frac{t_{w0}}{t_0} = g(a,b) = \sqrt{\frac{(a+1)\{n_1(ab+1) - (b+1)\}}{(a+b)(n_1(a+1) - 2)}} . \tag{5}$$

Note that $g(1,b) = g(a,1) = 1$. Hence, if either $n_1 = n_2$ or $V_1 = V_2$ holds, then $t_0 = t_{w0}$ holds. In practice, if the larger sample is no larger than 1.5 times the other, *or* if the larger variance is no larger than 1.5 times the other, t_0 and t_{w0} will differ by at most 20% or so [3]. As for the degrees of freedom, it can be shown that:

$$\frac{\phi^*}{\phi} = h(a,b) = \frac{(a+b)^2(n_1 - 1)(an_1 - 1)}{\{a^2(an_1 - 1) + b^2(n_1 - 1)\}\{(a+1)n_1 - 2\}} . \tag{6}$$

Since $h(1,1) = 1$ holds, having $n_1 = n_2$ *and* $V_1 = V_2$ is a sufficient condition for obtaining $\phi^* = \phi$. Also, it can be verified that $h(a,b) = \phi^*/\phi$ is much smaller than one if $b = V_2/V_1$ is close to one *and* $a = n_2/n_1$ is far from one. That is, Welch's t-test has relatively low statistical power (due to its degree of freedom ϕ^* being much smaller than Student's ϕ) when the variances are roughly equal but the sample sizes are quite different.

4. EXPERIMENTS

In order to compare Student's and Welch's t-tests in terms of reliability, we adopt a method similar to that of Webber *et al.* [11]: given a topic set of size n, with m runs that processed these topics, randomly partition the topics into two sets of size n_1 and n_2, respectively. For each of the m runs and a given evaluation measure, conduct a two-sided, two-sample test to see if the two means for the same run are statistically significant. The ground truth is that they are *not*, since the scores actually come from the same system. The random partitioning is done $B = 1000$ times, so a test collection with m runs will yield $Bm = 1000m$ p-values for each significance test type with a given evaluation measure.

Table 1: Test collections and runs used in this study.

	TREC99	NTCIR97
Topics (n)	601-700 minus 672 (99)	T41-385 minus 86, 331, 362 (97)
Runs (m)	TREC 2004 robust (110)	NTCIR-7 IR4QA Chinese (40)
Qrels	$L2$: relevant; $L1$: partially relevant; $L0$: judged nonrelevant	

Table 2: Sample size ratios experimented in this study.

Target ratio	Actual ratio (TREC99)	Actual ratio (NTCIR97)
50:50 ($a = 1.0$)	50:49	50:47
40:60 ($a = 1.5$)	40:59	40:57
30:70 ($a = 2.3$)	30:69	30:67
10:90 ($a = 9.0$)	10:89	10:87

Table 1 shows a summary of the two data sets used in this study. We chose them because (a) we wanted about $n = 100$ topics (or more if available) with graded relevance assessments; (b) we wanted data (with many runs) from different evaluation conferences to ensure generalisability. "TREC99" comprises 110 runs from the TREC 2004 robust track [9], with 99 robust track topics. While this data set has many runs, the 99 topics come from two robust track rounds: 50 from TREC 2003 and 49 from 2004. In contrast, "NTCIR97," which comprises 40 Simplified Chinese runs from the NTCIR-7 ACLIA IR4QA task [6], uses 97 topics that originate from a single round of the task.

For each data set with a given evaluation measure, we experimented with four different sample size ratios $a = n_2/n_1$ as shown in Table 2 to obtain a total of $4000m$ p-values. Recall that, according to Nagata [3], Student's and Welch's t statistics should not be vastly different for the $a = 1$ ($n_1 : n_2 = 50 : 50$) and $a = 1.5$ ($n_1 : n_2 = 40 : 60$) settings, regardless of how the two sample variances differ. We experimented with four evaluation measures: (binary) Average Precision (AP), Q-measure (Q), normalised Discounted Cumulative Gain (nDCG) and normalised Expected Reciprocal Rank (nERR). Unlike the other three measures, nERR is known to be suitable for navigational information needs due to its *diminishing return* property; for this very reason, it is known to be statistically less stable than the other measures [5].

5. RESULTS AND DISCUSSIONS

Figure 1 plots Welch's p-values against Student's p-values for the 110,000 two-sample t-tests conducted with the TREC99 data, for nDCG ((a)-(d)) and nERR ((e)-(h)) with different target sample size ratios. The graphs for TREC99 with AP and Q, as well all all graphs for NTCIR97, are omitted due to lack of space. However, the overall picture is the same for all evaluation measures and across the two data sets, and we believe that our findings are general. In each graph, the blue rectangle represents the situation where Student's t-test obtains a p-value smaller than $\alpha = 0.05$ (i.e., a false positive) while Welch's t-test does not; the red rectangle represents the opposite situation; the bottom left square represents the situation where both tests obtain a false alarm at $\alpha = 0.05$. It can be observed that when the target sample size ratio is $a = 1$ ($n_1 : n_2 = 50 : 50$), the two tests are indeed virtually identical and false alarms are very rare; as we gradually increase the sample size ratio until it reaches $a = 9.0$ ($n_1 : n_2 = 10 : 90$), we obtain more and more false alarms on both sides of the diagonal.

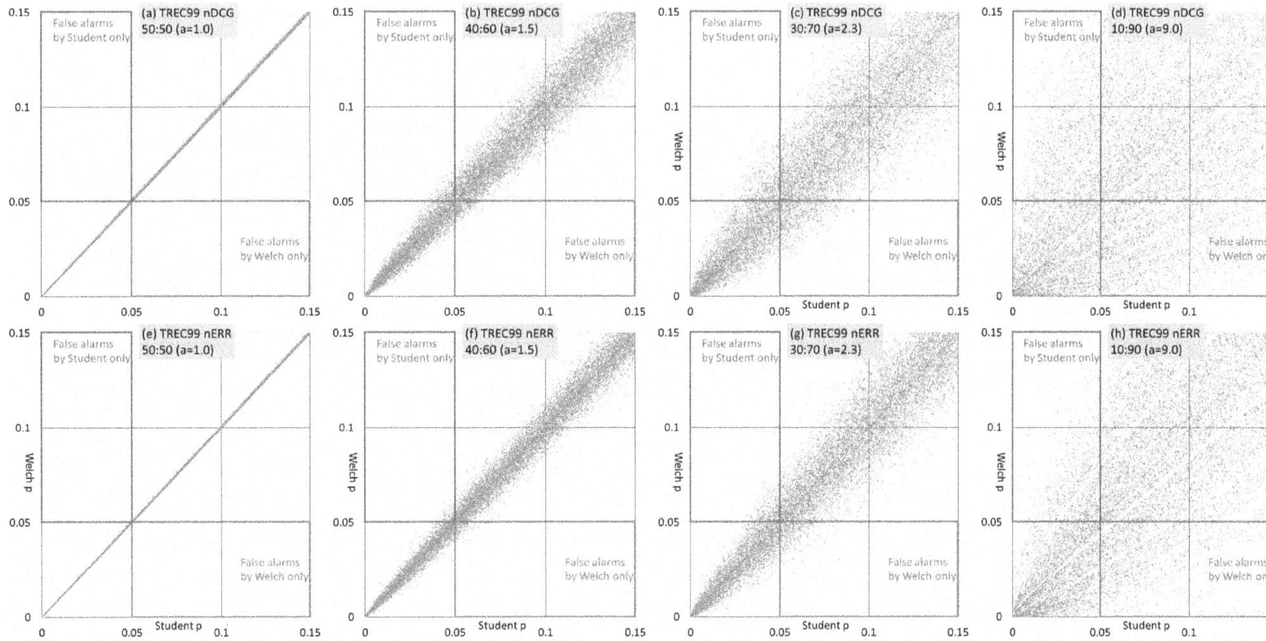

Figure 1: Welch's vs. Student's p-values: TREC99; 110 runs; nDCG (top) and nERR (bottom).

Tables 3 and 4 show the false positive rates for all of our TREC99 and NTCIR97 experiments, respectively. Based on the discussion provided in Section 3.3, we categorised the observations into three classes: the first is for those where the variance ratio satisfies $2/3 \leq b \leq 3/2$: recall that Student's and Welch's t statistics are expected to be similar to each other in this situation. The other two classes ($b < 2/3$ and $b > 3/2$) represent the situations where the sample variances are very different. For example, Table 3 Section (III) Column (d) provides the following information about our TREC99 experiments for nDCG with the sample size ratio $a = 9.0$ (with the actual sample sizes $n_1 = 10, n_2 = 89$ as shown in Table 1):

- For 64,447 out of the 110,000 observations, the sample variance ratio $b = V_2/V_1$ satisfied $2/3 \leq b \leq 3/2$; for these observations, the false positive rate was 4.0% for Student's t-test and 2.6% for Welch's t-test;
- For 16,614 out of the 110,000 observations, $b < 2/3$; for these observations, the false positive rate was 4.9% for Student's t-test and 0.7% for Welch's t-test;
- For 28,939 out of the 110,000 observations, $b > 3/2$; for these observations, the false positive rate was 5.6% for Student's t-test and 14.1% for Welch's t-test;
- Overall, for the 110,000 observations, the false positive rate was 4.6% for Student's t-test and 5.3% for Welch's t-test. Thus, Welch's t-test slightly underperforms Student's, due to its very high false positive rate for the $b > 3/2$ setting.

More generally, we can observe the following consistent trends from Tables 3 and 4:

- When the two sample sizes are equal (Column (a)), Student's and Welch's t-tests perform equally well, regardless of the range of b[3]. The overall false positive rates are 4.9-5.2%.
- When the two variances are similar ($2/3 \leq b \leq 3/2$), the false positive rates of the two tests are very small (1.0-4.8%), although, as discussed immediately below, Student's t-test yields more false positive than Welch's when the sample size ratio $a = n_2/n_1$ is extreme (Column (d));
- As we increase the sample size ratio $a = n_2/n_1$, Welch's t-test yields more and more false positives when $b = V_2/V_1 > 3/2$. That is, *if the sample sizes differ substantially and if the larger sample has a substantially larger variance, Welch's t-test may not be reliable for two-sample IR evaluation.* In particular, when $a = n_2/n_1 = 9$ (Column (d)), the false positive rates for Welch's t-test are 14.1-24.6% whereas those for Student's t-test are only 4.4-13.5%. Whereas, as we increase the sample size ratio a, Student's t-test yields more and more false positives when $b \leq 3/2$ (i.e., $2/3 \leq b \leq 3/2$ or $b < 2/3$), but this tendency is not as marked as Welch's for the $b > 3/2$ range. As a result, in terms of the overall false positive rates, Welch's t-test is actually slightly less reliable than the Student's t-test when a is very large.

The above results, based on real IR system runs from both TREC and NTCIR, suggest that the advice "Always use Welch's t-test instead of Student's t-test" should not be followed blindly in IR system evaluation.

6. CONCLUSIONS

For the purpose of reliable IR system evaluation, we compared two versions of two-sample t-tests: Student's t-test (which assumes homoscedasticity) and Welch's t-test (which relies on approximated distributions). Our topic set splitting experiments with runs from

[3]When $n_1 = n_2$, note that the variance ratio conditions $b < 2/3$ and $b > 3/2$ are equivalent: it is just a matter of swapping the two samples, since the two tests are symmetric with respect to the two samples. So we should expect similar results in Column (a) for these two ranges of b. The slight caveat is that we actually have $n_1 \simeq n_2$ rather than $n_1 = n_2$, as $n_1 + n_2 = 99$ or 97.

Table 3: TREC99 false positives at $\alpha = 0.05$: Student/Welch. The higher false positive rate in each condition is shown in bold. The total number of observations for each variance ratio is shown in parentheses.

	(a) 50:50 $a = 1.0$	(b) 40:60 $a = 1.5$	(c) 30:70 $a = 2.3$	(d) 10:90 $a = 9.0$
(I) AP				
$2/3 \leq b \leq 3/2$	3.5%/3.5% (91,286)	3.4%/3.4% (90,405)	**3.2%**/3.1% (87,833)	**2.8%**/1.6% (62,674)
$b < 2/3$	11.9%/**12.0%** (9,192)	**10.9%**/8.5% (8,887)	**9.7%**/5.7% (9,374)	**7.7%**/0.7% (16,938)
$b > 3/2$	**15.0%**/14.7% (9,522)	13.0%/**15.7%** (10,708)	9.9%/**15.9%** (12,793)	6.0%/**18.4%** (30,388)
All	5.2%/5.2% (110,000)	4.9%/**5.0%** (110,000)	4.5%/**4.8%** (110,000)	4.5%/**6.1%** (110,000)
(II) Q				
$2/3 \leq b \leq 3/2$	3.7%/3.7% (90,299)	3.5%/3.5% (89,563)	**3.5%**/3.4% (86,872)	**3.2%**/1.9% (61,402)
$b < 2/3$	11.1%/11.1% (9,620)	**10.5%**/7.9% (9,252)	**8.9%**/4.9% (9,763)	**7.6%**/0.7% (17,285)
$b > 3/2$	**13.3%**/13.2% (10,081)	11.6%/**14.3%** (11,185)	8.5%/**14.2%** (13,365)	5.5%/**16.9%** (31,313)
All	5.2%/5.2% (110,000)	4.9%/**5.0%** (110,000)	4.6%/**4.8%** (110,000)	4.5%/**6.0%** (110,000)
(III) nDCG				
$2/3 \leq b \leq 3/2$	4.4%/4.4% (94,936)	4.4%/4.4% (94,480)	4.2%/4.2% (90,837)	**4.0%**/2.6% (64,447)
$b < 2/3$	7.7%/7.7% (7,640)	**7.0%**/5.4% (7,076)	**6.6%**/4.0% (7,710)	**4.9%**/0.7% (16,614)
$b > 3/2$	**8.4%**/8.3% (7,424)	7.9%/**9.5%** (8,444)	7.6%/**12.1%** (11,453)	5.6%/**14.1%** (28,939)
All	4.9%/4.9% (110,000)	4.9%/4.9% (110,000)	4.7%/**5.0%** (110,000)	4.6%/**5.3%** (110,000)
(IV) nERR				
$2/3 \leq b \leq 3/2$	**4.8%**/4.7% (107,590)	4.4%/4.4% (107,161)	4.3%/4.3% (105,953)	**3.0%**/2.1% (87,017)
$b < 2/3$	10.5%/**10.8%** (1,165)	**10.4%**/8.3% (1,126)	**6.0%**/3.1% (1,196)	**1.7%**/0.1% (7,485)
$b > 3/2$	**13.9%**/13.5% (1,245)	14.4%/**16.8%** (1,713)	14.1%/**20.6%** (2,851)	13.5%/**24.2%** (15,498)
All	4.9%/4.9% (110,000)	4.6%/**4.7%** (110,000)	4.6%/**4.7%** (110,000)	4.4%/**5.1%** (110,000)

Table 4: NTCIR97 false positives at $\alpha = 0.05$: Student/Welch. The higher false positive rate in each condition is shown in bold. The total number of observations for each variance ratio is shown in parentheses.

	(a) 50:50 $a = 1.0$	(b) 40:60 $a = 1.5$	(c) 30:70 $a = 2.3$	(d) 10:90 $a = 9.0$
(I) AP				
$2/3 \leq b \leq 3/2$	4.3%/4.3% (33,683)	4.3%/4.3% (33,587)	4.2%/4.2% (32,716)	**3.6%**/2.3% (24,263)
$b < 2/3$	8.8%/**9.2%** (3,233)	**9.3%**/6.1% (2,965)	**10.7%**/5.1% (2,949)	**7.2%**/0.4% (6,277)
$b > 3/2$	**9.7%**/8.9% (3,084)	9.0%/**11.8%** (3,448)	7.5%/**14.8%** (4,335)	6.8%/**23.4%** (9,460)
All	**5.1%**/5.0% (40,000)	5.0%/**5.1%** (40,000)	5.0%/**5.4%** (40,000)	4.9%/**7.0%** (40,000)
(II) Q				
$2/3 \leq b \leq 3/2$	3.9%/3.9% (33,043)	4.1%/4.1% (33,085)	**4.1%**/4.0% (32,135)	**3.5%**/2.2% (23,172)
$b < 2/3$	9.0%/**9.3%** (3,575)	**10.3%/7.1%** (3,203)	**10.7%**/5.6% (3,300)	**7.6%**/0.4% (6,766)
$b > 3/2$	**10.4%**/9.9% (3,382)	9.5%/**11.9%** (3,712)	8.1%/**15.4%** (45,65)	6.4%/**23.2%** (10,062)
All	4.9%/4.9% (40,000)	5.1%/5.1% (40,000)	5.1%/**5.4%** (40,000)	4.9%/**7.2%** (40,000)
(III) nDCG				
$2/3 \leq b \leq 3/2$	1.8%/1.8% (29,136)	1.8%/1.8% (29,193)	**1.8%**/1.7% (27,739)	**2.2%**/1.1% (18,548)
$b < 2/3$	12.9%/**13.5%** (5,578)	**14.2%**/11.1% (5,076)	**14.9%**/8.2% (5,318)	**11.7%**/1.1% (8,533)
$b > 3/2$	**13.7%**/13.0% (5,286)	12.6%/**16.1%** (5,731)	9.9%/**17.7%** (6,943)	4.4%/**22.4%** (12,919)
All	4.9%/4.9% (40,000)	4.9%/**5.0%** (40,000)	4.9%/**5.3%** (40,000)	4.9%/**8.0%** (40,000)
(IV) nERR				
$2/3 \leq b \leq 3/2$	2.0%/2.0% (32,698)	1.7%/1.7% (32,303)	**1.5%**/1.4% (31,171)	**2.2%**/1.0% (21,570)
$b < 2/3$	17.9%/**18.5%** (3,715)	**18.0%**/14.7% (3,498)	**18.2%**/10.7% (3,625)	**12.4%**/1.7% (7,159)
$b > 3/2$	**20.1%**/19.2% (3,587)	18.7%/**23.2%** (4,199)	15.1%/**24.5%** (5,204)	5.0%/**24.6%** (11,270)
All	5.1%/5.1% (40,000)	4.9%/**5.1%** (40,000)	4.8%/**5.3%** (40,000)	4.9%/**7.8%** (40,000)

both TREC and NTCIR are consistent across different evaluation measures and across these two different IR venues. While neither our equal variance settings nor our equal sample size settings do not demonstrate any advantages of Student's t-test over Welch's t-test, our results do suggest that if the sample sizes differ substantially and if the larger sample has a substantially larger variance, Welch's t-test may be less reliable. Hence we argue that the advice "Always use Welch's t-test instead of Student's t-test" should not be followed blindly in IR system evaluation.

In practice, we recommend IR researchers to examine the sample sizes n_1, n_2 and the sample variances V_1, V_2 first and then make a conscious decision, rather than (say) relying on a default setting in the `t.test` function provided in R. We also recommend IR researchers to report explicitly which version of the two-sample t-test was used in their experiments, even if we may be able to spot a Welch's t-test when the degree of freedom reported is not an integer (Eq. 3).

Acknowledgement

I would like to thank Professor Yasushi Nagata for his helpful comments on my results.

7. REFERENCES

[1] D. J. Gans. Use of a preliminary test in comparing two sample means. *Communications in Statistics - Simuation and Computation*, 10(2):163–174, 1981.

[2] D. Hawking and N. Craswell. The very large collection and web tracks. In E. M. Voorhees and D. K. Harman, editors, *TREC: Experiment and Evaluation in Information Retrieval*, chapter 9. The MIT Press, 2005.

[3] Y. Nagata. *How to Understand Statistical Methods (in Japanese)*. Nikkagiren, 1996.

[4] T. Sakai. Evaluating evaluation metrics based on the bootstrap. In *Proceedings of ACM SIGIR 2006*, pages 525–532, 2006.

[5] T. Sakai. Metrics, statistics, tests. In *PROMISE Winter School 2013: Bridging between Information Retrieval and Databases (LNCS 8173)*, pages 116–163, 2014.

[6] T. Sakai, N. Kando, C.-J. Lin, T. Mitamura, H. Shima, D. Ji, K.-H. Chen, and E. Nyberg. Overview of the NTCIR-7 ACLIA IR4QA task. In *Proceedings of NTCIR-7*, pages 77–114, 2008.

[7] M. D. Smucker, J. Allan, and B. Carterette. A comparison of statistical significance tests for information retrieval evaluation. In *Proceedings of ACM CIKM 2007*, pages 623–632, 2007.

[8] J. Urbano, M. Marrero, and D. Martín. A comparison of the optimality of statistical significance tests for information retrieval evaluation. In *Proceedings of ACM SIGIR 2013*, pages 925–928, 2013.

[9] E. M. Voorhees. Overview of the TREC 2004 robust retrieval track. In *Proceedings of TREC 2004*, 2005.

[10] E. M. Voorhees. Topic set size redux. In *Proceedings of ACM SIGIR 2009*, pages 806–807, 2009.

[11] W. Webber, A. Moffat, and J. Zobel. Score standardization for inter-collection comparison of retrieval systems. In *Proceedings of ACM SIGIR 2008*, pages 51–58, 2008.

Uncovering Task Based Behavioral Heterogeneities in Online Search Behavior

Rishabh Mehrotra
Dept. of Computer Science
University College London
London United Kingdom
r.mehrotra@cs.ucl.ac.uk

Prasanta Bhattacharya
Dept. of Information Systems
National University of Singapore
prasanta@comp.nus.edu.sg

Emine Yilmaz
Dept. of Computer Science
University College London
London United Kingdom
emine.yilmaz@ucl.ac.uk

ABSTRACT

While a major share of prior work have considered search sessions as the focal unit of analysis for seeking behavioral insights, search tasks are emerging as a competing perspective in this space. In the current work, we quantify user search task behavior for both single- as well as multi-task search sessions and relate it to tasks and topics. Specifically, we analyze user-disposition, topic and user-interest level heterogeneities that are prevalent in search task behavior. Our results show that while search multi-tasking is a common phenomenon among the search engine users, the extent and choice of multi-tasking topics vary significantly across users. We find that not only do users have varying propensities to multi-task, they also search for distinct topics across single-task and multi-task sessions. To our knowledge, this is among the first studies to fully characterize online search tasks with a focus on user- and topic-level differences that are observable from search sessions.

CCS Concepts

•**Information systems → Task models;**

Keywords

Search tasks; Multitasking; User Behavior

1. INTRODUCTION

Users' information search behavior on search engines often span various motivations [2, 14]. While simple informational needs, such as "Adele's latest music" can be satisfied in a single search session, most other informational needs are complex and time-consuming. Consequently, users accomplish more complex information search tasks by issuing a series of search queries spanning multiple search sessions, possibly spread over multiple days. While a major portion of existing work have investigated search behavior using search sessions as the fundamental focus of search activity [6, 18, 19, 20, 24, 25], more recent studies suggest that users often seek to complete multiple search tasks within a single search session [14, 15, 22], while also taking multiple sessions to finish a single task at times. The emergence of multi-tasking behavior within a single search session makes it particularly complex to use user information from search sessions to personalize the user's search activity. This necessitates a shift in focus from search sessions to search tasks as a more accurate unit of analysis of human search behavior.

In our current analyses, we build upon search sessions to identify and characterize search tasks and topics. In characterizing these search tasks across sessions, we consider the possibility of three distinct forms of heterogeneity inherent in the search-task behavior. First, there could be *user-disposition* level heterogeneity wherein some users have a higher propensity to multi-task when searching for information, than other users. Second, there could be *topic* level heterogeneity wherein searchers have a higher (or lower) propensity to multi-task when searching information for specific kind of topics. Third, and finally, there could be *user-interest* level heterogeneity wherein users might have a higher or lower propensity to multi-task when searching for topics they are most or least interested in.

While recent work has highlighted the prevalence of multi-tasking behavior in online search [14, 15, 22], not much effort has been expended at fully characterizing online search tasks with an emphasis on such user- and topic-level differences. In the current study, we leverage a large dataset of real world search logs to perform a large scale characterization of search tasks with a focus on such differences. Specifically, we find that while most users (>50%) choose to multi-task in their search sessions, there exists significant differences in their choice of topics between single-task and multi-task sessions. Through our analyses we offer the following three insights:
(i) **Users' preference towards multitasking(3.2):** We find evidence that most users multi-task when searching for information with over 50% users completing more than 2 tasks within a single search session, and a minority of users even completing more than 5 tasks within a single session.
(ii) **Topic level heterogeneity(3.3):** For certain type of topics, users prefer to multi-task (e.g. kids, news, shopping etc.), while for certain others, users prefer to single-task (e.g. computers, games, adult etc.).
(iii) **User-interest level heterogeneity(3.4):** Users have different preferences towards multitasking depending on their level of interest in the specific search topic (e.g. some groups of users prefer to search about most-interested topics in single-tasking sessions and least-interested topics in mult-tasking sessions).

SIGIR '16, July 17-21, 2016, Pisa, Italy
© 2016 ACM. ISBN 978-1-4503-4069-4/16/07...$15.00
DOI: http://dx.doi.org/10.1145/2911451.2914755

No of Queries	620M
No of Sessions	190M
No of Users	2M
Avg No of queries per session	3.18
Avg no of sessions per user	76.01
Avg no of tasks per session	2.08

Table 1: Data summary

Time	Query	SessionID	TaskID	Topic
05/29/2012 14:06:04	adele songs	1	1	Arts
05/29/2012 14:11:49	wedding venue	1	2	Society
05/29/2012 14:12:01	video download	1	3	Arts
05/29/2012 14:06:04	Obama care	2	4	News
05/29/2012 14:11:49	running shoes	2	5	Shopping
05/29/2012 14:12:01	sports shoes	2	5	Shopping
05/29/2012 14:22:12	wedding cards	2	2	Society

Table 2: Sample search sessions

Analyzing such heterogeneities in online search behavior lends us a better understanding of how users interact with search systems when performing different tasks.

2. RELATED WORK

There has been a large body of work focused on the problem of segmenting and organizing query logs into semantically coherent structures. Many of these methods use the idea of a *timeout* cutoff between queries, where two consecutive queries are considered as two different sessions or tasks if the time interval between them exceeds a certain threshold, often 30 minutes [5, 9, 20]. However, the experimental results of these methods indicate that the timeouts, whatever their lengths, are of limited utility in predicting whether two queries belong to the same task, and unsuitable for identifying session boundaries. There have been attempts to extract in-session tasks [11, 14, 21], cross-session tasks [12, 23, 13] and hierarchies of tasks and subtasks [16] from query sequences based on classification and clustering methods. While existing research has investigated user behavior separately across sessions [1] and across tasks [10], in this work, we fully characterize search tasks with a focus on user and topic level differences, and jointly model user interactions across sessions, topics and tasks.

3. CHARACTERIZING SEARCH TASKS

We characterize online search sessions with a focus on the underlying user-level and topic level heterogeneities. As mentioned earlier, we investigate the prevalence of three related forms of search heterogeneity viz. (i) *user-disposition* level (do focused users behave differently than multi-taskers), (ii) *topic* level (are some topics more prone to multi-tasking?), and (iii) *user-interest* level differences in search behavior (do users' task behavior vary across their topical interests). We next describe our experimental setup (Section 3.1) based on which we discuss our findings in Section 3.2, 3.3 & 3.4.

3.1 Experimental Setup

3.1.1 Data Context

We use backend search logs for users of a major US-based search engine for a period of 30 days from May 1, 2015 to May 31, 2015 and choose a random sample of over 2 million users where each user is identified by a unique IP address. For our analysis, we filter out inactive users from our dataset who participate in <50 sessions, and focus instead on the more active user population. Table 1 presents a summary of the query, session and task information in our empirical context. Our dataset comprises 620 million queries spanning 190 million search sessions, with an average of 3 queries and 2 tasks per search session.

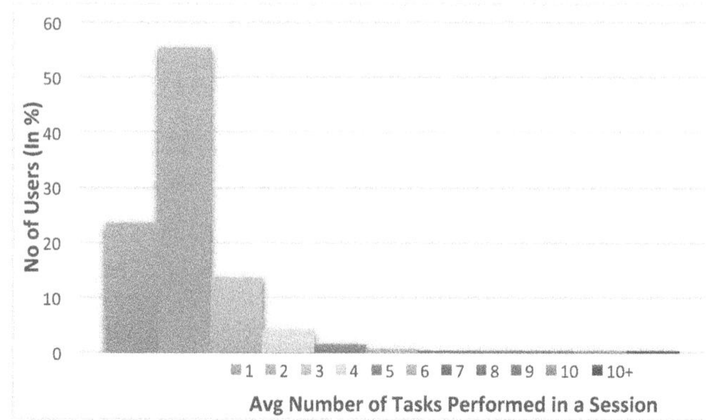

Figure 1: Quantifying the extent of multi-tasking within a session

3.1.2 Task Extraction

For our analysis, we make use of the Latent Structural SVM framework [23] for task identification. Given query sequences within sessions, search tasks are identified by clustering queries into tasks by find the strongest link between a candidate query and queries in the target cluster (*bestlink*). This is achieved by making use of a structural learning method with latent variables, i.e., latent structural SVMs, to utilize the hidden structure of query inter-dependencies to explore the dependency among queries within the same task.

Given a query sequence $Q = q_1, q_2, ..., q_M$, a feature vector for the task partition y is specified by the hidden best-link structure h as $\psi(Q, y, h)$. Based on $\psi(Q, y, h)$, the bestlink SVM is a linear model parameterized by w, and predicts the task partition by,

$$(y*, h*) = argmax_{y,h} w^T \psi(Q, y, h) \quad (1)$$

where Y and H represent the sets of possible structures of y and h respectively. $y*$ becomes the output for cross-session tasks and $h*$ is the inferred latent structure. Based on the best-link structure, $h(q_i, q_j) = 1$ if query q_i and q_j are directly connected in h; and otherwise, $h(q_i, q_j) = 0$, with the added clause that a a query can only link to another query in the past, or formally, $\sum_{i=0}^{j-1} h(q_i, q_j) = 1 \ \forall j \geq 1$. The feature vector for any particular task partition y is defined over the links in h as,

$$\psi(Q, y, h) = \sum_{i,j} h(q_i, q_j) \sum_{s=1}^{S} \phi_s(q_i, q_j) \quad (2)$$

where a set of symmetric pairwise features $\phi_s(q_i, q_j)$ is given to characterize the similarity between query q_i and q_j. Given a set of query logs with annotated tasks, the feature vector design and the directed linkage structure of h can be inferred in an SVM setting. A detailed overview of the approach can be found in Wang *et al.* [23].

3.2 Search Sessions to Search Tasks

Search sessions have been exploited in previous work on information search, as being the major focus for most analy-

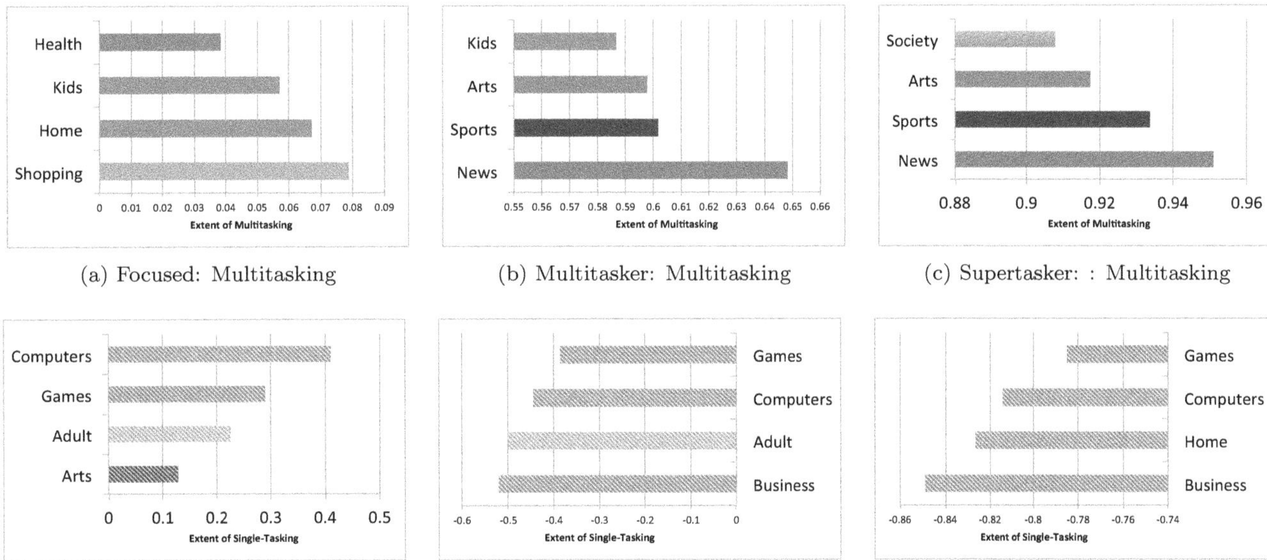

(a) Focused: Multitasking (b) Multitasker: Multitasking (c) Supertasker: : Multitasking

(d) Focused: Single-tasking (e) Multitasker: Single-tasking (f) Supertasker: Single-tasking

Figure 2: Top topics prone to multi-tasking (Top) and Single-tasking (Bottom) across different user groups.

sis of search behavior. The context of search activities within the current session has been used to build richer models of interests and improve how the search system interprets the user's current query. Session context has been used for modeling query and click sequences [4, 3], to disambiguate current search query [17], to build topical profiles for future interest prediction [24], to improve search quality [25, 6] to quantify struggling users [18], for understanding learning and expertise development [8] and for detecting atypicality in user behavior [7].

While search sessions are an important and convenient source for analysis, we contend that this conceptualization of sessions as focal units of analysis makes certain assumptions that are quite untenable in the general case. First, there exists no theoretical basis for bounding search sessions, as it is largely a data-driven subject. Previous research on the topic have adopted a time-out based strategy to bound search sessions [5, 9, 20]. However, it remains to be understood if such time-out based techniques have strong external validity across search contexts. Second, and most importantly, evidence from our own analysis of search logs show that users do indeed search for multiple unrelated topics within a single search session. Based on the task extracted within and across search sessions (3.1.2), our analysis hints at the presence of multiple search tasks within single session. This has been shown in Tables 1 and 2. In Table 2 we provide an illustration of a single search session (tagged session ID = 1) and the 2 different tasks that we have been able to identify from within the search session. Further, we also list the ODP topics that we could extract from the associated queries for each of the tasks. Since search sessions are inherently complex and often comprise a combination of multiple search tasks and topics, we shift our focus in the current study to analyze user- and topic-level differences across search tasks within and across sessions.

3.3 User-disposition and Topic Level Heterogeneity

Recent work on the topic of search multi-tasking has shown that a majority of users perform two or more tasks within a single search session [15]. Consistent with these studies, our analysis also uncovers that close to 55% of users perform two or more tasks within single sessions, with a minority of users even performing 5 or more tasks within the single session, as illustrated in Figure 1. Following Mehrotra *et al.* [15], we term these three discernible classes of users based on their frequency of multitasking behavior viz. focused (i.e. 1 task per session), multitaskers (i.e. 2-5 tasks per session) and supertaskers (i.e. >5 tasks per session). Having established that users vary on their disposition to single-task and multi-task, we now delve deeper into understanding whether users multi-task to varying extents depending on their topics.

To obtain such a topic representation for this study, we labeled each document with a vector of probabilities of categories from the top two levels of the ODP hierarchy using a text-based classifier. Each documents vector was restricted to the three most probable classes. The classifier has a micro-averaged F1 value of 0.60 and is described more fully in [24]. The most prominent topic among the top 3 returned results per query was used as the final tagged topic for that query.

We analyse topic level heterogeneity by investigating the level of multi-tasking in sessions filtered by topics. Our results are illustrated in Figure 2 wherein we highlight the top 4 most prevalent topics across multi-tasking and single-tasking sessions (top to bottom panels), for all three category of users (left to right panels). The length of the bars in each of the charts in the Figure 2 highlights the extent of multitasking (top panels) and the extent of single-tasking (bottom panels). The extent of multi-tasking is defined as $\frac{N_M - N_S}{N_{total}}$, which measures the difference between the proportion of times the topic featured in a multi-tasking session (N_M) and the proportion of times the topic featured in a single-tasking session (N_S). Conversely, the extent of single-tasking was calculated as the difference between the proportion of times the topic featured in a single-tasking session and the proportion of times the topic featured in a multi-tasking session.

We find that focused users primarily multi-task for top-

	Focused		Multi-taskers		Super-taskers	
	Single-Tasking	Multi-Tasking	Single-Tasking	Multi-Tasking	Single-Tasking	Multi-Tasking
Most Interested Topics	0.593	0.407	0.310	0.690	0.105	0.895
Least Interested Topics	0.458	0.542	0.249	0.751	0.081	0.919

Table 3: Relating User's Single/Multitasking Nature with their interest profiles.

ics related to shopping, home, kids, health and recreation. However, both multi- and super-taskers have a shared preference for multi-tasking on topics related to news, sports and arts. We also observe that focused users prefer to single task when searching for topics related to computers, games, adult and arts categories, while multi-taskers and super-taskers do not prefer to single-task when searching for their preferred topics. This is reflected by the negative scores on the extent of single-tasking in the bottom panel of Figure 2. These findings confirm our intuition that indeed certain topics are more prone to multi-tasking (e.g. news, sports) while others (e.g. computers, adult) usually witness single tasking sessions.

3.4 User-interest Level Heterogeneity

We next investigate whether users exercise any specific search preference when searching for topics that are of high vs. low interest to them. To analyze this, we compute the frequency of most and least searched topic categories from the search history of users in each of the three user groups viz. focused, multi-taskers and super-taskers [1]. Following this, we analyze their search behavior during single-tasking and multi-tasking sessions to investigate the distribution of high and low interest topic categories across these sessions. The results from this analysis are described in Table 3, and highlight that users exercise distinct preferences in search sessions for high vs. low interest topics.

Our results show that multi-taskers and super-taskers prefer to multi-task for a large majority of their search sessions (i.e. almost always >70%), irrespective of whether they are searching for high or low interest topics. In contrast, however, focused users prefer to search for high interest topics in single-tasking sessions (i.e. 59% of the time), and low interest topics in multi-tasking sessions (i.e. 54% of the time).

4. DISCUSSION AND CONCLUSION

We illustrate in this paper how a shift of focus from the idea of a search session to a search task raises a number of important questions. The most important of these is about fully characterizing the extent and underlying heterogeneities surrounding single-task and multi-task search sessions. While we draw on previous work as well as our own set of analyses to show that multi-tasking within a search session is fairly common, we also emphasize that the extent and nature of multi-tasking is strongly influenced by user dispositions (i.e. whether a user is naturally disposed to single vs. multi-tasking), topic preferences (i.e. users might prefer to multi-task when searching for certain topics than others), and interest preferences (i.e. users might prefer to multi-task about topics they are more or less interested in. Our findings have implications for understanding user preferences which in turn could impact the design of better personalization services for searchers.

[1]Note that this is different from the identification of top topics in the previous section which were identified at a session-level and not at a user-level.

5. REFERENCES

[1] E. Agichtein, E. Brill, and S. Dumais. Improving web search ranking by incorporating user behavior information. In *SIGIR 2006*.

[2] P. Bailey and Chen. User task understanding: a web search engine perspective. In *NII Shonan Meeting on Whole-Session Evaluation of IIR Systems*, 2012.

[3] H. Cao, D. H. Hu, D. Shen, D. Jiang, J.-T. Sun, E. Chen, and Q. Yang. Context-aware query classification. In *SIGIR 2009*.

[4] H. Cao, D. Jiang, J. Pei, Q. He, Z. Liao, E. Chen, and H. Li. Context-aware query suggestion by mining click-through and session data. In *KDD 2008*.

[5] L. D. Catledge and J. E. Pitkow. Characterizing browsing strategies in the world-wide web. *Computer Networks and ISDN systems*, 1995.

[6] M. Daoud, L. Tamine-Lechani, M. Boughanem, and B. Chebaro. A session based personalized search using an ontological user profile. In *Proceedings of the 2009 ACM symposium on Applied Computing*. ACM, 2009.

[7] C. Eickhoff, K. Collins-Thompson, P. N. Bennett, and S. Dumais. Personalizing atypical web search sessions. In *WSDM 2013*.

[8] C. Eickhoff, J. Teevan, R. White, and S. Dumais. Lessons from the journey: A query log analysis of within-session learning. In *WSDM 2014*.

[9] D. He, A. Göker, and D. J. Harper. Combining evidence for automatic web session identification. *Information Processing & Management*, 2002.

[10] J. Jiang, D. He, and J. Allan. Searching, browsing, and clicking in a search session: changes in user behavior by task and over time. In *SIGIR 2014*.

[11] R. Jones and K. L. Klinkner. Beyond the session timeout: automatic hierarchical segmentation of search topics in query logs. In *CIKM 2008*.

[12] Kotov, Bennett, White, Dumais, and Teevan. Modeling and analysis of cross-session search tasks. In *SIGIR 2011*.

[13] L. Li, H. Deng, A. Dong, Y. Chang, and H. Zha. Identifying and labeling search tasks via query-based hawkes processes. In *KDD 2014*.

[14] C. Lucchese, S. Orlando, R. Perego, F. Silvestri, and G. Tolomei. Identifying task-based sessions in search engine query logs. In *Proceedings of ACM WSDM 2011*.

[15] R. Mehrotra, P. Bhattacharya, and E. Yilmaz. Characterizing users' multi-tasking behavior in web search. In *Proceedings of the 2016 ACM on Conference on Human Information Interaction and Retrieval*, 2016.

[16] R. Mehrotra and E. Yilmaz. Towards hierarchies of search tasks & subtasks. In *WWW 2015*.

[17] L. Mihalkova and R. Mooney. Learning to disambiguate search queries from short sessions. In *Machine Learning and Knowledge Discovery in Databases*. 2009.

[18] D. Odijk, R. W. White, A. Hassan Awadallah, and S. T. Dumais. Struggling and success in web search. In *CIKM 2015*.

[19] F. Radlinski and T. Joachims. Query chains: learning to rank from implicit feedback. In *KDD 2005*.

[20] C. Silverstein, H. Marais, M. Henzinger, and M. Moricz. Analysis of a very large web search engine query log. In *ACm SIGIR Forum*, volume 33, pages 6–12. ACM, 1999.

[21] Spink, Koshman, Park, Field, and Jansen. Multitasking web search on vivisimo. com. In *ITCC 2005*.

[22] A. Spink, M. Park, B. J. Jansen, and J. Pedersen. Multitasking during web search sessions. *Information Processing & Management 2006*.

[23] H. Wang, Y. Song, M.-W. Chang, X. He, R. W. White, and W. Chu. Learning to extract cross-session search tasks. In *WWW 2013*.

[24] White, Bennett, and Dumais. Predicting short-term interests using activity-based search context. In *CIKM 2010*.

[25] B. Xiang, D. Jiang, J. Pei, X. Sun, E. Chen, and H. Li. Context-aware ranking in web search. In *SIGIR 2010*.

Understanding Website Behavior based on User Agent

Kien Pham
Computer Science and Engineering
New York University
kien.pham@nyu.edu

Aécio Santos
Computer Science and Engineering
New York University
aecio.santos@nyu.edu

Juliana Freire
Computer Science and Engineering
New York University
juliana.freire@nyu.edu

ABSTRACT

Web sites have adopted a variety of adversarial techniques to prevent web crawlers from retrieving their content. While it is possible to simulate users behavior using a browser to crawl such sites, this approach is not scalable. Therefore, understanding existing adversarial techniques is important to design crawling strategies that can adapt to retrieve the content as efficiently as possible. Ideally, a web crawler should detect the nature of the adversarial policies and select the most cost-effective means to defeat them. In this paper, we discuss the results of a large-scale study of web site behavior based on their responses to different user-agents. We issued over 9 million HTTP GET requests to 1.3 million unique web sites from DMOZ using six different user-agents and the TOR network as an anonymous proxy. We observed that web sites do change their responses depending on user-agents and IP addresses. This suggests that probing sites for these features can be an effective means to detect adversarial techniques.

Keywords

User-agent String, Web Crawler Detection, Web Cloaking, Stealth Crawling

1. INTRODUCTION

There has been a proliferation of crawlers that roam the Web. In addition to crawler agents from major search engines, there are shopping bots that gather product prices, email harvesters that collect address for marketing companies and spammers, and malicious crawlers attempting to obtain information for cyber-criminals. These crawlers can overwhelm web sites and degrade their performance. In addition, they affect log statistics leading to an overestimation of user traffic. There are also sites connected to illicit activities, such as selling illegal drugs and human trafficking, that want to avoid crawlers to minimize their exposure and eventual detection by law enforcement agents. A number of strategies can be adopted to prevent crawler access. Sites can use the Robot Exclusion Protocol (REP) to regulate what web crawlers are allowed to crawl. But since the REP is not enforced, crawlers may ignore the rules and access the forbidden information. Web sites may also choose what content to return based on the client identification included in the user-agent field of the HTTP protocol. However, this string is not reliable since the identification is not secure and one can easily spoof this information in the HTTP requests. More robust detection methods have been developed, including the use of web server logs to build classification models that learn the navigational patterns of web crawlers [7] and the adoption of mechanisms that detect human activity (e.g., embedding JavaScript code in pages to obtain evidence of mouse movement) [5].

From a crawler's perspective, this raises a new question: how to find and retrieve content from sites that adopt adversarial techniques. It is possible to automate a browser to simulate human actions, but this approach is not scalable. Since pages need to be rendered and the crawler must simulate a user's click behavior, crawler throughput would be significantly hampered. Ideally, this expensive technique should only be applied for sites that require it, provided that the crawler can identify adversarial techniques and adapt its behavior accordingly.

In this paper, we take a first step in this direction by studying how web sites respond to different web crawlers and user-agents. In addition, we are also interested in determining whether the response patterns are associated to specific topics or site types. We issued over 9M HTTP GET requests to more than 1.3M unique web sites (obtained from DMOZ) using different user agent. User agents included a web browser, different types of web crawlers (e.g., search engine providers, well-known and less-known crawlers), and an invalid user-agent string. We also issued requests in which we masked our IP address using proxies from the TOR network. To reduce the risk that sites can identify our experiment and to reduce the chance the content changes in between requests, requests with different user-agents were sent from independent machines (with different IP addresses) and concurrently. As we discuss in Section 3, the analysis of the responses uncovered many interesting facts and insights that are useful for designing adversarial crawling strategies at scale. For example, we observed that requests from less-known crawlers have a higher chance of success. In contrast, when a TOR proxy is used, not only are most requests unsuccessful, but there is also a large number of exceptions. Another important finding is that response patterns vary for different topics – sensitive topics result in a larger number of 403 (forbidden) responses.

SIGIR '16, July 17-21, 2016, Pisa, Italy

DOI: http://dx.doi.org/10.1145/2911451.2914757

The URLs used in the experiment, source code and response headers of all requests are available at https://github.com/ViDA-NYU/user-agent-study.

2. RELATED WORK

Many techniques have been proposed to detect web crawlers, for example log analysis, heuristic-based learning techniques, traffic pattern analysis and human-detection tests [1, 5, 6, 7]. Although relying on user-agent string is a naïve approach, our study shows that it is still used by web sites.

To regulate the behavior of crawlers, Web sites can implement the Robots Exclusion Protocol (REP) in a file called *robots.txt*. There have been studies that measured both REP adoption and the extent to which crawlers respect the rules set forth by sites [4, 2]. These studies found that while REP adoption is high, crawler compliance is low.

Cloaking is a technique whereby sites serve different content or URLs to humans and search engines. While there are legitimate uses for cloaking, this technique is widely used for spamming and presents a challenge for search engines [9, 8]. Cloaking detection usually requires a crawler to acquire at least two copies of the web pages: from a browser's view and from web crawler's view. In this paper, we also acquire multiple versions of pages returned to different user-agents.

3. EXPERIMENTS

3.1 Data Collection

We used DMOZ[1], a human-created directory of web sites, to collect URLs for our experiment. First, we selected URLs from all topics in DMOZ except the topic World, a non-English version URLs of DMOZ. This resulted in 1.9M URLs. Then, we grouped URLs by their web sites so that only one URL per web site is kept for the experiment. We do this to avoid hitting a web site multiple times, since this may lead a site to detect and potentially block our prober. After filtering, the original list was reduced to 1.3M URLs that were used in the experiment. Note that since each URL is associated with a DMOZ topic, we can analyze the behavior of web sites in particular topics.

3.2 Methodology

We spoofed the identity of our prober by changing the user-agent field in the header of an HTTP request. Table 1 shows 6 different user-agents corresponding to 5 different types of web crawlers. Besides well-known user-agents such as Chrome Web Browser, Google, and Bing, we used Nutch, ACHE and Empty (i.e., HTTP requests with an empty user agent). Nutch[2] is widely-adopted open-source web crawler. ACHE is focused crawler[3] and represents less-known system.

For each user-agent, we constructed an HTTP header with the corresponding user-agent string. The header was sent together with the HTTP GET requests for all URLs in our collection. We made roughly 7.8M requests for 1.3M URLs. Each URL received 6 requests (one per user-agent). Multiple requests to a URL with the same user-agent are only issued when an exception is raised (e.g., ConnectionError). To reduce the risk that sites can identify our experiment and to reduce the chance the content changes in between requests, these requests were sent simultaneously from machines with different IP addresses. For each request, we stored the entire response header and exception type.

We ran a second experiment in which our prober used a TOR[4] proxy. The HTTP requests were routed through the TOR network, and thus, the sites could not identify our IP address, although they could detect that the request was issued from within the TOR network. In this experiment, we used ACHE as the user-agent.

If a request fails and raises an exception, i.e., HTTPConnectionError or Timeout, we repeat the request at most 5 times until the web site responds. We set a delay of 20 minutes between each request to avoid web site detecting our actions by looking at request frequency.

3.3 Response Analysis

We analyzed the response headers received from all requests and DMOZ topics associated with each URL. In what follows, we present the results of this analysis.

Conflicting URLs. We call a URL *conflicting* if the status codes returned for the different user-agents are inconsistent, i.e., at least one status code that is different from the others. We discovered 85K conflicting URLs which represents 6.5% of our URL collection. This finding provides a partial answer to our first question, whether web sites behave differently to different user-agents. Figure 1 shows the distribution of conflicting URLs grouped by high-level topics. The topic *News* has the highest number of conflicting URLs (7.65%), while *Science* has the smallest number (4.36 %). The percentage of conflicting URLs is an indicator of how strictly crawler detection based on user agent is enforced by web sites in different topics.

Table 1: User-agent strings used in our experiments

ACHE	Ache
Bing	Mozilla/5.0 (compatible; bingbot/2.0; +http://www.bing.com/bingbot.htm)
Google	Mozilla/5.0 (compatible; Googlebot/2.1; +http://www.google.com/bot.html)
Browser	Mozilla/5.0 (X11; Linux x86_64) AppleWebKit/537.36 (KHTML, like Gecko) Chrome/42.0.2311.135 Safari/537.36
Nutch	Nutch
Empty	

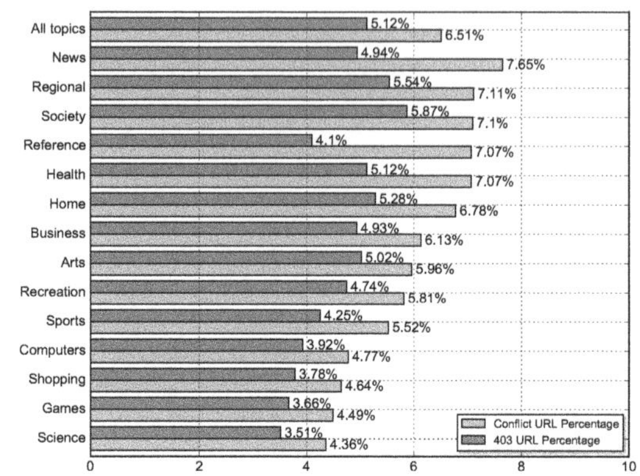

Figure 1: Percentage of URLs with conflicts and status code 403 for each topic

[1]http://www.dmoz.org
[2]http://nutch.apache.org/
[3]https://github.com/ViDA-NYU/ache
[4]https://www.torproject.org

Table 2: Number of exceptions by agents

	Connection Error	Timeout	Too Many Redirects
Google	46278	2768	165
Nutch	26494	1325	877
Bing	46410	2779	144
ACHE	45777	2581	135
Empty	47543	2238	292
Browser	45757	2335	129

Exceptions. Table 2 shows the number of exceptions raised by different user-agents. ConnectionError is the most frequent, accounting for 94.16% of all exceptions. Since this is a general exception, it could be caused either by the client or server due to network problems. Furthermore, ConnectionError exceptions happen at the network layers, therefore it does not reflect the web sites behavior on user-agents, which are handled at application layer. We have observed a few occurrences of Too-Many-Redirects exceptions, but most happen only for Nutch. This suggests that more sites block the Nutch crawler.

Status Codes. While the total number of distinct returned status codes is 56, in Table 3 we only show ones that present notable differences among our 6 user-agents. The definitions for these codes are given in Table 4[5]. Also, since most exceptions are not raised by application layer, we only take into account URLs that do not cause any exception to compute the status code statistics.

Note that the Nutch user-agent returns the highest number of status code 429 (Too Many Requests). Since Nutch is open source and has been widely adopted, it is possible that it is being misused, leading sites to block it. The Empty user-agent causes 407, 400, 403, 500, 503 which is reasonable because Empty is not a recognized user-agent string. (Service Unavailable) and 451 (Unavailable For Legal Reasons). A possible explanation is that some web sites do not want to be indexed in popular search engine, so they block Google. Another possibility is that the web sites do not respond with a 200 code because it detects spoofing in user-agent. Since Google publishes the IP addresses for its crawlers, it is easy for web sites to detect that our prober does not come for a Google address. Another interesting finding is that the ACHE user-agent returns the least number of 403 (Forbidden) codes. This suggests that sites are more permissive for less popular crawlers.

Overall, ACHE and Browser produce smaller numbers of unsuccessful status codes than Bing and Google. At a first glance, this is counter-intuitive. One possible reason is that web sites can easily detect spoofing if clients identify themselves as Google or Bing by verifying if the client's IP address is within the IP address range published by search engines. This observation suggests that to conduct a large-scale crawl, it might be a good idea to use a less popular crawler as the user-agent.

Finally, our results reveal that status codes may not provide the precise reasons for why web sites refuse access to their content. If a service is unavailable, it should return 503 to all requests, however in our experiment, the return codes differ for different user agents.

403 (Forbidden) Status Code. We found 66,911 URLs that returned 403 to at least one user-agent, we call these *403-URLs*. This represents 5.12% of all collected URLs. One question we investigated was whether there was a pattern for these URLs associated to the topics they belong to.

[5]Source: https://www.w3.org/Protocols/rfc2616/rfc2616-sec6.html

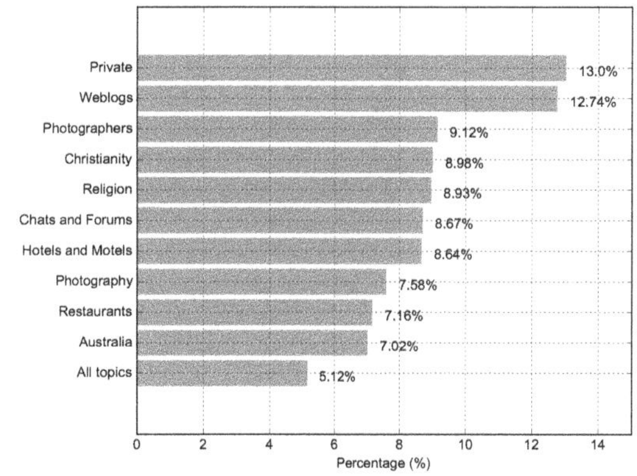

Figure 2: Topic distributions of 403-returned URLs

Since DMOZ topics are organized as tree, each URL is associated with a list of hierarchically connected topics. We grouped the 403-URLs by both lowest-level topics and highest-level topics separately. Each grouping provides different view: lowest-level topics tend to be specific while highest-level topics are more general. Figure 2 shows the top-10 lowest-level topics that have highest percentage of 403 URLs. We can easily see that topics which are more sensitive tend to return higher percentage of 403, e.g., Private, Weblogs, Religion or Chats and Forums. Note that we only take into account topics that consist of at least 100 URLs, so that the percentage values is more statistically representative. Figure 1 shows the percentage of 403 URLs over all highest-level topics. The pattern in this figure is not clear; the deviations from average percentage is not as significant as we observed in Figure 2. This is understandable since URLs from high-level topic are much more diverse than those from specific topics.

Using TOR as a Proxy. When we used TOR as routing proxy and ACHE as user-agent, we only got responses from 270K web sites out of 1.3M (20.7%); all other requests raised exceptions. This experiment indicates the ineffectiveness of using TOR to crawl anonymously. Furthermore, TOR seems to be overused for crawling, resulting in many web sites refusing access. Among the successful requests, only 29.07% of them got a 200 (OK) status code, the majority (69.17%) got a 503 (Service Unavailable) status code.

Content Difference. We analyzed the returned content by examining the content-length in the request response header. Although content-length does not show the precise differences in page content, it is cost-effective strategy to detect blocked pages [3]. Ideally, if a web site returns OK status code to all user-agents, we expect the returned content is the same as well as the content length in response header. Surprisingly, we discovered a significant difference in the returned content. We gathered 717K URLs with 200 status code returned to all user-agents. Out of these, 201K URLs, representing 28.96%, return content with different lengths. We computed the content length difference returned by each URL by subtracting length of the maximum content and that of minimum one. Figure 3 shows the histogram of content length difference, i.e., how many URLs return content with significantly different length. In the result, the length

Table 3: Number of URLs returning non-OK status code

	404	451	407	429	406	403	503	400	416	500	999	463	Total (excluding 200)
Google	24173	95	0	10	21	15365	6242	452	144	2239	1	0	49142
Bing	24734	11	0	39	72	16483	1161	383	145	2250	0	0	45275
Nutch	24319	11	0	8555	234	39147	883	450	164	2354	34	1	77168
ACHE	23583	11	0	12	14	2127	837	367	0	2192	0	0	29519
Empty	23636	11	466	10	297	16378	1921	9675	169	6976	36	418	60566
Browser	23552	11	0	17	13	4646	844	368	2	2108	0	0	31916

Table 4: Status code definitions

Status Code	Definitions
451	Unavailable For Legal Reasons
407	Proxy Authentication Required
429	Too Many Requests
406	Not Acceptable
403	Forbidden
503	Service Unavailable
400	Bad Request
416	Requested Range Not Satisfiable
500	Internal Server Error
999, 463	Undefined

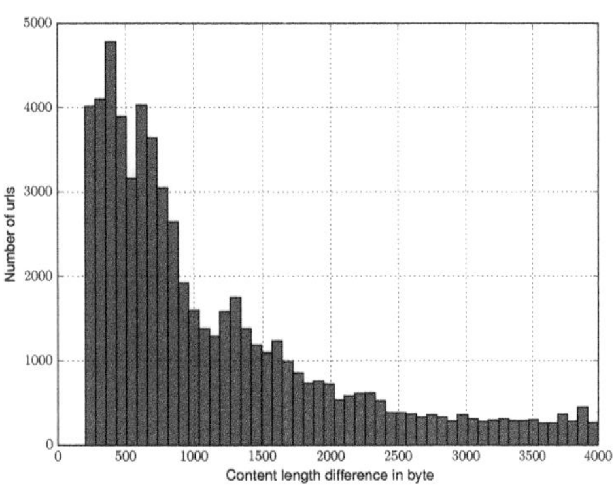

Figure 3: Content length difference in bytes

difference ranges from 1 byte to 3.6 MB, however in this figure, we omit the long tail since it is less informative. Also, we ignore cases where difference is less than 200 bytes. Although content length difference does not represent the semantic difference, it shows that web sites behaves differently to different user-agents.

4. CONCLUSIONS AND FUTURE WORK

We have carried out the first large-scale study of web site behavior based on their responses to different user-agents and to TOR proxies. The study shows that web sites respond with different content and status code to different user-agents and IP addresses. In addition, response patterns vary for different topics. The results also provide insights into potential strategies for adversarial crawling, including the use of a less popular user-agent.

There are several avenues we intend to pursue in future work. In particular, we plan to study in more detail the actual differences in the content returned to different agents as well as other aspects sites take into account for blocking crawlers (e.g., violation of the rules in robots.txt). Ultimately, our goal is to design effective techniques for adversarial crawling.

5. ACKNOWLEDGMENTS

This work was supported in part by NSF (awards CNS-1229185 and CI-EN-1405927) and the Defense Advanced Research Projects Agency (DARPA) MEMEX program award FA8750-14-2-023. We specially thank to Dr. Ari Juels for valuable feedback in the design of the experiment.

6. REFERENCES

[1] D. Doran and S. S. Gokhale. Web robot detection techniques: Overview and limitations. *Data Mining Knowledge Discovery*, pages 183–210, Jan. 2011.

[2] C. L. Giles, Y. Sun, and I. G. Councill. Measuring the web crawler ethics. In *roceedings of the 19th International Conference on World Wide Web*, pages 1101–1102, 2010.

[3] B. Jones, T.-W. Lee, N. Feamster, and P. Gill. Automated detection and fingerprinting of censorship block pages. In *Proceedings of the 2014 Conference on Internet Measurement Conference*, pages 299–304, New York, NY, USA, 2014. ACM.

[4] S. Kolay, P. D'Alberto, A. Dasdan, and A. Bhattacharjee. A larger scale study of robots.txt. In *Proceedings of the 17th International Conference on World Wide Web*, pages 1171–1172, 2008.

[5] K. Park, V. S. Pai, K.-W. Lee, and S. Calo. Securing web service by automatic robot detection. In *Proceedings of the Annual Conference on USENIX '06 Annual Technical Conference*, pages 23–23, 2006.

[6] A. Stassopoulou and M. D. Dikaiakos. Web robot detection: A probabilistic reasoning approach. *Computer Networks*, pages 265–278, 2009.

[7] P.-N. Tan and V. Kumar. Discovery of web robot sessions based on their navigational patterns. *Data Mining Knowledge Discovery*, pages 9–35, 2002.

[8] D. Y. Wang, S. Savage, and G. M. Voelker. Cloak and dagger: Dynamics of web search cloaking. In *Proceedings of the 18th ACM Conference on Computer and Communications Security*, pages 477–490, 2011.

[9] B. Wu and B. D. Davison. Cloaking and redirection: A preliminary study. In *Proceedings of the first International Workshop on Adversarial Information Retrieval on the Web*, Chiba, Japan, 2005.

Using Word Embedding to Evaluate the Coherence of Topics from Twitter Data

Anjie Fang[1], Craig Macdonald[2], Iadh Ounis[2], Philip Habel[2]
[1]a.fang.1@research.gla.ac.uk, [2]{firstname.secondname}@glasgow.ac.uk
University of Glasgow, UK

ABSTRACT

Scholars often seek to understand topics discussed on Twitter using topic modelling approaches. Several coherence metrics have been proposed for evaluating the coherence of the topics generated by these approaches, including the pre-calculated *Pointwise Mutual Information* (PMI) of word pairs and the *Latent Semantic Analysis* (LSA) word representation vectors. As Twitter data contains abbreviations and a number of peculiarities (e.g. hashtags), it can be challenging to train effective PMI data or LSA word representation. Recently, *Word Embedding* (WE) has emerged as a particularly effective approach for capturing the similarity among words. Hence, in this paper, we propose new Word Embedding-based topic coherence metrics. To determine the usefulness of these new metrics, we compare them with the previous PMI/LSA-based metrics. We also conduct a large-scale crowdsourced user study to determine whether the new Word Embedding-based metrics better align with human preferences. Using two Twitter datasets, our results show that the WE-based metrics can capture the coherence of topics in tweets more robustly and efficiently than the PMI/LSA-based ones.

1. INTRODUCTION

Topic modelling approaches can be used by scholars to capture the topics discussed in various corpora, including news articles, books [5] and tweets [4, 15]. Since typically for such scenarios no ground-truth exists to determine how well the topic modelling approach works, a number of topic coherence metrics have been proposed to assess the performance of the topic modelling approaches in extracting comprehensible and coherent topics from corpora. These metrics often capture the semantic similarity of words in a topic using external sources such as Wikipedia or WordNet.

To evaluate the coherence of a topic, a coherence metric averages the semantic similarity of words in topics. Recently, two effective coherence metrics, namely the *Pointwise Mutual Information* (PMI)-based [11] of word pairs and the *Latent Semantic Analysis* (LSA) word representation-based [3] metrics, have been adapted to tweet corpora [3]. Through a large crowdsourcing study, Fang et al. [3] found that a PMI-based metric using a Twitter background dataset aligned best with human preferences of topic coherence. However, some challenges remain, particularly because of the uniqueness of Twitter data, where unlike many other corpora, tweets contain abbreviations, several peculiarities (e.g. hashtags) and a vast vocabulary. For example, the PMI metric leverages the co-occurrence data of approx. 354 million word pairs [3], which is voluminous to store. Recently, *Word Embedding* (WE) has emerged as a more effective word representation than, among others, LSA [8, 9, 10]. Using WE word representation models, scholars have improved the performance of classification [6], machine translation [16], and other tasks. However, it remains to be seen whether Word Embedding can be effectively used to evaluate the coherence of topics in comparison with existing metrics.

In this paper, we propose a new Word Embedding-based metric, which we instantiate using 8 different Word Embedding models (trained using different datasets and different parameters). We also use as baselines two types of existing effective metrics based on PMI and LSA. We conduct a large-scale pairwise user study, comparing human judgements with the 8 WE-based and the 4 PMI/LSA-based baseline metrics. We generate the topic pairs using three topic modelling approaches (i.e. LDA, *Twitter LDA* and *Pachinko Allocation Model*). First, we rank the topic modelling approaches using each of the deployed coherence metrics. Second, we assess the extent to which the topical preferences emanating from the 12 metrics align with human assessments. Using two Twitter datasets, our results show that the new Word Embedding-based metrics outperform the PMI/LSA-based ones in capturing the coherence of topics in terms of robustness and efficientness.

2. BACKGROUND & RELATED WORK

In this paper, we use three topic modelling approaches to generate topics for Twitter data. They have been chosen because of their reasonable computational cost and scalability on high volumes of tweets. First, we use LDA [2], where each of K topics is represented by a term distribution ϕ, while each document has a topic distribution θ. Second, we experiment with an extension of LDA, the *Pachinko Allocation Model* (PAM) [7]. The topic layer in PAM is divided into a super-topic layer (distribution over sub-topics) and a sub-topic layer (distribution over terms). Third, we use a topic modelling approach tailored to tweet corpora, namely *Twitter LDA* (TLDA) [15], where a Bernoulli distribution is estimated and used to control the selection between "real" terms and background terms. PAM and TLDA are known

SIGIR '16, July 17-21, 2016, Pisa, Italy

DOI: http://dx.doi.org/10.1145/2911451.2914729

to generate more coherent topics than LDA on news corpora and tweets, respectively [7, 15].

There are two main existing types of effective topic coherence metrics. One metric, *Pointwise Mutual Information* (PMI), developed by Newman et al. [11], captures the semantic similarity of pairs of words in a topic, by examining how the word pairs co-occur in external sources such as Wikipedia. PMI has been tested on news articles and books. Fang et al. [3] showed that the PMI metric deployed using Twitter background datasets was closest to human judgements. Moreover, they also adapted a second type of metric, the LSA word representation metric, to evaluate the coherence of topics. The LSA-based coherence metric proved to be less aligned with human assessments than the PMI-based one on tweet corpora.

Turning to Word Embedding approaches, recently scholars have applied *Feed-Forward Neural Network* (FFNN) for Word Embeddings [1]. In this approach, similar to LSA, a word is represented as a continuous vector in a Word Embedding model. Based on FFNN, Mikolov et al. [8, 9] proposed a *skip-gram* model to generate Word Embeddings from large datasets more efficiently and effectively. Godin et al. [6] improved the performance of document classification via Word Embeddings. Indeed, Neural Networks were shown to generate more effective word representations than LSA [10]. Therefore, in this paper, we propose new Word Embedding-based metrics to capture the coherence of topics. We adopt the *skip-gram* approach to obtain our Word Embedding models. In the next section, we explain how we deploy the PMI, LSA, and WE-based metrics.

3. COHERENCE METRICS

We use three types of coherence metrics for Twitter data based on PMI and LSA, and Word Embeddings (WE), which are instantiated into 12 metrics. We first define the existing PMI & LSA-based metrics before introducing the new Word Embedding-based metric to evaluate the coherence of topics.

PMI & LSA metrics. A topic t can be represented by the top $n = 10$ words ($\{w_1, w_2, ..., w_{10}\}$) (selected by their probabilities ($p(w|z)$) in Φ for this topic). The coherence of a topic can be calculated by averaging the semantic similarity of pairs of words associated with that topic (Equation (1)). Both Newman et al. [11] and Fang et al. [3] showed that the PMI of pairs of words can capture the coherence of topics identified from both standard and tweet corpora. In particular, for the PMI metric, Equation (2) is used to measure the similarity of word w_i and w_j based on co-occurrence statistics obtained from a background corpus (e.g. Wikipedia or a large sample of tweets - detailed in Section 5) along with Equation (1). Note that the PMIs of word pairs need to be pre-calculated from these external datasets.

$$Coherence(t) = \frac{1}{\sum_{m=1}^{n-1} m} \sum_{i=1}^{n} \sum_{j=i+1}^{n} f_{ss}(w_i, w_j) \quad (1)$$

$$f_{ss}(w_i, w_j) = PMI(w_i, w_j) = log\frac{p(w_i, w_j)}{p(w_i) \times p(w_j)} \quad (2)$$

LSA can also be used to capture the semantic similarity of word pairs [13]. In applying LSA, each word is represented by a dense vector in the reduced LSA space, V_{m_i}, obtained by applying Singular Value Decomposition on a background corpus. Therefore, the LSA metric determines the similarity of two words by measuring the distance between the vectors of the words using a cosine function, by replacing Equation (2) in Equation (1) with:

$$f_{ss}(w_i, w_j) = cosine(V_{w_i}, V_{w_j}) \quad (3)$$

WE metric. Recently, as highlighted above, Word Embeddings have been shown to produce more effective word representations than LSA. Hence, we propose the use of WE vectors V_{w_i}, obtained from a pre-trained Word Embedding model on a large text dataset. If two words are semantically similar, the *cosine* similarity – as per Equation (3) – of their word vectors is higher. We describe how we train the Word Embedding models in Section 5.

We use the methodology explained in Section 4 to examine whether the WE-based metric can capture the coherence of topics from tweets, and how well WE, PMI, and LSA metrics compare with human judgements.

4. EVALUATION METHODOLOGY

We follow Fang et al. [3], and adopt a pairwise user study to gather human preferences to evaluate the effectiveness of the aforementioned metrics. Since it is difficult for humans to generate graded coherence scores of topics, we select a pairwise study, where a human is asked to choose which of two topics is more coherent. For our study, we first generate topic pairs using the three topic modelling approaches: LDA, PAM, and TLDA. We then determine whether the metrics can accurately identify the more coherent topics compared with human coherence assessments.

Ground Truth Generation. We use pairwise comparisons for the three topic modelling approaches, specifically: LDA vs. TLDA, LDA vs. PAM and TLDA vs. PAM. Each *comparison unit* consists of a certain number of topic pairs, where each pair contains a topic from topic models T_1 and T_2, respectively. Note that T_1 and T_2 are generated using any two topic modelling approaches among the three. In the pairwise user study, a human is asked to choose the more coherent topic among two topics presented in a given topic pair. For ease of assessment, we present the human with two similar topics in a topic pair. We first randomly select a number of topics from the topic model T_1. For each selected topic, we use Equation (4) to select its closest topic in T_2, where V_t is a vector representation using the term distribution of topic t. The selected topic pair is denoted as Pair($T_1 \rightarrow T_2$). Similarly, we also generate the same number of Pair($T_2 \rightarrow T_1$) for the comparison unit (T_1, T_2). Hence, for each comparison unit, we obtain a set of topic pairs. For example, we generate Pairs(LDA→TLDA & TLDA→LDA) for the comparison unit (LDA, TLDA).

$$closest_{t_j^{T_1}} = argmax_{i<K} \ (cosine(V_{t_j^{T_1}}, V_{t_i^{T_2}})) \quad (4)$$

A given coherence metric generates a coherence score for each topic in a topic pair. Thus for each comparison unit, we have a group of data pairs. We then apply the Wilcoxon signed-rank test to compute the statistical significance level of the difference between the two sets of data sampled in order to determine the better topic model between the two approaches utilised (e.g. TLDA > LDA). Therefore the outcomes of three comparison units gives the performance ranking order of the three topic modelling approaches. For instance, we obtain the ranking order LDA(1st)>TLDA(2nd) >PAM(3rd) from LDA>TLDA, LDA>PAM & TLDA>PAM. Similar to Fang et al., we do not observe a Condorcet paradox (e.g. TLDA>LDA, LDA>PAM & PAM>TLDA) in our experiments. Turning to our user study, a topic receives a vote if it is preferred by a human. Using the vote fraction of topics, we can also obtain an ordering of the three topic modelling approaches, i.e. the human ground-truth ranking.

Comparison of Coherence Metrics. A good metric should rank the three topic modelling approaches in a high

Table 1: Two used Twitter datasets.

Name	Time Period	Users#	Tweets#
(1) NYJ	20/05/2015-19/08/2015	2,853	946,006
(2) TVD	8pm-10pm 02/04/2015	121,594	343,511

agreement with humans. First, the three topic modelling approaches are ranked using each of the deployed coherence metrics. Second, the rankings are compared to the rankings from the generated ground-truth to identify which of the metrics agree most with the human assessments.

5. DATASETS & EXPERIMENTAL SETUP

Datasets. In this paper, we use the same two Twitter datasets from [3]. The first dataset[1] is comprised of the tweets of 2,852 newspaper journalists in the US state of New York posted from 20 May 2015 to 19 August 2015, denoted here as NYJ. The second dataset consists of tweets related to the first TV political leaders debate during the UK General Election held in April 2015, denoted as TVD[2]. Details of these two datasets are shown in Table 1.

Metrics Setup. We deploy 12 coherence metrics in total, which are implemented by two external sources: Wikipedia and a separate background Twitter dataset. The background Twitter dataset, which is also identical to the one used in [3], represents 1%-5% random tweets crawled from 01 Jan 2015 to 30 June 2015. Following [3], we remove stopwords, terms occurring in less than 20 tweets, and the retweets. The remaining tweets (30,151,847) are used to pre-calculate the PMI data, LSA word representation, and the WE models. The setup of the 12 metrics is described below:
Existing PMI/LSA metrics (4). We use the LSA word representation (1M tokens) and the PMI data (179M word pairs) from the *SEMILAR*[3] platform to implement the Wikipedia PMI/LSA-based metrics (W-PMI/W-LSA). For the Twitter PMI/LSA-based metrics (T-PMI/T-LSA), the Twitter background data contains 609k tokens and 354M word pairs.
WE metrics using GloVe (4). These metrics are instantiated using Word Embedding models from Wikipedia[4] and Twitter, pre-trained using the *GloVe* [12] tool. The metrics are denoted as G-W-WE$_{d=\{200,300\}}$ and G-T-WE$_{d=\{100,200\}}$, respectively, where $d = 100$ means that the size of word vectors in the WE model is 100.
WE metrics using word2vec (4). These metrics use Word Embedding models newly trained using the separate Twitter background dataset, but making use of the *word2vec*[5] tool. We denote the coherence metrics using our newly trained WE models (504K tokens) as T-WE$^{w=\{1,3\}}_{d=\{200,500\}}$, where w is the size of the context window size in the trained models.

We noticed that the unstemmed WE word representation performs poorly in our experiments. Hence, we stem the words in our 4 newly trained (*word2vec*) WE models. Note that the WE models of *GloVe* are not stemmed. We chose to use WE models with different pre-set parameters (e.g. context window and vector size) as we wish to examine whether these parameters affect the coherence evaluation task.

Topic Pairs Setup. Mallet[6] and Twitter LDA[7] are used to implement the three topic modelling approaches for the two Twitter datasets. The LDA parameters α and β are set to $50/K$ and 0.01 according to [14], and for TLDA $\gamma = 20$ according to [15]. Since the NYJ dataset contains many topics given the length of time and the fact that journalists discuss many issues, we use a high number of topics, $K = 100$. On the other hand, because the TVD dataset covers only one debate and the accompanying 2 hours' tweets, we use a smaller number of topic, $K = 30$. Each topic modelling approach is repeated 5 times. Therefore, for each topic modelling approach, we obtain 500 (150) topics in the NYJ (TVD) dataset, respectively. We use the methodology described in Section 4 to generate 100 topic pairs for each comparison unit. In total, we obtain 600 topic pairs from the two used Twitter datasets. In Section 6, we explain how we perform the pairwise user study using these 600 topic pairs.

[1] This dataset was collected by tracking the journalists' Twitter handles using Twitter Streaming API. [2] Collected by searching for debate-related hashtags using the Twitter Streaming API [3] semanticsimilarity.org [4] It also contains *English Gigaword V5*. [5] deeplearning4j.org [6] mallet.cs.umass.edu [7] github.com/minghui/Twitter-LDA

6. PAIRWISE USER STUDY

We now describe how we use CrowdFlower[8] workers to perform the topic preference task while ensuring job quality.

Job Description. We show a CrowdFlower worker the top 10 words (ranked by their probabilities in a topic) of 2 topics in a topic pair, and the 3 most retweeted tweets in these 2 topics. We ask the workers to select the more coherent topic among the two presented using these 10 words. We describe a more coherent topic as one that is less mixed and that can be easily interpreted. The workers are instructed to take into account: 1) the number of semantically similar words (e.g. Knicks & basketball) among the 10 shown words, 2) whether the presented words suggest a mixed topic (i.e. more than one discussion) and 3) whether the displayed words gives more information about a discussion. To reach a decision, a worker can also use three associated tweets for the two topics. We give two rules for using these tweets: 1) whether the 10 shown words are reflected by their tweets and 2) whether these tweets are related with the two topics. We collect 5 judgements from 5 different workers for each topic pair. For each judgement, we paid a worker $0.05.

Quality Control. To ensure quality control, only those workers who passed a test were allowed to enter the topic preference task. For the test, we choose a number of topic pairs. The topic preference of the selected topic pairs were verified in advance, and they were used to set the test questions for the quality control. The worker must have maintained more than 70% accuracy on the test questions through the whole task, otherwise their judgements were nullified. Overall, we used 168 trusted workers for this user study.

7. RESULTS

We first demonstrate whether the 12 used coherence metrics can differentiate the three topic modelling approaches in comparison with human assessments. We also show whether they can distinguish the more coherent topic from a topic pair in a manner similar to that of humans.

The column "Ranking Order Matching" in Table 2 shows the extent to which the ranking order of the 12 metrics exactly or partially matches that of human judgements for our two Twitter datasets. The human ground-truth ranking order is LDA^{1st}>TLDA^{2nd} >PAM^{3rd} for the NYJ dataset, and TLDA^{1st}>LDA$^{2nd/3rd}$>PAM$^{2nd/3rd}$ for the TVD one. If there are no significant differences between two topic modelling approaches, they share the same rank in the table. If a metric receives a ranking such as LDA^{1st}>TLDA$^{2nd/3rd}$ >PAM$^{2nd/3rd}$ in the NYJ dataset, we say that the ranking order partially matches the human ground-truth one.

We find, first, that the PMI-based metrics differentiate the three topic modelling approaches very well, with the ex-

[8] crowdflower.com

Table 2: The matching of the ranking order of the three topic modelling approaches from each metric and from humans, and the agreement of the topic preferences between each metric and humans.

Metrics	Ranking Order Matching		Preferences Agreement	
	NYJ	TVD	NYJ	TVD
(1) T-PMI	✔	✔	75.7%▲	51.0%
(2) W-PMI	✔	†	65.5%▲	56.0%
(3) T-LSA	✖	✖	47.6%	46.6%
(4) W-LSA	†	†	61.3%▲	47.3%
(5) G-T-WE$_{d=100}$	✖	✖	44.6%	39.3%
(6) G-T-WE$_{d=200}$	✖	✖	48.0%	39.3%
(7) G-W-WE$^{w=10}_{d=200}$	✖	✖	48.0%	43.3%
(8) G-W-WE$^{w=10}_{d=300}$	†	✖	50.6%	46.0%
(9) T-WE$^{w=1}_{d=200}$	†	†	65.3%▲	60.3%▲
(10) T-WE$^{w=1}_{d=500}$	†	†	66.7%▲	60.0%▲
(11) T-WE$^{w=3}_{d=200}$	†	†	64.3%▲	61.0%▲
(12) T-WE$^{w=3}_{d=500}$	†	†	70.7%▲	61.0%▲

"✔"/"†" means that the ranking order from a metric **exactly/partly** matches that from human judgements. "✖" indicates that the ranking order from a metric does not match that from human judgements or the metric cannot give a significant ranking order. "▲" represents that a metric have a high agreement ($\geq 60\%$) with humans.

ception of the W-PMI metric in the TVD dataset, whose ranking order only partially matches the ground-truth order. Second, all of our WE-based metrics using our trained WE models partially match the ground-truth ranking order. This finding indicates that the WE-based metrics have the ability to differentiate the three topic modelling approaches comparably to humans. However, the WE-based metrics using the *GloVe* pre-trained models do not differentiate well between the modelling approaches. One possible reason is that the words in those WE models are not stemmed. The coherence metric focuses on capturing the semantic similarity between words rather than their syntax. The other possible reason is that words on Twitter are different from the words in Wikipedia, as tweets contain abbreviations, misspellings and hashtags. Moreover, if the time period of the Twitter background dataset does not match that of the testing datasets form which we extract the topics, then the trained WE models may not adequately capture the semantic similarity of words, as is likely the case for *GloVe*.

The column "Preference Agreement" in Table 2 lists the agreement rate on choosing the preferred topics from 300 topic pairs in the two Twitter datasets between each metric and humans. As there are three options ("Topic 1", "Topic 2" and "No preference") in the topic preference task, the baseline agreement rate is 33.3%. We obverse that the WE-based metrics using our trained WE models have consistently high agreement rates across both datasets. In addition, while most of the metrics do not perform well on the TVD dataset, the WE-based metrics using our trained WE models have the hignest agreement with humans. We also find that a slightly higher dimension and context window are likely to get a better agreement rate, such as T-WE$^{w=3}_{500}$. It is interesting to note that unlike the newly trained WE models, the WE-based metric using WE models from *GloVe* do not have a high agreement with humans.

In summary, the WE-based metrics can effectively capture the coherence of topics from tweets, with a high agreement with humans. The WE-based metrics perform more robustly across the two Twitter datasets. Besides, the WE based metrics have an additional important benefit. In contrast to the PMI-based coherence that leverages the PMI data of a few hundreds millions of word pairs, the WE-based metrics use only a few hundred thousand (the size of vocabulary) words' vectors. Moreover, since *skip gram* is highly parallelizable, it is much faster to train a WE model than an LSA one [6]. Hence, we conclude that the WE-based metrics are more robust, efficient, and practical to use than the PMI/LSA-based ones.

8. CONCLUSIONS

We proposed a new *Word Embedding*-based topic coherence metric, and instantiated it using 8 different WE models. To identify the usefulness of these WE-based metrics, we conducted a large-scale pairwise user study to gauge human preferences. We examined which of the 8 WE-based metrics and the 4 existing PMI/LSA-based metrics align best with human assessments. We found that the WE-based metrics can effectively capture the coherence of topics from tweets. In addition, they performed more robustly and more efficiently than the PMI/LSA-based metrics. In future work, we will explore how the *Word Embedding* training parameters affect the coherence evaluation task.

9. REFERENCES

[1] Y. Bengio, R. Ducharme, P. Vincent, and C. Janvin. A neural probabilistic language model. *The Journal of Machine Learning Research*, 3, 2003.

[2] D. M. Blei, A. Y. Ng, and M. I. Jordan. Latent dirichlet allocation. *the Journal of machine Learning research*, 3:993–1022, 2003.

[3] A. Fang, C. Macdonald, I. Ounis, and P. Habel. Topics in tweets: A user study of topic coherence metrics for Twitter data. In *Proc. of ECIR*, 2016.

[4] A. Fang, I. Ounis, P. Habel, C. Macdonald, and N. Limsopatham. Topic-centric classification of Twitter user's political orientation. In *Proc. of SIGIR*, 2015.

[5] T. L. Griffiths and M. Steyvers. Finding scientific topics. In *Proc. of NAS*, 2004.

[6] R. Lebret and R. Collobert. N-gram-based low-dimensional representation for document classification. In *Proc. of ICLP*, 2015.

[7] W. Li and A. McCallum. Pachinko allocation: DAG-structured mixture models of topic correlations. In *Proc. of ICML*, 2006.

[8] T. Mikolov, K. Chen, G. Corrado, and J. Dean. efficient estimation of word representations in vector space. In *Proc. of ICLR workshop*, 2013.

[9] T. Mikolov, I. Sutskever, K. Chen, G. S. Corrado, and J. Dean. Distributed representations of words and phrases and their compositionality. In *Proc. of NIPS*, 2013.

[10] T. Mikolov, W. Yih, and G. Zweig. Linguistic regularities in continuous space word representations. In *Proc. of HLT-NAACL*, 2013.

[11] D. Newman, J. H. Lau, K. Grieser, and T. Baldwin. Automatic evaluation of topic coherence. In *Proc. of NAACL*, 2010.

[12] J. Pennington, R. Socher, and C. D. Manning. GloVe: Global vectors for word representation. In *Proc. of EMNLP*, 2014.

[13] G. Recchia and M. N. Jones. More data trumps smarter algorithms: Comparing pointwise mutual information with latent semantic analysis. *Behavior research methods*, 41:647–656, 2009.

[14] M. Steyvers and T. Griffiths. Probabilistic topic models. *Handbook of latent semantic analysis*, 427:424–440, 2007.

[15] W. X. Zhao, J. Jiang, J. Weng, J. He, E.-P. Lim, H. Yan, and X. Li. Comparing Twitter and traditional media using topic models. In *Proc. of ECIR*, 2011.

[16] W. Y. Zou, R. Socher, D. M. Cer, and C. D. Manning. Bilingual word embeddings for phrase-based machine translation. In *Proc. of EMNLP*, 2013.

Utilizing Focused Relevance Feedback

Elinor Brondwine
elinor@tx.technion.ac.il

Anna Shtok
annabel@tx.technion.ac.il

Oren Kurland
kurland@ie.technion.ac.il

Faculty of Industrial Engineering and Management
Technion, Israel

ABSTRACT

We present a novel study of ad hoc retrieval methods utilizing document-level relevance feedback and/or *focused relevance feedback*; namely, passages marked as (non-)relevant. The first method uses a novel mixture model that integrates relevant and non-relevant information at the language model level. The second method fuses retrieval scores produced by using relevant and non-relevant information separately. Empirical exploration attests to the merits of our methods, and sheds light on the effectiveness of using and integrating relevance feedback for textual units of varying granularities.

Keywords: focused relevance feedback

1. INTRODUCTION

Most previous work on using relevance feedback for ad hoc (query-based) document retrieval has focused on utilizing feedback provided at the document level. Utilizing information induced from relevant documents can significantly improve retrieval effectiveness [12, 13]. The effective utilization of non-relevant documents, on the other hand, has been demonstrated mainly for very difficult queries [16, 7].

Relevant documents can also contain non-relevant information. Thus, utilizing *focused relevance feedback*, that is, feedback for passages in relevant documents, can be of merit. For example, using information induced from relevant passages can improve retrieval effectiveness [14].

We present a study of methods that utilize positive and/or negative relevance feedback for documents and/or for passages. Our first method uses a novel mixture model that integrates, at the language model level, information induced from relevant and non-relevant units (documents and/or passages). Our second method fuses retrieval scores attained by using, separately, relevant and non-relevant units.

Empirical evaluation sheds light on the effectiveness of using information induced from relevant and non-relevant units of different granularities and their integration. For example, the best performance of our methods was attained using information induced from relevant passages and non-relevant documents.

Our main novel contribution is the development of methods that (i) use relevance feedback at both document and passage levels, and/or (ii) utilize non-relevant passages.

2. RELATED WORK

Methods using information induced from both relevant and non-relevant documents emphasize terms that appear in the former and downplay the importance of those appearing in the latter (e.g., [6, 12, 13, 16]). A similar principle, although implemented using different techniques, is applied in our methods that utilize also (non-)relevant passages.

Findings about the merits of using information induced from non-relevant documents have largely been inconclusive [6, 5, 13]. Notable exceptions are work on addressing very difficult queries [16, 7] and on the document routing task [15]. In contrast to our work, information induced from (non-)relevant passages in relevant documents was not used.

Shen and Zhai [14] showed the merits of using relevant (but not non-relevant) passages in the mixture model [17]. We extend the mixture model by using both relevant and non-relevant feedback units (documents and/or passages). Automatically identifying (non-)effective passages in (non-)relevant documents and using these for retrieval has shown no merit [11, 9]. In contrast, our methods utilize true relevance feedback for passages and documents.

A mixture model, different than ours, was used to induce a query model from *pseudo* relevant documents using non-relevant documents [10]. In contrast to our work, relevant documents and passage-level feedback were not used.

3. RETRIEVAL FRAMEWORK

Let D_{init} denote an initial list of documents retrieved from corpus C in response to query q by some retrieval method. Suppose that relevance feedback is provided for documents in D_F ($\subset D_{init}$); specifically, R_d and NR_d are the sets of relevant and non-relevant documents in D_F, respectively.

Relevant documents can also contain non relevant information. Accordingly, we further assume that *focused relevance feedback* is provided for relevant documents. Namely, non-overlapping variable length passages of documents in R_d are marked as relevant to q; unmarked passages are considered non-relevant. We concatenate all relevant and non-relevant passages in each relevant document into a single *relevant pseudo passage* and a single *non-relevant pseudo passage*, respectively; the order of concatenation has no effect since we use unigram language models that assume term

SIGIR '16, July 17-21, 2016, Pisa, Italy

DOI: http://dx.doi.org/10.1145/2911451.2914695

independence. R_p and NR_p are the sets of pseudo relevant and non-relevant passages in documents in R_d, henceforth simply referred to as relevant and non-relevant passages, respectively. Herein, R refers to the set of either relevant documents R_d or relevant passages R_p; NR is the set of non-relevant documents (NR_d) or non-relevant passages (NR_p).

Below we present two retrieval methods, based on unigram language models, that utilize the relevance feedback. The maximum likelihood estimate (MLE) of term w with respect to a set S of texts is $p_S^{MLE}(w) \stackrel{def}{=} \frac{\sum_{x \in S} c(w,x)}{\sum_{x \in S} \sum_{w' \in x} c(w',x)}$; $c(w,x)$ is the count of w in text x. We use $p_x^{Dir}(w)$ to denote the probability assigned to term w by a Dirichlet smoothed unigram language model induced from text x [17]. The similarity between two language models, $p_y(\cdot)$ and $p_z(\cdot)$, is measured using cross entropy, where higher values correspond to decreased similarity:

$$CE(p_y(\cdot) \mid\mid p_z(\cdot)) = -\sum_w p_y(w) \log p_z(w). \quad (1)$$

3.1 Distillation model

The goal of our first method is to "distill" the aspects most relevant to the information need from the feedback. For example, the premise of the mixture model [17] is that terms in relevant documents are generated either by a relevance topic language model or by the corpus language model. We generalize the mixture model to utilize both relevant and non-relevant feedback units (documents and/or passages).

We assume that terms in units in R (i.e., all relevant documents or all relevant passages) are generated by a mixture of (i) the relevance topic model, $p_{rel}(\cdot)$, which we want to estimate; (ii) the corpus language model, $p_C^{MLE}(\cdot)$, which is assumed to represent a *general* non-relevant document; and, (iii) a *query-specific* irrelevance topic model, $p_{NR}^{MLE}(\cdot)$, induced from the non-relevant units (NR). Following work on using negative relevance feedback, if w is a query term we set $p_{NR}^{MLE}(w) \stackrel{def}{=} 0$ and re-normalize the probabilities [16].

We estimate $p_{rel}(\cdot)$ by using the EM algorithm to maximize the log likelihood of units in R:

$$\sum_{x \in R} \sum_w c(w,x) \log \big((1-\lambda_1-\lambda_2)p_{rel}(w) + \lambda_1 p_{NR}^{MLE}(w) + \lambda_2 p_C^{MLE}(w)\big); \quad (2)$$

λ_1 and λ_2 are free parameters. As is common in work on query language models [17, 1], we interpolate $p_{rel}(\cdot)$ with the original query model:

$$p_{distill}(w) \stackrel{def}{=} \lambda_q p_q^{MLE}(w) + (1-\lambda_q)p_{rel}(w); \quad (3)$$

λ_q is a free parameter. We then rank the documents in the corpus using $-CE(p_{distill}(\cdot)||p_d^{Dir}(\cdot))$.

We instantiate Equation 2 using R ($\in \{R_d, R_p\}$) and NR ($\in \{NR_d, NR_p\}$). The resultant four models attained from Equation 3 are denoted **Distill(R,NR)**.

3.2 Score-based fusion

The second retrieval model is based on the principle that documents similar to the relevant units and dissimilar from the non-relevant units should be rewarded. Specifically, we apply a two-step approach inspired by work on using *only* the query and non-relevant documents [16]. First, a relevance topic model, $p_r(\cdot)$, is induced from the relevant units in R ($\in \{R_d, R_p\}$) using *some approach*. Then, the document corpus is ranked using $-CE(p_r(\cdot)||p_d^{Dir}(\cdot))$. Second, the top n documents are *re-ranked* by the similarity of their language models with $p_r(\cdot)$ and dissimilarity from the language models induced from non-relevant units in NR. Formally, documents d are ranked in descending order of the following score-based fusion:

$$-\alpha CE(p_r(\cdot)||p_d^{Dir}(\cdot)) + (1-\alpha) \min_{x \in NR} CE(p_x^{MLE}(\cdot)||p_d^{Dir}(\cdot)); \quad (4)$$

α is a free parameter. As in the distillation model, for query term w and non-relevant unit x ($\in NR$): $p_x^{MLE}(w) \stackrel{def}{=} 0$ and the probabilities are re-normalized[1].

Various methods can be used to induce $p_r(\cdot)$ from a set of relevant units, R ($\in \{R_d, R_p\}$). We use the standard mixture model [17] which is a special case of our distillation model from Equation 3 when setting $\lambda_1 = 0$ in Equation 2.[2] Equation 4 is then instantiated using a choice of NR ($\in \{NR_d, NR_p\}$). The four resultant score-based fusion methods are denoted **SF(R,NR)**.

4. EXPERIMENTAL SETUP

For experiments we used the INEX corpus[3] which contains 2,666,190 Wikipedia articles. We used the 120 queries from the ad hoc tracks of 2009 and 2010 for which binary document-level and (arbitrary-length) passage-level relevance judgments are available; unmarked text in relevant documents is considered non-relevant [2]. The average number of relevant documents per query is 86. The average percentage of relevant text in a relevant document is 41.5%; i.e., most text in relevant documents does not pertain to the query. We re-visit this important point below.

Krovetz stemming was applied to documents and queries and stopwords on the INQUERY list were removed. Indri 5.3 (http://www.lemurproject.org/indri) was used for experiments. The initial ranking from which D_{init} is derived is induced using standard language-model-based retrieval [17]: document d is scored by $-CE(p_q^{MLE}(\cdot)||p_d^{Dir}(\cdot))$ (see Equation 1). The Dirichlet smoothing parameter in document language models, μ, was set to 1000 in all methods [18].

The document feedback set, D_F, contains $2k$ documents: the k highest ranked relevant documents (R_d) and the k highest ranked non-relevant documents (NR_d) in D_{init}; $k \in \{1, 2, \ldots, 5\}$; each value entails an experimental setting. The goal was to ameliorate across-query effects that are due to varying numbers of (non-)relevant documents at top ranks.

Mean average precision at cutoff 1000 (MAP) serves as the retrieval evaluation measure. Two evaluation paradigms were employed: **standard** (regular) and **residual** collection. In the residual paradigm [3], all documents in D_F

[1]Equation 4 is conceptually reminiscent of the MultiNeg method from [16] that utilizes the query and non-relevant documents for re-ranking. Experiments — numbers are omitted due to space considerations — reveal the following. The approach in Equation 4 yields better performance in our setting when using min rather than average. The approach is also superior to using a single model, $p_{NR}^{MLE}(\cdot)$, induced from the non-relevant units; cf., the SingleNeg method [16].

[2]We found that using relevance model #3 (RM3) [8, 1] results in similar conclusions to those we present below. Actual results are omitted due to space considerations.

[3]http://www.mpi-inf.mpg.de/departments/databases-and-information-systems/software/inex

were removed from result lists and relevance judgments files; MAP is measured on result lists of 1000 documents. Statistically significant performance differences are determined using the paired two-tailed t-test with $p < 0.05$.

Free-parameter values are set using leave-one-out cross-validation performed over queries per experimental setting; MAP is the optimization measure. The value ranges are as follows: λ_q (Equation 3) is in $\{0.2, 0.5, 0.8\}$; λ_1 and λ_2 (Equation 2) are in $\{0, 0.1, 0.5, 0.9\}$; $\lambda_1 + \lambda_2 < 1$; α (Equation 4) is in $\{0, 0.2, \ldots, 1\}$; the number of documents re-ranked in the score-based fusion method, n, is set to 1000. As is common [17, 1], language models induced using relevance feedback are clipped to ν ($\in \{10, 25, 50\}$) terms.

As noted, the standard mixture model [17], henceforth MM, is a special instance of our distillation model when setting $\lambda_1 = 0$ in Equation 2 (i.e., non-relevant units are not used) and applying Equation 3. MM is also used to induce the relevance topic model, $p_r(\cdot)$, used in Equation 4. Hence, we use **MM(R_d)** which utilizes the relevant documents (R_d) and **MM(R_p)** (also used in [14]) which utilizes relevant passages (R_p) as reference comparisons. The EM algorithm used in the mixture and distillation models converged in 13-14 iterations.

5. EXPERIMENTAL RESULTS

Figure 1 depicts the performance results. We see that the more feedback documents are used (i.e., higher k), the more effective the retrieval. Specifically, for the residual evaluation paradigm (Figures 1(c) and 1(d)), where MAP values decrease with increasing k due to removing the given relevant documents from *all* rankings [4], the relative performance improvements of the feedback-based methods with respect to the initial ranking increase as a function of k.

Relevant units. Figure 1 shows that in *all* cases, using relevant passages ($R = R_p$) yields better performance than using relevant documents ($R = R_d$): compare a solid curve with white markers ($R = R_p$) to a dotted curve with gray markers of the same type ($R = R_d$). This finding can be attributed to the fact that relevant documents contain much non-relevant information as mentioned in Section 4.

The distillation model. Figures 1(a) and 1(c) show that in comparison to MM(R), which does not utilize non-relevant units, and regardless of the choice of R, using also non-relevant documents in our distillation model improves retrieval effectiveness in a vast majority of cases. For the standard evaluation, the distillation method yields improvements in 9 out of 10 cases (Distill(R_d,NR_d) vs. MM(R_d) and Distill(R_p,NR_d) vs. MM(R_p) over 5 values of k); in 7 cases the improvements are statistically significant. For the residual evaluation, effectiveness is improved in 7 out of 10 cases with 4 improvements being statistically significant.

The effectiveness of using $NR = NR_p$ depends on the relevant units used. Distill(R_d,NR_p) outperforms MM(R_d) in all cases (often statistically significantly) for both evaluation paradigms. Moreover, Distill(R_d,NR_p) outperforms Distill(R_d,NR_d) in all cases for the residual evaluation, although few improvements are statistically significant. The merits of using non-relevant passages ($NR = NR_p$) to distill a relevance topic model from relevant documents can be attributed to the fact that relevant documents contain much non-query-pertaining text (see Section 4). However, using the relevant passages alone, MM(R_p), is more effective than using relevant documents and non-relevant passages, Distill(R_d,NR_p), and is as effective as using non-relevant passages in addition to relevant passages, Distill(R_p,NR_p). That is, using non-relevant passages to distill a relevance topic model from either relevant documents or relevant passages has no merit over using only the relevant passages.

Distill(R_p,NR_d) is the most effective distillation model in a vast majority of cases; most improvements over other distillation models and the mixture models are statistically significant for both evaluation paradigms. Thus, in contrast to non-relevant passages in relevant documents, non-relevant documents can be effectively used to distill a relevance topic model from relevant passages[4].

The score-based fusion model. The performance of the score-based fusion model (Equation 4) is presented in Figures 1(b) and 1(d). The curves of SF(R,NR_p) (almost) coincide with the curves of MM(R) regardless of the choice of R. This means that using the similarity of a document to non-relevant passages has little merit. In contrast, SF(R,NR_d) outperforms MM(R), regardless of the choice of R. The improvements are statistically significant for all 10 cases (5 values of $k \times 2$ choices of R) for the standard evaluation, and in 4 out of 10 cases for the residual evaluation.

Overall, the most effective score-based fusion model for both evaluation paradigms is SF(R_p,NR_d). The improvements it posts over the other methods (specifically, MM) are statistically significant in a vast majority of the cases[5].

6. SUMMARY

Our distillation and score-based fusion methods use relevance feedback for documents and passages in different ways. The distillation model utilizes both relevant and non-relevant units in a mixture model to rank the entire corpus. The score-based fusion model re-ranks a list retrieved using information induced only from relevant units by using, in addition, dissimilarities with non-relevant units.

Despite these differences, the conclusions regarding the merits of using the different types of (non-)relevant units are similar in most cases. That is, using relevant passages is superior to using relevant documents regardless of the non-relevant units used. Yet, using non-relevant documents in addition to relevant passages is of much merit and results in the best performance for both methods. A noticeable difference between the two methods is the effectiveness of using non-relevant passages in addition to relevant documents in the distillation model. No such merits were observed for the score-based fusion method.

Acknowledgments. We thank the reviewers for their comments. This paper is based upon work supported in part by the German Research Foundation (DFG) via the German-Israeli Project Cooperation (DIP, grant DA 1600/1-1), the Israel Science Foundation under grant no. 433/12, and the Technion-Microsoft Electronic Commerce Research Center.

[4]Extending the distillation model to use both NR_p and NR_d showed merit over using each alone when relevant documents are used but not when relevant passages are used.

[5]We found that a score-based fusion method that extends Equation 4 by using both non-relevant documents and non-relevant passages does not statistically significantly outperform SF(R_d,NR_d) and SF(R_p,NR_d).

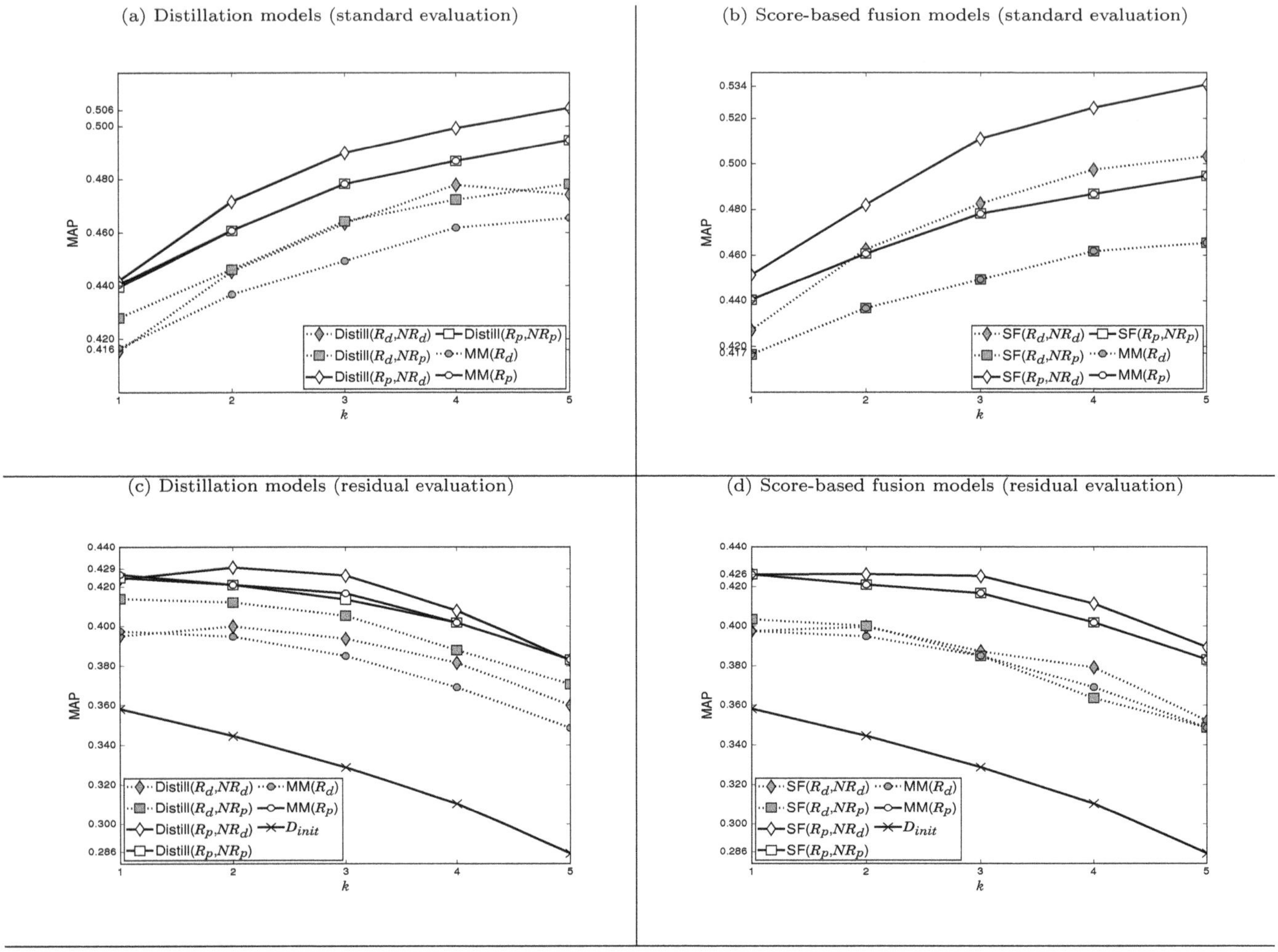

Figure 1: MAP as a function of k. The performance of MM(R) is presented for reference. The MAP of the initial result list (D_{init}) in the standard evaluation paradigm, which does not depend on k, is 0.368; the MAP in the residual evaluation is displayed. The color of the markers (white or gray) and curve style indicate the relevant units used (R_d or R_p). The type of the markers indicates the non-relevant units (NR_d or NR_p).

7. REFERENCES

[1] N. Abdul-Jaleel, J. Allan, W. B. Croft, F. Diaz, L. Larkey, X. Li, M. D. Smucker, and C. Wade. UMASS at TREC 2004 — novelty and hard. In *Proc. of TREC-13*, 2004.

[2] P. Arvola, S. Geva, J. Kamps, R. Schenkel, A. Trotman, and J. Vainio. Overview of the inex 2010 ad hoc track. In *Comparative Evaluation of Focused Retrieval - INEX*, pages 1–32. 2010.

[3] C. Buckley and S. Robertson. Relevance feedback track overview: TREC 2008. In *Proc. of TREC-17*, 2008.

[4] C. Cirillo, Y. K. Chang, and J. Razon. Evaluation of feedback retrieval using modified freezing, residual collection and test and control groups. *The SMART retrieval system-experiments in automatic document processing*, pages 355–370, 1971.

[5] M. D. Dunlop. The effect of accessing nonmatching documents on relevance feedback. *ACM Transactions on Information Systems*, 15(2):137–153, 1997.

[6] E. Ide. New experiments in relevance feedback. *The SMART retrieval system*, pages 337–354, 1971.

[7] M. Karimzadehgan and C. Zhai. Improving retrieval accuracy of difficult queries through generalizing negative document language models. In *Proc. of SIGIR*, pages 27–36, 2011.

[8] V. Lavrenko and W. B. Croft. Relevance-based language models. In *Proc. of SIGIR*, pages 120–127, 2001.

[9] Y. Li, X. Tao, A. Algarni, and S. Wu. Mining specific and general features in both positive and negative relevance feedback. In *Proc. of TREC*, 2009.

[10] Y. H. Peng Zhang and D. Song. Approximating true relevance distribution from a mixture model based on irrelevance data. In *Proc. of SIGIR*, pages 107–114, 2009.

[11] S. E. Robertson, H. Zaragoza, and M. J. Taylor. Microsoft cambridge at TREC-12: HARD track. In *Proc. of TREC*, pages 418–425, 2003.

[12] J. J. Rocchio. Relevance feedback in information retrieval. In G. Salton, editor, *The SMART Retrieval System: Experiments in Automatic Document Processing*, pages 313–323. Prentice Hall, 1971.

[13] I. Ruthven and M. Lalmas. A survey on the use of relevance feedback for information access systems. *Knowledge Engineering Review*, 18(2):95–145, 2003.

[14] X. Shen and C. Zhai. Active feedback-UIUC TREC-2003 HARD experiments. In *Proc. of TREC*, pages 662–666, 2003.

[15] A. Singhal, M. Mitra, and C. Buckley. Learning routing queries in a query zone. In *Proc. of SIGIR*, pages 25–32, 1997.

[16] X. Wang, H. Fang, and C. Zhai. A study of methods for negative relevance feedback. In *Proc. of SIGIR*, pages 219–226, 2008.

[17] C. Zhai and J. D. Lafferty. Model-based feedback in the language modeling approach to information retrieval. In *Proc. of CIKM*, pages 403–410, 2001.

[18] C. Zhai and J. D. Lafferty. A study of smoothing methods for language models applied to ad hoc information retrieval. In *Proc. of SIGIR*, pages 334–342, 2001.

What Makes a Query Temporally Sensitive?

Craig Willis, Garrick Sherman, and Miles Efron
Graduate School of Library and Information Science
University of Illinois at Urbana-Champaign
{willis8, gsherma2, mefron}@illinois.edu

ABSTRACT

This work takes an in-depth look at the factors that affect manual classifications of "temporally sensitive" information needs. We use qualitative and quantitative techniques to analyze 660 topics from the Text Retrieval Conference (TREC) previously used in the experimental evaluation of temporal retrieval models. Regression analysis is used to identify factors in previous manual classifications. We explore potential problems with the previous classifications, considering principles and guidelines for future work on temporal retrieval models.

1. INTRODUCTION

A growing body of information retrieval research argues that temporality should be modeled explicitly when scoring and ranking documents with respect to users' queries. Researchers have explored a variety of temporal retrieval models that explicitly incorporate time into document ranking [7, 2, 1]. They refer to general classes of "temporal queries" or "temporal information needs." Models have been proposed for "recency queries" [7, 2], "time-sensitive queries" [1], "implicitly temporal queries" [8], and "temporally biased queries" [5]. For evaluation, these studies rely on manual classifications of topics into temporal categories.

In this short paper, we take a deeper look into these manually classified topics to develop a clear understanding of *what makes a query temporally sensitive*? Previous manual classifications combine the temporal distribution of judged-relevant documents with common-sense notions of topic temporality without a clear explanation of the criteria or processes used in classification. If we cannot explain the processes being modeled, use of these manually classified topics for evaluation is of limited value.

To address this question, we analyze 660 topics from the Text Retrieval Conference (TREC) previously used in the experimental evaluation of temporal retrieval models. We employ qualitative and quantitative methods to identify topic characteristics that might affect the manual assessment of "temporal-sensitivity." The resulting coded topics are used in a set of regression analyses to assess the relationships between these characteristics and manually assigned categories. This paper's main contribution is an empirical assessment of the complexities that underpin temporal IR. This assessment helps us understand earlier temporal IR studies, while also suggesting novel ways to incorporate time effectively into retrieval.

SIGIR '16, July 17 - 21, 2016, Pisa, Italy

ISBN 978-1-4503-4069-4/16/07...$15.00
DOI: http://dx.doi.org/10.1145/2911451.2914703

2. TIME-SENSITIVE QUERIES

Topics	Collections	Studies
51-200 (Ad-hoc)	TREC Disks 1-2 AP (1988-89)	Jones & Diaz (2007)
301-450 (Ad-hoc)	TREC Disks 4-5 FT (1991-94); LA Times (1988-89)	Efron & Golovchinsky (2011); Dakka, Gravano & Ipeirotis (2012)
N1-100 (Novelty)	AQUAINT Xinhua (1996-2000); NYT (1999-2000)	Jones & Diaz (2007)
851-1050 (Blog)	Blog06 (Dec 6, 2005 - Feb 21, 2006)	Peetz, Meij & de Rijke (2013)
MB1-110 (Microblog)	Tweets 2011 (Jan 24, 2011 - Feb 8th, 2011)	Efron, Lin, de Vries (2014)

Table 1: TREC topics and collections analyzed by the authors and their use in prior temporal retrieval studies.

In this section, we review examples of studies focused on *temporal relevance*. The list of topics and collections used in each of the studies are listed in Table 1.

Jones and Diaz [5] define three classes of queries based on the manual analysis of topics: temporally ambiguous (requesting multiple events), temporally unambiguous (requesting a single event), and atemporal (having no preference). Jones and Diaz manually classify 100 TREC topics based only on their title, description, and narrative fields. They also include 2003 Novelty track topics because they include topics classified as "event" or "opinion," which the authors suggest correspond to the "temporally unambiguous" and "atemporal" categories, respectively.

Efron and Golovchinsky [2] investigate models for recency queries. Topics are classified as "recency" if at least 2/3 of the relevant documents occur after the median document time and the topic has a "bona fide temporal dimension" based on manual review, the specific criteria for which are not specified. The resulting classification consists of 61 recency queries.

Dakka, Gravano, and Ipeirotis [1] investigate a broad class of queries which they refer to as "time-sensitive." They hypothesize that there are queries for which more relevant documents are found at specific points in time, not just recently. They manually examine the title, description and narrative of each topic and identify queries associated with specific news events. If the topic information is insufficient to make a decision, they analyze the distribution of judged-relevant documents. The resulting classification consists of 86 temporally sensitive queries.

Finally, Peetz, Meij, and de Rijke [9] investigate the effect of temporal bursts in estimating query models. Building on the earlier studies, they evaluate their models using the previous manual classifications as well as a new collection based on TREC Blog06. As in the previous studies, the authors manually construct a subset of "temporal" queries based on topic descriptions and relevant document distributions. No specific criteria for classification are given.

3. WHAT MAKES A QUERY TEMPORALLY SENSITIVE?

Given the complex landscape described in the previous section, what in general makes a query temporally sensitive? Dakka et al [1] present a compelling definition. A query is *temporally sensitive* if "the relevant documents for the query are not spread uniformly over time, but rather tend to be concentrated at restricted intervals." This is an essential point, since many temporal retrieval models rely on the temporal distribution of results in document scoring. This is also why we do not include the topics developed for the NTCIR Temporalia test collections [4]: they are primarily concerned with *temporal topicality*, i.e. queries *about* a certain time, in contrast to our focus on temporal sensitivity, which relates to the unequal occurrence of relevant documents at certain points in time. Still, the distribution of relevant documents alone is not sufficient to determine true temporality. To address this, most of the studies listed above rely on common-sense notions of temporality based on the topic content considered independently of the distribution of relevant documents. A primary goal of the current study is to look deeper into these common-sense criteria with the aim of providing researchers a firmer basis for assessing which queries are likely to have a temporal dimension.

4. METHODS

4.1 Qualitative coding

We use content analysis [6] to identify characteristics of TREC topics potentially associated with temporal sensitivity. 660 topics were selected from the TREC Ad-hoc, Novelty, Blog, and Microblog tracks, all previously used by researchers to evaluate temporal retrieval models. The complete set of topics used in this study are listed in Table 1 along with the temporal constraints of each collection or sub-collection.

Two of the authors participated in the development of the codebook and subsequent coding of topics. Codes were defined based on characteristics of topics expected to be related to temporal sensitivity, informed by the literature. During this process, code definitions were refined and clarified. In the final coding, only topic title and description were used. Of the 660 topics, 330 were coded by both coders to allow for inter-rater consistency analysis. The final codebook is too large to publish in this short paper, but is available online[1]. Coding was completed using the Dedoose[2] service. After coding all 660 topics, the topic/code matrix was exported for subsequent reliability and regression analysis, as described in the following sections.

An example of a coded topic from the 2004 Novelty test collection is presented in Figure 1. This topic refers to a specific event and contains place entities as well as an explicit date. Topic N57 is categorized as an "event" by the TREC topic creator and is therefore an unambiguous temporal topic as defined by Jones and Diaz.

Title: $[(\text{East Timor})_{PlaceEntity}\text{Independence}]_{SpecificEvent}$

Description: $[(\text{East Timor})_{PlaceEntity}$ vote for independence from $(\text{Indonesia})_{PlaceName}$ in $(\text{August 1999})_{ExplicitDate}]_{SpecificEvent}$

Figure 1: TREC Novelty 2004 topic N57 example annotation

In addition to coding the topics based on the defined codes, the coders assigned a temporal designation to the distribution of relevant documents for each topic. Nonparametric densities were fit to the temporal distribution of relevant documents for topics with more than 20 relevant documents, following Dakka et al [1]. Each coder reviewed the relevant document distribution along with the total number of relevant documents for each topic and assigned one of four values based on subjective impressions about the degreee to which relevant documents were temporally constrained: too few observations (-1), low or no temporality (0), moderate temporality (1), and high temporality (2).

4.2 Reliability analysis

For this study, coder agreement is measured using Cohen's κ for the classification of the distribution of relevant documents. For the broader qualitative coding task, we use a variation of percent overlap, since coding is performed on arbitrary segments of text. We define *percent overlap* as:

$$overlap = \frac{m}{m + u_1 + u_2}$$

Where m is the number of excerpts assigned the same code by both coders, u_1 is the number of codes assigned to excerpts only by coder 1 and u_2 is the number of codes assigned to excerpts only by coder 2. If both coders assign no codes to a topic, it is considered perfect agreement. We report the macro (calculated over all topics) and micro (calculated as a per-topic average) overlaps. Per-code overlaps are used to characterize coder agreement within each code.

4.3 Relevant document distributions

In each of the four prior studies enumerated in Section 2, the authors acknowledge using the distribution of judged-relevant or pseudo-relevant documents in determining topic temporality. For this study, we use two different measures to analyze these distributions: the first-order time series autocorrelation (ACF) and the dominant power spectrum (DPS).

Jones and Diaz [5] use the ACF created by the temporal distribution of pseudo-relevant documents for a query as a predictor of query temporality. They note that queries with

[1]http://github.com/craig-willis/sigir-2016-queries/codebook
[2]http://www.dedoose.com

strong inter-day dependencies will have high ACF values, indicating predictability in the time series.

Similarly, He, Chang, and Lim [3] use the DPS as a predictor of the "burstiness" of temporal features for event detection. The DPS is the highest power spectrum, estimated using the periodogram.

In this study, both ACF and DPS measures are used to reduce the distribution of judged-relevant or pseudo-relevant documents to a single value for the regression analysis, as described in the next section.

4.4 Regression analysis

A primary goal of this study is to determine the characteristics that contribute to the manual judgment of topic temporality. We use logistic regression based on the generalized linear model (GLM) implementation in R. The predictors are binary presence indicators for each of the qualitative codes along with the ACF and DPS of the temporal distribution of true-relevant documents. The response variables are the binary temporal/non-temporal indicators manually assigned in the four studies. Model variables are selected using standard step-wise procedures based on the Akaike information criterion (AIC). Coefficients are reported using the log-odds and model fit is assessed using pseudo-R^2.

5. RESULTS

5.1 Codes

Code	% Agree
PersonEntity	0.94
PlaceEntity	0.91
ExplicitDate	0.89
PeriodicEvent	0.85
OrganizationEntity	0.76
SpecificEvent	0.64
OtherEntity	0.52
GenericEvent	0.45
IndirectEventReference	0.19

Table 2: Codes and percent agreement.

Our qualitative analysis suggests that three broad classes of features bear on query temporality: events, named entities, and explicit dates. It is intuitive that topics focused on specific and important events will have a higher degree of temporal relevance. Following the Topic Detection and Tracking definition, seminal events happen at specific times in specific places, often to individuals or other named entities (e.g., organizations). Perhaps the most essential code is the "SpecificEvent" – something important that happens at a particular time and place. Related to SpecificEvent is the "PeriodicEvent," which refers to an event that recurs periodically, such as the Super Bowl, World Cup, or Halloween. Jones and Diaz [5] note that many of the early ad-hoc queries were temporally ambiguous, referring to multiple events. We incorporate this concept through the "GenericEvent" code, which captures topics concerned with a class of specific events, such as earthquakes, elections, or strikes. While analyzing topics, it became apparent that some topics were likely to be inspired by a specific event, but without explicit reference in the topic description. This concept is captured through the "IndirectEventReference" code. The remaining codes are concerned with the identification of specific types of named entities, which are expected to have some association with topic temporality, and explicit dates.

Model Name	Model	R^2
Novelty	$-3.767 + 5.848 \cdot SpecEvt + 2.523 \cdot Other$	0.669
Novelty (Rel)	$-3.539+7.006 \cdot SpecEvt+2.530 \cdot Other- 7.343 \cdot ACF$	0.706
Dakka	$0.134 + 0.878 \cdot Place$	0.019
Dakka (Rel)	$-0.917 + 0.393 \cdot DPS^{\blacktriangle}$	0.263
Efron	$-1.765 + 2.353 * Place^{\blacktriangle} + 1.410 \cdot Other^{\circ}$	0.181
Efron (Rel)	$-2.727+1.965 \cdot Place^{\blacktriangle}+1.787 \cdot Other^{\triangle}+ 0.163 \cdot DPS^{\blacktriangle}$	0.377
Peetz	$-0.336 + 1.682 * SpecEvt^{\circ} + 0.982 \cdot PerEvt + 0.672 \cdot Person - 0.6175 \cdot Org$	0.127
Peetz (Rel)	$-1.245+1.218 \cdot SpecEvt+0.797 \cdot Period+ 2.835 \cdot ACF^{\circ} + 0.002 \cdot DPS$	0.223

Table 3: Logistic regression models predicting prior topic classifications for each test collection without and with (Rel) ACF/DPS predictors. Model fit reported based pseudo-R^2 after stepwise variable selection based on AIC. Variable significance indicated by $p < 0.05(^{\circ}), < 0.01(^{\triangle}), < 0.001(^{\blacktriangle})$

5.2 Code distributions

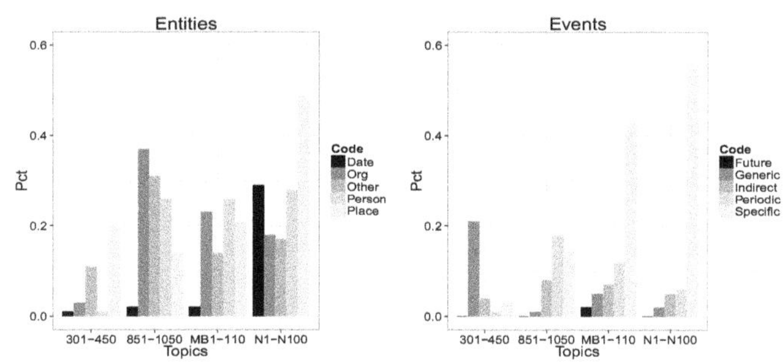

Figure 2: Percent of topics in each collection with codes assigned from the (a) entity code group and (b) events code group.

Figure 2 summarizes the percent of topics in each test collection with each code assigned. We can see that the Novelty and Microblog collections have a higher percentage of specific events than the Blog and ad-hoc collections. The ad-hoc collections have a higher number of generic events, which supports the findings of Jones and Diaz [5]. The Blog, Novelty, and Microblog test collections each have larger numbers of named entities in the topic titles and descriptions.

5.3 Reliability

To assess coding reliability, a total of 1,244 codes were assigned to 330 topics by the two coders. Higher overlap indicates greater agreement between coders. The macro percent overlap is 0.71 and micro percent overlap is 0.83, indicating that overall our codes may be applied with good consistency. The per-code overlap is reported in Table 2(c). As expected, some codes have higher agreement than others. Specifically, personal names (0.94), locations (0.91), and explicit dates (0.89) have very high agreement whereas indirect event references (0.19) and generic events (0.45) have lower agreement.

5.4 Regression analysis

In this section, we report the results of the logistic regression analysis, predicting the manually assigned categories for each test collection. The resulting models are reported in Table 3.

For the 2003-2004 Novelty collection, the response variable is the "opinion" (0) or "event" (1) classification of each

Collection	κ	ρ_{ACF}	ρ_{DPS}
AP	0.743	0.518	0.356
LA/FT	0.551	0.591	0.374
Blog	0.857	0.728	0.498
MB	0.806	0.692	0.354

Table 4: Cohen's κ for inter-coder agreement for classification of true-relevant document distributions. Pearson's ρ measuring correlation (average) between manual classifications and ACF/DPS values

topic, which is manually assigned by the TREC organizers. Following Jones and Diaz [5], we treat "event" as the temporal category. Logistic regression analysis is performed with and without the ACF and DPS predictors, as shown in Table 3. SpecificEvent and OtherEntity are significant predictors of the "event" category ($p < 0.01$), with a pseudo-R^2 of 0.669. Including the ACF of the true-relevant distribution is significant, with a minor improvement in model fit. The high pseudo-R^2 is unsurprising in this case, since the SpecificEvent code corresponds to the Novelty "event" category. It does, however, confirm our code definition.

Dakka et al manually classified "time-sensitive queries" for TREC topics 301-450. As reported in Table 3, only the PlaceEntity code is a significant predictor of the manual classification. However, the pseudo-R^2 is very low (0.019). Dakka et al acknowledge examining the relevant document distributions for the LA Times and Financial Times sub collections. Including the DPS of the true-relevant document distribution increases the pseudo-R^2 to 0.263, suggesting that the relevant document distribution played a significant role in the manual classification.

Efron and Golovchinsky also classified topics 301-450, in this case focusing on the identification of "recency" queries. As reported in Table 3, both PlaceEntity and OtherEntity are useful predictors of the temporal response. As with Dakka, including the DPS of the true-relevant distribution increases pseudo-R^2 from 0.181 to 0.377. This again suggests that the distribution of relevant documents played an important role in the determination of topic temporality.

Finally, we look at Peetz et al's classification of the Blog06-08 topics 850-1050. In this case, the SpecificEvent, PeriodicEvent, Person and Organization entities are useful predictors of the temporal category (pseudo-R^2=0.127). Including DPS improves model fit (pseudo-R^2=0.223), again suggesting that the distribution of relevant documents played a role in manual classification.

5.5 Relevant document distributions

As described in Section 3.1, non-parametric densities based on the temporal distribution of true-relevant documents are manually classified by two coders into four categories. The weighted Cohen's κ is calculated to assess agreement between the two coders. Average Pearson's correlation (ρ) measures the correlation between these manual classifications and the per-topic ACF/DPS values.

The results reported in Table 4 show moderate (0.40-0.60) to high (0.60-0.80) coder agreement and higher correlation between the ACF and the manual classifications. These findings show that ACF and DPS effectively capture the degree to which relevant documents are temporally constrained.

6. DISCUSSION AND CONCLUSIONS

In this study, we have tried to identify characteristics of TREC topics that can be used to explain manual classifications of "temporal sensitivity." Other researchers have classified topics without clear definitions or criteria. We have attempted to model these classifications by proposing features believed to indicate temporality. Features include the presence of different types of named entities, classes of events, and measures of the temporal distribution of judged relevant documents.

We were successful in modeling the "event" category in the Novelty track, based primarily on our "SpecificEvent" code. Event codes were also found to be useful predictors of the classification of Peetz et al [9]. However, we were generally unable to identify characteristics that fully explain the other manual classifications. They seem to consistently conflate two different concepts: the temporal distribution of judged-relevant documents and common-sense notions of topic temporality.

Since the first-order autocorrelation of the judged-relevant document distribution is highly correlated with manual judgements of temporality, we recommend using the ACF or other measure of distribution "burstiness" instead of manual assessment. In the future, common-sense notions of temporality should be clearly explicated.

If we cannot explain the process that determines the classifications, it raises questions about the value of these test collections for evaluation. Specifically, how can we be clear that the queries previously identified as "temporally sensitive" are truly so? This ambiguity also limits the utility of previous research, since it is unclear how to select queries for which the proposed models are well-suited.

7. ACKNOWLEDGMENTS

This work was supported in part by the US National Science Foundation under Grant No. 1217279. Any opinions, findings, conclusions, or recommendations expressed are those of the authors and do not necessarily reflect the views of the National Science Foundation.

8. REFERENCES

[1] W. Dakka, L. Gravano, and P. Ipeirotis. Answering General Time-Sensitive Queries. *IEEE Transactions on Knowledge and Data Engineering*, 24(2):220–235, 2012.

[2] M. Efron and G. Golovchinsky. Estimation methods for ranking recent information. *SIGIR 2011*, 2011.

[3] Q. He, K. Chang, and E.-P. Lim. Analyzing feature trajectories for event detection. *SIGIR 2007*, 2007.

[4] H. Joho, A. Jatowt, and R. Blanco. NTCIR Temporalia : A Test Collection for Temporal Information Access Research. In *Proceedings of WWW 2014*, 2014.

[5] R. Jones and F. Diaz. Temporal profiles of queries. *ACM Transactions on Information Systems*, 25(3), 2007.

[6] K. Krippendorff. *Content analysis: an introduction to its methodology.* Sage, Beverly Hills, CA, 1980.

[7] X. Li and W. B. Croft. Time-based language models. *CIKM 2003*, 2003.

[8] D. Metzler, R. Jones, F. Peng, and R. Zhang. Improving search relevance for implicitly temporal queries. *SIGIR 2009*, 2009.

[9] M.-H. Peetz, E. Meij, and M. de Rijke. Using temporal bursts for query modeling. *Information Retrieval*, 17(1):74–108, 2013.

Which Information Sources are More Effective and Reliable in Video Search

Zhiyong Cheng[‡], Xuanchong Li[§], Jialie Shen[‡], Alexander G. Hauptmann[§]
[‡]School of Information Systems, Singapore Management University, Singapore
[§]School of Computer Science, Carnegie Mellon University, USA
{jason.zy.cheng, jialie}@gmail.com, {xcli, alex}@cs.cmu.edu

ABSTRACT

It is common that users are interested in finding video segments, which contain further information about the video contents in a segment of interest. To facilitate users to find and browse related video contents, video hyperlinking aims at constructing links among video segments with relevant information in a large video collection. In this study, we explore the effectiveness of various video features on the performance of video hyperlinking, including subtitle, metadata, content features (i.e., audio and visual), surrounding context, as well as the combinations of those features. Besides, we also test different search strategies over different types of queries, which are categorized according to their video contents. Comprehensive experimental studies have been conducted on the dataset of TRECVID 2015 video hyperlinking task. Results show that (1) text features play a crucial role in search performance, and the combination of audio and visual features cannot provide improvements; (2) the consideration of contexts cannot obtain better results; and (3) due to the lack of training examples, machine learning techniques cannot improve the performance.

Keywords

Video Search, Video Hyperlinking

1. INTRODUCTION

With the explosive growth and the widespread accessibility of multimedia contents on the Web, video is becoming one of the most valuable sources to assess information and knowledge [4, 19]. When consuming video content, users are highly interested in finding further information on some aspects of the topics of interest associated with a video segment. Therefore, it is crucial to develop effective video search and hyperlinking to help users explore, navigate and search interesting video contents in audiovisual archives. *Video hyperlinking* aims at linking a video segment (or video anchor) to other video segments in a video collection, based on similarity or relatedness. Formally, the video hyperlinking task is defined as[1]: *given a set of test videos with metadata and a defined set of anchors, each defined by start time and end time in the video, return for each anchor a ranked list of hyperlinking targets.* Therefore, video hyperlinking enables users to navigate between video segments in a large video collection [3].

To facilitate the development and advancement of video hyperlinking systems, video hyperlinking has become a competition task since 2012 in MediaEval [6]. Standard test collections are provided and metrics are defined for the evaluation of developed systems. The task is defined to find *relevant anchors* or *short segments* (e.g., 2 minutes) of video contents given a set of query anchors. Thus, the hyperlinking is generally addressed within an information retrieval framework. As videos in the test collection could be in hours of length, video hyperlinking consists of two steps: (1) *video segmentation* - separate a video into a number of short video segments and (2) *video retrieval* - retrieval potential links to videos or video segments.[2] For video segmentation, many systems apply fixed-length segmentation to separate videos into fixed-length of segments. Other video segmentation methods have also been developed and studied, such as *video shot based* and *semantic-based segmentation*, however, no evidence shows that those segmentation methods are better than the fix-length segmentation method. More research efforts were devoted into the development of effective retrieval methods, including the explorations of different information sources (e.g., subtitle, metadata, transcriptions, segment surrounding context, name entity, enrichment of concept and synonyms, as well as audio and visual features [8]) and search strategies (e.g., combination with or re-ranking with visual features, combination of video-level and segment-level retrieval).

In this paper, we use the fixed-length video segmentation method and mainly focus on studying the effects of different types of information sources on the performance of video hyperlinking, including text (subtitle, metadata, transcription) and a variety of video content (audio, visual and motion) features. Nine different text-based retrieval methods are used based on the text information with and without the consideration of surrounding context (around the query or target segment). Besides, we also study the performance of multimodal feature combination using weighted linear combina-

SIGIR '16, July 17–21, 2016, Pisa, Italy.
© 2016 ACM. ISBN 978-1-4503-4069-4/16/07...$15.00
DOI: http://dx.doi.org/10.1145/2911451.2914765

[1]The definition is from TRECVID 2015 Video Hyperlinking task, http://www-nlpir.nist.gov/projects/tv2015/#lnk.

[2]The order of the two steps can be the reverse, retrieving relevant videos firstly and then extracting the most relevant segments from those videos identified in the first step [5].

tion. Further, we evaluate the performance of different combination weights over different categories of queries, which are classified according to their contents. Experiments show that surrounding context and video-content features have little contribution on the performance improvement.

2. VIDEO HYPERLINKING SYSTEM

In this study, we address the video hyperlinking as an ad-hoc retrieval problem. Given a query anchor indexed with certain features, video segments in the test collection are also indexed with the same features, and then a retrieval method is used to search and return the most relevant video segments to this query. In our experiments, we (1) first separate each video in the collections into *50s fixed-length* segments without overlapping, as this configure achieved good performance in the CUNI2014 video hyperlinking system [8]; (2) different types of features are extracted from each segment; (3) a variety of retrieval methods are explored; and (4) different strategies are used to combine the results obtained based on different features. In the next, we describe the features used and the retrieval methods considered in experiments.

2.1 Dataset

We first introduce the dataset used in the study. Our study is performed on the dataset of TRECVID 2015 Video Hyperlinking task. For the ease of understanding, we first clarify several terminologies: (1) *video* refers a long video clip (usually longer than 20 minutes); (2) both *video segment* (or *segment*) and *video anchor* (or *anchor*) refer to a short segment of a video (usually less than 2 minutes), defined by a start timestamp and an end timestamp; (3) *video metadata* (or *metadata*) contains the *title* and *a short program description* of a video; (4) *subtitle* is the manual annotation of the speech in a video; and (5) *transcript* refers to the annotation obtained by using automatic speech recognition (ASR) methods.

The TRECVID 2015 Video Hyperlinking dataset consists of around 2686 hours of BBC television broadcasts content from 05/12/2008 to 07/31/2008. The data is accompanied by metadata, subtitle, three kinds of ASR transcripts (generated by LIMSI [12], LIUM [16], and NST-Sheffield [14] respectively), two versions of key concepts (detected by two concept detectors), and the prosodic audio features [7].

The development set contains 30 query anchors. For each of them, a set of ground-truth anchors is provided. The number of positive segments for each query anchor varies from 17 to 122. Notice that many positive segments are from the same video from which the corresponding query anchor is extracted. The test set contains 135 query anchors, which are for the final evaluation in the competition.

2.2 Retrieval Methods

2.2.1 Text-based Methods

Text Features We explore the effectiveness of different sources of textual features, namely the subtitle and three kinds of ASR transcripts. For each type of the features, we also consider their combinations with metadata and surrounding contexts. The tested lengths of surrounding context include 50s, 100s, and 200s. Hence, for each of subtitle, LIMSI, LIUM, and NST-Sheffield, there are eight indexing methods.[3] For a video segment, the combination of *subtitle and metadata* is to concatenate *the subtitle of this segment* with *the metadata of the video* from which the segment is extracted. Similarly, the combination of *subtitle, metadata,* and *50s surrounding context* is the concatenation of *the subtitle of this segment, 50-seconds-length passage before and after the segment*, and *the metadata of the corresponding video*. All the textual sources are processed by punctuation & stop-words removal and capitalization normalization.

Retrieval Methods For each type of feature, we experiment with nine different retrieval models: (1) BM25, (2) DFR version of BM25(DFR-BM25) [9], (3) DLH hypergeometric DFR model (DLH13) [1], (4) DPH [2], (5) Hiemastra's Language Model (Hiemastra-LM) [11], (6) InL2 - inverse document frequency model for randomness, Laplace succession for first normalization, and normalization 2 for term frequency normalization [9], (7) TF-IDF, (8) LemurTF-IDF[4], and (9) PL2 - poisson estimation for randomness, Laplace succession for first normalization, and normalization 2 for term frequency normalization [9]. We used Terrier[5] IR system to run experiments with these retrieval methods (with default parameters) with different textual sources.

2.2.2 Content-based Method

For the content-based method, we use various video features in the retrieval task. These video features include motion features (e.g., improved dense trajectory [13]), audio features (e.g., MFCC) and visual semantic features [15]. After explicit feature mapping [18], the cosine similarity is used as the relevance score.

2.2.3 Multimodal-based Method

We explore the effects of the combination of different features, based on the assumption that different features can capture different aspects of video content.

Weighted Linear Combination (WLC) The relevant score of a video segment with respect to a query is computed by a weighted linear combination of the relevant scores obtained by different features. Let $wlc(q, v)$ be the final relevance score obtained by the weighted linear combination, and $rel(f_i)$ be the relevance score obtained based on feature f_i. Given the selected feature $\{f_1, f_2, \cdots, f_n\}$, the $wlc(q, v)$ is computed by:

$$wlc(q, v) = w_1 \cdot rel(f_1) + w_2 \cdot rel(f_2) + \cdots + w_n \cdot rel(f_n) \quad (1)$$

where $\{w_1, w_2, \cdots, w_n\}$ are the linear combination weights, which characterize the contribution of different features on the final performance. These weights are tuned on the training set. Due to the lack of training examples (refer to Table 1), we only used five features in our experiments. These features are selected based on on their individual performances and the consideration of feature heterogeneity. Specifically, the selected features are: *subtitle_metadata_LemurTF-IDF*[6], *subtitle_metadata_DPH*, *keyconcept_Lemur*

[3]Taken *subtitle* as an example, there are *subtitle, subtitle with 50s context, subtitle with 100s context, subtitle with 200s context, subtitle and metadata, subtitle and metadata with 50s context, subtitle and metadata with 100s context*, and *subtitle and metadata with 200s context.*

[4]http://www.lemurproject.org/

[5]http://www.terrier.org

[6]Subtitle_metadata_LemurTF-IDF denotes that the relevant score is obtained by LemurTF-IDF based on the subtitle and metatada. Similar definition is applied for other methods.

TF-IDF, *improved trajectory*, and *MFCC*. Keyconcept_Lemur TF-IDF denotes the TF-IDF method based on the key concepts of keyframes. The *key concepts* are the concepts detected in the keyframes with normalized scores greater than 0.7, using the Leuven's concept detectors of 1537 ImageNet concepts [17]. For a video segment, its key concept based representation is the concatenation of key concepts detected in all the keyframes of this segment.

For different types of videos, their contents or topics could be very diverse. Different types of features contribute to the representation of video contents differently. It would be useful to use different weights for different video categories. Thus we classify the videos into categories based on the programme category ontology of BBC news. Due to the limited query examples in the development dataset, we further group the videos into two broad categories:

- Category 1: news & weather; science & nature; music (religion & ethics); travel; politics news; life stories music; sport (tennis); food & drink; motosport.
- Category 2: history; arts, culture & the media; comedy (sitcoms), cars & motors; antiques, homes & garden, pets & animals; health & wellbeing, beauty & style.

In general, videos in the sub-categories of Category 1 enjoy more similar contents in text, audio, and visual features (such as news and music), and thus queries in Category 1 are easier to achieve better results. In contrast, for videos in the same sub-categories of Category 2, although their contents are about the same topic, the contents could be diverse in contents. For example, videos about *history* or *health* could be very different in words and scenes.

To evaluate the performance of this method, we randomly split the query anchors in the development set into training set and testing set. Table 1 presents the details of training set and testing set for global weighted linearly combination (GWLC - without the consideration of video categories) and categorized weighted linear combination (CWLC). Notice that the number of training examples is very small, especially for the CWLC method, which limits the performance of the weighted linear combination.

Table 1: Sizes of training set and testing set for the GWLC (whole) and CWLC (category 1 and category 2) methods.

Category	# Queries in the Training Set	# Queries in the Testing Set
GWLC	15	15
Category 1	9	9
Category 2	8	4

Learning to Rank [10] We also explored the use of learning to ranking techniques for refining the retrieval results. The retrieval scores obtained by different features are used as the input of different learning algorithms (e.g., linear regression, Naive Bayes, SVM, etc.). Unfortunately, these techniques cannot improve the performance, due to the lack of well-labeled data. Due to the space limitation, we have not reported the results of these methods in the following.

3. EXPERIMENTS

To evaluate the performance of video hyperlinking systems, the top ranking results of submissions are accessed using a mechanical turk (MT) crowdsourcing approach. A test assessment on a smaller part of the data by a local team of target users is used to identify potential discrepancies between the MT workers' judgments and those of the target user group. Descriptions given by the anchor creators (anchor descriptions, description and format requested targets) are used for evaluation purpose. In the generation of ground truth, only a subset of the submissions for each query will be used in evaluation. To reduce the workload of evaluators, for the anchors longer than 2 minutes, only the first two minutes will be used as the basis of relevance assessment. For more details about hyperlinking evaluation, please refer to [5]. The submissions are evaluated based on the precision at a certain rank measure, adapted to unconstrained time segments. In this paper, we report the performance on evaluation metrics of Precision@$\{5, 10, 20\}$ and MAP.

In the next, we report the experiment results of different methods on dataset. The results of content-based methods have not presented because of the overall poor performance.

Table 2: Results of using different transcripts, metadata, retrieval methods and contexts. In each row, the retrieval method is the best retrieval methods among the nine tested methods for the corresponding text source. 50s, 100s and 200s refer to the lengths of contexts. Please refer to Sect. 2.2.1 for the retrieval method in the "Method" column: (1) BM25, (3) DLH13, (4) DHP, (5) Hiemastra-LM, (8) LemurTF-IDF, and (9) PL2. NST refers to NST-Sheffield transcript.

Text Information	Method	MAP	P@5	P@10	P@20
Subtitle	(8)	**.162**	**.324**	**.297**	**.228**
LIMSI	(8)	.093	.215	.173	.137
LIUM	(1)	.056	.144	.124	.098
NST	(8)	.065	.164	.129	.102
Subtitle_Metadata	(8)	**.197**	**.293**	**.253**	**.205**
LIMSI_Metadata	(8)	.147	.200	.173	.147
LIUM_Metadata	(4)	.107	.147	.157	.132
NST_Metadata	(8)	.123	.153	.147	.128
Subtitle_50s	(9)	.114	.173	.137	.118
Subtitle_100s	(5)	.124	.220	.170	.132
Subtitle_200s	(3)	.128	.227	.160	.103
Subtitle_Metadata_50s	(3)	.124	.200	.147	.112
Subtitle_Metadata_100s	(5)	**.136**	.220	.180	**.135**
Subtitle_Metadata_200s	(3)	.134	**.247**	**.194**	.113

3.1 Performance on Development Data

Text-based Retrieval Method Table 2 shows the results of text-based retrieval methods using different text sources. For each type of text source, only the best performance obtained by the nine retrieval methods is reported. As a large set of text-based retrieval methods (different text sources and different retrieval methods) has been explored, we have not presented the results of all methods. The results are grouped into three groups in the table. As the performance of using subtitle is much better than the use of ASR transcripts (LIMSI, LIUM and NST-Sheffield), we did not show the performance of ASR transcripts with the consideration of context. The performance based on ASR transcripts is limited by the speech recognition accuracy. Among the three ASR transcripts, LIMSI obtains the best performance, followed by LIUM. Not surprising, with the consideration of metadata, the performance of ASR transcripts can be significant improved, as the metadata is manually annotated and summarizes the video contents. The combination of subtitle and metadata obtains higher MAP over subtitle while slightly lower precisions on top results. Recall that the metadata is a summary of the contents in a video. Supppose a query segment v_q is extracted from video V and a video segment v_s is extracted from V'; and V and V' is about the same topic, namely, their metadatas contain very similar content. The consideration of metadata in retrieval will increase the similarity score of v_s with respect to the query v_q, and thus move the video segment to a higher ranking position in the result list. If v_s is irrelevant, the consideration of metadata may cause the video segment v_s in a relatively high position, resulted in the decrease of precision; on the other hand, if v_s is indeed relevant to the query v_q, the resulted higher position due to metadata will lead to the increase of MAP.

From the results of the third group in the table, the consideration of context data makes the performance significantly decreased. The results imply that the incorporation of context data introduces noisy data, which misleads the search of relevant segment. By comparing the search methods of different text sources, it can be found that better performances are obtained by the vector space (LemurTF-IDF) method for text information without context (i.e., relatively short documents), and better performances are obtained by probabilistic methods with the consideration of contexts (i.e., relatively long documents).

Weighted Linear Combination Table 3 reports the performance of weighted linear combination methods. Because the performances of different queries varied in large ranges, we list the corresponding performance of the test queries using Subtitle_Metadata_LemurTF-IDF for comparisons. Obviously, the queries from Category 1 obtained much better results than queries from Category 2. By comparing with the performance of weighted linear combination methods, we can observe that the performance decreases with the combination of other features based on the simple late fusion method.

Table 3: Results of weighted linear combination methods.

Method	MAP	P@5	P@10	P@20
LemurTF-IDF	.305	.369	.339	.281
GWLC	.270	.400	.377	.327
LemurTF-IDF (category 1)	.432	.467	.456	.383
CWLC (category 1)	.381	.511	.489	.444
LemurTF-IDF (category 2)	.020	.150	.075	.050
CWLC (category 2)	.020	.150	.100	.0625

3.2 Performance on Test Data

In this section, we present the results of three methods on the test data in the final evaluation of the TRECVID 2015 Video Hyperlinking task: (1) Subtitle_Metadata_LemurTF-IDF (SM_LemurTF-IDF), (2) Global Weighted Linear Combination (GWLC), (3) Categorized Weighted Linear Combination (CWLC). Table 4 shows the results of the submitted runs on the test data. The same conclusions can be observed: the best performance is obtained by only using textual data. It is worth mentioning that the results of these methods achieved top positions in the competition.

Table 4: Performance on the test data.

Method	MAP	P@5	P@10	P@20
SM_LemurTF-IDF	.462	.654	.608	.438
GWLC	.316	.630	.534	.403
CWLC	.313	.630	.524	.401

4. CONCLUSION

In this paper, a large set of textual and video content features on the performance of video hyperlinking has been studied. The results show that the video hyperlinking performance relies on manual annotations (subtitle and metadata). The performance based on the ASR transcriptions is still far from the one achieved by manual annotations, while it is much better than audio, visual and motion features. The combination of surrounding context information will decrease the performance. The use of video content based features (audio, visual, and motion) has negative effects on the performance of textual features. Due to the limitation of well-labeled data, it is difficult to study the effectiveness of machine learning techniques on video hyperlinking task.

5. REFERENCES

[1] G. Amati. Frequentist and bayesian approach to information retrieval. In *Proc. of ECIR*, 2006.

[2] G. Amati, G. Amodeo, M. Bianchi, Ca. Gaibisso, and G. Gambosi. Fub, iasi-cnr and university of tor vergata at trec 2008 blog track. In *Proc. of TREC 2008*, 2008.

[3] C. Bhatt, N. Pappas, M. Habibi, and A. Popescu-Belis. Multimodal reranking of content-based recommendations for hyperlinking video snippets. In *Proc. of ACM ICMR*, 2014.

[4] X. Chang, Y. Yu, Y. Yang, and A. Hauptmann. Searching persuasively: Joint event detection and evidence recounting with limited supervision. In *Proc. of ACM MM*, 2015.

[5] M. Eskevich, G. Jones, and R. Aly. Multimedia information seeking through search and hyperlinking. In *Proc. of ACM ICMR*, 2013.

[6] M. Eskevich, G. Jones, S. Chen, R. Aly, R. Ordelman, and M. Larson. Search and hyperlinking task at mediaeval 2012. In *Proceedings of MediaEval Workshop*, 2013.

[7] F. Eyben, F. Weninger, F. Gross, and B. Schuller. Recent developments in opensmile, the munich open-source multimedia feature extractor. In *Proc. of ACM MM*, 2013.

[8] P. Galuščáková, P. Pecina, M. Kruliš, and J. Lokoc. Cuni at mediaeval 2014 search and hyperlinking task: visual and prosodic features in hyperlinking. In *Proceedings of the MediaEval Workshop*, 2014.

[9] A. Gianni. Probabilistic models for information retrieval based on divergence from randomness. *PhD Thesis, School of Computing Science, University of Glasgow*, 2003.

[10] L. Hang. A short introduction to learning to rank. *IEICE TRANSACTIONS on Information and Systems*, 94(10):1854–1862, 2011.

[11] D. Hiemstra. Using language models for information retrieval. *PhD Thesis, University of Twente*, 2001.

[12] L. Lamel. Multilingual speech processing activities in quaero: Application to multimedia search in unstructured data. In *Proc. of Baltic HLT*, pages 1–8, 2012.

[13] Z. Lan, M. Lin, X. Li, A. Hauptmann, and B. Raj. Beyond gaussian pyramid: Multi-skip feature stacking for action recognition. *arXiv preprint arXiv:1411.6660*, 2014.

[14] P. Lanchantin et al. Automatic transcription of multi-genre media archives. In *First Workshop on Speech, Language and Audio in Multimedia*, 2013.

[15] P. Over, J. Fiscus, G. Sanders, D. Joy, M. Michel, G. Awad, A. Smeaton, W. Kraaij, and G. Quénot. Trecvid 2014–an overview of the goals, tasks, data, evaluation mechanisms and metrics. In *Proceedings of TRECVID*, 2014.

[16] A. Rousseau, P. Deléglise, and Y. Estève. Enhancing the ted-lium corpus with selected data for language modeling and more ted talks. In *The 9th edition of the Language Resources and Evaluation Conference*, pages 3935–3939, 2014.

[17] T. Tommasi et al. Beyond metadata: searching your archive based on its audio-visual content. In *Proceedings of the 2014 International Broadcasting Convention*, 2014.

[18] A. Vedaldi and A. Zisserman. Efficient additive kernels via explicit feature maps. *IEEE Trans. Pattern Anal. Mach. Intell.*, 34(3):480–492, 2012.

[19] S. Yu, L. Jiang, Z. Xu, Y. Yang, and A. Hauptmann. Content-based video search over 1 million videos with 1 core in 1 second. In *Proc. of ACM ICMR*, 2015.

Why do you Think this Query is Difficult? A User Study on Human Query Prediction

Stefano Mizzaro
University of Udine
Via delle Scienze, 206
Udine, Italy
mizzaro@uniud.it

Josiane Mothe
Univ. de Toulouse, ESPE, IRIT
UMR5505 CNRS, 118 route de Narbonne
Toulouse, France
josiane.mothe@irit.fr

ABSTRACT

Predicting if a query will be difficult for a system is important to improve retrieval effectiveness by implementing specific processing. There have been several attempts to predict difficulty, both automatically and manually; but without high accuracy at a pre-retrieval stage. In this paper, we focus rather on understanding *why* a query is perceived by humans as difficult. We ran two separated but related experiments in which we asked humans to provide both a query difficulty prediction and reasons to explain their prediction. Results show that: (i) reasons can be categorized into 4 classes; (ii) reasons can be framed into closed questions to be answered on a Likert scale; and (iii) some reasons correlate in a coherent way with the human predicted numerical difficulty. On the basis of these results it is possible to derive hints to be provided to help users when formulating their queries and to avoid them to rely on their wrong perception of difficulty.

Keywords

Information retrieval; Query difficulty; difficulty understanding

1. QUERY DIFFICULTY PREDICTION

One of the outcomes of IR international evaluation campaigns is that system and query variability is high [5]. However, while there is some variability, some queries are difficult or easy for all the participants. For example in TREC Web 2014, which uses the ClueWeb 2012 corpus, the average ERR@20 for topic 278 "What are the lyrics to the theme song for "Mister Rogers' Neighborhood"?" is 0.0048 while the best run for that topic got 0.0820; this is a difficult topic for all systems. On the opposite, for topic 298 "medical care and jehovah's witnesses", the average ERR@20 is 0.5887 and the median is 0.5790; this is an easy topic.

The Reliable Information Access (RIA) workshop [5, 6] has been the first large scale attempt to try to *understand* query (and system) variability and difficulty. The two main conclusions of the failure analysis were: systems were missing an aspect of the query, generally the same aspect for all the systems, and "if a system can realize the problem associated with a given topic, then for well over half the topics studied, current technology should be able to improve results significantly" [6]. When considering failure analysis, 10 classes of topics were identified manually, but no indications were given on how to automatically assign a topic to a category.

Following these findings, there have been many attempts to automatically predict query difficulty. The purpose of a query difficulty predictor is to decide whether a system is able to properly answer the current query [2]. Different kinds of automatic predictors have been proposed in the literature both pre- [7] and post-retrieval [10], based on statistics only or considering some linguistic features [9]. Automatic predictors correlate with actual or observed system effectiveness, but the correlation is always weak, even if it is slightly higher when considering post-retrieval predictors than pre-retrieval ones (although post-retrieval predictors are less interesting, because more costly, than pre-retrieval) [7, 9, 10]. These results limit their practical use in real applications.

Another research direction is addressed by Hauff *et al.* who analyzed the relationship between predictions by non IR expert users and system effectiveness [8]. The authors considered various queries for a single topic or information need and measured the ability of users to judge the quality of query suggestions. They found that: (i) users are not good at predicting system failure; and (ii) the correlations between the users' prediction and both system effectiveness and automatic predictors are weak. We also had similar results when asking annotators to predict query difficulty, under several different experimental conditions, with different user groups, and both from the crowd and from participants in laboratory experiments.

In this paper, rather than focusing on query difficulty rating, we focus on reasons why users think a query is going to be easy or difficult for a search engine. We decided to consider users who are not necessarily IR experts since the latter know how systems work and may not be representative of a large variety of real search engine users. Therefore, when compared to RIA [5, 6], we ask to non experts to provide reasons that explain query difficulty (or ease). When compared to Hauff *et al.* [8], rather than just asking for ratings, we focus on explanations and comments on difficulty.

To know more on these reasons, we performed a user study made up of the two experiments described in the next two sections.

2. EXPERIMENT 1: ELICITING REASONS

The first experiment aimed at eliciting free text reasons why queries are perceived as difficult or easy by users.

2.1 Experimental Design

While we were interested mainly in the reasons why users think a query is going to be easy or difficult for a search engine, the task for human annotators was both to predict the difficulty a search engine may encounter to answer an information need and to explain

SIGIR '16, July 17-21, 2016, Pisa, Italy

DOI: http://dx.doi.org/10.1145/2911451.2914696

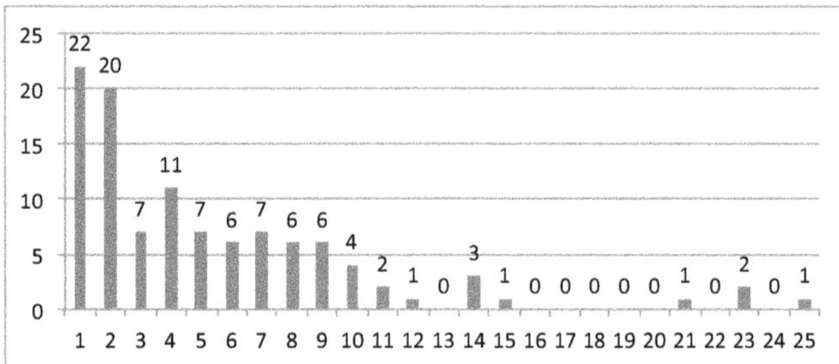

Figure 1: Number of queries by annotation frequency

the reasons of their prediction. Indeed, it is probably more natural for annotators to choose an explicit rating first and then to focus on providing the reasons for it. When asked to annotate the topic difficulty, the main question the annotators had to think of was: is the system going to succeed/fail when processing this query? Does the annotator think the system will retrieve relevant information (an easy query) or not (difficulty query)?

Annotators were provided with the query (TREC topic title); they had to decide the difficulty on, and to comment on the difficulty rating they chose, using the query only. Annotators were asked to use a three level numeric scale: 1 for easy query, 2 for medium query, and 3 for difficult queries. They also could use 0 when they did not know, although they were encouraged to decide on the difficulty. In addition to grading the query difficulty, annotators were asked to indicate the reasons why they thought the query was easy/difficult. For a query and whatever the grade they gave, they could indicate both comments, on its difficult and easy natures. We did not provide any guidance to write the comments apart from using the keyword "Easy:" or "Difficult:" before any comment they write. The tool we provided does not allow them to go back to an annotation they had done previously.

The group of annotators was composed of 38 Master's Students (25 1st and 13 2nd year) in *library and teaching studies*; although they had been trained to use specialized search engines, they had just an introduction class on how search engines work. Annotators could choose as many topics they wanted from a set of 150 TREC topics. Topics were displayed in different order to avoid any bias, as the first topics may be treated differently because the task was new for annotators. Moreover, annotators could skip some topics if they wish; this was done to avoid them to work on a topic they did not understand or felt uncomfortable with. Since the annotation process is difficult, we tried to provide to the annotators the most favorable conditions. The drawback is that the number of annotations varies over topics; this makes numerical analyses more difficult (for example, when computing an average difficulty score the averages are computed over different numbers of scores) but we were here more interested in the reasons, and this kind of qualitative data is less prone to such difficulties.

In this experiment, we used TREC 6, 7, and 8 adhoc task topics.Although these collections are old, we think that the elicitation of reasons will not differ much with other collections. Of course, the annotators knew that the document collection is composed of newspaper articles from the 90s even though it may be difficult for an annotator nowadays to get a picture of what were the popular topics in newspapers more than twenty years ago.

2.2 Results and Analysis

We analyzed the comments that the annotators associated with the evaluation of difficulty. The objectives were (i) to see if there were some recurrent patterns, and (ii) to extract some trends in the comments associated with classes of query difficulty as perceived by users/annotators.

Table 1: Distribution of grades used by annotators

Grade:	Easy	Medium	Difficult	Don't know
Frequency:	227	188	140	17

2.2.1 Descriptive Statistics

Figure 1 shows the number of queries as a function of the number of times it has been annotated by any of the 38 annotators. For example, 22 queries have been annotated a single time (left part of the figure); the most annotated query has been annotated 25 times (right side of the figure). In total 107 queries have been annotated at least by one annotator and 65 three times or more. Table 1 shows the distribution of grades, i.e., the number of times a given grade has been used (e.g., grade Easy has been used 227 times whatever the annotator and the query are).

We collected 460 annotations in total (one annotation count for one topic, one annotator). 107 topics have been graded by at least one annotator; a little fewer have been commented (6 topics have no comment associated with them). It is of course possible that other comments might be generated for the other topics, but with around 70% of the topics being annotated we can be rather confident that most of the reasons have been elicited in this experiment.

2.2.2 Recoding the Free Text Comments

We recoded the free text comments. Table 2 shows some examples of recoding that was made. Each comment could be recoded into more than one recoded phrases; for example the comment "terms are too general, there will be many documents retrieved" has been recoded into *Too-General-Words* and *Many-Documents*. We found out that there were mostly four types of comments, as shown in the table: T (on the topic itself), Q (on the query), W (on the words used), and D (on the documents or on the collection, e.g., if the annotator thinks that some document exists in the collection).

The table also shows how many comments were recoded in each category; however, notice that recoding is always subjective and another recoder may have recoded differently, thus these numbers just provide trends. In a few cases (about 5%), the comment was not explicitly associated with one of these classes. This was for example the case when annotators wrote *vague* without detailing if it was a query term which they found vague or the topic itself. A concrete example is the one of Query 417 (Title: *creativity*) for which the 5 annotators considered the query as difficult using comments such as "too broad, not enough targeted", "far too vague",

Table 2: Examples of recoding, grouped into four categories.

Free text comment	Recoded phrase
T: Topic (274 comments, 35 recoded phrases)	
"The topic is precise"	*Precise-Topic*
Q: Query (142 comments, 23 recoded phrases)	
"The query is formulated in a clear way"	*Clear-Query*
"The query is not precise at all"	*Broad-Query*
W: Words (180 comments, 28 recoded phrases)	
"A single word in the query"	*1-Word*
"The term 'exploration' is polysemous"	*Polysemous-Word*
D: Documents (143 comments, 15 recoded phrases)	
"Risk of getting too many results"	*Too-Many-Documents*
"There are many documents on this"	*Many-Documents*

Table 3: Most frequent comments.

Easy because		Difficult because	
Precise-Topic	66	*Risk-Of-Noise*	50
Many-Documents	45	*Broad-Topic*	43
No-Polysemous-Word	31	*Missing-Context*	34
Precise-Words	25	*Polysemous-Words*	22
Clear-Query	19	*Several-Aspects*	20
Usual-Topic	16	*Missing-Where*	16

"far too vague topic", "keyword used very broad, risk of noise", and "a single search term, risk of getting too many results". While the last comments are directed to one or the other class, the first two are not. We notice that the four categories are roughly equally distributed and have a good coverage.

After recoding, we got 740 annotations for 572 graded queries (each query could be annotated by various annotators; in addition several recoded phrases can be associated with a single comment). For recoding we used 105 different recoding phrases (4 of which are not associated with any of the four categories).

2.2.3 *Comments Associated with Ease and Difficulty*

Table 3 shows the most frequent recoded phrases associated with ease (left part) and difficulty (right part). Remember that a given query can be annotated by some comments associated with both. For example, while *Precise-Topic* is generally associated with ease (66 times), it is also associated with difficulty in 3 cases. In that case it is associated with other comments, e.g. "The topic is very precise but it may be too specific". In the same way, *Many-Documents* is mostly associated with ease and *Too-Many-Documents* to difficulty, although *Many-Documents* is also associated with difficulty (users may have in mind either a recall-oriented or a precision-oriented task). Also, when *Many-Documents* is used associated with difficulty, it is generally associated with *Risk-Of-Noise*.

2.2.4 *Annotator Effect*

It may be that some annotators are more likely to use some types of comments than others, either because of what they think about how systems work or because of their search experiences.

We analyzed the link between annotators and the four categories of comments, i.e., associated with Word (W), Query (Q), Topic (T), and Document (D). We grouped the recoded phrases belonging to each category and built a matrix that associates annotators and the four categories of comments associated with. We then used Correspondence Analysis (CA) [1] on that matrix to visualize in one shot the relationships. CA is close to Principal Component Analysis (PCA) in its principle and appropriate when analyzing categorical variables which is the case here. Compared to PCA, CA allows to display in the same space the variables and observations (rows and columns). The distance between objects of any kind is meaningful.

Figure 2 shows the two first axes of the corresponding CA. The horizontal axis divides the figure into two parts. The top part is more related to comments on W and T and so are the annotators in this part of the figure. The bottom part is related to Q and D categories; so are the annotators displayed in this part of the figure. Moreover, the bottom left corner of the figure is more related to comments on D, as the annotators who are in the same corner while the bottom right part is more associated with comments on Q. The annotators near the origin of the axes use annotations from all four categories, while the annotators in the top right corner are more inclined to use comments on Q (according to the horizontal axis) and on W (vertical axis), but do not use comments on D.

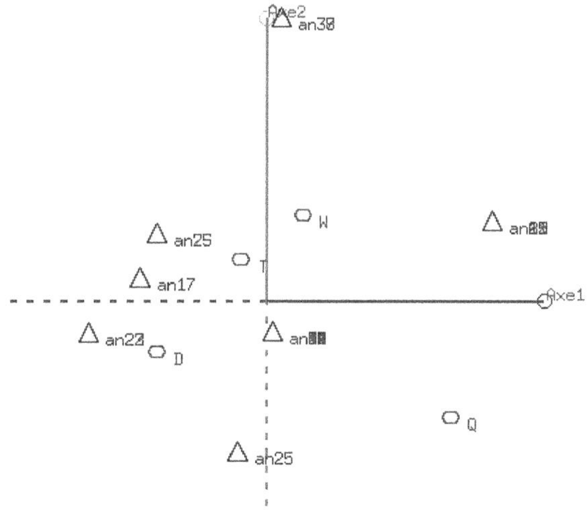

Figure 2: CA, first components: annotators (triangles) and comment categories (ellipses).

We went a step further to check if some annotators use some comments more than others by using the comments rather than the category of comments and found that it is indeed the case too.

3. EXPERIMENT 2: TESTING REASONS

The experiment described in the previous section allowed us to elicit reasons. However, free text questions have two drawbacks: first they need to be recoded and recoding is subjective, and second, annotators are sensitive to different features as we have shown in section 2.2.4. Based on these results, we decided to consider, rather than free text, closed and mandatory questions for the annotators to answer. Closed so that recoding will not be needed anymore, and mandatory so that the annotator effect will be less important. This is done in the second experiment, described in this section.

3.1 From Categories to Questions

We considered each of the 105 recoding phrases obtained in the previous experiment and transformed them into 32 closed questions (denoted with Qi in the following) that could be answered following a Likert scale. Examples of such questions are shown in the first column of Table 4. When recoding, we had tried to keep as most as possible the nuances annotators expressed. When rephrasing into questions, we removed these nuances to limit the number of questions and to remove some redundancy (e.g., precise, specific, focused, delimited, and clear were merged together).

3.2 Experimental Design

We performed a laboratory user study with 22 new volunteers mainly from our research institutes. They were recruited using generic emailing lists and they got a coupon for participating. Each of them was asked to annotate 10 queries (provided in a random order). We used 25 topics from TREC Web 2014 that uses ClueWeb 2012 corpus: we picked up the easiest 10, the most difficult 10, and the medium 5 according to the topic difficulty order presented in the overview paper [3]. We changed from TREC 6, 7, 8 to ClueWeb queries since the latter are more recent, might reflect more the types of current queries on the web, and are now more used in the IR community. Also, in the previous experiment some topics were not annotated: clearly the young students were not at ease with (some of the) old topics.

In order to make the statistical analysis more smooth and sound

Table 4: Examples of questions (column 1) with their Pearson's correlations with human predicted difficulty (col. 2) and actual difficulty (col. 3). Bold indicates a p-value < 0.05, * <0.005.

Question	Correl.	
Q1: The query contains vague word(s)	**.52**	-.30
Q3: The query contains word(s) relevant to the topic/query	**-.41**	.43
Q10: The topic is unusual/uncommon/unknown	**.52**	.26
Q13: The topic has several/many aspects	**.61***	-.07
Q17: The topic is usual/common/known	**.62***	-.25
Q18: The number of documents on the topic in the web is high	**-.69***	-.34
Q19: None or very few relevant documents will be retrieved	**.88***	.32
Q20: Only relevant documents will be retrieved	**-.47**	.09
Q23: Many of the relevant documents will be retrieved	**-.86***	-.20
Q24: Many relevant documents will be retrieved	**-.87***	-.21
Q26: The number of query words is too high	**.62***	**.45**
Q28: The query contains various aspects	**.46**	-.12
Q30: The query is clear	**-.53**	.30

we collected the same number of predictions for each query; we thus consider the same number of annotators for each topic. Annotators had to annotate the level of difficulty of the query, but rather than asking them to provide the reason of their grading in free text only, we asked to answer the 32 predefined questions Qi using a five level scale, from -2 "I strongly disagree" to +2 "I strongly agree". With 32 Qi by 25 topics by 8 annotators each, we collected a total of 6400 reason ratings. The free text reasons they provided has not been analyzed yet.

3.3 Results

Table 4 shows on the second column the Pearson's correlation between the questions and the human prediction of difficulty. Only the 13 Qi having a statistically significant correlation (p-value $<$ 0.05) are included. The seven Qi having values labeled with a * (Q13, Q17, Q18, Q19, Q23, Q24, Q26) have a correlation higher than 0.60 with a p-value < 0.005. These 13, and especially 7, Qi represent the reasons that, according to the users, correlate most with query difficulty. For example, users think a query is difficult because the topic has many aspects (Q13).

However, none of these 13 reasons that users think correlated with query difficulty, turns out to correlate with actual difficulty, with just one exception (Q26). This is shown in the third column in the table that reports the correlation with observed difficulty based on system effectiveness. We used the average ERR@20 as system effectiveness measure, calculated considering all the participant runs. Moreover, the correlation between the human prediction and actual difficulty is low (0.238, p-value 0.25), indeed a much lower value (and not statistically significant as well) than the correlation between Q26 and actual effectiveness, which is 0.45, p-value < 0.05. This means that to obtain a prediction of difficulty, it is much better to ask Q26 than to directly ask for a difficulty rating.

There is also the possibility that some Qi can be combined, maybe also with the difficulty prediction rating, and/or with automatic predictors, to obtain a more accurate numerical prediction. We do not have space here to present those results, but we note (see Figure 3) that some of the seven questions are redundant, and therefore there is no need to require the user to answer all of them.

4. DISCUSSION AND CONCLUSIONS

Other studies have shown that humans are bad query difficulty predictors [8] and generally think queries are easier for systems than they actually are. This paper is a first contribution to try to understand why users (rather than IR experts) think a query is easy

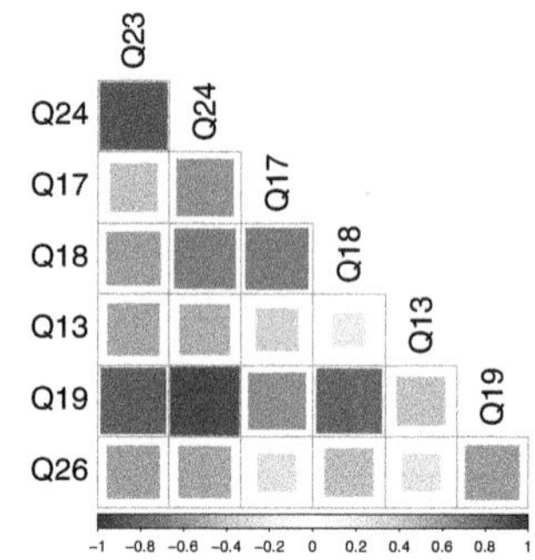

Figure 3: Pearson correlations between questions. Q18, Q19, Q23, and Q24 have a high correlation; they are redundant.

or difficult for a search engine. In a first user study, reasons were elicited from free text comments on query difficulty. After a manual recoding and a deep analysis, we found a set of 105 reasons classified into four categories. We then framed 32 closed questions that cover all the mentioned reasons and can be answered through a Likert scale. We used those 32 questions in a second user study, and showed that thirteen correlate with the human prediction of difficulty, and seven of them highly. On the other hand, these questions do not correlate with observed system difficulty. These questions can thus be seen as explanation why humans wrongly think queries are easy or difficult. These results can be useful when training search engine users [4], e.g., to help them to formulate queries and to provide them with hints about their wrong perception of system effectiveness. For example, a user can be told (by a teacher or a search engine) that the fact the query seems usual or common is not linked to system effectiveness.

References

[1] J.-P. Benzécri et al. *Correspondence analysis handbook.* Marcel Dekker New York, 1992.

[2] D. Carmel and E. Yom-Tov. *Estimating the query difficulty for information retrieval.* Morgan & Claypool, 2010.

[3] K. Collins-Thompson, C. Macdonald, P. Bennett, F. Diaz, and E. Voorhees. TREC 2014 Web Track Overview. In *Text REtrieval Conference*, 2015.

[4] E. Efthimiadis, J. M. Fernández-Luna, J. F. Huete, and A. MacFarlane. *Teaching and learning in information retrieval.* Vol. 31. Springer Science & Business Media, 2011.

[5] D. Harman and C. Buckley. The NRRC reliable information access (RIA) workshop. In *Conf. on Research and Development in Inf. Retrieval, SIGIR*, pages 528–529. ACM, 2004.

[6] D. Harman and C. Buckley. Overview of the reliable information access workshop. *Information Retrieval*, 12(6):615–641, 2009.

[7] C. Hauff, D. Hiemstra, and F. de Jong. A survey of pre-retrieval query performance predictors. In *Conf. on Information and Knowledge Manag., CIKM*, pages 1419–1420, 2008.

[8] C. Hauff, D. Kelly, and L. Azzopardi. A comparison of user and system query performance predictions. In *Conf. on Inf. and knowledge management, CIKM*, pages 979–988, 2010.

[9] J. Mothe and L. Tanguy. Linguistic features to predict query difficulty. In *Predicting query difficulty Wp, Conf. on Research and Development in IR, SIGIR*, pages 7–10, 2005.

[10] A. Shtok, O. Kurland, D. Carmel, F. Raiber, and G. Markovits. Predicting query performance by query-drift estimation. *ACM, TOIS*, 30(2):11, 2012.

A Platform for Streaming Push Notifications to Mobile Assessors

Adam Roegiest, Luchen Tan, Jimmy Lin, and Charles L. A. Clarke
David R. Cheriton School of Computer Science
University of Waterloo, Ontario, Canada
{aroegies, luchen.tan, jimmylin}@uwaterloo.ca, claclark@gmail.com

ABSTRACT

We present an assessment platform for gathering online relevance judgments for mobile push notifications that will be deployed in the newly-created TREC 2016 Real-Time Summarization (RTS) track. There is emerging interest in building systems that filter social media streams such as tweets to identify interesting and novel content in real time, putatively for delivery to users' mobile phones. In our evaluation design, all participants subscribe to the Twitter streaming API to identify relevant tweets with respect to a set of interest profiles. As the systems generate results, they are pushed in real time to our evaluation broker via a REST API. The broker then "routes" the tweets to assessors who have installed a custom app on their mobile phones. We detail the design of this platform and discuss a number of challenges that need to be tackled in this type of "Living Labs" setup. It is our goal that such an evaluation design will mitigate any issues that have arisen in traditional batch-style evaluations of this type of task.

1. INTRODUCTION

There is emerging interest in building push notification systems that filter social media streams, such as Twitter, to deliver relevant content to users' mobile phones. For example, the user might be a political news junkie interested in polls for the 2016 U.S. presidential elections and wishes to be notified whenever new results are posted on Twitter. She might also be interested in commentary by political pundits and reactions by the candidates. Such notifications must relevant (i.e., on topic), timely (i.e., the user desires poll results as soon as they are available), and novel (i.e., the user does not want tweets from multiple sources that cite the same poll). Techniques to address such information needs are becoming increasingly important as mobile devices continue to gain prominence for information access.

The TREC Microblog track in 2015 operationalized the push notification task in the so-called "scenario A" variant of the real-time filtering task [3]. Over the official evaluation period, which spanned ten days during July 2015, participating systems "listened" to Twitter's live tweet sample stream to identify relevant tweets with respect to 225 pre-defined "interest profiles" (each expressed through statements modeled after TREC *ad hoc* topics), 51 of which were later assessed. Each system identified up to ten tweets per day, which were ostensibly delivered to hypothetical users. In total, 14 groups submitted 37 runs to this evaluation.

As it was the first year, many aspects of the evaluation in 2015 represented substantial simplifications of the actual task. Instead of pushing notifications in real time, participating systems merely recorded the wall clock time at which the system *would have* pushed the notification. That is, all results were recorded locally and submitted in batch *after* the evaluation period ended. Thus, although the task itself is real time, the results were evaluated with standard batch protocols (pooling followed by semantic clustering; see Wang et al. [9] for more details). The goal of our work is to tackle this limitation: we present an assessment platform for gathering online relevance judgments for mobile push notifications. This platform will be deployed in the newly-created TREC 2016 Real-Time Summarization (RTS) track.

Real-Time Summarization at TREC 2016 represents a merger of the Microblog track, which ran from 2010 to 2015, and the Temporal Summarization track [1], which ran from 2013 to 2015. The creation of RTS was designed to leverage synergies between the two tracks in exploring prospective information needs over document streams containing novel and evolving information. Previously, Temporal Summarization evaluations operated by *simulating* a stream of documents using a static collection, which also represented a simplification of the underlying task model. We believe that by "joining forces", we could develop a more refined push notification task and associated evaluation infrastructure to support online user-in-the-loop evaluations, thereby growing the research community and pushing forward the state of the art.

2. GENERAL ARCHITECTURE

The TREC 2016 Real-Time Summarization track will operationalize a push notification task that largely follows the same task from the TREC 2015 Microblog track. Participants must deploy working systems that consume a live stream over a defined evaluation period. In 2016, this live stream will be comprised solely of tweets provided by the Twitter streaming API, but we are investigating the viability of alternate and additional sources, e.g., a stream of news stories or blog posts. The exact task definition is not

SIGIR '16, July 17 - 21, 2016, Pisa, Italy

ISBN 978-1-4503-4069-4/16/07... $15.00
DOI: http://dx.doi.org/10.1145/2911451.2911463

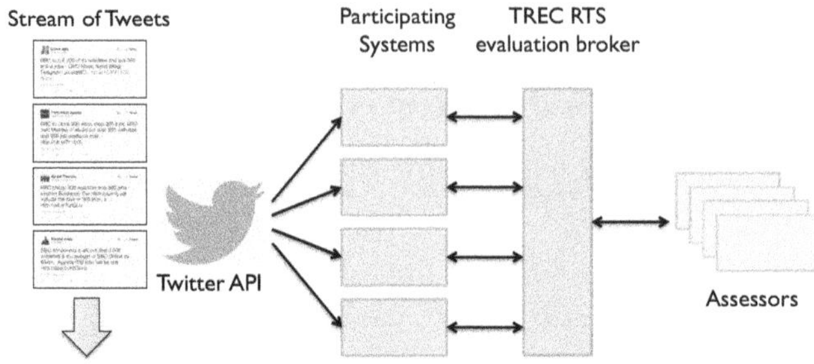

Figure 1: A high-level overview of the real-time push notification assessment platform.

relevant for the purposes of this work, which focuses on the assessment platform. The most substantial change from the previous evaluation is that systems now must submit their results in real time. This live submission is accomplished via a REST API and evaluation infrastructure that we have developed. The entire platform, including both server code and the mobile assessment app, is available open source.[1]

The high-level architecture of our assessment platform is shown in Figure 1. Our general approach builds on growing interest in so-called Living Labs [6] and related Evaluation-as-a-Service (EaaS) [2] approaches that attempt to better align evaluation methodologies with user task models and real-world constraints to increase the fidelity of research experiments. In our architecture, participating systems all subscribe to the Twitter streaming API (a sample stream is freely available to all registered users) to identify relevant tweets with respect to interest profiles. Since tweets are being posted in real time, the evaluation organizers do not distribute any data ahead of time—they listen to the stream just like all participants to gather an archival copy of the tweets. A pilot study in 2015 [4] confirmed that multiple geographically-distributed listeners to the public Twitter sample stream receive effectively the same tweets (Jaccard overlap of 0.999 across six independent crawls over a three day sample in March 2015). As the participating systems identify relevant tweets, they are pushed in real time to the evaluation broker, which then routes the tweets to assessors who have installed a custom app on their mobile phones. We intend to recruit students to serve as the assessors.

This setup has a number of distinct advantages:

- Gathering relevance judgments in an online fashion has the potential to yield more situationally accurate assessments, particularly for rapidly developing events. With post hoc batch evaluations, there is always a bit of disconnect as the assessor needs to "imagine" herself at the time the update was pushed. With our evaluation framework, we remove this disconnect.
- An online evaluation platform allows for the possibility of user-submitted information needs, thus giving assessors the ability to judge tweets for interest profiles they are genuinely interested in.
- An online evaluation platform opens the door to providing realistic, online feedback to participants, thus potentially facilitating active learning approaches. There are, of course, many additional complexities that remain unresolved (discussed below), and in the near term we do not anticipate providing this option.

[1] https://github.com/trecrts/trecrts-eval

Note that online evaluation using our assessment platform does not preclude the use of standard batch evaluation methodologies that have been well studied and appropriately validated. Indeed, it is the plan that the Real-Time Summarization track in TREC 2016 will also apply the batch evaluation methodology developed for the Microblog track in 2015 in a post hoc manner. This dual evaluation approach will help us validate the reliability and stability of our online mobile assessment platform.

3. PLATFORM COMPONENTS

3.1 Evaluation Workflow

We have designed our assessment platform around the following workflow:

1. Systems listen to the live Twitter sample stream to identify interesting and novel tweets with respect to a set of pre-defined interest profiles. Although we provide boilerplate code to get started, participants are responsible for building and running their own systems.
2. Whenever a system identifies a relevant tweet with respect to an interest profile, the system submits the result to the evaluation broker via a REST API, which records the submission time.
3. The broker routes the tweet to the mobile phone of an assessor, where it is rendered as a push notification containing both the text of the tweet and the corresponding interest profile.
4. The assessor may choose to judge the tweet immediately, or if it arrives at an inopportune time, to ignore it. Either way, the tweet is added to a judging queue in a custom app on the assessor's mobile phone, which she can access at any time to judge the queue of accumulated tweets.
5. As the assessor judges tweets, the results are relayed back to the evaluation broker and recorded.

While the information retrieval community is already familiar with a variety of batch relevance assessment approaches, our platform explores a largely untouched space in evaluation design. We anticipate that a number of experimental design decisions will need to be empirically verified:

- **Number of assessors**: The size of the assessor pool will be largely dependent on the number of topics, participating systems, and the incentive structure for providing judgments.
- **Topic assignment**: There are many possibilities for mapping between topics and assessors. As with standard pooled batch evaluations, assigning all tweets for a given topic to a single assessor increases the consistency of judgments, but might result in an unbalanced load across assessors. Alternatively, we could split each topic across multiple assessors, but this approach may increase inconsistency.
- **Assessor modeling**: It is likely that assessors will vary in quality, will respond to push notifications with varying degrees of latency, and will provide differing numbers of judgments in a given time period. We anticipate the need to construct post hoc assessor models in order to understand and account for these assessor differences.

- **Tweet interleaving**: It is unlikely that we will be able to devote an assessor to exclusively judge the output of a single system. Nor would this approach be desirable, since it would magnify the impact of assessor differences when performing system comparisons. Thus, assessors will see interleaved results from multiple systems. We have been separately investigating tweet interleaving strategies for evaluation [5], and we will apply the lessons learned from those experiments as appropriate.

3.2 Evaluation Broker

The evaluation broker (see Figure 1) serves as an intermediary between systems participating in the evaluation and the mobile assessors. The main role of the broker is to distribute interest profiles to participating systems, record system submissions, route submitted results to mobile assessors, and record judgments rendered by the assessors.

The broker is implemented in Node.js and backed by a MySQL database for persistent storage of result submissions and assessor judgments. Broker functionalities are implemented via different REST API endpoints. For example, systems submit a tweet for a particular interest profile using the following call:

```
POST /tweet/:topid/:tweetid/:clientid
```

where `:topid` specifies the topic (interest profile) identifier, `:tweetid` specifies the unique tweet identifier of the post, and `:clientid` specifies the client's unique identifier. The broker returns a 204 status code on success. It is expected that all participating systems will properly interface with the appropriate API endpoint during the evaluation period.

Currently, we have designed the broker to rate-limit the number of submissions by a system to ten tweets per topic per day, following the TREC 2015 Microblog track protocol. The broker further employs some common sense safeguards, e.g., to not bombard any individual assessor with an undue number of push notifications. The actual routing policy of how tweets are assigned to assessors is still currently under development, although we have already implemented a basic round robin approach.

3.3 Mobile Assessment App

For TREC 2016, we plan to recruit students from the University of Waterloo to serve as mobile assessors in a user study centered around the Real-Time Summarization task. As discussed, assessors will receive tweets as they are identified by participating systems in real time, on their mobile phones as push notifications through our custom app. A screenshot of the current app is shown in Figure 2. We envision the experimental study to proceed as follows:

- Assessors will be given a brief description of the task and an invitation to install the assessment app on their mobile phones.
- Assessors will log in to the app to indicate that they are ready to receive tweets. They may log out to stop receiving tweets when they unavailable (e.g., during an exam).
- Assessors will receive new tweets to judge as they become available (i.e., are pushed by participating systems). Tweets will be assessed with respect to the interest profile provided with the tweet.

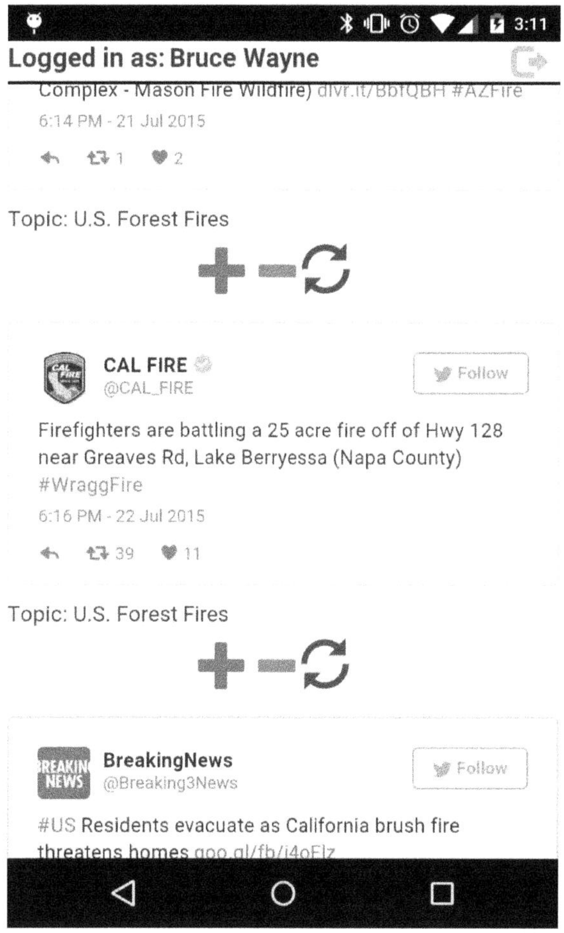

Figure 2: Screenshot of the mobile assessment app.

- At any point, assessors will be able to end their participation in the task and to opt out of further work. After ending participation they will receive a code that can be exchanged for remuneration (at a rate yet to be determined).
- Otherwise, assessors will be able to judge tweets until the end of the evaluation period, after which they will receive the renumeration code.

We have built the mobile assessment app for both iOS and Android using the Cordova framework. Cordova is designed to leverage existing web technologies for the creation of mobile apps without requiring extensive platform-specific API knowledge. This makes cross-platform development (Android and iOS) significantly less labor-intensive compared to writing two separate native apps. The tradeoff is performance, which is not a concern for us since our assessment task is not processing intensive.

Note that the broker does not directly deliver tweets to the assessors. Rather, tweet identifiers are sent to the mobile phone and tweets are rendered by the assessment app from these identifiers via Twitter's OEmbed API,[2] which displays any inline media content for the tweet. This mechanism was adopted to comply with the Twitter terms of service, which prohibit the distribution of tweet content, but

[2] https://dev.twitter.com/rest/reference/get/statuses/oembed

the mechanism also allows us to offload tweet rendering (including complex multimedia content) to the device. Using OEmbed, we can render a tweet natively with minimal effort yet still provide a user experience similar to that of the official Twitter client.

4. BASELINE SYSTEM

Although the main focus of this demonstration is the mobile assessment platform itself, we also present a baseline implementation to facilitate system development and participation in the track. Our baseline system, called YoGosling, is a modified and extended version of the system that generated the best performing automatic run in TREC 2015 [7]. Following TREC, we performed error analysis and ablation studies to distill the original system down to the components that contributed most to overall effectiveness [8]. This system is built on the Anserini project, which is the University of Waterloo's Lucene-based search framework. The system is able to incrementally index the Twitter sample stream and provide real-time search capabilities.

YoGosling converts the title field of interest profiles into queries for searching Lucene and applies a simple relevance scoring method to rank tweets. After relevance scoring, duplicate and near-duplicate tweets are identified by a novelty detection component (based on simple Jaccard similarity), so that users are not given repetitiously annoying information. One of the most important lessons learned in building YoGosling is the proper setting of score thresholds and ignoring tweets that fall below the thresholds. Our simple scoring model is amenable to a *global* threshold that yields reasonable effectiveness, thus obviating the need for per-topic tuning (difficult due to the paucity of training data). Another interesting feature of YoGosling is a simple relevance feedback mechanism whereby users assess tweets once a day, and these judgments are used to set the score threshold for the next day. We experimentally show that this technique can yield substantial gains in effectiveness [8].

5. FUTURE WORK

One of the main enhancements we are planning to add is the ability for assessors to supply their own interest profiles directly through an API, so that they can actually receive tweets of personal interest. In TREC 2016, we plan to develop interest profiles manually based on assessor input, but the profiles will be vetted by the track organizers before distribution to participating systems. An automatic API for interest profile submission creates several non-trivial problems, including near-duplicate detection, limiting the release of personal information, and topic termination (since some topics may only be important for a limited time). These issues are exacerbated if there is the expectation that behavioral traces will be released as part of a training set (as is the case with TREC evaluations), and ethics issues similar to the public release of web query logs come into focus.

At present, we have a few ideas of how to assign interest profiles to assessors, but lack concrete empirical evidence as to what strategy will actually "work". As discussed, foreseeable issues include inter-assessor consistency, assessor latency (how quickly they respond to push notifications), and assessment volume (how many judgments they ultimately provide). Related, the strategy used for interleaving tweets has the potential to affect the judgments rendered, and in turn the relative scoring of systems. Assessor differences introduce additional confounds. We have been exploring in parallel some of these questions via simulations [5], but the literature otherwise offers little guidance and we will have to make decisions about evaluation design for TREC 2016 based on limited empirical evidence.

6. CONCLUSIONS

In this demonstration, we described the architecture of an assessment platform for gathering online relevance judgments for mobile push notifications that will be deployed in the TREC 2016 Real-Time Summarization (RTS) track. Although the infrastructure is "feature complete" in terms of implementation, we freely admit that there are many unresolved issues regarding evaluation design. There is no substitute for operational experience in running a TREC evaluation, and we anticipate many lessons to be learned.

7. ACKNOWLEDGMENTS

This work was supported in part by the U.S. National Science Foundation under awards IIS-1218043 and CNS-1405688 and the Natural Sciences and Engineering Research Council of Canada (NSERC). Any opinions, findings, conclusions, or recommendations expressed are those of the authors and do not necessarily reflect the views of the sponsors.

8. REFERENCES

[1] J. Aslam, M. Ekstrand-Abueg, V. Pavlu, F. Diaz, R. McCreadie, and T. Sakai. TREC 2014 Temporal Summarization Track overview. *TREC*, 2014.

[2] A. Hanbury, H. Müller, K. Balog, T. Brodt, G. V. Cormack, I. Eggel, T. Gollub, F. Hopfgartner, J. Kalpathy-Cramer, N. Kando, A. Krithara, J. Lin, S. Mercer, and M. Potthast. Evaluation-as-a-Service: Overview and outlook. *arXiv:1512.07454*, 2015.

[3] J. Lin, M. Efron, Y. Wang, G. Sherman, and E. Voorhees. Overview of the TREC-2015 Microblog Track. *TREC*, 2015.

[4] J. H. Paik and J. Lin. Do multiple listeners to the public Twitter sample stream receive the same tweets? *SIGIR Workshop on Temporal, Social and Spatially-Aware Information Access*, 2015.

[5] X. Qian, J. Lin, and A. Roegiest. Interleaved evaluation for retrospective summarization and prospective notification on document streams. *SIGIR*, 2016.

[6] A. Schuth, K. Balog, and L. Kelly. Overview of the Living Labs for Information Retrieval Evaluation (LL4IR) CLEF Lab 2015. *CLEF*, 2015.

[7] L. Tan, A. Roegiest, and C. L. A. Clarke. University of Waterloo at TREC 2015 Microblog track. *TREC*, 2015.

[8] L. Tan, A. Roegiest, C. L. A. Clarke, and J. Lin. Simple dynamic emission strategies for microblog filtering. *SIGIR*, 2016.

[9] Y. Wang, G. Sherman, J. Lin, and M. Efron. Assessor differences and user preferences in tweet timeline generation. *SIGIR*, 2015.

A Visual Analytics Approach for What-If Analysis of Information Retrieval Systems

Marco Angelini
University of Rome
Rome, Italy

Nicola Ferro
University of Padua
Padua, Italy

Giuseppe Santucci
University of Rome
Rome, Italy

Gianmaria Silvello
University of Padua
Padua, Italy

ABSTRACT

We present the innovative visual analytics approach of the VATE^2 system, which eases and makes more effective the experimental evaluation process by introducing the what-if analysis. The what-if analysis is aimed at estimating the possible effects of a modification to an IR system to select the most promising fixes before implementing them, thus saving a considerable amount of effort.

VATE^2 builds on an analytical framework which models the behavior of the systems in order to make estimations, and integrates this analytical framework into a visual part which, via proper interaction and animations, receives input and provides feedback to the user.

1. INTRODUCTION

Understanding and interpreting the results produced by experimental evaluation is not a trivial task, which requires a lot of manual effort due to the complex interactions among the components of an *Information Retrieval (IR)* system. Moreover, after such activity, the researcher needs to come back to design and then implement the modifications that the previous analysis suggested as possible solutions to the identified problems. Afterwards, a new experimentation cycle needs to be started to verify whether the introduced modifications actually give the expected improvement. Therefore, the overall process of improving an IR system is extremely time and resource demanding and proceeds through cycles where each new feature needs to be implemented and experimented.

The goal of this paper is to introduce a new phase in this cycle: we call it *what-if analysis* and it falls between the experimental evaluation and the design and implementation of the identified modifications. What-if analysis aims at estimating what the effects of a modification to the IR system under examination could be before actually being implemented.

What-if analysis exploits *Visual Analytics (VA)* techniques to make researchers and developers: (i) interact with and explore the ranked result list produced by an IR system and the achieved performances; (ii) hypothesize possible causes of failure and their fixes; (iii) estimate the possible impact of such fixes through a powerful analytical model of the system behavior. This paper introduces the *Visual Analytics Tool for Experimental Evaluation (VATE^2)* prototype, which provides a proof-of-concept of how *what-if- analysis* works.

The paper is organized as follows: Section 2 summarizes our previous work on VA for performance and failure analysis, which constitutes the starting point for developing the what-if analysis; Section 3 gives an overview of the analytics framework defining the what-if analysis. Section 4 illustrates how the what-if analysis has been realized in the VATE^2 prototype and describes its main features. Finally, Section 5 draws some conclusions.

SIGIR '16, July 17-21, 2016, Pisa, Italy

DOI: http://dx.doi.org/10.1145/2911451.2911462

2. PERFORMANCE AND FAILURE ANALYSIS

In order to quantify the performances of an IR system, we realized *Visual Information Retrieval Tool for Upfront Evaluation (VIRTUE)* [1, 2] which adopts the *Discounted Cumulated Gain (DCG)* family of measures [4] which allow for graded relevance judgments and embed a model of the user behavior while he scrolls down the result list which also gives an account of its overall satisfaction.

We compare the result list produced by an experiment with respect to an *ideal* ranking created starting from the relevant documents in the ground-truth. In addition to what is typically done, we compare the result list with respect to an *optimal* one created with the same documents retrieved by the IR system but with an optimal ranking, i.e. a permutation of the results retrieved by the experiment aimed at maximizing its performances by sorting the retrieved documents in decreasing order of relevance.

Looking at a performance curve, as the DCG curve is, it is not always easy to spot what the critical regions in a ranking are. Indeed, DCG is a not-decreasing monotonic function which increases only when a relevant document is found in the ranking. However, when DCG stays constant, it is not immediately clear to understand whether this is due to a failure of the system which is not retrieving relevant documents while it would still be expected to do so, or whether the system is performing properly since there would be nothing to gain at that rank position.

To overcome this and similar issues, we introduce the *Relative Position (RP)* indicator, which allows us to quantify and explain what happens at each rank position and its paired with a visual counterpart which eases the explo-

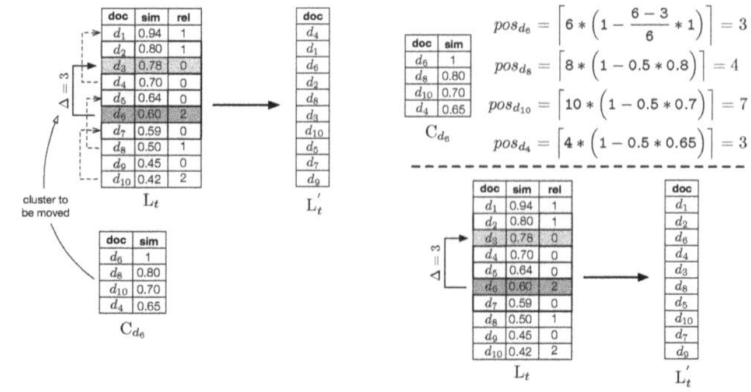

(a) Constant Movement Strategy. (b) Similarity-based Movement Strategy.

Figure 1: Document movement.

ration of the performances across the ranking, immediately grasping the most critical areas. RP quantifies the effect of misplacing relevant documents with respect to the ideal case, i.e. it accounts for how far a document is from its ideal position. RP eases the interpretation of the DCG curve since, for example, a constant value of DCG implies a negative value of RP, if this is due to a failure of the system which is not retrieving relevant documents while it would still be expected to do so, or a zero value of RP, if the system is performing properly since there would be nothing to gain at that rank position.

The RP indicator is paired with a visual counterpart that makes it even easier to quickly spot and inspect critical areas of the ranking. A bar is added on the left of the visualization where each rank position is represented with a box and, by using appropriate color coding to distinguish between zero, positive and negative values and shading to represent the intensity, each box represents the values of RP.

For example, in this way, looking at the bar and its colors, the developer can immediately identify not relevant documents which have been ranked in the positions of relevant ones. Then, the visualization allows them to inspect those documents and compare them with the topic at hand in order to make hypotheses about the causes of a failure.

3. WHAT-IF ANALYSIS

Suppose now that a query is about `personal computation devices` while a document talks about `personal computing devices`. If a system suffers from under-stemming, `computation` and `computing` may not be properly stemmed to `comput`. In this case, the previous document may be ranked lower because it matches the query only partially.

By performing failure analysis, the developer hypothesizes that the problem is the stemmer which does not conflate `computing` to `comput`. At the same time, the developer hypothesizes that if s/he fixes the failure, a given relevant document would be ranked higher than in the current system. What the visualization of Figure 2 offers to the developer is: (i) the possibility of dragging and dropping the target document in the estimated position of the rank; (ii) the estimation of which other documents would be affected by the movement of the target document and how the overall ranking would be modified; (iii) the computation of the system performances according to the new ranking. Indeed, if the stemmer is fixed, not only the target document identified by the developer would be affected by this modification but also other documents which, for example, contain the term `computable` and which were not examined by or known to the developer. Therefore, moving a single target document would actually cause the movement and repositioning of a whole set of documents that share features impacted by the same modification which will affect the target document selected by the developer. These complex interactions between documents may generate modifications on the ranking that go well beyond what the developer imagined when moving the single target document and which are definitely hard for her/him to guess. Thus, the contribution of the visualization and analytical engine of Figure 2 is to automatically point out to the developer all these complex interactions and how they affect the overall ranking.

In order to carry out the scenario just envisioned, VATE^2 needs: (i) to understand which documents would be affected by the movement of a target document indicated by the developer; and (ii) to adopt a strategy for simulating what the movement of the documents in the ranked list could be. Both of these items require a quite complex analytical model and computations. The complete description of the engine employed in VATE^2 is described in [3].

Document clustering is exploited in VATE^2 in order to understand which documents would be affected by the movement of a target document indicated by the developer, using a variation of the cluster hypothesis [5] that we could call the *failure hypothesis*: "closely associated documents tend to be affected by the same failures", stating the common intuition that a given failure will affect documents with common features (in our example all the documents where the term `computing` appears), and, consequently, that a fix for that failure will have an effect on the documents sharing those common features.

The movement of the document and the related document cluster happens according to two alternative strategies. The first is a straightforward algorithm that moves the documents in the cluster by the same amount of positions as the document dragged and dropped by the developer, as shown in Figure 1.(a). The second is a slightly more sophisticated algorithm that takes into consideration the similarity of the documents in the cluster to the document selected by the developer and then moves the documents in the cluster by an amount of positions proportional to their similarity to the document dragged and dropped by the developer, as shown in Figure 1.(b).

Once the new ranked list has been produced by using a clustering and movement strategy, the performances of this new ranked list are computed and the corresponding new line is shown to the developer so that s/he can assess whether the hypothesized modification may be beneficial or not. In the former case VATE^2 turns on a green light to indicate to the developer that s/he should go on with the fix of the system, otherwise it turns on a red light meaning that the fix may be useless or worsen the system.

4. THE VATE^2 PROTOTYPE

The prototype of VATE^2 is available online[1] and Figure 2 shows its main characteristics. The system is structured in three main parts:

(i) **Experimental collection information (A)**: this component is placed on the left side and it allows the devel-

[1] http://ims-ws.dei.unipd.it/vate_ui/

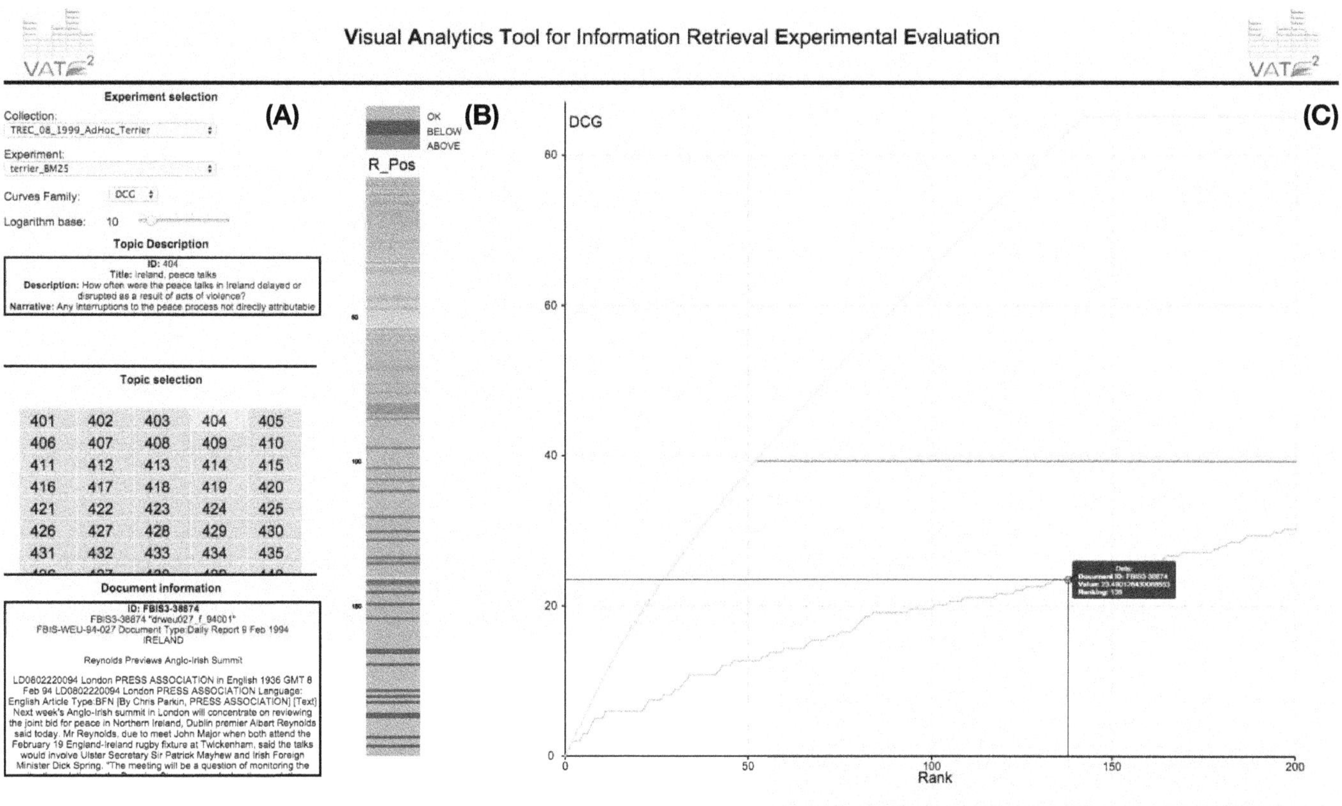

Figure 2: General overview of the VATE^2 system.

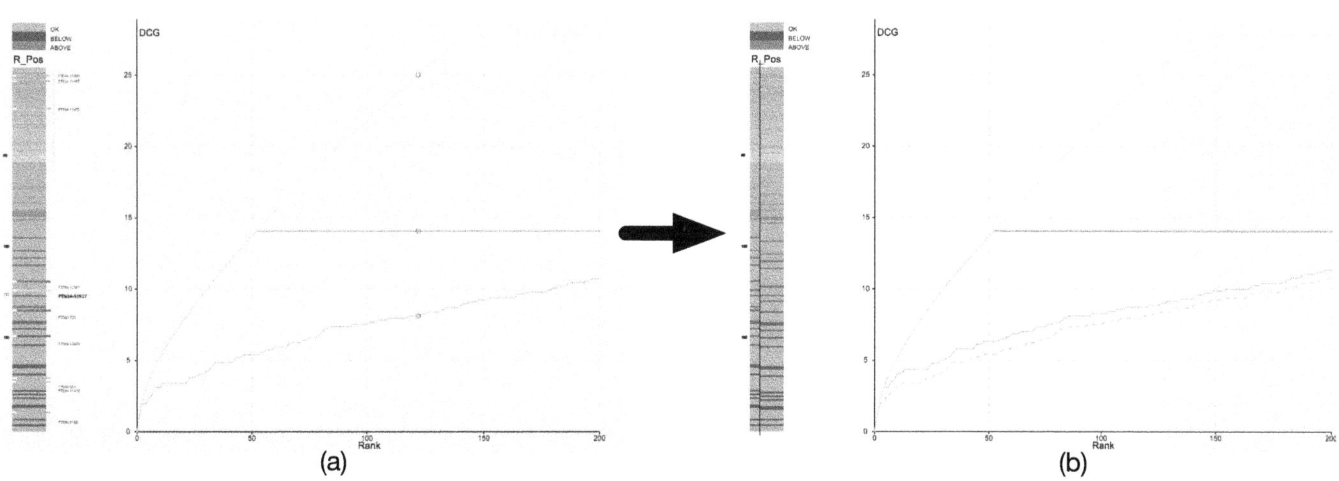

Figure 3: (a) selection of a document and highlight of its cluster; (b) the ranked list and the DCG curve after the movement.

oper to inspect and interact with the information regarding the experimental collection. More in detail, it is divided into three sub-components. The first is the "Experiment Selection" where the developer can select the experimental collection, the experiment to analyze and the evaluation measure and its parameters. The second sub-component is the "Topic Information" composed of the structured description of the topic and the topic selection grid. The third sub-component is the "Document Information" reporting the content of the document under analysis.

(ii) **Ranked list exploration (B)**: this component is placed on the center and shows a visual representation of the ranked list. More in detail, the documents are represented as rectangles ordered by rank from top to bottom where the color indicates the *RP* value; green rectangles indicate well-placed documents, blue rectangles indicate the documents placed below their ideal position and red rectangles indicate the documents placed above their ideal position. The intensity of the color encodes the severity of the misplacement, the more intense the worse the misplacement.

(iii) **Performance view (C)**: this component is placed on the right side and shows the performance curves of the selected experiment. The yellow curve is the ideal one, the magenta curve is the optimal one and the cyan curve is the experiment one. The developer can analyze the trend of the experiment by comparing the behavior of its curve with the ideal and optimal ranking by spotting the possible areas of improvement. Note that for simplicity we talk about "performances", even though we are considering the effectiveness of the evaluated systems.

The developer can interactively select the topic to be analyzed in the topic selection grid and the ranked list and the performance curves are updated accordingly to the selected topic for the given experiment. The user can select the effectiveness measure to be used among: *Cumulated Gain (CG)*, DCG, *Normalized Cumulated Gain (nCG)* and *Normalized Discounted Cumulated Gain (nDCG)*. The ranked list can be dynamically inspected by hovering the mouse over the documents: for each inspected document, the system shows its content on the left in the "Document information" area and marks with a circle the position of the document on the curves in the "Performance view". Moreover, the developer can interact with the "Performance view" by hovering the mouse over the curves which, by means of a tooltip, reports information about the document and the performance score. When a point in the DCG curve is selected, VATE^2 highlights the rectangle of the corresponding document in the ranked list giving a different perspective to the developer who can have a visual indication about the misplacement of the document thanks to the color of the rectangle.

Concerning what-if analysis, as shown in Figure 3.(a), once the developer selects a document, the system displaces on the right the rectangles corresponding to the documents in its similarity cluster and reports their identifiers also on the right. Moreover, a vertical yellow bar highlights the ideal interval in which the selected document should be placed. In Figure 3 Δ quantifies the movement of a document in terms of the number of positions it has been moved.

Once the developer selects a document, s/he can drag it to a new position in the ranked list; afterwards, the document along with its similarity cluster is moved in the new positions. This action is visually shown to the developer and it is represented with an animated movement of the corresponding rectangles to the new positions.

The effect of a movement is shown in Figure 3.(b). We can see an effect on the ranked list which is now split in two parts: on the left there is the old ranked list while on the right there is the new ranked list produced after the movement. In this way the developer can visually compare the effects of the movement and see what other documents have been affected by it. The effect of the movement can be also assessed in the "Performance view" where the new experiment curve (solid stroke) can be compared with the old one (dashed stroke). By analyzing both the ranked list and the performance curves the developer can understand whether their hypothesis about the fix leads to an improvement or deterioration in the performances.

All these operations can be iterated as many times as the developer needs to validate possible alternative fixes of the system.

From the design point-of-view, the adopted solutions reflect the way in which the system is typically used by experts. The "Performance view" part is as big as possible to allow experts a comfortable analysis of the system performances, which is the starting point of every investigation, and calls for handy tools for spotting each change in the DCG curve. Then, the interaction over the performance curve coordinated with the ranked list bar on the left facilitates developers in understanding the critical areas in the ranking, while the dynamic presentation of document content on the bottom left with respect to topic content on the top left supports the identification of possible failure causes.

5. FINAL REMARKS

In this paper we introduced the idea of what-if analysis as a new phase in experimental evaluation and we developed the VATE^2 prototype which demonstrates what what-if analysis is and how it works.

The identification of which documents are affected by a modification and the estimation of how the movement of one of them will cause the others to move is an extremely challenging problem. So, future work will concentrate on refining the techniques we have adopted to this end.

6. REFERENCES

[1] M. Angelini, N. Ferro, G. Santucci, and G. Silvello. A Visual Interactive Environment for Making Sense of Experimental Data. In *Proc. 36th European Conference on IR Research (ECIR 2014)*, pages 767–770. LNCS 8416, Springer, 2014.

[2] M. Angelini, N. Ferro, G. Santucci, and G. Silvello. VIRTUE: A visual tool for information retrieval performance evaluation and failure analysis. *Journal of Vis. Lang. & Comp. (JVLC)*, 25(4):394–413, 2014.

[3] N. Ferro and G. Silvello. What-If Analysis: A Visual Analytics Approach to Information Retrieval Evaluation. In *Proc. 7th Italian Information Retrieval Workshop (IIR 2016)*. CEUR Workshop Proc. (CEUR-WS.org), 2016.

[4] K. Järvelin and J. Kekäläinen. Cumulated Gain-Based Evaluation of IR Techniques. *ACM Trans. on Inf. Sys. (TOIS)*, 20(4):422–446, October 2002.

[5] C. J. van Rijsbergen. *Information Retrieval.* Butterworths, London, England, 2nd edition, 1979.

An Architecture for Privacy-Preserving and Replicable High-Recall Retrieval Experiments

Adam Roegiest
University of Waterloo

Gordon V. Cormack
University of Waterloo

ABSTRACT

We demonstrate the infrastructure used in the TREC 2015 Total Recall track to facilitate controlled simulation of "assessor in the loop" high-recall retrieval experimentation. The implementation and corresponding design decisions are presented for this platform. This includes the necessary considerations to ensure that experiments are privacy-preserving when using test collections that cannot be distributed. Furthermore, we describe the use of virtual machines as a means of system submission in order to to promote replicable experiments while also ensuring the security of system developers and data providers.

1. INTRODUCTION

The Total Recall track at TREC 2015 [15, 14] sought to investigate methods for achieving high-recall, with an assessor in the loop, through controlled simulation. The Total Recall track offered an online evaluation platform that allowed participants to produce systems that could request document assessments in a document-at-a-time manner, which is similar to the Microblog track's "evaluation as a service" methodology [11, 12]. This evaluation platform was primarily contained in a Web server (Section 3) that facilitated run creation, corpora distribution, the aforementioned document assessment process, and some basic online evaluation for training collections. Included in this platform was a baseline model implementation (the "BMI", Section 4.1), distributed as a VirtualBox virtual machine (VM), which participants could freely modify as they saw fit.

In developing this platform we sought to mitigate issues that have arisen in previous information retrieval research, and, in particular, high-recall retrieval experimentation. The primary issues we sought to address are as follows:

- Assessor-participant interaction and the effect on performance [9]

SIGIR '16, July 17 - 21, 2016, Pisa, Italy

ISBN 978-1-4503-4069-4/16/07...$15.00

DOI: http://dx.doi.org/10.1145/2911451.2911456

- Data anonymization and preserving the privacy of individuals in a corpus [1, 2]
- Re-usability of participant systems as on-going baselines for subsequent iterations of the track
- Lowering the barrier of participation in the track

We feel that we have successfully met these goals but we acknowledge that there are still improvements to be made. By controlling interaction through a simulated assessor (e.g., a system receives a binary judgement on a document), participant interaction does not rely on the ability of participants to get information out of the assessor but rather on the documents themselves. The BMI provides a working system to participants that they can use as a baseline for their experiments. Accordingly, there is less burden on participants to have an in-depth understanding of the Web server and can focus on their particular algorithms.

Furthermore, the track offered two modes of participation: an `At-Home` mode where interaction occurred over the Web; and a `Sandbox` mode where interaction occurred locally on a single machine. Participation in the `Sandbox` mode required participants to submit a working VM that would be ran, without Internet access, on test collections that were unknown to participants. Figure 1 provides a high-level conceptual depiction of how the live and sandbox modes differ.

We note that regardless of configuration, the data collections (the types and formats described in Section 2) are largely "plug-and-play", meaning that new data collections can, with little effort, be added to the platform. The result is that new experiments can be run on participant systems without necessitating participant action and without requiring participant effort — other than that required to run the system. Furthermore, the `Sandbox` mode of participation allows collections to be used that would otherwise be "too hot" to distribute or would require onerous and time consuming anonymization that may not work.

In the remainder of this work, we describe the major components of the Total Recall track's platform: the test collections and their format (Section 2); the Web server and its sandboxing (Section 3); the baseline system, participant systems, and their sandboxing (Section 4). We conclude with a discussion of limitations and future improvements to the platform (Section 5). Throughout these sections, we will provide the underlying reasoning as to why a particular approach was taken when another might have sufficed.

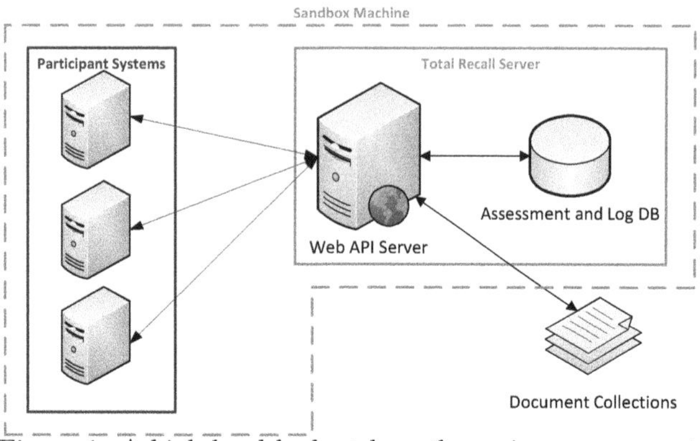

Figure 1: A high-level look at how the various components interact in live and sandbox environments. Note that the dashed blue line denotes the Total Recall server and participant VMs running on the same machine.

2. TEST COLLECTIONS

For our purposes, we consider a test collection to be a set of documents along with a set of qrels, which are tuples mapping documents and topics (information needs) to relevance assessments. Data collections are transmitted to participant clients through the Total Recall service first by transmitting the set of documents and then by having systems requests relevance assessments in a document-at-a-time manner. This simulates the interaction between participants and a gold standard assessor. that was present in previous TREC Legal tracks [10, 7], TREC Filtering tracks [13], and the TREC Spam tracks [4, 3, 8], while also controlling that interaction to ensure that it is equitable amongst all participants. Furthermore, to ease system development we curated each test collection so that a single file contained a single document. This is contrary to many past TREC collections where a file might contain multiple documents and was performed to simplify document parsing. We additionally translated each document into a plain text rendering from whatever native format it was originally stored in (e.g., PST, WARC, etc) to ease the burden of system design as participants would not have to worry about processing multiple filetypes.

By taking this controlled approach to high-recall retrieval experimentation, we hope to mitigate any bias that might be perceived by spending "too much time" with a topic authority (gold standard assessor) or the ability to ask the right questions. The focus is then on the algorithms used and less so on the human interaction between topic authorities and participants. This should not be construed to suggest that such interaction is bad but that we merely sought to eliminate the confound that different approaches to such interaction may have on system evaluation. Furthermore, this approach facilitates experimentation with more topics over more test collections since there is no requirement to provide access to a high-quality topic authority (that is willing to volunteer valuable time), which has previously limited how many topics and how much interaction could be performed [10, 7].

For the purposes of system development, we used three publicly available test collections: 20-Newsgroups[1]; Reuters-21758[2]; and, a variant of the Enron v2 e-mail collection[3]. The inclusion of the first two datasets is to facilitate rapid development and testing of participant systems as they both contain approximately 20,000 documents. Neither was meant to be representative of a valid test collection but were merely there to help participant's gain confidence that their system was working. Moreover, we offered samples of these first two corpora as a mechanism to ensure participants understood and could correctly interact with the Web server, but without requiring the extensive processing time of a larger corpus. The Enron collection was our attempt to provide a representative collection, as it had previously been used in the TREC 2009 Legal track [10], that would more accurately indicate the effectiveness of participant systems. For all of these collections, we provided an online mechanism to provide recall, effort, precision, and F1 scores for checking system performance.

At the beginning of July, the `At-Home` phase of participation began and three additional corpora were released to participants (after signing the appropriate usage agreements). These collections were the official test collections and so participants did not receive any explicit system performance feedback as a means of preventing any potential meta-learning by systems. Although, we acknowledge that some participants may have had internal quality assurance processes that would have helped determine their own performance.

Not all corpora can be distributed by the service due to usage agreements or the risk of divulging sensitive data to the public, and so, generally, such restricted corpora will be distributed only in the form of `Sandbox` participation (discussed in Section 3.1). This helps to ameliorate issues with imperfect anonymization and the inability to give all interested parties access to the data. While no system that emits any information (e.g., even summary evaluation metrics) can ever be entirely secure, we believe that structuring the release of collections in this way aids in preserving the privacy of all parties when private collections are used. For all test collections, we refer interested parties to the track overview [15] for in-depth descriptions.

3. THE SERVER

The Total Recall server operates as a Web service that participant systems interact with over HTTP requests (i.e., a REST(ful) API). There are three main types of interactions between systems and the service:

- Request for information on a corpus and a link to download the corpus. Such details include the type of corpus (e.g., e-mail, newswire) and the language of the corpus (English only for 2015).
- Request for information on a topic to process, which includes the corresponding corpus and a description of the information need.
- Request for relevance assessment of documents with respect to a particular topic.

Secondary interactions can occur, including: starting and finalizing a run; result generation for developmental test collections; error log checking; and, other track specific actions beyond the scope of this paper.

[1]http://qwone.com/~jason/20Newsgroups/
[2]http://www.daviddlewis.com/resources/testcollections/reuters21578/
[3]http://trec-legal.umiacs.umd.edu/corpora/trec/legal10/

Figure 2 provides the general workflow that a client system might be expected to perform. For brevity we omit the actual API that was used to interact with the service and instead direct interested parties to the API documentation[4]. Note that all requests and responses to and from the server are encoded in JSON format, which has become a standard format for passing data between a Web server and client software.

In terms of implementation the entirety of the Total Recall web server is written in Node.js[5], which is a Javascript runtime that uses an event-driven model for developing severside Web applications (e.g., REST(ful) APIs). Node.js is designed to be efficient and lightweight and is extremely popular in web development. While other architectures would have sufficed, Node.js was chosen due to its popularity and the opportunity to explore current state-of-the-art technologies in Web development. Where necessary (e.g., in storing judgments and a log of participant requests), the server relies on an installation of MySQL for persistant storage. As will be discussed in Section 5, using a default installation of MySQL was perhaps a poor choice and resulted in a small bottleneck near the end of the experimental period but has been corrected for following iterations. All code for the Total Recall track is available for public download in a git repository[6].

3.1 Sandboxing the Server

To facilitate the use of test collections that require complicated transmission protocols (e.g., transmitted by a third party, such as NIST) or are "too hot to handle" (e.g., raw versions of confidential email), we provided the **Sandbox** mode of participation. In this mode, participants submit their systems as a VM (more details in Section 4) which we run in a restricted environment with access to the data.

Test collections do not necessarily have to be stored directly on the sandbox machine; instead data providers will be able to distribute test collections via USB flashdrive or external hard drive. Once the test collection is loaded into the service (using some relatively simple shell scripts), the participant systems are can be ran with these collections much in the same way that they would in the live scenario. However, the participant's VM is prohibited from accessing the Internet or Web in any way. This is done so that we can prevent any blatant data leakage from the sandbox environment. This restriction is enforced by limiting access of the clients machines only to the service and (optionally) by airwalling the sandbox machine (i.e., never connecting it to the Internet once the test collections are present). Air-walling occurred for one of the **Sandbox** collections due to the nature of the of the collection.

By enforcing these restrictions on the sandbox machine, the data is protected from unintended transmission as well as unintended dissemination of personal or private data. Furthermore, we can limit the only output of the sandbox server to be only summary evaluation measures and statistics (discussed in the track overview [15, 14]) once all participant systems have been ran. In doing so, the goal would be to prevent accidental distribution of private data that may be contained in qrels and document identifiers.

[4]quaid.uwaterloo.ca:33333/#/api

[5]See https://nodejs.org/en/ for more information.

[6]http://repo.trec-total-recall.com

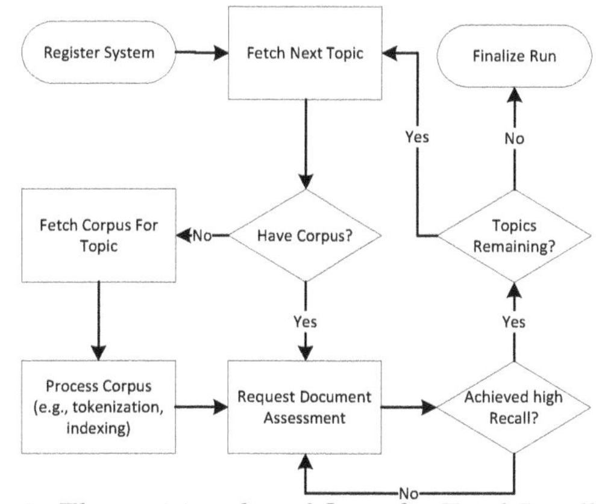

Figure 2: The envisioned workflow of a Total Recall participant system.

4. PARTICIPANT SYSTEMS

The envisioned workflow for a client system is depicted in Figure 2, and is implemented by the the Baseline Model Implementation (Section 4.1). Participants can construct several different systems to interact with the Total Recall service. Clients for `At-Home` experiments can be developed in several different ways: a purely automatic program (or set of programs) that performs the Total Recall task; a customized virtual machine that runs the above; as a "sidecar" (i.e., a directory containing additional scripts) supplied to the BMI's Virtual Machine. A "sidecar" submission can be run without any additional dependencies being added to the default BMI VM.

The Total Recall task is one that can be performed manually or through some combination of manual and automatic approaches. Accordingly, we allowed participants to submit a single manual run, which was to be performed before developing any automatic systems. Participants could submit manual runs using either the API, used by automatic systems, or a Web-based interface that we provided. The Web-based interface was quite simple and was largely just a pretty interface for the API. Out of the 3 manual teams, 2 used the Web interface and 1 directly communicated with the Web server via the API.

For sandbox submission, participants are required to submit systems that fall under the full VM or sidecar categories. This is done with the hope that systems would work out-of-the-box, which was mostly true for TREC 2015. Previous experience with running participant systems in a sandbox for the TREC Spam tracks [8, 3, 4] led us to believe that allowing the submission of arbitrary code would lead to wasted effort in getting code to run correctly. As coordinators would then have to debug and fix-up any code that was not compatible with the sandbox environment (e.g., installing libraries, having necessary compiler versions). By using a VM, we hoped to limit the necessity of such tasks and were successful in this by having only one system require major coordinator intervention (out of 11 different systems).

A final benefit to requiring submissions of VMs or sidecars is that it allows commercial vendors of high-recall retrieval software to submit their products without requiring source code submission (as was required in previous tracks that used sandboxing). Vendors can submit a fully compiled version of their software that runs on the VM and so do not expose their intellectual property to track coordinators, data providers, or any other parties that might come into contact with the software. Extra steps can also be taken, such as encrypting the VM and/or software so that outside parties cannot access the software at all (outside of the normal interaction between client and server).

4.1 Baseline Model Implementation (BMI)

Our primary baseline is an augmented version of the Continuous Active Learning (CAL) method originally presented by Cormack and Grossman [5], which is called AutoTAR [6]. Unlike the original version of CAL, AutoTAR uses exponentially increasing batches sizes, and unlike the reported results of the AutoTAR paper, we use a tuned version of `sofia-ml`[7] (based upon suggestions from the package's author).

This baseline is implemented as part of the virtual machine with sidecar approach, where the AutoTAR algorithm is refactored as a sidecar for a simple Debian VM. This was done to provide a model implementation of a sidecar and a meaningful working implementation that participants would be free to augment in the course of experimentation. The BMI is implemented using a combination of C++ and bash scripts (along with associated command line tools). The canonical implementation is available for download under GPL[8].

Cormack and Grossman have shown that AutoTar generally outperforms a simple CAL implementation. Accordingly, our intent was to provide a reasonable baseline that could "fast-track" participants to a working system, without requiring them to worry about API programming. We hoped that the BMI would provide ample opportunity for participants to improve upon its results or be inspired by the technique and devise original algorithms of their own. Several of the participants made use of the BMI in their own submissions.

5. DISCUSSION

As with the development and use of any long running software, issues were likely to arise throughout the course of the track and did. Primarily, the biggest issue was a bottleneck in document assessment requests near the submission deadline. This was primarily due to the vanilla installation of MySQL which became bogged down when there were many queries being ran. In hindsight, this issue is relatively easy to solve by configuring MySQL to handle queries more effectively and by adding additional connections to the Web server so that multiple requests are not held up by a single connection to the database.

Surprisingly, the use of a REST(ful) API did not appear to cause participants too much trouble, in spite of our fears that it might during development. These troubles were likely ameliorated by providing tools like the BMI and the manual participation interface.

Another design decision to consider for future iterations is the use of full virtual machines. There are many merits to the use of virtual machines, primarily the fact that the entire system is self-contained and so security issues are more manageable due to more complete isolation from other software on the machine. This isolation comes with performance setbacks. For example, we could only have one participant system running at a time due to the high overhead of both participant systems and the cost of virtualization on our sandbox machines. An alternative may be to use a more lightweight system, like Docker, which makes use of software containers. In short, software containers package an application together with its dependencies for running on an arbitrary (Linux) server. The easiest way to envision software containers is somewhere between virtual machines and auto-building tools (e.g., make, Maven). Accordingly, there is less emulation overhead that occurs with containers but at the expense greater exposure to the underlying system. A more thorough analysis of the costs and benefits is on-going and the inclusion of Docker containers may occur for TREC 2016.

6. CONCLUSIONS

We have presented a brief overview of the Total Recall track's online evaluation platform and the design decisions that went into its development. The use of this service is an attempt to develop a reusable system for evaluating information retrieval systems on both public and private data. In addition, we attempted to learn from issues that have arisen in previous TREC tracks dealing with high-recall retrieval and private collections. Interested parties are encouraged to read the track overview [15], visit the track website (trec-total-recall.org), join the mailing list[9] to follow the progress of the track, and contribute to the development of the platform.

7. REFERENCES

[1] http://www.securityfocus.com/news/11497.

[2] http://www.securitypronews.com/new-scam-tricking-people-by-offering-new-facebook-profile-look-2012-11.

[3] G. V. Cormack. TREC 2006 Spam Track Overview. In *Proc. TREC-2006*.

[4] G. V. Cormack. TREC 2007 Spam Track Overview. In *Proc. TREC-2007*.

[5] G. V. Cormack and M. R. Grossman. Evaluation of Machine-learning Protocols for Technology-assisted Review in Electronic Discovery. In *Proc. SIGIR 2014*.

[6] G. V. Cormack and M. R. Grossman. Autonomy and reliability of continuous active learning for technology-assisted review. *arXiv Preprint*, 2015.

[7] G. V. Cormack, M. R. Grossman, B. Hedin, and D. W. Oard. Overview of the TREC 2010 Legal Track. In *Proc. TREC-2010*.

[8] G. V. Cormack and T. R. Lynam. TREC 2005 Spam Track Overview. In *Proc. TREC-2005*.

[9] B. Hedin and D. W. Oard. Replication and automation of expert judgments: Information engineering in legal e-discovery. In *Proc. Systems, Man and Cybernetics*, 2009.

[10] B. Hedin, S. Tomlinson, J. R. Baron, and D. W. Oard. Overview of the TREC 2009 Legal Track. In *Proc. TREC-2009*.

[11] J. Lin and M. Efron. Evaluation as a service for information retrieval. *SIGIR Forum*.

[12] J. Lin and M. Efron. Overview of the trec-2013 microblog track. In *Proc. TREC-2013*.

[13] S. Robertson and I. Soboroff. The TREC 2002 Filtering Track Report. In *Proc. TREC 2002*.

[14] A. Roegiest and G. V. Cormack. Total recall track tools architecture overview. In *Proc. TREC-2015*.

[15] A. Roegiest, G. V. Cormack, C. L. Clake, and M. R. Grossman. TREC 2015 Total Recall Track overview. In *Proc. TREC-2015*.

[7] https://code.google.com/archive/p/sofia-ml/

[8] http://plg.uwaterloo.ca/~gvcormac/trecvm/

[9] Link available from track website.

Analysing Temporal Evolution of Interlingual Wikipedia Article Pairs

Simon Gottschalk
L3S Research Center
Hannover, Germany
gottschalk@L3S.de

Elena Demidova
Web and Internet Science Group, ECS
University of Southampton, UK
e.demidova@soton.ac.uk

ABSTRACT

Wikipedia articles representing an entity or a topic in different language editions evolve independently within the scope of the language-specific user communities. This can lead to different points of views reflected in the articles, as well as complementary and inconsistent information. An analysis of how the information is propagated across the Wikipedia language editions can provide important insights in the article evolution along the temporal and cultural dimensions and support quality control. To facilitate such analysis, we present MultiWiki – a novel web-based user interface that provides an overview of the similarities and differences across the article pairs originating from different language editions on a timeline. MultiWiki enables users to observe the changes in the interlingual article similarity over time and to perform a detailed visual comparison of the article snapshots at a particular time point.

1. INTRODUCTION

Wikipedia is a rich interlingual information source that often reflects cultural differences: Wikipedia articles describing real-world entities, topics, events and concepts evolve independently in different language editions, as there is no sophisticated support for multilingual collaboration when writing articles. Moreover, there is a social impact on multilingual article creation, as different communities of Wikipedia editors vary in their perception of the topics they are describing. As a result, there is a distributed evolution of Wikipedia articles that leads to semantic differences representing linguistic points of view on particular topics [3], as well as complementary or sometimes contradictory information between articles.

The temporal evolution of Wikipedia articles plays an important role when analysing the interlingual development of articles: For example, multilingual users actively transfer information from one language edition to others [4] and articles may be translated to complement missing information. Likewise, information on events impacting both language editions at a time could originate from one of the language editions and be adapted from the other article with some delay.

Our methods aim at supporting Wikipedia editors and readers in better understanding of how such changes propagate across the language editions. To this extent, we measure the similarity of the interlingual article snapshots at different time points and visualise them on a timeline.

Figure 1 gives an example of such a timeline generated by our tool, MultiWiki, for the English/German article pair "Codex Aureus of St. Emmeram", which visualises the following process: The English article was created in October 2003, nearly five years before the German one and consisted of a very few sentences for a long time. Then, in 2008, the German article was created and became immediately much longer than the English one. Hence, the timeline shows a very small similarity within the first two years after the creation of the German article. Then, parts of the German texts were adapted to enlarge the English article, which lead to a significant increase of their interlingual similarity. Finally, the texts evolved independently from each other and their similarity slightly decreased.

For each particular pair of snapshots derived from the timeline, our interface also provides a detailed comparison. This comparison clearly goes beyond existing tools (e.g. [1], [3]), in particular through visualising a detailed comparison of the similarities and differences of the article texts.

MultiWiki presented in this demonstration is a web-based tool[1] including the following functionalities:

- Computation of the interlingual similarity between the articles in an interlingual article pair. The features for this similarity computation include the similarity of the article texts, their media elements, entities and links, as well as Wikipedia editors and their locations;
- Tracking the changes of the interlingual similarity over time and visualisation of the similarity and its features on a timeline, tables and maps; and
- Visualisation of the textual similarities of an interlingual article pair given their snapshots.

These functions enable MultiWiki to: 1) Present an overview of the evolution of the interlingual article similarity over time; and 2) Enable users to perform a detailed article comparison at a certain time point.

[1] The demo is publicly available at: http://multiwiki.l3s.uni-hannover.de/demo.html.

SIGIR '16, July 17 - 21, 2016, Pisa, Italy

ISBN 978-1-4503-4069-4/16/07...$15.00

DOI: http://dx.doi.org/10.1145/2911451.2911472

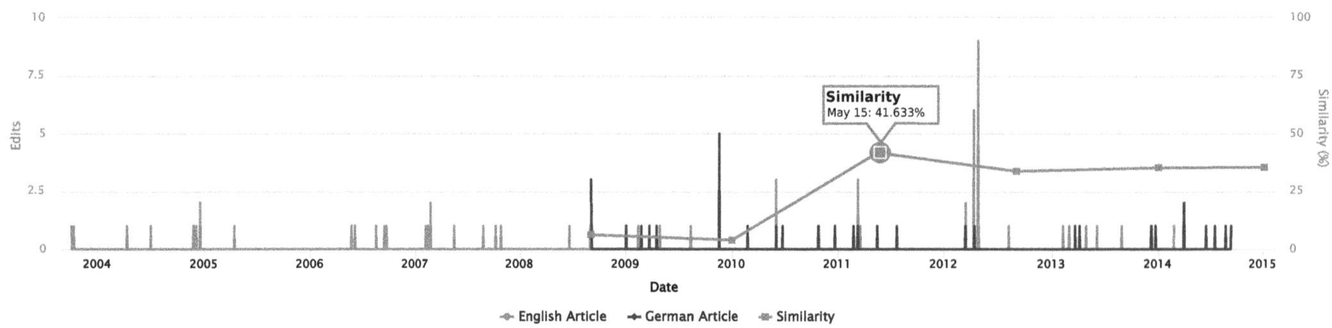

Figure 1: Timeline of the German/English article pair "Codex Aureus of St. Emmeram". The number of edits per article and the similarity of the article snapshots are plotted over time.

2. FEATURES & INTERFACE

MultiWiki provides users with an overview of how the relation between two articles that describe the same topic in different languages changes over time. To this extent, MultiWiki automatically generates a timeline that visualises the evolution of the semantic similarity of the articles over time and the corresponding number of edits for both articles.

In order to visualise this timeline and to enable a more fine-grained analysis of an article pair at a particular time point, we compute a semantic similarity score $Sim(A_1, A_2)$ for two article snapshots A_1 and A_2 from different Wikipedia language editions. This score is composed of several similarity functions $Sim_f(A_1, A_2) \in [0, 1]$ that are applied on different features $f \in F$.

We differentiate between the text-based features (F_{text}) and features using meta information like images and links (F_{meta}). The textual similarity Sim_{text} between two article snapshots A_1 and A_2 is computed as follows, where w_f denotes the weight assigned to one of the similarity functions:

$$Sim_{text}(A_1, A_2) = \sum_{f \in F_{text}} w_f \cdot Sim_f(A_1, A_2), \sum_{f \in F_{text}} w_f = 1.$$

Sim_{meta}, the similarity of the article snapshots computed using meta information, is defined analogously. We consider different feature categories, such as images, Wikipedia annotations (i.e. references to other Wikipedia articles in the text), external links and editors to be equally important. Therefore, we equally distribute the weights across these feature categories. Tables 1 and 2 provide an overview of the MultiWiki features and their weights.

The overall similarity $Sim(A_1, A_2) \in [0, 1]$ of a snapshot pair is the weighted sum of Sim_{text} and Sim_{meta}, where we set $\alpha = 0.5$ to balance the influence of both factor types:

$$Sim(A_1, A_2) = \alpha \cdot Sim_{text}(A_1, A_2) + (1-\alpha) \cdot Sim_{meta}(A_1, A_2).$$

In the following, we describe the features, the similarity functions based on them and how we present the results to the user: Our interface does not only show the numeric similarity scores, but also visualises the similarities based on particular features as illustrated in Figures 2 and 4.

Images

When comparing two Wikipedia articles, one of the main visual impressions is given by the images placed in them. Therefore, we compute the fraction of images used in both articles. In the interface, we oppose them in a table like the one shown in Figure 2(a).

External Links

Motivated by the findings in [4], MultiWiki aligns external links mentioned in the footnotes of the articles and their hosts. As illustrated in Figure 2(b), the host names of the external links are shown to the user ranked by their overlap frequency. Those at the top are frequently mentioned in both articles and are therefore good indicators for the topical overlap of the articles.

Wikipedia Links and Annotations

Two articles are similar if they refer to the same entities, concepts and topics [3]. To extract this kind of annotations, we rely on two sources: (1) Wikipedia links manually added to articles by Wikipedia editors; and (2) Wikipedia links automatically created by applying an entity annotation tool (DBpedia Spotlight). While the user-defined links are precise, but rather sparse and without repetitions, the automatic annotation raises the recall of the Wikipedia ref-

Name	Description	w_f
Images	Overlap of images in the articles	1/4
Wikipedia annotations	Overlap of Wikipedia annotations extracted from the articles	1/4
External links	Overlap of footnote links	1/8
External links (Hosts)	Overlap of the host names of footnote links	1/8
Editors	Overlap of editors	1/8
Editors (Locations)	Overlap of the editors' countries	1/8

Table 1: Similarity Measures based on Meta Features

Name	Description	w_f
Text length	Proportion of the number of characters	1/3
Text overlap	Jaccard overlap of the English texts	1/3
Text passage coverage	Percentage of characters that have been aligned with the other article	1/3

Table 2: Textual Similarity Measures

(a) Images (b) Links (Host Names) (c) Editor Locations

Figure 2: Selected Feature Similarities for the English/German article pair on "Lawrence Eagleburger"

erences. These references are aligned across languages by using interlingual article links provided by Wikipedia.

Wikipedia Editors

Wikipedia articles are thoroughly based on the input of the Wikipedia editors. Some multilingual editors tend to edit articles describing the same entity in different languages, such that similar content is spread across languages [4]. MultiWiki computes the overlap of the editors that contributed to the articles under comparison. Furthermore, the linguistic point of view (as defined in [3]) emphasises the cultural differences between language communities. Therefore, we determine the countries where anonymous editors come from and compute the similarity of the country distribution per article. As this location similarity Sim_{loc} ought to measure the similarity of the distribution, but should not be biased by differences in the number of anonymous editors, it is computed by Equation 2 (where L is the set of locations and each article A_i is assigned a set of editors $e \in E_i$): Before computing the overlap, the number of editors is matched by multiplying E_2 by $\frac{|E_1|}{|E_2|}$.

$$Sim_{\text{loc}}(A_1, A_2) = \frac{\sum\limits_{l \in L} min(|\{e \in E_1 | \text{e.loc} = l\}|, |\{e \in E_2 | \text{e.loc} = l\}| \cdot \frac{|E_1|}{|E_2|})}{|E_1|}$$

In the MultiWiki interface, two world maps like the one presented in Figure 2(c) are showing the editors' origins for a pair of article snapshots.

Textual Overlap

MultiWiki provides a fine-grained comparison of the article texts by aligning semantically similar text passages in an article pair as illustrated in Figure 4.

This alignment is facilitated by an bottom-up approach: At first, sentences with overlapping information are aligned using the following features: (1) Cosine similarity of the vectors representing text passages using terms (automatically translated to English); (2) Similarity of the Wikipedia entities metioned in the sentences; (3) Time similarity using temporal expressions automatically extracted from the sentences. Consequently, sentence pairs whose similarity score exceeds a pre-determined threshold value are merged in a bottom-up manner: As long as the similarity of an aligned text passage pair increases, the text passage is expanded by adding neighboured sentences from one of the articles or by merging two text passage pairs in a close neighbourhood. Given the aligned text passages, they are presented to the user by showing both articles side by side and connecting them as illustrated in Figure 4. With this visualisation approach, the user immediately obtaines an overview of the similarities and differences in the articles.

Textual Similarity

Regarding the textual similarity score of an article pair $Sim_{text}(A_1, A_2)$, three measures are derived from the article texts: 1) *Text passage coverage* is the percentage of text aligned as part of text passage pairs; 2) *Text length similarity* compares the length of the articles; and 3) *Text overlap similarity* is the Jaccard similarity of the English (machine-translated) texts.

3. SYSTEM ARCHITECTURE & PIPELINE

In order to facilitate the comparison of articles based on the proposed features and to analyse their temporal evolution, each article pair runs through a preprocessing pipeline. In a first step, we need to inspect the revision history in both languages to create a set of article snapshots pairs that fulfils the following condition: Both snapshots in an article pair must have been on-line at the same time. This ensures that dissimilarities between the articles are not based on temporal shifts. Besides, the selected article pairs should be evenly distributed over time to provide a better overview.

For each article snapshot, we collect meta information, extract the sentences and annotate them with the features

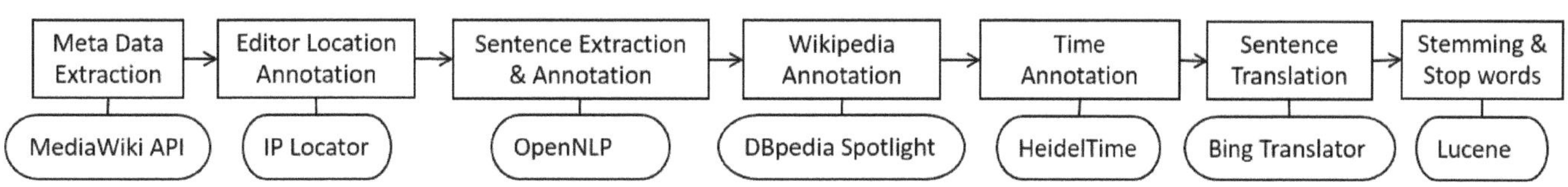

Figure 3: Processing Pipeline for a Wikipedia Article

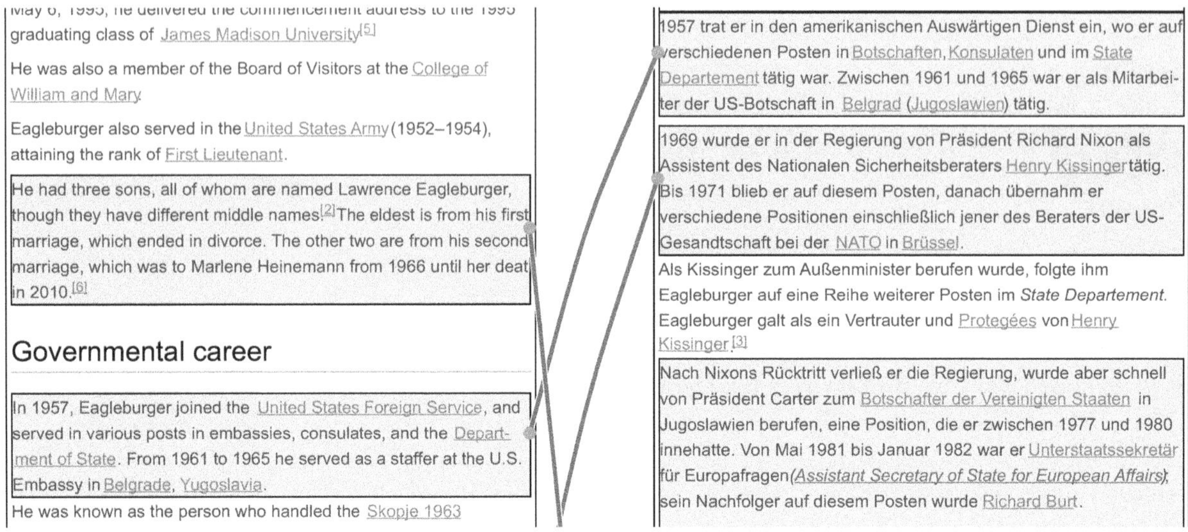

Figure 4: Text Comparison. The English article on "Lawrence Eagleburger" is on the left, the German one on the right. Aligned passages are marked green and connected with matching passages in the other article.

presented in Section 2 using state-of-the-art methods. The pipeline for extraction and annotation is depicted in Figure 3. At first, we fetch the texts of each article and collect its contributing editors from the revision history. For each of the unregistered, anonymous editors, the IP address is provided, which makes it possible to determine their country. To allow for the text passage alignment, the text is split into sentences; then the features needed for the sentence alignment are collected. The results of the preprocessing pipeline are stored in a database. Additionally, the complete set of interlingual Wikipedia links is stored, such that the final comparison of the article pair including the computation of similarity values and the text passage alignment can be performed at run time.

4. DATASET

To facilitate the demonstration of our methods, we extracted a set of 79 randomly selected article pairs to be investigated using MultiWiki. For each article pair, we collected eight snapshot pairs on average. The majority of 54 article pairs is German/English, 14 are Dutch/English and the remaining 11 pairs are Portuguese/English. As we extract multiple snapshots of each article to construct the timelines, a total of 637 snapshot pairs has been extracted and annotated. Among these article pairs, there is the politician "Lawrence Eagleburger", the German film "Der Stern von Afrika" (movie) and the "General Post Office".

5. RELATED WORK

The multilingual Wikipedia has been a research target for different disciplines. One area of interest in this context is the study of differences in the language points of view in Wikipedia [3]. In [4], Rogers conducts an intensive case study where he compares the highly controversial articles on the Srebrenica massacre in several Wikipedia language editions. In his work, all of the investigations like image alignment and a comparison of the table of contents are made manually. To simplify such tasks in future, some of the features mentioned in [4] have been implemented in MultiWiki.

Two of the few existing tools to support cross-lingual analytics in Wikipedia are Manypedia [3] that provides an automatic translation to English, article statistics and overlap of Wikipedia links, and Omnipedia [1], which can be used to compare the given Wikipedia links for up to 25 language editions simultaneously. Another tool that helps to explore the temporal development of a single article is Contropedia [2] that focusses on the interaction of Wikipedia editors. Unlike existing tools, MultiWiki excibits unique features such as temporal analysis of interlingual article similarity and detailed textual comparison of article snapshots.

6. CONCLUSIONS

In this paper we presented MultiWiki – a novel user interface to conduct a detailed visual analysis of the similarities and the differences across the Wikipedia articles on the same topic written in different languages. MultiWiki provides means to explore how information is propagated across the language editions by observing how the similarity of an article pair evolves over time. Moreover, it enables a detailed visual comparison of the article snapshots based on users, media elements, entities, and links as well as a detailed analysis of textual similarities.

7. ACKNOWLEDGMENTS

This work was partially funded by the ERC under ALEXANDRIA (ERC 339233) and H2020-MSCA-ITN-2014 WDAqua (64279).

8. REFERENCES

[1] P. Bao, B. Hecht, S. Carton, et al. Omnipedia: Bridging the Wikipedia Language Gap. In *Proceedings of CHI '12*.

[2] E. Borra, D. Laniado, E. Weltevrede, et al. A Platform for Visually Exploring the Development of Wikipedia Articles. *Proc. ICWSM*, 2015.

[3] P. Massa and F. Scrinzi. Manypedia: Comparing Language Points of View of Wikipedia Communities. In *Proceedings of the WikiSym '12*.

[4] R. Rogers. *Digital Methods*, chapter Wikipedia as Cultural Reference. The MIT Press, 2013.

Cobwebs from the Past and Present: Extracting Large Social Networks using Internet Archive Data

Miroslav Shaltev[1], Jan-Hendrik Zab[1] and
Philipp Kemkes[1], Stefan Siersdorfer, Sergej Zerr[2]
[1]L3S Research Center, Hannover, Germany
{shaltev,zab,kemkes}@L3S.de
siersdorfer@outlook.de
[2]Electronics and Computer Science, University of Southampton, Southampton, UK
s.zerr@soton.ac.uk

ABSTRACT

Social graph construction from various sources has been of interest to researchers due to its application potential and the broad range of technical challenges involved. The World Wide Web provides a huge amount of continuously updated data and information on a wide range of topics created by a variety of content providers, and makes the study of extracted people networks and their temporal evolution valuable for social as well as computer scientists. In this paper we present SocGraph - an extraction and exploration system for social relations from the content of around 2 billion web pages collected by the Internet Archive over the 17 years time period between 1996 and 2013. We describe methods for constructing large social graphs from extracted relations and introduce an interface to study their temporal evolution.

1. INTRODUCTION

The advances of the computer science and technology in the last decades enabled the extraction and analysis of social networks from various types of structured and unstructured data sources. Some sources provide explicit and easy to extract information about user relations. This includes online platforms such as Facebook, Twitter, or LinkedIn that maintain user databases and offer software interfaces for accessing contacts, friends, or followers. However, in many cases information about social connections is hidden within unstructured data such as Web pages and archives. In the past, personal relationships have been extracted from textual and multimedia sources such as books, historical repositories [3, 1, 9] and web search engines [5, 2, 6]. Despite the work towards increasing the efficiency of finding entity relations on the web [7] only recently in [8] a method suitable for mining of large graphs has been proposed.

SIGIR '16, July 17-21, 2016, Pisa, Italy
 ISBN 978-1-4503-4069-4/16/07...$15.00
DOI: http://dx.doi.org/10.1145/2911451.2911467

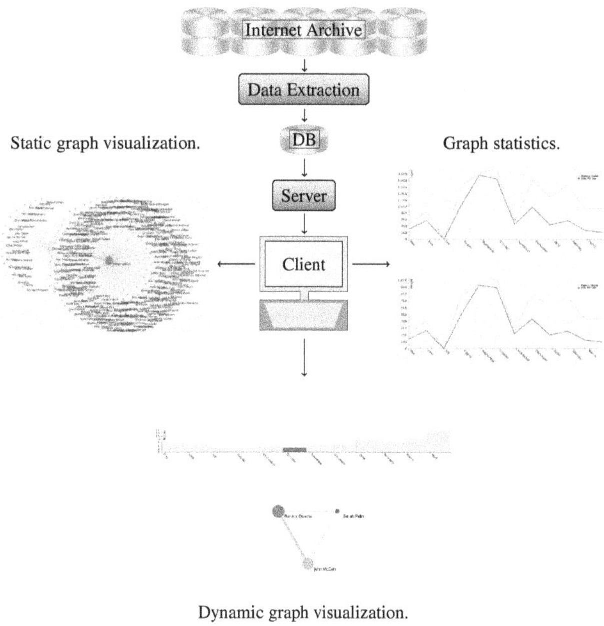

Figure 1: The overview over SocGraph system architecture and its main storage and visualization components.

In this work we introduce SocGraph[1] - a tool for the construction and analysis of social graphs extracted from the Internet Archive (IA) data and the exploration of the temporal evolution of communities in a variety of applications. The objectives of the analysis include, but are not limited to shedding light on financial and business relations on the internet, identifying ad-hoc communities centered in social media on different events, such as solar eclipse and "Earth Hour" that are concerned with artificial light pollution of the night skies of our cities,[2] or describing and profiling of working groups in citizen science projects, where volunteers are supporting scientists by classifying astronomic and biological phenomena in raw data photographs. Inspired by [8] we move a step further in that direction and provide an interface for studying the *temporal evolution* of the social networks extracted directly from archived web page content. For social

[1]http://socgraph.l3s.uni-hannover.de
[2]http://www.stars4all.eu/

and computer scientists our tool will provide a gateway to the information and knowledge about connections between people stored in the world wide web in the last few decades.

2. SYSTEM ARCHITECTURE

The architecture of our system is schematically shown in Fig. 1. First, we analyze the web archive to detect co-mentions of entities in the web pages. In the next step, at the server, we extract the temporal statistics and construct the social graph by connecting extracted entity pairs using detected edges.
Finally, the user can access the application and create, visualize, modify and interact with the graphs by issuing new queries via a web browser based user interface. In the following we provide an overview of the system components and show how results are presented to the user in more detail.

2.1 Data

The Internet Archive (IA) is a non-profit organization crawling the World Wide Web since 1996. For our application we have access to web pages from about 1.8×10^9 distinct URLs, collected by the IA in the time period of 17 years between 1996 and 2013. Extracting data even from a small sample of all archived web pages is a computationally intensive and requires parallelization of processes.

We used Hadoop and Spark [10] technology on a dedicated 25 node computing cluster with 1.3TB main memory and 268 CPU cores to extract co-mentions of persons directly from the archived documents. We stored extracted names, patterns, URLs, date of the crawl and additional miscellaneous information in a relational database, which can be accessed from the server process in real time. The crawled documents of MIME type text have been encapsulated in 346,000 Web ARChive (WARC) files.

2.2 Extraction of Entity Pairs

The entity pairs are extracted from the body of the archived documents first by splitting the documents into sentences using the Stanford CoreNLP library [4]. Then extracted sentences are scanned, detecting the constructs matching the template

$$< person1 >< pattern >< person2 >$$

such as <Barack Obama><and his rival><John McCain>, using a person names dictionary and a sliding window with a pattern length of three words. To reduce noise in the data we exclude pairs with identical names and discard overly long sentences and patterns. We computed the weight of the node as $1/n$, where n is the number of persons co-occurring in the sentence. In Fig.2a we plot the distribution of the weight per entry in the data set. The distribution of the number of extracted pairs per year is shown in Fig.2b.

2.3 Graph construction

For building the social graph, we select extracted pairs matching the user query and user defined parameters such as the time period T, and merge them into a network considering the node weight and the edge weight between two nodes as follows:

$$w = 1/n\,, \tag{1}$$

where n is the number of co-mentioned persons in a sentence.

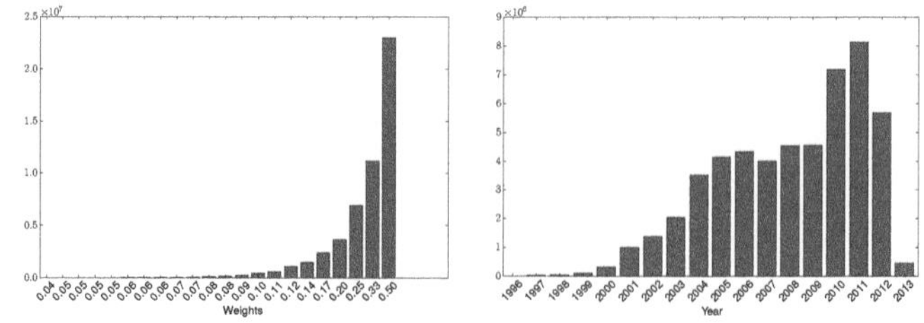

(a) (b)

Figure 2: The extracted data: (a) distribution of the weight per entry in the data set, (b) number of extracted edges per year.

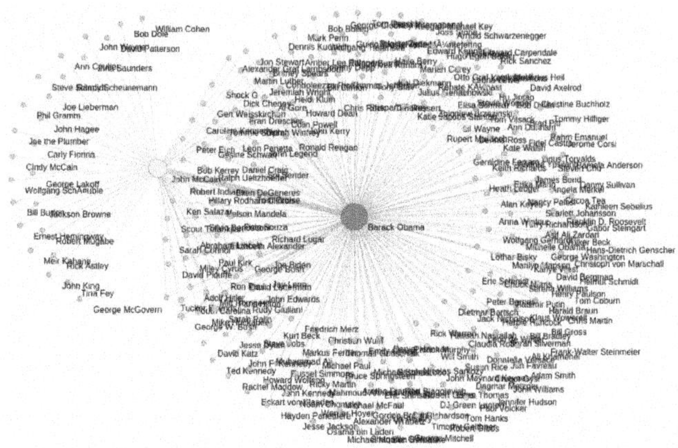

Figure 3: A static graph showing the extracted social network of Barack Obama and John McCain for the period May, 2008 to May, 2009.

We then define node weight $\mathcal{W}_N$ over all considered entries i as

$$\mathcal{W}_N = \sum_i w_i \tag{2}$$

and the edge weight $\mathcal{W}_{E,kl}$ between two nodes k and l as

$$\mathcal{W}_{E,kl} = \sum_i w_{k,i} + w_{l,i}\,, \tag{3}$$

where $w_{k,i}$ and $w_{l,i}$ are the individual node weights. We refer to such graphs as static graphs. To study the temporal evolution of the social networks we also construct dynamic graphs, consisting of sequences of static graphs for disjoint intervals of length ΔT within the time period T.

2.4 Graphical user interface

The graphical user interface of SocGraph is accessible through a web browser, see Fig. 5. The "Person" input field is expecting a query such as a name of a person or a list of person names. The "Time span" selectors can be used to choose a time period of interest. Three filters are exposed to the user. It is possible (a) to limit the maximum number of considered database entries through providing the value in the "Maximal number of entries“ input field, filter the nodes (b) by their weight through the adjustment of the "Weight per entry“ slider and filter the edges (c) by their weight through the "Edge weight“ slider.
The node weights are normalized in the range from zero to

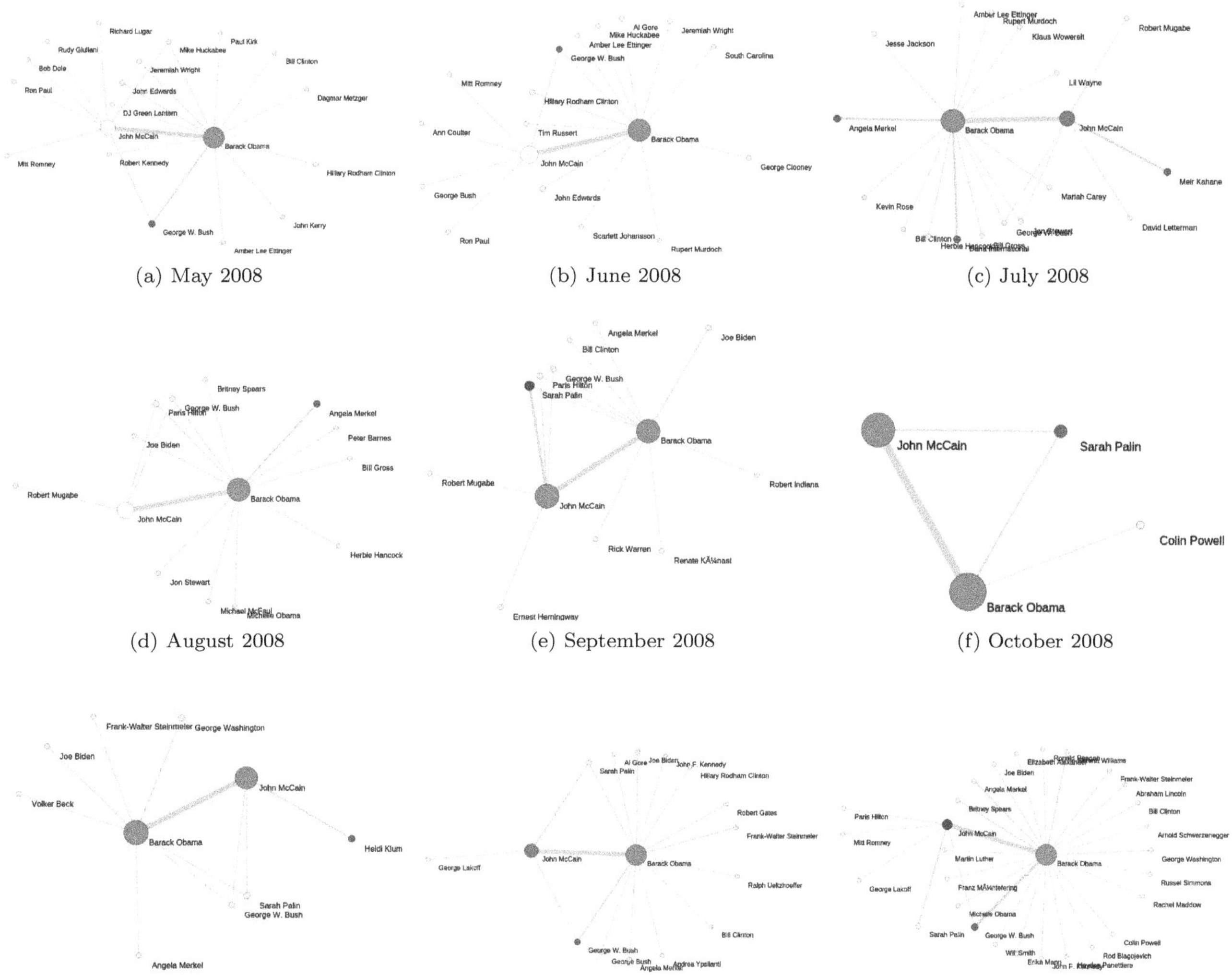

(a) May 2008 (b) June 2008 (c) July 2008

(d) August 2008 (e) September 2008 (f) October 2008

(g) November 2008 (h) December 2008 (i) January 2009

Figure 4: Temporal evolution of the social graph of Barack Obama and John McCain during the US election campaign 2008

one and a color scheme ranging from blue to red is utilized to indicate particular weight value from small to large, respectively. Overall, there are three modes of the SocGraph operation, namely:

(i) A static graph can be computed and visualized over the complete dataset, providing an overview of all comentions for the requested persons available in the Internet Archive. This mode is triggered by the "Graph View" button in the "Update" field of the control panel on the right.

(ii) For a specified sliding window a temporal statistical plot can be generated, showing the number of raw comentions as well as the weight of the persons of interest. This mode is triggered by the "Temporal statistic" button in the "Update" field of the control panel, the results are displayed in the "Temporal Statistic" tab of the demonstration interface.

(iii) Finally, SocGraph provides a functionality to construct and visualize the individual graphs for particular time periods as well as to create an animation of graph evolution over time. The length of particular periods (measured in days) can be entered in the "Sliding window" input of the "Animation" field of the control panel. The user obtains the dynamic graph by clicking on the "Refresh" button (left to the "Play" button) of the player control strip.
Once the data is loaded a time line with the number of edges in each sliding window period appears in the "Graph View" tab. To start the animation, the user should click the "Play" button. The animation speed can be controlled by the adjustment of the value (in seconds) in the "Speed" input. The playback can be paused with the "Pause button. Note, that the player also allows step by step forward and backward rendering of the graphs, triggered by the corresponding player control buttons.

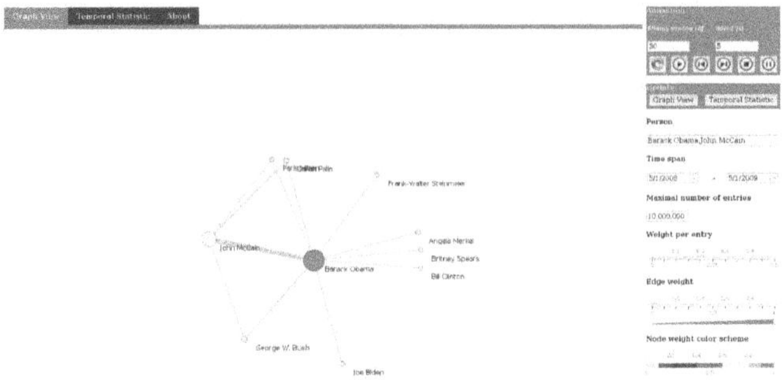

Figure 5: The graphical user interface of SocGraph as shown in a web browser.

3. DEMONSTRATION OVERVIEW

In the demonstration we will primarily show how the SocGraph time travel graph system works and how the social networks are constructed from the content of IA web pages. We will demonstrate the graphical interface usage for static and dynamic graph visualization. Additionally, we can elaborate in more detail on the person pair extraction process and explain the underlying parallelization algorithms.

We will explore the social networks of Barack Obama (node N_{BO}) and John McCain (node N_{MC}) for the one year period from May, 2008 to May, 2009, roughly corresponding to the US presidential election,as an example. The weight per entry has been set to 0.2, which means that we allow data records with up to four additional persons. The edge weight filter has been set to 0.025, in order to not overload the graphs and focus on the interesting entities. The static graph is plotted in Fig.3. A dynamic graph has been constructed with a sliding window of 30 days. The series of graphs are shown in Fig.4. For instance we observe that Hillary Clinton (N_{HC}) node was connected to (N_{BO}) from the beginning and disappeared in June 2008, corresponding to the time point, where Hillary Clinton endorsed Barack Obama and withdrew her candidacy. In following the sizes of both nodes, N_{BO} and N_{MC}, remain similar until November, where the actual election took place and N_{MC} drastically reduced the weight already in following month after Barack Obama became a president of the United States. Shortly before in September, Sarah Palins' (N_{SP}) talk on the side of John McCain had positive impact on the votes for this candidate. This fact is also reflected in our graph where N_{SP} appeared in September connected to N_{MC}.

4. DISCUSSION

In this paper we introduced a demonstration of SocGraph - a social graph extracting system for large networks from Internet Archive data. In contrast to other research concerned with graph construction from web related data, we are focused on the temporal evolution of social networks implicitly contained in the stored web pages. In our future work we plan to include pattern filtering techniques, integrate data from search engines and evaluate event identification, as well as sentiment analysis of the personal relationships and their evolution. Our system will be offered as a service within the EU Project Alexandria as part of a Web Observatory accessible to social and computer scientists as well as to general public for social network visualization and evolution analysis. The demonstration is available on our web page: `http://socgraph.l3s.uni-hannover.de` and can be used with any web browser. Additionally, the web page contains a summary of the demo applications as well as a short video tutorial.

5. ACKNOWLEDGMENTS

This work is partly funded by the European Research Council under ALEXANDRIA (ERC 339233), by the European Commission under grant agreements 619525 (QualiMaster) and 688135 (STARS4ALL).

6. REFERENCES

[1] C. Bird, A. Gourley, P. Devanbu, M. Gertz, and A. Swaminathan. Mining email social networks. In *MSR Workshop 2006.*

[2] X. Canaleta, P. Ros, A. Vallejo, D. Vernet, and A. Zaballos. A system to extract social networks based on the processing of information obtained from internet. In *ICC Association for Artificial Intelligence 2008.*

[3] D. K. Elson, N. Dames, and K. R. McKeown. Extracting social networks from literary fiction. In *Association for Computational Linguistics (ACL) System Demonstrations*, 2010.

[4] C. D. Manning, M. Surdeanu, J. Bauer, J. Finkel, S. J. Bethard, and D. McClosky. The Stanford CoreNLP natural language processing toolkit. In *Association for Computational Linguistics (ACL) System Demonstrations*, pages 55–60, 2014.

[5] Y. Matsuo, J. Mori, M. Hamasaki, K. Ishida, T. Nishimura, H. Takeda, K. Hasida, and M. Ishizuka. Polyphonet: An advanced social network extraction system from the web. In *Proceedings of World Wide Web Conference 2006, Semantic Web Track.*

[6] M. K. M. Nasution and S. A. Noah. Superficial method for extracting social network for academics using web snippets. In *RSKT '10.*

[7] R. Nuray-Turan, Z. Chen, D. V. Kalashnikov, and S. Mehrotra. Exploiting web querying for web people search in weps2. In *Web People Search Evaluation Workshop (WePS 2009).*

[8] S. Siersdorfer, P. Kemkes, H. Ackermann, and S. Zerr. Who with whom and how?: Extracting large social networks using search engines. In *CIKM '15*, pages 1491–1500. ACM.

[9] L. Wieneke, M. Düring, G. Sillaume, C. Lallemand, V. Croce, M. Lazzaro, F. S. Nucci, C. Pasini, P. Fraternali, M. Tagliasacchi, M. Melenhorst, J. Novak, I. Micheel, E. Harloff, and J. G. Moron. Building the social graph of the history of european integration - A pipeline for humanist-machine interaction in the digital humanities. In *SocInfo 2013 International Workshops.*

[10] M. Zaharia, M. Chowdhury, M. J. Franklin, S. Shenker, and I. Stoica. Spark: Cluster computing with working sets. In *Proceedings of the 2Nd USENIX Conference on Hot Topics in Cloud Computing*, HotCloud'10, pages 10–10, Berkeley, CA, USA, 2010. USENIX Association.

Context-Sensitive Auto-Completion for Searching with Entities and Categories

Andreas Schmidt
Karlsruhe Institute of Technology & University of Applied Sciences
Karlsruhe, Germany
andreas.schmidt@kit.edu

Johannes Hoffart
Max Planck Institute for Informatics
Saarbrücken, Germany
jhoffart@mpi-inf.mpg.de

Dragan Milchevski
Max Planck Institute for Informatics
Saarbrücken, Germany
dmilchev@mpi-inf.mpg.de

Gerhard Weikum
Max Planck Institute for Informatics
Saarbrücken, Germany
weikum@mpi-inf.mpg.de

ABSTRACT

When searching in a document collection by keywords, good auto-completion suggestions can be derived from query logs and corpus statistics. On the other hand, when querying documents which have automatically been linked to entities and semantic categories, auto-completion has not been investigated much. We have developed a semantic auto-completion system, where suggestions for entities and categories are computed in real-time from the context of already entered entities or categories and from entity-level co-occurrence statistics for the underlying corpus. Given the huge size of the knowledge bases that underlie this setting, a challenge is to compute the best suggestions fast enough for interactive user experience. Our demonstration shows the effectiveness of our method, and its interactive usability.

1. INTRODUCTION

Motivation. Searching in document collections by means of entities and semantic categories allows users to specify more precise search queries and improve retrieval effectiveness (e.g., [3, 9, 7]). The underlying assets, large knowledge bases (KBs) with entities organized in semantic types or categories (e.g., DBpedia YAGO or Wikidata), as well as methods for linking textual occurrences of entities to these KBs [14] are sufficiently mature to make this endeavor practically viable.

As an example, consider the screenshots of the STICS system [9] for news search, depicted in Figure 1. The user merely needs to start typing a name, and the system automatically suggests entities and categories that could be good completions of the input prefix. After making her choice (the politician Donald Trump in this case), the user may then select an entire category as a search criterion (here, the Simpsons characters), again after merely typing a prefix. The system will automatically match entities from that category and return documents with co-occurrences of the specified entities. Note that this interactive setting differs from traditional entity search where users merely enter ambiguous names and keywords [1].

SIGIR '16, July 17-21, 2016, Pisa, Italy

DOI: http://dx.doi.org/10.1145/2911451.2911461

Problem. Matching the user's input prefix against names of entities and categories (by prefix matching of individual tokens) often returns hundreds or thousands of auto-completion candidates. So the ranking of these candidates is crucial. A simple solution is to use the importance of entities as a criterion. However, the importance in the KB (e.g., derived from in-coming links in Wikipedia) is not necessarily in line with the frequency or prominence of an entity in the corpus. A good ranking thus needs to be *adaptive to the corpus.* In addition, the ranking should reflect the incremental nature of the user's input: after the first entity is chosen, the suggestions for the second one should be *sensitive to this context.* For example, after the user picked Donald Trump, an input prefix like "Sim" should not exactly prioritize famous singers like Paul Simon or Nina Simone, who are important but totally unrelated to Trump. Note that this incremental interpretation of the user's keystrokes and make this problem quite different from the traditional tasks of query segmentation (e.g., [8]) or entity linking for very short texts (e.g., [6]).

Solution. This demo paper presents a system that provides auto-completion suggestions for entities and categories in a corpus-adaptive and context-sensitive manner. Our solution builds on ideas from prior work on auto-completion (e.g., [4, 2]), but extends them to the underexplored realm of knowledge-driven search with interactive speed and usability. For corpus-adaptivity, the ranking of candidate entities is based on the importance in the underlying document collection, also taking into account the temporal dimension. For context-sensitivity, our ranking considers the semantic relatedness to other entities and categories already chosen by the user for her input so far. As basis for our solution we use the previously developed STICS [9], which ranks entity and category suggestions independently of the given context, purely based on statistics derived from the KB, not by statistics gathered form the document collection. Our demo is available online at **http://stics.mpi-inf.mpg.de**.

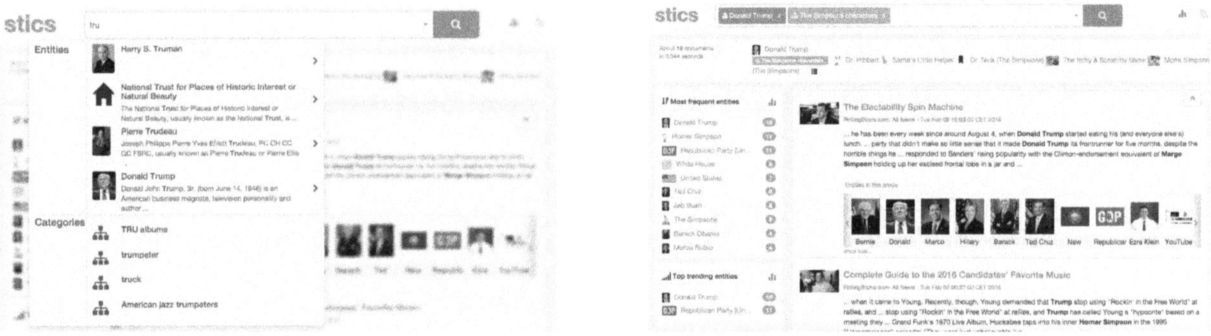

(a) Conventional Suggestion (b) Adaptive Suggestion

Figure 1: STICS news search with auto-completion suggestions for entities and categories.

2. KNOWLEDGE-DRIVEN SUGGESTIONS

The goal of the knowledge-driven auto-completion is to suggest, for a given prefix and specified entites and categories, only entities and categories that lead to non-empty results for the document collection being searched. Thus the suggestions depend on the retrieval model. In our system we retrieve documents that contain all specified entities and at least one entity of each category. Additionally, suggestions should be ranked so that entities and categories that are salient with respect to the collection are available for quick selection by the user.

Without any context, we should suggest entities and categories occurring frequently in the collection, this guide the user to useful queries for the collection. As soon as context is given in the form of entities or categories, there are multiple possibilities of what to suggest, and how to rank the suggestions. Given a category, an intuitive strategy could be to suggest categories that co-occurr in documents. However, categories are only present indirectly in the document, via the entity. Thus, we suggest categories that are associated with entities co-occurring with entities of the given category, in the same indirect manner.

More formally, the auto-completion should provide suggestions based on the input data (E, C, p), where E is the set of entities and C is the set of categories already specified by the user (both might be empty), and p is the current prefix that the user has already typed. An additional input is the type relation from the KB, which associates each entity with a set of categories (e.g. the entity `Hillary Clinton` has the categories `politician` and `lawyer`). The output is a tuple (E^*, C^*), containing two ordered lists of suggested entities and categories. For the actual ranking, we distinguish two cases:

E and C are empty: Without any KB context, E^* and C^* simply contain all entities and categories ranked by the global document frequency, where the frequency of a category is counted whenever an entity of the given category is present in a document. The more frequent an entity or category, the higher in the list. Both lists are then filtered by p to produce the final output.

E or C are non-empty: First the set of all context entities E_c is formed as the union of all entities in E and all entities in any category $c \in C$. E^* is then populated with all entities co-occuring with any $e \in E_c$, ranked by the maximum relatedness score (see Section 3). E^* is then filtered by p.

C^* is derived from E^* by adding for all of the categories of each $e \in E^*$. C^* is ranked by the sum of the relatedness scores of the contained entities, then filtered by p.

The filtering of entities and categories based on one or more prefixes is done in the following way: On average, every entity in the YAGO system is described by 2.7 words (category: 3.8 words). To match the given prefix(es), a prefix match between a single words describing the entity or category is done. If more than one prefix is given, each prefix must match at least one word from the description of the entity or category. The "coverage" of the prefixes is used as ranking criterium in a linear combination with the score described above.

Our system also supports "time travel" search. In this case, we are only interested in results appearing during an interval of time or at a specific point in time. This can easily be achieved by further filtering the set of documents that should be considered in a query. Restricting the news articles to consider automatically restricts the suggestions.

3. RELATEDNESS MEASURE

The relatedness between two or more entities is based on the distance of their occurrences in documents. The first step is to extract tuples of two or more entities occurring in a window of words of predefined size (e.g. 50 words). This is applied to all documents in the collection, and we derive an aggregated relatedness measure as follows.

Per document, each extracted n-tuple has a weight w that decreases with the maximum distance d between any two entities in the tuple: $w = \log \frac{1}{d}$. Across the entire collection, these weights are summed up over all documents where the n-tuple occurs.

4. INTERACTIVE PERFORMANCE

The auto-completion suggestions are always used in an interactive manner, where response times of below 100ms should be achieved. Consequently, a naive approach where in a first step all documents satisfying the previously entered entities and categories are retrieved, then co-occurring entities are extracted from this document set, is far to expensive. Thus we precompute the relatedness scores of all co-occurring entities. The starting point for building a datastructure supporting the suggestion lookup are the n-tuples

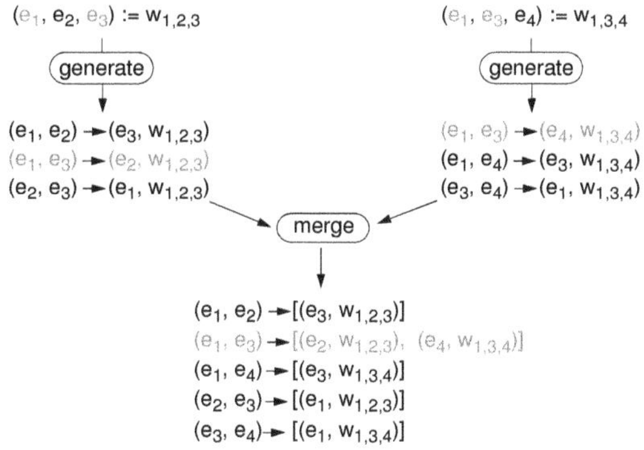

Figure 2: Data structure for generating entity suggestions.

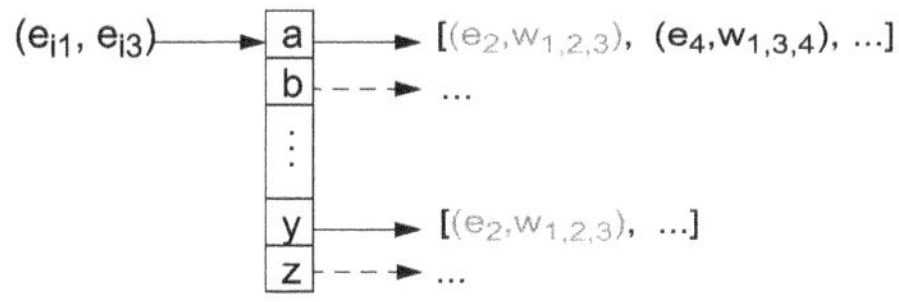

Figure 3: Splitting of entity-list along prefixes.

of entities extracted in Section 3. Consider for example the triple (e_1, e_2, e_3) with weight $w_{1,2,3}$. The existence of this triple states that there is at least one document in the collection in which the entities e_1, e_2, and e_3 occur.

Having a query with already specified entities e_1 and e_3, we can suggest entity e_2, as we know that there is at least one document satisfying this query. Having another pre-computed triple (e_1, e_3, e_4) we can further suggest e_4. The construction of the suggestion-datastructure is shown based on the two tuples (e_1, e_2, e_3) and (e_1, e_3, e_4) in Figure 2.

For every n-tuple $(e_1, ..., e_n)$ with weight $w_{1,...,n}$, from the relatedness measure, we generate a dictionary consisting of n entries, where the key is formed by $n-1$ entities and the value is the entity which is missing in the key, together with the weight $w_{1,...,n}$ of the origin n-tuple. This is done for all tuples from the entity-indexing step. After that, the dictionaries are merged, so that the values become lists, consisting of weighted entities.

To reduce the number of entities which must be filtered by prefix we split the value-list by the prefixes of the entities. Figure 3 shows the additional datastructure for key-entry (e_1, e_3) which splits the entries by a one-character prefix. The reason for $(e_2, w_{1,2,3})$ occurring twice is that the description of the entity consists of multiple words. The example shows one word starting with 'a' and another one with 'y' (e. g. Yello Air Taxi). The length of the character prefix can be varied to split entity lists that are too long into lists of shorter length that meet the performance requirement.

5. IMPLEMENTATION

For the implementation we use a MySQL 5.6 database with MyISAM tables. The core of the database are the tables storing the entity co-occurrence tuples, which are queried by dynamically created SQL statements. The structure of these table contains $n-1$ columns for the entity-ids (in ascending order) and two more columns for a related entity and the weight of this relationship, which is computed as explained in Section 3. On our demo dataset of more than 3 million documents nearly all queries can be answered in less than 100 ms. Some rare queries for one or two given entities with very high frequency (like `United_States`) and very short and popular prefixes (i.e. `'s'`, `'c'`) have runtime durations which are in the order of a second. However, as there are only a few thousand combinations like this, we generated another table which combines the critical entities and the corresponding prefixes. This way, the time constraint of 100 ms can be achieved.

The temporal adaptivity is integrated by splitting the entries in the co-occurence tables in slices of one month. This way, queries with time constraints only have to consider the entries satisfying the given time constraint.

6. DEMO SCENARIO

6.1 Dataset

As a demo dataset we use 3 million news articles from about 300 different news feeds which we have collected since mid 2013. In this dataset, about 57 million mentions have been linked to the YAGO [15] using the AIDA [10] entity linking system. YAGO contains 10 million entities, organized in over half a million categories organized in a taxonomy. For our data, about 600,000 distinct YAGO entities are marked up in documents. On average, a document contains 28 mentions of 9.5 distinct entities.

6.2 Auto-Completion Suggestions

Corpus-adaptive suggestions help users to explore corpora that they are – a priori - not familiar with. Consider a user searching for news about `Hillary Clinton`. If the suggestions were solely based on conventional ranking measures from the KB, typing "Cl" might lead to `Cleveland` or `Bill Clinton`. With our corpus-aware and time-adaptive suggestions, `Hillary Clinton` is now first, as she is featured prominently in news due to her presidential campaign.

Context-sensitive suggestions help to users to find entities that are specifically relevant for the user's current task. Consider again the user interested in `Hillary Clinton` and suppose the user subsequently types the prefix `'sa'`. In 2013 the top three suggestions are `Saudi Arabia` and `San Francisco`, reflecting that she was still the Secretary of State. This changed in 2015, as shown in Figure 4: now the top suggestions are `Bernie Sanders` and `Rick Santorum`, also candidates for the US presidential election.

Anecdotal examples for the improvements by corpus- and context-adaptivity are shown in Table 1.

7. RELATED WORK

A related field of research is entity search (aka. expert retrieval) [1], which, however, has a different computational model: queries are keywords or phrases, and answers are lists of entities. In our setting, the user input is a set of entities and the search engine returns a set of documents.

Entity recommendation is another related topic (e.g., [5, 13, 11]). Here the task is to identify related entities in the context of a user exploring a knowledge base or using a search engine. These recommendations are meant to guide the user; they are not intended to map the user's input to best fitting entities. In contrast, our focus is on interactive auto-completion at real-time speed.

Context-sensitive auto-completion has been well studied for keyword queries over web pages and text documents (e.g.

(a) conventional Suggestion (b) Adaptive Suggestion

Figure 4: Improving query formulation by adaptive auto-completion suggestions.

Input		**Suggested entities**		**Suggested categories**	
Prefix	Context	Conventional	Adaptive	Conventional	Adaptive
"do"	e: `Hillary Clinton`	Copa **do** Brasil Rio Grande **do** Sul Sport Club **do** Recife	**Do**nald Trump Patti Solis **Do**yle United States **do**llar	**do**cuments legal **do**cuments **do**cumentaries	**do**nor **do**ctor L.A. **do**dgers owners
"co"	c: `president`	**co**ld war **co**lumbia **co**nservative	Nationalist **co**ngress Party Indian National **co**ngress African National **co**ngress	dramatic **co**mposition **co**ding system physical **co**ndition	**co**untry **co**untries in Europe **co**mmunist states
"c"	c: `president` e: `Syria`	**c** (programming) **C**roatia **C**hurch of England	David **C**ameron Bill **C**linton **C**NN	English **c**ricketers dramatic **c**omposition **c**hampionship	Central Asian **c**ountries Near Eastern **c**ountries Former British **c**olonies

Table 1: Conventional vs. adaptive auto-completion suggestions for given Prefix, Entity (e), and Category (c).

[4, 2, 16]). Here, the context is given by previous queries, where in our case the context is given in a single query itself by multiple entities or categories.

Prior work on entity-level auto-completion includes the STICS [9], SEMEX [12] and Broccoli [3] systems. STICS is our baseline; its auto-completion is solely based on global importance. SEMEX is solely based on string similarity between the user input and the entity suggestions; there is no consideration of the relatedness between entities. Broccoli is closest to our setting; its auto-completion works for entities, categories, relations, and words or phrases. It is corpus-aware, but does not consider the temporal dimension of how importance and relatedness vary over time. Also, its context model currently only uses co-occurrence counts based on Wikipedia and Freebase.

8. REFERENCES

[1] K. Balog, M. Bron, and M. de Rijke. Query Modeling for Entity Search Based on Terms, Categories, and Examples. *ACM Transactions on Information Systems*, 29(4), 2011.

[2] Z. Bar-Yossef and N. Kraus. Context-sensitive query auto-completion. In *WWW 2011*, 2011.

[3] H. Bast, F. Bäurle, B. Buchhold, and E. Haußmann. Semantic full-text search with broccoli. In *SIGIR 2014*, 2014.

[4] H. Bast and I. Weber. Type less, find more: fast autocompletion search with a succinct index. In *SIGIR 2006*, 2006.

[5] B. Bi, H. Ma, B. P. Hsu, W. Chu, K. Wang, and J. Cho. Learning to recommend related entities to search users. In *WSDM 2015*, 2015.

[6] M. Cornolti, P. Ferragina, M. Ciaramita, H. Schütze, and S. Rüd. The SMAPH system for query entity recognition and disambiguation. In *ERD 2014*, 2014.

[7] J. Dalton, L. Dietz, and J. Allan. Entity query feature expansion using knowledge base links. In *SIGIR 2014*, 2014.

[8] M. Hagen, M. Potthast, A. Beyer, and B. Stein. Towards optimum query segmentation: in doubt without. In *CIKM 2012*, 2012.

[9] J. Hoffart, D. Milchevski, and G. Weikum. STICS: searching with strings, things, and cats. In *SIGIR 2014*, 2014.

[10] J. Hoffart, M. A. Yosef, I. Bordino, H. Fürstenau, M. Pinkal, M. Spaniol, B. Taneva, S. Thater, and G. Weikum. Robust Disambiguation of Named Entities in Text. In *EMNLP 2011*, 2011.

[11] J. Lee, A. Fuxman, B. Zhao, and Y. Lv. Leveraging knowledge bases for contextual entity exploration. In *KDD 2015*, 2015.

[12] J. Osterhoff, J. Waitelonis, and H. Sack. Widen the peepholes! entity-based auto-suggestion as a rich and yet immediate starting point for exploratory search. In *GI 2012*, 2012.

[13] R. Reinanda, E. Meij, and M. de Rijke. Mining, ranking and recommending entity aspects. In *SIGIR 2015*, 2015.

[14] W. Shen, J. Wang, and J. Han. Entity Linking with a Knowledge Base: Issues, Techniques, and Solutions. *IEEE Trans. Knowl. Data Eng.*, 27(2), 2015.

[15] F. M. Suchanek, G. Kasneci, and G. Weikum. Yago: A core of semantic knowledge. In *WWW 2007*, 2007.

[16] S. Vargas, R. Blanco, and P. Mika. Term-by-term query auto-completion for mobile search. In *WSDM 2016*, 2016.

EAIMS: Emergency Analysis Identification and Management System

Richard McCreadie, Craig Macdonald and Iadh Ounis
{firstname.lastname}@glasgow.ac.uk
University of Glasgow, UK

ABSTRACT

Social media has great potential as a means to enable civil protection and law enforcement agencies to more effectively tackle disasters and emergencies. However, there is currently a lack of tools that enable civil protection agencies to easily make use of social media. The Emergency Analysis Identification and Management System (EAIMS) is a prototype service that provides real-time detection of emergency events, related information finding and credibility analysis tools for use over social media during emergencies. This system exploits machine learning over data gathered from past emergencies and disasters to build effective models for identifying new events as they occur, tracking developments within those events and analyzing those developments for the purposes of enhancing the decision making processes of emergency response agencies.

1. INTRODUCTION

Social networks and social media have become some of the most prominent technologies currently in use today. Indeed, the number of different social media platforms continues to grow, accompanied by a steady increase in the number of users that either actively post or otherwise consume content shared using these platforms [5]. Furthermore, as these platforms continue to proliferate, the reach of these social networks and social media increases, particularly in rural areas where initial adoption was low.

Importantly, social media provide a wealth of real-time information, which, if used effectively can provide insights about what is happening in the world. In particular, during emergency situations such as natural disasters, information shared on social media has been shown to be valuable [19]. Indeed, experts in a variety of domains have developed tools to use social media to identify and track events [1, 12, 14, 16]. For instance, the Crisis Tracker system [16], uses a manually created set of search terms to crawl crisis-related content, which is then clustered automatically and manually annotated by volunteers. Such crisis tracking and analysis tools can collect, analyze and aggregate information from people involved in an event, enabling both the general public and emergency response agencies to monitor what is happening in real-time.

SIGIR '16, July 17 - 21, 2016, Pisa, Italy

ISBN 978-1-4503-4069-4/16/07... $15.00
DOI: http://dx.doi.org/10.1145/2911451.2911460

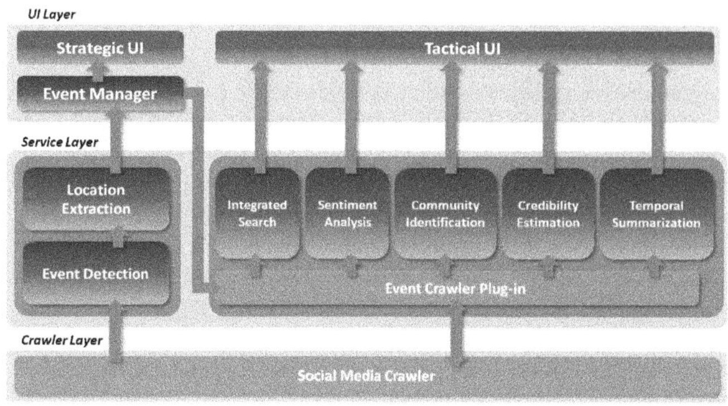

Figure 1: EAIMS architecture overview

In recent years, there have been notable technological advances in fields such as machine learning for sentiment and behavioral analysis [11], real-time event detection in social streams [10], temporal event summarization [8] and credibility estimation of social content [4]. These new technologies have the potential to provide richer information about crisis events based on social media content. However, to-date, there are few crisis tracking and analysis tools that make use of them.

We present a new crisis tracking and analysis toolkit, named: EAIMS (Emergency Analysis Identification and Management System). The goal of EAIMS is to provide an integrated toolkit for automatically identifying, tracking, summarizing and managing information about emergency events derived from social media. Unlike most crisis tracking and analysis systems, EAIMS provides automatic real-time detection of new emergency events. Furthermore, once an event is detected, EAIMS provides a rich suite of automatic tracking and analysis tools, namely: automatic timeline construction, targeted sentiment analysis, user-community identification and information credibility estimation.

EAIMS is designed for use by emergency management staff stationed at their operations center. In particular, we envisage the system being used by two different groups of people, representing strategic use across different events and tactical use within a single event. First, at a strategic level, the system can be used by emergency monitoring staff responsible for identifying new crisis events and initiating first response procedures. In particular, automatic event detection within EAIMS can automatically alert users to potential crisis events that they can then verify through existing channels. Using automatic tools to aid in crisis event identification has the potential to enable faster response times to unexpected crisis events. Second, at a tactical level, we envisage EAIMS being used by emergency analysts both during and after an event. Users can leverage the automatic tracking and analysis tools provided by EAIMS to more effectively monitor the event itself - using social media users as sensors. Furthermore, these tools can also be used to assess how the agency's response to the emergency is perceived - facilitating more informed communication with the public.

2. EAIMS ARCHITECTURE

A broad overview of the EAIMS architecture is illustrated in Figure 1. As we can see from Figure 1, EAIMS is comprised of three main architecture layers. The lowest layer is the crawling layer, which is responsible for collecting general, as well as event-specific social media content, which will be processed by the upper layers. The second architecture layer is the service layer. This layer is comprised of a series of plug-and-play services that provide the end-user with crisis tracking and analysis capabilities. In line with the vision of EAIMS, these services are divided into strategic and tactical services. Strategic services provide functionality to users working at the strategic level, i.e. when tracking different event reports across multiple regions. Meanwhile, tactical services provide functionality when working at the level of a single event. The tactical services also include the Event Crawler Plug-in, which is responsible for performing targeted collection of content for a particular event. The third layer of EAIMS is the UI (user interface) layer. This layer is responsible for managing and visualizing the strategic and tactical information provided by the service layer to the user. In particular, this layer contains three main components. First, the event manager component is responsible for maintaining the list of candidate events that have been identified. Second, the UI layer contains the strategic UI, that visualizes the different candidate events that have been detected on a map for the user. Finally, the tactical UI is responsible for visualizing the outputs from each of the tactical services for a selected event. We discuss the motivations and implementation of the tactical and strategic services/UI below.

3. STRATEGIC SERVICES AND UI

The aim of the strategic services is to provide automatic detection and annotation of new candidate events to the user. To provide this functionality, there are two notable components that are needed: 1) automatic identification of events of interest to the user; and 2) association of those events with locations. The output of these components are visualized within EAIMS's strategic UI, as illustrated in Figure 2, where each event is represented by a pin on the map. Clicking on a pin displays the earliest tweet identified for the event on the right hand side of the UI. Additionally, a map overlay is displayed which provides event controls. In particular, it enables the user to initialize tracking for the event[1] and to switch to the tactical view for this event. We discuss how we tackle the event detection and location identification components below.

[1] This triggers targeted crawling of social media posts based on tracking terms (named entities and #hashtags) extracted from each event cluster.

Figure 2: EAIMS: Strategic UI.

3.1 Event Detection

The aim of automatic event detection is to identify the first instance of a article/post that discusses a new emerging topic, e.g. a news article representing a new event. This is normally achieved by incremental clustering algorithms. However, such clustering approaches have been shown to be too computationally intensive to be applied to high volume streams, such as tweets. Hence subsequent approaches have focused on constant-time approximations to perform text clustering [13].

To enable EAIMS to identify events over high volume tweet streams, we use a recent distributed streaming event detection approach based on locality sensitive hashing [10]. Under this approach, when each post arrives, multiple locality sensitive hashing functions are used to generate hashes for that post. A locality sensitive hashing function is one where textually similar posts will receive similar hash codes with a high probability. Hash collisions with previous posts observed are used to determine whether a similar topic has been observed before. Clusters of similar posts are maintained, which represent different candidate events. Once a candidate event cluster reaches a predefined size (5 posts in our case), that cluster is emitted as a new event. This approach is both constant time and can be distributed over multiple machines to achieve parallelism for large events.

The above approach generates a relatively high volume of candidate events (hundreds per hour) over time, and are not specific to the interests of the user. Hence, for each cluster emitted as a candidate event, we apply an additional filtering step. In particular, we apply an SVM text classifier to filter out those events that are not about topics of interest to the user. We currently support two main use-cases, namely: flash flooding and large public demonstrations, with an associated event classifier for each.

3.2 Location Detection

Once a relevant event has been identified it is vital to identify a location for that event. Indeed, most response agencies are responsible only for particular geographical regions, hence it is important to only highlight events relevant to the user. A candidate event is represented by a cluster of social media posts, such as tweets. However, only about 2-3% of all tweets are geo-located [3]. Hence, there is a good chance that none of the posts within a cluster will have geolocations.

To tackle this issue, we use the Carmen location attribution approach [6]. Carmen aims to assign a location to a tweet from a database of known locations. To do so, it combines three types of information sourced from each tweet,

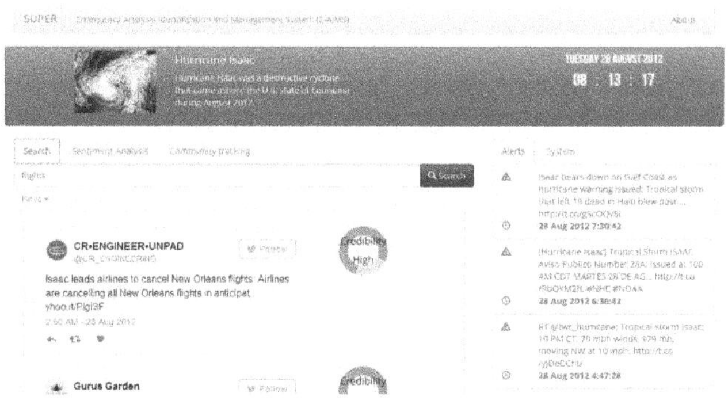

Figure 3: EAIMS: Tactical UI - Search Tab.

namely: place information encoded within the tweet; geo-coordinate information for the small number of tweets that have them; and location(s) extracted from parsing the user profile for the tweet author. An evaluation of Carmen's performance over a tweet dataset indicates that 22% of posts can be geo-located [6], although the granularity of the identification varies (e.g. in many cases location can only be narrowed down to the country of interest). This is often sufficient to identify the location for one or more posts in our event clusters.

4. TACTICAL SERVICES AND UI

In contrast to the strategic services, which identify and visualize multiple events, the aim of the tactical services are to provide a series of tools to enable a deeper analysis of a single event. When a user initiates tracking of an event within the strategic UI, the cluster of social media posts for that event are sent to the Event Crawler Plug-in. This plug-in then formulates a new tracking query to collect content specifically for that event. To do so, it extracts all named entities and hashtags from the event cluster. These query terms are passed to the crawler layer as a query.

The tactical UI is illustrated in Figure 3. As we can see from Figure 3, event-related information is displayed along the top of the page (this can be customized by the user). Below the event information is a series of tabs that provide access to the search, sentiment analysis and community identification functionalities (the search tab is selected in Figure 3). Down the right hand side, the output of the timeline generation service is displayed, showing the most recent updates automatically extracted from the social media content stream. We discuss each of these components in more detail below.

4.1 Integrated Search

The first of the tactical services is integrated search. This service provides dynamic indexing and retrieval of social media content crawled for the event. This service enables information exploration and discovery by emergency analysis staff during, as well as after the event. To provide social search capabilities, we build on top of the real-time indexing and retrieval functionality of the Terrier search engine platform [7]. In particular, using Terrier v4.1, we deploy a real-time distributed index using a temporal document-partitioning scheme. Under this setup, multiple mini-indices are constructed, each containing documents from a particular time period. For an emergency management scenario, this partitioning scheme has two major advantages. First, since many search requests will be time-orientated, we can

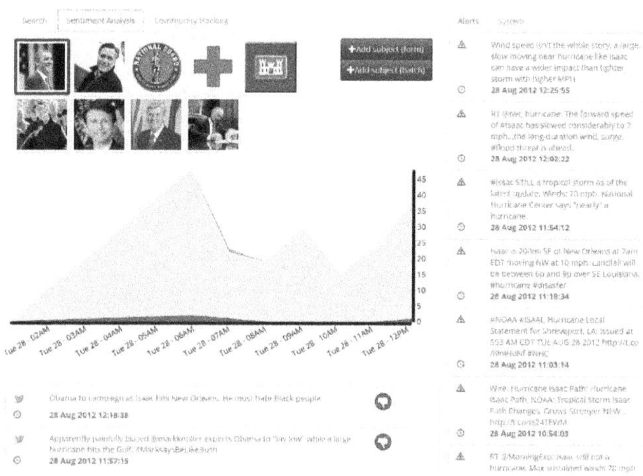

Figure 4: EAIMS: Tactical UI - Sentiment Tab.

limit the number of indices that have to be searched based on the user's search constraints. Second, for cases where the user wants results ranked by time, we initially need to only search the most recent indices to supply the most recent results. Indices containing older content can then be searched on-demand as the user scrolls down the search result page.

4.2 Credibility Estimation

When working with social media derived information, it is important to be able to judge the veracity/credibility of that information, if that information is to be actionable. To support this, EAIMS includes a credibility estimation service that works in parallel with the integrated search service. In particular, for each social media post ranked within a search engine result page, a credibility score is provided. To score the credibility of a post, we use the approach proposed by Castillo et al. [4], which uses a machine-learned regression model to score each post. This approach uses three main types of features to distinguish the credibility of posts, namely: text features (length of text, number of URLs/mentions/hashtags contained); information about the users who authored them (registration age, number of followers); and the general topics they refer to (such as the fraction of tweets in a topic containing URLs).

4.3 Sentiment Analysis

One of the areas where emergency management agencies see value in social media is as a means to track public opinions regarding the emergency response, i.e. as a means to judge how well the public think they are doing [9]. Prior work on sentiment analysis in social media during crises has applied well-known techniques for overall sentiment detection in posts [11]. However, we argue that sentiment analysis of the overall post might not always be suitable, as it may miss the presence of more targeted sentiments, e.g. about the people and organizations involved (which we refer to as sentiment targets). Hence, within EAIMS, we use a machine learned sentiment polarity text classification model designed to identify sentiment towards one or more named entities. In particular, we use crowdsourced sentiment labels for entity-tweet pairs to train a the classification model, using unigram and bigrams as features. The output of the sentiment analysis component is shown in Figure 4. In particular, the currently defined entities being tracked are displayed along the top of the UI, enabling the user to select which to view sen-

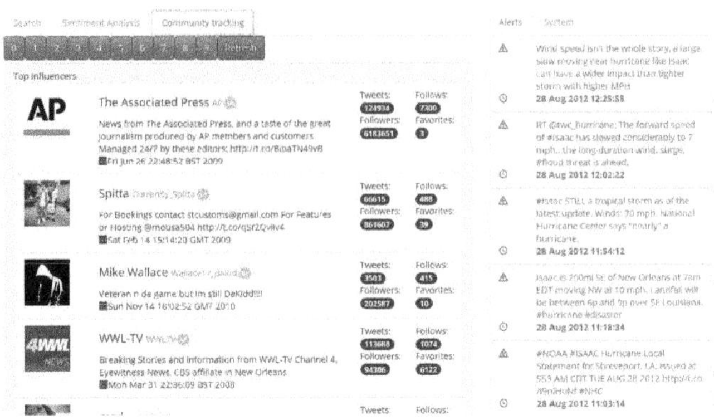

Figure 5: EAIMS : Tactical UI - Community Tab

timent for. Sentiment is then visualized in two ways. First, as a color-coded graph showing the sentiment polarity distribution for the currently selected entity over time. Second, a listing of recent posts expressing sentiment about that entity. The user can add new entities to track at any time.

4.4 Community Identification

Emergency management agencies typically maintain a social media presence as a communication channel with the general public. To make effective use of this channel, it is important to identify groups of stakeholders within the social network that can be messaged, such as local response volunteers or news agencies covering the event. To support this use-case, EAIMS provides an automatic community identification functionality. In particular, we use an approach based on topic modeling to identify communities as determined by the users' interaction patterns within the social network. User communities are visualized within the community tab of the tactical UI, as shown in Figure 5. In particular, the user can switch between any of the communities identified using the buttons displayed along the top of the UI. For the currently selected community, the top influencers are displayed, ranked by the number of social media connections they have within the network.

4.5 Timeline Generation

Finally, EAIMS provides a real-time timeline generation and notification functionality. In particular, the user can specify a series of information types to track, e.g. messages related to deaths or injuries. The timeline generation component monitors the social media content crawled for the event being tracked and extracts posts related to each of the specified information types to return to the user as updates. To achieve this, we build on recent works in the field of temporal summarization [8] to find relevant posts as they are crawled and then then apply explicit diversification with respect to the specified information types using the xQuAD framework [17]. In this way, we score a post based its relevance to the event, its coverage of information about the event, and its novelty with respect to specified information types. Posts that exceed a score threshold are displayed within the tactical UI as updates, as illustrated in Figure 3.

5. CONCLUSIONS

In this paper, we presented the Emergency Analysis Identification and Management System (EAIMS), a prototype service that provides real-time detection, monitoring and analysis tools for use over social media during emergencies. It combines state-of-the-art event detection, sentiment analysis, timeline generation, credibility analysis and community identification technologies to enable emergency monitoring staff to better leverage social media during crises. This prototype system is currently being deployed for flooding and public security use-cases within the FP7 SUPER Project.

6. ACKNOWLEDGMENTS

This work has been carried out in the scope of the EC co-funded SUPER Project (FP7-606853).

7. REFERENCES

[1] F. Abel, C. Hauff, G-J. Houben, R. Stronkman and K. Tao. Twitcident: Fighting Fire with Information from Social Web Streams. In *Proc. of WWW*, 2012.

[2] F. Aisopos, G. Papadakis, and T. Varvarigou. Sentiment analysis of social media content using n-gram graphs. In *Proc. of WSM*, 2011.

[3] S. H. Burton, K. W. Tanner, C. G. Giraud-Carrier and J. H. West. "Right time, right place" health communication on Twitter: Value and accuracy of location information. Journal of Medical Internet Research, 14(6), 2012.

[4] C. Castillo, M. Mendoza and B. Poblete. Information credibility on Twitter In *Proc. of WWW*, 2011.

[5] A. Datta, M. Dikaiakos, S. Haridi, and L. Iftode. Infrastructures for online social networking services [guest editorial]. *IEEE Internet Computing*, 16(3):10–12, 2012.

[6] M. Dredze, M. J. Paul, S. Bergsma and H. Tran. Carmen: A Twitter Geolocation System with Applications to Public Health. In *Proc. of HIAI*, 2013.

[7] C. Macdonald, R. McCreadie, R. L. Santos, and I. Ounis. From puppy to maturity: Experiences in developing terrier. *Proc. of OSIR*, 2012.

[8] R. McCreadie, C. Macdonald, and I. Ounis. Incremental update summarization: Adaptive sentence selection based on prevalence and novelty. In *Proc. of CIKM*, 2014.

[9] R. McCreadie *et al.* SUPER: Towards the use of Social Sensors for Security Assessments and Proactive Management of Emergencies. In *Proc. of SWDM*, 2015.

[10] R. McCreadie, C. Macdonald, I. Ounis, M. Osborne, and S. Petrovic. Scalable distributed event detection for Twitter. In *Proc. of IEEE Big Data*, 2013.

[11] S. Narr, M. Hülfenhaus, and S. Albayrak. Language-independent Twitter sentiment analysis. In *Proc. of KDML*, 2012.

[12] M. Osborne *et al.* Real-Time Detection, Tracking, and Monitoring of Automatically Discovered Events in Social Media. In *Proc. of ACL*, 2014.

[13] S. Petrovic, M. Osborne and V. Lavrenko. Streaming first story detection with application to Twitter. In *Proc. of NAACL*, 2010.

[14] H. Purohit and A. P. Sheth. Twitris v3: From Citizen Sensing to Analysis, Coordination and Action. In *Proc. of ICWSM*, 2013.

[15] J-C. Puras and C. A. Iglesias. Disasters2.0. Application of Web 2.0 technologies in emergency situations. In *Proc. of ISCRAM*, 2009.

[16] J. Rogstadius, M. Vukovic, C. A. Teixeira, V. Kostakos, E. Karapanos, J. A. Laredo. CrisisTracker: Crowdsourced social media curation for disaster awareness. IBM Journal of Research and Development, 57(5), 2013.

[17] R. L. T. Santos, C. Macdonald, and I. Ounis. Search Result Diversification. *Foundations and Trends in Information Retrieval*, 2015.

[18] H. Sayyadi, M. Hurst and A. Maykov. Event Detection and Tracking in Social Streams. In *Proc. of ICWSM*, 2009.

[19] J. Sutton, L. Palen, and I. Shklovski. Backchannels on the front lines: Emergent uses of social media in the 2007 southern California wildfires. In *Proc. of ISCRAM*, 2008.

Expedition: A Time-Aware Exploratory Search System Designed for Scholars

Jaspreet Singh, Wolfgang Nejdl, Avishek Anand
L3S Research Center, Leibniz Universität Hannover
Appelstr. 9a
30167 Hanover, Germany
{singh,nejdl,anand}@L3S.de

ABSTRACT

Archives are an important source of study for various scholars. Digitization and the web have made archives more accessible and led to the development of several time-aware exploratory search systems. However these systems have been designed for more general users rather than scholars. Scholars have more complex information needs in comparison to general users. They also require support for corpus creation during their exploration process. In this paper we present Expedition - a time-aware exploratory search system that addresses the requirements and information needs of scholars. Expedition possesses a suite of ad-hoc and diversity based retrieval models to address complex information needs; a newspaper-style user interface to allow for larger textual previews and comparisons; entity filters to more naturally refine a result list and an interactive annotated timeline which can be used to better identify periods of importance.

1. INTRODUCTION

Archives are an invaluable source of study for a variety of scholars like historians, social scientists, political scientists and journalists. The proliferation of such longitudinal corpora has seen significant strides made in Temporal IR - new retrieval models, temporal profiling techniques and various indexing methods have been proposed to address the challenges posed when searching such collections [7]. This in turn has led to the development of several specialized search and exploration systems where time is a first class citizen. Time-aware exploratory search systems primarily utilize either (i) temporal retrieval models to improve search result ranking [12] or (ii) timelines to detect trends and visually explore the collection [3, 14, 2]. However these systems are designed for more general users rather than the primary user group of digital archives - scholars.

Scholars differ from more general users in the following ways: (i) a scholar's information need tends to be more complex. A complex information need requires the user to issue several queries whose intent varies even during the exploration process. For instance, initially the user may want an overview and subsequently more focused results. (ii) While exploring the archive, scholars track relevant results to form a corpus of study (iii) scholars further analyze this corpus and then publish not only their results but also the corpus construction procedure.

Consider the scenario of a historian interested in the history of law enforcement in New York City. She has access to the New York Times news archive via a time-aware exploratory search system. Studies have shown that scholars often use general terms, names of people and places as search queries [6]. Lets say the user enters the terms 'police new york' as the initial query resulting in over 30,000 documents. It is infeasible for her to read all documents to get an overview. Using a diverse ranked list for such a query on the other hand can enable her to get an initial anecdotal overview of the query topic by reading just the top results. In doing so, she finds that Rudolph Giuliani was responsible for reforming the police in the 90s and filters her results to only include articles about Giuliani. While exploring the archive, it is also important to identify interesting time periods. Typically timelines are used to visualize periods of high and low activity in relation to the query. While even a simplistic timeline is useful for exploration, a more insightful visualization would also include annotations that explicitly highlight important periods and explain why they are important. Based on these annotations, she makes a more educated decision to further investigate the year 1994 - the year Giuliani came to power and vowed to reform the police. In this new list of documents she encounters several interesting articles which she would like to further analyze offline. She uses a simple save button to assign articles to an arbitrary corpus. The system also keeps track of which queries, retrieval models and filters she used when building the corpus. Using this documentation, she can easily share her corpus construction procedure and also revisit certain stages to explore in different directions.

To support such a scenario an ideal system should offer (i) a host of retrieval models, both diversity aware and ad-hoc, to support varying intents (ii) appropriate filters to refine the intent (iii) an insightful visual overview across time (iv) the ability to construct corpora and (v) the ability to document the exploration process. In this work we describe Expedition (Figure 1), a time-aware exploratory search system built for scholarly exploration in archives. Expedition allows users to enter keyword queries and vary the intent by choosing an appropriate retrieval model. The results are displayed using an adaptive layout that gives more screen

SIGIR '16, July 17-21, 2016, Pisa, Italy

DOI: http://dx.doi.org/10.1145/2911451.2911465

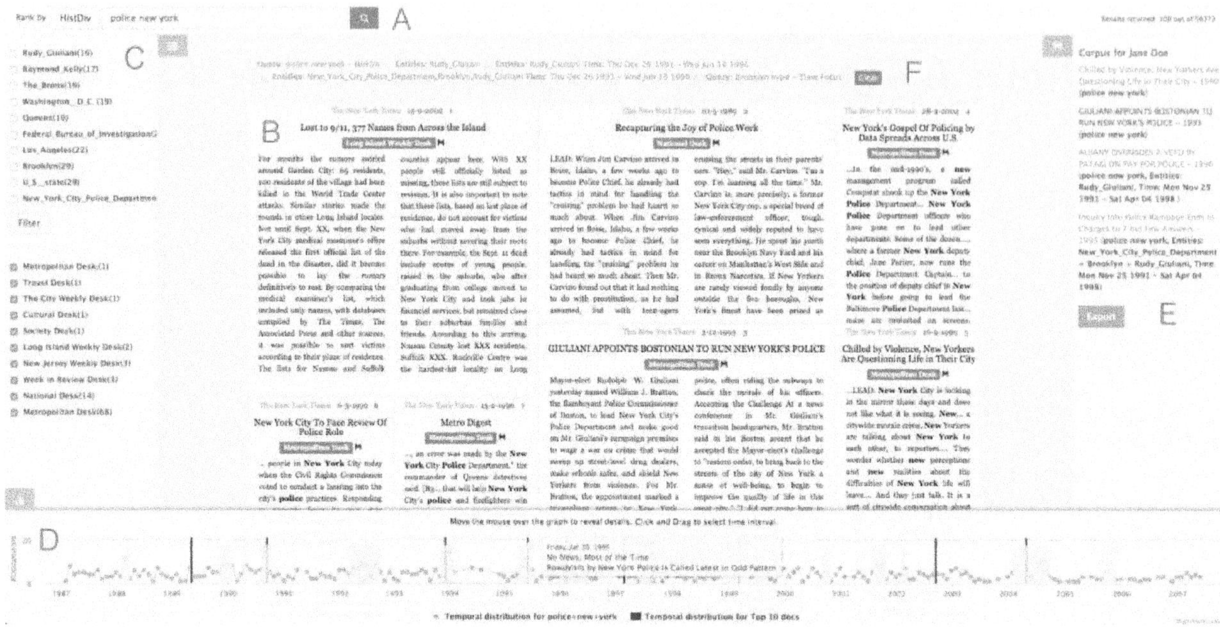

Figure 1: Expedition's User Interface: (A) Search box and retrieval model selector (B) Search result list (C) Left pane consisting of entity filter and article type filter (D) Timeline - shaded areas represent bursts (E) Corpus creation pane displaying the articles saved by the user (F) Search trail - tracks the user's actions during corpus creation (the gray text in the trail represents the current state of the user).

real estate to more relevant results. To aid exploration in time, the user is presented with a timeline which is annotated to indicate and describe important time periods of the query. Users are also presented with a list of salient entities to the query which serve as filters. Every query and subsequent refinement is stored and displayed in the search trail - documenting the user's progress. Users can also navigate back and forth through their exploration process by clicking on a particular state. Finally, users can add documents to their corpus and export it at any point.

2. SYSTEM DESIGN

The Expedition UI is shown in Figure 1. At the top of the interface the user can enter her keyword query and further specify her intent by selecting an appropriate retrieval model from a drop down list consisting of textual relevance, temporal relevance, topical diversity, temporal diversity and historical diversity. The search results are displayed using an adaptive newspaper layout where article real estate is directly proportional to its' rank. The timeline which is found at the bottom is generated using a combination of publication dates and temporal references from the pseudo-relevant documents. This timeline is further annotated with bursts which are labeled to provide the user with more insights. In the same timeline we also visualize the position of the top-k documents, allowing the user to examine the temporal scope of the top results. Furthermore, a list of salient entities can be found to the left of the results which can be used as filters. Every time the user re-specifies her intent, her actions are added to the search trail to help keep track of exploration process. Finally, the user can easily add documents to her corpus by clicking on the save button found below the article headline. Expedition can be accessed online at the following url: `http://bit.ly/archive-search`

In the remainder of this section we detail our system architecture and design choices made when creating Expedition.

2.1 Data Preparation

For the purpose of this prototype we used the New York Times Annotated Corpus which is a news archive consisting of 1.8M articles spread across 20 years. To support sophisticated retrieval models and generate insightful timelines, we first semantically enrich the corpus. Though the corpus already contains manual annotations for some entities, we additionally disambiguated all entities in the corpus using a state-of-the-art named entity disambiguation system [16] to improve coverage. We also extracted temporal expressions from all articles for timeline construction. The disambiguated entities are also useful for helping the user specify her intent during query time. For instance if the user is querying for **george bush**, she can specify whether she meant George Bush Sr. or George W. Bush to increase the accuracy of the result list. We indexed the entities, publication dates, article content from the augmented collection using Apache Lucene [1].

2.2 Architecture

We created a REST API with different end points to support the three major components of the system: retrieval and ranking, timeline generation and salient entity selection. This allows for the decoupling of the user interface which is simply a REST client that interacts with the API and visualizes data. The state of exploration displayed in the search trail and the corpus is maintained on the client side. In the remaining subsections we detail the algorithms used for each component.

[1] http://lucene.apache.org

2.3 Retrieval and Ranking

Expedition is equipped with three classes of retrieval models: textual relevance, temporal relevance and diversity. While textual and temporal relevance help users focus their results, the diversification algorithms are better suited to overviews and multifaceted queries. Depending on the intent, the user can use a combination of keywords and retrieval model to get the better results. [12] is another system that offers users a suite of temporal retrieval models to choose from. However, the retrieval models are designed for inputs consisting of both keywords and time expressions which is better suited to event exploration. To this end we include the following retrieval models:

Temporal Relevance: Textual relevance does not ensure that the user gets relevant results from the most important time periods. For instance, when searching for `world trade center`, results from 2001 are perceived to be more relevant than other years. We use the temporal language model suggested in [10] to help users focus their results to more important time periods.

Temporal Diversity: The algorithm suggested by [5] extends the temporal language model by adding an exponential decay to greedily select textually relevant documents from previously uncovered time periods. This retrieval model is particularly useful in getting an overview of a query across time. When searching for `world trade center`, results from both 2001 and the 1993 bombing are returned using this retrieval model.

Topical Diversity: Topical diversification is especially useful when the user wants a topical overview of the query. Topical diversity is generally used for ambiguous intents but it can also be used for queries with a multi-faceted information need. For example, when searching for `David Beckham`, the results should cover his career at Manchester United and Real Madrid. Topical diversity however is time agnostic which increases the likelihood of not getting a sufficient overview across time. We use Ia-Select [1] as our topical diversification algorithm. Ia-Select relies on modeling the content of a document using aspects. In our system we use entities as aspects.

Historical Diversity: To get a historical overview for a query we use HistDiv [15] - a diversification approach that jointly optimizes coverage of the most important aspects from the most important time periods. When searching for `David Beckham`, the top results include articles about his best achievements at Manchester United and Real Madrid when he was playing for them rather than articles that retrospectively looked back at his career. Such an overview serves as an ideal starting point to spur further exploration.

2.4 Timeline

For a more visual overview and to identify important time periods, we incorporate a timeline based visualization in Expedition. A timeline is an essential feature in all time-aware exploration systems. Timelines have been generated by plotting the number of documents in a result set aggregated by the publication date [11], temporal expressions found [3] or both. In [2], Alonso et al. devised a system with two timelines: a coarse global event timeline and a fine grained timeline plotting the top results. Matthews et al. [11] use a single timeline to visualize document changes across time as well as the change in entity mentions over time. A sliding window across this timeline can be used to zoom into a period. A second timeline is then used to visualize the headlines from top articles published in a selected period. [14] also uses a timeline to explore the collection, however they visualize only insightful time points rather than plotting a temporal profile of the query.

Estimating an insightful timeline is an important challenge. In Expedition, we use a combination of temporal references and publication dates to compute a more accurate timeline. While certain time periods experience high publication activity, some other periods maybe highly referred to and are also interesting to scholars. To generate a timeline, we first generate a probability distribution across time by discretizing time and aggregating the documents published in each time unit. We then smooth this distribution using the probability distribution generated by temporal references. We consider the top 1000 documents ranked by the unigram language model as pseudo relevant and utilize a monthly granularity for aggregations. To detect insightful periods or bursts we use the burst detection algorithm suggested in [13]. A burst is highlighted by a shaded region over the timeline. On mouse-over, the label of the burst is displayed. The burst label consists of the headlines of the top three articles published during the burst. This way users can make a more educated decision when selecting which period to focus on. Additionally, we plot the position in time of the top 10 articles. This gives the users an idea of the time periods that the top results cover and whether interesting periods have been represented in the top results or not.

2.5 Time and Entity Filters

We forsake standard filtering functionality for time and entity *selectors*. Applying a time period or entity filter causes a new query to be issued with the updated constraints. The result is a list of articles with filtered results from the previous search at the top followed by more articles matching these constraints. Consequently, a new timeline is generated and new entities are added to the left pane to spur further exploration.

Time Selector: The timeline doubles as an interactive time period selector. Users can select a time period by clicking on a burst directly or by clicking and dragging across the timeline. In its current state, Expedition supports document retrieval and ranking from a specific time period only based on publication dates which are time points rather than intervals. This scenario does not require temporal indexing techniques such as [4], which are more effective when utilizing temporal expressions, for faster retrieval. In principle, we could employ temporal indexing techniques for collections with documents with valid time intervals.

Entity Selector: We include a list of salient entities to the left of the result list. The entities give the user an overview from a different perspective and also allow the user to refine her intent. To compute the set of top-k salient entities (10 in our prototype) for a given query, we use the following steps: first we select the top 100 documents returned by the chosen retrieval model; we then compute the salient entities for each article using the method suggested in [8] and sort by document frequency; finally, we select the top 10 frequent entities from the sorted list.

2.6 Search Result Display

Typically scholars require more context compared to standard snippets when deciding which articles to add to their corpus. News Archive exploration systems like [11, 14] display the result headline and fixed-length snippet in a traditional list view. We, on the other hand, use the newspaper layout suggested in [9] - *a newspaper represents a mature information medium that is well suited to relatively short and loosely related pieces of text.* The newspaper style interface is well suited to exploring large archived collections since it supports: a multi-narrative scenario, comparison of articles side-by-side and varying degrees of importance by varying the article size. This type of result visualizations is also useful when displaying diversified results. In Expedition, we alter the size of the article depending on its' rank based on the assumption that more relevant results need larger previews. We compute these text previews using Lucene's built-in snippet generator. Clicking on the headline of any result brings up the full article. At the end of each article we add an entity selector consisting of the salient entities mentioned in the document. Lastly, each article also has a save button (floppy disk icon) so that scholars can create a corpus of study.

2.7 Search Trail and Corpus Building

The search trail is a series of consecutive stages that reflect the user's exploration. A new stage is appended to the trail each time the user selects a time period or entity, changes the retrieval model or alters the query. Each stage can be revisited by clicking on the corresponding entry in the search trail. To the right of the search result list is the corpus creation panel. When the user begins a new session, a new corpus is created automatically. The purpose of this panel is to display all documents the user saved. We display the headline of each saved article along with the query used to retrieve it. Clicking on a headline redirects the user to the full article. We also add an export button to this panel to allow users to download their corpora and search trail for offline analysis.

3. CONCLUSION & FUTURE WORK

In this paper we have described the design and implementation of Expedition - a time-aware exploratory search systems for scholars rather than general users. Expedition provides scholars with a multitude of retrieval models, an insightful timeline visualization, salient entity selectors and corpus creation facilities in a unified system. In the future, we plan to add query suggestions based on previously seen articles. We will also add support for multiple queries to be visualized in the same timeline to make temporal comparisons easier. At present Expedition supports only the manual selection of retrieval model. An interesting direction for further research is the automatic suggestion of retrieval models depending on the state of the user in the session. Expedition can also be used for a variety of different archives, not just news. Web archives are steadily gaining popularity among scholars yet access methods are lacking. Web archives also pose different problems when compared to news archives which are clean and consistent. We envisage that a version of Expedition designed to support various types of archives could benefit scholars immensely. With the amount of information being gathered in digital and web archives increasing rapidly, systems like Expedition can be commercialized for national libraries, archives and publishing houses. This work was carried out in the context of the ERC Grant (339233) ALEXANDRIA.

4. REFERENCES

[1] R. Agrawal, S. Gollapudi, A. Halverson, and S. Ieong. Diversifying search results. In *Proceedings of WSDM.* ACM, 2009.

[2] O. Alonso, K. Berberich, S. Bedathur, and G. Weikum. Neat: News exploration along time. Proc. of ECIR'2010.

[3] O. Alonso, M. Gertz, and R. Baeza-Yates. Clustering and Exploring Search Results Using Timeline Constructions. In *Proceedings of the 18th ACM Conference on Information and Knowledge Management*, CIKM '09, New York, NY, USA, 2009. ACM.

[4] A. Anand, S. Bedathur, K. Berberich, and R. Schenkel. Temporal index sharding for space-time efficiency in archive search. In *Proceedings of the 34th International ACM SIGIR*, SIGIR '11, 2011.

[5] K. Berberich and S. Bedathur. Temporal diversification of search results. In *Proceedings of the SIGIR 2013 workshop on time-aware information access*, 2013.

[6] G. Buchanan, S. J. Cunningham, A. Blandford, J. Rimmer, and C. Warwick. Information seeking by humanities scholars. In *Research and advanced technology for digital libraries.* Springer, 2005.

[7] R. Campos, G. Dias, A. M. Jorge, and A. Jatowt. Survey of temporal information retrieval and related applications. *ACM Comput. Surv.*, 47(2):15:1–15:41, Aug. 2014.

[8] B. Fetahu, K. Markert, and A. Anand. Automated news suggestions for populating wikipedia entity pages. *Proceedings of CIKM*, 2015.

[9] G. Golovchinsky and M. H. Chignell. The newspaper as an information exploration metaphor. *Information Processing & Management*, 33(5), 1997.

[10] X. Li and W. B. Croft. Time-based language models. In *Proceedings of the 12th international Conference on Information and knowledge management.* ACM, 2003.

[11] M. Matthews, P. Tolchinsky, R. Blanco, J. Atserias, P. Mika, and H. Zaragoza. Searching through time in the new york times. In *Proc. of the 4th Workshop on HCIIR.* Citeseer, 2010.

[12] A. Mishra and K. Berberich. EXPOSE: EXploring Past news fOr Seminal Events. In *In proceedings of WWW.* International World Wide Web Conferences Steering Committee, 2015.

[13] M.-H. Peetz, E. Meij, and M. de Rijke. Using temporal bursts for query modeling. *Information Retrieval*, 17(1), 2014.

[14] V. Setty, S. Bedathur, K. Berberich, and G. Weikum. Inzeit: efficiently identifying insightful time points. *Proc. of the VLDB Endowment*, 2010.

[15] J. Singh, W. Nejdl, and A. Anand. History by diversity: Helping historians search news archives. In *Proceedings of the 2016 ACM on Conference on Human Information Interaction and Retrieval*, CHIIR '16.

[16] M. A. Yosef, J. Hoffart, I. Bordino, M. Spaniol, and G. Weikum. Aida: An online tool for accurate disambiguation of named entities in text and tables. *Proceedings of the VLDB Endowment*, 4(12), 2011.

iGlasses: A Novel Recommendation System for Best-fit Glasses

Xiaoling Gu Lidan Shou Pai Peng Ke Chen Sai Wu Gang Chen
College of Computer Science and Technology, Zhejiang University, China
{belizabeth, should, pengpai_sh, ck, wusai, cg}@zju.edu.cn

ABSTRACT

We demonstrate *iGlasses*, a novel recommendation system that accepts a frontal face photo as the input and returns the best-fit eyeglasses as the output. As conventional recommendation techniques such as collaborative filtering become inapplicable in the problem, we propose a new recommendation method which exploits the implicit matching rules between human faces and eyeglasses. We first define fine-grained attributes for human faces and frames of glasses respectively. Then, we develop a recommendation framework based on a probabilistic graphical model, which effectively captures the correlation among these fine-grained attributes. Ranking of the frames (glasses) is done by their similarity to the query facial attributes. Finally, we produce a synthesized image for the input face to demonstrate the visual effect when wearing the recommended glasses.

Keywords

Eyeglasses Recommendation; Probabilistic Graphical Model

1. INTRODUCTION

People will not stop pursuing beauty and fashion. Everyone wants to be attractive and gains self-confidence in the presence of other people. Among all fashionable accessories, eyeglasses are probably one of the most important tools to show one's temperament. However, people often face the problem of selecting a right pair of eyeglasses that fit his/her face shape and hairstyle the most. The main difficulty is that everyone is unique and has distinctive appearance which makes it hard to refer to others' recommendations. Moreover, making the right choice requires prior knowledge of understanding style and color matching between glasses and one's face. For instance, rectangular shape of eyeglasses can make a round face appear thinner and longer. To address the above problem, we develop a novel mobile APP named *iGlasses*, which recommends the best-fit eyeglasses based on one's facial traits like a domain expert.

SIGIR '16, July 17-21, 2016, Pisa, Italy

DOI: http://dx.doi.org/10.1145/2911451.2911453

Most state-of-the-art recommender systems rely on collaborative filtering or content-based recommendation techniques [1], which either learn users' preferences from their ratings or identify user's interests based on item descriptions and historical data. For example, Netflix can recommend movies similar to those previously viewed by a user, while Amazon can recommend goods for one based on ratings given by similar users. Although these systems work well for items such as movies and books, their underlying techniques are not applicable in the context of eyeglasses recommendation, due to two reasons: First, unlike movies or books, the eyeglasses rating data and historical purchase data are hard to acquire. Second, learning user's preferences or interests is not suitable for eyeglasses recommendation, as people choose eyeglasses by considering their own appearences (face shape, hairstyle, skin color, etc.).

In this demonstration, we present *iGlasses*, a novel prototype which is able to automatically recommend personalized eyeglasses for users. *iGlasses* takes a face photo from a smartphone as input and returns a ranked list of eyeglasses. When the user selects a particular recommendation result, the prototype performs image synthesis to demonstrate the visual effect of the eyeglasses on the users's face. Specifically, we propose a novel recommendation method, which relies on a probabilistic graphical model capturing the correlation among facial attributes and eyeglasses attributes. Compared with conventional recommendation methods, our proposed method (1) does not require collecting user rating data or historical data as the training set; (2) does not suffer from cold start or sparsity problem; (3) provides personalized recommendation by mining the matching patterns between human faces and eyeglasses. Preliminary experiments show that our approach outperforms baseline methods in most cases.

2. SYSTEM STRUCTURE

The *iGlasses* recommendation framework is illustrated in Figure 1. Given a run-time query, namely a frontal face image, its *facial attributes* are predicted from a set of classifiers, which are pre-trained in the offline phase. The predicted facial attributes are then fed into the *recommendation model* to produce a set of matched attributes of frames (namely *frame attributes*). Such frame attributes are used to generate a ranked list of candidate glasses in the *retrieval module*. Finally, the *synthesis module* crafts synthesized images from the face image and candidate glasses images as the representation of final recommendation results. In what follows, we provide a brief overview of the major system components.

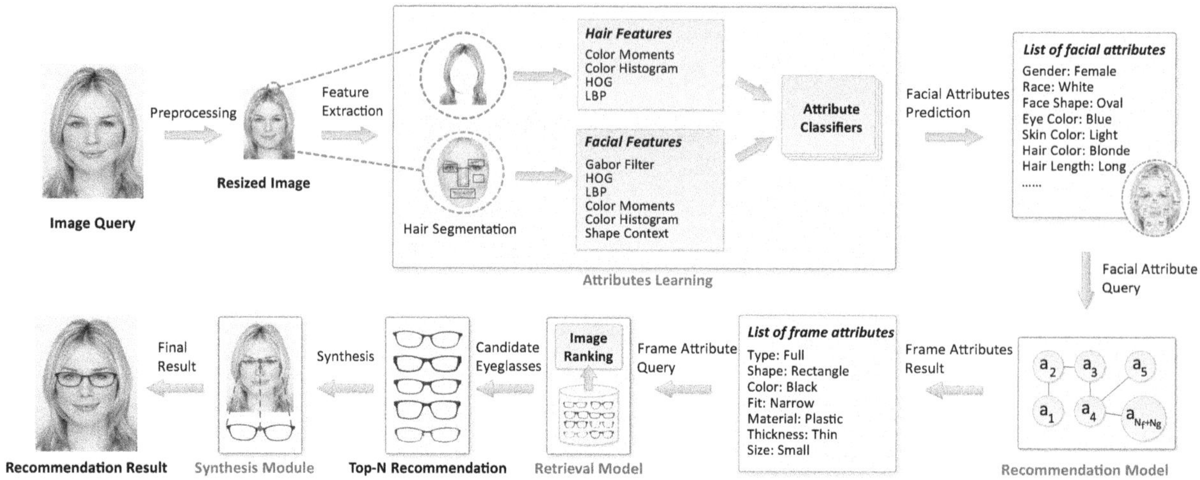

Figure 1: Framework Structure of *iGlasses*

2.1 Facial Attributes Learning

We utilize 17 fine-grained facial attributes to construct user profiles, including *gender, race, eyebrow thickness, eyebrow length, eyes shape, eyes color, nose bridge, mouth width, smiling, lip thickness, lip color, skin color, jaw shape, face shape, fatness, hair color* and *hair length.* We focus on the facial attributes as they include rich information of people and act as the main influence factors in the context of eyeglasses recommendation.

For facial attribute extraction and learning, we make use of the adaptive framework proposed by Kumar et al. [3], where SVM and Adaboost are combined to automatically select on screen space the face region and feature type for each facial attribute. Firstly, all face images are preprocessed before feature extraction. We align faces to a canonical pose by choosing the corners of both eyes as two fiducial points. Then, all face images are cropped and resized to a fixed width by running Viola Jones face detector [6]. To extract hair features, hair segmentation is done by using the GrabCut algorithm [5]. Once the feature extraction is completed, a set of SVM classifiers with an RBF kernel are trained for each attribute by extracting visual features (e.g., Gabor Filter, HOG, Color Moments, Color Histogram, LBP, Shape Context) from different face components (e.g., whole face, eyes, nose, mouth). Experiments on our face photo dataset achieve an average accuracy higher than 80% in detecting the facial attributes.

2.2 Recommendation Model

Our recommendation model is based on a probabilistic graphical model where complex relationships among facial attributes and frame attributes are explored. Similar to the facial attributes, we define 7 discriminative frame attributes, namely *type, shape, color, fit, material, thickness* and *size.* Specifically, we construct a tree-structured conditional random fields model[4] where each node represents an attribute, and each edge represents the mutual dependencies between two nodes. The reason for using tree model is that inference is easily tractable and can be learned efficiently.

A training image is denoted by a vector of attributes $\boldsymbol{\alpha} = \{\boldsymbol{\alpha}^f, \boldsymbol{\alpha}^g\}$, where $\boldsymbol{\alpha}^f = \{a_1^f, ..., a_{N_f}^f\}$, $\boldsymbol{\alpha}^g = \{a_1^g, ..., a_{N_g}^g\}$, N_f is the number of facial attributes (in our case is 17) and N_g is the number of frame attributes (in our case is 7). Each attribute a_i has multiple possible values, i.e. $a_i \in \{1, ..., n_i\}, i \geqslant 1$. Given an image $\boldsymbol{x}$, the joint probability of a specific configuration $\boldsymbol{\alpha}$ can be represented as:

$$p(\boldsymbol{\alpha}|\boldsymbol{x}) = p(\boldsymbol{\alpha}^f, \boldsymbol{\alpha}^g|\boldsymbol{x}) = \frac{1}{Z(\boldsymbol{x})} exp(-E(\boldsymbol{\alpha}^f, \boldsymbol{\alpha}^g, \boldsymbol{x}))) \quad (1)$$

where $Z(x) = \sum_{\boldsymbol{\alpha}^f, \boldsymbol{\alpha}^g} exp(-E(\boldsymbol{\alpha}^f, \boldsymbol{\alpha}^g, \boldsymbol{x}))$ is the partition function, and $E(\boldsymbol{\alpha}^f, \boldsymbol{\alpha}^g, \boldsymbol{x})$ is an energy function scoring the compatibility among an image $\boldsymbol{x}$, facial attributes $\boldsymbol{\alpha}^f$, and frame attributes $\boldsymbol{\alpha}^g$. The recommendation results can be obtained by the most likely joint attributes state $\hat{\boldsymbol{\alpha}^g} = \arg\max_{\boldsymbol{\alpha}^g} \max_{\boldsymbol{\alpha}^f} p(\boldsymbol{\alpha}^f, \boldsymbol{\alpha}^g|\boldsymbol{x})$.

2.3 Image Ranking

While the recommendation model generates a query vector of frame attributes $q = (q_1, q_2, ..., q_{N_g})$ (N_g=7), the image ranking module ranks the relevant eyeglasses images from the product database D, where each product image is labeled with frame attributes that annotated as $d^{(k)} = (d_1^{(k)}, d_2^{(k)}, ..., d_{N_g}^{(k)})$, $1 \leq k \leq |D|$. We define the similarity function between q and $d^{(k)}$ as follows:

$$f(q, d^{(k)}) = \sum_{i=1}^{N_g} w_i[q_i = d_i^{(k)}] \quad (2)$$

where $[\cdot]$ is the Iverson bracket notation, i.e. $[\cdot]$ equals 1 if the expression is true and 0 otherwise. We use Ridge Regression to learn a model w that represents the weight vector of frame attributes.

2.4 Synthesis

This module displays the recommended frame images synthesized with the input face image. To generate quality synthesis results, the frame should be placed on the face reasonably. We observe a variety of people wearing eyeglasses in real life and summarize some important rules. For example, the width of the frame should fit the face width, the height of the frame should be an appropriate proportion of the size of eyes, and the center of frame should be aligned at the nose bridge. There are mainly three key steps during the synthesis process. Firstly, active shape model [2] is used to

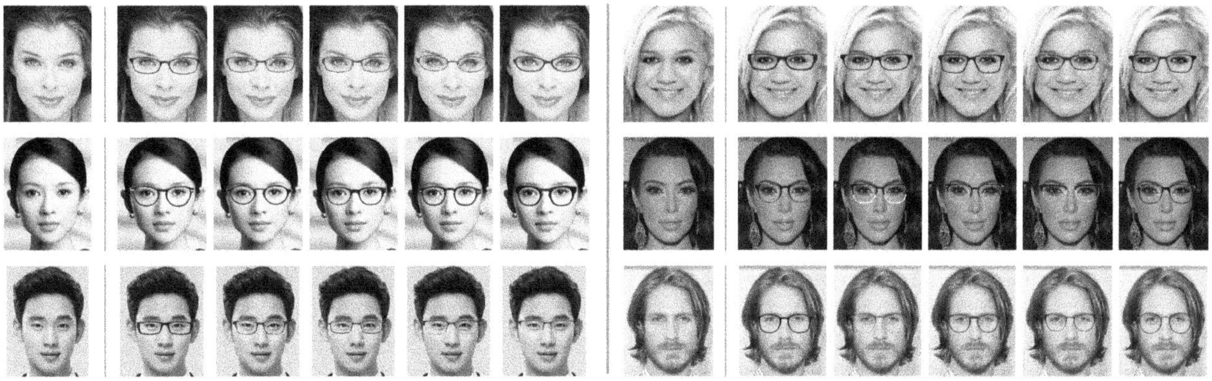

Figure 2: The final top 5 recommendation results on several testing faces

locate 77 feature points on the input face image to gain the size of eyes, the width of face and etc. Secondly, the frame image is scaled according to the human face width. Finally, the face photo is overlaid with the frame image by aligning the center of the face against the center of the frame.

3. EVALUATION

3.1 Dataset

We construct two datasets, including a face photo (FP) dataset and an eyeglasses product (GP) dataset, for evaluating the *iGlasses* system.

FP Dataset: We collect face photos, in which people wearing eyeglasses, from search engines and photo sharing web sites (e.g. Flicker, Pinterst) by using queries such as *celebrities with eyeglasses* and *stars with eyeglasses.* We use the images of movie stars and celebrities who wear eyeglasses as our training images, since those people always have a great sense of style. Viola Jones face detector [6] is utilized to remove those crawled images with no face detected. Then we retain 3039 face images where the eyeglasses is considered to match with the face. Each retained face image is annotated with both facial attributes and frame attributes. We leverage FP dataset to learn facial attributes and build our recommendation model.

GP Dataset: We collect eyeglasses product images from a variety of popular online eyewear stores (e.g. Warby Parker, Coastal, LensCrafters) for the recommendation results. In total, 2035 eyeglasses images are collected and each product image is labeled with frame attributes.

3.2 Baseline Methods

Our recommendation approach bridges the gap between low-level facial features and frame attributes by introducing facial attributes. To evaluate the effectiveness of intermediate facial attributes, we implement two alternative recommendation methods which directly predict the frame attributes with low-level features extracted from face images. More specifically, a set of classifiers are trained for each frame attribute with FP Dataset by using multi-class SVM and neutral network methods. Here different types of features (Gabor Filter, HOG, LBP, Color Moments, Color Histogram, Shape Context, etc.) are extracted from the whole face and concatenated to form a feature vector. Then the concatenated feature vectors are utilized to train a classifier

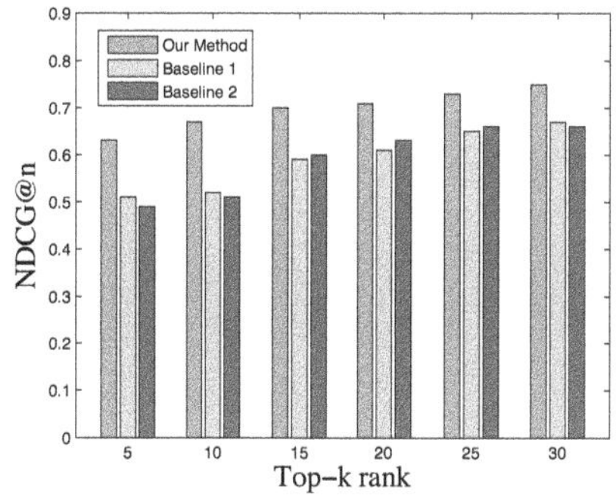

Figure 3: Performance of three recommendation methods measured with NDCG values

for each frame attribute. It is worthwhile to note that our recommendation approach and other two baseline methods share the same image ranking module and synthesis module.

3.3 Recommendation Results Evaluation

In order to qualitatively evaluate the final recommendation result, we conduct a user study with a crowdsourcing platform. We use 150 testing images to evaluate the performance of the two baseline methods and our approach. Given a testing face image, three top-k (k=30) ranked lists are generated by our method and other two baselines respectively. Every participant is asked to score the matching degree (1-5) between the recommended frame and query face for each ranked list. We collect scores for 150 $\times$ 3 ranked lists from 500 participants. Finally, the average scores are calculated for each ranked list as the ground truth.

The performance of our recommendation method is measured by Normalized Discounted Cumulative Gain (NDCG), which is widely used in ranking systems. Figure 3 reports the NDCG values of our recommendation method and other two baselines. From the results, we can observe that our model outperforms multi-class SVM and neural network, especially in the top 10 recommendations. This is mainly because that our model reserves the intrinsic relationship among frame attributes and captures the dependencies between frame attributes and facial attributes, while other two baseline methods neglect these correlations. Figure 2 presents the final top 5 recommendation results of our method on several testing faces.

4. DEMONSTRATION

4.1 Demonstration Setup

The *iGlasses* prototype includes an Android APP and a server backend. The mobile client is implemented on an Android smartphone and the web server is deployed with Apache Tomcat. The client is mainly in charge of displaying images, such as face images, eyeglasses images and synthesized images. While the server side is responsible for computing and communication with the client side. In the offline phase, the server builds facial attribute classifiers, constructs three recommendation models, and learns image ranking model. In the online phase, the server recognizes facial attributes and returns the synthesized images to the client.

4.2 Walkthrough Example

The *iGlasses* demo consists of the following steps, as illustrated in Figure 4:

Step 1: The user can either use *iGlasses* APP to take a photo or select an existing photo from his/her album as the input. Once the user chooses a photo, the query photo will be displayed at the client.

Step 2: As soon as the user submits the facial attribute query on the client, the above input photo is forwarded to the server. The server utilizes active shape model [2] to locate 77 feature points on the received face image and returns 17 fine-grained facial attributes by using the pre-trained SVM classifiers. Once the client obtains the facial attribute values, these facial attributes will be displayed along with face photo at the client.

Step 3: With the recognized/predicted facial attributes, *iGlasses* can recommend proper eyeglasses based on one's facial traits once the user submits a recommendation request. The server uses our probabilistic graphical model and image ranking model to recommend the best-fit eyeglasses. For comparison purpose, we also implement two alternative recommendation models on server using multi-class SVM and neural network methods, which can be configured in the APP.

Step 4: Once the ranked list of recommended eyeglasses are returned to the user, the *iGlasses* system can generate the synthesis result efficiently. Users can have a preview of how the recommended eyeglasses look on their faces. In most cases, our approach outperforms the baseline methods and produces high quality recommendation results.

5. CONCLUSION

In this demonstration, we presented *iGlasses*, a novel recommendation system for recommending the best-looking eyeglasses. *iGlasses* used a new recommendation approach based on a probabilistic graphical model, which exploited implicit matching rules between faces and eyeglasses. To qualitatively evaluate our recommendation method, we also implemented two baseline methods for comparison and conducted a user study. Experiments showed promising results from our approach.

6. ACKNOWLEDGEMENT

This research is supported by the National Key Basic Research Program of China (GrantNo. 2015CB352400). This research is also partially supported by the National Research Foundation, Prime Minister's Office, Singapore under its International Research Centre in Singapore Funding Initiative.

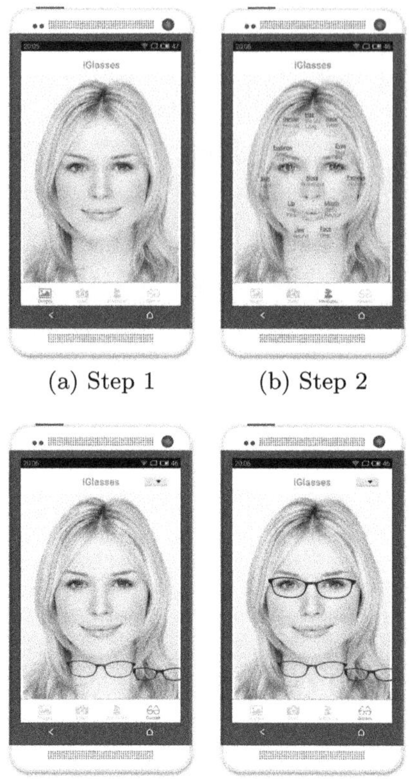

(a) Step 1 (b) Step 2

(c) Step 3 (d) Step 4

Figure 4: The Screenshots of *iGlasses* System

7. REFERENCES

[1] G. Adomavicius and A. Tuzhilin. Toward the next generation of recommender systems: A survey of the state-of-the-art and possible extensions. *IEEE Transactions on Knowledge and Data Engineering*, 17(6):734–749, 2005.

[2] T. F. Cootes, C. J. Taylor, D. H. Cooper, and J. Graham. Active shape models—their training and application. *Comput. Vis. Image Underst.*, 61(1):38–59, 1995.

[3] N. Kumar, A. C. Berg, P. N. Belhumeur, and S. K. Nayar. Describable visual attributes for face verification and image search. *IEEE Trans. Pattern Anal. Mach. Intell.*, 2011.

[4] T. Mensink, J. J. Verbeek, and G. Csurka. Tree-structured crf models for interactive image labeling. *IEEE Trans. Pattern Anal. Mach. Intell.*, 2013.

[5] C. Rother, V. Kolmogorov, and A. B. 0001. "grabcut": interactive foreground extraction using iterated graph cuts. *ACM Trans. Graph.*, 23(3):309–314, 2004.

[6] P. Viola and M. Jones. Robust real-time face detection. *International Journal of Computer Vision*, 57(2):137–154, 2004.

InfoScout

An interactive, entity centric, person search tool

Sean McKeown
School of Computing
Edinburgh Napier University
Edinburgh, Scotland
s.mckeown@napier.ac.uk

Martynas Buivys and Leif Azzopardi
School of Computing Science
University of Glasgow
Glasgow, Scotland
martynas.buivys@gmail.com
Leif.Azzopardi@glasgow.ac.uk

ABSTRACT

Individuals living in highly networked societies publish a large amount of personal, and potentially sensitive, information online. Web investigators can exploit such information for a variety of purposes, such as in background vetting and fraud detection. However, such investigations require a large number of expensive man hours and human effort. This paper describes InfoScout, a search tool which is intended to reduce the time it takes to identify and gather subject centric information on the Web. InfoScout collects relevance feedback information from the investigator in order to rerank search results, allowing the intended information to be discovered more quickly. Users may still direct their search as they see fit, issuing ad-hoc queries and filtering existing results by keywords. Design choices are informed by prior work and industry collaboration.

Keywords

Web Investigation; Open-Source Intelligence; People Searching; Professional Search; Entity Search

1. INTRODUCTION

The World Wide Web is an invaluable resource, providing access to a massive amount of information covering a wide variety of subjects. Ubiquitous access to the Internet has made this information more accessible than ever, while blogging, social media, and communication platforms allow users to be publishers of information, rather than simply consumers. Governments, businesses, and public bodies also contribute to this wealth of information, publishing census data, maps and financial documentation. One way in which these Big Data sources can be exploited is in a variety of Open-Source Intelligence (OSINT)[1] investigations, which make use of publicly available, heterogeneous, information to pursue particular goals. The types of OSINT investigation are varied, ranging from employee vetting [4], competitive intelligence [1], fraud detection [11] and copyright protection [1], to law enforcement [7] and counter-terrorism [3].

Open-Source information, particularly public social media data, is widely adopted for these purposes. Lexis Nexis indicates that 81% of law enforcement professionals in the United States make use of social media platforms as an investigative tool [7], with Facebook, Twitter and Youtube being the most frequented [7]. Similarly, CareerBuilder found that 43% of employers utilise social media to perform background checks on prospective employees, with half of them having rejected candidates as a result of their findings [4].

While such investigations are used in a variety of industries, they are time consuming and fraught with problems. This paper describes an application which is intended to reduce the time it takes for an investigator to find pages which are relevant to a given subject, the target of the investigation, and is based on findings from industry engagement.

2. BACKGROUND

While such types of search are prominent in a variety of industries, the literature in relation to the behaviour of Web investigators is sparse. High level descriptions of processes and techniques can be found in the NATO OSINT Handbook [9], which is set in the context of military like operations. Appel [1] provides a similar overview from the perspective of a professional Web investigator, while providing additional discussion pertaining to industry best practices and ethical considerations.

In order to better understand the requirements of investigators, McKeown et al. [8] conducted a qualitative study which compares and contrasts the behaviour of Web investigators with other search domains. It was found that the investigation is split into two major phases: *(i)* Background Verification and *(ii)* Open-Ended Search. The background verification stage primarily relies on fixed resources, such as resellers of the electoral roll, address information and company directories. The latter focuses more on expanding the knowledge of a subject, largely by way of general Web search engines and social media.

These investigators demonstrated low levels of search expertise, with minimal use of advanced search functionalities. However, a high level of domain expertise was evident. Contextual clues, personal knowledge and experience facilitate the discrimination of search results, as well as the assess-

[1]In this context, the term 'Open-Source' refers to the public availability of information, rather than a software licensing paradigm.

SIGIR '16, July 17 - 21, 2016, Pisa, Italy

ISBN 978-1-4503-4069-4/16/07...$15.00
DOI: http://dx.doi.org/10.1145/2911451.2911468

ment of the reliability and quality of pieces of information and sources. Investigators were aware of the notion of a digital footprint, but did not take any technical measures to conceal themselves online. Instead, they employ sensible strategies for avoiding contact with the subject of the investigation, such as carefully considering their interaction with social media profiles.

As a form of domain specific search, such investigations possess properties of exhaustive searches, as in the patent search [6] and E-Discovery domains [2], however, the end goal is not a complete enumeration of all relevant information. High recall is subordinate to high precision, with emphasis on finding the critical pieces of information required to fulfil the purpose of the investigation. The process, then, is more correctly characterised as a form of exploratory search.

However, such investigations are not without difficulty, with issues being highlighted in:

i Person disambiguation and name variants

ii Underutilization of technological solutions for case management and searching

iii Corroboration of findings and the reliability of evidence

iv Time constraints associated with the large volumes of data available on the Web.

2.1 Existing Tools

While investigators in McKeown et al. [8] typically only made use of a popular Web browser, general Web search engines and word processors to carry out the investigation, there are products available for such purposes.

Copernic Agent[2] is meta-search engine which allows search queries to be disseminated to a wide variety of sources for OSINT information gathering. External search engines and resources are categorised thematically, allowing the user to quickly execute searches for a given type of information. However, as of January 2014, this product is no longer supported, with many of the underlying calls to search engines being non-functional at the time of writing.

Maltego[3] is a proprietary OSINT and forensics tool which focuses on allowing the user to determine the links between entities. Maltego has a broad scope and can be used for a variety of OSINT purposes, providing the ability to visualise and discover real world links between entities in social or physical networks. This is achieved by combining meta-search functionality with an underlying graph, allowing the user to explore common nodes or expand the graph to new entities. The search interface differs greatly from that of standard Web search engines, with most actions populating, or operating, on the graph directly. As a result, non-technical users may find this tool difficult to use.

Oryon C Portable[4] is a portable Web browser based on Chromium which is pre-installed with a variety of add-ons and bookmarks for OSINT investigations. The default homepage provides tabs to select common search types, such as Web, Images, Blogs and Maps, while the bookmarks and other features are designed to give an investigator fast access to common resources. Specific resources are searched individually, and the browser itself is geared towards protecting the privacy of the user.

Person searching makes up a substantial portion of all Web searches [10, 5], and, as a result, several people search engines exist, such as *Pipl*[5] and *Spokeo*[6]. Such search engines typically behave like federated search systems, with details such as the individual's name and location fuelling queries to underlying social media, blogging and general Web searches. Disambiguation options are limited and there is often geographical confusion in the results, with the user being left to manually sift through the documents for the correct individual.

3. INFOSCOUT

Existing tools are insufficient because they do not adequately address the core problems faced by the investigator. Subject centric investigations rely heavily on disambiguating namesakes in order to acquire information about a particular individual, rather than people with the same name. This can be achieved with advanced query formulation, however this requires some degree of search expertise on the part of the investigator. Similarly, while existing solutions allow for faster and more convenient searching of multiple resources, the user must still manually inspect all documents, or their snippets, in order to identify relevant results, and extract the information, with minimal support for actually capturing evidence.

The requirements of the investigator can be described in simple economic terms: *they wish to maximise the recovery of information relating to the subject and the case, while minimising the amount of effort required.* InfoScout, the system described in this work, aims to address the investigator's difficulty with the large volumes of data found on the Web, allowing users to pinpoint information more readily, without the need for advanced query formulations or large quantities of existing knowledge.

InfoScout possesses the following features:

- Automatic page fetching and screenshot acquisition
- Content, entity and key term extraction
- User relevance feedback and re-ranking of search results
- Entity and term filtering of search results
- Case management

The core of InfoScout is designed around allowing the user to identify relevant documents quickly by re-ranking results based on user feedback. This allows the user to focus their time on extracting information from key documents, as opposed to locating such documents in the first place.

Initially, the user is presented with a simple interface which allows cases to be added, deleted, edited or continued. Each case has a subject as their focus, to which all search actions should pertain. The user enters ad-hoc queries and is then presented with a list of document screenshots, and links to said documents, for relevance judgements. This feedback

[2]https://www.copernic.com/en/products/agent/
[3]http://www.paterva.com/web6/products/maltego.php
[4]http://osintinsight.com/oryon.php
[5]https//pipl.com/
[6]http://www.spokeo.com/

is then used to build a ranking query which re-ranks the results using relevant terms and entities extracted from relevant documents. This inherently allows for person disambiguation as it allows for features of the users social network, location, hobbies and associated institutions to play a role in determining the order of documents. By marking a document with the entity *NASA* as relevant, it is more likely that further documents with this term are more highly ranked. Such re-ranking allows for results for *John Smith who works at NASA* to be distinguished from those of *John Smith who works for IBM*.

The interface for relevance feedback is simple, taking the form of a sequential suggestion of documents. The user is presented with a screenshot of the document and is given the option to mark the document as relevant, non-relevant, or to skip it altogether, see Figure 1. The re-ranking itself is transparent to the user.

The user must also be allowed to direct the search as they find relevant pieces of information about the subject. Adhoc queries can be submitted with new query terms, which will then be ranked using the information from previously judged documents. The user can choose to be presented with individual documents for judgement, or can explore the list of results as with a standard interface for Search Engine Results Pages (SERPs). Additionally, users may make use of extracted entities and terms in order to filter documents, as in Figure 2. This is useful in the case that the user wants to focus the investigation on a particular entities or keywords, such as the city or employer of the subject. Filters are applied on the standard SERP view.

Documents which are marked as relevant are also stored as part of the case, facilitating case management while also preserving the information as it appeared at the time of capture. This particular functionality mitigates the effort of manually tracking screenshots and documents in word processors, as with investigators in McKeown et al. [8] as well as mitigating later attempts at evidence obfuscation by the subject.

Search results are provided solely by the Bing search engine, as it allows for results from a wide range of Web results and includes publicly indexed social media pages. Early iterations of InfoScout used a federated approach, however this was discovered to be impractical, with API limitations and social media privacy settings negating the benefits. In practice, modern social media APIs are inherently privacy aware, such that less information is found programmatically than would otherwise be discovered by visiting the profile using a browser. Social media access in InfoScout leverages the Bing search engine, which may be tailored with appropriate queries[7]. Additionally, as was likely the case with Copernic Agent, the maintenance of a large number of APIs, which are likely to change over time, was considered an unnecessary overhead. Screenshots are provided to the user in order to facilitate rapid decision making of irrelevant documents while avoiding technical limitations of other means of directly displaying the document in the application, such as with iframes.

InfoScout facilitates the Open-Ended portion of the investigation, which is the most time consuming element of a case. In doing so, the cost of integrating existing, fixed, resources is mitigated, with the more constrained scope providing a cleaner and more focused solution. Similarly, no assumption is made about the financial position of the user or their subscriptions/access to popular industry resources, such as `192.com`.

[7]Such as searching for John Smith's Google+ profile with the query prefix: site:plus.google.com

Figure 1: User document feedback, documents are suggested for judgement one at a time from the top of the ranking.

3.1 Implementation

InfoScout is designed to be a Web application which can be run from any browser, with core components being hosted on the cloud as part of a distributed service. The core system is the OSINT API, which is both used to coordinate the various services and operations, as well as serve as the Web server which the user connects to. The API is implemented as a *Node JS* application, built using the *Express* framework. Re-ranking and filtering of Bing results is achieved by building an intermediate, local, index of Bing results, which makes use of the *ElasticSearch* platform. A consumer/provider pipeline in the OSINT API processes individual Bing result URLs using the *Alchemy Language* API[8], which allows the service to scale with large volumes of results. The parsed content of the documents, as well as their entities and most discriminative terms (within-document, ranked by their TFIDF) are stored in separate fields in the index. These fields facilitate later re-ranking and querying. Screenshots of the remote pages are captured using *Screenshotlayer*[9], which also stores the resulting images. Case information is stored using the *IBM's Compose MongoDB* service.

Document re-ranking is achieved by building ranking queries for submission to the ElasticSearch index. These ranking queries take the form of ElasticSearch Boosting Queries, which are comprised of a list of positive and negative document terms and entities. Modules within the OSINT API build this query in stages from the list of judged documents on the local index. The first stage aggregates scores for all terms and entities in the index for judged documents, with relative weights being calculated by within-document relevance, as determined by the Alchemy API. The second stage dynamically bins terms and entities by score, allowing for appropriate boosts to be applied to each bin. The final bins are then used to construct the re-ranking Boosting Query which is submitted to the ElasticSearch index for an updated document ranking. The result is that the most discriminative terms and entities from judged documents are used to weight

[8]http://www.alchemyapi.com/products/alchemylanguage
[9]https://screenshotlayer.com/

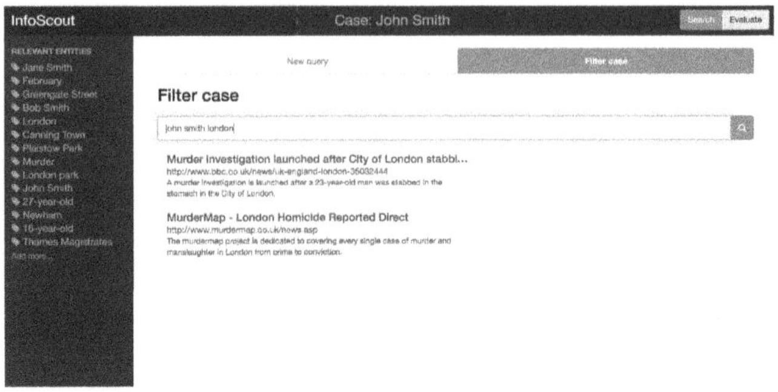

Figure 2: Filtering of search results by applying ad-hoc filters allows the user to focus the search within retrieved documents.

new documents for the investigator, facilitating discovery of pertinent information. While both terms and entities are present in the re-ranking query, the boost weightings are biased towards entities as these are fundamental to this kind of search. Similarly, filtering of results is achieved by building Bool(ean) Queries for the ElasticSearch index, making use of the extracted entities and document content.

4. SUMMARY AND FUTURE WORK

We have presented InfoScout, which is intended to reduce the time spent searching public resources for subject-centric information. The interface is minimalistic and the inner workings are transparent to the user, mitigating requirements for training and search expertise. Users can direct their search while reducing the number of irrelevant documents that they encounter as they pursue a particular subject or critical piece of information.

While this system is essentially a proof of concept, with enough resources it would be possible to build a new entity centric index in the same manner as the Bing search engine. This would mitigate the need for a secondary index and mid-investigation page fetching, while providing more flexibility. Additionally, more advanced relevance feedback and re-ranking methods could be employed, such as by maintaining language models for relevant/irrelevant documents. However, this would require further research into domain specific re-ranking in order to determine what is most effective in Web based, entity centric, environment.

Additional features to be implemented will further improve the time saving potential of the application by providing more intelligence via extended automatic document processing. Information extraction techniques and clustering can be utilised to generate entity profiles and associated documents, allowing the user to further focus their search on a particular namesake. Entity co-citation and query expansion using known name variants would further bolster the person disambiguation process. Case management features will also be expanded to allow for entity and document relationship handling, with a graph based visualisation of the investigation.

While Bing is a powerful search engine, the user must still have some degree of acquaintance with its advanced operators in order to be maximally effective. To this end, it may be useful to facilitate advanced query building for the user by automatically populating site and boolean operators based on user input.

Finally, an evaluation of the system should be conducted in order to quantify its effectiveness. This could be broken into two parts: i) An evaluation of effectiveness of the re-ranking and user feedback, which would require the generation of an appropriate ground truth corpus; ii) A usability and task-based assessment conducted with industry professionals. The former would allow offline tweaking and optimisation of the underlying mechanics, while the latter would investigate the appropriateness of the interface design and determine the real world impact on the time/effort investment of the investigator.

5. REFERENCES

[1] E. J. Appel. *Internet Searches for Vetting, Investigations, and Open-source Intelligence.* Taylor and Francis Group, 2011.

[2] S. Attfield and A. Blandford. Improving the cost structure of sensemaking tasks: Analysing user concepts to inform information system design. In *Proc. of INTERACT '09*, page 532–545, 2009.

[3] Department of Homeland Security. DHS terrorist use of social networking facebook case study | public intelligence, 2010.

[4] J. Grasz. Number of Employers Passing on Applicants Due to Social Media Posts Continues to Rise, According to New CareerBuilder Survey - CareerBuilder, June 2014.

[5] R. Guha and A. Garg. Disambiguating people in search. In *Proc. of the 13th World Wide Web Conference,*, 2004.

[6] H. Joho, L. A. Azzopardi, and W. Vanderbauwhede. A survey of patent users: An analysis of tasks, behavior, search functionality and system requirements. In *Proc. of IIix '10*, page 13–24, 2010.

[7] Lexis Nexis. Social Media Use in Law Enforcement: Crime prevention and investigative activities continue to drive usage., Nov. 2014.

[8] S. McKeown, D. Maxwell, L. Azzopardi, and W. B. Glisson. Investigating people: A qualitative analysis of the search behaviours of open-source intelligence analysts. In *Proceedings of the 5th Information Interaction in Context Symposium*, IIiX '14, pages 175–184, New York, NY, USA, 2014. ACM.

[9] NATO. NATO open source intelligence handbook, 2001.

[10] A. Spink, B. J. Jansen, and J. Pedersen. Searching for people on web search engines. *Journal of Documentation*, 60(3):266–278, 2004.

[11] L. Šubelj, Š. Furlan, and M. Bajec. An expert system for detecting automobile insurance fraud using social network analysis. *Expert Syst. Appl.*, 38(1):1039–1052, Jan. 2011.

InLook: Revisiting Email Search Experience

Pranav Ramarao, Suresh Iyengar, Pushkar Chitnis*, Raghavendra Udupa, B.Ashok
Microsoft Research, India
Bangalore, India
{t-prrama,supartha,pushkarc,raghavu,bash}@microsoft.com

ABSTRACT

Emails continue to remain the most important and widely used mode of online communication despite having its origins in the middle of last century and being threatened by a variety of online communication innovations. While several studies have predicted the continuous growth of volume of email communication, there is little innovation on improving the search in emails, an imperative part of the user experience. In this work, we present a lightweight email application codenamed **InLook**, that intends to provide a productive search experience.

Keywords

Email, search, productivity

1. INTRODUCTION

Email is the oldest modes of online communication and is used by more than 2.5 billion users today. Studies have predicted its continuous growth over the next few years [1]. Email **search** is an integral part of the user's experience. Studies also report that users search their mail data frequently and spend significant amount of time searching and re-searching [15].

Despite being an important activity, Email Search has not seen significant innovation in comparison to, say, Web Search. Web Search has evolved over the past decade from ten blue links to a more rich and task-oriented experience. Though email search has similar objectives to Web Search, there are some important distinctions:

- *Personalized*: Email Search is more personalized in nature as compared to web search.
- *Strong Intent*: As the document collection against which the user is querying is the user's own mail data, search queries generally have a strong intent.

*Currently working at Microsoft Research, Redmond, WA, USA

SIGIR '16, July 17-21, 2016, Pisa, Italy
© 2016 ACM. ISBN 978-1-4503-4069-4/16/07...$15.00
DOI: http://dx.doi.org/10.1145/2911451.2911458

- *Privacy Concerns*: As mail data is mostly private, so are queries that users issue against that data. Users are generally reluctant to share any data that is needed to build richer search experiences.
- *Absence of query logs*: One major impediment to email search is the absence of large volumes of query logs.

In this work, we present InLook, a light-weight email search tool, which is an amalgamation of different bodies of research related to email search. The underlying objective is to enhance the search experience of Email users.

The rest of the paper is structured as follows: Section 2 summarizes the various related work in the area of email search. Sections 3.1 through 3.3 show the varied features in InLook search experience. Section 4 describes the ranking algorithm used in InLook. We describe InLook application design in Section 5. Section 6 reports preliminary results of our user study of InLook. Section 7 briefly compares InLook with other email applications.

2. RELATED WORK

Email search can be tedious and frustrating experience, especially for older mails [13]. Researchers have tried various approaches to alleviate the problems related to email search. These can be broadly bucketed into following categories:

Organizing emails: Contrary to the popular belief, organizing emails into multiple folders might offer little help in search [20]. An alternative approach tries to organize emails into fewer categories like Social, Travel and Promotions [14] [3].

Email actions: Aberdeen *et al* [4] [8] predict the importance of an email based on the probability that it will be acted upon. A recent work by Dotan Castro *et al* [12] tries to predict actions on emails based on past user behavior. The actions considered in this work are: read, reply, delete and delete-without-read.

Order by relevance: To the best of our knowledge, there are only a handful of published research works in the area of email relevance. AbdelRahman *et al* [7] employ different features like email content, subject and sender to assign a score to an email. Ogilvie and Callan [18] use a language model based approach to rank emails. A recent work by Carmel *et al* [11] discuss the area of email relevance in great detail. The authors employ a wide range of features to rank emails, in a

Figure 1: Guided Search: Spell-Correct, Fuzzy person search, Auto-complete

learning to rank framework. The features include text similarity, folder information, attachments and sender behavior. Popular email applications like Google Inbox [4] and Thunderbird [6] display search results by relevance. But, these offerings have not divulged any related algorithmic details.

Other research areas in the context of emails search include generating suggestions [9] and spell-corrections [10] in the absence of query logs.

3. INLOOK SEARCH EXPERIENCE

This section details the email search experience offered by InLook. Some of the ideas below have been tried out before; InLook stitches them together in one application.

3.1 Guided search in InLook

One of the main contributors to the success of Web Search is guided search. In InLook we provide guided search for email users by means of the following search features:

1. *Auto-Completion and Spelling correction*: We employ the algorithm similar to the one described in [10] for auto-completion and spelling correction of both contacts and general search queries. Some of the features used in this algorithm to the rank the candidates are:
    - SubjectMatch: The maximum of fraction of candidate tokens appearing in any single subject line.
    - ContactMatch : The fraction of tokens in candidate which are present in at least one user contact.
    - Language Model Feature: Bigram language model score of the candidate. The raw bigram counts are discounted using Kneser-Ney technique.
2. *Fuzzy Search of People names*: We employ hashing-based people search algorithms developed in [17][19]. This approach learns hash functions that map similar names to similar binary code words in a language independent space. For example, "Chifa" $\sim$ "Qifa", "Lakshmi" $\sim$ "Laxmi", "Posansky" $\sim$ "Poznansky".

Figure 1 shows guided search instances in InLook.

3.2 InLook intent pane

In InLook, we present a mix of relevance and recency results for search queries. Showing results with either of the sort orders solely might not suffice for all queries. InLook introduces a notion of "Intent pane" which displays the best three emails based on relevance for a particular query. Rest of the mails in the result are shown in a traditional date order, we call this as the "Recency pane". Intent pane can be thought of as analogous to an "entity card" in Web Search. Section 4 describes the ranking model used. Additionally, this pane is not restricted to email results. It can also show relevant attachments, contact cards or links. Figure 2 shows Intent pane in action in InLook.

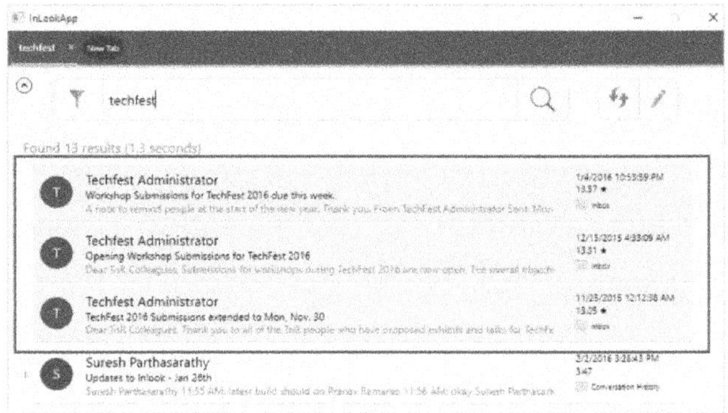

Figure 2: Intent Pane

3.3 Tabbed searching and commands

We take inspiration from web browsers and introduce the notion of tabs in InLook. This allows users to make multiple searches at the same time. We also provide a mechanism to pin a query to a tab. This becomes like an active channel or a standing query and the tab gets refreshed for this query periodically. Also, one can tear and dock tabs just like browsers and put them in multiple workspaces. This provides a very intuitive notion of segregating and searching through emails. Figure 3 shows InLook tabs in action. We plan to perform a detailed study on usage of tabs in the context of email search.

We introduce a notion of command box in InLook with an objective of faster task completion. The functionality of search box is over-ridden so that it morphs into a powerful command box. Users can think of this to be a shell on top of their email data. All these commands are powered by autocomplete to make it very easy to use. Some of the commands that can be executed are "*#compose* @person mailbody", "*#chat* @person" and "*#template* parameters".

Figure 3: Tabbed searches

4. RANKING OF EMAILS

Emails in the intent pane are ordered by relevance. Collecting training data for training email ranking models is a difficult task. It is tedious for a user to mark relevant mails for each query. Instead, we rely on a user's click log to give us partial relevance judgments and use it for ranking [16]. Also, it is much more plausible to infer that a particular mail is better than the other, instead of an absolute judgement. The learning to rank algorithm we discuss below is similar to the ranking discussed in [11].

For instance, let's say a user clicks on mails 1, 3 and 5. Given that the mail snippets are sufficiently informative, this gives some indication of the user's preferences. In this case, we may infer that the email at position 5 is more relevant than mails at positions 2 and 4. Likewise, we may infer that mail at position 3 is more relevant than the mail at position 2. We call such pairs of mails as discordant pairs, represented as $mail_j <_r mail_i$, which implies $mail_i$ is more relevant to user than $mail_j$. The sequence of clicks doesn't impose any ordering on mails 1, 3 and 5. We aggregate click logs from all users and train our ranking model using this data. For a given user, the logs consist of set of queries and for each query, the click sequence of mails. We log only the feature values as the mails can contain confidential information. We use a model based on logistic regression for our training. The objective function looks like:

$$Obj = min\left(\lambda * \frac{|w|^2}{2} + \frac{1}{n} * \sum_{(i,j)} Loss(mail_i, mail_j)\right) \quad (1)$$

where n is the number of discordant mail pairs (i, j) and $mail_i$ and $mail_j$ are the corresponding mails. w represents the weight vector we want to learn. This loss equation consists of a regularizer and sums up the loss over all the discordant pairs. $Loss(mail_i, mail_j)$ can be written as

$$\frac{1}{1 + exp(-(s_i - s_j))} \quad (2)$$

The score for i^{th} mail s_i is $\sum w_i * f_i$ where f_i is the feature value and w_i is the weight we want to learn. The optimal weights for the above optimization problem can be estimated using an algorithm like LBFGS [5]. Table 1 lists some of the features we use in ranking.

The above ranking model which we refer to as the global model is trained on click logs of multiple users. As the user interacts with the system, we build a local ranking model which makes it more personalized.

5. INLOOK DESIGN

InLook [1] is engineered as a C# WPF desktop application using a MVC framework. Figure 5 depicts the design of InLook. All the searches get routed by the mail manager to the appropriate stores. Caches are built-in at each stores to speed-up the retrieval. The index is built using Lucene.Net. Our design allows pluggable algorithms for Autocomplete, Spell correct and Ranking.

In addition to providing a fast and productive email experience, InLook also provides a test bed for new algorithms and experiences related to emails. InLook's modular design helps us experiment with other algorithms ranging from subject line auto-completion to varied UX experiences using the same code base. InLook provides us with an easy way to conduct user studies with emails and get their feedback.

[1] InLook can be downloaded from http://aka.ms/InLookApp

Figure 4: InLook Design

6. PRELIMINARY RESULTS

We instrument InLook and log various metrics like query response time, auto-complete usage and click positions. These metrics were collected from 50 users over a period of one month.

Average response time	**792 ms**
Auto-complete benefit (% key strokes saved)	**50.8%**
Intent pane had one mail $\notin$ recency pane	**65%**
Clicks on mail in intent pane $\notin$ recency pane	**58%**

While these numbers are encouraging, the scale of experiment is small. We plan to dogfood with a larger audience. We are exploring different UX layouts to remove any unconditional click bias.

7. COMPARISON WITH OTHER APPLICATIONS

We compare InLook with following commercial offerings: Gmail [2], Inbox by Google [4] and Thunderbird by Mozilla [6]. None of these provide all the features we described in one place.

Gmail provides guided search but does not provide Fuzzy name search and relevance results. Google Inbox provides relevance pane (though not for all queries) but provides minimal guided search. Thunderbird provides relevance results and minimal guided search. Thunderbird client makes uses

Feature Name	Feature Description
Body-Phrase-Match	Tokens (from Query) matched a phrase in the body of a mail
Subject-Phrase-Match	Tokens matched a phrase in the subject of a mail
URL-Match	Token matched a link in a mail
Filename-Prefix	Token matched prefix of a file name in an attachment
MailFrom-Match	Token matched (includes Fuzzy) a contact in "From" field of a mail
MailTo-Normalized	Token matched (includes Fuzzy) a contact in "To" field of a mail, normalized w.r.t. #recipients
Content-Match	Token matched a word in one of the attachments of a mail
Mail-Freshness	Decay feature which penalizes older mails

Table 1: Some of the features used in ranking

of tabs to display search results and emails. But, the algorithms employed in these offerings are not disclosed publicly making it hard to compare with quantitatively.

8. CONCLUSION

In this work, we presented InLook: a lightweight and productive email search experience. We have incorporated varied facets of email search into one single application. Specifically, we have incorporated guided search and have introduced an Intent pane for showing decorated/relevant results. Initial results suggest that a mix of relevant and time ordered mails is a good way to show search results. As future work, we plan to release InLook to a broader audience, to understand user behavior in detail. Exploring alternate UI layouts for displaying relevant and recent mails is an interesting future direction we want to pursue.

9. ACKNOWLEDGMENTS

We thank all our colleagues who helped dogfood InLook and gave us value feedback.

10. REFERENCES

[1] Email statistics. http://www.radicati.com/wp/wp-content/uploads/2015/02/Email-Statistics-Report-2015-2019-Executive-Summary.pdf.

[2] Gmail. https://mail.google.com.

[3] Gmail tabs. https://support.google.com/mail/answer/3055016?hl=en.

[4] Google's inbox. https://en.wikipedia.org/wiki/Inbox_by_Gmail.

[5] Lbfgs. https://en.wikipedia.org/wiki/Limited-memory_BFGS.

[6] Thunderbird. https://www.mozilla.org/en-US/thunderbird/.

[7] Samir AbdelRahman, Basma Hassan, and Reem Bahgat. A new email retrieval ranking approach. *International Journal of Computer Science and Information Technology*, 2010.

[8] Douglas Aberdeen, Ondrej Pacovsky, and Andrew Slater. The learning behind gmail priority inbox. In *in NIPS 2010 Workshop on Learning on Cores, Clusters and Clouds*, 2010.

[9] Sumit Bhatia, Debapriyo Majumdar, and Prasenjit Mitra. Query suggestions in the absence of query logs. In *SIGIR 2011, Beijing, China.*

[10] Abhijit Bhole and Raghavendra Udupa. On correcting misspelled queries in email search. In *AAAI, 2015, Austin, Texas, USA.*

[11] David Carmel, Guy Halawi, Liane Lewin-Eytan, Yoelle Maarek, and Ariel Raviv. Rank by time or by relevance?: Revisiting email search. In *CIKM 2015, Melbourne, VIC, Australia.*

[12] Dotan Di Castro, Zohar Shay Karnin, Liane Lewin-Eytan, and Yoelle Maarek. You've got mail, and here is what you could do with it!: Analyzing and predicting actions on email messages. In *WSDM, San Francisco, CA, USA, February 22-25, 2016.*

[13] David Elsweiler, Morgan Harvey, and Martin Hacker. Understanding re-finding behavior in naturalistic email interaction logs. In *SIGIR 2011, Beijing, China.*

[14] Mihajlo Grbovic, Guy Halawi, Zohar Shay Karnin, and Yoelle Maarek. How many folders do you really need?: Classifying email into a handful of categories. In *CIKM 2014, Shanghai, China.*

[15] Morgan Harvey and David Elsweiler. Exploring query patterns in email search. In *(ECIR), Barcelona, Spain, April 1-5, 2012.*

[16] Thorsten Joachims. Optimizing search engines using clickthrough data. In *ACM SIGKDD, 2002, Edmonton, Alberta, Canada.*

[17] Shaishav Kumar and Raghavendra Udupa. Multilingual people search. In *SIGIR 2010, Geneva, Switzerland.*

[18] Paul Ogilvie and Jamie Callan. Experiments with language models for known-item finding of e-mail messages. In *TREC 2005, Gaithersburg, Maryland, USA*, 2005.

[19] Raghavendra Udupa and Shaishav Kumar. Hashing-based approaches to spelling correction of personal names. In *EMNLP 2010, MIT Stata Center, Massachusetts, USA, A meeting of SIGDAT, a Special Interest Group of the ACL.*

[20] Steve Whittaker, Tara Matthews, Julian A. Cerruti, Hernan Badenes, and John C. Tang. Am I wasting my time organizing email?: a study of email refinding. In *CHI 2011, Vancouver, BC, Canada.*

Interacting with Financial Data using Natural Language

Vassilis Plachouras[1], Charese Smiley[2], Hiroko Bretz[2], Ola Taylor[1], Jochen L. Leidner[1], Dezhao Song[2], Frank Schilder[2]

[1] Thomson Reuters, Research & Development
1 Mark Square
London, EC2A 4EG, UK

[2] Thomson Reuters, Research & Development
610 Opperman Drive
Eagan, MN 55123, USA

firstname.lastname@thomsonreuters.com

ABSTRACT

Financial and economic data are typically available in the form of tables and comprise mostly of monetary amounts, numeric and other domain-specific fields. They can be very hard to search and they are often made available out of context, or in forms which cannot be integrated with systems where text is required, such as voice-enabled devices.

This work presents a novel system that enables both experts in the finance domain and non-expert users to search financial data with both keyword and natural language queries. Our system answers the queries with an automatically generated textual description using Natural Language Generation (NLG). The answers are further enriched with derived information, not explicitly asked in the user query, to provide the context of the answer. The system is designed to be flexible in order to accommodate new use cases without significant development effort, thus allowing fast integration of new datasets.

CCS Concepts

•Computing methodologies → Natural language generation; •Information systems → *Query intent;*

1. INTRODUCTION

Financial data, such as macro-economic indicator time series for countries, information about mergers and acquisition (M&A) deals between companies, or stock price time series, is typically stored in relational databases, requiring domain expertise to search and retrieve. For example, a financial analyst who is familiar with a particular database will be able to locate the information he or she is seeking quickly. However, for users who lack the necessary familiarity with the databases, it may be difficult and time-consuming to obtain the information they are looking for.

The retrieval of specific data points (e.g., India GDP 2010) may be useful for responding to a very specific information need. However, it will not present the wider picture and possibly ignore interesting wider trends or correlations. Providing a more comprehensive answer to the information seeker will draw in further dimensions that may easily be ignored if just a number is returned.

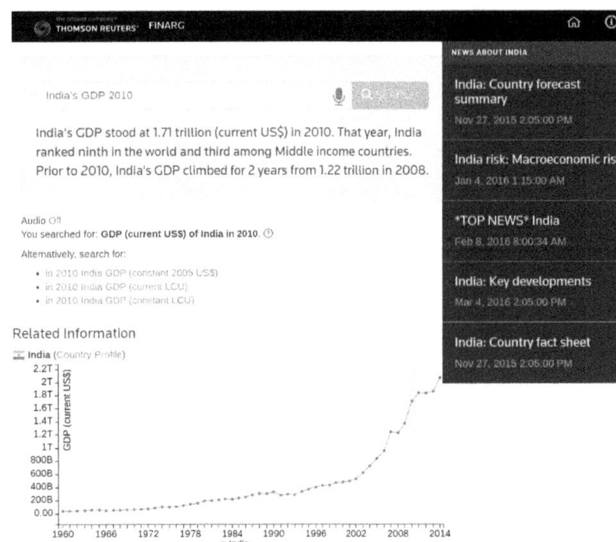

Figure 1: Screenshot of the system.

In this work, we introduce a system that enables financial domain experts and non-expert users to search financial data with natural language queries and uses Natural Language Generation (NLG) to produce human-readable answers from the data. The answers are automatically generated from the retrieved data and are put in context by performing comparisons with past data to identify trends and interesting data points. For the query "India's GDP 2010", the system retrieves the record that provides the GDP of India in 2010 and then produces the answer shown in Figure 1. For the query "India's GDP versus CO2 emissions 2000-2009", the system calculates the correlation between the two indicators and generates the sentence "For 2000-2009, CO2 emissions had a very strong correlation with GDP (0.97)."

The method was designed to be robust and avoid some of the issues that grammar-based Natural Language Interface (NLI) systems face, such as developing grammars for new domains. Furthermore, beyond just processing terse keyword-based queries the method is capable of handling

SIGIR '16, July 17-21, 2016, Pisa, Italy

© 2016 ACM. ISBN 978-1-4503-4069-4/16/07...$15.00

DOI: http://dx.doi.org/10.1145/2911451.2911457

many types of well-formed English questions like "China's CO2 emissions between 2009 and 2013" or "What is the GDP of India in 2010?" without complex linguistic processing. In addition, we have designed the system with the aim to be flexible and easily adaptable to different use cases, ranging from retrieving specific points from a time series of financial data to ranking entities or computing correlations, by supplying different configurations to the system. The output of the system has been integrated in Thomson Reuters Eikon, a platform for financial analysis.

The automatically generated textual description of answers enables the system to be used in desktop or smaller devices, where expressing the answer in a textual form can provide a succinct summary of multiple diagrams and charts, or in settings where text is required (e.g., in speech-enabled devices, where the answer can be spoken back to the user). To the best of our knowledge, this is the first system combining natural language search and NLG for financial data.

2. RELATED WORK

Keyword-Based Search Systems for Databases. The *BANKS* system [1] enables keyword search and navigation in structured and semi-structured datasets. The system performs an in-memory graph search and ranks answers by relevance and the a priori "prestige", inspired by PageRank. The *FRISK* system [15] uses a dynamic programming-based method for query segmentation and presents the possible interpretations so that users can select the one that is closest to the original intention. *Discover* [7] uses a greedy execution plan over a graph structure to provide efficient search over relational data without knowledge of the schema. The *Spark* system [12] assembles matching tuples from different tables together according to relationships such that the tuples are collectively relevant. *Keymantic* [2] and *Keyword++* [5] also belong to this family of systems.

Natural Language Interfaces to Databases (NLI). NLI systems convert user queries to the query language used by the underlying database. For example, both *DBSemSXplorer* [3] and *DEANNA* [21] systems translate a user query into a SPARQL query which is then processed by a triple store. *TR Discover* [19] is a general-purpose and domain-adaptable NLI for querying linked data. It uses a feature-based grammar to parse a natural language question into its first order predicate logic representation (FOL). The FOL of a question is further transformed into a SPARQL or SQL query to retrieve answers from a knowledge graph.

Question Answering Systems. Our system also relates to question answering, for which several systems have been produced, for example [8][22][10], the top-performing system entries [13][6][18] at the final (2007) open-domain QA factoid track of TREC, or IBM's *Watson* [4].

Natural Language Generation (NLG). Natural Language Generation has a long tradition in natural language processing [16]. More recently, statistical approaches where the text generation is informed by statistical properties of training corpora have been suggested [9].

Our system is different from keyword-based search systems for databases in the sense that we decouple the search process from a specific database technology by using a search engine instead. Compared to NLI systems, we avoid the expensive query execution on databases or knowledge graphs, possibly involving joins or graph traversals. Perhaps the systems that most closely resembles the present work are

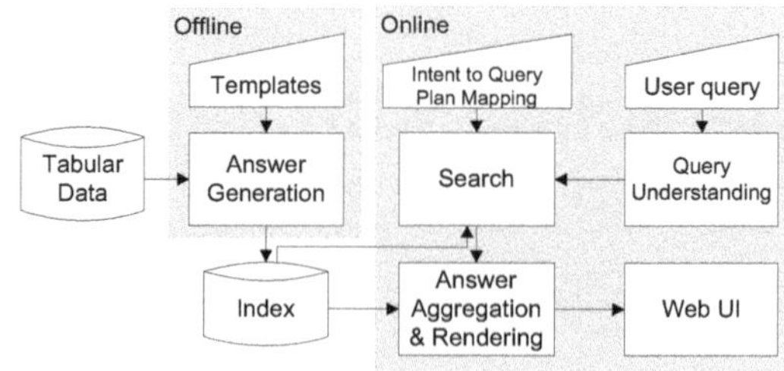

Figure 2: System architecture.

EKSO [20] which introduces the concept of offline indexing and *E-Mesh* [11], which also uses offline-generation to make answer retrieval robust in the light of linguistic variability. However, our system provides textual descriptions of the answers combined with useful context information, which has not been explicitly asked in user queries. *Mathematica*'s producer Wolfram Inc. created *WolframAlpha*[1], a commercial natural language search system over structured data, predominantly for the science and engineering domains. The technical details of this system have not been disclosed in any peer-reviewed publications to date. IBM Watson Analytics is an online platform that analyzes structured datasets to answer questions. Google also retrieves indicator values for a given country, macro-economic indicator and year. However, existing services such as WolframAlpha, IBM Watson Analytics and Google do not generate a textual description of the answers.

3. SYSTEM ARCHITECTURE

The architecture of the system is shown in Figure 2. At the preprocessing stage, the Answer Generation module transforms the data into virtual documents that can be indexed by a search engine, using parametric templates. The virtual documents, which represent the answers that the system returns, are indexed using Elasticsearch[2]. At query time, the Query Understanding module analyzes a user query and identifies entities that are relevant to the indexed data. From the identified entities, the module generates a ranked list of query intents, where each intent represents a group of entities in the query. The Search module iterates over the ranked list of intents and identifies the top-ranked intent that can be mapped to a predefined set of query plans. If such an intent is found, the query plan is populated with entities from the intent and one or more queries are sent to the underlying search engine. Next, the results are passed to the Answer Aggregation and Rendering module, which is responsible for generating a high quality human-readable description of the results, providing both an overview and the context of the result, as shown in Figure 1.

3.1 Template-based Answer Generation

The input for the Answer Generation module comprises the data and a set of templates, which transform the data into virtual documents that will be indexed by the search engine. A template consists of: 1) the type of the document, 2) the source of the data, either in the form of a path on disk or a SQL query that returns data from a database, and a mapping of the columns to field names in the index,

[1]http://www.wolframalpha.com/
[2]https://elastic.co

3) a document identifier, and 4) the caption, which is an array of constant strings and data values. When the Answer Generation module applies a template to a dataset, a virtual document is generated for each database record, comprising the named fields from the template, the document identifier and the caption field.

Since the templates control the format and data of the documents, the design of a template can be guided by the application requirements. For example, when developing an application about time-series of financial macro-economic indicators, where users can query for year ranges, two different design choices may be to create a separate virtual document per time-series point, or to aggregate k-year ranges of time-series points and present to the users precomputed results about trends and changes. In this work, we have precomputed the values for all 5 and 10 year intervals between 1960 and 2015 to speed up online query processing.

3.2 Query Understanding

Queries in financial search applications tend to be short and contain abbreviations or codes. While we can directly use the caption field of virtual documents to match against user queries, we have built a Query Understanding module that can extract entities relevant to the application in order to perform structured search more effectively. The query understanding module processes a query as follows.

Entity tagging. First, we identify entities in the query string. The type of entities depend on the application requirements. In the case of macro-economic indicators, we identify countries (e.g., US or United States), regions (e.g., South Asia), groups of countries (e.g., OECD), macro-economic indicators and their abbreviations (e.g., Gross national income, or GNI). In the case of merger and acquisition deals, we also identify companies, names of financial advisors such as investment banks, dates, industry sectors. We tag entities using a regular expression tagger, a trie-based tagger and a scalable n-gram tagger [14].

Intent generation and ranking. Next, from the set of all identified entities, we generate sets of non-overlapping entities, which we call intents. An intent I is a set of entities. For each intent I, we first apply a set of regular expressions to identify entities which have been tagged wrongly and remove them. In our setting, tagging errors occur where a token could be a 2-letter country code or not (e.g., the country code *IN* or the preposition *in*).

We also disambiguate entities when the presence of one entity can be used to disambiguate the tagged entities for another sequence of tokens. For example, there is more than one indicator for gross domestic product (GDP), which is expressed in different units, such as "current US$", or "constant 2005 US$". We consider the indicator units to be a distinct entity type and use them to disambiguate indicator entities tagged in queries.

Next, we compute a score $s(I) = \frac{\sum_{e \in I} s(e)}{(1+c)|I|}$, where $s(e)$ is a score associated with entity e adjusted by the prevalence of each identified entity, a measure, based on web counts, of how likely is one definition of an entity over another one with the same surface form, $|I|$ is the number of entities in I and c is the number of tokens not covered by any of the entities in I. The role of $(1 + c)$ and $|I|$ in the denominator is to decrease the score of intents which consist of many entities with poor coverage of the query. The output of the query understanding module is a ranked list of intents.

3.3 Search

The Search module receives as input the user query and the ranked list of intents and returns an answer obtained by querying the virtual document index. The first step in this process includes the mapping of intents to query plans. A query plan specifies the computational steps involved in answering the query and corresponds to a composition of elementary actions, such as searching, filtering results according to a specified condition, ranking results according to the values of a given field, aggregating values to compute the value of a function. Each query plan has one or more search steps, where a query is sent to the underlying search engine. The obtained results are compared to the user query, to identify if there is no or a partial match with the query.

The mapping of an intent I to a query plan, similar to a rule-based classifier, is performed by checking whether the entities in I are compatible with the entities required for a query plan. If no interval entity is provided, then the most recent result is returned. There is also a query plan which performs plain text search on the caption field of the virtual documents in the index in case that the user query cannot be mapped to a query plan. In this way, our system can robustly retrieve financial data exploiting either the data structure or their textual representation.

3.4 Answer Aggregation and Rendering

The Answer Aggregation and Rendering module generates human readable descriptions of the answers. The module accepts the output of the Search module as input. It then uses the intent chosen by the Query Understanding module to select from the template bank an appropriate set of templates for text generation, and populates the templates with the accompanying data. In this work, we cover several use cases for macro-economic indicators, such as country-year-indicator, country-multi-year-indicator, region-year-indicator, and group-year-indicator, as well as for M&A deals: company-company-deal, country-sector-year-deals, sector-year-deals, country-year-deals. Each use case relies on a separate template bank which contains multiple rephrasings for each sentence plan. Hence, the Answer Aggregation and Rendering module can generate variations of the same answer by selecting different templates. Three example templates are shown below.

- in [**year**], [**country**] [**indicator**] stand at [**amount**].
- [**country**] finish [**year**] with a [**indicator**] of [**amount**].
- [**country**] [**indicator**] end [**year**] at [**amount**].

The templates were generated semi-automatically from the Reuters News Archive (RNA), a large news corpus containing 14 million articles. We tag named entities (e.g., *countries, dates*), augmented with custom entities (e.g., economic indicators such as *GDP*) using variants derived from the RNA. Candidate sentences from the corpus not containing all pieces of information needed for the generation are discarded. Remaining sentences containing additional irrelevant information are then manually removed or altered.

Additional variation is achieved through verb selection at the lexical level. We use the RNA to extract verb choice patterns and found that verbs associated with smaller percentage changes (*inch, ease*) can be distinguished from those associated with larger changes (*skyrocket,plummet*). This stands in contrast to previous work (cf. [17]) which found verb choice to be largely idiosyncratic when analyzing a much smaller data sample. In the template example below, **verb_of_motion** is selected statistically based on the rate of change.

- [**country**] [**indicator**] for [**year**] averaged [**amount**] [**verb_of_motion**] [**percentage_change**] from [**from_value** in [**year_from**] to [**to_value**] in[**year_to**].

4. APPLICATIONS

We have applied our system to two datasets. The first dataset consists of macro-economic indicator data from the World Bank[3]. There are 1,319 indicators with a time frame from 1960 to 2015. For the macro-economic indicator dataset, the system processes queries requesting the indicator values for a specific country and year or range of years, the top ranked country according to an indicator for a region or group of countries (e.g., OECD), as well as the correlation between the indicator values for a given country. To this end, we created 2 answer generation and 36 answer rendering templates. The second dataset comprises more than 200K records about company M&A deals sampled from a proprietary database. For the M&A dataset, the system processes queries comprising company names, as well as queries for deals in a country, an industry sector, or their combinations for a given year, for which we prepared 4 answer generation and 15 answer rendering templates.

5. CONCLUSIONS

In this work, we have introduced a system that enables users to search financial data robustly using both keyword and natural language queries, and returns the answer in the form of an automatically generated textual description, enriched with additional derived information about the context of the answer. The textual description of the answers enables us to use the system both in desktop or smaller devices, including speech-enabled devices, where text may be the only way to deliver the answer. Moreover, the system was designed to be flexible and domain-adaptable, by using a template-based answer generation engine to convert data to virtual documents, which are indexed by a search engine, and a configurable mapping of user intents to query plans.

Acknowledgments

We thank Albert Lojko, Alex Tyrell, Sidd Shenoy, Rohit Mittal and Jessica Tran from Thomson Reuters F&R, and Khalid Al-Kofahi from Thomson Reuters R&D for their support and discussions. This work received financial support by Thomson Reuters Global Resources.

6. REFERENCES

[1] B. Aditya, Gaurav Bhalotia, Soumen Chakrabarti, Arvind Hulgeri, Charuta Nakhe, Parag, and S. Sudarshan. BANKS: Browsing and keyword searching in relational databases. VLDB '02, pages 1083–1086, 2002.

[2] Sonia Bergamaschi, Elton Domnori, Francesco Guerra, Mirko Orsini, Raquel Trillo Lado, and Yannis Velegrakis. Keymantic: Semantic keyword-based searching in data integration systems. *Proc. VLDB Endow.*, 3(1-2):1637–1640, 2010.

[3] Sina Fakhraee and Farshad Fotouhi. DBSemSXplorer: Semantic-based keyword search system over relational databases for knowledge discovery. KEYS '12, pages 54–62, 2012.

[4] David Ferrucci, Eric Brown, Jennifer Chu-Carroll, James Fan, David Gondek, Aditya A. Kalyanpur, Adam Lally, J. William Murdock, Eric Nyberg, John Prager, Nico Schlaefer, and Chris Welty. Building Watson: An overview of the DeepQA project. *AI Magazine*, 31(3):59–79, 2010.

[5] Venkatesh Ganti, Yeye He, and Dong Xin. Keyword++: A framework to improve keyword search over entity databases. *Proc. VLDB Endow.*, 3(1-2):711–722, 2010.

[6] Andrew Hickl, Kirk Roberts, Bryan Rink, Jeremy Bensley, Tobias Jungen, Ying Shi, and John Williams. Question answering with LCC's CHAUCER-2 at TREC 2007. TREC '07, 2007.

[7] Vagelis Hristidis and Yannis Papakonstantinou. DISCOVER: Keyword search in relational databases. VLDB '02, pages 670–681. Morgan Kaufmann, 2002.

[8] Boris Katz, Gary C. Borchardt, and Sue Felshin. Natural language annotations for question answering. FLAIRS '06, pages 303–306, 2006.

[9] Ravi Kondadadi, Blake Howald, and Frank Schilder. A statistical nlg framework for aggregated planning and realization. ACL '13, pages 1406–1415, 2013.

[10] Jochen L. Leidner, Johan Bos, Tiphaine Dalmas, James R. Curran, Stephen Clark, Colin J. Bannard, Mark Steedman, and Bonnie Webber. The QED open-domain answer retrieval system for TREC 2003. TREC '03, pages 595–599, 2003.

[11] Jochen L. Leidner and Darya Kamkova. Making structured data searchable via natural language generation – with an application to ESG data. FQAS '13, pages 495–506, 2013.

[12] Y. Luo, W. Wang, and X. Lin. Spark: A keyword search engine on relational databases. ICDE '08, pages 1552–1555, 2008.

[13] Dan Moldovan, Christine Clark, and Mitchell Bowden. Lymba's PowerAnswer 4 in TREC 2007. TREC '07, 2007.

[14] Naoaki Okazaki and Jun'ichi Tsujii. Simple and efficient algorithm for approximate dictionary matching. COLING '10, pages 851–859, 2010.

[15] K.Q. Pu and Xiaohui Yu. FRISK: Keyword query cleaning and processing in action. ICDE '09, pages 1531–1534, 2009.

[16] Ehud Reiter and Robert Dale. *Building Natural Language Generation Systems*. Cambridge University Press, 2000.

[17] Ehud Reiter, Somayajulu Sripada, Jim Hunter, Jin Yu, and Ian Davy. Choosing words in computer-generated weather forecasts. *Artif. Intell.*, 167(1-2):137–169, September 2005.

[18] Dan Shen, Michael Wiegand, Andreas Merkel, Stefan Kazalski, Sabine Hunsicker, Jochen L. Leidner, and Dietrich Klakow. The Alyssa system at TREC QA 2007: Do we need Blog06? TREC '07, 2007.

[19] Dezhao Song, Frank Schilder, Charese Smiley, Chris Brew, Tom Zielund, Hiroko Bretz, Robert Martin, Chris Dale, John Duprey, Tim Miller, and Johanna Harrison. TR Discover: A Natural Language Interface for Querying and Analyzing Interlinked Datasets. ISWC '15, pages 21–37, 2015.

[20] Qi Su and Jennifer Widom. Indexing relational database content offline for efficient keyword-based search. IDEAS '05, pages 297–306, 2005.

[21] Mohamed Yahya, Klaus Berberich, Shady Elbassuoni, Maya Ramanath, Volker Tresp, and Gerhard Weikum. Deep answers for naturally asked questions on the Web of data. WWW '12 Companion, pages 445–449, 2012.

[22] Zhiping Zheng. Question answering using Web news as knowledge base. EACL '03, pages 251–254, 2003.

[3] http://data.worldbank.org/

LONLIES: Estimating Property Values for Long Tail Entities

Mina Farid
University of Waterloo
mina.farid@uwaterloo.ca

Ihab F. Ilyas
University of Waterloo
ilyas@uwaterloo.ca

Steven Euijong Whang
Google Research
swhang@google.com

Cong Yu
Google Research
congyu@google.com

ABSTRACT

Web search engines often retrieve answers for queries about popular entities from a growing knowledge base that is populated by a continuous information extraction process. However, less popular entities are not frequently mentioned on the web and are generally interesting to fewer users; these entities reside on the long tail of information. Traditional knowledge base construction techniques that rely on the high frequency of entity mentions to extract accurate facts about these mentions have little success with entities that have low textual support.

We present LONLIES, a system for estimating property values of long tail entities by leveraging their relationships to head topics and entities. We demonstrate (1) how LONLIES builds communities of entities that are relevant to a long tail entity utilizing a text corpus and a knowledge base; (2) how LONLIES determines which communities to use in the estimation process; (3) how we aggregate estimates from community entities to produce final estimates, and (4) how users interact with LONLIES to provide feedback to improve the final estimation results.

1. INTRODUCTION

Search engines can provide direct answers to queries about popular entities, e.g., capitals of countries and birth dates of celebrities. These answers are obtained from structured knowledge bases that contain information about entities that are frequently queried and are generally interesting to a large number of users. Answering a user query becomes a matter of understanding and representing the user's intent in an meaningful way, then finding the corresponding nodes and edges in the knowledge base graph that contain the answer.

While some knowledge bases extend their content by allowing users to manually add information, many recent approaches [4, 7] have focused on automating the extraction of facts from unstructured data such as text. Most fact extraction techniques rely on the abundance of text and utilize the redundancy of information that is extracted from multiple data sources in order to statistically validate the newly extracted facts. For example, Google's Knowledge Vault [4] extracts fact triples using four different types of extraction systems, and the confidence of a triple increases as more extractors produce the same triple and more unique web sources contain the triple. The knowledge base is then augmented with facts that are extracted with high confidence, growing its size to cover a larger domain of information.

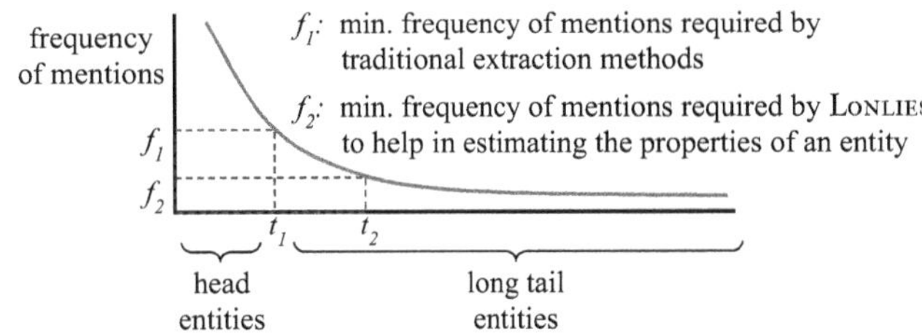

Figure 1: Mentions of Head and Long Tail Entities

Figure 1 models the frequency of entity mentions in the text as a distribution, representing the entities on the x-axis and the frequency of mentions of these entities on the y-axis. The "head" entities have many mentions (at least f_1 in the figure) that allow for efficient extraction using traditional methods. Entities that reside on the long tail (beyond the point t_1) pose a challenge to automatic knowledge base construction methods due to the insufficiency of relevant web content; the extracted facts cannot be verified and questions about them cannot be directly answered.

LONLIES estimates property values for long tail entities and does not rely on direct extraction of these values from text. LONLIES utilizes fewer mentions of these entities and information from a knowledge base to produce probabilistic estimates for the property values. In Figure 1, LONLIES can extract properties of long tail entities (between t_1 and t_2) that have enough frequency of mentions to assess their relationships to head topics, but do not have enough redundancy to allow for efficient traditional fact extraction. The intuition behind LONLIES is to leverage the text corpus to find occurrences of the long tail entity e_l with other head entities with known properties and exploit those head entities as an "information context" around e_l, which we call communities, to estimate a value for a property p of e_l. Communities are perceived as potential populations that e_l might be a member of, and they provide a more general context about e_l. The main insight behind LONLIES depends on two observations:

SIGIR '16, July 17-21, 2016, Pisa, Italy

DOI: http://dx.doi.org/10.1145/2911451.2911466

- Judging if e_l belongs to a particular community c_i requires less mentions in the relevant text than extracting an exact value for p.

- The ability to find an estimation for a property value p from a group of entities that form a community c_i depends on the p values of the entities in c_i and other statistical properties of c_i (e.g., its size and the variance of p values) but does not depend on e_l.

We combine these two notions in the following estimator for $e_l.p$:

$$e_l.\hat{p} = f_{\forall c_i \in C}(M(e_l, c_i), c_i.\hat{p})$$

where $M(e_l, c_i)$ measures the likelihood of e_l being a member of a community c_i, and $c_i.\hat{p}$ is an estimator for the property p that produces possible values for p using the p values of entities in c_i. $c_i.\hat{p}$ associates each estimate with a confidence interval that reflects the quality of the estimation. f is an aggregation function that combines estimates from a set of communities C.

The ability of LONLIES to find correct estimates for $e_l.p$ depends on (1) the estimation power of the constructed communities (i.e., how accurately $c_i.\hat{p}$ represents the values of p for entities in c_i); and (2) the confidence that e_l belongs to the communities used in the estimation. These two constraints together verify that estimates are produced from relevant communities that confidently produce representative p values. The error in estimating $e_l.p$ is the compound error of the membership assessment function M and the error in computing $c_i.\hat{p}$ estimates from communities.

LONLIES alleviates the risk of low-quality estimates for $e_l.p$ by being conservative in assessing the membership M and when producing estimates from c_i as we explain in Sections 2.3 and 2.4. LONLIES produces estimates only for results with high confidence. This, of course, lowers the recall of the long tail entities that LONLIES can handle, but maintains a high precision for the entities that are answered.

While this formula estimates $e_l.p$ from the p values of the constructed communities, the technique can be easily extended to leverage external rules and correlations of properties to estimate one property from another (e.g., to estimate *age* from *birth date* or *nationality* from *country_of_birth*).

2. THE LONLIES SYSTEM

Figure 3 illustrates the system architecture of LONLIES. We give an overview about the functionality of the four modules that constitute the stages of the estimation process and then discuss the details of each module separately. The modules rely on the availability of a text corpus and a knowledge base. The input to LONLIES is a long tail query entity, e_l, and a target property to estimate, p.

- The *KB Anchoring* module retrieves a set of documents that are relevant to the long tail query entity from the text corpus. It also extracts head entities that exist in the knowledge base that appear in the retrieved documents (Section 2.1).

- The *Community Construction* module builds a set of communities that may contain e_l as a member if e_l is added to the knowledge base (Section 2.2).

- The *Membership Assessment* module measures the similarity between e_l and a particular community in order to filter out irrelevant communities. It also filters out communities with low confidence of estimation (Section 2.3).

- The *Estimation* module aggregates estimates that are generated from the relevant communities and produces a distribution of estimates for the target property p (Section 2.4).

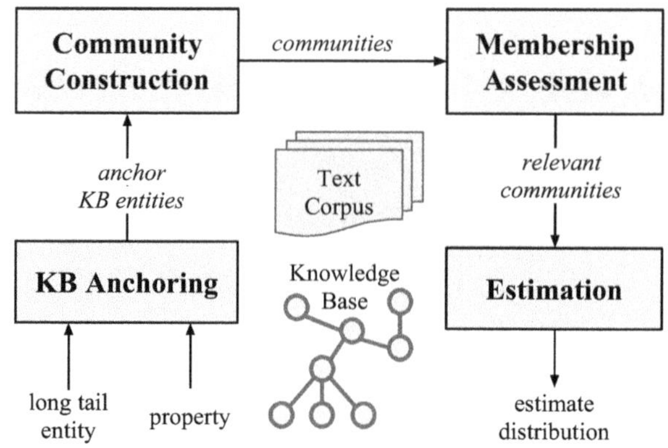

Figure 3: Lonlies System Architecture

2.1 Anchoring to Knowledge Base

The first step of LONLIES is retrieving a set of text documents that are relevant to the long tail query entity e_l. LONLIES extracts head entities that appear in the retrieved documents and exist in a knowledge base.

The co-occurrence of the long tail entity with head entities in text documents implies relationships to these entities in the knowledge base; the co-mentions represent what nodes in the knowledge base graph e_l might have been linked to if it was added to the knowledge base. Hence, we refer to these head entities as anchor KB entities E_H.

LONLIES does not classify the relationship between the long tail entity and anchor head entities that appear with it in the text. In fact, the co-occurrence merely indicates that a relationship between them exists. The *Membership Assessment* module validates these potential relationships.

2.2 Community Construction

Given the list of head entities that the long tail query entity is mentioned with, E_H, the goal of this module is to construct a set of communities C that can produce high-quality estimates for p.

Definition 2.1. A community c consists of a set of head entities that are retrieved from a knowledge base. Entities of a community c reflect nodes in the knowledge base graph.

Communities are constructed by traversing the knowledge base graph starting from E_H entity nodes. In LONLIES, we implemented two methods to construct communities.

Coherent community detection approach. We materialize a k-hop graph around all E_H entities from the knowledge base. We then run a community detection algorithm similar to [6] to detect communities in the materialized graph. We modified the *betweenness* function of the algorithm to separate communities that have coherent p values instead of dense connected subgroups. This method produces communities with consistent p values.

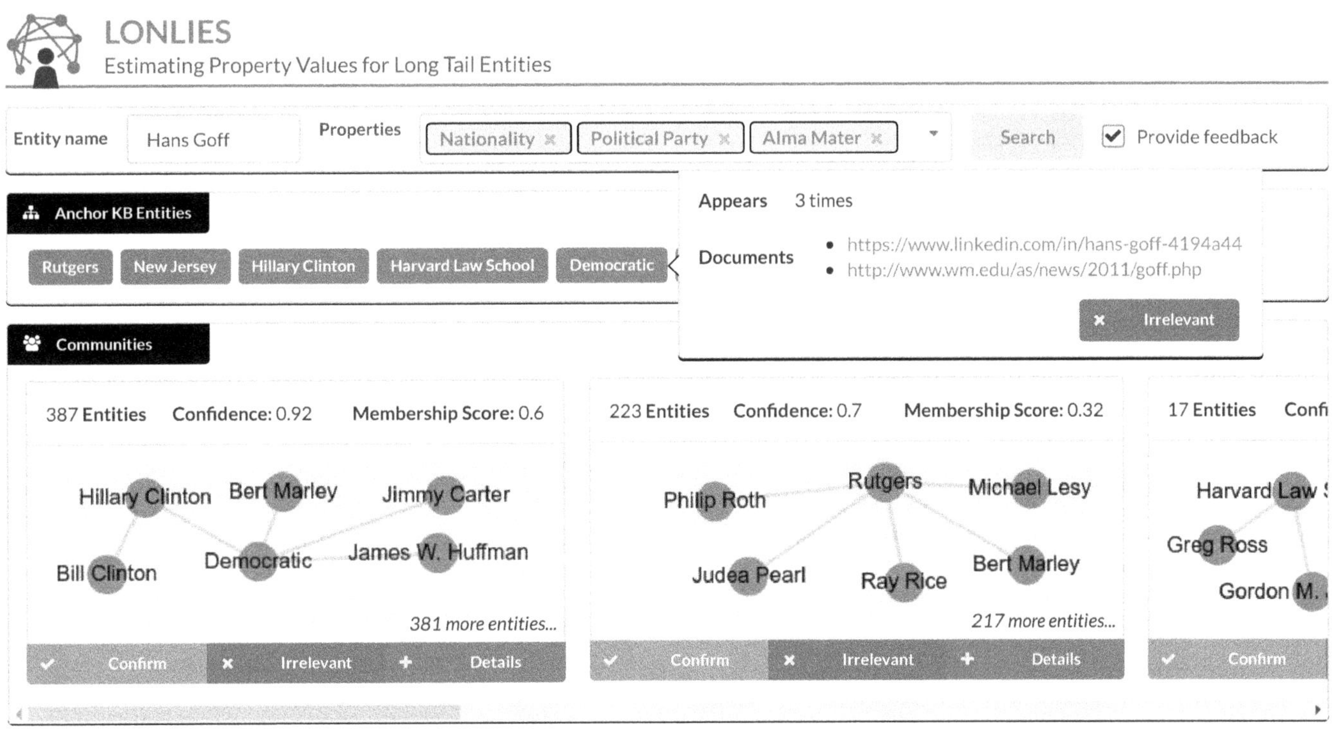

Figure 2: Lonlies GUI showing Anchor Head Entities and the Constructed Communities

Common KB relation approach. In this method, we start from each entity in E_H and construct a community from all entities in the KB graph that share a particular relationship to it. For example, a community c may include all entities that *work_at* the *University of Waterloo*. Not all constructed communities can produce high-quality, useful estimates, and the estimation power of a community depends on the property p that we are estimating. For example, a community that consists of people *born_in* the *United States* can confidently estimate the *nationality*, but the same community cannot help in estimating *age* or *occupation*.

After constructing a possibly large number of communities, LONLIES calculates multiple statistical features for each community, including the confidence of its produced estimates which depends on the size of the community and the homogeneity of the p values of its members, depending on the type of p. LONLIES computes the variance of the p values if p is a numerical property, or Simpson's diversity index[1] [8] of the p values for categorical properties. LONLIES associates a confidence score with the produced estimates and discards communities with low estimation confidence. This drastically reduces the number of communities to consider in the following stage.

2.3 Membership Assessment

As mentioned in Section 2.1, the co-occurrence of the long tail entity with another head entity does not necessarily indicate a strong relationship between them. Therefore, not all constructed communities are related to e_l.

This module produces a *membership score* that reflects the confidence in membership of e_l in a community c, $M(e_l, c)$, for each of the constructed communities. The membership in each community is determined independently from the membership in other communities.

We view this problem as a binary classification task where an entity is labeled "member" or "not member" in the community. LONLIES trains a classifier to compute the probability of an entity's membership in the community. To obtain training data, LONLIES retrieves documents from the text corpus where the community entities appear and extracts classification features from the text. Each entity in the community acts as a training data point. We run the trained classification model against the features extracted for e_l. LONLIES runs two classification tools, Stanford Classifier [5] and DeepDive [7], and assigns the higher score to the community.

2.4 Estimation

The *Estimation* module receives a set of estimates of p, together with their confidence and membership scores of the communities that produced them. LONLIES uses a straightforward method to aggregate these estimates, using the confidence and membership scores as weights. The result is a distribution of values for p with a final confidence score assigned for each estimate.

3. DEMONSTRATION OVERVIEW

The demonstration audience will be able to interact with the system by issuing queries about properties of long tail entities. The system will show the details of each step in the estimation to explain how it produced the final results. Users can provide feedback about the quality of each step and notice how the system employs the feedback in adjusting the estimation results. LONLIES uses Freebase [2] as its knowledge base and retrieves relevant text documents from Google Search and the ClueWeb09 [3] corpus that is indexed

[1]The index reflects the probability that two entities taken at random from the community have the same p value.

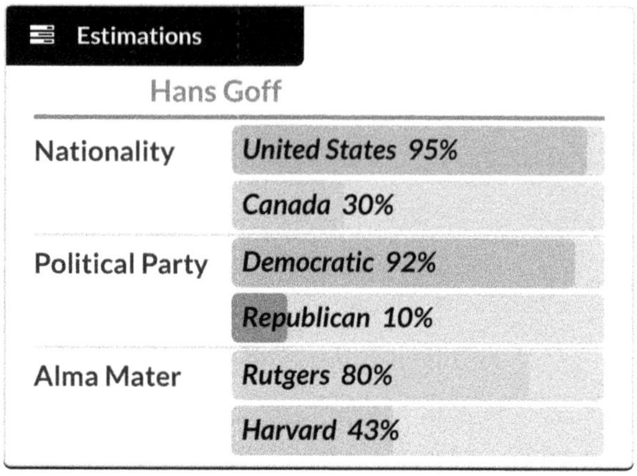

Figure 4: Example Estimation Results

by Apache Lucene. We provide a walk-through of an example query and explain what the audience may expect to see.

Users enter two inputs: the name of the long tail entity and properties of interest. As an example, assume that we are interested in the *Nationality*, *Political Party*, and *Alma Mater* of the entity *Hans Goff*, who is a member of Hillary Clinton's presidential campaign. Goff is considered a long tail entity since he does not exist in the knowledge base; however, he is frequently mentioned on the web with other head entities and topics.

Relevant documents and anchors to KB. In the first step, LONLIES retrieves a set of documents that are relevant to the query and provides a list of the anchor KB entities that are extracted from these documents. When the user clicks on an anchor entity, LONLIES shows how many times this head entity appears with the query entity and the list of documents where they appear together, as shown in Figure 2.

Constructed communities and their scores. Given the list of anchor entities, LONLIES constructs a set of communities. Users see a visualization of each community, which is represented as a set of (possibly connected) nodes that are retrieved from the knowledge base. The system presents some statistical details about the community including its confidence of estimating the target properties, the membership score that reflects how much the system believes that the query entity belongs to it, and its size (Figure 2).

When the user clicks on a community, LONLIES shows a detailed view of it. The details include the distribution of values within the community, the features used in determining the membership of entities in this community, and a justification of the produced score of membership.

Users can provide feedback about communities by confirming the membership of the query entity to them or by removing irrelevant communities from the estimation process. The communities are sorted by a score that combines the estimation confidence and the membership of the long tail entity. The higher the rank of a community, the more impact it has on the estimation results. Therefore, it is more valuable to present high-ranking communities to the user and get feedback about most influencing communities.

Estimates. Depending on the type of the property being estimated, LONLIES shows an appropriate visualization of the produced estimates. For categorical properties, LONLIES shows the top-k estimates ordered by their confidence scores (Figure 4 shows the top-2 estimates). For numerical properties, LONLIES shows a distribution of the property being estimated with its mean and variance.

4. RELATED WORK

Knowledge base construction methods, such as DeepDive [7] and Knowledge Vault [4], train property-specific extractors (e.g., using distant supervision) to extract specific relationships from text. Knowledge Vault also exploits a knowledge base to compute the prior of the extracted facts and predict links in the knowledge base graph. This prior is used together with extractions from multiple extraction systems on different data sources to validate the correctness of extracted facts. The success of these approaches relies heavily on the redundancy of information in the text in order to extract accurate property values.

Other question answering techniques [1] utilize query logs to find query-relevant web pages and paid crowd-sourcing to manually extract text snippets and author answers from the retrieved web pages.

5. CONCLUSION

We presented LONLIES, a system that estimates property values for long tail entities. LONLIES leverages the head entities that are co-mentioned with a long tail entity in a text corpus, together with information from a knowledge base, in order to construct a set of communities of entities. LONLIES aggregates the estimates that are produced from communities that (1) are relevant to the long tail entity, and (2) have high estimation power of its members, producing a distribution of the target property value.

6. ACKNOWLEDGMENTS

This work was generously supported by Google Faculty Research Award granted to Ihab F. Ilyas in 2014.

7. REFERENCES

[1] M. S. Bernstein, J. Teevan, S. Dumais, D. Liebling, and E. Horvitz. Direct Answers for Search Queries in the Long Tail. In *SIGCHI*, 2012.

[2] K. Bollacker, C. Evans, P. Paritosh, T. Sturge, and J. Taylor. Freebase: a collaboratively created graph database for structuring human knowledge. In *SIGMOD*, 2008.

[3] J. Callan, M. Hoy, C. Yoo, and L. Zhao. Clueweb09 data set, 2009.

[4] X. Dong, E. Gabrilovich, G. Heitz, W. Horn, N. Lao, K. Murphy, T. Strohmann, S. Sun, and W. Zhang. Knowledge Vault: A Web-scale Approach to Probabilistic Knowledge Fusion. In *SIGKDD*, 2014.

[5] C. Manning and D. Klein. Optimization, maxent models, and conditional estimation without magic. In *NAACL - Tutorials '03*, Stroudsburg, PA, USA, 2003. Association for Computational Linguistics.

[6] M. E. Newman and M. Girvan. Finding and evaluating community structure in networks. *Physical review E*, 69(2), 2004.

[7] F. Niu, C. Zhang, C. Ré, and J. W. Shavlik. Deepdive: Web-scale knowledge-base construction using statistical learning and inference. *VLDS*, 12:25–28, 2012.

[8] E. H. Simpson. Measurement of diversity. *Nature*, 1949.

Personalised News and Blog Recommendations based on User Location, Facebook and Twitter User Profiling

Gabriella Kazai
Lumi News
London
gabs@lumi.news

Iskander Yusof
Lumi News
London
iskander@lumi.news

Daoud Clarke
Lumi News
London
daoud@lumi.news

ABSTRACT

This demo presents a prototype mobile app that provides out-of-the-box personalised content recommendations to its users by leveraging and combining the user's location, their Facebook and/or Twitter feed and their in-app actions to automatically infer their interests. We build individual models for each user and each location. At retrieval time we construct the user's personalised feed by mixing different sources of content-based recommendations with content directly from their Facebook/Twitter feeds, locally trending articles and content propagated through their in-app social network. Both explicit and implicit feedback signals from the users' interactions with their recommendations are used to update their interests models and to learn their preferences over the different content sources.

CCS Concepts

•Information systems → Mobile information processing systems; Recommender systems;

Keywords

Lumi News, recommender system, mobile app

1. INTRODUCTION

Online content is being produced at an unprecedented rate, with thousands of news stories, blogs and videos added every day by a wide range of publishers, media outlets and Internet users. At the same time, in this accelerating supply-demand cycle, consumer behaviour is changing at an equally high pace [1, 7, 2]. Users increasingly consume news and media content on the go, using their smartphones, either via dedicated news apps or through social media. According to a survey by Mobiles Republic[1], a global news syndication company, 75% of readers with smartphones and 70% with tablets check the news more than once a day.

[1] `http://www.news-republic.com/infographic2013/`

SIGIR '16, July 17-21, 2016, Pisa, Italy

DOI: http://dx.doi.org/10.1145/2911451.2911464

The increasing use of mobiles for rich media consumption is reflected in the growing number of news apps available and their growing user base. For example, news aggregator apps, such as Flipboard, BuzzFeed, Yahoo News, Feedly, News360, Pulse and Apple News present news from a range of publishers, but either provide no personalisation, rely on the user's social networks or on the user selecting topics of interests. Research prototypes that experiment with more advanced recommendation techniques include Focal [4], PEN [3] and others, e.g. [9, 8, 6, 5]. This plethora of news portals and news apps is a clear sign of users' need for news consumption, but also a sign that the question of how to serve this content to users is still very much an open problem.

The goal of mobile news recommender systems is to help users find fresh content that is relevant to them or to their particular context (e.g. location, social) from a constant stream of publications and serve this content in ways that require minimal user interaction, given the limits of a device's form-factors. When considering the user's experience during a reading session, the feed of news stories recommended to the user should also cater for diversity and serendipity so that the user can discover new topics or stay informed on trending, but perhaps less personally relevant, events. This requires a different approach to those in traditional information retrieval, one that goes beyond optimising for relevance.

Another key challenge in recommender systems is the cold-start issue: how to recommend items to users for whom we have very little data. Typical approaches require the user to select from a list of predefined topics (e.g., Flipboard), making use of the user's location information or social network (e.g., Pulse) or learning the user's interests over time through interactions with the recommended content (e.g., [5]).

Our system, Lumi Social News[2], aims to provide users an out-of-the box personalised experience by leveraging both external and internal data and automatically building the user's profile from their location, their Facebook or Twitter feed, while also learning from the user's in-app interactions. The incoming streams of content are matched against the user's evolving profile to generate recommendations, where the scoring considers the item's relevance, popularity and freshness. The user's feed is then composed of items relevant to the user's interests, intermixed with locally trending stories, as well as content from other sources, such as the user's Twitter feed or stories from the user's social network on Lumi. Our approach thus aims to combine temporal, locational, social and preferential information to provide a

[2] `android.lumi.do`

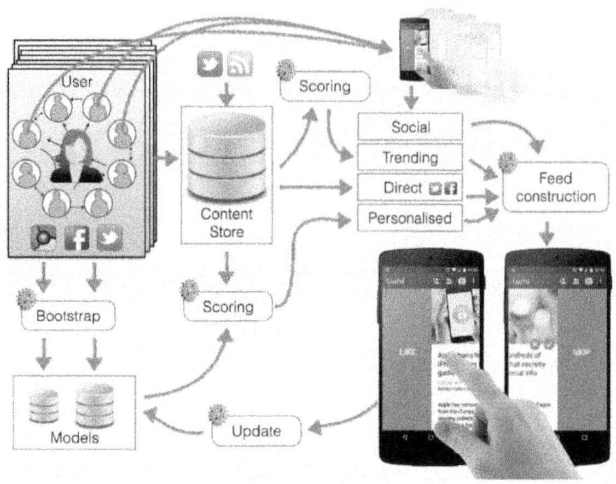

Figure 1: Lumi architecture data flow

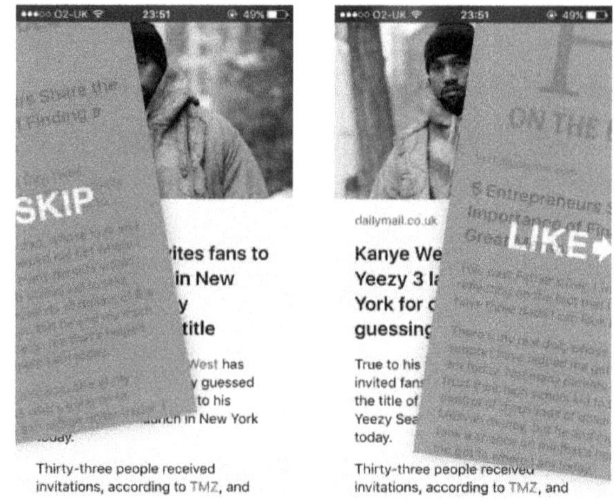

Figure 2: Screenshots of user swipe actions to skip or like an article

more fine-grained recommendation strategy.

Lumi is also different from other news recommender systems in that it is not limited to publishers, but presents users with a broad range of blogs and online publications, allowing much greater diversity and specialisation in the content delivered to users. This is achieved by leveraging user data to identify promising sources of content.

This paper presents the implementation of our solution to recommend news and more long tail media from a large crowd-curated content stream in a way that provides the user a diverse reading experience, combining topical, location-based and socially relevant content as well as breaking or trending news. Recommendations are presented to the user through an intuitive and easy-to-use, swiping interface, one story at a time. Users' interactions with their recommendations are then used to update their models and to tune their preferences over the various content sources.

2. SYSTEM FEATURES

Figure 1 shows a schematic overview of the data flow in Lumi. Content is ingested either via RSS or is contributed and curated by the users themselves. For example, users can sign up with Twitter and, in the process, bring the public content of those they follow on Twitter with them into Lumi. This content, after various quality filtering, becomes part of the content pool, from which recommendations can then be generated.

During the bootstrap process, Lumi automatically learns the user's interests from their location, from their public Twitter and/or Facebook feeds and from their in-app actions. The generated user models are then matched against the stream of incoming content and recommended to users based on a combination of their relevance and trending scores.

In addition to the model based recommendations, Lumi also serves content from a range of other sources to the user. In fact, a user's Lumi feed is made up of a mixture of content from any of the following sources, depending on availability for a given user: model-based recommendations, content pulled directly from the user's social media streams, e.g., Twitter/Facebook, as well as trending content with local or global relevance and content from the user's Lumi connections. The preferred composition of the feed across these sources is tuned based on the user's in-app interactions. For example, if a user spends longer on reading their model based recommendations than on content coming directly from their Twitter feed, Lumi updates the source weights and will include more model based recommendations in the user's feed.

Lumi also has a unique user interface in comparison to other news apps. Instead of showing the user a list of recommendations that is typical in recommender systems, Lumi displays only a single recommended item at any given time. This item is picked from the various ingested content streams, where the selection is based on the item's relevance to the user or the user's location as well as its recent popularity on social media, i.e., Twitter and Facebook. Figure 2 shows an example recommended article.

All articles are shown in the same style, providing a cohesive and smooth experience. The header image for an article is picked based on image quality and positioning in the original text, which is followed by the title and the full text of the article. In the case of a video, the video itself is positioned at the top, followed by the title and any textual description if available on the original site. There is a reactions bar at the bottom of each article, which lists users who liked the recommended item, ordered by social closeness or similarity to the user.

To get to the next recommendation, the user needs to either like or skip the current item by swiping left or right, respectively (see Figure 2). The metaphor used is that of a stack of cards, where the user has to flick the top card out of the way to see the next card. This provides a playful element to the reading experience.

All liked stories are saved by the system and can be accessed through the user's profile area and can also be read offline. The explicit feedback of the like/skip actions as well as implicit signals, such as the time the user spent on an article, are used to continually update the user's model, thus learning more about the user's evolving interests. The feedback is also applied to tune the user's preferences over the various sources that compose the user's feed.

3. SYSTEM OVERVIEW

The system is built using a microservices architecture, with separate services, for example, to perform ingestion of new content via Twitter, Facebook or RSS, content quality assessment (to determine whether to ingest a page), or generation of recommendations.

The front-end is implemented for Android phones in Java, which connects to the back-end via a restful API. User models and recommendations are generated using scikit-learn libraries and in-house developed services and methods.

Most components are deployed using Docker together with Amazon EC2 Container Service.

3.1 Ingestion

Ingestion components process a number of incoming streams of content from RSS, Twitter and Facebook. The content is rendered (HTML content of URLs downloaded), passed through a series of quality filters and subsequently a range of features and media are extracted. Exact duplicates, e.g., when the same article is tweeted by multiple people are removed at this stage. A fuzzy, content based filter is used later on in the pipeline, for example, to identify when the same story is published by multiple outlets, albeit with different details and in different editorial styles. Logistic Regression classifiers are used to assign topic labels, e.g., business, technology, football, etc., to the ingested articles. Content is then indexed and stored in Elasticsearch[3]. For each ingested page, we maintain our own social media share and like counts, tracking their popularity on the Web.

At the time of writing, with just over 100k installs, the system processes around 200 million tweets a day, resulting in over 100k articles curated by the Lumi users (after quality filtering and deduping), which then make it into the recommendable content pool.

3.2 Bootstrap

At signup, the public pages in a new user's Twitter or Facebook feeds (i.e., public pages published by those the user is following) are analysed and an initial user model is built. As some feeds may be noisy or not necessarily representative of the user's interests, we impose quality thresholds before a model can be built. While the model building is taking place in the background, the user is shown local and global trending stories. Stories explicitly liked by the user (swipe right) and stories that the user spent at least thirty seconds reading are also used as positive samples when training the user's model. A key stage of the model building is the feature extraction. We extract a wide range of features, including standard word features as well as categorical data and combine these within a single model in order to support users' topical interests and source preferences. We employ feature hashing to keep model sizes small. Once a model is built, the cache of stories already on the device is flushed and the new feed, containing personalised recommendations is sent to the device.

3.3 User model update

Users' respective models are updated based on their ongoing online activities, e.g. Twitter or Facebook, as well as based on their in-app actions, e.g. when they read, swipe to like or swipe to skip a story. For scalability, we follow an incremental model updating approach. Model updating happens as a background process, which loops through users in a staggered way, prioritising more active users first. This ensures that users ,who use Lumi multiple times a day always have up to date models and fresh recommendations.

3.4 Trending content

Trending content is identified by monitoring social media, e.g. likes on Facebook and tweets on Twitter. Locally trending stories in a given country or region are identified through content that is popular with users who share the same location. A particular challenge with trending content detection is that most social media share counts are heavily biased to US and UK interests, so we built our own location specific trending score method, which biases towards the sites and topics that are relevant to the user's location.

3.5 Model based recommendations

For each ingested page, each user's model is used to generate relevance scores, which are then stored in Amazon DynamoDB against the user. This is run as a background process, which generates recommendations for users even when they are not online, so that they don't miss out on interesting content. Relevance scores are calculated on batches of incoming pages, against all the user models, starting with more active users, similarly to how model updating is performed.

3.6 Social content

Lumi users can follow each other and discover interesting content that was liked by those they follow. Recommendations on who to follow are based on the relevance of the suggested user's liked items to the current user's interests as well as based on existing social links in the user's Twitter and Facebook networks.

When users follow other Lumi users, they also get to see stories that were liked by those they follow. The selection of these stories combines factors such as the user's closeness to the followed users, e.g., reciprocal relationship, similarity of interests, as well as the popularity of the liked story and its freshness. Similarly, stories liked by the user are shared to the user's followers in their Lumi social network. The reactions of their followers on these shared stories are then fed back to the user.

3.7 Direct Twitter/Facebook content

Similarly to social content, articles from the user's Twitter or Facebook feed are selected based on timeliness, social factors and popularity and are then mixed into the user's feed.

3.8 Feed construction

In order to provide diverse content, a user's feed is made up of content from the model-based recommendations, from local or global trending news, content that is directly streamed from their Twitter and/or Facebook feeds and social content that has been shared on Lumi by users that the current user is following. When a mobile client requests new recommendations, the top ranking items are returned from all the different sources that are available for the given user. The ranking function takes into account both the relevance of an item to the user's interests and its local or global popularity.

The preferences over the different sources are learnt and continually tuned based on the user's interactions. For this we use a Bayesian update process, normalised across the user's actions and across other users. Diversity across the

[3]`https://www.elastic.co/products/elasticsearch`

recommended content is ensured by optimising the order of stories from different sources in the feed as well as using the calculated similarity between articles. This is where the fuzzy deduping takes place, making sure that the user is recommended an article on a given story of interest from their preferred outlet, while ensuring that they are not recommended too similar articles related to the same story from other outlets.

4. EVALUATING RECOMMENDATIONS

Our ultimate goal is to make an app that people want to use every day: we want to optimise for user retention. However it takes a long time to measure the impact on retention, and we have found a metric that correlates closely with it, namely, the number of recommendations that a user spends over thirty seconds reading (from now on we refer to this just as "reading"). This is a natural metric to use for a news app, and it allows us to iterate much faster when trying out different recommendation algorithms.

To account for natural variations in the user-base, and different users' propensity for reading, we use split testing on individual recommendations, so that each user gets recommendations from a variety of sources or algorithms. This allows us to see how many users prefer one source or algorithm to another, giving a reliable way to identify when recommendations are working or not. If we were to split the recommendations across users so that some users got one type of recommendation and some users got another, it would be harder to trust our results because some users naturally read more than others.

We use a Bayesian formula due to Evan Miller[4] to compare two types of recommendations. Specifically, we assume that there is some probability p_A that a user will read a page of type A. For a new type of recommendation, B, we then estimate $P(p_B > p_A)$, the probability that the user reads a page of type B is greater than the probability that they read a page of type A. Given that the user has read r_A pages of type A and been presented with s_A pages of the same type that they have not read, then this probability can be estimated by

$$\sum_{i=1}^{r_B+1} \frac{B(r_A+i, s_A+s_B+2)}{(s_B+i)B(i, s_B+1)B(r_A+1, s_A+1)}$$

where B is the beta function. We evaluate this probability for each user, and look at the proportion of users where this probability exceeds a threshold of 0.9. If the proportion is high, we can be fairly certain that recommendations of type B are preferred by users.

5. CONCLUSIONS

Personalised recommendation of news and media content in general paves the way for solving the information overload and attention scarcity problem, especially in the face of the recent increase in content publishing, including citizen journalism and other user generated content. This demo paper presents the development of a personalised mobile news recommender system.

The presented system is the first in its class to provide personalised feeds by combining a number of different sources and model-based recommendations over a crowd curated content pool. The system non-intrusively learns users' interests from their Twitter or Facebook activities and responds to their feedback actions when reading recommended items.

It is a complex system with many moving parts that build on a combination of machine learning methods as well as information extraction and retrieval technologies to provide users with an experience of diverse, fresh, relevant content feed in a simple swiping user interface. The assessment of how recommender systems may perform in this setting with noisy and sparse data and online user feedbacks is a key challenge to deliver this service.

For future work, we will investigate combining topic based content streams into a user's feed to increase coverage across user's interest silos. In addition, we will experiment with various visualisations of the user's profile (their liked stories), for example, grouping liked stories by topics.

6. ACKNOWLEDGMENTS

Lumi is a result of the efforts of a great team, see `https://lumi.do/about/team`.

7. REFERENCES

[1] M. Constantinides, J. Dowell, D. Johnson, and S. Malacria. Exploring mobile news reading interactions for news app personalisation. MobileHCI '15, pages 457–462, New York, NY, USA, 2015. ACM.

[2] C. Esiyok, B. Kille, B.-J. Jain, F. Hopfgartner, and S. Albayrak. Users' reading habits in online news portals. In *Proceedings of the 5th Information Interaction in Context Symposium*, IIiX '14, pages 263–266, New York, NY, USA, 2014. ACM.

[3] F. Garcin and B. Faltings. Pen recsys: A personalized news recommender systems framework. NRS '13, pages 3–9. ACM, 2013.

[4] F. Garcin, F. Galle, and B. Faltings. Focal: A personalized mobile news reader. RecSys'14, pages 369–370. ACM, 2014.

[5] J. A. Gulla, A. D. Fidjestøl, X. Su, and H. Castejon. Implicit user profiling in news recommender systems. In *WEBIST (1)*, pages 185–192, 2014.

[6] I. Ilievski and S. Roy. Personalized news recommendation based on implicit feedback. In *Proceedings of the 2013 International News Recommender Systems Workshop and Challenge*, NRS '13, pages 10–15, New York, NY, USA, 2013. ACM.

[7] D. Lagun and M. Lalmas. Understanding user attention and engagement in online news reading. WSDM '16, pages 113–122, New York, NY, USA, 2016. ACM.

[8] A. Said, J. Lin, A. Bellogín, and A. de Vries. A month in the life of a production news recommender system. In *Proc. Workshop on Living Labs for IR Evaluation*, pages 7–10. ACM, 2013.

[9] M. Tavakolifard, J. A. Gulla, K. C. Almeroth, J. E. Ingvaldesn, G. Nygreen, and E. Berg. Tailored news in the palm of your hand: A multi-perspective transparent approach to news recommendation. WWW'13 Companion, pages 305–308, 2013.

[4] `http://www.evanmiller.org/bayesian-ab-testing.html`

PULP: A System for Exploratory Search of Scientific Literature

Alan Medlar[⋆] Kalle Ilves[○] Ping Wang[○] Wray Buntine[◇] Dorota Głowacka[○]

[○] Department of Computer Science, University of Helsinki [⋆] Institute of Biotechnology, University of Helsinki

[◇] Faculty of Information Technology, Monash University

[◇]alan.j.medlar@helsinki.fi, [⋆] Wray.Buntine@monash.edu [○] first.last@cs.helsinki.fi,

ABSTRACT

Despite the growing importance of exploratory search, information retrieval (IR) systems tend to focus on lookup search. Lookup searches are well served by optimising the precision and recall of search results, however, for exploratory search this may be counterproductive if users are unable to formulate an appropriate search query. We present a system called PULP that supports exploratory search for scientific literature, though the system can be easily adapted to other types of literature. PULP uses reinforcement learning (RL) to avert the user from context traps resulting from poorly chosen search queries, trading off between exploration (presenting the user with diverse topics) and exploitation (moving towards more specific topics). Where other RL-based systems suffer from the "cold start" problem, requiring sufficient time to adjust to a user's information needs, PULP initially presents the user with an overview of the dataset using temporal topic models. Topic models are displayed in an interactive alluvial diagram, where topics are shown as ribbons that change thickness with a given topics relative prevalence over time. Interactive, exploratory search sessions can be initiated by selecting topics as a starting point.

Keywords

Exploratory search; topic models; bandit algorithms; scientific literature search; query formulation

1. INTRODUCTION

Exploratory search is defined as a class of search activities performed to learn or discover new information [16]. Unlike lookup search, where a discrete set of results achieves a well-defined objective, exploratory search can involve unfamiliar subject areas and uncertainty regarding search goals. In exploratory tasks users are often uncertain how to formulate search queries [8] either because they are unfamiliar with the search topic or they have no clear search goals in mind. For these reasons exploratory search is considered to be challenging for the user and requires additional support from information retrieval (IR) systems.

Our work addresses the observation that IR systems primarily target lookup search, despite the increasing importance of exploratory search [5]. Most IR systems present a ranked list of documents in descending order of their relevance to the issued search query. This approach works very well for lookup tasks where the user has a discrete and well defined information need. However, retrieving the best matching results for the search query might trap the user in their initial query context and contribute to user perceptions that exploratory search is challenging. Moreover, for users attempting to acquire information in an unfamiliar domain where they lack the specific knowledge to formulate search queries, retrieving the best matching results to those queries may be counterproductive.

We address the issue of initial query formulation by visualizing what topics are covered by a given dataset and what keywords are associated with each topic, allowing the user to directly select a topic as their initial search query. In order to prevent the user from getting stuck in the context trap of the initial search query, we use reinforcement learning (RL) to trade off between exploration and exploitation throughout a search session.

2. BACKGROUND

Below, we briefly review the existing approaches to shed light on some of the open problems in exploratory search.

Relevance Feedback. The first key approach developed by the IR community was relevance feedback: users mark documents as relevant or non-relevant and the query model is updated accordingly. Initial studies showed that interactive IR systems benefited from relevance feedback [15], though later studies showed these features to be rarely used. The reasons are two-fold: (1) relevance feedback often leads to context traps, and (2) the cognitive load of selecting relevant documents is high compared to typing a new query [15]. Combining relevance feedback with user modelling techniques, such as reinforcement learning, would allow an IR system to suggest more relevant results and avoid getting stuck in context traps.

Faceted Search. Faceted search aims to avoid the context trap by using global features instead of contextual ones [21]. It organizes information according to a faceted classification system, allowing users to explore collections of documents by applying multiple filters. Such systems classify information elements along explicit global dimensions, enabling the classifications to be accessed and ordered in

SIGIR '16, July 17-21, 2016, Pisa, Italy

© 2016 ACM. ISBN 978-1-4503-4069-4/16/07...$15.00

DOI: http://dx.doi.org/10.1145/2911451.2911455

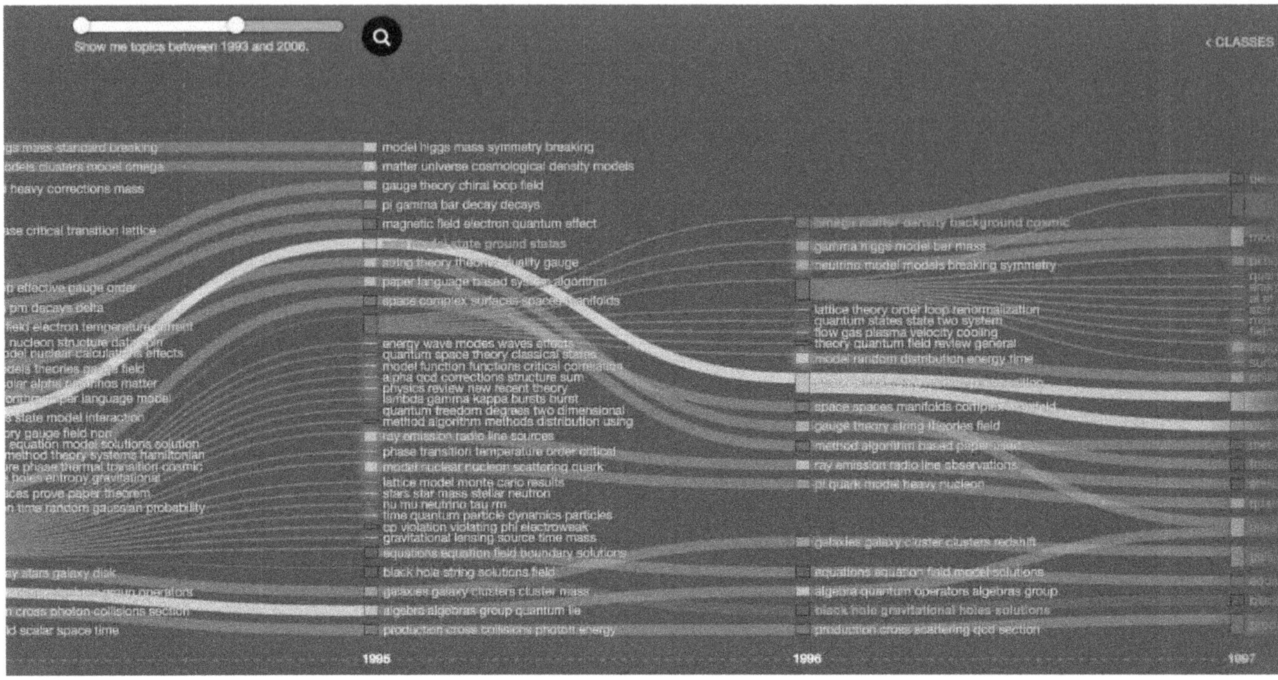

Figure 1: Interactive alluvial diagram showing what topics are present in each year and their relative abundance.

multiple ways. As the number of global features is often very large, the process, however, can quickly become overly demanding as users have to assess a large number of options [21]. Assisting the user in formulating the initial search query in combination with improved modeling of user needs would allow a reduction in the number of facets and thus enhance user experience.

Reinforcement Learning. In exploratory search, the information-needs of a user are constantly evolving, and hence modeling is crucial for acquiring information on search intent and query reformulation [20]. Recently, RL techniques have been applied to modeling exploratory search [14, 10]. RL allows a system to balance exploitation (moving towards more specific topics) and exploration (presenting alternative topics). The main disadvantage is the "cold start" problem: these systems need a number of sessions to adjust to a user's information needs. A recent study showed that systems employing RL techniques can optimally balance exploitation and exploration for a given set of users [2]. Assisting the user in formulating the initial query in an RL-based IR system would accelerate the user modeling aspect of such systems.

Exploratory Search Interfaces. The lack of success of relevance feedback is often attributed to user interface design failing to conveniently provide feedback at suitable levels of granularity. In response, a variety of systems were designed to support user feedback, including intelligent user interfaces that assist the user in comprehending an information space [7], visualizations that summarize results for faster relevance judgement [17], as well as interactive visualizations that allow the user to indicate the direction of exploration [10]. These systems are very useful but they usually do not take into consideration the evolving nature of user knowledge in exploratory search tasks and thus either fail to provide a good starting point for the search or lead to a context trap as the search progresses.

Models of Exploratory Search. Models of user behaviour in information search help us to provide personalized support [1]. Information Foraging Theory is a promising model of exploration that predicts the information seeker's decision from the expectation of information gain [18]. There are also models that assist the search systems in predicting user perception of the results from implicit interactions, including search satisfaction, disambiguating exploration and struggling scenarios [13], and predicting the user's domain knowledge [9]. We draw inspiration for the design of our system from models of user behaviour in exploratory search.

Search and Topic Models. While there has been extensive research on topic model visualisation, there has been less on their use for exploratory search. While there has been prior work using hierarchical topic models for document summarising and navigation [12], it did not present the dynamic aspect of time that is critical in scientific literature. Another study presented the graph of connections (institutions, subject areas, authors, *etc.*) [11]. In both of these examples, however, the intrinsic use of topics as an aid to IR was less developed.

3. SYSTEM OVERVIEW

PULP can be broadly divided into three parts: visualization of search topics, search engine interface, and search engine backend containing the document ranking algorithm. The current version of the system operates on ~1 million documents obtained from the arXiv repository, although the system can be easily adapted to other domains.

The search starts with the alluvial diagram of broad topics found in the arXiv dataset over the years (Figure 1). Each year is represented by a vertical list of research topics covered by papers added to arXiv in that particular year. Each research topic is labelled with the five most prominent keywords from that topic. The user can specify which years of the arXiv data should be visualised by using the slider in the upper left hand corner of the visualisation. The ribbons going between different years indicate how topics in different years are related to one another. When the search starts, all the ribbons representing the flow of the topics from year to year are light grey. The user can click on any of the existing topics to see its development over the years, at which point the ribbon representing that topic model will change colour. The user can click on as many topics as he likes. By clicking on the search button next to the slider, the top five keywords from the topics that the user clicked on will be sent to the search engine as a query. If none of the topics was selected, then by clicking on the search button, the user is directed to the query page of the search engine.

The search engine interface is presented in Figure 2. The query bar is at the top of the page. The keywords from the topics that the user clicked on in the alluvial diagram are shown in the search bar. The user can amend this query by deleting or adding keywords. If no topics in the alluvial diagram were selected, then the search bar is empty and the user can formulate their own query. After typing in the search query, the user is presented with 10 documents. The initial set of documents is ranked based on the Okapi BM25 algorithm [19]. Next, to see more documents the user can indicate which document interests them by clicking on the circle next to it and thus providing relevance score of 1 to that document. After clicking the "next" button in the top right corner of the page, a new set of documents is displayed based on the feedback provided by the user so far. The user can provide feedback to as many documents as he wishes.

The right margin of the page contains the topic model display with the distribution of topics in the presented search results and the rest of the dataset. The top most prominent topics for each document are shown. Each topic is represented with a consistent colour across all documents. The length of the bar representing a given topic corresponds to the relative prominence of this topic in a given document. By hovering the mouse cursor above a given topic, a tooltip appears with top five keywords associated with that topic. The topics representing the currently displayed search results are marked with a blue vertical line on the left side of the topic display bar. The remaining part of the topic model display shows how many potentially similar documents in terms of their topic distribution there are in the dataset. The topic model display can be scrolled down to cover the entire dataset. Below, we describe how the topic model visualisation was constructed and how the documents are ranked.

3.1 Temporal Topic Models

All documents in the dataset were preprocessed to remove stop-words and made lower case. They were then grouped by year of last update, with all documents prior to 1993 placed together. The standard, non-bursty, non-parametric topic model of Buntine and Mishra [6] is run on each group to produce 20 topics per group. For these topics, words are then ranked according to their "lift" over the background (the model estimates a "non-topical" background distribution as well [6]) and labelled with the top 5 ranked words.

Getting an estimate of topic flow is more challenging. The documents in year $Y{+}1$ are fit to the topics from year Y. The most likely topic for each word is then estimated using the topics from years Y and $Y{+}1$. This produces topic-to-topic mapping data from years Y to $Y{+}1$ for each word in year $Y{+}1$. We estimate the topic flows from this mapping data. We found this to be less noisy than heuristic estimates based on topic word-vector differences.

3.2 Document ranking

In order to help the user explore the document space, we use LinRel [4]. Suppose we have a matrix D, where each row d_i is a tf-idf (term frequency-inverse document frequency) feature vector representation of documents presented so far. Let $r = (r_1, r_2 ... r_t)^\top$ be the column vector of relevance scores received from the user up to time t. We estimate the expected relevance r_i of a document d_i as $\mathbb{E}[r_i] = d_i \cdot w$, where the vector w is estimated from user feedback. LinRel estimates $\hat{w}$ by solving $r = D \cdot w$ and estimates relevance score for each d_i as $\hat{r_i} = d_i \cdot \hat{w}$

In order to deal with the exploration-exploitation trade-off, we present documents not with the highest score $\hat{r_i}$, but with the largest upper confidence bound for the relevance score. Thus, if σ_i is an upper bound on standard deviation of relevance estimate $\hat{r_i}$, the upper confidence bound of document d_i is calculated as $r_i + \gamma\sigma_i$, where $\gamma > 0$ is a constant used to adjust the confidence level of the upper confidence bound. In each iteration, LinRel calculates $s_i = d_i \cdot (D^\top \cdot D + \lambda I)^{-1} D^\top$, where λ is the regularization parameter which is set to 1 if each of the feature vectors sums up to 1 (following [4]) and the documents that maximize $s_i \cdot r + \frac{\gamma}{2}\|s_i\|$ are selected for presentation. The first term $s_i \cdot r$ effectively ranks all the documents based on their similarity to the documents the user has selected so far and thus it narrows the area of the search space (exploitation). The second term $\frac{\gamma}{2}\|s_i\|$ ensures that the user is presented with a more diverse set of results. The exploration rate is controlled by the γ parameter. The higher the value of γ, the more diverse, or exploratory, the results are. The exploration rate in the current system is $\gamma = 1$, based on results from a previous experimental study [2].

3.3 Topic Model Representation

The same document preparation and topic model system discussed in Section 3.1 was used for the global topic representation. However, for the global model, more topics were used – 300 in the current version of the system. For this, we needed to estimate topic proportions per document, which was done using 500 cycles of the Gibbs sampler after an initial 1000 cycles. In the topic model visualisation in Figure 2 we used the top five topics proportions per document.

4. SUMMARY OF RESULTS

The search engine components of PULP (search interface and RL-based backend) were tested in a series of user experiments [2, 3]. The participants were researchers in various areas of computer science. Search results include more diverse results when users are exploring. Users found more useful results in exploratory tasks when compared to a baseline system, which was specifically tuned for lookup tasks. Overall, users gave higher ratings for documents retrieved during exploratory tasks using PULP compared to the base-

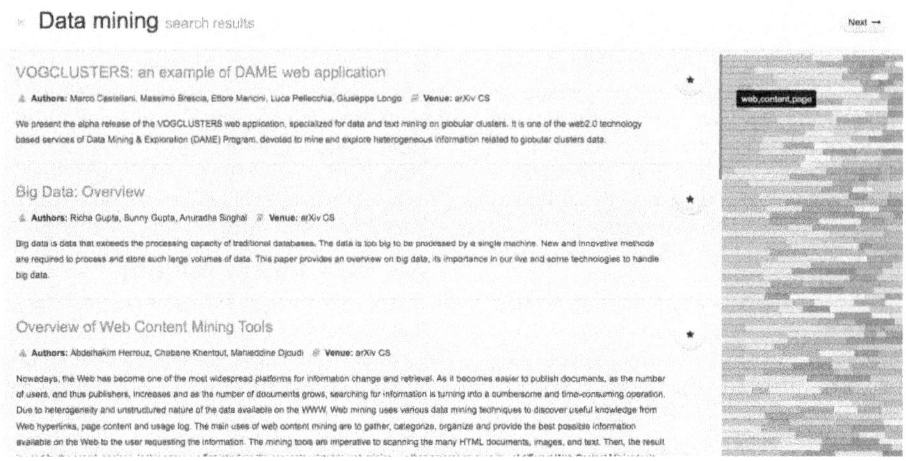

Figure 2: The search engine user interface.

line system. Additionally, in exploratory search tasks, there is a higher number of interactions, i.e. the number of search results users clicked or bookmarked in our system than in the baseline system. Currently, we are in the process of assessing exploratory searches initiated via our topic model visualisation versus free text search queries.

Acknowledgments. The work was supported by The Finnish Funding Agency for Innovation (projects Re:Know and D2I) and by Academy of Finland (project COIN).

5. REFERENCES

[1] K. Athukorala, D. Głowacka, A. Oulasvirta, J. Vreeken, and G. Jacucci. Is exploratory search different? a comparison of information search behavior for exploratory and lookup tasks. *JASIST*, 2015.

[2] K. Athukorala, A. Medlar, K. Ilves, and D. Głowacka. Balancing exploration and exploitation: Empirical parameterization of exploratory search systems. In *CIKM*, 2015.

[3] K. Athukorala, A. Medlar, A. Oulasvirta, G. Jacucci, and D. Głowacka. Beyond relevance: Adapting exploration/exploitation in information retrieval. In *IUI*. ACM, 2016.

[4] P. Auer. Using confidence bounds for exploitation – exploration trade-offs. *JMLR*, 3:397 – 422, 2002.

[5] N. J. Belkin. Some (what) grand challenges for information retrieval. In *ACM SIGIR Forum*, volume 42, pages 47–54. ACM, 2008.

[6] W. Buntine and S. Mishra. Experiments with non-parametric topic models. In *SIGKDD*, 2014.

[7] D. H. Chau, A. Kittur, J. I. Hong, and C. Faloutsos. Apolo: making sense of large network data by combining rich user interaction and machine learning. In *CHI*, 2011.

[8] S. Chowdhury, F. Gibb, and M. Landoni. Uncertainty in information seeking and retrieval: A study in an academic environment. *Information Processing & Management*, 47(2):157–175, 2011.

[9] M. J. Cole, J. Gwizdka, C. Liu, N. J. Belkin, and X. Zhang. Inferring user knowledge level from eye movement patterns. *Inf. Proc. Manag.*, 2012.

[10] D. Głowacka, T. Ruotsalo, K. Konyushkova, K. Athukorala, S. Kaski, and G. Jacucci. Directing exploratory search: Reinforcement learning from user interactions with keywords. In *IUI*, 2013.

[11] B. Gretarsson, J. O'Donovan, S. Bostandjiev, T. Höllerer, A. Asuncion, D. Newman, and P. Smyth. Topicnets: Visual analysis of large text corpora with topic modeling. *ACM Trans. Intell. Syst. Technol.*, 3(2):23:1–23:26, Feb. 2012.

[12] A. Haghighi and L. Vanderwende. Exploring content models for multi-document summarization. In *NAACL*, 2009.

[13] A. Hassan, R. W. White, S. T. Dumais, and Y. Wang. Struggling or exploring?: disambiguating long search sessions. In *WSDM*, 2014.

[14] S. Hore, L. Tyrvainen, J. Pyykko, and D. Glowacka. A reinforcement learning approach to query-less image retrieval. In *Symbiotic Interaction*, 2014.

[15] D. Kelly and X. Fu. Elicitation of term relevance feedback: an investigation of term source and context. In *SIGIR*, 2006.

[16] G. Marchionini. Exploratory search: from finding to understanding. *Com. ACM*, 49(4):41–46, 2006.

[17] J. Matejka, T. Grossman, and G. Fitzmaurice. Citeology: visualizing paper genealogy. In *CHI Extended Abstracts*, pages 181–190. ACM, 2012.

[18] P. Pirolli and S. Card. Information foraging. *Psych. rev.*, 106(4):643, 1999.

[19] K. Sparck Jones, S. Walker, and S. E. Robertson. A probabilistic model of information retrieval: Development and comparative experiments. *Info. Proc. & Manag.*, 36(6):779–840, 2000.

[20] R. W. White, P. N. Bennett, and S. T. Dumais. Predicting short-term interests using activity-based search context. In *CIKM*, 2010.

[21] K.-P. Yee, K. Swearingen, K. Li, and M. Hearst. Faceted metadata for image search and browsing. In *CHI*, 2003.

SECC: A Novel Search Engine Interface with Live Chat Channel

Cheng Zhang [1], Peng Zhang [*,1], Jingfei Li [1], Dawei Song [*,1,2]

[1]Tianjin Key Laboratory of Cognitive Computing and Application, Tianjin University, China

[2]School of Computing and Communications, The Open University, United Kingdom

zccode@gmail.com

{pzhang, jingfeili, dwsong}@tju.edu.cn

ABSTRACT

Traditional information retrieval systems rank documents according to their relevance to users' input queries. State of the art commercial search engines (SEs) train ranking models and suggest query refinements by exploiting collective intelligence implicitly using global users' query logs. However, they do not provide an explicit channel for users to communicate with each other in the search process. By asking or discussing with other users on the fly, a user could find relevant information more conveniently and gain a better search experience. In this paper, we present a demo of novel Search Engine with a live Chat Channel (SECC). SECC can group users automatically based on their input queries and allow them to communicate with each other in real time through a chat interface.

CCS Concepts

•Information systems → Search interfaces; •Software and its engineering → *Software design engineering;*

Keywords

Information Retrieval; Search Engine; Collective Intelligence; Chat Channel

1. INTRODUCTION

Users' collective intelligence, such as the collective users' query and interaction history recorded in search logs, has been widely used to support various important features, e.g., query recommendation [1], query completion [3] and webpage ranking [9], etc.

As shown in Figure 1, traditional search engines (TSEs) typically adopt a similar user interface, including a search control, display of search results and related searches. As an example, when a user inputs a query "information retrieval", popular TSEs such as Google, Bing and Baidu, all provide a list of related searches (as query recommendations), illustrated at the bottom of Figure 1.

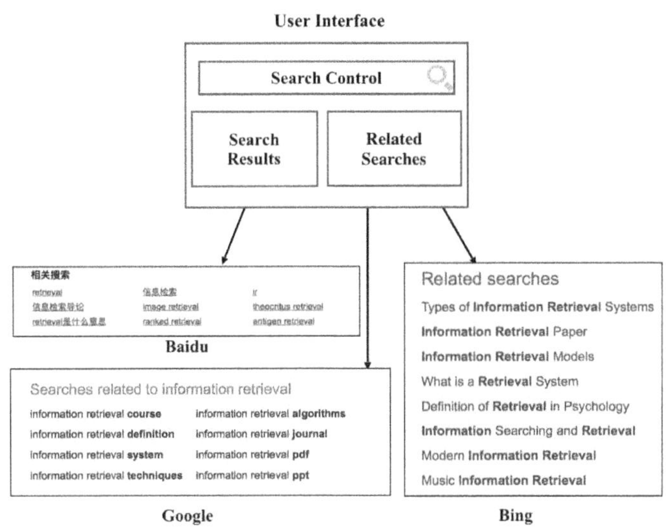

Figure 1: Common functionalities of popular search engines.

The components of query recommendation, query completion and webpage ranking are basic and important functionalities provided by the current search engines. These approaches are mostly trained with global query logs, which can be viewed as an implicit form of collective intelligence. Many search applications have utilized query logs to integrate the wisdom of other users, but the implicit methods could lead to estimation bias in inferring the user's intent [5].

Current TSEs provide little support to the situations where users want to readily communicate with other people to ask questions, especially when dealing with difficult search tasks. Recent attempts on collaborative search systems such as CoFox [4] , CoZapce [6] and SearchTogether [7], tackled this problem to some extent, but most of them focus on the collaboration between small groups of users, e.g., between specific people, colleagues and friends. It can be viewed as a kind of narrow collective intelligence.

In order to exploit global users' wisdom explicitly, we propose to add a live chat component in search engines to allow a user to request other users' help conveniently. In this ar-

*Corresponding Authors: Peng Zhang and Dawei Song

SIGIR '16, July 17-21, 2016, Pisa, Italy

© 2016 ACM. ISBN 978-1-4503-4069-4/16/07...$15.00

DOI: http://dx.doi.org/10.1145/2911451.2911454

ticle, we present a novel demo Search Engine with dynamically established live Chat Channels (SECC). SECC provides a socialized search function by implementing a user-friendly online chat interface for users who share similar search queries. Compared with TSEs, SECC allows similar users to communicate with each other to discuss about commonly concerned topics or problems. This new function will potentially benefit users' search experience.

The rest of the paper is organized as follows: In Section 2, we illustrate our motivation. The design and implementation of the demo is introduced in Section 3. Then, we demonstrate the SECC system in Section 4. Finally, Section 5 concludes the paper and discusses about future work.

2. MOTIVATION

In this section, we introduce our motivation from two perspectives: topology of search engine architecture and usage of collective intelligence. We first summarize the overall differences of SECC compared with TSE in Table 1.

	Topology	Collective Intelligence
TSE	single-center	implicit
SECC	multi-center	explicit

Table 1: Comparation between SECC and TSE in terms of topology and the usage of collective intelligence

2.1 Moving Towards a Multi-center Topology

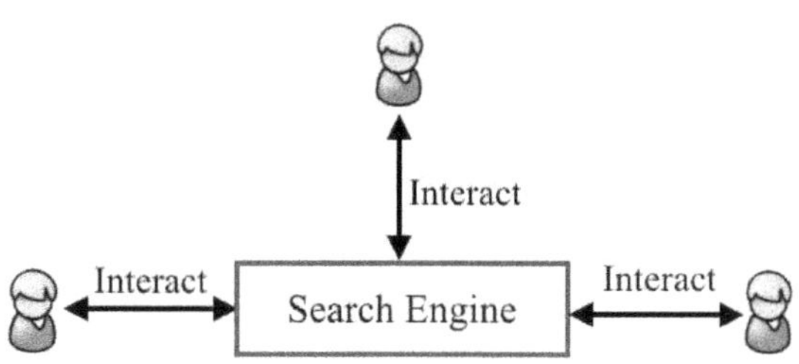

Figure 2: Single-Center interaction topology

Typical user interaction with a TSE can be summarized as follows: after a user submits a query, the SE returns a ranked list of documents to the user. Then, the user clicks on some results without any explicit communication with other people. This is a consequence of the TSE's single-center topology, as shown in Figure 2. In our opinion, TSE has a kind of star-like topology with a single center. All users communicate with the search engine. The feature of star-like topology is that it is easy to add new nodes (new users) into the network, but the failure of the central node will cause a halt of the entire network. If the center fails to provide satisfactory IR services (e.g., query recommendation), the users will be left no other choices to better satisfy their information needs, resulting in a poor user experience.

To address this issue, we propose a novel idea that moves from the single centered structure to a topology with multiple centers. To this end, we add a *Social Engine* to the original topology. As shown in Figure 3, the multi-center topology allows users to interact with the system through multiple channels, called *chat channels* in this paper, through the social engine. As a result, related users can be directly linked and they can instantly communicate with each other during a search session. This would improve the chance that users find desired information when the traditional search engine fails to do so.

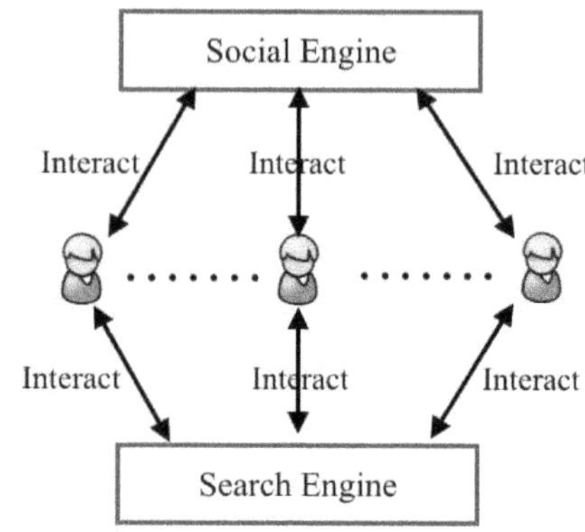

Figure 3: Multi-center interaction topology

2.2 Leveraging Explicit Collective Intelligence

In traditional search engines, collective intelligence has already been considered by mining historical and collective user behaviors, e.g., clicking, reading, query changing, etc. For instance, Boldi et al. [1] construct query flow graphs from global query logs to generate query recommendations. Duan et al. [3] propose to correct spelling errors for query completion based on the distribution of queries in the query log. A webpage re-ranking model is developed with the dynamically grouped users' query log data [9]. These approaches can be viewed as examples of applying implicit collective intelligence in the search process. However, as argued by Clark [2], it is still a challenge for machines to deeply and precisely understand the whole world to answer questions that go beyond the information exactly stated in text. For example, the implicit exploitation of collective intelligence may fail to solve some special problems, such as a mathematical problem described in Table 2 (an exercise that appeared in [8]). Therefore, there is a limitation for the use of implicit collective intelligence in search engines cover all possible search problems.

Consider the functions $f_n(x) = \sin ax$ ($n = 1, 2, 3, ..., -\pi \leq x \leq \pi$) as points of $\mathscr{L}^2$. Prove that the set of these points is closed and bounded, but not compact.

Table 2: A mathematical problem

To better exploit collective intelligence in SEs, we propose a practical solution by directly adding an explicit collective intelligence component (namely a social engine) into the SECC. The added component provides a live chat channel to a group of users who have similar search tasks. As shown in Figure 3, the dotted lines indicate the links among users. The user grouping should be dynamic with respect to the users' information need. Users in the same group will be provided a channel to communicate online with each other. When users face difficult problems (e.g., the mathematical problem presented in Table 2) which can not be solved by TSE, they can explicitly discuss the problems and share experiences through the chat channel. This would lead to a better chance for users to finally complete the search task through explicit collective intelligence, thus leading to a better user experience.

3. DESIGN AND IMPLEMENTATION

In this section, we design the framework of SECC and introduce its implementation details.

3.1 Framework

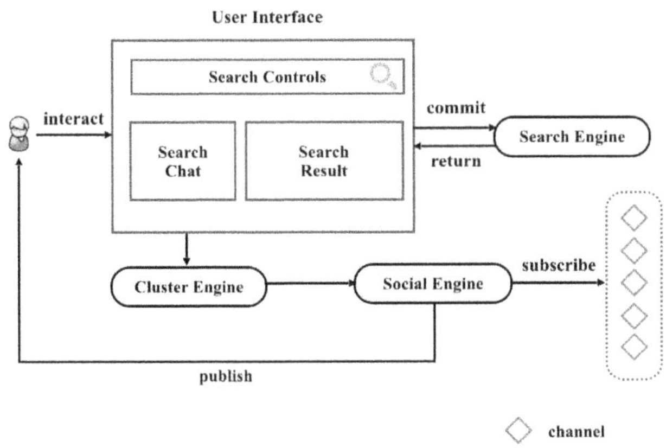

Figure 4: Framework

As shown in Figure 4, our system contains three main engines, i.e., a search engine, a cluster engine and a social engine. The search engine provides traditional functions (e.g., query completion, query suggestion and webpage ranking etc.) based on an indexed corpus. The cluster engine groups similar users dynamically based on overlapping of input queries. The social engine provides a chat channel for grouped users, which allows them to exploit collective intelligence. To facilitate these new functions, we designed a new layout of the user interface (Figure 6 (b)). On the left hand side is the chat panel, while the right hand side displays the search engine results page (SERP) returned by the search engine. The chat function is jointly supported by the cluster engine and the social engine.

When a user inputs a query, the search engine will represent the query with a language model, and then return webpages ranked according to estimated probabilities of relevance between the query language model and the language models of webpages. Meanwhile, the cluster engine will automatically run in background to dynamically group similar users according to users' query terms. Each group will correspond to a chat channel as shown in Figure 4. If a user is not satisfied with the search results, he/she can post questions on the chat channel, and then the social engine will broadcast the questions to all online users who are in the same channel.

It is worth noting that if a user changes his/her input query, the user's group (and chat channel) will change accordingly. The system detects the changes automatically and assists the user to establish another channel in real time.

3.2 Implementation

As shown in Figure 5, the SECC system consists of five modules, including user interface, web server, search engine, cluster engine and social engine.

SECC is coded with Python 2.7.x[1]. We develop the user interface with the bootstrap[2]. The web server is supported by Tornado[3] library which has the property of asynchronous and non-blocking network I/O. A fast full-text indexing and searching library implemented in Python, namely Whoosh[4], is utilized to develop the search engine module. The chat data are stored in the in-memory key-value database Redis[5] and accessible via the Python client for Redis[6]. Additionally, Ajax is used to request and post information for the chat engine. All modules and related technical information are illustrated in Figure 5.

When a user starts a search task, the search engine receives the input queries and return search results by HTTP request. The social engine, instead, uses long-polling to maintain the connection for users all the way through the search session and provides the users with necessary communication services.

In this version of demo, we focus on verifying the feasibility of the proposed framework. Therefore, we do not crawl webpages from the Internet. Instead, we use the TREC AP8889 as test corpus. In the future, we will enlarge the corpus by crawling webpages from the Internet and selected domains to make a more practical system.

4. DEMONSTRATION

We illustrate the demo in Figure 6. Figure 6 (a) shows the start page of our demo, which is in a typical search box style as used in the prominent TSEs. After we input a query into the search box, the system will detect the current user's search interest and cluster a set of users who shares similar search topics. Accordingly, the interface will change to another layout as shown in Figure 6 (b). The chat module is placed in the left side of the main page, while the search results are displayed in the right side (Figure 6 (b) and (c)). The user can communicate with others through live chat, which increases the interactivity among users.

An illustrative example is shown in Figure 6(b) and (c). Suppose two users, with nicknames 'zhang' and 'tju' respectively, share the same query words "Prime (Lending) Rate Moves". SECC will cluster them into the same chat channel, in which they can communicate conveniently. Similarly, if they both want to solve the mathematical problem mentioned in the previous section, they can discuss how to solve it through the chat channel and find the correct answer together. Note that, a user's chat channel will change dynamically in accordance with the change of the user's query words.

5. CONCLUSIONS AND FUTURE WORK

In this paper, we present a novel search engine with a live chat channel, which allows users sharing similar search

[1]https://www.python.org
[2]http://getbootstrap.com
[3]http://www.tornadoweb.org/en/stable
[4]http://bitbucket.org/mchaput/whoosh/wiki/Home
[5]http://redis.io
[6]http://pypi.python.org/pypi/redis

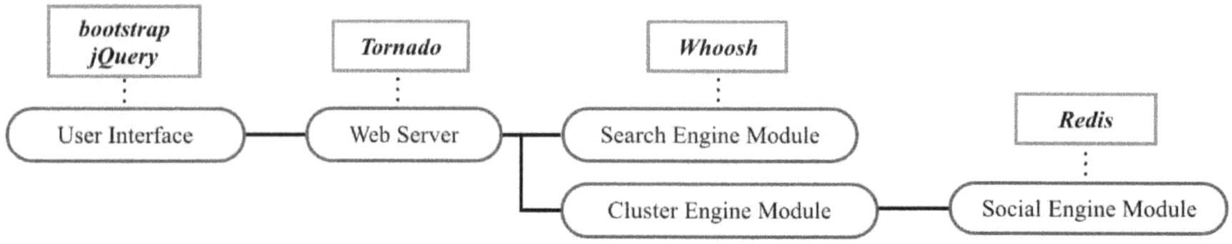

Figure 5: Modules and related technical dependencies

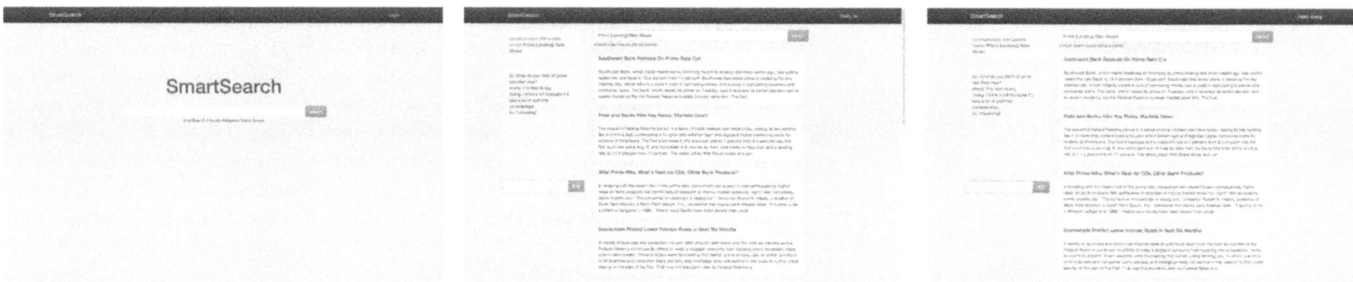

(a) (b) (c)

Figure 6: Demonstration of SECC

topics to interact with each other during search sessions and exploit collective intelligence explicitly. The system provides a live communication service besides traditional IR components.

The current version of the demo is for testing our initial ideas and has a large room for further improvements. Currently, the user cluster engine groups similar users based on overlapping of input queries. This query-based approach is insufficient for understanding the user's intent during a search task (or a session) and would cause too frequent updates of users' chat channels. Thus we will consider grouping users at the session/task level. Secondly, the size of indexed corpus is currently small. We should enlarge the corpus significantly by crawling webpages from the Internet (for selected domains) regularly, in order to make the search engine more practical. This will also attract more users to use our system, so as to improve our system by exploiting the collective intelligence explicitly and implicitly. Furthermore, we will investigate effective mechanisms, such as gamification, to promote the users' incentive to use the chat channels. Finally, we will carry out large scale user task-based evaluation and keep refining our interfaces and algorithms.

6. ACKNOWLEDGEMENTS

The work presented in this paper is sponsored in part by the Chinese National Program on Key Basic Research Project (973 Program, grant No. 2013CB329304, 2014CB744604), the Chinese 863 Program (grant No. 2015AA015403), the Natural Science Foundation of China (grant No. 61402324, 61272265), and the Tianjin Research Program of Application Foundation and Advanced Technology (grant No. 15JC-QNJC41700)..

7. REFERENCES

[1] P. Boldi, F. Bonchi, C. Castillo, D. Donato, A. Gionis, and S. Vigna. The query-flow graph: model and applications. In *Proceedings of the 17th ACM conference on Information and knowledge management*, pages 609–618. ACM, 2008.

[2] P. Clark. Elementary school science and math tests as a driver for ai: Take the aristo challenge. *to appear*, 2015.

[3] H. Duan and B.-J. P. Hsu. Online spelling correction for query completion. In *Proceedings of the 20th international conference on World wide web*, pages 117–126. ACM, 2011.

[4] R. P. Jesus, T. Leelanupab, and J. M. Jose. Cofox: A synchronous collaborative browser. In *Information Retrieval Technology*, pages 262–274. Springer, 2012.

[5] T. Joachims and F. Radlinski. Search engines that learn from implicit feedback. *Computer*, (8):34–40, 2007.

[6] H. Kruajirayu, A. Tangsomboon, and T. Leelanupab. Cozpace: a proposal for collaborative web search for sharing search records and interactions. In *Student Project Conference (ICT-ISPC), 2014 Third ICT International*, pages 165–168. IEEE, 2014.

[7] M. R. Morris and E. Horvitz. Searchtogether: an interface for collaborative web search. In *Proceedings of the 20th annual ACM symposium on User interface software and technology*, pages 3–12. ACM, 2007.

[8] W. Rudin. *Principles of mathematical analysis*, volume 3. McGraw-Hill New York, 1964.

[9] T. T. Vu, D. Song, A. Willis, S. N. Tran, and J. Li. Improving search personalisation with dynamic group formation. In *Proceedings of the 37th international ACM SIGIR conference on Research & development in information retrieval*, pages 951–954. ACM, 2014.

Simulating Interactive Information Retrieval

SimIIR: A Framework for the Simulation of Interaction

David Maxwell and Leif Azzopardi
School of Computing Science
University of Glasgow
Glasgow, Scotland
d.maxwell.1@research.gla.ac.uk
Leif.Azzopardi@glasgow.ac.uk

ABSTRACT

Simulation provides a powerful and cost-effective approach to explore and evaluate how interactions between a searcher and system influence search behaviour and performance. With a growing interest in simulation and an increasing number of papers using such an approach, there is a need for a flexible framework for simulation. Thus, we present *SimIIR*, an open-source toolkit for building and conducting *Interactive Information Retrieval (IIR)* experiments. The framework consists of a number of high level components, including the simulation, the searcher and the system, all of which must be configured. The SimIIR framework provides a series of interchangeable components. Examples of these components include the querying strategies (how simulated queries are formulated) and stopping strategies (the depth to which a searcher will examine snippets and documents) that a simulated searcher will employ. We have implemented various existing strategies so that they can be used by other researchers to not only replicate and reproduce past experiments, but also create new experiments. This paper describes the SimIIR framework and the different components that can be configured and extended as required.

Keywords: Simulation, Search Behavior, Strategy, Stopping Strategies, Continuation Strategies, Querying Strategies, User Modeling

1. INTRODUCTION

The process of search is inherently interactive. During a search session, a searcher can issue a number of queries, examine a number of snippets, and assess documents for relevance to their information need. Despite this, the *Information Retrieval (IR)* community has centred much of its research around the so-called *Cranfield Paradigm*. Revolving around the concept of standardised test collections and relevance judgements, the paradigm makes a number of key assumptions that are at odds with the interactive nature of search. Assumptions include a searcher: *(i)* issuing a single query; *(ii)* examining each document in turn and independently; and *(iii)* examining snippets and documents to a fixed depth. Simulation, as outlined by Keskustalo et al. [10], provides a means to go beyond the limitations presented by the Cranfield paradigm without conducting an expensive and time consuming user study. Simulation also offers a number of other benefits over user studies. The approach provides a rapid means to exploring *'what-if'* scenarios, and also facilitates a range of evaluations, such as a comparison between systems and understanding searcher behaviours [4]. Simulations enable a range and variety of searchers to be created who do not suffer from issues such as fatigue or learning effects, unless specifically coded to do so. Simulated searchers are therefore highly controlled, and can therefore yield reproducible results [4].

With a growing interest in simulation and a growing number of researchers employing the technique in their work (e.g. [1, 2, 3, 6, 7, 9, 13, 14, 15, 17]), we argue that there is a need for an IIR-based simulation toolkit. A toolkit freely available to the IIR community will ensure that experiments conducted with it can be easily reproduced, as well as reducing the major overheads for creating simulations. To address this issue, we introduce an open-source framework for the simulation of IIR (*SimIIR*). Over the past two years, we have been building the SimIIR framework and used it to produce a number of different simulations [13, 14] - with more to come. The framework can be configured in a variety of different ways to support different search processes, different searcher configurations, different experimental conditions, and different search engines.

2. SIMIIR

Previous studies employing simulation have either: *(i)* considered aspects of the IIR process in isolation, such as query generation (e.g. [11]); or *(ii)* considered the search process as a whole (e.g. [14]). SimIIR is designed to capture and broadly reflect the complex processes involved within the wider IIR process, and has been developed from the ground up in the *Python*[1] programming language using a highly modularised, class-based framework. Each component broadly represents a major stage in the IIR process[2],

SIGIR '16, July 17 - 21, 2016, Pisa, Italy

ISBN 978-1-4503-4069-4/16/07...$15.00

DOI: http://dx.doi.org/10.1145/2911451.2911469

[1] Python is a general purpose, high level programming language available at http://www.python.org. The SimIIR framework is presently designed to run on Python 2.7.x environments.

[2] The SimIIR framework, complete with a variety of example simulation configuration files, is freely available at http://git.io/vZ5mH.

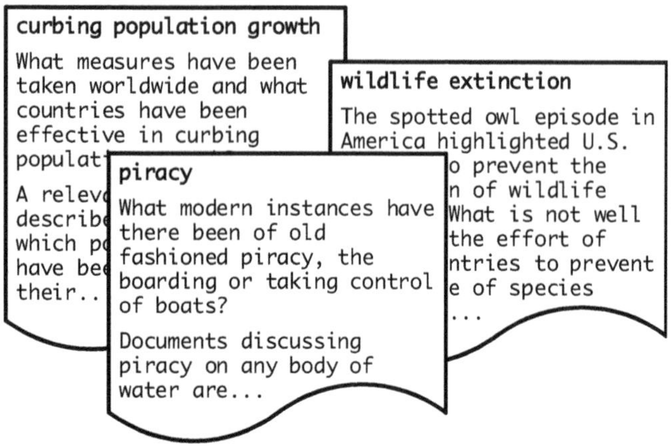

Figure 1: An example of three topic descriptions used within the SimIIR framework. The first line denotes the topic title, with everything following the title considered the topic description.

with new components simply inheriting from the relevant base class. This allows for the easy experimentation of different simulated searchers using a variety of test collections, querying strategies, stopping strategies, and more. This also highlights one of the main advantages of SimIIR in that it can be easily adapted to suit ever more advanced components as the research in this area progresses. SimIIR has already been employed in several publications investigating stopping strategies by Maxwell et al. [13, 14].

SimIIR Components: In order to successfully run an experiment on SimIIR, a *simulation* must first be defined. A simulation is comprised of a series of **topics**, a **search interface/engine**, an **output controller**, and a series of **simulated searchers** - all of which are elaborated on in subsequent sections. A simulation in essence is loosely associated with the concept of a real-world experiment, such as a user study. The experiment would be comprised of a series of searchers or subjects, examining documents for relevance over one or more topics. The parameters for each of these settings are specified in an XML *simulation configuration* file and passed to SimIIR. The experiment itself consists of a series of runs, the total number of which can be calculated by summing the combinations of the specified number of searchers and topics. The final component comprising a simulation is the list of simulated searchers. Every simulated searcher is specified within a separate XML *user configuration file*. Within this file, a host of additional components are defined, namely: a **querying strategy/generator**; a **classifier/decision maker** for both **snippets** and **documents**; a **stopping strategy**; a **logger**; and a **search context**. The components which comprise the searcher are encoded within the underlying **searcher model**, providing the various actions that are observed.

2.1 Topics

We define a topic as a description of what a simulated searcher is expected to find relevant. These are specified by a series of *topic description files*, consisting of a *title* and *description*. Figure 1 illustrates examples of such files. All the topic files that have been generated for SimIIR thus far are based upon the topics provided by various *TREC* tracks, such as the TREC *2005 Robust Track*.

ACTION	QUERY	1200.0	13.9	extinction wildlife	
ACTION	SERP	1200.0	15.4	EXAMINE_SERP	
ACTION	SNIPPET	1200.0	16.7	SNIPPET_REL	APW1998...
ACTION	DOC	1200.0	40.5	EXAMINING_DOC	APW1998...
ACTION	MARK	1200.0	43.1	CONSIDERED_REL	APW1998...
ACTION	SNIPPET	1200.0	44.4	SNIPPET_REL	XIE1998...
ACTION	DOC	1200.0	68.2	EXAMINING_DOC	XIE1998...
ACTION	SNIPPET	1200.0	69.5	SNIPPET_NR	NYT1999...
ACTION	QUERY	1200.0	83.4	efforts extinction wildlife	
ACTION	SERP	1200.0	84.9	EXAMINE_SERP	
ACTION	SNIPPET	1200.0	86.2	SEEN_PREV	XIE1998...

Figure 2: An example snippet of the output log file generated by SimIIR. Included is the action performed by the simulated searcher (e.g. QUERY, SNIPPET), the total time available (1200 seconds), the elapsed time of the simulated session, and the judgement for the action (if applicable), such as SNIPPET_REL for when a snippet is considered relevant.

2.2 Search Interface/Engine

We consider the search interface/engine component as an abstraction of a search engine and the *Search Engine Results Page (SERP)*. After issuing the search interface/engine with a query, the component provides SimIIR with access to the SERP - a ranked list of snippets and associated documents. As the interface is highly genericised, any search engine with a Python wrapper can be easily coupled to the SimIIR framework. Presently, only a wrapper for the *Whoosh* IR toolkit[3] has been implemented. Any additional configuration options for a particular search interface/engine can also easily be set in the simulation configuration file.

2.3 Output Controller

SimIIR also provides a flexible output controller with a variety of output options for the simulations that are run with the framework. Options are based upon the output files that are saved for each simulated run, and include options to save the interaction log of the simulated searchers (e.g. queries issued, snippets examined, documents examined), and whether to save the list of documents considered relevant by the simulated searchers. The file specified by the final option may then in turn be fed into an evaluation program such as `trec_eval`[4] to obtain the values for the various measures and metrics that can be computed.

For each run, output files include: a `.log` file, which contains the complete set of interactions undertaken by the simulated searcher (refer to Figure 2 for an example of an output log); a `.cfg` file, containing the configuration of components for a given simulated searcher; an `.out` file, containing output from an evaluation program such as `trec_eval` (if enabled); a `.queries` file, containing a line break separated list of queries issued; and a `.res` file, containing a list of the documents considered relevant (in the format of a standard TREC results file). Runs are identified by unique identifiers specified in the simulation configuration and searcher configuration files to avoid results being overwritten.

2.4 Querying Strategies/Generators

The querying strategy/generator is the component responsible for the generation and selection of queries. A variety

[3] *Whoosh* is a pure Python indexing and search library, available at https://pypi.python.org/pypi/Whoosh.

[4] The `trec_eval` program is freely available to download and compile at http://trec.nist.gov/trec_eval/.

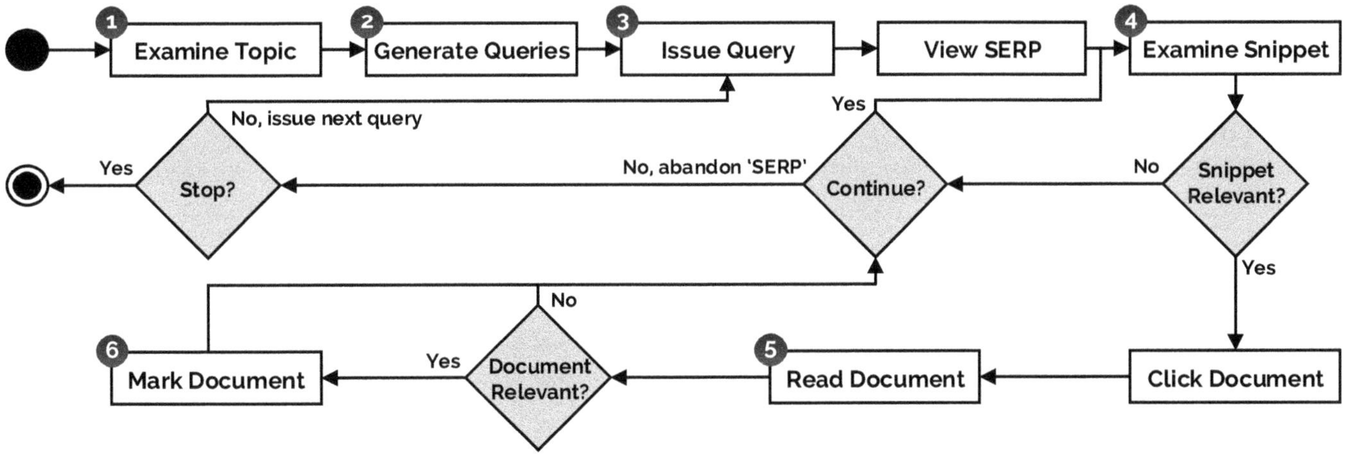

Figure 3: A flowchart of the *Complex Searcher Model (CSM)*, from Maxwell et al. [14] - presently used within SimIIR as the underlying searcher model. The flowchart illustrates the key components of the model (in white) and decisions (in grey) that simulated searchers consider. Numbers are associated with the steps as described in Section 2.9. The CSM is adapted from the works of Baskaya et al. [6] and Thomas et al. [19].

of different simulated query generation strategies exist, such as the approaches discussed by Baskaya [5] and Keskustalo et al. [11]. Queries also need not be generated - a list of queries issued by real-world searchers can be used, if desired. This functionality has been already implemented through a `PredeterminedQueryGenerator` class, which takes as input a list of queries to be issued. This is useful for comparing the performance of real-world searchers and simulated searchers under similar conditions, as used by Maxwell et al. [14].

In addition to the generator detailed above, a number of query generation strategies have been operationalised as SimIIR classes. Several of the querying strategies proposed by Baskaya [5] and Keskustalo et al. [11] have already been implemented, such as the `SingleTermQueryGenerator` that generates single term queries, the `BiTermQueryGenerator` that generates two term queries, and the `TriTermQueryGenerator` that generates three term queries. All of these classes generate queries from the provided topic title and description text. Work is also underway to incorporate terms from sources other than the topic title and description, such as previously examined snippets and documents. This will result in a wider potential vocabulary for query generation.

2.5 Snippet/Document Classifiers

We next describe another major component of the SimIIR framework - *classifiers.* These components are responsible for determining the attractiveness of a given snippet - or the relevancy of a document - to the provided topic that the simulated searcher is tasked to examine. Snippet and document classifiers can be specified individually to enable the simulator to take into account the fact that searchers may judge snippets differently from documents. As an example, a searcher may be more liberal when deciding the attractiveness of a snippet as opposed to a document's relevancy.

A series of snippet/document classifiers have already been implemented and are ready for use. These include: a *'TREC-style'* classifier, which judges everything to be relevant; an `InformedTrecTextClassifier` that uses TREC QRELS and probabilities (acting stochastically) to determine if a snippet/document should be considered attractive/relevant; and a `LMTextClassifier` which uses a language model (specified by optional configuration parameters) that acts deterministically to determine attractiveness and/or relevancy.

2.6 Stopping Strategies

The stopping strategy decides where a simulated searcher should stop examining a list of ranked documents. This concept is called *query stopping* [14], as opposed to *session stopping*, which is presently determined by the logger component (refer to Section 2.7). A variety of stopping strategies have been previously proposed in the literature, such as the *disgust* and *frustration point* rules [8, 12].

As two recent publications used the SimIIR framework to simulate the effects of stopping strategies [13, 14], a variety of strategies have already been implemented. As an example, these include: a `FixedDepthDecisionMaker`, implementing a naïve approach where simulated searchers will stop after examining x snippets regardless of relevance; a `NonrelDecisionMaker`, which operationalises the aforementioned disgust and frustration point rules [8, 12], where simulated searchers will stop after judging x snippets non relevant; and an `IftBasedDecisionMaker`, a stopping strategy which operationalises the implicit stopping rule encoded within *Information Foraging Theory (IFT)* [14, 16].

2.7 Loggers

A logger is the component of the SimIIR framework that determines the *costs* of interaction for the simulated searcher when performing actions, such as issuing a query. Interaction costs can be defined in the user configuration file. The logger therefore tracks and records all interactions that take place within a simulated search session, and is for example able to state when a predetermined time limit elapses - thus providing some form of session stopping. The details stored within the logger component can then be sent to the output controller component upon completion of the simulated search session to produce the `.log` output file.

To date, we have fully implemented a `FixedCostLogger` that considers each of the different actions undertaken by a simulated searcher, and as the name suggests, imposes a fixed cost upon each of them. Currently, a variable cost logger is in the early stages of development. This more advanced logger will for example provide the ability for SimIIR to impose variable costs that are dependent upon factors such as query or document length, for example [7, 18].

2.8 Search Contexts

The search context is the component of the SimIIR framework responsible for keeping a record of all issued queries, all examined snippets, documents (along with the judgements for each) and other interactions throughout a search session. The search context is in essence the 'memory' of the simulated searcher, and interacts closely with the specified logger component to record all events (refer to Section 2.7). By referring to the search context, a snippet classifier can for example determine what snippets the simulated searcher has previously seen, whether they were considered relevant or non-relevant, and what text was observed.

From the basic search context, we have derived a *relevance revision* search context, as used by Maxwell et al. [13, 14]. When considering a snippet relevant, a simulated searcher using the revised relevance search context can then revise its judgement of said snippet if the associated document is subsequently deemed to be not relevant. Such a technique can influence the stopping point of the simulated searcher if using a stopping strategy based upon the frustration point and disgust stopping rules [8, 12] (refer to Section 2.6) for instance. We envisage that as work in the area of IIR simulation progresses, more complex search contexts can be implemented. For example, one such approach could be a 'lossy' search context, where a simulated searcher would *forget* over time what snippets and documents have been examined.

2.9 The Searcher Model

When SimIIR is started, all the components are instantiated based upon the simulation and user configuration XML files. The process in which SimIIR simulates IIR is based upon the *Complex Searcher Model (CSM)*, a model of interaction proposed by Maxwell et al. [14]. The model, represented as a flowchart in Figure 3, is based upon the stochastic model presented by Baskaya et al. [6], but includes additional decision points as described by Thomas et al. [19]. While the CSM does not presently represent every aspect of the IIR process, it does provide a better representation than has been used previously. The model can be extended as research in this area progresses.

Essentially, the simulated searcher begins by ***(1)*** examining the given topic and title description. From the title and description, the simulated searcher then ***(2)*** generates a series of queries which are issued to the underlying search engine. The simulated searcher then ***(3)*** issues a query from the generated list, and then ***(4)*** proceeds to examine the first/next snippet in the ranked list provided. The simulated searcher can also decide to issue a new query, thus returning to *(3)*. If the snippet is considered relevant by the simulated searcher, ***(5)*** the document is then examined in full. If the document is also considered relevant, ***(6)*** the document is then marked relevant. If either the snippet or document are considered non-relevant, the simulated searcher then returns to *(4)* with the document unmarked.

3. SUMMARY

In this demonstration paper, we have described our new IIR simulation framework, SimIIR. The highly modularised architecture of the framework makes it straightforward to implement new simulation components, and will aid in pushing research forward in this area. Future work will see the development of more advanced components and the adaption of the CSM to facilitate this.

Acknowledgments We would like to thank Professor Kalervo Järvelin and Dr Heikki Keskustalo at the University of Tampere, Finland for their co-operation and participation in a STSM, funded by the ESF supported MUMIA Cost Action (reference `ECOST-STSM-IC1002-080914-049840`). The lead author is also financially supported by the EPSRC, grant number `1367507`. We would also like to thank Paul Thomas for his debugging efforts.

References

[1] L. Azzopardi. Query side evaluation: An empirical analysis of effectiveness and effort. In *Proceedings of the 32nd ACM SIGIR*, pages 556–563, 2009.
[2] L. Azzopardi. The economics in interactive information retrieval. In *Proc. 34th ACM SIGIR*, pages 15–24, 2011.
[3] L. Azzopardi, M. de Rijke, and K. Balog. Building simulated queries for known-item topics: An analysis using six european languages. In *Proc. 30th ACM SIGIR*, pages 455–462, 2007.
[4] L. Azzopardi, K. Järvelin, J. Kamps, and M.D. Smucker. Report on the sigir 2010 workshop on the simulation of interaction. *SIGIR Forum*, 44(2):35–47, 2011.
[5] F. Baskaya. *Simulating Search Sessions in Interactive Information Retrieval Evaluation.* PhD thesis, University of Tampere, School of Information Sciences, Finland, 2014.
[6] F. Baskaya, H. Keskustalo, and K. Järvelin. Modeling behavioral factors in interactive information retrieval. In *Proc. 22nd ACM CIKM*, pages 2297–2302, 2013.
[7] B. Carterette, A. Bah, and M. Zengin. Dynamic test collections for retrieval evaluation. In *Proc. 5th ACM ICTIR*, pages 91–100, 2015.
[8] W.S. Cooper. On selecting a measure of retrieval effectiveness part ii. implementation of the philosophy. *J. of the American Soc. for Info. Sci.*, 24(6):413–424, 1973.
[9] K. Järvelin. Interactive relevance feedback with graded relevance and sentence extraction: Simulated user experiments. In *Proc. 18th ACM CIKM*, pages 2053–2056, 2009.
[10] H. Keskustalo, K. Järvelin, and A. Pirkola. Evaluating the effectiveness of relevance feedback based on a user simulation model: Effects of a user scenario on cumulated gain value. *Information Retrieval*, 11(3):209–228, 2008.
[11] H. Keskustalo, K. Järvelin, A. Pirkola, T. Sharma, and M. Lykke. Test collection-based ir evaluation needs extension toward sessions — a case of extremely short queries. In *Proc. 5th AIRS*, pages 63–74, 2009.
[12] D.H. Kraft and T. Lee. Stopping rules and their effect on expected search length. *IPM*, 15(1):47 – 58, 1979.
[13] D. Maxwell, L. Azzopardi, K. Järvelin, and H. Keskustalo. An initial investigation into fixed and adaptive stopping strategies. In *Proc. 38th ACM SIGIR*, pages 903–906, 2015.
[14] D. Maxwell, L. Azzopardi, K. Järvelin, and H. Keskustalo. Searching and stopping: An analysis of stopping rules and strategies. In *Proc. 24th ACM CIKM*, pages 313–322, 2015.
[15] T. Pääkkönen, K. Järvelin, J. Kekäläinen, H. Keskustalo, F. Baskaya, D. Maxwell, and L. Azzopardi. Exploring behavioral dimensions in session effectiveness. In *Proc. 6th CLEF*, pages 178–189, 2015.
[16] P. Pirolli and S.K. Card. Information foraging. *Psychological Review*, 106:643–675, 1999.
[17] M.D. Smucker. An analysis of user strategies for examining and processing ranked lists of documents. In *Proc. of 5th HCIR*, 2011.
[18] M.D. Smucker and C.L.A. Clarke. Time-based calibration of effectiveness measures. In *Proc. 35th ACM SIGIR*, pages 95–104, 2012.
[19] P. Thomas, A. Moffat, P. Bailey, and F. Scholer. Modeling decision points in user search behavior. In *Proc. 5th IIiX*, pages 239–242, 2014.

The ComeWithMe System for Searching and Ranking Activity-Based Carpooling Rides

Vinicius Monteiro de Lira
CIN-UFPE, Recife, Brazil
vcml@cin.ufpe.br
ISTI-CNR, Pisa, Italy
lira@isti.cnr.it

Chiara Renso
ISTI-CNR, Pisa, Italy
renso@isti.cnr.it

Raffaele Perego
ISTI-CNR, Pisa, Italy
perego@isti.cnr.it

Salvatore Rinzivillo
ISTI-CNR, Pisa, Italy
rinzivillo@isti.cnr.it

Valeria Cesario Times
CIN–UFPE, Recife, Brazil
vct@cin.ufpe.br

ABSTRACT

ComeWithMe is an activity oriented carpooling service that enlarges the candidate destinations of a ride request by considering alternative places where the desired activity can be performed. It is based on the observation that individuals often move towards a place to perform an activity while the activity is often not strictly associated with a single place, as one may go for shopping or eating to many different locations. Activity-oriented carpooling hugely increases the number of rides matching a query, thus introducing requirements on system responsiveness and ranking effectiveness that are not common to traditional carpooling services. The demoed system implements the ComeWithMe service in almost its entirety, and includes the back-end and a user-friendly mobile application for smartphones aimed at achieving users' acceptance and usability.

Keywords

Carpooling; rides search; ranking

1. INTRODUCTION

The increasing of the vehicle fleet in major cities tends to worsen traffic congestion that in turn has negative effects on the environment due to the emission of pollutants. Traffic congestion becomes a factor of decision in the people's lifestyle: when planning their daily activities people consider not only the destination location, the time and the transportation facilities, but also the possible delay and stress due to traffic jams. Increasingly, people give priority to the traffic issue at the expenses of their preferences, sometimes changing the intended destination and/or the travelling time depending on the traffic forecasts.

On the other hand, economic development in large cities has increased the offers of venues where to carry on activities, allowing the users to choose among several alternative locations. For example, a person may choose among many different restaurants where to go for lunch, or different supermarkets where to go shopping. Additionally, each individual has a personal attitude to discover and try many different alternative locations [2]. ComeWithMe[1] exploits these attitudes offering a carpooling service that intercepts the willingness of users to delay/anticipate their movements and possibly change their final destination.

Previous work showed that ComeWithMe can boost the ride possibilities up to 80% [3, 5], thus providing a sustainable way to use the fleet of cars that performs daily routines in a city. A direct consequence of this huge increase is that when we apply this method to large cities with many users, each carpooling request can match hundreds of possible rides offers to several destinations at different temporal slots. It is clear that effectively ranking these offers is crucial for the passenger acceptance and the success of the system.

This paper presents a system to efficiently collect, index, retrieve and rank the carpooling rides offered by users. The demo presents the main features of the ComeWithMe prototype that manages both drivers (offering rides) and passengers (requesting rides), and matches the requests with offers with the objective of maximizing the passenger acceptance rate. The system we present tackles the scalability issue by exploiting an inverted index that optimizes query processing, while usability is achieved by exploiting the knowledge mined from drivers trajectory data collected from the smart-phone sensors, and by providing a user-friendly mobile interface running on smart-phones.

We show the ComeWithMe system for the driver and passenger profiles. The driver offers rides based on scheduled trips or the analysis of his travel history (routine trips) and also receives the requests of rides from the passengers. The passengers query the system by selecting the desired destination, the time and by setting the flexibility preferences. The system firstly expands the query to get alternative destinations while preserving the intended activity, then searches the possible rides offered by drivers and finally ranks the retrieved rides based on passengers preferences. From here, the user can select a ride and visualize its details, check the route on the map and send the request to the driver.

Carpooling is quite used today and many systems are available to users. We can recall Blablacar.com, CarpoolWorld.com, Djengo.be and Carpooling.com. These systems have all similar functionalities, such as the search for commuting rides (travelling between two cities) and regular rides

[1]http://comewithme.isti.cnr.it

SIGIR '16, July 17-21, 2016, Pisa, Italy

DOI: http://dx.doi.org/10.1145/2911451.2911459

(home to work). Part of them also provide search for rides for groups of users (groups in school, events or companies). In summary, almost all of them can be seen as complementary to ComeWithMe since they focus on fixed destinations, while our system is based on the idea that some destinations are flexible.

ComeWithMe has been introduced in [3] where an algorithm for the spatio-temporal reallocation has been proposed to test the system potential. This demo paper presents the implementation of the whole prototype system, based on scalable and efficient information retrieval techniques.

2. SYSTEM ARCHITECTURE

ComeWithMe is designed to answer efficiently and effectively activity-oriented carpooling queries.

Efficiency and scalability are needed since the possibility of reallocating space and time boosts the rides opportunities at a high rate. For example, the activity "eating Italian food" may result in hundreds of different destinations in a large city, which raises to thousands with a less specific activity is chosen, e.g., "eat at a restaurant". In general, the number of possible rides tends to exponentially increase with the generality of the activity performed. The additional flexibility in the management of the pickup-up points and the temporal constraints further increments the complexity of query answering.

Besides expanding the user query on the basis of the intended activity and then retrieving all possible rides, ComeWithMe ranks the candidate rides according to the user's context and preferences. A number of features affect ranking such as: user current location and schedule, her willingness to walk to reach the pick-up or destination points, her adaptability to anticipate or delay the preferred departure and arrival time. The personalization of ranking criteria is important to improve the quality of experience perceived by the user and increase the probability of the ride acceptance.

The architecture of ComeWithMe is illustrated in Figure 1. As we can see, it is organized into three main components detailed in the following subsections: the *Trip Manager* to handle trips data, the *Ride Search Engine* to answer activity-oriented queries, and the *Mobile app* to interact with the users.

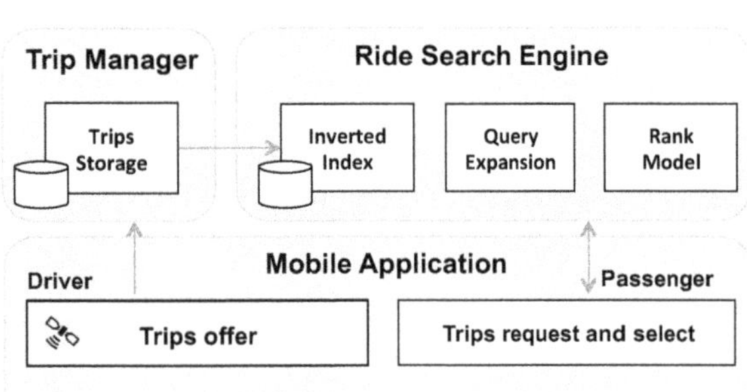

Figure 1: The architecture of the ComeWithMe system with three main components.

2.1 Trip Manager

This module is in charge of managing the drivers mobility data to model the ride offers. The region of interest covered by the carpooling service is simply modeled with a 2D spatial grid, and the path followed by each trip represented by the time-ordered sequence of cells visited [3]. The resolution of the grid is tuned to balance the number of activities per cell with the spatial accuracy of the rides.

The trips are associated with metadata specifying: the unique identifiers of the driver (*driverid*) and the trip (*tripid*), the date and the time t at which the trip will start, and the *ordered sequence* of cells visited along with their visiting time. Furthermore, each trip is annotated with additional information stating if the trip is routinely, and, if so, with its repetition pattern *(e.g., working days, week-end, Mondays, etc)*. An example of the conversion from the geospatial representation of the trip is exemplified in Figure 2.

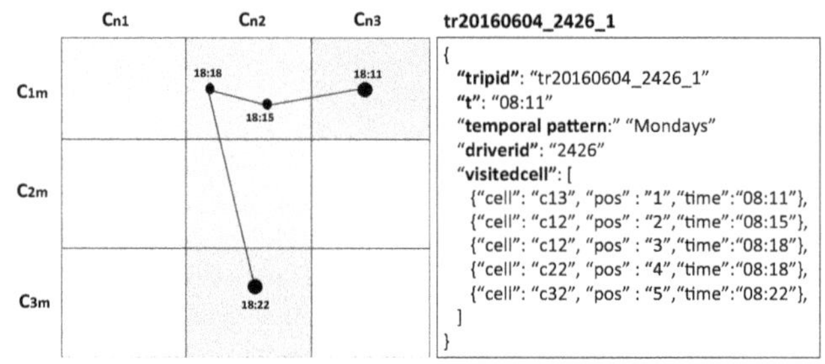

Figure 2: Example of trip representation.

ComeWithMe currently supports two different sources of trips: *routine trips* mined from historical GPS data collected by the ComeWithMe system, and *scheduled trips* explicitly offered by users through the mobile application.

Routine trips. ComeWithMe mobile app allows users to collect personal GPS data on a volunteer basis. These data are sent to the trip manager and stored in a spatial database. By applying the clustering method proposed in [4], we infer the drivers routine trips that are suggested as carpooling opportunities. The drivers have the option to decide whether to offer these rides to users.

Scheduled trips. These trips are made explicitly available by the user through the ComeWithMe mobile application specifying the path and the time of a specific planned trip she wants to share.

Additional functionalities provided by the Trip Manager module include the interactions with the mobile application, the requests of deletion of previously published trips, and the update of routine trips on a daily basis.

2.2 The Ride Search Engine

The main task of the *ride search engine* is to answer ComeWithMe passengers' queries by providing lists of ride opportunities ranked according to the user context and preferences. This task is accomplished by mean of three submodules: *Query Expansion, Inverted Index* and *Ranking Model.*

Query Expansion. This module boosts the possibilities of car rides by exploiting a query expansion technique. The use of query expansion generally increases recall and it is widely adopted in many application fields [1]. The queries in our context are carpooling requests expressing the passenger's intention to move to a venue to perform an activity. Given the destination *Point of Interest* (PoI) specified by the passenger, the query is automatically expanded with places related to the same activity by using a hierarchical thesaurus (an example is shown in Figure 3). The specific PoIs are the narrowest terms, while the intermediate layers represent different activities abstraction levels and thus possible query generalizations. For example, looking at Figure 3, when a passenger requests as destination "Da Gino", we see that it is an Italian Restaurant and expanding the query over Italian restaurants we have "Ristorante Giannino" as an alternative destination. Abstracting again up to "Eating" we have all the venues where they serve food corresponding to "Pizzeria", "Japanese restaurants", etc. The more we expand the query to broader terms, the more rides possibilities the passenger can select from the driver offers.

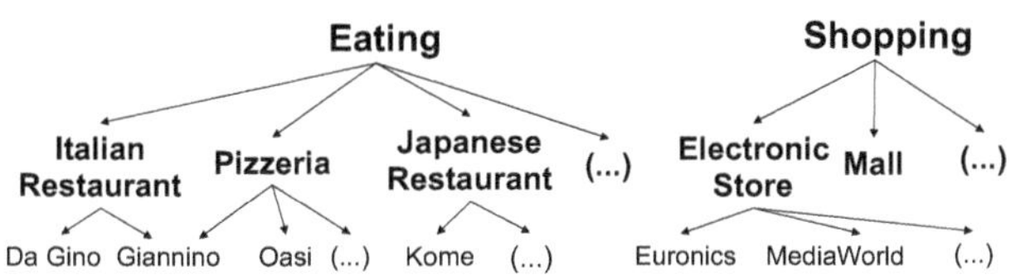

Figure 3: Structure of the thesaurus.

Each venue in the thesaurus is associated with a cell of the spatial grid indicating its location. Analogously, user queries are coded with the cells representing the pick-up area, the destination place, and a set of other cells representing alternative destinations. An example of the expansion process is illustrated in Figure 4: the destination PoI "Da Gino" is expanded with other possible venues (and cells) where the passenger can perform the activity "Eating".

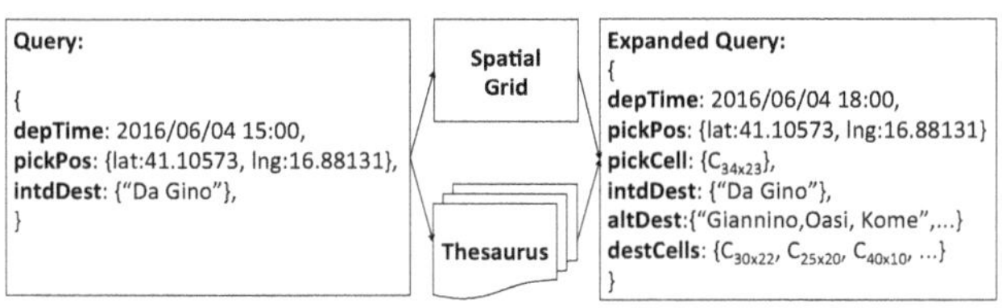

Figure 4: A query expansion example having Italian restaurant "Da Gino " as destination place is expanded into a list of cell containing alternative places for eating.

Inverted Index. Given the pick-up and the destination cells, and a time-window, ComeWithMe exploits an inverted index to retrieve the trips that cross these cells within the specified time window.

The index aims at speeding up query processing by improving the capability of ComeWithMe to handle an increasing number of ride opportunities, thus making the system scalable. We have a vocabulary entry for each cell of the spatial grid. In turn, each cell is associated with a list of postings, where each postings stores the *tripid* and the estimation of the time at which the car will cross the given cell. To speed up query processing, postings are organized into *buckets* where each bucket contains the postings referred to a specific coarse time window. Within each bucket, the postings are ordered by *tripid*. The organization in buckets avoids the scanning of the complete postings list when searching for trips, while the postings ordering within buckets allows to perform efficiently postings intersection operations.

To retrieve the candidate rides for a user query, ComeWithMe uses the pick-up cell, the time window for the ride (hint for accessing the right buckets), and the possible destination cells. The queries have the following semantics:

$$(pickCell\ AND\ (destCell_1\ OR\ destCell_2\ OR\ \cdots OR\ destCell_n))$$

Trips matching the above Boolean query are retrieved from the inverted index and the ones not respecting the correct order between pickup and destination cells, or the user-specified time constraints, are filtered out from the results list.

Ranking Model. We have already discussed how the query expansion consistently increases the possibilities of rides and, consequently, how crucial it is to propose to the user the rides that she is willing to accept.

The ranking score of candidate rides is thus computed as a linear combination of a set of features, mainly derived from the flexibility preferences the passenger can set through the mobile app: 1) a temporal tolerance indicating the delay of the departure time of the trip respect to the preferred time indicated in the query; 2) a temporal tolerance on the possible anticipation of the trip respect to the indicated preferred time; 3) a spatial tolerance indicating how much the passenger is willing to walk to reach the pick-up point and/or the destination location. Other information considered in the computation of the ride score include the trip duration and the semantic similarity between the actual destination of the ride and the one specified in the query. Intuitively, the duration of the trip should not be too long respect to the duration of the fastest of all the possible rides. On the other hand, the destination venue should be, in order of preference: close to the PoI chosen in the query; another PoI in the same thesaurus category (e.g., a different Italian restaurant when the requested venue was an Italian restaurant); a PoI in the more abstract category of the thesaurus.

The set of candidate rides retrieved from the index are thus ranked by considering:

1. the *distance* that the passenger is supposed to walk to reach the pick-up point and/or the destination location from the drop-off point. This distance is computed as the sum of the distance between the user location and the pick-up point, plus the distance between the drop off point and the destination. The obtained value is normalized with respect to the maximum distance the specific passenger declared to be willing to walk;

2. the *anticipation* of the trip respect to the desired pick-up time. This time is normalized with respect to the maximum time tolerance set in the user preferences;

3. the *delay* of the trip respect to the desired pick-up time (normalized as the previous feature);

4. the normalized *duration* of the trip. This feature has the value 1 when the duration is the minimum among all the retrieved rides, while it has the value 0 when the duration is close to the maximum duration of all the candidate rides;

5. the *semantic similarity* between the preferred destination PoI in the user query and the alternative PoI reached by the current ride. This value is set to 1 when the ride reaches the preferred destination, while it smoothly decreases to 0 as we consider PoIs in broader categories of the thesaurus.

For the first three features lower is better, while for the last two the opposite holds. Candidate rides are ranked using a linear combination of these five features where each feature is associated with a weight $\omega_i \in [-1, 1]$. Since no golden standard is available to optimize weights, the current prototype uses a uniform weighting schema $[-\frac{1}{5}, -\frac{1}{5}, -\frac{1}{5}, \frac{1}{5}, \frac{1}{5}]$. The effect in the result list of manually changing these weights will be shown during the demo.

2.3 The Mobile Application

ComeWithMe has two different profiles of users: the driver and the passenger. The passenger interface allows the user to request rides for a given destination, as shown in Figure 5. Once the required information is filled in, the user can submit the query and see the ranked list of rides offer.

In Figure 5, we see on the left our query example representing a user asking for a ride in the city of Pisa to go to the "Bella Napoli" pizzeria located in "via del Borghetto". The query specifies also the temporal tolerance (delay 30 minutes or anticipate 30 minutes) from the desired departure time at 19.00 and the spatial tolerance indicating the maximum distance the passenger is willing to walk (up to 600 meters).

ComeWithMe returns, for each query, a ranked list of rides where the best options are shown on the top. In our test dataset, during the specified temporal window (from 18:30 to 19:30), we have a total of 276 routine trips, 23 of which spatially matches the query from the pickup point to at least one "Pizzeria" among the 121 in the dataset. Since each trip can pass through many cells where "pizzeria" places are located, the ride search engine retrieves and ranks a total of 156 rides to "pizzeria" destinations (see Figure 5 on the right). Observing the results of the query, we notice that the first two rides are to the intended pizzeria "Bella Napoli", while other destination are "Panuozzo" and "La Greppia".

The passenger can select a ride from the ranked list and visualize some information about the driver and other details about the ride (e.g. the pickup address and time, the destination place, the estimated arrival, etc). Once the user selected and confirmed a ride, ComeWithMe notifies the driver about the upcoming request. Symmetrically, as shown in Figure 6, a driver can see the list of passenger requests and she can select one to visualize the details. From the details interface the driver can accept or decline the request, she can call the passenger, start a chat and visualize the trajectory on the map.

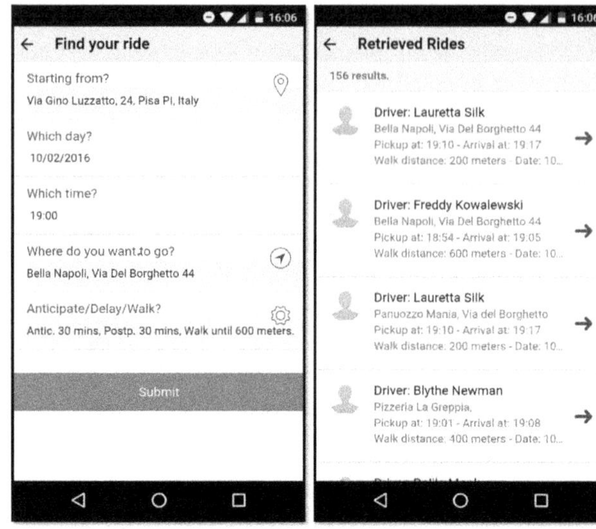

Figure 5: Passenger Interface.

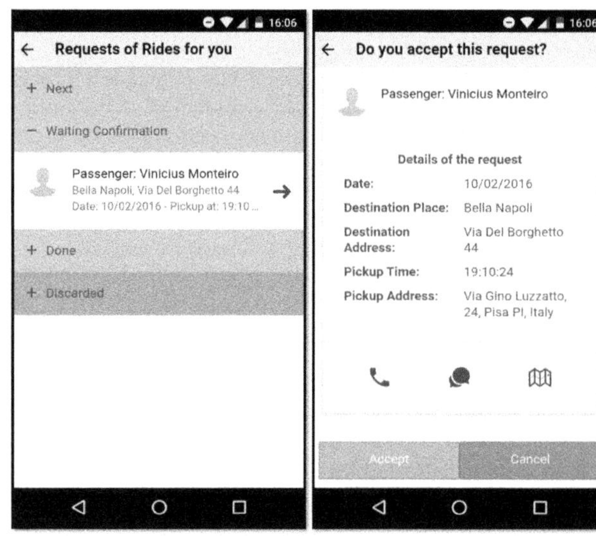

Figure 6: Driver Interface.

3. CONCLUSIONS

ComeWithMe is a carpooling system offering alternative destinations, thus boosting the number of available rides and requiring scalability besides efficiency and efficacy. The proposed demoed prototype has been implemented to meet these features showing promising results.

We are extending this prototype to support real usage features. For example, we plan to add the handling of the driver and passenger reputation, the management of groups of users and the optimization of the ranking function to maximize user satisfaction. As ongoing work, we are studying how to evaluate the system, and particularly the ranking function, by exploiting historical datasets. We also plan to conduct tailored user studies to further validate the acceptance of the system.

Acknowledgements. This work was partially supported by the EC H2020 Program INFRAIA-1-2014-2015 SoBigData: Social Mining & Big Data Ecosystem (654024).

4. REFERENCES

[1] C. Carpineto and G. Romano. A survey of automatic query expansion in information retrieval. *ACM Comput. Surv.*, 44(1):1:1–1:50, 2012.

[2] V. M. de Lira, S. Rinzivillo, C. Renso, V. C. Times, and P. C. A. R. Tedesco. Investigating semantic regularity of human mobility lifestyle. In *IDEAS 2014, Portugal, July 7-9*, 2014.

[3] V. Monteiro De Lira, V. C. Times, C. Renso, and S. Rinzivillo. ComeWithMe: An activity-oriented carpooling approach. In *IEEE 18th International Conference on Intelligent Transportation Systems*, 2015.

[4] R. Trasarti, F. Pinelli, M. Nanni, and F. Giannotti. Mining mobility user profiles for car pooling. In *Proceedings of the 17th ACM SIGKDD*. ACM, 2011.

[5] L. J. Young. A match.com for carpooling? http://goo.gl/pwTCVb.

ThingSeek: A Crawler and Search Engine for the Internet of Things

Ali Shemshadi, Quan Z. Sheng
School of Computer Science
The University of Adelaide, Australia
ali.shemshadi@adelaide.edu.au

Yongrui Qin
School of Computing and Engineering
University of Huddersfield, United Kingdom
y.qin2@hud.ac.uk

ABSTRACT

The rapidly growing paradigm of the Internet of Things (IoT) requires new search engines, which can crawl heterogeneous data sources and search in highly dynamic contexts. Existing search engines cannot meet these requirements as they are designed for traditional Web and human users only. This is contrary to the fact that things are emerging as major producers and consumers of information. Currently, there is very little work on searching IoT and a number of works claim the unavailability of public IoT data. However, it is dismissed that a majority of real-time web-based maps are sharing data that is generated by things, directly. To shed light on this line of research, in this paper, we firstly create a set of tools to capture IoT data from a set of given data sources. We then create two types of interfaces to provide real-time searching services on dynamic IoT data for both human and machine users.

1. INTRODUCTION

The Internet of Things (IoT) is an emerging paradigm, which aims to connect everyday physical objects to the Internet via wireless and identification technologies. It is revolutionizing numerous applications in a wide variety of real-world domains. Novel IoT-based solutions can provide competitive advantages in various key sectors of society. Some interesting examples are smart cities, smart homes, healthcare, security and surveillance [3]. Web services are now mature enough to enable sensors to automatically publish their data on the Internet. Unfortunately, traditional World Wide Web search engines currently do not cover existing IoT data on the Web. Therefore, a major milestone in boosting this area is to create tools to search IoT.

Some of the notable works in this area are as follows [11]: (1) Snoogle/Microsearch [7, 9]; (2) Dyser [4]; and (3) SPITFIRE [5]. Currently, to the best of our knowledge, all of the existing search engines have been examined only for small and/or unreal data. Furthermore, all of these search engines have been designed for human users only and it is neglected that smart objects may also require this service.

To the best of our knowledge, the only tangible result of initiating an IoT search engine is the *Thingful*[1] project. Thingful is a search engine for the IoT, providing a geographical index of connected objects around the world, including energy, radiation, weather, and air quality devices as well as seismographs, beacons, ships, aircraft and even wildlife trackers. The search engine indexes the data which is generated by publicly available sensors from different data sources. However, handling the data that should be indexed is a huge technical problem and the data on Thingful is mostly outdated. Moreover, the data collected by Thingful cannot be extracted by any means and the interface of the website presents raw data only. Thus, further improvements are required to convert the existing work to a good infrastructure for future works in this area.

Meanwhile, there is another search engine, namely *Shodan*[2] which also claims to be a search engine for IoT. Shodan is basically designed as a search engine for hackers as it identifies and hacks password protected devices such as servers and routers as well as any other object that is connected to the Internet. Shodan itself does not process sensor outputs and despite the size of its dataset, catching everyday objects on Shodan is still not straightforward as servers, routers and network devices constitute the majority of devices on its database.

We develop a data discovery engine to extract, analyze, visualize and export IoT data from publicly available data sources on the Internet. In our design, we focus on collecting publicly available real-time IoT data. The result of our work includes integrated tools for managing IoT data sources, a crawler engine to collect highly dynamic IoT data and two novel user interfaces to serve both human and machine users.

2. THINGSEEK: AN OVERVIEW

In this section, we present the framework of the ThingSeek crawler engine and specifications of the collected dataset.

2.1 ThingSeek Crawler Engine

2.1.1 ThingSeek Framework

To minimize the required amount of work when collecting data from a new source, we have broken down the crawling procedure into a certain set of steps in a unified framework.

[1]http://www.thingful.net
[2]https://www.shodan.io

SIGIR 2016 July 17-21, 2016 - Pisa, Italy
Copyright 2016 ACM ISBN 978-1-4503-4069-4/16/07
DOI: http://dx.doi.org/10.1145/2911451.2911471 ...$15.00.

Table 1: Example of selected parameters from a set of readings of a specific sensor

	id	title	private	status	updated	created	value	symbol
1	1213	house	false	public	2015-06-10T13:01:59.997058Z	2008-11-27T18:20:25.169483Z	77.46	F
2	1213	house	false	public	2015-06-10T20:31:00.777699Z	2008-11-27T18:20:25.169483Z	78.56	F
3	1213	house	false	public	2015-06-11T03:50:00.136106Z	2008-11-27T18:20:25.169483Z	79.5	F

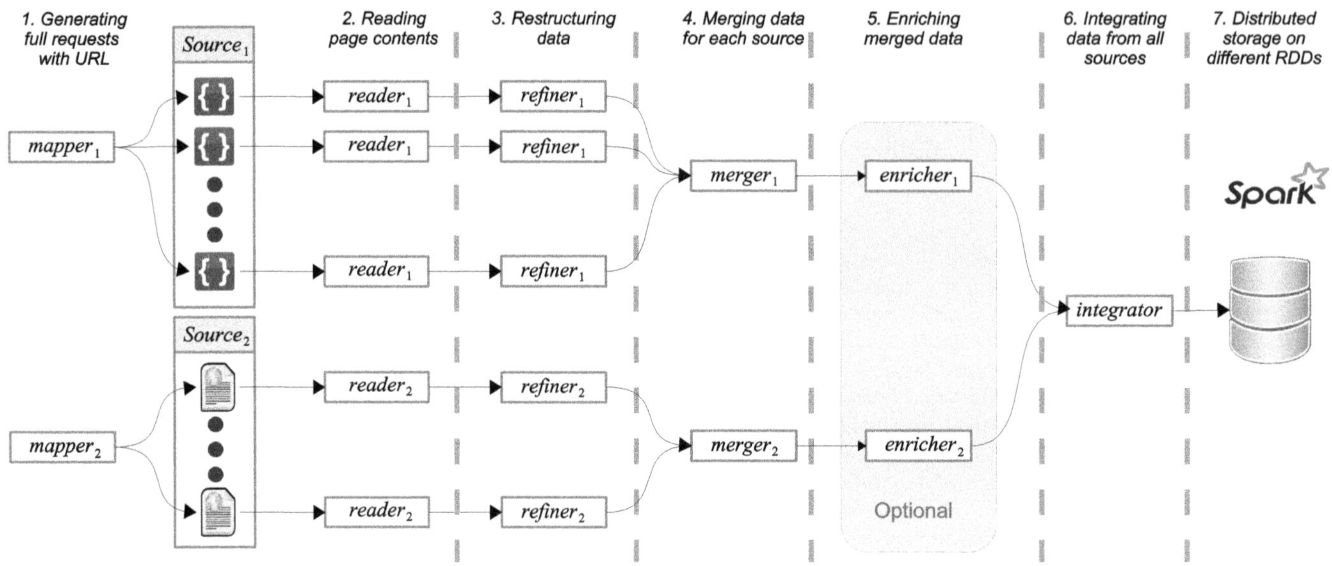

Figure 1: Architecture of the ThingSeek crawler engine

Figure 1 illustrates the main features of the ThingSeek crawler engine. In the first step, a URL generator initializes the queue of queries. Each entry in the queue is supplied with certain parameters to construct a query to a page or a specific location. The parameters can be the time window, the boundaries of the querying region and/or other parameters. Then for each entity in the queue, a reader function reads the selected part of the page, and the contents are converted to a set of vectors and refined using a refiner. The data for each subset is separately held until all subsets are refined where we merge all of the subsets of the resource's data. In this step, a specific enricher can be used to collect the missing information, if any, from other sources. This can, for example, fill the incomplete fields such as IP address by acquiring them from Shodan. Finally, the collected data from different sources are integrated and stored on a distributed backend.

Due to the size and dynamics of the sensor-generated data, IoT data sources often provide a subset of their data with a call to their API. Thus, pagination techniques such as location-based queries are deployed to present the data. We use the same mechanism through implementing the URL generator. The URL generator plays a key role in adjusting the workload on the data source. It converts a set of spatial segments to a sequence of queries which can be submitted via the API of the data source. Thus, a highly populated area can be placed multiple times in the processing queue while an empty area may appear only once (or not appear) in the queue. For example, through a URL generator, URL b will be repeated three times for others during a scan as it contains more dynamic objects than others:

$$\begin{bmatrix} a:1 & b:3 \\ c:1 & d:1 \end{bmatrix} \Longrightarrow [a, b, c, b, d, b] \quad (1)$$

We have developed ThingSeek using a set of tools to collect, process and visualize the dataset. Some of the tools we used are as follows: R programming language, SparkR, Apache Spark 1.4.1 and Rails framework.

We initialized the crawler with around 20 data sources. A sample of the collected data is shown in Table 1.

2.1.2 *Identifying IoT Data Sources*

We leverage Web Mapping such as Google Maps which is the most dominant way of visualizing spatial data on the Web, to achieve the goal. Thus, we limit our search scope to the sources which contain a map. We use a set of keywords to narrow our search results to find such sources such as "*real-time map [of application]*", "*live map [of application]*" and "*tracker map of [application]*". In the search query, the term "application" can be replaced with any application of IoT such as *flight*. We also include some of the available IoT platforms such as Xively[3] to the initial set of data sources.

2.2 Query Results Preparation

2.2.1 *Human User*

In this section, we propose our approach for query resolution and the indexing approach to enable large-scale search for IoT. Figure 2 shows the procedure of retrieving query results in ThingSeek. As the figure shows, the query processing workflow works as follows.

[3]https://xively.com/

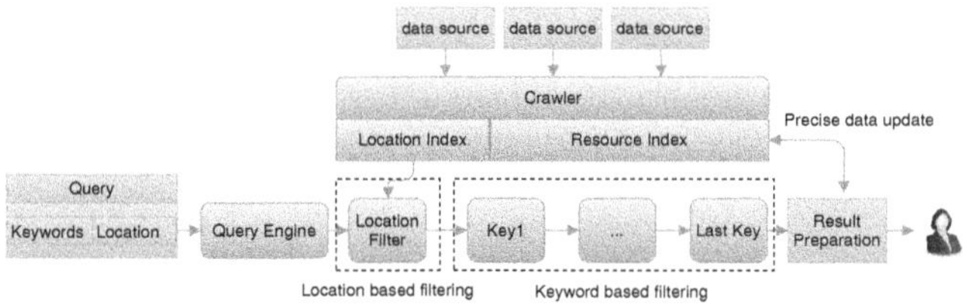

Figure 2: Query resolution and indexing in ThingSeek framework

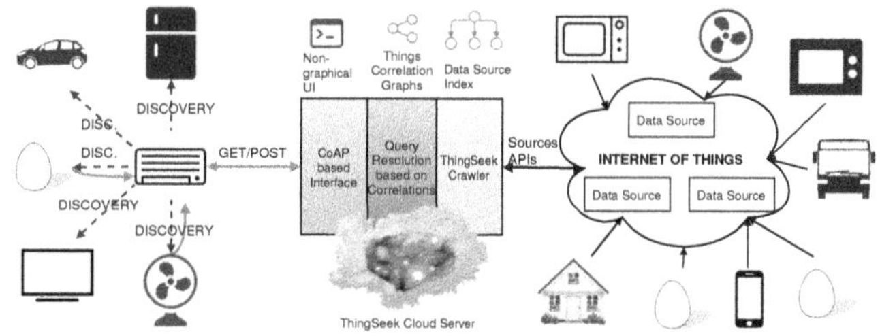

Figure 3: Query resolution for smart things in ThingSeek framework

1. Queries, which are formed as pairs of keywords and locations, are fed into the system. The query structure is inspired from the Thingful search engine.

2. The Queries are processed in two steps: location based filtering and keyword based filtering and finally the results are updated with the most recent values before being presented to the user.

3. We use approximate values based on indexed data in the location filtering step. The location filtering is facilitated using the R-Tree data structure to enhance the flexibility and the performance of the system.

4. In the keyword filtering, the results of location filtering are processed for each given keyword accordingly.

5. Before presenting the results to the user, we update the results with the most recent values using the data source index for each object in the result set. After preparing the final result set, we update the result continuously when presenting to the user. This would provide a better user experience of real-time data.

Due to the highly dynamic nature of the IoT data, analytical result may change promptly. In addition, raw IoT data are often meaningless and not very useful by themselves. Thus, we also designed a Web-based interface to visualize the IoT data as well as query the IoT data.

2.2.2 *Smart Objects Interface*

As objects are becoming smarter, they become the main producers and consumers of information. Thus, we created an interface for smart objects to enable them to query the dataset. To cope with the existing standards, we used Constrained Application Protocol (CoAP), which is a protocol for simple electronic devices to allow them to communicate interactively over the Internet. We initialize a CoAP based RESTful interface for smart objects to search for things in our database. Although CoAP contains a discovery tool, its scope is limited and lacks flexibility.

Figure 3 compares our architecture with CoAP discovery and illustrates how the ThingSeek's machine interface serves queries. For example, a smart air conditioning system searches objects related to air or weather to plan its cooling strategy. As shown, with the use of CoAP, a querying object can only enquire objects on the same network via distributing discovery messages to all objects on the network. Following this, the issuer gets objects' responses if they match to the query. However, this approach can limit the scope and effectiveness of the search. To resolve this issue, in our ThingSeek architecture, the smart object uses a service to send its query directly to the search engine with a POST or GET message. Due to the power, network and computing limits of things, ThingSeek should respond the query with a number of messages containing only a small number of results. In this regard, we use the *ECS* approach [6] (Extract-Cluster-Select) to provide the best response with limited size. The ECS approach extracts co-location (objects in the same location or very close to each other) and co-ownered (objects with the same owner) correlations between things and forms a unified Things Correlation Graph. Then, the nodes are clustered into k groups and finally a number of things from each cluster are selected and returned. It is designed to rank objects based on their correlations and responds the query with a limited number of the top-k results based on the weight of their correlations with the query issuer. Finally, the URI of the corresponding data source is located and crawled to get the latest sensor readings. If the object is not found in the index, the latest cached records will be supplied.

3. DEMONSTRATION

In this section, we demonstrate the functionality of the proposed ThingSeek framework. ThingSeek can extract IoT data from desired data sources by providing separate simple interfaces and effective search algorithms for users and machines. In particular, we demonstrate main functions through three main search scenarios: crawling an IoT data source, a human user searching IoT and a smart machine user searching IoT.

3.1 Crawling an IoT Data Source

Adding and removing data sources is a key to preserving the quality of the crawled data. To add a new data source, a new crawling procedure should be created in the system. Defining a new crawling procedure starts by initializing the link of the data source. Then, the following steps of the crawling procedure should be specified according to the steps in Figure 1. We have defined a universal module for each step which by default will be used. Otherwise, the user can introduce her own modules by defining new ones. Finally, a strategic crawling queue for the new data source will be specified by the user. For example, users can choose to crawl the new data source hourly and only update certain parts of the data.

3.2 IoT Search by Human Users

Through a Web-based user interface, a human user uses the search engine to acquire information from sensors. For example, a user would like to get information from nearby

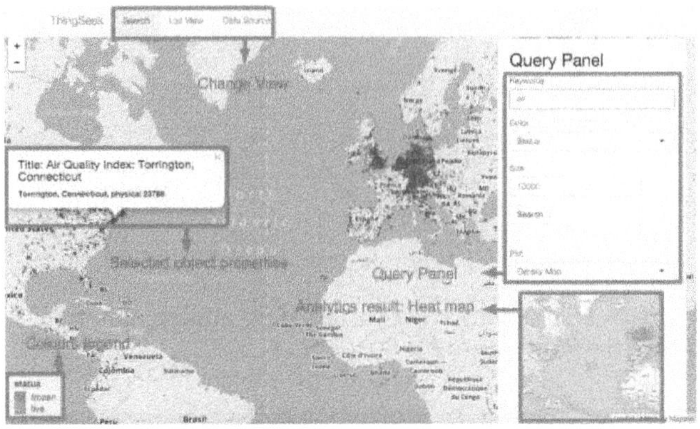

Figure 4: ThingSeek Web based visualization

weather sensors. Figure 4 shows a screen shot of our Web-based interface where each red spot denotes an object in the result set. Users can use the query panel to generate new queries and the result can be shown as a list of sensors or through an interactive map as shown. However, users would be more interested in acquiring knowledge from the data streams rather than finding the sensors. Thus, we added an interactive plot maker to generate real-time plots.

3.3 IoT Search by Smart Machines

In this scenario, we consider a smart object querying our search engine. We developed a Machine-to-Machine (M2M) interface based on the architecture in Figure 3 to enable things to use CoAP to connect to our server and submit their queries. To use the interface, on the client side, users can use any of CoAP implementations on CoAP website[4] to send a GET or POST message to our server. The message payload contains keywords followed the desired number of the result set at the end. The server would provide the results in response.

4. RELATED WORKS

To illustrate the future of search engines, [1] identified some of the challenging issues for searching within IoT as search locality and real-time search. Furthermore, based on IoT characteristics such as networked interconnection, real-time, semantic coherence and spontaneous interaction will result in raising issues such as architectural design, search locality, scalability and real-time for designing and implementing IoT search engines [2]. However, due to the existing differences in the nature of Web of Things (WoT) with the IoT, WoT may even strike additional different challenges.

In order to design the next generation of search engines, many components of current search engines from data collection methods to user experience and semantics should be redesigned. In this section, some of the previous initiations in this area are categorized and reviewed. MAX [10], Microsearch [8] and Snoogle [9] are developed based on this idea. In keyword search approach, keywords are extracted from a given term and top query results are ranked based on a score derived from the percentage of similarity between the given query term and the keyword-based description on sensors. The result is a list of sensors and thus, it might not be very useful particularly for human users.

[4]http://coap.technology/

5. CONCLUSION

Building future generation of crawlers and search engines is critical for research on IoT. In this paper, we demonstrate ThingSeek, a search engine with a crawler to hunt IoT data on the Web. We mainly focus on the sensor data that is published through Web Mapping. Our ThingSeek framework contains a crawler and two querying interfaces to cover both human and machine users, e.g., smart things. We discovered that a large portion of IoT data is shared using Web Mapping interfaces.

6. REFERENCES

[1] Christophe, B., Verdot, V., Toubiana, V.: Searching the web of things. In: Proceedings of the 5th IEEE International Conference on Semantic Computing (ICSC). pp. 308–315. IEEE (September 2011)

[2] Horowitz, D., Kamvar, S.: The anatomy of a large-scale social search engine. In: Proceedings of the 19th International World Wide Web Conference (WWW 2010). pp. 431–440. ACM (April 2010)

[3] Miorandi, D., Sicari, S., De Pellegrini, F., Chlamtac, I.: Internet of things: Vision, applications and research challenges. Ad Hoc Networks 10(7), 1497–1516 (2012)

[4] Ostermaier, B., Romer, K., Mattern, F., Fahrmair, M., Kellerer, W.: A real-time search engine for the web of things. In: Proceedings of the 2nd International Conference on the Internet of Things (IOT). pp. 1–8. IEEE (November 2010)

[5] Pfisterer, D., et al.: Spitfire: toward a semantic web of things. Communications Magazine, IEEE 49(11), 40–48 (2011)

[6] Shemshadi, A., Yao, L., Qin, Y., Sheng, Q.Z., Zhang, Y.: Ecs: A framework for diversified and relevant search in the internet of things. In: Intl. Conf. Web Information Systems Engineering (WISE 2015), pp. 448–462. Springer (2015)

[7] Tan, C.C., Sheng, B., Wang, H., Li, Q.: Microsearch: A search engine for embedded devices used in pervasive computing. ACM Transactions on Embedded Computing Systems (TECS) 9(4), 43 (2010)

[8] Tan, C., Sheng, B., Wang, H., Li, Q.: Microsearch: When search engines meet small devices. In: Proceedings of the 6th International Conference on Pervasive Computing. pp. 93–110. ACM, Sydney, Australia (2008)

[9] Wang, H., Tan, C., Li, Q.: Snoogle: A search engine for pervasive environments. IEEE Transactions on Parallel and Distributed Systems 21(8), 1188–1202 (August 2010)

[10] Yap, K.K., Srinivasan, V., Motani, M.: Max: human-centric search of the physical world. In: Proceedings of the 3rd International Conference on Embedded Networked Sensor Systems. pp. 166–179. SenSys '05, ACM, New York, NY, USA (2005)

[11] Zhang, D., Yang, L.T., Huang, H.: Searching in internet of things: Vision and challenges. In: Proceedings of the 9th International Symposium on Parallel and Distributed Processing with Applications (ISPA). pp. 201–206. IEEE (May 2011)

Tweetviz: Visualizing Tweets for Business Intelligence

Bas Sijtsma
University of Amsterdam
Amsterdam, The Netherlands
btsijtsma@gmail.com

Pernilla Qvarfordt Francine Chen
FX Palo Alto Laboratory, Inc.
Palo Alto, CA
{pernilla,chen}@fxpal.com

ABSTRACT

Social media offers potential opportunities for businesses to extract business intelligence. This paper presents Tweetviz, an interactive tool to help businesses extract actionable information from a large set of noisy Twitter messages. Tweetviz visualizes the tweet sentiment of business locations, identifies other business venues that Twitter users visit, and estimates some simple demographics of the Twitter users frequenting a business. A user study to evaluate the system's ability indicates that Tweetviz can provide an overview of a business's issues and sentiment as well as information aiding users in creating customer profiles.

CCS Concepts

•Human-centered computing → Visualization design and evaluation methods; *User studies;*

Keywords

Social Media Analytics; Information Visualization; Location Profiling; Sentiment Analysis

1. INTRODUCTION

Today's widespread use of social media offers new opportunities for businesses to extract business intelligence. Consumers freely share their opinions about products and services at a large scale on platforms such as Facebook and Twitter. This provides a valuable resource that businesses can leverage for a competitive advantage. Marketers can mine the vast amount of data to detect and discover new knowledge, such as insights into customer interests, competitors offers, or detecting problems with a service, and use these insights to realize value and competitive intelligence. Traditionally, businesses spend a lot of effort obtaining customer opinions through focus groups, interviews, and so on. Hence, social data monitoring tools that assess the consumers' opinion are of major interest to businesses that recognize the benefits of social media.

SIGIR '16, July 17-21, 2016, Pisa, Italy
© 2016 ACM. ISBN 978-1-4503-4069-4/16/07...$15.00
DOI: http://dx.doi.org/10.1145/2911451.2911470

Twitter is a social networking platform where users can send 140 character messages ('tweets'). Each day its users' generates over 500 million messages [1]. The large quantity of data necessitates automated tools to filter, order, mine and visualize it. In addition, the unstructured and noisy nature of social media data makes it difficult for companies to identify actionable areas of improvement.

We present Tweetviz, an interactive social media analytics system for exploring large collections of geo-tagged Twitter data. Tweetviz was developed based on requirements obtained from interviews with business owners and social media marketeers. Tweetviz addresses two major problems: 1) identifying potential issues at a company's location; and 2) finding information about visits to competitors among their customers. Tweetviz is designed to provide location-specific actionable information that can be used to improve a business.

2. RELATED WORK

A number of commercial social media tracking products such as Hootsuite[2] and Sproutsocial[3] focus on offering customer interaction statistics. They track metrics related to the number of responses to a company's messages, attempt to define the most successful response length, and other types of aggregated daily activity statistics. While this information is valuable from an on-line marketing perspective, this does not help businesses understand their customers' expressions at the venue level. Other systems such as Brandwatch[4] and Zignal Labs[5] focus in real-time event identification, e.g., identifying unhappy customers. Again, information at the venue level is not supported and analysts need to supply keywords of interest to provide to the system.

Several research systems have been developed for mining Twitter data. Diakopoulos' et al. developed a tool for mining current events from Twitter [2] which aimed to support journalists who wish to extract news from aggregated social media data. The user interface was specifically designed to allow for journalistic investigation of real-time responses to news events. Similarly, TwitInfo [3] allows users to explore real-time events occurring on Twitter. Both these systems are time-line based, and extract noteworthy elements based on tweet volume peaks and word-frequency based heuristics

[1]http://www.twitter.com/about
[2]https://hootsuite.com/
[3]http://sproutsocial.com/
[4]http://www.brandwatch.com
[5]zignallabs.com

within a small time frame. Tweetmotif [4] is an application for extracting topics and summarizing sentiment from Tweets. This system allows exploratory search of any query given by the user. All three systems contain elements that are potentially valuable for a business analyst. However, none of these systems consider the geographical origin of messages, thereby losing a substantial level of context that could be used to gather business intelligence. The goal of this research is to leverage the geographical information to provide actionable location specific information.

Conversely, Chen et al. [1] mined social media data to profile businesses at specific locations. They matched geo-tagged tweets to Foursquare venues by performing density-based clustering to identify a tweet's specific business location. Then, the average sentiment of tweets at each location was computed, thereby providing a sentiment profile of the business. Tweetviz provides and interactive visualization for mining this processed tweet data together with information extracted from related social media data.

3. TWEETVIZ

The aim of Tweetviz is to provide business owners with actionable information about business locations. To understand what information business owners desired, we conducted interviews with business owners involved in decision-making or social media management. Based on the interviews, we identified three issues these stakeholders have when analysing Twitter feeds: 1) It's difficult to prioritize issues because of the large amount of data generated. Is the opinion expressed on social media shared by a large number of customers? 2) Identifying problems as well as positive aspects during a customer's store experience helps businesses identify concrete improvements to their service; 3) Knowing who their customers are and what they like can help companies tweak their service and target the right customer.

Based on our stakeholder interviews, we identify two design requirements. First, Tweetviz should support the analyst to discover the most important topics discussed at their business, both positive and negative. Second, the system should help the analyst obtain a profile of their customers and their behavior. This must be supported irregardless of the volume of messages available.

3.1 Data used in Tweetviz

To support the functionality provided by Tweetviz, several datasets were collected. To present venue-level issues, the set of geo-tagged Twitter messages and automatically associated Foursquare business locations (i.e., *venues*) from [1] were used. The dataset contained around 24 million geo-tagged tweets from the San Francisco Bay Area, collected between June 4th, 2013 to March 23rd, 2015, with 656,098 distinct Twitter users. The dataset also included the estimated sentiment of each tweet, as described in [1].

The geo-tagged Twitter messages in the dataset were also used for estimating a customer's home location based on time and geo-location of the customer's tweets. In order to protect customers' privacy, the granularity of the estimation was reduced to neighborhoods using Zillow and Flickr neighborhood shapefiles rather than street address.

3.2 User Interface Design

Tweetviz was developed as a web application for modern web browsers. The front-end was built using the Angular JavaScript framework, supported by a back-end written in Node.js. All data is stored in a MySQL server. The system is designed to allow browsing of the available data with direct updates without reloading the page whenever an interaction is performed. Figure 1 displays a screen capture of the system.

3.2.1 Venue Selection and Filtering

One of our design principles was to allow users to both get an overview and details about business locations in the user interface. After selecting a company from the company dropdown (Figure 1, item 1), the user can view aggregated tweet statistics (item 4) at the city, neighborhood or branch levels (item 3). The user can group multiple branches together, or zoom into a single business to view its available Twitter data. For easier access of particular cities, neighborhoods or branches, an analyst can search (item 2) locations by name.

3.2.2 Tweet Sentiment at Business Locations

To support quick access and comparison of the sentiment at different branches, each branch is marked on the map with a color corresponding to the location's average sentiment (item 8). Tweets of selected cities, neighborhoods and/or branches, are displayed at the bottom of the user interface (item 11).

To assist in the identification of positive and negative aspects about the business' service repeatedly voiced on Twitter, Tweetviz displays tweets at selected venues grouped by keywords (item 10). Keywords were automatically identified as frequent nouns (each tweet was parsed using the Stanford NLP parser[6]).

When a keyword and sentiment is selected, the list of tweets (item 11) refreshes to only show tweets matching the selection. Since the sentiment classification is not perfect, a user can easily reclassify, with a single click, a tweet as the opposite sentiment, or mark it as irrelevant. This functionality allows an analyst to organize and improve the quality of their company's data in order.

3.2.3 Customer Demographics

An analyst can select the demographic information tab (item 6) to view summary statistics of the neighborhoods their customers live in to support customer profiling. This view shows neighborhoods ordered by most unique customers to selected venues and average home prices for the neighborhoods.

3.2.4 Visits to Competitor and Other Venues

A Tweetviz user can explore the other venues a business's customers tweet about (item 7). Although not all businesses are competitors, finding out what other businesses customers frequent can support creation of customer profiles.

To determine what other businesses a venue's customers visit, all tweets for each distinct customer are retrieved. Tweets not sent from a business location are discarded. Next, the number of visits to other businesses are extracted and aggregated. The system keeps track of both the unique number of customers visiting a business and the total number of visits. The results are filtered based on the list of selected venues (item 4).

[6] http://nlp.stanford.edu/software/lex-parser.shtml

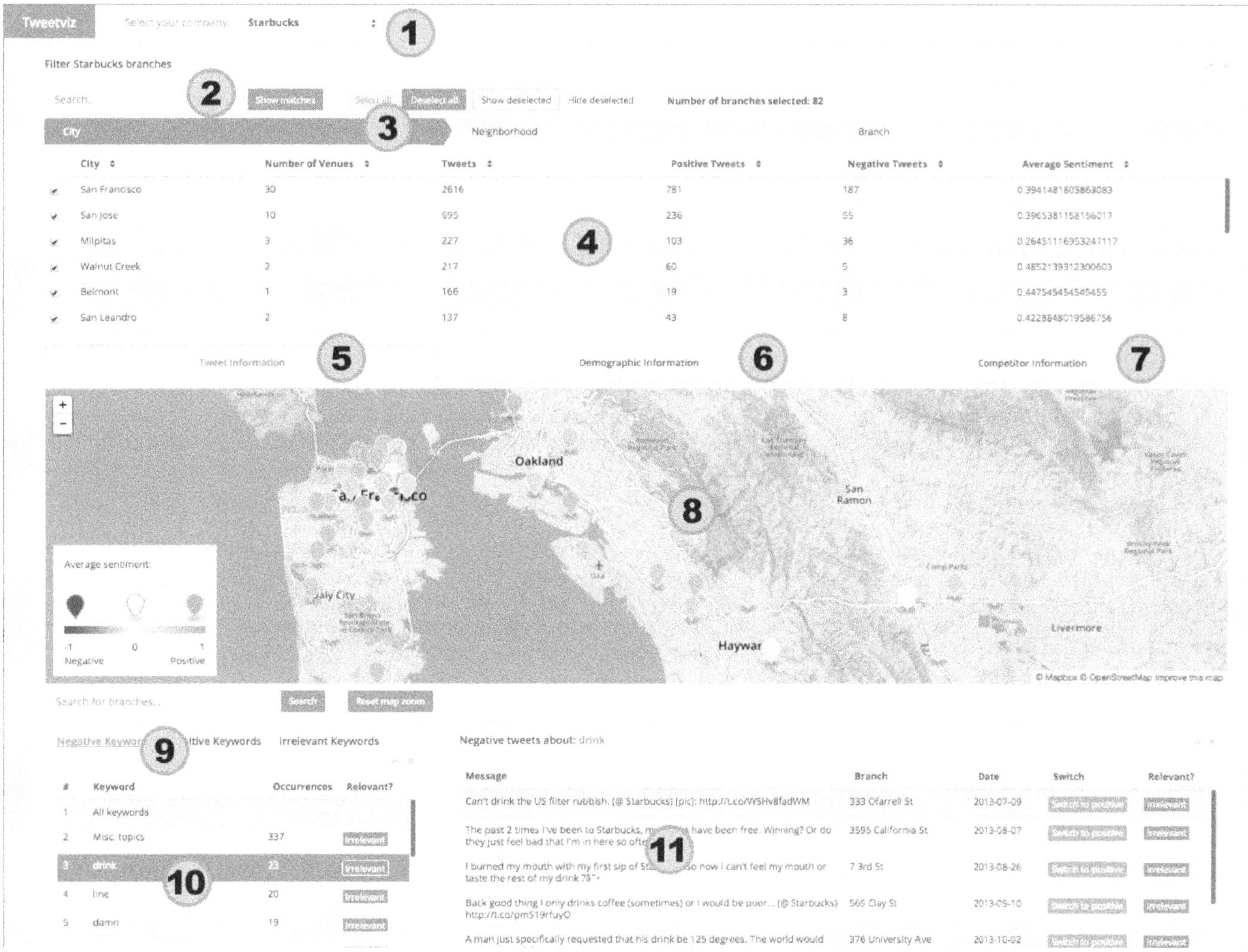

Figure 1: Screen capture of the Tweetviz user interface with elements marked with numbers in circles.

4. USER STUDY

We performed a user study to investigate users' experience of Tweetviz. We were in particular interested in understanding: 1) The system's ability to provide a valid overview of issues and sentiment voiced by customers; 2) The user experience; and 3) The type of inferences that participants draw given the available demographic and competitor information.

In order to assess the usefulness of automatic organization of noisy data by keyword, we compared Tweetviz as described above (aka experimental) with a version without automatic keyword identification (item 10 in Figure 1). In the baseline version, a list of all tweets for selected business were shown and the user could filter the list by typing a search query. Twelve participants used the experimental version of Tweetviz and another twelve participants used the baseline version. Of the 24 participants, 5 were women and 19 men and their ages ranged from 21 to 45 years. All the participants had experience of Twitter, and 20, or 83.3%, stated that they felt familiar or very familiar with Twitter.

Two types of tasks were designed: identification of business-related issues based on tweets (in total 4 tasks; 2 tasks using positive tweets and 2 using negative tweets) and profiling a business' customers using the available demographic and competitor information (in total 1 task). The experiment was designed to represent real scenarios a business analyst may be working towards, as indicated by interview subjects.

Ground-truth for the issue identification tasks was created by retrieving all tweets relevant to a task, and manually grouping the tweets based on negative and positive issues mentioned in the tweets. Keywords were ranked according to frequency, with the most frequent given a rank of 1.

Before the participants were given the tasks, they went through a training phase. During training, the participants were introduced to Tweetviz's features one at the time and asked to complete a simple task using the feature. Instructions were shown in a separate browser window located to the right of a browser window with Tweetviz. Next, the participants were given the five tasks one at the time starting with the issue identification tasks. The order of the issue identification tasks was balanced over all participants. The participants were free to choose how they worked with the tasks. After all tasks, the participants were asked about their impression of Tweetviz.

Table 1: TP-rate of ground truth top 1-3 issues

	Top 1	Top 2	Top 3
Baseline	0.625	0.500	0.368
Experimental	0.708	0.614	0.500

5. USER STUDY RESULTS

5.1 Issue Identification

For the first four tasks, identification of issues, we compared the performance between Tweetviz with (experimental condition) and without (baseline condition) automatically generated keyword classifications.

5.1.1 Task Completion Time

The total time spent on all four tasks for the experimental condition ranged from 556.5s to 1247.4s, with a mean (μ) of 947.5s and standard deviation (σ) of 209.3; versus the baseline condition with ranged from 519.7s to 1390.3s, $\mu = 1017.1s$ and $\sigma = 253.6$. Although on average the tasks were completed faster on the experimental interface, an independent samples t-test revealed that the difference is not statistically significant ($t(22) = 0,734, ns$).

5.1.2 Issue Identification Performance

The issues identified by the the participants were compared with the ground truth and assigned equivalent rank to matching ground truth issue. We found that the top three issues were more frequently found by participants using the experimental version of Tweetviz. Table 1 shows TP-rates for correctly identified issues with rank 1 (Top 1), rank 1 and 2 (Top 2) and top 3 ranks (Top 3). The TP-rate for Top3 was significant higher for participants using the experimental version compared with the baseline version (t(90)=2.6455, p<0.01). Many participants (7 out of 12) in the baseline condition requested that the tweets be better organized: *"It would be nice if there were a feature that grouped together tweets with similar semantics to make it easier to identify the top concerns or praise of customers, rather than requiring the user to examine every individual tweet when trying to find common trends in the data." (P3).*

5.1.3 Viewing Keywords and Searching Tweets

The two different versions of Tweetviz provided different functionality for parsing the tweets. In the baseline version the number of searches indicates that the search functionality was not well used, with $\mu = 1.0$ ($\sigma = 1.22$) searches performed per participant and task. A likely explanation is that instead of searching for possible terms, the participants scanned through all the tweets to identify business related issues.

In comparison, in the experimental version, tweets were automatically grouped by keyword. This functionality was heavily used by the participants; on average they clicked on 9.2 topics per task ($\sigma = 5.80$). We also found a strong significant correlation ($r = -0.7781, p < 0.05$) between the number of keyword clicks and issue identification performance. Hence, participants who clicked on more keywords found more of the top-ranked issues. This is confirmed by participants' comments, such as: *"[Tweetviz] was good at interacting with a bunch of tweets at once" (P6).* The implication is that showing tweets by keyword has the potential to be valuable for discovering the most important issues from a large collection of tweets, even with noisy classification and noisy tweets.

5.2 Creating User Profiles

Although our participants had no experience in user profiling, when examining the results of the user profiling task, we found that some participants were able to create rich descriptions of the customers.

For instance, three participants tried to find the average distance customers were traveling to reach business locations using the map. They experimented with selection and deselecting branches in various parts of the region to determine which branches had the most customers who lived further away from. Examples of richer descriptions from the user profiling task were: *"[..] middle/high-class income, heavy coffee-user "(P8)* and *"Customers are trendy and like to spend time in coffee shops, the park, and shops at Whole Foods"(P11)* and *"They have some brand loyalty (more check-ins at Philz than any other coffee companies), but they do also check in at competitors, such as [...]"(P6).*

These observations indicate that Tweetviz provides usable functionality to extract valuable information when effort is spent digging deeper into the data.

6. CONCLUSION

In this paper we present Tweetviz, a social media analytics tool designed to help businesses explore large volumes of geo-located Twitter data in order to extract actionable information. Tweetviz provides users with the ability to mine information about sentiment, possible competitors, and simple customer demographics at business locations. In a user study, we evaluated Tweetviz's ability to provide a valid overview of business related issues and sentiment expressed by its customers. We demonstrated that by interacting with the automatically generated keywords, a users' ability to discover the most important business-related issues in the noisy tweet data improves, and Tweetviz's data visualization allow its user to generate rich user profiles.

7. REFERENCES

[1] F. Chen, D. Joshi, Y. Miura, and T. Ohkuma. Social media-based profiling of business locations. In *Proceedings of the 3rd ACM Multimedia Workshop on Geotagging and Its Applications in Multimedia*, pages 1–6. ACM, 2014.

[2] N. Diakopoulos, M. Naaman, and F. Kivran-Swaine. Diamonds in the rough: Social media visual analytics for journalistic inquiry. In *Visual Analytics Science and Technology (VAST), 2010 IEEE Symposium on*, pages 115–122. IEEE, 2010.

[3] A. Marcus, M. S. Bernstein, O. Badar, D. R. Karger, S. Madden, and R. C. Miller. Twitinfo: aggregating and visualizing microblogs for event exploration. In *Proceedings of the SIGCHI conference on Human factors in computing systems*, pages 227–236. ACM, 2011.

[4] B. O'Connor, M. Krieger, and D. Ahn. Tweetmotif: Exploratory search and topic summarization for twitter. In *Proceedings of the International AAAI Conference on Weblogs and Social Media*, 2010.

Where the Event Lies: Predicting Event Occurrence in Textual Documents

Andrea Ceroni, Ujwal Gadiraju, Jan Matschke*, Simon Wingert†, and Marco Fisichella
L3S Research Center, Leibniz Universität Hannover, Appelstr. 9a, Germany
{ceroni, gadiraju, fisichella}@L3S.de
*jmatschke@gmx.de
†simon.wingert@gmx.net

ABSTRACT

Manually inspecting text in a document collection to assess whether an event occurs in it is a cumbersome task. Although a manual inspection can allow one to identify and discard false events, it becomes infeasible with increasing numbers of automatically detected events. In this paper, we present a system to automatize *event validation*, defined as the task of determining whether a given event occurs in a given document or corpus. In addition to supporting users seeking for information that corroborates a given event, event validation can also boost the precision of automatically detected event sets by discarding false events and preserving the true ones. The system allows to specify events, retrieves candidate web documents, and assesses whether events occur in them. The validation results are shown to the user, who can revise the decision of the system. The validation method relies on a supervised model to predict the occurrence of events in a non-annotated corpus. This system can also be used to build ground-truths for event corpora.

Keywords

Event Validation; Event Detection; Evaluation; Corpus Construction

1. INTRODUCTION

Event descriptions can provide concise summaries of news articles, making the seek for event related information more enjoyable for general readers and more effective for professionals like historians and journalists. We do not focus on how events are detected or extracted from text, but rather tackle the problem of assessing their occurrence within a given corpus. In line with both the basic definition of *event* given by the Topic Detection and Tracking (TDT) project [1] and with more recent works on event detection, e.g. [5, 6, 8], we model events as a set of participants related within a given time period. For instance, the event {(*Novak Djokovic*, *Roger Federer*, *US Open*), *2015-08-30 to 2015-09-15*} would represent the participation of two tennis players in the 2015 US Open.

Manually assessing whether an event occurs in a document collection becomes infeasible in scenarios where events are continuously and automatically detected from news streams on a large-scale. In this paper, we present a system to automatize the event validation process by predicting whether a given event has evidence within a set of unannotated documents retrieved from a corpus. Our system can find documents that corroborate the occurrence of an input event, thus simplifying the task of manually searching for event-related information to confirm or deny its verity. In more detail, the developed system allows to specify one event, retrieves candidate Web documents, and assesses what are the documents (if any) where it occurs. The validation judgments are shown to the user, who can explore the documents and possibly revise the decision of the system. Given the possibility for users to provide their own validation judgments, which are made persistent along with events and documents, the application can also be used to acquire ground truth data for a given set of input events. Event validation can also be applied as a post processing step of event detection to boost the precision within the detected set of events by reducing the number of false events with respect to a given corpus.

To validate events, the system relies on a state of the art method [4] that extracts features from events and documents and exploits them to train a model via supervised machine learning. Once trained, the model predicts event occurrence in terms of the mutual conformation of the event participants within the event timespan. Although our system uses the Web as a source for documents due to its easy accessibility and wide event coverage, any document collection could be used in principle owing to the lack of assumptions on the nature of events and documents within the validation model.

To the best of our knowledge our system is the first of its kind, showcasing automatic event validation and supporting users in looking for evidence corresponding to the verity of events.

2. RELATED WORK

The automatic detection of events within text has been widely studied, e.g. in [1, 5, 6]. However, event detection is different from event validation, since the output of the former (i.e., a set of *events*) constitutes the known input for the latter. Although the task of event validation with respect to a corpus can be modeled as the task of retrieving documents relevant to input events, checking the mere appearance of event participants in text has been proved to be insufficient to validate the occurrence of events in documents while establishing mutual relationships and temporal conformation [4].

Besides the method showcased by our system [4], which combines a wide set of features extracted from events and documents within a supervised model, another attempt to event validation has been proposed in [3], where the occurrence of events in documents is evaluated based on hand-crafted rules. Araki et al. [2] performed historical fact validation by casting the problem as *Passage Retrieval*: they assess event validity in terms of the textual similarity between facts and passages of fixed length.

SIGIR '16, July 17-21, 2016, Pisa, Italy
© 2016 ACM. ISBN 978-1-4503-4069-4/16/07... $15.00
DOI: http://dx.doi.org/10.1145/2911451.2911452

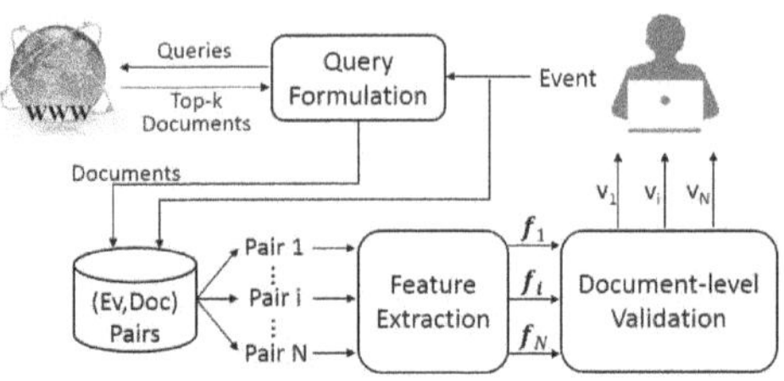

Figure 1: Approach overview of automatic event validation.

Available system implementations do not tackle event validation, but they rather consider other event-related applications like extraction [7], tracking [12], retrieval of event-related information [10], visualization [9], and retrospective exploration [11].

3. AUTOMATIC EVENT VALIDATION

The event validation process is depicted in Figure 1 and it consists of three phases. These are: *query formulation*, which generates queries from the event specified by the user and retrieves candidates documents from the Web; *feature extraction*, which extracts features from (event,document) pairs; *document-level validation*, to identify documents containing evidence of the event (if any).

3.1 Query Formulation

The Query Formulation phase takes an event specified by the user as input. An event is made of (i) a set of participants, representing the participants of the event, and (ii) a start and end date, indicating the timespan within which the event occurred. This is in line with event definitions used in previous works [5, 6, 8].

Given an event, queries are constructed by concatenating the event participants along with month and year of the event timespan (one distinct query for each month). The Bing Search API is used to perform queries and to retrieve the top-20 Web pages for each query in terms of URLs. We chose the Web as a source for documents due to its easy accessibility and wide event coverage, but any document collection could be used. After removing duplicates and discarding non-crawlable Web pages, plain text is extracted by using BoilerPipe[1]. Finally, events and documents are logically coupled and stored as *(event, document)* pairs for later use.

3.2 Feature Extraction

The features described in [4] are extracted from pairs to form the input to the validation model. These are logically split into three groups: *event features* describe the event without coupling it with any document; *document features* are extracted from the plain text of each document, independent of the event to be validated; *pair features* are extracted from pairs to give information about the extent to which a document contains evidence of the event. Stanford CoreNLP[2] is used for POS tagging, named entity recognition, and dates extraction. The features extracted from each pair p are concatenated in a feature vector $\boldsymbol{f}_p$ as input to the validation.

3.3 Document-level Validation

The last step of event validation consists of assessing the validity of pairs, i.e. whether the document in the pair contains *evidence* of the event. Note that we do not aim at stating whether an event is true or false in general, but whether it occurs in the retrieved documents. Formally, an event is said to be *valid* (i.e. to have evidence of its occurrence in a document) with a threshold $\tau, 0 < \tau \leq 1$, iff at least $\tau\%$ of the event participants conform together in an event reported in the document, strictly within the timespan of the event. This implies that an event can exhibit different degrees of evidence within the same document, depending on the imposed evidence threshold. For instance, if 75% of the participants relate together in a document and within the event timespan, then the event would have evidence in the document if a threshold $\tau = 50\%$ is considered, but would not have evidence for $\tau = 100\%$. Imposing an evidence threshold makes the validation a classification task and allows to have a more intuitive notion of document-level validity: a document (and then the corresponding pair) is judged as *valid* if the number of event participants that conform together within it is equal to or greater than the threshold, and *invalid* otherwise.

Given the feature vectors $\boldsymbol{f}_p$ extracted from (event,document) pairs p and an evidence threshold τ, an SVM with RBF Kernel trained considering τ as threshold is used to predict the validity $\gamma_p = SVM\left(\boldsymbol{f}_p, \tau\right)$ of each pair, where the validation judgment γ_p is binary and can assume the values $\{valid; invalid\}$. In our system, the user can choose among three evidence thresholds (50%, 65%, 100%) and the SVM trained with the chosen value is used accordingly. Refer to [4] for further details on the training process.

4. SYSTEM DEMONSTRATION

4.1 Implementation

We implemented a publicly available Web application[3,4] using the JSF framework. For a given input event, candidate documents are retrieved through the Bing Search API and then posed as input to the back-end validation model [4], implemented in Java. It uses the Stanford CoreNLP parser for feature extraction and SVM classifiers trained with the LibSVM library to validate each (event,document) pair. The user can review the documents and possibly revise the validity judgments given by the system. This feedback is stored in a MySQL database for future re-training of the validation model.

The user interface of our application is shown in Figure 2. The user can specify an input event by filling the form on the left-hand side. The required information consists in the event participants, it start and end dates, the validity threshold, and the number of candidate documents to retrieve. On the right-hand side is the list of retrieved documents along with their validation judgments (either *valid* or *invalid*), given with respect to the input event and evidence threshold. For each document, the user can inspect the plain textual content extracted with BoilerPipe and actually used for validation (Figure 3), as well as visit its original URL. When reviewing the text, the user has the chance of changing the original validation judgment, possibly marking cases of uncertainty. To simplify the review process of the user, the occurrences of event participants and dates detected by the Stanford CoreNLP parser are highlighted.

4.2 Scenarios

The main usage scenario that we consider consists of a user willing to retrieve information related to a given event, possibly provided by a certain news agency or an event detection algorithm, to either corroborate or deny its occurrence. Given the possibility for the users to provide and store their own validation judgments, the application can also be used to acquire ground truth data for a set of input events. The judgments about event validity are not absolute: they relate to the Web as ground truth and to the documents that have been thus retrieved. For instance, an event having no evidence in any retrieved Web pages might still occur in other documents

[1] http://code.google.com/p/boilerpipe/

[2] http://nlp.stanford.edu/software/corenlp.shtml

[3] http://forgetit.l3s.uni-hannover.de:8081/eventvalidation

[4] Video available here: www.l3s.de/~ceroni/SIGIR2016/Demo.mp4

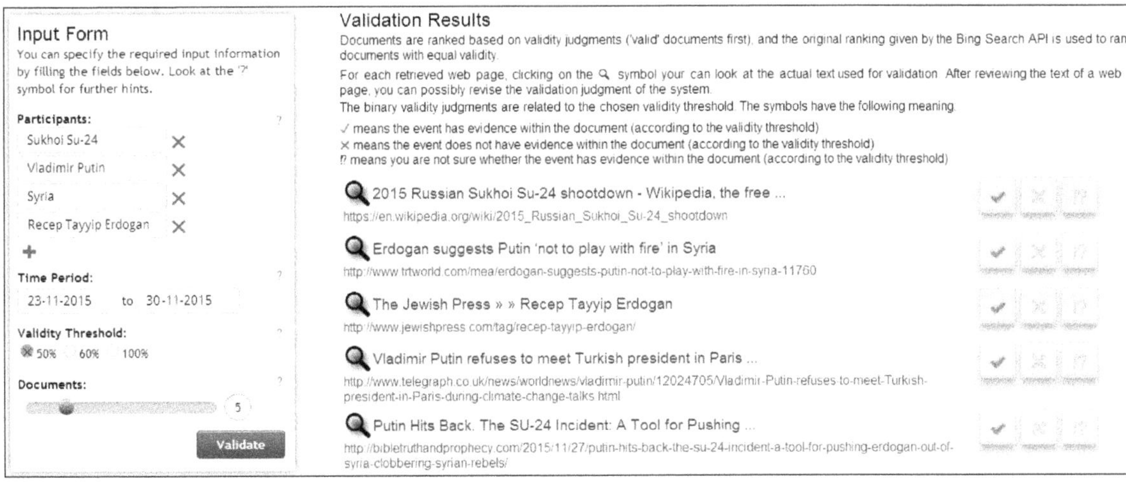

Figure 2: Example of a valid input event (left-hand side) and corresponding validation results (right-hand side).

in the Web that were not retrieved, or in corpora disjoint from the Web. In the rest of this section we discuss three examples of usages of the application, namely in presence of true, false, and less newsworthy input events. Since the system relies on the Bing Search API for retrieval and the set of documents populating the Web is continuously evolving, the set of documents shown in the figures and discussed in this section might be different from the ones got when performing the same queries at future points in time.

The validity judgments given for pairs always refer to the specified evidence threshold τ (Section 3.3). An (event, document) pair is said to be *valid* with a threshold τ if at least $\tau\%$ of the event participants relate together in the document, strictly within the event timespan. For instance, if 3 out of 4 participants conform together in a document, the occurrence of the event in it will be *valid* for $\tau = 50\%$ and $\tau = 65\%$, but *invalid* for $\tau = 100\%$ (all participants are required). We consider $\tau = 50\%$ in the rest of this section.

4.2.1 True Events

Let us assume that a user wants to check whether the entities *Sukhoi Su-24*, *Vladimir Putin*, *Syria*, and *Recep Tayyip Erdogan* have been related to each other within the period from 23-11-2015 to 30-11-2015. Actually they were, since on 24th November 2015 a Russian Sukhoi Su-24M bomber aircraft flying at the Syria-Turkey border was shot down by a Turkish fighter jet, leading to tensions between the two leaders Putin and Erdogan. The input form as well as the retrieved and validated Web pages representing this scenario are shown in Figure 2. The top-5 retrieved documents have been all judged as valid, which means that all of them are declared to contain evidence of the input event. Inspecting their content, one can observe that they report the description of the actual event as well as political discussions generated from it. An excerpt of the first document reporting the event is shown in Figure 3, where matching event participants and dates are highlighted in the application for sake of inspection and review.

Note that the mutual conformation of the event participants to the same event in the document is not a sufficient condition for the (event,document) pair to be declared as valid (i.e. the event occurs in the document). It has to be integrated by the temporal validity, which means that the event participants relate together strictly within the specified timespan of the event. As we will show in Section 4.2.2, (event,document) pairs exhibiting mutual occurrence and relation of event participants not explicitly within the event timespan are judged as *invalid*.

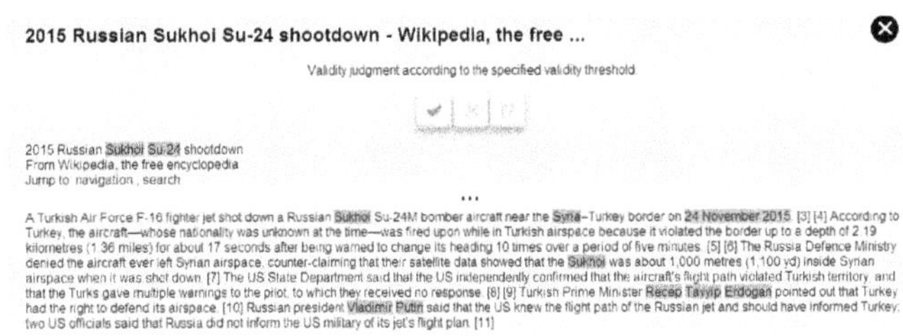

Figure 3: Excerpt of a retrieved document reporting the input event.

4.2.2 False Events

We focus on two reasons of event invalidity: (i) when event participants are not reported in the retrieved documents as they do not relate to each other, and (ii) when the participants did relate to each other but not within the specified event timespan.

Starting from the event mentioned in Section 4.2.1, let us modify the set of participants by replacing *Syria* and *Sukhoi Su-24* with two "intruders", namely *Spain* and *Foxtrot-class Submarine* (patrol submarines built in the Soviet Union). The retrieved documents along with their validation judgments are reported in Figure 4a, which shows that all retrieved documents have been judged as not containing the event. The input entities did not participate in a common event, and consequently, the system did not find any evidence.

To show temporal invalidity, let us keep the original participant set of the event in Section 4.2.1 and let us shift the event timespan one month in advance, namely from 23-10-2015 to 30-10-2015. The output of the system is shown in Figure 4b, where the result list differs from the one in Figure 2 because a different month has been used to formulate the query. All the retrieved documents have been declared as not containing the event, although participants actually occur in them, because no signal about temporal validity was found. As stated by the problem definition itself (Section 3.3), event validation strictly takes the temporal dimension of events into account when making decisions about their occurrence within documents.

4.2.3 Unpopular Events

Besides newsworthy events with a large amount of corroborating documents, as the one considered in Section 4.2.1, event validation also has to cope with less popular events, whose occurrences in documents might be less frequent or unclear. As an example, let us consider an event with participants *SIGIR*, *Chile*, *Ricardo Baeza-*

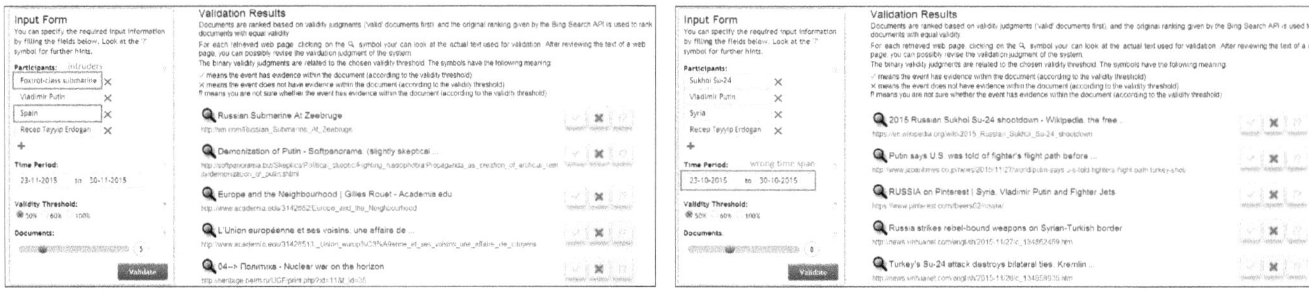

(a) Invalid event because of unrelated participants.

(b) Invalid event because of wrong time span.

Figure 4: Examples of invalid input events along with their validation results.

Figure 5: Top-5 retrieved documents for a low newsworthy event.

Yates from 04-08-2015 to 16-08-2015. This validation scenario is different from the previous ones because (i) the event has a high impact only for a particular community of researchers and (ii) the periodicity of the SIGIR conference might introduce documents referring to other venues outside the specified period. The top-5 retrieved documents and their validation judgments are shown in Figure 5, which shows that only a part of the documents contain evidence of the event. The others refer either to previous SIGIR venues, or contain works of Ricardo Baeza-Yates, or even completely unrelated documents.

4.2.4 User Feedback

Automatically determining whether an event occurs in a document collection is a challenging task. The usage of the Web itself as ground truth poses further challenges; due to its ubiquitous accessibility and wide event coverage, it can be regarded as a noisy source owing to the presence of unstructured and potentially untrustworthy sources (like blogs and forums) with questionable verity. Therefore, our application keeps users in the loop by allowing them to review the plain text extracted from the retrieved Web pages. By highlighting the event participants and dates detected in the text, our system simplifies the inspection and presents the user with the possibility of revising a potentially incorrect validity judgment deduced by the system (Figure 3). Such feedback is stored and can be used for future re-training of the validation model. Besides errors committed by the back-end classifier, other possible misclassifications can be caused by errors introduced during boilerplate removal and named entity or temporal expression extraction (e.g. important content of a Web page might not be included in the plain text or temporal expressions might not be detected by the NLP parser). Background information known to a user but not explicitly present in the text might be a further source of judgment discrepancy.

5. CONCLUSION

In this paper, we presented a system to automatize the event validation process by predicting whether a given event has evidence within a set of unannotated documents, thus simplifying the task of manually searching for event-related information to confirm or deny its verity. The developed system allows to specify an event, retrieves candidate web documents, and assesses what are the documents (if any) where it occurs. The validation method relies on a state of the art model for event validation. The user can review the documents and revise the validation judgments given by the system. Given the possibility for users to provide their own validation judgments, the application can also be used to acquire ground truth data for a given set of input events. By coupling our system with the powerful crowdsourcing paradigm, one can build large event corpora with corresponding ground truths in a scalable and cost-effective manner. Although we chose the Web as a source for documents, due to its easy accessibility and wide event coverage, other document collections could be explored and included in the system.

Acknowledgments This work was partially funded by the European Commission in the context of the FP7 project QualiMaster (grant No: 619525) and H2020 project AFEL (grant No. 687916).

6. REFERENCES

[1] J. Allan, R. Papka, and V. Lavrenko. On-line new event detection and tracking. In *SIGIR*, 1998.

[2] J. Araki and J. Callan. An annotation similarity model in passage ranking for historical fact validation. In *SIGIR*, 2014.

[3] A. Ceroni and M. Fisichella. Towards an entity-based automatic event validation. In *ECIR*, 2014.

[4] A. Ceroni, U. Gadiraju, and M. Fisichella. Improving event detection by automatically assessing validity of event occurrence in text. In *CIKM*, 2015.

[5] A. Das Sarma, A. Jain, and C. Yu. Dynamic relationship and event discovery. In *Proc. of WSDM '11*, 2011.

[6] Q. He, K. Chang, and E.-P. Lim. Analyzing feature trajectories for event detection. In *Proc. of SIGIR '07*, 2007.

[7] E. Kuzey and G. Weikum. Evin: Building a knowledge base of events. In *Proc. of WWW '14*, 2014.

[8] A. J. McMinn, Y. Moshfeghi, and J. M. Jose. Building a large-scale corpus for evaluating event detection on twitter. In *CIKM*, 2013.

[9] A. J. McMinn, D. Tsvetkov, T. Yordanov, A. Patterson, R. Szk, J. A. Rodriguez Perez, and J. M. Jose. An interactive interface for visualizing events on twitter. In *Proc. of SIGIR '14*, 2014.

[10] V. Milicic, G. Rizzo, J. L. Redondo Garcia, R. Troncy, and T. Steiner. Live topic generation from event streams. In *WWW '13*, 2013.

[11] A. Mishra and K. Berberich. ExposÉ: Exploring past news for seminal events. In *Proc. of WWW '15*, 2015.

[12] J. B. Vuurens, A. P. de Vries, R. Blanco, and P. Mika. Online news tracking for ad-hoc queries. In *Proc. of SIGIR '15*, 2015.

A Novel Approach to Define and Model Contextual Features in Recommender Systems

Parisa Lak
Ryerson University
Data Science Lab, Department of
Mechanical and Industrial Engineering
Parisa.Lak@ryerson.ca

ABSTRACT

Recommender Systems(RS) provide more accurate and more relevant recommendations using contextual feature(s). This accuracy improvement is at the cost of computational expenses. Therefore, finding and selecting the most relevant contextual features is an important problem. Moreover, modeling and incorporating the selected contextual features in RS algorithms has an impact on both the accuracy and computational cost. We are conducting a series of studies to detect, define, select, model and incorporate the most relevant contextual features for RS algorithms. The feature detection, definition and selection approach involves the evaluation of features derived from implicit and explicit information. The selected features from this approach can be modeled and incorporated in any selected RS algorithm. In our recent works, we also propose a series of algorithms that incorporates multiple contextual features in the baseline matrix factorization (MF) algorithm. We use the selected contextual features to modify user biases and item biases in the baseline MF.

Keywords

Context Aware Recommender Systems; Matrix Factorization; Recommender Systems; Contextual Feature Selection

1. RESEARCH PROPOSAL

Traditional RS consider only the information regarding the items and the users in order to provide recommendation. However, in some tasks user's opinion about an item might vary from one situation to another [1]. For these cases, it is important to consider contextual information as additional information to generate more relevant recommendations. Context Aware Recommender Systems (CARS) are one of the emerging topics of study in the field of RS. The studies in this field includes the investigations on how to model and incorporate contextual information in a traditional RS. Detecting, defining and selecting contextual features to be modeled and incorporated in RS algorithms is non-trivial. For this reason, it is important to carefully evaluate each contextual information to determine if it is relevant and ultimately if it can improve the accuracy of the system.

The general research question to be addressed in our proposed work is *How to detect, define, select, model and incorporate contextual information into RS algorithms?* This question is broken down into four specific questions: **RQ1.** *Which information can be considered as contextual information for a specific recommendation task?* In any recommendation task there is an interaction between the user and the system that provides recommendation. Through this interaction there are several user related foot prints that may reveal the characteristics of the situation that user interacts with the system. **RQ2.** *How to define contextual information as contextual features to be used in RS algorithms?* Contextual information, in their original format, often can not be incorporated in RS algorithms. **RQ3.** *How to select the most relevant contextual features to be used in RS algorithms?* Not all contextual features can increase the accuracy of prediction. It is important to select the most relevant contextual features. We proposed a novel contextual feature selection in a recent work. **RQ4.** *How to model and incorporate contextual features into a traditional RS algorithm?* Each RS algorithm has unique feature modeling and incorporation requirements. Selected contextual features should then be modeled to match the requirements of the selected RS algorithm. In our prior work [2] we evaluated baseline MF algorithm and its requirements. We propose an extension to MF algorithm that incorporates multiple "user-based" and "item-based" contextual features. In a recent work, we proposed and tested a context aware MF algorithm that incorporates multiple "user-based" contextual features.

Acknowledgments: This research is funded in part by IBM CAS Project no. 919, and NSERC CRD Grant no. 490782 2015.

SIGIR '16 July 17-21, 2016, Pisa, Italy

ACM ISBN 978-1-4503-4069-4/16/07.
DOI: http://dx.doi.org/10.1145/2911451.2911481

2. REFERENCES

[1] G. Adomavicius and A. Tuzhilin. Extending recommender systems: A multidimensional approach. In *Proceedings of the International Joint Conference on Artificial Intelligence (IJCAI-01), Workshop on Intelligent Techniques for Web Personalization (ITWP2001), Seattle, Washington, August*, pages 4–6. Citeseer, 2001.

[2] P. Lak, B. Caglayan, and A. B. Bener. The impact of basic matrix factorization refinements on recommendation accuracy. In *Proceedings of the 2014 IEEE/ACM International Symposium on Big Data Computing*, pages 105–112. IEEE Computer Society, 2014.

A Study of Information Seeking Behavior Using Physical and Online Explorations

Dongho Choi
Library & Information Science Department
School of Communication & Information (SC&I)
Rutgers, The State University of New Jersey
dongho.j.choi@rutgers.edu

ABSTRACT

People have their behavioral patterns, through which they determine how to seek and use information. People also exhibit established mobility pattern in their everyday lives. Meanwhile, the modern technologies such as smartphones, wearable devices, and eye trackers have allowed researchers to collect personal, contextual, and cognitive information of users, and create behavioral models from different perspectives. Considering the analogy between information exploration and geographical exploration, I want to identify the interconnections between these behaviors and predict individuals' search behavior using personal and contextual signals. The proposal uses a mixed-method approach that involves a four-week field study, a game study, and a lab study, collecting data from 40 participants through mobile device, eye tracker, online logs, and weekly diary.

Keywords

Information seeking behavior; geographical exploration; exploratory behavior

1. RESEARCH PROPOSAL

People develop their ways of information seeking over the life span regarding searching information in their everyday lives [3] and this behavior has been considered as an evolutionary instinct of individual [4]. Meanwhile, people show well-established mobility pattern in their daily life such as *returners* and *explorers* [1]. In this sense, interconnections between human information seeking behavior and foraging have been questioned. For example, Information Foraging theory [2] articulates that "information foragers use perceptual and cognitive mechanisms that carry over from the evolution of food-foraging adaptations".

Purpose of this work is to investigate and find hypothetical interconnections between geographical exploration and information seeking, with the following research questions: **(RQ1)** *To what extent, if any, do offline/physical exploration behavior relates to information seeking behavior?*; and **(RQ2)** *What aspects of offline/physical exploration can be used to explain and predict information seeking behavior?*

The dissertation work consists of three studies: field study, game study, and lab study. The field study will capture participants' physical exploration in everyday life and understand their information exploration both offline and online, installing an app on their phone and a Web browser plug-in on the computer. Along with the traces captured by GPS, participants' intention and context will be collected through weekly diary during the four weeks. Regarding offline information exploration, participants are doing a treasure-hunt task that requires moving around in a physical space, looking for clues and answers to complete the given task. Online exploratory behavior will be examined through searching/ browsing histories during assigned search task(s).

The game study is designed to monitor and compare people's information seeking behavior, bridging the possible gaps in findings from everyday life and controlled environment. Participants are playing a game that requires finding information and clues in a limited space, such as an "escape room" game. The main reason for the study is to understand people's cognitive process during information seeking in physical space, so we employ mobile eye tracker to observe their eye gaze during the game.

In the lab study, participants will be involved (1) an exploratory search [5] task, asking the participant to collect as much information as possible to write a report, and (2) problem-solving task that requires more than simple querying to find answers to given puzzles.

Acknowledgments: This work is supported by Google. Thanks to the ACM SIGIR for a Student Travel Grant.

SIGIR '16 July 17-21, 2016, Pisa, Italy

ACM ISBN 978-1-4503-4069-4/16/07.
DOI: http://dx.doi.org/10.1145/2911451.2911482

2. REFERENCES

[1] L. Pappalardo, F. Simini, S. Rinzivillo, D. Pedreschi, F. Giannotti, and A.-L. Barabási. Returners and explorers dichotomy in human mobility. *Nature communications*, 6, 2015.

[2] P. Pirolli. *Information foraging theory: Adaptive interaction with information*. 2007.

[3] R. Savolainen. Everyday life information seeking: Approaching information seeking in the context of "way of life". *Library & Information Science Research*, 17(3):259–294, 1995.

[4] A. Spink. *Information behavior: An evolutionary instinct*, volume 16. Springer Science & Business Media, 2010.

[5] R. White and R. Roth. *Exploratory Search: Beyond the Query-Response Paradigm*, volume 1. 2009.

Appearance-Based Retrieval of Mathematical Notation in Documents and Lecture Videos

Kenny Davila
Department of Computer Science
Rochester Institute of Technology
Rochester, New York, USA
kxd7282@rit.edu

ABSTRACT

Large data collections containing millions of math formulae in different formats are available on-line. Retrieving math expressions from these collections is challenging. Based on the notion that visually similar formulas are related, we propose a framework for appearance-based formula retrieval in two different modalities: symbolic for text documents and image-based for videos.

We believe that we can achieve high quality formula retrieval results using the visual appearance of math notation without complex formula semantic analysis.

We represent mathematical notation using different graph types to take advantage of the information available on each domain. For symbolic formula retrieval, math expressions in text formats like LaTeX are parsed to generate Symbol Layout Trees [4]. For image-based formula retrieval, image processing techniques are used to create a graph-based image content representation.

We store these graphs using an inverted index of pairs of primitives defined by the triplet (p, q, r), where p and q are the labels of two primitives connected in the graph by the path r [4].

Retrieval is a two-stage process: candidate selection and reranking. The first stage uses pairs of primitives from the query graph to find matches in the inverted index. Each match is given an initial score using the Dice coefficient of matched pairs of primitives [4].

The best top-K candidates from the first stage are selected for re-ranking using a detailed similarity metric. Two steps are performed for each candidate: matching and scoring. The **matching** step is done by searching for the largest common substructure between query and candidate graphs. Matching is related to the problem of finding the maximum common subgraph isomorphism (MCS) between two graphs. In addition, we consider label unification for symbolic formula retrieval, and our wildcard query nodes can match entire subgraphs. In the **scoring** step, multiple similarity criteria define a score vector used to sort candidates, either by lexicographic order or by a function of these scores.

In the next stage of our project, different datasets and benchmarks will be required to evaluate each modality. For symbolic formula retrieval, we will use the most recent versions of the NTCIR MathIR Tasks benchmarks [1]. To the best of our knowledge, there are no benchmarks for large scale image-based formula retrieval. However, the same collections used for symbolic formula retrieval could be adapted by rendering math expressions to images. In addition, we will use datasets of math lecture videos for image-based formula retrieval.

Traditional graded-scales of relevance used for evaluation of retrieval systems have been shown to have inconsistency issues [2]. We plan to use pairwise candidate comparisons during our evaluation phase. Some aggregation methods exist that generate relevance scores and ideal rankings using these pairwise candidate comparisons [3].

The proposed framework can be adapted to work for other domains like chemistry or technical diagrams where visually similar elements are usually related.

Keywords

Mathematical Information Retrieval, Content-Based Image Retrieval, Graph-Based Retrieval

Acknowledgments

This material is based upon work supported by the National Science Foundation (USA) under Grant No. HCC-1218801

1. REFERENCES

[1] A. Aizawa, M. Kohlhase, I. Ounis, and M. Schubotz. NTCIR-11 Math-2 task overview. In *Proceedings of NTCIR-11 Math-2 task Workshop Meeting [1]*, 2014.

[2] K. Radinsky and N. Ailon. Ranking from pairs and triplets: Information quality, evaluation methods and query complexity. In *WSDM*, pages 105–114, New York, NY, USA, 2011. ACM.

[3] M. N. Volkovs and R. S. Zemel. New learning methods for supervised and unsupervised preference aggregation. *JMLR*, 15(1):1135–1176, 2014.

[4] R. Zanibbi, K. Davila, A. Kane, and F. Tompa. Multi-stage math formula search: Using appearance-based similarity metrics at scale. *SIGIR*, 2016.

SIGIR '16 July 17-21, 2016, Pisa, Italy

ACM ISBN 978-1-4503-4069-4/16/07.

DOI: http://dx.doi.org/10.1145/2911451.2911477

Beyond Topical Relevance: Studying Understandability and Reliability in Consumer Health Search

Joao Palotti
Vienna University of Technology
Vienna, Austria
palotti@ifs.tuwien.ac.at

ABSTRACT

Nowadays people rely on search engines to explore, understand and manage their health. A recent study from Pew Internet states that one in each three adult American Internet users have used the Internet as a diagnosis tool [2].

Retrieving incorrect or unclear health information poses high risks as people may dismiss serious symptoms, use inappropriate treatments or escalate their health concerns about common symptomatology [1,9]. A number of studies have shown that the average user experiences difficulty in understanding the content of a large portion of the results retrieved by current search engine technology, for example, see [3]. Other studies have examined how poor the quality of health information on the web can be, for example, see [4].

In the context of consumer (non-experts) health search, search engines should not only retrieve relevant information, but also promote information that is understandable by the user and that is reliable/trustable and verified [9].

The focus of my Ph.D. is to go beyond topical relevance and study understandability and reliability as two important facets of relevance that must be incorporated into search systems to increase user satisfaction, especially in the context of consumer health search. For ease of comprehension, we divide this work into five steps to be accomplished:

1. Estimate the user expertise level.
2. Estimate how hard is to understand a document.
3. Estimate how reliable the content of a document is.
4. Integrate the understandability and reliability estimations in a personalised retrieval model.
5. Evaluate the relevance of documents not only concerning topical relevance, but also taking into account whether users can understand and rely on the content of the document.

The first step aims to promote easy-to-read material with reliable content to non-experts, while experts are not bothered with basic content. This step was completed in the first years of my Ph.D., using the logs of different search engines to better understand how and what users search in the medical domain, as well as to automatically infer user expertise based on user behaviour [5,8].

The second and third steps are bound to the document content, and need labor-intensive resources to be done (e.g., annotated data, assessments, user preferences). For that, I take advantage of CLEF eHealth task[1], which proposes to foster research in the consumer health search domain. In the 2015 task, besides the topical relevance assessment, we collected understandability assessments, asking assessors to judge whether they would recommend documents for their patients to read based on how technical documents were [6]. Given the success of the task, we are collecting assessments for reliability as well as topical relevance and understandability in 2016. These assessments provide the grounds for working in the fourth and fifth steps of the list above.

Our first experiments exploring the potential of integrating understandability in a personalised retrieval model (part of the fourth step) will be presented at this conference [7].

Finally, I aim to extend and explore the potential of evaluation metrics that integrate understandability and reliability into a single evaluation framework, based on very recent research [10].

SIGIR '16 July 17-21, 2016, Pisa, Italy

ACM ISBN 978-1-4503-4069-4/16/07.
DOI: http://dx.doi.org/10.1145/2911451.2911480

REFERENCES

[1] M. Benigeri and P. Pluye. Shortcomings of health information on the internet. *Health Prom. Inter.*, 2003.

[2] S. Fox and M. Duggan. Health online. Technical report, The Pew Internet & American Life Project, 2013.

[3] D. Friedman, L. Hoffman-Goetz, and J. Arocha. Readability of cancer information on the internet. *J Cancer Educ*, 2004.

[4] F. Hanif, J. Read, J. Goodacre, A. Chaudhry, and P. Gibbs. The role of quality tools in assessing reliability of the internet for health information. *Inform Health Soc Ca*, 2009.

[5] J. Palotti, A. Hanbury, and H. Muller. Exploiting health related features to infer user expertise in the medical domain. In *Proc. of WSCD*, 2014.

[6] J. Palotti, G. Zuccon, L. Goeuriot, L. Kelly, A. Hanbury, G. Jones, M. Lupu, and P. Pecina. CLEF eHealth Evaluation Lab 2015, Task2: Retrieving Information About Medical Symptoms. In *Proc. of CLEF 2015*, 2015.

[7] J. Palotti, L. Goeuriot, G. Zuccon, and A. Hanbury. Ranking health web pages with relevance and understandability. In *Proc. of SIGIR*, 2016.

[8] J. Palotti, A. Hanbury, H. Müller, and C. E. Kahn Jr. How users search and what they search for in the medical domain. *Information Retrieval Journal*, 2016.

[9] R. W. White and E. Horvitz. Cyberchondria: Studies of the escalation of medical concerns in web search. *TOIS*, 2009.

[10] G. Zuccon. Understandability biased evaluation for information retrieval. In *Proc. of ECIR*, 2016.

[1]https://sites.google.com/site/clefehealth/

Enhancing Information Retrieval with Adapted Word Embedding

Navid Rekabsaz
Vienna University of Technology
Favoritenstrasse 9/11
1040, Vienna, Austria
rekabsaz@ifs.tuwien.ac.at

Keywords

IR Models; word embeddings; similarity; related terms

ABSTRACT

Recent developments on word embedding provide a novel source of information for term-to-term similarity. A recurring question now is whether the provided term associations can be properly integrated in the traditional information retrieval models while preserving their robustness and effectiveness. In this paper, we propose addressing the question of combining the term-to-term similarity of word embedding with IR models. The retrieval models in the approach are enhanced by altering the basic components of document retrieval, i.e. term frequency (tf) and document frequency (df). In addition, we target the study of the meaning of the term relatedness of word embedding models and its applicability in IR. This research topic consists of first explore of reliable similarity thresholds of word embedding vectors to indicate "related terms" and second, identification of the linguistic types of the terms relatedness. In the following, we explain the mentioned research topics in more detail.

In Information Retrieval, terms are still the fundamental building blocks for establishing topical relevance relationships between documents and queries. The "basic" models to approximate this relationship, namely Vector Space Model (VSM), Probabilistic Retrieval Framework [4], and Language Model (LM) [3], have maintained a respectable command of the research and practice of IR. They are all fundamentally based on term frequency (tf) as a representation of importance of a term within a document and also a representation of the specificity of a term, usually realized by document frequency (df). These IR models are basically based on the underlying assumption of term independence.

As the first research topic, we challenge this assumption by conducting the idea of integrating word embedding into various IR models. As the basis of our approach, we consider the terms as concepts and define the relation between them based on the term-term similarity of word embedding models. In fact, the occurrence of a concept in a document is not only the frequency of the term (representing the concept) but also the partial frequency of the related terms. Considering this approach, we investigate the enhancement of various IR models, namely VSM, probabilistic, and language models with word embedding while preserving their robustness, and reliability.

Extending IR models with the embedded knowledge of word embedding particularly requires a deep understanding of its basic building block: term-term relatedness.

An issue in the word embedding methods is that they and their corresponding mathematical functions can provide approximation on the relatedness of any two terms, although this relatedness could be perceived as completely-meaningless in the language. Karlgren et al. [1] point it out by examples, showing that word embedding methods are too ready to provide answers to meaningless questions: *"What is more similar to a computer: a sparrow or a star?"*, or *"Is a cell more similar to a phone than a bird is to a compiler?"*.

In addition, as the relatedness of word embedding methods fundamentally consider the "close" terms as the terms with similar contexts, they generalize all different term relations e.g. antonyms, hypernymy, hyponyms, co-hyponyms, synonyms, antonyms, etc. into one notion of relatedness. However, using all these types bias the search to unrelated topics (e.g. searching for dog instead of cat!). Kruzewski and Baroni [2] notice this issue by an example: *animal*, *puppy*, and *cat* are all closely related to *dog*, but if you tell me that Fido is a dog, I will conclude that he is an animal, that he is not a cat, and that he might or might not be a puppy.

Therefore, as the second research direction, we address the mentioned issues by (1) exploring a threshold under which we would no longer consider two terms to be sufficiently related to the same concept (2) understanding the underlying notions of the terms' relations and adopting them for IR models.

Considering the mentioned research questions, the main goal of this Ph.D. is providing stable, reliable, and reusable information retrieval models, enhanced with adapted word embedding methods. The performance of the scoring models should be proofed by testing it on various IR domains i.e. ad hoc, news, health, patent, and social image sharing.

Acknowledge: This PhD is partly funded by two FWF projects MUCKE (I 1094-N23) and ADMIRE (P 25905-N23).

1. REFERENCES

[1] J. Karlgren, A. Holst, and M. Sahlgren. Filaments of meaning in word space. In *Proc. of ECIR*. 2008.

[2] G. Kruszewski and M. Baroni. So similar and yet incompatible: Toward automated identification of semantically compatible words. In *Proc. of NAACL*, 2015.

[3] J. M. Ponte and W. B. Croft. A language modeling approach to information retrieval. In *Proc. of SIGIR*, 1998.

[4] S. Robertson and H. Zaragoza. *The probabilistic relevance framework: BM25 and beyond*. Now Publishers Inc, 2009.

SIGIR '16 July 17-21, 2016, Pisa, Italy

ACM ISBN 978-1-4503-4069-4/16/07.

DOI: http://dx.doi.org/10.1145/2911451.2911475

Fairness in Information Retrieval

Aldo Lipani
Institute of Software Technology & Interactive Systems
Vienna University of Technology
Vienna, Austria
lipani@ifs.tuwien.ac.at

ABSTRACT

The offline evaluation of Information Retrieval (IR) systems is performed through the use of test collections. A test collection, in its essence, is composed of: a collection of documents, a set of topics and, a set of relevance assessments for each topic, derived from the collection of documents. Ideally, for each topic, all the documents of the test collection should be judged, but due to the dimensions of the collections of documents, and their exponential growth over the years, this practice soon became impractical. Therefore, early in IR history, this problem has been addressed through the use of the pooling method [5]. The pooling method consists of optimizing the relevance assessment process by pooling the documents retrieved by different search engines following a particular pooling strategy. The most common one consists on pooling the top d documents of each run. The pool is constructed from systems taking part in a challenge for which the collection was made, at a specific point in time, after which the collection is generally frozen in terms of relevance judgments. This method leads to a bias called *pool bias*, which is *the effect that documents that were not selected in the pool created from the original runs will never be considered relevant.* Thereby, this bias affects the evaluation of a system that has not been part of the pool, with any IR evaluation measures, making the comparison with pooled systems *unfair*.

IR measures have evolved over the years and become more and more complex and difficult to interpret. Witnessing a need in industry for measures that 'make sense', I focus on the problematics of the two fundamental IR evaluation measures, Precision at cut-off $P@n$ and Recall at cut-off $R@n$. There are two reasons to consider such 'simple' metrics: first, they are cornerstones for many other developed metrics and, second, they are easy to understand by all users. To the eyes of a practitioner, these two evaluation measures are interesting because they lead to more intuitive interpretations like, how much time people are reading useless documents (low precision), or how many relevant documents they are missing (low recall). But this last interpretation, due to the fact that recall is inversely proportional to the number of relevant documents per topic, is very difficult to be addressed if to be judged is just a portion of the collection of documents, as it is done when using the pooling method. To tackle this problem, another kind of evaluation has been developed, based on measuring how much an IR system makes documents accessible [1]. *Accessibility* measures can be seen as a complementary evaluation to recall because they provide information on whether some relevant documents are not retrieved due to an *unfairness* in accessibility.

The main goal of this Ph.D. is to increase the stability and reusability of existing test collections, when to be evaluated are systems in terms of precision, recall, and accessibility. The outcome will be: the development of a novel estimator to tackle the pool bias issue for $P@n$ [4], and $R@n$, a comprehensive analysis of the effect of the estimator on varying pooling strategies [3], and finally, to support the evaluation of recall, an analytic approach to the evaluation of accessibility measures [2].

SIGIR '16 July 17-21, 2016, Pisa, Italy

ACM ISBN 978-1-4503-4069-4/16/07.

DOI: http://dx.doi.org/10.1145/2911451.2911473

CCS Concepts

•**Information systems → Retrieval effectiveness;** *Test collections;*

Keywords

Pool Bias, Pooling Method, P@n, R@n, Accessibility

Acknowledgements

This research was supported by the Austrian Science Fund (FWF) project number P25905-N23 (ADmIRE).

REFERENCES

[1] L. Azzopardi and V. Vinay. Accessibility in information retrieval. In *Proc. of ECIR'08*, pages 482–489.

[2] A. Lipani, M. Lupu, A. Aizawa, and A. Hanbury. An initial analytical exploration of retrievability. In *Proc. of ICTIR'15*, pages 329–332.

[3] A. Lipani, M. Lupu, and A. Hanbury. The curious incidence of bias corrections in the pool. In *Proc. of ECIR'16*, pages 267–279.

[4] A. Lipani, M. Lupu, and A. Hanbury. Splitting water: Precision and anti-precision to reduce pool bias. In *Proc. of SIGIR'15*, pages 103–112.

[5] K. Spärck Jones and C. J. van Rijsbergen. Report on the need for and provision of an "ideal" information retrieval test collection. *British Library Research and Development Report No. 5266*, page 44.

Going Beyond Relevance: Incorporating effort in Information Retrieval

Manisha Verma
University College London
manisha.verma.13@ucl.ac.uk

ABSTRACT

Primary focus of Information retrieval (IR) systems has been to optimize for *Relevance*. Existing approaches used to rank documents or evaluate IR systems do not account for "user effort". At present, relevance captures topical overlap between document and user query. This mechanism does not take into consideration either time or effort of end user to satisfy information need. While a judge may spend time assessing a document, an end user may not thoroughly examine a document. We identified factors that are associated with effort for a single document and gathered judgments for same. We also investigated the role of several features in predicting effort on webpage. In future, we shall investigate role of effort on mobile and investigate effort based evaluation methodology that also takes into account user's search task.

1. INTRODUCTION

Search engines measure the estimate document relevance on basis of *Topicality*. A document is considered relevant to user's query if its content topically overlaps with user's information need. Information Retrieval (IR) systems are designed to optimize for relevance. It is assumed that relevant documents shall answer user's information need, which in turn will yield higher user satisfaction. Evaluation metrics are also designed to compare systems on basis of how many relevant documents are retrieved and where are they shown on SERPs.

At present, researchers rely on pre-designed small-scale test collections to evaluate effectiveness of IR systems known as *batch evaluation*. These test collections consist of some documents manually judged for relevance for pre-defined queries. Live users are also used to evaluate system's search effectiveness. *User based evaluation* relies on observing and measuring user's interaction with document to determine its relevance. One would expect that batch evaluation would agree with user-based evaluation of systems. However it has been shown in the past [1] that these two forms of evaluation do not agree with each other. Recently, Yilmaz *et al.* [4] proposed that this mismatch is due to the disagreement between what judges and users consider relevant. Trained judges are asked to identify document relevance regardless of how much time and effort it may take to consume it. While a judge can take significant time to evaluate a document, an end user may not be willing to spend as much time consuming it, even if it is relevant. They report that the primary reason of mismatch between explicit and implicit document judgments is a result of *effort* needed to find and consume required information from a given document.

Thus, we need to design systems and evaluation methodologies that consider both user effort and relevance to rank documents or compare systems. Effort would becomes crucial with change in device of information access. In mobile, where interaction is limited by screen size and restricted text-input, users are more likely to give up finding information via search engines. Thus, we need to characterize effort across devices. Finally, effort based evaluation of search engines would have to be designed around user's search tasks. For instance, systems that rank documents high effort documents on the top for easy tasks should be penalized more than those that rank low effort documents (on top) for relatively difficult task.

With the above mentioned motivations we wish to explore ways to accommodate *user effort* in IR evaluation. We shall focus on three research questions regarding effort. **RQ1:** What constitutes *user effort* in IR. What parameters are most representative of user effort. Given a document and user query, what features will be useful to predict effort based judgments. We identified three factors [3] to be associated with effort, gathered judgments (both explicit and preference based) and investigated their correlation with user satisfaction. Our findings suggest that ease of finding information dominates all other factors. **RQ2:** How can existing learning to rank framework be modified to optimize for both relevance and effort. **RQ3:** How does effort *vary* with user device. What factors characterize effort on mobile and desktop. We conducted a user study [2] to understand variation in relevance with device. We shall use this data to control for relevance and investigate role of effort on mobiles. **RQ4:** Finally, how can we design *effort based evaluation* methodology which takes into account user' search task while rewarding or penalizing systems.

2. REFERENCES

[1] M. Sanderson, M. L. Paramita, P. Clough, and E. Kanoulas. Do user preferences and evaluation measures line up? SIGIR '10. ACM.

[2] M. Verma and E. Yilmaz. Characterizing relevance on mobile and desktop. ECIR '16. Springer.

[3] M. Verma, E. Yilmaz, and N. Craswell. On obtaining effort based judgements for information retrieval. WSDM '16. ACM.

[4] E. Yilmaz, M. Verma, N. Craswell, F. Radlinski, and P. Bailey. Relevance and effort: An analysis of document utility. CIKM '14. ACM.

SIGIR '16 July 17-21, 2016, Pisa, Italy

ACM ISBN 978-1-4503-4069-4/16/07.
DOI: http://dx.doi.org/10.1145/2911451.2911487

Measuring Interestingness of Political Documents

Hosein Azarbonyad
h.azarbonyad@uva.nl

University of Amsterdam, Amsterdam, The Netherlands

ABSTRACT

Political texts are pervasive on the Web covering laws and policies in national and supranational jurisdictions. Access to this data is crucial for government transparency and accountability to the population. The main aim of our research is developing a ranking method for political documents which captures the interesting content within political documents. Text interestingness is a measure of assessing the quality of documents from users' perspective which shows their willingness to read a document. Different approaches are proposed for measuring the interestingness of texts. In this research we focus on measuring political texts' interestingness. As political data sources, we use publicly available parliamentary proceedings.

Keywords

Text Interestingness; Topical Diversity; Political Documents

1. RESEARCH PROPOSAL

Political texts such as parliamentary proceedings are valuable information sources for historians, politicians, and also the public. Access to this data is crucial for government transparency and accountability to the population [2]. Therefore, there is a need to develop techniques to access and analyze the content of political data sources. In this research we focus on measuring the interestingness of political documents. Interestingness of documents could be used for ranking these documents and help the users to not only find the documents that are related to their information need but also focus on more interesting documents. The availability of user-generated text-based reviews stimulated research in automatically computing the interestingness of texts [3, 4]. Our main research question is: **RQ1:** *What aspects of interesetingness are covered by current approaches? How can we incorporate the aspects related to documents content in text interestingness measures?* Our main goal is to design a measure for estimating the interestingness of debates. In [3] it is shown that text interestingness is highly correlated with topical diversity on e-books and e-commerce products description datasets. The current measures use either the topical diversity of documents to measure the interestingness of political debates [1] or the structural information of debates [6]. Both of these approaches do not use the main content of the debates for assessing their interestingness. We are aiming to propose text-based measures of interestingness for political debates and also leverage useful structural information of debates as well as the topical diversity of them.

We break **RQ1.1** down into three research questions. We first study whether interestingness of political debates is correlated with their topical diversity and answer the following question: **RQ1.2:** *Are topically diverse political documents also interesting?* Usually topical diversity of documents is measured by means of topic models. The main intuition is that if a document covers many dissimilar topics it is a diverse document. We propose a parsimonization technique [5] to extract salient information from topic models which makes them more suitable for the task of estimating diversity of documents compared to current topic models. The next research question is: **RQ1.3:** *What are the main deficiencies of current topic models in estimating topical diversity of documents? And how effective is the proposed parsimonious topic model in addressing these deficiencies?* We use the proposed parsimonious topic models to measure the topical diversity of documents. Then using the estimated diversity values for the debates, we analyze the impact of different sources of diversity on making the documents topically diverse. Our next research question is: **RQ1.4:** *What are the main sources of diversity of debates? And how they affect the topical diversity of debates?* As the sources of diversity, we study the effect of diversity of people participated in debates and the diversity of main topics of debates. We incorporate these sources of diversity in our proposed interestingness and diversity measures.

Acknowledgements This research was supported by the Netherlands Organization for Scientific Research (ExPoSe project, NWO CI # 314.99.108; DiLiPaD project, NWO Digging into Data # 600.006.014) and by the European Community's Seventh Framework Program (FP7/2007-2013) under grant agreement ENVRI, number 283465.

REFERENCES

[1] H. Azarbonyad, F. Saan, M. Dehghani, M. Marx, and J. Kamps. Are topically diverse documents also interesting? CLEF'15, 2015.
[2] M. Dehghani, H. Azarbonyad, M. Marx, and J. Kamps. Sources of evidence for automatic indexing of political texts. ECIR'15, 2015.
[3] M. Derzinski and K. Rohanimanesh. An information theoretic approach to quantifying text interestingness. In *NIPS MLNLP*, 2014.
[4] D. Ganguly, J. Leveling, and G. J. F. Jones. Automatic prediction of aesthetics and interestingness of text passages. COLING'14, 2014.
[5] D. Hiemstra, S. Robertson, and H. Zaragoza. Parsimonious language models for information retrieval. SIGIR'04, pages 178–185, 2004.
[6] A. Hogenboom, M. Jongmans, and F. Frasincar. Structuring political documents for importance ranking. NLDB'12, 2012.

SIGIR '16 July 17-21, 2016, Pisa, Italy

ACM ISBN 123-4567-24-567/08/06...$15.00
DOI: http://dx.doi.org/10.1145/2911451.2911485

Modeling User Feedback in Dynamic Search and Browsing

Jiyun Luo
Department of Computer Science
Georgetown University
Washington, DC, USA
jl1749@georgetown.edu

Categories and Subject Descriptors

•Information systems → Retrieval models and ranking; *Users and interactive retrieval;*

Keywords

Session Search; Dynamic Search; User Feedback Modeling

1. INTRODUCTION

Nowadays, searching for complicated information is a more and more common task. User's information needs are usually vague or consist of multiple sub-topics, and they must formulate many different queries to achieve their search's goal. A lot of work has been done to improve user satisfaction during the search process. Riccho etc. are developed to help find similar relevant documents. They help the user focus on and exploit the current search topic. xQuAD [5] etc. are efficient diversification algorithms that help the user explore multiple search topics. None of these approaches alone work well in session searches because none of them treat the search session as a whole. They can't answer the question of when to explore and when to exploit.

In our previous work [3], we argue that it is suitable to model session searches as a Dual-Agent Stochastic Game, which essentially is a Partially Observable Markov Decision Process (POMDP) [2] with two agents. Our model treats session search as a "trial-and-error" process and uses user feedback as learning signals to adjust its search strategies, such as exploration and exploitation.

The major feedback we considered in our previous works were query reformulations and user clickthrough datas. I first extend our work by introducing more user feedbacks into our framework. We implement a new search engine UI which allows users to explicitly mark out relevant passages and irrelevant documents. With these explicit feedbacks, I can improve the exploitation algorithm. I use the relevant text to reform a new query for retrieval. The irrelevant documents are then used to re-rank the retrieved documents. For exploration, my algorithm is inspired by xQuAD. The subtopics are found by the user during a search process. I run the algorithm n times in order to recommend n diversified documents. For each round, I sample one subtopic to recommend based on xQuAD.

The second research question I addressed is the decision of when to explore and when to exploit. In [6], the authors explore during the initial phase, and then choose one path to exploit based on user feedback. [4] applies exploration whenever it encounters a diversified query. I argue that their approaches only capture some specific user behavior models. [1] applies exploration as default behavior and interprets user click as a desire to exploit similar documents. However this assumption is not accurate. I use ϵ-greedy as a naive approach to balance Exploration and Exploitation. If the user has tried exploitation multiple times, then we should switch to exploration, and vice versa. Another possible solution could be to pick one search strategy at first, such as "exploitation", and if no positive feedback is received from the user, then we switch to the other search strategy.

The final challenge in this thesis is how to properly evaluate session search algorithms. We propose a new sophisticated evaluation metric, Cube Test. This new metric is able to emphasize subtopic coverage, novelty, and retrieval accuracy at the same time. It also emphasizes minimizing user effort by encouraging short sessions over long sessions. I plan to use this metric, MAP, nDCG, α-nDCG and nERR-IA to evaluate my algorithms as well as other well-known session based retrieval algorithms. I hope these metrics can reveal different aspects of retrieval algorithms and eventually help us to distinguish good session search algorithms from others.

SIGIR '16 July 17-21, 2016, Pisa, Italy

ACM ISBN 978-1-4503-4069-4/16/07.
DOI: http://dx.doi.org/10.1145/2911451.2911483

References

[1] C. Brandt, T. Joachims, Y. Yue, and J. Bank. Dynamic ranked retrieval. In *WSDM '11*.

[2] L. P. Kaelbling, M. L. Littman, and A. R. Cassandra. Planning and acting in partially observable stochastic domains. *Artificial intelligence*, 101(1):99–134, 1998.

[3] J. Luo, S. Zhang, and H. Yang. Win-win search: Dual-agent stochastic game in session search. In *SIGIR '14*.

[4] K. Raman, P. N. Bennett, and K. Collins-Thompson. Toward whole-session relevance: Exploring intrinsic diversity in web search. In *SIGIR '13*.

[5] R. L. Santos, C. Macdonald, and I. Ounis. Exploiting query reformulations for web search result diversification. In *WWW '10*.

[6] M. Sloan and J. Wang. Dynamic information retrieval: Theoretical framework and application. In *ICTIR '15*.

Modelling User Search Behaviour Based on Process

Mengdie Zhuang
Information School
University of Sheffield
Sheffield, UK
mzhuang1@sheffield.ac.uk

ABSTRACT

Typically, interactive information retrieval (IIR) system evaluations assess search processes and outcomes using a combination of two types of measures: 1. user perception (e.g. users' attitudes of the search experience and outcome); 2. user behaviour (e.g. time and counts of various actions including mouse and keyboard clicks). In general, we assume that they are indicative of the search outcomes (e.g. performance, opinion).

However, search is a dynamic process with changing outcomes. Therefore, neither measure solely provides a holistic way of evaluating search. On one hand, user behaviour measures are only descriptive of the outcome, and are not interpretive of the process. That is to say, they lack the rationale behind why those behaviours occurred. Another problem is that some mental activities may not reflect on user behaviour [1]. The challenge with logfiles, which contain behaviour data, is the voluminous number of data points and the need to find a reliable approach to define groups or sets based on behavioural patterns. Not all users are alike and nor do they all take the same approach to search for the same things, as evidenced by the TREC, INEX and CLEF interactive tracks. On the other hand, user perception measures are acquired in such small samples that do not scale to large participant populations, and are rarely measured constantly due to the laborious and time consuming data collection methods (e.g. questionnaire, interview). Moreover, not enough emphasis is put on assessing the reliability of individual perception measures, and the wide usage of likert-type scale limits the interpretation of answers. For a holistic understanding of the search process, we need both perception and behaviour measures. I speculate that user behaviour may predict user perception, and thus we should be able to analyse large-scale files for a greater understanding of the likely human responses.

This problem is a pervasive one that exists from small projects to large organisations. In addition, the evaluation of search systems based on the *entire search process* has not been investigated adequately. Although some models (e.g. Marchionini's model [3]) of the search process fits real-life search, it is still considered fundamental in describing mental activities in the search process, and the seemingly random iterations of mental status is not easily accessible. Previous studies (e.g. [5]) have used a short piece of action sequence to represent search trail, but it was measured in a short time period, rather than covering the whole search process.

The purpose of this research is to investigate the relationship between user perception and user behaviour during search; identify behaviour patterns across users' search process; investigate the validity of behavioural patterns and whether the patterns are indicative of user perception, which further implicate trends for either search success or failure. We will address the following research questions: ***Q1.*** *Which user behaviour measures are indicative of user perception?* ***Q2.*** *What behaviour patterns are represented in the search process when users use search systems for work task completion?* ***Q3.*** *What are the behaviour patterns of search process when users do not have a clear search task in mind (exploratory search)?* ***Q4.*** *How could these behaviour patterns be used to understand and produce a predictive model of user perception?*

The datasets I propose to use contain both user behaviour data from logfiles and user perception data from the results of the User Engagement Scale [4], which were collected in previous studies, and they covered different task types. Tackling such problems requires a mix of user- and system-centred approaches, and pattern recognition methodologies, such as time series analysis and Hidden Markov Model [2], will be applied. Our preliminary test [6] showed that although aesthetics and usability perceptions of search appear un-influenced by users interactions with system, attention, involvement and novelty were associated with general actions. Ultimately, this research will augment the development of a predictive model of search success, as well as a more cost-efficient interactive information retrieval evaluation method that enables automated data collection of essential measures, that would benefit both users and search engine developers.

SIGIR '16, July 17–21, 2016, Pisa, Italy.
ACM 978-1-4503-4069-4/16/07.
DOI: http://dx.doi.org/10.1145/2911451.2911486

Keywords

Search process; user behaviour; interactive information retrieval evaluation

REFERENCES

[1] Barreda-Ángeles, M., Arapakis, I., Bai, X., Cambazoglu, B.B., and Pereda-Baños, A., 2015. Unconscious Physiological Effects of Search Latency on Users and Their Click Behaviour. *Proc. SIGIR'15*, 203-212.

[2] Bishop, C.M., 2006. Pattern Recognition. Machine Learning.

[3] Marchionini, G., 1995. Information seeking in electronic environments. Cambridge University Press.

[4] O'brien, H.L. and Toms, E.G., 2008. What is user engagement? A conceptual framework for defining user engagement with technology. *JASIST*, 59, 6, 938-955.

[5] White, R.W. and Dumais, S.T., 2009. Characterizing and predicting search engine switching behavior. *Proc. CIKM'09*, 87-96.

[6] Zhuang, M., Toms, E.G., and Demartini, G., 2016. The Relationship Between User Perception and User Behaviour in Interactive Information Retrieval Evaluation. In Advances in Information Retrieval, Springer, 293-305.

Retrievability: An Independent Evaluation Measure

Colin Wilkie
School of Computing Science,
University of Glasgow
Glasgow, United Kingdom
c.wilkie.3@research.gla.ac.uk

ABSTRACT

Information Retrieval systems have traditionally been evaluated in terms of efficiency and performance. These aspects of retrieval systems, whilst very important, do not cover a crucial aspect of the system, the access it provides to the documents of the collection. Retrievability, a document centric evaluation measure, introduced by Azzopardi and Vinay, provides an alternative approach to evaluation [1]. Retrievability is the ease with which a document can be retrieved using a retrieval system. The more queries which retrieve the document, and the higher up the document is returned, the more retrievable it is. It can thus be used to describe how difficult it is to find documents in the collection given a particular configuration of a retrieval system. Unlike typical performance evaluations, performing a retrievability analysis can be done without recourse to relevancy judgements meaning there is no reliance on a test collection. This has major advantages when tuning a retrieval systems parameters as the tuning can be performed on the live collection.

Several applications of retrievability have been explored, however, many areas remain untouched or partially studied. Thus far, work in this PhD has explored the relationship between retrievability bias and performance in the context of ad hoc retrieval [2, 3, 5]. A benefit that would allow researchers in academia and industry to tune their system on their own collection and would save the resources of creating a test collection. Other aspects of retrievability also covered in this PhD have investigated the impact of query length on the estimation of Gini [6], investigating methods of computing retrievability more efficiently [4] and the application of various inequality metrics instead of the Gini Coefficient [7] when estimating the overall inequality of the system.

The remainder of this PhD aims to continue investigating the relationship between retrievability bias and performance, specifically to examine whether or not the relationship found thus far is generalisable to other domains and performance metrics. Applications of the theory of retrievability are also to be examined to see if there are alternative uses of retrievability to aid information retrieval outside of evaluation. Finally, due to the high cost of computing retrievability, another vein of research which is vital to moving retrievability more towards mainstream evaluation is to develop more efficient methods of estimating retrievability. Work in each of these areas will increase both the usefulness of retrievability by allowing demonstrating it can be applied to various domains and its attractiveness in both evaluation and general use for information retrieval.

Keywords

Retrievability; Bias; Effectiveness; Evaluation

1. REFERENCES

[1] Azzopardi, L., Vinay, V.: Retrievability: An evaluation measure for higher order information access tasks. In: Proc. of the 17th ACM CIKM. pp. 561–570 (2008)

[2] Wilkie, C., Azzopardi, L.: Relating retrievability, performance and length. In: Proc. of the 36th ACM SIGIR conference. pp. 937–940 (2013)

[3] Wilkie, C., Azzopardi, L.: Best and fairest: An empirical analysis of retrieval system bias. Advances in Information Retrieval pp. 13–25 (2014)

[4] Wilkie, C., Azzopardi, L.: Efficiently estimating retrievability bias. In: Advances in Information Retrieval. pp. 720–726 (2014)

[5] Wilkie, C., Azzopardi, L.: A retrievability analysis: Exploring the relationship between retrieval bias and retrieval performance. In: Proc. of the 23rd ACM CIKM. pp. 81–90 (2014)

[6] Wilkie, C., Azzopardi, L.: Query length, retrievability bias and performance. In: Proc. of the 24th ACM CIKM. pp. 1787–1790 (2015)

[7] Wilkie, C., Azzopardi, L.: Retrievability bias: A comparison of inequality measures. Advances in Information Retrieval pp. 209–214 (2015)

SIGIR '16 July 17-21, 2016, Pisa, Italy

ACM ISBN 978-1-4503-4069-4/16/07.

DOI: http://dx.doi.org/10.1145/2911451.2911478

Significant Words Representations of Entities

Mostafa Dehghani
Institute for Logic, Language and Computation
University of Amsterdam, The Netherlands
dehghani@uva.nl

ABSTRACT

Transforming the data into a suitable representation is the first key step of data analysis, and the performance of any data oriented method is heavily depending on it. We study questions on how we can best learn representations for textual entities that are: 1) precise, 2) robust against noisy terms, 3) transferable over time, and 4) interpretable by human inspection. Inspired by the early work of Luhn [4], we propose *significant words language models* of a set of documents that capture all, and only, the significant shared terms from them. We adjust the weights of common terms that are already well explained by the document collection as well as the weight of incidental rare terms that are only explained by specific documents, which eventually results in having only the significant terms left in the model.

KEYWORDS: Significant Words; Language Model.

1. SIGNIFICANT WORDS MODELS

Transformation of raw data to a representation that can be effectively exploited is motivated by the fact that data oriented methods often require input that is convenient to process. In this research, we introduce *significant words language models* (SWLM) as a family of models aiming to learn representations for the set of documents that are not affected by neither general properties nor specific properties. The general idea of SWLM is inspired by the early work of Luhn [4], in which he argues that to extract **significant words** by avoiding both common observations and rare observations (Figure1).

In order to estimate SWLM, we assume that terms in the each document in the set are drawn from three models: 1. *General model*, representative of common observation, 2. *Specific model*, representative of partial observation, and 3. *Significant Words model* which is a latent model representing the significant characteristics of the whole set. Then, we try to extract the latent significant words model.

1.1 Applications of the SWLM

The proposed approach is generally applicable to any system that requires the estimation of an effective model representing the significant features of a group of objects. Until now, we have employed the model in three main applications:

SIGIR '16 July 17-21, 2016, Pisa, Italy

ACM ISBN 978-1-4503-4069-4/16/07.
DOI: http://dx.doi.org/10.1145/2911451.2911474

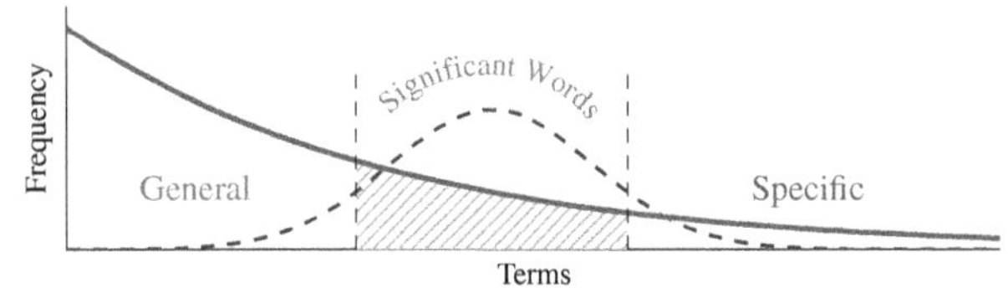

Figure 1: Establishing a set of "Significant Words" based on Luhn [4]

Group Profiling for Content Customization: We have proposed to use SWLM to extract the 'abstract' group level latent model from users group that captures all, and only, the essential features of the whole group. We employed the resulting models in the task of contextual suggestion [1, 3] and observed improvements in the performance of customization.

(Pseudo-)Relevance Feedback: We have presented a variant of SWLM, Regularized SWLM (RSWLM) for estimating a robust language model for a set of feedback documents by incorporating the information from the query. We have conducted extensive experiments on the effectiveness of RSWLM for (pseudo-)relevance feedback and demonstrated that it captures the essential terms representing the mutual notion of relevance.

Hierarchical Classification: We have also extended SWLM to be able to estimate proper models for hierarchical entities which take their position in the hierarchy into consideration [2]. We have employed SWLM on the task of hierarchical classification and observed that since estimated models of entities in the hierarchy are both horizontally and vertically separable, they are precise, robust and transferable over time.

2. REST OF THE JOURNEY

Besides applying the model in further applications, there are several other interesting directions to pursue in this research. These include using SWLM as an analytical tool to investigate and better understanding of the data, extending the method to be applicable to non-textual features, and employing the general idea of SWLM to the representation learning systems like embedding methods.

Acknowledgments This research is funded by the Netherlands Organization for Scientific Research (ExPoSe project, NWO CI # 314.99.108).

References

[1] M. Dehghani, H. Azarbonyad, J. Kamps, and M. Marx. Generalized group profiling for content customization. In *CHIIR '16*, pages 245–248, 2016.

[2] M. Dehghani, H. Azarbonyad, J. Kamps, and M. Marx. Two-way parsimonious classification models for evolving hierarchies. In *CLEF'16*, 2016.

[3] S. H. Hashemi, M. Dehghani, and J. Kamps. Parsimonious user and group profiling in venue recommendation. In *TREC 2015*. NIST, 2015.

[4] H. P. Luhn. The automatic creation of literature abstracts. *IBM J. Res. Dev.*, 2 (2):159–165, 1958.

Time-Quality Trade-offs in Search

Ryan Burton
University of Michigan School of Information
105 S. State St.,
Ann Arbor MI, 48109
ryb@umich.edu

ABSTRACT

This research explores the notion of *slow search*, where retrieval speed may be traded for improvements in result quality. This time-quality tradeoff leads to a number of implications for user interface and algorithm design. We will explore this space along various dimensions, including behavioral and qualitative analyses of interaction to investigate the value a user that is able to perceive when given the option to use *slow search* in addition to traditional search. We will also examine how different notions of 'quality' that a system might optimize may fit into this framework.

CCS Concepts

•Information systems → Search interfaces; Retrieval models and ranking; Personalization;

Keywords

Search behavior; interactive information retrieval; user interfaces; slow search

1. CONTEXT AND MOTIVATION

With the current popularity of Web search, users have become accustomed to information retrieval systems that are optimized to return the results of a search query within a fraction of a second. In order to be this fast, system implementors must make trade-offs between speed and quality. Traditionally, many IR systems make a number of simplifying assumptions about the linguistic complexity of queries and documents, and the time budget given to document matching, ranking, and additional distinguishing features such as personalization tends to be very small [4, 2]. With these simplifications, the scope of potential improvements may be limited for topic relevance, personalization, or ranking for diversity.

Proposed by Dörk et al. [1] and Teevan et al. [4] in 2013, *slow search* refers to the notion that a system may "take its time" to process results for additional effectiveness. Inspired by other "slow" movements such as slow food, slow travel, and slow technology [3], the authors posited that such a system may also lead to changes in how individuals and groups approach the process of search if a system emphasized slowness over speed. The authors proposed that users would be encouraged to be more mindful and reflective through revisiting previous journeys and exploring connections and relationships between search results.

In our work, we explore the space of time-quality trade-offs in search, and investigate the value that users perceive in the face of such trade-offs, as well as how users' search behaviors change when learning the capabilities of such systems. Primarily, this involves behavioral log analysis of new system designs as well as qualitative methods. Additionally, we are interested in the various ways in which we may improve quality with new algorithms that are flexible to dynamic time constraints.

2. RESEARCH GOALS

Our research goals center around understanding 1. how users' mental models are constructed as they become acclimatized to new search paradigms, 2. how individuals may use these novel systems depending on how much value they attribute to these systems, and 3. how we may use the lessons learned by addressing the aforementioned goals to design new algorithms and interfaces. The findings from this research will enable us to understand the ways in which we may build flexible IR systems that can address the underserved needs of users, being aware of contextual constraints such as time and urgency.

3. REFERENCES

[1] M. Dörk, P. Bennett, and R. Davies. Taking our sweet time to search. In *Proceedings of CHI 2013 Workshop on Changing Perspectives of Time in HCI*, 2013.

[2] M. L. Mauldin. Retrieval performance in FERRET: A conceptual information retrieval system. In *Proceedings of SIGIR 1991*, pages 347–355. ACM, 1991.

[3] L. Poirier and L. Robinson. Informational balance: slow principles in the theory and practice of information behaviour. *Journal of Documentation*, 70(4):687–707, 2014.

[4] J. Teevan, K. Collins-Thompson, R. W. White, S. T. Dumais, and Y. Kim. Slow search: Information retrieval without time constraints. In *Proceedings of HCIR 2013*, page 1. ACM, 2013.

SIGIR '16 July 17-21, 2016, Pisa, Italy

ACM ISBN 978-1-4503-4069-4/16/07.
DOI: http://dx.doi.org/10.1145/2911451.2911484

Torii: Attribute-based Polarity Analysis with Big Datasets

Fernando O. Gallego
University of Sevilla, ETSI Informática
Avda. Reina Mercedes, s/n, Sevilla E-41012, Spain
fogallego@us.es

ABSTRACT

Polarity analysis has become a key aspect of market analysis. The number of companies that are interested in the general opinion of the crowd regarding the items that they sell is increasing everyday. Attribute-based polarity analysis is a fine-grained approach that computes if the opinion about an attribute of (a component of) an item is positive, negative, or neutral. The existing techniques have a number of problems, namely: they do not take into account the conditions expressed in the opinions (e.g., when they hold and when they do not), they do not generally use any contextual information (e.g., past user opinions on the same attribute), and they are not validated on big datasets (e.g., billions of messages). In this paper, we present Torii, which is an attribute-based polarity analysis technique that takes both conditions and contextual information into account; we also present our approach to validate it on big datasets.

SIGIR '16 July 17-21, 2016, Pisa, Italy

ACM ISBN 978-1-4503-4069-4/16/07.

DOI: http://dx.doi.org/10.1145/2911451.2911479

Keywords

Attribute-based polarity analysis; Attribute conditions and contextual information; Big datasets validation.

Acknowledgements

Our work was supported the Spanish R&D&I programme by through grant TIN2013-40848-R. The work by Fernando O. Gallego was also partially supported by Dinamic Area, S.L. – Opileak.

User Interaction in Mobile Web Search

Jaewon Kim
Research School of Computer Science
The Australian National University
Canberra, ACT 0200, Australia
jaewon.kim@anu.edu.au

ABSTRACT

From previous studies, we believe that search behaviour on touch-enabled mobile devices is different from the behaviour with desktop screens. In the proposed research, we intend to explore user interaction while searching with the aim of improving search experience on mobile devices.

CCS Concepts

•**Information systems → Search interfaces; Web search engines;** •**Human-centered computing →** *Touch screens;*

Keywords

User interaction; web search; mobile device

1. RESEARCH AND RESULTS

Several studies have compared user behaviour and search performance between a desktop monitor and a mobile device (e.g., [3]), and it is believed that search engine developers need to provide a different presentation design for mobile web search. However, one remarkable trend of mobile devices is their enlargement of screen sizes during last a few years. Compared to early smartphones which have screens less than 4 inches across (diagonal), recently smartphones or *phablets* (a combined word of phone and tablet) have about 4.5 inches and over 5.5 inches, respectively. This led us to look for differences in search behaviour on different small screens, and if there are any, to suggest better presentation of search results for each screen size. Briefly, we found that participants in our experiment exhibited different search behaviours: less eye-movement within top links on the larger screen, fast reading with some hesitation before choosing a link on the medium, and frequent use of scrolling on the small screen. With this result, we suggested several ideas for presentation design for each screen size [4].

There are a number of studies which have investigated user interaction with search engine result pages (SERPs), and many of them indicated that the use of scrolling is closely related search behaviour (e.g., [2]), although people must still scroll through SERPs to see beyond the page folds. To the best of our knowledge, vertical scrolling is the only way to control viewport while searching, and is provided by all search engines. Because people are familiar with turning page horizontally when they read a book, and when controlling applications which provide horizontal switching interface (e.g., weather and shopping), it is worth investigating the effect of horizontal and vertical viewport control types (*pagination* versus *scrolling*) in mobile web search. This work has been completed, and our findings suggest that participants using pagination were more likely to find relevant documents despite spending less time on the SERPs overall.

Researchers have studied user interaction under manipulated elements of SERPs (e.g., length of snippets and rank order [1]) to investigate the effects of the contents on desktop monitors. Compared to effects on the desktop screens, searching with smartphones may be more affected by the elements of SERPs due to the smaller space to display search results. In addition, Google has started providing a mobile indicator, providing a small mark indicating that an item on a search results page links to a mobile optimized page instead of a full-size page for desktops as suggested by our earlier work [3]. We are currently investigating how the elements of SERPs interact with searchers, and how much these provide a better search experience, on small screens.

SIGIR '16 July 17-21, 2016, Pisa, Italy

ACM ISBN 978-1-4503-4069-4/16/07.

DOI: http://dx.doi.org/10.1145/2911451.2911476

2. REFERENCES

[1] E. Cutrell and Z. Guan. What are you looking for?: An eye-tracking study of information usage in web search. In *Proceedings of the SIGCHI conference*, pages 407–416. ACM, 2007.

[2] L. A. Granka, T. Joachims, and G. Gay. Eye-tracking analysis of user behavior in WWW search. In *Proceedings of the 27th annual international ACM SIGIR conference*, pages 478–479. ACM, 2004.

[3] J. Kim, P. Thomas, R. Sankaranarayana, T. Gedeon, and H.-J. Yoon. Eye-tracking analysis of user behavior and performance in web search on large and small screens. *Journal of the Association for Information Science and Technology*, 66(3):526–544, 2015.

[4] J. Kim, P. Thomas, R. Sankaranarayana, T. Gedeon, and H.-J. Yoon. Understanding eye movements on mobile devices for better presentation of search results. *Journal of the Association for Information Science and Technology*, 2016.

Collaborative Information Seeking: Art and Science of Achieving 1+1>2 in IR

Chirag Shah
School of Communication & Information
Rutgers University
4 Huntington St, New Brunswick, NJ 08873, USA
chirags@rutgers.edu

ABSTRACT

Traditional IR techniques, systems, and methods that assume an individual searcher are often shown to be inadequate for addressing search problems that are multi-faceted and/or too complex or difficult for individuals. The next big leap in information seeking/retrieval could happen by considering social and collaborative aspects of search. In this half-day tutorial, this concept, along with some of the foundational works and latest developments in the field of collaborative information seeking (CIS) will be presented. Specifically, the course will introduce the student to theories, methodologies, and tools that focus on information retrieval/seeking in collaboration. The student will have an opportunity to learn about the social aspect of IR with a focus on collaborative search or CIS situations, systems, and evaluation techniques. The three hours will be divided as: (1) introduction to group-based IR models, approaches, and systems; (2) back-end of CIS systems with system-focused mediation and front-end with user-focused mediation; and (3) evaluation of CIS systems/approaches, prediction and recommendations with collaborative aspects of IR, and future directions. The attendees will be given a course-pack that will include a reference list, an annotated bibliography of seminal works in the field, and depictions of relevant models/frameworks.

Length: Half day (3 hours)

Target Audience: Those interested in social and collaborative aspects of IR (from both academia and industry)

Prerequisite: A general understanding of web services, IR systems, and content analysis

SIGIR '16, July 17-21, 2016, Pisa, Italy

DOI: http://dx.doi.org/10.1145/2911451.2914801

Presenter: Chirag Shah

Affiliation: Rutgers University, USA

Address:
4 Huntington St, New Brunswick, NJ 08901
Phone: (848) 932-0887
Fax: (732) 932-6916
http://comminfo.rutgers.edu/ chirags
chirags@rutgers.edu

Bio:
Chirag Shah is an associate professor in both the School of Communication & Information (SC&I) and the Department of Computer Science at Rutgers University, USA. Shah received a PhD in Information Science from the University of North Carolina (UNC) at Chapel Hill. He holds an MTech, Computer Science & Engineering from IIT Madras, India and an MS, Computer Science from UMass Amherst. His research interests include various aspects of interactive information retrieval/seeking, especially in the context of online social networks and collaborations, resulting in two streams of works - Collaborative Information Seeking (CIS) and Social Information Seeking (SIS). This research is supported by grants from the US National Science Foundation (NSF), the Institute of Museum and Library Services (IMLS), Google, and Yahoo! At Rutgers, he directs the InfoSeeking Lab (http://infoseeking.org/). He has published two books on CIS - one as a solo author [9] and the other as a co-editor [5]. He was a guest editor for the IEEE Computer Special Issue on CIS published in March 2014.

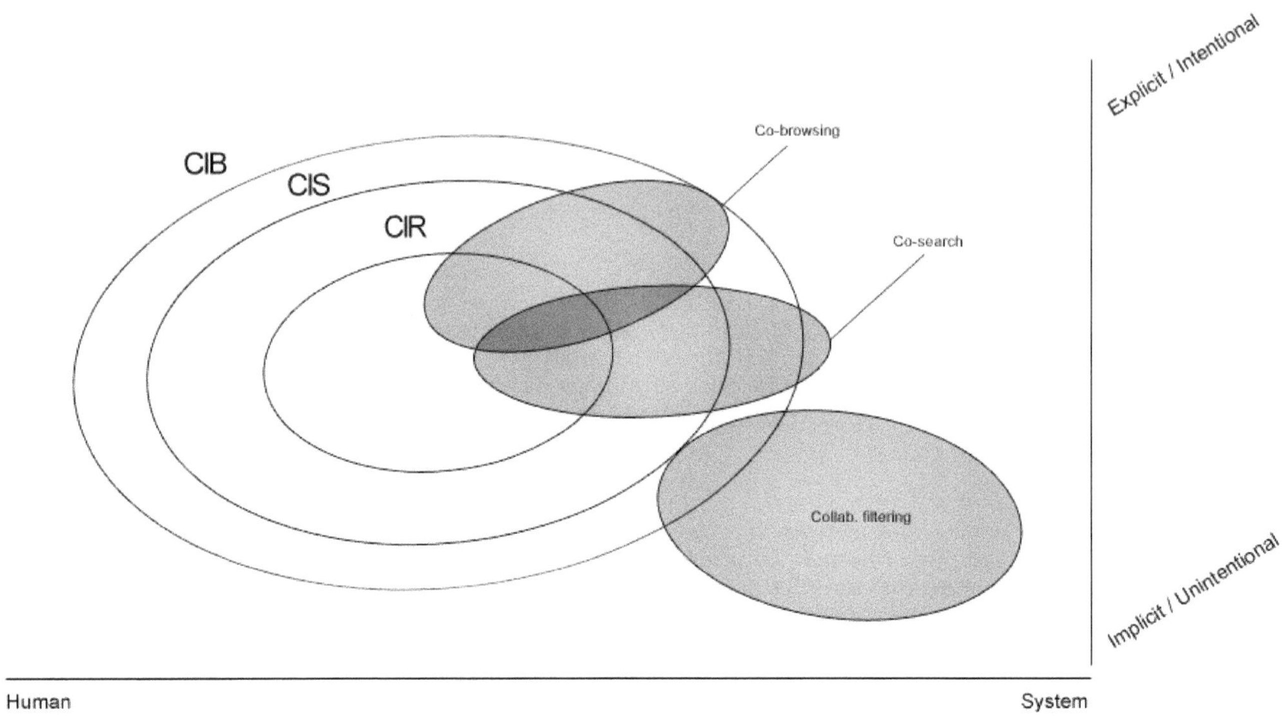

Figure 1: Depiction of CIS and related topics using the dimensions of human-system and explicit-implicit collaboration.

1. OVERVIEW AND RATIONALE

The course will introduce the student to theories, methodologies, and tools that focus on information retrieval/seeking in collaboration. The student will have an opportunity to learn about the social aspect of IR with a focus on collaborative search or collaborative information seeking (CIS) situations, systems, and evaluation techniques.

Traditionally, IR is considered an individual pursuit, and not surprisingly, the majority of tools, techniques, and models developed for addressing information need, retrieval, and usage have focused on single users. The assumption of information seekers being independent and IR problem being individual has been challenged often in the recent past. This course will introduce such works to the students, with an emphasis on understanding models and systems that support collaborative search or browsing. To put CIS in perspective, the course will show the students how various related concepts, such as collaborative information behavior (CIB), co-browsing, co-search, collaborative filtering, can be placed on the dimensions of human-system and explicitness-implicitness along with CIS and CIR (Figure 1) for exploration and developmental needs, as well as evaluation purposes.

Specifically, the course will (1) outline the research and latest developments in the field of collaborative IR, (2) list the challenges for designing and evaluating collaborative IR systems, and (3) show how traditional single user IR models and systems could be mapped to those for CIS. This will be achieved through introduction to appropriate literature, algorithms and interfaces that facilitate CIS, and methodologies for studying and evaluating them. Thus, the course will offer a balance between theoretical and practical elements of CIS.

2. COURSE OBJECTIVES

The course will have the following broad objectives:

1. Define collaborative information seeking (CIS) and differentiate it with related terms.
2. Identify situations and motivations for CIS.
3. List various dimensions of collaborative work/systems/meth
4. Discuss system-mediated and user-mediated CIS with examples.
5. Enumerate essential and desired features of CIS systems.
6. Outline an evaluation framework for CIS.

3. RELEVANCE TO THE IR COMMUNITY

With an increasing number of researchers from the fields of IR, HCI, and social media coming together, there has been an unprecedented interest to CIS/CIR and related issues in the recent years. While the concept of people working together in solving IR problems has been explored before, it has made its strong comeback in the past few years. This area has gained significant momentum through a number of workshops and other professional events, as well as special issues of journals. And yet, we have just scratched the surface. With the advent of social media and collaboratively generated content (CGC) everywhere, it is time the IR community takes a serious look at this topic that is increasingly achieving more relevance and importance. With its applicability to numerous domains including education, legal, health, and business, studying various issues relating to CIS/CIR is very timely and relevant to the IR community.

4. OUTLINE OF THE TUTORIAL

The three-hour course will follow a general structure given below.

- Hour-1: Discuss situations for CIS; Introduce a few group-based information seeking models and systems (e.g., Grudin's work [4]); Learn about the taxonomy for CIS systems and situations (e.g., Rodden [8], Golovchinsky [2]) and see how existing systems fit into this structure.
- Hour-2: Discuss the back-end of CIS systems; Look at the works by Pickens et al. [7], Shah et al. [11], and Soulier et al. [12] that focus on algorithmic mediation; Discuss the front-end of collaborative IR systems; Look at the works by Twidale et al. [13] and Morris [6] that focus on interface-based mediation.
- Hour-3: Learn about existing approaches to data mining and evaluation for CIS systems (e.g., Baeza-Yates & Pino [1]); See how system-based and user-based measurements could be used for a more holistic analysis (e.g., Shah & Gonzalez-Ibanez [10]); Understand how prediction and recommendation frameworks could be incorporated in collaborative search (e.g., Gonzalez-Ibanez et al. [3]).

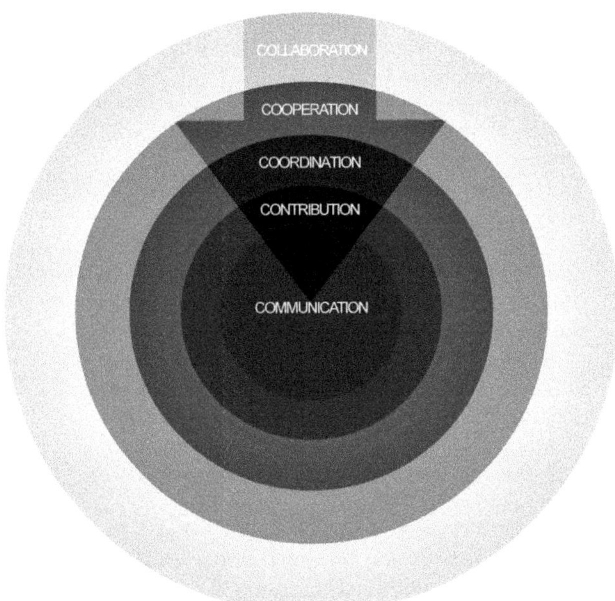

Figure 2: The *C5* model of collaboration.

Following is a more detailed outline of the tutorial presentation.

1. Collaboration - what and why
   (a) Requirement or setup
   (b) Division of labor
   (c) Diversity of skills
2. Defining collaboration - definitions from literature and our own understanding of various terms and terminology
   (a) The *C5* model (see Figure 2)
   (b) Interaction, intention, trust, awareness, etc. in defining collaboration
   (c) CIS in the context of collaboration, information seeking, and IR
3. Background - important people, works, and recent events relating to CIS/CIR
   (a) Various research groups around the world working on CIS/CIR
   (b) Conference events, social gatherings, workshops, etc.
4. Introducing collaboration in IR
   (a) Difference between CIS and CIR
   (b) CIS in the context of collaborative information behavior (CIB), co-browsing, co-search, and collaborative filtering
5. Studying group activities in time and space
   (a) Placement of various collaborative activities on time-space plane
   (b) Role of such placement in studying and/or evaluating CIS systems
6. Extended framework for collaborative activities with 12 different dimensions
   (a) Dimensions include intention, activeness, synchronous-asynchronous, co-located or remote, system-user, awareness, interactiveness, symmetry of roles, strength of the tie, symmetry of benefits, and nature of information activity
7. System-mediated CIS
   (a) Case study: Cerchiamo
   (b) Case study: Querium
8. User-mediated CIS
   (a) Case study: Ariadne
   (b) Case study: SearchTogether
   (c) Case study: Coagmento
9. Discuss generic features of a CIS/CIR system
   (a) Essential features
   (b) Desired features
10. Evaluation using system-focused and user-focused measures (see Figure 3)
   (a) Traditional measures: precision, recall, coverage, novelty, diversity
   (b) Productivity measures: effectiveness, efficiency
   (c) Usability measures: ease of learning, ease of use, satisfaction, cognitive load
   (d) Other: engagement, awareness

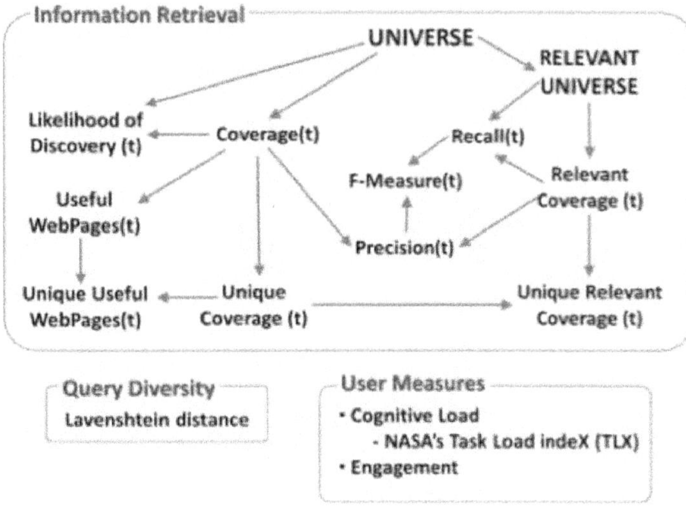

Figure 3: An example of an evaluation framework for collaborative search.

11. Creating synergic solutions for CIS
    (a) How does 1+1 become greater than 2 in collaboration
    (b) Issue of control in the context of system-mediated and user-mediated collaborations
    (c) Achieving selective collaboration to provide a balance of user-control and system-intelligence for synergy
12. Applications of CIS
    (a) Exploratory search (e.g., legal informatics, patent searching, healthcare)
    (b) Education
    (c) Product search (e.g., using selective collaboration method on Amazon and eBay)
    (d) Generalizing recommender systems for recommending people and processes
13. Future directions for research and development

5. COURSE MATERIALS

Course materials will be made available on a Web site hosted under http://collab.infoseeking.org/ two weeks prior to the tutorial. They will include links to relevant software; links to publications that will be discussed; and mechanisms for communication (Twitter hashtags, blog space, etc.) among the tutorial participants, before, during and after the tutorial.

Since this course is focused on introducing several relevant theories, models, approaches, and findings in the field of CIS/CIR, the participants will also be given an annotated bibliography that represents seminal works in this area.

6. REFERENCES

[1] R. Baeza-Yates and J. A. Pino. A First Step to Formally Evaluate Collaborative Work. In S. C. Payne and W. Prinz, editors, *Proceedings of ACM GROUP Conference*, pages 56–60, Phoenix, AZ, 1997.

[2] G. Golovchinsky, J. Pickens, and M. Back. A taxonomy of collaboration in online information seeking. In *Proceedings of JCDL 2008 Workshop on Collaborative Exploratory Search*, Pittsburgh, PA, June 2008.

[3] R. González-Ibáñez, C. Shah, and R. W. White. Capturing collabportunities: A method to evaluate collaboration opportunities in information search using pseudo-collaboration. *Journal of Association of Information Science and Technology (JASIST)*, 2014.

[4] J. Grudin. Groupware and social dynamics: eight challenges for developers. *Communications of the ACM*, 37(1):92–105, Jan. 1994.

[5] P. Hansen, C. Shah, and C.-P. Klas, editors. *Collaborative Information Seeking - Best Practices, New Domains, New Thoughts*. Springer, 2015.

[6] M. R. Morris and E. Horvitz. SearchTogether: An Interface for Collaborative Web Search. In *ACM Symposium on User Interface Software and Technology (UIST)*, pages 3–12, Newport, RI, Oct. 2007. New York, N.Y.: ACM Press.

[7] J. Pickens, G. Golovchinsky, C. Shah, P. Qvarfordt, and M. Back. Algorithmic Mediation for Collaborative Exploratory Search. In *Proceedings of the Annual ACM Conference on Research and Development in Information Retrieval (SIGIR)*, pages 315–322, Singapore, July 2008.

[8] T. Rodden. A Survey of CSCW Systems. *Interacting with Computers*, 3(3):319–353, 1991.

[9] C. Shah. *Collaborative Information Seeking: The Art and Science of Making The Whole Greater Than The Sum of All (The Information Retrieval Series)*. Springer, Berlin, Germany, 2012.

[10] C. Shah and R. Gonzalez-Ibanez. Evaluating the Synergic Effect of Collaboration in Information Seeking. In *Proceedings of the Annual ACM Conference on Research and Development in Information Retrieval (SIGIR)*, pages 913–922, Beijing, China, 2011.

[11] C. Shah, J. Pickens, and G. Golovchinsky. Role-based results redistribution for collaborative information retrieval. *Information Processing & Management*, 46(6):773–781, Nov. 2010.

[12] L. Soulier, C. Shah, and L. Tamine. User-driven system-mediated collaborative information retrieval. In *Proceedings of the 37th international ACM SIGIR conference on Research & development in information retrieval - SIGIR '14*, pages 485–494, New York, New York, USA, jul 2014. ACM Press.

[13] M. B. Twidale, D. M. Nichols, and C. D. Paice. Supporting collaborative learning during information searching. In *Proceedings of Computer Supported Collaborative Learning (CSCL)*, pages 367–374, Bloomington, Indiana, 1995.

Constructing and Mining Web-Scale Knowledge Graphs

Evgeniy Gabrilovich
Google Research
gabr@google.com

Nicolas Usunier
Facebook
usunier@fb.com

ABSTRACT

Recent years have witnessed a proliferation of large-scale knowledge graphs, from purely academic projects such as YAGO to major commercial projects such as Google's Knowledge Graph and Microsoft's Satori. Whereas there is a large body of research on mining homogeneous graphs, this new generation of information networks are highly heterogeneous, with thousands of entity and relation types and billions of instances of those types (graph vertices and edges). In this tutorial, we present the state of the art in constructing, mining, and growing knowledge graphs. The purpose of the tutorial is to equip newcomers to this exciting field with an understanding of the basic concepts, tools and methodologies, open research challenges, as well as pointers to available datasets and relevant literature. Knowledge graphs have become an enabling resource for a plethora of new knowledge-rich applications. Consequently, the tutorial will also discuss the role of knowledge bases in empowering a range of web applications, from web search to social networks to digital assistants. A publicly available knowledge base (Freebase) will be used throughout the tutorial to exemplify the different techniques.

1. OVERVIEW

This half-day tutorial will be composed of two parts. We will first present the main concepts of knowledge bases, as well as the main available datasets. Using the open-domain knowledge base Freebase (now moved to Wikidata) as our running example, we will describe the principles underlying the construction and the applications of large knowledge bases. In particular, we will describe how to automatically grow knowledge bases by extracting facts and events from text, and the research challenges of entity resolution, relation extraction and link prediction. We will also discuss the practical impact of knowledge bases on major Web applications such as search, question answering or digital assistants.

The second part will focus on the state-of-the-art and the open research challenges in growing and mining knowledge bases. The automatic extraction of facts from text with thousands of possible relations and millions of entities must be carried on with little to no explicit supervision, while prediction or infering clusters in the knowledge graph, poses the challenge of dealing with heterogeneous data and a large number of relationships. In this part of the tutorial, we will present the state-of-the-art in algorithms for link prediction and clustering in knowledge bases and relational data, with an emphasis on mdethods based on probabilistic models and representation learning. We will also discuss weakly learning algorithms for relation extraction from text.

SIGIR '16, July 17 - 21, 2016, Pisa, Italy

ISBN 978-1-4503-4069-4/16/07...$15.00

DOI: http://dx.doi.org/10.1145/2911451.2914807

2. OBJECTIVES

We believe the tutorial will appeal to two groups of SIGIR participants. The first group includes industry attendees working in related areas who want to acquire more scientific background and be apprised of the recent research results in the field. The second group includes established researchers as well as PhD students who are interested to work in this exciting area and who will benefit from the introduction to the main concepts, overview of main research challenges, and pointers to existing resources and datasets.

3. RELEVANCE TO THE IR COMMUNITY

Over the recent years, multiple large-scale knowledge bases have come to existence, from purely academic projects such as YAGO to major commercial projects such as Google's Knowledge Graph, and Microsoft's Satori. These knowledge bases are an enabling resource for a plethora of new knowledge-rich applications. The tutorial is designed to provide an overview of such applications and use-cases, as well as equip newcomers to this area with a solid understanding of the basic techniques, research challenges, and pointers to relevant literature. This tutorial will discuss the role of knowledge bases in empowering a range of web applications, from web search to social networks to digital assistants.

4. FORMAT AND DETAILED SCHEDULE

1. Overview
   - (a) Introduction
   - (b) A sampler of research problems (to be covered in detail later in the tutorial)
   - (c) Define the scope, outline the differences from prior works on mining homogeneous graphs
   - (d) Connections to related fields (e.g., data fusion)

2. Freebase as an example of a large-scale knowledge repository
    (a) Data types, schemas, triples
    (b) Data format and data availability
3. Constructing and growing knowledge graphs
    (a) Knowledge acquisition from text
        i. Entity recognition and disambiguation
        ii. Mining rules and regularities from the data
    (b) Link prediction (i.e., endogenous completion of missing knowledge)
4. Applications of knowledge graphs
    (a) Augmented search
        i. Proactively augmenting Web search results with structured knowledge
        ii. Query expansion
    (b) New knowledge-enabled applications
        i. Open-domain question answering
        ii. Towards a digital assistant: Siri, Cortana, Google Now, etc.
5. Methods and techniques
    (a) Using observable variables
        i. Random walk / path-based approaches
        ii. Probabilistic relational models / Markov logic networks
    (b) Using latent variables
        i. Matrix/tensor factorization
        ii. Block models and extensions
        iii. Energy and embedding-based models
6. Research challenges
    (a) Scaling the methods
    (b) Mining new entities
    (c) Knowledge representation
    (d) Knowledge acquisition from multiple modalities
    (e) Reasoning with commonsense knowledge
7. Resources
    (a) Pointers to additional relevant datasets
    (b) Pointers to relevant competitions and evaluations

5. TYPE OF SUPPORT MATERIALS TO BE SUPPLIED TO ATTENDEES

Tutorial slides will be provided online ahead of time. The slides from a previous edition of the tutorial at KDD'14 can be found online at http://www.cs.technion.ac.il/~gabr/publications/papers/KDD14-T2-Bordes-Gabrilovich.pdf

6. BRIEF BIOGRAPHIES

6.1 Evgeniy Gabrilovich

Evgeniy Gabrilovich is a senior staff research scientist at Google, where he works on improving healthcare. Prior to joining Google in 2012, he was a director of research and head of the natural language processing and information retrieval group at Yahoo! Research. Evgeniy is an ACM Distinguished Scientist, and is a recipient of the 2014 IJCAI-JAIR Best Paper Prize. He is also a recipient of the 2010 Karen Sparck Jones Award for his contributions to natural language processing and information retrieval. Evgeniy serves as a program co-chair for WWW 2017, and has served as a program co-chair for WSDM 2015. He also served as an area chair or senior program committee member at numerous major conferences, including SIGIR, WWW, WSDM, KDD, AAAI, IJCAI, ACL, EMNLP, CIKM, ICDM, and ICWSM. Evgeniy earned his PhD in computer science from the Technion — Israel Institute of Technology.

6.2 Nicolas Usunier

Nicolas Usunier is research scientist at Facebook AI Research. Before joining Facebook in 2015, he was associate professor at Université de Technologie de Compiègne (UTC, France) with a Higher-education chair from the CNRS, the French National Research Center. Prior to his position at UTC, he was associate professor at Université Pierre et Marie Curie in Paris, from where he received his PhD in computer science in 2006.

His main areas of research are large scale learning of embeddings and learning to rank, in particular with applications to knowledge bases. He served as an area chair for NIPS 2014 and is a reviewer for the major conference in machine learning and journals such as NIPS, ICML, JMLR and the Machine Learning journal.

7. REFERENCES

[1] M. Banko, M. J. Cafarella, S. Soderland, M. Broadhead, and O. Etzioni. Open information extraction for the web. In *IJCAI*, volume 7, pages 2670–2676, 2007.

[2] A. Bordes, N. Usunier, A. Garcia-Duran, J. Weston, and O. Yakhnenko. Translating embeddings for modeling multi-relational data. In *Advances in Neural Information Processing Systems*, pages 2787–2795, 2013.

[3] A. Bordes, J. Weston, R. Collobert, and Y. Bengio. Learning structured embeddings of knowledge bases. In *Conference on Artificial Intelligence*, number EPFL-CONF-192344, 2011.

[4] X. Dong, E. Gabrilovich, G. Heitz, W. Horn, N. Lao, K. Murphy, T. Strohmann, S. Sun, and W. Zhang. Knowledge vault: A web-scale approach to probabilistic knowledge fusion. In *Proceedings of the 20th ACM SIGKDD international conference on Knowledge discovery and data mining*, pages 601–610. ACM, 2014.

[5] X. L. Dong, E. Gabrilovich, G. Heitz, W. Horn, K. Murphy, S. Sun, and W. Zhang. From data fusion to knowledge fusion. *Proceedings of the VLDB Endowment*, 7(10):881–892, 2014.

[6] A. Fader, S. Soderland, and O. Etzioni. Identifying relations for open information extraction. In

Proceedings of the Conference on Empirical Methods in Natural Language Processing, pages 1535–1545. Association for Computational Linguistics, 2011.

[7] P. G. Ipeirotis and E. Gabrilovich. Quizz: Targeted crowdsourcing with a billion (potential) users. In *Proceedings of the 23rd international conference on World Wide Web*, pages 143–154. ACM, 2014.

[8] C. Kemp, J. B. Tenenbaum, T. L. Griffiths, T. Yamada, and N. Ueda. Learning systems of concepts with an infinite relational model. In *AAAI*, volume 3, page 5, 2006.

[9] N. Lao, T. Mitchell, and W. W. Cohen. Random walk inference and learning in a large scale knowledge base. In *Proceedings of the Conference on Empirical Methods in Natural Language Processing*, pages 529–539. Association for Computational Linguistics, 2011.

[10] M. Mintz, S. Bills, R. Snow, and D. Jurafsky. Distant supervision for relation extraction without labeled data. In *Proceedings of the Joint Conference of the 47th Annual Meeting of the ACL and the 4th International Joint Conference on Natural Language Processing of the AFNLP: Volume 2*, pages 1003–1011. ACL, 2009.

[11] M. Nickel, V. Tresp, and H.-P. Kriegel. A three-way model for collective learning on multi-relational data. In *Proceedings of the 28th international conference on machine learning (ICML-11)*, pages 809–816, 2011.

[12] M. Richardson and P. Domingos. Markov logic networks. *Machine learning*, 62(1-2):107–136, 2006.

[13] S. Riedel, L. Yao, B. M. Marlin, and A. McCallum. Relation extraction with matrix factorization and universal schemas. In *Joint Human Language Technology Conference/Annual Meeting of the North American Chapter of the ACL (HLT-NAACL '13)*, ACL, 2013.

[14] S. Riedel, L. Yao, A. McCallum, and B. M. Marlin. Relation extraction with matrix factorization and universal schemas. In L. Vanderwende, H. D. III, and K. Kirchhoff, editors, *HLT-NAACL*, pages 74–84. ACL, 2013.

[15] M. Schmitz, R. Bart, S. Soderland, O. Etzioni, et al. Open language learning for information extraction. In *Proceedings of the 2012 Joint Conference on Empirical Methods in Natural Language Processing and Computational Natural Language Learning*, pages 523–534. ACL, 2012.

[16] M. Surdeanu, J. Tibshirani, R. Nallapati, and C. D. Manning. Multi-instance multi-label learning for relation extraction. In *Proceedings of the 2012 Joint Conference on Empirical Methods in Natural Language Processing and Computational Natural Language Learning*, pages 455–465. ACL, 2012.

[17] R. West, E. Gabrilovich, K. Murphy, S. Sun, R. Gupta, and D. Lin. Knowledge base completion via search-based question answering. In *Proceedings of the 23rd international conference on World Wide Web*, pages 515–526. ACM, 2014.

Counterfactual Evaluation and Learning for Search, Recommendation and Ad Placement

Thorsten Joachims
Cornell University
Department of Computer Science
Ithaca, NY, USA
tj@cs.cornell.edu

Adith Swaminathan
Cornell University
Department of Computer Science
Ithaca, NY, USA
adith@cs.cornell.edu

ABSTRACT

Online metrics measured through A/B tests have become the gold standard for many evaluation questions. But can we get the same results as A/B tests without actually fielding a new system? And can we train systems to optimize online metrics without subjecting users to an online learning algorithm? This tutorial summarizes and unifies the emerging body of methods on counterfactual evaluation and learning. These counterfactual techniques provide a well-founded way to evaluate and optimize online metrics by exploiting logs of past user interactions. In particular, the tutorial unifies the causal inference, information retrieval, and machine learning view of this problem, providing the basis for future research in this emerging area of great potential impact.
Supplementary material and resources are available online at http://www.cs.cornell.edu/~adith/CfactSIGIR2016.

CCS Concepts

•**Information systems** → **Information retrieval; Retrieval models and ranking; Evaluation of retrieval results;**

Keywords

Learning to Rank; Counterfactual Estimation; Causal Inference; Batch Learning from Bandit Feedback

Motivation

How many clicks will a new ad placement system get? Will a different news-ranking algorithm increase the dwell times of my users? What ranking function will minimize abandonment? These and similar questions are crucial to consider when building good search engines, recommendation systems, ad placement systems and most other systems that interact with users.

SIGIR '16, July 17 - 21, 2016, Pisa, Italy

ISBN 978-1-4503-4069-4/16/07...$15.00
DOI: http://dx.doi.org/10.1145/2911451.2914803

One approach to address these questions is to field the new system in an A/B test. Unfortunately, this process is slow, costly and puts tight limits on the number of systems that can be fielded. However, we typically have large amounts of log-data from previous versions of our systems. Can we use this old data to evaluate new systems?

Trying to answer operational questions about a new system B with log-data from an old system A is essentially a counterfactual problem: how would system B have performed on some user-centered metric, if it had been operational instead of system A? (e.g. how many clicks would the new ad placement system have gotten, if it had been deployed in the past?) While it may seem like the logs from system A will be insufficient for estimating the properties of system B, research over the past years [21, 3, 7, 13, 23] has shown the opposite: the logs of system A can provide unbiased counterfactual estimates for the performance of system B, even though B has never been fielded.

This opens up a wide area of research on new evaluation and learning techniques for information retrieval. Unlike deploying new systems in weeks-long A/B tests to get unbiased performance estimates [10], counterfactual estimators can provide unbiased estimates from existing logs without delay. Analogously, counterfactual learning techniques can use existing log files for learning improved systems, without any need for online learning methods that require interactive control. In this way, this new approach to evaluation and learning can revolutionize the process of developing and optimizing systems that interact with users.

Research on counterfactual estimation (also called estimation of treatment effects and off-policy evaluation) and counterfactual learning (also called policy optimization) has made rapid progress in recent years [8, 3, 7, 6, 2, 13, 22, 9, 11, 14, 15, 19, 24, 12, 18], and it is starting to have impact in commercial applications. The recent workshop at WWW2015 on Online and Offline Evaluation of Web-based Services [8] highlights keen interest in these techniques from academia and industry alike. However, this research has happened in many rather disjoint fields, including statistics [16], economics [1], reinforcement learning [20], contextual bandit learning [21], Monte Carlo estimation [17] and information retrieval [23, 5, 4]. It is an excellent time to aggregate and unify the existing works into one coherent tutorial that is broadly accessible to an information retrieval audience.

Objectives

This tutorial will provide an overview of the rapidly growing body of research on offline evaluation and learning using online metrics. A confluence of developments in machine learning, causal inference, economics, and information retrieval has recently pushed these methods to be well-founded and practical. This tutorial will provide a unifying view that will enable newcomers to enter the field, enabling broader research and further adoption of these methods in practice. The objectives of the tutorial are:

1. Provide a unified view of counterfactual estimation and learning techniques as they apply to Information Retrieval evaluation and learning.
2. Translate the disparate terminology from economics, causal inference, and machine learning into a framework accessible to Information Retrieval researchers.
3. Give an overview of counterfactual evaluation techniques and how they apply to IR problems.
4. Give an overview of counterfactual learning techniques and how they apply to IR problems.
5. Demonstrate strengths and limitations of counterfactual techniques via case studies on IR problems.
6. Provide publicly available benchmark datasets to enable IR research in this area.
7. Outline directions for future research.

Prerequisites

This tutorial is aimed at an audience with intermediate experience with information retrieval. It assumes the following prerequisites:

- Familiarity with standard IR methods, applications and evaluation metrics is assumed and only briefly reviewed.
- Basic understanding of probability theory and introductory statistics is sufficient for understanding most of the tutorial.
- Some topics require basic understanding of machine learning.

All code samples demonstrating counterfactual analysis for IR will be in Python3. Participants who wish to run these demos locally must bring a device capable of running Python3 scripts. Supplementary material for this tutorial is available online at http://www.cs.cornell.edu/~adith/CfactSIGIR2016.

Presenters

Thorsten Joachims is a Professor in the Department of Computer Science and in the Department of Information Science at Cornell University. His research interests center on a synthesis of theory and system building in machine learning, with applications in information retrieval and recommendation. His past research focused on support vector machines, learning to rank, learning with preferences, and learning from implicit feedback, text classification and structured output prediction. He is an ACM Fellow, AAAI Fellow and Humboldt Fellow.

Adith Swaminathan is a PhD candidate in the Department of Computer Science at Cornell University, advised by Prof. Thorsten Joachims. His research interests are at the core of this tutorial, focusing on principles and algorithms for off-policy evaluation and learning for retrieval and recommendation systems. He received a BTech degree in Computer Science and Engineering from IIT Bombay in 2010 and MSc in Computer Science from Cornell University in 2014.

Acknowledgements

We acknowledge and thank for the support under NSF Awards IIS-1247637, IIS-1217686, and IIS-1513692, as well as a gift from Bloomberg.

1. REFERENCES

[1] S. Athey and G. Imbens. Recursive Partitioning for Heterogeneous Causal Effects. *ArXiv e-prints*, 2015.

[2] A. Beygelzimer and J. Langford. The offset tree for learning with partial labels. In *KDD*, pages 129–138, 2009.

[3] L. Bottou, J. Peters, J. Q. Candela, D. X. Charles, M. Chickering, E. Portugaly, D. Ray, P. Y. Simard, and E. Snelson. Counterfactual reasoning and learning systems: The example of computational advertising. *Journal of Machine Learning Research*, 14(1):3207–3260, 2013.

[4] B. Carterette, E. Kanoulas, V. Pavlu, and H. Fang. Reusable test collections through experimental design. In *SIGIR*, pages 547–554, 2010.

[5] B. Carterette, E. Kanoulas, and E. Yilmaz. Advances on the development of evaluation measures. In *SIGIR*, pages 1200–1201, 2012.

[6] M. Dudík, D. Erhan, J. Langford, and L. Li. Doubly robust policy evaluation and optimization. *Statistical Science*, pages 485–511, 2014.

[7] M. Dudík, J. Langford, and L. Li. Doubly robust policy evaluation and learning. In *ICML*, pages 1097–1104, 2011.

[8] N. Gupta, E. Koh, and L. Li. Workshop on online and offline evaluation of web-based services. In *WWW Companion*, 2015.

[9] K. Hofmann, A. Schuth, S. Whiteson, and M. de Rijke. Reusing historical interaction data for faster online learning to rank for IR. In *WSDM*, pages 183–192, 2013.

[10] R. Kohavi, R. Longbotham, D. Sommerfield, and R. M. Henne. Controlled experiments on the web: survey and practical guide. *Data Mining and Knowledge Discovery*, pages 140–181, 2009.

[11] J. Langford, A. Strehl, and J. Wortman. Exploration scavenging. In *ICML*, pages 528–535, 2008.

[12] L. Li, S. Chen, J. Kleban, and A. Gupta. Counterfactual estimation and optimization of click metrics in search engines: A case study. In *WWW Companion*, pages 929–934, 2015.

[13] L. Li, W. Chu, J. Langford, and X. Wang. Unbiased offline evaluation of contextual-bandit-based news article recommendation algorithms. In *WSDM*, pages 297–306, 2011.

[14] L. Li, R. Munos, and C. Szepesvari. Toward minimax off-policy value estimation. In *AISTATS*, 2015.

[15] J. Mary, P. Preux, and O. Nicol. Improving offline evaluation of contextual bandit algorithms via bootstrapping techniques. In *ICML*, pages 172–180, 2014.
[16] P. Rosenbaum and D. Rubin. The central role of the propensity score in observational studies for causal effects. *Biometrika*, 70(1):41–55, 1983.
[17] R. Rubinstein and D. Kroese. *Simulation and the Monte Carlo Method*. Wiley, 2008.
[18] T. Schnabel, A. Swaminathan, A. Singh, N. Chandak, and T. Joachims. Recommendations as treatments: Debiasing learning and evaluation. *ArXiv e-prints*, 2016.
[19] A. L. Strehl, J. Langford, L. Li, and S. Kakade. Learning from logged implicit exploration data. In *NIPS*, pages 2217–2225, 2010.
[20] R. S. Sutton and A. G. Barto. *Reinforcement Learning: An Introduction*. The MIT Press, 1998.
[21] A. Swaminathan and T. Joachims. Counterfactual risk minimization: Learning from logged bandit feedback. In *ICML*, pages 814–823, 2015.
[22] A. Swaminathan and T. Joachims. The self-normalized estimator for counterfactual learning. In *NIPS*, pages 3213–3221, 2015.
[23] E. Yilmaz, E. Kanoulas, and J. A. Aslam. A simple and efficient sampling method for estimating AP and NDCG. In *SIGIR*, pages 603–610, 2008.
[24] B. Zadrozny, J. Langford, and N. Abe. Cost-sensitive learning by cost-proportionate example weighting. In *ICDM*, pages 435–, 2003.

Deep Learning for Information Retrieval

Hang Li
Noah's Ark Lab, Huawei Technologies
Hong Kong Science Park
Shatin, Hong Kong
hangli.hl@huawei.com

Zhengdong Lu
Noah's Ark Lab, Huawei Technologies
Hong Kong Science Park
Shatin, Hong Kong
zhengdong.lu@huawei.com

ABSTRACT

Recent years have observed a significant progress in information retrieval and natural language processing with deep learning technologies being successfully applied into almost all of their major tasks. The key to the success of deep learning is its capability of accurately learning distributed representations (vector representations or structured arrangement of them) of natural language expressions such as sentences, and effectively utilizing the representations in the tasks. This tutorial aims at summarizing and introducing the results of recent research on deep learning for information retrieval, in order to stimulate and foster more significant research and development work on the topic in the future.

The tutorial mainly consists of three parts. In the first part, we introduce the fundamental techniques of deep learning for natural language processing and information retrieval, such as word embedding, recurrent neural networks, and convolutional neural networks. In the second part, we explain how deep learning, particularly representation learning techniques, can be utilized in fundamental NLP and IR problems, including matching, translation, classification, and structured prediction. In the third part, we describe how deep learning can be used in specific application tasks in details. The tasks are search, question answering (from either documents, database, or knowledge base), and image retrieval.

Keywords

Deep Learning, Information Retrieval, Search, Question Answering, Image Retrieval

1. INTRODUCTION

"Information retrieval (IR) is the activity of obtaining information resources relevant to an information need from a collection of information resources" -Wikipedia. Figure 1 gives an overview of the major tasks in IR, including search, question answering (from either documents, database, or knowledge base), and image retrieval. The user expresses her information need (intent) in keywords or a question and submits it to the information retrieval system; the system accesses the information and/or knowledge base (content), finds relevant result, and returns to the user. The key questions are how to represent the intent & content and how to conduct matching between the intent & content.

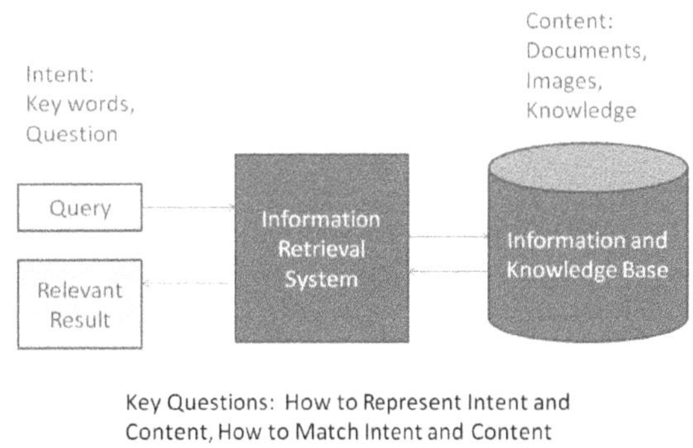

Figure 1: An overview of information retrieval.

The easiest task in IR would be document retrieval. In the traditional IR approach, the intent is represented as key words in a query, and the content consists of documents and each document is represented as a bag of words. Cosine similarity is calculated between the tf-idf vectors of the query and each document, and is viewed as the matching (relevance) score between them.

The traditional approach works well to some extent, but it also suffers from the term mismatch drawback. In fact, semantic matching between query and document is necessary in order to help the user to effectively find relevant information [21]. Deep learning techniques have been successfully employed to conduct semantic matching in web search, and significant improvement in relevance have been observed (e.g., [11, 31, 29]).

There are harder tasks in IR, such as question answering from documents, question answering from relational database, question answering from knowledge base, and image retrieval. The challenge is that the representations in the tasks are in different forms, for example, unstructured data, structured data, multimedia data, or mix of them, and it is very diffi-

SIGIR '16, July 17-21, 2016, Pisa, Italy
© 2016 ACM. ISBN 978-1-4503-4069-4/16/07...$15.00
DOI: http://dx.doi.org/10.1145/2911451.2914800

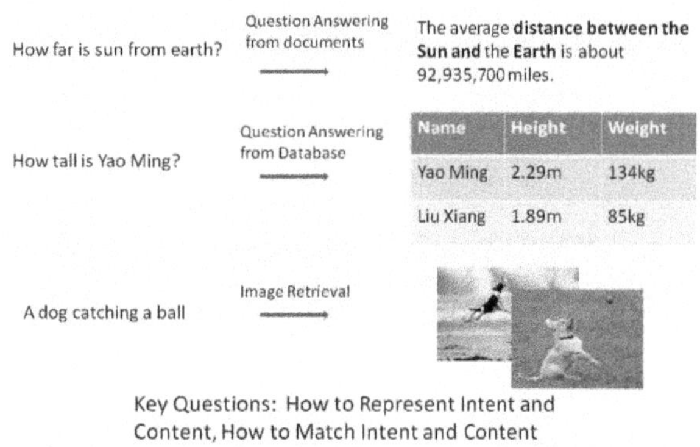

Figure 2: Hard problems in information retrieval and natural language processing.

cult or even impossible to perform direct matching between the intent and content in the tasks. Although some methods had been proposed for question answering, image retrieval, etc, they tended to be ad-hoc, and their performances were not satisfactory. Recently, significant progresses have been made in solving the hard problems in IR, with deep learning as the major machinery.

Deep learning is powerful, because it can help automatically learn representations of different data in different tasks [18]. The learned representations are all in the same form, namely real valued vectors, also referred to as distributed representations. In this way, the matching in IR can be conducted through the vector representations, and therefore the performance of some IR tasks can be significantly enhanced and the other tasks which were previously considered impossible can be successfully carried out.

For example, it is found possible to directly learn representations from images and their associated texts, exploit the representations in matching between questions and images, and achieve high accuracy in image retrieval (e.g., [15, 14, 17, 24, 36, 23]). Deep learning can also be employed to carry out question answering from database or knowledge base. Recent work shows that given only question answer pairs, a relational database or knowledge base, as well as the 'grounding' relations between the answers and the database or knowledge base, one can learn a deep neural network to automatically conduct question answering from the database or knowledge base. No human effort is needed in construction of a semantic parser for analyzing the questions and the performance can be even higher (e.g., [4, 28, 38, 41, 1, 43, 42]). It is also found that deep learning can improve traditional question answering from documents, which can be formalized as a problem of matching between two sentences (question and answer) each having a complicated syntactic and semantic structure. The advantage of the approach is that usually one does not need to use linguistic knowledge to build the system (e.g., [32, 22, 10, 37]). Another new and interesting finding is that with deep learning and a large amount of question answer pair data one can build a system which automatically *generates* an answer given a question in question answering, or in general in single turn dialogue (e.g.,[30, 35]). This was considered as a very hard problem.

Indeed, deep learning has opened many new opportunities to IR. There are a large number of new problems which one can try, and a large number of existing problems on which we can make improvement with deep learning. Certainly, there are also many challenges. The biggest question is how to combine neural computing (or deep learning) with traditional symbolic processing, both appears necessary for IR.

The objectives of the tutorial are as the following. First, to help the students and researchers who want to make further investigations on deep learning for IR to enhance the state of the art of the field; second, to help the practitioners who want to apply the existing deep learning for IR technologies into real world problems.

The tutorial is set at an intermediate level. It is assumed that the attendees have certain knowledge on machine learning and information retrieval. It is not a requirement, however, that the attendees know much about deep learning.

Several wonderful tutorials were given at related conferences, for example, Richard Socher, Chris Manning, Yoshua Bengio, Deep Learning for NLP, at ACL 2012 and NAACL 2013; Kevin Duh, Deep Learning for Natural Language Processing and Machine Translation, at CWMT 2014; Xiaodong He, Jianfeng Gao, and Li Deng, Deep Learning for Natural Language Processing: Theory and Practice, at CIKM 2014; Wen-tau Yih, Xiaodong He, and Jianfeng Gao, Deep Learning and Continuous Representations for NLP, at NAACL-HLT 2015. This tutorial is significantly different from the previous tutorials in the sense that it is organized from the viewpoint of IR.

2. OUTLINE OF TUTORIAL

The outline of the tutorial is as follows.

1. Basics of Deep Learning (50 minutes)
    - Word Embedding
    - Recurrent Neural Network
    - Convolutional Neural Network
    - Training of Models
2. Fundamental Problems in Deep Learning for IR and NLP (50 minutes)
    - Learning of Distributed Representation
    - Matching
    - Translation
    - Classification
    - Structured Prediction
3. Applications of Deep Learning to IR (50 minutes)
    - Search
    - Question Answering (from Documents)
        - Retrieval-based Question Answering
        - Generation-based Question Answering
    - Question Answering from Relational Database
    - Question Answering from Knowledge Base
    - Image Retrieval
4. Future Directions of Deep Learning for IR (10 minutes)

3. CONTENT OF TUTORIAL

The tutorial consists of four parts. We introduce the content of each part.

3.1 Basics of Deep Learning

We start with introducing the basic tools in deep learning for information retrieval and natural language processing, including word embedding [25, 27, 19, 20], recurrent neural network (RNN) [26, 9, 6], convolutional neural network (CNN) [7, 10, 13, 31], as well as training of deep neural network models.

3.2 Fundamental Problems in Deep Learning for IR and NLP

We formalize many tasks in IR and NLP into a number of fundamental problems including matching, translation, classification, and structured prediction, described below.

- Matching: matching two strings
  $s, t \rightarrow R^+$
- Translation: transforming one string to another
  $s \rightarrow t$
- Classification: assigning a label to a string
  $s \rightarrow c$
- Structured Prediction: mapping a string to its structure
  $s \rightarrow s'$

We first point out when we apply deep learning to the problems, we in fact learn representations of natural language in the problems. The learned representations can be used in realizing the tasks, with often enhanced performance. We explain methods that can be used for learning the representations in matching [22, 10, 37], translation [33, 6, 2, 8], classification [13, 16, 44], and structured prediction [7, 34, 5].

3.3 Applications of Deep Learning to IR and NLP

We introduce the recent work on applications of deep learning to IR tasks. First, we describe deep learning models which have been successfully applied to search to enhance relevance [11, 31, 29], as extensions of conventional linear models [3, 40, 39].

We also talk about deep learning for question answering including the retrieval-based setting in which answers are retrieved and returned from a large repository of question answer pairs [32, 22, 10, 12, 37], as well as the generation-based setting in which answers are automatically generated from a system which is trained with a large number of question answer pairs [30, 35].

We explain the work about question answering from database or knowledge base using deep learning in which only question answer pairs and the database or knowledge base are used in construction of the system [4, 28, 38, 41, 1, 43, 42]

We introduce the recent progress in image retrieval using deep learning in which only images and their associated texts (questions) are used as training data [15, 14, 17, 36, 24, 23].

3.4 Future Directions of Deep Learning for IR

We conclude the tutorial by summarizing the major challenges and opportunities in deep learning for information retrieval.

4. ACKNOWLEDGEMENT

The work is partially supported by China National 973 project 2014CB340301. The authors are grateful to Xin Jiang, Xi Zhang, Jun Xu, Shengxian Wan, and Liang Peng for providing related materials for this tutorial.

5. REFERENCES

[1] J. Andreas, M. Rohrbach, T. Darrell, and D. Klein. Learning to compose neural networks for question answering. *arXiv:1601.01705*, 2016.

[2] D. Bahdanau, K. Cho, and Y. Bengio. Neural machine translation by jointly learning to align and translate. In *Proceedings of ICLR'15*, 2015.

[3] B. Bai, J. Weston, D. Grangier, R. Collobert, K. Sadamasa, Y. Qi, O. Chapelle, and K. Weinberger. Supervised semantic indexing. In *Proceedings of CIKM'09*, 2009.

[4] A. Bordes, N. Usunier, S. Chopra, and J. Weston. Large-scale simple question answering with memory networks. *arXiv:1506.02075*, 2015.

[5] D. Chen and C. D. Manning. A fast and accurate dependency parser using neural networks. In *Proceedings of EMNLP'14*, 2014.

[6] K. Cho, B. van Merrienboer, C. Gulcehre, F. Bougares, H. Schwenk, and Y. Bengio. Learning phrase representations using rnn encoder-decoder for statistical machine translation. In *Proceedings of EMNLP'14*, 2014.

[7] R. Collobert, J. Weston, L. Bottou, M. Karlen, K. Kavukcuoglu, and P. Kuksa. Natural language processing (almost) from scratch. *Journal of Machine Learning Research*, 12:2493–2537, 2011.

[8] J. Gu, Z. Lu, H. Li, and V. O. K. Li. Incorporating copying mechanism in sequence-to-sequence learning. *arXiv:1603.06393*, 2016.

[9] S. Hochreiter and J. Schmidhuber. Long short-term memory. *Neural computation*, 9(8):1735–1780, 1997.

[10] B. Hu, Z. Lu, H. Li, and Q. Chen. Convolutional neural network architectures for matching natural language sentences. In *Proccedings of NIPS'14*, 2014.

[11] P.-S. Huang, X. He, and J. Gao. Learning deep structured semantic models for web search using clickthrough data. In *Proceedings of CIKM'13*, 2013.

[12] Z. Ji, Z. Lu, and H. Li. An information retrieval approach to short text conversation. *arXiv:1408.6988*, 2014.

[13] N. Kalchbrenner, E. Grefenstette, and P. Blunsom. A convolutional neural network for modelling sentences. In *Proceedings of ACL'14*, 2014.

[14] A. Karpathy, A. Joulin, and F. Li. Deep fragment embeddings for didirectional image sentence mapping. In *Proceedings of NIPS'14*, 2014.

[15] A. Karpathy and F. Li. Deep visual-semantic alignments for generating image descriptions. In *Proceedings of CVPR'15*, 2015.

[16] Y. Kim. Convolutional neural networks for sentence classification. In *Proceedings of EMNLP'14*, 2014.

[17] R. Kiros, R. Salakhutdinov, and R. S. Zemel. Unifying visual-semantic embeddings with multimodal neural language models. *arXiv:1411.2539*, 2014.

[18] Y. LeCun, Y. Bengio, and G. Hinton. Deep learning. *Nature*, 521(7553):436–444, 2015.

[19] O. Levy and Y. Goldberg. Neural word embedding as implicit matrix factorization. In *Proceedings of NIPS'14*, 2014.

[20] O. Levy, Y. Goldberg, and I. Dagan. Improving distributional similarity with lessons learned from word embeddings. *Transactions of Association for Computational Linguistics*, 3:211–225, 2015.

[21] H. Li and J. Xu. Semantic matching in search. *Foundations and Trends's in Information Retrieval*, 7(5):343–469, 2014.

[22] Z. Lu and H. Li. A deep architecture for matching short texts. In *Proceedings of NIPS'13*, 2013.

[23] L. Ma, Z. Lu, L. Shang, and H. Li. Multimodal convolutional neural networks for matching image and sentence. In *Proceedings of ICCV'15*, 2015.

[24] J. Mao, W. Xu, Y. Yang, J. Wang, and A. L. Yuille. Deep captioning with multimodal recurrent neural networks (m-rnn). *arXiv:1412.6632*, 2014.

[25] T. Mikolov, K. Chen, G. Corrado, and J. Dean. Efficient estimation of word representations in vector space. *arXiv:1301.3781*, 2013.

[26] T. Mikolov, M. Karafiát, L. Burget, J. Cernockỳ, and S. Khudanpur. Recurrent neural network based language model. In *Proceedings of InterSpeech'10*, 2010.

[27] T. Mikolov, I. Sutskever, K. Chen, G. Corrado, and J. Dean. Distributed representations of words and phrases and their compositionality. In *Proceedings of NIPS'13*, 2013.

[28] A. Neelakantan, Q. V. Le, and I. Sutskever. Neural programmer: Inducing latent programs with gradient descent. *arXiv:1511.04834*, 2015.

[29] A. Severyn and A. Moschitti. Learning to rank short text pairs with convolutional deep neural networks. In *Proceedings of SIGIR'15*, 2015.

[30] L. Shang, Z. Lu, and H. Li. Neural responding machine for short-text conversation. In *Proceedings of ACL'15*, 2015.

[31] Y. Shen, X. He, J. Gao, L. Deng, and G. Mesnil. A latent semantic model with convolutional-pooling structure for information retrieval. In *Proceedings of CIKM'14*, 2014.

[32] R. Socher, E. H. Huang, and A. Y. Ng. Dynamic pooling and unfolding recursive autoencoders for paraphrase detection. In *Proceedings of NIPS'11*, 2011.

[33] I. Sutskever, O. Vinyals, and Q. V. Le. Sequence to sequence learning with neural networks. In *Proceedings of NIPS'14*, 2014.

[34] O. Vinyals, L. Kaiser, T. Koo, S. Petrov, I. Sutskever, and G. Hinton. Grammar as a foreign language. *arXiv:1412.7449*, 2014.

[35] O. Vinyals and Q. V. Le. A neural conversational model. *arXiv:1506.05869*, 2015.

[36] O. Vinyals, A. Toshev, S. Bengio, and D. Erhan. Show and tell: a neural image caption generator. *arXiv:1411.4555*, 2014.

[37] M. Wang, Z. Lu, H. Li, and Q. Liu. Syntax-based deep matching of short texts. In *Proceedings of IJCAI'15*, 2015.

[38] J. Weston, S. Chopra, and A. Bordes. Memory networks. In *Proceedings of ICLR'15*, 2015.

[39] W. Wu, H. Li, and J. Xu. Learning query and document similarities from click-through bipartite graph with metadata. In *Proceedings of WSDM'13*, 2013.

[40] W. Wu, Z. Lu, and H. Li. Learning bilinear model for matching queries and documents. *The Journal of Machine Learning Research*, 14(1):2519–2548, 2013.

[41] W. Yih, M. Chang, X. He, and J. Gao. Semantic parsing via staged query graph generation: Question answering with knowledge base. In *Proceedings of ACL'15*, 2015.

[42] J. Yin, X. Jiang, L. Shang, Z. Lu, H. Li, and X. Li. Neural generative question answering. In *Proceedings of IJCAI'16*, 2016.

[43] P. Yin, Z. Lu, H. Li, and B. Kao. Neural enquirer: Learning to query tables. In *Proceedings of IJCAI'16*, 2016.

[44] H. Zhao, Z. Lu, and P. Poupart. Self-adaptive hierarchical sentence model. In *Proceedings of IJCAI'15*, 2015.

From Design to Analysis: Conducting Controlled Laboratory Experiments with Users

Diane Kelly and Anita Crescenzi
School of Information and Library Science
University of North Carolina at Chapel Hill
Chapel Hill, NC, USA
[dianek I amcc]@email.unc.edu

ABSTRACT

This full-day tutorial provides general instruction about the design of controlled laboratory experiments that are conducted in order to better understand human information interaction and retrieval. Different data collection methods and procedures are described, with an emphasis on self-report measures and scales. This tutorial also introduces the use of statistical power analysis for sample size estimation and introduces and demonstrate two data analysis procedures, Multilevel Modeling and Structural Equation Modeling, that allow for examination of the whole set of variables present in interactive information retrieval (IIR) experiments, along with their various effect sizes. The goals of the tutorial are (1) to increase participants' understanding of the uses of controlled laboratory experiments with human participants; (2) to increase participants' understanding of the technical vocabulary and procedures associated with such experiments and (2) to increase participants' confidence in conducting and evaluating IIR experiments. Ultimately, we hope our tutorial will increase research capacity and research quality in IR by providing instruction about best practices to those contemplating interactive IR experiments.

1. BACKGROUND AND MOTIVATION

The controlled laboratory experiment is one of the most important methods used in interactive information retrieval (IIR) to study users. Controlled laboratory experiments are useful in a number of different situations. They help us to: (1) examine search behavior (e.g., How does task complexity impact search behavior?) and the relevance judgment process (e.g., How does document order impact relevance assessments?); (2) evaluate system and interface designs (e.g., Is my new interface any good? Is my query expansion technique any good?); and (3) test and develop theory (e.g., To what extent does Information Foraging Theory explain people's stopping behaviors in search?).

The controlled laboratory experiment is especially important for examining causal relationships and evaluating theory. Shadish, Cook and Campbell elucidate criteria for establishing causal relationships in experiments: an experimenter must observe the outcome after a manipulation of the (intended) cause, observe covariation between cause and effect, and reduce the plausible alternative explanations for the variation through experimental design and analysis [18]. Experiments also allow for interaction with participants so that specialized data collection instruments can be used, contextual aspects can be measured, and additional feedback can be gathered. Finally, controlled laboratory experiments give researchers the ability to determine *a priori* which constructs they want to study and how they will measure these constructs. The emphasis is not only on predicting behavior, but also explaining it.

The inclusion of humans introduces many potential threats to the internal validity of experiments; fortunately, many of these threats can be addressed through experimental design techniques that have been pioneered by researchers from the behavioral sciences. IR researchers often lack formal training in the behavioral sciences and have a difficult time understanding and incorporating this perspective into their IIR experiments. Educating researchers and students how to conduct IIR experiments from a behavioral science perspective is critical if we want more valid and reliable evaluations of interactive IR systems and more basic knowledge about how people interact with IR systems. In this tutorial, we will emphasize the behavioral science aspects of experimental design. We elaborate our motivations below.

User Experience Measures and Scales

One of the most crucial types of data in IIR experiments are user experience measures. These measures are typically gathered through self-report questionnaires and scales. These types of measures can be used as dependent variables (e.g., engagement, usability), as well as independent and moderating variables (e.g., pre-task difficulty, past knowledge, level of search experience). These types of data are central to studies of IIR as users are the only ones who can tell us about their attitudes, feelings and experiences. Self-report measures offer a critical perspective to understanding IIR, and when properly constructed, can provide both a valid and reliable signal.

Researchers often group all self-report measures together and dismiss them because they are subjective and somehow biased, or create questions and response sets that introduce measurement error. However, it is important to distinguish between previously validated measures, which have undergone extensive psychometric testing, and sets of ad-hoc questions researchers ask that have not been tested. In general, there is a lack of understanding of psychometric theory in our field and of techniques for good question/item design, many of which have been developed to reduce measurement error [6, 7, 20, 21]. Introducing some of these practices to our field can potentially increase the quality and reusability of this important class of measures.

Sample Sizes for Experiments

Another motivation for this tutorial is a general lack of understanding in our community about how to determine an appropriate sample size [12]. At present, there are no published guidelines about how sample sizes are determined in IIR studies.

SIGIR'16, July 17-July 21, 2016, Pisa, Italy.

ACM 978-1-4503-4069-4/16/07...$15.00.
DOI: http://dx.doi.org/10.1145/2911451.2914809

Instead, researchers often assume more is better and evaluate the goodness of sample sizes using criteria that were not developed in the context of controlled laboratory studies. It can be challenging to infer acceptable sample sizes by scanning the literature because reported sample sizes vary and researchers rarely justify their numbers. Furthermore, researchers often confuse sample sizes needed to generalize results with sample sizes needed to show causal relationships. These are two different issues.

Identifying an appropriate sample size is important for a number of reasons, not the least of which is to avoid making inappropriate conclusions about one's research ideas. It is common for researchers to claim a study without significant findings was "underpowered," meaning there were not enough participants to detect significance. Specifically, underpowered studies are associated with larger risks for Type II errors. Thus, an underpowered study primary affects the researcher and the state of research in a field since it potentially inhibits discovery. Identifying a sample size that gives the researcher the greatest potential for finding differences if they are present without overspending is an important issue.

Data Analysis Techniques

A final motivation for this tutorial is that in the past, researchers have faced challenges analyzing aspects of the experimental design in a single model, including (1) experimental variables, (2) potentially ancillary variables like task number and task order, (3) demographics variables, (4) process variables like search behaviors and (5) outcome variables like user experience measures and performance measures. Kelly and Sugimoto [14] reviewed forty years of IIR experiments and found the most common statistical tools used to analyze data were t-tests and ANOVAs, with little use of modeling techniques that allow for the investigation of larger numbers of variables in a single analysis. The convergence on these types of statistical methods was likely a function of the standard IIR experimental design that emerged from the 1970s. Both Kelly and Sugimoto [14] and Toms and O'Brien [19] call for the use of more sophisticated statistical modeling techniques to better understand IIR.

In our recent work, we demonstrated the usefulness of multilevel modeling (MLM) as a technique for analyzing data from IIR experiments [5]. MLM is similar to many other modeling techniques, such as regression, where there exists several predictor variables and one outcome (or dependent) variable [17]. MLM allows for analysis of data to multiple levels. In an IIR context, repeated-measures (e.g., task) would be modeled at Level 1 and the group variable (e.g., individual) would be modeled at Level 2. A multilevel model provides multiple advantages over a repeated-measures ANOVA: (a) the ability to explicitly model the effect of variables at the task-level (e.g., task sequence or topic) as well as variables at the individual-level (e.g., demographics), (b) coefficient estimates indicate the magnitude, direction and significance of effects of each variable while partialing out the effects of other covariates in the model, and (c) effect size estimates of variance attributable to different variables. A final advantage of MLM is it allows for easier analysis of between- and within-subject variables. While one can run mixed factor ANOVAs, anyone with experience setting-up these types of analyses appreciates the challenges in doing so, many of which are specific to IIR studies – for example, there are many things that almost always vary (e.g., task) even if researchers are not interested in including such variance in their experiments.

2. AUDIENCE AND OBJECTIVES

The audience for this tutorial includes students and researchers who are interested in conducting laboratory experiments with human participants. We will assume participants have had little formal experience learning about experimental design in the context of laboratory user studies, but have a basic understanding of some terminology such as variables and hypotheses. With respect to the data analysis section, we will assume participants have a basic understanding of descriptive and inferential statistics, and hypotheses testing.

- Provide general instruction about the *design* of controlled laboratory IIR experiments with human participants.
- Increase participants' understanding of the *technical vocabulary* and *procedures* associated with IIR experiments.
- Describe different *data collection methods and procedures*, with an emphasis on self-report measures and scales.
- Introduce the use of *statistical power analysis* for sample size estimation in experiments with users.
- Introduce and demonstrate two *data analysis procedures*, *Multilevel Modeling* [17] and *Structural Equation Modeling* [2], that allow for examination of the whole set of variables present in IIR experiments, including their various *effect sizes*.
- Increase participants' *confidence* in understanding and conducting IIR experiments.

3. RELEVANCE

As described above, the laboratory experiment with users is one of the primary methods used to understand search behavior and evaluate systems and interfaces. It is also one of the best ways to test and develop theories and hypotheses. During the past few years, there has been a huge growth in the number of researchers who are interested in studying and understanding users. This can be seen in the increases in IIR-focused papers and workshops at SIGIR, as well as the creation of the new SIGIR-sponsored *Conference on Human Information Interaction and Retrieval (CHIIR)*. We believe our tutorial will increase research capacity and research quality in this area by providing instruction about best practices to those contemplating their own IIR experiments. We also believe the data analysis section of the tutorial will highlight new data analysis tools to those already familiar with IIR experiments.

4. TOPICS AND ORGANIZATION

The basic approach of this tutorial is to use the morning session to present issues relating to experimental design using published studies to illustrate experimental design decisions and their impact. In the afternoon, we will use a dataset from a published study [5], the design of which will be discussed in the morning session, to illustrate different approaches to experimental data analysis.

The tutorial will start by putting the IIR experiment in context. Specifically, we will discuss its history and legacy as one of the most essential methods for understanding IR interactions and evaluating systems [13]. We will then compare and contrast this approach with other common approaches, and identify and describe research scenarios for which the laboratory experiment is a good choice and those for which it is not [8]. Next, we will introduce some factors that make laboratory experiments with users challenging, including individual differences in relevance judgments, the iterative nature of searching, and search tasks [3, 13].

Various kinds of experimental designs, including within- and between- subjects designs and factorial designs will be presented [10, 13]. The relationship between experimental design and one's research questions and hypotheses will be discussed, with examples drawn from actual studies. Different types of hypothesis will also be briefly reviewed including null, alternative, directional and non-directional since they are connected to data analysis. The concepts of Type I and Type II errors will also be reviewed since they provide the foundation for some of the material we will present later, in particular, sample sizing and statistical power [1, 9, 16]. The importance of using experimental design to control for unwanted effects, random assignment to conditions and other techniques for maximizing internal validity will be emphasized.

In the next section of the tutorial, we will introduce various components of IIR experiments [13]. We will start by discussing search tasks, as these are a required part of a laboratory user study [3, 4, 15, 22]. We will discuss the advantages and disadvantages of using open or closed collections. We will also introduce a number of data collection techniques [11, 13]. Special attention will be given to self-report measures. Psychometric theory will be briefly described to help participants better distinguish between measures that have demonstrated validity and reliability, and measures that are comprised of ad-hoc sets of questions that may or may not be valid [6, 21]. Several relevant scales will be presented and participants will be provided with some guidelines for constructing their own items (since we are often in the situation where we need to create ad-hoc sets of questions!). We will cover methods for reliability assessment for data reduction purposes (i.e., collapsing multiple variables into a composite variable). This step is especially critical for data analysis so as not to increase the risk of Type I errors. It also simplifies analysis and presentation issues.

In the final part of the morning session, we will discuss one of the most important components of IIR experiments: research participants. We will introduce *statistical power analysis* for sample size estimation, which helps researchers consider sample size and the risks associated with Type I and Type II errors [1, 16]. In doing so, we will explain effect size and introduce one tool for performing power analysis, G*Power, which is freely available online [9]. We will also distinguish between sample size and representativeness, which people often conflate, and explain why it is not just a numbers game.

In the afternoon session, we walk through the process of analyzing an experimental study using the dataset from one of our own studies to provide a concrete example [5]. The study used a mixed experimental design with between- and within-subjects factors in which participants completed multiple search tasks.

In the first part of the afternoon, we will introduce the dataset and its variables, their operational definitions, how they were measured and their ranges. The dependent variables in the dataset are self-reported responses to post-task questionnaire and multiple questions were asked for each construct of interest. The independent variables include those experimentally manipulated as well as covariates that may also influence the dependent variable (demographics such as age and education level; task variables such as order and topic; pre-task questionnaire responses such as expected difficulty and topic interest; search interactions such as task time and number of queries).

Next, we will show, interpret and compare the results from a series of statistical tests selected to illustrate how to analyze repeated measurements (e.g., multiple tasks completed by each participant) with experimental variables and covariates at the task level (e.g., topic) and at the individual level (e.g., participant's prior search experience). The statistical tests will focus on multilevel regression models [17] as well as repeated-measures analysis of variance (ANOVA) and covariance (ANCOVA).

We will also examine multiple methods for analyzing a construct of interest measured by multiple questions: using multiple tests, one for each question; creating a composite variable; and statistical tests for analyzing a dependent variable with multiple measures. Statistical tests covered include repeated-measures multivariate analysis of variance (RM-MANOVA) and covariance (RM-MANCOVA) as well as a brief introduction to structural equation modeling focusing on confirmatory factor analysis and structural equations with latent variables [2]. We will finish with best practices for reporting experimental study results.

5. PRESENTER BIOGRAPHIES

Diane Kelly is a Professor at the School of Information and Library Science at the University of North Carolina at Chapel Hill. Her research and teaching interests are in interactive information search and retrieval, information search behavior, and research methods. Kelly is the recipient of a *Francis Carroll McColl Term Professorship* at UNC, the 2014 *ASIST Research Award* and the 2013 *British Computer Society's IRSG Karen Spärck Jones Award.* She is the recipient of two teaching awards: the 2009 *ASIST/Thomson Reuters Outstanding Information Science Teacher Award* and the 2007 *SILS Outstanding Teacher of the Year Award.* She is the current *ACM SIGIR* treasurer and was co-chair of the inaugural *ACM SIGIR Conference on Human Information Interaction and Retrieval (CHIIR).* She is an associate editor for *Transactions on Information Systems,* and serves on the editorial boards of *Information Processing & Management*, *Information Retrieval Journal* and *Foundations and Trends in Information Retrieval.*

Anita Crescenzi is a PhD student at the School of Information and Library Science at the University of North Carolina at Chapel Hill. Her research interests are in interactive information retrieval, information behavior, decision-making and research methods. Crescenzi also has a special interest in statistical analysis methods including multilevel modeling and structural equation modeling. Crescenzi has over eight years of experience in applied user research, usability evaluation and user experience design in the health insurance and medical library domains. She has also taught pre-algebra and social studies to middle school students as well as conducted technical and software training classes for adults. She has reviewed papers for the *SIGIR* conference and *CHIIR, and* was a member of the 2016 *CHIIR* local organizing committee.

6. REFERENCES

[1] Bausell, R. B. & Li, Y. F. (2002). *Power analysis for experimental research: A practical guide for the biological, medical and social sciences.* New York: Cambridge Press.

[2] Bollen, K. (1989). *Structural equation modeling with latent variables.* New York: Wiley & Sons.

[3] Borlund, P. (2003). The IIR evaluation model: A framework for the evaluation of interactive information retrieval systems. *Information Research, 8*(3), paper 152.

[4] Byström, K. & Hansen, P. (2005). Conceptual framework for tasks in information studies. *JASIST, 56*(10), 1050–1061.

[5] Crescenzi, A., Kelly, D. & Azzopardi, L. (2016). Impacts of time constraints and system delays on user experience. To appear in *Proc. of CHIIR 2016,* 141-150.

[6] DeVillis, R. F. (2012). *Scale development: Theory and applications*. Thousand Oaks, CA: Sage Publications.

[7] Dillman, D. A., Smyth, J. D., & Christian, L. M. (2009). *Internet, Mail and Mixed-Mode Surveys (3rd Edition)*. John Wiley & Sons, Inc.: Hoboken, NJ.

[8] Dumais, S., Jeffries, R., Russell, D. M., Tang, D. & Teevan, J. (2014). Understanding user behavior through log data and analysis. In J.S. Olson & W. Kellogg (Eds.), *Human Computer Interaction Ways of Knowing*. NY: Springer.

[9] Faul, F., Erdfelder, E., Lang, A.-G., & Buchner, A. (2007). G*Power 3: A flexible statistical power analysis program for the social, behavioral, and biomedical sciences. *Behavior Research Methods, 39*, 175-191.

[10] Field, A. & Hole, G. (2003). *How to Design and Report Experiments*. Thousand Oaks, CA: Sage Publications.

[11] Hornbæk, K. (2013). Some whys and hows of experiments in human–computer interaction. *Foundations and Trends in Human-Computer Interaction, 5(4), 299-373.*

[12] Kelly, D. (2015). Statistical power analysis for sample size estimation in information retrieval experiments with users (tutorial). *Proceedings of ECIR 2015*, 822-825.

[13] Kelly, D. (2009). Methods for evaluating interactive information retrieval systems with users. *Foundations and Trends in Information Retrieval, 3(1-2).*

[14] Kelly, D. & Sugimoto, C. R. (2013). A systematic review of interactive information retrieval evaluation studies, 1967 - 2006. *JASIST, 64*(4), 745-770.

[15] Li, Y. & Belkin, N. J. (2008). A faceted approach to conceptualizing tasks in information seeking. *IP&M, 44*, 1822-1837.

[16] Murphy, K. R. (2009). *Statistical power analysis: A simple and general model for traditional and modern hypothesis tests (3rd edition).* New York: Routledge.

[17] Rabe-Hesketh, S. & Skrondal, A. (2012). *Multilevel and longitudinal modeling using Stata.* Stata Press, College Station, TX, 3rd edition.

[18] Shadish, W., Cook, T. & Campbell, D. (2002). *Experimental and Quasi-Experimental Designs for Generalized Causal Inference*. Wadsworth Cenage Learning.

[19] Toms, E. & O'Brien, H. (2009). The ISSS Measurement Dilemma. *IEEE Computer, 42*(3), 48.

[20] Tourangeau, R., Rips, L. J., & Rasinski, K. (2000). *The Psychology of Survey Response*. Cambridge University Press.

[21] Spector, P. E. (1992). *Summated rating scale construction: An introduction*. Thousand Oaks, CA: Sage Publications.

[22] Wildemuth, B. W., Freund, L. & Toms, E. G. (2014). Untangling search task complexity and difficulty in the context of interactive information retrieval studies. *Journal of Documentation, 70*(6), 1118-1140.

Instant Search - A Hands-on Tutorial

Ganesh Venkataraman, Abhimanyu Lad, Viet Ha-Thuc, Dhruv Arya
LinkedIn Corporation
Mountain View, CA, USA
{ghvenkat,alad,vhathuc,darya}@linkedin.com

MOTIVATION

Instant search has become a common part of the search experience in most popular search engines and social networking websites. The goal is to provide instant feedback to the user in terms of query completions ("instant suggestions") or directly provide search results ("instant results") as the user is typing their query. The need for instant search has been further amplified by the proliferation of mobile devices and services like *Siri* and *Google Now* that aim to address the user's information need as quickly as possible. Examples of instant results include web queries like *"weather san jose"* (which directly provides the current temperature), social network queries like searching for someone's name on Facebook or LinkedIn (which directly provide the people matching the query). In each of these cases, instant search constitutes a superior user experience, as opposed to making the user complete their query before the system returns a list of results on the traditional search engine results page (SERP).

We consider instant search experience to be a combination of instant results and instant suggestions, with the goal of satisfying the user's information need as quickly as possible with minimal effort on the part of the user. We first present the challenges involved in putting together an instant search solution at scale, followed by a survey of IR and NLP techniques that can be used to address them. We will also conduct a hands-on session aimed at putting together an end-to-end instant search system using open source tools and publicly available data sets. These tools include typeahead.js from Twitter for the frontend and Lucene/elasticsearch for the backend. We present techniques for prefix-based retrieval as well as injecting custom ranking functions into elasticsearch. For the search index, we will use the dataset made available by Stackoverflow [2].

This tutorial is aimed at both researchers interested in knowing about retrieval techniques used for instant search as well as practitioners interested in deploying an instant search system at scale. The authors have worked extensively on building and scaling LinkedIn's instant search experience. To the best of our knowledge, this is the first tutorial that covers both theoretical and practical aspects of instant search.

SIGIR '16, July 17 - 21, 2016, Pisa, Italy

ISBN 978-1-4503-4069-4/16/07...$15.00

DOI: http://dx.doi.org/10.1145/2911451.2914806

Keywords

Information Retrieval; Instant Search; Query Understanding

1. OBJECTIVES

Over the years search has become more focused on *getting results as you type.* Instant search has become a common part of the user experience in nearly all popular search engines, including web search engines (like Google), verticalized search engines (like Kayak) as well as social search engines (like Facebook, LinkedIn). The two broad categories of instant search include:

1. **Instant Results** (Figure 1). Here the actual result is provided while the query is being typed out.
2. **Instant Suggestions** (Figure 2). Here the user is guided to complete the query and the results will be presented after the suggestion is clicked.

For the rest of this proposal, **instant search** refers to both the above aspects unless otherwise stated. From an information need perspective, it is useful to think about queries as belonging to two categories:

1. **Navigational search**. Here the user has a single entity in mind and there exists a single document which would satisfy their information need. Classic example of navigational query in social networks is name search.
2. **Exploratory search**. Here multiple results can satisfy the information need. Example: "software engineer new york" could have several good results.

The general approach for navigational search is to provide the result right away – most often in a typeahead dropdown box. As illustrated in Figure 1, this means providing the current temperature for San Jose, or presenting the people search results for the query *"sh"*. For exploratory queries where the need can be met by multiple documents, the goal is not to provide results in the typeahead box, but instead guide the user in framing their query before they end up on the search engine results page (SERP).

For a great instant search experience, we will need the following aspects to work in tandem:

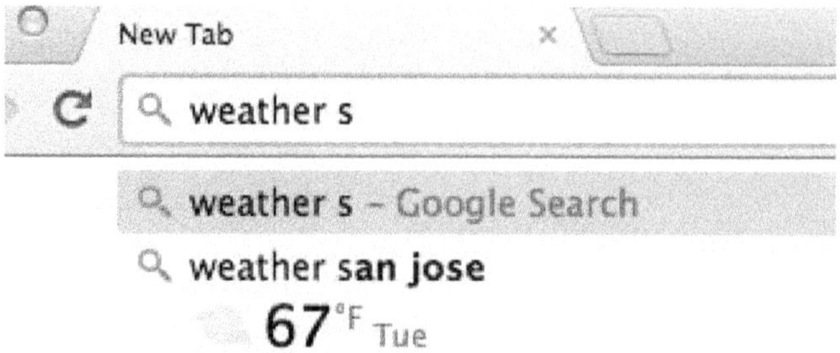

(a) Example from Google search

(b) Example from LinkedIn

Figure 1: Instant result experience

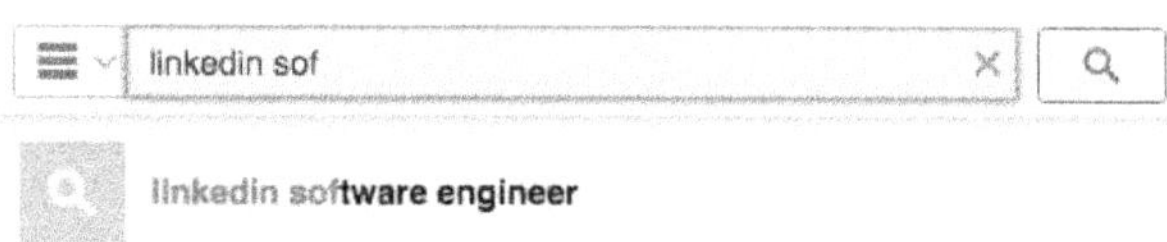

Figure 2: Instant suggestions

1. Frontend (client side) and decoration of search results
2. Offline data analysis
3. Offline indexing
4. Online retrieval within strict latency limits
5. Online Ranking within strict latency limits
6. Spell correction
7. Query suggestions

This tutorial is aimed at going over the theoretical and practical aspects of all the above issues. Our tutorial would be useful for both academics interested in expanding their knowledge as well as practitioners keen on putting together a working solution. We will make all our code available on GitHub and leverage the following tools - typeahead.js [4] from Twitter, Elasticsearch [1]/Lucene [14] for backend. We will use the Stackoverflow user-generated data [2] to construct the index and build an instant search experience on this dataset.

2. RELEVANCE TO INFORMATION RETRIEVAL AND RELATED WORK

Instant search is increasingly becoming an important part of the search experience. While there has been decades of research effort spent on optimizing the traditional "SERP" experience, building a scalable instant search experience poses its own unique set of challenges in terms of indexing, retrieval, and ranking. We believe the information retrieval researchers and practitioners would greatly benefit from an overview of these challenges, potential solutions and alternatives, as well as the various trade offs involved.

Our goal in this tutorial is to provide an overview of the challenges involved, the various pieces of technology and relevance components that need to work together, and then walk the audience through the process of building a scalable system end-to-end. **To the best of our knowledge, such a tutorial has not been presented before in the information retrieval community.** That said, there's prior research that attempts to address various challenges posed by instant search – although in a piecemeal manner.

2.1 Related Work

In the area of indexing and retrieval, Bast et al. [9] proposed a block-based index to improve retrieval speed by reducing random accesses to posting lists. But this does not address the problem of efficiently finding candidate completions of the partially typed query. Li et al. [16] describe a trie based approach to represent prefixes, with posting lists at the leaf nodes. While such an approach works well for query autocomplete systems with few million entries, it's much harder to scale further without additional retrieval techniques like early termination [7, 21, 22].

Early termination is a retrieval technique that avoids exhaustively scoring all matching documents; this is achieved by reorganizing the index such that documents with high prior probability of relevance (generally referred to as "static rank") appear first. Commonly used scores include within-document term frequencies [18], or some notion of document quality or popularity [10, 17]. Needless to say, the effectiveness of early termination hinges on the choice of "static rank", which in turn is highly dependent on the problem domain.

Fuzzy search is an area of research that aims to build retrieval systems that are tolerant to minor spelling errors or variations. While full word spelling correction is a well-studied problem [15, 13, 6], fixing spelling errors in partial queries as the user is typing is a relatively new area of research [11, 12].

In the area of personalized query suggestions, Bar-Yossef et al. [8] propose an approach that biases query completions towards previous queries in the same session. But this does not address single-query sessions, which are very common in navigational search use cases. Weber et al. [20] focused on how query likelihoods differ by demographics. Milad [19] provides a machine learning framework that can combine demographic and user features for generating personalized query completions.

In terms of open source technologies, there are several JavaScript libraries for implementing client side autocomplete, e.g. typeahead.js [4] and Bootstrap [3]. For the search backend, Apache Lucene [14] is a search engine library with support for full text search via a fairly expressive query language, extensible scoring, and high performance indexing. Elastic Search [1] is a search server based on Lucene that provides the ability to quickly build scalable search engines. It provides a distributed, multitenant-capable search engine with a HTTP web interface.

In this tutorial, we aim to bring together the best ideas from prior research and leverage open source technologies to put together a working end to end instant search experience over a publicly available dataset.

3. FORMAT AND DETAILED SCHEDULE

All code and scripts needed will be made available on GitHub

1. Quick hitter – End-to-end instant search experience using Python and typeahead.js (20 min)
    - This will serve as an ice-breaker.
    - We will show how easy it is to put together a basic autocomplete service within 40 lines of python.
    - The time will also be used to make sure the developer environment is set up.
2. Literature and tools survey. Cover various aspects of instant search referenced in Section 2.1. These include:
    - Performance and Retrieval (30 min).
        - Using indexing techniques like early termination and static rank to retrieve and rank fewer documents while maintaining recall.
        - Using FST or Trie based retrieval. Theory covering aspects of Lucene FST [5].
        - Prefix indexing based retrieval.
        - Trade offs between prefix indexing and FST.
    - Tolerance to Errors. We will cover various aspects of fixing common spelling errors in autocomplete (20 min).
    - Relevance (20 min).
        - Ranking autocomplete suggestions using session data.
        - Personalizing suggestions.
        - Using custom scoring function inside Lucene.
3. Walking through a real example (90 min)
    (a) Overview and an End-to-End Prototype (15 min)
    - Understanding and familiarizing ourselves with the dataset
        - Essential fields
        - Tokenization needs
    - Understanding the tools (elasticsearch [1], python etc.)
    - Given a particular open data set and a schema, create an search index using elasticsearch [1]. Sample curl queries would be provided to test if the index is working (specific queries with expected results)

    (b) Designing Prefix Index (30 min)
    - Retrieval and Ranking. Given an open data set.
        - Decide which fields to index and create an index which can handle prefixes
        - Send sample prefix query and get results
    - Decide fields to index for retrieval (Analyzers, N-Grams etc.)
    - Decide fields to be used for ranking

    (c) Building front end (15 min)
    - Integrate front end components to build end-to-end experience
    - Use typeahead.js [4] to query the backend built using tools built in previous sections

    (d) Ranking and Query Rewriting (30 min)
    This will be the creative section of the tutorial where attendees have the opportunity to extent what had been built in the last one hour towards their own custom search experience. Examples would be provided. Sample problems handled:
    - Blending results between different query types like mixing query suggestions and results for the same prefix. Example: query like "ha" can have a mix of results like "Tag: hadoop" (suggesting to search via tag "hadoop") as well as instant results like the question "How to learn Hadoop".
    - Integrating metadata into ranking (like number of upvotes for a Q&A site)

4. PRESENTER INFORMATION

Ganesh Venkataraman currently leads jobs relevance at LinkedIn. His contributions at LinkedIn include, leading end to end re-architecture of job search, machine learned ranking for people search typeahead, introducing machine learned ranking towards skills search at LinkedIn. He co-authored a paper on personalized ranking which won the best paper award at the IEEE Big Data Conference 2015. He holds a Ph.D. from Texas A&M in Electrical & Computer Engineering where he was the recipient of the Dean's graduate merit scholarship.

Abhimanyu Lad Abhimanyu (Abhi) Lad leads query understanding efforts at LinkedIn. His contributions include major improvements to query intent prediction, query suggestions, spelling correction, name search and leading a major re-architecture of LinkedIn people search stack. He holds a Ph.D. in Language and Information Technologies from Carnegie Mellon University, where he was the recipient of the Yahoo! Ph.D. Fellowship. He has several publications in the field of information retrieval and machine learning with over 130 citations.

Viet Ha-Thuc leads machine learning efforts for improving search quality at LinkedIn. He has played a key role in designing and implementing machine learned ranking for personalized search and federation across several verticals at LinkedIn. His work on LinkedIn search has been published at conferences such as CIKM, Big Data and WWW. One of the publications received the Best Application Paper Award at 2015 IEEE Big Data. Prior to LinkedIn, he was a scientist in the Content Understanding group at Yahoo! Labs, where he developed a machine learning system for extracting relevant entities and concepts in text documents. The system was deployed to annotate every email and news article in the Yahoo! ecosystem. He received a Ph.D. in Computer Science from the University of Iowa in 2011.

Dhruv Arya currently leads job search quality at LinkedIn. His goal is to apply machine learning and data mining approaches to build talent matching algorithms that connect job seekers to the most relevant jobs. Apart from this, he has made key contributions to query understanding and rewriting, whole page optimization, as well as personalized federated search, which was presented at CIKM 2015. He received a Master's degree in Computer Science from University of Pennsylvania in 2013.

5. REFERENCES

[1] Elasticsearch documentation, https://www.elastic.co/guide/index.html.

[2] Stackoverflow creative commons data dump, http://blog.stackoverflow.com/2009/06/stack-overflow-creative-commons-data-dump/.

[3] Twitter bootstrap library. http://getbootstrap.com.

[4] typeahead.js library. https://twitter.github.io/typeahead.js.

[5] Using finite state transducers in lucene, http://blog.mikemccandless.com/2010/12/using-finite-state-transducers-in.html.

[6] F. Ahmad and G. Kondrak. Learning a spelling error model from search query logs. In *Proceedings of the conference on Human Language Technology and Empirical Methods in Natural Language Processing*, pages 955–962. Association for Computational Linguistics, 2005.

[7] V. N. Anh, O. de Kretser, and A. Moffat. Vector-space ranking with effective early termination. In *Proceedings of the 24th annual international ACM SIGIR conference on Research and development in information retrieval*, pages 35–42. ACM, 2001.

[8] Z. Bar-Yossef and N. Kraus. Context-sensitive query auto-completion. In *Proceedings of the 20th international conference on World wide web*, pages 107–116. ACM, 2011.

[9] H. Bast and I. Weber. Type less, find more: fast autocompletion search with a succinct index. In *Proceedings of the 29th annual international ACM SIGIR conference on Research and development in information retrieval*, pages 364–371. ACM, 2006.

[10] S. Brin and L. Page. The anatomy of a large-scale hypertextual web search engine, 1998. In *Proceedings of the Seventh World Wide Web Conference*, 2007.

[11] S. Chaudhuri and R. Kaushik. Extending autocompletion to tolerate errors. In *Proceedings of the 2009 ACM SIGMOD International Conference on Management of data*, pages 707–718. ACM, 2009.

[12] H. Duan and B.-J. P. Hsu. Online spelling correction for query completion. In *Proceedings of the 20th international conference on World wide web*, pages 117–126. ACM, 2011.

[13] J. Gao, X. Li, D. Micol, C. Quirk, and X. Sun. A large scale ranker-based system for search query spelling correction. In *Proceedings of the 23rd International Conference on Computational Linguistics*, pages 358–366. Association for Computational Linguistics, 2010.

[14] E. Hatcher and O. Gospodnetic. Lucene in action. 2004.

[15] M. D. Kernighan, K. W. Church, and W. A. Gale. A spelling correction program based on a noisy channel model. In *Proceedings of the 13th conference on Computational linguistics-Volume 2*, pages 205–210. Association for Computational Linguistics, 1990.

[16] G. Li, J. Wang, C. Li, and J. Feng. Supporting efficient top-k queries in type-ahead search. In *Proceedings of the 35th international ACM SIGIR conference on Research and development in information retrieval*, pages 355–364. ACM, 2012.

[17] X. Long and T. Suel. Optimized query execution in large search engines with global page ordering. In *Proceedings of the 29th international conference on Very large data bases-Volume 29*, pages 129–140. VLDB Endowment, 2003.

[18] M. Persin, J. Zobel, and R. Sacks-Davis. Filtered document retrieval with frequency-sorted indexes. *JASIS*, 47(10):749–764, 1996.

[19] M. Shokouhi and K. Radinsky. Time-sensitive query auto-completion. In *Proceedings of the 35th international ACM SIGIR conference on Research and development in information retrieval*, pages 601–610. ACM, 2012.

[20] I. Weber and C. Castillo. The demographics of web search. In *Proceedings of the 33rd international ACM SIGIR conference on Research and development in information retrieval*, pages 523–530. ACM, 2010.

[21] H. Yan, S. Shi, F. Zhang, T. Suel, and J.-R. Wen. Efficient term proximity search with term-pair indexes. In *Proceedings of the 19th ACM international conference on Information and knowledge management*, pages 1229–1238. ACM, 2010.

[22] F. Zhang, S. Shi, H. Yan, and J.-R. Wen. Revisiting globally sorted indexes for efficient document retrieval. In *Proceedings of the third ACM international conference on Web search and data mining*, pages 371–380. ACM, 2010.

Online Learning to Rank for Information Retrieval

SIGIR 2016 Tutorial

Artem Grotov
University of Amsterdam
Amsterdam, The Netherlands
a.grotov@uva.nl

Maarten de Rijke
University of Amsterdam
Amsterdam, The Netherlands
derijke@uva.nl

ABSTRACT

During the past 10–15 years offline learning to rank has had a tremendous influence on information retrieval, both scientifically and in practice. Recently, as the limitations of offline learning to rank for information retrieval have become apparent, there is increased attention for *online* learning to rank methods for information retrieval in the community. Such methods learn from user interactions rather than from a set of labeled data that is fully available for training up front.

Below we describe why we believe that the time is right for an intermediate-level tutorial on online learning to rank, the objectives of the proposed tutorial, its relevance, as well as more practical details, such as format, schedule and support materials.

Keywords

Online learning to rank; Bandit algorithms; Exploration vs. exploitation

1. INTRODUCTION

Today's search engines have developed into complex systems that combines hundreds of ranking criteria with the aim of producing the optimal result list in response to users' queries. For automatically tuning optimal combinations of large numbers of ranking criteria, learning to rank [22, LTR] has proved invaluable. For a given query, each document is represented by a feature vector. The features may be query dependent, document dependent or capture the relationship between the query and documents. The task of the learner is to find a model that combines these features such that, when this model is used to produce a ranking for an unseen query, user satisfaction is maximized.

Traditionally, learning to rank algorithms are trained in batch mode, on a complete dataset of query and document pairs with their associated manually created relevance labels. This setting has a number of disadvantages and is impractical in many cases. First, creating such datasets is expensive and therefore infeasible for smaller search engines, such as small web-store search engines [24]. Second, it may be impossible for experts to annotate documents, as in the case of personalized search [18]. Third, the relevance of documents to queries can change over time, like in a news search engine [7].

Online learning to rank addresses all of these issues by incrementally learning from user feedback in real time [34]. Online learning is closely related to active learning, incremental learning, and counterfactual learning. However, online learning is more difficult because the agent has to balance exploration and exploitation: actions with unknown performance have to be explored to learn better solutions [11].

There is a growing body of established methods for online learning to rank for information retrieval (see the schedule below for a broad range of examples). The time is right to organize and present this material to a broad audience of interested information retrieval researchers, whether junior or senior, whether academic or industrial. The online learning to rank methods available today have been proposed by different communities, in machine learning and information retrieval. A key aim of the tutorial is to bring these together and offer a unified perspective. To achieve this we illustrate the core and state of the art methods in online learning to rank, their theoretical foundations and real-world applications, as well as existing online learning algorithms that have not been used by information retrieval community so far.

We expect the tutorial to be useful for both academic and industrial researchers who either want to develop new online learning to rank methods, use them in their own research, or apply the methods described in the tutorial to improve search and recommendation systems.

2. OBJECTIVES

Online learning to rank from user interactions is fundamentally different from currently dominant supervised learning to rank approaches for information retrieval, where training data is assumed to be randomly sampled from some underlying distribution, and where absolute and reliable labels are provided by professional annotators [15]. When learning from user interactions, a system has no control over which queries it receives, it only receives feedback on the result lists it presents to users, and it has to present high quality result lists while learning, to satisfy user expectations.

Following Hofmann et al. [11], in this tutorial we formulate online learning to rank as a reinforcement learning problem, in which an *agent*, the search engine, learns from interactions with an *environment*, the user and their interactions, by trying out actions (e.g., returning a ranked list of items) and observing rewards (e.g., interpreting user feedback as absolute or relative feedback) in multiple rounds or discrete time steps; see Figure 1.

Particularly relevant to this tutorial are methods for tackling so-called *contextual bandit problems* (also known as bandits with side information) [1]. A contextual bandit problem is a special case of

SIGIR '16, July 17 - 21, 2016, Pisa, Italy

ISBN 978-1-4503-4069-4/16/07...$15.00

DOI: http://dx.doi.org/10.1145/2911451.2914798

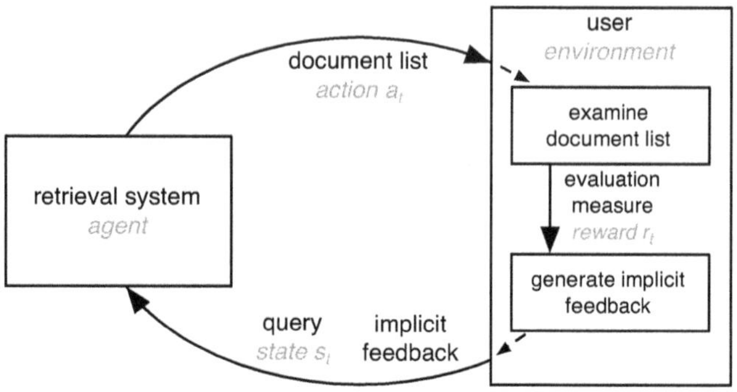

Figure 1: The information retrieval problem modeled as a contextual bandit problem, with information retrieval terminology in black and the corresponding reinforcement terminology in green and italics. (Figure taken from [11].)

a reinforcement learning problem in which states are independent of the agent's actions. In information retrieval terms, the context could consist of the user and the query and the actions are the search engine result pages. A difference between typical contextual bandit formulations and online learning to rank for information retrieval is that in information retrieval (absolute) rewards cannot be observed directly. Instead, feedback for learning is inferred from observed user interactions as noisy preference indications.

As we will demonstrate in the tutorial, an important benefit of reducing IR problems to bandit approaches is that the rich body of work on bandit approaches can be used. At the same time, information retrieval poses unique challenges that inspire additional research on bandit algorithms.

The objectives of the tutorial are as follows:

- To describe existing online LTR algorithms in a unified way, i.e., using common notation and terminology, so that different models can easily be related to each other.
- Explain the importance of balancing exploration and exploitation in an online LTR setting.
- To explain how to analyse the performance of online LTR algorithms and why it is worth the effort.
- To present appropriate experimental and evaluation methodologies for online LTR in both synthetic and real world settings.
- To describe how to deploy online LTR algorithms in an industrial setting.
- To present online learning algorithms that have not been used yet for learning to rank and indicate how IR researchers might go about using them.
- To discuss future directions of research in online LTR.

These objectives are meant to give participants a thorough understanding of existing learning to rank for information retrieval methods and to present online learning methods that have so far not been applied to learning to rank, let alone to learning to rank for information retrieval.

3. DETAILED SCHEDULE

The tutorial will be organized in two halves of 90 minutes each, each mixing theory and experiment, with formal analyses of online learning to rank methods interleaved with discussions of code and of experimental outcomes. Part I is aimed at familiarizing participants with the key concepts and algorithms. In Part II we select a small number of topics to provide a more in-depth technical treatment.

Part I

[10 minutes] Introduction, aims and historical notes

Here we discuss the context in which online LTR is applied and the most important historical milestones in its development.

[10 minutes] LTR in IR.

- The task of ranking documents, its importance, relationship to other machine learning tasks, and the unique challenges of LTR [22].
- Current approaches to LTR and argue that they all have issues that have to be addressed, such as the cost of producing labelled data and the mismatch between manually curated labels and user intent [34].

[15 minutes] Online LTR: balancing exploration and exploitation.

- How does online LTR addresses the shortcomings of offline LTR [11, 34]?
- How does online LTR relate to, and differ from, other tasks such as learning from labelled data, active learning and learning from logged interactions [30]?
- We explain the importance of balancing exploration and exploitation [13].

[5 minutes] Introduction to bandits and reinforcement learning.

- An important formalism behind many online LTR methods: bandit algorithms [1, 20]
- Connection to reinforcement learning [11, 29]
- Illustrate the importance of formal analysis and present k-armed bandits [1], contextual bandits [20] and cascading bandits [19] as ways to formalize the online LTR setting.

[10 minutes] Online signals to learn from.

- Close connection with online and logged based IR Evaluation [9, 14], because in both settings one needs to make the connection between observed user feedback and the hidden quality of the system.
- How to use observed user feedback to train the ranking models? The observed user feedback includes clicks, absence of clicks, dwell times, abandonment and many other signals [17, 21].
- Signals can be interpreted in a number of ways, for example, clicks can be interpreted in the form of absolute click through rates, or as relative preferences between documents or retrieval systems or using click models [16].

[20 minutes] Dueling bandit gradient descent.

- Dueling bandit gradient descent [34, DBGD], one of the core methods used in online LTR. We present the theory behind this method and discuss under which conditions it is guaranteed to work.
- More advanced methods that build on DBGD such as Probabilistic Multileave Gradient Decent [23, 27] and DBGD with Candidate Preselection [12].

[5 minutes] Real world applications.

- Real world applications of online LTR.
- Practical considerations such as what kind of infrastructure is required and what is important to log during online LTR.

[15 minutes] Discussion.

Part II

In this part we dig deeper into the foundations of some of the concepts introduced in Part I.

[5 minutes] Introduction.

- Focus on deepening the participants' understanding of the concepts introduced in part one.
- Connecting to online learning to rank methods not yet used in information retrieval.

[30 minutes] Online LTR in K-armed bandits setting.

- How to perform online LTR with a finite population of candidate rankers, framing it as a K-armed bandits problem [6].
- Challenges associated with deciding which ranker is the best among a population, the concept of Condorcet winner and Relative Upper Confidence Bound algorithm [35–38].

[20 minutes] Current problems: non-linear models, better exploration, safety guarantees, combining offline and online.

- State of the art in online LTR and ways to improve it [10].
- Non-linear neural network and tree ensemble-based ranking models [3], exploration strategies based on uncertainty estimations [31].

[10 minutes] Existing online algorithms not used in information retrieval.

- Online learning algorithms that have not been used in the LTR settings with the goal of inspiring researchers to adapt those algorithms for use in the IR community [4, 5]

[10 minutes] Datasets and resources.

- How to run online LTR experiments at home [25]
- CLEF LL4IR: Living Labs for IR Evaluation [26]
- TREC OpenSearch – Academic Search [32]

[15 minutes] Discussion and conclusion.

- Change the world!

4. TYPE OF SUPPORT MATERIALS TO BE SUPPLIED TO ATTENDEES

- Slides
- Draft survey on online learning to rank for information retrieval [8]
- Code and data samples to follow experimental segments of the tutoral
- Lerot – experimental environment for online learning to rank [25]

Acknowledgements

This research was supported by Ahold, Amsterdam Data Science, the Bloomberg Research Grant program, the Dutch national program COMMIT, Elsevier, the European Community's Seventh Framework Programme (FP7/2007-2013) under grant agreement nr 312827 (VOX-Pol), the ESF Research Network Program ELIAS, the Royal Dutch Academy of Sciences (KNAW) under the Elite Network Shifts project, the Microsoft Research Ph.D. program, the Netherlands eScience Center under project number 027.012.105, the Netherlands Institute for Sound and Vision, the Netherlands Organisation for Scientific Research (NWO) under project nrs 727.011.005, 612.001.116, HOR-11-10, 640.006.013, 612.066.930, CI-14-25, SH-322-15, 652.002.001, 612.001.551, the Yahoo Faculty Research and Engagement Program, and Yandex. All content represents the opinion of the authors, which is not necessarily shared or endorsed by their respective employers and/or sponsors.

REFERENCES

[1] Peter Auer. Using confidence bounds for exploitation-exploration trade-offs. *Journal of Machine Learnng Research*, 3:397–422, 2003.

[2] Alexey Borisov, Pavel Serdyukov, and Maarten de Rijke. Using metafeatures to increase the effectiveness of latent semantic models in web search. In *WWW 2016: 25th International World Wide Web Conference*. ACM, April 2016.

[3] Christopher J.C. Burges. From ranknet to lambdarank to lambdamart: An overview. Technical Report MSR-TR-2010-82, June 2010.

[4] Giuseppe Burtini, Jason Loeppky, and Ramon Lawrence. A survey of online experiment design with the stochastic multi-armed bandit. *CoRR*, abs/1510.00757, 2015. URL http://arxiv.org/abs/1510.00757.

[5] Róbert Busa-Fekete and Eyke Hüllermeier. A survey of preference-based online learning with bandit algorithms. In *Algorithmic Learning Theory: 25th International Conference, ALT 2014, Bled, Slovenia, October 8-10, 2014. Proceedings*, pages 18–39, Cham, 2014. Springer International Publishing.

[6] Róbert Busa-Fekete and Eyke Hüllermeier. A survey of preference-based online learning with bandit algorithms. In *ALT '14*, number 8776 in LNCS, pages 18–39. Springer, 2014.

[7] Susan T. Dumais. The web changes everything: Understanding and supporting people in dynamic information environments. In *Research and Advanced Technology for Digital Libraries, 14th European Conference, ECDL 2010*, 2010.

[8] Artem Grotov and Maarten de Rijke. Online learning to rank for information retrieval: A survey. *Draft*, 2016.

[9] Artem Grotov, Shimon Whiteson, and Maarten de Rijke. Bayesian ranker comparison based on historical user interactions. In *SIGIR 2015: 38th international ACM SIGIR conference on Research and development in information retrieval*. ACM, August 2015.

[10] Artem Grotov, Maarten de Rijke, and Shimon Whiteson. Online LambdaRank. In *Submitted*, 2016.

[11] Katja Hofmann, Shimon Whiteson, and Maarten de Rijke. Balancing exploration and exploitation in learning to rank online. In *ECIR 2011: 33rd European Conference on Information Retrieval*. Springer, April 2011.

[12] Katja Hofmann, Anne Schuth, Shimon Whiteson, and Maarten de Rijke. Reusing historical interaction data for

faster online learning to rank for information retrieval. In *WSDM 2013: International Conference on Web Search and Data Mining*. ACM, February 2013.

[13] Katja Hofmann, Shimon Whiteson, and Maarten de Rijke. Balancing exploration and exploitation in listwise and pairwise online learning to rank for information retrieval. *Information Retrieval Journal*, 16(1):63–90, February 2013.

[14] Katja Hofmann, Shimon Whiteson, and Maarten de Rijke. Fidelity, soundness, and efficiency of interleaved comparison methods. *ACM Transactions on Information Systems*, 31(3): Article 18, October 2013.

[15] Katja Hofmann, Shimon Whiteson, Anne Schuth, and Maarten de Rijke. Learning to rank for information retrieval from user interactions. *ACM SIGWEB Newsletter*, (Spring): 5:1–5:7, April 2014.

[16] Thorsten Joachims. Optimizing search engines using clickthrough data. In *Proceedings of the Eighth ACM SIGKDD International Conference on Knowledge Discovery and Data Mining*, KDD '02, pages 133–142, New York, NY, USA, 2002. ACM.

[17] Youngho Kim, Ahmed Hassan, Ryen W. White, and Imed Zitouni. Modeling dwell time to predict click-level satisfaction. In *Proceedings of the 7th ACM International Conference on Web Search and Data Mining*, WSDM '14, pages 193–202, New York, NY, USA, 2014. ACM.

[18] Ron Kohavi, Roger Longbotham, Dan Sommerfield, and Randal M. Henne. Controlled experiments on the web: Survey and practical guide. *Data Mining and Knowledge Discovery*, 18(1):140–181, 2009.

[19] Branislav Kveton, Csaba Szepesvári, Zheng Wen, and Azin Ashkan. Cascading bandits. *CoRR*, abs/1502.02763, 2015. URL http://arxiv.org/abs/1502.02763.

[20] John Langford and Tong Zhang. The epoch-greedy algorithm for multi-armed bandits with side information. In J. C. Platt, D. Koller, Y. Singer, and S. T. Roweis, editors, *Advances in Neural Information Processing Systems 20*, pages 817–824. Curran Associates, Inc., 2008.

[21] Damien Lefortier, Pavel Serdyukov, and Maarten de Rijke. Online exploration for detecting shifts in fresh intent. In *CIKM 2014: 23rd ACM Conference on Information and Knowledge Management*. ACM, November 2014.

[22] Tie-Yan Liu. Learning to rank for information retrieval. *Foundations and Trends in Information Retrieval*, 3(3): 225–331, March 2009.

[23] Harrie Oosterhuis, Anne Schuth, and Maarten de Rijke. Probabilistic multileave gradient descent. In *ECIR 2016: 38th European Conference on Information Retrieval*, LNCS. Springer, March 2016.

[24] Mark Sanderson. Test collection based evaluation of information retrieval systems. *Foundations and Trends in Information Retrieval*, 4(4):247–375, 2010.

[25] Anne Schuth, Katja Hofmann, Shimon Whiteson, and Maarten de Rijke. Lerot: an online learning to rank framework. In *Living Labs for Information Retrieval Evaluation workshop at CIKM'13.*, 2013.

[26] Anne Schuth, Krisztian Balog, and Liadh Kelly. Overview of the living labs for information retrieval evaluation (ll4ir) clef lab 2015. In *Experimental IR Meets Multilinguality, Multimodality, and Interaction*, pages 484–496. Springer, 2015.

[27] Anne Schuth, Harrie Oosterhuis, Shimon Whiteson, and Maarten de Rijke. Multileave gradient descent for fast online learning to rank. In *WSDM 2016: The 9th International Conference on Web Search and Data Mining*. ACM, February 2016.

[28] Aleksandrs Slivkins, Filip Radlinski, and Sreenivas Gollapudi. Ranked bandits in metric spaces: learning optimally diverse rankings over large document collections. Technical report, arXiv preprint arXiv:1005.5197, 2010.

[29] Richard S. Sutton and Andrew G. Barto. *Reinforcement Learning: An Introduction*. MIT Press., 1998.

[30] Adith Swaminathan and Thorsten Joachims. Counterfactual risk minimization: Learning from logged bandit feedback. *CoRR*, abs/1502.02362, 2015. URL http://arxiv.org/abs/1502.02362.

[31] Aibo Tian and Matthew Lease. Active learning to maximize accuracy vs. effort in interactive information retrieval. In *Proceedings of the 34th International ACM SIGIR Conference on Research and Development in Information Retrieval*, SIGIR '11, pages 145–154, New York, NY, USA, 2011. ACM.

[32] TREC. OpenSearch track. http://trec-open-search.org, 2016.

[33] Aleksandr Vorobev, Damien Lefortier, Gleb Gusev, and Pavel Serdyukov. Gathering additional feedback on search results by multi-armed bandits with respect to production ranking. In *Proceedings of the 24th International Conference on World Wide Web*, pages 1177–1187. ACM, 2015.

[34] Yisong Yue and Thorsten Joachims. Interactively optimizing information retrieval systems as a dueling bandits problem. In *ICML '09*, 2009.

[35] Masrour Zoghi, Shimon Whiteson, Maarten de Rijke, and Remi Munos. Relative confidence sampling for efficient on-line ranker evaluation. In *7th ACM WSDM Conference (WSDM2014)*. ACM, February 2014.

[36] Masrour Zoghi, Shimon Whiteson, Remi Munos, and Maarten de Rijke. Relative upper confidence bound for the k-armed dueling bandit problem. In *ICML 2014: International Conference on Machine Learning*, June 2014.

[37] Masrour Zoghi, Shimon Whiteson, and Maarten de Rijke. Mergerucb: A method for large-scale online ranker evaluation. In *WSDM 2015: The Eighth International Conference on Web Search and Data Mining*. ACM, February 2015.

[38] Masrour Zoghi, Shimon Whiteson, Zohar Karnin, and Maarten de Rijke. Copeland dueling bandits. In *NIPS 2015*, December 2015.

[39] Masrour Zoghi, Tomáš Tunys, Lihong Li, Damien Jose, Junyan Chen, Chun Ming Chin, and Maarten de Rijke. Click-based hot fixes for underperforming torso queries. In *SIGIR 2016: 39th international ACM SIGIR conference on Research and development in information retrieval*. ACM, July 2016.

Question Answering with Knowledge Base, Web and Beyond

Wen-tau Yih
Microsoft Research
One Microsoft Way
Redmond, WA, USA
scottyih@microsoft.com

Hao Ma
Microsoft Research
One Microsoft Way
Redmond, WA, USA
haoma@microsoft.com

ABSTRACT

In this tutorial, we give the audience a coherent overview of the research of question answering (QA). We first introduce a variety of QA problems proposed by pioneer researchers and briefly describe the early efforts. By contrasting with the current research trend in this domain, the audience can easily comprehend what technical problems remain challenging and what the main breakthroughs and opportunities are during the past half century. For the rest of the tutorial, we select three categories of the QA problems that have recently attracted a great deal of attention in the research community, and present the tasks with the latest technical survey. We conclude the tutorial by discussing the new opportunities and future directions of QA research.

1. INTRODUCTION

Developing a Question Answering (QA) system to automatically answer natural-language questions has been a long-standing research problem since the dawn of AI, for its clear practical and scientific value. For instance, whether a system can answer questions correctly is a natural way to evaluate a machine's understanding of a domain. Providing succinct and precise answers to informational queries is also the direction pursued by the next generation of search engines that aim to incorporate more "semantics", as well as the basic function in digital assistants like Siri and Cortana. The tutorial starts from the historical background, but puts more emphasis on recently emerging approaches, such as leveraging structured and semi-structured information sources, in addition to a large-scale corpus. We select three categories of the QA problems that have recently attracted a great deal of attention in the research community. The first two categories regard answering factoid questions, where the main difference of the problem settings is the information source used for extracting answers. QA with knowledge base aims to answer natural language questions using real-world facts stored in an existing, large-scale database. Examples of the most recent KB-based QA systems include [1, 2, 4, 18, 22, 25, 24]. The representative approach for this task is to develop a semantic parser (of questions), which is the main focus. Other approaches like text matching in the embedding space and those driven by information extraction are also discussed. The other category, QA with the Web [3, 7, 11, 19, 17], targets answering questions using mainly from the facts extracted from general text corpora derived from the Web. In addition to the common components and techniques used in this setting, including passage retrieval, entity recognition and question analysis, we also introduce latest work on how to leverage and incorporate additional structured and semi-structured data to improve the performance. The third category of the QA problems that we highlight is the non-factoid questions. Due to its broad coverage, we briefly cover three exemplary topics: story comprehension [15], reasoning questions [21, 12] and paragraph QA [10].

This tutorial aims to present the current state of research in the emerging question answering field. After the completion of the tutorial, the expected learning outcomes are:

1. The audience will acquire the basic understanding and overview of the emerging topics of question answering.
2. The audience will learn and understand some of the current research work, as well as industry practices using IR, NLP and ML techniques in question answering. The audience will also be able to incorporate some aspects of what has been learned into their own work.
3. The audience will be able to identify a few research directions that could have big impact in the near future.

2. RELEVANCE

The topic of Question Answering is timely for the IR community. QA has again emerged in the past few years, as the trend in the web development and growth is clearly to make search results more semantic. Many research papers published in SIGIR [11, 19], WWW [16, 17, 20] and ACL [2, 3, 5, 23, 24] studied QA-related problems in-depth recently.

To our knowledge, no recent Question Answering tutorial has been delivered in related venues, such as SIGIR, WWW and ACL. Earlier tutorials on corpus-based QA methods were presented by Sanda Harabagiu and Dan Moldovan in NAACL-2001 [9] and by Jimmy Lin and Boris Katz in EACL-2003 [13]. Tutorials dedicated to the IBM Watson system were given more recently [8, 6], although they did not intend to cover more general topics in QA research. In a related WWW-2015 tutorial titled "An Introduction to Entity Recommendation and Understanding" [14], the presenters Hao

SIGIR '16, July 17-21, 2016, Pisa, Italy

DOI: http://dx.doi.org/10.1145/2911451.2914804

Ma and Yan Ke briefly introduced Question Answering in the context of Entity Recommendation and Understanding. In comparison, this tutorial covers more in-depths introduction to QA-related problems and solutions.

3. FORMAT AND DETAILED SCHEDULE

The main content of this tutorial consists of the historical background of the question answering research, detailed description of open-domain factoid question answering approaches using structured and unstructured information sources, and introduction to recent, non-factoid question answering tasks. The outline is listed below.

Part I. Overview of Question Answering Research.

- Overview of early Question Answering research
  - Natural language understanding problems proposed at the dawn of AI
  - Early representative QA systems
  - Key developments and milestones
- Current Question Answering research trend
  - Categories of QA problems and settings studied recently
  - Data sources, technical problems and solutions
  - Main challenges and opportunities
- Demos of some existing QA systems

Part II. Question Answering with Knowledge Base.

- Introduction to modern large-scale knowledge base
- Task setting and benchmark datasets
- State-of-the-art approaches
  - Semantic parsing (of questions)
  - Matching questions and answers in embedding space
  - Information extraction and text matching

Part III. Question Answering with the Web.

- Problem setting and the general system architecture
- Essential natural language analysis: entity and answer type
- Leveraging additional information sources
  - Usage data (e.g., search query logs or browsing logs)
  - Knowledge bases
  - Semi-structured data (e.g., Web tables)

Part IV. Non-Factoid Question Answering.

- Story comprehension (e.g., MC-Test)
- Reasoning questions (e.g., bAbI dataset & task)
- Paragraph QA (e.g., quiz bowl competition)

Part V. Conclusion.

- Summary of the tutorial
- Directions of future research

4. REFERENCES

[1] J. Berant, A. Chou, R. Frostig, and P. Liang. Semantic parsing on freebase from question-answer pairs. In *EMNLP*, pages 1533–1544, 2013.

[2] J. Berant and P. Liang. Semantic parsing via paraphrasing. In *Proceedings of ACL*, 2014.

[3] E. Brill, S. Dumais, and M. Banko. An analysis of the askmsr question-answering system. In *Proceedings of the ACL-02 conference on Empirical methods in natural language processing-Volume 10*, pages 257–264. Association for Computational Linguistics, 2002.

[4] A. Fader, L. Zettlemoyer, and O. Etzioni. Open question answering over curated and extracted knowledge bases. In *Proceedings of the 20th ACM SIGKDD international conference on Knowledge discovery and data mining*. ACM, 2014.

[5] A. Fader, L. S. Zettlemoyer, and O. Etzioni. Paraphrase-driven learning for open question answering. In *ACL (1)*, pages 1608–1618, 2013.

[6] J. Fan and K. Barker. Natural language processing in watson. In *AAAI-2015: Tutorials*, 2015.

[7] D. Ferrucci, E. Brown, J. Chu-Carroll, J. Fan, D. Gondek, A. A. Kalyanpur, A. Lally, J. W. Murdock, E. Nyberg, J. Prager, et al. Building watson: An overview of the deepqa project. *AI magazine*, 31(3):59–79, 2010.

[8] A. M. Gliozzo, A. Kalyanpur, and J. Fan. Natural language processing in watson. In *Proceedings of the 2012 Conference of the North American Chapter of the Association for Computational Linguistics: Human Language Technologies: Tutorials*, page 4. Association for Computational Linguistics, 2012.

[9] S. Harabagiu and D. Moldovan. Open-domain textual question answering. In *Proceedings of the 2001 Conference of the North American Chapter of the Association for Computational Linguistics: Tutorials*. Association for Computational Linguistics, 2001.

[10] M. Iyyer, J. L. Boyd-Graber, L. M. B. Claudino, R. Socher, and H. Daumé III. A neural network for factoid question answering over paragraphs. In *EMNLP*, pages 633–644, 2014.

[11] J. Ko, E. Nyberg, and L. Si. A probabilistic graphical model for joint answer ranking in question answering. In *Proceedings of the 30th annual international ACM SIGIR conference on Research and development in information retrieval*, pages 343–350. ACM, 2007.

[12] M. Lee, X. He, W. tau Yih, J. Gao, L. Deng, and P. Smolensky. Reasoning in vector space: An exploratory study of question answering. In *Proceedings of the International Conference on Learning Representations (ICLR) 2016*, 2016.

[13] J. Lin and B. Katz. Question answering techniques for the world wide web. *EACL-2003 Tutorial*, 2003.

[14] H. Ma and Y. Ke. An introduction to entity recommendation and understanding. In *Proceedings of the 24th International Conference on World Wide Web Companion*, pages 1521–1522. International World Wide Web Conferences Steering Committee, 2015.

[15] M. Richardson, C. J. Burges, and E. Renshaw. Mctest: A challenge dataset for the open-domain machine comprehension of text. In *EMNLP*, volume 1, page 2, 2013.

[16] H. Sun, H. Ma, X. He, W.-t. Yih, Y. Su, and X. Yan. Table cell search for question answering. In *Proceedings of the 25th International Conference on World Wide Web*, 2016.

[17] H. Sun, H. Ma, W.-t. Yih, C.-T. Tsai, J. Liu, and M.-W. Chang. Open domain question answering via semantic enrichment. In *Proceedings of the 24th International Conference on World Wide Web*, pages 1045–1055, 2015.

[18] C. Unger, L. Bühmann, J. Lehmann, A.-C. Ngonga Ngomo, D. Gerber, and P. Cimiano. Template-based question answering over rdf data. In *Proceedings of the 21st international conference on World Wide Web*, pages 639–648. ACM, 2012.

[19] E. M. Voorhees and D. M. Tice. Building a question answering test collection. In *Proceedings of the 23rd annual international ACM SIGIR conference on Research and development in information retrieval*, pages 200–207. ACM, 2000.

[20] R. West, E. Gabrilovich, K. Murphy, S. Sun, R. Gupta, and D. Lin. Knowledge base completion via search-based question answering. In *Proceedings of the 23rd international conference on World wide web*, pages 515–526, 2014.

[21] J. Weston, A. Bordes, S. Chopra, and T. Mikolov. Towards AI-complete question answering: A set of prerequisite toy tasks. In *Proceedings of the International Conference on Learning Representations (ICLR) 2016*, 2016.

[22] M. Yahya, K. Berberich, S. Elbassuoni, M. Ramanath, V. Tresp, and G. Weikum. Natural language questions for the web of data. In *Proceedings of the 2012 Joint Conference on Empirical Methods in Natural Language Processing and Computational Natural Language Learning*, pages 379–390. Association for Computational Linguistics, 2012.

[23] X. Yao and B. Van Durme. Information extraction over structured data: Question answering with freebase. In *ACL*, 2014.

[24] W.-t. Yih, M.-W. Chang, X. He, and J. Gao. Semantic parsing via staged query graph generation: Question answering with knowledge base. In *Proceedings of the 53rd Annual Meeting of the Association for Computational Linguistics and the 7th International Joint Conference on Natural Language Processing (Volume 1: Long Papers)*, pages 1321–1331, Beijing, China, July 2015. Association for Computational Linguistics.

[25] L. Zou, R. Huang, H. Wang, J. X. Yu, W. He, and D. Zhao. Natural language question answering over rdf: a graph data driven approach. In *Proceedings of the 2014 ACM SIGMOD international conference on Management of data*, pages 313–324. ACM, 2014.

Scalability and Efficiency Challenges in Large-Scale Web Search Engines

B. Barla Cambazoglu
Independent Researcher
Barcelona, Spain
barla@berkantbarlacambazoglu.com

Ricardo Baeza-Yates
Universitat Pompeu Fabra, Barcelona, Spain &
Universidad de Chile, Santiago, Chile
rbaeza@acm.org

ABSTRACT

Commercial web search engines need to process thousands of queries every second and provide responses to user queries within a few hundred milliseconds. As a consequence of these tight performance constraints, search engines construct and maintain very large computing infrastructures for crawling the Web, indexing discovered pages, and processing user queries. The scalability and efficiency of these infrastructures require careful performance optimizations in every major component of the search engine.

This tutorial aims to provide a fairly comprehensive overview of the scalability and efficiency challenges in large-scale web search engines. In particular, the tutorial provides an in-depth architectural overview of a web search engine, mainly focusing on the web crawling, indexing, and query processing components. The scalability and efficiency issues encountered in these components are presented at four different granularities: at the level of a single computer, a cluster of computers, a single data center, and a multi-center search engine. The tutorial also points out some open research problems and provides recommendations to researchers who are new to the field.

Keywords

Web search engines; crawling; indexing; query processing; efficiency; scalability

1. OUTLINE

The tutorial has four sections. The first section provides the main concepts. Each of the remaining sections covers a particular architectural component of a web search engine.

1.1 Main Concepts

In this section, we provide the necessary background for the following sections. First, we explain the main challenges posed by the Web and its characteristics. Second, we present the main components of a search engine and possible software/hardware architectures. Finally, we summarize the interactions among the three main components: crawler, indexer, and query processor.

SIGIR '16, July 17-21, 2016, Pisa, Italy
© 2016 ACM. ISBN 978-1-4503-4069-4/16/07...$15.00
DOI: http://dx.doi.org/10.1145/2911451.2914808

1.2 Web Crawling

The web crawler is responsible for discovering new web pages and downloading their content while refreshing the content of previously downloaded pages [42]. The main performance objective for a web crawler is to achieve high page download rates. The efficiency of a sequential crawler is mainly determined by the selection and implementation of proper data structures [36]. Scalability is achieved through multi-threading [30] and parallelization [23]. In addition to such techniques, our tutorial covers the URL reordering [46] and web repository refreshing [43] problems.

1.3 Indexing

The indexing process involves various parsing, extraction, and classification tasks, through which certain features are extracted and the textual content of downloaded pages are converted into an inverted index [51]. The main performance metrics for an indexer are the length of deployment cycles, compactness, and the speed of index updates. So far, most algorithmic improvements are concentrated on index compression [44], duplicate detection [29], and document reordering [12, 47]. At the architectural level, the efficiency and scalability are improved via online index construction [38], index partitioning [20], and static index pruning [2, 41]. Our tutorial also covers the indexing strategies for geographically distributed web search engines [33].

1.4 Query Processing

Query processing involves generating the set of best-matching results for a given user query [9]. The success of a query processor is mainly assessed by its throughput and average response latency. A large body of research work on relevance ranking assume relatively standard processing techniques using an inverted index while large-scale search engines rely on more sophisticated techniques. In addition to the state-of-the-art ranking techniques employed in web search engines, our tutorial covers a variety of problems including query processing on multi-core architectures [48], pipelined query processing [31], response latency prediction [40], selective search [35], query forwarding [21, 49], query scheduling [26], power/energy cost efficiency [27, 34], multi-site web search [7, 25], and green search engines [13]. We also briefly present learning-to-rank optimizations in web search [22, 39, 50] and discuss the impact of efficiency improvements on user engagement [3, 4, 11].

This section also covers caching in web search engines [6, 24]. The idea behind caching is to speed up query response times by storing precomputed query results, also reducing the computational workload of backend search systems. Caching happens at different architectural layers in a web search engine [45]. The tutorial covers common challenges in caching, such as admission [8], eviction [28], and prefetching [37]. It also focuses on the freshness problem, which attracted much research attention [1, 10, 12, 19, 32].

2. LEARNING OBJECTIVES

The following are the main objectives of the tutorial.

- To provide an in-depth background on the architectural components of a web search engine.
- To present the fundamental scalability and efficiency issues which have been often addressed in the information retrieval literature.
- To shed some light into the techniques used in large-scale commercial search engines and bridge the gap between the industry and academia.
- To identify open research problems in the context of web search engine scalability and efficiency, promoting further research on the topic.

3. PREVIOUS EDITIONS

The initial structure of this tutorial series is based on a book chapter published by the presenters [14]. Earlier versions of the tutorial were presented in SIGIR'13 [15], WWW'14 [5], SIGIR'14 [16], WSDM'15 [17], and CIKM'15. The tutorial was also given in three different summer schools: the 2nd COST 804 Training School on Energy Efficiency in Large Scale Distributed Systems, the 3rd MUMIA Training School on Information Retrieval and Interactive Information Access, and more recently, the 10th European Summer School in Information Retrieval. The presenters have also published a short book whose structure and content is based on these tutorials [18].

4. TARGET AUDIENCE

Efficiency has been one of the main research topics in the previous editions of the SIGIR conference. The topics covered in this tutorial have a fairly high overlap with those encountered in the efficiency-related paper sessions in SIGIR. As a supporting fact, the presenters of the tutorial co-authored a large number of papers in recent years' efficiency sessions. A subset of the topics covered in the tutorial are taken from the papers presented in the efficiency sessions of related conferences, such as WSDM and WWW.

Since the tutorial was already presented in SIGIR before, this edition of the tutorial aims to come with a major content update. Unlike the previous editions, which all targeted intermediate audiences, this edition targets an advanced audience. Therefore, the introductory sections of the tutorial are compressed, making space for relatively new and more technical material. We aim to go into more depth in selected topics in the context of web search efficiency, such as machine-learned ranking systems, user impact of efficiency optimizations, and energy-efficient and green web search engines. Although the attendees are expected to have a solid understanding of fundamental concepts related to web search, parts of the presented material should be easy to follow by beginner and intermediate audiences as well.

5. PRESENTERS' SHORT BIOGRAPHIES

Berkant Barla Cambazoglu received his B.S., M.S., and Ph.D. degrees, all in computer engineering, from the Computer Engineering Department of Bilkent University in 1997, 2000, and 2006, respectively. After getting his Ph.D. degree, he worked as a postdoctoral researcher in Bilkent University for a short period of time. In 2006, he joined the Biomedical Informatics Department of the Ohio State University as a postdoctoral researcher. In 2008, he joined Yahoo Labs as a postdoctoral researcher. He received research scientist and senior research scientist positions at the same institution, in 2010 and 2012, respectively. Between 2013 and 2015, he was a senior manager, heading the web retrieval group in Yahoo Labs Barcelona. His main research interests are distributed information retrieval and web search efficiency. In 2010, 2011, 2014, and 2015, he co-organized the LSDS-IR workshop. He was the proceedings chair for WSDM'09 and the poster and proceedings chairs for ECIR'12. He served as an area chair in SIGIR'13 and SIGIR'14. He regularly serves on the program committees of SIGIR, WWW, and KDD conferences. He is a member of the editorial board of IP&M. He has many papers published in prestigious journals including IEEE TPDS, JPDC, JASIST, Inf. Syst., ACM TWEB, and IP&M, as well as papers and tutorials presented at top-tier conferences, such as SIGIR, CIKM, WSDM, WWW, and KDD.

Ricardo Baeza-Yates' areas of expertise are information retrieval, web search and data mining, data science and algorithms. He was VP of Research at Yahoo Labs, based in Sunnyvale, California, from August 2014 to February 2016. Before he founded and led from 2006 to 2015 the Yahoo labs in Barcelona and Santiago de Chile. Between 2008 and 2012 he also oversaw the Haifa lab, and started the London lab in 2012. He is part time Professor at the Dept. of Information and Communication Technologies (DTIC) of the Universitat Pompeu Fabra (UPF), in Barcelona, Spain, as well as in the Dept. of Computing Science (DCC) of Universidad de Chile at Santiago. During 2005 he was an ICREA research professor at UPF. Until 2004 he was Professor and founding director of the Center for Web Research at Universidad de Chile. He obtained a Ph.D. in CS from the University of Waterloo, Canada, in 1989. Before he obtained two masters (M.Sc. CS & M.Eng. EE) and the electronics engineer degree from the University of Chile in Santiago. He is co-author of the best-seller Modern Information Retrieval textbook, published in 1999 by Addison-Wesley with a second enlarged edition in 2011, which won the ASIST 2012 Book of the Year award. He is also co-author of the 2nd edition of the Handbook of Algorithms and Data Structures, Addison-Wesley, 1991; and co-editor of Information Retrieval: Algorithms and Data Structures, Prentice-Hall, 1992, among more than 500 other publications. From 2002 to 2004 he was elected to the board of governors of the IEEE Computer Society and in 2012 he was elected for the ACM Council. He has received the Organization of American States award for young researchers in exact sciences (1993), the Graham Medal for innovation in computing given by the University of Waterloo to distinguished ex-alumni (2007), the CLEI Latin American distinction for contributions to CS in the region (2009), and the National Award of the Chilean Association of Engineers (2010), among other distinctions.

In 2003 he was the first computer scientist to be elected to the Chilean Academy of Sciences and since 2010 is a founding member of the Chilean Academy of Engineering. In 2009 he was named ACM Fellow and in 2011 IEEE Fellow.

6. REFERENCES

[1] S. Alici, I. S. Altingovde, R. Ozcan, B. B. Cambazoglu, and O. Ulusoy. Timestamp-based result cache invalidation for web search engines. In *Proceedings of the 34th International ACM SIGIR Conference on Research and Development in Information Retrieval*, pages 973–982, 2011.

[2] I. S. Altingovde, R. Ozcan, and O. Ulusoy. Static index pruning in web search engines: Combining term and document popularities with query views. *ACM Transactions on Information Systems*, 30(1):2:1–2:28, 2012.

[3] I. Arapakis, X. Bai, and B. B. Cambazoglu. Impact of response latency on user behavior in web search. In *Proceedings of the 37th International ACM SIGIR Conference on Research and Development in Information Retrieval*, pages 103–112, 2014.

[4] L. Azzopardi, D. Kelly, and K. Brennan. How query cost affects search behavior. In *Proceedings of the 36th International ACM SIGIR Conference on Research and Development in Information Retrieval*, pages 23–32, 2013.

[5] R. Baeza-Yates and B. B. Cambazoglu. Scalability and efficiency challenges in large-scale web search engines. In *Proceedings of the 23rd International Conference on World Wide Web*, pages 185–186, 2014.

[6] R. Baeza-Yates, A. Gionis, F. Junqueira, V. Murdock, V. Plachouras, and F. Silvestri. The impact of caching on search engines. In *Proceedings of the 30th Annual International ACM SIGIR Conference on Research and Development in Information Retrieval*, pages 183–190, 2007.

[7] R. Baeza-Yates, A. Gionis, F. Junqueira, V. Plachouras, and L. Telloli. On the feasibility of multi-site web search engines. In *Proceedings of the 18th ACM Conference on Information and Knowledge Management*, pages 425–434, 2009.

[8] R. Baeza-Yates, F. Junqueira, V. Plachouras, and H. Witschel. Admission policies for caches of search engine results. In *String Processing and Information Retrieval*, volume 4726 of *Lecture Notes in Computer Science*, pages 74–85. Springer Berlin / Heidelberg, 2007.

[9] R. Baeza-Yates and B. Ribeiro-Neto. *Modern Information Retrieval*. Addison-Wesley Publishing Company, USA, 2nd edition, 2011.

[10] X. Bai and F. P. Junqueira. Online result cache invalidation for real-time web search. In *Proceedings of the 35th International ACM SIGIR Conference on Research and Development in Information Retrieval*, pages 641–650, 2012.

[11] M. Barreda-Ángeles, I. Arapakis, X. Bai, B. B. Cambazoglu, and A. Pereda-Baños. Unconscious physiological effects of search latency on users and their click behaviour. In *Proceedings of the 38th International ACM SIGIR Conference on Research and Development in Information Retrieval*, pages 203–212, 2015.

[12] R. Blanco, E. Bortnikov, F. Junqueira, R. Lempel, L. Telloli, and H. Zaragoza. Caching search engine results over incremental indices. In *Proceedings of the 33rd International ACM SIGIR Conference on Research and Development in Information Retrieval*, pages 82–89, 2010.

[13] R. Blanco, M. Catena, and N. Tonellotto. Exploiting green energy to reduce the operational costs of multi-center web search engines. In *Proceedings of the 25th International Conference on World Wide Web*, pages 1237–1247, 2016.

[14] B. B. Cambazoglu and R. Baeza-Yates. Scalability challenges in web search engines. In *Advanced Topics in Information Retrieval*, volume 33 of *The Information Retrieval Series*, pages 27–50. Springer Berlin Heidelberg, 2011.

[15] B. B. Cambazoglu and R. Baeza-Yates. Scalability and efficiency challenges in commercial web search engines. In *Proceedings of the 36th International ACM SIGIR Conference on Research and Development in Information Retrieval*, page 1124, 2013.

[16] B. B. Cambazoglu and R. Baeza-Yates. Scalability and efficiency challenges in large-scale web search engines. In *Proceedings of the 37th International ACM SIGIR Conference on Research and Development in Information Retrieval*, page 1285, 2014.

[17] B. B. Cambazoglu and R. Baeza-Yates. Scalability and efficiency challenges in large-scale web search engines. In *Proceedings of the 8th ACM International Conference on Web Search and Data Mining*, pages 411–412, 2015.

[18] B. B. Cambazoglu and R. A. Baeza-Yates. *Scalability Challenges in Web Search Engines*. Synthesis Lectures on Information Concepts, Retrieval, and Services. Morgan & Claypool Publishers, 2015.

[19] B. B. Cambazoglu, F. P. Junqueira, V. Plachouras, S. Banachowski, B. Cui, S. Lim, and B. Bridge. A refreshing perspective of search engine caching. In *Proceedings of the 19th International Conference on World Wide Web*, pages 181–190, 2010.

[20] B. B. Cambazoglu, E. Kayaaslan, S. Jonassen, and C. Aykanat. A term-based inverted index partitioning model for efficient distributed query processing. *ACM Transactions on the Web*, 7(3):15:1–15:23, 2013.

[21] B. B. Cambazoglu, E. Varol, E. Kayaaslan, C. Aykanat, and R. Baeza-Yates. Query forwarding in geographically distributed search engines. In *Proceeding of the 33rd International ACM SIGIR Conference on Research and Development in Information Retrieval*, pages 90–97, 2010.

[22] B. B. Cambazoglu, H. Zaragoza, O. Chapelle, J. Chen, C. Liao, Z. Zheng, and J. Degenhardt. Early exit optimizations for additive machine learned ranking systems. In *Proceedings of the 3rd ACM International Conference on Web Search and Data Mining*, pages 411–420, 2010.

[23] J. Cho and H. Garcia-Molina. Parallel crawlers. In *Proceedings of the 11th International Conference on World Wide Web*, pages 124–135, 2002.

[24] T. Fagni, R. Perego, F. Silvestri, and S. Orlando. Boosting the performance of web search engines: Caching and prefetching query results by exploiting

historical usage data. *ACM Transactions on Information Systems*, 24(1):51–78, 2006.

[25] G. Francès, X. Bai, B. B. Cambazoglu, and R. Baeza-Yates. Improving the efficiency of multi-site web search engines. In *Proceedings of the 7th ACM International Conference on Web Search and Data Mining*, pages 3–12, 2014.

[26] A. Freire, C. Macdonald, N. Tonellotto, I. Ounis, and F. Cacheda. Hybrid query scheduling for a replicated search engine. In *Proceedings of the 35th European Conference on Advances in Information Retrieval*, pages 435–446, 2013.

[27] A. Freire, C. Macdonald, N. Tonellotto, I. Ounis, and F. Cacheda. A self-adapting latency/power tradeoff model for replicated search engines. In *Proceedings of the 7th ACM International Conference on Web Search and Data Mining*, pages 13–22, 2014.

[28] Q. Gan and T. Suel. Improved techniques for result caching in web search engines. In *Proceedings of the 18th International Conference on World Wide Web*, pages 431–440, 2009.

[29] M. Henzinger. Finding near-duplicate web pages: a large-scale evaluation of algorithms. In *Proceedings of the 29th Annual International ACM SIGIR Conference on Research and Development in Information Retrieval*, pages 284–291, 2006.

[30] A. Heydon and M. Najork. Mercator: a scalable, extensible web crawler. *World Wide Web*, 2(4):219–229, 1999.

[31] S. Jonassen and S. Bratsberg. A combined semi-pipelined query processing architecture for distributed full-text retrieval. In *Web Information Systems Engineering*, volume 6488 of *Lecture Notes in Computer Science*, pages 587–601. Springer Berlin / Heidelberg, 2010.

[32] S. Jonassen, B. B. Cambazoglu, and F. Silvestri. Prefetching query results and its impact on search engines. In *Proceedings of the 35th International ACM SIGIR Conference on Research and Development in Information Retrieval*, pages 631–640, 2012.

[33] E. Kayaaslan, B. B. Cambazoglu, and C. Aykanat. Document replication strategies for geographically distributed web search engines. *Information Processing & Management*, 49(1):51–66, 2013.

[34] E. Kayaaslan, B. B. Cambazoglu, R. Blanco, F. P. Junqueira, and C. Aykanat. Energy-price-driven query processing in multi-center web search engines. In *Proceedings of the 34th International ACM SIGIR Conference on Research and Development in Information Retrieval*, pages 983–992, 2011.

[35] A. Kulkarni and J. Callan. Selective search: Efficient and effective search of large textual collections. *ACM Transactions on Information Systems*, 33(4):17:1–17:33, 2015.

[36] H.-T. Lee, D. Leonard, X. Wang, and D. Loguinov. IRLbot: scaling to 6 billion pages and beyond. In *Proceedings of the 17th International Conference on World Wide Web*, pages 427–436, 2008.

[37] R. Lempel and S. Moran. Predictive caching and prefetching of query results in search engines. In *Proceedings of the 12th International Conference on World Wide Web*, pages 19–28, 2003.

[38] N. Lester, A. Moffat, and J. Zobel. Efficient online index construction for text databases. *ACM Transactions on Database Systems*, 33(3):1–33, 2008.

[39] C. Lucchese, F. M. Nardini, S. Orlando, R. Perego, N. Tonellotto, and R. Venturini. Quickscorer: A fast algorithm to rank documents with additive ensembles of regression trees. In *Proceedings of the 38th International ACM SIGIR Conference on Research and Development in Information Retrieval*, pages 73–82, 2015.

[40] C. Macdonald, N. Tonellotto, and I. Ounis. Learning to predict response times for online query scheduling. In *Proceedings of the 35th International ACM SIGIR Conference on Research and Development in Information Retrieval*, pages 621–630, 2012.

[41] A. Ntoulas and J. Cho. Pruning policies for two-tiered inverted index with correctness guarantee. In *Proceedings of the 30th Annual International ACM SIGIR Conference on Research and Development in Information Retrieval*, pages 191–198, 2007.

[42] C. Olston and M. Najork. Web crawling. *Foundations and Trends in Information Retrieval*, 4(3):175–246, 2010.

[43] C. Olston and S. Pandey. Recrawl scheduling based on information longevity. In *Proceedings of the 17th International Conference on World Wide Web*, pages 437–446, 2008.

[44] G. Ottaviano and R. Venturini. Partitioned elias-fano indexes. In *Proceedings of the 37th International ACM SIGIR Conference on Research and Development in Information Retrieval*, pages 273–282, 2014.

[45] R. Ozcan, I. S. Altingovde, B. B. Cambazoglu, F. P. Junqueira, and Özgür Ulusoy. A five-level static cache architecture for web search engines. *Information Processing & Management*, 48(5):828–840, 2012.

[46] S. Pandey and C. Olston. Crawl ordering by search impact. In *Proceedings of the International Conference on Web Search and Data Mining*, pages 3–14, 2008.

[47] F. Silvestri, S. Orlando, and R. Perego. Assigning identifiers to documents to enhance the clustering property of fulltext indexes. In *Proceedings of the 27th Annual International ACM SIGIR Conference on Research and Development in Information Retrieval*, pages 305–312, 2004.

[48] S. Tatikonda, B. B. Cambazoglu, and F. P. Junqueira. Posting list intersection on multicore architectures. In *Proceedings of the 34th International ACM SIGIR Conference on Research and Development in Information Retrieval*, pages 963–972, 2011.

[49] A. Teymorian, O. Frieder, and M. A. Maloof. Rank-energy selective query forwarding for distributed search systems. In *Proceedings of the 22nd ACM International Conference on Information and Knowledge Management*, pages 389–398, 2013.

[50] L. Wang, J. Lin, and D. Metzler. Learning to efficiently rank. In *Proceeding of the 33rd International ACM SIGIR Conference on Research and Development in Information Retrieval*, pages 138–145, 2010.

[51] J. Zobel and A. Moffat. Inverted files for text search engines. *ACM Computing Surveys*, 38(2), 2006.

Simulation of Interaction: A Tutorial on Modelling and Simulating User Interaction and Search Behaviour

Leif Azzopardi
School of Computing Science, University of Glasgow
Glasgow, United Kingdom
Leif.Azzopardi@glasgow.ac.uk

ABSTRACT

Search is an inherently interactive, non-deterministic and user-dependent process. This means that there are many different possible sequences of interactions which could be taken (some ending in success and others ending in failure). Simulation provides a low cost, repeatable and reproducible way to explore a large range of different possibilities. This makes simulation very appealing, but it also requires care and consideration in developing, implementing and instantiating models of user behaviour for the purposes of experimentation.

In this tutorial, we aim to provide researchers with an overview of simulation, detailing the various types of simulation, models of search behavior used to simulate interaction, along with an overview of the various models of querying, stopping, selecting and marking. Through the course of the tutorial we will describe various studies and how they have used simulation to explore different behaviours and aspects of the search process. The final section of the tutorial will be dedicated to "best practice" and how to build, ground and validate simulations. The tutorial will conclude with a demonstration of an open source simulation framework that can be used develop various kinds of simulations.

CCS Concepts

•Information systems → Task models; Search interfaces; Test collections; •Human-centered computing → User models; Web-based interaction;

Keywords

Simulation, Evaluation, Performance, Information Retrieval

1. INTRODUCTION

Simulation provides a complementary approach to traditional forms of evaluation i.e. TREC style batch evaluations and user studies. Recently, there has been a growing interest in developing user models and developing simulations to augment these traditional forms of evaluation [31] in order to explore more possibilities and draw deeper insights into search and search behaviour [12, 25]. This is because simulation provides a low cost means of experimentation that enables repeatable and reproducible evaluations to be conducted that include interaction. However for the results of such simulations to be credible the models used need to be validated. And so it is important and timely to discuss the state of the art in simulation and how to build credible and valid simulations. In this tutorial, we will cover: (i) the what, why, when of simulation, (ii) the high level interaction models used for simulation, (iii) simulating the different components: (a) query generation, (b) stopping strategy, (c) decision making, etc, and (iv) how to build and evaluate valid simulations and what-if simulations.

SIGIR '16, July 17 - 21, 2016, Pisa, Italy

ISBN 978-1-4503-4069-4/16/07...$15.00

DOI: http://dx.doi.org/10.1145/2911451.2914799

1.1 Tutorial Overview

First we will provide an overview of simulation in IR and describe the different ways in which simulation has been used (e.g. simulated work tasks and tracks [22, 47], simulated and synthetic data collections [1, 10, 29, 44], and simulated interaction [12, 24, 25, 34, 48].) The focus of this tutorial will be on how to use simulation to undertake interactive-based evaluations and explorations to determine:

1. how well an IR system performs, and

2. how performance changes under different conditions and behaviours.

We will describe and explain the benefits and drawbacks of simulation and how it fits with other evaluations type (i.e. TREC style, user studies, etc).

High Level Interaction Models

In the next part of the tutorial, we will focus on explaining the different high level models used to simulate the interaction between the user and the search system [21, 37, 38, 39, 45, 24].

Here we will cover the state-based stochastic model of the user [21] and the process oriented: Searcher Model [39, 45] and the Complex Searcher Model [37, 38] as shown in Figure 1,. This will provide the necessary background for understanding how the search process is modelled, and what components need to be instantiated when developing a simulation. We will point out the types of tasks that are currently modelled and what we can evaluate with them along with pointing out their limitations and describing avenues for further development.

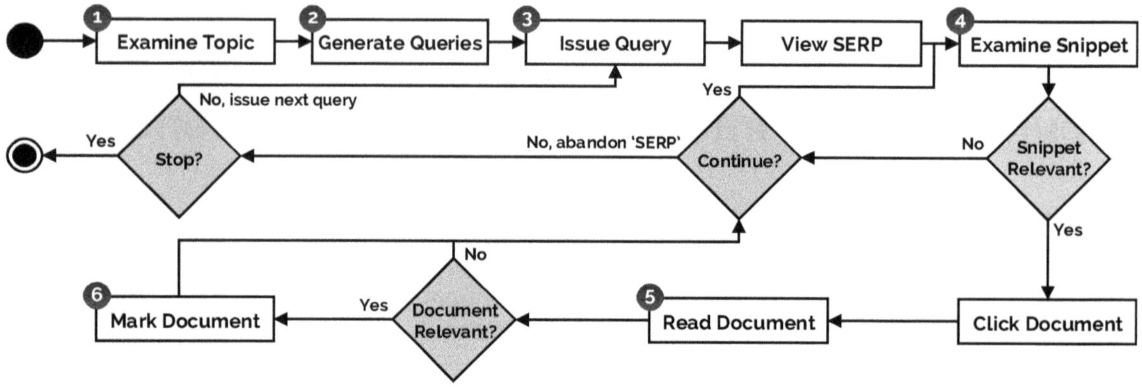

Figure 1: A flow chart of the high level interactions that are simulated.

Components

The core actions/components in most high level interaction models are:

1. the application of query (re)formulation strategies;
2. snippet scanning and assessment;
3. snippet clicking;
4. document reading;
5. document assessment; and
6. session stopping.

So in this part of the tutorial, we will explore in detail each of the components within the high level interaction models and describe and explain the different methods and models used to: (i) generate/formulate queries and query suggestions [1, 10, 21, 23, 29, 33, 46], (ii) determine when users stop and how they browse [24, 23, 37, 38, 45], (iii) interact and provide feedback [19, 27, 28, 32, 33, 35, 41] and (iv) encode the cost of actions [13, 20, 40, 42, 43]. Here we will explain a number of these different studies, and how they have examined the influence of the different components on search performance and/or search behaviors.

Putting it all together

The final part of the tutorial is how to put all the components together to build a credible and valid simulation, or to create reasonable "what-if" simulations. To build a simulation, we will explain the typical method undertaken:

- specify the search goal and stopping criteria, i.e. search until the simulated user reaches a certain level of gain, reaches a time limit, or meets some other stopping condition,
- specify the high level interaction model, and specify each of the different low level components,
- then, vary the parameters and components of interest in order to ask particular research questions.

This will be followed up by discussion on how to ground and validate simulations - and how simulations can guide empirical research and illuminate theory. We will conclude the day by providing a demonstration of a toolkit for simulating interaction [36].

1.2 Intended Audience

This tutorial will be focused at an introductory to intermediate level. We assume the participant has a good knowledge of Information Retrieval i.e. knowledge about the TREC style evaluation and the IR process. The tutorial is aimed at masters, graduate students and researchers wanting to know more about the variety of simulation methods, techniques and tools and how they can use them to enhance their research.

1.3 Intended Learning Outcomes

By the end of the tutorial, participants should be able to:

- Explain the benefits and drawbacks of simulations
- Describe the different high level interaction models
- Discuss and compare the different querying, stopping and decision making components
- Evaluate and measure the performance of systems and behaviours using simulation
- Design and construct grounded simulations and what-if simulations

1.4 Biography

Leif Azzopardi is a Senior Lecturer within the School of Computing Science at the University of Glasgow, within the Glasgow Information Retrieval Group. His research focuses on building formal models for Information Retrieval - usually drawing upon different disciplines for inspiration, such as Quantum Mechanics, Operations Research, Microeconomics, Transportation Planning and Gamification. Central to his research is the theoretical development models for Information Seeking and Retrieval, where his research interests include:

- Models for the retrieval of documents, sentences, experts and other information objects [18, 26];
- Probabilistic models of user interaction and the simulation of users for evaluation [1, 9, 11];
- Economic and optimization of models of interaction [3, 5, 6, 16], specifically how cost and effort affect interaction and performance with search systems [13, 30];

- Methods which assess the impact of search technology on society in application areas such as, search engine bias and the accessibility of e-Government information [14, 15], and;
- Searching for fun (i.e. the SINS of users) [4].

Over the past ten years, he has developed a number of techniques, tools and methods for simulated evaluations, including: (i) query generation methods [9, 11, 1], (ii) stopping strategies [37, 38] (iii) interaction styles and search strategies [3, 6, 2]. In 2010, he co-organized an ACM SIGIR Workshop on the Simulation of Interaction and delivered a keynote on the 'Assimilation of Users' at the ACM SIGIR 2013 Workshop Modeling User Behaviour for Evaluation. He has also given numerous lectures and invited talks on simulation at various universities and at the Information Foraging Summer School (2010-2012). He has also given a series of tutorials on Retrievability [7, 8] (ACM SIGIR 2014, ECIR 2015, ACM ICTIR 2015) and on Formal Models of Information Seeking, Search and Retrieval [17] (ACM SIGIR 2015, ACM CIKM 2015).

2. REFERENCES

[1] L. Azzopardi. Query side evaluation: An empirical analysis of effectiveness and effort. In *Proceedings of the 32nd ACM SIGIR*, pages 556–563, 2009.

[2] L. Azzopardi. Usage based effectiveness measures: Monitoring application performance in information retrieval. In *Proceedings of the 18th ACM CIKM Conference*, pages 631–640, 2009.

[3] L. Azzopardi. The economics in interactive information retrieval. In *Proc. 34th ACM SIGIR*, pages 15–24, 2011.

[4] L. Azzopardi. Searching for unlawful carnal knowledge. In *Proceedings of the SIGIR Workshop: Search for Fun*, volume 11, pages 17–18, 2011.

[5] L. Azzopardi. Economic models of search. In *Proceedings of the 18th Australasian Document Computing Symposium*, pages 1–1, 2013.

[6] L. Azzopardi. Modelling interaction with economic models of search. In *Proc. 37th ACM SIGIR*, pages 3–12, 2014.

[7] L. Azzopardi. The retrievability of documents. In *Proceedings of the 37th International ACM SIGIR Conference*, SIGIR '14, pages 1291–1291, 2014.

[8] L. Azzopardi. Theory of retrieval: The retrievability of information. In *Proceedings of the 2015 International Conference on The Theory of Information Retrieval*, ICTIR '15, pages 3–6, 2015.

[9] L. Azzopardi and M. de Rijke. Automatic construction of known-item finding test beds. In *Proceedings of SIGIR '06*, pages 603–604, 2006.

[10] L. Azzopardi, M. de Rijke, and K. Balog. Building simulated queries for known-item topics: An analysis using six european languages. In *Proc. 30th ACM SIGIR*, pages 455–462, 2007.

[11] L. Azzopardi, M. de Rijke, and K. Balog. Building simulated queries for known-item topics: an analysis using six european languages. In *Proceedings of the 30th annual international ACM SIGIR conference*, pages 455–462, 2007.

[12] L. Azzopardi, K. Järvelin, J. Kamps, and M. Smucker. Report on the sigir 2010 workshop on the simulation of interaction. *SIGIR Forum*, 44(2):35–47, 2011.

[13] L. Azzopardi, D. Kelly, and K. Brennan. How query cost affects search behavior. In *Proceedings of 36th ACM SIGIR Conference*, pages 23–32, 2013.

[14] L. Azzopardi and V. Vinay. Accessibility in information retrieval. In *Proceedings of the 30th European Conference on Advances in Information Retrieval*, pages 482–489, 2008.

[15] L. Azzopardi and V. Vinay. Retrievability: An evaluation measure for higher order information access tasks. In *Proc. of the 17th ACM CIKM Conference*, pages 561–570, 2008.

[16] L. Azzopardi and G. Zuccon. An analysis of theories of search and search behavior. In *Proceedings of the 2015 International Conference on The Theory of Information Retrieval*, ICTIR '15, pages 81–90, New York, NY, USA, 2015. ACM.

[17] L. Azzopardi and G. Zuccon. Building and using models of information seeking, search and retrieval: Full day tutorial. In *Proceedings of the 38th International ACM SIGIR Conference on Research and Development in Information Retrieval*, SIGIR '15, pages 1107–1110, 2015.

[18] K. Balog, L. Azzopardi, and M. de Rijke. Formal models for expert finding in enterprise corpora. In *Proceedings of the 29th Annual International ACM SIGIR Conference on Research and Development in Information Retrieval*, SIGIR '06, pages 43–50, 2006.

[19] F. Baskaya, H. Keskustalo, and K. Järvelin. Simulating simple and fallible relevance feedback. In *Advances in Information Retrieval*, pages 593–604. Springer Berlin Heidelberg, 2011.

[20] F. Baskaya, H. Keskustalo, and K. Järvelin. Time drives interaction: Simulating sessions in diverse searching environments. In *Proc. 35th ACM SIGIR*, pages 105–114, 2012.

[21] F. Baskaya, H. Keskustalo, and K. Järvelin. Modeling behavioral factors in interactive information retrieval. In *Proc. 22nd ACM CIKM*, pages 2297–2302, 2013.

[22] P. Borlund. The iir evaluation model: a framework for evaluation of iir systems. *Info. research*, 8(3), 2003.

[23] B. Carterette, A. Bah, and M. Zengin. Dynamic test collections for retrieval evaluation. In *Proc. 5th ACM ICTIR*, pages 91–100, 2015.

[24] B. Carterette, E. Kanoulas, and E. Yilmaz. Simulating simple user behavior for system effectiveness evaluation. In *Proc. 20th ACM CIKM*, pages 611–620, 2011.

[25] C. Clarke, L. Freund, M. Smucker, and E. Yilmaz. Report on the sigir 2013 mube workshop. *SIGIR Forum*, 47(2):84–95, 2013.

[26] R. T. Fernández, D. E. Losada, and L. A. Azzopardi. Extending the language modeling framework for sentence retrieval to include local context. *Information Retrieval*, 14(4):355–389, 2011.

[27] D. Harman. Relevance feedback revisited. In *Proc. 15th ACM SIGIR Conference*, pages 1–10, 1992.

[28] K. Järvelin. Interactive relevance feedback with graded relevance and sentence extraction: Simulated user experiments. In *Proc. 18th ACM CIKM Conference*, pages 2053–2056, 2009.

[29] C. Jordan, C. Watters, and Q. Gao. Using controlled query generation to evaluate blind relevance feedback algorithms. In *Proc. 6th ACM/IEEE-CS JCDL*, pages 286–295, 2006.

[30] D. Kelly and L. Azzopardi. How many results per page?: A study of serp size, search behavior and user experience. In *Proceedings of the 38th International ACM SIGIR Conference*, pages 183–192, 2015.

[31] H. Keskustalo and K. Järvelin. Simulations as a means to address some limitations of laboratory-based ir evaluation. *The Janus Faced Scholar: A Festschrift in Honour of Peter Ingwersen, Informationsvidenskabelige Akademi, Copenhagen*, pages 69–86, 2010.

[32] H. Keskustalo, K. Järvelin, and A. Pirkola. The effects of relevance feedback quality and quantity in interactive relevance feedback: A simulation based on user modeling. In *Advances in IR*, volume 3936 of *LNCS*, pages 191–204. 2006.

[33] H. Keskustalo, K. Järvelin, and A. Pirkola. Evaluating the effectiveness of relevance feedback based on a user simulation model: Effects of a user scenario on cumulated gain value. *Information Retrieval*, 11(3):209–228, 2008.

[34] A. Leuski. Relevance and reinforcement in interactive browsing. In *Proc. 9th ACM CIKM*, pages 119–126, 2000.

[35] J. Lin and M. D. Smucker. How do users find things with pubmed?: towards automatic utility evaluation with user simulations. In *SIGIR'08 Proceedings of the 31st annual international ACM SIGIR conference*, pages 19–26, 2008.

[36] D. Maxwell and L. Azzopardi. Simulating interactive information retrieval with simiir: A framework for the simulation of interaction. In *Proceedings of the 39th annual international ACM SIGIR conference*, 2016.

[37] D. Maxwell, L. Azzopardi, K. Järvelin, and H. Keskustalo. An initial investigation into fixed and adaptive stopping strategies. In *Proc. 38th ACM SIGIR*, pages 903–906, 2015.

[38] D. Maxwell, L. Azzopardi, K. Järvelin, and H. Keskustalo. Searching and stopping: An analysis of stopping rules and strategies. In *Proc. 24th ACM CIKM*, pages 313–322, 2015.

[39] A. Moffat, P. Thomas, and F. Scholer. Users versus models: What observation tells us about effectiveness metrics. In *Proc. 22nd ACM CIKM*, pages 659–668, 2013.

[40] T. Pääkkönen, K. Järvelin, J. Kekäläinen, H. Keskustalo, F. Baskaya, D. Maxwell, and L. Azzopardi. Exploring behavioral dimensions in session effectiveness. In *Proc. 6th CLEF*, pages 178–189, 2015.

[41] I. Ruthven. Re-examining the potential effectiveness of interactive query expansion. In *Proc. 26th ACM SIGIR Conference*, pages 213–220, 2003.

[42] M. Smucker. An analysis of user strategies for examining and processing ranked lists of documents. In *Proc. of 5th HCIR*, 2011.

[43] M. D. Smucker and C. L. Clarke. Modeling optimal switching behavior. In *Proceedings of the 2016 ACM on Conference on Human Information Interaction and Retrieval*, pages 317–320. ACM, 2016.

[44] J. Tague, M. Nelson, and H. Wu. Problems in the simulation of bibliographic retrieval systems. In *Proc. 3rd ACM SIGIR*, pages 236–255, 1980.

[45] P. Thomas, A. Moffat, P. Bailey, and F. Scholer. Modeling decision points in user search behavior. In *Proc. 5th IIiX*, pages 239–242, 2014.

[46] S. Verberne, M. Sappelli, K. Järvelin, and W. Kraaij. User simulations for interactive search: Evaluating personalized query suggestion. In *Advances in Information Retrieval*, volume 9022 of *LNCS*. 2015.

[47] E. Voorhees and D. Harman. *TREC: Experiment and Evaluation in Information Retrieval*. The MIT press, 2005.

[48] R. White, J. Jose, C. van Rijsbergen, and I. Ruthven. A simulated study of implicit feedback models. In *Advances in Information Retrieval*, volume 2997 of *LNCS*, pages 311–326. 2004.

Succinct Data Structures in Information Retrieval: Theory and Practice

Simon Gog
Institute of Theoretical Informatics, Karlsruhe Institute of Technology
Am Fasanengarten 5
76131 Karlsruhe, Germany
gog@kit.edu

Rossano Venturini
Department of Computer Science,University of Pisa
Largo Bruno Pontecorvo 3
I-56127 Pisa, Italy
rossano.venturini@unipi.it

ABSTRACT

Succinct data structures are used today in many information retrieval applications, e.g., posting lists representation, language model representation, indexing (social) graphs, query auto-completion, document retrieval and indexing dictionary of strings, just to mention the most recent ones. These new kind of data structures mimic the operations of their classical counterparts within a comparable time complexity but require much less space. With the availability of several libraries for basic succinct structures – like SDSL, Succinct, Facebook's Folly, and Sux – it is relatively easy to directly profit from advances in this field.

In this tutorial we will introduce this field of research by presenting the most important succinct data structures to represent set of integers, set of points, trees, graphs and strings together with their most important applications to Information Retrieval problems. The introduction of the succinct data structures will be sustained with a practical session with programming handouts to solve. This will allow the attendees to directly experiment with implementations of these solutions on real datasets and understand the potential benefits they can bring on their own projects.

1. MOTIVATION

The current growth and availability of massive amounts of data gathered and processed by applications – Web search engines, textual and biological databases, just to cite a few – has changed the algorithmic requirements of basic processing and mining tools and provide ample motivation for a great deal of new theoretical and practical research on algorithms and data structures.

Not surprisingly, the last decades have seen a massive research in the field of the so-called succinct and compressed data structures. These new kind of data structures mimic the operations of their classical counterparts within a comparable time complexity but requiring much less space. These solutions usually resort to a careful combination of ideas born both in algorithmic and data compression fields. As a concrete example consider trees which are probably among the most used data structure in practice. Everybody is familiar with the classical way to represent the structure of a tree in memory: each node is connected to its children by means of pointers. This representation immediately allows simple navigational operations on the tree. One can also augment the structure with auxiliary information in order to answer queries such as: Who is the parent of a given node? How many nodes are in a given subtree? Who is the lowest common ancestor of a given pair of nodes? and so on. The main drawback of this solution is its space occupancy which can be very optimistically estimated in 32 bits per node. Not surprisingly the problem of repesenting trees space efficiently has been one of the first problems to be addressed. The current best succinct tree representation requires *provably* no more than 2 bits per node and is able to answer in constant time a large set of queries [9]. The practical consequence of the use of this succinct data structure is immediate: applications can store in main memory trees whose sizes would be prohibitive with the classical representation.

These efficient tree representations are just an example of succinct data structures and, even if the research field is relatively new, a large fraction of classical data structures have their succinct counterpart [1, 2, 6, 10, 14, 25, 31]. Most of these results are of practical interest and several implementations exist, for example we mention SDSL[1], Succinct[2], Facebook's Folly[3], and Sux[4].

Several authors are successfully applying the ideas at the basis of the succinct data structures to solve problems in other fields of research. Information retrieval community profits a lot from these data structures as there exist several applications in which they play a central role, e.g., posting lists representation [22, 28, 29, 35], language model representation [34], indexing (social) graphs [8], query auto-completion [21], document retrieval [15, 16, 19, 26, 30] and indexing dictionary of strings [11, 18, 36], just to mention the most recent ones.

The tutorial will introduce this field of research by presenting the most important succinct data structures to represent set of integers, set of points, trees, graphs and strings together with their most important applications to Informa-

SIGIR '16, July 17-21, 2016, Pisa, Italy

DOI: http://dx.doi.org/10.1145/2911451.2914802

[1]https://github.com/simongog/sdsl-lite
[2]https://github.com/ot/succinct
[3]https://github.com/facebook/folly
[4]http://sux.di.unimi.it

tion Retrieval problems. The introduction of the succinct data structures will be sustained with a practical session with programming handouts to solve. This will allow the attendees to directly experiment with implementations of these solutions on real datasets and understand the potential benefits they can bring on their own projects.

2. OBJECTIVES AND RELEVANCE TO THE IR COMMUNITY

Indexing is the key to efficient query processing in the vast majority of IR applications. The use of inverted indexes in web search engines is probably one of the most prominent examples in Information Retrieval.

While index compression is a relatively old and established method in IR and covered by all relevant text books the new data structures which combine compression and efficient execution of operations – like random access – are a relatively new field of which many IR researchers are not yet aware of. However, this field of research is highly relevant for IR as, for example, we have already seen that techniques from the succinct data structure field are able to improve inverted indexes systematically [29, 35]. Succinct data structures often *extend the functionality* of traditional structures or reduce query time. For example, while inverted indexes are restricted in handling phrase queries, new document retrieval frameworks based on succinct structures allow to efficiently answer top-k queries for phrases of arbitrary length [19], and it is also possible to determine the document frequency of any phrase in constant time by just spending at most 2 bits per element in the collection [32]. Unfortunately, succinct structures per se are not easy to implement from scratch and especially the implementation of the latter two results is very complex. However, as more and more implementations of basic succinct structures become available via libraries, it is possible to combine these pieces to obtain more advanced solutions. While other fields like Bioinformatics already actively profit from using succinct structures after engineering the theoretical proposals to their applications, e.g., the FM-Index is used in DNA read mapping, the IR community does not yet fully exploit the new possibilities of succinct structures. With this tutorial we do not only inform the audience about succinct data structures but also point out engineering challenges and encourage the participants to use the potential of these solutions in IR. Therefore the objectives of this tutorials are (1) to introduce the audience to the world of succinct data structures, (2) to teach the basic techniques of succinct structures, (3) to present the practical impact of the structures to selected applications in IR, and (4) to show the participants how they can implement their own succinct structures on top of existing basic structures provided by the succinct data structure library.

3. DETAILED SCHEDULE

The tutorial is subdivided in two parts. The goal of the first part is to describe the most important succinct data structures. We will present the theoretical achievements in this field of research by focusing our attention to the ones that have demonstrated their relevance in practice. The introduction of each of these solutions will be sustained by presenting a selection of Information Retrieval problems in which they have an immediate application.

The goal of the second part is to present ready-to-use implementations of these data structures. This is done by introducing the Succinct Data Structure Library (SDSL).This library covers all the data structures presented in the previous part and has one of the presenters as its creator and one of its main developers. The speakers will also prepare a set of programming handouts which will allow the attendees to experiment with the learned concepts. The ultimate objective of the tutorial is to demonstrate to the attendees the potential benefit that succinct data structures can bring in their applications at a tiny implementation cost.

Schedule of the tutorial.

- **Part I**
  - Introduction to succinct data structures;
  - Basic operations on binary vectors [25, 31];
  - Elias-Fano representation [4, 5, 8, 27, 28, 29, 35];
  - Succinct representations of trees and range minimum/maximum queries [3, 9, 12, 33];
  - Wavelet trees [2, 13, 17, 24];
  - Compressed Full-Text indexes [7, 25];
  - Structures for IR [8, 11, 14, 20, 21, 23].
- **Part II**
  - Overview about SDSL components and concepts;
  - Detailed presentation of components via small code examples;
  - Exploration of practical performance of structures;
  - Presentation of benchmarking facilities;
  - Programming handouts.

4. ACKNOWLEDGEMENT

This tutorial was partially supported by the EU H2020 Program under the scheme *INFRAIA-1-2014-2015: Research Infrastructures* grant agreement #654024 *SoBigData: Social Mining & Big Data Ecosystem.*

References

[1] J. Barbay. Succinct and compressed data structures for permutations and integer functions. In *Encyclopedia of Algorithms*. 2015.

[2] J. Barbay and J. I. Munro. Succinct encoding of permutations: Applications to text indexing. In *Encyclopedia of Algorithms*. 2008.

[3] D. Benoit, E. Demaine, J. I. Munro, R. Raman, V.Raman, and S. S. Rao. Representing trees of higher degree. *Algorithmica*, 43(4):275–292, 2005.

[4] P. Elias. Efficient storage and retrieval by content and address of static files. *Journal of the ACM*, 21:246–260, 1974.

[5] R. M. Fano. On the number of bits required to implement anassociative memory. *Memorandum 61, Computer Structures Group, Project MAC*, 1971.

[6] P. Ferragina, R. González, G. Navarro, and R. Venturini. Compressed text indexes: From theory to practice. *ACM Journal of Experimental Algorithmics*, 13, 2008.

[7] P. Ferragina and G. Manzini. Indexing compressed text. *Journal of the ACM*, 52(4):552–581, 2005.

[8] P. Ferragina, F. Piccinno, and R. Venturini. Compressed indexes for string-searching in labeled graphs. In *Proceedings of the 24th International Conference on World Wide Web (WWW)*, pages –, 2015.

[9] P. Ferragina and S. S. Rao. Tree compression and indexing. In *Encyclopedia of Algorithms*. 2008.

[10] P. Ferragina and R. Venturini. Indexing compressed text. In *Encyclopedia of Database Systems*, pages 1442–1448. 2009.

[11] P. Ferragina and R. Venturini. The compressed permuterm index. *ACM Transactions on Algorithms*, 7(1):10, 2010.

[12] J. Fischer and V. Heun. Space-efficient preprocessing schemes for range minimum queries on static arrays. *SIAM Journal on Computing*, 40(2):465–492, 2011.

[13] L. Foschini, R. Grossi, A. Gupta, and J. S. Vitter. When indexing equals compression: Experiments with compressing suffix arrays and applications. *ACM Transactions on Algorithms*, 2(4):611–639, 2006.

[14] S. Gog, T. Beller, A. Moffat, and M. Petri. From theory to practice: Plug and play with succinct data structures. In *Proceedings of the 13th International Symposium Experimental Algorithms (SEA)*, pages 326–337, 2014.

[15] S. Gog and G. Navarro. Improved single-term top-k document retrieval. In *Proceedings of the Seventeenth Workshop on Algorithm Engineering and Experiments, ALENEX*, pages 24–32, 2015.

[16] S. Gog and M. Petri. Compact indexes for flexible top-k retrieval. In *Combinatorial Pattern Matching - 26th Annual Symposium, CPM*, pages 207–218, 2015.

[17] R. Grossi, A. Gupta, and J. S. Vitter. High-order entropy-compressed text indexes. In *Proceedings of the Fourteenth Annual ACM-SIAM Symposium on Discrete Algorithms (SODA)*, pages 841–850, 2003.

[18] R. Grossi and G. Ottaviano. Fast compressed tries through path decompositions. *ACM Journal of Experimental Algorithmics*, 19(1), 2014.

[19] W. Hon, R. Shah, and J. S. Vitter. Space-efficient framework for top-k string retrieval problems. In *50th Annual IEEE Symposium on Foundations of Computer Science, FOCS*, pages 713–722, 2009.

[20] W. Hon, R. Shah, and J. S. Vitter. Space-efficient framework for top-k string retrieval problems. In *Proceedings of the 50th Annual IEEE Symposium on Foundations of Computer Science (FOCS)*, pages 713–722, 2009.

[21] B. P. Hsu and G. Ottaviano. Space-efficient data structures for top-k completion. In *Proceedings of the 22nd International World Wide Web Conference (WWW)*, pages 583–594, 2013.

[22] R. Konow, G. Navarro, C. L. A. Clarke, and A. López-Ortiz. Faster and smaller inverted indices with treaps. In *Proceedings of the 36th Annual International ACM SIGIR Conference on Research and Development in Information Retrieval (SIGIR)*, pages 193–202, 2013.

[23] G. Navarro. Spaces, trees and colors: The algorithmic landscape of document retrieval on sequences. *ACM Computing Surveys*, 46(4):article 52, 2014. 47 pages.

[24] G. Navarro. Wavelet trees for all. *Journal Discrete Algorithms*, 25:2–20, 2014.

[25] G. Navarro and V. Mäkinen. Compressed full text indexes. *ACM Computing Surveys*, 39(1), 2007.

[26] G. Navarro and Y. Nekrich. Top-k document retrieval in optimal time and linear space. In *Proceedings of the Twenty-Third Annual ACM-SIAM Symposium on Discrete Algorithms, SODA*, pages 1066–1077, 2012.

[27] D. Okanohara and K. Sadakane. Practical entropy-compressed rank/select dictionary. In *Proceedings of the Nine Workshop on Algorithm Engineering and Experiments, ALENEX*, 2007.

[28] G. Ottaviano, N. Tonellotto, and R. Venturini. Optimal space-time tradeoffs for inverted indexes. In *Proceedings of the 8th Annual International ACM Conference on Web Search and Data Mining (WSDM)*, pages –, 2015.

[29] G. Ottaviano and R. Venturini. Partitioned elias-fano indexes. In *Proceedings of the 37th Annual International ACM SIGIR Conference on Research and Development in Information Retrieval (SIGIR)*, pages 273–282, 2014.

[30] M. Patil, S. V. Thankachan, R. Shah, W. Hon, J. S. Vitter, and S. Chandrasekaran. Inverted indexes for phrases and strings. In *Proceeding of the 34th International ACM SIGIR Conference on Research and Development in Information Retrieval, SIGIR*, pages 555–564, 2011.

[31] N. Rahman and R. Raman. Rank and select operations on binary strings. In *Encyclopedia of Algorithms*. 2008.

[32] K. Sadakane. Succinct data structures for flexible text retrieval systems. *J. Discrete Algorithms*, 5(1):12–22, 2007.

[33] K. Sadakane and G. Navarro. Fully-functional succinct trees. In *Proceedings of the 21st Annual ACM-SIAM Symposium on Discrete Algorithms (SODA)*, pages 134–149, 2010.

[34] E. Shareghi, M. Petri, G. Haffari, and T. Cohn. Compact, efficient and unlimited capacity: Language modeling with compressed suffix trees. In *Proceedings of the 2015 Conference on Empirical Methods in Natural Language Processing, EMNLP*, pages 2409–2418, 2015.

[35] S. Vigna. Quasi-succinct indices. In *Proceedings of the Sixth ACM International Conference on Web Search and Data Mining (WSDM)*, pages 83–92, 2013.

[36] S. Yata. Marisa trie, https://code.google.com/archive/p/marisa-trie/. 2011.

Temporal Information Retrieval

Nattiya Kanhabua
Department of Computer Science
Aalborg University, Denmark
nattiya@cs.aau.dk

Avishek Anand
L3S Research Center
Leibniz Universität Hannover, Germany
anand@L3S.de

ABSTRACT

The study of temporal dynamics and its impact can be framed within the so-called *temporal IR approaches*, which explain how user behavior, document content and scale vary with time, and how we can use them in our favor in order to improve retrieval effectiveness.

This half-day tutorial will outline research issues with respect to temporal dynamics, and provide a comprehensive overview of temporal IR approaches, essentially regarding processing dynamic content, temporal information extraction, temporal query analysis, and time-aware retrieval and ranking. The tutorial is structured into two sessions. During the first session, we will explain the general and wide aspects associated to temporal dynamics by focusing on the web domain, from content and structural changes to variations of user behavior and interactions. We will begin with temporal indexing and query processing. Next step, we will explain current approaches to time-aware retrieval and ranking, which can be classified into different types based on two main notions of relevance with respect to time, namely, recency-based ranking, and time-dependent ranking.

In the latter session, we will describe research issues centered on determining the temporal intent of queries, and time-aware query enhancement, e.g., temporal relevance feedback, and time-aware query reformulation. In addition, we present applications in related research areas, e.g., exploration, summarization, and clustering of search results, as well as future event retrieval and prediction. To this end, we conclude our tutorial and outline future directions.

This tutorial targets graduate students, researchers and practitioners in the field of information retrieval. The goal is to provide an overview as well as an important context that enables further research on and practical applications within this area.

1. INTRODUCTION

The time dimension has strong influence in many domains, e.g., Topic Detection and Tracking (TDT) [1], and Emerging Trend Detection (ETD) [12]. In our context, we focus on the impact of time on search processes seen by the evolution of the Web [30] that can be categorized with respect to its changes of 1) content and structure, and 2) user querying behavior. The content of the Web changes constantly over time, e.g., documents are added, modified or deleted continuously. Similarly, the link structure of the Web also evolves [16]. Content and structure changes affect basic processes like crawling and indexing, but also the computation of graph-based authority measures that typically are used for document ranking.

Another web evolution aspect is the change of user querying behavior, which can be observable at least in two ways. First, search traffic for particular queries varies over time and presents certain temporal patterns, such as, spikes, periodicity (e.g., weekly or monthly), seasonality and trends [32]. Second, many queries are time-sensitive, which contain underlying temporal information needs that do not exhibit a temporal pattern in search streams [38]. Understanding temporal search intent is a challenging task before applying an appropriate time-aware ranking method.

Temporal IR has received a large share of attention in the last decade. For example, there are at least two main research challenges related to temporal IR that have been organized recently: the TREC Temporal Summarization Track and Temporalia (Temporal Information Access) [24]. In this tutorial, we will give a comprehensive overview of the important aspects of temporal information retrieval, which intends to support participants with basic knowledge who want to get acquainted with the research area, and for more advanced researchers aiming to understand in more detail this field of research. This tutorial complements previous work, such as, an overview of challenges and opportunities in temporal IR [3], a tutorial [41], and a recent survey [14] as follows:

- We categorize temporal IR research challenges into three main topics, i.e., temporal indexing and query processing, temporal query analysis, and time-aware ranking;
- We provide a review of most recent state-of-the-art and best practices in the topics related to the research challenges;
- We present a number of interesting application areas in order to open new horizons for research and innovations;
- We provide detailed description of the approaches in order to make it suitable as a teaching material.

2. TOPIC

This section outlines the topics that our tutorial will cover.

SIGIR '16, July 17 - 21, 2016, Pisa, Italy

ISBN 978-1-4503-4069-4/16/07... $15.00
DOI: http://dx.doi.org/10.1145/2911451.2914805

2.1 Temporal Indexing and Query Processing

Evolving web content has an impact on several components of a search engine. In this section, we revisit three main building blocks of the search system, namely *crawling*, *indexing*, and *query processing*.

We will explain how to index versioned archives, which requires even more complex indexing and maintenance procedures. Several works have been proposed in the area of versioned indexing and query processing [7, 10, 13, 21, 37, 53]. Two general approaches to text indexing, which have been employed, are either based on index compression (by exploiting the redundancy between consecutive versions) [20, 21, 22], or based on index partitioning for faster temporal selections [5, 6, 7, 10]. We will present recent works on indexing, query processing and index maintenance efforts towards supporting temporally qualified queries, i.e., [5, 6, 7, 10], in more detail.

2.2 Temporal Query Analysis

Understanding search intent behind a user's query is the first step before applying a suitable retrieval and ranking model. In the temporal search realm, a system should be able to identify a query that contains an underlying temporal information need, so-called a *temporal query* [24]. We categorize temporal queries into two main classes. The first class of temporal queries can be observed through *temporal patterns* of user search behavior in query logs, whereas the second class of temporal queries may not exhibit such temporal patterns in a query stream, but can be referred to specific time or a particular event.

In this tutorial, we will explain current approaches to understanding temporal query intent [32], as well as methods for detecting and predicting time-sensitive queries, such as, spiky, periodic or seasonal queries [43, 45]. In addition, we will explain how to determine the underlying temporal information needs for a given temporal query by analyzing temporal document collections [25, 29, 54].

We will address the problem of *multi-faceted temporal queries* and its impact on result diversification [36, 46, 51, 56]. Finally, we will describe query enhancement techniques applied to temporal queries, which include *time-based pseudo-relevance feedback* [31, 40], and time-aware query reformulation [18, 26, 49].

2.3 Time-aware Ranking

Existing works on time-aware ranking can be classified into different types based on two main notions of relevance with respect to time: 1) recency-based ranking [16, 17, 19, 33], and 2) time-dependent ranking [11, 29]. Recency-based ranking methods promote documents that are recently created or updated. The preference of freshness is quite common in a general web search, where a user looks for recent information, e.g., about breaking news. On the other hand, time-dependent ranking methods takes into account the relevant time periods underlying a given temporal query, which this type of ranking explicitly adjusts the score of a document with respect to the time of queries, for example, by assuming that documents with creation dates close to the query's time are more relevant and thus must be ranked higher.

In addition to the aforementioned classification of time-aware methods, we also outline existing works that explicitly model entities and events into retrieval and ranking processes [9, 27, 44]. Note that, entity and event-based retrieval returns events instead of documents, whereas time-aware ranking methods use a very simple notion of events.

2.4 Applications of Temporal IR

Some applications have taken time-based exploration of textual archives beyond just searching over time, e.g., Time Explorer [34], and time-aware exploration search [39]. Filtering and displaying information might benefit from presenting time information conveniently in some domains, for instance, generating a timeline summary for a specific news story [35, 52, 55] and for a given entity [50]. Arguably, the most widespread summarization technology is the (query) focused summaries produced by search engines, or search results snippets using temporal expressions, which include the most frequent units of time appearing in search result pages [2, 15, 48]. There exists another form of temporal summary in terms of landmark documents, authors, and topics [47].

A series of temporal applications are the ones based on *prediction of events*, e.g., [8, 23, 27]. The most challenging task is the actual *forecast* of forthcoming events. A method to turn a standard IR engine into a future event predicting machine is proposed in [4], whereas an approach to forecasting real-life events by extracting information from a corpus comprised of 22 years of news stories is presented in [42].

3. DETAILED SCHEDULE

A tentative schedule, which is aimed to meet a high-quality presentation within the chosen time period, is as follows.

- 9:00 - 10:30 Part I (**1.5 hour**)
  - Introduction to Temporal IR (*20 minutes*)
  - Temporal Indexing and Query Processing (*35 minutes*)
  - Time-aware Retrieval and Ranking (*35 minutes*)
- 10:30 - 11:00 Coffee break
- 11:00 - 12:30 Part II (**1.5 hour**)
  - Temporal Query Analysis (*40 minutes*)
  - Applications of Temporal IR (*40 minutes*)
  - Conclusions and Future Directions (*10 minutes*)

4. INTENDED AUDIENCE AND MATERIAL

This tutorial targets graduate students, junior researchers and practitioners in the field of information retrieval. Our prospective participants should have a basic knowledge of search processes, essentially regarding web crawling, document indexing, query analysis, and retrieval and ranking. A prerequisite skill about other research areas, e.g., natural language processing, is required but not mandatory. The participants can download slides and a survey on temporal information retrieval [28] from the authors' homepages.

5. BIOGRAPHY

Nattiya Kanhabua is an assistant professor at the Department of Computer Science, Aalborg University, Denmark. Her research interests are information retrieval, data mining, machine learning, and spatial and temporal analytics. She did her PhD at the Department of Computer and

Information Science, Norwegian University of Science and Technology (NTNU). She was a postdoctoral researcher at the L3S Research Center Hannover, Germany. At L3S, she worked in several research projects, e.g., 1) EU Project ForgetIT: Concise Preservation by Combining Managed Forgetting and Contextualized Remembering, 2) ALEXANDRIA, an ERC Advanced Grant Project on Foundations for Temporal Retrieval, Exploration and Analytics in Web Archives, and 3) Medical Ecosystem: Personalized Event-based Surveillance. She has published her research work in top-tier conferences, e.g., SIGIR, WSDM, CIKM, JCDL and ECIR.

Avishek Anand is a postdoctoral researcher at the L3S Research Center in Hannover, Germany. His research interests lay in the intersection of retrieval, mining, and data management aspects of temporal Web collections like Web archives, Wikipedia and news collections. He did his PhD at the Department of Databases and Information Systems, Max Planck Institute for Informatics, Saarbruecken, Germany, where he worked on indexing and query processing approaches for supporting temporal text workloads. Currently, he is working on retrieval models for historical intents, tag-based search over Archives and mining methods for enriching Wikipedia using news collections. He has published his research in several top-tier conferences, such as, SIGIR, WSDM, CIKM, ICDE and EDBT.

6. REFERENCES

[1] J. Allan, R. Papka, and V. Lavrenko. On-line new event detection and tracking. In *Proceedings of the 21st Annual International ACM SIGIR Conference on Research and Development in Information Retrieval*, SIGIR '98, pages 37–45, 1998.

[2] O. Alonso, M. Gertz, and R. A. Baeza-Yates. Clustering and exploring search results using timeline constructions. In *Proceedings of the 18th ACM conference on Information and knowledge management*, CIKM '09, pages 97–106, 2009.

[3] O. Alonso, J. Strötgen, R. A. Baeza-Yates, and M. Gertz. Temporal information retrieval: Challenges and opportunities. In *Proceedings of the 1st International Temporal Web Analytics Workshop (TWAW 2011)*, 2011.

[4] G. Amodeo, R. Blanco, and U. Brefeld. Hybrid models for future event prediction. In *Proceedings of the 20th ACM International Conference on Information and Knowledge Management*, CIKM '11, pages 1981–1984, 2011.

[5] A. Anand, S. Bedathur, K. Berberich, and R. Schenkel. Efficient temporal keyword search over versioned text. In *Proceedings of the 19th ACM International Conference on Information and Knowledge Management*, CIKM '10, pages 699–708, 2010.

[6] A. Anand, S. Bedathur, K. Berberich, and R. Schenkel. Temporal index sharding for space-time efficiency in archive search. In *Proceedings of the 34th International ACM SIGIR Conference on Research and Development in Information Retrieval*, SIGIR '11, pages 545–554, 2011.

[7] A. Anand, S. Bedathur, K. Berberich, and R. Schenkel. Index maintenance for time-travel text search. In *Proceedings of the 35th International ACM SIGIR Conference on Research and Development in Information Retrieval*, SIGIR '12, pages 235–244, New York, NY, USA, 2012. ACM.

[8] C.-m. Au Yeung and A. Jatowt. Studying How the Past is Remembered: Towards computational history through large scale text mining. In *Proceedings of the 20th ACM International Conference on Information and Knowledge Management*, CIKM '11, pages 1231–1240, 2011.

[9] R. A. Baeza-Yates. Searching the future. In *Proceedings of SIGIR workshop on mathematical/formal methods in information retrieval MF/IR*, SIGIR '05, 2005.

[10] K. Berberich, S. Bedathur, T. Neumann, and G. Weikum. A time machine for text search. In *Proceedings of the 30th annual international ACM SIGIR conference on Research and development in information retrieval*, SIGIR '07, pages 519–526, 2007.

[11] K. Berberich, S. J. Bedathur, O. Alonso, and G. Weikum. A language modeling approach for temporal information needs. In *Proceedings of the 32nd European Conference on IR Research on Advances in Information Retrieval*, ECIR '10, pages 13–25, 2010.

[12] M. Berry. *Survey of Text Mining: Clustering, Classification, and Retrieval.* Springer, Sep. 2003.

[13] A. Z. Broder, N. Eiron, M. Fontoura, M. Herscovici, R. Lempel, J. McPherson, R. Qi, and E. J. Shekita. Indexing shared content in information retrieval systems. In *Proceedings of the 10th International Conference on Extending Database Technology*, EDBT '06, pages 313–330, 2006.

[14] R. Campos, G. Dias, A. M. Jorge, and A. Jatowt. Survey of temporal information retrieval and related applications. *ACM Comput. Surv.*, 47(2):15:1–15:41, Aug. 2014.

[15] R. Campos, A. M. Jorge, G. Dias, and C. Nunes. Disambiguating implicit temporal queries by clustering top relevant dates in web snippets. In *Proceedings of the The 2012 IEEE/WIC/ACM International Joint Conferences on Web Intelligence and Intelligent Agent Technology - Volume 01*, WI-IAT '12, pages 1–8, 2012.

[16] N. Dai and B. D. Davison. Freshness matters: in flowers, food, and web authority. In *Proceedings of the 33rd international ACM SIGIR conference on Research and development in information retrieval*, SIGIR '10, pages 114–121, 2010.

[17] A. Dong, Y. Chang, Z. Zheng, G. Mishne, J. Bai, R. Zhang, K. Buchner, C. Liao, and F. Diaz. Towards recency ranking in web search. In *Proceedings of the third ACM international conference on Web search and data mining*, WSDM '10, pages 11–20, 2010.

[18] M. Efron. Query representation for cross-temporal information retrieval. In *Proceedings of the 36th International ACM SIGIR Conference on Research and Development in Information Retrieval*, SIGIR '13, pages 383–392, 2013.

[19] J. L. Elsas and S. T. Dumais. Leveraging temporal dynamics of document content in relevance ranking. In *Proceedings of the third ACM international conference on Web search and data mining*, WSDM '10, pages 1–10, 2010.

[20] J. He and T. Suel. Faster temporal range queries over versioned text. In *Proceeding of the 34th International ACM SIGIR Conference on Research and Development in Information Retrieval*, SIGIR '11, pages 565–574, 2011.

[21] J. He, H. Yan, and T. Suel. Compact full-text indexing of versioned document collections. In *Proceedings of the 18th ACM Conference on Information and Knowledge Management*, CIKM '09, pages 415–424, 2009.

[22] J. He, J. Zeng, and T. Suel. Improved index compression techniques for versioned document collections. In *Proceedings of the 19th ACM Conference on Information and Knowledge Management*, CIKM '10, pages 1239–1248, 2010.

[23] A. Jatowt, É. Antoine, Y. Kawai, and T. Akiyama. Mapping temporal horizons: Analysis of collective future and past related attention in twitter. In *Proceedings of the 24th International Conference on World Wide Web*, WWW '15, pages 484–494, 2015.

[24] H. Joho, A. Jatowt, and B. Roi. A survey of temporal web search experience. In *Proceedings of the 22nd International Conference on World Wide Web (Companion)*, WWW '13, pages 1101–1108, 2013.

[25] R. Jones and F. Diaz. Temporal profiles of queries. *ACM Trans. Inf. Syst.*, 25, July 2007.

[26] A. C. Kaluarachchi, A. S. Varde, S. Bedathur, G. Weikum, J. Peng, and A. Feldman. Incorporating terminology evolution for query translation in text retrieval with association rules. In *Proceedings of the 19th ACM*

international conference on Information and knowledge management, CIKM '10, pages 1789–1792, 2010.

[27] N. Kanhabua, R. Blanco, and M. Matthews. Ranking related news predictions. In *Proceedings of the 34th international ACM SIGIR conference on Research and development in Information Retrieval*, SIGIR '11, pages 755–764, 2011.

[28] N. Kanhabua, R. Blanco, and K. Nørvåg. Temporal information retrieval. *Foundations and Trends in Information Retrieval*, 9(2):91–208, 2015.

[29] N. Kanhabua and K. Nørvåg. Determining time of queries for re-ranking search results. In *Proceedings of the 14th European conference on Research and advanced technology for digital libraries*, ECDL'10, pages 261–272, 2010.

[30] Y. Ke, L. Deng, W. Ng, and D.-L. Lee. Web dynamics and their ramifications for the development of web search engines. *Computer Networks*, 50(10):1430–1447, July 2006.

[31] M. Keikha, S. Gerani, and F. Crestani. TEMPER: A temporal relevance feedback method. In *Proceedings of the 33rd European Conference on IR Research on Advances in Information Retrieval*, ECIR '11, pages 436–447, 2011.

[32] A. Kulkarni, J. Teevan, K. M. Svore, and S. T. Dumais. Understanding temporal query dynamics. In *Proceedings of the Forth International Conference on Web Search and Web Data Mining*, WSDM '11, pages 167–176, 2011.

[33] X. Li and W. B. Croft. Time-based language mmdels. In *Proceedings of the 12th international conference on Information and knowledge management*, CIKM '03, pages 469–475, 2003.

[34] M. Matthews, P. Tolchinsky, R. Blanco, J. Atserias, P. Mika, and H. Zaragoza. Searching through time in the new york times. In *HCIR Workshop on Bridging Human-Computer Interaction and Information Retrieval*, HCIR '10, 2010.

[35] R. McCreadie, C. Macdonald, and I. Ounis. Incremental update summarization: Adaptive sentence selection based on prevalence and novelty. In *Proceedings of the 23rd ACM International Conference on Conference on Information and Knowledge Management*, CIKM '14, pages 301–310, 2014.

[36] T. N. Nguyen and N. Kanhabua. Leveraging dynamic query subtopics for time-aware search result diversification. In *Proceedings of the 36th European Conference on Advances in Information Retrieval*, ECIR '14, pages 222–234, 2014.

[37] K. Nørvåg and A. O. Nybø. Dyst: Dynamic and scalable temporal text indexing. In *Proceedings of the 13th International Symposium on Temporal Representation and Reasoning*, TIME '06, pages 204–211, 2006.

[38] S. Nunes, C. Ribeiro, and G. David. Use of temporal expressions in web search. In *Proceedings of the 30th European Conference on IR Research on Advances in Information Retrieval*, ECIR '08, pages 580–584, 2008.

[39] D. Odijk, G. Santucci, M. d. Rijke, M. Angelini, and G. Granato. Time-aware exploratory search: Exploring word meaning through time. In *SIGIR 2012 Workshop on Time-aware Information Access*, TAIA '12, 2012.

[40] M.-H. Peetz, E. Meij, and M. Rijke. Using temporal bursts for query modeling. *Information Retrieval*, 17(1):74–108, 2014.

[41] K. Radinsky, F. Diaz, S. T. Dumais, M. Shokouhi, A. Dong, and Y. Chang. Temporal web dynamics and its application to information retrieval. In *Proceedings of the Sixth ACM International Conference on Web Search and Data Mining*, WSDM '13, pages 781–782, 2013.

[42] K. Radinsky and E. Horvitz. Mining the web to predict future events. In *Proceedings of the Sixth ACM International Conference on Web Search and Data Mining*, WSDM '13, pages 255–264, 2013.

[43] K. Radinsky, K. Svore, S. Dumais, J. Teevan, A. Bocharov, and E. Horvitz. Modeling and predicting behavioral dynamics on the web. In *Proceedings of the 21st international conference on World Wide Web*, WWW '12, pages 599–608, 2012.

[44] D. Shan, W. X. Zhao, R. Chen, B. Shu, Z. Wang, J. Yao, H. Yan, and X. Li. Eventsearch: A system for event discovery and retrieval on multi-type historical data. In *Proceedings of the 18th ACM SIGKDD International Conference on Knowledge Discovery and Data Mining*, KDD '12, pages 1564–1567, 2012.

[45] M. Shokouhi. Detecting seasonal queries by time-series analysis. In *Proceedings of the 34th International ACM SIGIR Conference on Research and Development in Information Retrieval*, SIGIR '11, pages 1171–1172, 2011.

[46] J. Singh, W. Nejdl, and A. Anand. History by diversity: Helping historians search news archives. In *Proceedings of the 1st International ACM SIGIR Conference on Human Information Interaction and Retrieval (CHIIR)*, 2016.

[47] R. Sipos, A. Swaminathan, P. Shivaswamy, and T. Joachims. Temporal corpus summarization using submodular word coverage. In *Proceedings of the 21st ACM International Conference on Information and Knowledge Management*, CIKM '12, pages 754–763, 2012.

[48] K. M. Svore, J. Teevan, S. T. Dumais, and A. Kulkarni. Creating temporally dynamic web search snippets. In *Proceedings of the 35th International ACM SIGIR Conference on Research and Development in Information Retrieval*, SIGIR '12, pages 1045–1046, 2012.

[49] N. Tahmasebi, G. Gossen, N. Kanhabua, H. Holzmann, and T. Risse. NEER: An Unsupervised Method for Named Entity Evolution Recognition. In *Proceedings the 24th International Conference on Computational Linguistics*, COLING '12, pages 2553–2568. ACL, 2012.

[50] T. A. Tran, C. Niederée, N. Kanhabua, U. Gadiraju, and A. Anand. Balancing novelty and salience: Adaptive learning to rank entities for timeline summarization of high-impact events. In *Proceedings of the 24th ACM International on Conference on Information and Knowledge Management*, CIKM '15, pages 1201–1210, 2015.

[51] S. Whiting, K. Zhou, J. Jose, and M. Lalmas. Temporal variance of intents in multi-faceted event-driven information needs. In *Proceedings of the 36th International ACM SIGIR Conference on Research and Development in Information Retrieval*, SIGIR '13, pages 989–992, 2013.

[52] R. Yan, X. Wan, J. Otterbacher, L. Kong, X. Li, and Y. Zhang. Evolutionary timeline summarization: A balanced optimization framework via iterative substitution. In *Proceedings of the 34th International ACM SIGIR Conference on Research and Development in Information Retrieval*, SIGIR '11, pages 745–754, 2011.

[53] J. Zhang and T. Suel. Efficient search in large textual collections with redundancy. In *Proceedings of the 16th International Conference on World Wide Web*, WWW '07, pages 411–420, 2007.

[54] R. Zhang, Y. Konda, A. Dong, P. Kolari, Y. Chang, and Z. Zheng. Learning recurrent event queries for web search. In *Proceedings of the 2010 Conference on Empirical Methods in Natural Language Processing*, EMNLP '10, pages 1129–1139, 2010.

[55] X. W. Zhao, Y. Guo, R. Yan, Y. He, and X. Li. Timeline generation with social attention. In *Proceedings of the 36th International ACM SIGIR Conference on Research and Development in Information Retrieval*, SIGIR '13, pages 1061–1064, 2013.

[56] K. Zhou, S. Whiting, J. M. Jose, and M. Lalmas. The impact of temporal intent variability on diversity evaluation. In *Proceedings of the 35th European Conference on Advances in Information Retrieval*, ECIR '13, pages 820–823, 2013.

Third International Workshop on *Gamification* for Information Retrieval (GamifIR'16)

Michael Meder
Technische Universität Berlin
michael.meder@dai-labor.de

Frank Hopfgartner
University of Glasgow
frank.hopfgartner@glasgow.ac.uk

Gabriella Kazai
Semion Ltd
gabs@lumi.do

Udo Kruschwitz
University of Essex
udo@essex.ac.uk

ABSTRACT

Stronger engagement and greater participation is often crucial to reach a goal or to solve an issue. Issues like the emerging employee engagement crisis, insufficient knowledge sharing, and chronic procrastination. In many cases we need and search for tools to beat procrastination or to change people's habits. Gamification is the approach to learn from often fun, creative and engaging games. In principle, it is about understanding games and applying game design elements in a non-gaming environments. This offers possibilities for wide area improvements. For example more accurate work, better retention rates and more cost effective solutions by relating motivations for participating as more intrinsic than conventional methods. In the context of Information Retrieval (IR) it is not hard to imagine that many tasks could benefit from gamification techniques. Besides several manual annotation tasks of data sets for IR research, user participation is important in order to gather implicit or even explicit feedback to feed the algorithms. Gamification, however, comes with its own challenges and its adoption in IR is still in its infancy. Given the enormous response to the first and second GamifIR workshops that were both co-located with ECIR, and the broad range of topics discussed, we now organized the third workshop at SIGIR 2016 to address a range of emerging challenges and opportunities.

1. BACKGROUND AND MOTIVATION

The purpose of the GamifIR workshop series is to bring together researchers and practitioners from a wide range of areas including game design, IR, human-computer interaction, computer games, and natural language processing in order to promote the development and exchange of research ideas and results relating to emerging areas of gamification within the context of IR.

Many research challenges in the field of IR rely on tedious manual labour. For example, manual feedback is required to assess the relevance of documents to a given search task, to annotate documents or to evaluate interactive IR approaches. A recent trend to perform these tasks is the use of crowdsourcing techniques, i.e., obtaining relevance labels from anonymous crowd workers via an open call. Although research indicates that such techniques can be useful, they fail when *motivated* users are required to perform a task for reasons other than just being paid per click, document judged or time spent on the task.

A promising approach to increase user motivation is by employing gamification methods, which has been applied in various environments and for different purposes such as marketing, education, pervasive health care, enterprise workplaces, e-commerce, human resource management and many more. The definition of gamification is still under discussion, e.g., it is still debated whether it covers methods "to facilitate and support the users' overall value creation" [7] or if it aims to enhance user experience using game design elements "regardless of specific usage intentions, contexts [...]" [1] or environments. Definitions pursuing the increase of user experience and overall value indicate that the application of gamification is goal oriented. Although several studies indicate that gamification can lead to increased user activity, a detailed analysis of users' personal perception of gamification principles has barely been studied. In the last few years, several frameworks on how to 'gamify' were proposed, but there are still many open questions on how to start (e.g., [9, 2]). We argue that a particular challenge of applying gamification is to find an elegant and subtle way of adopting and adapting game design patterns, mechanisms and elements to a particular problem or scenario.

Given the interest in the first and second GamifIR workshops[1] [4, 6] and the discussions emerging at these events, we are convinced that we are only at the start of seeing gamification becoming an established methodology to support and push forward IR in a variety of ways.

2. WORKSHOP GOALS & PROMOTION

By hosting a workshop in conjunction with SIGIR 2016, we intented to promote this area of research by bringing together IR and games researchers and practitioners. Potential topics for papers included:

[1]For a detailed summary of the 2015 edition of the workshop series, we refer to [8].

SIGIR '16 July 17-21, 2016, Pisa, Italy

ACM ISBN 978-1-4503-4069-4/16/07.
DOI: http://dx.doi.org/10.1145/2911451.2917759

- Gamification approaches in a variety of contexts, including document annotation and ground-truth generation; interface design; information seeking; user modelling; knowledge sharing
- Gamification in Crowdsourcing
- Gamification for teaching IR
- Gamification in recommender systems and Apps
- User engagement and motivational factors of gamification
- Player types, contests, cooperative gamification
- Long-term user engagement
- Search challenges
- Gamification design
- Applied game principles, elements and mechanics

The workshop was advertised via various Call for Papers that were distributed to relevant mailing lists, forums, and social media platforms. A website[2] was set up to provide further information and the Twitter account *@GamifIR* was used to promote the workshop.

3. WORKSHOP SUMMARY

All submitted papers went through a semi-blind peer-reviewing process where each submission was reviewed by at least three experts in the field. The workshop proceedings have been published by CEUR.[3]

Papers were presented at the workshop on 21 July 2016 in Pisa, Italy. Given the co-location of the workshop with the SIGIR conference, the event mainly attracted researchers working in the field of IR who presented their preliminary work on applying gamification to perform various IR related tasks such as crowdsourced document annotation, relevance assessment or interactive search.

4. ACKNOWLEDGMENTS

We acknowledge the efforts of the programme committee, namely Raian Ali (Bournemouth University, UK), Omar Alonso (Microsoft, USA), Leif Azzopardi (University of Glasgow, UK), Jon Chamberlain (University of Essex, UK), Sebastian Deterding (University of York, UK), Carsten Eickhoff (ETH Zurich, CH), Christopher Harris (State University of New York, USA), Hideo Joho (University of Tsukuba, JP), Till Plumbaum (Technische Universität Berlin, GER), Ashok Ranchod (University of Southampton, UK), Thomas Springer (Technische Universität Dresden, GER), Susanne Strahinger (Technische Universität Dresden, GER), Albert Weichselbraun (University of Applied Sciences Chur, CH), and Lincoln Wood (University of Auckland, NZ).

We acknowledge financial support by the European Commissiion via the European Union Seventh Framework Programme FP7/2007-2013, grant agreement number 610594 (CrowdRec).

[2]http://gamifir.com/

[3]Past editions of the workshop have been published by ACM [3] and CEUR [5].

5. REFERENCES

[1] S. Deterding, D. Dixon, R. Khaled, and L. Nacke. From game design elements to gamefulness: defining gamification. *Proceeding of the 15th International Academic MindTrek Conference*, pages 9–15, 2011.

[2] J. Hamari, J. Koivisto, and H. Sarsa. Does gamification work? - a literature review of empirical studies on gamification. In *In proceedings of the 47th Hawaii International Conference on System Sciences*, 2014.

[3] F. Hopfgartner, G. Kazai, U. Kruschwitz, and M. Meder, editors. *GamifIR '14: Proceedings of the First International Workshop on Gamification for Information Retrieval*, New York, NY, USA, 2014. ACM.

[4] F. Hopfgartner, G. Kazai, U. Kruschwitz, and M. Meder. Workshop on gamification for information retrieval (gamifir'14). In *Advances in Information Retrieval - 36th European Conference on IR Research, ECIR 2014, Amsterdam, The Netherlands, April 13-16, 2014. Proceedings*, pages 806–809, 2014.

[5] F. Hopfgartner, G. Kazai, U. Kruschwitz, and M. Meder, editors. *Proceedings of the Second International Workshop on Gamification for Information Retrieval co-located with the 37th European Conference on Information Retrieval (ECIR 2015), Vienna, Austria, March 29, 2015*, volume 1345 of *CEUR Workshop Proceedings*. CEUR-WS.org, 2015.

[6] F. Hopfgartner, G. Kazai, U. Kruschwitz, M. Meder, and M. Shovman. Second international workshop on gamification for information retrieval (gamifir'15). In *Advances in Information Retrieval - 37th European Conference on IR Research, ECIR 2015, Vienna, Austria, March 29 - April 2, 2015. Proceedings*, pages 838–840, 2015.

[7] K. Huotari and J. Hamari. Defining gamification: a service marketing perspective. *Proceeding of the 16th International Academic MindTrek Conference*, pages 17–22, 2012.

[8] G. Kazai, Lumi, F. Hopfgartner, U. Kruschwitz, and M. Meder. ECIR 2015 workshop on gamification for information retrieval (gamifir'15). *SIGIR Forum*, 49(1):41–49, 2015.

[9] B. Morschheuser, J. Hamari, and J. Koivisto. Gamification in crowdsourcing: A review. In *proceedings of the 49th Annual Hawaii International Conference on System Sciences (HICSS), Hawaii, USA*, 2016.

HIA'16: The 2nd International Workshop on Heterogeneous Information Access at SIGIR 2016

Ke Zhou
Yahoo Research
London, U.K.
kezhou@yahoo-inc.com

Yiqun Liu
Tsinghua University
Beijing, China
yiqunliu@tsinghua.edu.cn

Roger Jie Luo
Snapchat
Venice Beach, USA
roger.luo@snapchat.com

Joemon Jose
University of Glasgow
Glasgow, U.K.
Joemon.Jose@glasgow.ac.uk

ABSTRACT

Information access is becoming increasingly heterogeneous. Especially when the user's information need is for exploratory purpose, returning a set of diverse results from different resources could benefit the user. For example, when a user is planning a trip to China, retrieving and showing results from vertical search engines like travel, flight information, map and Q2A sites can satisfy the user's rich and diverse information need. This heterogeneous search paradigm is useful in many contexts and brings many new challenges.

Categories and Subject Descriptors: H.3.3 [Information Retrieval][Information Search and Retrieval]
Keywords: Heterogeneous; Federated search; Aggregated search; Composite retrieval; Card recommendation.

1. INTRODUCTION

The environment where users interact within is becoming increasingly heterogeneous. On the Web, we have now many search engines, so-called *verticals*, each targeting a specific type of information (e.g. image, news, video) to satisfy the user's information need [3]. Aggregating search results from those heterogeneous verticals has become de-facto search paradigm (aggregated search) in commercial search engines [1, 8]. It is also common that users search their own desktop (e.g. Spotlight) to re-find or browse different types of files (codes, documents, emails) when aiming to fulfill a given work task [5]. More recently, systems such as Google Now, Apple Siri and Microsoft Cortana aim to proactively recommend heterogeneous cards (e.g. weather, stocks, news, calendar) to the users, even without users to issue the query [7]. Due to the rising heterogeneous nature of the information that users can access, numerous challenges have arisen.

SIGIR '16 July 17-21, 2016, Pisa, Italy

ACM ISBN 978-1-4503-4069-4/16/07.
DOI: http://dx.doi.org/10.1145/2911451.2917760

The main objective of the workshop is to draw researchers' attention to this rising field as well as to inspire them to collaborate in order to further promote the research area of heterogeneous information access. Although many studies have been conducted in the past on distributed information retrieval (homogeneous search federation) [6], there are multiple challenges emerging in the heterogeneous information access space. The new challenges include but are not limited to: How to select the most relevant resources and present them concisely in order to best satisfy the user; How to model the complex user behaviors while interacting with heterogeneous search systems; How to evaluate the performance of these systems; How to optimize the system for the increasing popular mobile experience. We would like to create a forum to encourage discussion and exchange of ideas on heterogeneous information access in different contexts. To facilitate the discussion, we encourage submissions on ideas and results from different aspects of heterogeneous information access, including aggregated search [1], composite retrieval [2], personal search [5], structured search [4], proactive heterogeneous card recommendation [7], etc. Another objective of the workshop is to encourage submissions with novel ideas (e.g. new applications) on heterogeneous information access and potential future research directions.

2. REFERENCES

[1] J. Arguello, F. Diaz, J. Callan, and J.-F. Crespo. Sources of evidence for vertical selection. In *SIGIR '09*, pages 315–322.

[2] H. Bota, K. Zhou, J. Jose, and M. Lalmas. Composite retrieval of heterogeneous web search. In *WWW'14*, pages 119–130.

[3] T. Demeester, D. Trieschnigg, D. Nguyen, K. Zhou and D. Hiemstra. Overview of the TREC 2014 Federated Web Search Track. In *TREC'14*. Proceedings of Text REtrieval Conference.

[4] D. Herzig, and T. Thanh. Heterogeneous web data search using relevance-based on the fly data integration. In *WWW '12*, pages 141–150.

[5] K. Jinyoung, and W. B. Croft. Ranking using multiple document types in desktop search. In *SIGIR'10*, pages 50–57.

[6] M. Shokouhi and S. Luo. Federated search. In *FTIIR'11*, Foundations and Trends in Information Retrieval, pages 1-102.

[7] M. Shokouhi and Q. Guo. From Queries to Cards, Re-ranking Proactive Card Recommendations Based on Reactive Search History. In *SIGIR'15*, pages 695–704.

[8] K. Zhou, R. Cummins, M. Lalmas and J. Jose. Evaluating Aggregated Search Pages. In *SIGIR'12*, pages 115–124.

Medical Information Search Workshop (MEDIR)

Steven Bedrick
Oregon Health State University
US
bedricks@ohsu.edu

Lorraine Goeuriot
LIG - Université Grenoble Alpes
France
lorraine.goeuriot@imag.fr

Gareth J. F. Jones
Dublin City University
Ireland
gjones@computing.dcu.ie

Anastasia Krithara
NCSR Demokritos
Greece
akrithara@iit.demokritos.gr

Henning Mueller
HES-SO
Switzerland
henning.mueller@hevs.ch

George Paliouras
NCSR Demokritos
Greece
paliourg@iit.demokritos.gr

1. WORKSHOP OVERVIEW

Medical information search refers to methodologies and technologies that seek to improve access to medical information archives via a process of information retrieval (IR). Such information is now potentially accessible from many sources including the general web, social media, journal articles, and hospital records. Health-related content is one of the most searched-for topics on the internet, and as such this is an important domain for research in information retrieval.

Medical information is of interest to a wide variety of users, including patients and their families, researchers, general practitioners and clinicians, and clinicians with specific expertise such as radiologists. There are several dedicated services that seek to make this information more easily accessible, such as Health on the Net's medical search systems for the general public and medical practitioners[1]. Despite the popularity of the medical domain for users of search engines, and current interest in this topic within the information retrieval research community, development of search and access technologies remains particularly challenging. One of the central challenges in medical information search is diversity of the users of these services. These challenges can be summarized as follows:

1. Varying information needs: Understanding various types of users and their information needs is one of the cornerstones of medical information search, while adapting information retrieval to best address these needs to develop effective, potentially personalized systems is one of its greatest challenges.

2. Varying medical knowledge: The different categories of users of medical information search systems have different levels of medical knowledge, and indeed the medical knowledge of different individuals within a category can also vary greatly.

3. Varying language skills: Given that much of medical content is written in the English language, research to date in medical information search has predominantly focused on monolingual English retrieval. However, given the large number of non-English speakers on the Internet and the lack of content in their native language, effective support for them to search the English sources is highly desirable.

The objective of this workshop is to provide a forum to enable the progression of research in medical information retrieval to provide enhanced search services for all users with interest in medical information search.

This workshop aims to bring together researchers interested in medical information search with the goal of identifying specific research challenges that need to be addressed to advance the state-of-the-art and to foster interdisciplinary collaborations towards the meeting of these challenges. To enable this, we will encourage participation from researchers in all fields related to medical information search including mainstream information retrieval, but also natural language processing, multilingual text processing, and medical image analysis.

Topics of interest include but are not limited to: Users and information needs; Semantics and NLP for medical IR; Reliability and trust in medical IR; Personalised search; Evaluation of medical IR; Multilingual questions in medical IR; Multimedia technologies in medical IR; The role of social media in medical IR.

The workshop programme includes an invited presentation by Pr Bill Hersh, and short research and position papers describing approaches or challenges on the topics of the workshop. The programme aims to encourage interaction and discussion to develop a shared understanding of the research challenges facing the area of medical information retrieval. The workshop will seek to identify specific actions necessary to advance this field, and to hopefully foster further collaborations between the participants.

Acknowledgement

We would like to thanks the European Science Foundation project ELIAS for supporting this workshop.

[1]http://www.hon.ch/

SIGIR '16 July 17-21, 2016, Pisa, Italy

ACM ISBN 978-1-4503-4069-4/16/07.

DOI: http://dx.doi.org/10.1145/2911451.2917761

Neu-IR: The SIGIR 2016 Workshop on Neural Information Retrieval

Nick Craswell
Microsoft
Bellevue, US
nickcr@microsoft.com

W. Bruce Croft
University of Massachusetts
Amherst, US
croft@cs.umass.edu

Jiafeng Guo
Chinese Academy of Sciences
Beijing, China
guojiafeng@ict.ac.cn

Bhaskar Mitra
Microsoft
Cambridge, UK
bmitra@microsoft.com

Maarten de Rijke
University of Amsterdam
Amsterdam, The Netherlands
derijke@uva.nl

Keywords

Neural networks; deep learning; information retrieval

Website: http://research.microsoft.com/neuir2016

1. MOTIVATION

In recent years, deep neural networks have yielded significant performance improvements on speech recognition and computer vision tasks [4, 7], as well as led to exciting breakthroughs in novel application areas such as automatic voice translation [8], image captioning [2, 12], and conversational agents [11]. Despite demonstrating good performance on natural language processing (NLP) tasks (e.g., language modelling [6] and machine translation [1]), the performance of deep neural networks on information retrieval (IR) tasks has had relatively less scrutiny. Recent work in this area has mainly focused on word embeddings [3, 9, 14] and neural models for short text similarity [5, 10].

The lack of many positive results in this area of information retrieval is partially due to the fact that IR tasks such as ranking are fundamentally different from NLP tasks, but also because the IR and neural network communities are only beginning to focus on the application of these techniques to core information retrieval problems. Given that deep learning has made such a big impact, first on speech processing and computer vision and now, increasingly, also on computational linguistics, it seems clear that deep learning will have a major impact on information retrieval and that this is an ideal time for a workshop in this area.

Neu-IR (pronounced "*new IR*") will be a forum for new research relating to deep learning and other neural network based approaches to IR. The purpose is to provide an opportunity for people to present new work and early results, compare notes on neural network toolkits, share best practices, and discuss the main challenges facing this line of research.

SIGIR '16 July 17-21, 2016, Pisa, Italy

ACM ISBN 978-1-4503-4069-4/16/07.

DOI: http://dx.doi.org/10.1145/2911451.2917762

2. SCOPE

The Neu-IR workshop will be a gathering of academic and industrial researchers working at the intersection of IR and neural networks. We solicit submission of papers of two to six pages, representing reports of original research, preliminary research results, proposals for new work, descriptions of neural network based toolkits tailored for IR, and position papers. Papers presented at the workshop will be required to be uploaded to arXiv.org but will be considered non-archival, and may be submitted elsewhere (modified or not), although the workshop site will maintain a link to the arXiv versions. This makes the workshop a forum for the presentation and discussion of current work, without preventing the work from being published elsewhere. We are interested in submissions relevant to the following main themes:

- The application of neural network models in IR tasks, including but not limited to:
  - Full text document retrieval, passage retrieval, question answering
  - Web search, searching social media, distributed information retrieval, entity ranking
  - Learning to rank combined with neural network based representation learning
  - User / task modelling, personalization, diversity
  - Query formulation assistance, query recommendation, conversational search
  - Multimedia retrieval
- Fundamental modelling challenges faced in such applications, including but not limited to:
  - Learning dense representations for long documents
  - Dealing with rare queries and rare words
  - Modelling text at different granularities (character, word, passage, document)
  - Compositionality of vector representations
  - Jointly modelling queries, documents, entities and other structured/knowledge data
- Best practices for research and development in the area, dealing with concerns such as:
  - Finding sufficient publicly-available training data
  - Baselines, test data, avoiding overfitting
  - Neural network toolkits
  - Real-world use cases, deployment at scale

3. INTERACTION FORMAT

Neu-IR will be a highly interactive full day workshop, featuring a mix of presentation and interaction formats, appropriate for the main themes identified in §2. The workshop will feature presentations of the following types:

- Invited keynotes
- Invited toolkit walkthrough on CNTK [13]
- Contributed paper presentations
- An interactive "Lessons from the Trenches" session to share best practices and lessons learned
- Breakout sessions and panel discussions on issues that emerge from the contributed papers

4. ORGANIZERS

Nick Craswell is a Principal Lead Researcher in Microsoft Bing, working on core relevance. And leads a small team of Applied Researchers who are embedded in Microsoft Research Cambridge in the UK. He has published a number of papers relating to clicks and their use, and he ran the first successful WSDM workshop on Web Search Click data in 2009, and co-organized WSCD workshops in 2012 and 2013.

Bruce Croft is a Distinguished Professor in the College of Information and Computer Sciences at the University of Massachusetts Amherst. He leads the Center for Intelligent Information Retrieval, which has produced results in many areas of IR for the past 25 years.

Jiafeng Guo is an Associate Professor at Institute of Computing Technology, Chinese Academy of Sciences. He has worked on a number of topics related to Web search and data mining, including query representation and understanding, learning to rank, and topic modelling. His current research is focused on representation learning and deep models for information retrieval and information filtering.

Bhaskar Mitra is a Senior Applied Scientist at Bing in Microsoft Research Cambridge. He started at Bing in 2007 (then called Live Search) at the Search Technology Center in India. He is currently pursuing a (part-time) doctorate at University College London. His research interests include representation learning and neural networks, and in particular their application to modern day information retrieval.

Maarten de Rijke is a Professor of Computer Science at the Informatics Institute of the University of Amsterdam. Together with a team of PhD students and postdocs he works on problems on semantic search and on- and offline learning to rank for information retrieval. Some of their recent work uses deep neural networks for text similarity, entity search, product search, session analysis, and click modelling.

5. PROGRAM COMMITTEE

- Carsten Eickhoff, ETH Zurich
- Debasis Ganguly, Dublin City University
- Katja Hoffman, Microsoft Research
- Hang Li, Huawei Technologies
- Piotr Mirowski, Google DeepMind
- Alessandro Moschitti, Qatar Computing Research Inst.
- Pavel Serdyukov, Yandex
- Fabrizio Silvestri, Yahoo Labs
- Alessandro Sordoni, University of Montreal

References

[1] D. Bahdanau, K. Cho, and Y. Bengio. Neural machine translation by jointly learning to align and translate. *arXiv preprint arXiv:1409.0473*, 2014.

[2] H. Fang, S. Gupta, F. Iandola, R. Srivastava, L. Deng, P. Dollár, J. Gao, X. He, M. Mitchell, J. Platt, et al. From captions to visual concepts and back. *arXiv preprint arXiv:1411.4952*, 2014.

[3] D. Ganguly, D. Roy, M. Mitra, and G. J. Jones. Word embedding based generalized language model for information retrieval. In *Proc. SIGIR*, pages 795–798. ACM, 2015.

[4] G. Hinton, L. Deng, D. Yu, G. E. Dahl, A.-r. Mohamed, N. Jaitly, A. Senior, V. Vanhoucke, P. Nguyen, T. N. Sainath, et al. Deep neural networks for acoustic modeling in speech recognition: The shared views of four research groups. *Signal Processing Magazine, IEEE*, 29(6):82–97, 2012.

[5] P.-S. Huang, X. He, J. Gao, L. Deng, A. Acero, and L. Heck. Learning deep structured semantic models for web search using clickthrough data. In *Proc. CIKM*, pages 2333–2338. ACM, 2013.

[6] R. Jozefowicz, O. Vinyals, M. Schuster, N. Shazeer, and Y. Wu. Exploring the limits of language modeling. *arXiv preprint arXiv:1602.02410*, 2016.

[7] Y. LeCun, Y. Bengio, and G. Hinton. Deep learning. *Nature*, 521(7553):436–444, 2015.

[8] W. D. Lewis. Skype translator: Breaking down language and hearing barriers. In *Translating and the Computer (TC37)*, 2015.

[9] B. Mitra, E. Nalisnick, N. Craswell, and R. Caruana. A dual embedding space model for document ranking. *arXiv preprint arXiv:1602.01137*, 2016.

[10] A. Severyn and A. Moschitti. Learning to rank short text pairs with convolutional deep neural networks. In *Proc. SIGIR*, pages 373–382. ACM, 2015.

[11] O. Vinyals and Q. Le. A neural conversational model. *arXiv preprint arXiv:1506.05869*, 2015.

[12] O. Vinyals, A. Toshev, S. Bengio, and D. Erhan. Show and tell: A neural image caption generator. *arXiv preprint arXiv:1411.4555*, 2014.

[13] D. Yu, A. Eversole, M. Seltzer, K. Yao, et al. An introduction to computational networks and the computational network toolkit. Technical report, Tech. Rep. MSR, Microsoft Research, 2014, https://cntk.ai/, 2014.

[14] G. Zheng and J. Callan. Learning to reweight terms with distributed representations. In *Proc. SIGIR*, pages 575–584. ACM, 2015.

Privacy-Preserving IR 2016: Differential Privacy, Search, and Social Media

Hui Yang
Georgetown University, USA
huiyang@cs.georgetown.edu

Ian Soboroff
NIST, USA
ian.soboroff@nist.gov

Li Xiong
Emory University, USA
lxiong@emory.edu

Charles L. A. Clarke
University of Waterloo, Canada
claclark@plg.uwaterloo.ca

Simson L. Garfinkel
NIST, USA
simson.garfinkel@nist.gov

ABSTRACT

Due to lack of mature techniques in privacy-preserving information retrieval (IR), concerns about information privacy and security have become serious obstacles that prevent valuable user data to be used in IR research such as studies on query logs, social media, and medical record retrieval. In SIGIR 2014 and SIGIR 2015, we have run the privacy-preserving IR workshops exploring and understanding the privacy and security risks in information retrieval. This year, we continue the efforts of connecting the two disciplines of IR and privacy/ security by organizing this workshop. We target on three themes, differential privacy and IR dataset release, privacy in search and browsing, and privacy in social media. The workshop include panels with researchers from both fields on these three themes, as well as invite industry speakers for real-world challenges. The goals of this workshop include (1) bringing together the two research fields, and (2) yielding fruitful collaborations.

Keywords

Privacy-Preserving Information Retrieval

1. MOTIVATION

Information retrieval and information privacy/security are two fast-growing computer science disciplines. Information retrieval provides a set of information seeking, organization, analysis, and decision-making techniques. Information privacy/security defends information from unauthorized or malicious use, disclosure, modification, attack, and destruction. The two disciplines often appear as two areas with opposite goals: one is to seek information from large amounts of materials, the other is to protect (sensitive) information from being found out. On the other hand, there are many synergies and connections between these two disciplines. For example, information retrieval researchers or practitioners often need to consider privacy or security issues in designing solutions for information processing and management, while researchers in information privacy and security often utilize information retrieval techniques when they build the adversary models to simulate how the adversary can actively seek sensitive information. However, there have been only limited efforts to connect the two important disciplines.

Due to lack of mature techniques in privacy-preserving information retrieval, concerns about information privacy and security have become serious obstacles that prevent valuable user data to be used in IR research such as studies about query logs, social media, tweets, session analysis, and medical record retrieval. For instance, the recent TREC Medical Record Retrieval Tracks are halted because of the privacy issue and the TREC Microblog Tracks could not provide participants with a standard testbed of tweets for system development. The situation needs to be improved in a timely manner.

In addition, with the emergence of online social networks and the growing popularity of digital communication, more and more information about individuals is becoming available on the Internet. While much of this information is not sensitive, it is not uncommon for users to publish sensitive information online, especially on social networking sites. The availability of this publicly accessible and potentially sensitive data can lead to abuse and expose users to stalking and identity theft. User privacy is at risk whenever owners of publicly available network resources can be traced and recorded, and their user activities can be mined and inferred. The digital ecosystem involves not only such threats to personal privacy but also promising cures. For example, information-theoretic protocols may decompose each user's query into several sub-queries, ensuring they include no information about the user's intent.

All these motivate us to propose this "privacy-preserving IR" workshop in SIGIR.

2. PAST WORKSHOPS

Since 2014, the privacy workshop has been running in SIGIR. The first privacy-preserving IR workshop (PIR 2014) [5] received active participation. There were three keynotes given in the workshop. Most workshop attendees agreed that

SIGIR '16 July 17-21, 2016, Pisa, Italy

ACM ISBN 978-1-4503-4069-4/16/07.

DOI: http://dx.doi.org/10.1145/2911451.2917763

we need to continue to collaborate on this topic, and to seek both general and specific solutions to the privacy and security issues in various IR tasks. The second workshop (PIR 2015) [7] started to receive solutions to the problems that we identified in the previous year. It featured a keynote on differential privacy and a heated debate on "privacy would be resolved if the search is not personalized". Both years' workshop reports can be found in SIGIR forum too.

3. WHAT'S NEW

This year, the workshop organizers formed a team spanning across IR, Privacy, and the government sector. We focus on forming IR and privacy research bridges and partnerships and thus organizing panels by themes. For each theme, we invite researchers from IR and researchers from Privacy/Security to form pairs. The panel discussion not only focus on presenting problems but more on seeking solutions and achieving a mutual understanding of the research problem. Among many challenges in privacy-preserving IR, this year we focus on three major themes: *differential privacy for IR data release*, *privacy-preserving search/browsing* and *privacy and social media.*

4. THEMES

The three main themes of this year including the following.

- Differential privacy for IR data release [1, 2]: How to preserve privacy when releasing internal data. For instance, web query logs and medical records could not be shared without privacy concerns. Another challenge is how to anonymize the datasets and make sure that they can be shared with a certain degree of privacy guaranteed while preserving the utility of the data. We focus on the latest technology of differential privacy in particular.
- Privacy preserving search/browsing [3]: How to recognize and communicate privacy concerns to users of search engines. It is important to develop effective and efficient solutions to protect users' privacy in information retrieval applications while they are searching or surfing the net. We also plan to discuss softwares such as TunnelBear[1].
- Privacy and social media [4, 6]: New information retrieval and natural language processing technologies are needed to quickly identify components and/or attributes of a user's online activities on social media that may reduce the user's privacy, and warn users about their vulnerability on the Web. For instance, authorship attribution.

5. ACTIVITIES AND SCHEDULE

This full day workshop includes invited speakers, panels, short contributed talks and a poster session. It ends with a breakout session. The activities are scheduled as the following:

09:00-09:30 Welcome and Introduction.
09:30-10:30 Invited speaker #1 (Differential privacy)
10:30-11:00 Coffee
11:00-11:45 Contributed talks (session #1)
11:45-12:30 Posters flowing into Lunch
12:30-13:30 Lunch
13:30-14:30 Invited speaker #2 (Industry)
14:30-15:15 Contributed talks (session #2)
15:15-16:30 Panel and breakout planning
16:30-17:30 Breakouts (research challenges)
17:30-18:00 Summary of breakouts

[1] https://www.tunnelbear.com/

6. WEBSITE

The website of the workshop can be found at privacypreservingir org.

7. ACKNOWLEDGMENTS

This research was supported by NSF grant CNS-1223825, DARPA grant FA8750-14-2-0226, and NSF student travel grant. Any opinions, findings, conclusions, or recommendations expressed in this paper are of the authors, and do not necessarily reflect those of the sponsor. We also express our special thanks to our student organizer, Sicong Zhang.

References

[1] L. Fan, L. Bonomi, L. Xiong, and V. Sunderam. Monitoring web browsing behavior with differential privacy. In *Proceedings of the 23rd International Conference on World Wide Web*, WWW '14, 2014.

[2] M. Gaboardi, E. J. G. Arias, J. Hsu, A. Roth, and Z. S. Wu. Dual query: Practical private query release for high dimensional data. In *ICML 2014, Beijing, China, 21-26 June 2014.*

[3] W. Jiang, L. Si, and J. Li. Protecting source privacy in federated search. In W. Kraaij, A. P. de Vries, C. L. A. Clarke, N. Fuhr, and N. Kando, editors, *SIGIR*, pages 761–762. ACM, 2007.

[4] W. Luo, Q. Xie, and U. Hengartner. Facecloak: An architecture for user privacy on social networking sites. In *CSE '09 - Volume 03*, pages 26–33, Washington, DC, USA, 2009. IEEE Computer Society.

[5] L. Si and H. Yang. Pir 2014 the first international workshop on privacy-preserving ir: When information retrieval meets privacy and security. *SIGIR Forum*, 48(2):83–88, Dec. 2014.

[6] L. Singh, G. H. Yang, M. Sherr, A. Hian-Cheong, K. Tian, J. Zhu, and S. Zhang. Public information exposure detection: Helping users understand their web footprints. In *ASONAM 2015, Paris, France.*

[7] H. Yang and I. Soboroff. Privacy-preserving IR 2015: When information retrieval meets privacy and security. In *SIGIR'15 , Santiago, Chile, August 9-13, 2015.*

Search as Learning (SAL) Workshop 2016

Jacek Gwizdka
University of Texas Austin, USA
sigir2016@gwizdka.com

Preben Hansen
Stockholm University, Sweden
preben@dsv.su.se

Claudia Hauff
Delft University of Technology, the Netherlands
c.hauff@tudelft.nl

Jiyin He
Centrum Wiskunde & Informatica, the Netherlands
jiyinhe@acm.org

Noriko Kando
National Institute of Informatics, Japan
kando@nii.ac.jp

ABSTRACT

The "Search as Learning" (SAL) workshop is focused on an area within the information retrieval field that is only beginning to emerge: supporting users in their learning whilst interacting with information content.

Keywords

Search, learning, human information interaction

1. MOTIVATION

Search systems to date are viewed more as tools for the retrieval of content to satisfy immediate information needs, than as part of larger complex information environments in which humans *learn* while interacting with information content. As users increasingly learn informally while searching as well as use search systems as tools for self-study, there is a growing recognition of the importance to address the challenges of *designing*, *developing*, and *evaluating* search systems that foster discovery and enhance learning outside of formal educational settings.

The research agenda of "Search as Learning" aims to bring together these challenges and opportunities by reaching out to researchers with backgrounds in information science (IS), human computer interaction (HCI), and information retrieval (IR), with the goal of integrating conceptual, experimental, and simulation-based approaches and methodologies from within these different fields. This will allow the transformation of search systems as isolated information access tools into systems that provide support for learning directly and that consider the broader outcomes of searching beyond a set of search results.

Studies in IS have always focused on the broader context of search with the aim to understand, conceptualise, and form theories of the relations between user behavior and the users' information environment. Earlier work identified search as not to be an isolated activity but part of a larger information seeking process, i.e., "a process, in which humans purposefully engage in order to change their state of knowledge" [12]. Further work proposed that the information seeking processes should be thought of as driven by higher-level human needs or the user environment, e.g, in the context of a work task [1]. The importance of learning has resurfaced as noted by Jansen et al. [10]: "a learning theory may better describe the information searching process than more commonly used paradigms of decision making or problem solving". Connecting learning theory and IS perspectives [13] suggests that "the use of information as the fundamental building block for learning". In the first edition of this workshop (SAL'14) Freund et al. [7] presented a conceptual framework for the role of search in informal learning and Byström [2] discussed the social, individual and techno-material dimensions of search as a learning activity in the context of real-life work tasks and how this leads to future research topics and methodological implications for interactive information retrieval. These conceptual models and frameworks provide theoretical foundations for exploratory analyses of log data as well as the development of empirical models to validate the proposed theories. Recently, Vakkari [17] and Rieh et al. [15] reviewed relevant research so far and discussed future directions from both theoretical and empirical perspective [8].

Within the IR and HCI community studies addressing different aspects of learning during search are gaining traction, while following a more empirical, data-driven methodology, e.g., studies that analyse user learning behaviour from commercial search logs [5, 18], and that investigate behavioural indicators of the evolving status of users' knowledge during search [4, 6, 19]. Further, the need to develop evaluation paradigms that go beyond individual query interaction has been noted by many IR researchers. A number of directions have been proposed, e.g., towards whole session based evaluation, user-centric evaluation methods and metrics [3, 9, 14, 16], as well as evaluation of search outcome in broader contexts such as work tasks [11]. The effort of integrating whole-session and task based evaluation of IR systems with IR's test-collection driven simulation based evaluation paradigm is reflected by the recent editions of the TREC Session Track and Tasks Track. The interactive and context-rich nature of learning as both a process and outcome of information seeking is the next frontier in the evaluation of information systems and is a natural fit for the strong evaluation focussed IR community.

Together, the theory from IS and empirical models from IR studies have the necessary prerequisites to shed light on how local evaluation of ranking and system design within a particular part of the search process can be combined with more global assessments of system-user performance. On the one hand, conceptual models and frameworks of the cognitive process of searching and learning would provide guidance to use the empirical results in appropriate contexts; and on the other hand, empirical predictive models and simulation based evaluation would provide means to translate the

SIGIR '16 July 17-21, 2016, Pisa, Italy

ACM ISBN 978-1-4503-4069-4/16/07.
DOI: http://dx.doi.org/10.1145/2911451.2917766

conceptual models and frameworks into operations at an algorithmic level. However, it is not yet well understood how the results of these different lines of research should be put together and operationalised for the design and evaluation of IR systems that support learning activities.

SIGIR is a key venue that brings together researchers from IS, HCI, and IR, and the SAL workshop provides the opportunity where theory meets empirical studies. The discussion in the workshop will not only identify and prioritise the problems and solutions on the topic of search as learning, but also contribute to the future of IR research in seeking integrated cognitive and empirical approaches to the theory, modelling, and evaluation of information seeking processes and information systems.

2. THEME AND PURPOSE

The Search as Learning Workshop aims to flesh out research directions and methodologies and survey state-of-the-art approaches in this important emerging research area. We are particularly interested in engaging researchers across the IR, IS, HCI and learning science fields.

Topics of interest include the following but not limited to:

- Understanding searching as a human learning process;
- Learning process in the context of work tasks;
- System features and functionalities to foster learning;
- The implications of searching for learning for different populations: children, low literacy searchers, non-experts;
- The role of affect and engagement on learning during search;
- Evaluation of learning performance and experience;
- Learning analytics for search contexts;
- Collaborative aspects of searching as learning;
- Interaction monitoring, modelling, and optimization for learning outcomes.

3. WORKSHOP FORMAT AND PLANNED ACTIVITIES

The workshop includes two keynotes presentations (Kevyn Collins-Thompson from University of Michigan and Andreas Nuernberger from University of Magdeburg), presentations of selected papers, and interactive sessions in the format of breakout groups.

The focus of the workshop is to encourage interaction and collaboration among attendees. With the interactive sessions, we expect to identify and define the major challenges from the perspective of different research areas, and to explore and discover interdisciplinary challenges. Overall, we expect the workshop to foster new research directions for search and learning and future collaborations such as joint projects and publications.

4. REFERENCES

[1] P. Borlund. The IIR evaluation model: a framework for evaluation of interactive information retrieval systems. *Information research*, 8(3), 2003.

[2] K. Byström. Searching as a learning activity in real life workplaces. In *Workshop on Search as Learning (SAL) 2014.*, 2014.

[3] M. Cole, J. Liu, N. Belkin, R. Bierig, J. Gwizdka, C. Liu, J. Zhang, and X. Zhang. Usefulness as the criterion for evaluation of interactive information retrieval. *Proc. HCIR*, pages 1–4, 2009.

[4] M. J. Cole, J. Gwizdka, C. Liu, N. J. Belkin, and X. Zhang. Inferring user knowledge level from eye movement patterns. *Inf. Process. Manage.*, 49(5):1075–1091, Sept. 2013.

[5] C. Eickhoff, J. Teevan, R. White, and S. Dumais. Lessons from the journey: a query log analysis of within-session learning. In *Proceedings of the 7th ACM international conference on Web search and data mining*, pages 223–232. ACM, 2014.

[6] C. Eickhoff, S. Dungs, and V. Tran. An eye-tracking study of query reformulation. In *Proceedings of the 38th International ACM SIGIR Conference on Research and Development in Information Retrieval*, pages 13–22. ACM, 2015.

[7] L. Freund, H. O'Brien, and R. Kopak. Getting the big picture: supporting comprehension and learning in search. In *Workshop on Search as Learning (SAL) 2014.*, 2014.

[8] P. Hansen and S. Y. Rieh. Editorial: Recent advances on searching as learning: An introduction to the special issue. *Journal of Information Science*, 42(1):3–6, 2016.

[9] J. He, M. Bron, A. de Vries, L. Azzopardi, and M. de Rijke. Untangling result list refinement and ranking quality: a framework for evaluation and prediction. In *Proceedings of the 38th International ACM SIGIR Conference on Research and Development in Information Retrieval*, pages 293–302. ACM, 2015.

[10] B. J. Jansen, D. Booth, and B. Smith. Using the taxonomy of cognitive learning to model online searching. *Information Processing & Management*, 45(6):643–663, 2009.

[11] K. Järvelin and P. Ingwersen. Information seeking research needs extension towards tasks and technology. *Information Research*, 10(1), 2004.

[12] G. Marchionini. *Information seeking in electronic environments*. Cambridge university press, 1997.

[13] D. Neuman. Learning in information-rich environments. In *Encyclopedia of the Sciences of Learning*, pages 1908–1910. Springer, 2012.

[14] K. Raman, P. N. Bennett, and K. Collins-Thompson. Toward whole-session relevance: Exploring intrinsic diversity in web search. In *Proceedings of the 36th international ACM SIGIR conference on Research and development in information retrieval*, pages 463–472. ACM, 2013.

[15] S. Y. Rieh, K. Collins-Thompson, P. Hansen, and H.-J. Lee. Towards searching as a learning process: A review of current perspectives and future directions. *Journal of Information Science*, 42(1):19–34, 2016.

[16] M. D. Smucker and C. L. Clarke. Time-based calibration of effectiveness measures. In *Proceedings of the 35th international ACM SIGIR conference on Research and development in information retrieval*, pages 95–104. ACM, 2012.

[17] P. Vakkari. Searching as learning: A systematization based on literature. *Journal of Information Science*, 42(1):7–18, 2016.

[18] R. W. White, S. T. Dumais, and J. Teevan. Characterizing the influence of domain expertise on web search behavior. In *Proceedings of the Second ACM International Conference on Web Search and Data Mining*, pages 132–141. ACM, 2009.

[19] X. Zhang, M. Cole, and N. Belkin. Predicting users' domain knowledge from search behaviors. In *Proceedings of the 34th International ACM SIGIR Conference on Research and Development in Information Retrieval*, pages 1225–1226. ACM, 2011.

SIGIR 2016 Workshop WebQA II: Web Question Answering Beyond Factoids

Alessandro Moschitti, Lluís Màrquez, Preslav Nakov
Qatar Computing Research Institute, HBKU, Qatar
{amoschitti, lmarquez, pnakov}@qf.org.qa

Eugene Agichtein
Emory University, Atlanta, USA
eugene.agichtein@emory.edu

Charles Clarke
University of Waterloo, Canada
claclark@gmail.com

Idan Szpektor
Yahoo Research, Haifa, Israel
idan@yahoo-inc.com

1. OVERVIEW

Web search engines have made great progress in answering factoid queries, such as

How many people live in Australia?

They can provide a succinct answer, up to a few words in length, and can sometimes offer additional information such as related facts or entities. However, Web search engines are currently not well-tailored for managing more complex questions, especially when they require explanation or description, e.g.,

Can I get a Qatar residence permit for my wife while she is currently in Doha with a tourist visa?

Given a question like this, currently, search engines resort to returning a link to a detailed Web document, which does not make sure the user can find an answer. Alternatively, such a question might be posted on a Community Question Answering (CQA) site, e.g., Qatar Living,[1] hoping to get a human-authored and detailed response. Other questions submitted on the Web can be short and ambiguous (such as Web queries to a search engine). These issues make the WebQA task more challenging than traditional question answering, and finding the most effective approaches for it remains an open question.

This workshop is a second edition of the successful WebQA workshop, which was held at SIGIR'2015 [1]. The new edition continues the exploration of the boundaries of Web question answering for better understanding the spectrum of approaches and possible responses that are more detailed than a short fact, yet are more useful than a full document. In particular, we also focus on methods that can handle complex questions involving the interdependencies between different entities and facts.

[1]http://www.qatarliving.com/forum

SIGIR '16 July 17-21, 2016, Pisa, Italy

ACM ISBN 978-1-4503-4069-4/16/07...$15.00

DOI: http://dx.doi.org/10.1145/2911451.2917767

2. THEME AND GOAL

This workshop aims to explore diverse approaches to answering questions on the Web. Unlike the more formal format of conferences, the aim of this workshop is to bring together researchers in diverse areas working on this problem, including those from natural language processing, information retrieval, social media and recommender systems communities. Yet, it is designed to be of interest for the SIGIR audience. However, due to its format, its goal, as compared to the main conference, is to conduct a more focused and open discussion. Both academic and industrial stakeholders were welcome to the workshop, including keynotes and invited speakers. In particular, we encouraged the discussion of ongoing research and late–breaking, preliminary results on the following topics:

- Social and user generated question analysis
- Identifying question intent in Web queries
- Answer aggregation from various sources
- Answer summarization from various sources
- Using collaboratively generated content for QA
- Inferring answers for Web questions using knowledge bases or graphs
- Answering opinion questions, including sentiment analysis
- Answering complex, multi-sentence questions
- Evaluation of question answering systems (e.g., via crowd-sourcing)

3. RELEVANCE TO SIGIR

Web question answering is a central topic in information retrieval. However, answering Web queries poses challenges harder than in traditional Web search, as the expectation of the user is much higher when the system promises an answer, not just 10 blue links to click.

While an active area of research exists, this workshop provides a more focused forum addressing specific challenges such as query understanding, answer extraction, and source selection, that are more critical to Web QA compared to traditional web search.

We believe that a continuation of the first WebQA workshop is important as many relevant publications have continued to be disseminated across conferences. See for example, [6, 12, 13, 17, 18, 19, 20, 21, 23], also given the advent of neural networks, e.g., [5, 8, 9, 22, 24]. WebQA offers a forum to researchers and practitioners to discuss and possibly collaborate, thus helping advance the state of the art.

This workshop also coincides and complements the LiveQA track at TREC 2015 and 2016 [2]. LiveQA is a revival of the TREC Question Answering track. The track provides a challenge and data for answering *real user questions*, posted live to the Yahoo! Answers site. The TREC 2016 LiveQA challenge evaluation was held around the time of the workshop, which would provide both the active and the potential participants a way to discuss ideas and approaches.

Another relevant activity is the challenge on CQA organized in 2015 and 2016 at SemEval, i.e., Task 3 [14, 15], which focused on answering new questions using a CQA forum (Qatar Living). In particular, participants were asked to rerank the results returned by a search engine, and in addition to select the good answers from a community forum (see for example the systems developed in [3, 10, 16]). Additionally, the challenge proposed a question-question similarity and an answer selection subtasks (see e.g., [4, 7, 11]).

The WebQA II workshop was held shortly after SemEval 2016, and thus it allowed the participants to discuss its outcome as well as further ideas in more detail. It is valuable for two more reasons: (*i*) there is still a lot of disagreement regarding the goals and the nature of Web question answering, mostly related to the *question intent* (what kind of queries benefit from question answering compared to other methods); and (*ii*) leading search engines are eager to provide question answering services, especially for mobile devices.

4. REFERENCES

[1] E. Agichtein, D. Carmel, C. L. Clarke, P. Paritosh, D. Pelleg, and I. Szpektor. Web question answering: Beyond factoids: SIGIR 2015 workshop. In *SIGIR*, 2015.

[2] E. Agichtein, D. Carmel, D. Harman, D. Pelleg, and Y. Pinter. Overview of the TREC 2015 LiveQA track. In *TREC*, 2015.

[3] A. Barrón-Cedeño, S. Filice, G. Da San Martino, S. Joty, L. Màrquez, P. Nakov, and A. Moschitti. Thread-level information for comment classification in community question answering. In *ACL*, 2015.

[4] A. Barrón-Cedeño, G. D. S. Martino, S. Joty, A. Moschitti, F. A. A. Obaidli, S. Romeo, K. Tymoshenko, and A. Uva. ConvKN at SemEval-2016 Task 3: Answer and question selection for question answering on Arabic and English fora. In *SemEval*, 2016.

[5] A. Bordes, S. Chopra, and J. Weston. Question answering with subgraph embeddings. In *EMNLP*, 2014.

[6] L. Braunstain, O. Kurland, D. Carmel, I. Szpektor, and A. Shtok. Supporting human answers for advice-seeking questions in CQA sites. In *ECIR*, 2016.

[7] S. Filice, D. Croce, A. Moschitti, and R. Basili. KeLP at SemEval-2016 Task 3: Learning semantic relations between questions and answers. In *SemEval*, 2016.

[8] F. Guzmán, L. Màrquez, and P. Nakov. Machine translation evaluation meets community question answering. In *ACL*, 2016.

[9] M. Iyyer, J. Boyd-Graber, L. Claudino, R. Socher, and H. Daumé III. A neural network for factoid question answering over paragraphs. In *EMNLP*, 2014.

[10] S. Joty, A. Barrón-Cedeño, G. Da San Martino, S. Filice, L. Màrquez, A. Moschitti, and P. Nakov. Global thread-level inference for comment classification in community question answering. In *EMNLP*, 2015.

[11] T. Lei, H. Joshi, R. Barzilay, T. S. Jaakkola, K. Tymoshenko, A. Moschitti, and L. Màrquez. Semi-supervised question retrieval with gated convolutions. In *NAACL-HLT*, 2016.

[12] Q. Liu, E. Agichtein, G. Dror, Y. Maarek, and I. Szpektor. When web search fails, searchers become askers: Understanding the transition. In *SIGIR*, 2012.

[13] Q. Liu, T. Jurczyk, J. Choi, and E. Agichtein. Real-time community question answering: Exploring content recommendation and user notification strategies. In *IUI*, 2015.

[14] P. Nakov, L. Màrquez, W. Magdy, A. Moschitti, J. Glass, and B. Randeree. SemEval-2015 task 3: Answer selection in community question answering. In *SemEval*, 2015.

[15] P. Nakov, L. Màrquez, A. Moschitti, W. Magdy, H. Mubarak, A. A. Freihat, J. Glass, and B. Randeree. SemEval-2016 task 3: Community question answering. In *SemEval*, 2016.

[16] M. Nicosia, S. Filice, A. Barrón-Cedeño, I. Saleh, H. Mubarak, W. Gao, P. Nakov, G. Da San Martino, A. Moschitti, K. Darwish, L. Màrquez, S. Joty, and W. Magdy. QCRI: Answer selection for community question answering - experiments for Arabic and English. In *SemEval*, 2015.

[17] A. Omari, D. Carmel, O. Rokhlenko, and I. Szpektor. Novelty based ranking of human answers for community questions. In *TREC*, 2016.

[18] B. Petersil, A. Mejer, I. Szpektor, and K. Crammer. That's not my question: Learning to weight unmatched terms in CQA vertical search. In *SIGIR*, 2016.

[19] A. Severyn and A. Moschitti. Structural relationships for large-scale learning of answer re-ranking. In *SIGIR*, 2012.

[20] A. Severyn and A. Moschitti. Learning to rank short text pairs with convolutional deep neural networks. In *SIGIR*, 2015.

[21] G. Tsur, Y. Pinter, I. Szpektor, and D. Carmel. Identifying web queries with question intent. In *WWW*, 2016.

[22] K. Tymoshenko, D. Bonadiman, and A. Moschitti. Convolutional neural networks vs. convolution kernels: Feature engineering for answer sentence reranking. In *NAACL-HLT*, 2016.

[23] K. Tymoshenko and A. Moschitti. Assessing the impact of syntactic and semantic structures for answer passages reranking. In *CIKM*, 2015.

[24] W.-T. Yih, M.-W. Chang, C. Meek, and A. Pastusiak. Question answering using enhanced lexical semantic models. In *ACL*, 2013.

Author Index

www.ingramcontent.com/pod-product-compliance
Ingram Content Group UK Ltd.
Pitfield, Milton Keynes, MK11 3LW, UK
UKHW051418290926
15471UKWH00009B/1659

9 781450 346146